WINDOWS USER'S GUIDE TO DOS

USING THE COMMAND LINE IN WINDOWS 2000 PROFESSIONAL

CAROLYN Z. GILLAY
SADDLEBACK COLLEGE

BETTE A. PEAT
SOLANO COMMUNITY COLLEGE

FRANKLIN, BEEDLE & ASSOCIATES, INC. • 8536 SW ST. HELENS DRIVE, SUITE D
WILSONVILLE, OREGON • 97070 • 503-682-7668

President and Publisher	Jim Leisy (jimleisy@fbeedle.com)
Production	Jeni Lee Tom Sumner Stephanie Welch
Proofreader	Stephanie Welch
Cover	Ian Shadburne
Marketing	Chris Collier
Order Processing	Krista Hall

Printed in the U.S.A.

Names of all products herein are used for identification purposes only and are trademarks and/or registered trademarks of their respective owners. Franklin, Beedle & Associates, Inc., makes no claim of ownership or corporate association with the products or companies that own them.

©2002 Franklin, Beedle & Associates Incorporated. No part of this book may be reproduced, stored in a retrieval system, transmitted, or transcribed, in any form or by any means—electronic, mechanical, telepathic, photocopying, recording, or otherwise—without prior written permission of the publisher. Requests for permission should be addressed as follows:

Rights and Permissions
Franklin, Beedle & Associates, Incorporated
8536 SW St. Helens Drive, Suite D
Wilsonville, Oregon 97070

Library of Congress Cataloging-in-Publication Data

Gillay, Carolyn Z.
Windows user's guide to DOS : using the command line in Windows 2000 Professional / Carolyn Z. Gillay, Bette A. Peat.
p. cm.
ISBN 1-887902-72-4
1. MS-DOS (Computer file) 2. PC-DOS (Computer file) 3. Microsoft Windows (Computer file) 4. Operating systems (Computers) I. Peat, Bette A. II. Title

QA76.76.O63 G564 2002
005.4'469--dc21

2001040684

DEDICATION

To Christopher, Milton, Loren, and Kevin Smith—
not of my blood, but of my heart. You all bring such joy to me.

—C. Z. G.

For Tammy, who is my strength and my pride.

—B. A. P.

Campbell University Library
Buies Creek, NC 27506

CONTENTS

CHAPTER 1
GETTING STARTED WITH THE OPERATING SYSTEM 28

PREFACE

This textbook introduces the hardware, software, and operating system concepts of today's computer systems. Students gain system-level experience through problem-solving exercises at the command line. It is written for use as the core textbook for a course that focuses exclusively on DOS, for the DOS portion of a network or programming class, as a supplement to a Windows 2000 Professional course, or for a class that follows an introduction to Windows 2000 Professional.

WHY LEARN DOS WHEN IT'S A WINDOWS WORLD?

Students with no computer experience believe DOS is "dead." However, the rise of network computing and the vast number of businesses running legacy DOS applications make knowledge of DOS and the Windows 2000 command line essential. Command syntax, parameters, parsing commands, and troubleshooting are all handled better from the command line interface rather than the graphical user interface.

The command line interface exists in Windows 95, Windows 98, Windows Me, Windows NT 4.0, Windows NT 4.5, Windows 2000, Windows XP, and Novell. Batch files are useful in all these operating systems. Batch file skills are critical in the networking world, as well as on the stand-alone computer system.

BEGINS WITH THE BASICS AND LEADS TO THE ADVANCED

This text leads students from a basic to a sophisticated use of the command line interface. Each chapter has questions for both novice and advanced students, so it challenges advanced students without sacrificing the needs of beginning students. Furthermore, while this text does teach the various character-based commands, it also stresses the concepts, theory, and understanding of operating systems in general.

The text demonstrates the command line interface and explains when and why one would use it instead of the graphical user interface of Windows 2000. It provides numerous examples to allow students to master operating systems. This text teaches these concepts using the Command Prompt window, referred to as the MS-DOS Prompt window in earlier versions of Windows. Though this text deals primarily with those commands and functions that are available at the command prompt, it also deals with commands and functions necessary to understand, maintain, and troubleshoot a system that are available only in the GUI.

Pipes, filters, and redirection used with batch files are covered in a thorough, step-by-step methodology. Advanced batch files are covered in detail, building on programming logic in a comprehensible way. Students cover all batch file commands and are introduced to DEBUG.

Setting up computer systems, optimizing performance, and troubleshooting require students to have good command line skills. To this end, the student learns how to create an Emergency Repair disk (ERD), boot into Safe Mode, and create a set of floppy disks to boot the system into Windows 2000 Professional.

This text also covers two major forms of connectivity: networking and the Internet. We have found that there is a gap in too many students' knowledge of networks. Students often take a Windows and/or DOS class and then, if on a networking career path, jump into a large-systems networking class. This can be an intimidating jump. There are many other students who work in small offices that do not have network administrators; others may work in environments where they only need to access a network or share files, folders, and devices on their own systems at home. These students are not going to follow the networking program. To address the needs of all these students, this text introduces some basic networking concepts and then leads the students into setting up a peer-to-peer network (where possible) and shows them how to share files, folders, and devices. Students also learn general networking techniques, such as mapping drives, which will serve them in good stead if they are on the networking career path.

Another connectivity topic is the Internet. In our textbook, students learn various ways to connect to the Internet and then do some simple activities using Internet Explorer. A brief introduction to TCP/IP concepts is included because, when using the Internet, so many students are lost at the first mention of such terms as "protocol" and "IP address." This overview gives them an understanding of some of these important terms so that they have a better comprehension of online activities. Students learn how to use simple Internet-related commands that can be run at the command line, such as FTP. In addition, certain troubleshooting commands such as ping and Telnet are covered.

The last two chapters cover a much too neglected topic—troubleshooting. These chapters include backing up a computer system and recovering a damaged system using such tools as Recovery Console and Safe Mode. Recovery Console is a command line repair tool. Safe Mode gives the computer user options to repair a damaged system. In addition, the students learns the purpose, function, and structure of the Registry. They learn advanced troubleshooting concepts, looking at the CMOS setup utility as well as looking at memory and the paging file. They learn about the tools in Windows such as Regedit and RegEdt32. They use Regedit to do simple tasks.

This book takes up where other Windows books leave off. Although no prior knowledge or experience with computers, software, operating systems, or Windows 95/98/2000 is necessary, it helps if the students have completed a basic Windows 95/98/2000 class.

ACTIVITIES DISK WITH SHAREWARE PROGRAMS AND DATA FILES

The esoteric nature of operating systems is one of the biggest obstacles in teaching the command line interface to students. Many students find the material interesting and stimulating. However, there is always a group that asks, "What good is DOS? It doesn't do anything." Using discussion and example, this text demonstrates the importance of the command line interface.

Often, when teaching the command line interface, instructors attempt to use a complex application program, such as Word, and it costs them time teaching the application, not the operating system. To resolve this problem, two simple shareware applications are provided for students to work with: a simple database (Home Phone Book) and a simple spreadsheet (Thinker). Students have the opportunity to load an application program and prewritten data files, as well as create simple data files. In doing so, students better understand the differences between data files and program files and are able to use operating system commands to manipulate both types of files. In addition, the text includes several educationally sound shareware games that reinforce certain DOS concepts in an enjoyable manner.

These shareware files are on the ACTIVITIES disk along with data files students use for the exercises in the book. The ACTIVITIES disk's files are easily installed on a computer system's hard disk or network server. The exercises do not direct students to save files to the hard disk or network server. Early on, students create a DATA disk, and all files are written to the DATA disk. This approach provides real-life experience in working with the hard disk or server without risking damage to either. There are numerous warnings and cautions alerting students to when a possible network conflict could arise.

AN INTEGRATED PRESENTATION OF CONCEPTS AND SKILLS

Each section of the book is presented in a careful, student-oriented, step-by-step approach. Interspersed between the steps in the exercises are the reasons for and results of each action. At the end of each chapter, there are application assignments that allow students to apply their knowledge and prove mastery of the subject area through critical-thinking skills. Each command is presented in a syntactically correct manner so that when the students have finished the course, they will be able to not only use software documentation, but also be comfortable in a network/Internet environment that requires the use of syntax and commands. This also assists the students in their ability to learn how to solve problems using the documentation at hand. This skill also transfers to the use of application packages and other operating system environments. No matter what changes are made to future versions of the operating system, students will be able to use the new commands.

USES A SELF-MASTERY APPROACH

Each chapter includes a chapter overview, a list of key terms, a chapter summary, discussion questions, true-and-false questions, completion questions, multiple-choice questions, and problems where students are asked to write the commands. Each chapter also includes three sets of application assignments that focus on the skills learned in the chapter. The first two require the use of the computer. The first problem set requires students to complete activities on the computer and write the resulting answers on a Scantron form; the second problem set requires students to use the computer and print out the answers.

For the second problem set, the student results are sent to a batch file provided with the ACTIVITIES disk. The batch file is an easy-to-follow program. The students supply their solutions to the problems, and the batch file formats the answers in a consistent manner and includes the students' names and other instructor-directed identifying information. The printouts typically print on two pages or less.

The last set of application assignments are brief essay questions that encourage students to integrate what they have accomplished in the chapter with their improved understanding of the command line interface of the Windows 2000 operating system. All three types of assignments reinforce critical-thinking skills. These application assignments can be turned in as homework. Where hands-on assignments are not possible, such as dealing with the Registry, students still have an opportunity to answer brief essay questions that encourage them to explain their understanding of the topic at hand.

SUPPLEMENTARY MATERIAL

This book comes with an instructor's manual that includes teaching suggestions for each chapter as well as the answers for every question and application exercise. A complete PowerPoint presentation for each chapter is included as well. There are additional chapter tests. A midterm and a final are included.

REFERENCE TOOLS

This text is useful as a reference for MS-DOS commands. The first appendix provides instructions to install the subdirectory containing the shareware programs and data files to the hard disk. This feature is particularly useful for students who work at home or in an office. The rest of the appendices include a complete command reference (including DOS commands that are no longer available in Windows), an ANSI table, and FDISK. There is also a glossary.

ACKNOWLEDGMENTS

A project of this scope is difficult to complete successfully without the contributions of many individuals. Thank you to all who contributed. A special thanks to:

- David Robinson (Pioneer Pacific College) for contributing a high-quality test bank to the Instructor's CD.
- Mike Estes, for sharing his time, his extensive computer and network knowledge and his willingness to always go the extra mile for not only me but for the students and faculty at Saddleback College.
- Kathryn Maurdeff for providing questions, answers, and PowerPoint presentations.
- All the authors of the shareware included with this textbook.
- My students at Saddleback College, who make writing worthwhile.
- My colleagues in the Computer Information Management Department at Saddleback College.
- The California Business Education Association and the National Business Education Association for providing forums for professional growth as well as inviting me to make presentations sharing my teaching experiences.
- A big thanks to everyone at Franklin, Beedle & Associates: Christine Collier and Krista Brown, who do a great job of running marketing and distribution; Jeni Lee, who made the first draft of this book possible; Tom Sumner and Stephanie Welch, who somehow make sense of all the pieces of manuscript I send them and produce a coherent whole; Ian Shadburne for an eye-catching cover, and Sue Page for a fine job of overseeing and producing the instructor's materials. Thank you also to Jim Leisy, publisher and friend, who always manages to find more books for me to write.
- To Bette Peat, my wonderful co-author, and now good friend. Your knowledge, patience, and troubleshooting abilities make our writing so much easier.
- And, as always, to Frank Panezich, who travels the world with me and makes not only traveling, but my life, so much fun.

Anyone who wants to offer suggestions or improvements or just share ideas can reach me at *czg@bookbiz.com*.

—*C.Z.G.*

My thanks to everyone who helped along the way. Special thanks to:

- My family; Parkers, Peats, and Farneths; for their continuous encouragement and their "you can do it" attitude. They believed when it wasn't practical to believe, and supported me through some rough roads.
- My friends and colleagues at Solano Community College, especially Jane Thompson, Donna Anderson, and Mary Ann Harris for their unending support and friendship.
- The CIS students at Solano for making me find answers for questions I never thought of, most particularly Jonathan Cerkoney and Janice Larsen.
- The "Covelo connection," Jean and Manny Macaraeg, for adjusting their schedule to accommodate mine so many times.
- All the crew at Franklin, Beedle & Associates for their patience and flexibility.
- And once again, most of all, to Carolyn—for the opportunity. Thank you, my dear, dear friend.

Anyone who wants to offer suggestions, improvements, or just share ideas can reach me at *bpeat@solano.cc.ca.us* or *wugbook@pacbell.net*.

—*B.A.P.*

We would both like to thank the following instructors, whose contributions, insights, and suggestions were indispensable:

David Robinson	*Pioneer Pacific College*
Dale Farris	*Lamar State College*
Glen Johannson	*Spokane Community College*
Jeff Brown	*Montana State University—Great Falls*
Joann Luukkonen	*Central Lakes College—Brainerd*
Ken Conway	*Arapahoe Community College*
Callie Moore	*Bristol Community College*
Victor Mendez	*San Antonio College*
Rodger Wein	*San Antonio College*
Wendy Bailey	*Wilson Technical Community College*
Ron West	*Umpqua Community College*
Vernene Scheurer	*Highline Community College*
Wayne Hine	*College of Southern Idaho*

REVIEW CHAPTER

MICROCOMPUTER SYSTEMS

HARDWARE, SOFTWARE, AND THE OPERATING SYSTEM

LEARNING OBJECTIVES

1. Categorize the latest types of computers in use today.
2. Identify and explain the functions of basic hardware components.
3. Explain how a CPU functions.
4. Compare and contrast RAM, cache, and ROM.
5. Explain how the use of adapter boards increases the capabilities of a computer.
6. List and explain the functions of the various peripheral input and output devices of a computer.
7. Explain what external storage devices are.
8. Explain how to measure the capacity of a disk.
9. Explain how disk drives write information to and read information from a disk.
10. Explain the purpose and function of a hard disk.
11. Compare the purposes and functions of disks.
12. Explain how and why a disk is divided.
13. Explain how disk drives derive their names.
14. Compare and contrast system software and application software.
15. Explain the functions of an operating system.
16. Explain the advantages of using a network.

CHAPTER OVERVIEW

It is impossible to live today without being affected by computers. Computers are used in public and private industry and are found in every sector of the business world. Computer software is what makes computers useful for all types of applications. There is specialized software for sophisticated scientific applications such as nuclear and atomic physics and for all forms of engineering and industrial research. The greatest use of application software is in business, with all types of word-processing, accounting, and marketing packages. Computer use only continues to grow.

Application software makes a computer useful, but you must first understand how the operating system of a computer works. Foremost, the operating system manages all the basic functions of the computer and allows the computer to run application programs. When new technology appears in hardware and software, the operating system must keep pace. Thus, you must have a basic understanding of computer hardware to understand the role and function of the operating system. Hardware and technology are constantly changing, so new versions of operating systems also appear. The operating system of choice today is Windows 2000 Professional.

R.1 AN INTRODUCTION TO COMPUTERS

At the most basic level, computers are calculators; but this definition is very narrow. Computers are used to handle accounting chores (spreadsheets), write books (word-processing documents), organize and retrieve information (databases), create and manipulate graphics, and communicate with the world (the Internet). In the visual arts, computers have revolutionized the way films are made, games are played, and reality is perceived (virtual reality).

R.2 CATEGORIES OF COMPUTERS

Computers are categorized by a variety of factors, such as size, processing speed, information storage capacity, and cost. In the ever-changing technical world, these classifications are not absolute. Technical advancements blur some categories. For instance, the capabilities of many microcomputers today exceed those of mainframes manufactured five years ago. In addition, the microcomputer now is the dominant computer used by most businesses. These computers are available in sizes ranging from desktop to subnotebook. Table R.1 shows the major categories of computers.

Computer	Applications
Supercomputer: Very large computer	Sophisticated scientific applications such as nuclear physics, atomic physics, and seismology.
Mainframe: Large computer	General-purpose business machines. Typical applications include accounting, payroll, banking, and airline reservations.
Minicomputer: Small mainframe computer	Specialized applications such as engineering and industrial research.
Microcomputer: Small, general-purpose computer	General applications such as word processing, accounting for small businesses, and record keeping. Today, these computers are also known as desktops, PCs, notebooks, subcompacts, and laptops.

TABLE R.1 COMPUTER TYPES

R.3 COMPUTER COMPONENTS

Although the number of computer types continue to grow, computers operate the same way, regardless of their category. Information is input, processed, and stored and the resulting information is output. Figure R.1 is a graphic representation of this process.

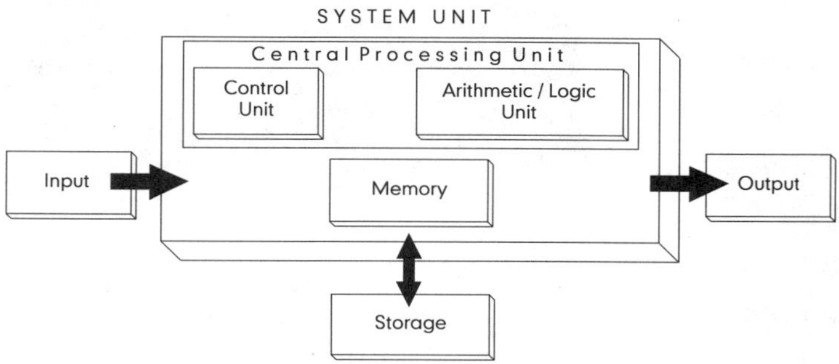

FIGURE R.1 COMPONENTS OF A COMPUTER SYSTEM

Figure R.1 shows the physical components of a computer system, referred to as ***hardware***. All computer systems, from mainframes to notebooks, have the same basic hardware. Hardware by itself can do nothing; a computer system needs software. ***Software*** is a set of detailed instructions, called a ***program***, that tells the hardware what operations to perform. ***Data***, in its simplest form, is related or unrelated numbers, words, or facts that, when arranged in a particular way, provide information. Software applications turn raw data into information.

R.4 MICROCOMPUTER HARDWARE COMPONENTS

This textbook is devoted to single-user computers—microcomputers. Microcomputers are also called micros, subcompacts, home computers, laptops, notebooks, personal computers (PCs), or desktop computers. Microcomputers are comprised of hardware components. Much like a stereo system, the basic components of a complete system, also called a system configuration, include an input device (typically a keyboard), a pointing device (a mouse or trackball), a system unit that houses the electronic circuitry for storing and processing data and programs (the central processing unit/CPU, adapter cards, power supply, and memory/RAM and ROM), an external storage unit that stores data and programs on disks (a disk drive), and an output device such as a visual display unit (a monitor). Most people also purchase a printer for producing a printed version of the results. Typically today, a system also includes speakers for multimedia activities. Figure R.2 represents a typical microcomputer system.

FIGURE R.2 A TYPICAL MICROCOMPUTER SYSTEM

If you look at the back of a computer, you can see the input/output devices, called peripherals. Since they are "peripheral," or outside the case, they must communicate with what is inside the computer through cables attached to connections that are called ***ports***. Figure R.3 shows some examples of these connections.

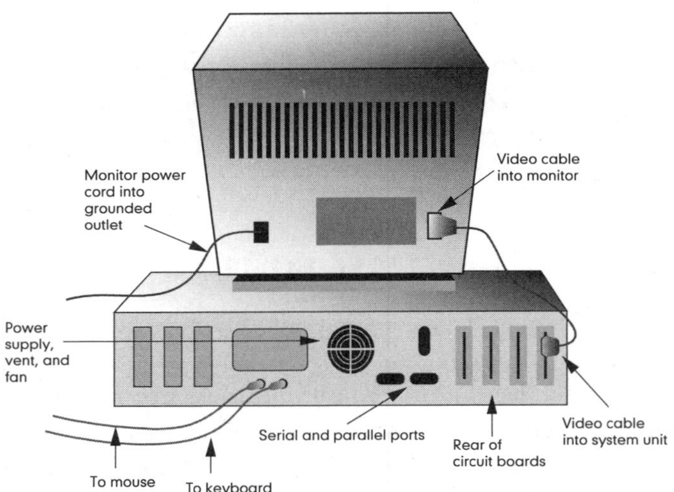

FIGURE R.3 CABLES ATTACHED TO A CASE

R.5 THE SYSTEM UNIT

The system unit, as shown in Figure R.4, is the "black box" that houses the electronic and mechanical parts of the computer. It contains many printed electronic circuit boards, also called ***interface cards***, ***cards***, or ***adapter cards***. One of these is a special printed circuit board called the ***system board*** or the ***motherboard***. Attached to the system board is a microprocessor chip that is the central processing unit (CPU), random access memory (RAM), and read-only memory (ROM). The system unit is also referred to as the chassis or case. With the outer case removed, the unit looks like the diagram in Figure R.4.

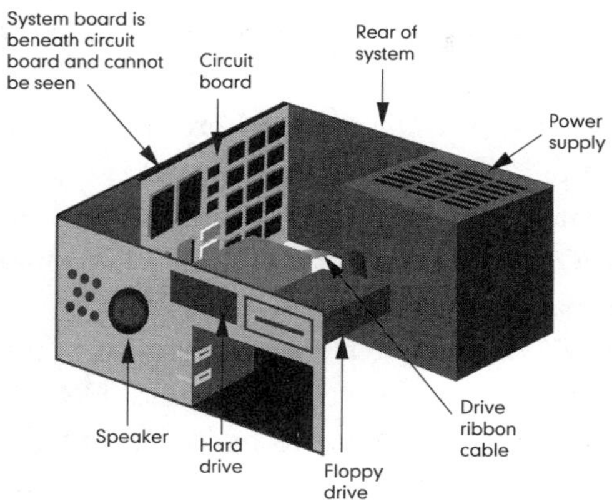

FIGURE R.4 INSIDE THE SYSTEM UNIT

Inside the typical system unit, you find the following:

- A system board or motherboard that contains components such as a CPU, RAM, ROM, a chipset, and a system clock
- Expansion slots that contain adapter cards such as a video card, a sound card, and a network interface card
- Secondary storage units (disk drives)
- A power supply

A system unit has a power supply (to get power to every single part in the PC), disk drives (including CD-ROM drives, floppy disk drives, removable drives, and hard disk drives), and circuit boards. The motherboard, also called the system board, is the core of the system. Everything in the PC is connected to the motherboard so that it can control every part of the system. Figure R.5 shows a system board.

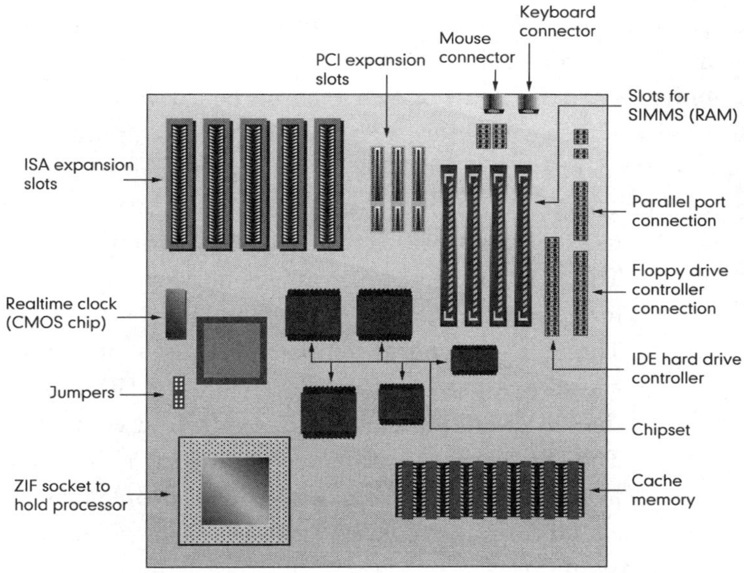

FIGURE R.5 COMPONENTS ON A SYSTEM BOARD

Most modern system boards have several components built in, including various sockets, slots, connectors, chips, and other components. Most system boards have the following components:

- A processor socket/slot is the place where the CPU is installed.
- A chipset is a single chip that integrates all the functions of older system chips such as the system timer, the keyboard controller, and so forth.
- A Super Input/Output chip integrates devices formerly found on separate expansion cards in older systems.
- All system boards must have a special chip containing software that is called BIOS (Basic Input Output System) or ***ROM-BIOS***. (***ROM*** is ***read-only memory***.) This chip contains the startup programs and drivers that are used to get your system up and running and acts as the interface to the basic hardware in your system. BIOS is a collection of programs embedded into a chip, called a flash ROM chip. It is non-volatile, which means that when you turn off the computer, none of the information stored in ROM is lost. ROM-BIOS has four main functions: POST (power-on self test), which tests a computer's critical hardware components such as the processor, memory, and disk controllers; the bootstrap loader, which finds the operating system and loads or boots your computer; BIOS, which is the collection of actual drivers used to act as a basic interface between the operating system and the hardware (when you run the Windows operating system in safe mode, you are running solely on BIOS drivers); and the CMOS (complementary metal-oxide semiconductor) setup, which contains the system configuration and setup programs. CMOS is usually a menu-driven program that allows you to configure the motherboard and chipset settings along with the date and time and passwords. You usually access the CMOS settings by pressing a special keystroke combination before the operating system loads. The keystroke, such as **F2**, depends on the computer. Most ROM is located on the system board, but some ROM is located on adapter boards.
- SIMM/DIMM (single inline memory module/dual inline memory module) slots are for the installation of memory modules. These modules are small boards that plug into special connectors on the motherboard or memory card and replace individual memory chips. If one chip goes bad, the entire module must be replaced.
- System buses are the heart of every motherboard. A ***bus*** is a path across which data can travel within a computer. A data path is the communication highway between computer elements. The main buses in a system include the following:
    - The processor bus, the highest-speed bus in the system, is primarily used by the processor to pass information to and from memory.
    - The AGP (accelerated graphics port) bus is a high-speed bus specifically for a video card.
    - The PCI (peripheral component interconnect) bus is a collection of slots that high-speed peripherals such as SCSI (small computer system interface) adapters, network cards, and video cards can be plugged into.
    - The ISA (industry standard architecture) bus is an old bus that appeared in the first computers. Most people use it for plug-in modems, sound cards, and various other low-speed peripherals.
- The voltage regulator is used to drop the power supply signal to the correct voltage for the processor.
- A battery supplies power for the CMOS chip, which holds the system configuration information.

R.6 CENTRAL PROCESSING UNIT

A ***central processing unit,*** most commonly referred to as a ***CPU,*** is the brain of a computer and is composed of transistors on a silicon chip. It comprehends and carries out instructions sent to it by a program and directs the activity of the computer. The CPU is plugged into the motherboard. The CPU is described in terms of its central processing chip and its model designation. Intel manufactures many of the CPU chips in Windows-based PCs. Intel processors running Windows are commonly called ***Wintel*** machines. These chips were, for many years, designated by a model number such as 80386 or 80486. Typically the first two numbers were dropped, so people referred to a computer as a 386 or 486. With the introduction of the 80586, Intel began referring to its chips as Pentiums, such as the Pentium 350. Since that time, Intel has released the Pentium II, the Pentium III, and the Pentium IV. The major competitors to Intel are AMD and Cyrix. A CPU is rated by the following items:

1. Speed. The system clock on the system board times the activities of the chips on the system board. This clock provides a beat that synchronizes all the activities. The faster the beat, the faster the CPU can execute instructions. This is measured in ***megahertz (MHz)***, where one MHz is equal to 1,000,000 beats of the clock per second. The original 8088 CPU had a MHz rating of 4.77 MHz. Today, 500 is a common speed, and speeds are available up to 866 MHz or more. In fact, a 1-GHz CPU has been developed and even faster CPUs are coming.
2. Efficiency of the program code built into the CPU chip.
3. Internal data path size (word size), the largest number of bits the CPU can process in one operation. Word sizes range from 16 bits (2 bytes) to 64 bits (8 bytes).
4. Data path, the largest number of bits that can be transported into the CPU. It ranges from 8 bits to 64 bits.
5. Maximum number of memory addresses that the CPU can assign. The minimum is 1 megabyte and the maximum is 4,096 megabytes (4 gigabytes).
6. Internal cache, which is memory included in the CPU. It is also referred to as primary cache or level 1 (L1) cache.
7. Multiprocessor ability. Some chips can accomplish more than one task at a time and thus are multiprocessors.
8. Special functionality. Some chips are designed to provide special services. For example, the Pentium MMX chip is designed to handle multimedia features especially well.

R.7 INPUT/OUTPUT (I/O) BUSES

Adapter cards are printed circuit boards, as mentioned previously. They are installed in a system unit either when the unit is purchased or later. Adapter cards allow a user to use a special video display or use a mouse, a modem, or a fax-modem. These items are considered ***peripheral devices*** and are installed within a system unit in expansion slots. The number of adapter card options you can install depends on how many slots your system unit has. Inexpensive system units usually have only one or two expansion slots, but a costly system unit, especially one designed to be a network server, can have seven, eight, or more.

I/O buses allow your CPU to communicate with your peripheral devices. A peripheral device connected to your computer is controlled by the CPU. Examples of peripherals (also called peripheral devices or devices) include such items as a disk drive, a printer, a mouse, or a modem. The original personal computers had nothing built into the computer except a CPU, memory, and a keyboard. Everything else, such as floppy disk drives, hard disk drives, printers, and modems, were provided by add-in cards. Nowadays, computer manufacturers have found that it is less expensive to build the most common peripherals into the motherboard. Connectors to which you connect the cables for your devices are called ports. Today, most computers include a parallel port for a printer, two serial ports for devices such as an external modem or a serial mouse, and controllers for up to two floppy drives and two hard disk drives.

However, not every peripheral has a built-in connection. Data paths often stop at an expansion slot. An ***expansion slot*** is a slot or plug where you can add an interface card to enhance your computer system. An interface card is a printed circuit board that enables a personal computer to use a peripheral device, such as a CD-ROM drive, modem, or joystick, for which it does not already have the necessary connections, ports, or circuit boards. Interface cards are also called cards, adapter cards, or adapter boards. The size and shape of the expansion slot is dependent on the kind of bus your computer uses.

Remember, a bus is a set of hardware lines (conductors) used for data transfer among the components of the computer system. A bus is essentially a shared information highway that connects different parts of the system—including the CPU, the disk drive controller, and memory. Buses are characterized by the number of bits that they can transfer at one time, which is equivalent to the number of wires within a bus. A computer with a 32-bit address bus and a 16-bit data bus can transfer 16 bits of data at a time from any of 2^{32} memory locations. Buses have standards—technical guidelines that are used to establish uniformity in an area of hardware or software development. Common bus standards include ISA (industry standard architecture), PCI (peripheral component interconnect), local bus, PC card slots—formerly known as PCMCIA (Personal Computer Memory Card International Association)—primarily used on notebook computers, and VESA (Video Electronics Standards Association) local bus.

The newest bus standard is ***USB (universal serial bus)***. It is an external bus standard that brings the plug-and-play standard capability of hardware devices outside the computer, eliminating the need to install cards into dedicated computer slots and reconfigure the system. Most new computers today include a USB connection. The advantage of USB is that you may daisy-chain devices. This connectivity feature means that your first device plugs into the USB connector, then the next device plugs into the first device, and so forth. You need only one USB connection, but can use it for many devices. In addition, USB devices can be "hot-plugged" or unplugged, which means that you can add or remove a peripheral device without needing to power down the computer. The device, however, must be USB-compatible.

FireWire is a new bus technology. This bus was derived from the FireWire bus originally developed by Apple and Texas Instruments. It is now known as IEEE 1394 rather than FireWire. This bus is extremely fast and suits the demands of today's audio and video multimedia, which must move large amounts of data quickly.

R.8 RANDOM ACCESS MEMORY

RAM (random access memory) is the workspace of the computer. It is often referred to simply as ***memory***. The growth in the size of RAM in the last few years has been phenomenal. Whereas 4 MB of memory was more than satisfactory just a few years ago, the demand based on software needs has made 128 MB of RAM commonplace, and 256 or more MB of RAM desirable. Physically, RAM is contained in many electrical circuits. However, a computer's memory is not like a person's memory. RAM is not a permanent record of anything. RAM is the place where the programs and data are placed while the computer is working. Computer memory is temporary (volatile) and useful only while the computer is on. When the computer is turned off, what is in memory is lost.

There are two types of RAM, ***dynamic RAM (DRAM)*** and ***static RAM (SRAM)***. Dynamic RAM chips hold data for a short time, whereas static RAM chips can hold data until the computer is turned off. DRAM is much less expensive than SRAM; thus most memory on a motherboard consists of DRAM. Dynamic RAM chips do not hold their data long and must be refreshed about every 3.86 milliseconds. "Refresh" means rewrite the data to the chip. The direct memory access (DMA) controller takes care of refreshing RAM. The DMA controller is on the system board and is part of the chipset. It provides faster memory access because it moves data in and out of RAM without involving the CPU. Today, you also see extended data output (EDO) memory on newer computers. This RAM module works about 20 percent faster then conventional RAM, but the system board must support EDO memory. Since the speed at which you and your computer work is driven by RAM, you can expect improvements in RAM speed to continue.

R.9 CACHE MEMORY

Caching is a method used to improve processing speed. It uses some of the more expensive static RAM chips to speed up data access. Basically, ***cache memory*** stores frequently used RAM data, thereby speeding up the process of data access. Whenever the CPU needs data from RAM, it visits the cache first to see if the data is available there. If it is, then rapid action occurs. If not, the CPU goes to RAM proper.

The cache holds data or programming code that is often used or anticipated. This way the CPU has the instructions it needs ready and waiting without having to refresh RAM. Caches can be found in video and printer memory systems as well.

R.10 CONTROLLERS

A ***controller*** is a device on which other devices rely for access to a computer subsystem such as a disk drive. A disk controller, for example, controls access to one or more disk drives. What kind of controller interface you have determines the number and kinds of devices you can attach to your computer. A common disk drive controller is the Integrated Device Electronics (IDE), which resides on the drive itself, eliminating the need for a separate adapter card. Another type is the small computer system interface (SCSI, pronounced "skuzzi"), which is a very high-speed interface and is used to connect computers to many SCSI peripheral devices such as hard disks and printers. The original SCSI standard is now called SCSI-I, and the new enhanced SCSI standard is called SCSI-II. In addition, new developments include Fast SCSI, Fast/Wide SCSI, and UltraSCSI.

R.11 CONNECTORS

Most computers have both a serial port and a parallel port. See Figure R.6. These connections allow devices to be plugged in. ***Serial ports*** communicate in series, one data bit after another, and service serial devices such as modems and mouses. ***Parallel ports*** communicate in parallel, eight data bits at a time, and service parallel devices such as printers. The most common configuration for a personal computer is two serial ports and one parallel port. Serial ports are referred to as COM ports, and on a standard computer they are designated as COM1 and COM2. Parallel ports are called LPT ports. The first LPT port is called LPT1. COM stands for *com*munications and LPT stands for *l*ine *p*rin*t*er.

A personal computer can have up to five I/O ports, usually three serial and two parallel. Although computers are limited to five ports, there can actually be more than five peripheral devices. Today, many devices that plug into parallel ports, such as Zip drives and scanners, have a "through port" so that one LPT port can service two devices. If you have a SCSI interface, you may also connect a series of devices, creating a daisy chain.

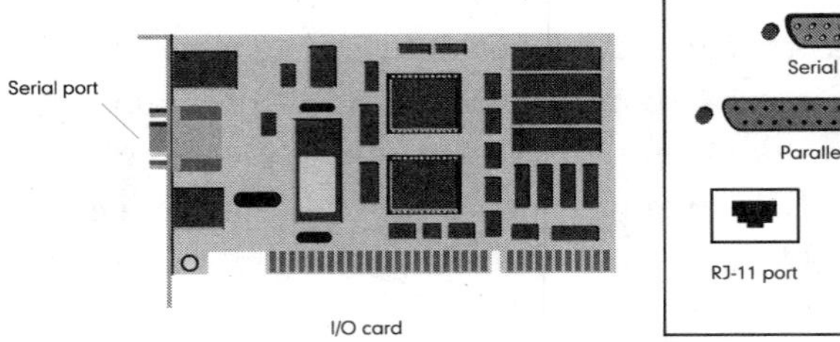

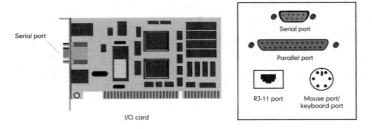

FIGURE R.6 I/O PORTS

Today, many computers come with a built-in modem. If that is the case, you have a connector called an RJ-11 telephone plug, which is identical to the plug on the back of a telephone. Having an RJ-11 connector frees up a serial port.

R.12 PERIPHERALS—INPUT DEVICES

How do software programs and data get into RAM? The answer is input devices. The most common input device is the keyboard, which is attached to a system unit with a cable. By keying in instructions and data, you communicate with the computer. The computer places the information into RAM. Again, most modern computers have a keyboard port to connect the keyboard (see Figure R.6).

You can also input using a pointing device, such as a ***mouse, trackball,*** track pointer, or touchpad, to get to the place to enter data. (In this textbook, all such devices will be collectively referred to as a mouse.) Data manipulation is as easy as moving the cursor to where you want it on the screen and pressing one of the mouse buttons. Most computers today have a connector for the mouse, most commonly called the PS/2 connector. See Figure R.6.

Other input devices include modems, with which data can be downloaded directly into the computer, and scanners, for inserting text through optical character recognition (OCR) software and graphics. Disk drives are both input and output devices.

R.13 PERIPHERALS—OUTPUT DEVICES

In addition to getting information into the CPU, you also want to get it out. You may want to see what you keyed in on the monitor, or you might desire a printed or "hard" copy of the data. These processes are known as output. Output devices refer to where information is sent. Thus, you read information in and write information out, commonly known as I/O for input and output.

R.14 OUTPUT DEVICES—MONITORS

A ***monitor***, also called a terminal display screen, screen, cathode-ray tube (CRT), or video display terminal (VDT), looks like a television. The common monitor size standard used to be 14 inches (measured diagonally). However, today most users opt for at least a 15-inch monitor. The new standard is becoming the 19-inch monitor, with the 21-inch monitor gaining ground. In addition, the liquid crystal display (LCD) used on notebook computers is now becoming available as a stand-alone monitor to accompany your desktop computer. These monitors take far less space since they are completely flat, but at this time, they are very new and very costly.

Another important facet of a monitor is the sharpness of its image, referred to as its ***resolution***. Resolution is a measure of how many ***pixels*** (dots) on the screen are addressable by software. A resolution of 800 by 600 means 800 pixels per line horizontally and 600 pixels vertically. Multiplying 800 by 600 will give you the total number of pixels available (480,000 pixels). The resolution must be supported by the video card controller, and the software you are using must make use of the resolution capabilities of the monitor.

To determine the sharpness of your image, you must also know the dot pitch of the pixels. ***Dot pitch*** is the measurement in millimeters between pixels on the screen. The smaller the dot pitch, the sharper the image. Common sizes range from .25 to .31. A dot pitch of .28 or .25 will give you the best results.

Another factor in choosing a monitor is the interlace factor. An ***interlaced*** monitor begins at the top of the screen and redraws (refreshes) every other line of pixels, then returns to the top and refreshes the rest of the lines. A ***noninterlaced*** monitor refreshes all the lines at one time, eliminating the wandering horizontal line and the flickering screen. Thus, a noninterlaced monitor is the preferred choice. The refresh rate (vertical scan rate) is the time it takes for the electronic beam to fill the screen with lines from top to bottom. Video Electronics Standards Association (VESA) has set a minimum refresh rate standard of 70 Hz (70 complete vertical refreshes per second) as one requirement of Super VGA monitors. Multiscan monitors are also available. These monitors offer a variety of vertical and horizontal refresh rates but cost much more than other monitors.

Information written to the screen by the CPU needs a special kind of circuit board—a video display adapter card, commonly called a video card or a graphics adapter card. In the early days of computing, the video adapters were monochrome. The color graphics adapter (CGA) and the enhanced graphics adapter (EGA) came next, but only in 16 colors. Next was the video graphics array (VGA), which generated 256 colors. Today, most people have the Super VGA format, which generates sharper resolution and can display an almost unbelievable 16 million colors. Commonly, a video card has its own "on-board" memory, which is physically on the card. Today, four megabytes of memory on a video card is common, and soon eight megabytes will be the standard.

R.15 OUTPUT DEVICES—PRINTERS

A printer is attached to a system unit with a cable, usually to a parallel port. A printer allows a user to have a hard copy (unchangeable because it is on paper) of information. In the past, ***impact printers***, such as dot-matrix printers, were used. An impact printer works like a typewriter. The element strikes some kind of ribbon, which in turn strikes the paper and leaves a mark. A dot-matrix printer forms characters by selecting dots from a grid pattern on a movable print head and permits printing in any style of letters and graphics (pictures). Dot-matrix printers are still used today for multiple-part forms that use carbon paper.

Today, ***nonimpact printers*** are in general use. This category includes thermal printers that burn images into paper using a dot-matrix grid and ***inkjet printers*** that spray ionized drops of ink to shape characters. Today, inkjet printers that produce very good quality black and white as well as color images have become the most popular personal printer. The ***laser printer*** is more expensive, but produces fine quality black and white printing. Although laser color is available, it remains very costly. Laser printers uses a laser beam instructed by the computer to form characters with powdered toner fused to the page by heat, like a photocopying machine. Laser printers operate noiselessly at speeds up to 900 characters per second (cps), equivalent to 24 pages per minute.

R.16 MODEMS

A ***modem*** (*mo*dulator/*dem*odulator) translates the digital signals of the computer into the analog signals that travel over telephone lines. The speed at which the signal travels is called the baud rate—the unit of time for a signal to travel over a telephone line. The rate of transmission has increased to 56,000 baud, and will soon be even faster. The speed at which data packets travel is measured in bits per second (bps) and is usually very near the baud rate. For this transmission to occur, the party on the other end must also have a modem that translates the analog signals back into digital signals. In addition, the computer needs special instructions in the form of a software communication program.

Cable modems are also available in some areas. In this case, the cable company lays high-speed cable lines that require a special modem as well as a network interface card. This greatly increases the transmission speed. Another alternative is an Integrated Services Digital Network (ISDN) line—a high-speed telephone data line that also greatly increases speed. A digital subscriber line (DSL) is yet another choice, if available. Here users can purchase bandwidth that is potentially 10 times faster than ISDN lines but still slower than cable. ***Bandwidth*** can simply be described as a pipe that moves data from point A to point B. It is the data transfer capacity of a digital communications system.

Another choice for organizations such as businesses or educational institutions is a dedicated leased line that provides digital service between two locations at high speeds. A leased line is a permanent 24-hour connection to a specific location that can only be changed by the telephone company. Leased lines are used to connect local area networks to remote locations or to the Internet through a service provider. Leased lines include T1 and T3 connections. T1 is a digital connection running at 1.55 megabits per second (Mbps) and costs several thousand dollars per month. A T3 connection is equivalent to 30 T1 lines and connections can run up to 45 Mbps. The cost limits the use to major companies or large universities. There are even satellite modems (wireless) that are incredibly fast and at this time quite costly.

The growth of online services has made a modem or a digital connection a necessity. CompuServe, America Online, and Internet service providers—all leading to the information superhighway—make all kinds of information available. These services are the libraries of the future.

R.17 CAPACITY MEASUREMENT—BITS AND BYTES

A computer is made primarily of switches. All it can do is turn a switch on or off: 0 (zero) represents an off state and 1 (one) represents an on state. A ***bit*** (short for *bi*nary digi*t*) is the smallest unit a computer can recognize. Bits are combined in meaningful groups, much as letters of the alphabet are combined to make words. A common grouping is eight bits, called a ***byte***. A byte can be thought of as one word.

Computer capacities, such as RAM and ROM, are measured in bytes, originally grouped by thousands of bytes or ***kilobytes (KB)***, but now by millions of bytes or ***megabytes (MB***, sometimes called ***megs)*** and ***gigabytes (GB***, sometimes called ***gigs)***. A computer is binary, so it works in powers of 2. A kilobyte is 2 to the tenth power (1,024), and K or KB is the symbol for 1,024 bytes. If your computer has 64KB of memory, its actual memory size is 64 x 1,024, or 65,536 bytes. For simplification, KB is rounded off to 1,000, so that 64KB of memory means 64,000 bytes. Rapid technological growth has made megabytes the measuring factor.

You should know the capacity of your computer's memory because it determines how much data the computer can hold. For instance, if you have 32 MB of RAM on your computer and you buy a program that requires 64 MB of RAM, your computer will not have the memory capacity to use that program. Furthermore, if your computer has a hard disk capacity of 100 MB and the application program you buy requires at least 125 MB of space on the hard disk, you won't be able to install the program. Today, of course, a computer that has a hard disk of only 100 MB is very unusual, but the principle remains the same—you have a specific amount of space on your hard disk and you can exceed the size of your hard disk if you have many large programs.

Disk capacity is also measured in bytes. A 3½-inch double-density disk holds 720KB. Because high-density and hard disks hold so much more information, they are also measured in megabytes. A 3½-inch high-density disk holds 1.44 MB. Hard disks vary in size, commonly ranging from 1.2 GB to over 20 GB. Today, most people consider an 8-GB hard disk a very minimum requirement for hard disk space; it has a capacity of over eight billion bytes. Most computer users, when referring to gigabytes, use the term ***gig***. An 8.2-GB hard drive is referred to as an "eight point two gig" hard drive.

R.18 DISKS

Since RAM is volatile and disappears when the power is turned off, ***secondary storage media*** or external storage media are necessary to save information permanently. Disks and disk drives are magnetic media that store data and programs in the form of magnetic impulses. Such media include floppy disks, hard disks, compact discs (CD-ROMs), digital videodiscs (DVDs), removable drives such as Zip and Jaz drives, tapes, and tape cartridges. In the microcomputer world, the most common secondary storage media are floppy disks and hard disks, with removable drives rapidly becoming a standard for most users.

Storing information on a disk is equivalent to storing information in a file cabinet. Like file cabinets, disks store information in files. When the computer needs the information, it goes to the disk, opens a file, reads the information from the disk file into RAM, and works on it. When the computer is finished working on that file, it closes the file and returns (writes) it back to the disk. In most cases, this process does not occur automatically. The application program in use will have instructions that enable the user to save or write to the disk.

R.19 FLOPPY DISKS

Floppy disks serve a dual purpose. First, disks provide a permanent way to hold data. When power is turned off, the disk retains what has been recorded on it. Second, floppy disks are transportable. Programs or data developed on one computer can be used by another merely by inserting the disk into the other computer. If it were not for this capability, programs such as the operating system or other application packages could not be used. Each time you wanted to do some work, you would have to write your own instructions.

Floppy disks come in two sizes: 3½ inch and 5¼ inch. The standard size used to be the 5¼ inch, but now the 3½ inch is the standard. The 5¼-inch floppy disk, technically known as a minifloppy diskette, is rarely used today. The 3½-inch diskette is a microfloppy diskette, but both are commonly referred to as floppy disks. Like a phonograph record, the 5¼-inch floppy disk has a hole (called a hub) in the center so that it can fit on the disk drive's spindle.

The disk drive spins the disk to find information on it or to write information to it. Once a disk is locked into a disk drive, it spins at about 300 revolutions per minute. The 3½-inch disk, made of a circular piece of plastic, polyurethane, or Mylar covered with magnetic oxide, is enclosed in a rigid plastic shell. The 3½-inch 720KB diskette has a plastic shutter–covered hole in the upper-right corner. When the plastic shutter covers the opening, the disk can be written to. When it does not cover the opening, the disk is "write protected" and cannot be written or saved to. The 3½-inch 1.44 MB disk works the same way. It has an opening in the upper-left corner, although this opening does not have a plastic shutter. There is a metal shutter over the area of the disk where the computer writes to the disk. The computer's disk drive opens the shutter only when it needs access. When the disk is not in the drive, the metal shutter is closed. Figure R.7 shows a 3½-inch disk.

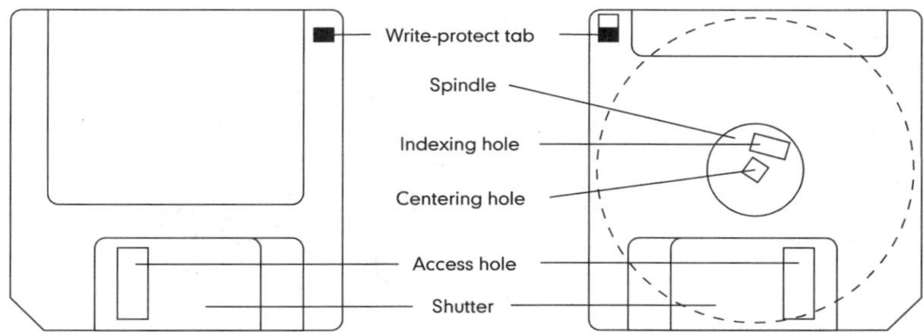

FIGURE R.7 A FLOPPY 3½-INCH DISK

R.20 CD-ROMS

Today, a common transport device for software is a ***compact disc–read-only memory (CD-ROM)***. Borrowed from the music recording business, this disc can hold up to 600 MB of data and retrieves information by laser. Although originally a read-only device, CD-ROM drives are now readily available that both read from and write to a CD (CDRWs). CD-ROM drives are commonplace, and most software companies are distributing their software via compact disc. The newest technology is ***DVD***. It is an enhancement of CD-ROM technology. It provides a new generation of optical-disc storage technology. It encompasses audio, video, and computer data. DVD was designed for multimedia applications with a key goal of being able to store a full-length feature film. DVD is not an acronym. It is a trademark name owned by the DVD Consortium.

R.21 REMOVABLE DISKS

Recently, another type of external storage media has been developed—the removable disk. There are now hard disks that you can remove from a computer, making data portable. There are also other types of removable disk media. Two of the most common are Zip drives and Jaz drives. Zip drives come in two forms: permanent drives that are inside the computer, like a floppy drive, and portable drives that attach to the computer and can be moved from computer to computer easily. Zip drives use a diskette that is somewhat like a floppy disk in appearance. It can hold 100 MB of information—equivalent to more than 70 3½-inch floppy disks. Jaz drives use a cartridge rather than a disk. Currently, Jaz cartridges hold up to two gigabytes of data. The advent of these new disk types makes large amounts of data portable. Zip and Jaz drives read and write data more slowly than a hard disk. Zip drives in particular are becoming the popular alternative to floppy disks for storing and backing up user data.

R.22 HARD DISKS

A ***hard disk***, also known as a fixed disk or a hard drive, is a nonremovable disk that is permanently installed in a system unit (see Figure R.8). A hard disk holds much more information than a removable floppy disk. If a floppy disk can be compared to a file cabinet that holds data and programs, a hard disk can be compared to a room full of file cabinets.

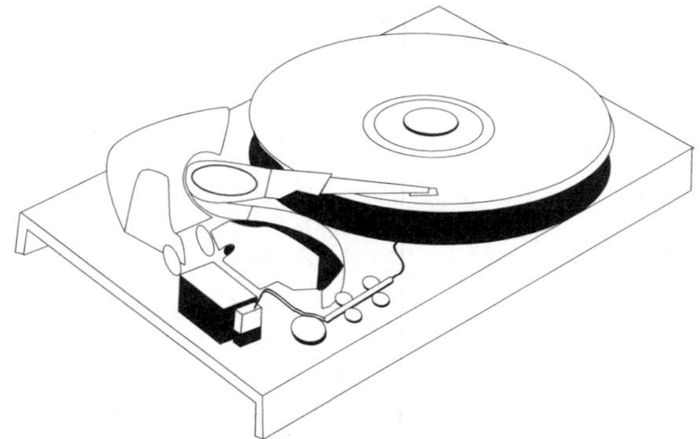

FIGURE R.8 A HARD DISK

A hard disk is composed of two or more rigid platters, usually made of aluminum and coated with oxide, that allow data to be encoded magnetically. Both the platters and the read/write heads are permanently sealed inside a box; the user cannot touch or see the drive or disks. These platters are affixed to a spindle that rotates at about 3,600 revolutions per minute (rpm), although this speed can vary. A hard disk drive is much faster than a standard floppy disk drive. The rapidly spinning disks in the sealed box create air pressure that lifts the recording heads above the surface of the platters. As the platters spin, the read/write heads float on a cushion of air.

Since a hard disk rotates faster than a floppy disk and since the head floats above the surface, the hard disk can store much more data and access it much more quickly than a floppy disk. Today, a common hard disk storage capacity is eight gigabytes.

R.23 DIVIDING A DISK

A disk's structure is essentially the same whether it is a hard disk or a floppy disk. Data is recorded on the surface of a disk in a series of numbered concentric circles known as ***tracks,*** similar to the grooves in a phonograph record. Each track on the disk is a separate circle divided into numbered ***sectors***. The amount of data that can be stored on a disk depends on the density of the disk—the number of tracks and the size of the sectors. Since a hard disk is comprised of several platters, it has an additional measurement, a ***cylinder***. Two or more platters are stacked on top of one another with the tracks aligned. If you connect any one track through all the platters, you have a cylinder (see Figure R.9).

A ***cluster*** is the basic unit of disk storage. Whenever a computer reads from or writes to a disk, it always reads from and writes to a cluster, regardless of the space the data needs. Clusters are always made from adjacent sectors, from one to eight sectors or more. The location and number of sectors per cluster are determined by the software in a process known as formatting.

A disk is a random access medium, which does not mean that the data or programs are randomly arranged on the disk. It means that the head of the disk drive, which reads the disk, does not have to read all the information on the disk to get a specific item. The CPU instructs the head of the disk drive to go directly to the track and sector that holds a specific item.

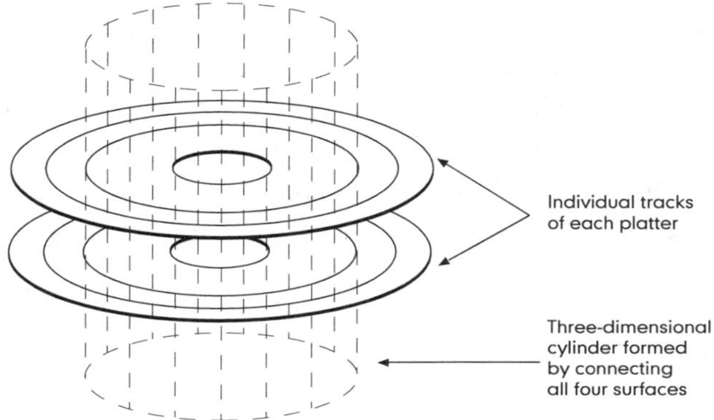

FIGURE R.9 HARD DISK CYLINDERS

R.24 DISK DRIVES

A ***disk drive*** allows information to be written to and read from a disk. All disk drives have read/write heads, which read and write information back and forth between RAM and the disk, much like the ones on tape or video recorders.

A floppy disk drive is the device that holds a floppy disk. The user inserts a floppy disk into a disk drive (see Figure R.10). The hub of the disk fits onto the hub mechanism, which grabs the disk. When the disk drive door is shut, the disk is secured to the hub mechanism. The disk cover remains stationary while the floppy disk rotates. The disk drive head reads and writes information back and forth between RAM and the disk through the exposed head slot. Older disk drives are double-sided and can read from and write to both sides of a disk, but cannot read from or write to a high-density floppy disk. The current generation of high-density disk drives read from and write to both the old style floppy disk and the new style high-density disk.

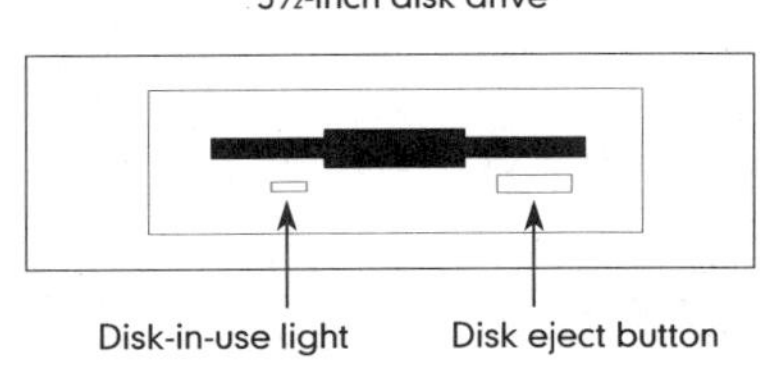

FIGURE R.10 A FLOPPY DISK DRIVE

R.25 DEVICE NAMES

A ***device*** is a place (a piece of hardware) for a computer to send information (write to) or a place from which to receive information (read from). In order for the system to know which device it is supposed to be communicating with at any given time, each device is given a specific and unique name. Device names, which are also known as reserved names, cannot be used for any other purpose. Disk drives are devices. A disk drive name is a letter followed by a colon.

Drive A: is the first floppy disk drive. Drive C: is the first hard disk drive. All other drives are lettered alphabetically from B: to Z:. You must be able to identify which disk drive you are using. There are certain rules that are *usually* followed. If you have two floppy drives that are stacked, the top one is Drive A. If you have two floppy drives side by side, the one on the left is Drive A. Often users have one floppy disk (Drive A), one hard drive (Drive C), a removable drive (Drive D), and a CD-ROM drive (Drive E—although often the CD-ROM drive has an assigned letter near the end of the alphabet, such as R:, to allow for the addition of more drives, both hard and removable, or for network drives). Some common examples are illustrated in Figure R.11.

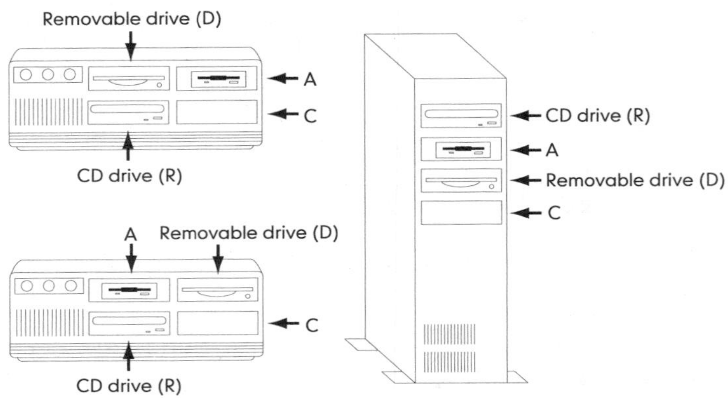

FIGURE R.11 DISK DRIVE CONFIGURATIONS

R.26 SOFTWARE

Up to this point, hardware is what has been discussed. However, software is what makes a computer useful. In fact, without software, hardware has no use. You can think of hardware as a box to run software. Software is the step-by-step instructions that tell the computer what to do. These instructions are called programs. Programs need to be installed or loaded into RAM, so that the CPU can execute them. Programs usually come stored on disks. A program is read into memory from a floppy disk, CD-ROM, or hard disk. Software can also be divided into categories. The most common division is between application software and system software.

Application software, as its name suggests, is a set of instructions, a complete program, that directs the computer to solve a particular problem. Application software solves problems and handles information. It is a program designed to assist the user in the performance of a specific task, such as word processing, accounting, money management, or even games. Application software may also be called software packages, off-the-shelf software, canned software, or just software. There are thousands of commercially available application packages. You may have heard of application software by brand names such as WordPerfect (word processing), Excel (spreadsheet), Quicken (money management), or Doom (game). The reason most people purchase a computer is the availability of application software.

System software is also a set of instructions or programs. These programs coordinate the operations of all the various hardware components. System software is usually supplied by the computer manufacturer because it is necessary to run application software. System software is always computer-oriented rather than user-oriented;

that is, it takes care of what the computer needs so the computer can run application software.

When you purchase a computer, you usually also purchase the operating system with it, preinstalled on the hard disk. The operating system supervises the processing of application programs and all the input/output of the computer. Running a computer is somewhat analogous to producing a concert. The hardware is like the musicians and their instruments. They do not change. The application software is like the score the musicians play, anything from Bach to Ricky Martin. The computer hardware can play any application software from an accounting program to a game. Like the conductor who tells the violins or trumpets when to play and how loudly, the operating system makes the computer work. It is the first and most important program on the computer and *must* be loaded into memory (RAM) before any other program.

Typically, operating systems are comprised of several important programs stored as system files. These include a program that transfers data to and from the disk and into and out of memory and performs other disk-related tasks. Other important programs handle hardware-specific tasks. These programs check such things as whether a key has been pressed, and if it has, they encode it so that the computer can read it and then decode it so that it may be written to the screen. This program also encodes and decodes bits and bytes into letters and words.

The term *operating system* is generic. Brand names for microcomputer operating systems include System 7, Unix, Linux, MS-DOS, and UCSD-P. The most popular operating system for microcomputers is Windows, which Microsoft Corporation developed and owns. Windows is licensed to computer manufacturers, who tailor it to their specific hardware. In addition, users purchase Windows 98 commercially either as an upgrade to Windows 95 or as a complete package (if the user has purchased a computer with no operating system on it).

In 2000, Microsoft introduced both Windows 2000 and Windows Millennium Edition (Windows Me). Windows Me is designed for the home computer user and can be considered an upgrade from Windows 98. Windows 2000 is a family of operating systems that consists of Windows 2000 Server, Windows 2000 Advanced Server, Windows 2000 Datacenter Server, and Windows 2000 Professional. Windows 2000 Server replaces Windows NT 4.0. Incorporating many new features and functions, Windows 2000 Server is powerful, yet easy to manage, and is designed for the small or medium-sized business organization with many computers that need to share data and resources. Windows 2000 Advanced Server is Microsoft's newest version of the Enterprise Edition of Windows NT Server. It is the choice for organizations involved in e-commerce, high-end business applications, a company Internet site, intranet sites, and database programs. Windows 2000 Datacenter Server is the newest member of the Windows server family. It is the operating system for businesses that need the highest degree of scalability. It is intended for those businesses and Internet service providers (ISPs) that manage large Internet and intranet sites. Windows 2000 Professional replaces Windows NT 4.0 Workstation, incorporating many new features and functions. Windows 2000 Professional is an operating system that is designed for corporate and high-end users who want a robust and powerful operating environment. It is powerful and easy to use, and provides a great deal of flexibility for the corporate desktop. It is especially strong in the area of mobile computing (for those with notebook computers).

Most people who use a computer are interested in application software. They want programs that are easy to use. If you are going to use a computer and run application packages, you are going to need to know how to use the operating system first. No application program can be used without an operating system. Since Windows 2000 Professional is the newest microcomputer operating system in use for high-end and business users today, this textbook is devoted to teaching the concepts of the operating system in general and Windows 2000 Professional operations in particular.

R.27 OPERATING SYSTEM FUNDAMENTALS

Windows 2000 Professional is a program that is always working. No computer hardware can work unless it has an operating system in RAM. When you ***boot the system***, you load the operating system software into RAM.

Some of the operating system (OS) software is built into the hardware. When you turned on the computer or "powered up," the computer would not know what to do if there were no program directing it. The read-only memory chip called ROM-BIOS (read-only memory–Basic Input Output System), abbreviated to RIOS, is built into the hardware of the microcomputer system. ROM-BIOS programs provide the interface between the hardware and the operating system.

When you turn on the computer, the power goes first to ROM-BIOS. The first set of instructions is to run a self-test to check the hardware. The program checks RAM and the equipment attached to the computer. Thus, before getting started, the user knows whether or not there is a hardware failure. Once the self-test is completed successfully, the program loads the operating system.

When the operating system loads, ROM-BIOS checks to see if a disk drive is installed. In today's computers, it is possible to tell the computer where you want it to load the operating system from. It can go first to the A drive to see if there is a disk there. If it finds none, it can then go to the C drive. The OS looks for a special program called the ***boot record***. A computer can also be set up to boot from a CD-ROM or from another peripheral disk drive, such as a Zip or Jaz drive. These drives are attached to the computer by an internal interface card or a parallel port. If ROM-BIOS does not find the boot record in any of the drives it was set to look at or if there is something wrong with the boot record, you get an error message. If the ROM-BIOS program does find the proper boot record, it reads the record from the disk into RAM and turns control over to this program. The boot record is also a program that executes. Its job is to read into RAM the rest of the operating system, in essence, pulling the system up by its bootstraps. Thus, one "boots" the computer instead of merely turning it on.

The operating system files loaded into RAM manage the resources and primary functions of the computer, freeing application programs from worrying about how the document gets from the keyboard to RAM and from RAM to the screen. This whole process can be considered analogous to driving an automobile. Most of us use our cars to get from point A to point B. We would not like it if every time we wanted to drive we first had to open the hood and attach the proper cables to the battery and to all the other parts that are necessary to start the engine. The operating system is the engine of the computer that lets the user run the application as if driving a car.

R.28 WHY WINDOWS 2000 PROFESSIONAL?

Previously, the most popular operating system was MS-DOS. MS-DOS is a character-based operating system. In order to use it, you had to key in commands and could not use a pointing device such as a mouse. Each application program running under this operating system was installed as a separate entity—there was no sharing of resources, such as a printer, and no ability to run more than one application at a time.

In 1990 Microsoft released the first successful version of Windows, version 3.0—an "environment" that worked between the operating system and application programs. Windows introduced the PC user to a ***graphical user interface***, referred to as a ***GUI***. In the 3.0 version of Windows, commands could be issued by clicking a mouse. Peripheral devices such as printers were installed in Windows and were thus available to all the applications. Application programs were written to run under Windows. Windows offered the advantage of being able to run more than one program at a time in order to share data between programs. Windows for Workgroups was next introduced, which had built-in networking features for a peer-to-peer network. The last releases of these versions of Windows were Windows 3.1 and Windows for Workgroups 3.11.

In 1995, Microsoft introduced the Windows 95 operating system, an operating system that no longer required DOS as a stand-alone operating system. DOS and Windows became integrated into one operating system. The change from Windows 3.x to Windows 95 was dramatic. One of the biggest improvements was the change from a 16-bit operating system to a 32-bit operating system. This change took advantage of the power and speed of new microprocessors. Built with a new architecture (design), Windows 95 was faster, handled computer resources better, improved the system capacity to run more applications, and was more robust. Being robust means, among other things, that if an application program does not work, the system does not crash (cease to function). Instead, Windows 95 allowed you the opportunity to close an aberrant program so that you could continue your work.

Windows 95 introduced plug and play. Prior to the introduction of the Windows 95 plug-and-play standard, adding devices to a PC was a painful process. A lack of coordination between the hardware and software caused devices to conflict with one another. Furthermore, application software had no idea what devices were on the system. The different bus standards for different devices complicated the issue further. Plug and play let devices "talk" to Windows 95, which then handled how programs used the devices. This feature allowed users to buy new devices, plug them into the computer, and allow Windows 95 to handle the "dirty work."

Although the design of Windows 95 was important in terms of new hardware, for most users the change that they saw was in the user interface. The Windows 95 user interface was intended to be more intuitive and easier to use. Features like wizards led you through things you did not know how to do. Windows 95 also allowed you to use both the right and left mouse buttons and provided context-sensitive menus at a mere click of the mouse.

The move to Windows 98 from Windows 95 was less drastic. Although the core operating system was improved for better performance, Windows 98 was essentially the same. In many ways it looked the same as Windows 95. What Windows 98 did was point the user into a new direction—the Internet. A basic design consideration for Windows 98 was a consistent visual and functional view of your computer system. Windows 98 and Internet Explorer version 5.0 (the Windows 98 Web browser) were intended to be integrated, so that many of the Windows 98 functions worked like a Web browser. This feature was designed to make users' transitions from their local computers to the Internet seamless and easy. There was another release of Windows called Windows 98 SE (Special Edition).

Windows Millennium Edition is designed specifically for home users. Windows Me is intended to make using a computer easier. Now that it is more common for home users to have more than one computer, Windows Me gives you the ability to network all of your home computers. It also lets you communicate more efficiently over the Internet, and allows you to work with multimedia content such as photos, videos, and music. There are many wizards, and Help has been improved, which makes troubleshooting problems easier. It includes a movie-maker that lets you transfer video. It supports Universal Plug and Play, a developing technology that will allow future intelligent devices (such as specialized VCRs and thermostats) to be controlled from your computer.

Windows 2000 Professional is the mainstream Microsoft desktop operating system for businesses of all sizes. Its key features include better reliability, ease of use, security, networking capabilities, and mobile computing. Windows 2000 Professional is considered to have industrial-strength, rock-solid reliability. It rarely crashes. Not only is it easier to use with the desktop interface, with the best features incorporated from Windows 98 and Windows NT Workstation, but also it is much easier to install hardware and software to. The security feature is very important, as it provides a secure file system. It also provides a built-in safeguard called Windows File Protection, which prevents system files from being deleted or altered by users. It has increased networking capability. And it is much easier to use for mobile users.

The Windows 2000 Professional GUI is highly customizable. The user can choose to have the desktop look identical to that of Windows 95/98 or to have it totally customized to each user's preferences. This textbook is a guide to understanding and using the command line in the Windows 2000 Professional operating system.

R.29 HARDWARE REQUIREMENTS FOR WINDOWS 2000 PROFESSIONAL

Windows 2000 Professional is a powerful operating system. Although you can run most of your old programs under Windows 2000 Professional, you will find yourself buying the new, improved versions of your favorite application programs. These programs will be powerful and large. To run Windows 2000 Professional, you need at least a 133-MHz or faster processor, at least 64 MB of memory, a high-density disk drive, a CD-ROM or DVD drive, and at least a 2-GB hard disk drive with at least 650 MB available. Furthermore, you need a VGA monitor and VGA display adapter. You also need a pointing device such as a mouse or trackball. With this hardware, you can run Windows 2000 Professional and applications written for Windows 2000 Professional. This configuration is the absolute minimum.

A desirable configuration for Windows 2000 Professional is listed below:

Processor	Intel Pentium III 500 MHz or better
Cache	512KB internal L2 cache
RAM	128 MB
Hard drive	14.4 GB with at least 1.5 GB free

Floppy drive	3½ inch
Removable drive	Zip drive
Monitor	SVGA, 19 inch, high resolution, noninterlaced
Graphics	Video card with at least 32 MB of memory
CD	48X CD-ROM or better, DVD if you play many games
Modem	56K, unless you choose to use a cable or DSL modem
Sound system	Sound card and speakers
Input devices	Keyboard and mouse

In computers, and especially in Windows 2000 Professional, more is better—a faster processor, more memory, and more disk space.

R.30 NETWORKS

Today, it is likely that you will be using a network in a work or lab environment. A ***network*** is two or more connected computers, and it usually has various peripheral devices such as printers. A network allows users to communicate with each other and to share information and devices. Special operating system software and hardware are required for networking. Network software permits information exchange among users; the most common uses are electronic mail (email) and the sharing of files. With email, users can send and receive messages within the network system. Sharing files allows users to share information.

There are two kinds of networks. A ***local area network (LAN)*** encompasses a small area such as one office. The hardware components, such as the server, the terminals, and the printers, are directly connected by cables. (See Figure R.12.) A ***wide area network (WAN)*** connects computers over a much larger area such as from building to building, from state to state, or even worldwide. Hardware components of a WAN communicate over telephone lines, fiber-optic cables, or satellites. The Internet is an example of a WAN.

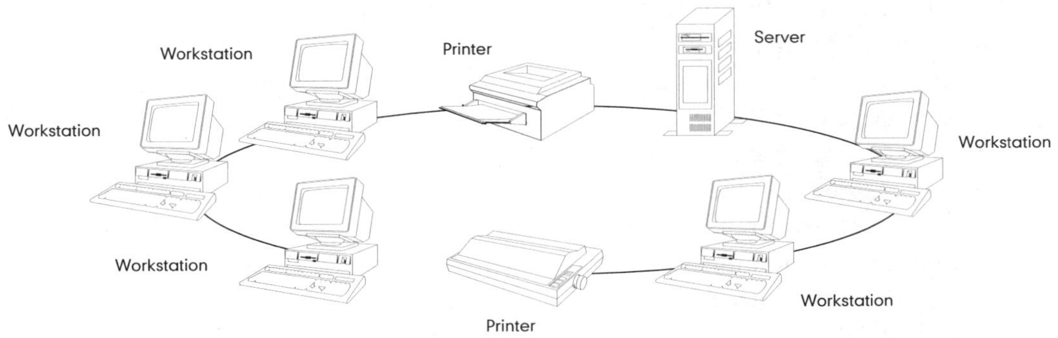

FIGURE R.12 A TYPICAL NETWORK CONFIGURATION

CHAPTER SUMMARY

This chapter discussed the fundamental operations of a computer. All computers function the same way. Data is input, processed, and stored. The results are the output. Hardware components include the system unit, the monitor, the keyboard, and the printer. The central processing unit (CPU) is the brain of the computer and can comprehend and carry out instructions sent to it by a program. RAM (random access memory) is the workspace of the computer. RAM is volatile. Cache memory is high-speed memory that stores the most recently used data. ROM (read-only memory) is a chip with programs written on it. ROM is not volatile. It usually holds the startup routines of a computer. CD-ROM drives are used to import data and install software from compact discs.

Adapter cards are printed circuit boards that allow a user to add various peripheral devices to a computer. Peripherals are devices that are attached to the system unit. All of these features are integrated by I/O buses, which are the connections through which data travels. The most common input devices are the keyboard and the mouse. The most common output devices are the monitor and the printer. Modems allow the transmission of data over telephone lines and allow computers to communicate.

Floppy disks, hard disks, removable disks, and compact discs are means of permanent storage for data and programs. A floppy disk is a piece of plastic inside a jacket. A hard disk is made of rigid platters that are permanently sealed inside a box. A compact disc can handle up to 600 MB of data, which makes it a great device for transporting information. All disks are divided into numbered tracks and sectors so that a computer can locate information.

A floppy disk drive is the device into which a floppy disk is inserted so that a computer can read from or write to it. Disk drives have reserved names that consist of a letter of the alphabet followed by a colon. The left or top disk drive is known as Drive A:. The first hard disk drive is known as Drive C:.

A byte represents a single character. The capacity of some floppy disks is measured in bytes, usually thousands of bytes, or kilobytes (KB). The capacity of RAM, ROM, and high-density floppy disks is measured in millions of bytes, or megabytes (MB), often referred to as megs. Hard drive capacity is referred to in gigabytes (GB).

Software is step-by-step instructions that tell the computer what to do. These instructions are called programs. Programs are loaded into RAM, where the CPU executes each instruction. When a program is working in RAM, the program is being run or executed. Programs are stored on disks and loaded into RAM from disks. Software is divided into application software and system software. Application software solves problems, handles information, and is user-oriented. System software coordinates the operation of the hardware, is mandatory for running application software, and is computer-oriented. An operating system is comprised of programs, called system software, that perform the functions necessary to control the operations of the computer. The operating system interfaces with the user and tells the computer what to do.

Networks are two or more computers connected together that usually share peripheral devices such as printers. There are two basic types of networks: LANs and WANs. A LAN (local area network) is usually connected by cables within a small area. A WAN (wide area network) connects computers over a much larger area, from building to building or worldwide.

Windows 2000 Professional, the newest business operating system in use today, is a graphical operating system that is user friendly, which makes the use of operating system commands easier.

KEY TERMS

adapter card
application software
bandwidth
bit
boot record
boot the system
bus
byte
cache memory
card
central processing unit (CPU)
cluster
compact disc–read-only memory (CD-ROM)
controller
cylinder
data
device
disk drive
dot pitch
DVD
dynamic RAM (DRAM)
expansion slot
floppy disk
gig
gigabyte (GB)
graphical user interface (GUI)
hard disk
hardware
impact printer
inkjet printer
interface card
interlaced
kilobyte (KB)
laser printer
local area network (LAN)
megabyte (MB)
megahertz (MHz)
memory
modem
monitor
motherboard
mouse
network
nonimpact printer
noninterlaced
parallel port
peripheral device
pixel
port
program
random access memory (RAM)
read-only memory (ROM)
resolution
ROM-BIOS
secondary storage media
sector
serial port
software
static RAM (SRAM)
system board
system software
track
trackball
universal serial bus (USB)
wide area network (WAN)
Wintel

DISCUSSION QUESTIONS

1. Define hardware.
2. Define software.
3. What is data?
4. What is meant by the system configuration?
5. Describe a typical microcomputer configuration.
6. What are interface cards? How may they be used?
7. What is the purpose and function of a bus?
8. Compare and contrast RAM, cache, and ROM.
9. Why are parallel and serial ports necessary? What are they used for?
10. List two input devices and two output devices and briefly explain how these work.
11. What purposes do disks serve?
12. What is the difference between disk storage and memory capacity?
13. What is a CD-ROM? A DVD?
14. What is the difference between a hard disk and a floppy disk?
15. What are tracks and sectors? Where are they found?
16. What is a cluster? What is it comprised of?
17. What is a device? Give three examples of devices.

18. Identify and define two types of modem connections.
19. Compare and contrast floppy disks, removable disks, CD-ROMs, DVDs, and hard disks.
20. Define an operating system.
21. Compare and contrast application software and system software.
22. Can application packages run without an operating system? Why or why not?
23. What is the function of an operating system?
24. What are the advantages of using Windows 2000 Professional?
25. What is the purpose and function of a network?

TRUE/FALSE QUESTIONS

For each question, circle the letter T if the statement is true or the letter F if the statement is false.

T F 1. The system board contains components such as the CPU and RAM.

T F 2. An interface card is a printed circuit board that enables a computer to use a peripheral device.

T F 3. A monitor is a common input device.

T F 4. A hard disk is a read-only device.

T F 5. By themselves, the hardware components of a computer can do nothing.

COMPLETION QUESTIONS

Write the correct answer in each blank space.

6. A(n) ________________ is a common path across which data can travel within a computer.
7. The components of a complete computer system are also called the ________________.
8. Frequently used RAM data is stored in ________________, which speeds up the process of data access.
9. The two most common ports available on computers are ________________ and ________________ ports.
10. People purchase a computer because of the availability of ________________.

MATCHING QUESTIONS

Match each term in the left-hand column with the proper definition in the right-hand column.

11. Hardware
12. Software
13. Floppy disk drive
14. RAM
15. Booting the system

a. Instructions that tell a computer what operations to perform
b. Self-diagnostic routine
c. Measures a disk's capacity
d. Tangible, physical part of a computer
e. Device where a floppy disk is inserted
f. Powering on a computer and loading the operating system
g. Workspace of a computer

MULTIPLE CHOICE QUESTIONS

For each question, write the letter for the correct answer in the blank space.

16. The physical components of a computer are called
    - a. software.
    - b. firmware.
    - c. hardware.
    - d. none of the above

17. Memory that disappears when the computer's power is turned off is considered
    - a. volatile.
    - b. nonvolatile.
    - c. vital.
    - d. nonvital.

18. The central processing unit
    - a. is the workspace of the computer.
    - b. comprehends and carries out instructions sent to it by a program.
    - c. both a and b
    - d. neither a nor b

19. Disks are divided into numbered
    - a. tracks and sectors.
    - b. bits and bytes.
    - c. RAM and ROM.
    - d. none of the above

20. An example of an input device is a
    - a. monitor.
    - b. keyboard.
    - c. mouse.
    - d. both b and c

APPLICATION ASSIGNMENT—BRIEF ESSAY

You are going to buy a computer system. You have a budget of $2,500. Write a report listing the features and specifications of the computer system you would like to purchase. (Do not include a printer in your system.) Be very specific in regards to the amount of RAM, the size of the hard drive or drives, the number and type of floppy drives and removable drives, the monitor type, etc.

CHAPTER

1

GETTING STARTED WITH THE OPERATING SYSTEM

LEARNING OBJECTIVES

After completing this chapter, you will be able to:

1. Define "operating system."
2. Define "enhancements."
3. Explain the function and purpose of OS version numbers.
4. List some of the types of system configurations.
5. Explain the need and procedure for booting the system.
6. Explain the function of disk files.
7. Explain the function of and rules for file specifications.
8. List and explain the importance of the two types of computer files.
9. Describe the function and purpose of commands.
10. Compare and contrast internal and external commands.
11. Describe four key groups and explain the purpose of each group of keys.
12. Explain the function and purpose of the DIR, VER, and CLS commands.
13. Explain the purpose of and the procedure for using the DATE and TIME commands.
14. Explain the legal and ethical ramifications of copying disks that were not purchased.
15. Explain the purpose and function of the DISKCOPY command.
16. Explain the necessary steps to end a work session.

STUDENT OUTCOMES

1. Identify your system configuration.
2. Boot the system.
3. Use the DIR command to display the files on the screen.
4. Cancel a command.

5. Use the VER command to determine which version of DOS is being used.
6. Use the CLS command to clear the screen.
7. Use the DATE and TIME commands to set or change the date and time on the computer.
8. Make a copy of a disk.
9. End a computer work session.

CHAPTER OVERVIEW

Most people who use computers are really interested in application software. They want programs that are easy to use and that help them solve specific problems. However, before you can use application software, you must know at least the basics of using the operating system. No computer can work without an operating system in RAM. The Windows operating system takes care of mandatory functions for computer operations such as handling the input and output of the computer, managing computer resources, and running application software. It enables the user to communicate with the computer.

In this chapter you will learn about loading the operating system into the computer, familiarize yourself with the keyboard, use some basic commands, make a copy of the ACTIVITIES disk to use in future activities, learn your system configuration, and identify the version of Windows you are using.

1.1 WHAT IS AN OPERATING SYSTEM?

An ***operating system*** is a software program. If you have a microcomputer, commonly referred to as a PC, that conforms to the standards developed by IBM and uses a microprocessor in the Intel family, you are probably using a version of the Windows operating system. In fact, these computers are sometimes called Wintel machines because they use the Intel processor and run the Windows operating system.

You need to load the Windows operating system (the OS) into memory (RAM) before you can use other software programs. The OS is in charge of the hardware components of the computer. You, the user, communicate what you want the computer to do through the OS. These commands are issued by pointing and clicking in the GUI or by keying in commands such as TYPE or CLS at the command line prompt.

1.2 VERSIONS OF THE OPERATING SYSTEM (OS)

Microsoft periodically releases new versions of the OS to take advantage of new technology. These new upgrades contain enhancements. The term ***enhancements*** simply means that more functions and/or commands are available. In addition, new versions of software and operating systems fix problems, called ***bugs***, that appeared in earlier versions. To keep track of these versions, each new version is assigned a number. The first version of Windows 95 was Windows 95 4.00.950, released in 1995. The last Windows 95 version was 95 4.00.1111, known as Windows 95B or OSR2. Also available is a major update of Windows 95 called Windows 98, SE version 4.10.1998. The most recent version of Windows is Windows Millennium Edition, referred to as Windows Me (Version 4.90.3000). These versions of Windows are and were primarily used on personal desktop computers.

Windows NT Workstation was a desktop operating system designed primarily for software developers and "power users," such as engineers who worked on large, powerful applications such as CAD (Computer-Aided Design). Microsoft's network operating system, Windows NT Server, was primarily used in large corporate environments where it provided network administrators with the ability to manage many networked computers with various security needs.

Windows 2000 Professional is the replacement for Windows NT Workstation 4. It can be used as a desktop operating system in a networked environment or as a standalone operating system. Windows 2000 Server and Windows 2000 Advanced Server are replacing Windows NT Server in the corporate environment.

This text will focus on Windows 2000 Professional, though it is generally applicable to all versions of the Windows operating system. It is assumed in this textbook that Windows 2000 Professional is installed on your computer. If you are working on your own computer and have not installed or upgraded to Windows 2000 Professional, refer to the documentation that came with the Windows software so you can initiate the installation or upgrade. If you are in a laboratory environment, a version of Windows will be available for you.

1.3 OVERVIEW OF FILES AND DISKS

You need a way to store information permanently. In the microcomputer world, the primary way to save data and programs permanently is to store them on a disk. After you have booted your computer, the OS reads the programs or data it needs from the disk into its memory. However, in order for Windows to find this information, it has to have a way of organizing it, which it does by keeping programs and data in files on the disk. Just as you organize your written work in files, Windows organizes computer information in disk files.

A ***disk file*** is much like a file folder stored in a file cabinet. The file cabinet is the floppy disk or the hard disk. A file consists of related information stored on the disk in a "folder" or directory with a unique name. Information with which a computer works is contained and stored in files on the disk. (See Figure 1.1.)

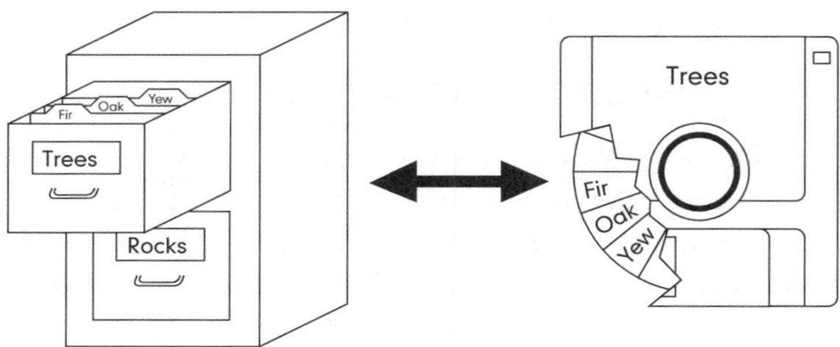

FIGURE 1.1 DISKS AND FILES

1.4 FILE NAMES, FILE TYPES, AND FOLDERS

Because computers must follow very specific rules, there is a specific format for file names. Technically, a file name is called the ***file specification***. The first rule is that the file specification must be unique. Second, the file specification is broken into two parts, a ***file name*** and a ***file extension***. The file name typically describes or identifies the file, and the file extension typically identifies the kind of data in the file. Since the term "file specification" is rather awkward, most people simply refer to the file name, meaning both the file name and its extension. In versions of the OS before Windows, referred to simply as DOS, the file name size was limited by what was called the 8.3 (eight-dot-three) rule, which was a limit of eight characters for the file name and three characters for the file extension). In Windows, the 8.3 rule is gone. Now file names can have a maximum of 255 characters, referred to as LFNs (long file names). The three-letter file extension, known as the file type, remains in Windows. However, some software does not recognize long file names (LFNs), and some network operating systems have difficulty dealing with them. Because storing long file names takes additional space, consider using the 8.3 rule when saving to floppy disks with limited capacity.

There are two major types of computer files: ***data files*** and ***program files***. Data files contain information that is usually generated by an application program. Most often, only an application program can use a data file directly. Program files are application programs that allow a user to perform specific tasks, for example, a payroll program that lets you create and maintain a payroll system for a company.

You do not purchase a computer to run the Windows operating system. You purchase a computer so that you may use application packages to help with tasks such as gaining access to the Internet, writing letters, managing your checkbook, doing your taxes, or creating a budget. If you needed to employ someone to do these tasks for you, you might go to a temporary employment agency and hire a secretary to write your letters or an accountant to manage your checkbook and taxes.

In the computer world, you purchase application packages, so that you can do the work. These application packages fall into generic categories such as word-processing or spreadsheet programs. In the same way you would choose a specific temporary employee such as Mr. Woo for your letter writing, in the computer world, you choose application packages by their names. They have brand names such as WordPerfect, Quicken, or Lotus 1-2-3. These application packages are "employees" you choose to do the work.

In order for these application programs to do work, they must be copied from where they are installed (usually the hard drive, or perhaps the network drive) into RAM, the workspace of the computer. They are "temporary" employees because you call on them only when you need to do a specific task that they can accomplish. Windows is like an office manager who goes to the disk to get the correct file and place it in RAM. This process is known as loading the program from disk into memory. Windows then lets the program do its job. This process is known as executing the program. Program files are step-by-step instructions that direct the computer to do something.

Even though WordPerfect can create letters for anyone, you are interested only in the letters *you* create—the information that *you* want. Once you create your data, you also want to keep it. Remember, all the work occurs in RAM, and RAM is volatile (temporary). In order to keep information permanently, you direct WordPerfect to write (save) the information to a disk as a data file. WordPerfect actually does not save the data; instead, it turns to the operating system, which does the actual work of writing the file to disk. When you need to retrieve the information to alter it, WordPerfect again turns to the OS to retrieve the file. Windows then reads the disk to retrieve the appropriate data file and gives it to WordPerfect.

A unique name must be assigned to each file so that it can be identified by the OS. Program files have predetermined names such as WPWIN.EXE for WordPerfect, QW.EXE for Quicken, or 123.EXE for Lotus 1-2-3. WPWIN is the file name and .EXE is the file extension. Clicking on the application icon tells Windows to retrieve the program from the disk and place it in memory so you may work. When you install the application program you wish to use, it creates the icon, which actually is a reference to the name and location of the program file so that Windows can find and load it. Data files, on the other hand, are named by you, the user. You may call the files anything you want. For instance, a file name for a letter to your sister might be SISTER.LET or a name for your budget file might be BUDGET97.WK1. Typically, in the Windows environment, application programs assign a file extension such as .DOC or .WK1 to identify the data file as a document file belonging to a specific application program.

The above file specifications conform to the older DOS limitations of eight characters for a name and three characters for an extension. In Windows, the data file could have been named BUDGET FOR 1997.WK1. However, if you had an older version of Lotus 1-2-3 that was not able to handle long file names, Lotus would have generated an error message to you saying that the file name was invalid.

A file name is mandatory, but a file extension is not. A file name typically identifies the file, such as WP for word processing or SISTER for your letter. The file name tells you about the file, and the file type (extension) identifies the kind of data in a file. For instance, .EXE is reserved for programs so that Windows knows the file is a worker; in a program like WPWIN.EXE, the extension .EXE stands for executable code.

Data files are generated by specific application programs, and the information or data in them can be altered or viewed only within the application package. You would not give your tax information to an administrative assistant to make changes. You would give that data to the accountant, who knows how to make the changes.

Data files do not stand alone. They can be used only in conjunction with an application program. Again, the job of the operating system is to fetch and carry both program files and data files in and out of memory and to and from the disk (reading and writing). In addition, since the OS is the "office manager," you may also use it to do office-related tasks such as copying or deleting a file. The OS does not know what is in the file folder, nor can it make changes to the information in the file folder. It can manipulate the file folder by such tasks as copying the information in it or throwing it away.

To assist you in organizing your information further, the OS can divide or structure your disks into what are called folders or directories. Technically they are subdirectories, but the terms *directory, subdirectory,* and *folder* are used interchangeably. Folders allow you to group related program or data files so they will be easy to locate later. For instance, all the files related to a spreadsheet program such as Lotus 1-2-3 could be stored in a folder named LOTUS. You might then group any data files you created with Lotus, such as BUDGET93.WK1 and APRIL97.WK1, in another folder called BUDGETS.

A primary directory (root) is automatically created when you prepare a disk to store information. It is named and called the root directory, but its symbol is \ (the backslash). You can create additional folders (subdirectories) for storing related files. Directories, including the root, will be discussed in full detail in later chapters.

1.5 IDENTIFYING YOUR SYSTEM CONFIGURATION

All computers come with disk drives: the floppy disk drive, the hard or fixed disk drive, usually a CD-ROM drive, and sometimes a large capacity removable drive, such as a Zip drive or a DVD drive. Today there are many ways that computer systems can be configured:

- One hard disk drive, one CD-ROM drive, and one floppy disk drive.
- One hard disk drive, one CD-ROM drive, one floppy disk drive, and one Zip drive.
- Two hard disk drives, one CD-ROM drive, and one floppy disk drive.
- One hard disk drive, one CD-ROM drive, one read-write CD-ROM drive, and one floppy disk drive.

The possibilities are numerous. Computers can be configured to suit the needs of the individual user.

1.6 COMPUTER CONFIGURATION GUIDE

This textbook is based on a specific computer configuration, the one that is most common to PC users.

Hard disk	C:
Floppy disk drive to be used	A:
Location of Windows utility files	C:\WINNT\SYSTEM32
Windows files	C:\WINNT
Windows Profiles	C:\WINNT\PROFILES or C:\Documents and Settings
Displayed screen prompt for Drive C	C:\>
Activities folder on Drive C	C:\WINDOSBK
Displayed prompt for floppy disk	A:\>

Note: If you install Windows 2000 Professional as an upgrade from another version of Windows, your system files may be in the WINDOWS directory, not in the WINNT directory as shown here. Your Windows directory could have another name as well such as WIN2K or WINDOWS2000, depending on who installed the software.

If your computer configuration conforms to the above, you can follow the textbook without making any adjustments. However, computer configuration setups vary, particularly on network systems. Thus, your system configuration may be different, and you might have to substitute what is on your system for the setups used in this textbook. Complete the following table so that the substitutions will be readily identifiable for your computer:

Description	Book Reference	Your System
Hard drive	C:	
Floppy drive	A:	
Location of OS utility files	C:\WINNT\SYSTEM32	
Windows 2000 Professional files	C:\WINNT\PROFILES or C:\Documents and Settings	
Displayed prompt for Drive C	C:\>	
Activities folder on Drive C	C:\WINDOSBK	
Prompt for floppy disk	A:\>	

1.7 BOOTING THE SYSTEM

You need to know how to get the operating system files from the bootable disk into memory (RAM) so that you can use the computer. With the Windows operating system, this happens automatically when you turn the system on. This process is known as ***booting the system***. These files reside on the hard disk; however, these files can be placed on floppy disks so that you can boot the computer with minimum system files from Drive A. The following activity allows you to have your first hands-on experience with the computer. You are going to load Windows or "boot the system."

Note: Since laboratory procedures will vary, check with your instructor before proceeding with these activities. A special process may be needed to boot the system if you are on a network.

1.8 ACTIVITY: BOOTING THE SYSTEM

Step 1 Check to see if the monitor has a separate on/off switch. If it does, turn on the monitor.

Step 2 Be sure there is no disk in Drive A. If your Drive A has a door that shuts or latches, be sure it is open. (Remember that your instructions may be different if you are booting to a network. You will need to get your user name and password from your instructor if you are in a lab environment.) Power on the computer by locating the **Power** button and pressing it. The **Power** button location can vary, depending on the design of the computer.

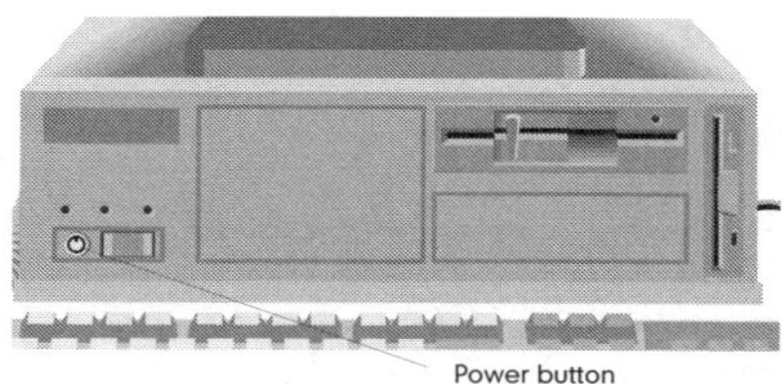

FIGURE 1.2 POWERING ON THE COMPUTER

WHAT'S HAPPENING? In Windows 2000 Professional, the startup sequence is as follows:

- Power-on self-test (POST)
- Initial startup process
- Bootstrap loader process
- Operating system selection if the user has more than one operating system installed
- Hardware detection
- Hardware configuration selection if the user is using more than one hardware profile
- Kernel loading
- Operating system logon process

The POST determines the amount of memory and checks that the hardware devices are present and working. Then the computer system BIOS (Basic Input Output System) begins the process of starting the operating system. The normal search order is for the system to first look in Drive A and then, if no disk is present in Drive A, to look to Drive C. The BIOS looks for the active partition of the hard drive and reads the MBR (Master Boot Record) into memory. The MBR then looks for the system partition information. The Windows 2000 partition boot sector reads the file system to find the bootstrap loader. It then loads the bootstrap loader into memory and starts the bootstrap loader (ntldr—NT loader). The hidden system file NTLDR uses another file, BOOT.INI, which identifies the location of the default operating system to load or gives you a choice of which operating system you wish to use if you have multiple operating systems installed. The NTLDR loads and executes another hidden system file called NTDETECT.COM. This file checks your hardware so that Windows 2000 Professional can configure the computer correctly. Then the core components of the operating system are loaded into memory, such as the kernel (NTOSKRNEL.EXE) and the Hardware Abstraction Layer (HAL.DLL). Lastly, the Windows subsystem automatically starts WINLOGON.EXE, which presents the dialog box for you to enter your user name and password. Depending on how your system is configured, you may first have to press **Ctrl** + **Alt** + **Delete** in order to log on to the system.

Step 3 Press **Ctrl** + **Alt** + **Delete** if necessary.

Step 4 Enter your user name and password.

Step 5 Click **OK**.

WHAT'S HAPPENING? You have successfully booted the system.

1.9 SHUTTING DOWN THE SYSTEM

It is very important that you shut down Windows 2000 Professional computers correctly every time. When you go through the shut-down process, Windows writes certain information to the disk. If you simply turn off the computer, Windows will not have an opportunity to take care of the process it needs to go through to shut down. Simply turning off the computer could "crash" the system and it might be unable to boot the next time it is turned on.

1.10 ACTIVITY: THE WINDOWS SHUT-DOWN PROCEDURE

Step 1 Click the **Start** button on the lower-left corner of the screen. ("Click" means to place the point of the arrow over the word **Start** and press the left button on the mouse once.)

Step 2 Click **Shut Down**.

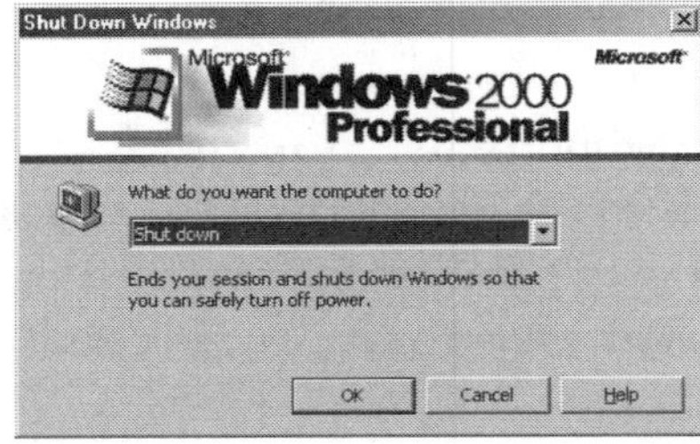

WHAT'S HAPPENING? Your dialog box may vary, depending on the version of Windows you are using or if you are on a network or have set up profiles. If Shut down does not appear in the drop-down window, click and hold on the down arrow and slide down to shut down.

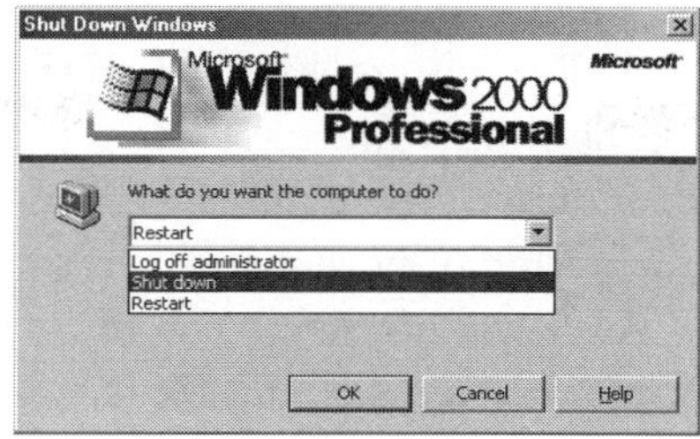

Step 3 Click **OK**.

On many computers today, the power will shut off automatically. On a computer that automatically shuts down, the screen will simply go blank, and you may not have to complete Step 4. On others, you will see a screen similar to the following:

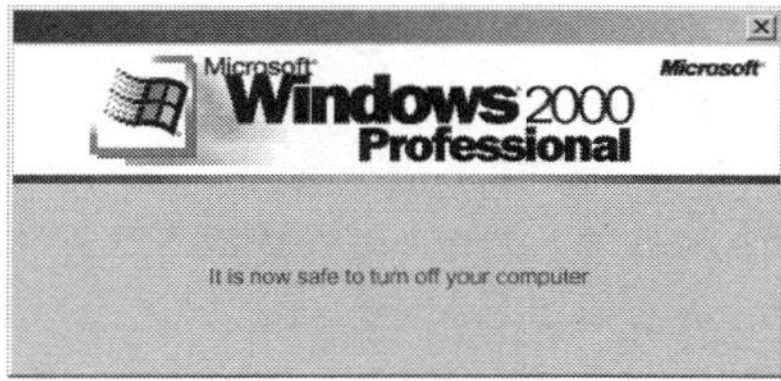

Step 4 Turn off the **Power** switch. Turn off the monitor.

WHAT'S HAPPENING? You have successfully shut down Windows.

1.11 WHY DOS?

Since Windows is a GUI (graphical user interface), when you boot the system, you open the desktop with icons, menus, and pictures. You will run your programs and open your data files by clicking or double-clicking icons or menu choices. You accomplish tasks such as copying a file by opening the Windows Explorer window, selecting a file with your mouse, and dragging it to a different location, a procedure known as drag-and-drop. These are the reasons why a GUI is so popular. It is "user friendly."

In character-based operating systems, with DOS being the most common, all you would see on the screen after you booted would be a prompt such as C:\>—no picture, no icons, no drag-and-drop. In order to accomplish any task, you need to know what command to use. For instance, to copy a file in a character-based operating system, you would need to key in **COPY *THIS.FIL THAT.FIL***. This means you would need to know the command and how to use it. Hardly as easy as a drag-and-drop operation!

Why then, you may ask yourself, would you ever need to learn the "hard, archaic way" of using your computer when you can easily use the new, improved way? In fact, if you talk to many people, they would say to you, "DOS is dead; long live Windows." They would also say, "You don't need to know DOS anymore because it is all Windows." Those people are only somewhat right. They are correct in saying that DOS as a stand-alone operating system is dead. A new computer comes with Windows as its operating system, not DOS. But they are wrong in assuming that you do not need to know DOS.

What they do not understand, and you will after completing this text, is that what they refer to as DOS is really the command line interface. In fact, the GUI is simply a pretty face on top of what is really going on under the hood. Windows is like the gauges on the dashboard of an automobile. When the red light goes on, there is trouble under the hood. The red light only alerts you to a problem. Sometimes, you may fix the problem simply by responding to the evidence given. For instance, if you see the red oil light come on, that information only requires you to put oil in your engine. Other times, you must dig deeper to solve the problem. You must go to the engine and run diagnostic tests to identify the problem. Then you can fix the problem.

The same is true in Windows. Windows will alert you to a problem like the red light on the dashboard. Sometimes you can fix it at the GUI level, and other times you must open the hood and go to the command line interface to run diagnostic software to identify the problem. Once you have identified the problem, you can fix it either by running the problem-solving software you are given with Windows or by making small fixes at the system level.

Microsoft, even though it expects you to use the GUI for your day-to-day computer operations, still knows the importance of a character-based interface—the command line. That is why, with Windows 95, Windows 98, Windows Me, Windows NT, Windows 2000 Server, and Windows 2000 Professional, one of the choices is the availability of the command line interface. In Windows Me, it is a menu choice called the MS-DOS Prompt. In Windows 2000 Server and Windows 2000 Professional, it is simply called the Command Prompt. You open what used to be called a DOS window and is now called a Command Prompt window, but where you really are is right back to a character-based interface.

Why, then, did Microsoft leave this option available to the user? There are many reasons. For instance, you will find that there are many tasks that still cannot be accomplished from the GUI. In addition, Windows provides utility programs that can only be run at the command line to help you solve problems with Windows itself. Furthermore, there are other tasks that, although they can be done from the GUI, are accomplished easier and faster from the command line, and most users will use the command line in those instances. You will also find that even in the Windows environment, there is an assumption that the user "knows" DOS. For instance, you will find that error messages you receive are couched in DOS terms, such as "Path not found. Please check the location of your program and correct the path." Likewise, you will still find that there are programs, especially if you are involved in developing Web pages for use on the Internet, that can only be run from the *DOS system level* (another way of saying *command line interface* or *command line prompt*).

Additionally, if you are a user of the Internet, which often runs on Unix- or Linux-based computers, you often will be once again at the command line. Although Unix and Linux (both of which are command line interface operating systems—Linux is based on Unix-like commands) do not use commands identical to DOS commands, they are in fact similar enough that, if you know one, you can figure out the other.

If you work with networks or plan a career in network administration, knowledge of the command line is a necessity. Network operating systems, such as Novell, rely on the command line interface. Even the Windows 2000 family of operating systems, Microsoft's GUI networking operating system, absolutely relies on command line interfaces. Windows 2000 Professional provides you with an expanded list of commands that are available to you from the command line. In addition, Novell, Windows 2000 Professional, and Windows allow you to write batch files, which are usually written, tested, and run at the command line interface, to automate many routine tasks. In fact,

Windows 2000 Professional has even more powerful batch file commands available to you than Windows Me. Furthermore, if a career in a computer-related field is in your future, you must know the command line interface. Almost all networking classes have as a prerequisite a working knowledge of DOS. Remember that "DOS" is a shorthand way of saying "command line interface."

You will also find that the knowledge that you gain in this text by learning the command line interface will help you understand what is going on in the Windows environment. Perhaps an analogy might be your automobile. Most of us are not auto mechanics and do not know how to do engine repair. Nonetheless, if you have an understanding of what is going on under the hood, you may be able to do minor repairs and preventative maintenance so you can avoid more costly major repairs. At the very least, you will be able to explain problems to professional auto technicians in intelligent terms that will allow them to identify problems so that they may spend their expensive time fixing, not identifying, problems. In this text, you are going to use the command line prompt, and you will learn what's under the hood of Windows. This will give you, as with an automobile, the ability to do minor repairs and preventative maintenance as well as to explain complex problems to a software technician.

1.12 ACCESSING THE COMMAND LINE PROMPT

In order to use the command line interface, you first need to access it. You must open the DOS window from a menu, or you may create a shortcut to it.

One thing you must remember is not to turn off the computer when you are in a DOS window. You must exit the window and then follow the Windows shut-down procedure.

Note: What you see on your screen may differ from the examples shown in this book. While almost all of the examples shown are done on a computer with Windows 2000 Professional, some may be from another version of Windows. You can ignore these minor differences. If there is a significant difference, it will be noted and explained.

1.13 ACTIVITY: THE COMMAND LINE PROMPT

Step 1 Boot the system.

Step 2 Click **Start**. Click **Programs**. Click **Accessories**. Click **Command Prompt**.

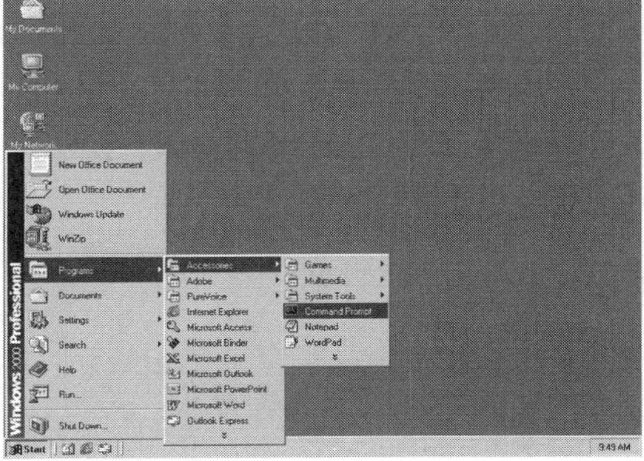

Note: If you do not see the title bar, press **Alt** + **Enter**

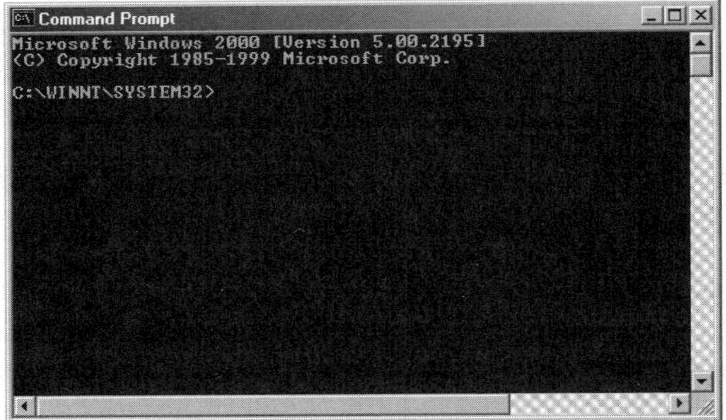

WHAT'S HAPPENING? You have opened the Command Prompt window. This is the character-based interface. You may close this window and return to the desktop.

Step 3 Click the ☒ on the title bar in the right corner.

WHAT'S HAPPENING? You have returned to the desktop. You can also create a shortcut to the command line. A shortcut is an icon on the desktop that points to an application or command.

Note: If you are in a lab environment, check with your administrator or lab technician to see if there are any special instructions for creating shortcuts.

Step 4 Right-click the desktop.

Step 5 Point to **New**.

Step 6 Click **Shortcut**.

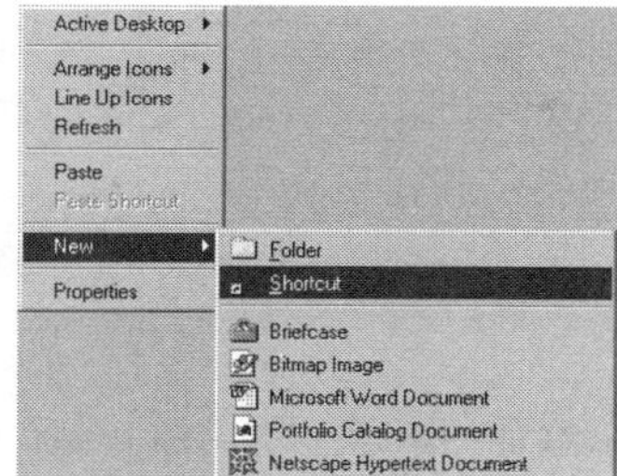

WHAT'S HAPPENING? You opened the dialog box for the Create Shortcut wizard. A wizard is a tool that leads you through the steps you need to take to accomplish your goal. In order to create a shortcut, you need to know the name and location of the program of interest.

Step 7 In the text box, key in the following (remember that the WINNT directory is called the WINDOWS directory if you installed Windows 2000 Professional as an upgrade from another version of Windows):
C:\WINNT\SYSTEM32\CMD.EXE

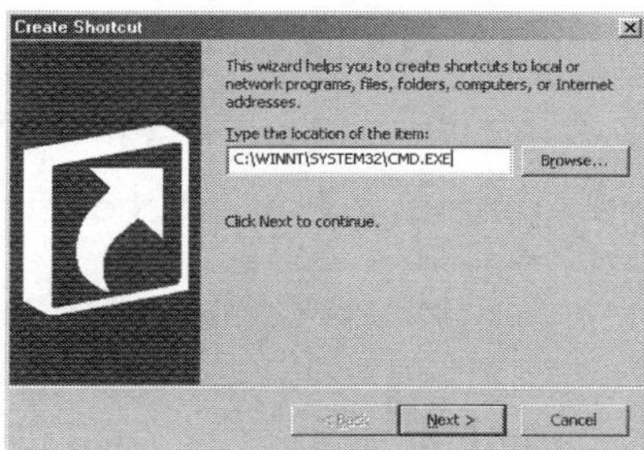

Step 8 Click **Next**.

WHAT'S HAPPENING? You may use any name you wish for your shortcut. However, in this example, Windows automatically gives the shortcut the name of **CMD.EXE**. In this way, Windows is telling you that **CMD.EXE** is the Command Prompt.

Step 9 Key in the following: **Command Prompt**

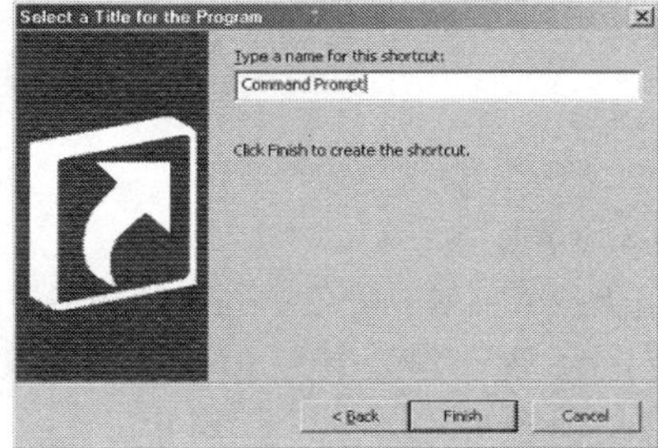

Step 10 Click **Finish**.

WHAT'S HAPPENING? You have created a shortcut and placed it on the desktop. By double-clicking it, you can go to the command line, referred to as the "Command Prompt."

Step 11 Double-click the **Command Prompt** shortcut.

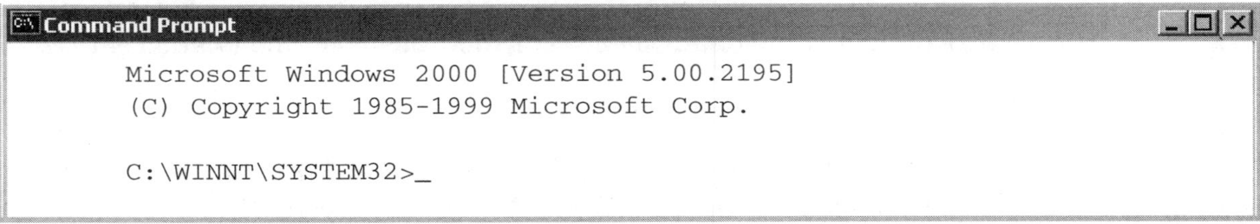

WHAT'S HAPPENING? The Command Prompt window opens with **C:\WINNT\SYSTEM32** as the default drive and directory. You would prefer it to open in the root of **C:**. You may alter the start location.

Step 12 Click the ☒ on the title bar in the right corner.

Step 13 Right-click the **Command Prompt** shortcut. Click **Properties**.

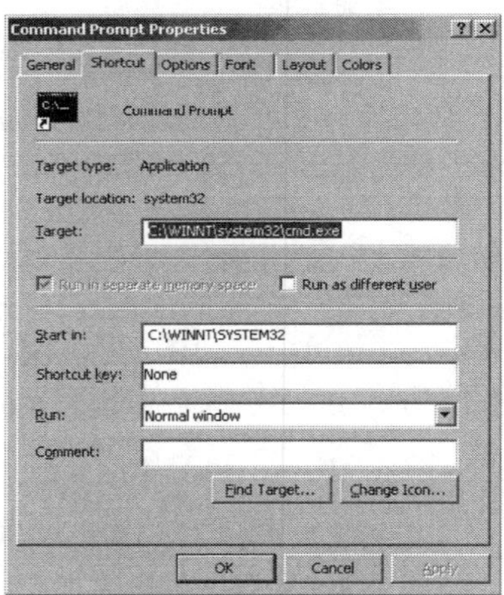

WHAT'S HAPPENING? In Windows 2000 Professional, when you open the shortcut, you may be taken to either **C:\WINNT\SYSTEM32** or to **C:**, depending on what the setup was (the **WINNT** directory is called the **WINDOWS** directory if you installed Windows 2000 Professional as an upgrade from another version of Windows). This is determined by the entry in the Start in: text box. In this example, the Command Prompt window will open in **C:\WINNT\SYSTEM32**.

Step 14 Select the text in the **Start in:** text box.

Step 15 Key in the following: **C:**

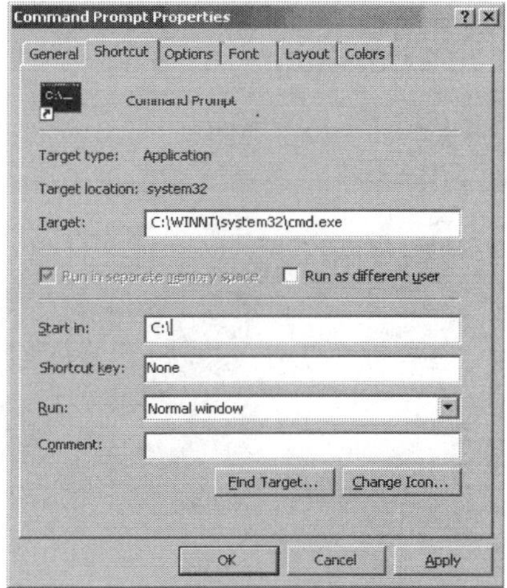

WHAT'S HAPPENING? You have altered the properties of the Command Prompt window so that it will always start at **C:**.

Step 16 Click **OK**.

Step 17 Double-click the **Command Prompt** icon.

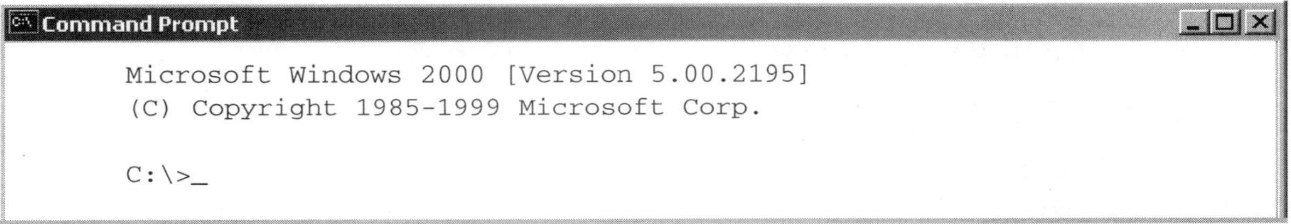

WHAT'S HAPPENING? Now your shortcut will always open with **C:\>** as the default.

Step 18 Click the [X] on the title bar in the right corner.

1.14 CONTROLLING THE APPEARANCE OF THE COMMAND LINE WINDOW

In Windows, everything initially appears in a window with a title bar and a toolbar, but this look can be changed. You can leave the Command Prompt in a window. When it is in a window, you can use the Minimize button, the Maximize button, or the Restore button, all on the right side of the title bar. The Minimize button will make the window a button on the taskbar. The Maximize button will fill the entire screen with the window, and the Restore button will return the window to its previous size. While in window view, you may alter the size of the text in the window. You may also dispense with the window altogether and view the command line in full-screen mode by clicking on the icon on the far left side of the title bar, selecting Properties, selecting Options, and selecting Full Screen under Display Options. To toggle (switch) between a window and full-screen mode, you may press the **Alt** and **Enter** keys.

1.15 ACTIVITY: ALTERING THE COMMAND LINE WINDOW

Step 1 Double-click the **Command Prompt** shortcut on the desktop.

Step 2 Place and hold your mouse pointer over the Minimize button in the upper-right corner of the Command Prompt window.

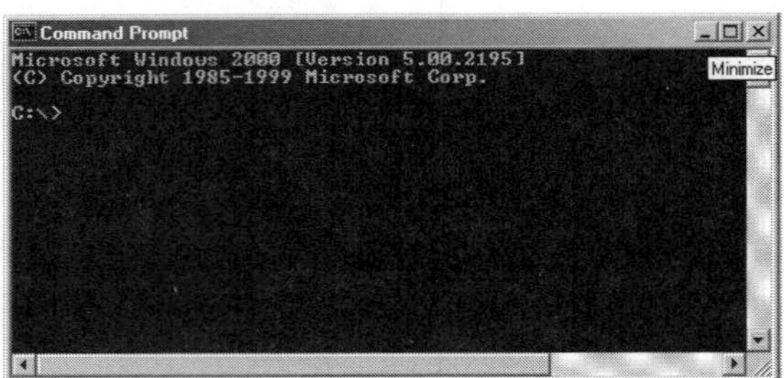

WHAT'S HAPPENING? When you do not know what an icon represents, placing the mouse pointer over the object causes a brief description of the object to appear. This description is called a ***ToolTip***.

Step 3 Click the Minimize button on the title bar.

WHAT'S HAPPENING? The Command Prompt window has become a button on the toolbar. It is still open but not active.

Step 4 Click the **Command Prompt** button on the toolbar.

Step 5 Click the Maximize button on the title bar.

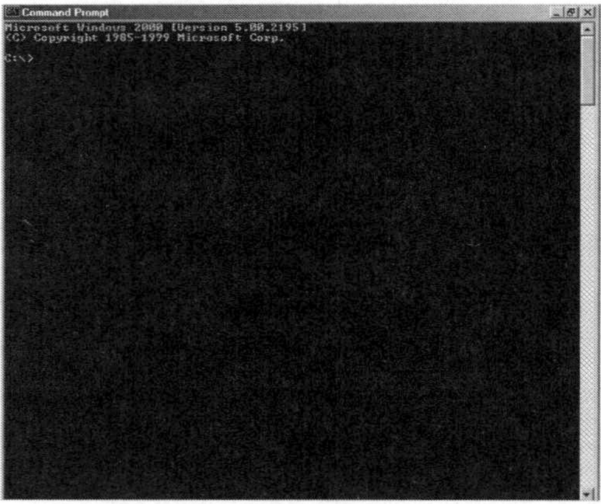

WHAT'S HAPPENING? Now the Command Prompt window is at its maximum size. Depending on the resolution of your monitor and the text size setting, the display may fill the entire screen.

Step 6 Click the Restore button.

Step 7 Click on the icon in the upper-left corner of the Command Prompt screen, C:\. You will open a menu.

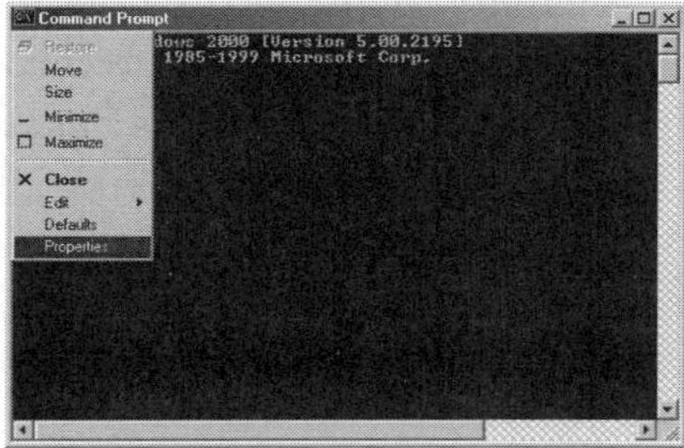

Step 8 Select **Properties** from the menu. Click on **Font**.

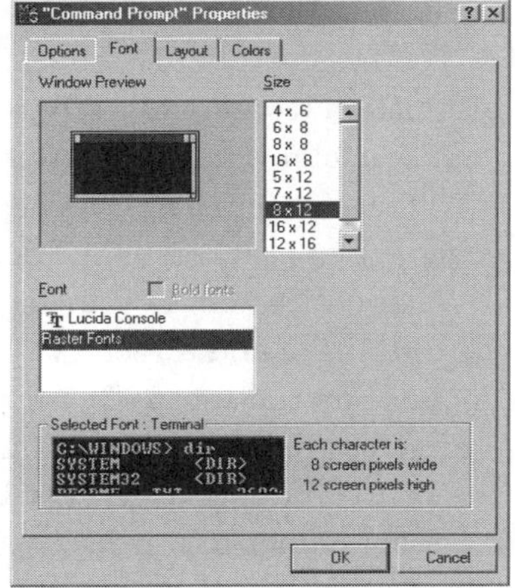

WHAT'S HAPPENING? While you are in this window, you may choose a font size. The fonts that have Tт in front of them are called TrueType fonts. The other choice is raster or bit-mapped fonts. Typically, a bit-mapped font will be clearer and sharper in a Command Prompt window, and a TrueType font is better for use in application programs such as Word or Excel. Your choices of font sizes will depend on your monitor and available resolutions.

Step 9 Click **Cancel** to close the Properties box.

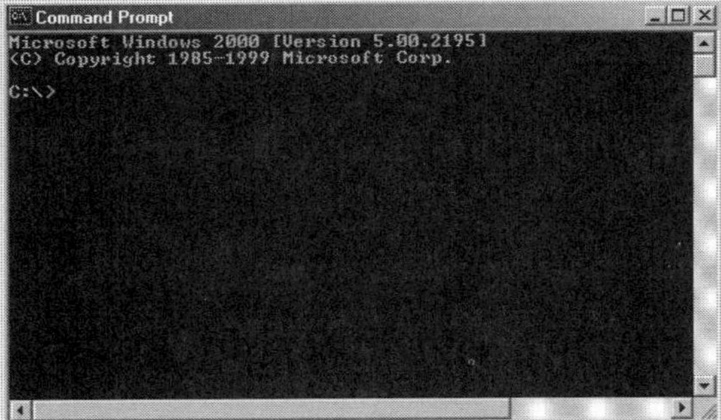

WHAT'S HAPPENING? You have returned the display to a window. The actual displays you will see on the screen are white text on a black background, but in this text, dark text on a lighter background will be used for easier reading. Remember *never*

turn off the computer when at the Command Prompt. You must first close the Command Prompt window and return to the Windows desktop or type EXIT at the prompt to return to the desktop. Then you must shut down the computer using the Windows shut-down procedure, learned previously.

Step 10 Key in the following: C:\>**EXIT** Enter

WHAT'S HAPPENING? You have closed the Command Prompt window and returned to the desktop.

1.16 THE DEFAULT DRIVE AND DEFAULT DIRECTORY

The command prompt is where you key in your commands. You normally do not use a pointing device when in command prompt mode. Command prompt mode is character-based, which means that you must explicitly tell the operating system what you want it to do by keying in the instruction (command). Where you key in your command is indicated by a blinking ***cursor*** following the prompt. The prompt usually looks like C:\>_ or sometimes [C:\]_. (The _ represents the blinking cursor.) The letter and colon behind the greater-than sign or in brackets is the default drive. The \ is the default directory. The default drive and directory is your location. This will change depending on where you are. The default drive and directory that is displayed when you go to the command line prompt depends on the setup of your particular computer, how many hard drives you have, and what software is currently running. The most common prompt will be C:\>; C:\WINDOWS>, or C:\WINNT\SYSTEM32>, but many other variations are possible. The operating system names drives using a letter followed by a colon, such as A:, C:, or J:. All drives, no matter the type—CD-ROM drives, floppy drives, removable drives such as Zip drives or Jaz drives, and hard drives—follow this naming rule. The default drive is the one where the operating system is currently pointing. It can be changed easily.

1.17 ACTIVITY: CHANGING THE DEFAULT DRIVE

Note 1: You should be at the Windows desktop.
Note 2: In this text, the prompt used will be C:\>.

Step 1 Click **Start,** point to **Programs,** point to **Accessories,** and click **Command Prompt** or double-click the **Command Prompt** shortcut on the desktop.

Step 2 Get the disk labeled ACTIVITIES that came with the textbook.

Step 3 To insert a 3½-inch disk properly into the disk drive, place your thumb on the label with the metal shutter facing away from you and toward the floppy disk drive (see Figure 1.3). Slip the disk into the slot and gently push the disk into the drive until you hear it click and/or feel it snap into place. When the disk is properly in place, the small rectangular button on the floppy drive will pop out.

FIGURE 1.3 INSERTING A DISK

Note 1: Remember, when you see the notation Enter, it means to press the Enter key located towards the right side of the keyboard and labeled Enter and/or Return.

Note 2: The prompt will be in the following font: C: What you key in will be in the following font: **C:** Key in only what follows the prompt, not the prompt itself.

Note 3: You will need to refer to your Configuration Table in Chapter 1.6 from time to time to ensure that your operating procedures for this, and all other activities, are correct for the computer you are using.

Step 4 Key in the following: C:\>**A:** Enter

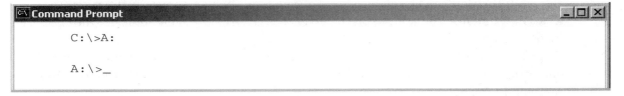

WHAT'S HAPPENING? You have changed the default drive to the A drive.

1.18 UNDERSTANDING COMMANDS

Windows operating system ***commands*** are programs and, like application programs, they perform specific tasks. OS commands are of two types: internal or external. When you boot the system, internal commands are automatically loaded and stored into memory (RAM). These internal commands are built into the command processor, CMD.EXE. This file, and hence, these internal commands, are always placed in memory and remain in RAM the entire time your computer is on.

To use an internal command, you key in the command name at the command line or click the icon. For an internal command, Windows checks memory, finds the program, loads it into RAM, and executes it. These are called internal or resident commands because they reside in memory or inside the computer. Internal commands are limited in number because they take up valuable space in memory.

External commands are stored as files on a disk. When you wish to use an external command, you call upon the operating system to load the program into RAM by keying in the program's name or clicking its icon. Since it is an external command, the OS cannot find the program internally, so it must go to the disk, locate the file, load it into RAM, and then execute it. If the OS cannot find the file, the program cannot be run. These commands are called external or transient commands because they reside in a file on a disk and must be read into RAM each time you key them in.

Windows loads and executes programs such as Word or Quicken. Clicking or double-clicking a program icon or choosing a program from a menu loads an external command. You do not have to key in a command name, but the process is the same. For instance, the icon for Word stores the location and name of the program file such as C:\PROGRAM FILES\MICROSOFT OFFICE\WINWORD.EXE. The operating system looks first for the program in memory. When it cannot find it in memory, it goes to the specified location, including the disk drive as well as the directory. In the example given, Windows looks to Drive C in a folder called MICROSOFT OFFICE in a folder called PROGRAM FILES for a file called WINWORD.EXE. When it finds it, it loads it, and you have Word available to you. You are letting the GUI do the work. You could do the work yourself at the command prompt by simply keying in WINWORD.EXE. The end result would be the same. The OS would find and load Word for you. If the icon were set up incorrectly, Windows would not load (execute) the program you wanted, no matter how often you chose the icon or the menu choice. The icon or menu choice is only a pointer to the program file.

If the icon had stored incorrect information, such as an incorrect program location, Windows would give you the error message that it could not load Word because it could not find it. If you did not understand this process, you would not be able to use Word because all you would see would be the error message. If you did understand the operating system process, you would either correct the pointer or run Word from the command prompt.

Although all program files are external, including application programs, the term *external command* is reserved for the group of programs that perform operating system functions. These programs are files that come with Windows and are copied to a subdirectory called C:\WINNT\SYSTEM32 on the hard disk when Windows is installed. This group of files is generically referred to as the command line utility files or system utility files.

In the Command Prompt window, unlike the Windows GUI environment, you have no icons. In order to use commands, you must know their file names. The DIR command, an internal command that stands for directory, is provided so that you may look for files on a disk from the command line. In Windows, Explorer is the equivalent of the DIR command. When you key in DIR and press the **Enter** key, you are asking the operating system to run the directory program. The purpose or task of the DIR command is to display the names of all the files in a directory on the disk onto the screen. You see what could be described as a table of contents of the disk. The DIR command is the first internal command you will use.

1.19 ACTIVITY: USING THE DIR COMMAND

Note: Be sure the disk labeled ACTIVITIES is in Drive A.

Step 1 Key in the following: A:\>**DIR** **Enter**

```
Command Prompt

04/23/2000  04:03p                  71 MAR.TMP
04/23/2000  04:03p                  71 MARCH.TMP
04/23/2000  04:18p                  72 APR.TMP
07/31/1999  12:53p               2,672 NEWPRSON.FIL
08/12/2000  04:12p                   3 Y.FIL
11/16/2000  12:00p                  53 Sandy and Nicki.txt
11/16/2000  12:00p                  59 Sandy and Patty.txt
01/31/2000  12:09p                 294 EXP00JAN.DAT
07/03/2000  01:50p    <DIR>            DATA
07/03/2000  01:50p    <DIR>            TEST
07/03/2000  01:50p    <DIR>            GAMES
07/03/2000  01:51p    <DIR>            PHONE
07/03/2000  01:51p    <DIR>            FINANCE
07/03/2000  01:52p    <DIR>            LEVEL-1
07/03/2000  01:52p    <DIR>            SPORTS
07/03/2000  01:53p    <DIR>            MEDIA
07/03/2000  01:53p    <DIR>            WORKING
05/27/2001  10:08p                  76 LONGFILENAME
05/27/2001  10:08p                  81 LONGFILENAME.TXT
05/27/2001  10:09p                 122 LONGFILENAME.EXTENSION
05/27/2001  10:42p                  97 LONGFILENAMING.TXT
05/27/2001  10:43p                  95 LONGFILENAMED.TXT
              90 File(s)         29,381 bytes
               9 Dir(s)         292,864 bytes free

A:\>_
```

This graphic represents the last part of the screen you will see (90 files and 9 directories will be listed). You will see text moving vertically on the screen. This movement is known as ***scrolling***, the result of executing the DIR command. The operating system is displaying, or listing, all the files on the root of the disk in Drive A and stops scrolling when the list ends. The last subdirectory on the list is **WORKING**. You can tell it is a subdirectory by the **<DIR>** entry to the left of the name. One file on the list, just above the DATA directory, is called **EXP00JAN.DAT**. The file name is **EXP00JAN**. The file extension is **DAT**.

The order of the file information differs significantly from other versions of Windows. You will use the file **EXP00JAN.DAT** as your example. First, you will see the date that the file was created, **01/31/2000**; and the time, **12:09p**. The date and time indicate either when this file was created or when it was last modified. Next is the number **294**, the size of the file in bytes. Then you will see the file name.

Now look at the bottom two lines of the screen. One line states: **90 File(s) 29,381 bytes**. This line indicates how many files are in the current directory and how much room they occupy. The next line, **9 Dir(s) 292,864 bytes free**, indicates first how many directories are below the current directory and second how much room is left on the disk for more files. All the files listed on the disk are practice files so that you may practice using the operating system commands without harming any of your own files.

1.20 SOFTWARE VERSIONS

Software companies regularly release new versions of software to take advantage of new technology. These upgrades also contain enhancements. The term *enhancements* simply means more features. In addition, new versions of software fix problems in older versions. This process is known as fixing bugs. To keep track of the versions, companies assign them version numbers. For instance, there is WordPerfect 8 and WordPerfect 9 and Word 97 and Word 2000.

As previously explained, version numbers are also assigned to operating systems. For MS-DOS, 1.0 was the first version, released in 1981, and DOS 6.22 was the last stand-alone, character-based operating system. Windows 95 replaced DOS 6.22. Windows Millennium Edition replaced Windows 98 and Windows 95, and Windows 2000 Professional replaced Windows NT. Beginning with Windows 95, DOS has been integrated into the Windows operating system.

1.21 ACTIVITY: USING THE VER COMMAND

Step 1 Key in the following: A:\>**VER** Enter

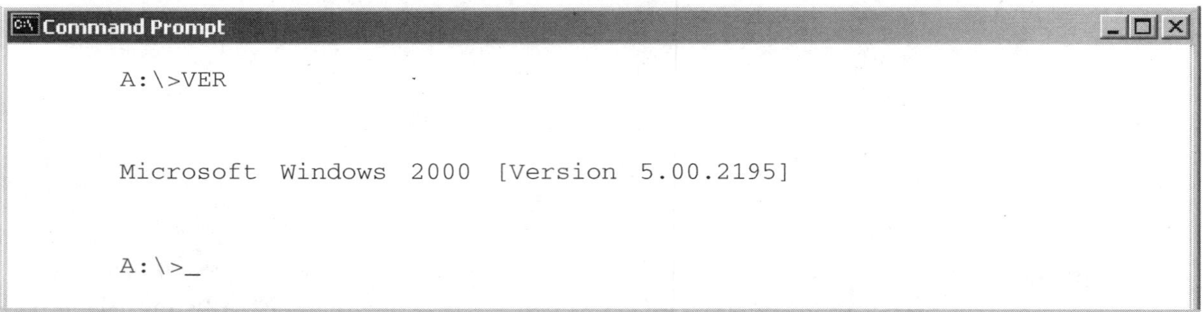

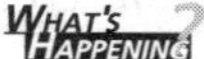

In this example, the computer is running the operating system Windows 2000 [Version 5.00.2195]. The version number you see depends on the version of Windows you have on your computer.

1.22 THE KEYBOARD

The keyboard on a microcomputer is similar to a typewriter keyboard, but it has at least 40 additional keys, many with symbols rather than alphabetic characters. Generally, the keyboard can be broken down into four major categories:

- **Alphanumeric keys.** These keys, located in the center of the keyboard, are the standard typewriter keys. They consist of the letters of the alphabet and Arabic numerals.

- **Function keys.** Keys labeled F1, F2 etc., located across the top or on the left side of the keyboard, are known as **Function** keys. These keys are program-dependent, which means that their functions are dependent on the software in use. Often a notebook computer will have the function keys located in different spots on the keyboard due to space limitations.
- **Directional keys.** These keys, located between the alphanumeric keys and the number pad, are also known as the **cursor** keys. These keys are also program-dependent and allow you to move the cursor in the direction of the arrows. There are additional keys labeled **Insert**, **Delete**, **Home**, **End**, **Page Up**, **Page Down**, **Num Lock**, **Print Screen**, and **Pause**, as well as others, depending on the keyboard and system. Notebook computers often have separate directional keys, but **Home**, **Page Up**, and other such keys share locations in the interest of saving space.
- **Numeric keys.** These keys, located to the right of the directional keys, are known as the number keypad or numeric keypad. Numeric keys can be used in two ways: like a calculator keypad or with the directional arrows and other commands. The directional arrows in combination with other commands are program-dependent. The user must activate the mode desired (numeric keypad or directional arrows) with the **Num Lock** key, which acts as a toggle switch. A ***toggle switch*** acts like an on/off switch. Press the key once and the numbers are turned on. Press the same key again and the numbers are turned off. Other toggle keys will be discussed later.

In addition, some of the newer keyboards come with what are called **Windows Logo keys**. These keys perform certain functions in the Windows environment. They cannot be used at the Command Prompt. Some keyboards now also come with special keys for use with the Internet. These keys also cannot be used at the Command Prompt.

The following activity will familiarize you with some of the special keys and features of a computer keyboard. Figure 1.4 shows one of the major types of keyboards used today.

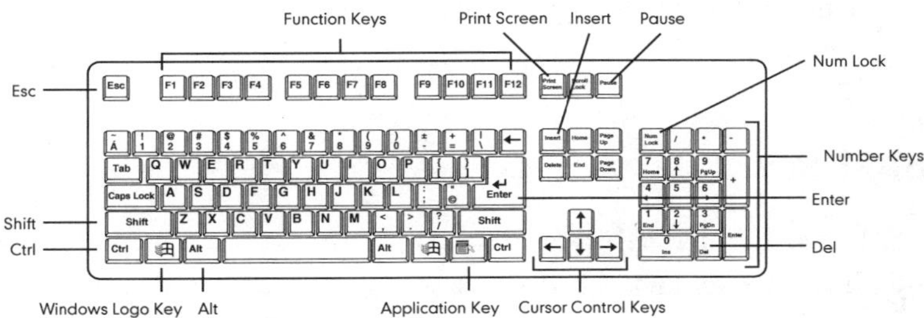

FIGURE 1.4 SAMPLE KEYBOARD LAYOUT FOR A WINDOWS NATURAL KEYBOARD

1.23 THE BACKSPACE KEY

The Backspace key, labeled Backspace or just the symbol ←, allows you to erase characters you have keyed in prior to pressing Enter.

1.24 ACTIVITY: CORRECTING ERRORS USING THE BACKSPACE KEY

Step 1 At the A prompt (A:\>), key in the following: **The quick brown fox**

Step 2 Press the **Backspace** key until you reach the A prompt (A:\>). As you see, each time you press this key, you delete a character.

1.25 THE ESCAPE KEY

Esc is an abbreviation for Escape. Look for the key labeled **Esc**. When you press this key, it cancels a line you have keyed in, provided you have not yet pressed **Enter**. When you press the **Esc** key, the operating system eliminates the line of text and waits for you to key in something else.

1.26 ACTIVITY: USING THE ESCAPE KEY

Step 1 Key in the following: A:\>**The quick brown fox**

WHAT'S HAPPENING? To erase this line, you could repeatedly press the **Backspace** key. However, you can use the **Esc** key to cancel the line instead.

Step 2 Press the **Esc** key.

Notice that the cursor is blinking after the A:\>. As stated previously, results will vary slightly, depending on the version of Windows you are using. In this text, the results shown will be from Windows 2000 Professional.

1.27 THE SHIFT KEY

The Shift key is labeled **Shift** with an up-arrow symbol or just the up-arrow symbol. This key allows the user to shift to uppercase letters and special characters such as the * above the number 8 key. There are usually two **Shift** keys, one on either side of the alphabet keys. To activate, you need only press one **Shift** key.

1.28 ACTIVITY: USING THE SHIFT KEY

Step 1 Press the key on the keyboard for the letter **m**.

Step 2 Hold down the **Shift** key and press the letter **m**.

Step 3 Press either **Backspace** or **Esc** to delete the letters.

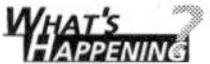

Windows is case *aware*, but not case *sensitive*. If you name a file **MyFile**, and later try to find it using **MYFILE** or **myfile**, the system will have no problem locating it. However, it will remember the case you used, and, when you use the DIR command, it will show you the file in the same case you used when you created it.

1.29 THE PRINT SCREEN KEY

In versions of DOS previous to Windows 95, the Print Screen key was used to send copy to the printer. Pressing this key along with the **Shift** key gave you a hard copy or printed version of what the screen displayed, like a snapshot of the screen at a specific moment in time. The **Print Screen** key in Windows does not function in this way. Pressing the **Print Screen** key still takes a snapshot of the screen, but you do not need to press the **Shift** key. You simply press the **Print Screen** key. Also, what you are capturing is a picture or graphic—not text to send to a printer. Pressing **Print Screen** captures an image of the entire screen. Pressing the **Print Screen** key once in conjunction with the **Alt** key captures an image of the active window only, not the entire screen. The image is copied to memory and can be pasted into a document to be printed, but it cannot be printed directly to the printer.

1.30 ACTIVITY: USING THE PRINT SCREEN KEY IN WINDOWS

Step 1 Click the Close button (**X**) on the title bar of the Command Prompt window.

You have closed the Command Prompt window and returned to the Windows desktop.

Step 2 Click **Start**. Point to **Programs**. Point to **Accessories**. Click **WordPad**.

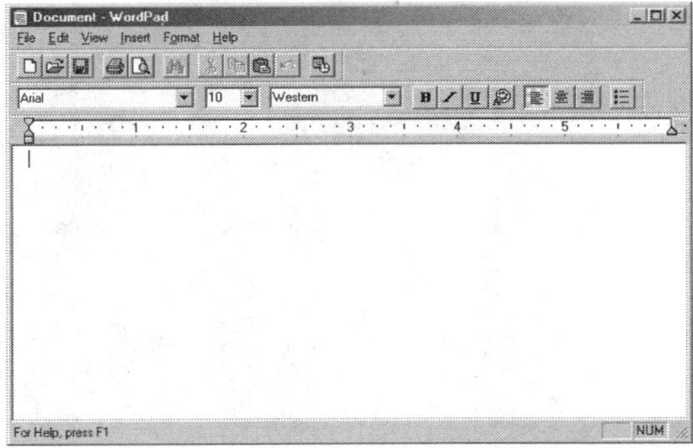

You have opened the mini word-processing program WordPad that comes with Windows.

Step 3 Click the Minimize button (**_**) on the WordPad title bar.

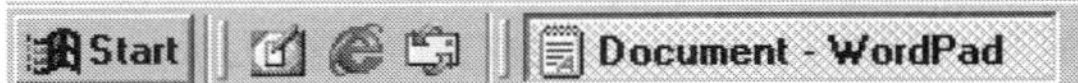

WHAT'S HAPPENING? You have minimized the WordPad program to a button on the taskbar. WordPad is still open and still running, but the window it is operating in has been minimized.

Step 4 Click **Start**. Point to **Programs**. Point to **Accessories**. Click **Command Prompt**.

Step 5 Size the command line window to about four inches tall by five or six inches wide. Exact measurement is not important.

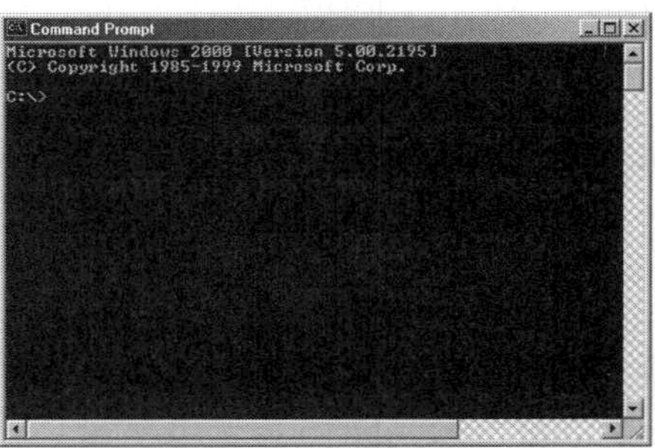

WHAT'S HAPPENING? You have opened the Command Prompt window.

Step 6 Hold down the key labeled **Alt** and while holding it down, press the **Print Screen** key once. Be sure you do not hold down the **Print Screen** key—just press it once.

Step 7 Open WordPad by clicking once on the **WordPad** button on the taskbar.

Step 8 On the WordPad menu bar, click **Edit**. Click **Paste**.

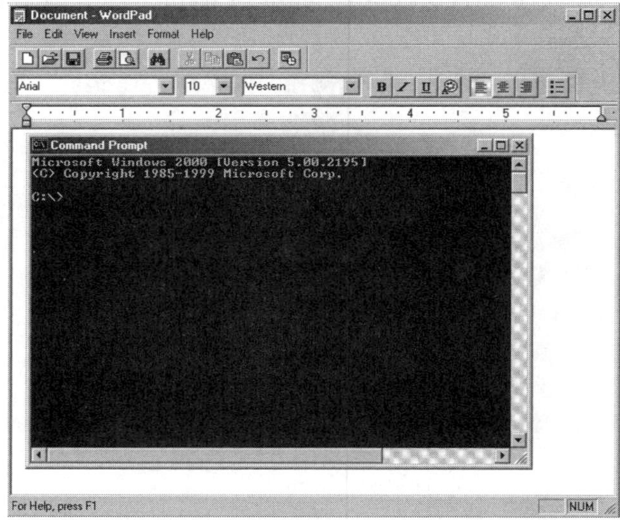

WHAT'S HAPPENING? You have captured a graphic image of the Command Prompt screen and pasted it into a document. You could save, print, or add text to this document.

Step 9 On the WordPad menu bar, click **File**. Click **Exit**.

Step 10 When asked to save changes, click **No**.

Step 11 Click the command line window to make it active.

Step 12 Key in the following: C:\ >**EXIT** Enter

WHAT'S HAPPENING? You have returned to the desktop.

1.31 FREEZING THE DISPLAY AND CANCELING A COMMAND

You have already seen that, when you use the DIR command, the display scrolls by so quickly on the screen that it is very difficult to read. There is a way to stop displays from rapidly scrolling on the screen. The Windows Operating System allows you to read a long display by temporarily halting the scrolling. How you do it depends on what kind of computer you have. Most new computers have a key labeled Pause; all you need to do is press Pause. Nearly every kind of computer will let you use Ctrl + **S** for freezing the display. Most computers today are so fast that chances are the data will process much faster than you can manually pause the display, unless you have a long display of data. Furthermore, if you keyed in a command and pressed Enter, but you either made an error or changed your mind about executing the command, you can, in theory, cancel the command or cause it to stop executing. In reality, most computers execute commands so quickly that they cannot be canceled. To cancel an ongoing command after you have pressed Enter, press the Ctrl key in conjunction with the Break key or the letter **C**. Look for the key labeled Break. It is often paired with the Pause key. This command is not the same as Esc, which is used prior to pressing Enter. As previously stated, with today's fast computers, by the time you press these halting keys, the command will have already been completed.

1.32 ACTIVITY: USING THE PAUSE, CONTROL, AND BREAK KEYS

Step 1 Double-click the **Command Prompt** shortcut on the desktop.

Step 2 Key in the following: C:\>**DIR /S** Enter

Step 3 Press the Pause key.

```
Command Prompt
        12/07/1999  12:00p              26,384 actmovie.exe
        12/07/1999  12:00p              58,368 secpol.msc
        12/07/1999  12:00p              71,952 Channel Screen Saver.scr
        12/07/1999  12:00p              72,464 actxprxy.dll
        12/07/1999  12:00p              39,184 admparse.dll
        12/07/1999  12:00p              27,408 adptif.dll
        12/07/1999  12:00p             121,616 adsldp.dll
        12/07/1999  12:00p             130,832 adsldpc.dll
        12/07/1999  12:00p              62,224 adsmsext.dll
        12/07/1999  12:00p             164,112 adsnds.dll
        12/07/1999  12:00p             198,928 adsnt.dll
        12/07/1999  12:00p             112,400 adsnw.dll
        12/07/1999  12:00p             357,648 advapi32.dll
        12/07/1999  12:00p              88,848 advpack.dll
```

```
12/07/1999  12:00p           18,192 alrsvc.dll
12/07/1999  12:00p           64,784 amstream.dll
12/07/1999  12:00p            9,029 ansi.sys
12/07/1999  12:00p          107,792 apcups.dll
12/07/1999  12:00p           12,498 append.exe
12/07/1999  12:00p          120,592 appmgmts.dll
12/07/1999  12:00p          222,992 appmgr.dll
12/07/1999  12:00p          296,208 appwiz.cpl
12/07/1999  12:00p           19,728 arp.exe
12/07/1999  12:00p          103,184 asctrls.ocx
```

WHAT'S HAPPENING? Pressing this key halts or "freezes" the display on the screen (your display will be different depending on when your display freezes). If you do not have a **Pause** key, repeat Step 3, but press the **Ctrl** + **S** keys instead of the **Pause** key for Step 4. The display stops and the cursor remains blinking when you press these two keys. When you press **Enter**, the display will continue scrolling. If you want to "break" out of the command or stop it from executing, you can use the **Ctrl** + **C** or the **Ctrl** + **Break** keys to interrupt the command.

Step 4 Press the **Enter** key. As soon as the directory starts displaying on the screen, hold the **Ctrl** key down. While holding down the **Ctrl** key, press the **Break** key.

```
Command Prompt

12/07/1999  12:00p          153,360 cards.dll
12/07/1999  12:00p           34,064 ccfgnt.dll
12/07/1999  12:00p          142,608 cdfview.dll
12/07/1999  12:00p           68,368 cdm.dll
12/07/1999  12:00p          402,704 cdonts.dll
12/07/1999  12:00p        2,450,192 cdosys.dll
12/07/1999  12:00p          135,440 certcli.dll
12/07/1999  12:00p          419,088 certmgr.dll
12/07/1999  12:00p           48,640 certmgr.msc
12/07/1999  12:00p           17,168 cfgmgr32.dll
12/07/1999  12:00p           47,888 secur32.dll
12/07/1999  12:00p               75 View Channels.scf
12/07/1999  12:00p            8,464 chcp.com
12/07/1999  12:00p           13,072 chkdsk.exe
12/07/1999  12:00p           13,072 chkntfs.exe
12/07/1999  12:00p          156,944 ciadmin.dll
12/07/1999  12:00p           53,248 ciadv.msc
12/07/1999  12:00p          101,648 cic.dll
12/07/1999  12:00p            9,488 cidaemon.exe
12/07/1999  12:00p           68,368 ciodm.dll
12/07/1999  12:00p           18,704 cipher.exe
12/07/1999  12:00p            5,392 cisvc.exe
12/07/1999  12:00p            9,488 ckcnv.exe

C:\>_
```

The operating system stops running or executing the DIR /S command. You are returned to the C:\> prompt. You interrupted or stopped the program or the command from running, and therefore you see only a partial directory display. (Don't be concerned if you cannot pause the display because the scroll action is too fast.) **Ctrl** + **C** has the same function and meaning as **Ctrl** + **Break**.

Step 5 Key in the following:C:\>**DIR /S** **Enter**

Step 6 As soon as the directory information starts displaying on the screen, hold the **Ctrl** key down and then simultaneously press the letter **C**.

```
Command Prompt
   12/07/1999  12:00p          59,664 gcdef.dll
   12/07/1999  12:00p          24,576 gdi.exe
   12/07/1999  12:00p         234,256 gdi32.dll
   12/07/1999  12:00p           1,591 getstart.gif
   12/07/1999  12:00p         297,744 glmf32.dll
   12/07/1999  12:00p         119,568 glu32.dll
   12/07/1999  12:00p         304,912 gpedit.dll
   12/07/1999  12:00p          53,248 gpedit.msc
   12/07/1999  12:00p          93,456 gpkcsp.dll
   12/07/1999  12:00p           8,192 gpkrsrc.dll
   12/07/1999  12:00p         118,544 gptext.dll
   12/07/1999  12:00p          34,576 graftabl.com
   12/07/1999  12:00p          19,694 graphics.com
   12/07/1999  12:00p          21,232 graphics.pro
   12/07/1999  12:00p          41,232 grpconv.exe
   12/07/1999  12:00p         251,152 h323.tsp
   12/07/1999  12:00p         156,944 h323msp.dll
   12/07/1999  12:00p          15,442 hardware.inf
   12/07/1999  12:00p         128,272 hdwwiz.cpl
   12/07/1999  12:00p          11,536 help.exe
   12/07/1999  12:00p         503,056 hhctrl.ocx
   12/07/1999  12:00p          67,856 hhsetup.dll
   12/07/1999  12:00p          17,168 hid.dll

   C:\>_
```

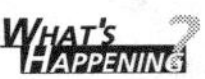

This procedure worked exactly like **Ctrl** + **Break**. The system ceased executing the program or the DIR command and returned you to the C:\> prompt, ready for the next command.

1.33 THE CLS COMMAND

Your screen is filled with the display of the directory and other commands that you have keyed in. You may want to have a "fresh" screen, with nothing displayed except the C:\> prompt and the cursor in its "home" position (the upper left-hand corner of the screen). The internal command CLS clears the screen. Whatever is displayed on the screen will go away, as if you erased a chalkboard. The command erases the screen display, not your files.

1.34 ACTIVITY: USING THE CLS COMMAND

Step 1 Key in the following: C:\>**CLS** Enter

The screen is now cleared, and the C:\> is back in the upper left-hand corner.

1.35 THE DATE AND TIME COMMANDS

The computer, via a battery, keeps track of the current date and time. Date and time are known as the ***system date*** and the ***system time***. The system date and time are the date and time the computer uses when it opens and closes files (last date/time accessed) or when another program asks for the date and time. Today's computers have a built-in clock. It is simply a built-in, 24-hour, battery-operated clock that sets the date and time automatically when you boot the system. You can change or check the system date and system time whenever you wish by using the internal DATE and TIME commands at the command line, or from within the Windows desktop by clicking the time displayed at the far right of the taskbar.

1.36 ACTIVITY: USING DATE/TIME COMMANDS AT THE COMMAND LINE

Step 1 Key in the following: C:\>**DATE** Enter

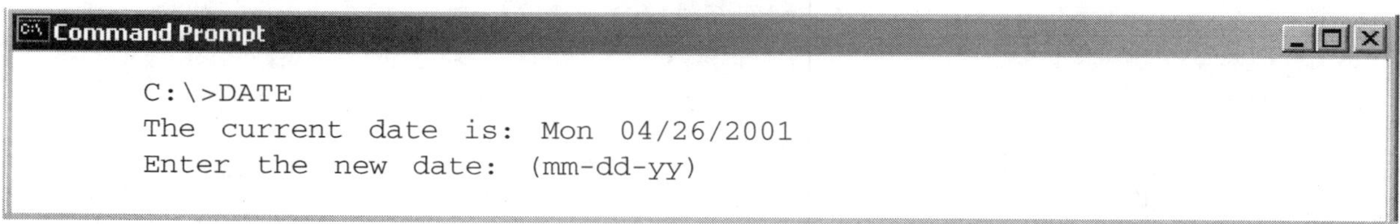

Command Prompt
C:\>DATE
The current date is: Mon 04/26/2001
Enter the new date: (mm-dd-yy)

The date displayed on your screen is the current date, not the above example. If you did not wish to change the date, you would just press Enter, retaining the date displayed and returning you to C:\>. However, if you do want to change the date, respond to the prompt. You must key in the date in the proper format, such as **11-15-01**. You may not key in character data such as **November 15, 2001**. Furthermore, you are allowed to use some other separators that are not stated. You may key in **11/15/01** using the forward slash, or you may use periods such as **11.15.01**. No other characters can be used.

Step 2 Key in the following: **12-31-01** Enter

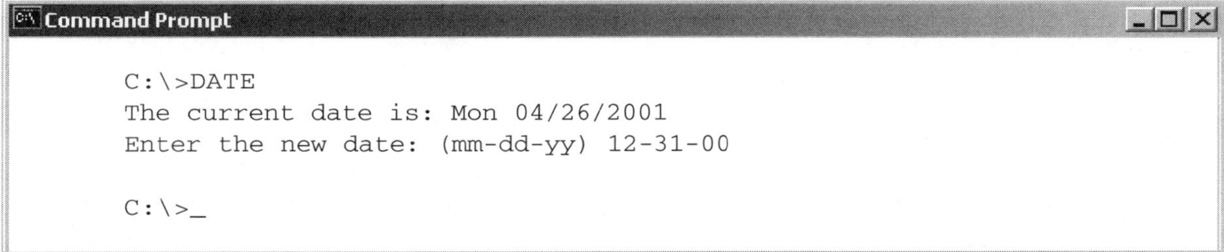
Command Prompt
C:\>DATE
The current date is: Mon 04/26/2001
Enter the new date: (mm-dd-yy) 12-31-00
C:\>_

WHAT'S HAPPENING? You did change the date, and we will examine this change in a moment. You can also change the time in the same fashion with the TIME command.

Step 3 Key in the following: C:\>**TIME** Enter

```
Command Prompt

C:\>TIME
The current time is: 1:12:13.78
Enter the new time:
```

WHAT'S HAPPENING? The time displayed on your screen is the current time, not the above example. If you did not wish to change the time, you would just press Enter, retaining the time displayed and returning you to C:\>. However, if you do want to change the time, you respond to the prompt. You may use only the colon (:) to separate the numbers. Although in this case you are going to key in the seconds, most people usually key in only the hour and minutes. If you wish the time to be in the P.M., you add a "p" after the time. You may also use a 24-hour clock.

Step 4 Key in the following: **23:59:59** Enter

```
Command Prompt

C:\>TIME
The current time is: 1:12:13.78
Enter the new time: 23:59:59

C:\>_
```

WHAT'S HAPPENING? You have just reset the computer clock with the DATE and TIME commands. These are internal commands. How do you know the system date and time have been changed? You can check by keying in the commands using a parameter that displays only the date and time.

Step 5 Key in the following: C:\>**DATE /T** Enter

Step 6 Key in the following: C:\>**TIME /T** Enter

```
Command Prompt

C:\>DATE /T
Tue 01/01/2002

C:\>TIME /T
```

```
12:00a

C:\>_
```

Your time display numbers may be slightly different. What have you done? You have changed the system date and time. You entered the date of December 31, 2001 (12-31-01), prior to changing the time. The date now displayed is Tuesday, January 1, 2002. How did that happen? Why is the displayed date different from the keyed-in date? After you entered the date of 12/31/01, you entered the time of 11:59 p.m. (23:59:59). Seconds went by; the time passed midnight, and, when you are passed midnight, you are into a new day. Hence, the day "rolled over" from December 31, 2001 to January 1, 2002. In other words, the system keeps the date and time current based on the information you give. The /T parameter used with the DATE and TIME commands displayed the system date and time.

The day of the week is displayed in the date. You can experiment with the DATE and TIME commands. For instance, you can find the day of your birthday in any future or past year by using the DATE command and entering your birthday.

Step 7 Key in the following: C:\>**DATE** Enter

Step 8 At the prompt on the screen key in your birthday for 2001. In this example, I will use my birthday, **12-11-01**.
Key in the following: **12-11-01** Enter

Step 9 Key in the following: C:\>**DATE** Enter

Step 10 Key in the following: C:\>Enter

```
Command Prompt

C:\>DATE
The current date is: Mon 01/01/2002
Enter the new date: (mm-dd-yy) 12-11-01

C:\>DATE
The current date is: Tue 12/11/2001
Enter the new date: (mm-dd-yy)

C:\>_
```

If you are using Windows 95 and have not added the Y2K patch, the OS will not know if you are referring to the year 1901 or the year 2001, and you will get an error message. In that case, you are required to enter a 4-digit year, 12-11-2001. However, if you have Windows 2000 Professional or Windows 98/ Millennium, the OS knows that you mean the year 2001 and does not give an error message. The screen display shows you the day of your birthday in 2001. In this case, my birthday falls on a Tuesday in 2001. If you wish to see or change the system date or time, you can also use the clock on the taskbar.

Step 11 Click the Close button in the Command Prompt window.

1.37 ACTIVITY: CHANGING THE DATE AND TIME USING THE TASKBAR

Step 1 Right-click the time display on the right of the taskbar. Click **Adjust Date/ Time**.

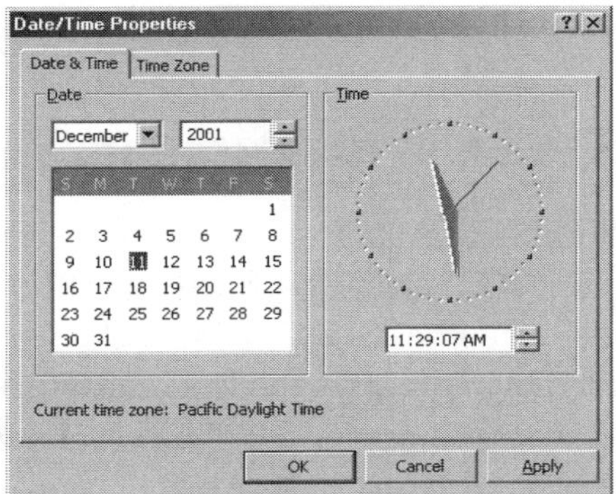

You have opened the Date/Time Properties dialog box. You can change the date by clicking on any one of the numbers in the calendar. You can change the time either by clicking in the box under the clock, deleting any part of the time, and keying in the correct time, or by using the up and down arrows. This type of data-entry box is called a spin box, because the values go both up and down. You can change the year in the same way: key in the new value or use the spin box arrows. You can change the month by keying in the correct month or by using the down arrow and selecting the correct month. This type of data-entry box is called a drop-down list box.

Step 2 Change the date, month, and time to the current values.

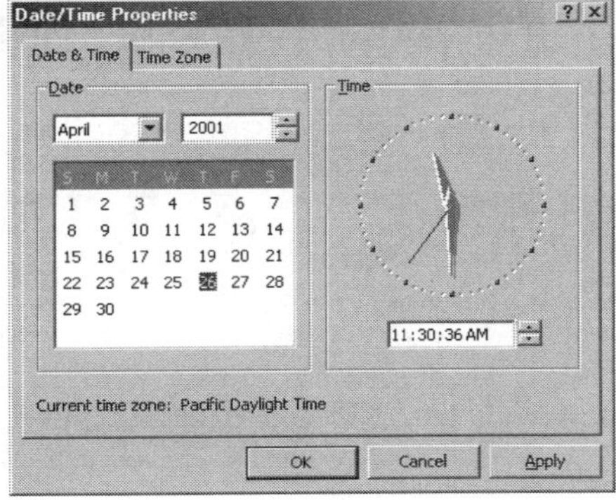

You have returned the system time and date to the current values. Another feature of the clock on the taskbar is to show you the current date without opening the dialog box.

Step 3 Click **OK**.

Step 4 Place the mouse pointer over the time on the taskbar. Do not click, just point the arrow.

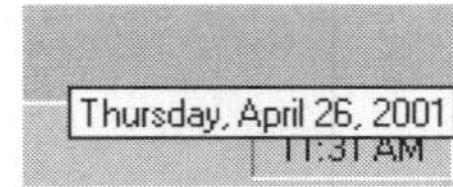

WHAT'S HAPPENING? The day and date are briefly displayed. The display remains only for a few seconds and then disappears.

1.38 MEDIA OBJECTS: THEIR PROPERTIES AND VALUES

What is an object? What is a property? To Windows, *everything* is an object. A file, the keyboard, a disk drive—all are objects. Each object has properties, and the properties may have values.

To explain the object-property-value relationship, you can use a person. A person is an object. All objects of that same type (human) have the same properties. Some properties of this person object are *name*, *height*, and *eye color*. The values of person objects, however, differ. One person's name property value is John Jones; another person's name property value is Olivia Wu. A newborn person has the property of name, but no value has been assigned to that property.

To discover information about an object in Windows, you examine that object's property sheet. Most objects' property sheets can be displayed by right-clicking on the object icon and choosing Properties from the shortcut menu. For example, when you copy a disk, it is very important that you know what type of media you are using. Furthermore, it is important to know what type of floppy disk drive or hard drive you have on your system. You need to know the "native" format of the disk drive, whether or not you have a high-density disk drive, and which drive is Drive A. In Windows, this information is ascertained by examining a drive's property sheet.

1.39 ACTIVITY: EXAMINING DISK PROPERTIES AND VALUES

Step 1 Double-click the **My Computer** icon on the desktop.

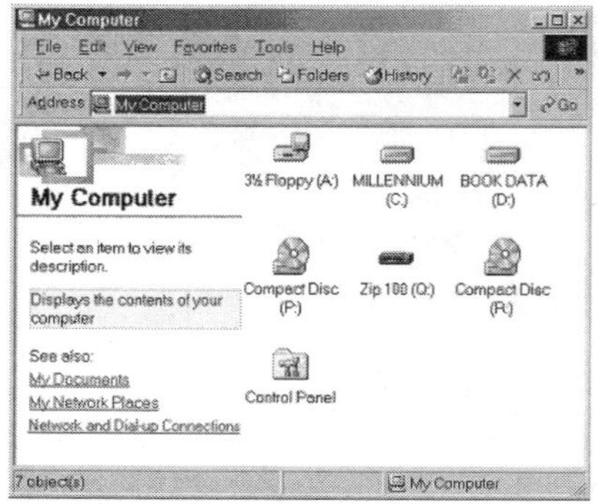

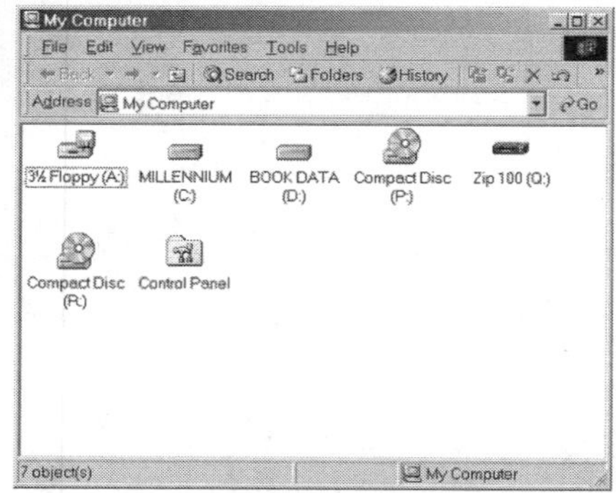

WHAT'S HAPPENING? You have opened the My Computer window. The view on the left is the default for Windows 2000 Professional. This view enables Web contents in folders—it emulates what you see on the Web. In the view on the right, this feature is turned off, and you see only the contents as objects and folders. In this text, we will use the view on the right, without Web contents view enabled.

All the drives available to your system are displayed. On this system, there is one floppy drive: A. There are two hard drives or hard drive partitions, C and D. There is one removable drive and two CD-ROM drives.

You are going to examine the properties of the A drive on your system, the drive where the ACTIVITIES disk is presently located.

Step 2 Right-click the A drive icon.

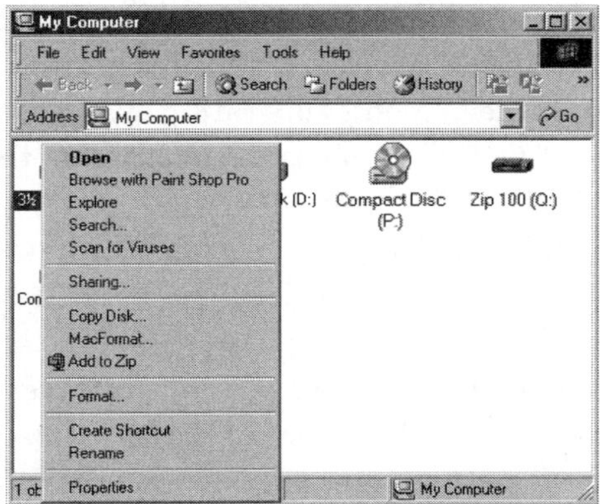

WHAT'S HAPPENING? A menu with options has "dropped down" from the A drive icon.

Step 3 Click **Properties**.

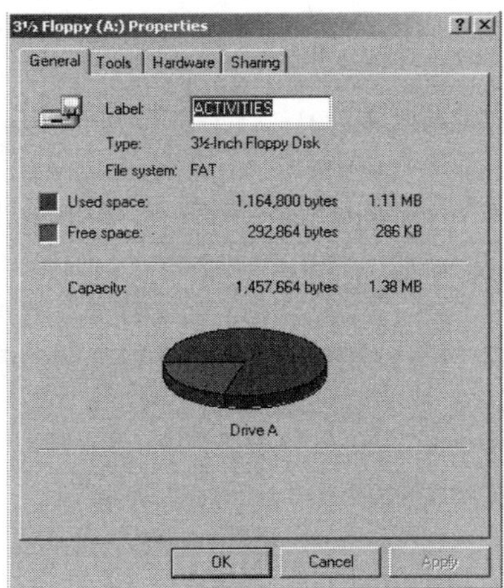

WHAT'S HAPPENING? The property sheet for the A drive displays the properties of the ACTIVITIES disk. You can see many things about the disk: the label or electronic name, the amount of used space, and the amount of free space displayed in numbers and in a graphic pie chart. You can also see the disk type and its total capacity. This is a 3½-inch diskette with a total capacity of 1,457,664 bytes.

Step 4 Click **Cancel**.

Step 5 Close My Computer.

1.40 ETHICAL CONSIDERATIONS IN COPYING DISKS

It is unethical and illegal to make a copy of a program or a disk that you did not purchase and do not own. Making a copy of a program or receiving a copy of a program is stealing someone else's work. If you did not personally purchase the program, even if you are using it at work, it is still illegal to copy it and use it. However, most software manufacturers allow you and encourage you to make backup copies of program disks for your own personal use in case something happens to the original. Remember, however, you need to have purchased the program or have permission to copy the disk in order for the copy to be both legal and ethical. If your program came on a CD-ROM, as is usually the case (such as with the Windows operating system), it is possible to copy it if you have a recording CD-ROM (CDRW) drive, but, again, this is legal *only if you purchased the CD*.

In the following activity, you are going to copy the ACTIVITIES disk that comes with this book so that you have a working copy of it. You will work from a copy of the ACTIVITIES disk so that, if anything happens, you can use the original ACTIVITIES disk to make another copy. Whenever possible, always work from a copy, never an original. This copy of the ACTIVITIES disk will be used in all future exercises. It is legal to make a copy for your personal use only. If you are in a computer lab, check with your instructor for the procedures in your specific lab.

1.41 MAKING A COPY OF THE ACTIVITIES DISK: DISKCOPY

When making an exact copy of a disk, you must have like media. This means the disk you are copying from and the disk you are copying to must be *exactly* the same type and capacity. You are now going to make a working copy of the ACTIVITIES disk. You will use an external program called DISKCOPY. It is stored as a file called DISKCOPY.COM in the WINNT\SYSTEM32 subdirectory. It does exactly what it says; it copies all the information from one floppy disk to another. Before it copies a disk, it formats it. You can never use the DISKCOPY command to copy from a hard disk to a floppy disk or from a floppy disk to a hard disk. You could copy the disk from the desktop. Notice the menu in the previous Activity 1.39, Step 2. One of the options is Copy Disk. In the following activity, you will use the command line method. Please follow the instructions precisely. The ACTIVITIES disk is a high-density, 3½-inch floppy disk. Your blank disk must be the same media type in order to do the next activity.

1.42 ACTIVITY: USING DISKCOPY

Note: If you are in a lab environment, check with your instructor to see if there are any special procedures in your lab.

Step 1 Get a new label. On the label write "ACTIVITIES Disk—Working Copy" and your name. Get a new disk or one that you no longer want the information on that is the same type and capacity as the ACTIVITIES disk. Affix the label to the disk. See Figure 1.5 for the correct location of the label.

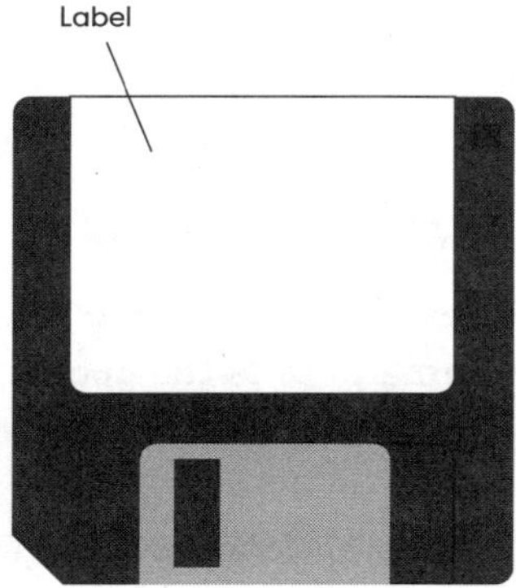
Label

FIGURE 1.5 FLOPPY DISK LABEL PLACEMENT

Step 2 Place the ACTIVITIES disk that came with the textbook in Drive A.

Step 3 Click **Start**. Point to **Programs**. Point to **Accessories**. Click **Command Prompt**.

Step 4 Key in the following: C:\ >**CD \WINNT\SYSTEM32** Enter

Note: Refer to your configuration table, if necessary, to locate the correct directory.

Step 5 Key in the following: C:\WINNT\SYSTEM32>**DISKCOPY A: A:** Enter

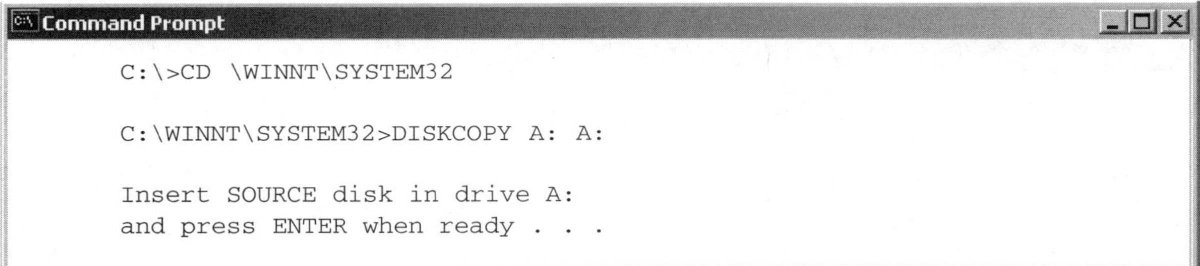
Command Prompt
C:\>CD \WINNT\SYSTEM32
C:\WINNT\SYSTEM32>DISKCOPY A: A:
Insert SOURCE disk in drive A:
and press ENTER when ready . . .

WHAT'S HAPPENING

By keying in **DISKCOPY**, you asked the command processor to find a program called DISKCOPY. It first looked in memory in the internal table of commands. When it could not find a match, it went to the disk in Drive **C** and the subdirectory **WINNT\SYSTEM32**, found the program, loaded it into memory, and started executing it. This program has some prompts, which are instructions to follow. The program asks you to put the SOURCE disk that you wish to copy in Drive A. In this case, the ACTIVITIES disk, which you want to copy, is already in Drive A.

You are telling the operating system to make a copy from the disk in Drive A to the disk in Drive A. To make the copy or begin executing the command DISKCOPY, press the Enter key.

Step 6 Press Enter

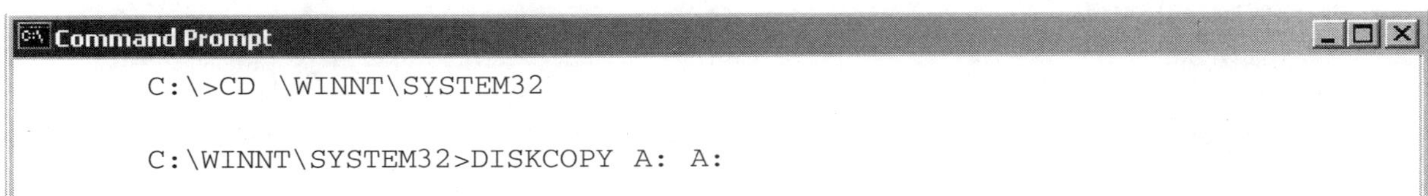
Command Prompt
C:\>CD \WINNT\SYSTEM32
C:\WINNT\SYSTEM32>DISKCOPY A: A:

```
Insert SOURCE disk in drive A:
and press ENTER when ready . . .

Copying 80 tracks
18 sectors per track, 2 side(s)
```

Track and sector numbers will vary depending on the type of disk used. The DISKCOPY command tells the operating system to copy everything on the disk in Drive A (the SOURCE) to RAM. While this program is doing the copying, the cursor flashes onscreen. When the command is completed or the copying is finished, you will need to take another step. You see the following prompt:

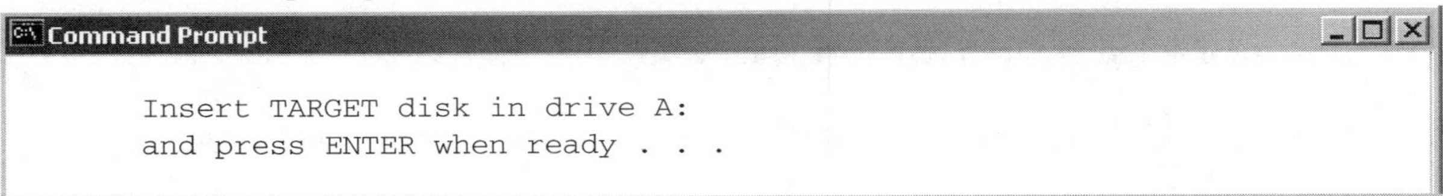

Command Prompt

```
Insert TARGET disk in drive A:
and press ENTER when ready . . .
```

This prompt tells you to remove the SOURCE disk from Drive A and insert the blank or TARGET disk in Drive A so the operating system has a place to copy the information.

Step 7 Remove the master ACTIVITIES disk from Drive A. Insert the blank disk labeled "ACTIVITIES Disk—Working Copy" into Drive A. Close or latch the drive door. Press **Enter**

Command Prompt

```
C:\>CD \WINNT\SYSTEM32

C:\WINNT\SYSTEM32>DISKCOPY A: A:

Insert SOURCE disk in drive A:
and press ENTER when ready . . .

Copying 80 tracks
18 sectors per track, 2 side(s)

Insert TARGET disk in drive A:
and press ENTER when ready . . .
```

Again, you see the flashing cursor. After DISKCOPY formats the TARGET disk, whatever was copied into RAM is copied or written to the blank disk in Drive A. When the process is complete, you will see the following message:

Command Prompt

```
Volume Serial Number is 1508-0C25

Copy another disk (Y/N)?
```

WHAT'S HAPPENING? The system wants to know if you wish to make multiple copies of the floppy diskette already in Drive A.

Step 8 Press **N** **Enter**

WHAT'S HAPPENING? The prompt tells you that the program has finished executing. The volume serial number changes with each DISKCOPY command and will not be the same as the example.

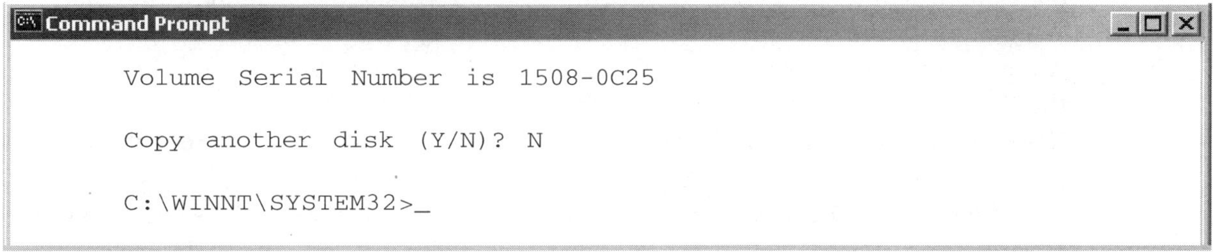

WHAT'S HAPPENING? You are returned to the C:\WINNT\SYSTEM32> prompt. The operating system is now ready for a new command.

Step 9 Close the Command Prompt window.

1.43 HOW TO END THE WORK SESSION

You can stop working with the computer at any time. Since your programs are stored on disks, you will not lose them. However, you must always exit Windows properly and completely; otherwise you could do serious, sometimes irreparable, damage to the system.

1.44 ACTIVITY: ENDING THE WORK SESSION

Note: Check with your lab instructor to see what special procedures you might need to follow in your lab environment.

Step 1 Close any remaining open windows, including the Command Prompt window.

Step 2 Click **Start**.

Step 3 Click **Shut Down**. Be sure Shut down is the choice on the drop-down menu.

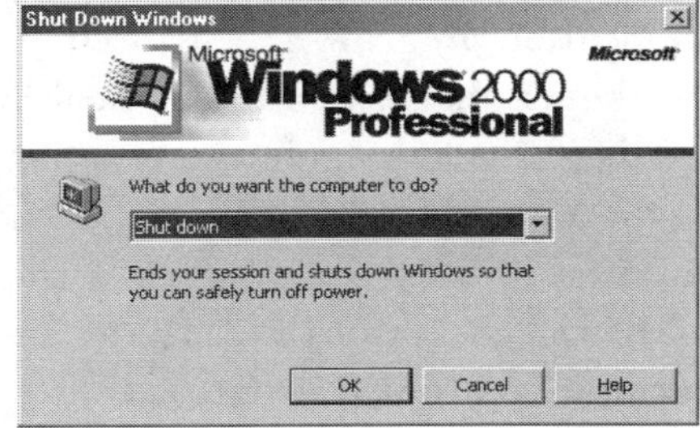

Step 4 Click **OK**.

WHAT'S HAPPENING? You have initiated the shut-down procedure.

Step 5 New computers will power down automatically, but if this does not happen, wait until you see the screen telling you it is safe to turn off the computer.

Step 6 Turn off the monitor and the system unit (if necessary).

CHAPTER SUMMARY

1. An operating system is a software program that is required in order to run application software and to oversee the hardware components of the computer system.
2. Windows is the major operating system in use today on Wintel microcomputers.
3. All microcomputers come with disk drives. There are three basic types of disk drives: the floppy disk drive, the hard disk drive, and the CD-ROM drive.
4. Computer systems are configured in various ways, such as: 1) one hard disk drive, one CD-ROM drive, and one floppy disk drive, 2) one hard disk drive, one CD-ROM drive, one floppy disk drive, and one Zip drive, 3) two hard disk drives, one CD-ROM drive, and one floppy disk drive, or 4) one hard disk drive, one CD-ROM drive, one read-write CD-ROM drive, and one floppy disk drive.
5. Booting the system, also known as a cold start, means more than powering on the system. It loads the operating system into memory and executes the self-diagnostic test routine.
6. Internal commands are programs loaded in CMD.EXE with the operating system. They remain in memory until the power is turned off.
7. External commands are stored on a disk and must be loaded into memory each time they are used. They are transient and do not remain in memory after being executed.
8. Programs and data are stored on disks as files. The formal name for this is *file specification*, which includes the file name and the file extension.
9. A command is a program. A program is the set of instructions telling the computer what to do.
10. Programs (commands) must be loaded into memory in order to be executed.
11. To load a program into memory, the user can key in the command name at the system prompt or click on the command's icon.
12. The DIR command is an internal command that displays the directory (table of contents) of a disk.
13. The **Backspace** key deletes characters to the left of the cursor.
14. The **Esc** key ignores what was previously keyed in before **Enter** is pressed.
15. The **Shift** key shifts letters to upper case.
16. The **Print Screen** key can be used to "dump" an image of the screen so that it can be pasted into an application program and printed.
17. A toggle switch is like a light switch. In one position, the function is turned on. By pressing the same toggle switch again the function is turned off.
18. The **Ctrl** key and the **Pause** key, when held down together, freeze the screen display on older computers. Newer computers use the **Pause** key.
19. The **Ctrl** key and the **Break** key or the **Ctrl** key and the letter **C** when held down together cancel a command that was entered.

20. Minor internal commands include VER, CLS, DATE, and TIME.
    - VER displays the current version of the OS that is in memory
    - CLS clears the screen.
    - DATE and TIME allow you to look at and/or change the system date and system time, a process that can also be done from the desktop taskbar. Using the /T parameter with the DATE or TIME command will display the system date or time.
21. DISKCOPY is an external command that makes an identical copy of any disk, track for track, sector for sector. It was used to make a working copy of the ACTIVITIES disk but can be used to make exact copies with any two floppy disks that are the same media type. It formats a disk prior to copying to it.
22. To end a work session with the computer, Windows must be shut down in the proper sequence and shouldn't be turned off until a message on the screen tells you it is safe to do so.

KEY TERMS

alphanumeric key	disk file	operating system
booting the system	enhancement	program file
bug	file extension	scrolling
command	file name	system date
cursor	file specification	system time
data file	function key	toggle switch
directional key	numeric key	ToolTip

DISCUSSION QUESTIONS

1. What is an operating system?
2. What are enhancements?
3. Define system configuration.
4. List two common ways that computer systems are configured.
5. Why is it necessary to boot the system?
6. How would you boot the system?
7. What is an object?
8. What is a property?
9. What is a value?
10. Identify and explain the function and purpose of the two parts of a file specification.
11. What is the difference between a command and a program?
12. Compare and contrast internal and external commands.
13. What is the purpose of the DIR command?
14. Name and describe the functions of the four parts of a keyboard.
15. What is the purpose and function of a toggle switch?
16. Identify one way to print what is on the screen.
17. How can you stop the display from rapidly scrolling on the screen?
18. How can you cancel a command after you have pressed **Enter**?
19. What is the function of the VER command?
20. What is the function of the CLS command?
21. How can you set the date and time?
22. How do you set the time when using the TIME command?

23. What is the purpose of making a backup copy of a program?
24. Why should you work with a copy of a program rather than with the original?
25. Why is it important to know what type of media you are using when copying disks?
26. What is the purpose of the DISKCOPY command?
27. What are the necessary steps to ending a work session?

TRUE/FALSE QUESTIONS

For each question, circle the letter T if the statement is true and the letter F if the statement is false.

T F 1. To identify what version of the operating system you are using, you could, at the command line, use the VER command.

T F 2. A correct way to key in a date would be **2/4/01**.

T F 3. When you see the computer notation Ctrl + **C**, it means you should key in the word **Control** and then the letter **C**.

T F 4. LFN is an acronym for Last File Noted.

T F 5. DISKCOPY.COM is a program that is stored on the disk as a file.

COMPLETION QUESTIONS

Write the correct answer in each blank space.

6. One way to communicate with the computer is by __________ commands on the keyboard.
7. Programs, data, and text are stored on disks as _______.
8. The operating system is in charge of the ________ components of the computer.
9. If you wanted to see the table of contents of a disk in the Command Prompt window, you would key in _______.
10. If you wished to cancel a command line you keyed in prior to pressing Enter, you would press the ______ key.

MULTIPLE CHOICE QUESTIONS

For each question, write the letter for the correct answer in the blank space.

11. To display the contents of a disk, key in the following command:
    a. TOC
    b. DIR
    c. DIS
    d. Directory
12. To change the date to May 7, 2001, after you key in DATE, you could key in:
    a. 5/7/01
    b. 5-7-01
    c. 5.7.01
    d. all of the above

13. To clear the screen, key in:
    a. CLS
    b. CLR
    c. CLEAR
    d. Clear the screen
14. Which of the following is a type of disk drive?
    a. hard disk drive
    b. soft disk drive
    c. both a and b
    d. neither a nor b
15. To copy all the information from one floppy disk to another, you may use the command:
    a. DISKCOPY
    b. COPY
    c. DISKCMP
    d. D-COPY

APPLICATION ASSIGNMENTS

PROBLEM SET I—AT THE COMPUTER

PROBLEM A

A-a Boot the system, if it is not booted.

A-b Go to the Command Prompt window.

A-c Make sure the prompt is **C:\>**.

A-d Change the date to 5/8/01.

A-e Re-enter the same command.

1. The day of the week that appears on the screen is:
    a. Tue
    b. Wed
    c. Thu
    d. Fri

A-f Change the date to the current date.

2. The command you used was:
    a. DATE
    b. TIME
    c. DISKCOPY
    d. none of the above

A-g Key in **TIME** Enter

A-h At the time prompt, key in **27:00** Enter

☐ 3. What error message is displayed on the screen?
   a. Not a valid time.
   b. The system cannot accept the time entered.
   c. Please key in the correct time.
   d. Do not use a colon.

A-i Press Enter

PROBLEM B

B-a Place the working copy of the ACTIVITIES disk in Drive A.

B-b Key in C:\>**A:** Enter

B-c Key in A:\>**DIR** Enter

☐ 4. What date is listed for **Y.FIL**?
   a. 8/12/1999
   b. 8/12/2001
   c. 8/12/1998
   d. 8/12/2000

B-d Press the F3 key.

☐ 5. What appeared on the screen?
   a. DATE
   b. DIR
   c. Y.FIL
   d. none of the above

B-e Press the Backspace key twice.

☐ 6. What is displayed on the screen?
   a. DIR
   b. DI
   c. D
   d. <Enter>

B-f If the Command Prompt is not in a window, place it in one now.

B-g Click on the icon at the left of the title bar. Select **Properties**.

☐ 7. What Property sheet is on the top?
   a. Options
   b. Font
   c. Layout
   d. Colors

B-h Click **Cancel**.

PROBLEM C

C-a Close the Command Prompt window.

8. You may close the Command Prompt window by clicking the
   a. [minimize] button on the title bar.
   b. [restore] button on the title bar.
   c. [maximize] button on the title bar.
   d. [X] on the title bar.

C-b Exit Windows properly.

9. The fastest way to exit Windows correctly is to
   a. turn off the computer.
   b. click Start, then click Shut Down.

C-c Be sure to remove your ACTIVITIES Disk—Working Copy from Drive A.

PROBLEM SET II—BRIEF ESSAY

1. When DOS was a stand-alone operating system, file specifications were limited to the 8.3 file-naming rules. Windows 95 introduced the use of LFNs. Compare and contrast these two sets of rules. List any reasons for still retaining the use of 8.3 file names.
2. You can change the system time and date either from the command line or from Windows. List the advantages and disadvantages of each method. Which do you prefer? Explain your answer.

CHAPTER

2

COMMAND SYNTAX

USING THE DIR COMMAND WITH PARAMETERS AND WILDCARDS

LEARNING OBJECTIVES

After completing this chapter you will be able to:

1. Define command syntax.
2. Explain what parameters are and how they are used.
3. Explain the purpose and use of the DIR command.
4. Define prompts and explain how they are used.
5. Explain the purpose of the CD command.
6. Explain the purpose and function of a device.
7. Explain the purpose and function of device names.
8. Explain the purpose and function of defaults.
9. Explain the function and purpose of subdirectories (paths).
10. Explain the use and purpose of wildcards.
11. Define global specifications and identify their symbols.
12. Explain the purpose and function of redirection.

STUDENT OUTCOMES

1. Read a syntax diagram and be able to name and explain what each part signifies.
2. Use both fixed and variable parameters with the DIR command.
3. Give the names of the disk drives on your computer.
4. Change the default drive and the directory.
5. Use subdirectories (paths) with the DIR command.
6. Use global specifications with the DIR command.
7. Use wildcards with the DIR command.
8. Redirect the output of the DIR command to either a file or a printer.
9. Use online Help.

CHAPTER OVERVIEW

To communicate with the computer at the command line prompt, you need to learn the computer's language. You must follow the syntax of the language and use punctuation marks the computer understands. As in mastering any new language, new vocabulary words must be learned, word order (syntax) must be determined, and the method of separating statements into syntactic units must be understood. The computer has a very limited use of language, so it is exceedingly important to be precise when you are speaking to it.

In this chapter, you will learn some basic computer commands, the syntax or order of these commands, and where the commands begin and end. You will learn how to make your commands specific, how to use wildcards to affect a command, and how to determine which disk you want to write to or read from. You will also learn how to use the online Help feature.

2.1 COMMAND SYNTAX

All languages have rules or conventions for speaking and writing. The syntax, or word order, and punctuation of a language is important. For example, in English the noun (person, place, or thing) is followed by the verb (the action). In Latin the verb most often ends a sentence, because Latin had no punctuation marks and the subject could be anywhere in the sentence, even within the verb. When you learn a language, you learn its syntax.

Anything you key into the computer must be a word the computer understands. The words you key in are actually commands ordering the computer to perform a specific task. These commands must also be in the correct order; that is, they must have the proper syntax. The computer cannot guess what you mean. People can understand "Going I store," but if you key in an incorrect word or put correct words in the wrong order, a computer will not understand.

In computer language, a command can be compared to a verb, the action you wish to take. In Chapter 1, you used the command DIR. In other words, when you keyed in DIR, you were asking the system to take an action: run the program called DIR that lets you see the directory (table of contents) of a disk.

Using the graphical user interface in the Windows OS does not change things—there are still syntax and rules. An icon that points to a program is based on the rules of syntax. Certainly, it is easier from a user's perspective to click an icon to accomplish a task rather than having to know the command and the appropriate syntax. However, when things do not work, you the user need to know how to go under the hood, so to speak, and fix the problem so that you can "click" on your desktop successfully.

2.2 WHAT ARE PARAMETERS?

A ***parameter*** is information you can use to modify or qualify a command. Some commands require parameters, while other commands let you add them when needed. Some parameters are variable. A ***variable parameter*** is one to which you the user supply the value. This process is similar to a math formula. For instance, $x + y = z$ is a simple formula. You can plug in whatever values you wish for x and y. If $x = 1$ and $y = 2$, you know the value of z, which is 3. These values can change or are *variable* so that x can equal 5 and y can equal 3, which makes z equal to 8. These variables can have any other numerical value you wish. You can also have $z = 10$, $x = 5$, and mathematically establish the value of y. No matter what numbers x, y, or z are, you will be able to establish the value of each.

Other parameters are ***fixed***. For instance, if the formula reads $x + 5 = z$, then x is the variable parameter and 5 is the fixed parameter. You can change the value of x but not the value of 5.

When you are working with some command line commands, you are allowed to add one or more parameters to make the action of a command more specific. This process is the same in English. If I give my granddaughter my Visa card and tell her, "Go buy," I have given her an open-ended statement—she can buy anything (making her one happy camper!). However, if I add a qualifier, "Go buy shoes," I have limited what she can do. The word "shoes" is the parameter. This pattern exemplifies precisely what parameters do to a command.

2.3 READING A SYNTAX DIAGRAM

A command line interface is a language that has a vocabulary, grammar, and syntax. To use the language of the command line, you must learn the vocabulary (commands) and understand the grammar (punctuation) and syntax (order). The syntax information is provided through online Help. The ***command syntax*** diagrams tell you how to enter a command with its optional or ***mandatory parameters***. However, you need to be able to interpret these ***syntax diagrams***.

Here is the formal command syntax diagram for the DIR command you used earlier:

```
DIR [drive:][path][filename] [/A[[:]attributes]] [/B] [/C] [/D] [/L] [/N]
  [/O[[:]sortorder]] [/P] [/Q] [/S] [/T[[:]timefield]] [/W] [/X] [/4]
```

The first entry is the command name, DIR. You must use this name only. You cannot substitute another word such as DIRECTORY or INDEX. The parameters that follow the command are in brackets [ ]. Brackets indicate that these parameters are optional—not required for the command. The DIR command has ***optional parameters*** only. There are no required, or mandatory, parameters for the DIR command.

2.4 USING FIXED PARAMETERS WITH THE DIR COMMAND

DIR is a command with optional parameters. Most often, a fixed parameter is referred to as a ***switch*** and typically begins with / (the slash).

In the **DIR** command syntax diagram, **/W** and **/P** are in brackets. You never key in the brackets, only / (the forward slash or slash) and the **W** or **P**. You must be careful; there is only one slash—the forward slash /. The \ is a ***backslash*** and is always referred to as the backslash. When a mark is referred to as a slash, it always means the forward slash.

When you key in **DIR** and the files scroll by, they move so quickly that you cannot read them. In the previous chapter, you learned that you could halt the display by pressing the **Pause** key or the **Ctrl** and **S** keys. However, there is a more efficient way to solve this problem by using the **/P** parameter. The **/P** parameter will display one screen of information at a time. It will also give you a prompt that you must respond to before it will display another screenful of information.

Note 1: There are times you may find it necessary to quit before you have completed the entire chapter. Each activity begins with a note indicating which diskette is in the drive and the current directory and drive. Thus, if you complete an activity, you may pick up where you left off. When you stop working, be sure to return to the Windows desktop and initiate the Windows shut-down procedure.

Note 2: Be sure you know what your computer laboratory procedures are.

Note 3: If your system varies from the textbook, refer to the Configuration Table in Chapter 1.6.

2.5 ACTIVITY: USING FIXED PARAMETERS WITH THE DIR COMMAND

Note: Whenever the textbook refers to the ACTIVITIES disk, you will use the working copy that you made in Chapter 1 and labeled "ACTIVITIES Disk—Working Copy."

Step 1 If it is not on, turn on the computer.

Step 2 Open a **Command Prompt** window.

Step 3 Key in the following: C:\>**CD ** Enter

Step 4 Key in the following: C:\>**CLS** Enter

Command Prompt
C:\>_

WHAT'S HAPPENING? You have successfully booted the system. To ensure that you were at the root of Drive C, you keyed in **CD **. You are at the root directory of Drive C. You have also cleared the screen.

Step 5 Insert the "ACTIVITIES Disk—Working Copy" in Drive A. (Remember, this means your working copy.)

Step 6 Key in the following: C:\>**A:** Enter

Command Prompt
C:\>A:
A:\>_

WHAT'S HAPPENING? The default drive is now Drive A. The default directory is the root of A.

Step 7 Key in the following: A:\>**DIR /P** Enter

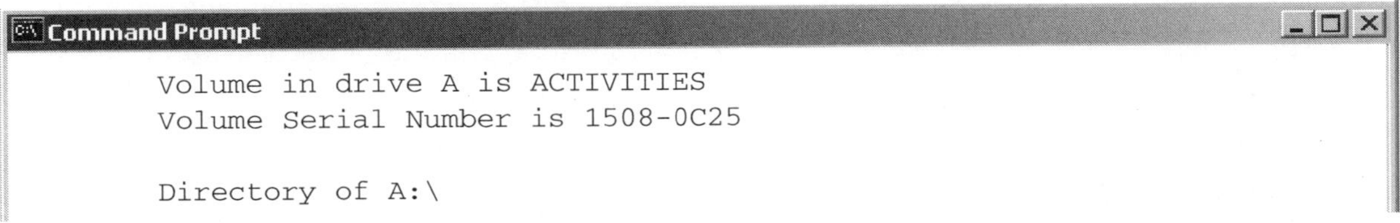
Command Prompt
Volume in drive A is ACTIVITIES
Volume Serial Number is 1508-0C25
Directory of A:\

```
05/30/2000  04:32p                 45 BYE.TYP
08/12/2000  04:12p                314 CASES.FIL
04/23/2000  04:03p                 72 APRIL.TMP
04/23/2000  04:03p                 53 BONJOUR.TMP
04/23/2000  04:03p                 75 FEB.TMP
01/01/2002  04:32a                 34 GOODBYE.TMP
05/30/2000  04:32p                 75 FEBRUARY.TMM
05/30/2000  04:32p                 98 OLIVE.OIL
12/06/2000  02:45p                 19 FILE3.FP
12/06/2000  02:45p                 19 FILE3.SWT
12/06/2000  02:45p                 19 FILE4.FP
12/31/2001  04:32p                181 WILDONE.DOS
10/01/2000  04:12p                 29 MIDDLE.UP
01/01/2002  04:32a                 34 GOODBYE.TXT
10/01/2000  04:12p                 26 RIGHT.UP
10/01/2000  04:12p                 26 DRESS.UP
06/16/2000  04:32p                 72 APRIL.TXT
06/16/2000  04:32p                 73 JANUARY.TXT
06/16/2000  04:32p                 75 FEBRUARY.TXT
Press any key to continue . . .
```

WHAT'S HAPPENING? You keyed in the command **DIR** followed by a slash / and the parameter **P**. The slash, which must be included with a fixed parameter, is commonly referred as a switch. However, the slash (/) is really a ***delimiter***. A delimiter is a signal that one thing is ending and another is beginning. The number of files on your screen may differ from the figure above, depending on the size of your open Command Prompt window. Command line commands use different punctuation marks, such as delimiters, but the punctuation marks that they use are very specific. Remember, / is used only with fixed parameters.

In this example, the slash is the signal to the DIR command that additional instructions follow. The parameter P is the additional instruction. There can be no space between the slash and the P. The slash and the P stop the directory from scrolling. Thus, /P told the DIR command to fill the screen and then pause until the user takes some action. The message at the bottom of the screen tells you to press any key to continue.

Step 8 Press **Enter**

Command Prompt

```
06/16/2000  04:32p                 71 MARCH.TXT
07/31/1999  12:53p                 46 STEVEN.FIL
05/30/2000  04:32p                 53 HELLO.TXT
12/06/2000  02:45p                 19 FILE2.CZG
01/31/2001  12:09p                304 EXP01JAN.DAT
02/28/2001  12:10p                307 EXP01FEB.DAT
03/31/1999  12:11p                294 EXP99MAR.DAT
10/01/1999  02:53p                 73 JAN.NEW
05/30/2000  04:32p                 45 BYE.TXT
05/14/2001  11:28a              4,842 GO.BAT
07/31/2000  04:32p              1,228 STATES.USA
04/23/2000  04:03p                 73 JANUARY.TMP
```

```
12/31/2001  04:32p              64 WILD2.YYY
12/31/2001  04:32p              64 WILD3.ZZZ
12/31/2001  04:32p              93 WILDONE
12/31/2001  04:32p             181 WILDTHR.DOS
10/01/1999  02:53p              74 APR.NEW
12/31/2001  04:32p             182 WILDTWO.DOS
11/22/1989  10:35p           7,269 RNS.EXE
01/31/1999  12:09p             294 EXP99JAN.DAT
03/31/2001  12:11p             302 EXP01MAR.DAT
03/31/2000  12:11p             292 EXP00MAR.DAT
11/06/2000  04:12p              53 EMPLOYEE.ONE
11/06/2000  04:12p              57 EMPLOYEE.THR
Press any key to continue . . .
```

WHAT'S HAPPENING? When you pressed Enter, the display continued scrolling. Because there are still more files, the DIR command asks you to press any key again to continue the display. As you can see, the display stops each time the screen fills.

Step 9 Press Enter

Step 10 Press Enter

Step 11 Continue pressing Enter until you reach the end of the display.

Command Prompt

```
07/03/2000   01:52p     <DIR>              SPORTS
07/03/2000  01:53p      <DIR>              MEDIA
07/03/2000  01:53p      <DIR>              WORKING
05/27/2001  10:08p                  76     LONGFILENAME
05/27/2001  10:08p                  81     LONGFILENAME.TXT
05/27/2001  10:09p                 122     LONGFILENAME.EXTENSION
05/27/2001  10:42p                  97     LONGFILENAMING.TXT
05/27/2001  10:43p                  95     LONGFILENAMED.TXT
              90 File(s)         29,382 bytes
               9 Dir(s)         292,864 bytes free

A:\>_
```

WHAT'S HAPPENING? You kept pressing Enter until there were no more files to display. The system prompt (A:\>) appears to signal that there are no more files on this disk and that the OS is waiting for you to key in the next command. There is another way to display the files on the screen. You may use the /W parameter to display the directory in a wide format.

Step 12 Key in the following: A:\>**DIR /W** Enter

Command Prompt

```
A:\>DIR /W
 Volume in drive A is ACTIVITIES
 Volume Serial Number is 1508-0C25

 Directory of A:\
```

```
BYE.TYP                    CASES.FIL                  APRIL.TMP
BONJOUR.TMP                FEB.TMP                    GOODBYE.TMP
FEBRUARY.TMM               OLIVE.OIL                  FILE3.FP
FILE3.SWT                  FILE4.FP                   WILDONE.DOS
MIDDLE.UP                  GOODBYE.TXT                RIGHT.UP
DRESS.UP                   APRIL.TXT                  JANUARY.TXT
FEBRUARY.TXT               MARCH.TXT                  STEVEN.FIL
HELLO.TXT                  FILE2.CZG                  EXP01JAN.DAT
EXP01FEB.DAT               EXP99MAR.DAT               JAN.NEW
BYE.TXT                    GO.BAT                     STATES.USA
JANUARY.TMP                WILD2.YYY                  WILD3.ZZZ
WILDONE                    WILDTHR.DOS                APR.NEW
WILDTWO.DOS                RNS.EXE                    EXP99JAN.DAT
EXP01MAR.DAT               EXP00MAR.DAT               EMPLOYEE.ONE
EMPLOYEE.THR               APR.99                     FEB.99
CAROLYN.FIL                MAR.99                     MIDDLE.RED
LEFT.RED                   RIGHT.RED                  SECOND.FIL
PERSONAL.FIL               DANCES.TXT                 MARK.FIL
GREEN.JAZ                  EMPLOYEE.TWO               AWARD.MOV
STATE.CAP                  EXP00FEB.DAT               GRAMMY.REC
FRANK.FIL                  FEB.NEW                    OLDAUTO.MAK
MAR.NEW                    FILE2.FP                   FILE2.SWT
BLUE.JAZ                   FILE3.CZG                  EXP99FEB.DAT
NAME.BAT                   NEWAUTO.MAK                STATE2.CAP
JAN.TMP                    JAN.99                     TEST.TXT
GETYN.COM                  WILD1.XXX                  MAR.TMP
MARCH.TMP                  APR.TMP                    NEWPRSON.FIL
Y.FIL                      Sandy and Nicki.txt        Sandy and Patty.txt
EXP00JAN.DAT               [DATA]                     [TEST]
[GAMES]                    [PHONE]                    [FINANCE]
[LEVEL-1]                  [SPORTS]                   [MEDIA]
[WORKING]                  LONGFILENAME               LONGFILENAME.TXT
LONGFILENAME.EXTENSION     LONGFILENAMING.TXT         LONGFILENAMED.TXT
              90 File(s)         29,381 bytes
               9 Dir(s)         292,864 bytes free

A:\>_
```

WHAT'S HAPPENING? The directory display is now across the screen, three columns wide. In addition, the information about the files is not as comprehensive. All you see is the file specification—the file name and its extension. You do not see the file size, date, or time, but you still see the total number of files and the number of bytes free. You can also identify the directories by the brackets around them such as **[MEDIA]**. Thus, /W allows you to see the files side by side. You can use more than one parameter at a time. Since there are so many files on this disk, the entire directory does not fit on one screen.

Step 13 Key in the following: A:\>**DIR /P /W** Enter

Command Prompt
A:\>DIR /P /W
Volume in drive A is ACTIVITIES

```
 Volume Serial Number is 1508-0C25

 Directory of A:\

BYE.TYP                  CASES.FIL                APRIL.TMP
BONJOUR.TMP              FEB.TMP                  GOODBYE.TMP
FEBRUARY.TMM             OLIVE.OIL                FILE3.FP
FILE3.SWT                FILE4.FP                 WILDONE.DOS
MIDDLE.UP                GOODBYE.TXT              RIGHT.UP
DRESS.UP                 APRIL.TXT                JANUARY.TXT
FEBRUARY.TXT             MARCH.TXT                STEVEN.FIL
HELLO.TXT                FILE2.CZG                EXP01JAN.DAT
EXP01FEB.DAT             EXP99MAR.DAT             JAN.NEW
BYE.TXT                  GO.BAT                   STATES.USA
JANUARY.TMP              WILD2.YYY                WILD3.ZZZ
WILDONE                  WILDTHR.DOS              APR.NEW
WILDTWO.DOS              RNS.EXE                  EXP99JAN.DAT
EXP01MAR.DAT             EXP00MAR.DAT             EMPLOYEE.ONE
EMPLOYEE.THR             APR.99                   FEB.99
CAROLYN.FIL              MAR.99                   MIDDLE.RED
LEFT.RED                 RIGHT.RED                SECOND.FIL
PERSONAL.FIL             DANCES.TXT               MARK.FIL
GREEN.JAZ                EMPLOYEE.TWO             AWARD.MOV
Press any key to continue . . .
```

By using these parameters together, you could see the files in a wide display, one screenful at a time.

Step 14 Press **Enter**

Command Prompt

```
STATE.CAP                EXP00FEB.DAT             GRAMMY.REC
FRANK.FIL                FEB.NEW                  OLDAUTO.MAK
MAR.NEW                  FILE2.FP                 FILE2.SWT
BLUE.JAZ                 FILE3.CZG                EXP99FEB.DAT
NAME.BAT                 NEWAUTO.MAK              STATE2.CAP
JAN.TMP                  JAN.99                   TEST.TXT
GETYN.COM                WILD1.XXX                MAR.TMP
MARCH.TMP                APR.TMP                  NEWPRSON.FIL
Y.FIL                    Sandy and Nicki.txt      Sandy and Patty.txt
EXP00JAN.DAT             [DATA]                   [TEST]
[GAMES]                  [PHONE]                  [FINANCE]
[LEVEL-1]                [SPORTS]                 [MEDIA]
[WORKING]                LONGFILENAME             LONGFILENAME.TXT
LONGFILENAME.EXTENSION   LONGFILENAMING.TXT       LONGFILENAMED.TXT
              90 File(s)          29,381 bytes
               9 Dir(s)          292,864 bytes free

A:\>_
```

You have returned to the system prompt.

2.6 USING FILE NAMES AS VARIABLE PARAMETERS

In the previous activities, you used the DIR command with two different optional fixed parameters, /P and /W. These optional fixed parameters have specific meanings. There is another parameter you can use with the DIR command: the name of the file.

File names are formally called file specifications. A file specification is broken into two parts, the file name and the file extension. When people refer to a ***file*** or file name, they really mean the file specification: the file name and file extension together. It is much like a person's name. When someone refers to Ramon, he usually means someone specific such as Ramon Rodreiquez. In the computer world, when you refer to a file name, you must give both its first name (file name) and its last name (file extension). When you create files in an application program, you are allowed to name the file. On this disk the files already exist and are already named. You cannot call them anything else. However, when you have the opportunity for naming files, you must follow the rules. Windows has rules called *conventions* for naming files. These are:

1. All files in a directory (subdirectory) must have unique names.
2. File names are mandatory. All files must have file names less than but no more than 255 characters long. However, it is recommended that you do not use very long file names, as most programs cannot interpret them.
3. File extensions are usually three characters long.
4. The following characters are illegal, and may *not* be used in a file name:

   \ / : * ? " < > |

5. All other characters, including periods and spaces, are legal in Windows file names.

Typically, a file name reflects the subject of the file, for example, EMPLOYEE or TAXES. The file extension is usually given by the application creating the file. For example, Microsoft Word uses .DOC for its extension, Lotus 1-2-3 uses .WK1, and Microsoft Excel uses .XLS.

Keep in mind that many older, 16-bit application packages created before Windows 95 cannot deal with long file names, spaces in file names, or periods in file names. These packages adhere to the older DOS rules, which limit the name to eight characters and the optional extension to three characters. You will also find that files on the Internet tend to adhere to the older DOS rule—also called the 8.3 rule.

When you key in the DIR command, you get the entire table of contents of the disk, known as the directory. Usually, you do not care about all the files. Most often, you are interested only in whether or not one specific file is located or stored on the disk. If you use one of the parameters, /P or /W, you still have to look through all the files. You can locate a specific file quickly by using the file name. Simply give the DIR command specific information about what file you seek. Look at the syntax diagram:

```
DIR [drive:][path][filename] [/P] [/W]
```

The file name, indicated above in brackets, is a variable optional parameter. To use the optional parameter, you must plug in the value or the name of the file for [filename]. In some syntax diagrams, you will see [filename[.ext]]. The .ext is in separate brackets within the file name brackets because it is part of the file name syntax. A file may not have an extension, but if it does have an extension, you must include it. When you include it, there must be no spaces between the file name and the file extension.

The delimiter that is used between a file name and a file extension is a period, or what is called the ***dot***. A dot, as a delimiter, is used between a file name and a file extension. A file name is keyed in as MYFILE.TXT. To verbalize the name of this file, you would say "MY FILE dot TEXT."

2.7 ACTIVITY: USING A FILE NAME AS A VARIABLE PARAMETER

Note: You should be at the command line at the A:\> prompt.

Step 1 Key in the following: A:\>**DIR STEVEN.FIL** Enter

```
Command Prompt

A:\>DIR STEVEN.FIL
 Volume in drive A is ACTIVITIES
 Volume Serial Number is 1508-0C25

 Directory of A:\

07/31/1999  12:53p                  46 STEVEN.FIL
               1 File(s)             46 bytes
               0 Dir(s)         292,864 bytes free

A:\>_
```

WHAT'S HAPPENING? The DIR command returned exactly what you asked for—a single file that met your criteria. This command did find the file **STEVEN.FIL** on the disk in Drive A. Furthermore, **STEVEN.FIL** is the variable parameter. You substituted **STEVEN.FIL** for [filename]. You are told the Volume name is ACTIVITIES. The date and time **STEVEN.FIL** was last updated appears first (**07/31/1999 12:53p**), then the size of the file is listed in bytes (**46**) followed last by the file name (**STEVEN.FIL**). The line beneath (**1 File(s) 46 bytes**) told you that you only have one file that matched that criteria. The last line states that there are no directories (**0 Dir (s)**) and how much space is free on the disk for more data (**292,864 bytes free**). What if the system could not find the file you asked for?

Step 2 Key in the following: A:\>**DIR NOFILE.TXT** Enter

```
Command Prompt

A:\>DIR NOFILE.TXT
 Volume in drive A is ACTIVITIES
 Volume Serial Number is 1508-0C25
```

```
 Directory of A:\

File Not Found

A:\>_
```

WHAT'S HAPPENING? **File Not Found** is a system message. Sometimes it is referred to as an error message. DIR is telling you that it looked through the entire list of files in the root directory of the disk in Drive A and could not find a "match" for the file called **NOFILE.TXT**. You may also enter more than one file specification with the DIR command.

Step 3 Key in the following: A:\>**DIR STEVEN.FIL CAROLYN.FIL** Enter

```
Command Prompt

A:\>DIR STEVEN.FIL CAROLYN.FIL
 Volume in drive A is ACTIVITIES
 Volume Serial Number is 1508-0C25

 Directory of A:\

07/31/1999  12:53p                  46 STEVEN.FIL

 Directory of A:\

07/31/1999  12:53p                  47 CAROLYN.FIL
               2 File(s)             93 bytes
               0 Dir(s)         292,864 bytes free

A:\>_
```

WHAT'S HAPPENING? The Command Prompt allows you to enter more than one parameter at a time when using the DIR command. This feature was introduced in Windows 2000 Professional. Here you asked to display two files. Both were displayed with their individual file names and file information as well as their location (**Directory of A:**). Now the last line tells you that you found two files that take up a total of 93 bytes (the total of 46 for **STEVEN.FIL** and 47 for **CAROLYN.FIL**).

Step 4 Key in the following: A:\>**DIR LONGFILENAME** Enter

```
Command Prompt

A:\>DIR LONGFILENAME
 Volume in drive A is ACTIVITIES
 Volume Serial Number is 1508-0C25

 Directory of A:\
```

```
05/27/2001  10:08p                76 LONGFILENAME
               1 File(s)           76 bytes
               0 Dir(s)       292,864 bytes free

A:\>_
```

As you can see, you may use the DIR command with long file names.

Step 5 Key in the following: A:\>**DIR LONGFILENAME.EXTENSION** Enter

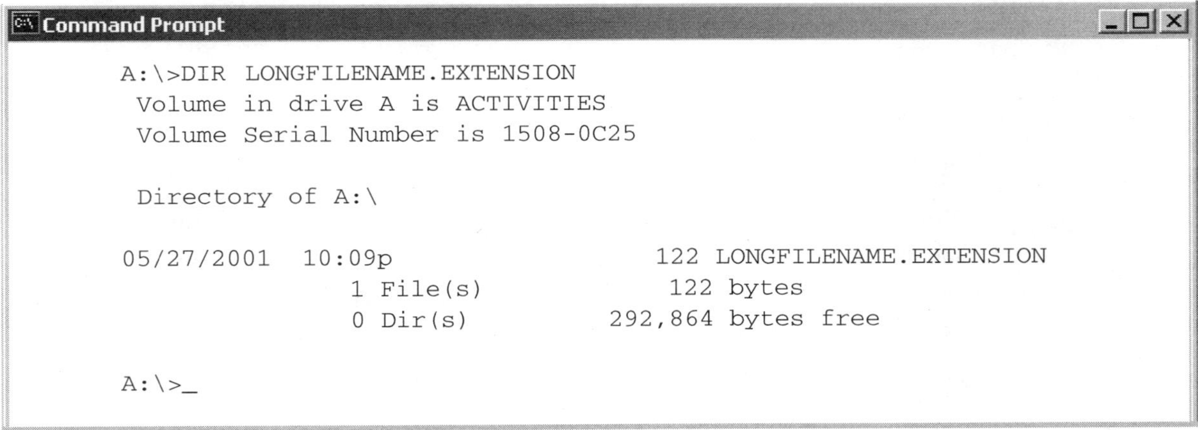

```
Command Prompt
A:\>DIR LONGFILENAME.EXTENSION
 Volume in drive A is ACTIVITIES
 Volume Serial Number is 1508-0C25

 Directory of A:\

05/27/2001  10:09p               122 LONGFILENAME.EXTENSION
               1 File(s)          122 bytes
               0 Dir(s)       292,864 bytes free

A:\>_
```

You may also have a file extension that is longer than three characters, as is shown here.

Step 6 Key in the following: A:\>**DIR Sandy and Patty.txt** Enter

```
Command Prompt
A:\>DIR Sandy and Patty.txt
 Volume in drive A is ACTIVITIES
 Volume Serial Number is 1508-0C25

 Directory of A:\


 Directory of A:\


 Directory of A:\

File Not Found

A:\>_
```

It appears that the file you requested could not be found. Note that Directory of A:\ appears three times. This is a long file name with spaces in it. The DIR command read or parsed (interpreted the parameters) as three separate files—first "Sandy," then "and," and last "Patty.txt." It could find no files by those names. If you want a long file name with spaces in it treated as one unit, you must enclose the file name in quotation marks.

Step 7 Key in the following: A:\>**DIR "Sandy and Patty.txt"** Enter

```
Command Prompt

A:\>DIR "Sandy and Patty.txt"
 Volume in drive A is ACTIVITIES
 Volume Serial Number is 1508-0C25

 Directory of A:\

11/16/2000  12:00p                 59 Sandy and Patty.txt
               1 File(s)           59 bytes
               0 Dir(s)       292,864 bytes free

A:\>_
```

Now that the DIR command knows to treat the file name as one unit, it could locate the file. Every file with a long file name also gets a file name, an alias, that follows the 8.3 rule. Windows assigns this automatically. If you want to see the 8.3 file names, you need to use the /X parameter.

Step 8 Key in the following: A:\>**DIR /X** Enter

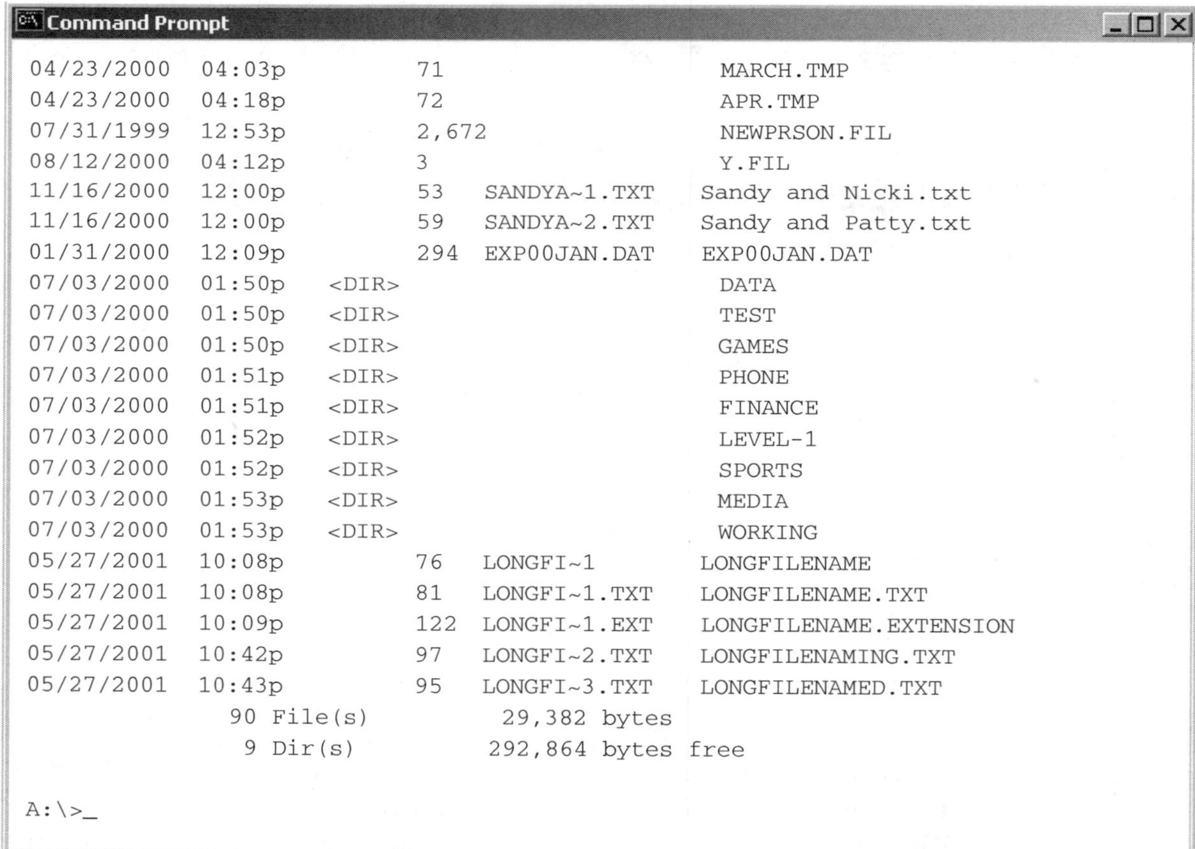

```
Command Prompt
04/23/2000  04:03p            71                 MARCH.TMP
04/23/2000  04:18p            72                 APR.TMP
07/31/1999  12:53p         2,672                 NEWPRSON.FIL
08/12/2000  04:12p             3                 Y.FIL
11/16/2000  12:00p            53  SANDYA~1.TXT  Sandy and Nicki.txt
11/16/2000  12:00p            59  SANDYA~2.TXT  Sandy and Patty.txt
01/31/2000  12:09p           294  EXP00JAN.DAT  EXP00JAN.DAT
07/03/2000  01:50p    <DIR>                      DATA
07/03/2000  01:50p    <DIR>                      TEST
07/03/2000  01:50p    <DIR>                      GAMES
07/03/2000  01:51p    <DIR>                      PHONE
07/03/2000  01:51p    <DIR>                      FINANCE
07/03/2000  01:52p    <DIR>                      LEVEL-1
07/03/2000  01:52p    <DIR>                      SPORTS
07/03/2000  01:53p    <DIR>                      MEDIA
07/03/2000  01:53p    <DIR>                      WORKING
05/27/2001  10:08p            76  LONGFI~1      LONGFILENAME
05/27/2001  10:08p            81  LONGFI~1.TXT  LONGFILENAME.TXT
05/27/2001  10:09p           122  LONGFI~1.EXT  LONGFILENAME.EXTENSION
05/27/2001  10:42p            97  LONGFI~2.TXT  LONGFILENAMING.TXT
05/27/2001  10:43p            95  LONGFI~3.TXT  LONGFILENAMED.TXT
              90 File(s)         29,382 bytes
               9 Dir(s)         292,864 bytes free

A:\>_
```

In addition to the long file name, the file also has an eight-dot-three name preceding the actual file name on the directory display. The 8.3 file name is always derived from the long file name by removing any spaces from the file name, taking the first six characters of the file name, and adding a tilde (~) and a number. When there is more than one file with the same first six characters in its name, Windows handles it. If you look at the display for the two files that begin with "Sandy" (**Sandy and Nicki.txt** and **Sandy and Patty.txt**), the first file placed on the disk is given the number 1 following the tilde, and the second file, the number 2. There are three files that begin with **LONGFILE** and end with the **TXT** (**LONGFILENAME.TXT**, **LONGFILENAMING.TXT**, and **LONGFILENAMED.TXT**). The first file, **LONGFLENAME.TXT**, is assigned the 8.3 name of **LONGFI~1.TXT**. The second file, **LONGFILENAMING.TXT**, is assigned the next number—**LONGFI~2.TXT**. And the last file, **LONGFILENAMED.TXT**, is assigned the next number—**LONGFI~3.TXT**.

If you cannot see the long file names, these names become very confusing, as it is difficult to distinguish one file from another. You want to be able to identify the contents of a file quickly by looking at the file names. Older versions of DOS and older application software will not allow you to use or view long file names. In the real world, the more you have to key in, the more likely you will make a typographical error. Thus, even though you can use spaces and long names, it may be a better idea to keep the file names short and concise. This is especially important when using floppy disks. Long file names take up needed room on floppies.

2.8 COMMAND LINE EDITING

You may reuse the last command you keyed in on a line without rekeying it. When you key in a command, it is stored in a memory buffer until it is replaced by the next keyed in command. The last command line you keyed in can be recalled to the screen so you may edit it. To recall the command line one letter at a time, press the F1 key once for each keystroke you wish to repeat. To recall the entire command line, press the F3 key. In addition, Windows 2000 Professional lets you use the up and down arrow keys to recall commands used in a command prompt session. Furthermore, you may also recall command lines by number, edit them, keep a command history, find commands by number, and so on. The following table illustrates the keys you may use to edit a command history.

Key	Editing Function
F7	Displays a list of commands.
Alt + F7	Clears the list of commands.
↑	Allows you to scroll up through the commands.
↓	Allows you to scroll down through the commands.
F8	Searches the list for the command that starts with the text you provide.
F9	Selects the command from the list by number.

PgUp	Displays the oldest command in the list.
PgDn	Displays the newest command in the list.
Esc	Erases the displayed command from the screen.
Home	Moves the cursor to the beginning of the displayed command.
End	Moves the cursor to the end of the displayed command.
←	Moves the cursor back one character.
→	Moves the cursor forward one character.
Ctrl + ←	Moves the cursor back one word.
Ctrl + →	Moves the cursor forward one word.
Backspace	Moves the cursor back one character and deletes the character preceding the cursor.
Delete	Deletes the character at the cursor.
Ctrl + End	Deletes all characters from the cursor to the end of the line.
Ctrl + Home	Deletes all characters from the cursor to the beginning of the line.
Insert	Toggles between insert and overstrike mode.

TABLE 2.1 EDITING KEYS COMMAND SUMMARY

2.9 ACTIVITY: USING COMMAND EDITING

Note: The "ACTIVITIES Disk—Working Copy" is in Drive A. You are at the Command Prompt screen. A:\> is the default drive and directory.

Step 1 Key in the following, including the error: A:\>**DIIR /p** Enter

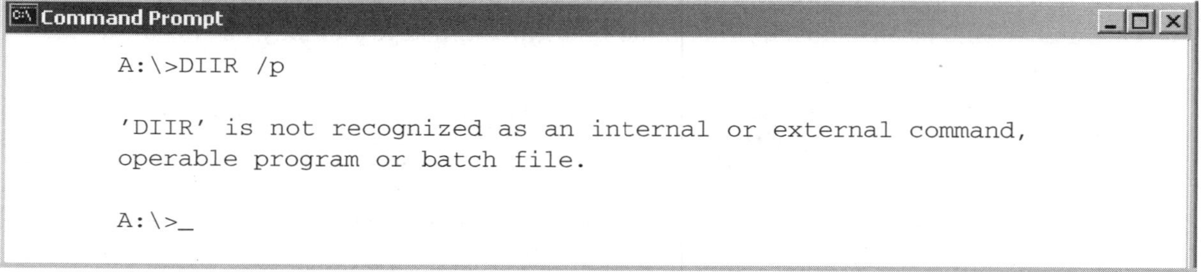
Command Prompt
A:\>DIIR /p
'DIIR' is not recognized as an internal or external command,
operable program or batch file.
A:\>_

WHAT'S HAPPENING

Your command was keyed in incorrectly and was not understood by the system. You received the error message "'DIIR' is not recognized as an internal or external command, operable program or batch file." This error message informs you that the OS did not understand what it is you asked for. It is important to read the messages so that you understand what is happening.

Step 2 Press the F1 key twice.

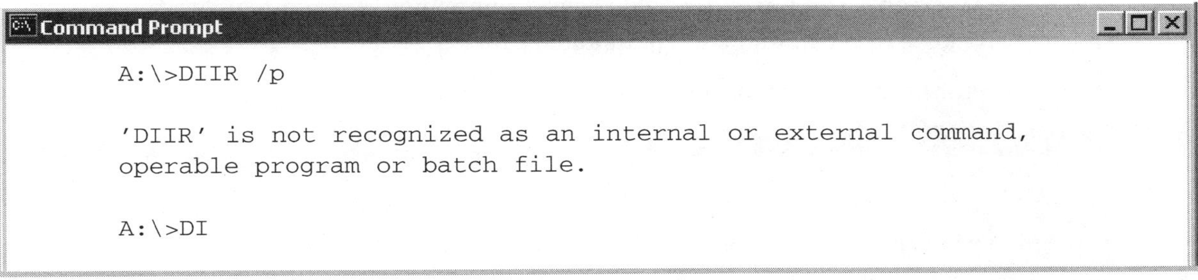

```
A:\>DIIR /p

'DIIR' is not recognized as an internal or external command,
operable program or batch file.

A:\>DI
```

WHAT'S HAPPENING? The characters that you keyed in previously are being recalled from the buffer. If you were to press the F1 key once more, the incorrectly entered second "I" would appear, the character error you want to eliminate.

Step 3 Press the Esc key to cancel the command.

Step 4 Key in the following: A:\>**CLS** Enter

Step 5 Key in the following: A:\>**DIR FRANK.FIL** Enter

Step 6 Key in the following: A:\>**DIR JAN.99** Enter

Step 7 Key in the following: A:\>**VOL** Enter

Step 8 Key in the following: A:\>**DIR MAR.99** Enter

Step 9 Key in the following: A:\>**DIR OLIVE.OIL** Enter

Step 10 Key in the following: A:\>**DIR DRESS.UP RIGHT.UP** Enter

```
A:\>DIR OLIVE.OIL
 Volume in drive A is ACTIVITIES
 Volume Serial Number is 1508-0C25

 Directory of A:\

05/30/2000  04:32p                 98 OLIVE.OIL
               1 File(s)             98 bytes
               0 Dir(s)         292,864 bytes free

A:\>DIR DRESS.UP RIGHT.UP
 Volume in drive A is ACTIVITIES
 Volume Serial Number is 1508-0C25

 Directory of A:\

10/01/2000  04:12p                 26 DRESS.UP

 Directory of A:\

10/01/2000  04:12p                 26 RIGHT.UP
               2 File(s)             52 bytes
               0 Dir(s)         292,864 bytes free

A:\>_
```

(This graphic represents the tail end of what you see scroll by on your screen.) You have executed several commands and can now use the editing keys to recall and edit commands.

Step 11 Press the ↑ key two times.

You have recalled, in descending order, the commands you previously entered.

Step 12 Press the ↓ key one time.

You recalled, in ascending order, the last command you keyed in.

Step 13 Press **Ctrl** + ← one time.

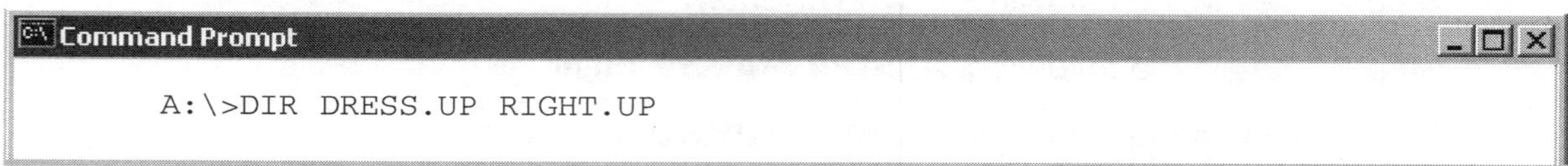

Your cursor is now on the **R** in **RIGHT.UP**. Using the **Ctrl** and ← keys moved you back one word.

Step 14 Press the **Insert** key.

When you pressed the **Insert** key, you toggled into what is called overstrike mode. Overstrike will replace each character as you key in data. The cursor also changed to an underline.

Step 15 At the cursor, key in **FILE3.FP**.

Notice how you did not have to delete the **RIGHT.UP** characters. As you keyed in data, it replaced what was there.

Step 16 Press **Enter**. Press ↑ two times.

You recalled the prior command you keyed in.

Step 17 Press the [Ctrl] + [←] one time. Key in **FILE3.FP**.

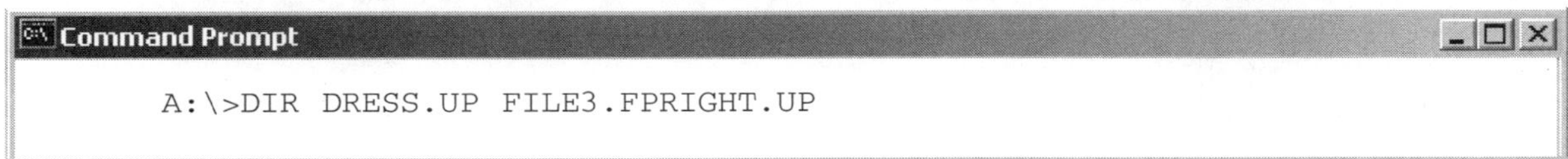

When you are in insert mode, you are "inserting" data at the cursor.

Step 18 Press [F7]

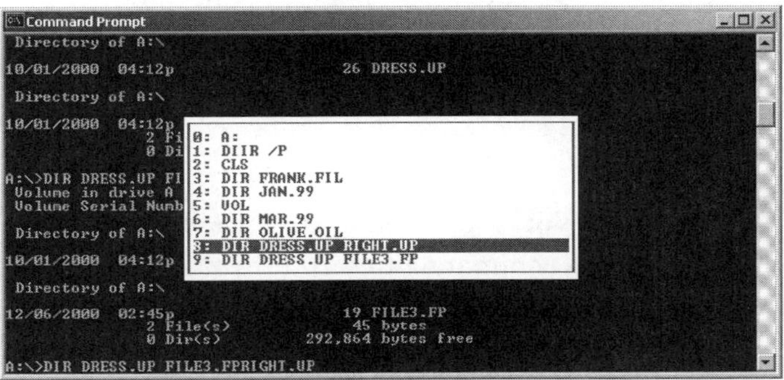

Pressing the [F7] key lists all the commands that you have keyed in. You may edit any line you wish by selecting the line number, but you must press the [F9] key first.

Step 19 Press [F9]. Press the number that appears before **DIR JAN.99**. In this example, it is **4**.

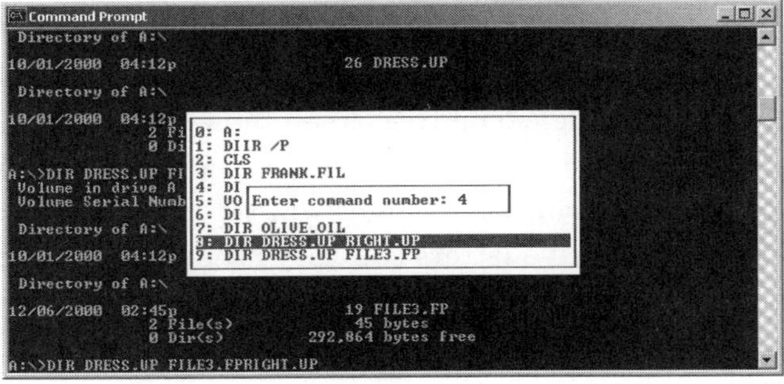

By pressing [F9], you saw the **Enter command number:** prompt. You then keyed in the line number (**4**) of the command you wished to edit.

Step 20 Press [Enter]

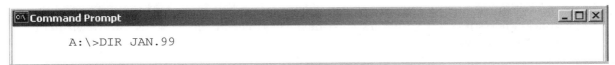

You can edit this line or simply execute it again. If you wish to delete a line quickly, there is a shortcut—the **Esc** key. You can also search for a previously entered command by pressing the first letter or letters of the command you are interested in.

Step 21 Press **Esc**. Press **D**. Press **F8**

WHAT'S HAPPENING? You selected a command by keying in the first letter and then pressing **F8**. If you continued to press **F8**, you would cycle through all the commands that begin with D.

Step 22 Press **Esc**. Press **Alt** + **F7**. Press **↑** one time.

WHAT'S HAPPENING? By pressing **Alt** + **F7**, you cleared the commands that were in the buffer. There are no commands to scroll through or to edit. When you are working at the Command Prompt, remember these editing commands. They can save you many keystrokes.

Step 23 Close the Command Prompt window.

WHAT'S HAPPENING? You have returned to the desktop.

2.10 DRIVES AS DEVICE NAMES

A disk drive is an example of a device. A device is a place to send information (write) or a place from which to receive information (read). Disk drives have assigned ***device names***. These are letters of the alphabet followed by a colon. Using these names, Windows knows which disk drive to read from or write to. When you are at the command prompt, the prompt displayed on the screen tells you where the system is currently "pointing" and from which device data will be read from or written to. If you are using a stand-alone computer, your drive names will typically be A: or B: or C:. However, if you are on a network, disk drive letters can vary. They can include such drive letters as J: or P: or W:. Again, the displayed prompt will tell you on what drive (device) the operating system is going to take an action. Disk drives are not the only places where the system sends or receives information. Other common devices are the keyboard, the printer, and the monitor.

2.11 DEFAULTS

In addition to understanding names of devices, it is also important to understand the concept of ***defaults***. Computers must have very specific instructions for everything they do. However, there are *implied* instructions that the system falls back to or defaults to in the absence of other instructions. Default, by computer definition, is the value used unless another value is specified. If you do not specify what you want, the system will make the assumption for you. For example, when A:\> is displayed on the screen, it is called the A prompt, but it is also the ***default drive***. When you want any activity to occur but do not specify where you want it to happen, the system assumes the activity will occur on the default drive, the A:\> that is displayed on the screen.

When you key in DIR after A:\>, how does the operating system know that you are asking for a table of contents of the disk in Drive A? When a specific direction is given, the operating system must have a specific place to look. A:\>, the default drive, is displayed on the screen. Since you did *not* specify which disk you wanted DIR to check, it defaulted to the default drive—the drive displayed in the prompt on the screen. It deduced that you want the table of contents or directory listing for the default drive, the disk in Drive A.

The prompt displayed on the screen is also known as the ***designated drive*** or the ***logged drive***. All commands, if given no other instructions to the contrary, assume that all reads and writes to the disk drive must take place on the default drive, the drive indicated by the prompt on the screen. When you are not in the Command Prompt window, the same rules apply. There is indeed a default drive, and in Windows Explorer it is indicated on the title bar, if you have set the Folder option to "Display the full path in the title bar."

2.12 ACTIVITY: WORKING WITH DEFAULTS

Note: The "ACTIVITIES Disk—Working Copy" should be in Drive A. You should be at the Windows desktop.

Step 1 Click **Start**. Point at **Programs**. Point at **Accessories**. Click **Command Prompt**.

Step 2 Key in the following: C:\>**A:** Enter

Command Prompt

```
Microsoft Windows 2000 [Version 5.00.2195]
(C) Copyright 1985-1999 Microsoft Corp.

C:\>A:

A:\>_
```

WHAT'S HAPPENING? You have opened the Command Prompt window. Opening this window is often referred to as "shelling out to DOS" or "shelling out to the command line."

Step 3 Key in the following: A:\>**DIR** Enter

Command Prompt

```
05/30/2000  01:46p          157 NEWAUTO.MAK
07/31/2000  04:32p          265 STATE2.CAP
04/23/2000  04:03p           73 JAN.TMP
10/10/1999  04:53p           73 JAN.99
```

```
12/11/1999  04:03p                65 TEST.TXT
05/02/1994  12:57a                26 GETYN.COM
12/31/2001  04:32p                64 WILD1.XXX
04/23/2000  04:03p                71 MAR.TMP
04/23/2000  04:03p                71 MARCH.TMP
04/23/2000  04:18p                72 APR.TMP
07/31/1999  12:53p             2,672 NEWPRSON.FIL
08/12/2000  04:12p                 3 Y.FIL
11/16/2000  12:00p                53 Sandy and Nicki.txt
11/16/2000  12:00p                59 Sandy and Patty.txt
01/31/2000  12:09p               294 EXP00JAN.DAT
07/03/2000  01:50p    <DIR>          DATA
07/03/2000  01:50p    <DIR>          TEST
07/03/2000  01:50p    <DIR>          GAMES
07/03/2000  01:51p    <DIR>          PHONE
07/03/2000  01:51p    <DIR>          FINANCE
07/03/2000  01:52p    <DIR>          LEVEL-1
07/03/2000  01:52p    <DIR>          SPORTS
07/03/2000  01:53p    <DIR>          MEDIA
07/03/2000  01:53p    <DIR>          WORKING
05/27/2001  10:08p                76 LONGFILENAME
05/27/2001  10:08p                81 LONGFILENAME.TXT
05/27/2001  10:09p               122 LONGFILENAME.EXTENSION
05/27/2001  10:42p                97 LONGFILENAMING.TXT
05/27/2001  10:43p                95 LONGFILENAMED.TXT
              90 File(s)         29,382 bytes
               9 Dir(s)         292,864 bytes free

A:\>_
```

Displayed on the screen is the result of the DIR command you executed. (The graphic represents the tail end of that listing.) Since you did not specify which disk drive DIR should look into, it assumed or defaulted to the disk in Drive A. Review the syntax diagram: The syntax diagram has [*drive*:], which is another optional variable parameter. You can substitute the letter of the drive you wish DIR to look into.

Step 4 Key in the following: A:\>**DIR A:** Enter

```
Command Prompt

05/30/2000  01:46p               157 NEWAUTO.MAK
07/31/2000  04:32p               265 STATE2.CAP
04/23/2000  04:03p                73 JAN.TMP
10/10/1999  04:53p                73 JAN.99
12/11/1999  04:03p                65 TEST.TXT
05/02/1994  12:57a                26 GETYN.COM
12/31/2001  04:32p                64 WILD1.XXX
04/23/2000  04:03p                71 MAR.TMP
04/23/2000  04:03p                71 MARCH.TMP
04/23/2000  04:18p                72 APR.TMP
07/31/1999  12:53p             2,672 NEWPRSON.FIL
08/12/2000  04:12p                 3 Y.FIL
```

```
        11/16/2000  12:00p                   53 Sandy and Nicki.txt
        11/16/2000  12:00p                   59 Sandy and Patty.txt
        01/31/2000  12:09p                  294 EXP00JAN.DAT
        07/03/2000  01:50p      <DIR>           DATA
        07/03/2000  01:50p      <DIR>           TEST
        07/03/2000  01:50p      <DIR>           GAMES
        07/03/2000  01:51p      <DIR>           PHONE
        07/03/2000  01:51p      <DIR>           FINANCE
        07/03/2000  01:52p      <DIR>           LEVEL-1
        07/03/2000  01:52p      <DIR>           SPORTS
        07/03/2000  01:53p      <DIR>           MEDIA
        07/03/2000  01:53p      <DIR>           WORKING
        05/27/2001  10:08p                   76 LONGFILENAME
        05/27/2001  10:08p                   81 LONGFILENAME.TXT
        05/27/2001  10:09p                  122 LONGFILENAME.EXTENSION
        05/27/2001  10:42p                   97 LONGFILENAMING.TXT
        05/27/2001  10:43p                   95 LONGFILENAMED.TXT
                      90 File(s)         29,382 bytes
                       9 Dir(s)         292,864 bytes free

A:\>_
```

WHAT'S HAPPENING? You substituted **A:** for the variable optional parameter, [*drive*:]. The display, however, is exactly the same as DIR without specifying the drive because A:\> is the default drive. It is unnecessary to key in **A:** but not wrong to do so. (The graphic represents the tail end of your listing.) If you want to see what files are on Drive C or Drive R, you must tell DIR to look on the drive you are interested in.

Note: Remember that if you are on a network, your hard drive letter may not be C:. Refer to your Configuration Table in Chapter 1.6 for the correct drive letter for your system.

Step 5 Key in the following: A:\>**C:** Enter

Step 6 Key in the following: C:\>**CD ** Enter

WHAT'S HAPPENING? You have changed the default drive to the hard disk, Drive C. You then changed the directory to the root of C. In this example, you were already at the root of C. Keying in **CD ** confirmed that location.

Step 7 Key in the following: C:\>**DIR A:** Enter

```
Command Prompt

       05/30/2000  01:46p                  157 NEWAUTO.MAK
       07/31/2000  04:32p                  265 STATE2.CAP
       04/23/2000  04:03p                   73 JAN.TMP
       10/10/1999  04:53p                   73 JAN.99
       12/11/1999  04:03p                   65 TEST.TXT
       05/02/1994  12:57a                   26 GETYN.COM
       12/31/2001  04:32p                   64 WILD1.XXX
       04/23/2000  04:03p                   71 MAR.TMP
       04/23/2000  04:03p                   71 MARCH.TMP
       04/23/2000  04:18p                   72 APR.TMP
       07/31/1999  12:53p                2,672 NEWPRSON.FIL
       08/12/2000  04:12p                    3 Y.FIL
       11/16/2000  12:00p                   53 Sandy and Nicki.txt
       11/16/2000  12:00p                   59 Sandy and Patty.txt
       01/31/2000  12:09p                  294 EXP00JAN.DAT
       07/03/2000  01:50p      <DIR>          DATA
       07/03/2000  01:50p      <DIR>          TEST
       07/03/2000  01:50p      <DIR>          GAMES
       07/03/2000  01:51p      <DIR>          PHONE
       07/03/2000  01:51p      <DIR>          FINANCE
       07/03/2000  01:52p      <DIR>          LEVEL-1
       07/03/2000  01:52p      <DIR>          SPORTS
       07/03/2000  01:53p      <DIR>          MEDIA
       07/03/2000  01:53p      <DIR>          WORKING
       05/27/2001  10:08p                   76 LONGFILENAME
       05/27/2001  10:08p                   81 LONGFILENAME.TXT
       05/27/2001  10:09p                  122 LONGFILENAME.EXTENSION
       05/27/2001  10:42p                   97 LONGFILENAMING.TXT
       05/27/2001  10:43p                   95 LONGFILENAMED.TXT
                     90 File(s)         29,382 bytes
                      9 Dir(s)         292,864 bytes free

C:\>_
```

WHAT'S HAPPENING? (The graphic represents the tail end of your listing.) The display of files, which scrolled by quickly, is still of the files on Drive A, but this time you *had* to specify the drive because the default drive was no longer A. Keying in **DIR** and a drive letter, **A:**, told the command line, "I want a display of the directory (DIR), but this time I don't want you to display the files on the default drive. I want you to look only on the disk that is in Drive A." As long as you tell the command DIR where you want it to look, you can work *with* and *from* any drive you wish. If you are not specific, the command will execute on the default drive shown by the prompt on the screen (A:\>, B:\>, C:\>, etc.).

Step 8 Key in the following: C:\>**DIR HELLO.TXT** Enter

```
Command Prompt

C:\>DIR HELLO.TXT
 Volume in drive C is 2000 PRO
 Volume Serial Number is C4A7-8571
```

```
 Directory of C:\

File Not Found

C:\>_
```

Step 9 Key in the following: C:\>**DIR A:HELLO.TXT** Enter

Command Prompt

```
C:\>DIR A:HELLO.TXT
 Volume in drive A is ACTIVITIES
 Volume Serial Number is 1508-0C25

 Directory of A:\

05/30/2000  04:32p                  53 HELLO.TXT
               1 File(s)             53 bytes
               0 Dir(s)         292,864 bytes free

C:\>_
```

WHAT'S HAPPENING?

You first asked DIR to look on the default drive for a file called **HELLO.TXT**. The default drive is Drive C. The prompt displayed on the screen, C:\>, is the default drive. Since you did not specify which drive to check for the file called **HELLO.TXT**, DIR assumed the default drive. DIR could not find the **HELLO.TXT** file on the default drive, so it responded with **File Not Found**. The operating system is not smart enough to say, "Oh, this file is not on the default drive. Let me go check the ACTIVITIES disk in a different disk drive." The operating system followed your instructions exactly.

Your next step was more specific. You made a clearer request: "Look for a file called HELLO.TXT." However, you first told DIR what disk drive to look into—A:. The drive designator (**A:**) preceded the file name (**HELLO.TXT**) because you always tell DIR which "file cabinet" to look in (the disk drive **A:**) before you tell it which "folder" you want (**HELLO.TXT**). By looking at the syntax diagram, you see that you can combine optional variable parameters. You gave DIR [*drive*:][*path*][*filename*] some specific values—**DIR A:HELLO.TXT**. The **A:** was substituted for the [*drive*:], and **HELLO.TXT** was substituted for [*filename*]. So far, you have used the optional variable parameters [*drive*:] and [*filename*] and the optional fixed parameters [/P] and [/W]. You have not used [*path*].

2.13 A BRIEF INTRODUCTION TO SUBDIRECTORIES—THE PATH

Subdirectories are used primarily, but not exclusively, with hard disks and any other large storage media such as RW-CDs or Zip disks. Hard disks have a large storage capacity (current common values are from 8 to 20 GB or more), and are therefore more difficult to manage than floppy disks. This is also true of RW-CDs and Zip disks. In general, users like to have similar files grouped together. Subdirectories allow a disk to be divided into smaller, more manageable portions. Windows refers to *subdirectories* as *folders*, and they are graphically represented with folder icons. In the command line shell, folders are referred to as directories and subdirectories.

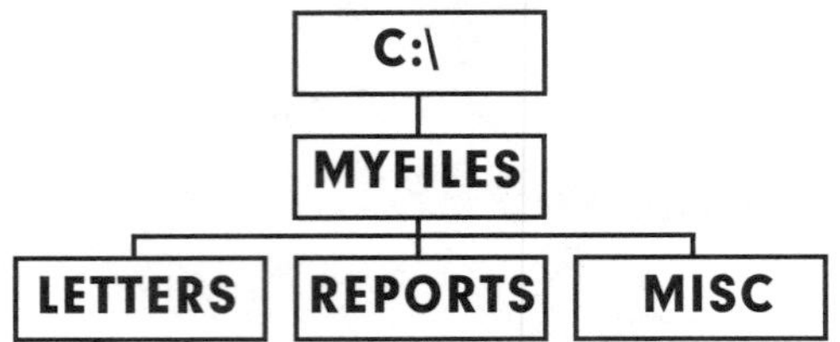

The full path name of a file called REP.DOC that is in the REPORTS directory is C:\MYFILES\REPORTS\REP.DOC. The first \ (backslash) always represents the root directory. The following backslashes without spaces are delimiters—separators between elements in the path, elements being subdirectories and the ending file.

Subdirectories can be used on floppy disks. If you think of a disk as a file cabinet, a subdirectory can be thought of as a drawer in the file cabinet. These file cabinet drawers (subdirectories) also hold disk files. Just as disk drives have a name, such as A:, B:, or C:, subdirectories must also have names so the system will know where to look. Since subdirectories are part of a disk, their names should not be a single letter of the alphabet. Single letters of the alphabet should be reserved for disk drives.

Every disk comes with one directory that is named by the operating system. This directory is called the ***root directory*** and is indicated by the backslash (\). The prompt displays the default directory as well as the default drive, as in A:\> or C:\>. Technically, there is only one *directory* on any disk—the root directory, referred to only as \. All others are *subdirectories*. However, the terms *directories* and *subdirectories, folders* and *subfolders* are used interchangeably. This textbook will also use the terms *directory* and *subdirectory* interchangeably. All subdirectories on a disk have names such as UTILITY or SAMPLE, or any other name you choose or a program chooses. The rules for naming subdirectories are the same as for naming files, although subdirectory names do not usually have extensions.

When working with files on a disk, you need to perform certain tasks that can be summarized as finding a file, storing a file, and retrieving a file. Because there are subdirectories on a disk, simply supplying the DIR command with the drive that the file might be on is insufficient information. You must also tell DIR the path to the file. The ***path*** is the route followed by the operating system to locate, save, and retrieve a file. Thus, in a syntax diagram, the path refers to the course leading from the root directory of a drive to a specific file. Simply stated, when you see *path* in a syntax diagram, you substitute the directory name or names. In essence, you are being very specific by telling the DIR command not to go just to the file cabinet (the disk) but to go to a drawer (subdirectory) in the file cabinet.

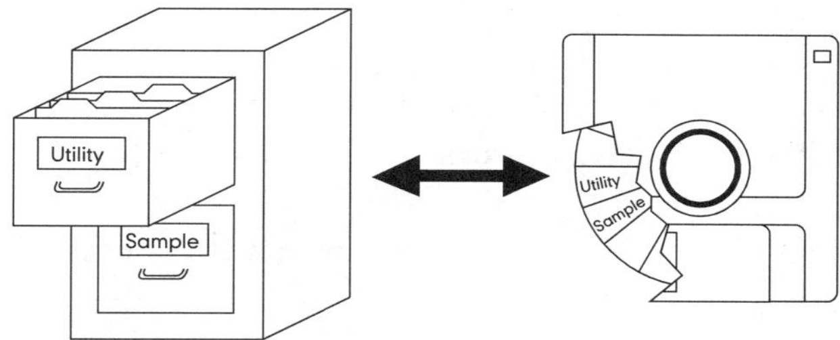

FIGURE 2.1 FILE CABINETS AND SUBDIRECTORIES

2.14 ACTIVITY: USING PATH WITH THE DIR COMMAND

Note: You are at the command line screen. The "ACTIVITIES Disk—Working Copy" is in Drive A. C:\> is displayed as the default drive and the default directory.

Step 1 Key in the following: C:\>**DIR A:** Enter

```
Command Prompt
        05/30/2000  01:46p                157 NEWAUTO.MAK
        07/31/2000  04:32p                265 STATE2.CAP
        04/23/2000  04:03p                 73 JAN.TMP
        10/10/1999  04:53p                 73 JAN.99
        12/11/1999  04:03p                 65 TEST.TXT
        05/02/1994  12:57a                 26 GETYN.COM
        12/31/2001  04:32p                 64 WILD1.XXX
        04/23/2000  04:03p                 71 MAR.TMP
        04/23/2000  04:03p                 71 MARCH.TMP
        04/23/2000  04:18p                 72 APR.TMP
        07/31/1999  12:53p              2,672 NEWPRSON.FIL
        08/12/2000  04:12p                  3 Y.FIL
        11/16/2000  12:00p                 53 Sandy and Nicki.txt
        11/16/2000  12:00p                 59 Sandy and Patty.txt
        01/31/2000  12:09p                294 EXP00JAN.DAT
        07/03/2000  01:50p     <DIR>          DATA
        07/03/2000  01:50p     <DIR>          TEST
        07/03/2000  01:50p     <DIR>          GAMES
        07/03/2000  01:51p     <DIR>          PHONE
        07/03/2000  01:51p     <DIR>          FINANCE
        07/03/2000  01:52p     <DIR>          LEVEL-1
        07/03/2000  01:52p     <DIR>          SPORTS
        07/03/2000  01:53p     <DIR>          MEDIA
        07/03/2000  01:53p     <DIR>          WORKING
        05/27/2001  10:08p                 76 LONGFILENAME
        05/27/2001  10:08p                 81 LONGFILENAME.TXT
        05/27/2001  10:09p                122 LONGFILENAME.EXTENSION
        05/27/2001  10:42p                 97 LONGFILENAMING.TXT
        05/27/2001  10:43p                 95 LONGFILENAMED.TXT
                      90 File(s)         29,382 bytes
                       9 Dir(s)         292,864 bytes free

        C:\>_
```

(The graphic represents the tail end of your listing.) On the screen display there are entries with **<DIR>** following their name, indicating subdirectories. How do you know what files are inside a subdirectory? Look at the beginning of the syntax diagram: DIR [*drive*:][*path*][*filename*]. You will substitute the specific drive letter for [*drive*:] and substitute the specific subdirectory name for [*path*]. You include \ to indicate that you want to begin at the top of the directory and look down. You want to see what is in the **DATA** subdirectory.

Step 2 Key in the following: C:\>**DIR A:\DATA** Enter

```
Command Prompt

C:\>DIR A:\DATA
 Volume in drive A is ACTIVITIES
 Volume Serial Number is 1508-0C25

 Directory of A:\DATA

07/03/2000  01:50p      <DIR>          .
07/03/2000  01:50p      <DIR>          ..
08/12/2000  04:36p                  33 GOOD.TXT
08/12/2000  04:36p                  32 HIGHEST.TXT
05/10/2000  04:38p                 221 MOTHER.LET
07/04/2000  11:29a                  83 THIN.EST
07/04/2000  04:37p                  52 TEA.TAX
07/04/2000  11:29a                 250 THANK.YOU
07/03/2000  04:36p                  26 BONJOUR.TXT
               7 File(s)            697 bytes
               2 Dir(s)         292,864 bytes free

C:\>_
```

WHAT'S HAPPENING? You keyed in the command you wanted to execute, the drive letter you were interested in, the backslash to indicate that you wanted to start at the root directory, and finally the name of the subdirectory. Remember, the first backslash always indicates the root directory. The screen display shows you only what files are in the subdirectory (file drawer) called **DATA**. The third line of the display (**Directory of A:\DATA**) tells you the subdirectory you are looking in. What if you wanted to look for a specific file in a subdirectory? Once again, look at the syntax diagram: DIR [*drive*:][*path*][*filename*]. You will substitute the drive letter, the path name, and the file name you wish to locate. You need to use a delimiter to separate the file name from the directory name. The delimiter reserved for path names is the backslash. It separates the path name from the file name so that DIR knows which is which.

Note: It is very important to remember that the first backslash always represents the root directory, and any subsequent backslashes are delimiters separating file names from directory names.

Step 3 Key in the following: C:\>**DIR A:\DATA\THIN.EST** Enter

```
Command Prompt

C:\>DIR A:\DATA\THIN.EST
 Volume in drive A is ACTIVITIES
 Volume Serial Number is 1508-0C25

 Directory of A:\DATA

07/04/2000  11:29a                  83 THIN.EST
               1 File(s)             83 bytes
               0 Dir(s)         292,864 bytes free

C:\>_
```

You keyed in the command you wanted to execute, the drive letter you were interested in, the first backslash indicating the root directory, the name of the subdirectory, then a backslash used as a delimiter, and finally the name of the file. The screen display shows you only the file called **THIN.EST** located on the ACTIVITIES disk in the subdirectory **DATA**.

2.15 CHANGING DEFAULTS

Since you generally work on a specific drive, instead of keying in the drive letter every time, you can change the default drive so that the operating system *automatically* uses the drive displayed on the screen as the default drive.

Refer to your Configuration Table in Chapter 1.6, or consult your instructor to see where the Windows system utility files are located. If they are in a subdirectory other than C:\WINNT\SYSTEM32, you will have to know the name of that location, and you will have to substitute that path for C:\WINNT\SYSTEM32. For example, if your system command files are located on a network in F:\APPS\WINNT\SYSTEM32, you would substitute that drive and path each time you see C:\WINNT\SYSTEM32 in this text. If you have not filled out the information on your Configuration Table in Chapter 1.6, you may wish to do so at this time.

2.16 ACTIVITY: CHANGING THE DEFAULT DRIVE

Note: You are in the Command Prompt window. The "ACTIVITIES Disk—Working Copy" is in Drive A. C:\> is displayed as the default drive and the default directory.

Step 1 Key in the following: C:\> **A:** Enter

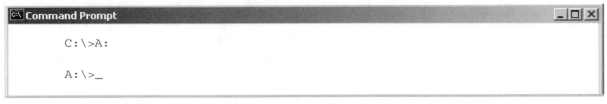

```
Command Prompt

C:\>A:

A:\>_
```

By keying in a letter followed by a colon, you are telling the system that you want to change your work area to that designated drive. Thus, when you keyed in **A:**, you changed the work area from the hard disk, Drive C, to the floppy disk in Drive A. You have now made A: the default drive. The assumption the DIR command will make is that all files will come from the disk in Drive A. It will not look at the hard disk, Drive C.

Step 2 Key in the following: A:\>**DIR** Enter

```
Command Prompt

05/30/2000  01:46p                157 NEWAUTO.MAK
07/31/2000  04:32p                265 STATE2.CAP
04/23/2000  04:03p                 73 JAN.TMP
10/10/1999  04:53p                 73 JAN.99
12/11/1999  04:03p                 65 TEST.TXT
05/02/1994  12:57a                 26 GETYN.COM
12/31/2001  04:32p                 64 WILD1.XXX
04/23/2000  04:03p                 71 MAR.TMP
04/23/2000  04:03p                 71 MARCH.TMP
04/23/2000  04:18p                 72 APR.TMP
07/31/1999  12:53p              2,672 NEWPRSON.FIL
08/12/2000  04:12p                  3 Y.FIL
11/16/2000  12:00p                 53 Sandy and Nicki.txt
11/16/2000  12:00p                 59 Sandy and Patty.txt
01/31/2000  12:09p                294 EXP00JAN.DAT
07/03/2000  01:50p    <DIR>          DATA
07/03/2000  01:50p    <DIR>          TEST
07/03/2000  01:50p    <DIR>          GAMES
07/03/2000  01:51p    <DIR>          PHONE
07/03/2000  01:51p    <DIR>          FINANCE
07/03/2000  01:52p    <DIR>          LEVEL-1
07/03/2000  01:52p    <DIR>          SPORTS
07/03/2000  01:53p    <DIR>          MEDIA
07/03/2000  01:53p    <DIR>          WORKING
05/27/2001  10:08p                 76 LONGFILENAME
05/27/2001  10:08p                 81 LONGFILENAME.TXT
05/27/2001  10:09p                122 LONGFILENAME.EXTENSION
05/27/2001  10:42p                 97 LONGFILENAMING.TXT
05/27/2001  10:43p                 95 LONGFILENAMED.TXT
              90 File(s)         29,382 bytes
               9 Dir(s)         292,864 bytes free

A:\>_
```

DIR does not display the directory of the hard disk. It displays the directory of the ACTIVITIES disk in Drive A. (The graphic represents the tail end of your listing.) You have changed the assumption, or default, and, since you did not specify which drive you wanted, the default directory was displayed. Since the default is now A:\>, if you wish to locate any information on any other disk, you must specify the parameters and include the letter of the drive and the subdirectory, if necessary, where the file is located.

Step 3 Key in the following: A:\>**DIR DISKCOPY.COM** Enter

```
Command Prompt

A:\>DIR DISKCOPY.COM
 Volume in drive A is ACTIVITIES
 Volume Serial Number is 1508-0C25

 Directory of A:\

File Not Found

A:\>_
```

WHAT'S HAPPENING? Because the default drive is the drive with the ACTIVITIES disk, DIR looked for this file only on the ACTIVITIES disk in Drive A. You must be aware of where you are (what the default drive and subdirectory are) and where your files are located.

Step 4 Key in the following: A:\>**DIR C:\DISKCOPY.COM** Enter

```
Command Prompt

A:\>DIR C:\DISKCOPY.COM
 Volume in drive C is 2000 PRO
 Volume Serial Number is C4A7-8571

 Directory of C:\

File Not Found

A:\>_
```

WHAT'S HAPPENING? Although you did tell DIR to look on Drive C, you were not specific enough. DIR looked only in the root directory of C and could not find the file of interest.

Step 5 Key in the following: A:\>**DIR C:\WINNT\SYSTEM32\DISKCOPY.COM** Enter

Note: Substitute your drive and/or subdirectory that contains your system utility files if it is different from this example.

```
Command Prompt

A:\>DIR C:\WINNT\SYSTEM32\DISKCOPY.COM
 Volume in drive C is 2000 PRO
 Volume Serial Number is C4A7-8571

 Directory of C:\WINNT\SYSTEM32

12/07/1999  07:00a              8,464 diskcopy.com
               1 File(s)          8,464 bytes
               0 Dir(s)   7,401,742,336 bytes free

A:\>_
```

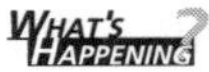

Your dates and times may vary depending on which version of Windows you are using. In this case, because you specified the drive and subdirectory as well as the file name, DIR knew where to look and located the file. You asked DIR not only to look on Drive C, but more specifically to look on Drive C in the subdirectory called **\WINNT\SYSTEM32** for the file called **DISKCOPY.COM**.

2.17 CHANGING DIRECTORIES

In addition to changing drives, you can also change directories. When you work on a hard disk, it is usually divided into subdirectories. Once you establish your default drive, you can also establish your default directory. Then, instead of keying in the path name every time, you can change the default directory so that the operating system will use the directory displayed on the screen as the default directory. To change directories, you key in the command CD (which stands for "change directory") followed by the directory (path) name. The partial command syntax is: CD [/D] [drive:][path].

If you key in **CD** with no parameters, it tells you the directory that is currently the default directory. If you wish to change the default, you follow CD with a path name such as **CD \WINDOWS\SYSTEM32**. If you wish to change drives at the same time you change directories, you use the /D parameter. Thus, if your default prompt were A:\> and you keyed in **CD /D C:\WINNT\SYSTEM32**, you would change drives as well as directories.

2.18 ACTIVITY: CHANGING DIRECTORIES

Note: You are at the command line screen. The "ACTIVITIES Disk—Working Copy" is in Drive A. A:\> is displayed as the default drive and the default directory.

Step 1 Key in the following: A:\>**C:** Enter

Step 2 Key in the following: C:\>**CD** Enter

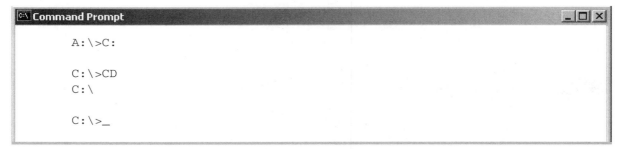

When you keyed in **CD**, C:\ displayed, telling you that your current default drive is C and the current default directory is the root or \. In the last activity, when you wanted to locate the file called **DISKCOPY.COM**, you had to precede it with the path name **\WINNT\SYSTEM32**. If you change to that directory, the only place that DIR will look for that file is in the current default directory.

Step 3 Key in the following: C:\>**CD \WINNT\SYSTEM32** Enter

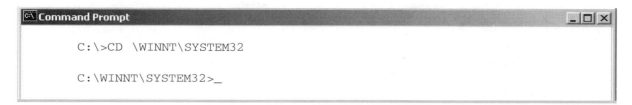

You told Windows to change from the current directory to a directory called **SYSTEM32** under a directory called **WINNT** under the root (\) of the default drive (**C:**). You changed directories so that **WINNT\SYSTEM32** is now the default directory. Notice how the prompt displays both the default drive and directory. Whenever you execute any command, the command will look only in the current directory for the file of interest.

Step 4 Key in the following: C:\WINNT\SYSTEM32>**DIR DISKCOPY.COM** Enter

Command Prompt

```
C:\WINNT\SYSTEM32>DIR DISKCOPY.COM
 Volume in drive C is 2000 PRO
 Volume Serial Number is C4A7-8571

 Directory of C:\WINNT\SYSTEM32

12/07/1999  07:00a                8,464 diskcopy.com
               1 File(s)          8,464 bytes
               0 Dir(s)   7,401,742,336 bytes free

C:\WINNT\SYSTEM32>_
```

The command DIR looked only in the **\WINNT\SYSTEM32** directory and located the file called **DISKCOPY.COM**. Look at the line that states **Directory of C:\WINNT\SYSTEM32**. DIR always tells you where it has looked. This procedure works with any directory.

Step 5 Key in the following: C:\WINNT\SYSTEM32>**CD ** Enter

Whenever you key in **CD **, it always takes you to the root directory of the drive you are on.

Step 6 Key in the following: C:\>**CD /D A:\DATA** Enter

Step 7 Key in the following: A:\DATA>**DIR** Enter

Command Prompt

```
C:\>CD /D A:\DATA

A:\DATA>DIR
 Volume in drive A is ACTIVITIES
 Volume Serial Number is 1508-0C25

 Directory of A:\DATA

07/03/2000  01:50p      <DIR>          .
07/03/2000  01:50p      <DIR>          ..
08/12/2000  04:36p                  33 GOOD.TXT
08/12/2000  04:36p                  32 HIGHEST.TXT
05/10/2000  04:38p                 221 MOTHER.LET
07/04/2000  11:29a                  83 THIN.EST
07/04/2000  04:37p                  52 TEA.TAX
07/04/2000  11:29a                 250 THANK.YOU
07/03/2000  04:36p                  26 BONJOUR.TXT
               7 File(s)            697 bytes
               2 Dir(s)         292,864 bytes free

A:\DATA>_
```

WHAT'S HAPPENING? You used two commands. With the first command, you changed the default drive to A and the default directory to **DATA** on Drive A. You could do this because you used the /D parameter. Then you changed from the root of the A drive to the **DATA** directory. With the second command, you executed the DIR command. All files in the **DATA** directory are displayed. You could have looked for a particular file, but, since there are only a few files in the **DATA** directory, you could find any file you are looking for easily.

Step 8 Key in the following: A:\DATA>**CD ** Enter

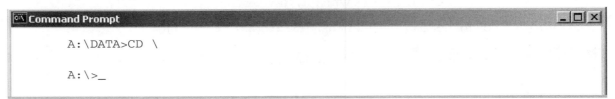

Command Prompt

```
A:\DATA>CD \

A:\>_
```

WHAT'S HAPPENING? You have now returned to the root directory of Drive A.

2.19 GLOBAL FILE SPECIFICATIONS: WILDCARDS, THE ?, AND THE *

Using the DIR command and a file specification, you can find one specific file that matches what you keyed in. Every time you wish to locate a file, you can key the entire file specification. Often, however, you wish to work with a group of files that have similar names or a group of files whose names you do not know. There is a "shorthand" system that allows you to operate on a group of files rather than a single file. This system is formally called ***global file specifications***; informally, it is called using ***wildcards***. Sometimes it is referred to as using ambiguous file references. Conceptually, they are similar to playing cards, where the joker can stand for another card of your choice. In Windows, the question mark (?) and the asterisk (*) are the wildcards. These symbols stand for unknowns. The * represents or substitutes for a group or *string* of characters; the ? represents or substitutes for a *single* character. Many commands allow you to use global file specifications. You will use the DIR command to demonstrate the use of wildcards. You will find that the techniques you learn here will also apply when you use Search in the GUI (the Windows desktop).

2.20 ACTIVITY: DIR AND WILDCARDS

Note: The "ACTIVITIES Disk—Working Copy" is in Drive A. A:\> is displayed as the default drive and the default directory.

Step 1 Key in the following: A:\>**C:** Enter

Step 2 Key in the following: C:\>**CD \WINNT\SYSTEM32** Enter

Note: Remember that if the system utility files are in a subdirectory with a different name, you will have to substitute your subdirectory name.

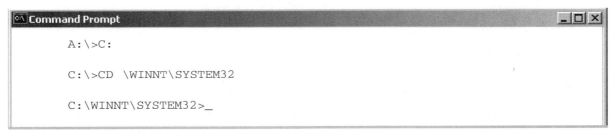

WHAT'S HAPPENING? You have changed the default directory to where the system utility files are located. If you wanted to locate a file and all you remembered about the file name was that it began with the letter G and that it was located on the default drive and subdirectory, you would not be able to find that file. You have insufficient information.

Step 3 Key in the following: C:\WINNT\SYSTEM32>**DIR G** Enter

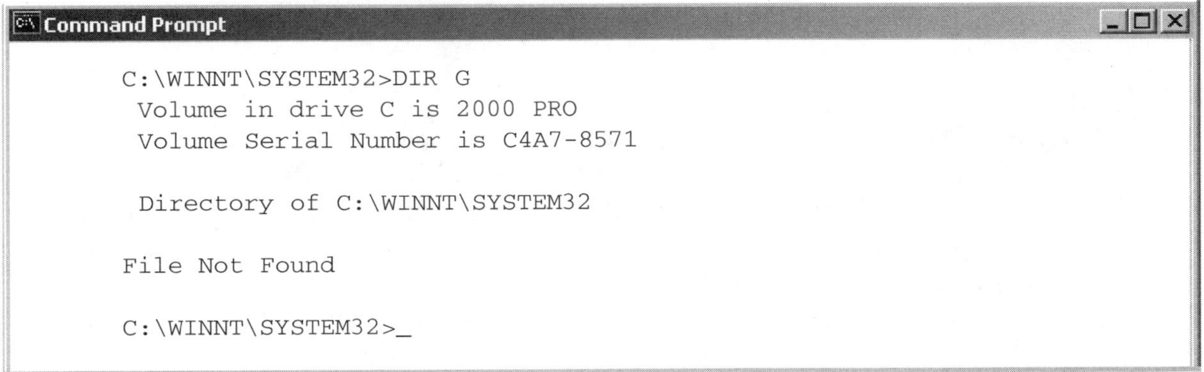

First, note how the prompt reflects the subdirectory **\WINNT\SYSTEM32**. When you keyed in **DIR G**, you were correct, but only somewhat. You first entered the work you wanted done, the command DIR. You did not need to

enter the drive letter. DIR assumed both the default drive and default subdirectory. However, DIR specifically looked for a file called G. There was no file called G; that was simply the first letter of the file name. You could find files that begin with G by using the wildcard symbol * to represent all other characters—both the file name (*) and the file extension (.*).

Step 4 Key in the following: C:\WINNT\SYSTEM32>**DIR G*.*** Enter

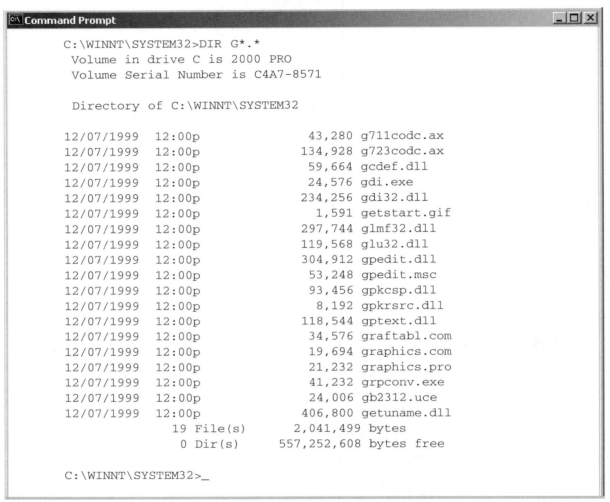

```
Command Prompt

C:\WINNT\SYSTEM32>DIR G*.*
 Volume in drive C is 2000 PRO
 Volume Serial Number is C4A7-8571

 Directory of C:\WINNT\SYSTEM32

12/07/1999  12:00p              43,280 g711codc.ax
12/07/1999  12:00p             134,928 g723codc.ax
12/07/1999  12:00p              59,664 gcdef.dll
12/07/1999  12:00p              24,576 gdi.exe
12/07/1999  12:00p             234,256 gdi32.dll
12/07/1999  12:00p               1,591 getstart.gif
12/07/1999  12:00p             297,744 glmf32.dll
12/07/1999  12:00p             119,568 glu32.dll
12/07/1999  12:00p             304,912 gpedit.dll
12/07/1999  12:00p              53,248 gpedit.msc
12/07/1999  12:00p              93,456 gpkcsp.dll
12/07/1999  12:00p               8,192 gpkrsrc.dll
12/07/1999  12:00p             118,544 gptext.dll
12/07/1999  12:00p              34,576 graftabl.com
12/07/1999  12:00p              19,694 graphics.com
12/07/1999  12:00p              21,232 graphics.pro
12/07/1999  12:00p              41,232 grpconv.exe
12/07/1999  12:00p              24,006 gb2312.uce
12/07/1999  12:00p             406,800 getuname.dll
              19 File(s)      2,041,499 bytes
               0 Dir(s)     557,252,608 bytes free

C:\WINNT\SYSTEM32>_
```

The files listed in the subdirectory vary, depending on the release or version of the OS, so do not worry if your screen display is different. You asked DIR to find files beginning with the letter G on the default drive and default subdirectory. You did not know anything else about the file names or even how many files you might have that begin with the letter G. You represented any and all characters following the letter G with the asterisk, separated the file name from the file extension with a period, and represented all the characters in the file extension with the second asterisk. Thus, **G*.*** (read as "G star dot star") means all the files that start with the letter G having any or no characters following the letter G, and can have any or no file extension. Now DIR could look for a match.

In this example, the first file DIR found that had the G you specified was **g711codc.ax**. DIR returned this file because the asterisk (*) following the G matched the remainder of the file name, **711codc**. Remember, * represents any group of characters. The second *, representing the file extension, matched **ax** because, again, the * represents any group of characters. The second file DIR found that began with G was **g723codc.ax**. DIR displayed this file because the * following the G matched the remainder of the file name, **723codc**. The second * representing the file extension matched **ax** because, again, the * represents any group of characters. The third file matches **G*.*** for the same reasons. You could have more or fewer files depending on how your system is set up.

There are other ways of requesting information using the *. If all you know about a group of files on the disk in the default drive is that the group has the common file extension **.SYS**, you could display these files on the screen using wildcards.

Step 5 Key in the following: C:\WINNT\SYSTEM32>**DIR *.SYS** Enter

Command Prompt

```
C:\WINNT\SYSTEM32>DIR *.SYS
 Volume in drive C is 2000 PRO
 Volume Serial Number is C4A7-8571

 Directory of C:\WINNT\SYSTEM32

12/07/1999  07:00a               9,029 ansi.sys
03/29/2000  06:24a               4,557 atiicdxx.sys
12/07/1999  07:00a              27,097 country.sys
12/07/1999  07:00a               4,768 himem.sys
12/07/1999  07:00a              42,793 key01.sys
12/07/1999  07:00a              42,521 keyboard.sys
12/07/1999  07:00a              27,866 ntdos.sys
12/07/1999  07:00a              29,146 ntdos404.sys
12/07/1999  07:00a              29,370 ntdos411.sys
12/07/1999  07:00a              29,274 ntdos412.sys
12/07/1999  07:00a              29,146 ntdos804.sys
12/07/1999  07:00a              33,808 ntio.sys
12/07/1999  07:00a              34,528 ntio404.sys
12/07/1999  07:00a              35,632 ntio411.sys
12/07/1999  07:00a              35,392 ntio412.sys
12/07/1999  07:00a              34,528 ntio804.sys
12/07/1999  07:00a             187,024 spcmdcon.sys
12/07/1999  07:00a           1,726,256 win32k.sys
              18 File(s)      2,362,735 bytes
               0 Dir(s)   7,401,226,240 bytes free

C:\WINNT\SYSTEM32>_
```

The * represented any file name, but all the files must have **.SYS** as a file extension. Again, the number of files displayed may vary. The next activities will demonstrate the differences between the two wildcards, * and ?.

Step 6 Key in the following: C:\WINNT\SYSTEM32>**DIR A:*.TXT** Enter

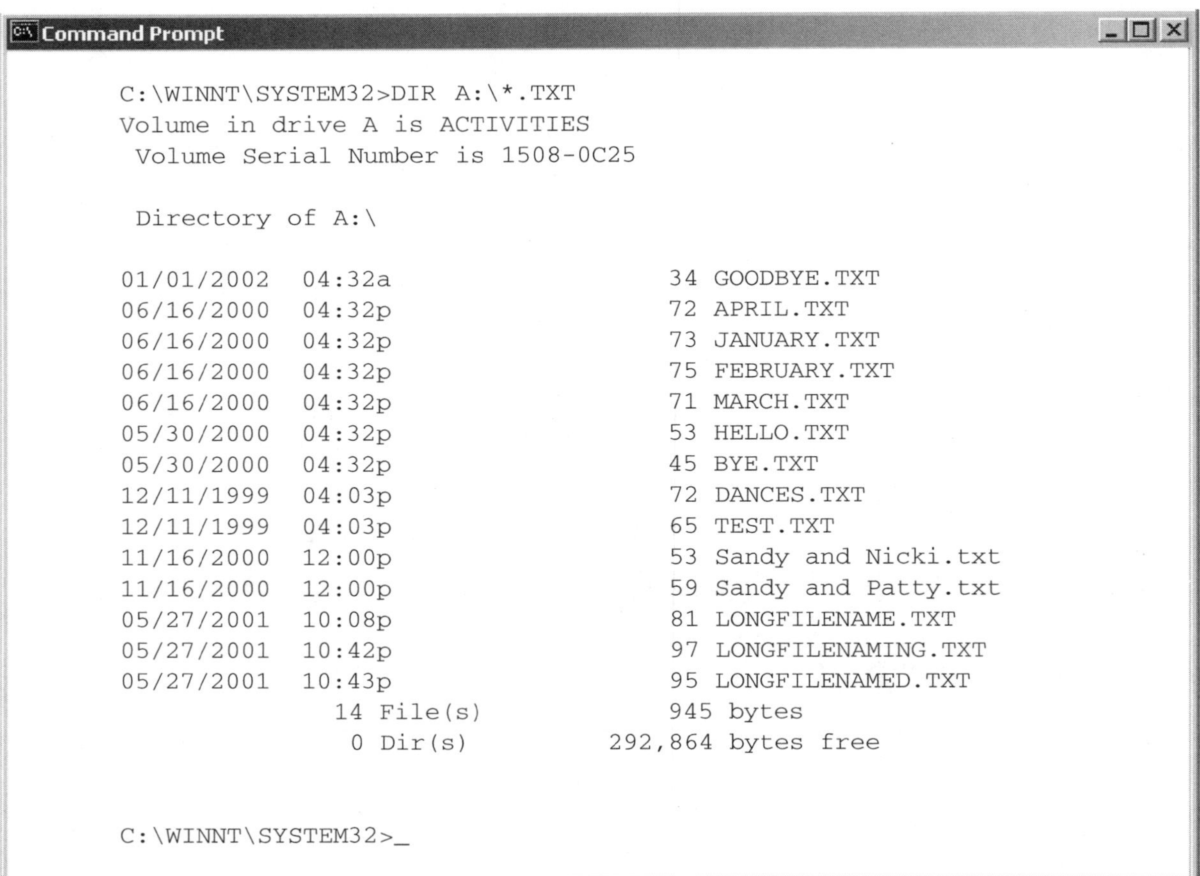
Command Prompt

```
C:\WINNT\SYSTEM32>DIR A:\*.TXT
Volume in drive A is ACTIVITIES
 Volume Serial Number is 1508-0C25

 Directory of A:\

01/01/2002  04:32a              34 GOODBYE.TXT
06/16/2000  04:32p              72 APRIL.TXT
06/16/2000  04:32p              73 JANUARY.TXT
06/16/2000  04:32p              75 FEBRUARY.TXT
06/16/2000  04:32p              71 MARCH.TXT
05/30/2000  04:32p              53 HELLO.TXT
05/30/2000  04:32p              45 BYE.TXT
12/11/1999  04:03p              72 DANCES.TXT
12/11/1999  04:03p              65 TEST.TXT
11/16/2000  12:00p              53 Sandy and Nicki.txt
11/16/2000  12:00p              59 Sandy and Patty.txt
05/27/2001  10:08p              81 LONGFILENAME.TXT
05/27/2001  10:42p              97 LONGFILENAMING.TXT
05/27/2001  10:43p              95 LONGFILENAMED.TXT
              14 File(s)        945 bytes
               0 Dir(s)     292,864 bytes free


C:\WINNT\SYSTEM32>_
```

WHAT'S HAPPENING? You asked DIR what files had an extension of **.TXT** and were located on the ACTIVITIES disk. You did not know anything about the file names, only the file extension. DIR searched the table of contents in Drive A since you placed an **A:** prior to ***.TXT**. It looked only in the root directory of the disk since you preceded ***.TXT** with \. The command found 14 files that matched ***.TXT**. Now, how does the question mark differ from the asterisk?

Step 7 Key in the following: C:\WINNT\SYSTEM32>**DIR A:\?????.TXT** Enter

Command Prompt

```
C:\WINNT\SYSTEM32>DIR A:\?????.TXT
 Volume in drive A is ACTIVITIES
 Volume Serial Number is 1508-0C25

 Directory of A:\

06/16/2000  04:32p              72 APRIL.TXT
06/16/2000  04:32p              71 MARCH.TXT
05/30/2000  04:32p              53 HELLO.TXT
05/30/2000  04:32p              45 BYE.TXT
12/11/1999  04:03p              65 TEST.TXT
               5 File(s)        306 bytes
               0 Dir(s)     292,864 bytes free

C:\WINNT\SYSTEM32>_
```

This time you asked your question differently. You still asked for files that had the file extension of **.TXT** in the root directory of the ACTIVITIES disk. However, instead of using the asterisk representing "any number of characters," you used the question mark (?) five times. You asked for a file name with five characters and DIR displayed files with five characters or fewer in their file name. You then separated the file name from the file extension with a period saying that the file not only needed to have that size name, but also the extension **.TXT**. This time five files matched your request. Note how the above screen display differs from the screen display in Step 6. This time you do not see the files **GOODBYE.TXT**, **JANUARY.TXT**, **FEBRUARY.TXT**, **DANCES.TXT**, **Sandy and Nicki.txt**, **Sandy and Patty.txt**, **LONGFILENAME.TXT**, **LONGFILENAMING.TXT**, or **LONGFILENAMED.TXT** on the screen. Those file names were longer than five characters.

Step 8 Key in the following: C:\WINNT\SYSTEM32>**DIR A:\EXP*.*** Enter

```
Command Prompt

C:\WINNT\SYSTEM32>DIR A:\EXP*.*
 Volume in drive A is ACTIVITIES
 Volume Serial Number is 1508-0C25

 Directory of A:\

01/31/2001  12:09p                 304 EXP01JAN.DAT
02/28/2001  12:10p                 307 EXP01FEB.DAT
03/31/1999  12:11p                 294 EXP99MAR.DAT
01/31/1999  12:09p                 294 EXP99JAN.DAT
03/31/2001  12:11p                 302 EXP01MAR.DAT
03/31/2000  12:11p                 292 EXP00MAR.DAT
02/28/2000  12:10p                 297 EXP00FEB.DAT
02/28/1999  12:10p                 295 EXP99FEB.DAT
01/31/2000  12:09p                 294 EXP00JAN.DAT
               9 File(s)          2,679 bytes
               0 Dir(s)         292,864 bytes free

C:\WINNT\SYSTEM32>_
```

This time you asked to see all the files located on the ACTIVITIES disk (Drive A) in the root directory (\) that start with the letters EXP (**EXP*.***). The ***.*** following the **EXP** represents the rest of the file name and the file extension. These file names were created with a pattern in mind. Budget files start with EXP, which stands for "expenses," followed by the last two digits of the year (99, 00, or 01), followed by the month (JANuary, FEBruary, or MARch). The file extension is .DAT to indicate these are data files, not program files. However, often you are not interested in all the files. You want only some of them. For example, you might want to know what expense files you have on the ACTIVITIES disk for the year 1999.

Step 9 Key in the following: C:\WINNT\SYSTEM32>**DIR A:\EXP99*.*** Enter

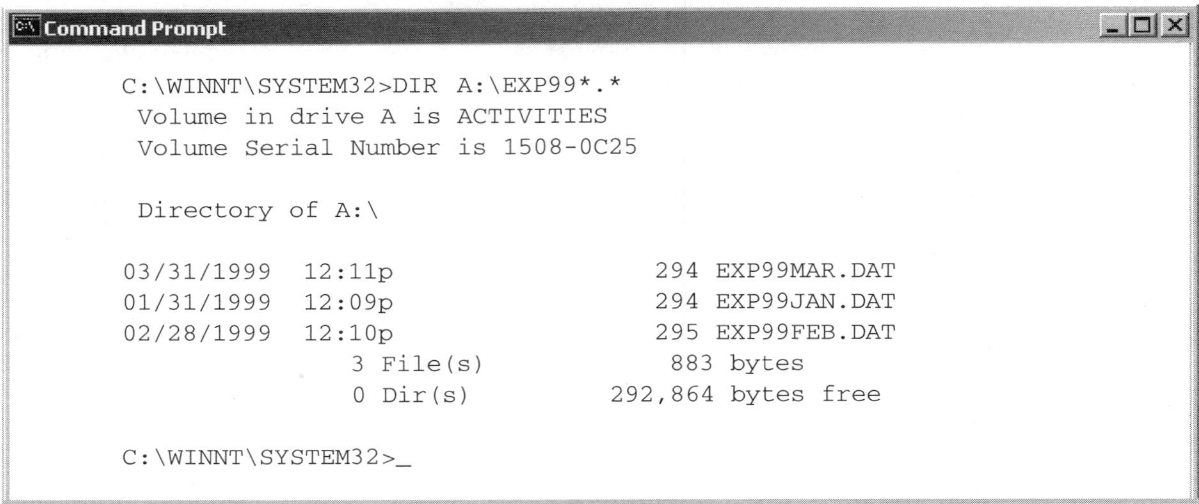

```
Command Prompt

C:\WINNT\SYSTEM32>DIR A:\EXP99*.*
 Volume in drive A is ACTIVITIES
 Volume Serial Number is 1508-0C25

 Directory of A:\

03/31/1999  12:11p                 294 EXP99MAR.DAT
01/31/1999  12:09p                 294 EXP99JAN.DAT
02/28/1999  12:10p                 295 EXP99FEB.DAT
               3 File(s)            883 bytes
               0 Dir(s)        292,864 bytes free

C:\WINNT\SYSTEM32>_
```

Here you asked for all the files (**DIR**) on the ACTIVITIES disk in Drive A in the root directory that were expense files for 1999 (**EXP99**). The rest of the file names were represented by ***.***. On your screen display you got only the 1999 files. However, suppose your interest is in all the January files. You no longer care which year, only which month.

Step 10 Key in the following: C:\WINNT\SYSTEM32>**DIR A:\EXP??JAN.*** Enter

```
Command Prompt

C:\WINNT\SYSTEM32>DIR A:\EXP??JAN.*
 Volume in drive A is ACTIVITIES
 Volume Serial Number is 1508-0C25

 Directory of A:\

01/31/2001  12:09p                 304 EXP01JAN.DAT
01/31/1999  12:09p                 294 EXP99JAN.DAT
01/31/2000  12:09p                 294 EXP00JAN.DAT
               3 File(s)            892 bytes
               0 Dir(s)        292,864 bytes free

C:\WINNT\SYSTEM32>_
```

The two question marks represented the two characters within the file name. The characters could have been any characters, but they would be limited to two characters. You could have also keyed in **DIR A:\exp*jan.*** because Windows will recognize characters entered after a wildcard. Previous versions of the operating system would have ignored all characters after the asterisk, allowing any and all characters to fill the remaining spaces. The command **DIR *JAN.*** would have resulted in the same display as **DIR *.***. Windows 2000 Professional, however, does recognize characters following the asterisk wildcard, and the resulting display shows you the files you were looking for. However, if you had files such as **EXP2001JAN.DAT** and

EXP01JAN.DAT, using **DIR EXP*JAN.DAT** would display both files but using **DIR EXP??JAN.DAT** would only display the **EXP01JAN.DAT** file.

Step 11 Key in the following: C:\WINNT\SYSTEM32>**CD ** [Enter]

```
Command Prompt

C:\WINNT\SYSTEM32>CD \

C:\>_
```

WHAT'S HAPPENING? You have returned to the root directory of C.

2.21 REDIRECTION

The system knows what you want to do when you key in commands. In the Command Prompt window, input is expected from the keyboard, which is considered the ***standard input*** device. In addition, the results of a command's execution are written to the screen. The screen, or monitor, is considered the ***standard output*** device.

You can change this through a feature called ***redirection***. Redirection allows you to tell the operating system to, instead of writing the output to the standard output device (the screen), write the information somewhere else. Typically, this is to a file or to a printer. For redirection to work with a printer, the printer must be a local printer and not a network printer. A local printer is a printer that is physically attached to your computer. Redirection does not work with all commands, only with commands that write their output to standard output. Redirection does work with the DIR command because DIR gets its input from the standard input device, the keyboard, and writes to the standard output device, the screen. The syntax for redirection is COMMAND > DESTINATION. The command is what you key in, such as DIR *.TXT. You then use the greater-than symbol (>) to redirect the results of that command to where you specify, instead of to the screen. The command would be keyed in as DIR *.TXT > MY.FIL to send the results, or output of the DIR command, to a file named MY.FIL. The command would be keyed in as DIR *.TXT > LPT1 if you wanted the output to go to the printer attached to the first printer port. You must use the device name for the printer, PRN, for the default printer or LPT1, LPT2, or LPT3 for a printer attached to a specific port on your computer. If you are using a network printer, you cannot redirect unless you know the name of the network printer.

2.22 ACTIVITY: REDIRECTING OUTPUT TO A FILE

Note: The system is booted. You have shelled out to the command prompt screen. The "ACTIVITIES Disk—Working Copy" is in Drive A. C:\> is displayed as the default drive and the default directory.

Step 1 Key in the following: C:\>**A:** [Enter]

Step 2 Key in the following: A:\>**DIR *.NEW** [Enter]

Command Prompt

```
C:\>A:

A:\>DIR *.NEW
 Volume in drive A is ACTIVITIES
 Volume Serial Number is 1508-0C25

 Directory of A:\

10/01/1999  02:53p                  73 JAN.NEW
10/01/1999  02:53p                  74 APR.NEW
10/01/1999  02:53p                  75 FEB.NEW
10/01/1999  02:53p                  71 MAR.NEW
               4 File(s)            293 bytes
               0 Dir(s)         292,864 bytes free

A:\>_
```

WHAT'S HAPPENING? You changed the default drive to the A drive. You then asked for all the files on the ACTIVITIES disk that have the file extension of **.NEW**. You saw the output displayed on the screen. You have four files that meet the criteria. You keyed in a command and the results were sent to the screen.

You are now going to create a file on your "ACTIVITIES Disk—Working Copy" using redirection. Remember that when the instructions in this text say "ACTIVITIES disk" they mean the copy of the ACTIVITIES disk you made in Chapter 1. It is this disk that is in the A drive.

Step 3 Key in the following: A:\>**DIR *.NEW > MY.HW** Enter

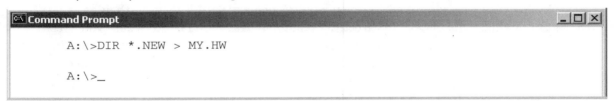

WHAT'S HAPPENING? This time you instructed the system to send the output of the DIR command to a file called **MY.HW**, instead of sending the output to the screen. Redirection is an "instead of" procedure. You either have the results of the DIR command displayed on the screen, or you send it to a file.

Note: If you see a dialog box that says "The disk cannot be written to because it is write protected. Please remove the write protection from the volume ACTIVITIES in drive A:," your disk is write protected. Remove the disk and move the sliding tab to cover the small hole in the corner to unprotect it. Reinsert the disk and click **Try Again** in the dialog box to complete the task.

Step 4 Key in the following: A:\>**DIR MY.HW** Enter

```
Command Prompt

A:\>DIR MY.HW
 Volume in drive A is ACTIVITIES
 Volume Serial Number is 1508-0C25

 Directory of A:\

04/30/2001  12:09p                 384 MY.HW
               1 File(s)            384 bytes
               0 Dir(s)         292,352 bytes free

A:\>_
```

WHAT'S HAPPENING? You now have a file that contains the output from the DIR command.

2.23 REDIRECTING OUTPUT TO THE PRINTER

You have seen that you can redirect output to a file. You can also redirect output to a local printer. Since the DIR command normally writes to the screen, you can redirect the output of the DIR command to the printer to get a printout of what normally would be written to the screen. However, you cannot use just any name with a device, as you can with a file name. Windows has very specific names for its devices. You already know that a letter of the alphabet followed by a colon (:) is always a disk drive. Printers have names also. The printer device names are PRN, LPT1, LPT2, and sometimes LPT3. PRN is the default printer, usually LPT1. These are the names for local printers. Network printers also have specific names. The network administrator assigns the network printer name. Unless you know your network printer name, you may not be able to redirect output to the printer.

CAUTION: BEFORE DOING THE NEXT ACTIVITY, CHECK WITH YOUR LAB INSTRUCTOR TO SEE IF YOU HAVE A LOCAL PRINTER. IF YOU HAVE ACCESS TO ONLY A NETWORK PRINTER, YOU MAY NOT BE ABLE TO DO THE NEXT ACTIVITY UNLESS YOU HAVE RECEIVED OTHER INSTRUCTIONS. IF YOU DO HAVE A LOCAL PRINTER, AND YOU USE LPT1, BE SURE TO USE THE NUMBER ONE, NOT THE LOWERCASE L.

2.24 ACTIVITY: REDIRECTING THE OUTPUT TO THE PRINTER

Note 1: DO NOT do this activity until you have checked with your lab instructor for any special instructions. In fact, you may be unable to do the activity. If you cannot do it, read the activity.

Note 2: The "ACTIVITIES Disk—Working Copy" is in Drive A. A:\> is displayed as the default drive and the default directory. Be sure the printer is turned on and online before beginning this activity.

Step 1 Key in the following: A:\>**DIR *.TXT** Enter

Command Prompt

```
A:\>DIR *.TXT
 Volume in drive A is ACTIVITIES
 Volume Serial Number is 1508-0C25

 Directory of A:\

01/01/2002  04:32a                34 GOODBYE.TXT
06/16/2000  04:32p                72 APRIL.TXT
06/16/2000  04:32p                73 JANUARY.TXT
06/16/2000  04:32p                75 FEBRUARY.TXT
06/16/2000  04:32p                71 MARCH.TXT
05/30/2000  04:32p                53 HELLO.TXT
05/30/2000  04:32p                45 BYE.TXT
12/11/1999  04:03p                72 DANCES.TXT
12/11/1999  04:03p                65 TEST.TXT
11/16/2000  12:00p                53 Sandy and Nicki.txt
11/16/2000  12:00p                59 Sandy and Patty.txt
05/27/2001  10:08p                81 LONGFILENAME.TXT
05/27/2001  10:42p                97 LONGFILENAMING.TXT
05/27/2001  10:43p                95 LONGFILENAMED.TXT
              14 File(s)         945 bytes
               0 Dir(s)      292,352 bytes free

A:\>_
```

WHAT'S HAPPENING? You asked for all the files on the ACTIVITIES disk that had the file extension of **.TXT**.

Step 2 Key in the following: A:\>**DIR *.TXT > PRN** Enter

WHAT'S HAPPENING? You instructed the operating system to send the output to an alternate output device, specifically the printer, instead of displaying it on the screen. The printer should be printing, and nothing should be on the screen. Remember, redirection is an "instead of" procedure. You either display the results of the DIR command on the screen, or send the results to the printer. See Figure 2.2.

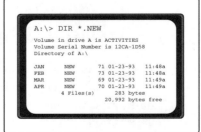

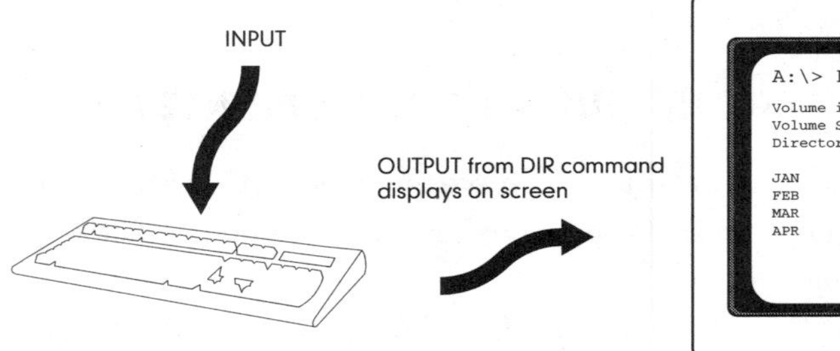
INPUT
OUTPUT from DIR command displays on screen
A:\> DIR *.NEW
Volume in drive A is ACTIVITIES
Volume Serial Number is 12CA-1D58
Directory of A:\
JAN NEW 71 01-23-93 11:48a
FEB NEW 73 01-23-93 11:48a
MAR NEW 69 01-23-93 11:49a
APR NEW 70 01-23-93 11:49a
4 Files(s) 283 bytes
20,992 bytes free

FIGURE 2.2 REDIRECTED OUTPUT

Your page may not have ejected from your local printer. If you have a dot-matrix printer, it printed the lines in the file and then it stopped. The printer did not advance to the beginning of a new page.

You have to go to the printer and roll the platen until the perforated line appeared so that you could tear off the page. If you have an inkjet printer or a laser printer, the situation is even stranger. No paper appears at all. In order to feed the paper manually with an inkjet printer, you have to press the **Reset** button. With a laser printer, you have to go to the printer, turn the **Online** button off, press the form feed (**FF**) button, and then turn the **Online** button back on. In all these cases, you are doing what is called a *hardware solution* to a problem. You are manipulating the hardware to get the desired results.

2.25 GETTING HELP

As you begin to use commands, their names, purposes, and proper syntax become familiar. Initially, however, these commands are new to users. Prior to DOS 5.0, the only way to become familiar with a command or to check the proper syntax was to locate the command in the manual. The reference manual that comes with any software package is called ***documentation***. The completeness of the documentation can vary from software package to software package. The documentation that comes with an operating system consists of at least the installation instructions and occasionally a command reference manual, which is a list of commands with a brief description and syntax for each. For the Windows operating systems, documentation is in the form of text files on the CD. In DOS 6.0 and above, the documentation has been provided less and less in written form, and more and more online. There is a very good database of information that can be accessed via the Help choice on the Start menu from the desktop, but this help is for procedures and methods used in the Windows GUI. You may also get help on command line commands in the GUI help. But to get help with a command and its syntax within the DOS environment, key in the name of the command followed by a space, a forward slash (/), and a question mark (?). You may also use HELP followed by the command name, such as HELP DIR. For reference, the commands and syntax are listed in Appendix B.

2.26 ACTIVITY: GETTING HELP WITH A COMMAND

Note: The "ACTIVITIES Disk—Working Copy" is in Drive A. A:\> is displayed as the default drive and the default directory.

Step 1 Key in the following: A:\>**DIR /?** Enter

```
Command Prompt

Displays a list of files and subdirectories in a directory.

DIR [drive:][path][filename] [/A[[:]attributes]] [/B] [/C] [/D] [/L] [/N]
  [/O[[:]sortorder]] [/P] [/Q] [/S] [/T[[:]timefield]] [/W] [/X] [/4]

  [drive:][path][filename]
              Specifies drive, directory, and/or files to list.

  /A          Displays files with specified attributes.
  attributes   D  Directories            R  Read-only files
```

```
              H  Hidden files       A  Files ready for archiving
              S  System files       -  Prefix meaning not
  /B          Uses bare format (no heading information or summary).
  /C          Display the thousand separator in file sizes.  This is
                 the default.  Use /-C to disable display of separator.
  /D          Same as wide but files are list sorted by column.
  /L          Uses lowercase.
  /N          New long list format where filenames are on the far
              right.
  /O          List by files in sorted order.
  sortorder   N  By name (alphabetic)       S  By size (smallest first)
              E  By extension (alphabetic)  D  By date/time (oldest
                                               first)
              G  Group directories first    -  Prefix to reverse
                                                   order
  /P          Pauses after each screenful of information.
  /Q          Display the owner of the file.
  /S          Displays files in specified directory and all
              subdirectories.
  /T          Controls which time field displayed or used for sorting
  timefield   C  Creation
              A  Last Access
              W  Last Written
  /W          Uses wide list format.
  /X          This displays the short names generated for non-8dot3
                 file names.  The format is that of /N with the short
                 name inserted before the long name. If no short name is
                 present, blanks are displayed in its place.
  /4          Displays four-digit years

Switches may be preset in the DIRCMD environment variable. Override
preset switches by prefixing any switch with - (hyphen)-for example,
/-W.

A:\>_
```

WHAT'S HAPPENING? On your screen, the first lines of text probably will have scrolled off the screen. In this text, you see the entire display. This display is a complete syntax explanation for the DIR command. Previously, we looked at only a partial syntax diagram for the DIR command. Notice the first line of the complete diagram: **DIR [drive:][path][filename] [/A[[:]attributes]] [/B] [/C] [/D] [/L] [/N]**. Notice that the entire line is in brackets, **[ ]**, meaning that all of the parameters or switches are optional. The DIR command can stand alone—it requires no parameters. You may include the drive, path, and file name, and you may specify the order (**/O**) in which you wish the files displayed. Look at the diagram at the line that begins with **/O List by files in sorted order**. Below that are the orders available. **N** is by name, **S** by size, **E** by extension, **D** by date, and so on.

Step 2 Key in the following: A:\>**DIR /ON** Enter

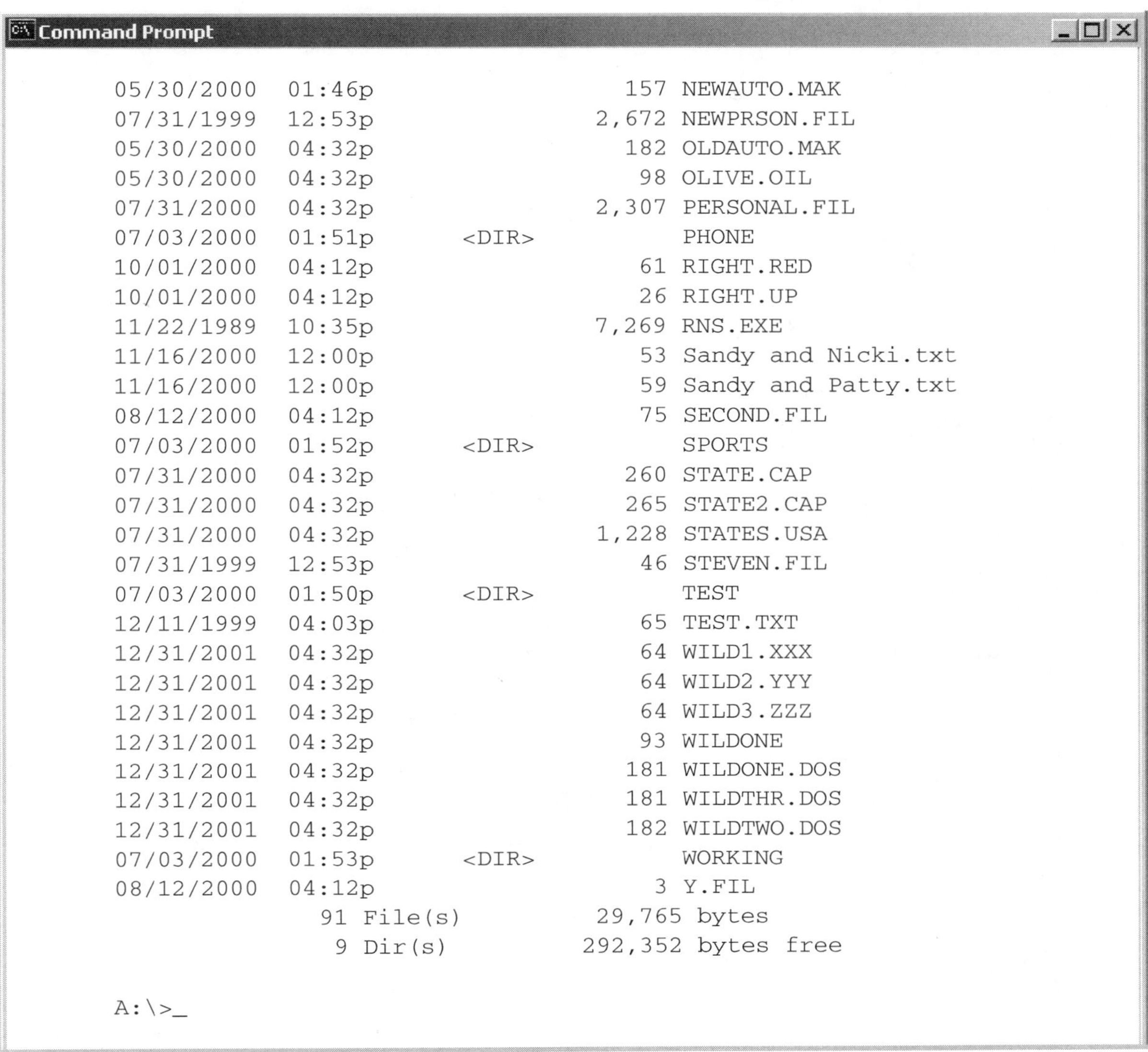

```
Command Prompt

05/30/2000  01:46p                 157 NEWAUTO.MAK
07/31/1999  12:53p               2,672 NEWPRSON.FIL
05/30/2000  04:32p                 182 OLDAUTO.MAK
05/30/2000  04:32p                  98 OLIVE.OIL
07/31/2000  04:32p               2,307 PERSONAL.FIL
07/03/2000  01:51p      <DIR>          PHONE
10/01/2000  04:12p                  61 RIGHT.RED
10/01/2000  04:12p                  26 RIGHT.UP
11/22/1989  10:35p               7,269 RNS.EXE
11/16/2000  12:00p                  53 Sandy and Nicki.txt
11/16/2000  12:00p                  59 Sandy and Patty.txt
08/12/2000  04:12p                  75 SECOND.FIL
07/03/2000  01:52p      <DIR>          SPORTS
07/31/2000  04:32p                 260 STATE.CAP
07/31/2000  04:32p                 265 STATE2.CAP
07/31/2000  04:32p               1,228 STATES.USA
07/31/1999  12:53p                  46 STEVEN.FIL
07/03/2000  01:50p      <DIR>          TEST
12/11/1999  04:03p                  65 TEST.TXT
12/31/2001  04:32p                  64 WILD1.XXX
12/31/2001  04:32p                  64 WILD2.YYY
12/31/2001  04:32p                  64 WILD3.ZZZ
12/31/2001  04:32p                  93 WILDONE
12/31/2001  04:32p                 181 WILDONE.DOS
12/31/2001  04:32p                 181 WILDTHR.DOS
12/31/2001  04:32p                 182 WILDTWO.DOS
07/03/2000  01:53p      <DIR>          WORKING
08/12/2000  04:12p                   3 Y.FIL
              91 File(s)         29,765 bytes
               9 Dir(s)         292,352 bytes free

A:\>_
```

(This graphic represents the tail end of your listing.) Notice that the files are displayed in alphabetical order. You can reverse the order.

Step 3 Key in the following: A:\>**DIR /O-N** Enter

```
Command Prompt

10/10/1999  04:53p                  75 FEB.99
03/31/1999  12:11p                 294 EXP99MAR.DAT
01/31/1999  12:09p                 294 EXP99JAN.DAT
02/28/1999  12:10p                 295 EXP99FEB.DAT
03/31/2001  12:11p                 302 EXP01MAR.DAT
01/31/2001  12:09p                 304 EXP01JAN.DAT
02/28/2001  12:10p                 307 EXP01FEB.DAT
03/31/2000  12:11p                 292 EXP00MAR.DAT
01/31/2000  12:09p                 294 EXP00JAN.DAT
02/28/2000  12:10p                 297 EXP00FEB.DAT
11/06/2000  04:12p                  54 EMPLOYEE.TWO
11/06/2000  04:12p                  57 EMPLOYEE.THR
11/06/2000  04:12p                  53 EMPLOYEE.ONE
```

```
10/01/2000  04:12p                26 DRESS.UP
07/03/2000  01:50p    <DIR>          DATA
12/11/1999  04:03p                72 DANCES.TXT
08/12/2000  04:12p               314 CASES.FIL
07/31/1999  12:53p                47 CAROLYN.FIL
05/30/2000  04:32p                45 BYE.TYP
05/30/2000  04:32p                45 BYE.TXT
04/23/2000  04:03p                53 BONJOUR.TMP
05/30/2000  04:32p                19 BLUE.JAZ
05/30/2000  04:32p                86 AWARD.MOV
06/16/2000  04:32p                72 APRIL.TXT
04/23/2000  04:03p                72 APRIL.TMP
04/23/2000  04:18p                72 APR.TMP
10/01/1999  02:53p                74 APR.NEW
10/10/1999  04:53p                72 APR.99
              91 File(s)         29,765 bytes
               9 Dir(s)         292,352 bytes free

A:\>_
```

WHAT'S HAPPENING? The file names scrolled by quickly, but they were in reverse alphabetical order, from Z to A. (This graphic represents the tail end of your listing.) Thus, by using the parameters **/O-N** (**O** for order, the **-** for reverse, and **N** for file name), you accomplished your task.

Step 4 Key in the following: A:\>**DIR /S** Enter

```
Command Prompt

08/08/2000  01:39p               184 AME-LIT.BKS
08/08/2000  01:39p               662 PULITZER.BKS
               3 File(s)          1,079 bytes

 Directory of A:\MEDIA\TV

07/03/2000  01:53p    <DIR>          .
07/03/2000  01:53p    <DIR>          ..
03/05/2000  04:41p               232 COMEDY.TV
07/03/2000  01:24p               213 DRAMA.TV
               2 File(s)            445 bytes

 Directory of A:\MEDIA\MOVIES

07/03/2000  01:53p    <DIR>          .
07/03/2000  01:53p    <DIR>          ..
10/17/2000  01:40p               255 DRAMA.MOV
10/17/2000  01:40p               231 MUSIC.MOV
10/17/2000  01:40p               255 OTHER.MOV
               3 File(s)            741 bytes

 Directory of A:\WORKING

07/03/2000  01:53p    <DIR>          .
07/03/2000  01:53p    <DIR>          ..
```

```
               0 File(s)              0 bytes

     Total Files Listed:
             158 File(s)      1,098,945 bytes
              48 Dir(s)         292,352 bytes free

A:\>_
```

WHAT'S HAPPENING? Again, the file names scrolled by quickly, but this time, all the files on the disk, including those in the subdirectories, were displayed. (This graphic represents the tail end of your listing.) The /S parameter displays all the files from the specified directory and all its subdirectories.

Using the different parameters available with the DIR command, you can display files sorted by their *attributes* (covered in a later chapter), display only the names of the files with no additional information (/B), or display the information in lower case (/L). However, if you use more than one parameter, each parameter must begin with the slash.

Step 5 Key in the following: A:\>**DIR /BLP** Enter

```
Command Prompt

A:\>DIR /BLP
Parameter format not correct - "BLP".

A:\>_
```

WHAT'S HAPPENING? As you can see, although B, L, and P are all valid parameters, they must be separated.

Step 6 Key in the following: A:\>**DIR /B /L /P** Enter

```
Command Prompt

A:\>DIR /B /L /P
bye.typ
cases.fil
april.tmp
bonjour.tmp
feb.tmp
goodbye.tmp
february.tmm
olive.oil
file3.fp
file3.swt
file4.fp
wildone.dos
middle.up
goodbye.txt
right.up
dress.up
april.txt
january.txt
february.txt
```

```
march.txt
steven.fil
hello.txt
file2.czg
exp01jan.dat
Press any key to continue . . .
```

WHAT'S HAPPENING? Now that you have separated the parameters, you have the directory listing you wanted—a bare listing in lower case letters that is paused.

Step 7 Press Ctrl + **C** to break out of the command.

Step 8 Key in the following: A:\>**EXIT** Enter

Step 9 Initiate and complete the Windows shut-down procedure.

CHAPTER SUMMARY

1. Command syntax means the correct command and the proper order for keying in commands.
2. A parameter is some piece of information that you want to include in a command. It allows a command to be specific.
3. A delimiter indicates where parts of a command begin or end. It is similar to punctuation marks in English.
4. Some commands require parameters. They are called mandatory or required parameters. Other commands allow parameters; these are called optional parameters.
5. A variable parameter or switch is one that requires the user to supply a value. A fixed parameter or switch has its value determined by the OS.
6. A syntax diagram is a representation of a command and its syntax.
7. The DIR command is an internal command that displays the directory (table of contents) of a disk.
8. DIR has many parameters, all of which are optional.
9. A file specification has two parts, the file name and the file extension. A file name is mandatory; however, a file extension is optional. If you use a file extension, separate it from the file name by a period, called a dot.
10. A valid file name contains legal characters, most often alphanumeric characters. It cannot contain illegal characters.
11. You may use keys such as ↑ or ↓ to perform command line editing.
12. Every device attached to the computer has a reserved, specific, and unique name so that the operating system knows what it is communicating with.
13. Disk drives are designated by a letter followed by a colon, as in A:. A local printer has the device name of PRN, LPT1, LPT2, or LPT3.
14. Defaults are implied instructions the operating system falls back to when no specific instructions are given.
15. The root directory's name is \ (backslash).
16. Subdirectories allow a disk to be divided into areas that can hold files. Subdirectories are named by the user or by an application program.
17. The system prompt displayed on the screen is the default drive and directory.
18. You can change the default drive and default subdirectory.

19. To change the default drive, you key in the drive letter followed by a colon, as in A: or C:.
20. To change the default subdirectory, you key in CD followed by the subdirectory name, such as CD \DATA or CD \WINNT\SYSTEM32.
21. To change directories and drives at the same time, you use the /D parameter, such as CD /D A:\DATA.
22. The subdirectory that contains the system utility files is usually \WINNT\SYSTEM32.
23. You can look for files on drives and subdirectories other than the default if you tell the OS where to look by prefacing the file names with a drive designator and/or path name.
24. If the file is in a subdirectory, the file name must be prefaced by the drive designator and followed by the subdirectory name. A user must include the subdirectory name in the command, as in C:\WINNT\SYSTEM32\FILENAME.EXT.
25. Global file specifications (* or ?) allow a user to substitute a wildcard for unknown characters.
26. The ? represents one character in a file name; the * matches a string of characters.
27. A command's output that normally is displayed on the screen may be redirected to a file. You key in the command, add the redirection symbol (>), and then key in the file name.
28. A command's output that is normally displayed on the screen may be redirected to a local printer or a network printer, if you know the network printer name. You key in the command, add the redirection symbol (>), and then key in the device name (PRN or LPT*n* if it is a local printer).
29. To get help on a command, key in the name of the command followed by a forward slash and a question mark, such as DIR /?.
30. The DIR command allows you to sort the directory listing by use of the parameter /O followed by the sort order letter you are interested in. For instance, to sort by name, you would key in DIR /ON.

KEY TERMS

backslash
command syntax
default
default drive
delimiter
designated drive
device name
documentation
dot
file
fixed parameter
global file specifications
logged drive
mandatory parameter
optional parameter
parameter
path
redirection
root directory
standard input
standard output
subdirectory
switch
syntax
syntax diagram
variable parameter
wildcard

DISCUSSION QUESTIONS

1. Define *command syntax*.
2. Why is syntax important when using a command?
3. Define *parameters*.

4. What is the difference between a variable and a fixed parameter?
5. How would you use a syntax diagram? Why is the diagram important?
6. Name two parameters that can be used with the DIR command. Explain why you would use the parameters.
7. Define *delimiters*. Give an example of a delimiter.
8. Define *file specifications*.
9. How do you separate a file name and a file extension?
10. What is used to separate a file specification from a path name?
11. What is the function and purpose of a device?
12. Explain the function and purpose of the default drive.
13. How can you tell which drive is the default drive?
14. Define *default subdirectory*.
15. How can you tell which directory is the default subdirectory?
16. What steps must be done to change the default drive? Why would you change drives?
17. What does A:\> mean?
18. If you keyed in 10 commands and wanted to reuse a command previously keyed in, what could you do?
19. What steps must be done to change a directory? Why would you change a directory?
20. What is the significance of the first backslash in a command?
21. Define *global file specifications*.
22. How are wildcards used?
23. If you see C:\WINNT\SYSTEM32> on the screen, what does it mean?
24. What is the purpose and function of redirection?
25. What would you do if you forgot the parameter for a wide DIR display?

TRUE/FALSE QUESTIONS

For each question, circle the letter T if the statement is true and the letter F if the statement is false.

T F 1. Command syntax is the proper order or sequence for keying in commands.
T F 2. When working at the Command Prompt, you are allowed to add one parameter to every command.
T F 3. A device is a place to send information to (write) or receive information from (read).
T F 4. The # is a wildcard that represents a group of characters.
T F 5. If you see brackets in a syntax diagram, you do not use the parameters.

COMPLETION QUESTIONS

Write the correct answer in each blank space.

6. A variable parameter is one in which the _________ provides the value.
7. A mark that separates characters (much like a punctuation mark in English) is known as a(n) ___________.
8. All files in a directory must have a(n) ________ name.
9. The \ symbol represents the ______.
10. If you keyed in _________, you would see all the files displayed across the screen, rather than down the screen.

MULTIPLE CHOICE QUESTIONS

For each question, write the letter for the correct answer in the blank space.

11. Which of the following is a global file specification?
    a. "
    b. /
    c. *
    d. .
12. In a Command Prompt window, the prompt displayed on the screen is
    a. the only drive the computer can ever use.
    b. the default drive.
    c. always the floppy disk drive.
    d. always the hard disk drive.
13. To display the directories for Drive A and Drive C at the same time, key in:
    a. DIR A: C:
    b. DIR A:/C
    c. DIR A: /DIR C:
    d. none of the above
14. The default drive can be changed by
    a. pressing **Enter** twice.
    b. using the DIR command.
    c. entering the new drive letter followed by a colon.
    d. The default drive cannot be changed.
15. If the system prompt is A:\> and you wanted to display all the files that are in the subdirectory called **CHAIRS** on Drive C, you would key in:
    a. CHAIRS
    b. DIR C:\CHAIRS
    c. DIR CHAIRS
    d. DIR A:\CHAIRS

WRITING COMMANDS

Write the correct steps or commands to perform the required action *as if you were at the computer*. The scenarios do not necessarily represent actual files on the disk. The prompt will indicate the default drive and directory.

16. A directory of all files that have the extension of **.TXT** on the root of Drive A.

17. A directory listing of the file called **MYFILE.TXT** located in the subdirectory **NEWS** on Drive C.

18. Clear the screen.

19. Display all the file names on the default drive and directory so only the file names and extensions are listed. (*Hint:* See the syntax diagram.)

20. Display all the files on the default drive that begin with the letter E, are five or fewer characters in length, and have no extension.

APPLICATION ASSIGNMENTS

PROBLEM SET I—AT THE COMPUTER

Open a Command Prompt window. Insert the ACTIVITIES Disk—Working Copy in Drive A.

☐ 1. On the ACTIVITIES disk in the root directory, find the file called **PERSONAL.FIL**. What is its size in bytes?
   a. 3
   b. 315
   c. 2307
   d. 3055

☐ 2. On the ACTIVITIES disk in the root directory, find all the files that have the file extension **.NEW**. How many files are there?
   a. one
   b. two
   c. three
   d. four

☐ 3. On the ACTIVITIES disk in the subdirectory called **GAMES**, find the file called **LS.PAS**. What is the file date?
   a. 6-23-89
   b. 8-13-98
   c. 3-1-97
   d. none of the above

4. Do a paused, wide display of the root directory of the ACTIVITIES disk. The fourth file down in the second column is:
   a. FILE2.FP
   b. MAR.NEW
   c. FILE4.FP
   d. DRESS.UP

5. Display the syntax diagram and help for the DIR command. What command did you use?
   a. DIR /HELP
   b. HELP DIR
   c. DIR /?
   d. either b or c

6. From the root of the ACTIVITIES disk, change the default directory to **SPORTS**. What command did you use?
   a. CD :
   b. CD ..
   c. CD SPORTS or CD \SPORTS
   d. DIR \SPORTS

7. On the ACTIVITIES disk, change back to the root from the **SPORTS** directory. What command did you use?
   a. CD ROOT
   b. CD \
   c. CD \ROOT
   d. none of the above

8. On the hard disk in the **WINNT\SYSTEM32** subdirectory, locate the file called **MEM**. What is the file extension?
   a. .BAT
   b. .COM
   c. .EXE
   d. .SYS

9. On the ACTIVITIES disk in the root directory, find all the files that have a file name that is at most four characters long and have the file extension **.TXT**. Which of the following files is among those displayed?
   a. YOUR.TXT
   b. MINE.TXT
   c. TEST.TXT
   d. NAME.TXT

10. On the ACTIVITIES disk in the root directory, how many files have a file name that is two characters or fewer in length and have any file extension?
    a. two
    b. three
    c. six
    d. none of the above

11. On the ACTIVITIES disk in the subdirectory **\DATA**, find all the files that have names beginning with the letter T and have any extension. What files are displayed?
    a. THIN.EST and TEA.TAX
    b. TEA.TAX and THANK.YOU
    c. THIN.EST and TEA.TAX and THANK.YOU
    d. none of the above

12. On the hard disk in the **WINNT\SYSTEM32** subdirectory, what file extension does *not* appear?
    a. .CZG
    b. .SYS
    c. .COM
    d. .EXE

13. When using the sort order parameter (/O), what additional parameter lets you sort files by file extension?
    a. X
    b. N
    c. D
    d. E

14. On the ACTIVITIES disk in the root directory, display all the files by file name in alphabetical order and pause the display. Which file appears first?
    a. APR.TXT
    b. BELLE.TXT
    c. APRIL.TXT
    d. APR.99

15. Key in the command to display the syntax and help for the DATE command. What is the last sentence to appear on the screen?
    a. Displays or sets the date.
    b. If Command Extensions are enabled the DATE command supports the /T switch which tells the command to just output the current date, without prompting for a new date.
    c. Press ENTER to change the date.
    d. DATE [date]

PROBLEM SET II—AT THE COMPUTER

Note 1: Before proceeding with these assignments, check with your lab technician or instructor to see if there are any special procedures for your lab environment.

Note 2: The ACTIVITIES Disk—Working Copy disk is in Drive A. The A:\> prompt is displayed as the default drive and directory. All work will occur from the root of the ACTIVITIES disk. You may not change drives or directories.

Note 3: The first homework activity may seem confusing and unclear. It is just a way to create a file containing your name and class information, which you will use for turning in your homework.

Step 1 Key in the following: **NAME** Enter

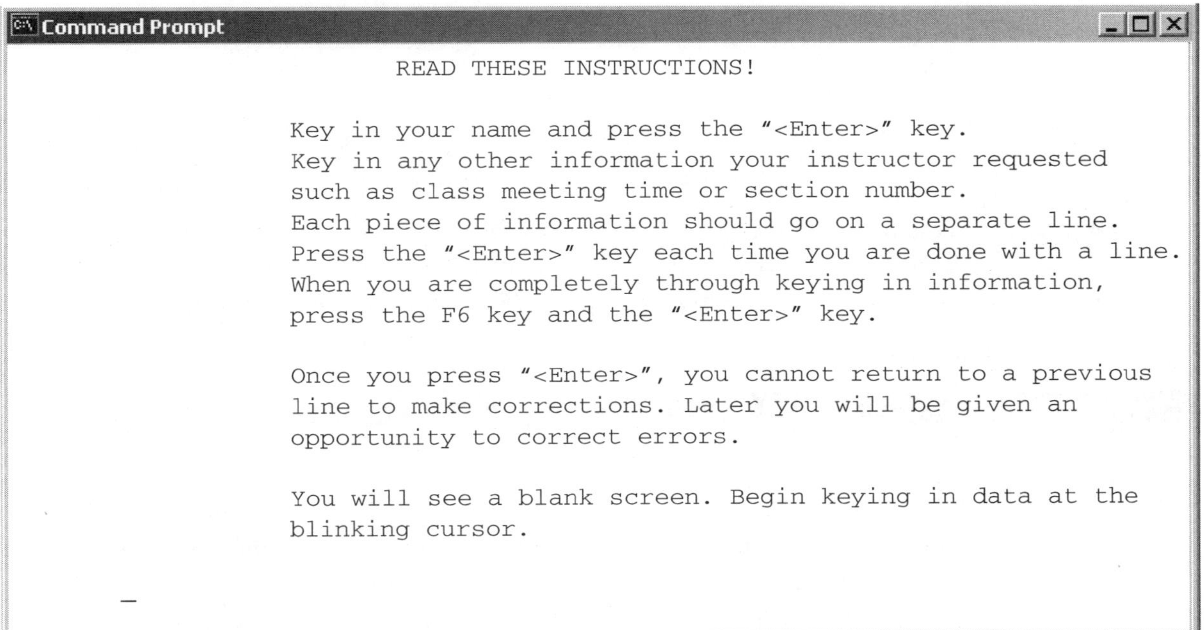

Command Prompt
READ THESE INSTRUCTIONS!
Key in your name and press the "<Enter>" key.
Key in any other information your instructor requested
such as class meeting time or section number.
Each piece of information should go on a separate line.
Press the "<Enter>" key each time you are done with a line.
When you are completely through keying in information,
press the F6 key and the "<Enter>" key.
Once you press "<Enter>", you cannot return to a previous
line to make corrections. Later you will be given an
opportunity to correct errors.
You will see a blank screen. Begin keying in data at the
blinking cursor.

Step 2 Here is an example to key in, but your instructor will have other specific information that applies to your class. Key in the following:

Bette Peat Enter (*Your* name goes here)

CIS 55 Enter (*Your* class goes here)

M-W-F 8-9 Enter (*Your* day and time go here)

Chapter 2 Enter (*Your* assignment goes here)

Step 3 Press F6 Enter

WHAT'S HAPPENING? You will see the following on the screen:

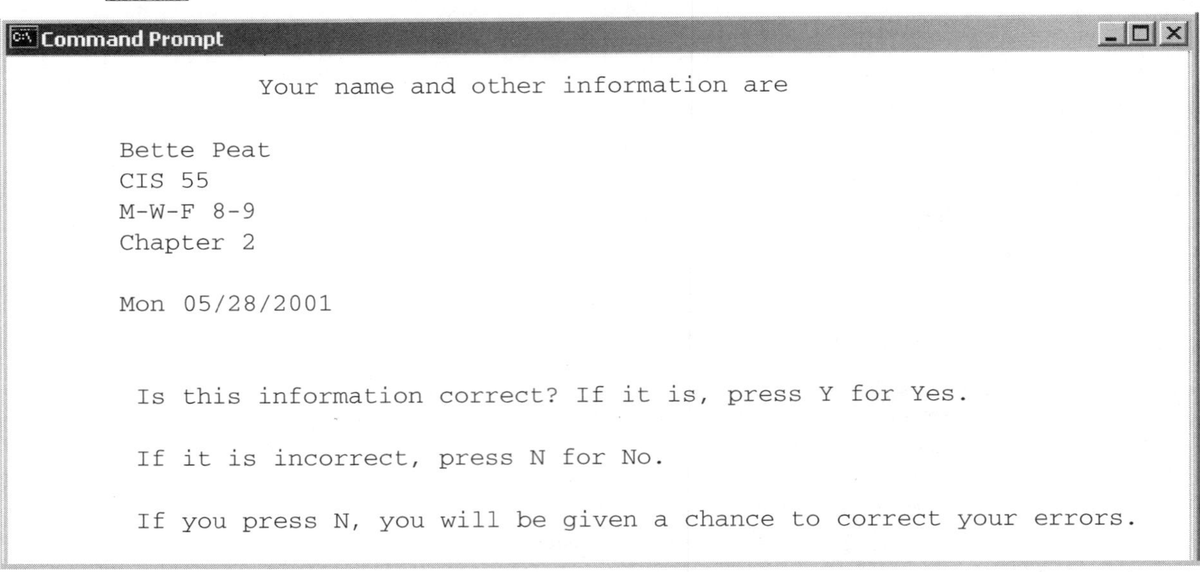

This program gives you a chance to check your data entry—what you have keyed in. The current date is inserted automatically. If it is correct, you press **Y**. If it is incorrect, you press **N**. In this case, the printout was correct.

Step 4 Press **Y**.

You have completed the program and returned to the command line prompt. You now have a file called **NAME.FIL** in the root directory of the working copy of the ACTIVITIES disk that contains the above data. (*Hint:* Remember redirection; see 2.21 and 2.22 to refresh your memory.) Now you are ready to complete Problem Set II. Remember to pay attention to the default directory. All the homework files need to be created in the root directory of the ACTIVITIES disk. If you do not create them there, you will not be able to find or print them.

TO CREATE 1.HW

- The root directory of the ACTIVITIES disk is the default.
- Locate all the files in the root directory that have a **.99** file extension.
- Place the output in a file called **1.HW**.

TO CREATE 2.HW

- The root directory of the ACTIVITIES disk is the default.
- Locate all the files in the **GAMES** directory that begin with the letter A and

have any file extension.

- Place the output in a file called **2.HW**.

TO CREATE 3.HW

- The root directory of the ACTIVITIES disk is the default.
- Find the files in the root directory that have file names up to five characters in length and have the file extension of **.TMP**.
- Place the output in a file called **3.HW**.

TO CREATE 4.HW

- The root directory of the ACTIVITIES disk is the default.
- Display all the files in the **PHONE** directory across the screen.
- Place the output in a file called **4.HW**.

TO CREATE 5.HW

- The root directory of the ACTIVITIES disk is the default.
- Display all the files with the file extension of **.TXT** in order by file name.
- Place the output in a file called **5.HW**.

CAUTION: DO NOT PROCEED WITH THIS STEP UNLESS IT IS OKAYED BY YOUR LAB INSTRUCTOR.

TO PRINT YOUR HOMEWORK

Step 1 Be sure the printer is on and ready to accept print jobs from your computer.

Step 2 Key in the following (be very careful to make no typing errors):

GO NAME.FIL 1.HW 2.HW 3.HW 4.HW 5.HW Enter

If the files you requested, **1.HW**, **2.HW**, etc., do not exist in the default directory, you will see the following message on the screen:

Command Prompt

```
File Not Found
The system cannot find the file specified.

    Is there a message that says "File Not Found. The system cannot
    find the file specified."

    If so, press Y to find out what could be wrong.

    Otherwise, press N to continue.
```

The operating system is telling you that the file cannot be found. If you see this screen, press **Y** to see what could be wrong, and repeat the print procedure after you have corrected the problem.

If the default directory contains the specified files, the following message will appear on the screen:

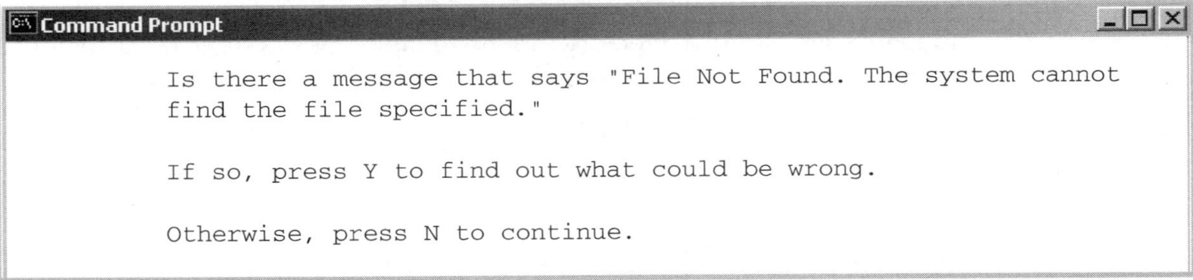

Step 3 Keep pressing **N**, and follow the messages on the screen until the Notepad program opens with a screen similar to the following:

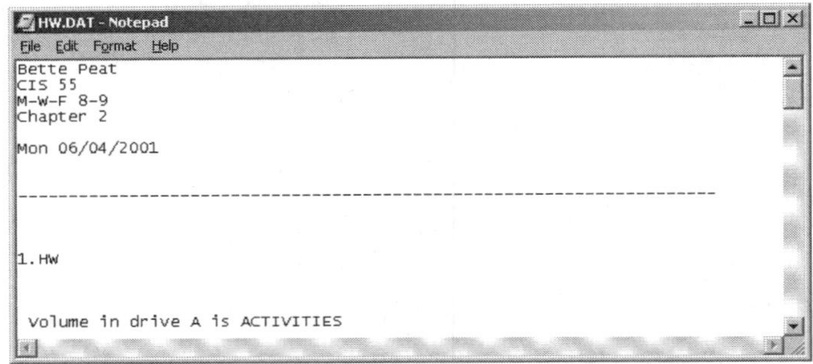

WHAT'S HAPPENING? All the requested files have been found and placed in a Notepad document. Your homework is now ready to print.

Step 4 On the Notepad menu bar, click **File**. Click **Print**.

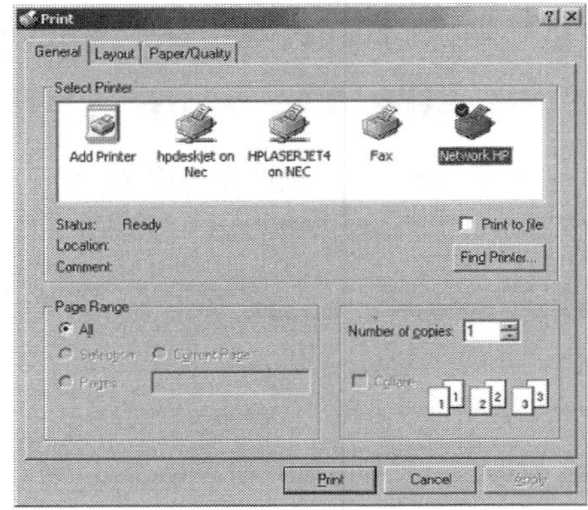

WHAT'S HAPPENING? The print dialog box opens. If you have more than one printer, all your printer choices will be displayed. The default printer is the highlighted printer.

Step 5 Click the **Print** button. Click **Close**.

Step 6 In the Notepad window, click **File**. Click **Exit**.

WHAT'S HAPPENING? The following will appear on the Command Prompt screen:

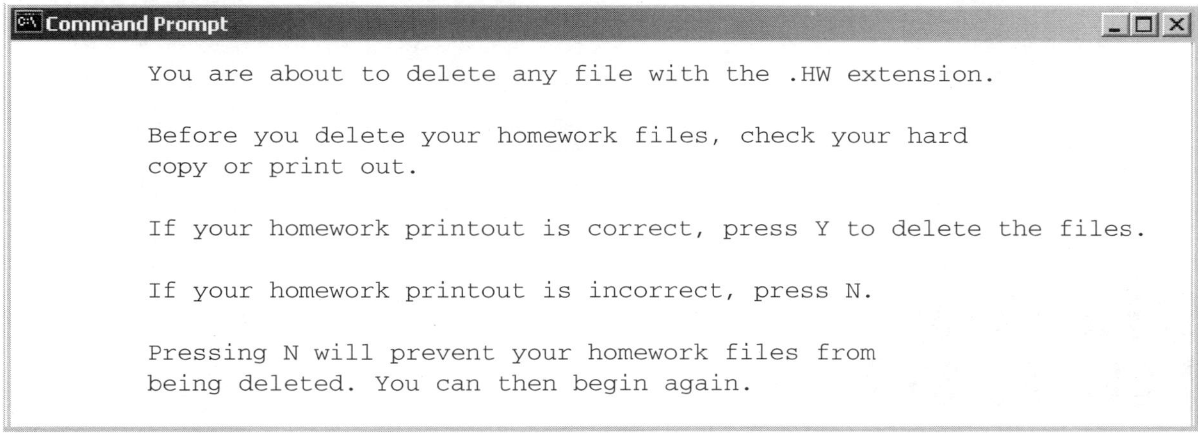
Command Prompt
You are about to delete any file with the .HW extension.
Before you delete your homework files, check your hard copy or print out.
If your homework printout is correct, press Y to delete the files.
If your homework printout is incorrect, press N.
Pressing N will prevent your homework files from being deleted. You can then begin again.

WHAT'S HAPPENING? At this point, look at your printout. If it is correct, you can press **Y** to delete the homework files for this chapter. If your printout is incorrect, you can press **N**. That will preserve your homework and you will need to redo only the problem that was incorrect, not all the homework assignments.

Step 7 Press **Y** Enter

WHAT'S HAPPENING? You have returned to the default prompt.

Step 8 Close the Command Prompt session.

Step 9 Execute the shut-down procedure.

PROBLEM SET III—BRIEF ESSAY

1. *Although the Windows operating system is a graphical user environment, it is still important to learn how to use the command line interface.*

   Agree or disagree with the above statement and explain your answer.

2. You have keyed in the following commands:

   C:\WINNT>**CD **

   C:\>**A:**

   A:\>**DIR HOUSE*.TXT**

   Describe the output and purpose of each command you keyed in. Could you have accomplished this task by using any other commands? If so, write the command(s).

CHAPTER

3

DISKS AND FORMATTING

LEARNING OBJECTIVES

After completing this chapter you will be able to:

1. Explain the need for formatting a disk.
2. Describe the structure of a disk.
3. Name and explain the purpose of each section of a disk.
4. Define *formatting*.
5. Explain the difference between internal and external commands.
6. List and explain the steps in formatting a floppy disk.
7. Explain the purpose and function of the /Q parameter and other parameters used with the FORMAT command.

STUDENT OUTCOMES

1. Format a floppy disk.
2. Use the LABEL command to change the volume label on a disk.
3. View the current volume label using the VOL command.
4. Use the /Q parameter to format a disk.

CHAPTER OVERVIEW

Disks are the mainstays of the computer workstation. They are used for storing data and programs and for distributing data from one computer to another. In order to be used, disks must be formatted, a process by which an operating system sets up the guidelines for reading from and writing to a disk. In Windows, you can still format a disk by using the FORMAT command from the command line.

In this chapter you will learn how a disk is structured, how the operating system uses disks, and how to format and electronically label a disk. In addition, you will learn how to change the electronic label. Throughout, remember that formatting a disk is a dangerous operation because it removes all the data from a disk.

3.1 WHY FORMAT A DISK?

So far, the disks you have used with this text have been already prepared for your environment. Although most floppy disks come preformatted, you may still purchase unformatted disks. And if you purchase a new hard disk, it too must be formatted. When you want to prepare a disk for use, you will use a system utility command called FORMAT.COM. But prior to using the format command (which can also be accessed from the GUI), you should have some understanding of what this process is all about.

3.2 PARTITIONING AND FORMATTING DISKS

Before Windows 2000 Professional can use a disk, the disk must be prepared for use. A hard disk requires a special process. It must first be partitioned, or divided, into one or more logical divisions and then formatted with a file system. A ***primary partition*** is a section of a hard disk. When a disk is partitioned, it allocates a fixed amount of space for each primary partition. This information is stored in what is called a ***partition table*** that is located in the first physical sector of a hard disk. The partition table tells where each partition begins and ends. The physical locations of the partitions are given as the beginning and ending head, sector, and cylinder number. In addition, the partition table identifies the type of file system used for each partition and identifies whether the partition is bootable.

One partition is marked as the ***active partition***, and you may boot from only the active partition. Hard disks are limited to a maximum of four primary partitions per physical disk. Only one primary partition can be designated as an extended partition. An ***extended partition*** can contain logical drives (volumes). Thus, if you had two physical drives, each could be partitioned as one primary partition and would be assigned the drive letters C and D. Drive C would be partitioned, formatted, and bootable. Drive D would be partitioned and formatted but not bootable. If you had one hard drive, as many users do, the hard drive might be partitioned as only one primary partition, Drive C, that, of course, would be bootable. In another instance, the single hard drive could be partitioned with one primary partition and an extended partition. In that case, you would then have Drive C (the bootable drive) and logical drive D. Each drive would have to be formatted.

Only one operating system can be active at a time. If you had a dual-booting system and were using two operating systems, such as Windows 2000 Professional and Linux, you could create a ***partition*** for each operating system. You would then choose and boot the computer from the active partition where the operating system you wished to use was located. Each operating system formats disks in its own, unique way. Depending on the operating system you use and the file system you select, the operating system you are using might be able to recognize the other drive, but not read the files on it.

Each operating system has a unique way of recording information on a disk. The organizational scheme is known as a ***file system***. One factor that makes one computer compatible with another is not the brand name such as Apple, IBM, or Compaq, but rather the operating system, part of which is the file system that each operating system brand uses. Disk formatting is based almost entirely on which operating system the computer uses. Operating systems prepare disks so that information can be read from and written to them. The disk manufacturers cannot prepare a disk in advance without knowing what kind of operating system will be used. The process of preparing a disk so that it will be compatible with an operating system is known as ***formatting*** or ***initializing the disk***.

Since this textbook is for Windows 2000 Professional users, the only kind of formatting that you are interested in is Windows-based. Although there are many file systems in use for readable/writable disks, such as Unix and HPFS (OS2), Windows 2000 Professional supports four file systems for readable/writable disks, the NTFS file system and three FAT file systems (FAT12, FAT16, and FAT32). FAT12 is used only on floppy disks. Essentially, you have two choices—FAT and NTFS. FAT is an acronym for ***file allocation table***, and ***NTFS*** is an acronym for ***New Technology File System***. Windows 2000 also supports two types of file systems on CD-ROM and DVD (Compact Disc File systems [CDFS] and Universal Disk Format [UDF]). The CDFS and UDF file systems are beyond the scope of this text.

All disks, including hard disks, must be formatted. In general, when you purchase a computer, the hard drive or drives have already been partitioned and formatted. When you purchase floppy disks for a Wintel computer (a computer that has an Intel or clone-Intel processor and is running the Windows operating system), the floppy disks are also preformatted, although nonformatted disks are also available and are usually less expensive. Even if you purchase preformatted disks, it is inevitable that you will want to reuse them. Disks that have been used and possess information that is no longer needed can be erased or re-prepared with the FORMAT command. Hard disks are typically formatted once, when they are new, and are rarely reformatted because formatting eliminates what is on the disk. Although you may format both hard and floppy disks, this textbook deals only with formatting floppy disks using the FORMAT command in Windows 2000 Professional.

Windows 2000 provides two types of disk storage configurations, basic disk and dynamic disk. ***Basic disk*** is a physical disk that contains primary partitions and/or extended partitions with logical drives and a partition table. Windows 2000, by default, initializes all disks as basic. New to Windows 2000 are dynamic disks. ***Dynamic disks*** are physical disks that have been upgraded by and are managed by the Disk Management utility program. Dynamic disks do not use partitions or logical drives, and only computers running Windows 2000 can use dynamic disks. Dynamic disks are beyond the scope of this text. Discussion will be limited to basic disks.

3.2.1 THE STRUCTURE OF A DISK

Formatting a disk consists of two parts: ***low-level formatting***, or ***physical formatting***, and ***high-level formatting***, or ***logical formatting***. Low-level (physical) formatting creates and sequentially numbers tracks and sectors for identification purposes. Tracks are concentric circles on a disk. Each track is divided into smaller units called sectors. A sector, which is the smallest unit on a disk, is usually 512 bytes, the industry standard. The number of tracks and sectors varies depending on the type of disk. When data needs to be written to or read from a disk, the identification number of the track and sector tells the read/write head where to position itself. This process accounts for every space on the disk. It is similar to assigning every house a unique address so that it can be instantly identifiable. However, even after a disk is physically prepared to hold data, it is not ready for use.

The second part of formatting is high-level (logical) formatting. In logical formatting, the operating system creates a file system on a disk so it can keep track of the location of files. Formatting a hard disk involves only logical formatting. Low-level formatting of a hard disk is usually done as part of the manufacturing process. Low-level formatting can also be done by the computer system vendor, or you may purchase special software programs to low-level format your hard disk, although this is a rare occurrence. Most commonly, when you purchase a computer system, the high-level and low-level formatting of the hard disk are done. However, when you format a floppy disk, both the physical and logical formatting processes occur.

Logical formatting determines how the operating system uses a disk by building a structure to manage files on the disk so they can be easily saved and retrieved. The FORMAT command performs both high- and low-level formatting on a floppy disk. On a hard disk, only high-level formatting is performed.

Windows 2000 Professional needs to monitor the status of all of a disk's data sectors so it can answer critical questions. Does a sector already have information in it? Is it damaged? In either case, it cannot be used. Is it an empty sector, available for data storage? Since there can be many sectors on a disk, particularly on a hard disk, it would be too time-consuming for Windows 2000 Professional to manage them one sector at a time. Instead, it combines one or more sectors into logical units called ***clusters,*** also called ***allocation units*** since these units allocate disk space. When Windows 2000 Professional writes a file to a disk, it copies the file's contents to unused clusters in the data sectors. The smallest unit that Windows 2000 Professional works with when reading or writing to a disk is a cluster. To be able to read from and write files to a disk, Windows 2000 Professional tracks locations in the file system you have chosen, either the FAT file system or the NTFS file system.

Floppy disks only use FAT. Thus, since the smallest unit Windows 2000 Professional can deal with is a cluster, a file that is only 100 bytes long saved to a 3½-inch, 1.44-MB disk will actually occupy 512 bytes on the floppy disk. If you were using the FAT file system and the file were saved to a 2-MB hard disk, it would actually occupy 32,768 bytes. The portion of a cluster that is not being used by the data in the file is still allocated to the file; that space can be claimed by no other file. It is wasted space on your disk and is called ***cluster overhang***. Furthermore, as you can imagine, a data file is rarely ever *exactly* one cluster in size, nor would its size necessarily be an even number. How the data is managed depends on whether you are using FAT or NTFS.

3.2.2 THE MASTER BOOT RECORD AND THE BOOT SECTOR

The first part of any hard disk is the ***master boot record (MBR)***. The master boot record is the mechanism required to find a hard disk and launch any necessary code to load drivers located on the boot record. The MBR of a hard disk resides at the first physical sector of the disk. The ***boot sector*** is the first sector on every logical drive. It contains a table of that drive's characteristics and contains a short program, called the bootstrap loader, that begins loading Windows 2000 Professional, copying the necessary system files from the disk into memory. If you are using FAT, and the disk the system is trying to boot from is not a system disk, you see the message:

```
Non-System disk or disk error
Replace the disk and press any key when ready
```

If you are using NTFS, and the disk the system is trying to boot from is not a system disk, you see one of the following messages:

- Invalid partition table
- Error loading operating system
- Missing operating system

If you have a floppy disk in Drive A that is not a system disk, you may see the message

```
NTLDR is missing
Press any key to restart
```

Even if a disk is not a system disk (one capable of booting the system), it still has a boot sector. (There is no MBR on a floppy disk. The first sector on a floppy disk is the boot sector.) On any disk, the boot sector contains information about the physical characteristics of the disk: the number of tracks, the number of bytes per sector, the number of sectors per track, the version of the operating system used to format the disk, the root directory, the volume serial number, etc. The boot sector allows Windows 2000 Professional to identify the type of disk.

3.2.3 FAT16, VFAT, AND FAT32

When you format a disk using FAT, the formatting program creates three critical elements: the boot record, the file allocation table (two copies), and the root directory. These elements occupy the first portion of the disk and take only about one to two percent of the disk space. The remainder of the disk is used for file storage. See Figure 3.1.

BOOT RECORD
FILE ALLOCATION TABLE (FAT)
FILE ALLOCATION TABLE (FAT)
ROOT DIRECTORY
FILES AREA (DATA SECTORS)

FIGURE 3.1 THE LOGICAL STRUCTURE OF A DISK

The order of the sections is always the same. The boot record, two copies of the FAT, and the root directory table are always located in the first sectors. These elements control how the files are stored on a disk and how Windows 2000 Professional saves and retrieves files. The data sectors are where the data or files are actually stored.

A map of a disk's data clusters, the FAT, is made up of entries that correspond to every cluster on the disk. The number of clusters varies from one type of disk to another. Cluster size on a hard disk is not determined by the disk's overall capacity, but by the partition size. Table 3.1 indicates the relationship between cluster size and disk size.

Disk Size	Number of Sectors in a Cluster	Cluster Size in Bytes	Cluster size in KB
3½-inch 1.44 MB	1 sector	512 bytes	½KB
3½-inch 2.88 MB	2 sectors	1,024 bytes	1KB
3½-inch 720KB	2 sectors	1,024 bytes	1KB
5¼-inch 1.2 MB	1 sector	512 bytes	½KB
5¼-inch 360KB	2 sectors	1,024 bytes	1KB
32 MB–63 MB	2 sectors	1,024 bytes	1KB
64 MB–127 MB	4 sectors	2,048 bytes	2KB
128 MB–255 MB	8 sectors	4,096 bytes	4KB
256 MB–511 MB	16 sectors	8,192 bytes	8KB
512 MB–1,023 MB	32 sectors	16,384 bytes	16KB
1,024 MB–2,048 MB	64 sectors	32,768 bytes	32KB

TABLE 3.1 CLUSTER SIZE AND DISK SIZE

To manage the data, each entry in the FAT is a number that indicates the status of a cluster. A 0 (zero) in the FAT means the cluster is empty and available for use. Other specific numbers indicate that a cluster is reserved (not available for use) or bad (also not available for use). Any other number indicates that a cluster is in use.

To follow the trail of a data file longer than one cluster, the number in the FAT is a pointer to the next cluster that holds data for that file. That entry becomes a pointer to the next cluster that holds data in the same file. A special entry in the FAT indicates where the file ends and that no more data is in the file. Thus, the numbers in the FAT are used to link, or chain, clusters that belong to the same file. The FAT works in conjunction with the root directory table. Since the FAT is used to control the entire disk, two copies of the FAT are kept on the disk in case one is damaged. The FAT occupies as many sectors as it needs to map the disk. The FAT is always located on the first sectors of the disk.

Windows 95 introduced a special version of FAT called ***VFAT***, or ***virtual file allocation table***, which allowed Windows 95 to maintain backward compatibility and to accommodate long file names. VFAT is a variation of the original 16-bit FAT. It is a virtual 32-bit FAT, meaning that it is not really a 32-bit FAT. A reserved area of the VFAT keeps directory block information for long file names. In Windows 2000 Professional, the 32-bit

VFAT is the primary file system. The VFAT is still referred to as the FAT and you rarely hear the term "VFAT." The FAT file system can maintain a maximum of 65,536 clusters, which means that the largest hard drive that can be supported is 2.1 GB. When you purchase a new computer today, it is common to have a hard drive of 10, 18, 20, or more GB. Manufacturers of computer systems can get around this limitation by partitioning a hard drive into 2-GB sizes and creating the logical drive letters C, D, E, and F (for an 8-GB drive, for instance).

To overcome this limitation, FAT32 was introduced in Windows 95 OSR2, which is also referred to as Windows 95 B. It was enhanced in Windows 98. FAT32 is an enhancement of the FAT file system and is based on 32-bit file allocation table entries, rather than the 16-bit file entries the FAT file system used in DOS and the first version of Windows 95. FAT16 is usually referred to simply as FAT on disks greater than 5 MB. As a result, FAT32 will support larger hard drives (up to 2 terabytes). A terabyte is a trillion bytes, or 1,000 billion bytes. An 8-GB drive would simply be Drive C under FAT32. FAT32 also uses smaller clusters than the FAT file system. However, FAT32 is for drives over 512 MB and does not apply to floppy disks. See Table 3.2 for a comparison.

Drive Size	FAT Cluster Size	FAT32 Cluster Size
256 MB–511 MB	8KB	Not supported
512 MB–1,023 MB	16KB	4KB
1,024 MB–2 GB	32KB	4KB
3 GB–8 GB	Not supported	4KB
9 GB–16 GB	Not supported	8KB
17 GB–32 GB	Not supported	16KB
Greater than 32 GB	Not supported	32KB

TABLE 3.2 COMPARISON OF FAT AND FAT32

FAT32 provides some further enhancements. It allows a moveable root directory, the ability to use the backup copy of the file allocation table (FAT maintains two copies of the table but can use only one of them), and an internal backup copy of some critical FAT data structures. Unlike FAT, FAT32 does impose a restriction on the number of entries in the root directory table, but the number is over 64,000 and thus, does not restrict users as the 512 file limit did. It also allows the root directory table to be located anywhere on the hard disk.

There are advantages and disadvantages to both FAT and FAT32. With FAT32, you have smaller clusters. Therefore, there are more clusters on a partition, and you can store more data on your hard disk. However, the more clusters there are, the bigger the FAT must be. It takes Windows longer to search the table in order to find the information that it needs so it can access a file. On the other hand, with larger clusters, the table is much smaller and Windows needs less time to search to locate the information it needs to access a file. Unfortunately, you also increase the amount of wasted disk space from cluster overhang.

If you have many small files, using FAT32 is probably best. If you have mostly large files such as graphics or video files, then FAT is fine. You could have one drive FAT and another FAT32, depending on your needs. Remember, FAT32 can be used only on drives larger than 512 MB. In addition, DOS, Windows 3.1, Windows NT, and the original version of Windows 95 will *not* recognize FAT32 and cannot boot or use files on any drive that has FAT32. However, Windows 2000 can recognize FAT 32. If, for example, your C drive used FAT32 and you wanted to use another operating system such as DOS 6.22 to boot from the A drive, you would not be able to "see" the C drive at all. Remember as well, floppy disks are always FAT and can be read by all of the above operating systems.

3.2.4 THE ROOT DIRECTORY

The root directory is a table that records information about each file on a disk. When you use Windows Explorer or My Computer, the information displayed on the screen comes from this root directory table.

In order to make Windows 2000 Professional compatible with older Windows and DOS programs, some changes had to be made in the root directory table. The DOS directory structure only recognized 8.3 file names. Windows 95, Windows 98, and then Windows 2000 Professional, needed to allow long file names while still permitting the use of DOS or Windows 3.1 or 3.11 programs with the 8.3 file name limitation. The DOS root directory stores information in a table about every file on a disk, including the file name, the file extension, the size of the file in bytes, the date and time the file was last modified, and the file's attributes. The Windows 2000 Professional root directory table still includes this information, but it also uses previously unused areas in the table, particularly the file attribute, to handle long file names. In addition to the file attributes you have learned about, Windows 2000 Professional uses a special combination of attributes to signal that an entry is the first of a series of directory entries. This feature allows a series of directory entries to be chained together so that long file names can be used.

To maintain compatibility with DOS or Windows 3.1 or 3.11 programs, Windows 2000 Professional gives every file both a long file name and a short file name. The short file name, an alias, is based on the long file name and is stored in the first directory entry using the DOS 8.3 name. Neither a user nor an application can control the name created by the alias process.

Another critical entry in the root directory table is the starting cluster number. This number indicates which cluster holds the first portion of the file, or the first FAT address. In this way, the root directory tells Windows 2000 Professional what is on the disk, and the FAT tells Windows 2000 Professional where data is on the disk.

3.2.5 THE FAT AND THE ROOT DIRECTORY

Imagine a book on computers with a table of contents. Like the root directory, the table of contents tells you what is in the book. One chapter could be listed as "The Hard Disk" starting on page number 30. The page number is a pointer to the place you must go to find the information about the hard disk. The page number is similar to the FAT.

You must turn to page 30 to begin reading about the hard disk. However, the information about the hard disk is not located only on page 30. You must read page 31, then page 32, and so on, until you have all the information about the hard disk. The pages are linked, or have a trail. If a book were like a disk, the table of contents (the root directory) would be followed by a chart (the FAT) instructing you to begin on page 30, then go to page 31, then to page 32, and so on. The number in the FAT is a pointer to the next cluster that holds data in the file, enabling the system to follow the trail of a file longer than one cluster. A special entry in the FAT, called an ***EOF (end-of-file) marker***, indicates when there is no more data in the file. Other data indicates when the cluster is available or has bad sectors in it. See Figure 3.2.

ROOT DIRECTORY

File Name	File Extension	Date	Time	File Size	Starting Cluster
MYFILE	TXT	1/23/98	11:13 PM	41,364	1
YOUR	XLS	11/7/99	1:00 AM	98,509	3
THIS	DOC	5/7/00	2:13 AM	38,949	7

FAT

Cluster	Pointer	Data in Cluster
1	2	MYFILE.TXT
2	EOF	MYFILE.TXT
3	4	YOUR.XLS
4	5	YOUR.XLS
5	6	YOUR.XLS
6	EOF	YOUR.XLS
7	8	THIS.DOC
8	EOF	THIS.DOC
9	0	Unused
10	BAD	Contains bad sectors

FIGURE 3.2 THE ROOT DIRECTORY AND THE FAT

The FAT works in conjunction with the root directory table. The FAT can occupy as many sectors as it needs to map out the disk.

3.2.6 THE DATA PORTION OR THE FILES AREA

The rest of the disk, which is the largest part, is used for storing files or data. As far as Windows 2000 Professional is concerned, all files, programs, and data are chains of bytes laid out in sequence. Space is allocated to files on an as-needed basis, one cluster at a time. When a file is written to a disk, Windows 2000 Professional begins writing to the first available cluster. It writes in adjacent, or ***contiguous***, clusters if possible, but, if any adjacent sectors are already in use (allocated by the FAT), Windows 2000 Professional skips to the next available (unallocated) space. Thus, a file can be ***noncontiguous***, physically scattered around a disk.

3.2.7 UNDERSTANDING THE FAT AND THE ROOT DIRECTORY TABLE

To illustrate how the root directory table and the FAT work, imagine you want to create a file called MYFILE.TXT, which will occupy three clusters on a disk. Let us say that clusters 3, 4, and 6 are free. The operating system first creates an entry in the root directory table and fills in the file information (file name, file extension, date, time, etc.). Then data is written to the first free cluster, number 3, as the starting cluster number in the root directory table. Windows 2000 Professional knows it will need three clusters and must link or chain them. It does this by placing a 4 (a pointer) in the number 3 cluster pointing to the next available cluster. When it gets to cluster 4, it places a 6 (another pointer) pointing to the next available cluster. The FAT continues to cluster 6. When it gets to cluster 6, it places an end-of-file marker, a note indicating that the file ends there.

To make an analogy, imagine a self-storage facility comprised of storage bins that hold things (the data). The front office that manages the self-storage facility does not care what is in the bins. The front office only has to know how many bins there are, where they are located, and if they are in use. The front office has a map of all its numbered storage bins (the FAT). The bins are numbered so that the front office knows where the bins are located. The front office also needs a list (the root directory) of all the people who have rented bins. Thus, I walk in and say that I want the boxes stored for Gillay. The front office first looks up Gillay in the list to be sure they have stored my boxes. In this case, they find the name Gillay, so they know I have rented at least one bin. Besides having my name in their directory, their list points to another list that says to go to the map (the FAT), starting with bin 3. The front office goes to the map (the FAT) and sees that storage bin 3 is linked to storage bin 4, which is linked to storage bin 6. Storage bin 6 has no links. Now the front office knows that Gillay has bins 3, 4, and 6 full of boxes. The front office can send someone (rotate the disk) to bins 3, 4, and 6 to retrieve the boxes. To look at this process graphically, see Figure 3.3.

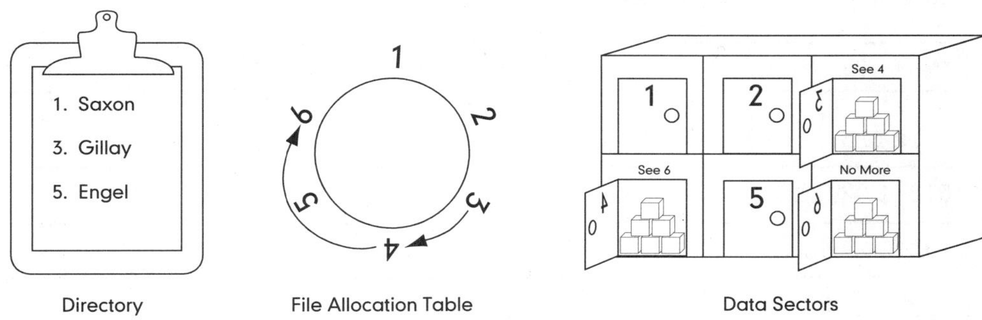

FIGURE 3.3 STORING FILES

This analogy gives you some of the basic information you need in order to understand the FAT structure of a disk.

3.2.8 NTFS

The file system that you use with Windows 2000 determines which of the operating system's advanced features that you can use. If you are concerned with disk security, performance, and efficiency, you would choose to use the NTFS file system. The NTFS file system, first introduced in Windows NT, is the preferred file system to FAT, VFAT, and FAT32. What NTFS offers, besides the performance needed for the much larger disk drives seen today, is a secure file system. With the NTFS file system, you can manage the security of files and folders for your machine. In addition to the ability to have a secure file system, NTFS also offers other major advantages. These include:

- A secure file system with the ability to assign permissions to each file and folder on the disk.
- More efficient storage of data on large hard disks.
- Faster access to files and folders.
- Better data recovery because a log file is kept of disk activities. Thus, if there is a disk failure, Windows 2000 can restore the disk based on the log file.
- Ability to compress files, allowing more data to be stored on a disk.
- Ability to assign disk quotas, which allow you to set limits on how much disk space a user may have.
- Encryption of files for better security.

3.2.9 CLUSTERS AND NTFS

NTFS uses the cluster scheme that you have seen in FAT for allocating data, but for a given drive, it has less overhead. Every business has expenses that do not directly make a profit, such as rent or utilities, and the business must pay these costs so it can stay in business. These expenses are known as overhead. A computer system's overhead is its cost of doing business because it must use processing time and memory to run the operating system. Computer overhead does not directly relate to the task at hand, but is mandatory so that the computer system can operate. In business, reducing overhead means that you can make a larger profit. With computers, reducing operating overhead means that you can allocate more computer resources to the work you wish to do. Table 3.3 shows the cluster sizes for NTFS volumes.

Partition Size	Cluster Size in Bytes	Sectors in a Cluster
–512 MB	512	1
513–1,024 MB	1,024	2
1,025–2,048 MB	2,048	4
2,049–4,096 MB	4,096	8
4,097–8,192 MB	8,192	16
8,193–16,384 MB	16,384	32
16,385–32,768 MB	32,768	64
–16 exabytes*	65,536	128

*An exabyte is roughly one quintillion bytes or a billion billion bytes and is abbreviated EB.

TABLE 3.3 NTFS CLUSTER SIZE

The structure of an NTFS volume looks similar to FAT, but there are differences, as you can see in Figure 3.4.

Partition boot information	Master File Table (MFT)	System Files and Folders

FIGURE 3.4 STRUCTURE OF AN NTFS VOLUME

3.2.10 MASTER FILE TABLE (MFT)

Instead of using the FAT, NTFS uses a special file called the ***Master File Table (MFT)*** that tracks all the files and directories in a volume. The MFT is really a database file of all the files on the system. A database is a way of finding information quickly. For instance, libraries, long before computers, used databases. The card catalog was a database. The card catalog did not have books in it, but it instead had a card that pointed to the physical location of the book on a shelf. Databases are used heavily in the computer world. When using NTFS, the MFT is dynamic and will change size when necessary. The first 16 records, called the metadata files, contain information about the volume itself and are considered the overhead for maintaining the file system. The MFT has an entry for the MFT itself (just another file) and other metadata files such as the log file, marked bad clusters, and the root directory.

After the volume information, each record in the MFT corresponds to one file or one folder in the file system. The record for the file or folder contains the attributes of the file or folder, including such attributes as the file name, the status of the read-only bit, the file creation and last accessed date, and so on. One major attribute that MFT adds to the file system is the security descriptor. The security descriptor provides information on who has what access to what files or folders and what they can or cannot do to the file or folder, i.e., who can read the file, write to the file, and so on. NTFS is considered a secure file system, and you can assign a permission for every file and folder on your system.

In addition, and very different from FAT, the data in the file is considered just an attribute in the file and, if the amount of data is small enough, the entire file will fit in the MFT. This feature not only allows very fast access to files but also eliminates file fragmentation. However, there is a limit to how much data will fit into the MFT (about 750 bytes) and most files are too large to have all their data fit into the MFT. In that case, NTFS also allocates files in cluster units. If any attribute (usually the data) does not fit into the MFT record, NTFS stores it a new, separate set of clusters, called a ***run*** or an ***extent***. Any attribute stored in the MFT is considered a resident attribute and any attribute forced out to an extent is called a nonresident attribute. When the extent needs to become larger (usually because data is added to a file), NTFS again tries to allocate contiguous clusters to the same extent. If that is not possible, then NTFS will allocate an extent somewhere else on the disk. This process continues as the file becomes larger.

Folders (directories) are treated much as files are in NTFS. If the folder is small enough, the index to the files in the folder is kept in its entirety in the MFT. This too is an attribute called the Index Root attribute. If the folder entries are larger than what will fit into the MFT, then NTFS creates a new extent with a nonresident attribute called an index buffer. The index buffer contains a data structure called a b-tree. A b-tree stores indexes to information in a sorted order. This makes locating information on the volume much quicker because the entry is more easily found.

3.2.11 DECIDING ON A FILE SYSTEM

You may choose your file system when you install Windows 2000 Professional. You may also convert a FAT file system to FAT32 or NTFS at any time with special utility programs that come with Windows 2000 Professional. However, these are one way conversions. You cannot convert from NTFS or FAT32 to FAT. When you format a floppy disk, it will always be the FAT file system. With a hard disk, you make the decision. Remember, every disk has a file system assigned to it. If you look at the properties of a disk, you will see which file system has been assigned to it.

3.3 CLARIFYING PROCEDURES

1. **System utility files subdirectory.** You will be at the command prompt screen. You may have to change your directory so that you are in the subdirectory that has the system utility files. Remember to refer to your Configuration Table in Chapter 1.6 to ensure that all substitutions have been made before you begin this activity.
2. **A blank or new disk.** Whenever a new or blank disk is referred to, you may use a brand new disk or an old disk containing information you no longer wish to keep. Any information will be written over in the format process.
3. If you are in a lab environment, you need to check with your instructor to see if there are any particular procedures that need to be followed in your lab. For instance, in some networked environments, you cannot format a floppy disk in Drive A.

3.4 ACTIVITY: FORMATTING A FLOPPY DISK

WARNING! Never format an application disk or a disk that has data you wish to keep. Also, if you have a hard disk, you must be *exceedingly* careful. **Never, *never* key in** C:\>**FORMAT C:.** If you do, you may completely erase, forever, all the information on the hard disk.

Step 1 Shell out to the command prompt screen. (This means to open a Command Prompt window.) Make certain that you have no disk in your A drive.

Note: Your starting prompt may differ from the examples in this text. Your initial prompt upon shelling out to the Command Prompt screen may be C:\WINNT\SYSTEM32> or perhaps a network drive, such as G:\>.

Step 2 Key in the following: C:\>**CD \WINNT\SYSTEM32** Enter

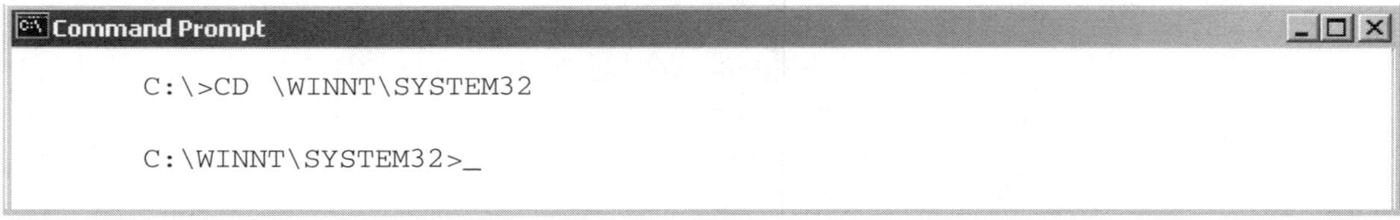
Command Prompt
C:\>CD \WINNT\SYSTEM32
C:\WINNT\SYSTEM32>_

WHAT'S HAPPENING

You have changed the default directory to the **\WINNT\SYSTEM32** subdirectory. The prompt should now display **C:\WINNT\SYSTEM32>**.

To format a disk, you use the FORMAT command. FORMAT is another example of a system utility program, also called an external command, stored as a file in the **WINNT\SYSTEM32** subdirectory. The default drive and subdirectory, in this situation, become very important. Whenever you use an external command, you are telling the operating system to look for a file that matches what you keyed in.

Remember that the prompt on the screen represents the default drive and subdirectory. When the operating system looks for an external command, it will look on the default drive only (in this case, Drive C) and in the default subdirectory (in this case, **\WINNT\SYSTEM32**) for the command or file name that you keyed in. You can instruct the operating system to look or do something on a different disk drive or different subdirectory, but you must specify that disk drive and/or subdirectory. In this case, you are looking for the command FORMAT. You can see whether or not this command, stored as a file called **FORMAT.COM**, is located on the disk in the default drive and in the default subdirectory.

Step 3 Key in the following: C:\WINNT\SYSTEM32>**DIR FORMAT.COM** Enter

Command Prompt

```
C:\WINNT\SYSTEM32>DIR FORMAT.COM
 Volume in drive C is 2000 PRO
 Volume Serial Number is C4A7-8571

 Directory of C:\WINNT\SYSTEM32


12/07/1999  12:00p              34,064 FORMAT.COM
               1 File(s)         34,064 bytes
               0 Dir(s)     456,032,256 bytes free

C:\WINNT\SYSTEM32>_
```

WHAT'S HAPPENING? The screen display tells you that the FORMAT command, stored as the file named **FORMAT.COM**, is located on the default drive, Drive C. In addition, since your system utility files are in a subdirectory, you will not only be on Drive C but also in a subdirectory called **\WINNT\SYSTEM32**. To use (or execute or run) the FORMAT program, you key in the name of the command.

Step 4 Key in the following (be sure to include the drive letter A):
C:\WINNT\SYSTEM32>**FORMAT A:** Enter

Command Prompt

```
C:\WINNT\SYSTEM32>FORMAT A:
Insert new disk for drive A:
and press ENTER when ready...
```

In Step 3 you used the DIR command to locate the file. You called the program by keying in the name of the file. When you do that, you are asking the

operating system to find the file called **FORMAT.COM** and load it into memory. FORMAT is the command that tells the system what work you want it to do. The **A:** tells the system that the disk you want to format is in Drive A. If you did not specify a lettered drive, A:, B:, or C:, you would receive a message that you were missing a parameter—the drive letter. In earlier versions of DOS, the FORMAT command would not ask for a drive letter and would format the default drive. Since the default drive is C and C is the hard disk, FORMAT would have unintentionally erased everything on the hard disk. You never want this to happen. *Never!*

In addition, you get a message or prompt that tells you what to do. Before you get involved in the following activity, it is exceedingly important that you know what kind of disk drive you have so that you can choose the correct disk with the correct format. It is assumed that you have a 3½-inch high-density disk drive and floppy disk. If you have any other type of floppy disk or drive, ask your instructor for further instructions. If you are not sure, refer to your Configuration Table in Chapter 1.6. If you do not use the correct floppy disk, you will have problems.

Step 5 Get a blank disk out and prepare a sticky paper label for it. Do not use either the ACTIVITIES disk or the ACTIVITIES Disk—Working Copy. Write your name and the words "DATA disk" on the label. Place the label on the disk. Insert the disk into Drive A. Be sure that this disk either is blank or contains data you no longer want. Everything on the disk will be eliminated after you press **Enter**.

Step 6 Press **Enter**

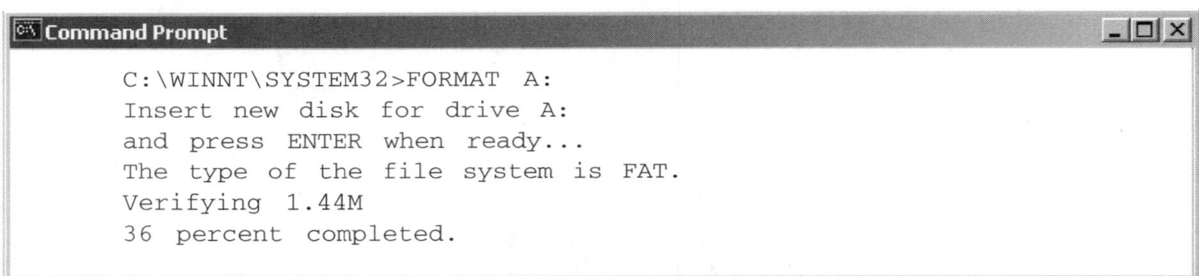
Command Prompt
C:\WINNT\SYSTEM32>FORMAT A:
Insert new disk for drive A:
and press ENTER when ready...
The type of the file system is FAT.
Verifying 1.44M
36 percent completed.

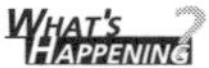
WHAT'S HAPPENING

The light on the floppy disk drive is glowing, indicating that activity is taking place on the disk. The FORMAT command displays what media type it is formatting. The message will vary depending on whether the disk has or has not been formatted before. The **Verifying 1.44M** that appears in the above screen display will vary depending on the type of floppy disk you are formatting.

The message "*nn* percent completed" tells you that the formatting is taking place and, at that moment, *nn* percent of the formatting process is completed (the *nn* represents a number that changes as the disk is formatted) until it reaches 100 percent. Do not do anything until you see the following message displayed on the screen:

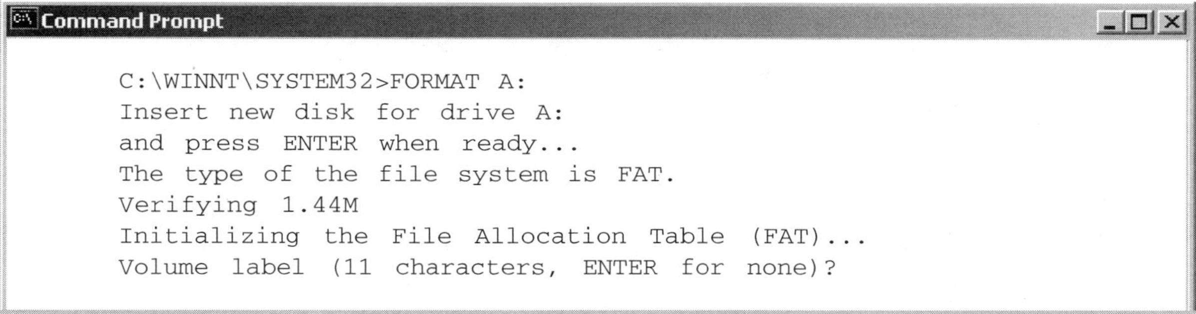

```
Command Prompt

C:\WINNT\SYSTEM32>FORMAT A:
Insert new disk for drive A:
and press ENTER when ready...
The type of the file system is FAT.
Verifying 1.44M
Initializing the File Allocation Table (FAT)...
Volume label (11 characters, ENTER for none)?
```

You are informed that your file system is FAT. In addition, you are being asked for a volume label, an electronic name. However, you are not going to place a volume label on the disk at this time.

Step 7 Press **Enter**

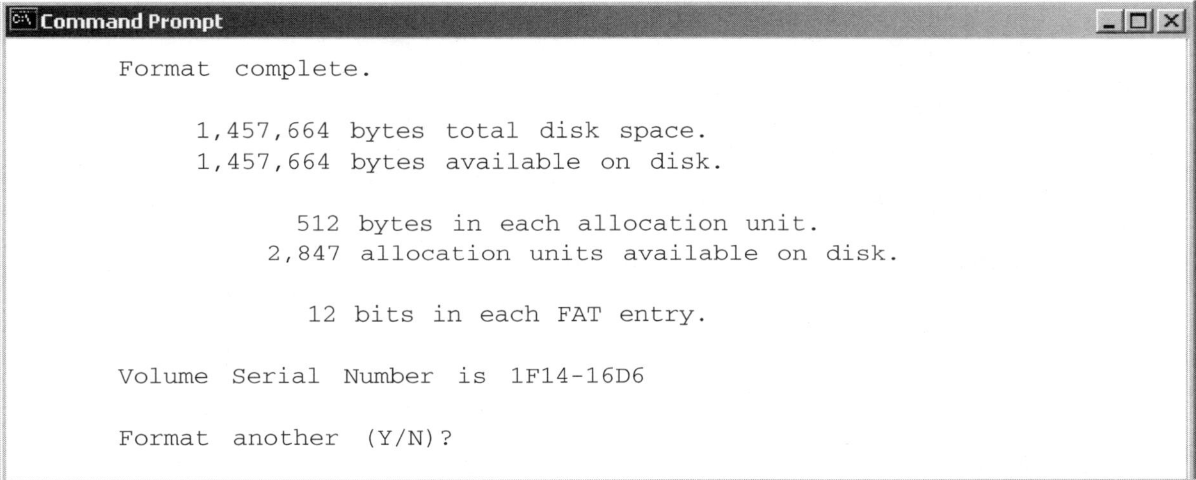

```
Command Prompt

Format complete.

     1,457,664 bytes total disk space.
     1,457,664 bytes available on disk.

           512 bytes in each allocation unit.
         2,847 allocation units available on disk.

            12 bits in each FAT entry.

Volume Serial Number is 1F14-16D6

Format another (Y/N)?
```

Step 8 Press **N**. Press **Enter**

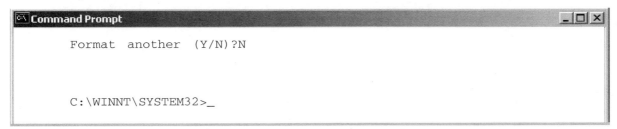

```
Command Prompt

Format another (Y/N)?N


C:\WINNT\SYSTEM32>_
```

You have completed formatting your disk. The FORMAT command was executed, formatting the disk in Drive A. The bytes available will vary depending on what your disk capacity is. You also see a report that FAT12 is being used. You also receive a status report that tells you how many spots were bad on the disk, if any. In addition, the report tells you about the allocation units on the disk. In this case, the allocation unit—the cluster—is 512 bytes, so you know that one sector on a 3½-inch high-density disk is a cluster. If you multiplied the size of the allocation unit by the number of allocations units available, you would come up with the number of available bytes (512 * 2,847 = 1,457,664 bytes). The OS can now read from and write to this disk because it has set up the tracks and sectors, the boot record, the FAT, the root directory, and the data section as needed. Notice the line **Volume Serial Number is 1F14-16D6**. This is a hexadecimal number, randomly generated by the formatting process. It is used for disk identification by application programs. For example, if you open a WordPerfect document file from a floppy disk and, while it is in memory, replace that disk with another, WordPerfect will be aware of the disk change by virtue of this number. Programmers can use ***volume serial numbers*** to identify the disks they use to distribute their programs.

Step 9 Key in the following: C:\WINNT\SYSTEM32>**CD ** Enter

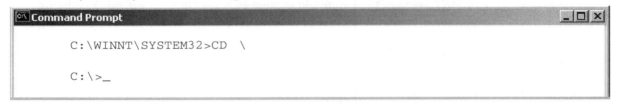

WHAT'S HAPPENING? You have returned to the root directory. The root directory of any disk is always the \.

3.5 FORMATTING A DISK WITH A VOLUME LABEL

You can use parameters other than the disk drive letter with the FORMAT command. The FORMAT command has many parameters, some of which are used more than others. The syntax for the FORMAT command is:

```
FORMAT volume [/FS:file-system] [/V:label] [/Q] [/A:size] [/C] [/X]
FORMAT volume [/V:label] [/Q] [/F:size]
FORMAT volume [/V:label] [/Q] [/T:tracks /N:sectors]
FORMAT volume [/V:label] [/Q] [/1] [/4]
FORMAT volume [/Q] [/1] [/4] [/8]

  volume          Specifies the drive letter (followed by a colon),
                  mount point, or volume name.
  /FS:filesystem  Specifies the type of the file system (FAT, FAT32, or
                  NTFS).
  /V:label        Specifies the volume label.
  /Q              Performs a quick format.
  /C              Files created on the new volume will be compressed by
                  default.
  /X              Forces the volume to dismount first if necessary. All
                  opened handles to the volume would no longer be valid.
  /A:size         Overrides the default allocation unit size. Default
                  settings are strongly recommended for general use.
                  NTFS supports 512, 1024, 2048, 4096, 8192, 16K, 32K, 64K.
                  FAT supports 512, 1024, 2048, 4096, 8192, 16K, 32K, 64K,
                  (128K, 256K for sector size > 512 bytes).
                  FAT32 supports 512, 1024, 2048, 4096, 8192, 16K, 32K,
64K,
                  (128K, 256K for sector size > 512 bytes).

                     Note that the FAT and FAT32 file systems impose
                     the following restrictions on the number of clusters
                     on a volume:
```

```
                  FAT: Number of clusters <= 65526
                  FAT32: 65526 < Number of clusters < 268435446

                  Format will immediately stop processing if it decides
                  that the above requirements cannot be met using the
                  specified cluster size.

                  NTFS compression is not supported for allocation unit
                  sizes above 4096.
/F:size           Specifies the size of the floppy disk to format (160,
                  180, 320, 360, 640, 720, 1.2, 1.23, 1.44, 2.88, or 20.8).
/T:tracks         Specifies the number of tracks per disk side.
/N:sectors        Specifies the number of sectors per track.
/1                Formats a single side of a floppy disk.
/4                Formats a 5.25-inch 360K floppy disk in a
                  high-density drive.
/8                Formats eight sectors per track.
```

Although this syntax diagram may look intimidating, it really is not. The parameters that are important to remember are as follows:

```
FORMAT volume [/V:label] [/Q]
```

The other versions of the syntax show parameters that still work but have been superseded. Beginning with MS-DOS version 3.3, the volume: or drive letter is mandatory. It must be included. This mandatory drive letter prohibits you from accidentally formatting the disk in the default drive. In addition, many of the options such as /C (compressed), /X (dismount), and /A (cluster size) are really only relevant when managing a network.

The /V allows you to place a volume label on a disk, but as you have already seen, the FORMAT command asks you for a volume label even if you don't include the /V. The /Q performs a quick format, but a quick format can be used only on a disk that has been previously formatted. It is "quick" because it simply deletes the entries from the FAT and the root directory and essentially leaves the files area untouched.

The /F:*size* parameter is an easy way to format floppy disks that do not match the capacity of a floppy disk drive. For instance, if you have a high-density disk drive but wish to format a 720KB disk, you would inform the FORMAT command using /F:720. However, /F:*size* does not solve all your mismatching problems. If you have a 720KB disk drive, you cannot format a high-density, 1.44-MB floppy disk in that drive. The 720KB disk drive is older technology and does not recognize the new high-density media type. Do not format a floppy disk at a size higher than it was designed for. This means, for example, if you have a 720KB disk, do not format it as a 1.44-MB disk. Table 3.4 shows the valid numbers that can be used. In general, however, the older capacity disks are disappearing and you will rarely, if ever, have the need to use these numbers.

Disk Capacity	Number to Use with /F
160KB	160
180KB	180
360KB	360

720KB	720
1.2 MB	1.2
1.44 MB	1.44
2.88 MB	2.88

TABLE 3.4 VALID DISK SIZES

In the next activity, you are going to use the /V parameter to place a volume label on the disk you are formatting. A ***volume label*** is an electronic name. It is very much like labeling a file drawer so you know what it contains. The switch is /V, which tells the FORMAT command that it is to format a disk and place an electronic volume label on it. Whenever you format a disk in recent versions of the OS, you are automatically asked for a volume label, even if you do not include /V, so why use the parameter at all? When you don't use it, the formatting process stops and asks you for the volume label. When you use the /V (a fixed parameter), you can provide the label itself (a variable parameter) at the time you enter the command, rendering it unnecessary for the FORMAT command to ask you to enter it after the formatting process. In the partial command diagram, **FORMAT A: /V[*:label*]** notice that the bracketed item [:label] includes both the colon and the label with no spaces between.

3.6 ACTIVITY: USING THE /V OPTION

Note: Your default directory is the root of C and C:\> is displayed. The disk just formatted is in Drive A.

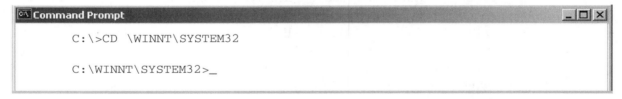

Step 1 Key in the following: C:\>**CD \WINNT\SYSTEM32** Enter

WHAT'S HAPPENING? You made **\WINNT\SYSTEM32** the default subdirectory.

Step 2 Key in the following:
C:\WINNT\SYSTEM32>**FORMAT A: /V:SAMPLEDATA** Enter

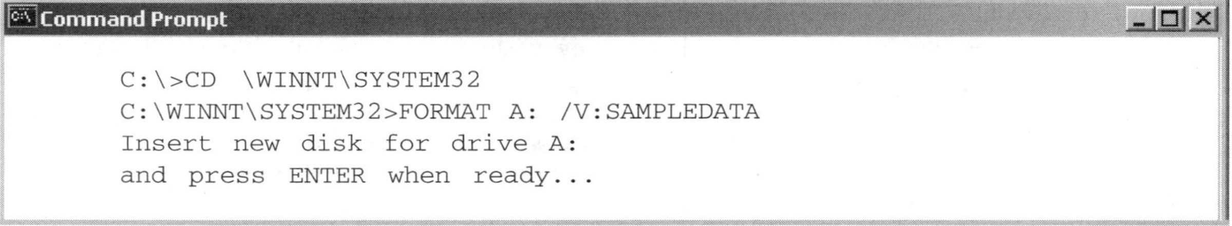

Command Prompt
C:\>CD \WINNT\SYSTEM32
C:\WINNT\SYSTEM32>FORMAT A: /V:SAMPLEDATA
Insert new disk for drive A:
and press ENTER when ready...

WHAT'S HAPPENING? The FORMAT command was loaded from the disk into memory. The data contained in any files on the disk is not actually deleted, but instead the FAT and the root directory table are "zeroed out." Also, the disk area is scanned for bad surfaces that might have appeared since the last time you formatted the disk.

Step 3 Press **Enter**

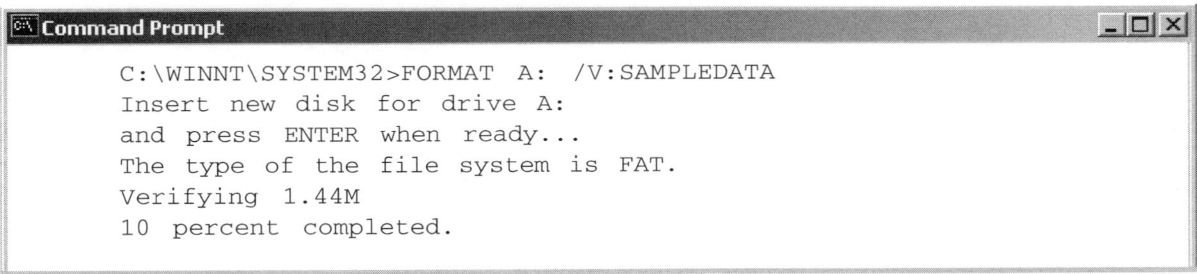

Command Prompt
C:\WINNT\SYSTEM32>FORMAT A: /V:SAMPLEDATA
Insert new disk for drive A:
and press ENTER when ready...
The type of the file system is FAT.
Verifying 1.44M
10 percent completed.

WHAT'S HAPPENING? You have begun the process of formatting the DATA disk.

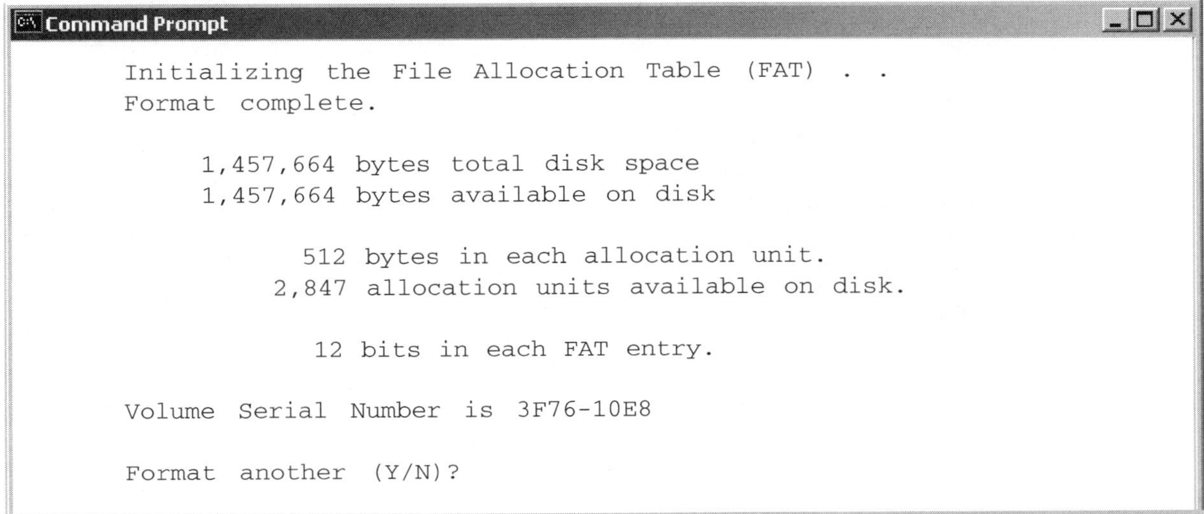

Command Prompt
Initializing the File Allocation Table (FAT) . .
Format complete.
1,457,664 bytes total disk space
1,457,664 bytes available on disk
512 bytes in each allocation unit.
2,847 allocation units available on disk.
12 bits in each FAT entry.
Volume Serial Number is 3F76-10E8
Format another (Y/N)?

WHAT'S HAPPENING? You were not asked to enter the volume label, as the label was provided within the command.

Step 4 Key in the following: **N** **Enter**

WHAT'S HAPPENING? Since you do not want to format another disk, you pressed **N** for "no." You named your disk SAMPLEDATA because on this disk you are going to store samples. Whenever you use a volume label, make it as meaningful as possible so that you do not have to look at all the files on the disk to know what is on the disk. Examples of meaningful names (volume labels) could include ENGLISH to indicate the disk is for your English homework or INCOMETAX for a disk that contains your income tax data. There are two ways to see your volume label.

Step 5 Key in the following: C:\WINNT\SYSTEM32>**DIR A:** Enter

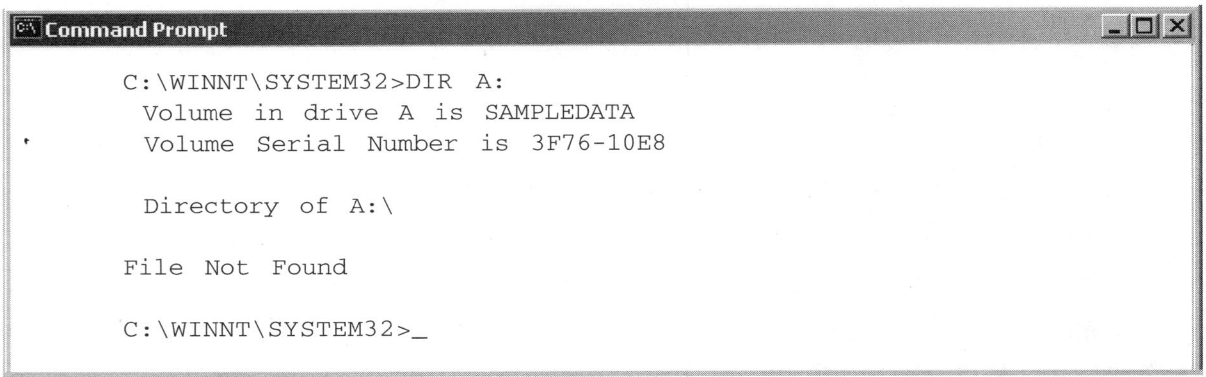


```
C:\WINNT\SYSTEM32>DIR A:
 Volume in drive A is SAMPLEDATA
 Volume Serial Number is 3F76-10E8

 Directory of A:\

File Not Found

C:\WINNT\SYSTEM32>_
```

WHAT'S HAPPENING? You can see displayed the label you entered, SAMPLEDATA. The internal command VOL lets you look at the volume label on any disk or check to see if there is a label. By using this command, you can quickly see what is on a disk without having to execute the directory command. The syntax is:

```
VOL [drive:]
```

Step 6 Key in the following: C:\WINNT\SYSTEM32>**VOL** Enter

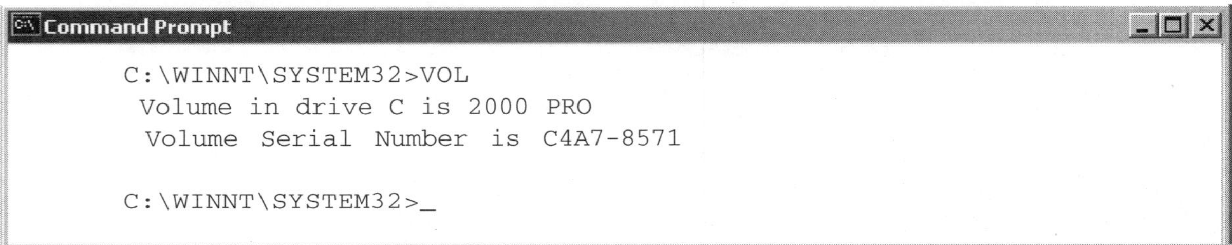


```
C:\WINNT\SYSTEM32>VOL
 Volume in drive C is 2000 PRO
 Volume Serial Number is C4A7-8571

C:\WINNT\SYSTEM32>_
```

WHAT'S HAPPENING? The volume label on your hard disk may well be different depending on whether a volume label was entered when the hard disk was formatted. In this example, a volume label was placed on the hard disk, so you see the message **Volume in drive C is 2000 PRO**. When you used the VOL command, the operating system looked only on Drive C, the default drive. To look at the volume label on Drive A, you must specifically request Drive A by giving VOL another parameter, the variable parameter [*drive*:], which represents the drive letter.

Step 7 Key in the following: C:\WINNT\SYSTEM32>**VOL A:** Enter

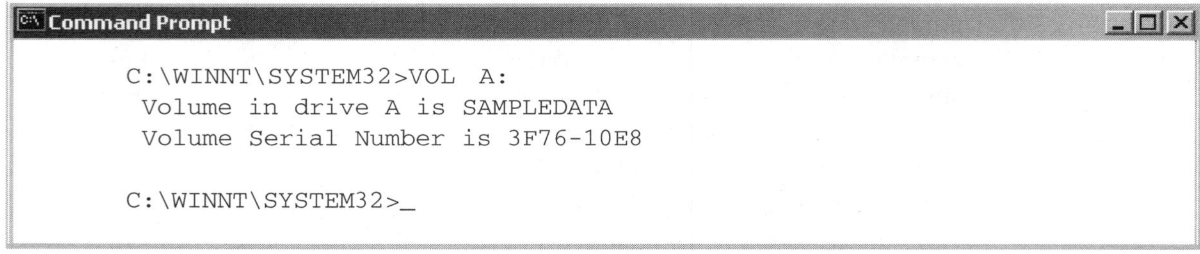


```
C:\WINNT\SYSTEM32>VOL A:
 Volume in drive A is SAMPLEDATA
 Volume Serial Number is 3F76-10E8

C:\WINNT\SYSTEM32>_
```

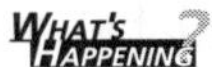

Since you placed a volume label on the DATA disk, you can see it with the VOL command. If a volume label is meaningful, it clearly identifies what files are on the disk.

3.7 THE LABEL COMMAND

It would be very inconvenient if every time you wanted to change the volume label on a disk you had to reformat the disk. Not only is this fatal to your data, but it takes time to format disks. In MS-DOS version 3.3, the LABEL command was introduced. It is an external command that lets you change the volume label without reformatting the disk. Remember, VOL, an internal command, lets you *see* the volume label, but LABEL lets you *change* the volume label. Bracketed items are always optional. The partial syntax is:

```
LABEL [drive:][label]
```

3.8 ACTIVITY: USING THE LABEL COMMAND

Note: Your default directory is the **\WINNT\SYSTEM32** subdirectory on Drive C, and you have C:\WINNT\SYSTEM32> displayed. The disk you just formatted is in Drive A.

Step 1 Key in the following: C:\WINNT\SYSTEM32>**LABEL A:** Enter

Note: Be certain to include the A: parameter, or the OS will assume you want to change the electronic name of the C drive. This action can cause problems on networked computers.

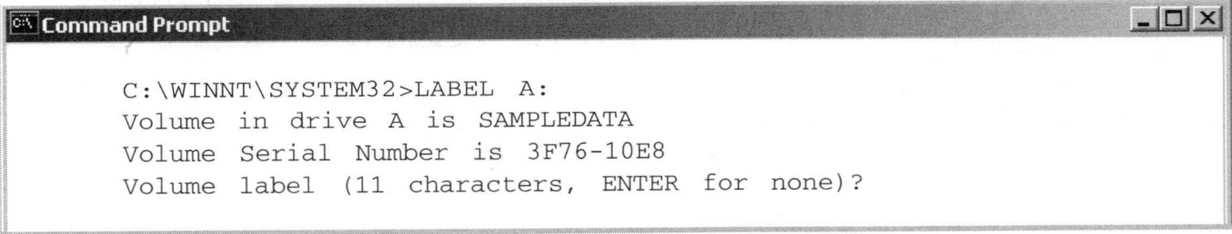
Command Prompt
C:\WINNT\SYSTEM32>LABEL A:
Volume in drive A is SAMPLEDATA
Volume Serial Number is 3F76-10E8
Volume label (11 characters, ENTER for none)?

This message looks exactly like the one you saw when you used the FORMAT command without the /V parameter. At this point, you can key in a new volume label.

Step 2 Press Enter

```
Command Prompt
C:\WINNT\SYSTEM32>LABEL A:

Volume in drive A is SAMPLEDATA
Volume Serial Number is 2436-14CD
Volume label (11 characters, ENTER for none)?

Delete current volume label (Y/N)?
```

The LABEL command knows that you already have a volume label, so it is asking you if you want to remove it.

Step 3 Key in the following: **Y** Enter

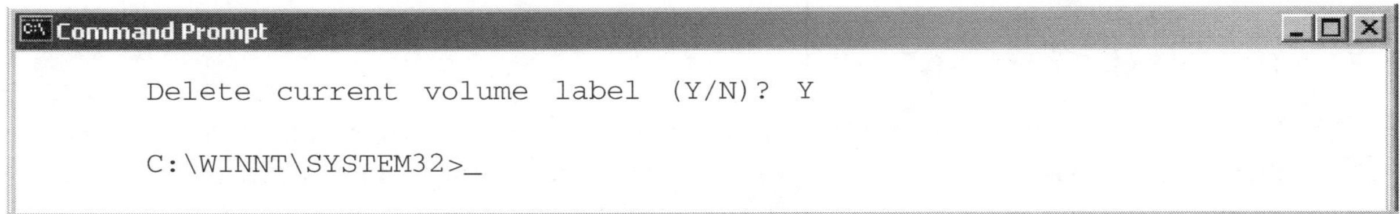
Command Prompt
Delete current volume label (Y/N)? Y
C:\WINNT\SYSTEM32>_

WHAT'S HAPPENING? You deleted the current volume label.

Step 4 Key in the following: C:\WINNT\SYSTEM32>**VOL A:** Enter

Command Prompt
C:\WINNT\SYSTEM32>VOL A:
Volume in drive A has no label
Volume Serial Number is 3F76-10E8
C:\WINNT\SYSTEM32>_

WHAT'S HAPPENING? You no longer have a volume label on the disk. In the next step you are going to place a volume label on the DATA disk, but you are going to take a shortcut. You are going to use the volume label SAMPLE DATA. Since you already know what you want to key in, you do not have to wait for the LABEL command to ask you what label you want. The LABEL command allows the use of spaces, whereas the /V parameter with FORMAT does not allow spaces.

Step 5 Key in the following: C:\WINNT\SYSTEM32>**LABEL A:SAMPLE DATA** Enter

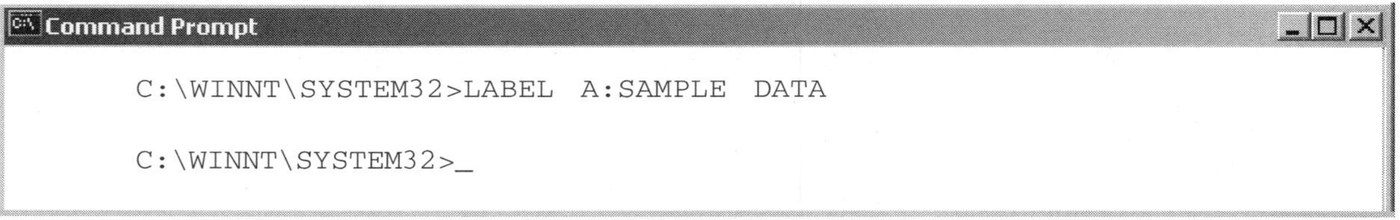
Command Prompt
C:\WINNT\SYSTEM32>LABEL A:SAMPLE DATA
C:\WINNT\SYSTEM32>_

WHAT'S HAPPENING? You are returned to the system level prompt. Did your volume label change on the DATA disk?

Step 6 Key in the following: C:\WINNT\SYSTEM32>**VOL A:** Enter

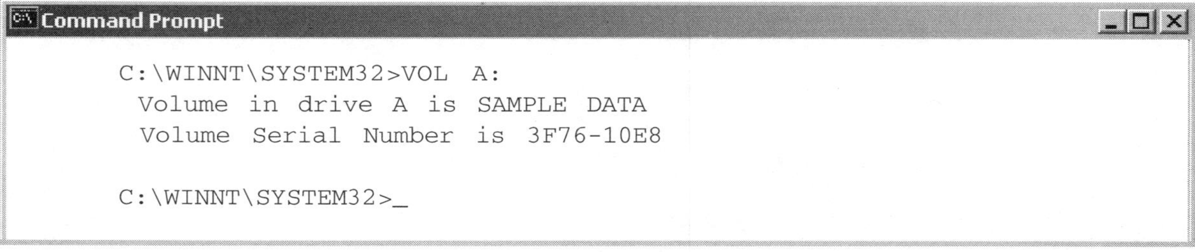
Command Prompt
C:\WINNT\SYSTEM32>VOL A:
Volume in drive A is SAMPLE DATA
Volume Serial Number is 3F76-10E8
C:\WINNT\SYSTEM32>_

WHAT'S HAPPENING? Using the VOL command, you can see the new volume label.

3.9 FORMATTING A DISK USING THE /Q PARAMETER

Often you will want to clear a disk totally to ensure that there is really nothing on the disk and you know the tracks and sectors are already there from a previous formatting. There is no need to take the time to reformat the disk. You can use the /Q parameter. The /Q parameter stands for "quick" format. The /Q works *only* on a disk that has been previously formatted. It works like the usual FORMAT command, but skips the low-level formatting. It clears the FAT and root directory as it prepares a disk for new files. However, in order to clear the disk rapidly, /Q will not check for ***bad sectors*** on a disk. Using /Q is a very fast way to erase a disk.

3.10 ACTIVITY: USING THE /Q PARAMETER

Note: Your default directory is the **\WINNT\SYSTEM32** subdirectory on Drive C, and C:\WINNT\SYSTEM32> is displayed. The SAMPLE DATA disk is in Drive A.

Step 1 Key in the following: C:\WINNT\SYSTEM32>**FORMAT A: /Q** Enter

Command Prompt

```
C:\WINNT\SYSTEM32>FORMAT A: /Q
Insert new disk for drive A:
and press ENTER when ready...
```

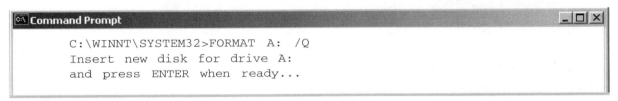

WHAT'S HAPPENING? FORMAT is asking you for a disk to format. Since you already have a disk in the drive, you may proceed.

Step 2 Be sure the SAMPLE DATA disk is in Drive A. Then press Enter

Command Prompt

```
C:\WINNT\SYSTEM32>FORMAT A: /Q
Insert new disk for drive A:
and press ENTER when ready...
The type of the file system is FAT.
QuickFormatting 1.44M
Initializing the File Allocation Table (FAT) . . .
Volume label (11 characters, ENTER for none)?
```

WHAT'S HAPPENING? Notice how fast the formatting occurred. FORMAT is asking you for a volume label.

Step 3 Press Enter

Step 4 Key in **N** Enter (you do not want to quick format another disk).

Command Prompt

```
Volume label (11 characters, ENTER for none)?
Format complete.

     1,457,664 bytes total disk space
    1,457,664 bytes available on disk
```

```
         512 bytes in each allocation unit.
       2,847 allocation units available on disk.

          12 bits in each FAT entry.

Volume Serial Number is 0C3D-10F7

QuickFormat another (Y/N)?N

C:\WINNT\SYSTEM32>_
```

The FORMAT command wanted to know if you had any more disks to quick format. You responded **N** for "no." You returned to the system prompt. What happened to the SAMPLE DATA volume label?

Step 5 Key in the following: C:\WINNT\SYSTEM32>**VOL A:** Enter

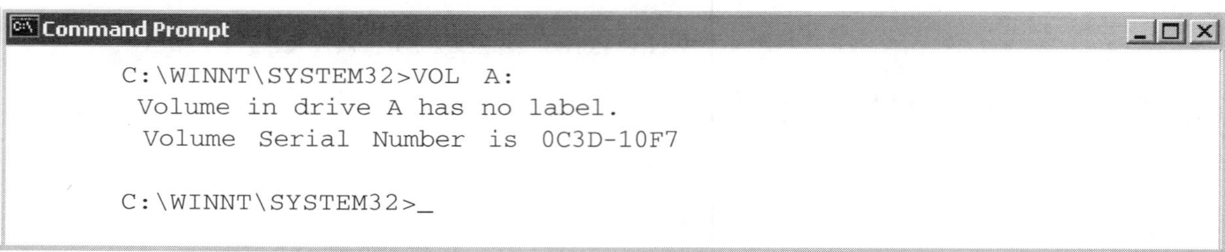
Command Prompt
C:\WINNT\SYSTEM32>VOL A:
Volume in drive A has no label.
Volume Serial Number is 0C3D-10F7
C:\WINNT\SYSTEM32>_

WHAT'S HAPPENING? As you did not enter a new volume label, but just pressed Enter when you formatted the disk, the previous volume label was eliminated.

Step 6 Key in the following: C:\WINNT\SYSTEM32>**CD ** Enter

Command Prompt
C:\WINNT\SYSTEM32>CD \
C:\>_

WHAT'S HAPPENING? You returned to the root directory of the hard disk.

3.11 MAKING A DATA DISK

Step 1 Place your new disk in the A drive.

Step 2 Open up a Command Prompt window. Key in the following: C:\WINNT\SYSTEM32>**FORMAT A: /V:DATA** Enter

Command Prompt

```
C:\WINNT\SYSTEM32>FORMAT A: /V:DATA
Insert new disk for drive A:
and press ENTER when ready...
```

WHAT'S HAPPENING? You are prompted to insert a disk, but a disk is already in the drive.

Step 3 Press **Enter**

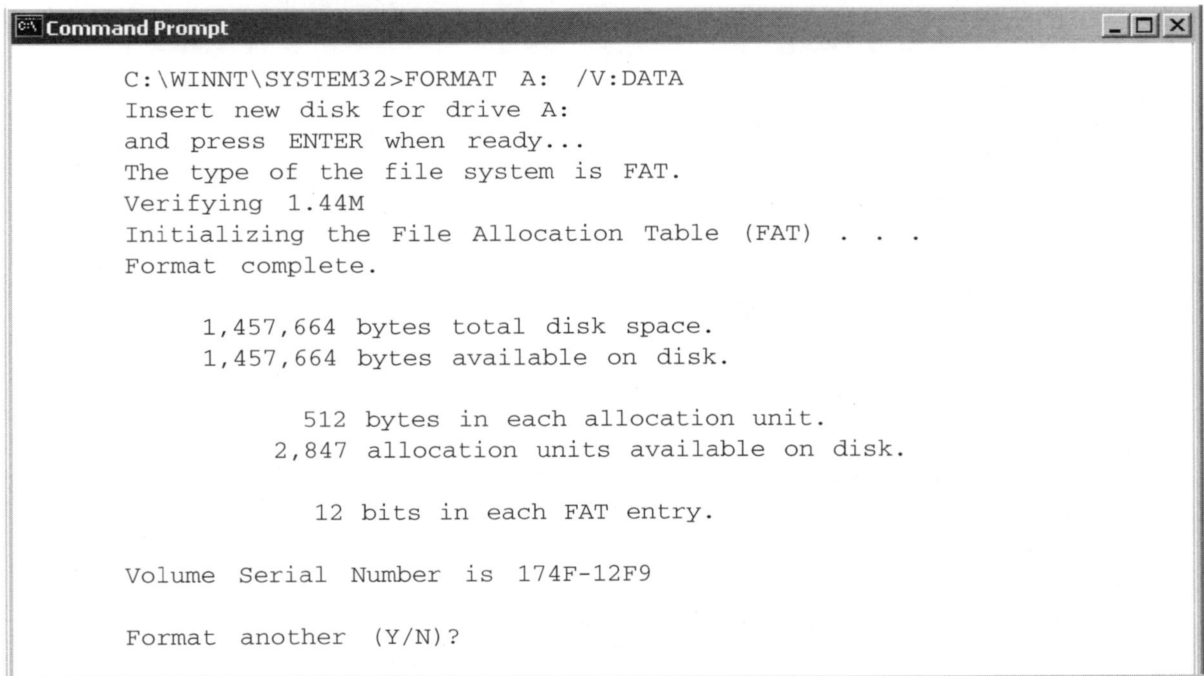
```
C:\WINNT\SYSTEM32>FORMAT A: /V:DATA
Insert new disk for drive A:
and press ENTER when ready...
The type of the file system is FAT.
Verifying 1.44M
Initializing the File Allocation Table (FAT) . . .
Format complete.

    1,457,664 bytes total disk space.
    1,457,664 bytes available on disk.

          512 bytes in each allocation unit.
        2,847 allocation units available on disk.

           12 bits in each FAT entry.

Volume Serial Number is 174F-12F9

Format another (Y/N)?
```

WHAT'S HAPPENING? You have formatted a disk and assigned a label, DATA, to the disk.

Step 4 Key in the following: **N** **Enter**

Step 5 Key in the following: C:\WINNT\SYSTEM32>**DIR A:** **Enter**

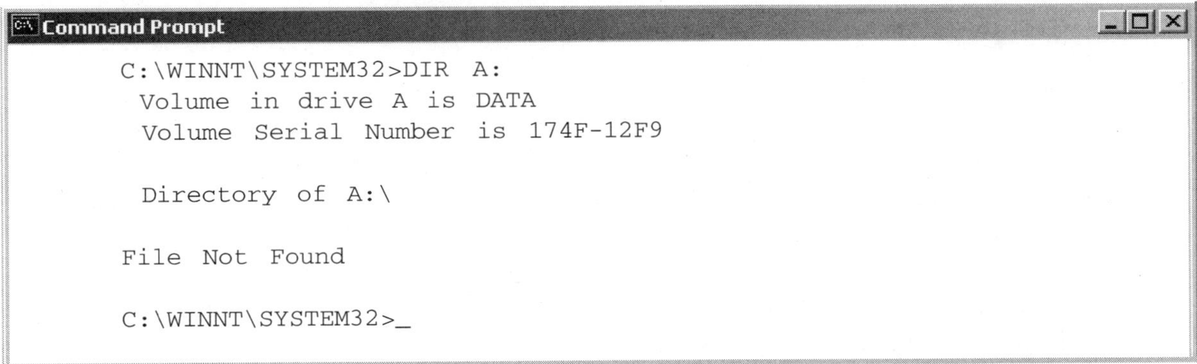
```
C:\WINNT\SYSTEM32>DIR A:
 Volume in drive A is DATA
 Volume Serial Number is 174F-12F9

 Directory of A:\

File Not Found

C:\WINNT\SYSTEM32>_
```

WHAT'S HAPPENING? As you can see, the label or "name" on the disk is DATA, and there are no files on the disk.

3.12 ACTIVITY: SHUTTING DOWN WINDOWS

Step 1 Key in the following: C:\WINNT\SYSTEM32>**EXIT** **Enter**

WHAT'S HAPPENING? You have closed the Command Prompt window and have returned to the desktop. Remember, the appearance of the desktop will differ from computer to computer.

Step 2 Click **Start**. Click **Shut Down**. Be sure the **Shut down** option is showing in the drop-down list.

Step 3 Click the **OK** button and wait for the safe message before you turn off the power.

WHAT'S HAPPENING? You have completed the Windows shut-down procedure.

3.13 HIGH-DENSITY DISKS AND DISK DRIVES

If you have a newer computer, you have what are called high-capacity or high-density 3½-inch disk drives. If so, the FORMAT command will format any disk placed in the drive in its "native" format; it will assume that the disk to be formatted is a blank high-density disk. However, if you happened to have a 3½-inch, 720KB, double-density disk and placed it in a 3½-inch high-density drive, FORMAT would prepare it as a high-density disk. Because a DS/DD (double-sided/double-density) disk was not designed as a DS/HD (double-sided/high-density) disk, it does not have as many magnetic particles and should not be formatted as a high-density disk. In fact, you will get an error message that will show many bytes as bad sectors.

If you have high-density disk drives and use only high-density disks, you will have no problems. The problems begin to occur when you try to mix and match different density disks with different density drives.

Double-density disk drives are found on older computers—most likely you will not run into these drives today. However, should you happen to have an older computer, you do need to be aware of their limitations. A double-density disk drive *cannot* read from or write to a high-density diskette. High-density drives *can* both read from and write to either the DS/DD or DS/HD disks. This feature is one of the ways that hardware and software maintain what is called ***downward compatibility***—something that was developed on an old computer can still be used on a new computer. The only problem you run into is in formatting disks. You can format a 720KB disk in a DS/HD drive by using the following syntax:

```
FORMAT /F:720
```

When you format a diskette, the FORMAT command report will tell you how many bytes it formatted. You can then place the information on your Configuration Table in Chapter 1.6. The important thing is to be aware of the type of floppy disk drive you have and what media type floppy disks you are using.

This text will refer to 3½-inch diskettes. If you are using 5¼-inch diskettes, double-density disks have a capacity of 360KB and high-density diskettes have a capacity of 1.2 MB. For formatting a double-density diskette in a high-density drive, the syntax is:

```
FORMAT /F:360
```

CHAPTER SUMMARY

1. Floppy disks that are purchased are sometimes not ready to use. They must first be prepared for use.
2. Each type of computer has its own specific way of recording information on a disk. This text is only concerned with Windows-based computers.
3. Disks are the means to store data and programs permanently.
4. All disks must be formatted by a utility program stored as a file called FORMAT.COM so that data and programs can be read from and written to them.
5. Disks that have information on them can be formatted again.
6. If a disk has files on it, formatting the disk will remove all of those files.
7. Since the FORMAT command removes all data, formatting a hard disk can be dangerous.
8. Formatting a disk means that the physical layout of the disk is defined to determine how the information is stored on the disk so that the OS can locate what is stored.
9. Each operating system has a unique way of recording information on a disk. This is known as a file system.
10. The OS uses sections of a disk, whether it is a hard disk or a floppy disk. A disk is divided into concentric circles called tracks. Each track is divided into sectors. The number of tracks, sectors, and sides of a disk determine the capacity of the disk.
11. The two major types of files systems that Windows 2000 Professional supports is FAT and NTFS.
12. All floppy disks are formatted as FAT disks.
13. The smallest unit that the operating system will read from or write to is a cluster. A cluster is made up of one or more adjacent sectors, depending on the type of disk.
14. Each disk that is formatted with FAT has a root directory and two copies of a file allocation table (FAT).
15. All disks that are formatted with FAT have a boot record, a FAT, a directory, and data sectors.
16. All FAT-formatted disks use the file allocation table. The FAT (file allocation table) is a map of every track and sector on the disk. The FAT tells the OS where files are on the disk. The FAT links a file together by pointing to the next cluster that holds the file's data.

17. On a FAT-formatted disk, the root directory has information about files including the file name and the file's starting cluster entry in the FAT.
18. The data sectors are where files are actually stored.
19. Files are chains of bytes laid out in sequence.
20. NTFS is the preferred file system for Windows 2000 Professional.
21. Major advantages of using NTFS include that it is a secure file system that provides more efficient storage of data on hard disks and faster access to files and folders.
22. Insead of using FAT, NTFS uses a special file called the Master File Table (MFT) that tracks all the files and directories in a volume. It is a database of all the files on the system.
23. Files are written to a disk in the first available cluster and, if possible, in adjacent or contiguous clusters. If the adjacent clusters are already in use, the OS skips to the next available noncontiguous cluster.
24. A disk is formatted with the FORMAT command, an external utility program.
25. The basic syntax of the FORMAT command is:

    ```
    FORMAT volume: [/V:label] [/Q] [/F:size]
    ```

26. The internal VOL command allows you to view the internal electronic label.
27. The external LABEL command allows you to change the internal electronic label.
28. The /Q parameter performs a quick format that does not check for bad sectors on a disk. In addition, it can be used only on a disk that has been previously formatted.
29. Always use the correct media type when formatting disks.

KEY TERMS

active partition
allocation unit
bad sectors
basic disk
boot sector
cluster
cluster overhang
contiguous
downward compatibility
dynamic disk
end-of-file (EOF) marker
extended partition
extent
file allocation table (FAT)
file system
formatting
high-level formatting
initializing the disk
logical formatting
low-level formatting
master boot record (MBR)
master file table (MFT)
noncontiguous
New Technology File System (NTFS)
partition
partition table
physical formatting
primary partition
run
virtual file alloction table (VFAT)
volume label
volume serial number

DISCUSSION QUESTIONS

1. What purpose do disks serve?
2. Why must you format a disk?
3. Compare and contrast physical (low-level) formatting with logical (high-level) formatting of a disk.

4. Define *tracks, sectors,* and *clusters.*
5. What is the purpose and function of the boot record?
6. Define *FAT*. How is it used on a disk?
7. Compare and contrast FAT, FAT32, and NTFS.
8. What is the purpose and function of the root directory in a FAT file system?
9. How is space allocated to files in FAT? In NTFS?
10. FORMAT can be a dangerous command. Explain.
11. What does the prompt on the screen represent?
12. Compare and contrast internal and external commands.
13. What steps can you take when you see error messages ?
14. What is a volume label?
15. When formatting a disk, the drive letter is a mandatory parameter. Why?
16. Give the basic syntax for the FORMAT command and explain each item.
17. Explain the purpose and function of a quick format.
18. When using the FORMAT command, what are the purpose and function of the parameter /V?
19. What is the purpose and function of the VOL command?
20. What is the purpose and function of the LABEL command?
21. When using the FORMAT command, when would you use the /Q parameter?

TRUE/FALSE QUESTIONS

For each question, circle the letter T if the statement is true or the letter F if the statement is false.

T F 1. The root directory table keeps track of where files are located, while the FAT keeps track of what is in files.
T F 2. You may format any disk with the FORMAT command.
T F 3. DIR FORMAT.COM will execute the command FORMAT and format a disk.
T F 4. Each disk is divided into tracks, which are then next divided into clusters.
T F 5. All floppy disks are formatted as FAT.

COMPLETION QUESTIONS

Write the correct answer in each blank space.

6. The smallest unit of disk space the operating system will work with is called a(n) ________.
7. The information in files is stored in the _______ sectors of a disk.
8. In a FAT-formatted disk, where a file is located is kept track of by the ________, while the ________________ keeps track of the files and attributes.
9. NTFS keeps track of all its files and directories in the _______________.
10. In order to be usable, a disk must first be ____________.

MULTIPLE CHOICE QUESTIONS

For each question, write the letter for the correct answer in the blank space.

11. When you format a disk, you
    a. erase everything on that disk.
    b. prepare it so the operating system can read from and write to it.
    c. both a and b
    d. neither a nor b
12. On a hard disk, you may only boot from the _____ partition.
    a. active
    b. extended
    c. expanded
    d. primary
13. To name a disk when you are formatting it, you can use
    a. the LABEL command.
    b. the VOL command.
    c. /V for volume label.
    d. /N for name.
14. NTFS and FAT are examples of
    a. operating systems.
    b. partition tables.
    c. file systems.
    d. none of the above
15. To change the volume label of the disk currently in Drive A without eliminating any information on it, key in:
    a. LABEL A:
    b. VOL A:
    c. VOLUME A:
    d. none of the above

WRITING COMMANDS

Write the correct steps or commands to perform the required action as if you were at the computer. The prompt will indicate the default drive and directory.

16. View the name of the disk in the default drive.

```
A:\>
```

17. Format and place the volume label MYDISK on the disk in Drive A.

```
C:\WINNT\SYSTEM32>
```

18. Display the volume label on Drive A.

```
C:\>
```

19. Locate the FORMAT command on the hard drive.

```
A:\>
```

20. Change the label on the disk in Drive A from DATA to ACTION.

```
C:\WINNT\SYSTEM32>
```

APPLICATION ASSIGNMENTS

PROBLEM SET I—AT THE COMPUTER

Note 1: Your DATA disk is in Drive A. C:\> is displayed as the default drive and the default directory.

Note 2: Remember, be very careful when using the FORMAT command. *Never* issue the command without a drive parameter specified, A: or B:, and do not use the C drive as a parameter.

PROBLEM A

A-a Format the DATA disk the fastest way.

A-b Key in the following at the volume label prompt: **MYDATA DISK**

☐ 1. In addition to the drive letter, what parameter did you use with the FORMAT command?
   a. /U
   b. /Q
   c. /S
   d. none of the above

A-c Display the volume label of the DATA disk.

☐ 2. In addition to the drive letter, what command did you use?
   a. VOL
   b. NAME
   c. FORMAT
   d. all of the above

☐ 3. What volume label is displayed?
   a. MY DATA DISK
   b. MYDISK
   c. MYDATADISK
   d. none of the above

PROBLEM B

B-a Change the name of the disk in the A drive without using the FORMAT command.

B-b Use the name **CLASSDISK**.

4. Which command did you use?
   a. NAME
   b. LABEL
   c. VOL
   d. none of the above

B-c Check to see that the name has actually changed.

5. What volume label is displayed?
   a. DATA
   b. CLASSDISK
   c. MYDATADISKVERY_OWN
   d. none of the above

B-d Change the volume label to **DATA DISK**.

6. In addition to the drive letter, what command did you use?
   a. VOL
   b. FORMAT
   c. LABEL
   d. none of the above

PROBLEM SET II—BRIEF ESSAY

1. You have taught a friend how to format a disk, and she is happy to find that the process is simple. However, she does not understand why she must format a disk and what is happening when it is formatted. Briefly answer her questions. Include an explanation of the purpose of the boot record, the directory table, the FAT, and the data sectors.

2. You have just keyed in **FORMAT A:/V:CLEAN**. What is it that you did, and why did you do it?

CHAPTER 4

PROGRAM FILES, DATA FILES, AND SUBDIRECTORIES

LEARNING OBJECTIVES

After completing this chapter you will be able to:

1. List and explain the major reasons for learning about the operating system.
2. Explain the difference between program files and data files.
3. Explain the difference between freeware and shareware programs.
4. Define "real mode" and "protected mode" operations.
5. Explain the hierarchical filing system of a tree-structured directory.
6. Define the CD, MD, and RD commands.
7. Explain the purpose and function of a root directory and tell how and when it is created.
8. Explain what subdirectories are and tell how they are named, created, and used.
9. Explain the purpose and use of subdirectory markers.
10. Identify the commands that can be used with subdirectories.
11. Explain the purpose of the PROMPT command.
12. Explain the purpose and function of the MOVE command.
13. List the steps to remove a directory.
14. Explain the function of the PATH command.

STUDENT OUTCOMES

1. Load and use an application program.
2. Create subdirectories using the MD command.
3. Display the default directory using the CD command.
4. Change directories using the CD command.

5. Use subdirectory markers with commands.
6. Use the PROMPT command to change the display of the prompt.
7. Rename a directory using the MOVE command.
8. Use the RD command to eliminate a directory.
9. Explain how to remove an entire tree structure.
10. Use the PATH command.

CHAPTER OVERVIEW

You do not purchase a computer to use the operating system. You purchase a computer to help you be more efficient in doing work you want to do. Work on a computer is comprised of two aspects—the programs that do the work and the information you create. When you work with a computer, you accumulate many programs and data files. If you are going to be an efficient user, you must have a way to manage these files. Part of the power of the Windows operating system is its ability to manage files. From the desktop, you can use Windows Explorer and My Computer to view the location of your files and to manage them. In this text, you will learn how to manage your files from the command prompt. There are things that you cannot do easily (and some things you cannot do at all) from the Windows GUI.

In this chapter you will learn to use a program file and a data file. You will also learn the subdirectory commands to help you manage your files.

4.1 WHY USE THE COMMAND PROMPT SCREEN?

So far, you have used commands to prepare a disk for use (FORMAT), to copy a disk (DISKCOPY), to see what files are on a disk (DIR), and to clear the screen (CLS). Each of these commands is useful, but no one buys a computer to use the operating system. You purchase a computer to assist you in work, and the way you work on a computer is by using application programs. The four major categories of application programs include word processors to make writing easier, spreadsheets to manage budgets and do financial projections, databases to manage and manipulate collections of data, and graphics to create artistic drawings and designs. The application programs that use graphics include CAD (computer-aided design), desktop publishing, photo-editing programs, and scanning or camera programs. Each program has its own instructions that must be learned. If this is true, why are you learning about the operating system? There are two important reasons.

First and foremost, you cannot run an application program without Windows. It is the manager of the system, supervising the hardware and software components and allowing you to load and execute specific application packages. All application programs run under the supervision of the operating system.

The second reason for learning about the operating system is that application programs are stored as files on disks and usually generate data files. Windows has a variety of commands that allow you to manage and manipulate program and data files. Be aware that the operating system manages the files—their location, movement, etc.—but not the information you put *into* files.

4.2 PROGRAM FILES, DATA FILES, AND THE OPERATING SYSTEM

On the hard disk is a subdirectory called WINDOSBK. This subdirectory was created by installing the files and directories from the ACTIVITIES disk to the hard disk. It was placed on the hard disk or network server by the lab technician or the instructor. If you are using your own computer, you will have to create the directory and place the files there yourself—see Appendix A for instructions on how to do this. The subdirectory WINDOSBK contains other subdirectories, among which are PHONE and FINANCE. These subdirectories have application programs, one called HPB and the other called Thinker, which will help you understand how operating systems work in the "real world."

HPB (Home Phone Book) is a simple application program that works much like a Rolodex. It is a database that allows you to keep track of names, addresses, and phone numbers. Designed to work under DOS, Thinker is a spreadsheet program that allows you to manipulate numbers in columns and rows. The Windows operating system, because it is downward compatible, allows for the use of older software, referred to as ***legacy software***. You are going to use the Command Prompt window to execute these programs by loading the program and data files and listing the files that are there.

Using the command line helps you understand how the operating system works in conjunction with various types of files. An application or program file is an executable file that is loaded from disk into memory. The operating system then turns control over to the application program. With software written for DOS or earlier versions of Windows, when the application program needed to interface with the hardware, such as when it wanted to write a character to the screen, print, or respond to mouse movement, there were two choices. The application program could "talk" directly to the device or it could talk to DOS and let DOS do the actual labor of writing to the screen or sending a job to the printer. This is called ***real mode*** operation. With software written for the Windows 2000 Professional operating system, this is not the case. Windows software runs in protected mode. In ***protected mode***, no communication exists between the application software and the actual hardware itself. ***Device drivers*** (the software that comes with peripheral devices, such as a mouse or a modem) are called mini-drivers. Instead of having the manufacturer's device drivers talk to the hardware or to the core of the operating system itself, these drivers talk to virtual device drivers, which are part of the Windows operating system. These virtual device drivers are outside of the core operations of the operating system, which remains "protected" from the actions of the devices and device drivers.

As an example, assume you bought a fancy ACME video card with all the new bells and whistles. It has the magic words "Plug and Play" on the package. When you install it, you may have to insert the disk that came with it in order to install a mini-driver that talks to the Windows virtual video card driver and tells it how to blow the whistles and ring the bells. The core of the Windows operating system, however, is *not* touched by the software driver written by ACME. The Windows virtual video driver will make sure nothing gets through to the core of the operating system that could cause problems. Thus the term "protected mode."

An application program cannot load itself into memory. The operating system is the means by which the application program gets loaded into memory. Remember that work takes place only in memory. The operating system also assists in loading the data file into memory so that the application program can use the data. Ensuring the cooperative effort between the OS and the application program and its data files is the work of the operating system. You, the user, do not directly interface with the operating system at the application level.

There is another component: the command line commands that Windows provides. Commands are also programs. These commands allow you, the user, to interface directly with the operating system to manage your program and data files.

4.3 SHAREWARE

Some of you may have already purchased commercial application packages such as WordPerfect, Word, or PageMaker. There are hundreds of different programs to choose from that will meet almost any computer user's needs, from managing a checkbook (Quicken) to playing a game (Flight Simulator).

The subdirectory WINDOSBK contains data files, freeware programs, and shareware programs. Freeware and shareware programs are available from a wide variety of sources. One of the most common sources today is the Internet. Friends and acquaintances may pass programs to you; members of computer clubs share their programs; or you can receive them from a source such as this textbook.

Freeware is software that is in the public domain. The authors (programmers) of these programs have donated the programs to anyone who wants to use them with the understanding that people will use them but not alter them. The programmers do not expect to be paid in any way—although sometimes they will ask for a small donation for expenses.

Shareware is a trial version of a program. The program is not distributed through commercial channels, thus saving the programmer the costs of marketing and distribution. After you purchase commercial software, if you do not like it or it does not meet your needs, you usually cannot return it. On the other hand, shareware is something you can try out. If you like it, you then register it with the programmer for a nominal fee. If you do not like it, you simply delete the file or files from your disk. Trying these programs costs you nothing. If you decide to retain and use the program, the programmer *does* expect to be paid. The programmer or programmers who write shareware are professional programmers, students, and people who just enjoy programming.

Sometimes, to encourage people to register, the program will be a limited version without all the features of the shareware program. Sometimes called "crippleware," it may lose features after a certain date or have annoying screens that pop up to remind you to register it. When you do register it, you receive the full version or the latest version of the program, the documentation (a manual of commands and instructions), and notices of updates and technical support. The update notices will provide you with the latest version of corrections to the program. Technical support means you can call the programmer(s) for help if something is not working correctly.

This textbook includes both freeware and shareware. Appendix A lists all the shareware programs with the fees and addresses necessary to register them. If, after you complete the textbook, you wish to continue using the shareware programs, please pay the appropriate fees and register the programs. Otherwise, delete the files. Shareware provides some really great programs and by registering them, you are encouraging the programmer to write shareware. Who knows, you may be assisting the next Bill Gates or Steve Jobs.

4.4 ACTIVITY: USING DIR TO LOCATE THE HPB PROGRAM

Note 1: Check with your lab technician or network administrator to be sure that the subdirectory **WINDOSBK** has been installed for you, either on the C:\ drive or on a network drive. Be sure to fill in your Configuration Table in Chapter 1.6 with your specific location of this subdirectory. This text is written with the assumption that the **WINDOSBK** subdirectory is directly off the root of the C drive. If you are working on your own computer, you will have to install the subdirectory **WINDOSBK**. Complete instructions on how to do this are in Appendix A.

Note 2: It is assumed that your computer is booted and Windows is loaded. You have shelled out to the Command Prompt. You have changed the directory to the root directory of C. C:\> is displayed on the screen as the default drive and directory.

Note 3: When keying in commands, you may use the command line editing keys to correct typographical errors, as shown in Chapter 2.

Step 1 Key in the following: C:\>**DIR WINDOS*.*** Enter

```
Command Prompt

C:\>DIR WINDOS*.*
 Volume in drive C is 2000 PRO
 Volume Serial Number is C4A7-8571

 Directory of C:\

04/24/2001  09:38a      <DIR>          WINDOSBK
               0 File(s)              0 bytes
               1 Dir(s)    445,775,872 bytes free

C:\>
```

You are verifying that you have a subdirectory called **WINDOSBK**. In this example, only one entry matches the criterion you requested. You asked DIR to find any file or any directory on the hard disk that begins with **WINDOS** and has any other characters in the file name and any file extension. Your display may vary depending on how many other files you have that begin with **WINDOS**. If the entry named **WINDOSBK** is not displayed, refer to Appendix A and take the necessary steps before continuing.

Step 2 Key in the following: C:\>**CD \WINDOSBK\PHONE** Enter

Step 3 Key in the following: C:\WINDOSBK\PHONE>**DIR HPB.EXE** Enter

```
Command Prompt

C:\>CD\WINDOSBK\PHONE

C:\WINDOSBK\PHONE>DIR HPB.EXE
 Volume in drive C is 2000 PRO
 Volume Serial Number is C4A7-8571

 Directory of C:\WINDOSBK\PHONE
```

```
01/04/1999  03:48a              164,420 HPB.EXE
               1 File(s)        164,420 bytes
               0 Dir(s)     445,317,120 bytes free

C:\WINDOSBK\PHONE>_
```

You changed the default directory to **WINDOSBK** and then to the **PHONE** subdirectory where the HPB program is located. You used the DIR command to see if the file called **HPB.EXE** is on the hard disk C: off of the ***root directory*** (\) in the subdirectory called **WINDOSBK\PHONE**. DIR is the command, **WINDOSBK\PHONE** is the ***path***, and **HPB.EXE** is the file name of the program. The DIR command just allows you to see if the file is on the disk; it does not let you use the program. The name of the file is **HPB**. HPB stands for Home Phone Book. The name of the extension is **.EXE**. The **.EXE** file extension has a special meaning: executable code. This informs the OS the file is a program. The file extension **.EXE** always indicates an executable program.

Step 4 Key in the following: C:\WINDOSBK\PHONE>**DIR HPB.DAT** Enter

Command Prompt

```
C:\WINDOSBK\PHONE>DIR HPB.DAT
 Volume in drive C is 2000 PRO
 Volume Serial Number is C4A7-8571

 Directory of C:\WINDOSBK\PHONE

01/04/1999  03:48a                4,368 HPB.DAT
               1 File(s)          4,368 bytes
               0 Dir(s)     445,317,120 bytes free

C:\WINDOSBK\PHONE>_
```

You used the DIR command to see if the file called **HPB.DAT** is in this subdirectory. DIR is the command, **HPB** is the file name, and **DAT** is the file extension. DIR does not let you use the data; it just lets you see if it is there.

4.5 USING APPLICATION PROGRAMS AND DATA FILES

In the above activity, you used the command DIR to see if there were two files on the disk, HPB.EXE and HPB.DAT. All DIR did was let you know that these files exist. To make use of these files, you have to load them into memory. Remember that the application program is HPB.EXE, which has the instructions to tell the computer what to do. The HPB.DAT data file cannot be used by itself. You must load the application program first; then you can get to the data.

4.6 ACTIVITY: USING APPLICATION PROGRAMS AND DATA FILES

Note: C:\WINDOSBK\PHONE> is displayed on your screen.

Step 1 Key in the following: C:\WINDOSBK\PHONE>**HPB.DAT** Enter

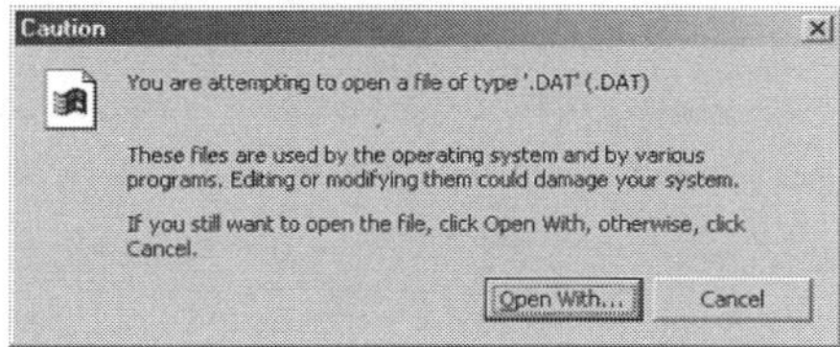

WHAT'S HAPPENING? You opened up a dialog box that warned you against trying to open the file. The file called **HPB.DAT** is a data file. It is not a program, so it cannot execute. It does not have a program file extension **.EXE**, **.COM**, or **.BAT**. It is a data file. Data files cannot execute.

Step 2 Click **Cancel**. Key in the following: C:\WINDOSBK\PHONE>**HPB** Enter

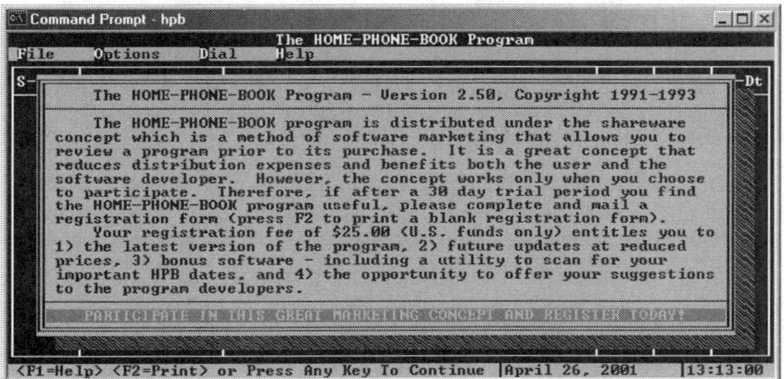

WHAT'S HAPPENING? When you keyed in **HPB**, the operating system looked for a file with the name of **HPB** and an extension of **.COM**, **.EXE**, or **.BAT** because those are the extensions that mean "execute." Because **HPB** is a file with an **.EXE** file extension, it was found. The operating system took an image copy of the program from the disk and loaded it into memory. Control was turned over to the HPB program. HPB is a shareware program with its own commands and instructions. You are looking at the registration information for the HPB program.

Step 3 Press Enter

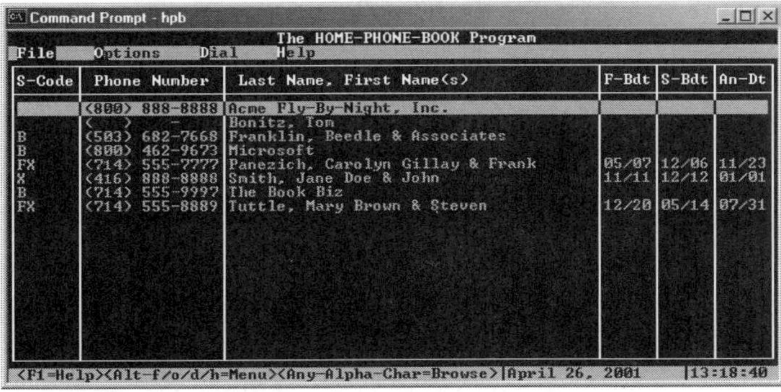

You interfaced with the operating system when you keyed in the command **HPB**, and, by doing so, loaded the program. Control was given over to the HPB program. HPB can work with only one data file at a time. **HPB.EXE** asked the operating system to load its data file, **HPB.DAT**. The information on the screen, such as "Acme Fly-By-Night, Inc." with a phone number, is the data. If you wanted to add your own data, you would have to learn how to use the program.

Step 4 Press **Alt** + **O**.

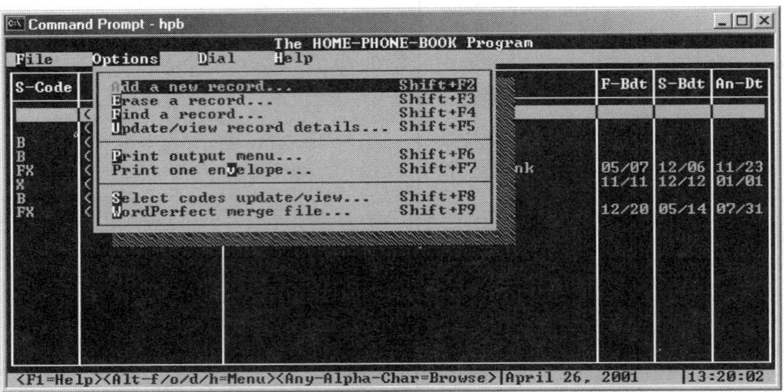

You have dropped down a menu that tells you how to perform tasks (Add, Erase, Find, etc.) with the information in this data file.

Step 5 Press **Esc**

Step 6 Press **Alt** + **F**. Press **X**.

```
C:\WINDOSBK\PHONE>_
```

You have exited the HPB program and returned to the Command Prompt screen. You did not make any changes to the data file.

Step 7 Key in the following:
C:\WINDOSBK\PHONE>**CD \WINDOSBK\FINANCE** **Enter**

```
C:\WINDOSBK\PHONE>CD \WINDOSBK\FINANCE

C:\WINDOSBK\FINANCE>_
```

You have changed to another directory, **FINANCE**, which is under the **WINDOSBK** directory. It has different programs and data files.

Step 8 Key in the following: C:\WINDOSBK\FINANCE>**DIR TH*.EXE** **Enter**

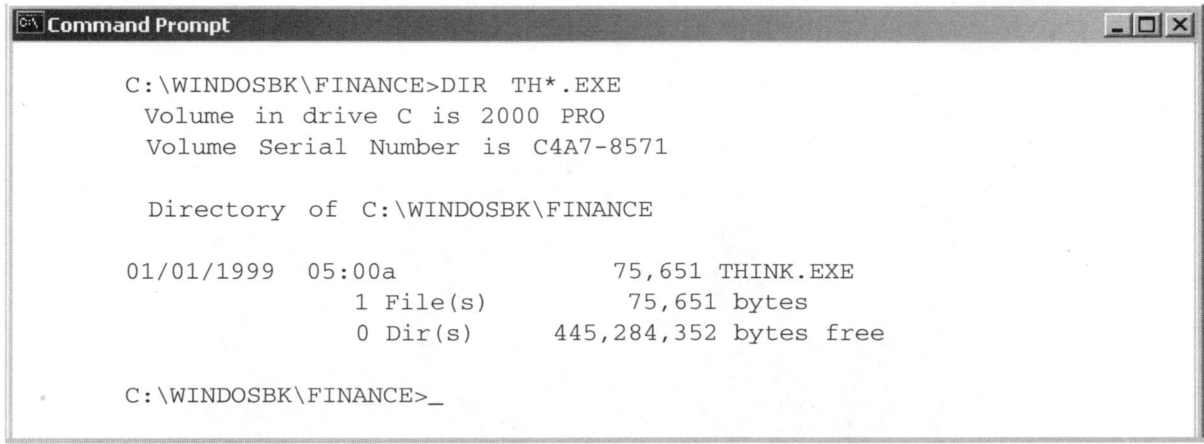

```
Command Prompt

C:\WINDOSBK\FINANCE>DIR TH*.EXE
 Volume in drive C is 2000 PRO
 Volume Serial Number is C4A7-8571

 Directory of C:\WINDOSBK\FINANCE

01/01/1999  05:00a              75,651 THINK.EXE
               1 File(s)         75,651 bytes
               0 Dir(s)     445,284,352 bytes free

C:\WINDOSBK\FINANCE>_
```

WHAT'S HAPPENING? You are looking at another program file called **THINK.EXE**.

Step 9 Key in the following: C:\WINDOSBK\FINANCE>**DIR *.TKR** Enter

```
Command Prompt

C:\WINDOSBK\FINANCE>DIR *.TKR
 Volume in drive C is 2000 PRO
 Volume Serial Number is C4A7-8571

 Directory of C:\WINDOSBK\FINANCE

01/01/1999  05:00a               6,656 BALANCE.TKR
01/01/1999  05:00a              18,304 BUDGET.TKR
01/01/1999  05:00a              10,624 MORTGAGE.TKR
01/01/1999  05:00a               8,064 HOMEBUD.TKR
               4 File(s)         43,648 bytes
               0 Dir(s)     445,284,352 bytes free

C:\WINDOSBK\FINANCE>_
```

WHAT'S HAPPENING? This program uses the file extension **.TKR** to identify data files that belong to it. You have your choice of what data file you want to look at. Do not be concerned if the files are displayed in a different order.

Step 10 Key in the following: C:\WINDOSBK\FINANCE>**THINK** Enter

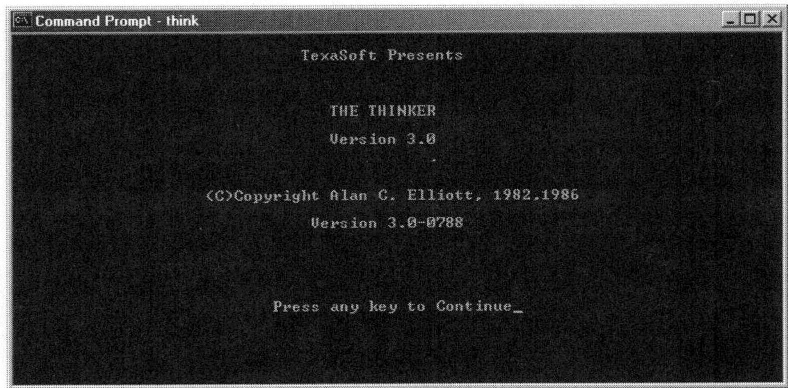

This is also a shareware program.

Step 11 Press **Enter**

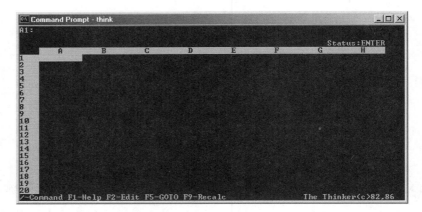

This spreadsheet program allows you to manipulate numerical data. It has its own set of commands. You must tell it what data file you want to load. Each of the following keys you press will execute a command in this program. Be sure you begin by pressing the forward slash (/), not the backslash (\).

Step 12 Press **/**.

Step 13 Press **F**.

Step 14 Press **R**.

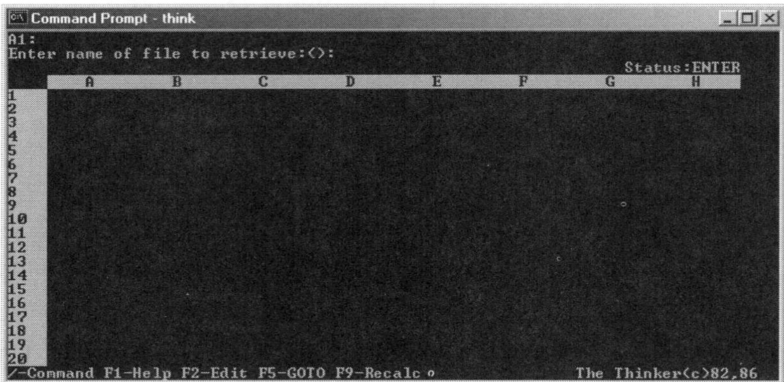

You went through a series of steps to get to the Retrieve command in this program. Programs that involve user-created data have different commands to load the data files. But in all cases, when you key in a data file name, the program will turn to the operating system to locate the data file and load it into memory.

Step 15 Key in the following: **HOMEBUD** **Enter**

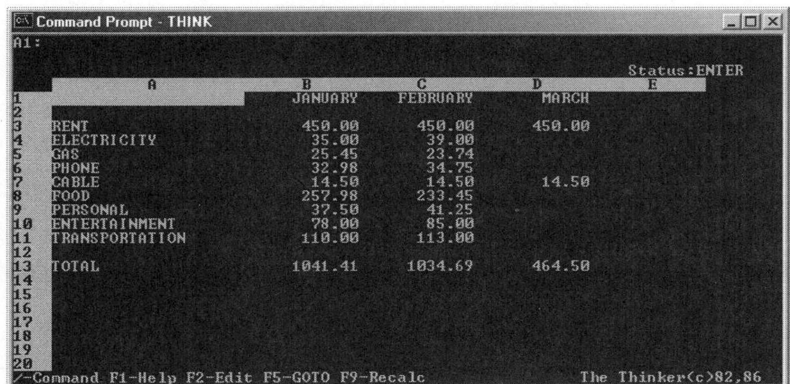

	A	B	C	D	E
1		JANUARY	FEBRUARY	MARCH	
2					
3	RENT	450.00	450.00	450.00	
4	ELECTRICITY	35.00	39.00		
5	GAS	25.45	23.74		
6	PHONE	32.98	34.75		
7	CABLE	14.50	14.50	14.50	
8	FOOD	257.98	233.45		
9	PERSONAL	37.50	41.25		
10	ENTERTAINMENT	78.00	85.00		
11	TRANSPORTATION	110.00	113.00		
12					
13	TOTAL	1041.41	1034.69	464.50	
14					
15					
16					
17					
18					
19					
20					

You have loaded the data file called **HOMEBUD.TKR**. The numbers and text displayed on the screen are the data you want to see.

Step 16 Press **/**.

Step 17 Press **F**.

Step 18 Press **R**.

By using the correct commands in this program, you have the opportunity to load another data file with different information. The data file that you are currently looking at is **HOMEBUD.TKR**. There are three other files, **BUDGET**, **MORTGAGE**, and **BALANCE**, that you could look at.

Step 19 Press **Enter**

Step 20 Press **/**.

Step 21 Press **Q**.

Step 22 Press **Y**.

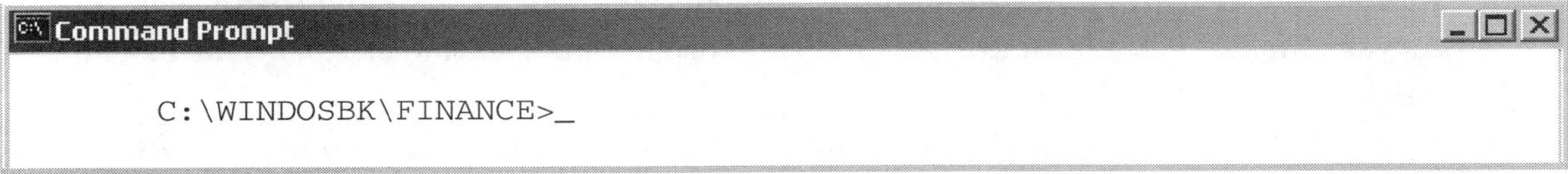

Step 23 Key in the following: C:\WINDOSBK\FINANCE>**CD ** **Enter**

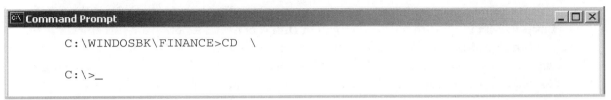

You exited the program Thinker and returned to the system prompt. You are now back to the system level. Next, you returned to the root directory. Thus, you used the operating system to load the application program called HPB, which can work with only one data file at a time, which you also loaded. You used the OS again to change to the directory where the Thinker program was located. You then used the commands of the Thinker program to load the data file, **HOMEBUD.TKR**. When you used the commands in Thinker, Thinker told the operating system to get the data files you specified so that Thinker could place the data files in memory to let you work with the information in them. You followed the instructions of the programs HPB and Thinker. When you were finished with each program, you returned to the Command Prompt window.

4.7 MANAGING PROGRAM AND DATA FILES AT THE COMMAND PROMPT

In the last few activities, you moved around the hard disk and loaded both program files and data files. Although you did not spend much time working with each program, the experience should give you some idea of how many different types of programs there are. With each new program, you generate new data files. Windows does a very good job managing your program files so that you can launch them from the Start/Programs menu. You need to manage the data files you create in these programs so that you can quickly locate what you need and get to work.

As an example of what you are faced with, imagine that you own 10 books. By reading each spine, you can quickly peruse the authors and titles and locate the book you wish to read. Suppose your library grows, and you now have 100 books. You do not want to read every author and title looking for just one book, so you classify the information. A common classification scheme is to arrange the books alphabetically by the author's last name. Now you have shortened your search time. If you are looking for a book by Peat, you go to the letter P. You may have more than one book by an author that begins with P, but, by going to the letter P, you have narrowed your search. Now imagine you have 10,000 books—arranging alphabetically by author is still not enough. You may have 200 books by authors whose last names begin with P. So you further classify your books. You first divide them into categories like computer or fiction. Then, within the category, you arrange alphabetically by last name. So, if you wanted a computer book by Peat, you would first go to the computer section, then to the letter P. If you wanted a novel by Peters, you would first go to the fiction section and then the letter P. As you can see, you are classifying and categorizing information so that you can find it quickly.

This process is exactly what you want to do with files. Remember, you have many data files. You want to be able to locate them quickly by grouping them logically. The way you do this in the OS is by the means of subdirectories.

Some programs, upon installation, create a directory for your files. For example, Lotus 1-2-3 may create a directory called DATA beneath its program directory. Assuming Lotus resides in C:\123, your files would all go to C:\123\DATA. However, do you want all of your files together? What happens in a year or two, when you have created 200 more files? Some sort of organization becomes necessary.

4.8 HIERARCHICAL FILING SYSTEMS OR TREE-STRUCTURED DIRECTORIES

As shown in Chapter 3, every disk must be formatted. Formatting a disk automatically creates a directory known as the root directory. Every disk must have a root directory so that files can be located on the disk. The root directory table is the area of the disk that contains information about what is stored there. It is like an index to the disk. However, there is a limit to the number of files or entries that can be placed in the root directory table if your disk is formatted as FAT16. See Table 4.1. Under FAT16, the root directory is a fixed size and location on the disk. This is no longer true with FAT32. Under FAT32 the root directory is now free to grow as necessary and can be located anywhere on a disk. There is no longer a limit on the number of directory entries in the root directory because the root directory is now an ordinary cluster chain and can grow as large as needed, limited only by the physical size of your disk.

Disk Size	Number of Root Directory Entries
3½-inch and 5¼-inch DS/DD disks	112
3½-inch and 5¼-inch DS/HD disks	224
Hard disk	512

TABLE 4.1 FAT16 ROOT DIRECTORY FILE LIMITS

Although the limits of the root directory table on a floppy disk may be adequate, the limits on a FAT16 root directory of a hard disk were not. If you had a 1-GB hard disk, 512 entries were not enough space to store all the files the drive can accumulate. Normally, people work more efficiently when they group files and programs together logically. Subdirectories give you the capability of "fooling" the system so that you can create as many file entries as you need. The only limitation is the capacity of the disk. Even though FAT32 no longer limits the size of the root directory, subdirectories are still an important part of organizing a disk.

This capability is called the hierarchical or tree-structured filing system. In this system, the root directory has entries not only for files but also for other directories called subdirectories, which can contain any number of entries. Windows refers to the subdirectories as folders.

The root directory is represented by a backslash. (Do not confuse the backslash \ with the forward slash /.) All directories other than the root directory are technically called subdirectories, yet the terms *directory* and *subdirectory* are used interchangeably. Windows uses the terms *folders* and *subfolders*. All of these terms—*folders, subfolders, directories,* and *subdirectories*—are used interchangeably. Subdirectories are not limited to a specific number of files. Subdirectories may have subdirectories of their own. Subdirectories divide the disk into different areas.

The directory structure of a disk is like an inverted family tree with the root directory at the top and the subdirectories branching off from the root. The root directory is the point of entry in the hierarchical directory structure. In Figure 4.1, the example on the left is a family tree showing a parent who has two children; the one on the right is a root directory with two subdirectories. The two subdirectories contain all files and programs having to do with sales and accounting. Again, what you are doing is classifying and further classifying information.

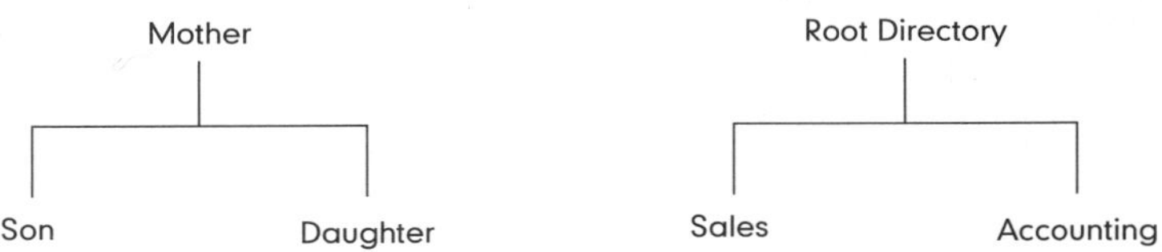

FIGURE 4.1 A DIRECTORY IS LIKE A FAMILY TREE

A child can have only one biological mother, but a child can become a parent and have children. Those children can also become parents and have children. Likewise, ACCOUNTING can be a ***child directory*** of the root directory, but also a parent directory to subdirectories beneath it (see Figure 4.2).

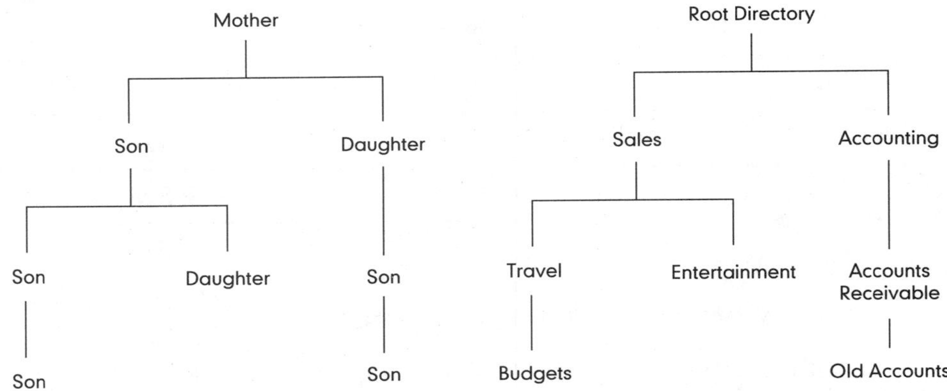

FIGURE 4.2 HIERARCHICAL STRUCTURE OF A DIRECTORY

The children are dependent on the parent above. Each subdirectory is listed in its ***parent directory,*** but not in any directory above the parent. Note the absolute ***hierarchical structure***. You cannot skip a subdirectory any more than you can have a grandparent and grandchild with no parent in between. You move around in the directories via the path that tells the operating system where to go for a particular file.

Think of a disk as a building. When a structure is built, it has a finite size, which is also true of a disk. For example, you can have a 1.44-MB floppy disk or a 2-GB hard disk. The size is fixed. You cannot make it larger or smaller, but you can divide it into rooms. However, you first have to get inside. To open the door, you need a drive letter. Once inside, you are in a room that is equivalent to the fixed size of a disk. This undivided room is the root directory. Every disk has a root directory that may or may not be subdivided. The name of the root directory is always \ (backslash). Thus, the structure could look like Figure 4.3.

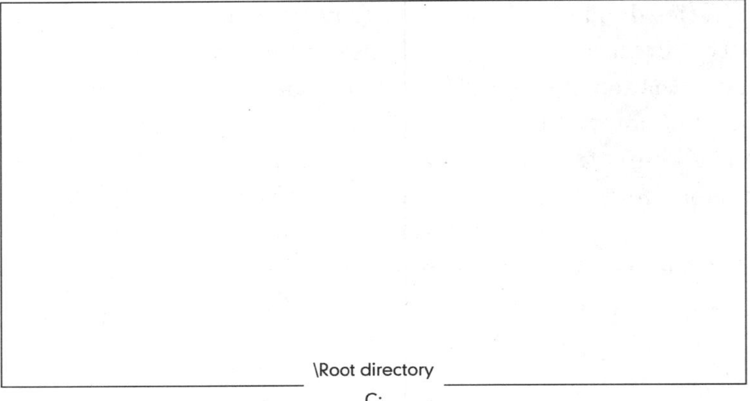

FIGURE 4.3 A DISK AS A BUILDING

Since it is difficult to find things when they are scattered about a large room, you want to put up walls (subdirectories) so that like things can be grouped together. When the walls go up, the root directory becomes the main lobby—backslash (\). In the rooms (subdirectories) you plan to have games, names and addresses in phone books, and the operating system commands. You post a sign (label) indicating what you plan to put inside each room (see Figure 4.4).

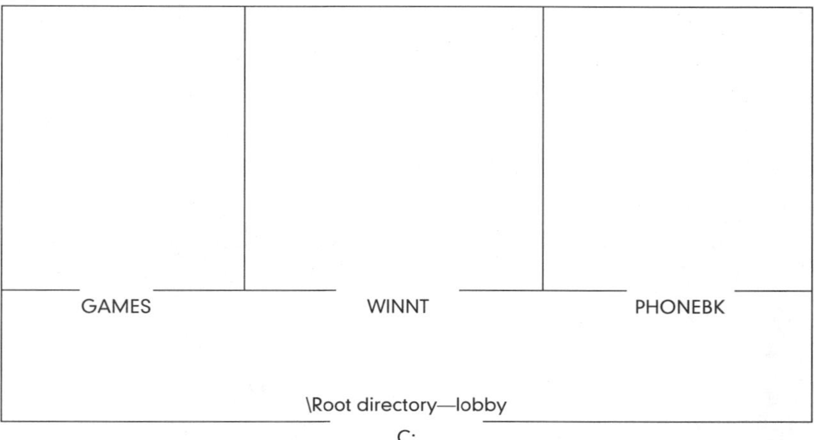

FIGURE 4.4 SUBDIRECTORIES AS ROOMS

Each room is off the main lobby, the \. You cannot go from the GAMES room to the PHONEBK room without first going through the main lobby (\). Furthermore, the lobby (\) sees only the entryways to the rooms. It does not know what is in the rooms, only that there are rooms (subdirectories). In addition, each room can be further divided (see Figure 4.5).

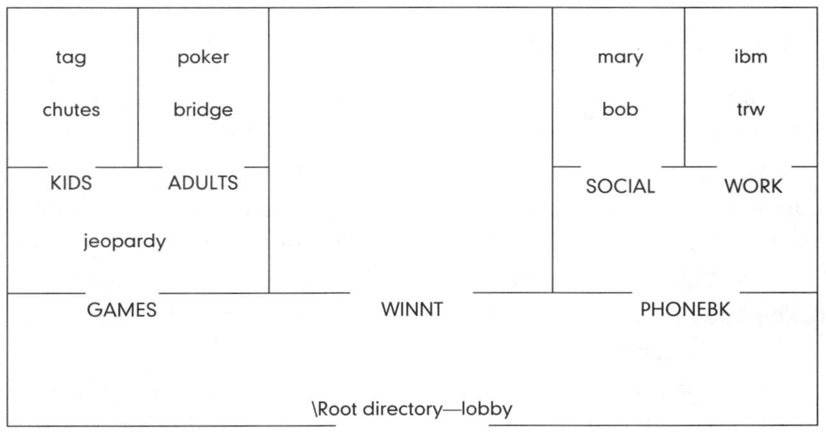

FIGURE 4.5 MORE SUBDIRECTORIES

Each new room (subdirectory) is off another room (subdirectory). The GAMES room, for example, now has two new rooms—KIDS and ADULTS. The GAMES room (subdirectory) now becomes a lobby. You can get to the KIDS and ADULTS rooms (subdirectories) only through the GAMES lobby. Furthermore, in order to get to the GAMES room, you must pass through the main lobby \ (root directory).

The GAMES lobby knows that there are two new rooms but does not know what is inside each. The main lobby (\) knows the GAMES room but does not know what is inside GAMES. The KIDS and ADULTS rooms know only the GAMES lobby.

The same relationship exists for all other new rooms (subdirectories). A subdirectory knows only its parent lobby and any children it may create. There are no shortcuts. If you are in the KIDS room and wish to go the SOCIAL room, you must return to the GAMES lobby, then you must pass through the main lobby (root directory) to the PHONEBK lobby. Only then can you enter the SOCIAL room.

You do not have to subdivide rooms. GAMES is subdivided, while WINNT is not. Remember, you are not changing the size of the structure; you are merely organizing it. Presently, these rooms have nothing in them, but they are ready to receive something. That something is files. The files are like the furniture (see Figure 4.6).

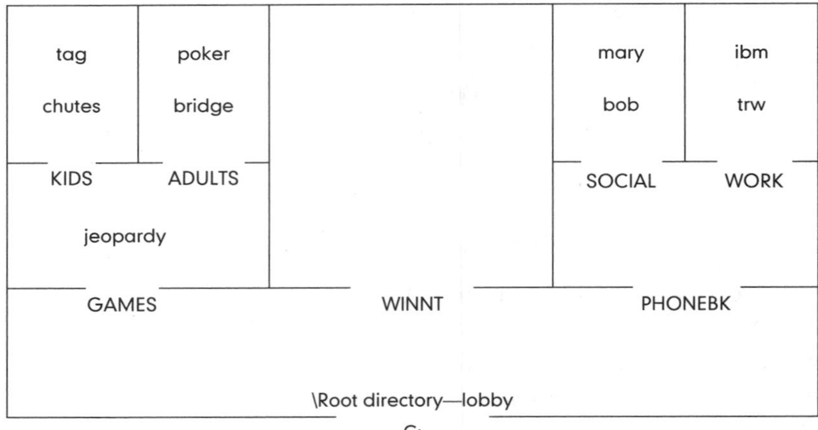

FIGURE 4.6 FILES IN SUBDIRECTORIES

You now have not only created the rooms (subdirectories), but you have also filled them with furniture (files). Thus, using subdirectories is a way to manage the numerous files and programs you collect and create. Again, this is a classification scheme, and you expect there to be some logic to it. Just as you would not expect to find a stove in a room called bedroom, you would not expect to find a file called ADDRESS.EXE in a subdirectory called GAMES. This does not mean there cannot be a mistake—that someone could, indeed place the stove in the bedroom—but that would make the stove *very* hard to find.

There is another component to using subdirectories. When you use subdirectories, you can change your work area, much like using a room. If you are going to cook, you will go to the kitchen because you expect the tools that you need to be in that location. You expect not only the stove to be there but also all the tools you need—the sink, the spices, and the pots and pans. If you want to go to sleep, you will go to the bedroom because that is where you expect to find the bed. Subdirectories have names that you or a program choose. The only exception is the root directory, which is created when you format the disk and is always known as \ (backslash). The root directory *always* has the same name on every disk (\).

Because computers are so rigid, they must follow certain rules when naming anything. Subdirectories follow the same naming conventions as files. Usually, subdirectory names do not have extensions. Although the Windows operating system treats subdirectories as files, the subdirectories themselves cannot be manipulated with the standard file manipulation commands. Subdirectories have their own special commands. Table 4.2 lists the directory management commands.

Command	Function
CHDIR or CD	Changes a directory.
MKDIR or MD	Makes or creates a directory.
RMDIR or RD	Removes or erases a directory and its subdirectories.
PATH	Defines the search paths.
PROMPT	Changes the look of the prompt to identify what subdirectory is the default.
MOVE	Allows you to rename a directory.

TABLE 4.2 DIRECTORY MANAGEMENT COMMANDS

4.9 CREATING SUBDIRECTORIES

When you create a subdirectory, you are setting up an area where files can be stored. There is nothing in the subdirectory initially. The internal MD command creates a subdirectory. When you format a disk, you are preparing it to hold files. When you set up a subdirectory, you are preparing it to hold a logical group of files. The syntax of the command is:

```
MKDIR [drive:]path
```

or

```
MD [drive:]path
```

MD and MKDIR perform exactly the same function. You will use MD, because it requires fewer keystrokes. In the following activity, you will create two subdirectories under the root directory on the DATA disk. These subdirectories will be for two classes: one in political science and the other in physical education.

4.10 ACTIVITY: HOW TO CREATE SUBDIRECTORIES

Note: You are at the Command Prompt. C:\> is displayed as the default drive and directory.

Step 1 Place the DATA disk created in Chapter 3 into Drive A.

Step 2 Key in the following: C:\> **FORMAT A:/Q/V:DATA** Enter

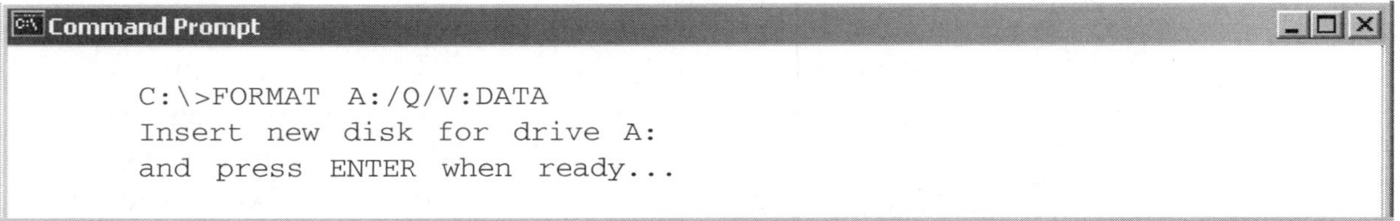

```
Command Prompt

C:\>FORMAT A:/Q/V:DATA
Insert new disk for drive A:
and press ENTER when ready...
```

WHAT'S HAPPENING? You are going to format the DATA disk again. In addition to using the /Q parameter to format the disk quickly, you also used a shortcut to place a volume label on the disk, so you do not have to wait for the volume label prompt. If you want to include a volume label on a disk, you can do it at the time of issuing the FORMAT command. However, when you use /V (followed by a colon), you cannot have spaces in the volume label name.

Step 3 Press **Enter**

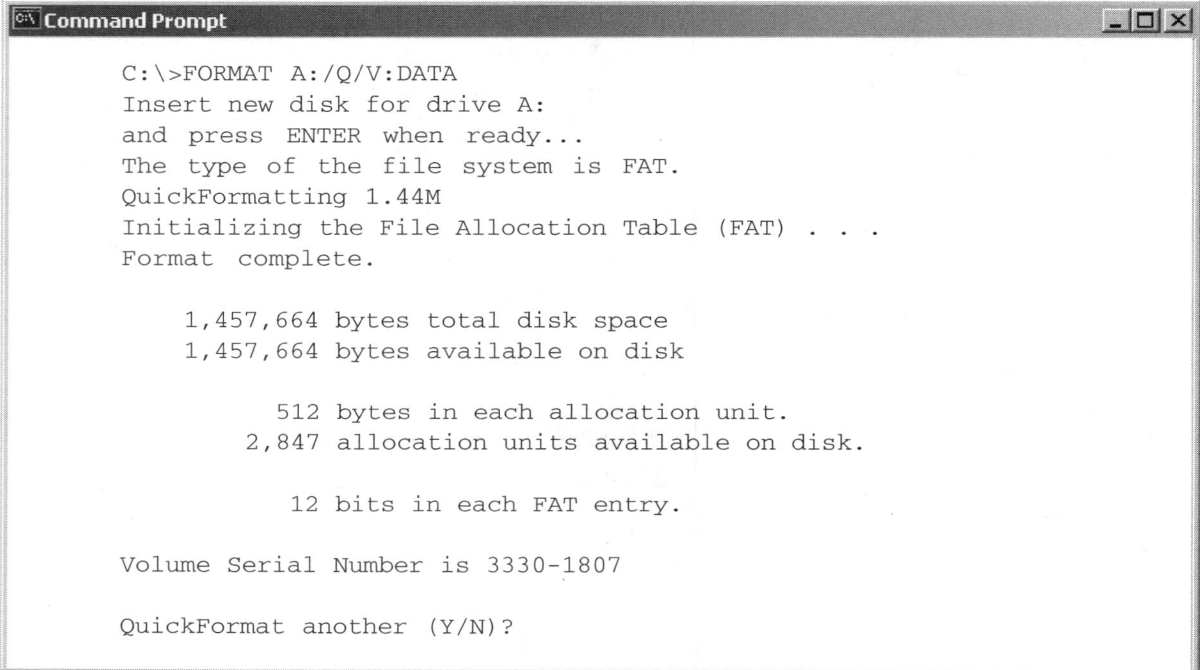

```
Command Prompt

C:\>FORMAT A:/Q/V:DATA
Insert new disk for drive A:
and press ENTER when ready...
The type of the file system is FAT.
QuickFormatting 1.44M
Initializing the File Allocation Table (FAT) . . .
Format complete.

    1,457,664 bytes total disk space
    1,457,664 bytes available on disk

          512 bytes in each allocation unit.
        2,847 allocation units available on disk.

           12 bits in each FAT entry.

Volume Serial Number is 3330-1807

QuickFormat another (Y/N)?
```

WHAT'S HAPPENING? You formatted the disk and placed a volume label on it.

Step 4 Press **N** **Enter**

Step 5 Key in the following: C:\>**A:** **Enter**

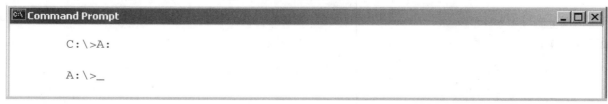

```
Command Prompt

C:\>A:

A:\>_
```

WHAT'S HAPPENING? You have changed the default drive. However, you are in more than a default *drive,* you are in a default *directory*—the root of A. This is the only directory on this disk and was created when you formatted it. You can tell that you are in the root directory because when you look at the prompt, it displays not just A: but also \, indicating the root.

Step 6 Key in the following: A:\>**MD POLYSCI** Enter

Step 7 Key in the following: A:\>**MD PHYSED** Enter

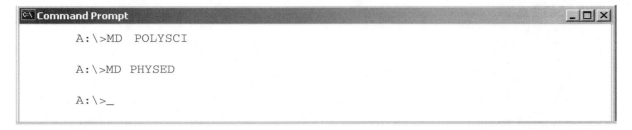

You created two subdirectories called **POLYSCI** and **PHYSED** under the root directory on the DATA disk. **POLYSCI** will hold all the files that involve classes in political science, and **PHYSED** will hold files that involve classes in physical education. Although you have created the subdirectories to hold the files, they are now "empty" file cabinets. When you used the MD command, all you saw on the screen was the system prompt. How do you know that you created subdirectories? You can see the subdirectories you just created by using the DIR command.

Step 8 Key in the following: A:\>**DIR** Enter

```
Command Prompt
A:\>DIR
 Volume in drive A is DATA
 Volume Serial Number is 3330-1807

 Directory of A:\



04/30/2001  11:15a      <DIR>          POLYSCI
04/30/2001  11:15a      <DIR>          PHYSED
               0 File(s)              0 bytes
               2 Dir(s)       1,456,640 bytes free
A:\>_
```

WHAT'S HAPPENING?

The DIR command displayed the contents of the disk. In this case, there are only the two subdirectory files you just created. It is the <DIR> after each file name that indicates a subdirectory. **POLYSCI** and **PHYSED** are subdirectories. It is also important to note that the \ following the **Directory of A:** on the screen indicates the root directory of the disk.

One of the parameters for the DIR command is /A for attributes. The only attribute you are interested in is D for directories. If you look at the syntax diagram, it indicates the /A followed by a list of the attributes you can request. The D is for directories:

```
/A           Displays files with specified attributes.
 attributes  D  Directories         R  Read-only files
             H  Hidden files        A  Files ready for archiving
             S  System files        -  Prefix meaning not
```

Step 9 Key in the following: A:\>**DIR /AD** Enter

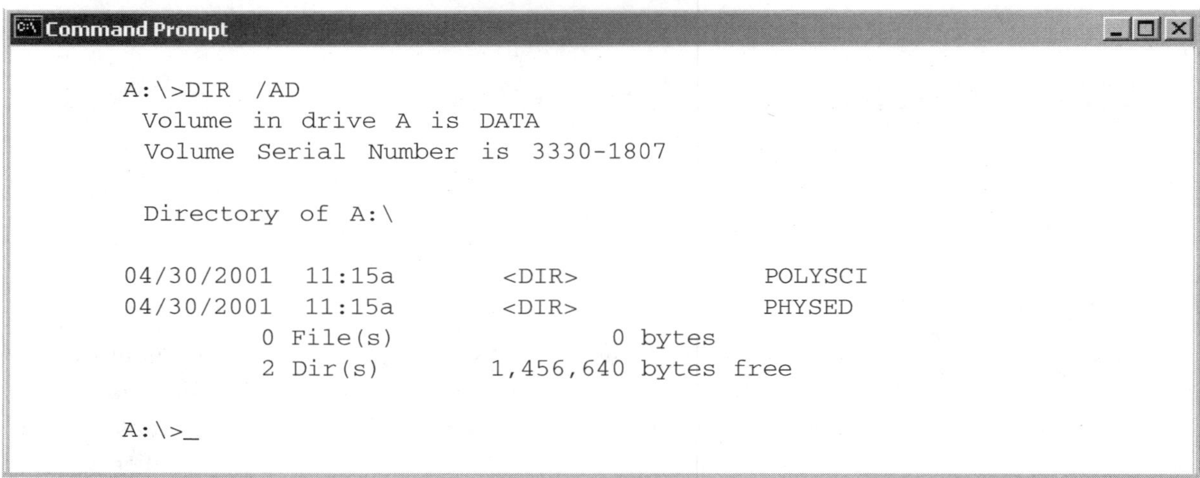

```
Command Prompt

A:\>DIR /AD
 Volume in drive A is DATA
 Volume Serial Number is 3330-1807

 Directory of A:\

04/30/2001  11:15a      <DIR>          POLYSCI
04/30/2001  11:15a      <DIR>          PHYSED
        0 File(s)             0 bytes
        2 Dir(s)      1,456,640 bytes free

A:\>_
```

WHAT'S HAPPENING? You see displayed only the directories on the DATA disk because that is all that the disk contains. What if you want to look at a disk that already has directories and files on it?

Step 10 Key in the following: A:\>**DIR C:\WINDOSBK** Enter

```
Command Prompt

05/30/2000  01:46p                 157 NEWAUTO.MAK
07/31/1999  12:53p               2,672 NEWPRSON.FIL
05/30/2000  04:32p                 182 OLDAUTO.MAK
05/30/2000  04:32p                  98 OLIVE.OIL
07/31/2000  04:32p               2,307 PERSONAL.FIL
07/03/2000  01:51p      <DIR>          PHONE
10/01/2000  04:12p                  61 RIGHT.RED
10/01/2000  04:12p                  26 RIGHT.UP
11/22/1989  10:35p               7,269 RNS.EXE
11/16/2000  12:00p                  53 Sandy and Nicki.txt
11/16/2000  12:00p                  59 Sandy and Patty.txt
08/12/2000  04:12p                  75 SECOND.FIL
07/03/2000  01:52p      <DIR>          SPORTS
07/31/2000  04:32p                 260 STATE.CAP
07/31/2000  04:32p                 265 STATE2.CAP
07/31/2000  04:32p               1,228 STATES.USA
07/31/1999  12:53p                  46 STEVEN.FIL
07/03/2000  01:50p      <DIR>          TEST
12/11/1999  04:03p                  65 TEST.TXT
12/31/2001  04:32p                  64 WILD1.XXX
12/31/2001  04:32p                  64 WILD2.YYY
12/31/2001  04:32p                  64 WILD3.ZZZ
12/31/2001  04:32p                  93 WILDONE
12/31/2001  04:32p                 181 WILDONE.DOS
12/31/2001  04:32p                 181 WILDTHR.DOS
12/31/2001  04:32p                 182 WILDTWO.DOS
07/03/2000  01:53p      <DIR>          WORKING
08/12/2000  04:12p                   3 Y.FIL
```

```
                    90 File(s)          29,382 bytes
                    11 Dir(s)    6,895,611,904 bytes free

A:\>_
```

(This graphic represents the tail end of your listing.) As you can see, using DIR with no parameters shows you all files, not just directories.

Step 11 Key in the following: A:\>**DIR C:\WINDOSBK /AD** Enter

```
Command Prompt

A:\>DIR C:\WINDOSBK /AD
 Volume in drive C is 2000 PRO
 Volume Serial Number is C4A7-8571

 Directory of C:\WINDOSBK

04/24/2001  09:38a      <DIR>          .
04/24/2001  09:38a      <DIR>          ..
07/03/2000  01:50p      <DIR>          DATA
07/03/2000  01:51p      <DIR>          FINANCE
07/03/2000  01:50p      <DIR>          GAMES
07/03/2000  01:52p      <DIR>          LEVEL-1
07/03/2000  01:53p      <DIR>          MEDIA
07/03/2000  01:51p      <DIR>          PHONE
07/03/2000  01:52p      <DIR>          SPORTS
07/03/2000  01:50p      <DIR>          TEST
07/03/2000  01:53p      <DIR>          WORKING
               0 File(s)              0 bytes
              11 Dir(s)     445,218,816 bytes free

A:\>_
```

The above command listed only the directories on the hard disk in the subdirectory called **WINDOSBK**. Do not be concerned if the order is different on your computer. What if you wish to see the names of the files inside the directory? Since **POLYSCI** is a subdirectory, not just a file, you can display the contents of the directory with the DIR command. Remember, the terms *directory* and *subdirectory* are interchangeable. Actually there is only one directory—the root directory. Although others may be called directories, they are really subdirectories. Again, the syntax of the DIR command is DIR [*drive*:][*path*]. You use the subdirectory name for *path*.

Step 12 Key in the following: A:\>**DIR POLYSCI** Enter

```
Command Prompt

A:\>DIR POLYSCI

 Volume in drive A is DATA
 Volume Serial Number is 3330-1807

 Directory of A:\POLYSCI
```

```
04/30/2001  11:15a      <DIR>          .
04/30/2001  11:15a      <DIR>          ..
          0 File(s)              0 bytes
          2 Dir(s)       1,456,640 bytes free

A:\>_
```

WHAT'S HAPPENING? The directory line, **Directory of A:\POLYSCI**, tells you the path. You are looking from the root directory into the subdirectory called **POLYSCI**. Even though you just created the subdirectory **POLYSCI**, it seems to have two subdirectories in it already, . (one period, also called the ***dot***) and . . (two periods, also called the ***double dot***). Every subdirectory, except the root directory, has two named subdirectories, always. The subdirectory named . is another name or abbreviation for the current directory, **POLYSCI**. The subdirectory name . . is an abbreviation for the parent directory of the current directory, in this case the root directory \. The . (dot) and . . (double dot) are called ***subdirectory markers*** or ***dot notation***. This always holds true—the single dot is the name of the subdirectory you are currently in, the default directory, and the double dot is the name of the directory immediately above the current directory, the parent directory.

Step 13 Key in the following: A:\>**DIR PHYSED** Enter

```
Command Prompt

A:\>DIR PHYSED
 Volume in drive A is DATA
 Volume Serial Number is 3330-1807

 Directory of A:\PHYSED

04/30/2001  11:15a      <DIR>          .
04/30/2001  11:15a      <DIR>          ..
          0 File(s)              0 bytes
          2 Dir(s)       1,456,640 bytes free

A:\>_
```

WHAT'S HAPPENING? The line that reads **Directory of A:\PHYSED** tells you the path. You are looking from the root directory into the subdirectory called **PHYSED**, the same way you looked when you asked for a directory on another drive. If, for instance, you asked for a directory of the disk in Drive B, that line would read **Directory of B:**. If you had asked for a directory of Drive C, that line would have read **Directory of C:**. It tells you not only what drive but also what subdirectory is displayed on the screen.

4.11 THE CURRENT DIRECTORY

Just as the operating system keeps track of the default drive, it also keeps track of the ***current directory,*** or default directory of each drive. When you boot the system, the default drive is the drive you load the operating system from, usually C, and the default directory is the root directory of the current drive. You can change the directory just as you can change the drive. Doing so makes a specific subdirectory the default. In previous chapters you used the CD command to change the default directory to the \WINNT\SYSTEM32 subdirectory on the hard disk. It was important to have that as the default subdirectory so that you could use the external commands.

The change directory command (CHDIR or CD) has two purposes. If you key in CD with no parameters, the name of the current default directory is displayed. If you include a parameter after the CD command, the default directory will be changed to the directory you request. The CD command does not use spaces as delimiters, so it is possible to change to a directory that contains a space in its name, such as My Documents, without using quotes. This process is similar to changing drives by keying in the desired drive letter followed by a colon, e.g., A:, B:, and C:.

However, do not be fooled. If your default drive and directory is the root of A so that the displayed prompt is A:\> and you key in CD C:\WINDOSBK, you *will not* change drives. What you will do is change the default directory on Drive C to \WINDOSBK. Your current default drive and directory will still be the root of A and your displayed prompt will still be A:\>. However, if you change to the C drive by keying in C:, you will go to the current default directory on the C drive, which is now C:\WINDOSBK. But if you use the /D parameter with the CD command, you will change drives and directories with one command. The command would be CD /D C:\WINDOSBK. The commands CHDIR and CD are exactly the same. You will use CD because it requires fewer keystrokes. The syntax for the CD command is as follows:

```
CD  [/D]  [drive:][path]
```

4.12 ACTIVITY: USING THE CD COMMAND

Note: The DATA disk is in Drive A. The default drive is Drive A, and A:\> is displayed on the screen.

Step 1 Key in the following: A:\>**CD** Enter

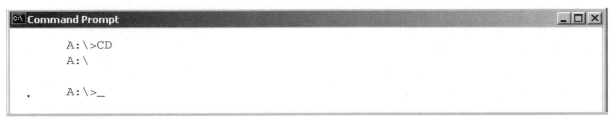

This display tells you that you are in the root directory of the DATA disk and that any command you enter will apply to this root directory, which is also the default directory. You can change this default using the CD command. You are going to change the default subdirectory from the root to the subdirectory called **POLYSCI**.

Step 2 Key in the following: A:\>**CD POLYSCI** Enter

Step 3 Key in the following: A:\POLYSCI>**CD** Enter

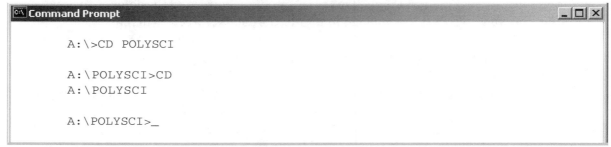

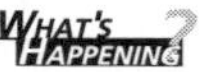

In Step 2, CD followed by the name of the subdirectory changed the default from the root directory to the subdirectory **POLYSCI**. Since you changed the default directory, the prompt then said A:\POLYSCI>. However, you can always confirm that you changed the default directory by keying in **CD**. CD with no parameters always displays the default drive and default subdirectory. When you keyed in **CD**, it displayed **A:\POLYSCI**, which tells you that you are in the subdirectory **\POLYSCI** on the DATA disk in Drive A and that any command you enter with no parameters will apply to this default subdirectory. You can think of the command this way: CD with no parameters shows you the current drive and directory; CD followed by a subdirectory name changes the subdirectory. CD *cannot* be used to change drives.

Step 4 Key in the following: A:\POLYSCI>**DIR** Enter

```
Command Prompt

A:\POLYSCI>DIR
 Volume in drive A is DATA
 Volume Serial Number is 3330-1807

 Directory of A:\POLYSCI

04/30/2001  11:15a      <DIR>          .
04/30/2001  11:15a      <DIR>          ..
               0 File(s)              0 bytes
               2 Dir(s)       1,456,640 bytes free

A:\POLYSCI>_
```

You are displaying the contents of the current default directory, **\POLYSCI**. When you use a command, in this case DIR, it always assumes the default drive and default subdirectory, unless you specify another drive and/or subdirectory.

Step 5 Key in the following: A:\POLYSCI>**CD ** Enter

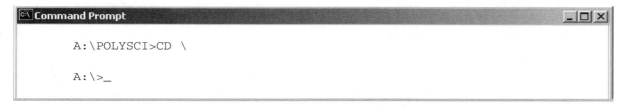

WHAT'S HAPPENING? By keying in **CD **, you moved to the root directory of the DATA disk. The first backslash always means the root directory.

4.13 RELATIVE AND ABSOLUTE PATHS

You are going to add subdirectories to the ***tree structure*** so that the levels will look like those in Figure 4.7. To create these additional subdirectories, you use the MD, or make directory, command. The command syntax allows these parameters: MD [*drive*:]*path*.

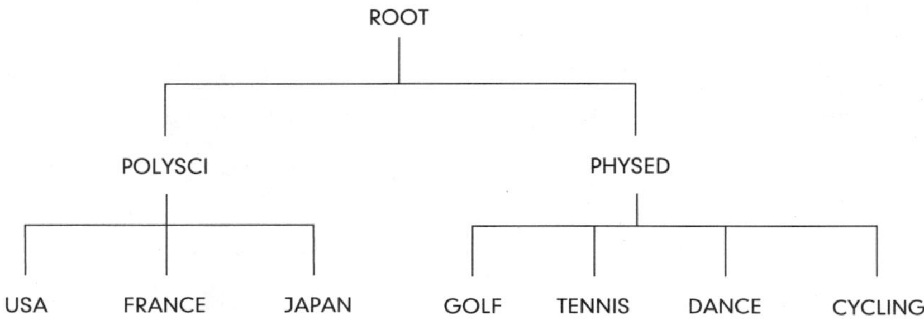

FIGURE 4.7 DIRECTORY WITH SUBDIRECTORIES

The *drive:* is the letter of the drive that contains the disk on which the subdirectory is to be created (such as A:, B:, or C:). If you omit the drive designator, the subdirectory will be created on the default or current drive. The path is the path name of the directory in which the subdirectory is to be created. If you omit the path name, the subdirectory is created in the default or current subdirectory.

It is important to understand the concept of ***absolute path*** and ***relative path***. The absolute path is the complete and total hierarchical structure. You start at the top and work your way down through every subdirectory without skipping a directory. The absolute path is *always* absolutely correct.

As an analogy, if you were living in Los Angeles, California, you could get a bus ticket to Santa Barbara. It would not be necessary to use the absolute path to ask for a ticket—the United States, California, Los Angeles, and then Santa Barbara—you could use the relative path of just Santa Barbara. If you were in London, England, and were flying to Los Angeles and needed to buy your connecting bus ticket from the airport to Santa Barbara before you left England, you would indeed need to give the English ticket broker complete information about the ticket that you wanted. You would need to give the absolute path of where you wanted to leave from and where you wanted to go to—you would ask for a ticket to the United States, state of California, city of Los Angeles, and then a bus ticket from the airport to the city of Santa Barbara.

Just as the ticket salesperson in Los Angeles knows where Santa Barbara is, the current directory also knows information about its immediate surroundings. However, a directory knows *only* about the files and subdirectories within itself and the files and directory immediately above it. There can be many directories beneath it (many child directories) but only one directory above it (the parent directory). Each directory knows only its immediate child directories and its parent directory—no more. If you want to move to a different parent subdirectory, you must return to the root. The root is the common "ancestor" of all the directories on the disk.

Thus, if you wanted to go from the subdirectory GOLF in the above figure to the subdirectory FRANCE, you would need to go via ROOT. Once you get to the root, you can choose where you want to go. There are many places to go. It is like a subway—you must pass through all the stations along the path to get to your destination.

4.14 ACTIVITY: CREATING MORE SUBDIRECTORIES

Note: The DATA disk is in Drive A. A:\> is displayed as the default drive and the default directory.

Step 1 Key in the following: A:\>**CD** Enter

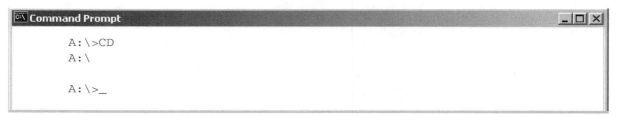

WHAT'S HAPPENING? You confirmed that the default directory is the root of the DATA disk. To create three subdirectories under **POLYSCI**, you will use the MD command along with the subdirectory names. The subdirectories will be called **USA**, **JAPAN**, and **FRANCE**. You will begin with an absolute path and then use a relative path.

Step 2 Key in the following: A:\>**MD A:\POLYSCI\USA** Enter

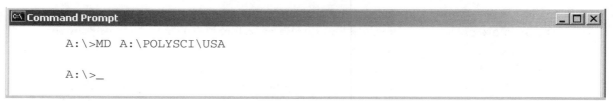

WHAT'S HAPPENING? You have given absolute instructions as to where to create the directory. You issued the command MD (make a directory) followed by the location (go to Drive A, under the root directory (\), under the directory called **POLYSCI**). The next backslash is a delimiter to separate **POLYSCI** from the next entry. Then you can add your new subdirectory called **USA**. You could not create **USA** until you created **POLYSCI** because it is a hierarchy. Looking at the screen, however, nothing seems to have happened.

Step 3 Key in the following: A:\>**DIR POLYSCI** Enter

```
Command Prompt

A:\>DIR  POLYSCI
 Volume in drive A is DATA
 Volume Serial Number is 3330-1807

 Directory  of  A:\POLYSCI

04/30/2001  11:15a     <DIR>          .
04/30/2001  11:15a     <DIR>          ..
04/30/2001  11:17a     <DIR>          USA
          0 File(s)              0 bytes
          3 Dir(s)       1,456,128 bytes free

A:\>_
```

You indeed have a subdirectory called **USA** under the root, under **POLYSCI**. You are now going to create the subdirectory called **JAPAN**. Here you can use a relative path. The default prompt shows you that you are already in Drive A. If you are already in Drive A, it is the default directory. Therefore, you do not need to include the drive letter because the operating system assumes the default drive, unless you tell it otherwise. The default directory is the root. The \ is shown in the prompt, which tells you that you are in the root directory and that it is your default. Since you are already in the root, you do not need to include it. The first backslash is implied.

Step 4 Key in the following: A:\>**MD POLYSCI\JAPAN** Enter

Step 5 Key in the following: A:\>**DIR POLYSCI** Enter

```
Command Prompt

A:\>MD POLYSCI\JAPAN

A:\>DIR  POLYSCI
 Volume in drive A is DATA
 Volume Serial Number is 3330-1807

 Directory of A:\POLYSCI
04/30/2001  11:15a     <DIR>          .
04/30/2001  11:15a     <DIR>          ..
04/30/2001  11:17a     <DIR>          USA
04/30/2001  11:18a     <DIR>          JAPAN
          0 File(s)              0 bytes
          4 Dir(s)       1,455,616 bytes free

A:\>_
```

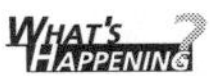

You created the subdirectory **JAPAN** under **POLYSCI** and then you used the DIR command to see that **JAPAN** was, indeed, created. As you can see, in Step 2, you used the absolute path to create the directory. In Step 4, you used the default values and created a subdirectory using the relative path.

Step 6 Key in the following: A:\>**CD POLYSCI** Enter

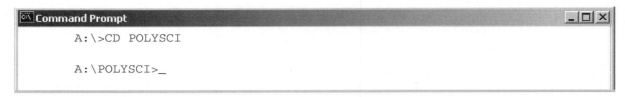

WHAT'S HAPPENING? You have changed the default directory to **POLYSCI**, which is under the root directory. Using the relative path, you are going to create one more subdirectory, **FRANCE**, under **POLYSCI**. Remember, you are in **POLYSCI** under the root on the DATA disk, so all you need to use is a relative path name—relative to where you are.

Step 7 Key in the following: A:\POLYSCI>**MD FRANCE** Enter

Step 8 Key in the following: A:\POLYSCI>**DIR** Enter

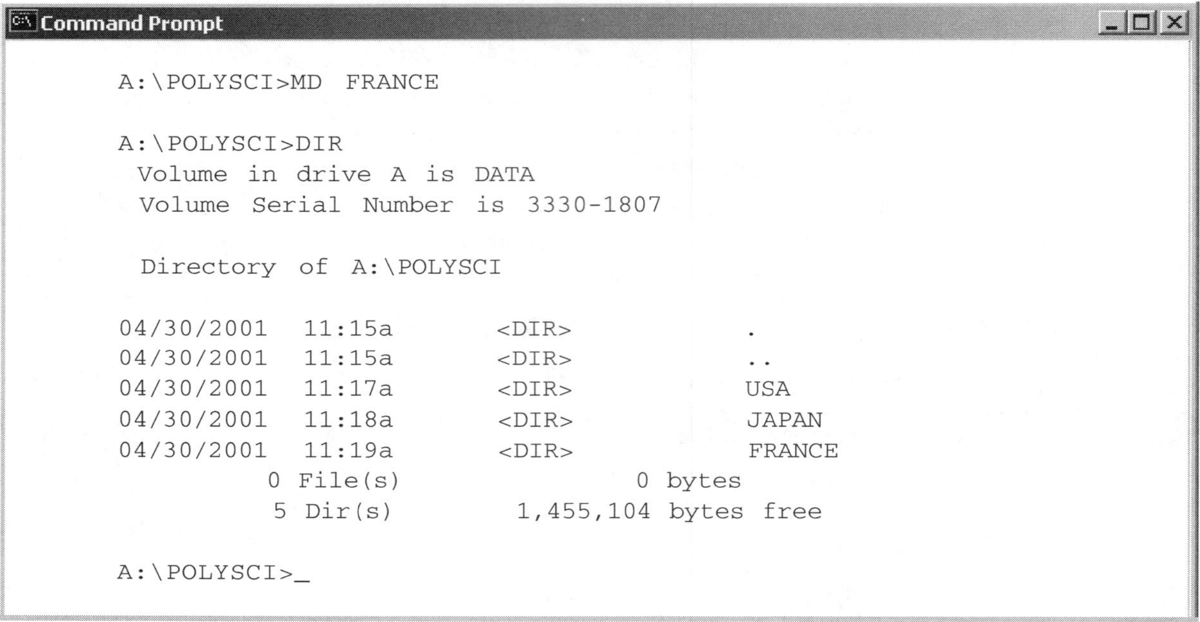

WHAT'S HAPPENING? You needed only to key in **FRANCE**. The path was assumed from the position relative to where you were. In other words, as the current directory displayed, **A:\POLYSCI** was where the new directory **FRANCE** was added. Because you gave no other path in your command, the default drive and directory were assumed.

Step 9 Key in the following: A:\POLYSCI>**MD \MEXICO** Enter

Step 10 Key in the following: A:\POLYSCI>**DIR** Enter

Command Prompt

```
A:\POLYSCI>MD \MEXICO

A:\POLYSCI>DIR
 Volume in drive A is DATA
 Volume Serial Number is 3330-1807
```

```
 Directory of A:\POLYSCI

04/30/2001  11:15a      <DIR>          .
04/30/2001  11:15a      <DIR>          ..
04/30/2001  11:17a      <DIR>          USA
04/30/2001  11:18a      <DIR>          JAPAN
04/30/2001  11:19a      <DIR>          FRANCE
          0 File(s)              0 bytes
          5 Dir(s)       1,454,592 bytes free

A:\POLYSCI>_
```

You created the subdirectory **MEXICO**, but where is it? Here is a common mistake users make. When you keyed in **\MEXICO**, you were keying in an absolute path. Remember, the first backslash always means the root. You created the directory called **MEXICO** under the root (\), not under **POLYSCI**. The term *first backslash* can be misleading. In the path statement **POLYSCI\USA**, some users would think that the first backslash is the one separating **POLYSCI** from **USA**. This is not true. You are separating **POLYSCI** from **USA**; hence, this backslash is a delimiter. The first backslash is the one that begins any path statement such as **\POLYSCI\USA**. The backslash preceding **POLYSCI** is the first backslash.

Step 11 Key in the following: A:\POLYSCI>**DIR **Enter

```
Command Prompt
A:\POLYSCI>DIR \
 Volume in drive A is DATA
 Volume Serial Number is 3330-1807

 Directory of A:\

04/30/2001  11:15a      <DIR>          POLYSCI
04/30/2001  11:15a      <DIR>          PHYSED
04/30/2001  11:20a      <DIR>          MEXICO
          0 File(s)              0 bytes
          3 Dir(s)       1,454,592 bytes free

A:\POLYSCI>_
```

By keying in **DIR **, you asked to look at the root directory. As you can see, looking at the screen display of the DATA disk, **MEXICO** is under the root directory. Windows simply followed your instructions. Remember, there are no files in the newly created subdirectories. You have made "rooms" for "furniture." As of now, they are empty. You can create subdirectories wherever you wish as long as the proper path is included. You *must* pay attention to where you are and whether you are keying in an absolute path or a relative path. If you key in an absolute path of the directory you want to create, you will always be correct. If you key in a relative path, you must remember that you will create the subdirectory *relative* to where you are.

Step 12 Key in the following: A:\POLYSCI>**MD \PHYSED\TENNIS** Enter

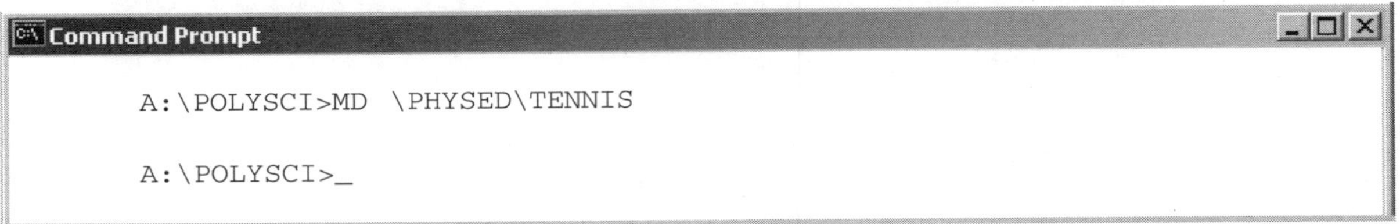

Since the default, or current, directory is **POLYSCI**, you first had to tell the operating system to return to the root (\) and then go to the subdirectory called **PHYSED**. Remember, the relative path only looks down or under **POLYSCI**. Thus, the path is **\PHYSED**. You told the system that under **PHYSED** the name for the new subdirectory was **TENNIS**. The second backslash (**PHYSED\TENNIS**) is a separator or delimiter, separating the first subdirectory name from the second subdirectory name. The first backslash indicates the root. Any other backslash in the line is a delimiter. This is *always* true. The MD command does not change the current or default directory. You can verify that you created the subdirectory **TENNIS** under the subdirectory **\PHYSED** by using the DIR command with the path name.

Step 13 Key in the following: A:\POLYSCI>**DIR \PHYSED** Enter

Command Prompt

```
A:\POLYSCI>DIR \PHYSED
 Volume in drive A is DATA
 Volume Serial Number is 3330-1807

 Directory of A:\PHYSED

04/30/2001  11:15a      <DIR>          .
04/30/2001  11:15a      <DIR>          ..
04/30/2001  11:21a      <DIR>          TENNIS
           0 File(s)              0 bytes
           3 Dir(s)       1,454,080 bytes free

A:\POLYSCI>_
```

The subdirectory **PHYSED** is displayed with the **TENNIS** subdirectory listed. It was very important to key in the backslash in **\PHYSED** in order to tell DIR to go up to the root and then down to the subdirectory **PHYSED**. If you had not included the backslash (\) and had keyed in **DIR PHYSED** only, you would have seen the message "File not found" because DIR would have looked below **POLYSCI** only. **PHYSED** is under the root directory, not under the subdirectory **POLYSCI**.

4.15 KNOWING THE DEFAULT DIRECTORY

Since Windows, and any operating system, always uses default values unless you specify otherwise, knowing the current default is very important. Recognizing the default drive and directory is easy because the screen displays the prompt or disk drive letter, A:\ or

C:\. You know the default directory or subdirectory the same way. The screen displays the full path, but that was not always the case. In versions of DOS prior to DOS 6, the default prompt did not display the path—only the drive. If you were currently in C:\WINNT\SYSTEM32>, all you would have seen was C>—no path indicators at all. You change the way the prompt appears with the PROMPT command. The PROMPT command, issued without any parameters, still returns only the current drive and the greater-than sign (>). It eliminates the path display from the prompt. You also could key in the CD command, which would display the default or current drive*and* the directory you are in, but it is much easier to have the default subdirectory as well as the default drive always displayed in the prompt on the screen, which is the default setup in Windows.

4.16 THE PROMPT COMMAND

The system or command prompt is a letter of the alphabet designating the default or disk drive, followed by the greater-than sign, such as A> or C>. This was the prompt displayed automatically in versions of DOS prior to DOS 6.0. Since the introduction of DOS 6.0, if no prompt is specified, the prompt includes the path as well as the greater-than sign, such as A:\> or C:\>. However, the prompt can be changed to reflect what you want displayed. All you are changing with the PROMPT command is the way the prompt *looks*, not the function of the prompt. PROMPT is an internal command—it is contained in CMD.EXE. The syntax for the PROMPT command is as follows:

```
PROMPT [text]

text     Specifies a new command prompt.
```

The PROMPT command also has some special characters, called ***metastrings***, that mean specific things. When you include one of these metastrings, it establishes a specific value. Metastrings always have the syntax $x where *x* represents any of the values in the following table:

Character	Description
$A	& (ampersand)
$B	| (pipe)
$C	((left parenthesis)
$D	Current date
$E	Escape code (ASCII code 27)
$F	) (right parenthesis)
$G	> (greater-than sign)
$H	Backspace (erases previous character)
$L	< (less-than sign)
$N	Current drive
$P	Current drive and path
$Q	= (equal sign)
$S	Blank space
$T	Current time
$V	Windows 2000 version number
$_	Carriage return and line feed
$$	$ (dollar sign)

The following activity allows you to change the prompt and use text data as well as metastrings. PROMPT, when keyed in without any parameters, returns the displayed prompt to the old default value (A:\>, B:\>, or C:\>) and will include the path.

4.17 ACTIVITY: CHANGING THE PROMPT

Note 1: The DATA disk is in Drive A. The default drive is Drive A. The default subdirectory is POLYSCI. The prompt A:\POLYSCI> is displayed.

Note 2: This uses the letter **G**, not the letter **Q**.

Step 1 Key in the following: A:\POLYSCI>**PROMPT HELLO$G** **Enter**

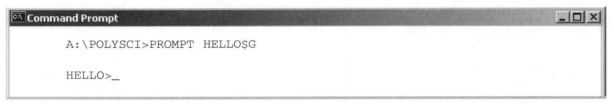

WHAT'S HAPPENING? You changed the way the prompt looks. You no longer see A:\POLYSCI> but, instead, the text you supplied, HELLO. The greater-than sign, **>**, appeared because you keyed in **$G**. When the operating system sees **$G**, it returns the metastring value for G, which is **>**. The function of the prompt has not changed, only its appearance. The new prompt works just as if A>, B>, or C> were displayed. Any command keyed in works the same way.

Step 2 Key in the following: HELLO>**VOL** **Enter**

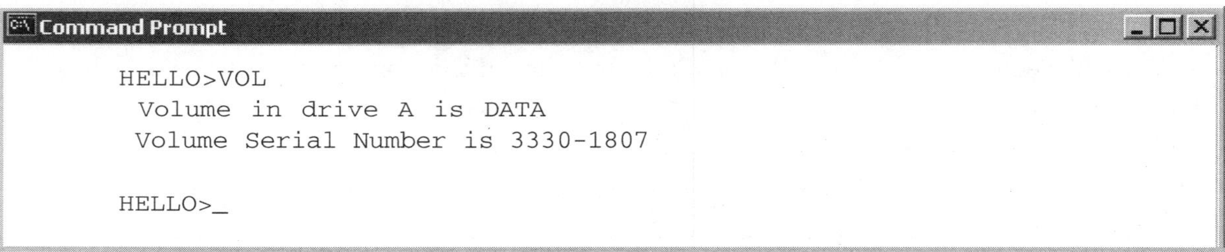

WHAT'S HAPPENING? As you can see, the VOL command works the same way. What if you change drives?

Step 3 Key in the following: HELLO>**C:** **Enter**

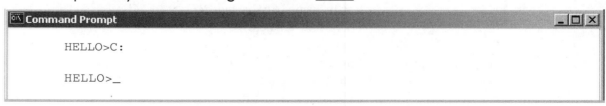

WHAT'S HAPPENING? You changed the default drive to C, but, by looking at the screen, there is no way to tell what the default drive is.

Step 4 Key in the following: HELLO>**VOL** **Enter**

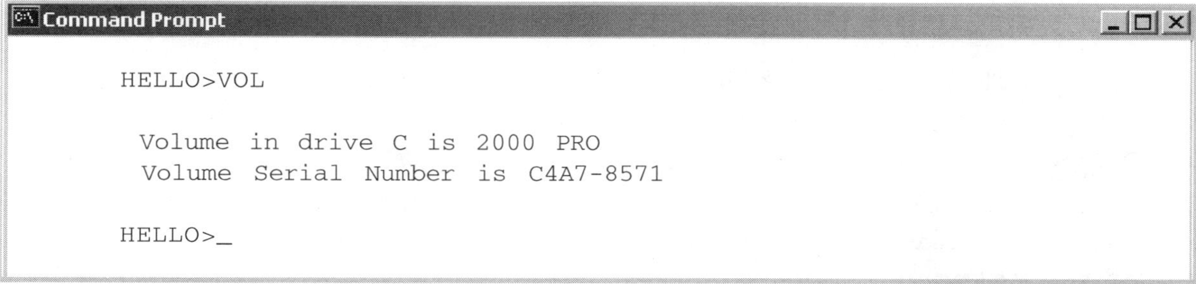

You changed the designated drive. You can see, however, that having the default drive letter displayed on the screen is very important. You can return the prompt to the default value by keying in the command with no parameters.

Step 5 Key in the following: HELLO>**PROMPT** Enter

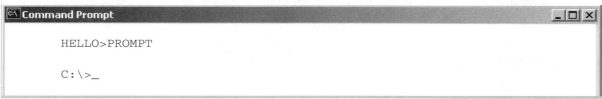

Now you know what drive you are in. You can see the default drive, which is Drive C, displayed in the prompt.

Step 6 Key in the following: C:\>**A:** Enter

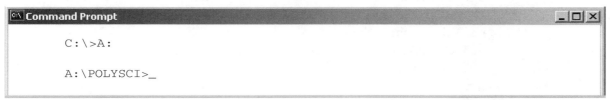

You know what drive you are in, and you know what subdirectory you are in.

4.18 SUBDIRECTORY MARKERS

The single **.** (one period) in a subdirectory is the specific name of the current directory, which is a way to refer to the current subdirectory. The **..** (two periods) is the specific name of the parent directory of the current subdirectory. The parent directory is the one immediately above the current subdirectory. You can use **..** as a shorthand version of the parent directory name to move up the subdirectory tree structure. You can move up the hierarchy because a child always has only one parent. However, you cannot use a shorthand symbol to move down the hierarchy because a parent directory can have many child directories, and the operating system will have no way of knowing which child directory you are referring to.

4.19 ACTIVITY: USING SUBDIRECTORY MARKERS

Note: The DATA disk is in Drive A. The default drive is Drive A. The default subdirectory is **POLYSCI**. The prompt A:\POLYSCI> is displayed.

Step 1 Key in the following: A:\POLYSCI>**CD ..** Enter

Note: With the CD or MD commands, the space after the command (CD) and before the backslash (\) or the directory marker (. or ..) is optional.

WHAT'S HAPPENING? You used **..** to move up to the root directory. The root directory is the parent of the subdirectory **\POLYSCI**.

Step 2 Key in the following: A:\>**MD PHYSED\GOLF** Enter

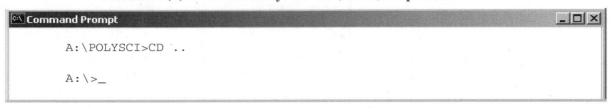

WHAT'S HAPPENING? You created a subdirectory called **GOLF** under the subdirectory called **PHYSED**. Since you were at the root directory of the DATA disk, you needed to include the relative path name, **PHYSED\GOLF**. Had you keyed in **MD \GOLF**, the **GOLF** subdirectory would have been created in the root directory because the root directory is the default directory. However, you do not need to include the path name of **PHYSED** if you change directories and make **PHYSED** the default directory.

Step 3 Key in the following: A:\>**CD PHYSED** Enter

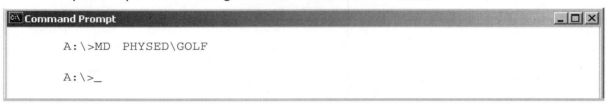

WHAT'S HAPPENING? **PHYSED** is now the default directory. Any activity that occurs will automatically default to this directory, unless otherwise specified. You may use a relative path name.

Step 4 Key in the following: A:\PHYSED>**MD DANCE** Enter

Step 5 Key in the following: A:\PHYSED>**DIR** Enter

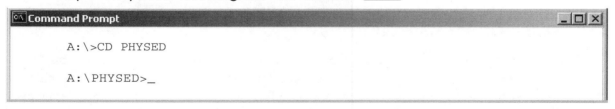

```
 Volume in drive A is DATA
 Volume Serial Number is 3330-1807

 Directory of A:\PHYSED

04/30/2001  11:15a      <DIR>          .
04/30/2001  11:15a      <DIR>          ..
04/30/2001  11:21a      <DIR>          TENNIS
04/30/2001  11:22a      <DIR>          GOLF
04/30/2001  11:22a      <DIR>          DANCE
         0 File(s)              0 bytes
         5 Dir(s)       1,453,056 bytes free

A:\PHYSED>_
```

You used the relative path name. You did not have to key in the drive letter or the first backslash (the root), only the name of the directory **DANCE** that now is under the subdirectory called **PHYSED**.

Step 6 Key in the following: A:\PHYSED>**CD DANCE** Enter

```
Command Prompt

A:\PHYSED>CD  DANCE

A:\PHYSED\DANCE>_
```

You used the relative path to move to the subdirectory **DANCE** under **PHYSED**, which is under the root. You are going to create one more directory under **PHYSED** called **CYCLING**, but you are going to use the subdirectory markers.

Step 7 Key in the following: A:\PHYSED\DANCE>**MD ..\CYCLING** Enter

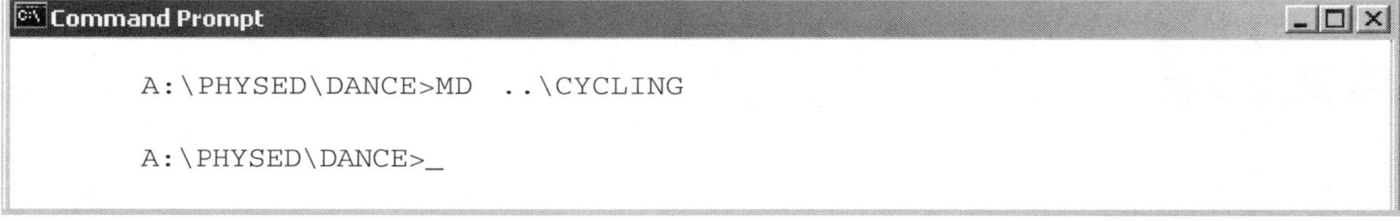

```
Command Prompt

A:\PHYSED\DANCE>MD  ..\CYCLING

A:\PHYSED\DANCE>_
```

You used the markers to move up to the parent directory of DANCE, which is PHYSED, and you created the directory CYCLING in that directory.

Step 8 Key in the following: A:\PHYSED\DANCE>**DIR** Enter

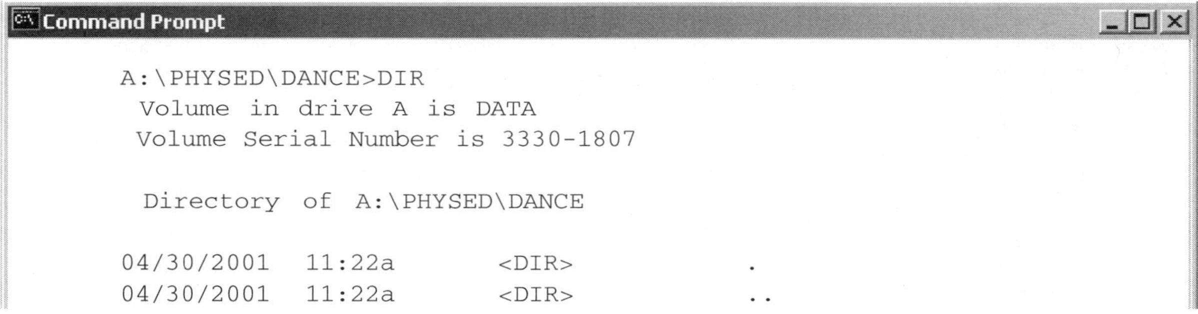

```
Command Prompt

A:\PHYSED\DANCE>DIR
 Volume in drive A is DATA
 Volume Serial Number is 3330-1807

 Directory of A:\PHYSED\DANCE

04/30/2001  11:22a      <DIR>          .
04/30/2001  11:22a      <DIR>          ..
```

```
               0 File(s)              0 bytes
               2 Dir(s)       1,452,544 bytes free

A:\PHYSED\DANCE>_
```

WHAT'S HAPPENING? When you keyed in the DIR command, you were looking at the default directory **DANCE**. **CYCLING** does not appear there because you did not put it there.

Step 9 Key in the following: A:\PHYSED\DANCE>**DIR ..** Enter

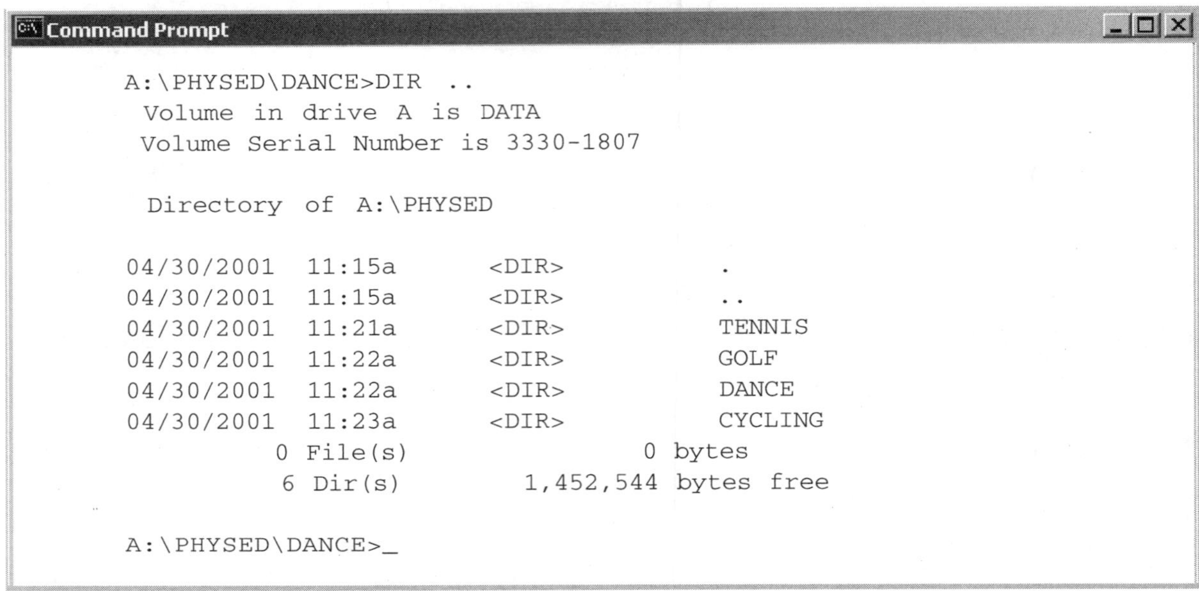

```
Command Prompt

A:\PHYSED\DANCE>DIR ..
 Volume in drive A is DATA
 Volume Serial Number is 3330-1807

 Directory of A:\PHYSED

04/30/2001  11:15a      <DIR>          .
04/30/2001  11:15a      <DIR>          ..
04/30/2001  11:21a      <DIR>          TENNIS
04/30/2001  11:22a      <DIR>          GOLF
04/30/2001  11:22a      <DIR>          DANCE
04/30/2001  11:23a      <DIR>          CYCLING
               0 File(s)              0 bytes
               6 Dir(s)       1,452,544 bytes free

A:\PHYSED\DANCE>_
```

WHAT'S HAPPENING? When you keyed the DIR command followed by **..** you looked at the parent directory of **DANCE**, which was **PHYSED**. **CYCLING**, indeed, appears there.

Step 10 Key in the following: A:\PHYSED\DANCE>**CD ..** Enter

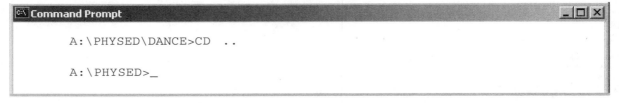

```
Command Prompt

A:\PHYSED\DANCE>CD ..

A:\PHYSED>_
```

WHAT'S HAPPENING? You used the subdirectory marker to move to the parent of **DANCE**, which is **PHYSED**.

Step 11 Key in the following: A:\PHYSED>**CD** Enter

```
Command Prompt

A:\PHYSED>CD\

A:\>_
```

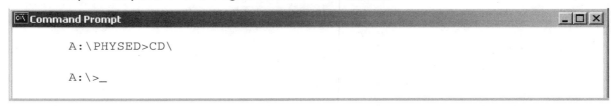

You moved to the root directory of the DATA disk. (You did not use a space between CD and \, as you did in the prior example; the space is optional.) Using the command **CD** or **CD ** will always take you to the root directory of the default disk. The following figures demonstrate what the DATA disk now looks like.

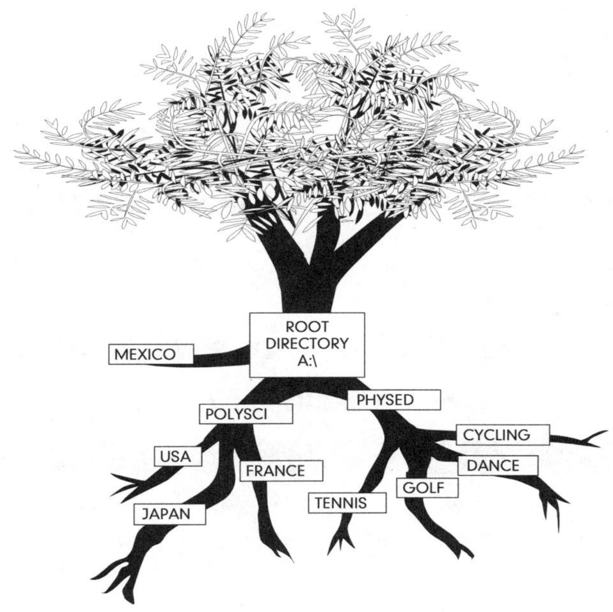

FIGURE 4.8 STRUCTURE OF THE DATA DISK

Another way to illustrate the subdirectory structure pictorially is as follows:

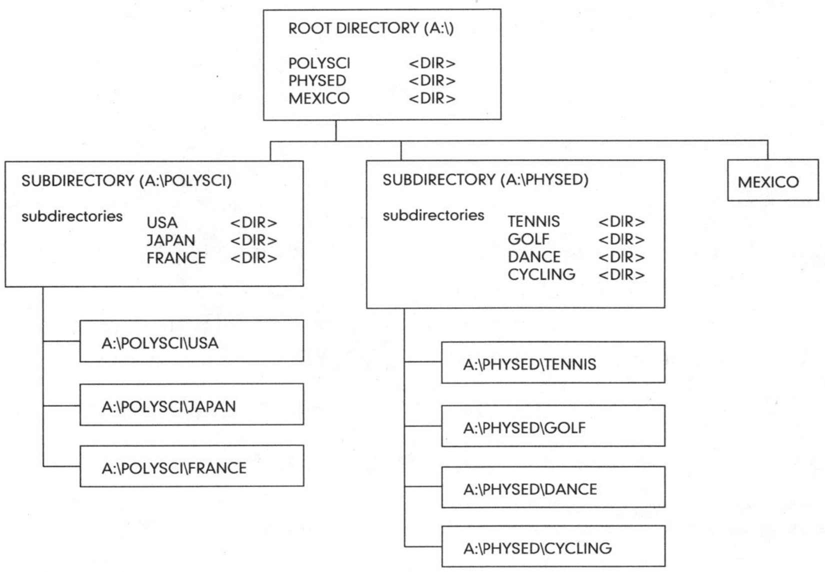

FIGURE 4.9 SUBDIRECTORIES: ANOTHER VIEW

4.20 CHANGING THE NAMES OF DIRECTORIES

Prior to MS-DOS version 6.0, the only way the operating system had to rename a directory was to eliminate the old directory and create a new one. Beginning with MS-DOS version 6.0, you could use the MOVE command. In the Windows operating system, you can rename a file or a directory from Windows Explorer. To rename a directory from the Command Prompt, you can still use the MOVE command. The syntax of the MOVE command to rename a directory is:

```
To rename a directory:
MOVE [/Y | /-Y] [drive:][path]dirname1 dirname2
```

4.21 ACTIVITY: USING MOVE TO RENAME A DIRECTORY

Note: The DATA disk is in Drive A. A:\> is displayed as the default drive and the default directory.

Step 1 Key in the following: A:\>**MOVE PHYSED GYM** Enter

Step 2 Key in the following: A:\>**DIR** Enter

```
Command Prompt

A:\>MOVE PHYSED GYM
          1 file(s) moved.

A:\>DIR
 Volume in drive A is DATA
 Volume Serial Number is 3330-1807

 Directory of A:\

04/30/2001  11:15a      <DIR>          POLYSCI
04/30/2001  11:15a      <DIR>          GYM
04/30/2001  11:20a      <DIR>          MEXICO
           0 File(s)              0 bytes
           3 Dir(s)       1,452,544 bytes free

A:\>_
```

WHAT'S HAPPENING? You used the MOVE command to change the name of the **PHYSED** directory to **GYM**. You got a confirmation message on the screen that the renaming process was successful. You then used DIR to confirm that the directory name was changed. Indeed, **PHYSED** is no longer there, but **GYM** is.

Step 3 Key in the following: A:\>**MOVE GYM\CYCLING GYM\BIKING** Enter

Step 4 Key in the following: A:\>**DIR GYM** Enter

```
Command Prompt

A:\>MOVE GYM\CYCLING GYM\BIKING
          1 file(s) moved.
```

```
A:\>DIR GYM
 Volume in drive A is DATA
 Volume Serial Number is 3330-1807

 Directory of A:\GYM

04/30/2001  11:15a      <DIR>          .
04/30/2001  11:15a      <DIR>          ..
04/30/2001  11:21a      <DIR>          TENNIS
04/30/2001  11:22a      <DIR>          GOLF
04/30/2001  11:22a      <DIR>          DANCE
04/30/2001  11:23a      <DIR>          BIKING
          0 File(s)              0 bytes
          6 Dir(s)       1,452,544 bytes free

A:\>_
```

You used the MOVE command to change the name of the **CYCLING** directory under **GYM** to **BIKING**. Although the message says **1 file(s) moved**, you actually renamed the directory. As long as you give the correct path name, either absolute or relative, you can be anywhere and rename a directory. You got a confirmation message on the screen that the renaming process was successful. You then used DIR to confirm the name change. Indeed, **CYCLING** is no longer there, but **BIKING** is.

4.22 REMOVING DIRECTORIES

In the same way a disk can be cluttered with files, so can it be cluttered with subdirectories. Removing subdirectories requires a special command, the remove directory command (RD or RMDIR). As with CD and CHDIR, RD and RMDIR are exactly the same. RD is used because it requires fewer keystrokes. You cannot use the RD command to delete a directory that contains hidden or system files. Using it alone, without parameters, limits its use to empty subdirectories. In addition, you can never remove the default directory—the current directory. In order to remove a subdirectory, you must be in another directory. Furthermore, since you created the directories from the top down, you must remove them from the bottom up. This means using RD one directory at a time unless you use the /S parameter. The /S parameter allows you to traverse the directory tree from the top down. You cannot use wildcards with RD. The command syntax is:

```
Removes (deletes) a directory.

RMDIR [/S] [/Q] [drive:]path
RD  [/S]  [/Q]  [drive:]path

    /S     Removes all directories and files in the specified directory
           in addition to the directory itself. Used to remove a directory tree.

    /Q     Quiet mode, do not ask if ok to remove a directory tree with /S
```

If you do not include the drive designator, the default drive will be used. The remove directory command will not remove the directory you are currently in (the default directory), nor can it ever remove the root directory.

4.23 ACTIVITY: USING THE RD COMMAND

Note: The DATA disk is in Drive A. A:\> is displayed as the default drive and the default directory.

Step 1 Key in the following: A:\>**RD MEXICO** Enter

Step 2 Key in the following: A:\>**DIR** Enter

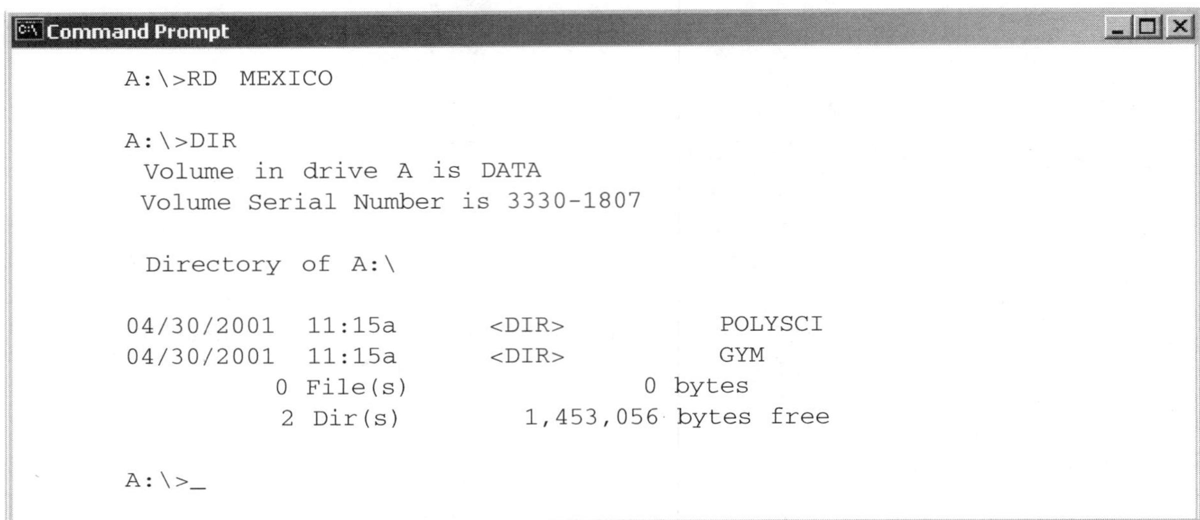

What's Happening? You, indeed, removed the directory called **MEXICO** from the root directory of the DATA disk.

Step 3 Key in the following: A:\>**CD POLYSCI\JAPAN** Enter

Step 4 Key in the following: A:\POLYSCI\JAPAN>**RD JAPAN** Enter

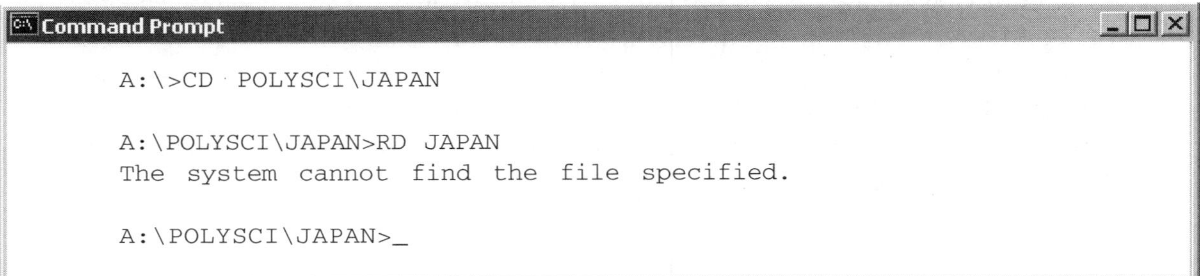

Command Prompt
A:\>CD POLYSCI\JAPAN
A:\POLYSCI\JAPAN>RD JAPAN
The system cannot find the file specified.
A:\POLYSCI\JAPAN>_

What's Happening? RD did not remove the directory **\POLYSCI\JAPAN**. You got an error message. In this case, the path is valid. **JAPAN** is a directory. A directory is simply a special type of file. But the OS is looking for a directory (file) named **JAPAN** in the current directory. There is no directory by that name. You cannot remove a directory you are in. RD will never remove the default directory. Remember, the root directory can also never be removed.

Step 5 Key in the following: A:\POLYSCI\JAPAN>**CD ..** Enter

Step 6 Key in the following: A:\POLYSCI>**DIR** Enter

Step 7 Key in the following: A:\POLYSCI>**RD JAPAN** Enter

Step 8 Key in the following: A:\POLYSCI>**DIR** Enter

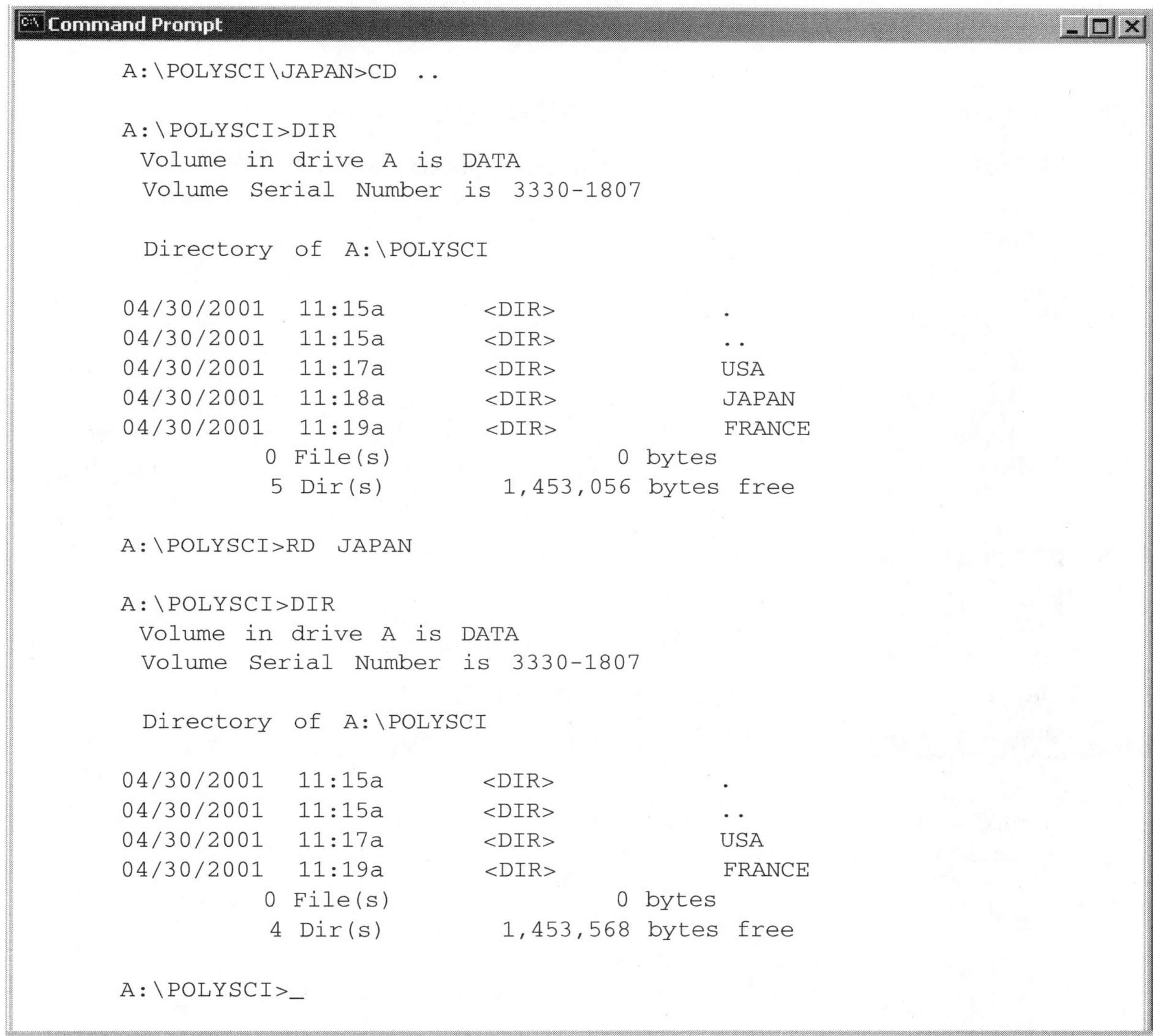

```
Command Prompt

A:\POLYSCI\JAPAN>CD ..

A:\POLYSCI>DIR
 Volume in drive A is DATA
 Volume Serial Number is 3330-1807

 Directory of A:\POLYSCI

04/30/2001  11:15a      <DIR>          .
04/30/2001  11:15a      <DIR>          ..
04/30/2001  11:17a      <DIR>          USA
04/30/2001  11:18a      <DIR>          JAPAN
04/30/2001  11:19a      <DIR>          FRANCE
          0 File(s)              0 bytes
          5 Dir(s)       1,453,056 bytes free

A:\POLYSCI>RD JAPAN

A:\POLYSCI>DIR
 Volume in drive A is DATA
 Volume Serial Number is 3330-1807

 Directory of A:\POLYSCI

04/30/2001  11:15a      <DIR>          .
04/30/2001  11:15a      <DIR>          ..
04/30/2001  11:17a      <DIR>          USA
04/30/2001  11:19a      <DIR>          FRANCE
          0 File(s)              0 bytes
          4 Dir(s)       1,453,568 bytes free

A:\POLYSCI>_
```

WHAT'S HAPPENING? You moved to the parent of **JAPAN**, which is **POLYSCI**. You used the DIR command to see that **JAPAN** was there. You then used the RD command and the DIR command again. The subdirectory entry **JAPAN** was not displayed. You did, indeed, remove it. Remember, you create directories in a hierarchical fashion, top down, and you must remove directories bottom-up using RD without parameters. If **JAPAN** had a subdirectory beneath it, such as **JAPAN\INDUSTRY**, you would have needed to remove the **INDUSTRY** subdirectory before you could remove the **JAPAN** subdirectory.

Step 9 Key in the following: A:\POLYSCI>**CD ** Enter

```
A:\POLYSCI>CD \

A:\>_
```

WHAT'S HAPPENING? You have moved to the root directory of the DATA disk.

4.24 DELETING A DIRECTORY AND ITS SUBDIRECTORIES

The RD command is useful for deleting an empty directory, but what if you want to delete a directory and its contents with a single command? This can be done by using the parameter /S with the RD command. The syntax is as follows:

```
RMDIR [drive:]path [/S] [/Q]
```

or

```
RD [drive:]path [/S] [/Q]
```

The variable /S will remove the specified directory and all subdirectories, including any files. It is used to remove a tree. The variable /Q means to run RD in quiet mode. Adding this variable will make your system delete directories without confirmation.

4.25 ACTIVITY: USING RD WITH THE /S PARAMETER

Note: The DATA disk is in Drive A. The Command Prompt window is open, and A:\> is displayed as the default drive and the default directory.

Step 1 Key in the following: A:\>**DIR GYM /S** Enter

```
A:\>DIR GYM /S
 Volume in drive A is DATA
 Volume Serial Number is 3330-1807

 Directory of A:\GYM

05/02/2001  07:28a      <DIR>          .
05/02/2001  07:28a      <DIR>          ..
05/02/2001  08:19a      <DIR>          TENNIS
05/02/2001  08:54a      <DIR>          GOLF
05/02/2001  08:55a      <DIR>          DANCE
05/02/2001  08:57a      <DIR>          BIKING
               0 File(s)              0 bytes

 Directory of A:\GYM\TENNIS

05/02/2001  08:19a      <DIR>          .
05/02/2001  08:19a      <DIR>          ..
               0 File(s)              0 bytes

 Directory of A:\GYM\GOLF

05/02/2001  08:54a      <DIR>          .
```

```
05/02/2001  08:54a      <DIR>          ..
               0 File(s)              0 bytes

 Directory of A:\GYM\DANCE

05/02/2001  08:55a      <DIR>          .
05/02/2001  08:55a      <DIR>          ..
               0 File(s)              0 bytes

 Directory of A:\GYM\BIKING

05/02/2001  08:57a      <DIR>          .
05/02/2001  08:57a      <DIR>          ..
               0 File(s)              0 bytes

     Total Files Listed:
               0 File(s)              0 bytes
              14 Dir(s)       1,453,568 bytes free

A:\>_
```

WHAT'S HAPPENING? You can see that there are no files in **GYM** or any of its subdirectories. (You may not be able to view the entire listing; some of it may scroll off the screen.) Therefore, there is nothing in **GYM** that you wish to keep.

Step 2 Key in the following: A:\>**RD GYM /S** Enter

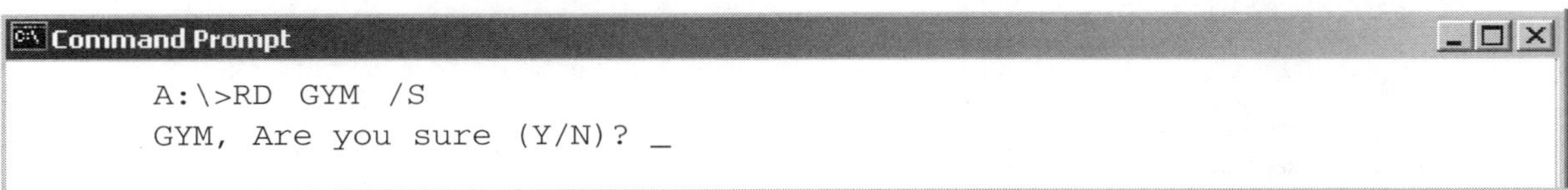

```
Command Prompt
A:\>RD GYM /S
GYM, Are you sure (Y/N)? _
```

WHAT'S HAPPENING? You get a chance to back out of the RD /S command by pressing **N** for "No." In this case, you do want to proceed.

Step 3 Press **Y** Enter

```
Command Prompt
A:\>_
```

WHAT'S HAPPENING? The RD /S command deleted **GYM**. You can use the DIR command to confirm that **GYM** is gone.

Step 4 Key in the following: A:\>**DIR** Enter

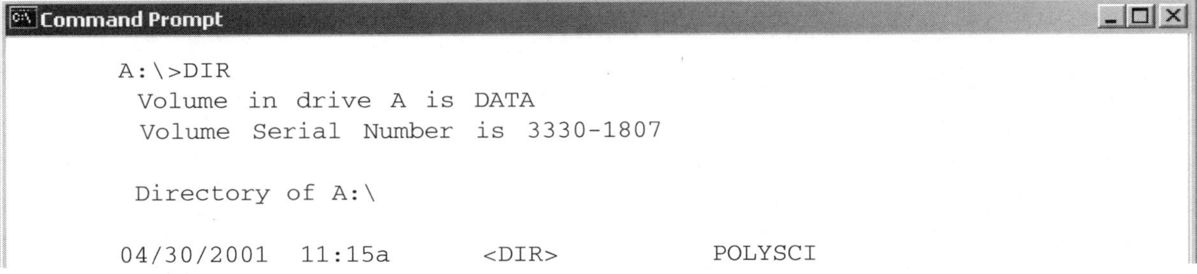

```
Command Prompt
A:\>DIR
 Volume in drive A is DATA
 Volume Serial Number is 3330-1807

 Directory of A:\

04/30/2001  11:15a      <DIR>          POLYSCI
```

```
                 0 File(s)              0 bytes
                 1 Dir(s)       1,456,128 bytes free

A:\>_
```

WHAT'S HAPPENING? You removed **GYM** and all its subdirectories with one command. RD /S is very useful, very fast, very powerful, and *very dangerous*.

4.26 USING MULTIPLE PARAMETERS WITH MD AND RD

You can make or remove more than one directory on the same command line. Both RD and MD allow you to create or remove more than one directory with one command line. In addition, the MD command allows you to create a parent and a child directory with one command. If the parent directory does not exist, the OS will create the child directories and any necessary intermediate directories.

4.27 ACTIVITY: USING MULTIPLE PARAMETERS WITH MD AND RD

Step 1 Key in the following: A:\>**MD FIRST SECOND** Enter

Step 2 Key in the following: A:\>**DIR** Enter

```
Command Prompt

A:\>MD FIRST SECOND

A:\>DIR
 Volume in drive A is DATA
 Volume Serial Number is 3330-1807

 Directory of A:\

04/30/2001  11:15a      <DIR>          POLYSCI
05/27/2001  09:46p      <DIR>          FIRST
05/27/2001  09:46p      <DIR>          SECOND
               0 File(s)              0 bytes
               3 Dir(s)       1,454,592 bytes free

A:\>_
```

WHAT'S HAPPENING? Both subdirectories were created.

Step 3 Key in the following: A:\>**RD FIRST SECOND** Enter

Step 4 Key in the following: A:\>**DIR** Enter

```
Command Prompt

A:\>RD FIRST SECOND

A:\>DIR
 Volume in drive A is DATA
 Volume Serial Number is 3330-1807
```

```
 Directory of A:\

04/30/2001  11:15a       <DIR>          POLYSCI
               0 File(s)              0 bytes
               1 Dir(s)       1,456,128 bytes free

A:\>_
```

WHAT'S HAPPENING? Both subdirectories were removed.

Step 5 Key in the following: A:\>**MD THIS\THAT\WHAT** Enter

Step 6 Key in the following: A:\>**DIR THIS /S** Enter

```
Command Prompt

 Directory of A:\THIS

05/29/2001  08:25a      <DIR>          .
05/29/2001  08:25a      <DIR>          ..
05/29/2001  08:25a      <DIR>          THAT
               0 File(s)              0 bytes

 Directory of A:\THIS\THAT

05/29/2001  08:25a      <DIR>          .
05/29/2001  08:25a      <DIR>          ..
05/29/2001  08:25a       <DIR>         WHAT
               0 File(s)              0 bytes

 Directory of A:\THIS\THAT\WHAT

05/29/2001  08:25a      <DIR>          .
05/29/2001  08:25a      <DIR>          ..
               0 File(s)              0 bytes

     Total Files Listed:
               0 File(s)              0 bytes
               8 Dir(s)       1,454,592 bytes free

A:\>_
```

WHAT'S HAPPENING? When you created the child directory **WHAT**, it had no existing parent directories (**THIS\THAT**). Since **THIS** and **THAT** had to exist before WHAT could be created, the OS created them for you.

Step 7 Key in the following: A:\>**RD /S /Q THIS** Enter

Step 8 Key in A:\>**DIR** Enter

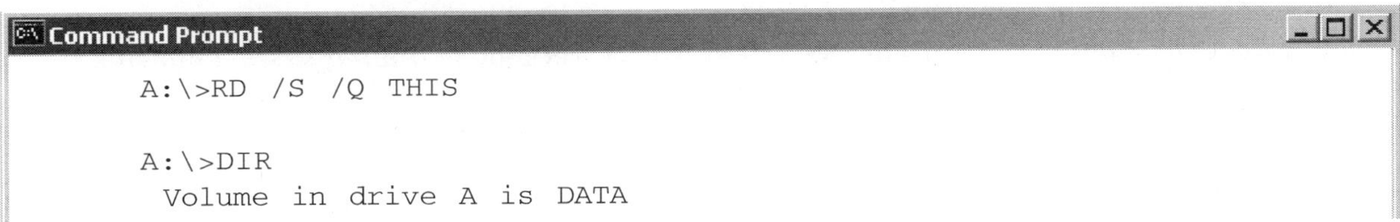

```
Command Prompt

A:\>RD /S /Q THIS

A:\>DIR
 Volume in drive A is DATA
```

```
 Volume Serial Number is 3330-1807

 Directory of A:\

04/30/2001  11:15a      <DIR>          POLYSCI
               0 File(s)              0 bytes
               1 Dir(s)       1,456,128 bytes free

A:\>_
```

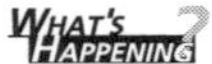

You used the /S parameter to remove the entire directory structure for the **THIS** directory. In addition, you used the /Q parameter so that you would not be prompted for confirmation of the deletion of the directories.

4.28 UNDERSTANDING THE PATH COMMAND

You have, so far, changed the current or default subdirectory using the CD command, which works well for locating various data files. In addition, in this chapter you executed two application programs, HPB and Thinker. You changed to the subdirectory where program files were located. You needed to do this in order to execute or run the programs.

The process of executing a program is simple and always the same. You key in the file name of the program, and the operating system looks for the file first in memory. If you keyed in DIR, for example, that program is in memory, and, since it is an internal program, the OS would look no further. If you keyed in THINK, it would not find it in memory, and the operating system would look for the file only in the current default drive and directory. First, it would look for THINK.COM. If no file by that name existed, it would look for THINK.EXE. If it found no file by that name, its last search would be for THINK.BAT. If it found no file by any of those names, it would return an error message. That would be the operating system's way of telling you it could not find a file by one of those names in the current drive or directory.

If the OS found a file with the correct name, as it did with THINK.EXE, it would take a copy of the file, place it in memory, and turn control over to that application program. A program is executed at the command prompt in this way. In the Windows GUI, you double-click the icon or choose an item off a menu to execute a program. However, the GUI is just a pretty face that does *exactly* what you did from the command prompt. When you work from the Windows interface, the Windows operating system first looks in memory and then on the disk for the program. The only difference is that when a program is installed, it tells the Windows operating system where it is being installed and what the path to the program is. Windows then keeps track of the location of the file. If there were an error in installation or a program file was somehow moved, Windows would not be able to execute the program because the path would be incorrect. Windows has a hard time fixing its mistakes; that is why managing Windows at the system level is so important.

The operating system's search for the correct file is limited to the following file extensions in the order listed:

Extension	Meaning
.COM	Command file
.EXE	Executable file
.BAT	Batch file
.CMD	Command script file
.VB	VBScript file (Visual Basic)
.VBE	VBScript Encoded Script file (Visual Basic)
.JS	JScript file (JavaScript)
.JSE	JScript Encoded Script file (JavaScript)
.WSF	Windows Script file
.WSH	Windows Script Host Settings file

If the command interpreter does not find any of these in your default drive and directory, it then searches your search path as set in the PATH statement, in the file extension order listed above. If your file name does not meet any of these criteria, then you see the error message, "Filename is not recognized as an internal or external command, operable program or batch file."

These are the only file extensions that indicate programs and are sometimes called ***executables***. You have previously executed programs. You have also used external commands such as FORMAT, DISKCOPY, and MOVE, which, being external commands, are also programs stored as files with either a .COM or .EXE file extension. These are examples of the system's utility files. They are just programs you want to execute (executables). When you use these programs, you do not have to key in C: and then CD\WINNT\SYSTEM32 in order to execute them.

Why, then, when the root of the directory was the default drive and default directory, did those commands work? The files were not on the DATA disk. Based on this information, since those files were not in the default drive and subdirectory, you should have seen an error message. Why didn't this happen? Because of the PATH command.

The PATH command sets a ***search path*** to other drives and directories. This command tells the system what other drives and directories you want it to look in for a program file not in the current drive or directory. The PATH command looks only for program files that can be executed. All this means is that, when you key in a command and you have set the path, the operating system will search for the program first in memory, second in the current directory, and then in the subdirectories you have specified with the PATH command. When it finds the program, it will load and execute it. You can set the path for command files to another subdirectory or disk drive. In the Windows operating system, the default PATH includes the subdirectory where the system utility files are located—C:\WINNT\SYSTEM32. The command syntax for the path command is as follows:

```
PATH [[drive:]path[;...][;%PATH%]]
PATH ;

Type PATH ; to clear all search-path settings and direct cmd.exe to
search only in the current directory.
Type PATH without parameters to display the current path.
Including %PATH% in the new path setting causes the old path to be
appended to the new setting.
```

PATH is the command. PATH with no parameters displays the current path. Choosing a *drive*: indicates which drive designator you want the path to follow. If you omit the drive designator, the default drive will be used. You can have more than one subdirectory in the search path by using the semicolon (;) between each path element (with no spaces between the semicolon and the paths). The semicolon (;) used as the only parameter, without the drive or path, cancels any paths you have set. The current path is represented by %PATH%.

4.29 ACTIVITY: USING THE PATH COMMAND

CAUTION!!! DO NOT DO THIS ACTIVITY IF YOU ARE ON A NETWORK UNLESS INSTRUCTED TO DO SO.

Note: The DATA disk is in Drive A. A:\> is displayed as the default drive and the default directory.

Step 1 Key in the following: A:\>**PATH > HOLDPATH.BAT** Enter

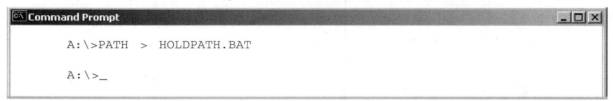

You have captured the current path and placed it in a batch file called **HOLDPATH.BAT**. Doing activities with the PATH command will destroy the path that is set up in your lab environment. By placing the current path in a batch file, you will be able to return to the proper path when the activities are done. Batch files will be discussed later in this text.

Step 2 Key in the following: A:\>**DIR** Enter

Command Prompt

```
A:\>DIR
 Volume in drive A is DATA
 Volume Serial Number is 3330-1807

 Directory of A:\
```

```
04/30/2001  11:15a      <DIR>          POLYSCI
05/29/2001  11:30a                  56 HOLDPATH.BAT

         1 File(s)             36 bytes
         1 Dir(s)       1,455,616 bytes free

A:\>_
```

WHAT'S HAPPENING? You now have the file **HOLDPATH.BAT** on the root of the DATA disk. With this file, you will later be able to return the path to where it was set by your lab administrator.

Step 3 Key in the following: A:\>**PATH** Enter

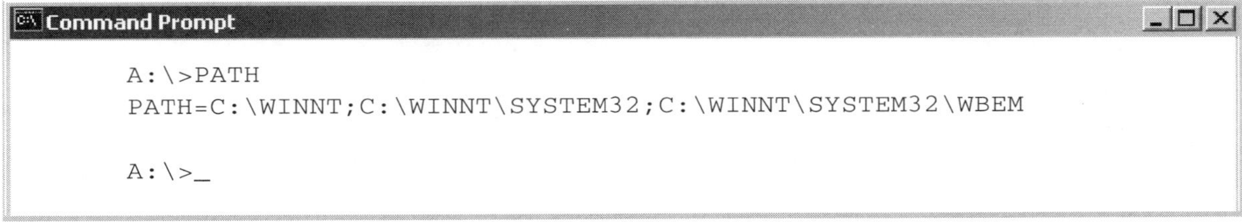

```
A:\>PATH
PATH=C:\WINNT;C:\WINNT\SYSTEM32;C:\WINNT\SYSTEM32\WBEM

A:\>_
```

WHAT'S HAPPENING? You have displayed the current search path. Your display may be different depending on what programs you have on your disk and their locations.

Step 4 Note that a semicolon follows the command PATH in this step.
Key in the following: A:\>**PATH;** Enter

Step 5 Key in the following: A:\>**PATH** Enter

```
A:\>PATH;

A:\>PATH
PATH=(null)

A:\>_
```

WHAT'S HAPPENING? By using the semicolon (;) following the command word PATH, you eliminated all possible existing search paths. The second PATH command, with no parameters, showed that there is now no path set.

Step 6 Key in the following: A:\>**PATH C:\WINNT\SYSTEM32** Enter

Note: Remember, if the system utility programs are in a subdirectory on the hard disk other than **C:\WINNT\SYSTEM32**, you must key in the appropriate path name. Refer to your Configuration Table in Chapter 1.6.

Step 7 Key in the following: A:\>**PATH** Enter

```
Command Prompt

A:\>PATH C:\WINNT\SYSTEM32

A:\>PATH
```

```
PATH=C:\WINNT\SYSTEM32

A:\>_
```

When you first keyed in the **PATH C:\WINNT\SYSTEM32** command, it appeared that nothing happened, but something did. The second PATH command shows that you have set a path the operating system will search. If it does not find a command (file) in the default drive and subdirectory, in this case A:\, it will go to the path set, the subdirectory called **\WINNT\SYSTEM32** under the root directory of Drive C.

Step 8 Key in the following: A:\>**THINK** **Enter**

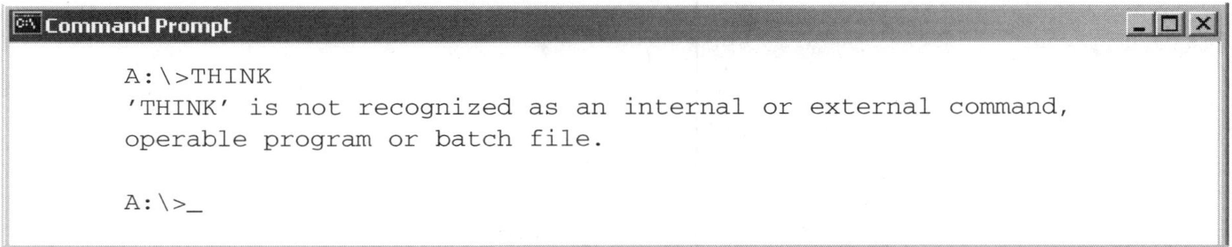

Command Prompt
A:\>THINK
'THINK' is not recognized as an internal or external command,
operable program or batch file.
A:\>_

WHAT'S HAPPENING?

Thinker is an application program, but it is not located in the root of the A drive nor in the **\WINNT\SYSTEM32** subdirectory. So, even though the search path is set, it is not set to the directory that holds the **THINK.EXE** file. In the beginning of this chapter, you found that this program was located in the **C:\WINDOSBK\FINANCE** directory and was called **THINK.EXE**. You had to change drives and directories in order to execute the program. If you do not want to change the default drive and subdirectory to use this program, you can use the PATH command instead.

Step 9 Key in the following: A:\>**PATH C:\WINDOSBK\FINANCE** **Enter**

Step 10 Key in the following: A:\>**PATH** **Enter**

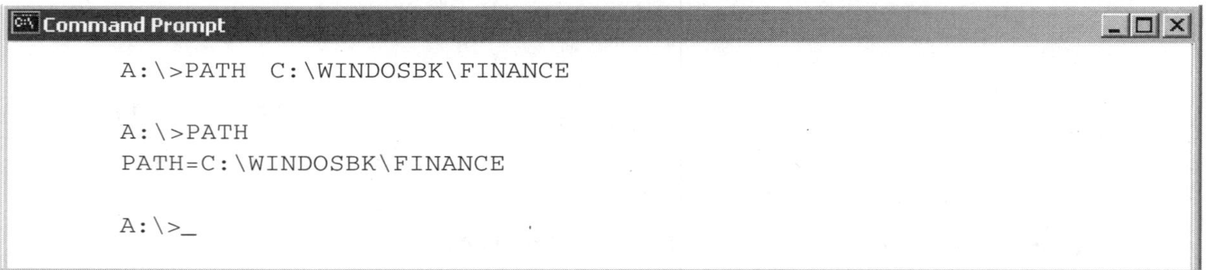

You set the search path to the **C:\WINDOSBK\FINANCE** subdirectory on the hard disk, but, by doing so, you canceled the path to the **C:\WINNT\SYSTEM32** subdirectory. In this example, you wanted to keep both search paths. In other words, instead of just searching the default drive and directory for the necessary program, you wanted the operating system to continue the search in the **C:\WINNT\SYSTEM32** subdirectory and then to look in the **C:\WINDOSBK\FINANCE** directory. To instruct the operating system to do these two tasks, you have to include all the directories you want searched in your PATH command and separate the directories with a semi-colon.

Step 11 Key in the following:
A:\>**PATH C:\WINNT\SYSTEM32;C:\WINDOSBK\FINANCE** Enter

Step 12 Key in the following: A:\>**PATH** Enter

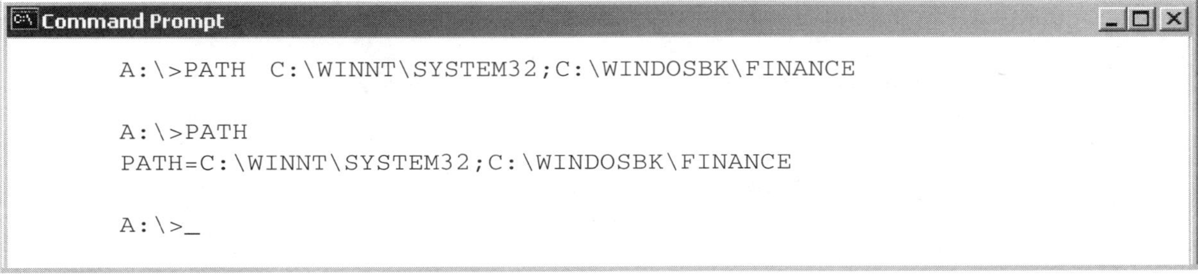

WHAT'S HAPPENING? You set the path so that, if the operating system does not find the program you wish to execute in memory or in the default drive and subdirectory (A:\), it next will look in the **C:\WINNT\SYSTEM32** directory on the hard disk. If it does not find the file there, it will look on the hard disk in the subdirectory **C:\WINDOSBK\FINANCE**.

Step 13 Key in the following: A:\>**THINK** Enter

Step 14 Press Enter

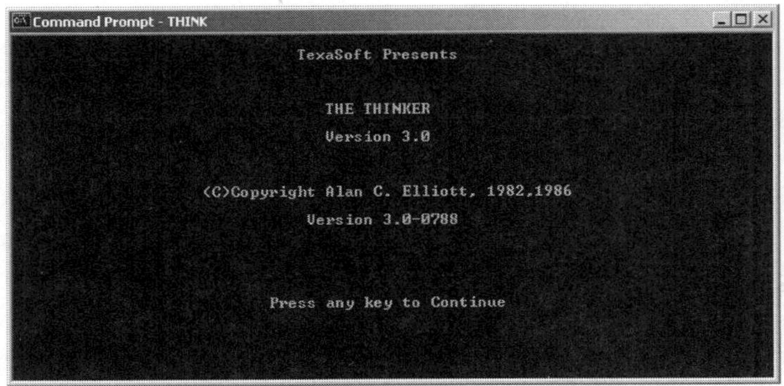

WHAT'S HAPPENING? The operating system still did not find the **THINK.EXE** file in the default directory of the DATA disk. However, since you set the search path to the **C:\WINNT\SYSTEM32** subdirectory, it looked there, but **THINK.EXE** was not there either. The search continued on to **C:\WINDOSBK\FINANCE** where the Thinker program, **THINK.EXE**, is located. Once the operating system found the program file, it loaded it.

Step 15 Press Enter. Press **/**.

Step 16 Press **Q**.

Step 17 Press **Y**.

WHAT'S HAPPENING? You are back at the system level. Now you want to return the path to its original setting.

Step 18 Key in the following: A:\>**HOLDPATH** Enter

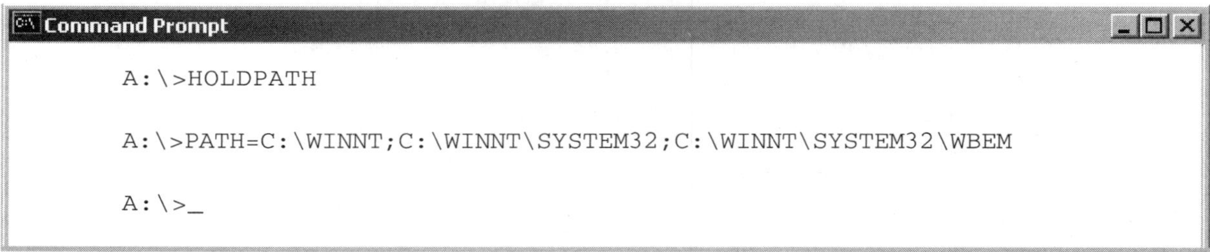

WHAT'S HAPPENING? The PATH has been returned to its original setting. The path is set for the duration of the time the computer is on or until the user changes it. You can now eliminate the **HOLDPATH.BAT** file from the DATA disk.

Step 19 Key in the following. A:\>**DEL HOLDPATH.BAT** Enter

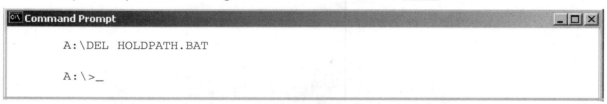

WHAT'S HAPPENING? You have deleted the **HOLDPATH.BAT** file.

Step 20 Execute the Windows shut-down procedure.

CHAPTER SUMMARY

1. Software designed for use with Windows operates in protected mode.
2. When running software created for older versions of DOS or Windows 3.x, Windows operates in real mode.
3. Subdirectories are created to help organize files on a disk as well as to defeat the number-of-files limitation of the root directory imposed by FAT16.
4. Whenever a disk is formatted, one directory is always created. It is called the root directory.
5. MD is an internal command that allows the user to create a subdirectory.
6. Subdirectory-naming conventions follow Windows file-naming conventions. Programs written for previous versions of DOS and Windows follow the "eight-dot-three" file-naming convention.
7. A <DIR> next to a file name indicates that it is a subdirectory.
8. CD is an internal command that, when keyed in by itself, will show the user the current or default directory.

9. CD followed by a directory name will change the current directory to the named directory.
10. CD used with the /D parameter will allow you to change drives at the same time you change directories.
11. When managing subdirectories and file names, you must use the backslash (\) as a delimiter to separate subdirectory and/or file names.
12. You may use either an absolute path name or a relative path name. The absolute path name is the entire subdirectory name or names. The relative path requires only the path name relative to your current directory.
13. The way the prompt looks can be changed using the PROMPT command. The PROMPT command followed by a text string will show that text.
14. The PROMPT command has metastrings. When included following the PROMPT command, the metastrings will return a value. For instance, the metastrings PG will set the prompt to display the default drive and subdirectory. To return the prompt to the default value, key in PROMPT with no parameters.
15. Subdirectory markers, also called dot notation, are shortcuts to using subdirectories. The single dot (.) represents the current directory itself. The double dot (..) represents the name of the parent directory.
16. You can move up the tree with subdirectory markers, but not down the tree.
17. The MOVE command allows you to rename subdirectories.
18. RD is an internal command that allows users to eliminate subdirectories.
19. Subdirectories must be empty of files before you can use the RD command without parameters.
20. The root directory can never be eliminated.
21. RD used with the /S parameter allows you to remove an entire directory, including all its files and subdirectories, with one command.
22. PATH is an internal command that allows you to tell the operating system on what disk and in what subdirectory to search for command files.
23. PATH keyed in by itself will display the current path.
24. PATH keyed in with a semicolon following it will cancel the path.

KEY TERMS

absolute path
child directory
current directory
device driver
dot (.)
dot notation
double dot (..)
executable
hierarchical structure
legacy software
metastring
parent directory
path
protected mode
real mode
relative path
root directory
search path
subdirectory marker
tree structure

DISCUSSION QUESTIONS

1. List three of the major categories of application software and briefly explain their functions.
2. What is the purpose and function of a program file (application program)?

3. Explain the purpose and function of the operating system when working with program files and data files.
4. Briefly explain the difference between real-mode and protected-mode operation.
5. Explain documentation, update notices, and technical support.
6. What file extensions indicate an executable program?
7. What is the purpose and function of the root directory? What symbol is used to represent the root directory?
8. What is a subdirectory?
9. Why would you want to create a subdirectory?
10. What is a parent directory?
11. Explain the purpose and function of three directory management commands.
12. Give the syntax for creating a subdirectory.
13. Give the syntax for the CD command.
14. What is the difference between an absolute path and a relative path?
15. If you wanted to create a subdirectory called JAIL under the subdirectory called COURT on Drive A:, would you get the same result by keying in either MD A:\COURT\JAIL or MD A:\JAIL? Why or why not?
16. What are subdirectory markers? How can they be used?
17. What are metastrings?
18. How can you return the prompt to the default value? Would you want to? Why or why not?
19. Explain the purpose and function of the MOVE command. Explain each part of the syntax.
20. Why will the RD command without parameters not remove a directory if there is a file in it?
21. What steps must be followed to remove a directory with RD?
22. What is the purpose and function of the PATH command?
23. How can you undo the path?
24. How can you set a multiple search path?
25. What is the difference between the path to a file and using the PATH command?

TRUE/FALSE QUESTIONS

For each question, circle the letter T if the statement is true and the letter F if the statement is false.

T F 1. A subdirectory can hold a maximum of 112 files.

T F 2. The RD /S command deletes a specified directory structure and all the files and subdirectories beneath it.

T F 3. The MOVE command allows you to delete subdirectories.

T F 4. If the default directory is the root directory, you do not need to include the path name for creating a new subdirectory under a subdirectory called **MEDIA**.

T F 5. The double dot is a shorthand name for the parent directory.

COMPLETION QUESTIONS

Write the correct answer in each blank space.

6. Two files can have the same name on the same disk so long as they are in ________ subdirectories.
7. When using MOVE to rename a directory, you need to use two parameters: the old directory name and the ________ directory name.
8. If the current default subdirectory is MEDIA, the directory above MEDIA is known as the ________ directory.
9. When looking at a directory display, you can identify a subdirectory because the name appears with ________ by it.
10. To place the current path in a batch file called HOLDPATH.BAT, you would key in ____________________.

MULTIPLE CHOICE QUESTIONS

For each question, write the letter for the correct answer in the blank space.

11. Formatting a floppy disk automatically creates
    a. subdirectories.
    b. a root directory.
    c. command files.
    d. none of the above
12. A subdirectory is created by using the
    a. MD command.
    b. CD command.
    c. MAKEDIR command.
    d. both a and c
13. When you create subdirectories under existing subdirectories,
    a. omitting the drive designator or path name means that the operating system will perform the task using the default values.
    b. omitting the new subdirectory name means that the operating system will name the new subdirectory after its parent directory.
    c. you must return to the root directory.
    d. no more than 32 subdirectories may be contained in any one subdirectory.
14. One of the major purposes in creating subdirectories is to be able to
    a. use the DIR command.
    b. use relative and absolute paths.
    c. group files together logically.
    d. none of the above
15. When you create subdirectories, you are allowed
    a. eight characters in the subdirectory name.
    b. to use the same naming conventions as for files.
    c. to save as many files as the disk space will allow.
    d. both b and c

WRITING COMMANDS

Write the correct steps or commands to perform the required action as if you were at the computer. The prompt will indicate the default drive and directory. Use the relative path whenever possible.

16. Locate the file called **BETTE.TXT** in the **ARCHIE** directory that is under **COMICS**.

    `A:\COMICS>`

17. Display the name of the current directory.

    `A:\TEXT>`

18. Change the prompt to = followed by the greater-than sign.

    `A:\>`

19. Locate the file called **FISH.FIL** in the parent directory of the default directory using subdirectory markers.

    `C:\ZOO\AQUARIUM>`

20. Set up a search path that will look in the root directory of Drive C, and then the **\BOOK** directory also located on Drive C.

    `A:\TEXT>`

APPLICATION ASSIGNMENTS

Note 1: Remember, if you are logged on to a network, do not use the PATH command without instructions and/or assistance from your lab administrator.

Note 2: You will format a new disk, the APPLICATION disk.

CAUTION!!! YOU WILL NOT USE THE DATA DISK. THE DATA DISK WILL BE USED ONLY FOR THE CHAPTER ACTIVITIES. YOU WILL FORMAT A NEW DISK, CALLED THE APPLICATION DISK, AND THIS DISK WILL BE USED FOR THE APPLICATION ASSIGNMENTS.

Note 3: The homework problems will use Drive A as the drive where the APPLICATION disk is located.

Note 4: The homework problems will use the **WINNT\SYSTEM32** subdirectory as the directory where the operating system utility files are located. If you have a different drive or directory, substitute that drive or directory.

Note 5: Windows is running, and you have shelled out to the Command Prompt window. The visible prompt is C:\>.

PROBLEM SET I—AT THE COMPUTER

PROBLEM A

A-a **_Do not use the DATA disk for these application problems._**

A-b Write your name and the word "APPLICATION" on a label for a blank disk or a disk you no longer want; then insert the disk in Drive A. Be *sure* either the disk is blank or you no longer need the data that it contains. Everything on it will be eliminated after you press the **Enter** key.

A-c Key in the following: C:\>**FORMAT A: /V:APPLICATION** **Enter**

A-d Press **Enter**

A-e When the message appears asking if you wish to format another disk, press **N** **Enter**

A-f Key in the following: C:\>**A:** **Enter**

A-g With the root directory of the APPLICATION disk as the default, use the relative path to create a directory called **NEW** on the APPLICATION disk.

☐ 1. What command did you use to create the directory?
   a. MD NEW
   b. MD C:\NEW
   c. CD NEW
   d. CD C:\NEW

A-h Using the relative path, make **NEW** the default directory.

☐ 2. What command did you use to make NEW the default directory?
   a. MD NEW
   b. MD C:\NEW
   c. CD NEW
   d. CD C:\NEW

A-i Do a directory listing of the default directory.

☐ 3. Look at the directory display. How many bytes do the two directories occupy?
   a. 2,048
   b. 1,024
   c. 512
   d. none of the above

A-j Remove the **NEW** directory.

☐ 4. What command did you execute *first*?
   a. RD NEW
   b. CD NEW
   c. RD \
   d. CD \

PROBLEM B

B-a Change the prompt so it reads only **HELLO THERE**.

5. What command did you use?
   a. PROMPT PG
   b. PROMPT HELLO THERE
   c. PROMPT $HELLO $THERE
   d. none of the above

B-b Key in the following: **PROMPT VG** Enter

6. What word is included in the prompt?
   a. Version
   b. Date
   c. Time
   d. Volume

B-c Key in the following: **PROMPT PG** Enter

PROBLEM C

C-a Get help on the PROMPT command.

7. What symbol will display the = sign in the prompt?
   a. $D
   b. $E
   c. $Q
   d. $T

C-b Key in the following: **PROMPT D_PG** Enter

8. What appears in the prompt?
   a. the current OS version
   b. the current date
   c. the current time
   d. the current volume label

C-c Key in the following: **PROMPT PG** Enter

C-d Key in the following: **CD POLY** Enter

9. What message appears?
   a. Incorrect DOS version.
   b. Invalid subdirectory.
   c. The system cannot find the path specified.
   d. Invalid command.

PROBLEM D

D-a With the root directory of the APPLICATION disk as the default, create a directory called **HISTORY** off the root.

D-b With the root directory of the APPLICATION disk as the default, create two subdirectories under **HISTORY**. One will be called **US**, and the other will be called **EUROPE**.

D-c With the root directory of the APPLICATION disk as the default, create a directory called **OLD** off the root.

D-d Make **OLD** the default directory.

D-e With **OLD** as the default directory, create a subdirectory called **LETTERS** under the **\HISTORY\US** subdirectory.

10. What command did you use?
    a. MD LETTERS
    b. MD HISTORY\LETTERS
    c. MD HISTORY\US\LETTERS
    d. MD \HISTORY\US\LETTERS

D-f With **OLD** as the default directory, remove the subdirectory called **LETTERS** that you just created.

11. The command you used was:
    a. CD LETTERS
    b. CD HISTORY\LETTERS
    c. RD HISTORY\US\LETTERS
    d. RD \HISTORY\US\LETTERS

D-g Use the subdirectory markers to move to the parent directory of **OLD**.

12. The command you used was:
    a. CD ..
    b. CD \
    c. MD..
    d. MD \

13. The parent of OLD is:
    a. HISTORY
    b. LETTERS
    c. the root of the APPLICATION disk—the \
    d. the root of the hard disk—the \

D-h Remove the directory **OLD**.

14. Which of the following command(s) could you have used?
    a. RD OLD
    b. RD \OLD
    c. both a and b
    d. neither a nor b

PROBLEM E

E-a Create a directory called **PHONE** under the root directory of the APPLICATION disk.

E-b With the root directory as the default directory, create two subdirectories under the **PHONE** directory called **BUSINESS** and **PERSONAL**.

15. The command you used to create **PERSONAL** was:
    a. MD PERSONAL
    b. MD \PERSONAL
    c. MD PHONE\PERSONAL or MD \PHONE\PERSONAL
    d. MD PERSONAL\PHONE or MD \PERSONAL\PHONE

E-c Do a directory listing of the **PHONE** directory.

16. How many files and directories are listed?
    a. 0 File(s) 2 Dir(s)
    b. 0 File(s) 4 Dir(s)
    c. 4 File(s) 4 Dir(s)
    d. 2 File(s) 2 Dir(s)

E-d Using the relative path, change the default directory to **PHONE**.

17. The command you used was:
    a. CD PHONE
    b. MD PHONE
    c. RD PHONE

E-e With **PHONE** as the current default directory, use the relative path to change the default directory to **BUSINESS**.

18. The command you used was:
    a. CD \PHONE
    b. CD \BUSINESS
    c. CD BUSINESS
    d. RD BUSINESS

E-f Use the subdirectory markers to move to the parent directory of **BUSINESS**.

19. The command you used was:
    a. CD ..
    b. CD \
    c. MD ..
    d. MD \

20. The parent of **BUSINESS** is:
    a. PERSONAL
    b. PHONE
    c. the root directory of the APPLICATION disk—the \
    d. none of the above

E-g Move to the root directory of the APPLICATION disk.

21. The command you used was:
    a. CD ROOT
    b. CD \..
    c. CD ..\
    d. CD \

PROBLEM F

F-a With the root directory as the default directory, create a directory called **BOOKS** under the root of the APPLICATION disk.

22. Which of the following command(s) could you have used?
    a. MD BOOKS
    b. MD \BOOKS
    c. either a or b
    d. neither a nor b

F-b With the root directory as the default directory, create two subdirectories under the **BOOKS** directory called **MYSTERY** and **SCIFI**.

23. Which of the following command(s) could you have used to create the **MYSTERY** subdirectory?
    a. MD BOOKS\MYSTERY
    b. MD \BOOKS\SCIFI\MYSTERY
    c. either a or b
    d. neither a nor b

F-c With the root directory as the default directory and using the method learned in this chapter, rename the **SCIFI** directory to **HORROR**.

24. Which of the following command(s) could you have used to rename **SCIFI**?
    a. MOVE \BOOKS \BOOKS\HORROR
    b. MOVE SCIFI MYSTERY
    c. MOVE BOOKS\SCIFI BOOKS\HORROR
    d. either a or c

F-d Use the RD command to remove the **BOOKS** directory in one step.

25. What parameter did you use?
    a. /N
    b. /O
    c. /S
    d. none

26. If you wanted to know what the current path was on your system, what command would you use?
    a. DIR
    b. PATH
    c. PATH /?
    d. PATH ?/

PROBLEM SET II—AT THE COMPUTER

PROBLEM A

A-a With the root directory of the APPLICATION disk as the default, create a directory called **CLASS**.

1. Write the command(s) you used to create the directory.

A-b Make **CLASS** the default directory.

2. Write the command(s) you used to change the default directory to **CLASS**.

A-c Change the default directory to the root of the APPLICATIONS disk.

A-d With the root of the APPLICATIONS disk as the default directory, using the relative path, rename **CLASS** to **ORDERS**.

3. Write any message(s) that appeared on the screen.

4. Write the command(s) you used to rename the directory.

A-e Remove the directory called **ORDERS**.

5. Write the command(s) you used to remove the directory.

PROBLEM B

B-a Key in the following: A:\>**PROMPT TP$G** Enter

6. Look at the screen display and write the displayed prompt.

B-b Key in the following: **PROMPT PG** Enter

7. Look at the screen display and write the displayed prompt.

PROBLEM SET III—BRIEF ESSAY

1. A friend is watching you work at the command line. You key in the following:

   C:\WINNT>**CD **

   C:\\>**A:**

   A:\\>**CD HOUSE\UTILS**

   A:\HOUSE\UTILS>**DIR**

   A:\HOUSE\UTILS>**DIR \HOMEWORK\PROBLEM**

   Your friend asks you how you know when and where to place the backslashes. Explain to her how to determine the positioning of the backslashes and the differences between the placements. Include a brief description of relative and absolute paths.

2. Windows, and thus the command prompt, uses a hierarchical filing system. Briefly describe this system and justify why it is used.

CHAPTER

5

INTERNAL COMMANDS

COPY AND TYPE

LEARNING OBJECTIVES

After completing this chapter you will be able to:

1. Explain the purpose and function of internal commands.
2. Explain the purpose and function of the COPY command.
3. List the file-naming rules.
4. Explain the purpose and function of the TYPE command.
5. Explain when and how to use wildcards with the COPY command.
6. Explain the purpose and use of subdirectory markers.
7. Identify the commands that can be used with subdirectories.
8. Explain when and how files are overwritten.
9. Explain the function, purpose, and dangers of concatenating files.
10. Compare and contrast printing files using the TYPE and COPY commands.

STUDENT OUTCOMES

1. Copy a file on the same disk using the COPY command.
2. Use wildcards with the COPY command to copy files on the same disk.
3. Display a text file using the TYPE command.
4. Use the COPY command to make additional files on the same disk but in different subdirectories.
5. Use wildcards with the COPY command to copy files on the same disk to a different subdirectory.
6. Use the COPY and DIR commands with subdirectories.
7. Use subdirectory markers with commands.
8. Overwrite a file using the COPY command.

9. Combine the contents of two or more files using the COPY command.
10. Print files.

CHAPTER OVERVIEW

In this chapter you will review the Windows operating system rules used to create unique names for files and learn some essential internal commands that will help you manage and manipulate your files. You will learn about the COPY command, which allows you to make additional copies of files and to back up files by copying them to another disk or directory. You will learn the consequences of overwriting files and of combining the contents of files. You will copy dummy files that are in the WINDOSBK directory to your DATA disk so that you can have experience in naming, managing, manipulating, viewing, and printing files.

5.1 WHY LEARN COMMAND LINE COMMANDS?

In the last chapter, you learned how to manipulate subdirectories. You learned MD, CD, and RD, which are directory management commands that handle subdirectories. However, directories are places to hold files. With the directory management commands, you have built the bookshelves, but you have not as yet put any books on them. If shelves are directories, books are files. In a library, you are interested in locating, reading, and using books, not admiring the shelves. In the same way, on your computer, you are interested in locating, reading, and using files, not admiring the directories you created.

You will have many files and directories on a disk. The directories will be used to organize both your program and data files. Directories are the largest units of information management, but you need to manage information in smaller quantities—at the file level. You will generate many data files with your programs. You will need a way to perform "housekeeping tasks" such as copying files from one directory or one disk to another and eliminating files you no longer need. These tasks are different from creating or changing the data within the files. You must use the application program that created a data file to change the data in that file.

For instance, if you are the accountant who created Ms. Woo's tax return, you know how to manage the information correctly in her tax return. You also have other clients for whom you perform the same service. You, the accountant, are analogous to an application program such as TurboTax. The data for Ms. Woo's tax return is in a data file created by TurboTax. The other clients such as Mr. Rodriguez and Mr. Markiw need separate data files, also generated in TurboTax. Those data files have to be named according to the rules of the operating system in which TurboTax works. If your version of TurboTax was created for the Windows OS, you will be able to use up to 255 characters in a file name, including blank spaces. If your version was created for DOS 6.22 or older operating systems, you will be limited to eight-character names with three-character extensions.

In addition to the accounting work, there are other tasks that must be performed. For instance, Ms. Woo might get married and want her data file under her married name. This does not require a change to the accounting data itself. You, as the accountant, do not need to perform these low-level tasks. You hire a clerk to perform them. In the computer world, you use the operating system to perform these tasks.

In Windows, you can use Windows Explorer and My Computer to manage your files. You can drag files from one place to another, cut and paste them, rename them, and delete them with the click of a mouse button. Using the command line will help you understand file manipulation as well as disk and subdirectory structure. You will also learn that there are some tasks that you can accomplish more easily and quickly at the command line than in the GUI. For instance, in the GUI, in order to copy a file and give it a new name, you must take two steps—first copy the file, second rename it. At the command line, you can accomplish this task with one step. The COPY command allows you to change the name of the destination file as it is copied.

In addition, several major internal commands will help manage your files on disks and in directories. These file-management commands include DIR, COPY, REN, DEL, and TYPE. These commands are internal, meaning that once you have booted the system, they are always available to use. They are in the booting file CMD.EXE; they are not separate files in the WINNT\SYSTEM32 directory. These commands deal only with files as objects; you are not working with the *contents* of files, just manipulating the files. The commands allow you to see what files you have on a disk or in a directory (DIR), copy files from here to there (COPY), change their names (REN), throw files away (DEL), and take a quick peek at what is inside a file (TYPE). The following activities in this chapter will show you how to use the COPY and TYPE commands.

5.2 THE COPY COMMAND

COPY, one of the most frequently used internal commands, is used to copy files from one place to another. COPY does exactly what it says—it takes an original ***source file,*** makes an identical copy of that file, and places the copy where you want it: its destination. In a sense, it is similar to a photocopy machine. You place your original on the copy plate, press the appropriate button, and receive a copy of your document. Nothing has happened to your original document. If it has a smudge on it, so does your copy. The same is true with the COPY command—it makes an exact copy of the file, and the original file remains intact. Copying a file *does not* alter the original file in any way.

Why might you want to copy files? You might want to copy a file from one disk to another. For example, you might create an inventory of all your household goods for your homeowner's insurance policy. It would be stored as a file on your disk. If your home burned down, so would your disk with your inventory file. It makes sense to copy this file to another disk and store it somewhere else, perhaps in a safe-deposit box.

You might want to make a second copy of an existing file on the same disk. Why would you want to do this? If you are going to be making changes to a data file with the program that created it, you might like a copy of the original just in case you do not like the changes you make. You cannot have two files with the same name in the *same* directory, but you can have them in *different* directories.

You might want to copy a file to a device. One of the most common devices is the printer. You can use the COPY command to copy a file to the printer to get a hard copy, but the file must be an ASCII file, a special kind of text file that contains no codes such as bold or italic—just keyed in characters.

You have used the HPB program and the Thinker program. You might wish to make another copy of those program files in case something happens to the original, presuming you are the legal owner. Those programs also had data files with information in them. You might like to have another copy, a backup copy of the various data files, so that if anything goes wrong, you still have a copy to work with.

COPY has a very specific syntax. Its basic syntax is always:

```
COPY [drive:][path]filename  [drive:][path]filename
```

or conceptually:

```
COPY source  destination
```

COPY is the command or the work you want the system to do. The *source* is what you want copied, your original. The *destination* is where you want it copied to. The command, the source, and the destination are separated by spaces. In the formal syntax, the variables are as follows: *[drive:]* stands for the drive letter where the file is located; *[path]* is the subdirectory where the file is located; and *filename* is the name of the file you wish to copy. The file name is made up of two parts: the file name and the file extension. If a file has an extension, it is separated from the file name by the period or dot at the command line. If you are using a version of the operating system prior to Windows 95, when you key in a file name, you must have no spaces between the file name and the file extension. In Windows, if you wish to use a long file name that includes spaces, you must enclose the entire name in quotes. All three portions of the command—COPY, source, and destination—are mandatory. Drive and path do not need to be specified if you are using the default drive and subdirectory.

You use file-management commands to manage files. When you are learning how to use these commands, you do not want to worry about harming "real" programs or "real" data files. The WINDOSBK subdirectory, therefore, contains practice data files and program files. In the following activities, you will write data to your DATA disk only. You will never write to the hard disk. In this way you can enjoy the next activities and not worry about making mistakes. Mistakes are part of the learning process.

5.3 REVIEW OF FILE-NAMING RULES

To name any file, whether it is an application or a data file, you must follow the operating system file-naming rules. A file name is technically called a file specification. The file specification is comprised of two parts: the file name itself and the file extension. The file-naming rules are:

1. The names of files in a directory must be unique.
2. No file name can be longer than 255 characters, including the file extension.
3. File extensions are optional.
4. A file name must be separated from its extension with a period, called a dot.
5. All alphanumeric characters can be used in file names and file extensions except the following nine illegal or forbidden characters:

```
"   /   \   :   ¦   <   >   *   ?
```

You cannot alter the rules. Usually, you will not get an opportunity to name program files. You purchase these programs, and the file names are those that were assigned by a programmer. Remember, a program file commonly has the file extension of .COM, .EXE, or .BAT. However, you will be naming your data files all the time. You name a data file from within the application program, usually when you save it to a disk.

You should apply some common sense when you are naming files. For instance, naming a file ABCDEF.GHI does not tell you much about the contents of the file, but a file named TAXES99.TKR does give you a clear idea of what is in the data file. File names should reflect file contents. However, you must know how your application program works. Most application programs let you assign the file name, but not the file extension. The programs themselves usually assign the extension to data files.

5.4 ACTIVITY: MAKING COPIES OF FILES

Note 1: The DATA disk is in Drive A. Be sure it is the DATA disk and not the APPLICATION disk.

Note 2: You have opened a Command Prompt window, and C:\WINNT\SYSTEM32> is displayed as the default drive and the default directory. Remember to check your Configuration Table in Chapter 1.6 if your system configuration varies from the textbook.

Note 3: It is assumed that the **WINDOSBK** directory with its files has been installed on the hard disk. If it has not, refer to Appendix A for instructions on how to install it at home or see your lab administrator.

CORRECTING KEYSTROKE ERRORS

Note 4: When keying in commands, you may use the editing keys to correct typographical errors and to recall previously used commands. Refer to Chapter 2 for details.

Step 1 Key in the following: C:\WINNT\SYSTEM32>**CD \WINDOSBK** Enter

Step 2 Key in the following: C:\WINDOSBK>**DIR *.TMP** Enter

```
Command Prompt

C:\WINNT\SYSTEM32>CD \WINDOSBK

C:\WINDOSBK>DIR *.TMP
 Volume in drive C is 2000 PRO
 Volume Serial Number is C4A7-8571

 Directory of C:\WINDOSBK

04/23/2000  04:03p                  72 APRIL.TMP
04/23/2000  04:03p                  53 BONJOUR.TMP
04/23/2000  04:03p                  75 FEB.TMP
01/01/2002  04:32a                  34 GOODBYE.TMP
04/23/2000  04:03p                  73 JANUARY.TMP
04/23/2000  04:03p                  73 JAN.TMP
04/23/2000  04:03p                  71 MAR.TMP
04/23/2000  04:03p                  71 MARCH.TMP
04/23/2000  04:18p                  72 APR.TMP
               9 File(s)            594 bytes
               0 Dir(s)   1,149,108,224 bytes free

C:\WINDOSBK>_
```

You changed the default directory to **WINDOSBK**. You then used the DIR command to see what files had a **.TMP** file extension in this directory. You want to make a copy of the file called **JAN.TMP** and place it on the DATA disk. You are going to use the absolute path for both the source file and the ***destination file***.

Step 3 Key in the following:
C:\WINDOSBK>**COPY C:\WINDOSBK\JAN.TMP A:\JAN.TMP** Enter

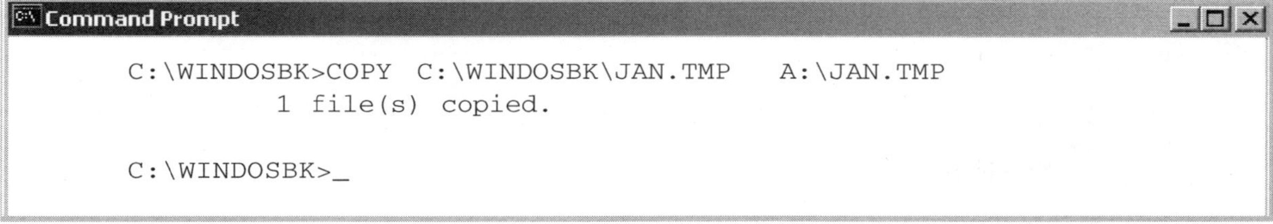

```
Command Prompt

C:\WINDOSBK>COPY C:\WINDOSBK\JAN.TMP   A:\JAN.TMP
        1 file(s) copied.

C:\WINDOSBK>_
```

You see a message on the screen telling you that the file was copied. If you look at your command, following the syntax diagram, **COPY** is the command and **JAN.TMP** is the source file or what you want to copy. It is located in the subdirectory called **WINDOSBK**, which is under the root directory of the hard disk. **C:** was substituted for *[drive:]*. The subdirectory name **\WINDOSBK** was substituted for *[path]* (remembering that \ indicates the root directory). The next \ is a delimiter separating the subdirectory name from the file name. The second backslash (\) is only a separator. **JAN.TMP** was substituted for *filename*. A **.** (dot), not a space, separates the file name from the file extension.

The destination file also followed the syntax diagram. **A:** was substituted for *[drive:]*; \ was substituted for *[path]*; **JAN.TMP** was substituted for *filename*. Each file followed the file-naming rules; each is a unique name with no illegal characters. Each file extension has no illegal characters. You used a period to separate the file name from the file extension. The period is not part of the file specification. It is a delimiter telling the operating system that you are done with the file name; get ready for the file extension. Thus, **JAN** is the source file name and **.TMP** is the source file extension. **JAN** is the destination file name, and **.TMP** is the destination file extension.

Step 4 Key in the following: C:\WINDOSBK>**DIR A:** Enter

```
Command Prompt

C:\WINDOSBK>DIR A:

 Volume in drive A is DATA
 Volume Serial Number is 3330-1807

 Directory of A:\

04/30/2001  11:15a      <DIR>          POLYSCI
04/23/2000  04:03p                  73 JAN.TMP
```

```
        1 File(s)            73 bytes
        1 Dir(s)      1,455,616 bytes free

C:\WINDOSBK>_
```

You used the DIR command to confirm that you copied **JAN.TMP** to the DATA disk. You have one file and one subdirectory in the root directory of the DATA disk. In Step 3, you used the absolute path name. You can save yourself a lot of time by using relative path names.

Step 5 Key in the following: C:\WINDOSBK>**COPY FEB.TMP A:** Enter

Step 6 Key in the following: C:\WINDOSBK>**COPY MAR.TMP A:** Enter

Step 7 Key in the following: C:\WINDOSBK>**COPY APR.TMP A:** Enter

Step 8 Key in the following: C:\WINDOSBK>**DIR A:** Enter

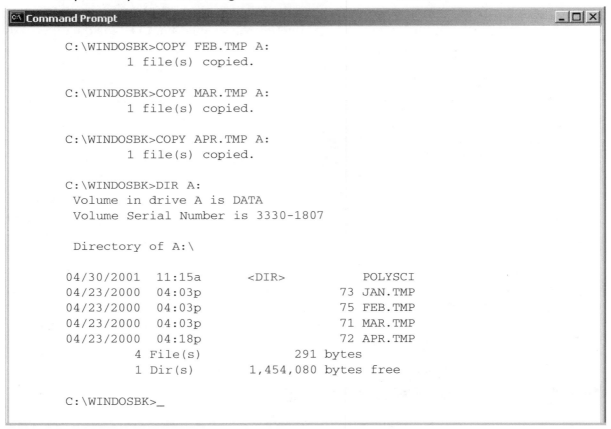

```
Command Prompt

C:\WINDOSBK>COPY FEB.TMP A:
        1 file(s) copied.

C:\WINDOSBK>COPY MAR.TMP A:
        1 file(s) copied.

C:\WINDOSBK>COPY APR.TMP A:
        1 file(s) copied.

C:\WINDOSBK>DIR A:
 Volume in drive A is DATA
 Volume Serial Number is 3330-1807

 Directory of A:\

04/30/2001  11:15a      <DIR>          POLYSCI
04/23/2000  04:03p                  73 JAN.TMP
04/23/2000  04:03p                  75 FEB.TMP
04/23/2000  04:03p                  71 MAR.TMP
04/23/2000  04:18p                  72 APR.TMP
        4 File(s)            291 bytes
        1 Dir(s)      1,454,080 bytes free

C:\WINDOSBK>_
```

You executed several COPY commands and used DIR to confirm that you copied the files. You copied the file called **FEB.TMP** to the root directory of the DATA disk, but you did not need to key in all the information. Since the default drive and directory are already **C:\WINDOSBK**, the command will always look in the default drive and directory and no place else, unless you tell it otherwise. Since the destination you wanted the file copied to was the DATA disk, which in this case is Drive A, you had to key in the drive letter followed by a colon. The colon lets the operating system know the destination is a drive. If you just keyed in **A**, the COPY command would think that you wanted to name the file A. You did not give the destination file a name, because if you do not supply a file name, the COPY command will use the source file name as the destination file name. In this case the source file name was **FEB.TMP**, and that is what the copy of the file on the DATA disk is called. You then proceeded to perform the same task with **MAR.TMP** and **APR.TMP**. Next, you will give the destination file a different name and override the defaults. Remember, in Windows Explorer or My Computer, you can copy files, but you cannot give them a new name when you copy them. Hence, you must copy the files, then rename each one. At the command line, you can copy and give the files a new name in one command. This is one of the reasons users like the command line.

Step 9 Key in the following: C:\WINDOSBK>**COPY MAR.TMP A:\MARCH.FIL** Enter

Step 10 Key in the following: C:\WINDOSBK>**DIR A:** Enter

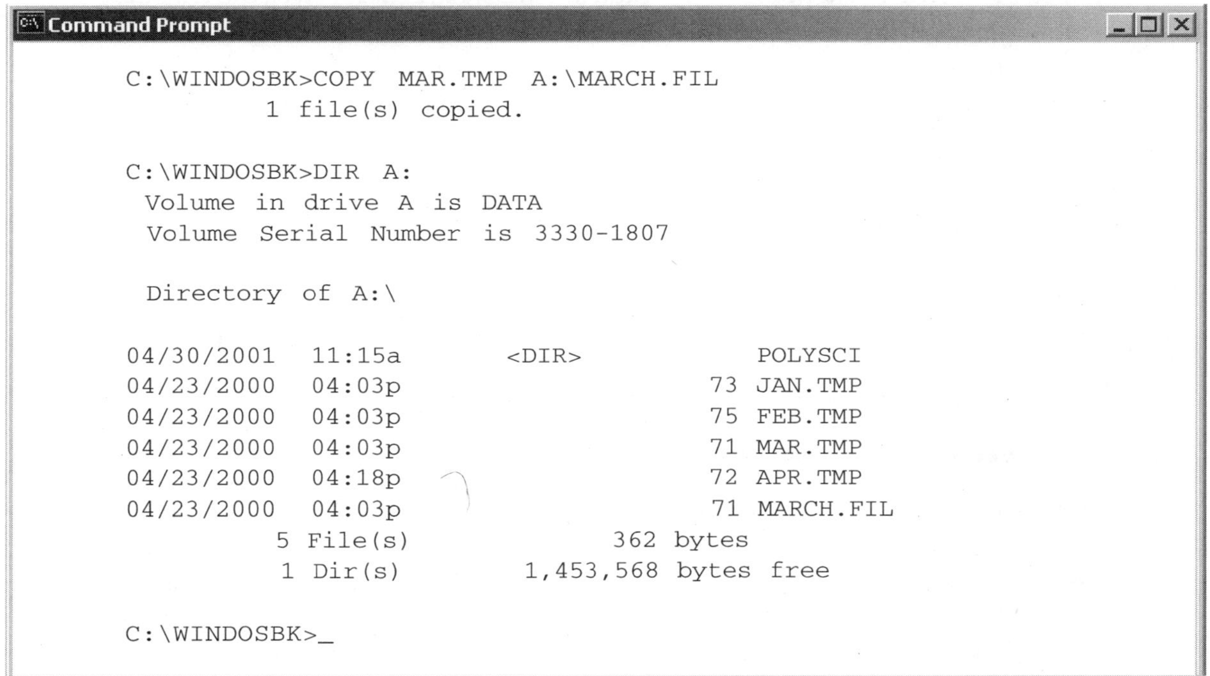

```
Command Prompt

C:\WINDOSBK>COPY MAR.TMP A:\MARCH.FIL
        1 file(s) copied.

C:\WINDOSBK>DIR A:
 Volume in drive A is DATA
 Volume Serial Number is 3330-1807

 Directory of A:\

04/30/2001  11:15a      <DIR>          POLYSCI
04/23/2000  04:03p                  73 JAN.TMP
04/23/2000  04:03p                  75 FEB.TMP
04/23/2000  04:03p                  71 MAR.TMP
04/23/2000  04:18p                  72 APR.TMP
04/23/2000  04:03p                  71 MARCH.FIL
               5 File(s)            362 bytes
               1 Dir(s)       1,453,568 bytes free

C:\WINDOSBK>_
```

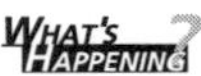

You executed the COPY command and used DIR to confirm that you copied the file. Following the syntax diagram, **COPY** is the command. **MAR.TMP** is the source file or what you want to copy. **MARCH.FIL** is the new destination file name. The destination file name followed the file-naming rules; it is a unique name with no illegal characters. You used a period to separate the file name from the file extension. The period is a delimiter, not part of the file specification. You did not need to use the drive letter or path name (subdirectory name) in the source file, but you did need to specify the drive letter in the destination. The default drive and subdirectory are always assumed unless you specify otherwise. In this case, you overrode the defaults by telling the COPY command to call the destination file on the DATA disk **MARCH.FIL**.

5.5 USING LONG FILE NAMES

You may consider using long files names (LFNs) with files on floppy disks, but only when really necessary. On a 1.44-MB floppy disk, the directory entry table has room for only 224 file names. Floppy disks use the old FAT filing system. In reality, you can rarely save more than 212 actual files or subdirectory names on the root of a floppy disk. Floppy disks were "designed" to hold files that complied with the old eight-dot-three naming convention based on the FAT. Even if the files are very small (without much data in them) and there is still ample room in the data sectors on the diskette for information, once the directory entry table is filled, you can no longer place more files on the disk, even though there is room. Once the root directory table is full, as far as the operating system is concerned, the disk is full regardless of how much actual space remains on the disk.

For example, assume you saved two files to the root of a floppy disk. One file is named FIRST.FIL, and the second is named TWENTY.FIL. If you saved the same files to another floppy disk, but with the names FIRST.FIL and TWENTYFIRST.FIL, the amount of space taken up by the actual data files would be the same. However, there would be a difference in the root directory table entries. Compare the two directory entry tables in Figure 5.1.

Disk 1 Directory Table	Disk 2 Directory Table
FIRST.FIL	FIRST.FIL
TWENTY.FIL	TWENTYF
	IRST.FIL

FIGURE 5.1 TWO DIRECTORY ENTRY TABLES

Notice that on the second disk, the long file name took two entries in the directory entry table. Disk 2 will "fill" faster than Disk 1, even though the amount of data is identical! A file with 20 characters in its name can take the space of three eight-dot-three named files. Although it is possible to have files with up to 255 characters in their names, you can see how quickly the root directory entry table of a floppy disk could be filled, thus limiting your ability to save files to a disk.

When referring to files that contain spaces in their long file name at the command line, you need to enclose the entire file specification in quotes. To see both the short and long name in a directory listing, you need to use the /X parameter with DIR. See Figure 5.2.

```
11/16/2000   12:00p                53 SANDYA~1.TXT     Sandy and Nicki.txt
11/16/2000   12:00p                59 SANDYA~2.TXT     Sandy and Patty.txt
```

FIGURE 5.2 DIRECTORY LISTING SHOWING SHORT AND LONG FILE NAMES

Notice the second file listed. The file Sandy and Nicki.txt has an alias of SANDYA~1.TXT. The digit is assigned by the operating system. The Sandy and Patty.txt file is assigned the digit 2 following the tilde. The digit is assigned by the operating system. If you had a third file, Sandy and Brian.txt, in the same directory, it would get another digit. See Figure 5.3.

```
11/16/2000  12:00p          53 SANDYA~1.TXT   Sandy and Nicki.txt
11/16/2000  12:00p          59 SANDYA~2.TXT   Sandy and Patty.txt
11/20/2001  12:00p          75 SANDYA~3.TXT   Sandy and Brian.txt
```

FIGURE 5.3 DIRECTORY LISTING CONTAINING THREE SIMILAR FILE NAMES

When dealing with long file names, it is helpful to have meaningful, unique characters within the first six characters of the name to avoid this confusion when using short file names.

5.6 ACTIVITY: COPYING FILES WITH LONG FILE NAMES

Note: The DATA disk is in Drive A. C:\WINDOSBK is displayed.

Step 1 Key in the following:
C:\WINDOSBK>**COPY "SANDY AND NICKI.TXT" A:** Enter

```
Command Prompt

C:\WINDOSBK>COPY "SANDY AND NICKI.TXT" A:
        1 file(s) copied.

C:\WINDOSBK>_
```

WHAT'S HAPPENING? You have successfully copied the file to the DATA disk.

Step 2 Key in the following: C:\WINDOSBK>**DIR A: /X** Enter

```
Command Prompt

Directory of A:\


04/30/2001  11:15a        <DIR>               POLYSCI
04/23/2000  04:03p          75                FEB.TMP
04/23/2000  04:03p          73                JAN.TMP
04/23/2000  04:03p          71                MAR.TMP
04/23/2000  04:18p          72                APR.TMP
04/23/2000  04:03p          71                MARCH.FIL
11/16/2000  12:00p          53 SANDYA~1.TXT   Sandy and Nicki.txt
               6 File(s)            415 bytes
               1 Dir(s)       1,453,056 bytes free
C:\WINDOSBK>_
```

Notice the display on the right contains the entire file name **Sandy and Nicki.txt**, whereas the display in the center does not. The operating system has assigned the file **Sandy and Nicki.txt** an alias in the eight-dot-three file name format.

5.7 USING WILDCARDS WITH THE COPY COMMAND

In Chapter 2, you used global file specifications, or wildcards (* and ?), with the DIR command so that you could display a group of files. You can also use wildcards to copy files. In the previous activity you copied one file at a time. You then proceeded to key in a command line for each file you copied. Since each of the files you wished to copy had the same file extension, instead of keying in each source file and destination file, you could have used the wildcards to key in the command line and reduced three commands to one. You can also use wildcards when changing the destination name.

5.8 ACTIVITY: USING WILDCARDS WITH THE COPY COMMAND

Note: The DATA disk is in Drive A. C:\WINDOSBK> is displayed.

Step 1 Key in the following: C:\WINDOSBK>**COPY *.TMP A:*.NEW** Enter

```
Command Prompt

C:\WINDOSBK>COPY *.TMP  A:*.NEW
APRIL.TMP
BONJOUR.TMP
FEB.TMP
GOODBYE.TMP
JANUARY.TMP
JAN.TMP
MAR.TMP
MARCH.TMP
APR.TMP
        9 file(s) copied.

C:\WINDOSBK>_
```

As each file is copied, it is displayed on the screen. Your command line instructed the operating system to copy any file in the **WINDOSBK** subdirectory that has the file extension **.TMP**, regardless of its file name, to a new set of files that will have the same file name but a different extension, **.NEW**. The * represented any file name. The operating system knew that you were referring to file extensions because you preceded the file extension with the delimiter, the period. These files will be copied to the DATA disk.

You could have keyed in the absolute path name,

COPY C:\WINDOSBK*.TMP A:*.NEW

but once again, it is unnecessary to specify the source drive (default drive) and source subdirectory (default directory). Since you did not tell it otherwise, the COPY command assumed the default drive and subdirectory for the source. You needed to key in the destination drive and the destination file extension since you were not using the default values.

Step 2 Key in the following: C:\WINDOSBK>**DIR A:*.NEW** Enter

Command Prompt

```
C:\WINDOSBK>DIR A:*.NEW
 Volume in drive A is DATA
 Volume Serial Number is 3330-1807

 Directory of A:\

04/23/2000  04:03p                  72 APRIL.NEW
04/23/2000  04:03p                  53 BONJOUR.NEW
04/23/2000  04:03p                  75 FEB.NEW
01/01/2002  04:32a                  34 GOODBYE.NEW
04/23/2000  04:03p                  73 JANUARY.NEW
04/23/2000  04:03p                  73 JAN.NEW
04/23/2000  04:03p                  71 MAR.NEW
04/23/2000  04:03p                  71 MARCH.NEW
04/23/2000  04:18p                  72 APR.NEW
               9 File(s)            594 bytes
               0 Dir(s)       1,448,448 bytes free

C:\WINDOSBK>_
```

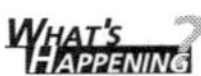

You keyed in the command **DIR A:*.NEW**. You used the wildcards to display the **.NEW** files, instead of displaying the entire directory. You also used the wildcard * to make copies of the **.TMP** files. The file names are identical, but the extensions are different. You successfully copied nine files with the extension **.TMP** to nine new files with the extension **.NEW** from the hard disk to the DATA disk. However, the directory display merely shows that the files are there. How can you tell if the contents of the files are the same? You can use the TYPE command.

5.9 THE TYPE COMMAND

The DIR command allowed you to determine that, indeed, there are files with the .TMP and .NEW extensions on the DATA disk. Using the DIR command is like opening your file drawer (the disk) and looking at the labels on the files. DIR does not show you what is in the files. An internal command called TYPE opens a file and displays the contents of the file on the screen. However, although the TYPE command will display the contents of any file on the screen, a file must be an ASCII file for the data to be meaningful. The TYPE command displays the file on the screen without stopping (scrolling). If the file is longer than one full screen, you can stop the scrolling by pressing the **Pause** key. The syntax is:

```
TYPE  [drive:][path]filename
```

TYPE is the command (the work) you want the system to perform. The brackets [ ] indicate that what is between the brackets is optional. You do not key in the brackets, only what is inside them. *[drive:]* represents the drive letter. You must substitute the drive letter where the file is located (A:, B:, or C:). Another name for the drive letter is the "designated disk drive." This letter tells the command on which disk drive to look for the information. *[path]* is the name of the subdirectory where the file is located. You do not key in "path." You substitute the name of the path or subdirectory name, as in \WINNT\SYSTEM32 or \PHONE. The file name is mandatory. If the file has an extension, it must be included as part of the file name. You do not key in "filename" but substitute the actual name of the file. *Filename* is the parameter that the TYPE command expects. In addition, the file must be a text file to be readable. The TYPE command will not display the contents of a document file created with a word-processing program such as WordPerfect or Word.

5.10 ACTIVITY: DISPLAYING FILES USING THE TYPE COMMAND

Note: The DATA disk is in Drive A. C:\WINDOSBK> is displayed.

Step 1 Key in the following: C:\WINDOSBK>**TYPE** Enter

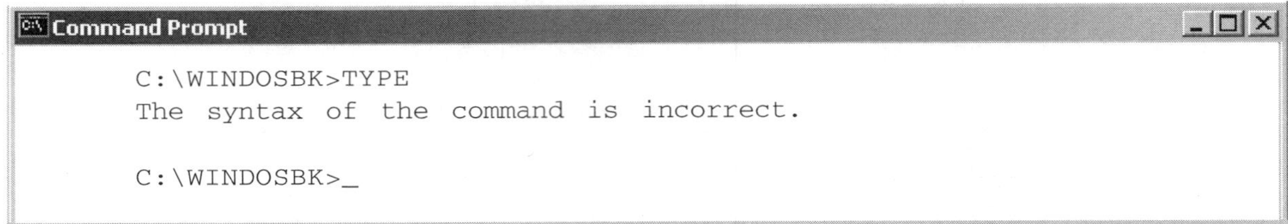
Command Prompt

```
C:\WINDOSBK>TYPE
The syntax of the command is incorrect.

C:\WINDOSBK>_
```

WHAT'S HAPPENING? The message displayed on the screen tells you that TYPE does not know what to do. The operating system is asking you, "TYPE or display what?" Since you did not give a file name, as the syntax mandates, the TYPE command cannot show the contents of a file.

Step 2 Key in the following: C:\WINDOSBK>**TYPE PHONE\HPB.EXE** Enter

Command Prompt

```
C:\WINDOSBK>TYPE PHONE\HPB.EXE
MZD B_     á3__¥[Ç    _ _&-    _







                                   Ui_+  Ü+_~_VWÜ_ W        Ü4__
                                                              â>__t__
Ä_µ &¦_- ¶  Ü   _+_Ä_µ &¦_- ¶ Ä__ &¦_¦e   +   PÜ14+
C:\WINDOSBK>_
```

WHAT'S HAPPENING? Your display may be slightly different, depending on your system. What you see on screen is, indeed, the contents of a file named **HPB.EXE** in the **PHONE** subdirectory—a program you executed in Chapter 4. This program or executable code is in machine language and not meaningful to you in this format. However, the TYPE command will display the contents of any file, even if it looks like nonsense characters to you. Remember, when you keyed in HPB, the program executed and allowed you to look at some data—names and addresses, but when you used TYPE, looking at the contents of the program was not meaningful. Because HPB is a program file and not a text file, using the TYPE command has no value.

Programs or executable code files are recognized by their file extensions, such as **.COM**, **.EXE**, or **.SYS**, as well as those extensions listed in Chapter 4. **COM** stands for command file. **EXE** stands for executable code. **SYS** stands for system file. There are also other support files that programs need such as those files that have the .DLL (dynamic link library) extension. These types of files are not text files and not readable using the TYPE command. However, the TYPE command will do whatever you ask, even if it means displaying nonsense. Remember, a file must be a text file to be readable.

Another name for a text file is an ASCII (pronounced "ask-ee") file. ***ASCII*** is an acronym for American Standard Code for Information Interchange. ASCII is a code that translates the bits of information into readable letters. All you need to remember is that an ASCII file is a readable text file. Another name for an ASCII file is an ***unformatted text file***. ASCII files are in a common language that almost all programs can recognize.

The data files that programs generate are usually not readable either. Each program has a special way of reading and writing the information in a data file so that the program knows what to do with the data. Usually, no other program can read the data file except the program that generated it. It would be like wanting to write a letter in Japanese if you didn't speak, read, or write Japanese. You would hire a translator (the program). He would write the letter (the data file). You still could not read the letter. You would give it to the translator to know what is in the letter. Furthermore, if you had another translator—say a French translator (another program)—you could not give your Japanese letter (data file) to the French translator. She would not be able to read it either.

Step 3 Key in the following: C:\WINDOSBK>**TYPE PHONE\HPB.DAT** Enter

```
Command Prompt

04231994
           Smith                              Jane Doe
11111951416222333334444Joh
n              12121952416555666677771 23 Sunset Road
                                                      Toronto

ON5H5 6Y2    Cana
da                  41688888880 1011975Dear John & Jane,    X      Sample
record for co
uple with different last namesDelete it for practice!
Joe                01011971Joan              02021972
                                                                 07041993

The
Book Biz
                        498 North Street
                                   Orange               CA92669      USA
  7145559997                                  B



                                                      04231994

Tuttle
```

```
              Mary Brown     12201963              Steven
0514196371455593
77      444  Sweetheart  Lane
                  Tustin               CA92670      USA
714555888907
311994                    FX
                                                          Walter
10121995

                                12121996
C:\WINDOSBK>_
```

You are looking at the data file for the **HPB.EXE** program in its rawest form when you key in **TYPE PHONE\HPB.DAT**. This program has its data in a somewhat recognizable form, in that you can at least read some of it. But, as you can see, the format of the data is not correctly laid out as it is when you use the data file with the program file, **HPB.EXE**.

Format, in this case, does not mean format as in format a disk but format in the sense of how the data is arranged. Only the program **HPB.EXE** knows how to arrange this data so it is meaningful to you. TYPE can be useful with data files like these because it gives you an idea of what information the file actually holds. Nearly all the files in the **WINDOSBK** directory are ASCII files, which means that you can read them using the TYPE command.

Step 4 Key in the following: C:\WINDOSBK>**TYPE JAN.TMP** Enter

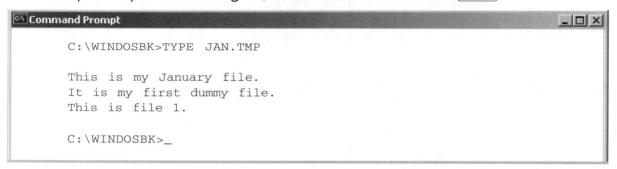

```
Command Prompt

C:\WINDOSBK>TYPE  JAN.TMP

This  is  my  January  file.
It  is  my  first  dummy  file.
This  is  file  1.

C:\WINDOSBK>_
```

In this case, the above is a text file (ASCII file), so you can read it. Using the TYPE command, you "opened" your file, **JAN.TMP**, and saw the contents displayed on the screen. Whenever a file is readable on the screen, as this one is, you know it is an ASCII file. You did not need to include the drive or path since **JAN.TMP** was on the hard disk in the **WINDOSBK** subdirectory and the TYPE command used the default values. You copied this file to the DATA disk in Activity 5.4. Is the content of the file the same on the DATA disk as it is in the **WINDOSBK** subdirectory? If it is, you will know that the COPY command makes no changes to any information in a file when it copies it.

Step 5 Key in the following: C:\WINDOSBK>**TYPE A:JAN.TMP** Enter

```
Command Prompt

C:\WINDOSBK>TYPE A:JAN.TMP

This is my January file.
It is my first dummy file.
This is file 1.

C:\WINDOSBK>_
```

The contents of the two files are the same. Copying the file from one disk to another had no impact on the contents. This is also true no matter what type of file you copy. But you would still need to include the drive designator **A:** in front of the file name **JAN.TMP** because that told the operating system which disk drive to select. Had you not included the drive designator, the operating system would have looked for the file **JAN.TMP** on the default hard disk and in the default subdirectory **\WINDOSBK**. After the TYPE command has executed, you are returned to the system prompt, ready for the next command.

Step 6 Key in the following: C:\WINDOSBK>**CD ** Enter

You have returned to the root directory of the hard disk.

5.11 DUMMY FILES

You are going to use some dummy files. "Dummy" refers to the fact that these files have no particular meaning and are of no importance. You can use these files to practice file-management commands without worrying about harming your "real" program and data files. The concept of dummy files and/or dummy data is common in data processing. Often data-processing professionals wish to test different portions of systems or programs. For instance, if you were writing a program about employee benefits, rather than looking at every employee, you would create dummy files and data in order to have a smaller representative sample that is manageable and easily tested. Not only are the files smaller, they are samples. If the data gets harmed in any way, it has no impact on the "real" data.

The following activities allow you to do the same. Following the instructions, you will use the COPY command to make copies of different files either on the DATA disk or from the WINDOSBK subdirectory to the DATA disk. You will then display the contents of the file on the screen with the TYPE command.

5.12 ACTIVITY: USING THE COPY AND TYPE COMMANDS

Note 1: C:\> is displayed and the DATA disk is in Drive A.

Note 2: Remember that if your DATA disk is in a drive other than A, you will have to substitute the proper drive letter. Check your Configuration Table in Chapter 1.6 for the appropriate substitutions.

Step 1 Key in the following: C:\>**A:** [Enter]

```
Command Prompt

C:\>A:

A:\>_
```

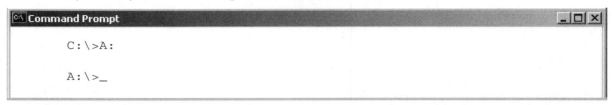

WHAT'S HAPPENING? You changed the default drive so that all activities will automatically occur or default to the DATA disk.

Step 2 Key in the following: A:\>**COPY JAN.TMP JAN.OLD** [Enter]

```
Command Prompt

A:\>COPY JAN.TMP JAN.OLD
        1 file(s) copied.

A:\>_
```

WHAT'S HAPPENING? You keyed in the command and its required parameters to accomplish the work you wanted done. You did not need to specify the drive letter or the path name preceding either the source file or the destination file name. Because you did not, the COPY command automatically read **JAN.TMP** from and wrote **JAN.OLD** to the default drive and directory, which is the root directory of the DATA disk.

Step 3 Key in the following: A:\>**TYPE JAN.TMP JAN.OLD** [Enter]

```
Command Prompt

A:\>TYPE JAN.TMP JAN.OLD

JAN.TMP



This is my January file.
It is my first dummy file.
This is file 1.

JAN.OLD



This is my January file.
It is my first dummy file.
```

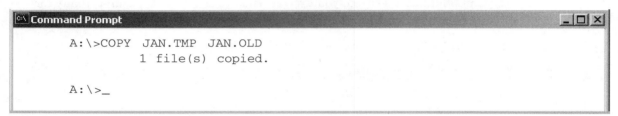

```
This is file 1.

A:\>_
```

WHAT'S HAPPENING? You can see that you made a copy of the **JAN.TMP** file to a new file called **JAN.OLD**, but the contents of the files are identical. Also, rather than keying in the TYPE command twice, TYPE allows you use more than one parameter.

Step 4 Key in the following: A:\>**COPY MAR.TMP MAR.TMP** Enter

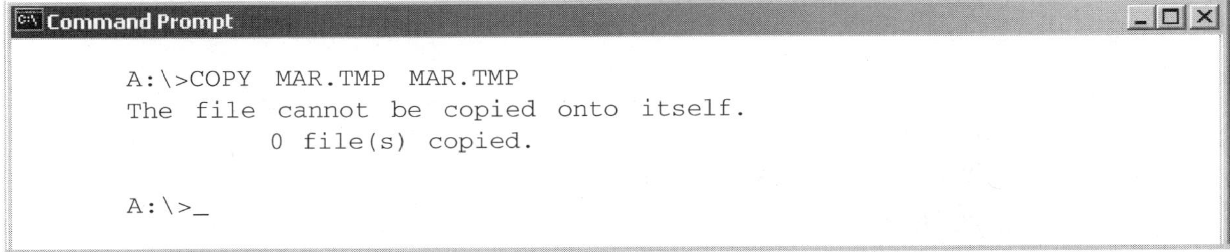

```
A:\>COPY MAR.TMP MAR.TMP
The file cannot be copied onto itself.
        0 file(s) copied.

A:\>_
```

WHAT'S HAPPENING? You must give new files on the same disk and in the same subdirectory unique names. Just as you should not label two file folders the same in a file drawer, you would not label two disk files with the same names.

Step 5 Key in the following: A:\>**COPY MAR.TMP MARCH.TXT** Enter

```
Command Prompt
A:\>COPY MAR.TMP MARCH.TXT
        1 file(s) copied.

A:\>_
```

WHAT'S HAPPENING? Here you are making a copy of the contents of the file on the DATA disk called **MAR.TMP**, copying the contents to the DATA disk, and calling this new file **MARCH.TXT**. You could have used the absolute path and file name by keying in **COPY A:\MAR.TMP A:\MARCH.TXT**. Either is correct, but it is not necessary to specify the disk drive since the default drive is assumed. Nor is it necessary to specify the path or directory because the root directory (\) is the default directory.

Step 6 Key in the following: A:\>**TYPE MARCH.TXT MAR.TMP** Enter

```
Command Prompt
A:\>TYPE MARCH.TXT MAR.TMP

MARCH.TXT



This is my March file.
It is my third dummy file.
This is file 3.
```

```
MAR.TMP



This is my March file.
It is my third dummy file.
This is file 3.

A:\>_
```

WHAT'S HAPPENING? The contents of each file are identical even though the file names are different. The COPY command does nothing to the original; the contents of the original file remain the same. As far as the system is concerned, what makes a file different is its unique file name. To the operating system, **MAR.TMP** and **MARCH.TXT** are unique, separate files.

Step 7 Key in the following: A:\>**COPY JAN.TMP JANUARY.TXT** Enter

Step 8 Key in the following: A:\>**COPY FEB.TMP FEBRUARY.TXT** Enter

Step 9 Key in the following: A:\>**COPY APR.TMP APRIL.TXT** Enter

Command Prompt

```
A:\>COPY JAN.TMP JANUARY.TXT
        1 file(s) copied.

A:\>COPY FEB.TMP FEBRUARY.TXT
        1 file(s) copied.

A:\>COPY APR.TMP APRIL.TXT
        1 file(s) copied.

A:\>_
```

Step 10 Key in the following: A:\>**DIR *.TMP *.TXT** Enter

Command Prompt

```
A:\>DIR *.TMP *.TXT
 Volume in drive A is DATA
 Volume Serial Number is 3330-1807

 Directory of A:\

04/23/2000  04:03p                 73 JAN.TMP
04/23/2000  04:03p                 75 FEB.TMP
04/23/2000  04:03p                 71 MAR.TMP
04/23/2000  04:18p                 72 APR.TMP

 Directory of A:\

11/16/2000  12:00p                 53 Sandy and Nicki.txt
04/23/2000  04:03p                 71 MARCH.TXT
04/23/2000  04:03p                 73 JANUARY.TXT
```

```
04/23/2000  04:03p                75 FEBRUARY.TXT
04/23/2000  04:18p                 72 APRIL.TXT
               9 File(s)           635 bytes
               0 Dir(s)     1,445,888 bytes free
```

You had four files with the extension **.TMP**. You still have those files, but, in addition, you now have four more files you just "created" with the copy command that have the extension **.TXT**. It is the operating system that keeps track of all these files.

5.13 MAKING ADDITIONAL FILES ON THE SAME DISK

You often want to have extra copies of files on the same disk but in a different subdirectory. You may want to keep your backup files in the same file cabinet (disk) but in a different drawer (subdirectory). In this way you can group similar files together. When you make a copy of a file on the same disk, in a different subdirectory, it may have the same file name. Every file on a disk must have a unique name. However, a copy of a file in a different subdirectory, even though the file name is the same, has a different path name and is therefore unique.

You sometimes want to have extra copies of the same files on the same disk. Often, you may wish to make copies of files created when you use other software application packages. You choose to make copies because you want to leave your original files intact. For instance, if you created an extensive client list with a database-management package and needed to update it, rather than working on the original file, you could re-key in the entire client list. If you made a mistake, you would still have your original list.

However, an easier method would be to copy the client list, stored as a file, to a new file with a new name and make changes to the new file. When you make a copy of a file on the same disk in the same subdirectory, you must give it a different name. Every file name in a directory must be unique.

5.14 ACTIVITY: USING THE COPY COMMAND

Note: The DATA disk is in Drive A. A:\> is displayed.

Step 1 Key in the following: A:\>**MD \CLASS** Enter

```
A:\>MD \CLASS

A:\>_
```

You created a subdirectory called **CLASS** on the DATA disk. Remember, MD, which means "make directory," is the command to create a place for additional files. The first backslash (\) is the name of the root directory. **CLASS** is the name of the subdirectory. The only reserved name for a directory is \. You may use any name for the subdirectory you create, provided that you follow the file-naming rules.

Step 2 Key in the following: A:\>**DIR** Enter

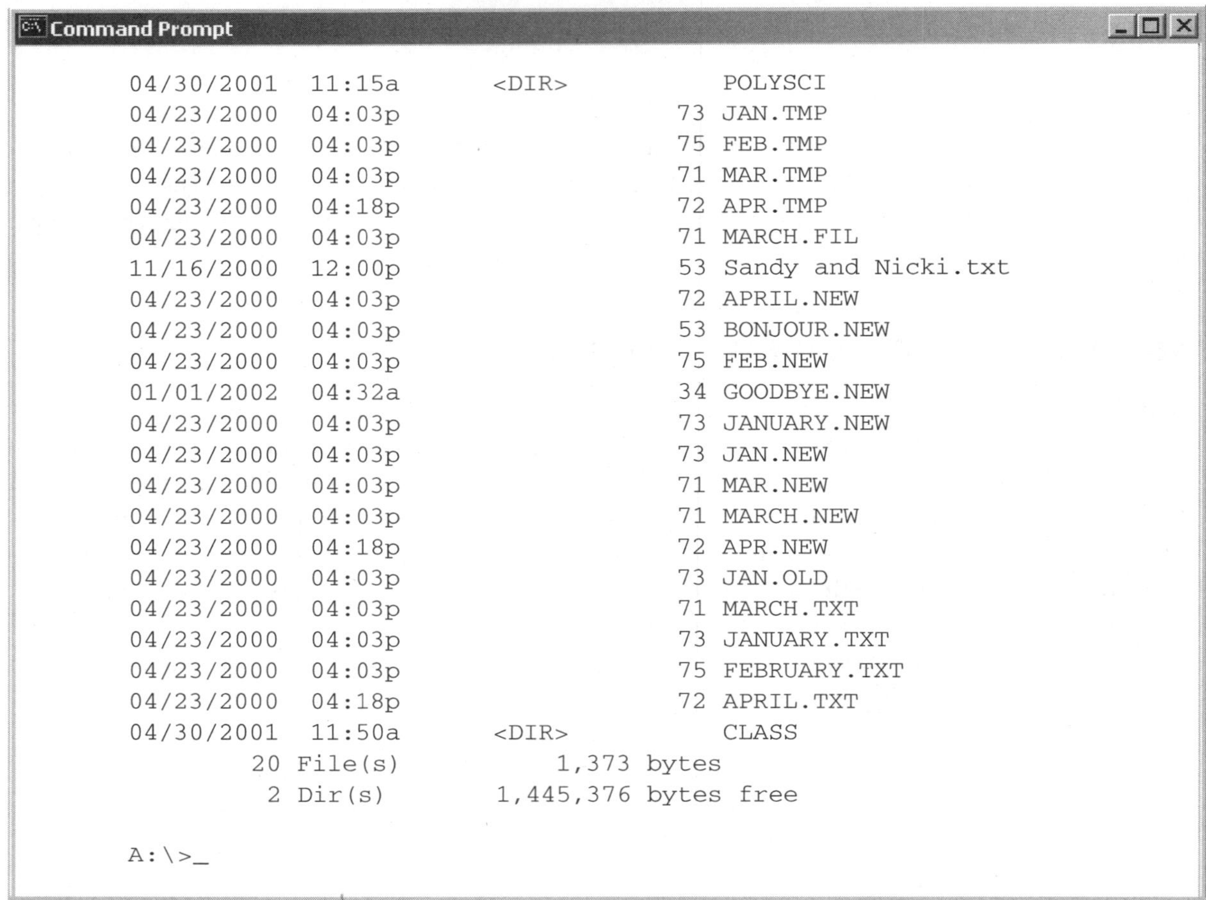

Command Prompt

```
04/30/2001  11:15a    <DIR>          POLYSCI
04/23/2000  04:03p               73 JAN.TMP
04/23/2000  04:03p               75 FEB.TMP
04/23/2000  04:03p               71 MAR.TMP
04/23/2000  04:18p               72 APR.TMP
04/23/2000  04:03p               71 MARCH.FIL
11/16/2000  12:00p               53 Sandy and Nicki.txt
04/23/2000  04:03p               72 APRIL.NEW
04/23/2000  04:03p               53 BONJOUR.NEW
04/23/2000  04:03p               75 FEB.NEW
01/01/2002  04:32a               34 GOODBYE.NEW
04/23/2000  04:03p               73 JANUARY.NEW
04/23/2000  04:03p               73 JAN.NEW
04/23/2000  04:03p               71 MAR.NEW
04/23/2000  04:03p               71 MARCH.NEW
04/23/2000  04:18p               72 APR.NEW
04/23/2000  04:03p               73 JAN.OLD
04/23/2000  04:03p               71 MARCH.TXT
04/23/2000  04:03p               73 JANUARY.TXT
04/23/2000  04:03p               75 FEBRUARY.TXT
04/23/2000  04:18p               72 APRIL.TXT
04/30/2001  11:50a    <DIR>          CLASS
        20 File(s)          1,373 bytes
         2 Dir(s)       1,445,376 bytes free

A:\>_
```

WHAT'S HAPPENING? The directory display shows the subdirectory called **CLASS**. You know it is a subdirectory because it has **<DIR>** by the file name. To see what is inside that subdirectory, or "file cabinet," you must use DIR with the path name. A review of the syntax is:

```
DIR [drive:][path][filename]
```

You do not need to include the drive letter since the default drive is where the DATA disk is. Nor do you need to include \ for the root directory, since the root directory of the DATA disk is the default. You do need to include the path name. The path name is the subdirectory name, **CLASS**.

Step 3 Key in the following: A:\>**DIR CLASS** Enter

Command Prompt

```
A:\>DIR CLASS
 Volume in drive A is DATA
 Volume Serial Number is 3330-1807

 Directory of A:\CLASS

04/30/2001  11:50a    <DIR>          .
04/30/2001  11:50a    <DIR>          ..
```

```
          0 File(s)              0 bytes
          2 Dir(s)       1,445,376 bytes free

A:\>_
```

This directory listing is not for the root directory. The display tells you what you are looking at. The third line of the display reads **Directory of A:\CLASS**, telling you that you are looking at the subdirectory called **CLASS** on the DATA disk. There is nothing yet in this subdirectory. The **.** and the **..** are created when you create a subdirectory. The **.** tells the operating system that this is a subdirectory. The **..** is a shorthand name for the directory above **CLASS**, in this case the root directory (\). How do you copy a file into this subdirectory? You can always use the absolute path. You do this by following the syntax of the COPY command:

```
COPY [drive:][path]filename   [drive:][path]filename
```

Step 4 Key in the following: A:\>**COPY A:\JAN.TMP A:\CLASS\JAN.PAR** Enter

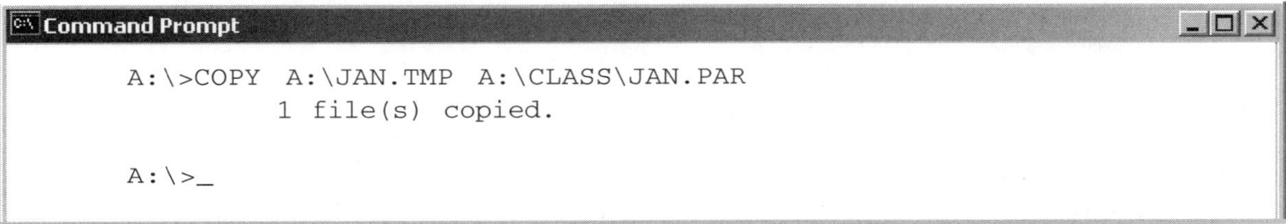

```
A:\>COPY A:\JAN.TMP A:\CLASS\JAN.PAR
          1 file(s) copied.

A:\>_
```

You copied the source file, **JAN.TMP**, from the root directory on the DATA disk, to the destination, the subdirectory **CLASS**; you also gave the destination file a new name, **JAN.PAR**. By looking at the syntax diagram, you can follow how you substituted the values you wanted:

```
COPY [drive:] [path]   [filename]  [drive:]  [path]     [file name]
COPY   A:       \       JAN.TMP      A:      \CLASS\     JAN.PAR
```

In the destination syntax, what is the second backslash? The first backslash is the name of the root directory. The second backslash is used as a delimiter between the subdirectory name and the file name. This delimiter tells the operating system that the subdirectory name is over and the file name is about to begin. Backslashes are used as delimiters separating subdirectory and file names.

Keying in the absolute path is not as easy as using the relative path. With the relative path, you don't have to key in the default drive and directory. The system will make these assumptions for you. You must include the command COPY. Since the DATA disk is the default drive, you do not need to include the drive letter, and, since the root directory is the default directory, you do not need to include the first \. However, you do need to include the source file name.

The same is true with the destination file. You do not need to include the drive letter or root directory, but you must include the path name and the new file name. The shorthand way of copying is done in Step 5.

Step 5 Key in the following: A:\>**COPY FEB.TMP CLASS\FEB.PAR** Enter

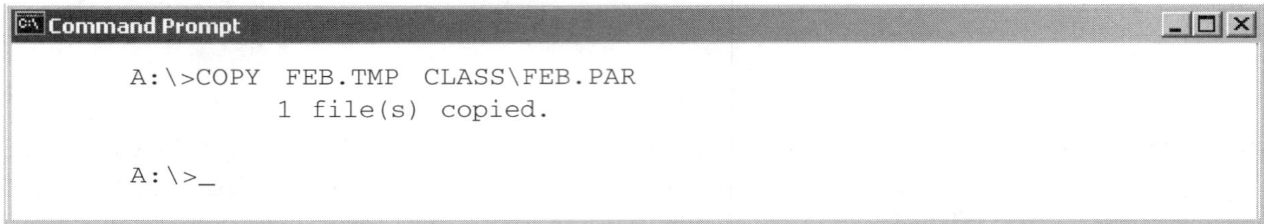

Command Prompt
A:\>COPY FEB.TMP CLASS\FEB.PAR
1 file(s) copied.
A:\>_

WHAT'S HAPPENING? In this case, you kept your typing to a minimum by using the relative path, observing your default drive and directory and keying in only what was necessary to execute the command.

Step 6 Key in the following: A:\>**DIR CLASS** Enter

```
Command Prompt

A:\>DIR CLASS
 Volume in drive A is DATA
 Volume Serial Number is 3330-1807

 Directory of A:\CLASS

04/30/2001  11:50a     <DIR>          .
04/30/2001  11:50a     <DIR>          ..
04/23/2000  04:03p                 73 JAN.PAR
04/23/2000  04:03p                 75 FEB.PAR
            2 File(s)           148 bytes
            2 Dir(s)      1,444,352 bytes free

A:\>_
```

WHAT'S HAPPENING? You copied the files **JAN.TMP** and **FEB.TMP** from the root directory to the subdirectory **CLASS** on the DATA disk. You gave the copies new names, **JAN.PAR** and **FEB.PAR**. Are the files the same? You can use the TYPE command to compare the contents visually, TYPE supports wildcards, but since the files are in different directories, you must look at each file individually. Again, since you want to look at the contents of two files in different subdirectories, you must follow the TYPE syntax:

```
TYPE [drive:][path]filename[.ext]
```

Step 7 Key in the following: A:\>**TYPE JAN.TMP CLASS\JAN.PAR** Enter

```
Command Prompt

A:\>TYPE JAN.TMP CLASS\JAN.PAR

JAN.TMP



This is my January file.
It is my first dummy file.
```

```
This is file 1.

CLASS\JAN.PAR



This is my January file.
It is my first dummy file.
This is file 1.

A:\>_
```

The contents of the files are the same, even though they are in different directories. The same is true for the **FEB** files.

Step 8 Key in the following: A:\>**TYPE FEB.TMP** Enter

Step 9 Key in the following: A:\>**TYPE CLASS\FEB.PAR** Enter

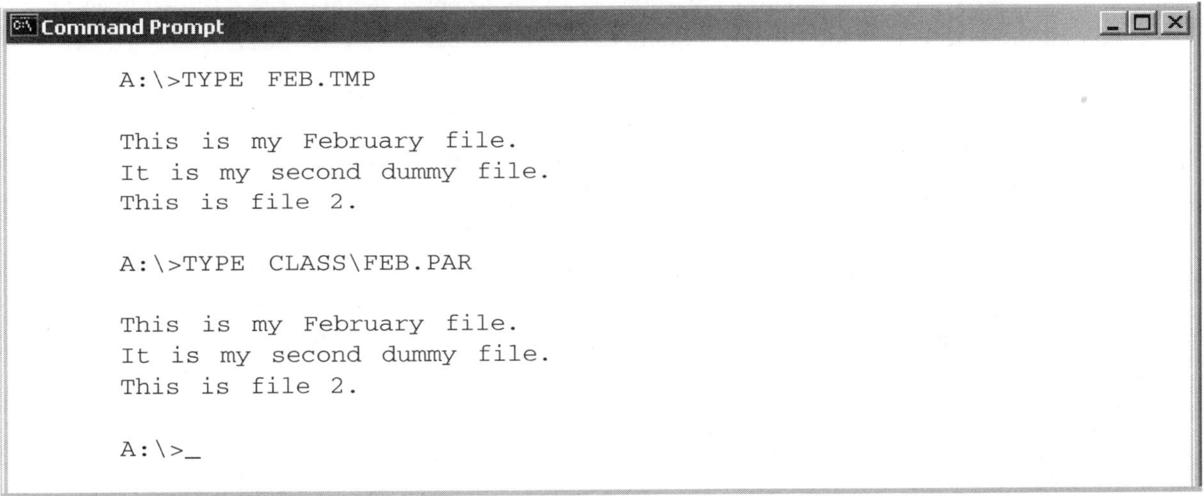

```
Command Prompt

A:\>TYPE FEB.TMP

This is my February file.
It is my second dummy file.
This is file 2.

A:\>TYPE CLASS\FEB.PAR

This is my February file.
It is my second dummy file.
This is file 2.

A:\>_
```

The file contents are the same.

5.15 USING WILDCARDS WITH THE COPY COMMAND

You can also use wildcards to copy files on the same drive to a different subdirectory. Again, the important point to remember when using the command line is that you can never violate syntax. It is always COPY *source destination*. Computers and commands always do what you tell them to. Users sometimes think that the "computer lost their files." More often than not, files are misplaced because the user gave an instruction that he or she thought meant one thing but, in reality, meant something else. For instance,when the default drive and directory was A:\>, you keyed in COPY THIS.FIL YOUR.FIL. You wanted YOUR.FIL to be copied to the root of Drive C. Since you did not key that in (C:\YOUR.FIL), the default drive and directory were used, and YOUR.FIL was copied to the default drive and directory (A:\) instead of where you wanted it to go.

5.16 ACTIVITY: USING WILDCARDS WITH THE COPY COMMAND

Note: The DATA disk is in Drive A. A:\> is displayed.

Step 1 Key in the following: A:\>**COPY *.TMP CLASS*.ABC** Enter

```
Command Prompt

A:\>COPY *.TMP CLASS\*.ABC
JAN.TMP
FEB.TMP
MAR.TMP
APR.TMP
        4 file(s) copied.

A:\>_
```

As each file is copied, it is displayed on the screen. Your command line says COPY any file on the DATA disk in the root directory (the default directory) that has the file extension **.TMP**, regardless of its file name, to a new set of files that will have the same file name but a different extension, **.ABC**. These files were copied to the subdirectory called **CLASS** on the DATA disk.

You could have keyed in **COPY A:*.TMP A:\CLASS*.ABC**. Once again, for the source files (***.TMP**), it is unnecessary to specify the designated drive and directory. Since you did not tell it otherwise, the default drive and default directory were assumed. However, for the destination you had to include the subdirectory name, **CLASS**; otherwise, the files would have been copied to the default drive and directory instead of to the subdirectory **CLASS**.

This is another area where using the command line is much quicker and easier than using the GUI. In order to accomplish what you did with one command, you would have had to take many more steps in Windows Explorer. You would have had to select the files individually, drag them to their new location, and then rename each file individually. You can see why users like the command line for certain tasks.

Step 2 Key in the following: A:\>**DIR *.TMP** Enter

Step 3 Key in the following: A:\>**DIR CLASS*.ABC** Enter

```
Command Prompt

A:\>DIR *.TMP
 Volume in drive A is DATA
 Volume Serial Number is 3330-1807

 Directory of A:\

04/23/2000  04:03p                  73 JAN.TMP
04/23/2000  04:03p                  75 FEB.TMP
04/23/2000  04:03p                  71 MAR.TMP
04/23/2000  04:18p                  72 APR.TMP
            4 File(s)            291 bytes
            0 Dir(s)       1,442,304 bytes free
```

```
A:\>DIR CLASS\*.ABC
 Volume in drive A is DATA
 Volume Serial Number is 3330-1807

 Directory of A:\CLASS

04/23/2000  04:03p                  73 JAN.ABC
04/23/2000  04:03p                  75 FEB.ABC
04/23/2000  04:03p                  71 MAR.ABC
04/23/2000  04:18p                  72 APR.ABC
               4 File(s)           291 bytes
               0 Dir(s)      1,442,304 bytes free

A:\>_
```

You keyed in two commands, **DIR *.TMP** and **DIR CLASS *.ABC**, although you could have used one command. You used wildcards to display the **.ABC** files in the subdirectory **CLASS** and the **.TMP** files in the root directory. You also used the wildcard * to make copies of the **.TMP** files. The file names are identical, but the extensions are different. The files were copied to the subdirectory **CLASS**. However, the directory display merely shows that the files are there. To see that the contents of the original files and copied files are the same, use the TYPE command. Remember, you must specify the subdirectory where the **.ABC** files are located.

Step 4 Key in the following: A:\>**TYPE FEB.TMP** **Enter**

Step 5 Key in the following: A:\>**TYPE CLASS\FEB.ABC** **Enter**

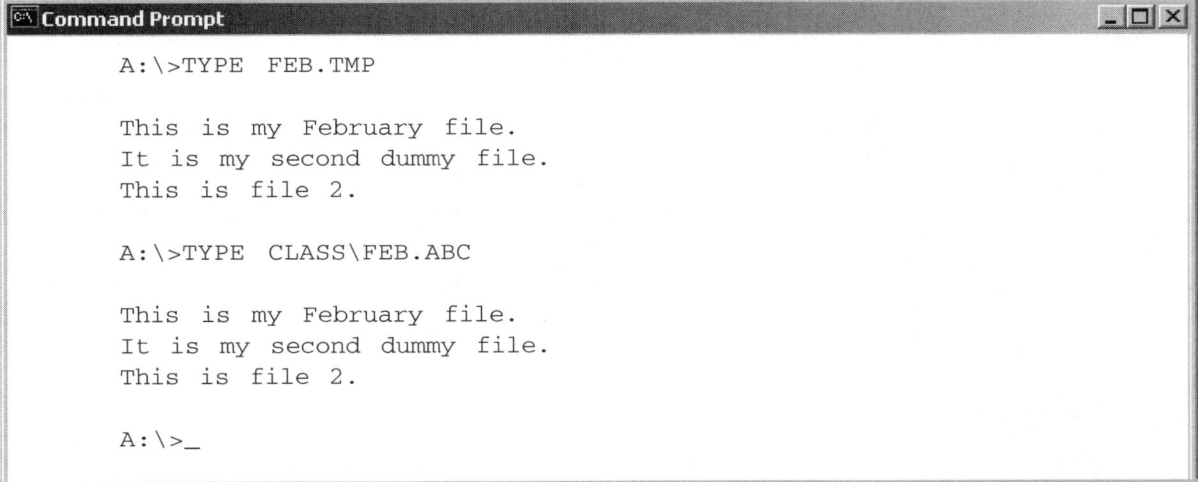

Command Prompt
A:\>TYPE FEB.TMP
This is my February file.
It is my second dummy file.
This is file 2.
A:\>TYPE CLASS\FEB.ABC
This is my February file.
It is my second dummy file.
This is file 2.
A:\>_

The file contents are identical, even though the file names are different and the files are in different directories.

5.17 USING COPY AND DIR WITH SUBDIRECTORIES

You are going to see how commands work with subdirectories by using the COPY command to place files in the subdirectories and by using the DIR command to see that the files were copied.

5.18 ACTIVITY: USING COPY WITH SUBDIRECTORIES

Note: The DATA disk is in Drive A. A:\> is displayed.

Step 1 Key in the following: A:\>**CD POLYSCI\USA** Enter

Step 2 Key in the following: A:\POLYSCI\USA>**DIR** Enter

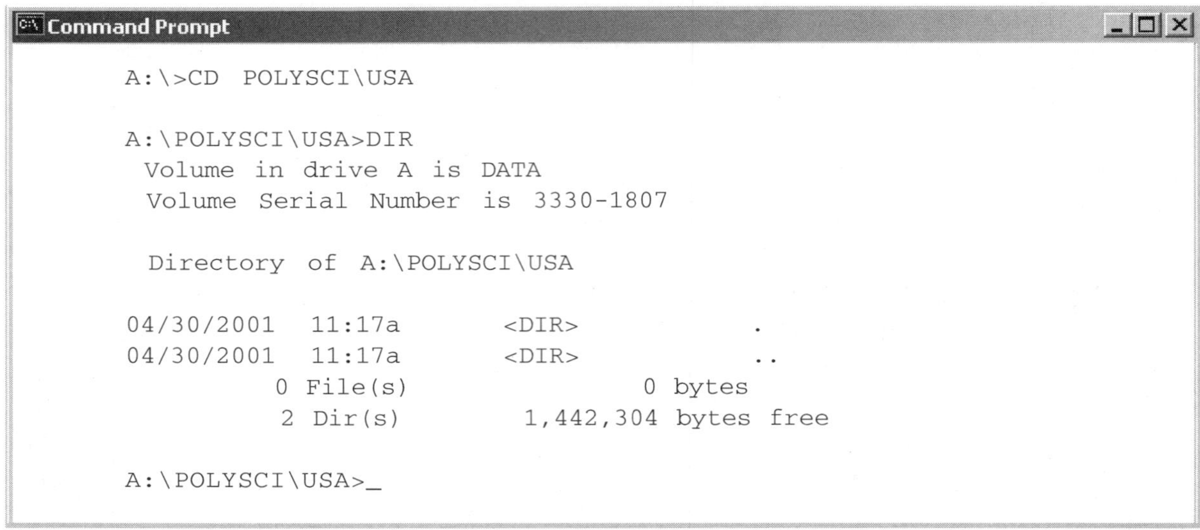

```
Command Prompt

A:\>CD POLYSCI\USA

A:\POLYSCI\USA>DIR
 Volume in drive A is DATA
 Volume Serial Number is 3330-1807

 Directory of A:\POLYSCI\USA

04/30/2001  11:17a    <DIR>          .
04/30/2001  11:17a    <DIR>          ..
          0 File(s)              0 bytes
          2 Dir(s)       1,442,304 bytes free

A:\POLYSCI\USA>_
```

You changed the default directory to the **USA** directory, which is under the **POLYSCI** directory under the root of the DATA disk. The prompt should display **A:\POLYSCI\USA>** as the default drive and subdirectory. The prompt is quite lengthy because it shows you the default drive as well as the default subdirectory. *Remember:* All activities will occur in the subdirectory **\POLYSCI\USA**, unless you specify another path. When you keyed in DIR, it showed you the contents of only the current default directory. The directory is empty of files but has the two subdirectory markers, dot and double dot.

Step 3 Key in the following:
A:\POLYSCI\USA>**COPY \CLASS\JAN.PAR FINAL.RPT** Enter

```
Command Prompt

A:\POLYSCI\USA>COPY \CLASS\JAN.PAR FINAL.RPT
        1 file(s) copied.

A:\POLYSCI\USA>_
```

The file called **JAN.PAR** in the subdirectory **\CLASS** was successfully copied to the subdirectory **\POLYSCI\USA**, but is now called **FINAL.RPT**. Spacing is very important when keying in commands.

```
Command  Space  Source (no spaces)  Space  Destination (no spaces)
COPY              \CLASS\JAN.PAR             FINAL.RPT
```

The syntax of the COPY command remained the same—COPY *source destination*. First, you issued the COPY command, but it was not enough to list just the file name **JAN.PAR** as the source. You had to include the path so that the operating system would know in which subdirectory the file was located; hence, the source was **\CLASS\JAN.PAR**. Users often get confused when using \. Here is a simple rule: The first \ in any command line always means the root directory. Any other \ in the command is simply a delimiter.

Thus, in the example, the first \ tells the operating system to go to the root and then go down to **CLASS**. The second \ is the delimiter between the subdirectory name and the file name, **JAN.PAR**. The destination is a file called **FINAL.RPT**. You did not have to key in the path for the destination because the default (**\POLYSCI\USA**) was assumed. Remember, you can always key in the command using the absolute path. In this instance, the command would have read as follows:

```
COPY   A:\CLASS\JAN.PAR   A:\POLYSCI\USA\FINAL.RPT
```

Next, you are going to make a copy of the file in the current directory, so you do not need to include the absolute path name; here, you can use the relative path name.

Step 4 Key in the following: A:\POLYSCI\USA>**COPY FINAL.RPT NOTE2.TMP** Enter

Step 5 Key in the following: A:\POLYSCI\USA>**COPY FINAL.RPT NOTE3.TMP** Enter

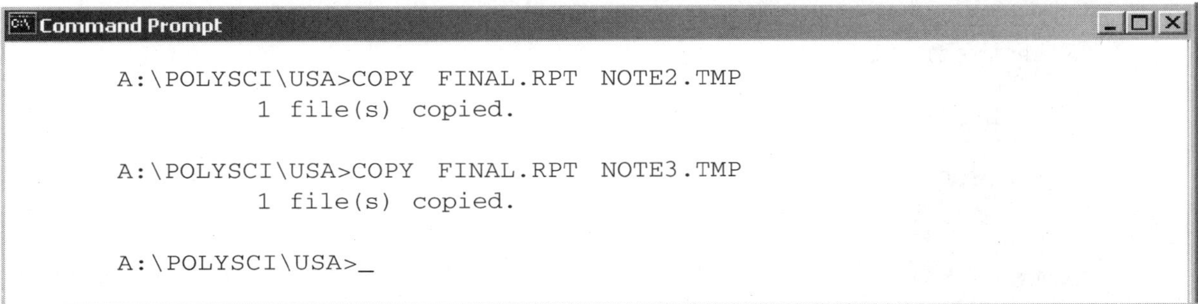
Command Prompt
A:\POLYSCI\USA>COPY FINAL.RPT NOTE2.TMP
1 file(s) copied.
A:\POLYSCI\USA>COPY FINAL.RPT NOTE3.TMP
1 file(s) copied.
A:\POLYSCI\USA>_

WHAT'S HAPPENING?

You copied two files. You did not have to include the absolute path name because the default path was assumed. You used the relative path name. The operating system always assumes the default drive and directory, unless you tell it otherwise. Technically, the commands looked like this:

```
COPY   A:\POLYSCI\USA\FINAL.RPT   A:\POLYSCI\USA\NOTE2.TMP
COPY   A:\POLYSCI\USA\FINAL.RPT   A:\POLYSCI\USA\NOTE3.TMP
```

You can see that using the relative path eliminates a lot of keystrokes.

Step 6 Key in the following: A:\POLYSCI\USA>**DIR** Enter

```
Command Prompt
A:\POLYSCI\USA>DIR
 Volume in drive A is DATA
 Volume Serial Number is 3330-1807

 Directory of A:\POLYSCI\USA
```

```
04/30/2001  11:17a      <DIR>          .
04/30/2001  11:17a      <DIR>          ..
04/23/2000   04:03p                 73 FINAL.RPT
04/23/2000   04:03p                 73 NOTE2.TMP
04/23/2000   04:03p                 73 NOTE3.TMP
           3 File(s)            219 bytes
           2 Dir(s)       1,440,768 bytes free

A:\POLYSCI\USA>_
```

You see only the files that are in the default subdirectory. You can create subdirectories from the current directory. Do not forget about the command line editing keys. As you use them, you become familiar with how they work and you save yourself unneeded keystrokes.

Step 7 Key in the following: A:\POLYSCI\USA>**MD \WORK** Enter

Step 8 Key in the following: A:\POLYSCI\USA>**MD \WORK\CLIENTS** Enter

Step 9 Key in the following: A:\POLYSCI\USA>**MD \WORK\ADS** Enter

```
Command Prompt

A:\POLYSCI\USA>MD  \WORK

A:\POLYSCI\USA>MD  \WORK\CLIENTS

A:\POLYSCI\USA>MD  \WORK\ADS

A:\POLYSCI\USA>_
```

You had to include the first backslash so that the **WORK** directory would be under the root instead of under POLYSCI\USA. **WORK** had to be created before you could create its subdirectories, **CLIENTS** and **ADS**. However, you could have created **WORK** and **CLIENTS** with one command by keying in **MD\WORK\CLIENTS**. Now that you have created the directories of interest, you can use wildcards to copy files to them.

Step 10 Key in the following: A:\POLYSCI\USA>**COPY *.* \WORK\CLIENTS** Enter

```
Command Prompt

A:\POLYSCI\USA>COPY  *.*  \WORK\CLIENTS
FINAL.RPT
NOTE2.TMP
NOTE3.TMP
          3 file(s) copied.

A:\POLYSCI\USA>_
```

As the files were copied to the **\WORK\CLIENTS** subdirectory, they were listed on the screen. Again, the syntax is the same: the command (COPY), the source (***.*** meaning all the files in the default subdirectory **\POLYSCI\USA**), the destination (**\WORK\CLIENTS**). You had to

include the absolute path name in the destination. The first \ in the destination is very important because it tells the OS to go to the top of the tree structure and *then* go down to the **\WORK\CLIENTS** subdirectory. If you had not included that first backslash, the operating system would have looked under the subdirectory **\POLYSCI\USA**. Since you wanted to have the files with the same name in the destination subdirectory, **\WORK\CLIENTS**, you did not have to specify new file names. The operating system used or *defaulted* to the current file names.

Step 11 Key in the following: A:\POLYSCI\USA>**DIR \WORK\CLIENTS** Enter

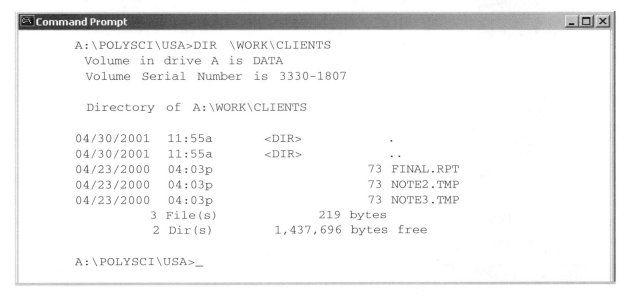

```
Command Prompt

A:\POLYSCI\USA>DIR \WORK\CLIENTS
 Volume in drive A is DATA
 Volume Serial Number is 3330-1807

 Directory of A:\WORK\CLIENTS

04/30/2001  11:55a      <DIR>          .
04/30/2001  11:55a      <DIR>          ..
04/23/2000  04:03p                  73 FINAL.RPT
04/23/2000  04:03p                  73 NOTE2.TMP
04/23/2000  04:03p                  73 NOTE3.TMP
               3 File(s)            219 bytes
               2 Dir(s)      1,437,696 bytes free

A:\POLYSCI\USA>_
```

WHAT'S HAPPENING? You can copy files from anywhere to anywhere, provided you give the source and destination locations. If you use the relative path, be sure you are aware of the current default drive and directory.

Step 12 Key in the following:
A:\POLYSCI\USA>**COPY \WORK\CLIENTS\NOTE?.TMP \WORK\ADS\EXAM?.QZ** Enter

```
Command Prompt

A:\POLYSCI\USA>COPY \WORK\CLIENTS\NOTE?.TMP \WORK\ADS\EXAM?.QZ
\WORK\CLIENTS\NOTE2.TMP
\WORK\CLIENTS\NOTE3.TMP
          2 file(s) copied.

A:\POLYSCI\USA>_
```

WHAT'S HAPPENING? The operating system displayed the entire path name as it copied all the **.TMP** files from the subdirectory **\WORK\CLIENTS** to the subdirectory **\WORK\ADS**. So that you could retain the number in the source file name in the destination file names, you used the **?** wildcard as a place holder. Thus, **NOTE2.TMP** copied as **EXAM2.QZ**, and **NOTE3.TMP** copied as **EXAM3.QZ**. To see if the files were copied correctly, you will use the DIR command.

Step 13 Key in the following: A:\POLYSCI\USA>**DIR \WORK\ADS** Enter

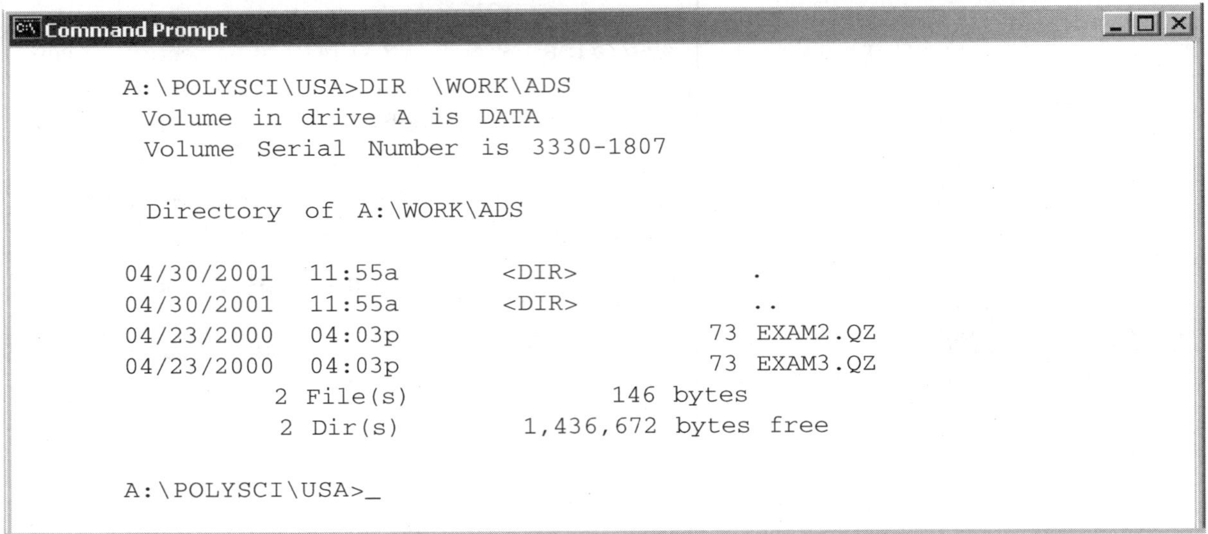

Command Prompt

```
A:\POLYSCI\USA>DIR  \WORK\ADS
 Volume in drive A is DATA
 Volume Serial Number is 3330-1807

 Directory of A:\WORK\ADS

04/30/2001  11:55a      <DIR>          .
04/30/2001  11:55a      <DIR>          ..
04/23/2000  04:03p                  73 EXAM2.QZ
04/23/2000  04:03p                  73 EXAM3.QZ
               2 File(s)            146 bytes
               2 Dir(s)       1,436,672 bytes free

A:\POLYSCI\USA>_
```

WHAT'S HAPPENING? You successfully copied the files because you used the proper path name. You have been using the COPY and DIR commands to exemplify how to use the path. Any command will work if you use the proper syntax and the proper path.

Step 14 Key in the following: A:\POLYSCI\USA>**C:** Enter

Step 15 Key in the following: C:\>**CD \WINDOSBK** Enter

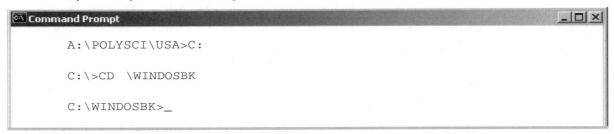

Command Prompt

```
A:\POLYSCI\USA>C:

C:\>CD  \WINDOSBK

C:\WINDOSBK>_
```

Note: The prompt you saw as you began Step 15 (**C:\ >**) may be different on your system if you have been interrupted while following the steps in this chapter. It does not matter; the command **CD \WINDOSBK** specifies to change directories to the root (\) of the current drive, and *then* to the subdirectory **WINDOSBK**. Regardless of what directory you went to when you keyed in Step 14, you will end up in **C:\WINDOSBK** after Step 15.

WHAT'S HAPPENING? You changed the default drive to C. In this example, you were in the root directory of C. You then changed the default directory to **WINDOSBK**. Note that it took two steps. You must first change drives, then change directories.

Step 16 Key in the following: C:\WINDOSBK>**COPY DRESS.UP A:** Enter

Command Prompt

```
C:\WINDOSBK>COPY  DRESS.UP   A:
        1 file(s) copied.

C:\WINDOSBK>_
```

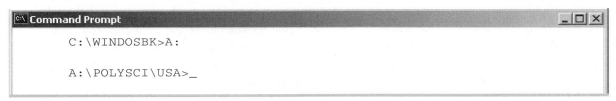

WHAT'S HAPPENING? You executed a simple COPY command. You asked the OS to copy the file called **DRESS.UP** from the **\WINDOSBK** directory to the DATA disk in the A drive, but where on the DATA disk did the file get copied? Since the last place you were on the DATA disk was the **USA** subdirectory (under **POLYSCI**, under the root), that is where the file was copied. You did not specify a destination directory and consequently, the current default directory was used. If you wanted the file copied to the root directory of the DATA disk, you would have had to key in **COPY DRESS.UP A:**.

Step 17 Key in the following: C:\WINDOSBK>**DIR A:DRESS.UP** Enter

Step 18 Key in the following: C:\WINDOSBK>**DIR A:\DRESS.UP** Enter

Command Prompt

```
C:\WINDOSBK>DIR A:DRESS.UP
 Volume in drive A is DATA
 Volume Serial Number is 3330-1807

 Directory of A:\POLYSCI\USA

10/01/2000  04:12p                  26 DRESS.UP
               1 File(s)             26 bytes
               0 Dir(s)       1,436,160 bytes free

C:\WINDOSBK>DIR A:\DRESS.UP
 Volume in drive A is DATA
 Volume Serial Number is 3330-1807

 Directory of A:\

File Not Found

C:\WINDOSBK>_
```

WHAT'S HAPPENING? The last place you were on the DATA disk was in the subdirectory **\POLYSCI\USA**. The operating system "remembered" where you last were and copied the file to the **USA** subdirectory (currently, the default directory), not to the root directory. When you asked DIR to locate the file **DRESS.UP** and preceded **DRESS.UP** only with **A:**, the operating system looked in the default directory of **A:**, which was **\POLYSCI\USA**. In order to look at the root directory, you had to request **A:\DRESS.UP**. When you did, the file was not found because that was not where it was copied.

Step 19 Key in the following: C:\WINDOSBK>**A:** Enter

Your default drive is now the A drive, where the DATA disk is located. Look at the default directory. Note that you are not in the root directory of the DATA disk but were returned to the **USA** subdirectory (under **POLYSCI**, under the root directory). As you can see, if you change drives during various activities, Windows will remember the last default subdirectory of the drive you were on. On the hard disk, the default directory is still **\WINDOSBK**.

Step 20 Key in the following: A:\POLYSCI\USA>**CD C:** Enter

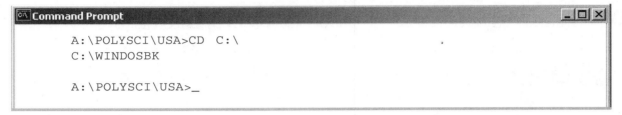

```
Command Prompt

A:\POLYSCI\USA>CD C:\
C:\WINDOSBK

A:\POLYSCI\USA>_
```

You issued the command to change the directory to the root on the hard disk, in this case Drive C, but your prompt shows that you are still in the **USA** subdirectory on the DATA disk. Did you accomplish anything with the command?

Step 21 Key in the following: A:\POLYSCI\USA>**DIR C:ZZZ*.*** Enter

```
Command Prompt

A:\POLYSCI\USA>DIR C:ZZZ*.*
 Volume in drive C is 2000 PRO
 Volume Serial Number is C4A7-8571

 Directory of C:\

File Not Found

A:\POLYSCI\USA>_
```

You used a made-up file name to see the current default directory on the C drive. Notice the directory line **Directory of C:**. You did, indeed, change directories on C drive. When you issued the command **CD C:**, you changed the default directory from **\WINDOSBK** to the root of C on the hard disk without leaving the DATA disk.

5.19 USING SUBDIRECTORY MARKERS WITH THE COPY COMMAND

Because the command line can get unwieldy, using the subdirectory markers dot and double dot is a convenient shorthand way of writing commands. The **..** represents the parent of the current directory. The only directory that does not have a parent is the root directory because it is the ultimate parent of all the directories on a disk. You are going to use COPY as an example, but any system command works with subdirectory markers. Subdirectory markers are sometimes also called “dot notation.”

5.20 ACTIVITY: USING SHORTCUTS: THE SUBDIRECTORY MARKERS

Note: The DATA disk is in Drive A. A:\POLYSCI\USA> is displayed.

Step 1 Key in the following: A:\POLYSCI\USA>**COPY FINAL.RPT ..\FIRST.TST** Enter

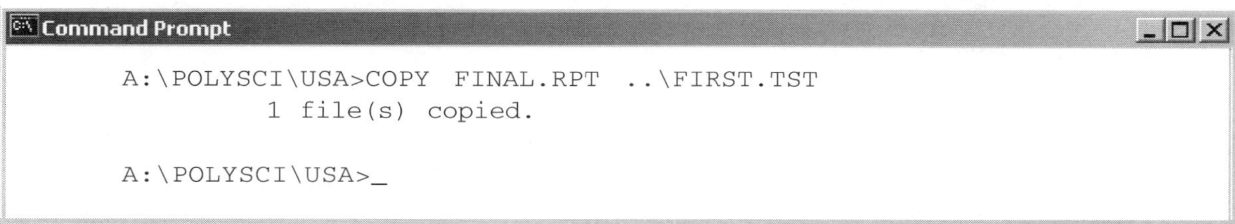
Command Prompt
A:\POLYSCI\USA>COPY FINAL.RPT ..\FIRST.TST
1 file(s) copied.
A:\POLYSCI\USA>_

WHAT'S HAPPENING? You copied the file called **FINAL.RPT** located in the current directory, **USA**, to the parent of **USA**, which is **POLYSCI**. You gave it a new name, **FIRST.TST**. Instead of having to key in **\POLYSCI\FIRST.TST**, you used the shorthand name for **\POLYSCI**, which is **..**. This means the parent of **USA**. You included \ between **..** and **FIRST.TST** as a delimiter.

Step 2 Key in the following:
A:\POLYSCI\USA>**COPY ..\FIRST.TST ..\FRANCE\LAST.TST** Enter

Command Prompt

```
A:\POLYSCI\USA>COPY  ..\FIRST.TST  ..\FRANCE\LAST.TST
        1 file(s) copied.

A:\POLYSCI\USA>_
```

WHAT'S HAPPENING? You copied the file called **FIRST.TST** from the **POLYSCI** subdirectory to the **FRANCE** subdirectory, which is a child directory of **POLYSCI**. The long way to key in the command is to use the absolute path. If you issued the command using the absolute path, it would look like the following:

```
COPY A:\POLYSCI\FIRST.TST A:\POLYSCI\FRANCE\LAST.TST
```

In the source file, the first **..** represented the parent of USA. You did not have to key in **\POLYSCI**. However, you did need to key in the delimiter \ preceding the file name. You also did not need to key in **\POLYSCI** in the destination file. Instead you used the subdirectory marker **..** (double dot). You did need to key in \ preceding **FRANCE** and \ preceding **LAST.TST** because they were needed as delimiters to separate subdirectory names and file names. You can use subdirectory markers to save keystrokes. You can now verify that the files are in the **FRANCE** subdirectory.

Step 3 Key in the following: A:\POLYSCI\USA>**DIR ..\FRANCE** Enter

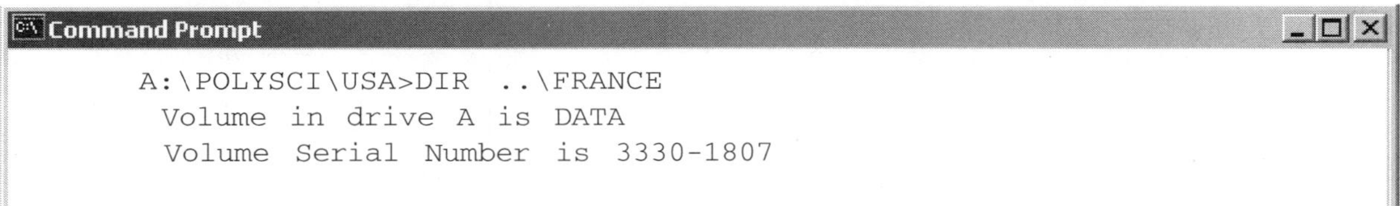
Command Prompt
A:\POLYSCI\USA>DIR ..\FRANCE
Volume in drive A is DATA
Volume Serial Number is 3330-1807

```
 Directory of A:\POLYSCI\FRANCE

04/30/2001  11:19a      <DIR>          .
04/30/2001  11:19a      <DIR>          ..
04/23/2000   04:03p                   73 LAST.TST
         1 File(s)              73 bytes
         2 Dir(s)        1,435,136 bytes free

A:\POLYSCI\USA>_
```

You used the DIR command with the subdirectory markers to verify that you successfully copied the file using subdirectory markers. The double dot (..) represents the immediate parent directory. If you want to move up the tree structure by two levels, you can use a triple dot (...) to accomplish this.

Step 4 Key in the following: A:\POLYSCI\USA>**CD ** Enter

You returned to the root of the DATA disk.

5.21 OVERWRITING FILES WITH THE COPY COMMAND

When you made copies of files, you gave the files on the same disk and in the same subdirectory unique names. One of the reasons for doing this is that, when you tried to use the same file name on the same disk and directory, you got an error message:

```
File cannot be copied onto itself,
     0 file(s) copied.
```

The operating system would not permit you to make that error. However, the rule of unique file names is true only if the files are on the same disk and in the same subdirectory. If you are using more than one disk or more than one subdirectory, the system *will* let you use the same file name. There have been no problems so far because, when you copied the source file from one disk to the destination file on another disk, it was a new file on the destination disk.

Overwrite means just what it says; it writes over or replaces what used to be in a file. If the contents of the source file are different from the contents of the destination file, when you overwrite the destination file this will change. Both files will now have not only the same file *name* but also the same file *contents*. The previous contents of the destination file will be gone. Overwriting also happens on the same disk when the destination file name already exists. The same rules apply to subdirectories. See Figure 5.4 for a graphic representation of this.

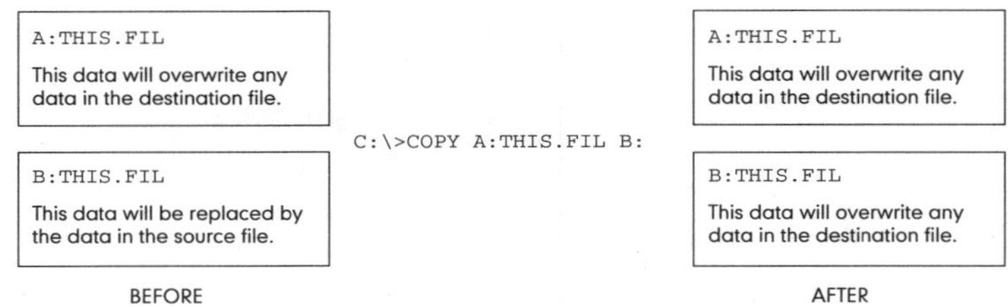

FIGURE 5.4 OVERWRITING FILES

The overwrite process seems dangerous because you will lose the data in the destination file when you replace it with the source file. Why are you not protected from this error? Because, when working with computers, this is typically *not* an error. Usually, you *do* want to overwrite files. That is, you want to replace the old contents of a file with the new, revised contents.

Data changes all the time. For example, if you have a customer list stored as a file named CUSTOMER.LST on a disk, the information in the file (the data) changes as you add, delete, and update information about customers. When you have completed your work for the day, you want to back up your file or copy it to another disk because you are working with it on a daily basis. Thus, you have a file called CUSTOMER.LST on your source disk and a file called CUSTOMER.LST on your destination disk. Since CUSTOMER.LST is clearly a descriptive file name, you really do not want to create a new file name every time you copy the file to the destination disk because creating new file names and then tracking current files can be time-consuming and confusing. In addition, if you are working with a file on a daily basis, you could end up with hundreds of files. In reality, you do not care about last week's or yesterday's customer information or the old file; you care about the current version and its backup file. When copying a file for backup purposes, you do want the source file to overwrite the destination file. Windows warns you that this is an overwrite—that you are about to overwrite the data in the older file. The same is true at the command line. In earlier versions of the operating system, prior to DOS 6.2, you were not made aware of the existence of a file on the destination disk that has the same name—DOS simply overwrote the destination file contents with the source file contents without a warning.

5.22 ACTIVITY: OVERWRITING FILES USING THE COPY COMMAND

Note: The DATA disk is in Drive A. A:\> is displayed.

Step 1 Key in the following: A:\>**TYPE GOODBYE.NEW** Enter

Step 2 Key in the following: A:\>**TYPE JAN.OLD** Enter

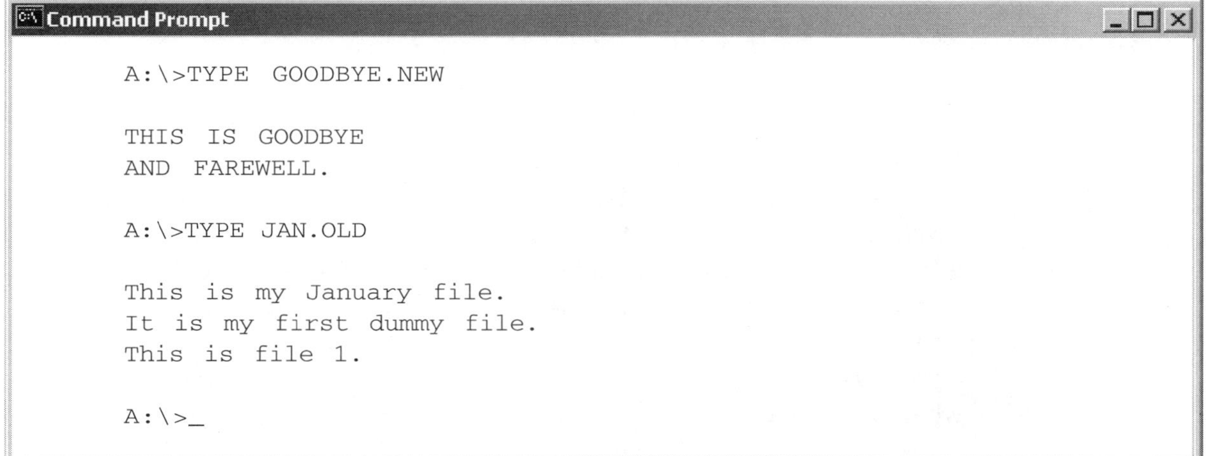

Command Prompt
A:\>TYPE GOODBYE.NEW
THIS IS GOODBYE
AND FAREWELL.
A:\>TYPE JAN.OLD
This is my January file.
It is my first dummy file.
This is file 1.
A:\>_

You have displayed the contents of two files and can see that each file contains different data.

Step 3 Key in the following: A:\>**COPY GOODBYE.NEW JAN.OLD** Enter

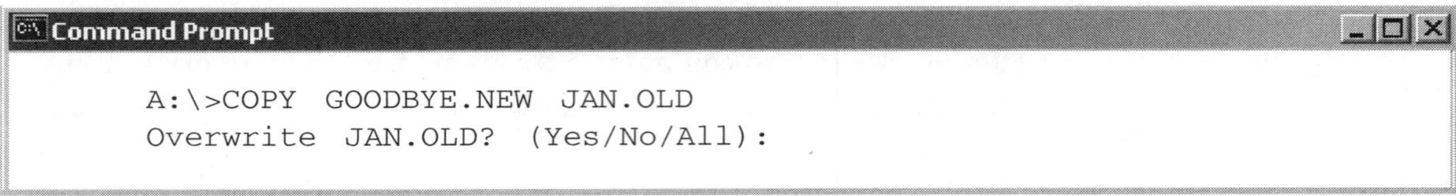

Overwrite JAN.OLD? (Yes/No/All):

WHAT'S HAPPENING? You get a message telling you that you already have a file by the name of **JAN.OLD**.

Step 4 Key in the following: **Y** Enter

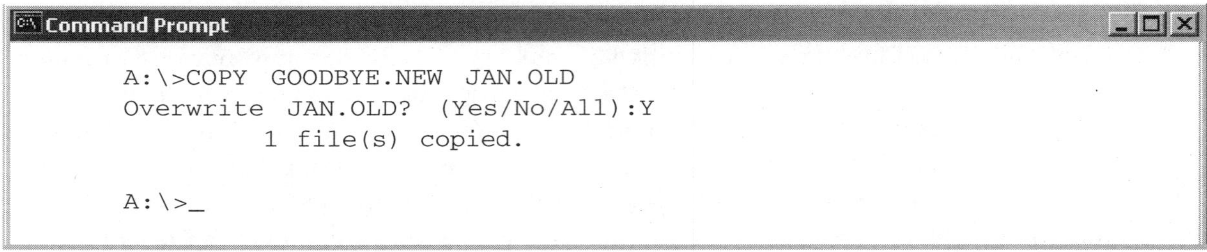

Overwrite JAN.OLD? (Yes/No/All):Y

WHAT'S HAPPENING? The file **GOODBYE.NEW** was successfully copied to the file called **JAN.OLD**, but what about the contents of the file? Did anything change?

Step 5 Key in the following: A:\>**TYPE GOODBYE.NEW** Enter

Step 6 Key in the following: A:\>**TYPE JAN.OLD** Enter

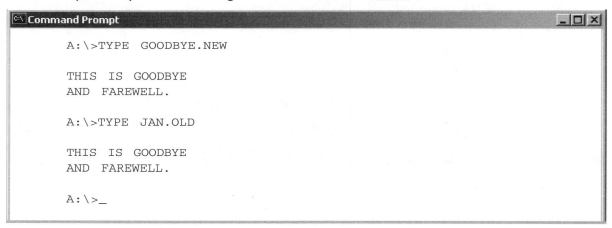

WHAT'S HAPPENING? The file contents are now identical. What used to be inside the file called **JAN.OLD** located on the DATA disk was overwritten or replaced (i.e., is gone forever) by the contents of the file called **GOODBYE.NEW**. You need to be aware of how this procedure works so that you do not accidentally overwrite a file.

The operating system does not allow you to overwrite or copy a file when the source file and the destination file are on the same disk and in the same subdirectory and have exactly the same file name.

Step 7 Key in the following: A:\>**COPY JAN.OLD JAN.OLD** Enter

Command Prompt

```
A:\>COPY JAN.OLD JAN.OLD
The file cannot be copied onto itself.
        0 file(s) copied.

A:\>_
```

WHAT'S HAPPENING? You tried to copy (overwrite) a file onto itself and got an error message. This process works the same when you are dealing with subdirectories.

In Activity 5.14, you copied **JAN.TMP** and **FEB.TMP** to the **CLASS** directory with the same file names but different extensions, so that in the **CLASS** directory the files were now called **JAN.PAR** and **FEB.PAR**. You are going to use wildcards to copy the rest of the **.TMP** files to the **CLASS** directory. In the process, you will overwrite the existing files.

Step 8 Key in the following: A:\>**COPY *.TMP CLASS*.PAR** Enter

Command Prompt

```
A:\>COPY *.TMP CLASS\*.PAR
JAN.TMP
Overwrite CLASS\JAN.PAR? (Yes/No/All):
```

WHAT'S HAPPENING? The OS does not know the contents of the file; it only knows you already have a file by that name. Rather than prompting you each time, one of the choices is A for "all." Thus, if you intend to overwrite all the **.TMP** files, you can choose A.

Step 9 Key in the following: **A** Enter

Command Prompt

```
A:\>COPY *.TMP CLASS\*.PAR
JAN.TMP
Overwrite CLASS\JAN.PAR? (Yes/No/All):A
FEB.TMP
MAR.TMP
APR.TMP
        4 file(s) copied.

A:\>_
```

WHAT'S HAPPENING? The OS has overwritten the **JAN.PAR** and **FEB.PAR** files in the **CLASS** directory with the **JAN.TMP** and **FEB.TMP** files in the root directory. You can prove this occurred by using the TYPE command.

Step 10 Key in the following: A:\>**TYPE JAN.TMP** Enter

Step 11 Key in the following: A:\>**TYPE CLASS\JAN.PAR** Enter

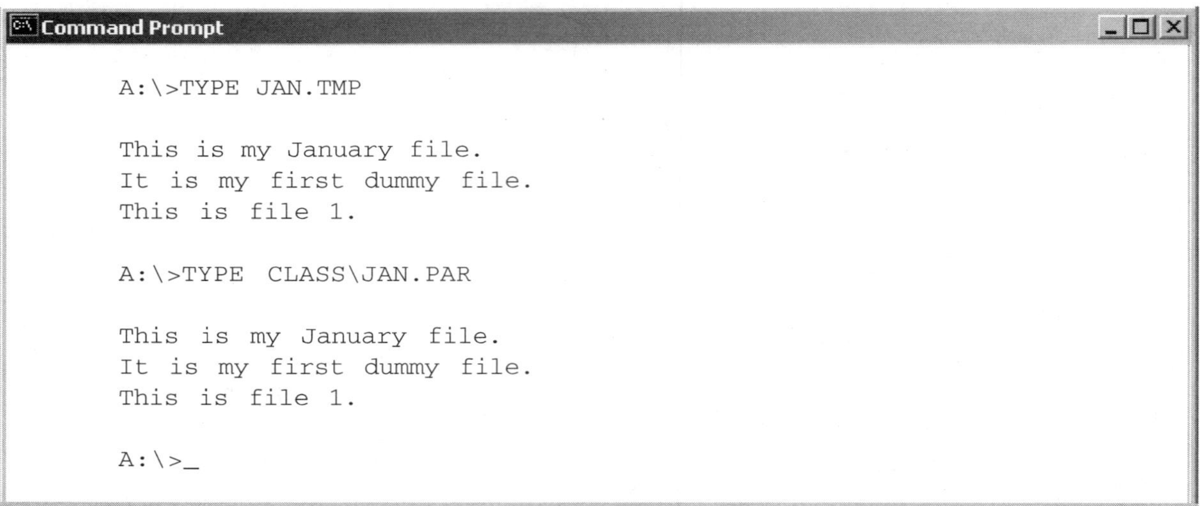

```
Command Prompt

A:\>TYPE JAN.TMP

This is my January file.
It is my first dummy file.
This is file 1.

A:\>TYPE CLASS\JAN.PAR

This is my January file.
It is my first dummy file.
This is file 1.

A:\>_
```

WHAT'S HAPPENING? As you can see, the contents of the two files are identical. You did overwrite the destination file with the contents of the source file. You can verify that all the files have been copied by using the DIR command.

Step 12 Key in the following: A:\>**DIR CLASS*.PAR** Enter

```
Command Prompt

A:\>DIR CLASS\*.PAR
 Volume in drive A is DATA
 Volume Serial Number is 3330-1807

 Directory of A:\CLASS

04/23/2000  04:03p                  73 JAN.PAR
04/23/2000  04:03p                  75 FEB.PAR
04/23/2000  04:03p                  71 MAR.PAR
04/23/2000  04:18p                  72 APR.PAR
               4 File(s)           291 bytes
               0 Dir(s)      1,434,112 bytes free

A:\>_
```

WHAT'S HAPPENING? Now all the **.TMP** files are in the **CLASS** directory. They have the same file names but different file extensions.

5.23 COMBINING TEXT FILES WITH THE COPY COMMAND

Sometimes, but rarely, it is useful to combine the contents of two or more text (ASCII) files. This process is known as the ***concatenation*** of files. To concatenate means to "put together." You might wish to concatenate when you have several short text files that would be easier to work with if they were combined into one file. When you combine files, nothing happens to the original files; they remain intact. You just create a new file from the original files.

However, most often users concatenate files accidentally and are unaware of it until they attempt to retrieve the file. ***Concatenation should never be done with***

either program files or the data files generated by programs. Programs are binary code and combining any of these files makes the binary code useless and the program incapable of being executed. The same is true for the data files that programs generate. When you create a data file with a program, that program "formats" the data in such a way that the program knows how to interpret that data. That data file format is different for each program. A data file can be read only by the program that created it. If another program can read a foreign data file, it is because the program converts the foreign data into its own native format. The classic example of that is converting data files created in WordPerfect so that these files can be used in Word and the reverse.

Why learn concatenation if you should not use it? You need to learn concatenation because accidental concatenation of files can occur. The clue is to read the messages displayed on the screen. In the following activity you will see the results of concatenation. The COPY command never changes. The syntax never changes. It is always COPY *source destination*. Look at the syntax diagram:

```
COPY [/V] [/N] [/Y ¦ /-Y] [/Z] [/A ¦ /B ] source [/A ¦ /B]
   [+ source [/A ¦ /B] [+ ...]] [destination [/A ¦ /B]]
```

/A indicates an ASCII file, whereas /B indicates a binary file. In addition, whenever you see the notation in a syntax diagram of two or more items separated by the pipe symbol (¦) as in [/A ¦ /B], it is an either/or choice. Either you may use /A or you may use /B, but you may not use both.

5.24 ACTIVITY: COMBINING FILES USING THE COPY COMMAND

Note: The DATA disk is in Drive A. A:\> is displayed.

Step 1 Key in the following: A:\>**TYPE C:\WINDOSBK\EMPLOYEE.ONE** Enter

Step 2 Key in the following: A:\>**TYPE C:\WINDOSBK\EMPLOYEE.TWO** Enter

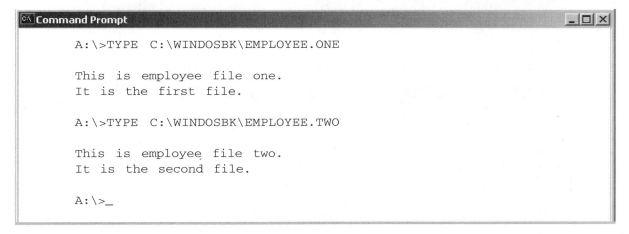

```
Command Prompt

A:\>TYPE C:\WINDOSBK\EMPLOYEE.ONE

This is employee file one.
It is the first file.

A:\>TYPE C:\WINDOSBK\EMPLOYEE.TWO

This is employee file two.
It is the second file.

A:\>_
```

You have displayed the contents of two files on the screen. Each file is unique with a different file name and different file contents. You are going to place the contents of these two files into a new file called **JOINED.SAM** that will consist of the contents of the first file, **EMPLOYEE.ONE**, followed by the contents of the second file, **EMPLOYEE.TWO**. The new file will reside on the DATA disk.

Note: In the following step, there are spaces between COPY and the source file specification (**C:\WINDOSBK\EMPLOYEE.ONE**), before and after the **+** sign, and before the destination file name, (**JOINED.SAM**). Though it appears here that the command is on two different lines, the entire command must go on one line.

Step 3 Key in the following (press the Enter key only when you see **Enter**):
A:\>**COPY C:\WINDOSBK\EMPLOYEE.ONE + C:\WINDOSBK\EMPLOYEE.TWO JOINED.SAM** **Enter**

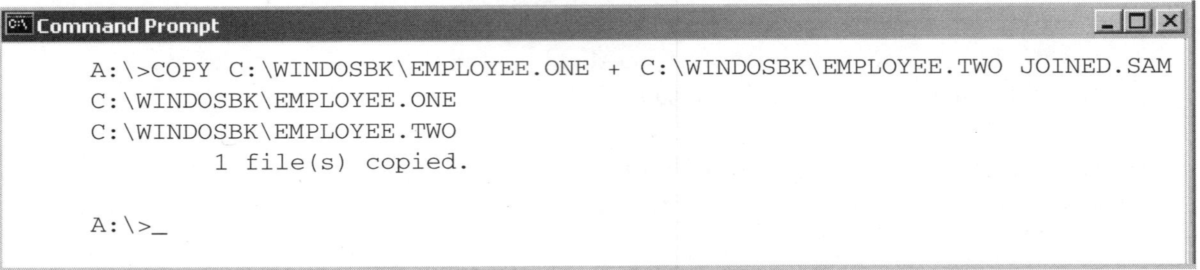
Command Prompt

```
A:\>COPY C:\WINDOSBK\EMPLOYEE.ONE + C:\WINDOSBK\EMPLOYEE.TWO JOINED.SAM
C:\WINDOSBK\EMPLOYEE.ONE
C:\WINDOSBK\EMPLOYEE.TWO
        1 file(s) copied.

A:\>_
```

WHAT'S HAPPENING? The message is **1 file(s) copied**. It seems as if you have too many parameters because the syntax is COPY *source destination*. However, you are still following the correct syntax for the COPY command. You are creating one destination file out of two source files. What you did here was say COPY (the command) the contents of the file called **C:\WINDOSBK\EMPLOYEE.ONE** *and* the contents of the file called **C:\WINDOSBK\EMPLOYEE.TWO** (the source) to a new file called **JOINED.SAM** that will reside on the DATA disk (the destination). The plus sign (**+**) told the operating system that the source had more to it than just one file. It also told the OS that you were joining files. The destination file is the last file name on the command line that does not have a plus sign in front. Look at Step 3 and note that **JOINED.SAM** has just a space in front of it, not a plus sign, making **JOINED.SAM** the destination. Source and destination files in the copy command are separated by a single space delimiter. Multiple source files are separated by a <space>+<space> delimiter.

Step 4 Key in the following: A:\>**TYPE JOINED.SAM** **Enter**

Command Prompt

```
A:\>TYPE JOINED.SAM

This is employee file one.
It is the first file.

This is employee file two.
It is the second file.

A:\>_
```

The file **JOINED.SAM** consists of the contents of the file **EMPLOYEE.ONE** followed by the contents of the file **EMPLOYEE.TWO**. The contents in **JOINED.SAM** do not show any file names. You do not know where one file ended and the next began. **JOINED.SAM** is a new file, but you did not destroy or in any way alter the two original source files, **EMPLOYEE.ONE** and **EMPLOYEE.TWO**. You can prove this by using the TYPE command.

Step 5 Key in the following: A:\>**TYPE C:\WINDOSBK\EMPLOYEE.ONE** Enter

Step 6 Key in the following: A:\>**TYPE C:\WINDOSBK\EMPLOYEE.TWO** Enter

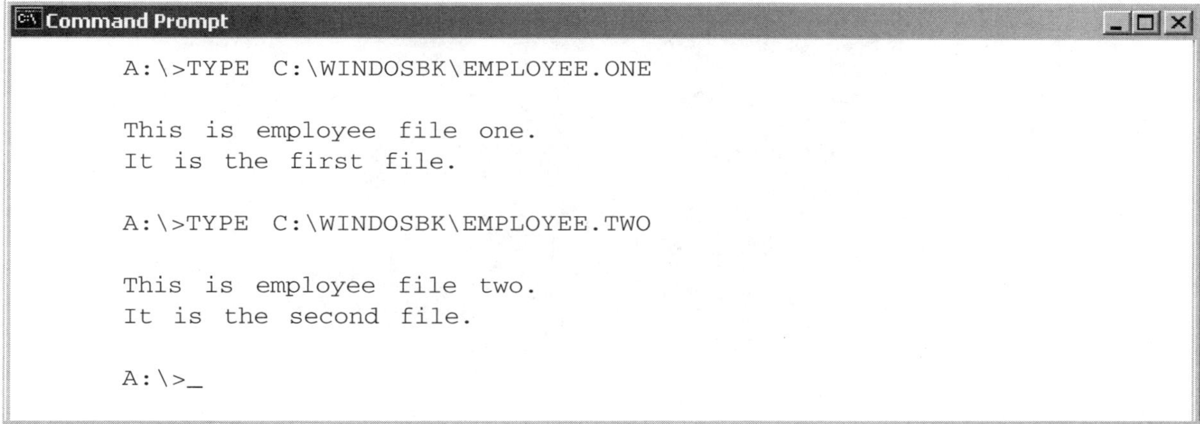

Command Prompt

```
A:\>TYPE C:\WINDOSBK\EMPLOYEE.ONE

This is employee file one.
It is the first file.

A:\>TYPE C:\WINDOSBK\EMPLOYEE.TWO

This is employee file two.
It is the second file.

A:\>_
```

As you can see, the source files remain unchanged. You merely created a third file from the contents of two files. You can join many files with the plus sign, but this is useful for text files *only*. If you try to join two data files created by an application program using the COPY command, the application program will no longer be able to read the combined data file.

Step 7 Key in the following: A:\>**CD /D C:\WINDOSBK\FINANCE** Enter

Step 8 Key in the following (in the next step, do not press the Enter key until you see Enter):

C:\WINDOSBK\FINANCE>**COPY BUDGET.TKR + HOMEBUD.TKR A:\TEST.TKR** Enter

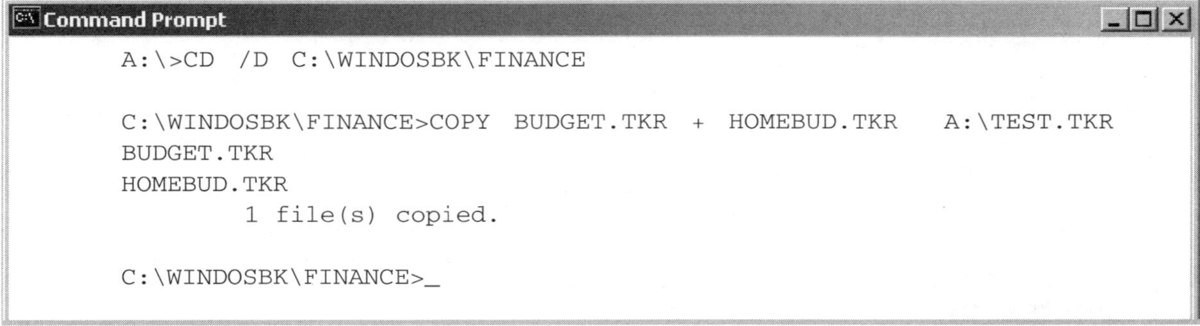

Command Prompt

```
A:\>CD /D C:\WINDOSBK\FINANCE

C:\WINDOSBK\FINANCE>COPY BUDGET.TKR + HOMEBUD.TKR  A:\TEST.TKR
BUDGET.TKR
HOMEBUD.TKR
        1 file(s) copied.

C:\WINDOSBK\FINANCE>_
```

You have changed the drive and directory to the **FINANCE** directory under the **WINDOSBK** directory on the hard disk. You then concatenated, or combined, the contents of two data files, **BUDGET.TKR** and **HOMEBUD.TKR**, generated by the Thinker program and placed the contents on the DATA disk in one file called **TEST.TKR**. Notice the message on the screen, **1 file(s) copied**. You are now going to try to retrieve this joined file, **TEST.TKR**, in the Thinker program.

Step 9 Key in the following: C:\WINDOSBK\FINANCE>**THINK** Enter

Step 10 Press Enter

Step 11 Press /.

Step 12 Press **F**.

Step 13 Press **R**.

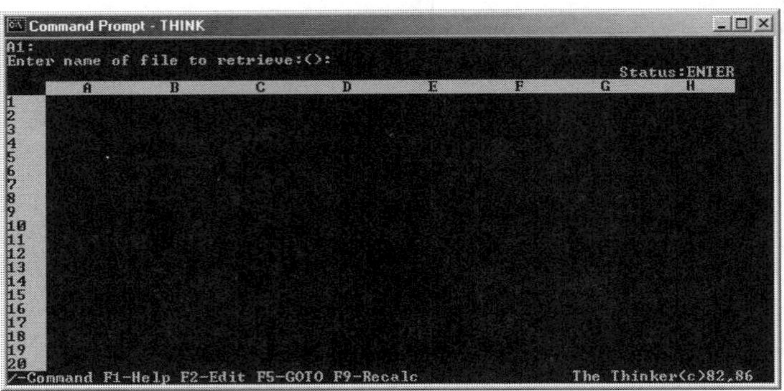

You have loaded the Thinker program and have issued the command to load a data file. A prompt asks you what data file you wish to load. You are going to try to load the **TEST.TKR** file on the DATA disk.

Step 14 Key in the following: **A:\TEST.TKR** Enter

ERROR IN TRYING TO GET FILE, TRY AGAIN... Status:ENTER

The Thinker program cannot recognize the joined data file and informs you of this with the above message. (*Note:* Sometimes the program finds the error so severe, it kicks you out of the program and returns you to the system level. If that happens to you, simply press Enter and proceed to Step 19.)

Step 15 Press Enter

Note: Complete Steps 16 through 18 if you have not returned to the command line prompt.

Step 16 Press /.

Step 17 Press **Q**.

Step 18 Press **Y**.

WHAT'S HAPPENING You have exited the program and returned to the Command Prompt window.

Step 19 Key in the following: C:\WINDOSBK\FINANCE>**CD ** Enter

Step 20 Key in the following: C:\>**A:** Enter

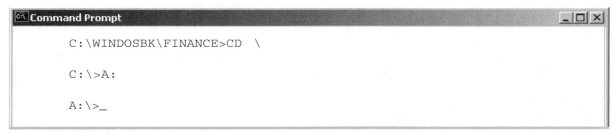

You have demonstrated that you should not combine program files or data files created with application programs. You may say to yourself that by never including **+**, you cannot make that mistake. However, there is more to the story. You can also use wildcards to concatenate files, which eliminate the need to use **+** as well as the need to key in all the file names separately. If you wanted to join all the files with a **.TMP** file extension and place them into a new file called **MONTHS.SAM**, located on the DATA disk, you would have to key in

```
COPY JAN.TMP + FEB.TMP + MAR.TMP + APR.TMP A:MONTHS.SAM
```

You can save many keystrokes by using wildcards.

Step 21 Key in the following: A:\>**COPY *.TMP MONTHS.SAM** Enter

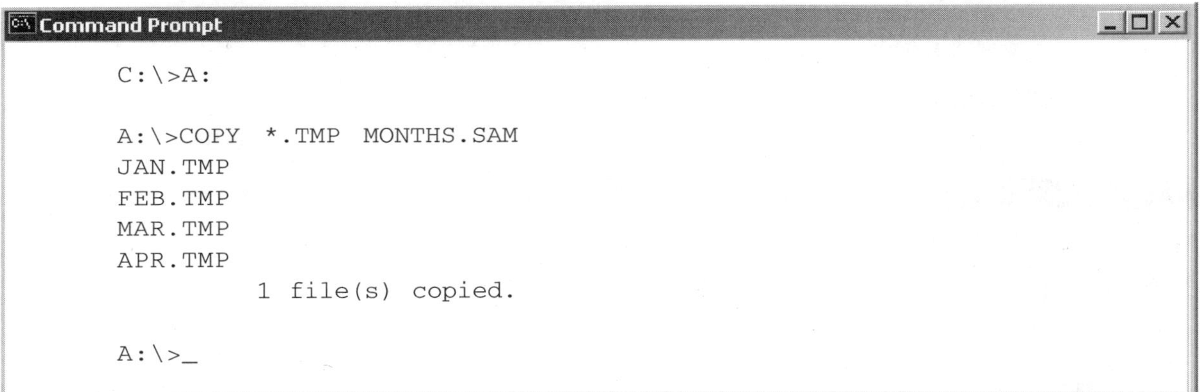

Using the wildcard has the same effect as keying in all the file names and connecting the source files with plus signs. The operating system found each file with a **.TMP** file extension and wrote the contents of those files to a new file called **MONTHS.SAM**. Note the message **1 file(s) copied**. Four files were combined into one.

Step 22 Key in the following: A:\>**TYPE MONTHS.SAM** Enter

Command Prompt

```
A:\>TYPE MONTHS.SAM

This is my January file.
It is my first dummy file.
This is file 1.
```

```
This is my February file.
It is my second dummy file.
This is file 2.

This is my March file.
It is my third dummy file.
This is file 3.

This is my April file.
It is my fourth dummy file.
This is file 4.

A:\>_
```

As you can see, you joined together the contents of all the **.TMP** files into a new file called **MONTHS.SAM**. Again, since the **.TMP** files are ASCII files, the text is readable on the screen. How then can you make an error? A typical activity is to copy files from a hard disk to a floppy disk or removable disk such as a Zip drive for backup purposes. Wildcards are very useful for backing up groups of files. You may choose to place the copies in a subdirectory. If you make only a one-character error, you will combine the files into one file, making the file useless. Let's say you want to copy all the files in **C:\WINDOSBK\FINANCE** that begin with a B to the **CLASS** subdirectory, but you make a typographical error (a "typo") when keying in **CLASS**.

Step 23 Key in the following:
A:\>**COPY C:\WINDOSBK\FINANCE\B*.TKR CLASX** Enter

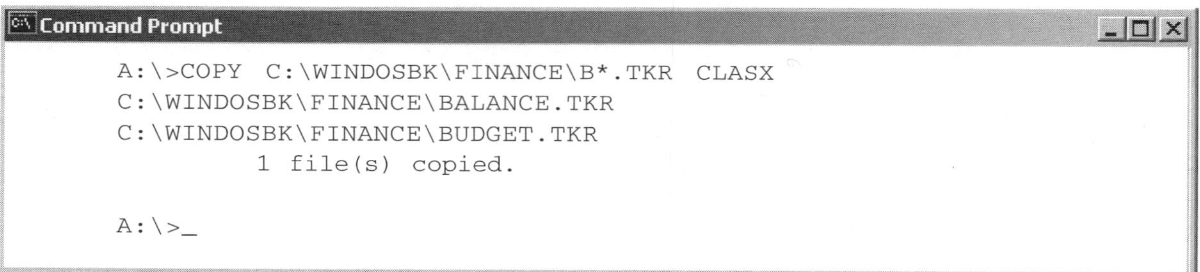

```
Command Prompt

A:\>COPY C:\WINDOSBK\FINANCE\B*.TKR CLASX
C:\WINDOSBK\FINANCE\BALANCE.TKR
C:\WINDOSBK\FINANCE\BUDGET.TKR
        1 file(s) copied.

A:\>_
```

The first hint that you made an error is in the message telling you that only one file has been copied. Your intention was to copy the **.TKR** files that begin with B to the **CLASS** directory so you have a backup copy of each file. You made that one, small typographical error, keying in **CLASX** instead of **CLASS**, so instead of having the BALANCE and BUDGET files backed up into the **CLASS** directory, you now have one useless file called **CLASX**.

Step 24 Key in the following: A:\>**DIR CLASS\B*.*** Enter

Step 25 Key in the following: A:\>**DIR CLASX** Enter

```
Command Prompt

A:\>DIR CLASS\B*.*
 Volume in drive A is DATA
 Volume Serial Number is 3330-1807
```

```
 Directory of A:\CLASS

File Not Found


A:\>DIR CLASX
 Volume in drive A is DATA
 Volume Serial Number is 3330-1807

 Directory of A:\

04/30/2001  12:09p                15,108 CLASX
               1 File(s)          15,108 bytes
               0 Dir(s)        1,400,832 bytes free

A:\>_
```

There are no files that begin with B in the **CLASS** subdirectory, but there is one file called **CLASX** in the root directory. Once again, the operating system did exactly what you told it to do. In this case, however, what you *said* is not what you *meant*. This is why reading the messages on the screen is so important. The message you should have seen, if you had not made an error, was **2 file(s) copied**. The minute you see the message **1 file(s) copied**, you should realize that you joined the files into one file instead of copying each to the subdirectory called **CLASS**.

5.25 PRINTING FILES

So far, you have not printed the contents of any files. You may have redirected the output of the DIR command to the printer, but this printed only file *names*, not file *contents*. You could redirect the output of the TYPE command to the printer by keying in TYPE MY.FIL > PRN, if you were not on a network that prevented it. You may also copy a file to a printer by keying in COPY MY.FIL PRN. Note here that there is no redirection, but merely copying a file to a device. Again, if you are printing to a network printer, this may not work. However, using either redirection or the COPY command, you need to manually eject the paper from the printer. The PRINT command makes it easier to print the contents of text files. The PRINT command will print the contents of files, not their names, and it will automatically eject the page. However, these techniques work only for ASCII files. Again, data files generated by application programs can be printed only from within the application program because the application program must send special signals to the printer so that the data prints correctly.

There are times you wish to print an ASCII file. You often will want a hard copy of configuration information on your computer. There are also other reasons for printing text files; for instance, if you have a printer problem from within an application program, the first thing you want to do is verify that it is a software problem, not a hardware problem. To test this, you return to the command line interface level and print an ASCII file. If the ASCII file prints, you now know you have a software problem within the application program and not a connection problem with your printer.

There are three ways to print a text file from the command line:

- Use the PRINT command. The syntax of the PRINT command is as follows:

```
PRINT [/D:device] [[drive:][path]filename[...]]

    /D:device   Specifies a print device.
```

- Use redirection as you did in Chapter 2 with the DIR command.
- Copy the contents of a file to a printer. The destination is a device, not a file. The device is the printer. Since the printer is a device, it has a reserved name: PRN. Sometimes this name causes problems when you are printing on a network, so you will use LPT1 for Line Printer 1. When you use LPT1, be sure to key in the letter L, the letter P, the letter T, and the number 1. You cannot use the letter l ("ell") as the number 1. These are the names for local printers. Network printers also have specific names. The network administrator assigns the network printer name. Unless you know your network printer name, you may not be able to copy a file to the printer.

Note : Before doing the next activity, check with your lab instructor to see if you have a local printer. If you have access to only a network printer, you MAY NOT be able to do the next activity unless your instrutor has given you other instrutions It is probable that you will have special needs in your own lab environment for printing from the Command line. The steps below work in many, but not all, circumstances.

5.26 ACTIVITY: PRINTING FILES

CAUTION!!! DO NOT DO THIS ACTIVITY IF YOU ARE ON A NETWORK UNLESS INSTRUCTED TO DO SO.

Note 1: The DATA disk is in Drive A. **A:\>** is displayed.

Note 2: Check with your lab instructor for any special instructions.

Note 3: Remember, many times in a lab environment, you can use **LPT1,** the hardware name of the printer port. When **LPT1** does not work, you may try **PRN**. Other times, you need to use the printer object's ***URL (Uniform Resource Locator)***, such as **\\SERVER\HP**. Once again, check with your lab instructor for what is needed in your lab.

Step 1 Key in the following: A:\>**TYPE FEB.TMP** Enter

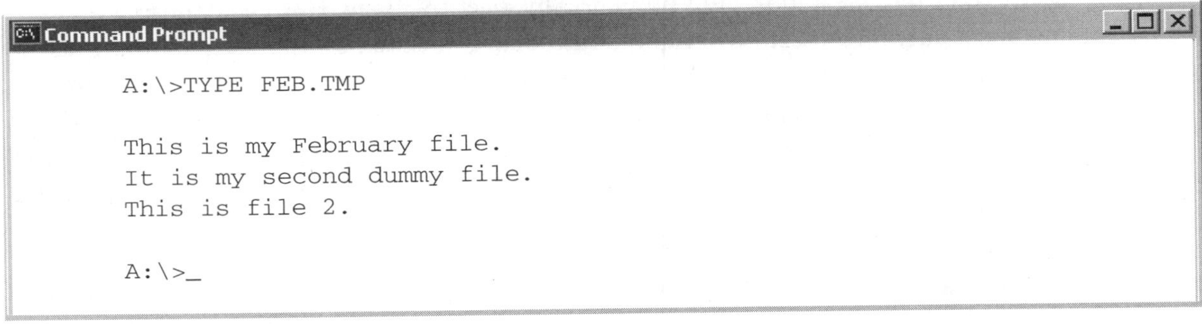

Command Prompt
A:\>TYPE FEB.TMP
This is my February file.
It is my second dummy file.
This is file 2.
A:\>_

WHAT'S HAPPENING? You see the contents of the file. To print it, you may use the PRINT command.

Step 2 Key in the following: A:\>**PRINT FEB.TMP** Enter

Command Prompt
A:\>PRINT FEB.TMP
A:\FEB.TMP is currently being printed
A:\>_

The PRINT command tells you the status of your print job. A print job is something that you sent to the printer to be printed. If you check your printer, you should have a hard copy of the contents of the file **FEB.TMP**. Note that you see only the contents of the file, not any of the file information such as its name or size. Another advantage of the PRINT command is that you may use wildcards.

Step 3 Key in the following: A:\>**PRINT *.TMP** Enter

```
Command Prompt

A:\>PRINT *.TMP
A:\JAN.TMP is currently being printed
A:\FEB.TMP is currently being printed
A:\MAR.TMP is currently being printed
A:\APR.TMP is currently being printed

A:\>_
```

Again, you see a status report. Each file's contents will have printed on a separate piece of paper and each page was automatically ejected. You may also key in multiple files names as in **PRINT APR.TMP JAN.99**, and so on. You may also use redirection.

Step 4 Key in the following: A:\>**TYPE JANUARY.TXT** <Enter>

```
Command Prompt

A:\>TYPE JANUARY.TXT

This is my January file.
It is my first dummy file.
This is file 1.

A:\>_
```

The contents of the TYPE command are written to the standard output device, the screen. You can redirect the output to another device—the printer.

Step 5 Turn the printer on. Make sure the printer is online.

Step 6 Key in the following: A:\>**TYPE JANUARY.TXT > LPT1** Enter

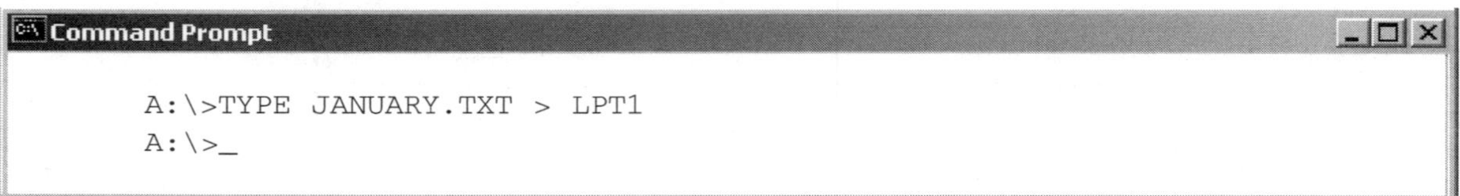

```
A:\>TYPE JANUARY.TXT > LPT1
A:\>_
```

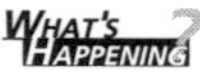

Nothing was written to the screen because you redirected the output to the printer. Now you want to eject the page. Depending on how your printer is set up, it may automatically eject the page without your having to take the next step. Check your printer to see if your page printed and ejected; otherwise, manually eject the page. See Activity 2.24 for the steps to take to manually eject a page. It would seem that, if this works as it did, you could also use redirection with the COPY command, but you cannot. The only output that is actually a *product* of the copy command itself is **1 file(s) copied**. If you redirected that output, you would have only the printed message **1 file(s) copied**, not the contents of the file. Instead of using redirection, you copy the file to a device, the printer.

Step 7 Key in the following: A:\>**COPY JANUARY.TXT LPT1** Enter

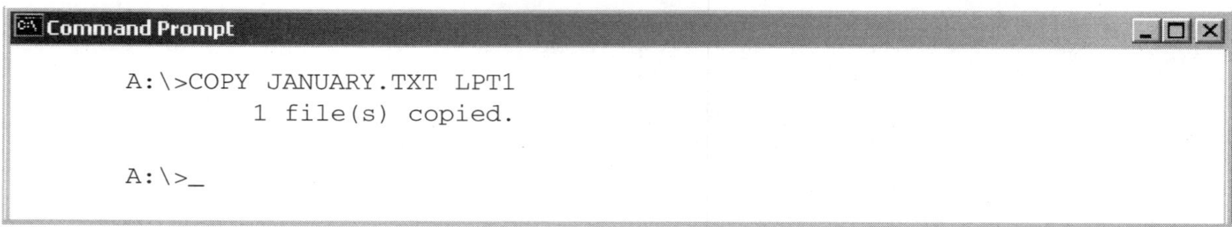

```
A:\>COPY JANUARY.TXT LPT1
        1 file(s) copied.

A:\>_
```

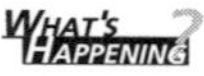

Even though you are using a device, the syntax for the COPY command remains the same. COPY is the command, the work you want done. **JANUARY.TXT** is the source, the file you want copied. You do not need to enter a drive designator in front of the file name because the operating system will assume the default. **LPT1** is the device name for the printer. The printer is the destination, where you want the contents of the file to go. As soon as you press Enter, you may hear and see the printer begin to print. If your page does not eject, manually eject it. You then see your hard copy:

```
This is my January file.
It is my first dummy file.
This is file 1.
```

CHAPTER SUMMARY

1. One of the major reasons people buy computers is for using application programs that assist people in different tasks.
2. Application software usually generates data. Both application software and data are stored as disk files.
3. Usually, only a program can use the data files it creates. A data file without the application program cannot be used.
4. Another component of the operating system is the commands that allow the user to manage and manipulate program and data files.
5. The internal commands DIR, COPY, and TYPE allow you to manage the files on a disk.

6. The file extensions .COM (command file) and .EXE (executable code) tell the operating system that the file is a program.
7. COPY allows you to copy files selectively.
8. The syntax of the copy command is:

```
COPY  [drive:][path] filename [drive:][path] filename
```

   A simple way to remember the COPY syntax is

```
COPY source destination
```

   Source is what you want to copy. Destination is where you want it copied.
9. The COPY command never changes the source file.
10. When naming files, it is best to stick to alphanumeric characters. Certain characters are illegal, such as the colon (:) and the asterisk (*).
11. When copying a file to a subdirectory, you must include the path name. The path name and the file name are separated by the backslash, which is used as a delimiter. The one exception is that the root directory's name is \ (backslash).
12. Wildcards may be used with the COPY command.
13. Files must have unique names when on the same drive and in the same subdirectory, but files that are copied to different subdirectories may have identical names because the path makes those file names unique.
14. TYPE allows you to display the contents of a file on the screen. The syntax is:

```
TYPE [drive:][path]filename
```

15. Wildcards may be used with the TYPE command.
16. You may use subdirectory markers with the DIR, COPY, and TYPE commands.
17. If you use *.* with a command, it chooses all the files. Thus, DIR *.* would display all the files. COPY C:\WHAT*.* A:\ would copy all the files in the WHAT directory to the disk in Drive A.
18. When you move between drives, the operating system remembers the last directory you were in.
19. Overwriting files with the COPY command is the process in which the contents of the source file copy over the contents of the destination file.
20. Concatenation means combining the contents of files using the COPY command with either + or a wildcard. There is only one destination file. You should not concatenate program files or data files generated from program files.
21. You may print the contents of an ASCII file by using the PRINT command with the name of the file or files. You may use multiple file names or use wildcards. Usually the PRINT command automatically ejects the pages.
22. You may also print the contents of an ASCII file by keying in TYPE filename > LPT1 or TYPE filename > PRN. If you are on a network, you may need to know the name of your device. You will probably have to manually eject the page.
23. You may also print the contents of an ASCII file by keying in COPY filename LPT1 or TYPE filename PRN. If you are on a network, you may need to know the name of your device. You will probably have to manually eject the page.

KEY TERMS

ASCII
concatenation
destination file
LPT1
overwrite
PRN
source file
unformatted text file
Uniform Resource Locator (URL)

DISCUSSION QUESTIONS

1. Explain the function and purpose of internal commands.
2. Give two reasons for making a copy of a file on the same disk.
3. Give the syntax for the COPY command and explain each part of the syntax.
4. Is a file extension mandatory when naming a file?
5. What is the maximum number of characters that may be used when naming a file?
6. List three characters that cannot be used when naming files.
7. List three examples of legal file names.
8. When would you use a wildcard with the COPY command?
9. What is the purpose and function of the TYPE command? Explain each part of the syntax diagram.
10. How can you recognize an executable file?
11. What are ASCII files?
12. What is the purpose and function of dummy files?
13. Every file on a disk must have a unique name. Yet, when you make a copy of a file on the same disk in a different subdirectory, it may have the same file name. Explain.
14. Under what circumstances could a user think that the computer has "lost" its files?
15. Can you use wildcards with the TYPE command? Why or why not?
16. What does the first \ in any command line mean?
17. What does it mean to "overwrite" a file? What are some of the dangers of overwriting files?
18. Why would you make a copy of a file on the same disk? On another disk?
19. What would happen if you tried to copy a file from one disk to another and the destination disk already had a file with the same name?
20. How would you combine the contents of two files? Why would you?
21. What happens to the original files when you combine two or more files?
22. What are some of the dangers of concatenating program files or data files?
23. What message on the screen informs you that you have concatenated several files?
24. Name two ways that you may print the contents of an ASCII file.
25. Identify two advantages to using the PRINT command to print the contents of ASCII files.

TRUE/FALSE QUESTIONS

For each question, circle the letter T if the statement is true and the letter F if the statement is false.

T F 1. The contents of two files on the same disk can be identical even though the file names are different.

T F 2. It is a good idea to concatenate text files and program files.

T F 3. The COPY command is an internal command.

T F 4. The contents of files are not affected by displaying them with the TYPE command.

T F 5. To save time when copying multiple files to a different disk, you can use wildcards.

COMPLETION QUESTIONS

Write the correct answer in each blank space.

6. There are two mandatory parameters for the COPY command. They are the _________ and the _________ .
7. When you replace the contents of a file with the contents of a different file, this process is known as __________.
8. You can differentiate between a program file and a data file by the file _________.
9. If you wish to display the contents of a text file on the screen, you would use the ________ command.
10. The delimiter that is used to separate a file name from a file extension is ________.

MULTIPLE CHOICE QUESTIONS

For each question, write the letter for the correct answer in the blank space.

11. The COPY command can be used to
    a. copy a file from one disk to another.
    b. make a second copy of an existing file on the same disk.
    c. copy a file from one directory to another directory.
    d. all of the above
12. Files may be copied to another disk in order to
    a. make backup copies.
    b. copy a program to another disk.
    c. share data files with others.
    d. all of the above
13. To display the contents of an ASCII file on the screen, you use the
    a. DIR command.
    b. TYPE command.
    c. VIEW command.
    d. SEE command.
14. COPY *.TXT THE.FIL will result in
    a. joining together all files with the .TXT extension to a file called THE.FIL.
    b. joining THE.FIL to all files with the .TXT extension.
    c. creating a new set of files with the same file name having .FIL as an extension.
    d. none of the above
15. COPY MY.TXT \DATA\OLD.TXT will
    a. copy the file MY.TXT to a new file called DATA.
    b. copy the file MY.TXT to a new file called OLD.TXT in the subdirectory DATA.
    c. copy the file OLD.TXT to a file called MY.TXT in the subdirectory DATA.
    d. copy the file called DATA to a file called MY.TXT in the subdirectory called OLD.TXT.

WRITING COMMANDS

Write the correct steps or commands to perform the required action as if you were at the computer. The prompt will indicate the default drive and directory.

16. Copy the file called OLD.FIL from the root of Drive C to the root of Drive A, keeping the same file name.

    A:\>

17. Copy all files in the default directory with the .TXT file extension to files with the same names but with the .DOC file extension.

    A:\>

18. Copy the file JOE from the root directory to the INFO directory, and call the new file NAMES on the default drive.

    A:\>

19. Copy the contents of two files, one named DOG *and* one named CAT from the default directory to a file called ANIMALS in the \MYFILES directory.

    A:\>

20. Copy all files from the default directory with the extension .TXT to the subdirectory TXTFILES.

    A:\>

APPLICATION ASSIGNMENTS

Note 1: Place the APPLICATION disk in Drive A. Be sure to work on the APPLICATION disk, not the DATA disk.

Note 2: The homework problems will assume Drive C is the hard disk and the APPLICATION disk is in Drive A. If you are using another drive, such as floppy Drive B or hard Drive D, be sure to substitute that drive letter when reading the questions and answers.

Note 3: All subdirectories will be created under the root directory unless otherwise specified.

PROBLEM SET I

PROBLEM A

Note: If the DATA disk is in Drive A, remove it and place it in a safe place. *Do not* use the DATA disk for these application problems.

A-a Insert the APPLICATION disk into Drive A.

A-b Copy the file called **GRAMMY.REC** from the **WINDOSBK** subdirectory to the root directory of the APPLICATION disk keeping the same file name.

A-c Copy the file called **GRAMMY.REC** from the **WINDOSBK** subdirectory to the root directory of the APPLICATION disk but call the new file **GRAMMY.TAP**.

A-d Execute the DIR command to display only the **GRAMMY** files on the APPLICATION disk.

☐ 1. What date is listed for the files?
   a. 10-02-00
   b. 10-10-99
   c. 10-10-00
   d. 10-02-99

☐ 2. What are the sizes of the GRAMMY files in bytes?
   a. GRAMMY.REC = 569 and GRAMMY.TAP = 339
   b. GRAMMY.REC = 596 and GRAMMY.TAP = 496
   c. both files are 569 bytes
   d. GRAMMY.REC = 569 and GRAMMY.TAP = 596

A-e While in the root of the APPLICATION disk, copy the file **GRAMMY.REC** to **GRAM:.REC**.

☐ 3. What message appears on the screen?
   a. File(s) copied
   b. Invalid file name
   c. The filename, directory name, or volume label syntax is incorrect.
   d. no message was displayed

PROBLEM B

B-a Copy any files with the file extension **.99** from the **WINDOSBK** subdirectory to the root directory of the APPLICATION disk keeping the same file names.

☐ 4. How many files were copied?
   a. two
   b. four
   c. six
   d. eight

B-b Execute the DIR command to display only the files with the extension of **.99** on the APPLICATION disk.

☐ 5. What date is displayed for the files?
   a. 11/23/98
   b. 10/23/98
   c. 11/11/99
   d. 10/10/99

B-c Create a subdirectory on the APPLICATION disk called **FILES**.

B-d Copy all the files with the extension of **.99** from the root directory of the APPLICATION disk into this subdirectory but give them the new extension of **.FIL**.

B-e Do a directory display of the **FILES** directory.

6. There is a line in the resulting display that states
   a. 2 File(s) 291 bytes
   b. 4 File(s) 291 bytes
   c. 6 File(s) 291 bytes
   d. 8 File(s) 291 bytes

B-f Create a subdirectory on the APPLICATION disk called **BOOKS**.

B-g Copy all the files in the **WINDOSBK\MEDIA\BOOKS** directory to the **BOOKS** directory keeping the same file name(s).

7. How many files were copied?
   a. one
   b. three
   c. five
   d. seven

PROBLEM C

C-a Display the contents of the **GRAMMY.REC** file located in the root directory of the APPLICATION disk.

8. What artist is listed for 1989?
   a. Eric Clapton
   b. Whitney Houston
   c. Bette Midler
   d. Paul Simon

C-b Display the contents of the **MUSIC.MOV** file located in the **C:\WINDOSBK\MEDIA\MOVIES** directory.

9. What movie title is displayed?
   a. Carousel
   b. Paint Your Wagon
   c. Star Wars
   d. Evita

C-c Display the contents of the **MYSTERY.BKS** file located in the **BOOKS** directory of the APPLICATION disk.

10. What author's name is NOT displayed?
    a. Sue Grafton
    b. Robert Parker
    c. Elmore Leonard
    d. Donald Westlake

PROBLEM D

D-a Create a subdirectory called **ROOM** on the APPLICATION disk under the **FILES** directory created in Problem B.

D-b On the APPLICATION disk change the default directory to **ROOM**.

D-c Using subdirectory markers, copy the file called **APR.FIL** from the **FILES** directory to the **ROOM** directory keeping the same name but giving it the new extension of **.RMS**.

☐ 11. Which command did you use?
- a. COPY \..\APR.FIL \APR.RMS
- b. COPY ..\APR.FIL APR.RMS
- c. COPY ..\APR.FIL \APR.RMS
- d. COPY ..\APR.FIL ..\APR.RMS

PROBLEM E

E-a Change to the root directory of the APPLICATION disk.

Note: The root directory of the APPLICATION disk is the default drive and directory.

E-b Copy any file with a **.TMP** extension from the **WINDOSBK** directory to the root of the APPLICATION disk, keeping the same file names but giving them the extension of **.TRP**.

E-c Copy the file called **APR.99** from the root directory of the APPLICATION disk to the subdirectory called **HISTORY** giving the file the new name of **APR.ICE**.

E-d Copy any files with a **.99** file extension from the root directory of the APPLICATION disk to the **HISTORY** subdirectory, but give the files the new extension of **.ICE**.

☐ 12. Which command did you use?
- a. COPY *.99 HISTORY
- b. COPY *.99 HISTORY*.ICE
- c. COPY *.99 *.ICE
- d. COPY .ICE \HISTORY\.99

☐ 13. What message was displayed?
- a. 1 file(s) copied
- b. Overwrite HISTORY\APR.ICE? (Yes/No/All):
- c. Overwrite APR.ICE (Yes/No/All)?
- d. no message was displayed

E-e Take any steps necessary to copy the files.

Note: The root directory of the APPLICATION disk is the default drive and directory.

E-f Overwrite the file **A:\BONJOUR.TRP** with the contents of the file called **RIGHT.UP**, which is located in the **WINDOSBK** directory.

☐ 14. Which command did you use?
- a. COPY C:\BONJOUR.TRP RIGHT.UP
- b. COPY C:\WINDOSBK\RIGHT.UP BONJOUR.TRP
- c. COPY C:\WINDOSBK\BONJOUR.TRP C:\WINDOSBK\RIGHT.UP
- d. COPY C:\WINDOSBK\RIGHT.UP RIGHT.UP

E-g Display the contents of the file called **BONJOUR.TRP** on the APPLICATION disk.

15. What is the first line in the file?
    a. This is a file for me.
    b. This is a file for you.
    c. HELLO, EVERYONE.
    d. BONJOUR, EVERYONE.

PROBLEM F

Note: The root directory of the APPLICATION disk is the default drive and directory.

F-a Copy all the files that begin with **EMP** and have any file name and extension from the **WINDOSBK** directory to the root directory of the APPLICATION disk.

F-b Copy all the files that have a **.MAK** extension from the **WINDOSBK** directory to the root directory of the APPLICATION disk.

F-c Concatenate the files called **EMPLOYEE.THR** and **EMPLOYEE.TWO** (in that order) to the root directory of the APPLICATION disk, calling the new file **EMPLOYEE.FIL**.

16. Which command did you use?
    a. COPY EMPLOYEE.THR + EMPLOYEE.TWO EMPLOYEE.FIL
    b. COPY EMPLOYEE*.* EMPLOYEE.FIL
    c. COPY EMPLOYEE.FIL EMPLOYEE.THR
    d. COPY EMP*.* EMP*.*

F-d Display the contents of the file **EMPLOYEE.FIL** on the APPLICATION disk.

17. What is the first line in the file?
    a. This is employee file one.
    b. This is employee file two.
    c. This is employee file three.
    d. There are no employees.

Note: The root directory of the APPLICATION disk is the default drive and directory.

F-e Concatenate all the files that have the extension **.MAK** from the root directory of the APPLICATION disk to the subdirectory **FILES** on the APPLICATION disk. The new file should be named **AUTOMOB.ILE**. Use a wildcard.

18. Which command did you use?
    a. COPY MAK AUTOMOB.ILE
    b. COPY ?.MAK FILES
    c. COPY *.MAK FILES/AUTOMOB.ILE
    d. COPY *.MAK FILES\AUTOMOB.ILE

Note: The root directory of the APPLICATION disk is the default drive and directory.

F-f Display the contents of the file called **AUTOMOB.ILE**.

19. Which make of automobile is displayed?
    a. Lexus LS400
    b. Dodge Caravan
    c. Ford Aerostar
    d. Chevrolet Astrovan

PROBLEM G

Note 1: Check with your lab instructor prior to proceeding with this problem.
Note 2: Remember, use the method of printing (LPT1, PRN, or the URL of your printer) that works in your particular lab environment.
Note 3: You may not be able to do this activity in your lab enviroment. Check with your instructor to see if you should proceed.
Note 4: The root directory of the APPLICATION disk is the default drive and directory.

Print the file called **AME-LIT.BKS** located in the **BOOKS** directory. Use redirection. (*Note:* If you used **PRN** or a URL instead of **LPT1**, substitute what you use for **LPT1** in the answers.)

20. Which command did you use? (*Note:* If you are in a lab environment that uses a URL, assume that LPT1 is your URL.)
    a. PRINT BOOKS\AME-LIT.BKS > LPT1
    b. PRINT BOOKS\AME-LIT.BKS LPT1
    c. COPY PRN\BOOKS\AME-LIT.BKS
    d. COPY BOOKS\AME-LIT.BKS > LPT1

PROBLEM H

Note: The root directory of the APPLICATION disk is the default drive and directory.

H-a Copy all the files from the **WINDOSBK** directory that have the file extension of **.BAT**.

21. How many files were copied?
    a. two
    b. four
    c. six
    d. eight

H-b Copy the file called **MARK.FIL** and the file called **GETYN.COM** from the **WINDOSBK** directory to the root of the APPLICATION disk.

22. Is there a way use one command to copy both of these files simultaneously?
    a. yes
    b. no

23. What is the size, in bytes, of GETYN.COM?
    a. 326
    b. 226
    c. 126
    d. 26

24. What kind of file is GETYN.COM?
    a. data
    b. text
    c. program
    d. none of the above

PROBLEM SET II—AT THE COMPUTER

Note 1: Before proceeding with these assignments, check with your lab instructor to see if there are any special procedures you should follow.

Note 2: The APPLICATION disk is in Drive A. A:\> is displayed as the default drive and the default directory. All work will occur on the APPLICATION disk.

Note 3: Make sure that **NAME.BAT**, **MARK.FIL**, **GETYN.COM**, and **GO.BAT** are all present in the root directory of the APPLICATION disk before proceeding with these problems.

Note 4: All files with the **.HW** extension *must* be created in the root directory of the APPLICATION disk.

Step 1 Key in the following: A:\>**NAME** Enter

Step 2 Here is an example to key in, but your instructor will have other information that applies to your class. Key in the following:

Bette A. Peat Enter (*Your* name goes here.)

CIS 55 Enter (*Your* class goes here.)

T-Th 8-9:30 Enter (*Your* day and time go here.)

Chapter 5 Applications Enter

Step 3 Press F6 Enter

Step 4 If the information is correct, press **Y** and you are back to A:\>.

WHAT'S HAPPENING? You have returned to the system level. You now have a file called **NAME.FIL** with your name and other pertinent information. *Hint*: Remember redirection.

TO CREATE 1.HW

- Create a subdirectory called **MOVIES** under the root directory of the APPLICATION disk.
- Copy all the files in the **WINDOSBK\MEDIA\MOVIES** directory to the **MOVIES** directory on the APPLICATION disk and keep the same file names.
- Locate all the files in the **MOVIES** directory on the APPLICATION disk.
- Place the names of the files in a file called **1.HW**.

TO CREATE 2.HW

- On the APPLICATION disk, make a copy of all the files in the **MOVIES** directory in the **MOVIES** directory, keeping the same file names but having a new extension of **.FLM**.

- Locate only the files in the **MOVIES** directory that have the extension of **.FLM** on the APPLICATION disk.
- Place the names of the files with only an extension of **.FLM** in a file called **2.HW**.

TO CREATE 3.HW

- Redirect the contents (not the file name) of the file called **DRAMA.FLM** in the **MOVIES** directory on the APPLICATION disk to a file called **3.HW**.

TO CREATE 4.HW

- Overwrite the file called **DRAMA.FLM** in the **MOVIES** directory on the APPLICATION disk with the contents of the file called **APR.99** located in the root directory of the APPLICATION disk.
- Redirect the contents (not the file name) of the file called **DRAMA.FLM** in the **MOVIES** directory on the APPLICATION disk to a file called **4.HW**.

TO CREATE 5.HW

- Concatenate all the files that have the extension **.RED** from the **WINDOSBK** directory to the **MOVIES** directory on the APPLICATION disk.
- Call the new file **MYRED.FIL**.
- Redirect the contents (not the file name) of the file called **MYRED.FIL** to a file called **5.HW**.

TO PRINT YOUR HOMEWORK

Step 1 Be sure the printer is on and ready to accept print jobs from your computer.

Step 2 Key in the following (be very careful to make no typing errors):
GO NAME.FIL 1.HW 2.HW 3.HW 4.HW 5.HW Enter

- If the files you requested, **1.HW, 2.HW**, etc., do not exist in the default directory, you will see the following message on the screen:

```
Command Prompt

File Not Found
The system cannot find the file specified.

Is there a message that says "File Not Found. The system cannot
find the file specified."

If so, press Y to find out what could be wrong.

Otherwise, press N to continue.
```

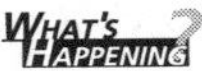

The operating system is telling you that the file cannot be found. If you see this screen, press **Y** to see what could be wrong, and repeat the print procedure after you have corrected the problem.

If the default directory contains the specified files, the following message will appear on the screen:

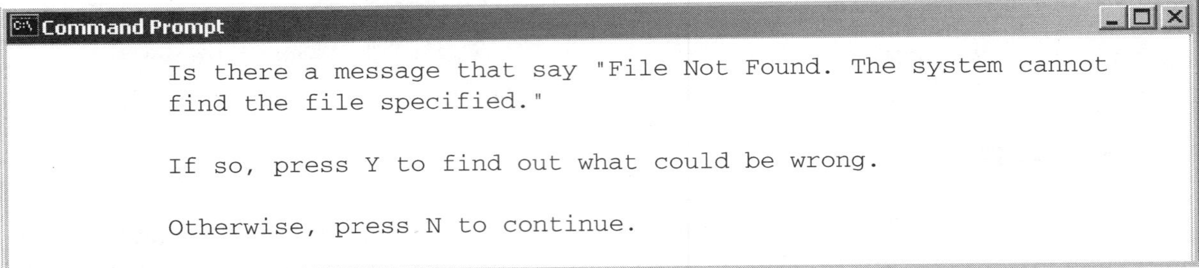

WHAT'S HAPPENING? You will need to press **N** once for each file you are printing.

Step 3 Follow the messages on the screen until the Notepad program opens with a screen similar to the following:

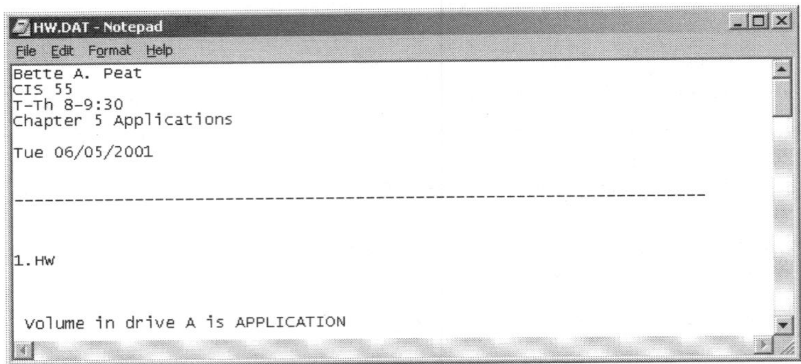

WHAT'S HAPPENING? All the requested files have been found and placed in a Notepad document. Your homework is now ready to print.

Step 4 On the Notepad menu bar, click **File**. Click **Print**.

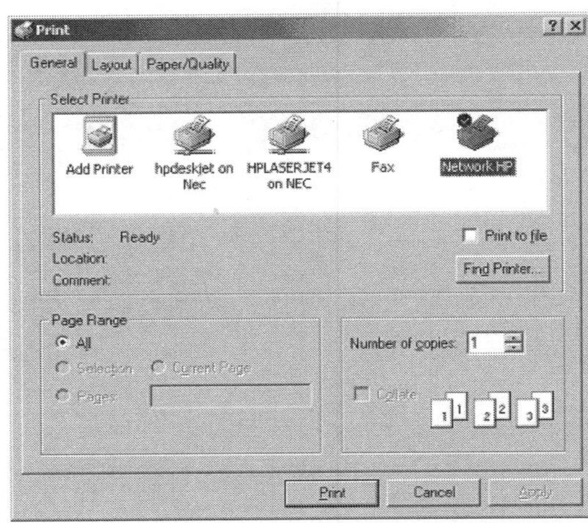

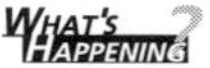

The print dialog box opens. If you have more than one printer, all your printer choices will be displayed. The default printer is the highlighted printer.

Step 5 Click the **Print** button.

Step 6 In the Notepad window, click **File**. Click **Exit**.

WHAT'S HAPPENING? The following will appear on the Command Prompt screen:

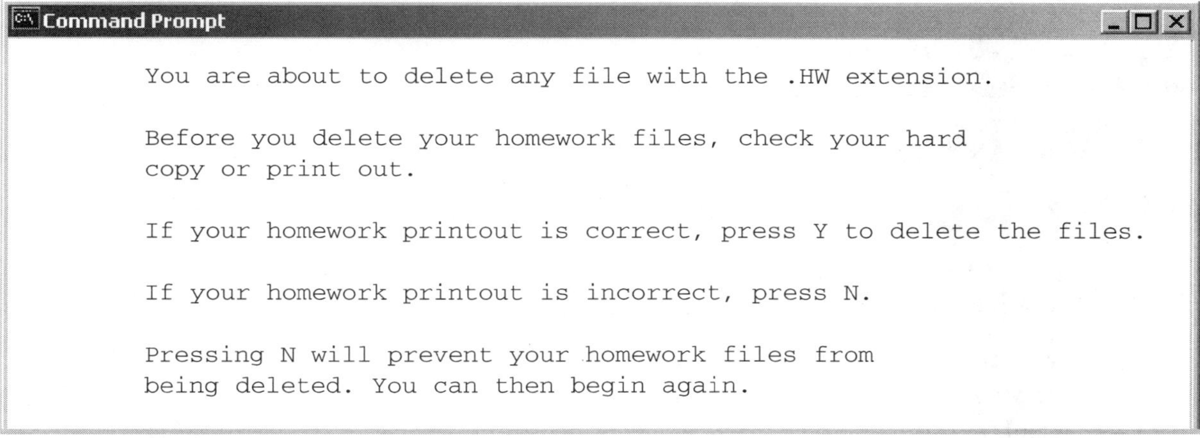

```
Command Prompt

You are about to delete any file with the .HW extension.

Before you delete your homework files, check your hard
copy or print out.

If your homework printout is correct, press Y to delete the files.

If your homework printout is incorrect, press N.

Pressing N will prevent your homework files from
being deleted. You can then begin again.
```

WHAT'S HAPPENING? At this point, look at your printout. If it is correct, you can press **Y** to delete the homework files for this chapter. If your printout is incorrect, you can press **N**. That will preserve your homework and you will need to redo only the problem that was incorrect, not all the homework assignments.

Step 7 Press **Y** **Enter**

WHAT'S HAPPENING? You have returned to the default prompt.

Step 8 Close the Command Prompt session.

Step 9 Execute the shut-down procedure.

PROBLEM SET III—BRIEF ESSAY

1. Copying and printing files can be done from My Computer or Windows Explorer. Why or why not might you use the command line to accomplish these tasks?

2. Briefly explain the purpose and function of subdirectory markers. Give three examples of how you would use subdirectory markers. Include commands that can be used with subdirectory markers.

CHAPTER

6

USING DEL, REN, MOVE, AND RD /S

LEARNING OBJECTIVES

After completing this chapter you will be able to:

1. Explain why it is necessary to eliminate files from a disk.
2. Explain when and how to use wildcards with the DEL command.
3. Explain the use of the /P parameter with the DEL command.
4. Explain the purpose and function of the RENAME/REN command.
5. Explain the purpose and function of the MOVE command.
6. Explain the purpose and function of the RD /S command.
7. Explain the importance of backing up data.

STUDENT OUTCOMES

1. Use the DEL command to eliminate files on disks and in directories.
2. Use wildcards appropriately with the DEL command.
3. Use parameters with the DEL command.
4. Use the RENAME/REN command to change the names of file and subdirectories.
5. Use the RENAME/REN command with wildcards to change the names of files and subdirectories.
6. Use the MOVE command to move files and subdirectories.
7. Use the RD command without parameters to delete empty directories.
8. Use the RD command with parameters to delete directories with files and other directories.
9. Back up a data disk using the DISKCOPY command.
10. Back up files using the COPY command.

CHAPTER OVERVIEW

The more work you do with computers, the more files you create, and the harder it is to manage them. It becomes increasingly difficult to keep track of what disks have which files and which files are needed. In addition, as new data is keyed into existing files, the names given to the files may no longer be appropriate. It is also important to be able to make a copy of an entire disk or specific files on a disk so that data is not lost due to a power failure, a power surge, or a bad disk.

In this chapter, you will continue to work with commands that help you manage and manipulate your files. This chapter will focus on the DEL command, which allows you to delete files you no longer need or want; the RENAME command, which is used to rename files; and the MOVE command, which allows you to move files and subdirectories from one location to another. In addition, you will look at the RD /S command, which allows you to quickly eliminate a subdirectory and all its files. You will also learn why and how to back up specific files or an entire disk so that you do not lose important data.

6.1 ELIMINATING FILES WITH THE DEL COMMAND

In the various activities completed previously, you copied many files. The DATA disk began as a disk absent of files. As you have been working, the number of files on the disk has increased dramatically. This is typical when working with computers. There is a kind of Murphy's Law that says you create as many files as you have disk space. However, you do not want to keep files forever. The more files and/or disks you have, the harder it is to keep track of what disks have which files and which files are the ones you need. If you have floppy disks, you end up with many floppies, and if you have a hard disk, you end up with many subdirectories and many files. Often, you are not quite sure what files are where. By keeping only the files you need on your disk, you will decrease the number of files you have to manage.

Logic tells you that, if you can copy and create files, you should be able to eliminate files by deleting or erasing them. You can do these tasks with the DEL command, which is identical to another command, ERASE (for the purposes of this book, we will discuss the DEL command with the understanding that ERASE works the same way). This command is internal, always resident in memory. You do need to be careful with this command. Once you press **Enter** after the DEL command, the file is gone forever. The operating system does not ask you if this is really the file you want to get rid of; it simply obeys your instructions.

When a file is deleted at the command line, it cannot be recovered except by certain special utility programs. Even then, recovery is not necessarily complete or even possible. Technically, when you delete a file, the file is not actually physically removed from the disk. Instead, the first character of the file name is replaced with a special byte—the symbol **σ**—that marks the file as deleted in the directory entry table. Then a 0 is placed in each cluster entry in the FAT (file allocation table). The value of 0 in each cluster means to the operating system that the space is now available for reuse by other files, even though, in fact, the data is still on the disk. When you create the next file, the operating system sees that there is space available in the directory entry table and the FAT and assigns the new file to that space. The old file is overwritten by the new file.

Special utility programs, such as Norton Utilities, can occasionally help you recover deleted files, particularly if you realize immediately that you inadvertently erased a file. In versions of the operating system from MS-DOS version 5.0 through MS-DOS version 6.22, the UNDELETE command was available. UNDELETE was an operating system utility supplied to recover deleted files. However, once a file was overwritten by new data, nothing could recover the previous data. It was gone forever. When you use the DEL command in the Windows operating system, you cannot recover deleted files. UNDELETE is no longer supported by Windows 2000 Professional. Thus, you should consider that, for all practical purposes, when you use DEL, you have indeed removed the file or files.

When you delete a file from a hard drive using My Computer or Windows Explorer (using the Windows GUI), the file goes to the Recycle Bin and is then recoverable. You can open the Recycle Bin, select the file you deleted, and restore it. However, if you never empty your Recycle Bin, eventually it becomes full and Windows begins deleting the oldest files in the Recycle Bin. Files are not recoverable if you delete them from a removable disk, such as a Zip drive or a floppy disk. Files deleted from the command prompt bypass the Recycle Bin and cannot be recovered by the operating system.

The syntax of the DEL command (identical to ERASE) is:

```
DEL  [/P]  [/F]  [/S]  [/Q]  [/A[[:]attributes]]  names
ERASE  [/P]  [/F]  [/S]  [/Q]  [/A[[:]attributes]]  names
```

The /P parameter prompts you before each file is deleted. /F forces the deletion of read-only files. /S deletes specified files from the current directory and all subdirectories. /Q puts the command in quiet mode; you are not prompted to confirm the deletion. /A deletes files based on specified attributes. The attributes are abbreviated as follows: R, read-only; A, archive; s, system; h, hidden; -, a prefix meaning “not.”

6.2 ACTIVITY: USING THE DEL COMMAND

Note 1: When keying in commands, you may use the editing keys to correct typographical errors.

Note 2: Be sure the DATA disk, not the APPLICATION disk, is in Drive A.

Note 3: C:\> is displayed as the default drive and directory.

Step 1 Key in the following: C:\>**A:** Enter

Step 2 Key in the following: A:\>**COPY C:\WINDOSBK*.DOS *.AAA** Enter

```
Command Prompt

C:\>A:

A:\>COPY  C:\WINDOSBK\*.DOS  *.AAA
C:\WINDOSBK\WILDONE.DOS
C:\WINDOSBK\WILDTHR.DOS
C:\WINDOSBK\WILDTWO.DOS
        3 file(s) copied.

A:\>_
```

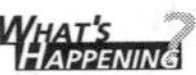

You changed the default drive to A. You then copied the files with a **.DOS** extension from the **\WINDOSBK** directory, keeping the same file names but giving them a different extension (**.AAA**), to the root of the DATA disk.

Step 3 Key in the following: A:\>**DIR *.AAA** Enter

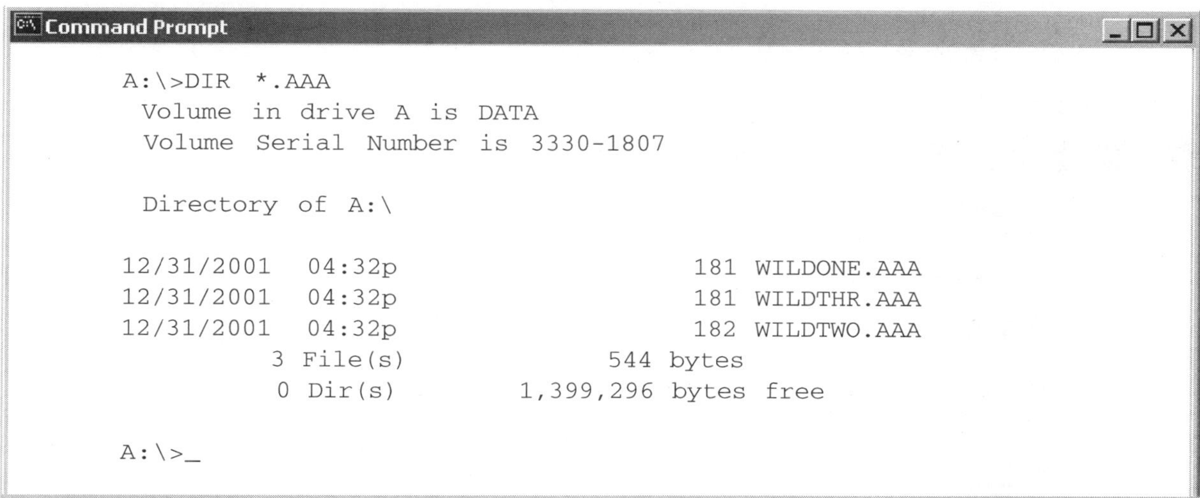

```
Command Prompt

A:\>DIR *.AAA
 Volume in drive A is DATA
 Volume Serial Number is 3330-1807

 Directory of A:\

12/31/2001  04:32p                181 WILDONE.AAA
12/31/2001  04:32p                181 WILDTHR.AAA
12/31/2001  04:32p                182 WILDTWO.AAA
               3 File(s)            544 bytes
               0 Dir(s)       1,399,296 bytes free

A:\>_
```

WHAT'S HAPPENING? You used the DIR command to confirm that the **.AAA** files are on the DATA disk. The work you wish to do is delete files. The DEL command is an internal command and was installed in memory (RAM) when you booted the system. It will remain in memory until you turn off the power.

Step 4 Key in the following: A:\>**DIR WILDONE.AAA** Enter

```
Command Prompt

A:\>DIR WILDONE.AAA
 Volume in drive A is DATA
 Volume Serial Number is 3330-1807

 Directory of A:\

12/31/2001  04:32p                181 WILDONE.AAA
               1 File(s)            181 bytes
               0 Dir(s)       1,399,296 bytes free

A:\>_
```

WHAT'S HAPPENING? The DIR command verified that the file called **WILDONE.AAA** is located on the DATA disk.

Step 5 Key in the following: A:\>**DEL WILDONE.AAA** Enter

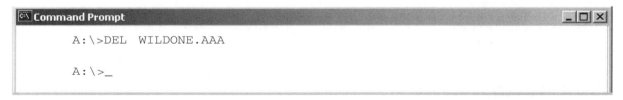

```
Command Prompt

A:\>DEL WILDONE.AAA

A:\>_
```

WHAT'S HAPPENING? You are asking the DEL command to eliminate the file called **WILDONE.AAA**, located on the DATA disk. You did not need to include the drive letter or \ because the operating system assumed the default drive and directory and looked only for the file called **WILDONE.AAA** on the DATA disk in the root. However, it appears that nothing happened. All you got on the screen was the system prompt.

Step 6 Key in the following: A:\>**DIR WILDONE.AAA** Enter

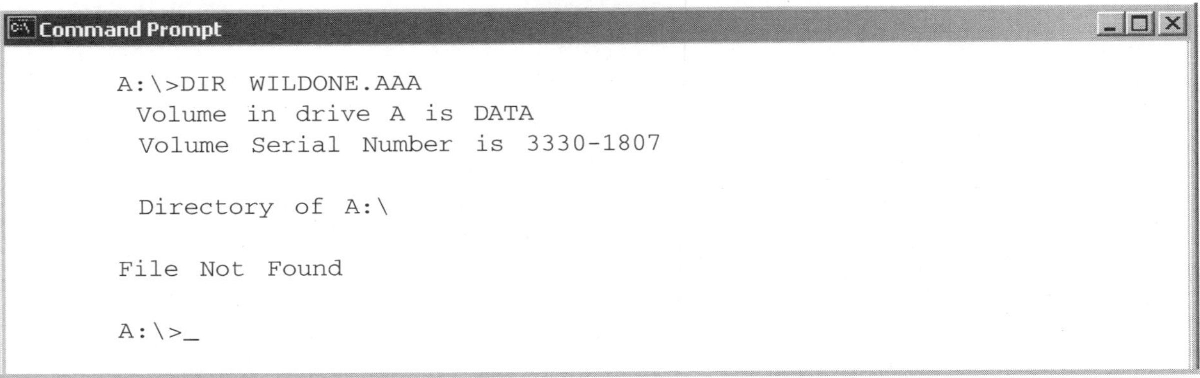

The DIR command confirmed that the file is gone. You now know that the DEL command was executed and that it removed the file called **WILDONE.AAA**. It is no longer on the DATA disk. What if the file you wanted to delete was not on the disk?

Step 7 Key in the following: A:\>**DEL NOFILE.XXX** Enter

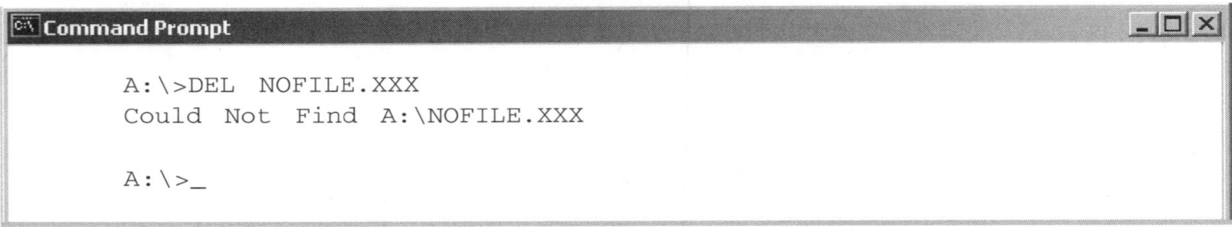

Command Prompt
A:\>DEL NOFILE.XXX
Could Not Find A:\NOFILE.XXX
A:\>_

In order for the DEL command to execute, it must be able to find the file to delete. Here, the file was not found.

Step 8 Key in the following: A:\>**DEL** Enter

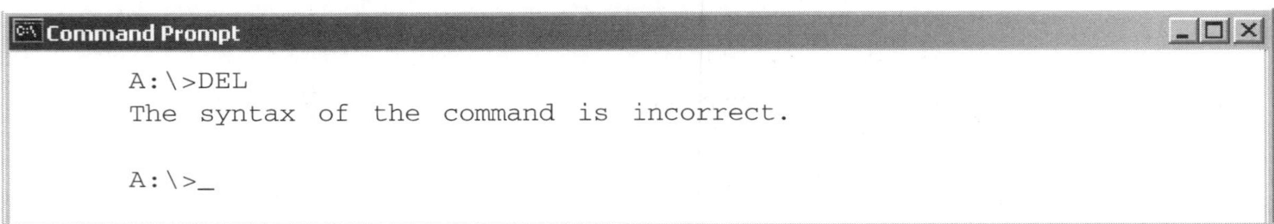

Not only must the operating system find the file but it also must know what file to look for. Remember, the syntax is DEL *names*.

6.3 DELETING MULTIPLE FILES

You can delete more than one file at a time with the DEL command. List the files you want to delete after the DEL command, separated by spaces.

6.4 ACTIVITY: USING DEL WITH MULTIPLE PARAMETERS

Step 1 Key in the following: A:\>**COPY C:\WINDOSBK*.DOS *.BBB** Enter

Step 2 Key in the following: A:\>**DIR *.BBB** Enter

```
Command Prompt

A:\>COPY  C:\WINDOSBK\*.DOS  *.BBB
C:\WINDOSBK\WILDONE.DOS
C:\WINDOSBK\WILDTHR.DOS
C:\WINDOSBK\WILDTWO.DOS
        3 file(s) copied.

A:\>DIR  *.BBB
 Volume in drive A is DATA
 Volume Serial Number is 3330-1807

 Directory of A:\

12/31/2001  04:32p                 181 WILDONE.BBB
12/31/2001  04:32p                 181 WILDTHR.BBB
12/31/2001  04:32p                 182 WILDTWO.BBB
               3 File(s)            544 bytes
               0 Dir(s)       1,398,272 bytes free

A:\>_
```

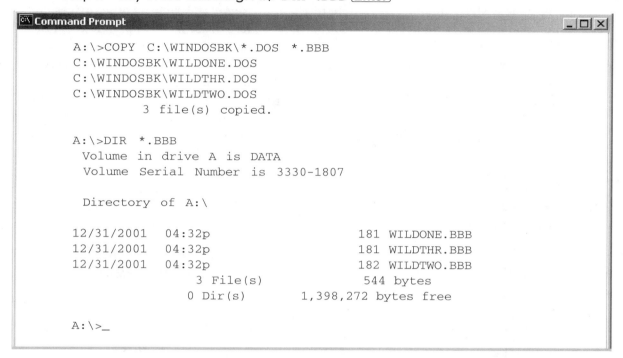

WHAT'S HAPPENING? You copied the same files from the previous exercise and used the DIR command to verify their presence on the DATA disk.

Step 3 Key in the following:
A:\> **DEL WILDONE.BBB WILDTWO.BBB WILDTHR.BBB** Enter

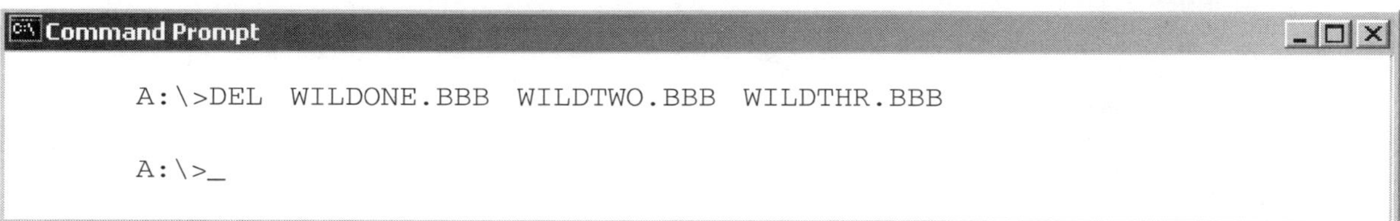
Command Prompt
A:\>DEL WILDONE.BBB WILDTWO.BBB WILDTHR.BBB
A:\>_

WHAT'S HAPPENING? No message appears on the screen. Were the files in fact deleted?

Step 4 Key in the following: A:\>**DIR *.BBB** Enter

```
Command Prompt

A:\>DIR  *.BBB
 Volume in drive A is DATA
 Volume Serial Number is 3330-1807

 Directory of A:\

File Not Found

A:\>_
```

The DIR command has confirmed that the files were deleted.

6.5 DELETING FILES ON OTHER DRIVES AND DIRECTORIES

Using the DEL command to eliminate files works exactly the same on other drives and subdirectories as it did in the previous activities. The syntax of the command remains DEL *names*. The only difference is that you must specify which disk drive and which directory you want to look on. Once again, the operating system follows your instructions exactly as keyed in; it does not check with you to see if you are deleting the correct file. One of the most common mistakes computer users make is placing the drive designator or subdirectory in the wrong place, which can completely change the meaning and results of an instruction. Again, the syntax of the command is:

```
DEL names
```

DEL is the command; *names* represents the designated drives, subdirectories, and names of the files you wish to delete. Notice that DEL and names are not in brackets, so they are required parts of the command.

6.6 ACTIVITY: USING THE DEL COMMAND WITH INDIVIDUAL FILES

Note: The DATA disk is in Drive A. A:\> is displayed.

Step 1 Key in the following: A:\>**MD TRIP** Enter

Step 2 Key in the following: A:\>**COPY C:\WINDOSBK*.99 TRIP** Enter

Step 3 Key in the following: A:\>**COPY C:\WINDOSBK*.JAZ TRIP** Enter

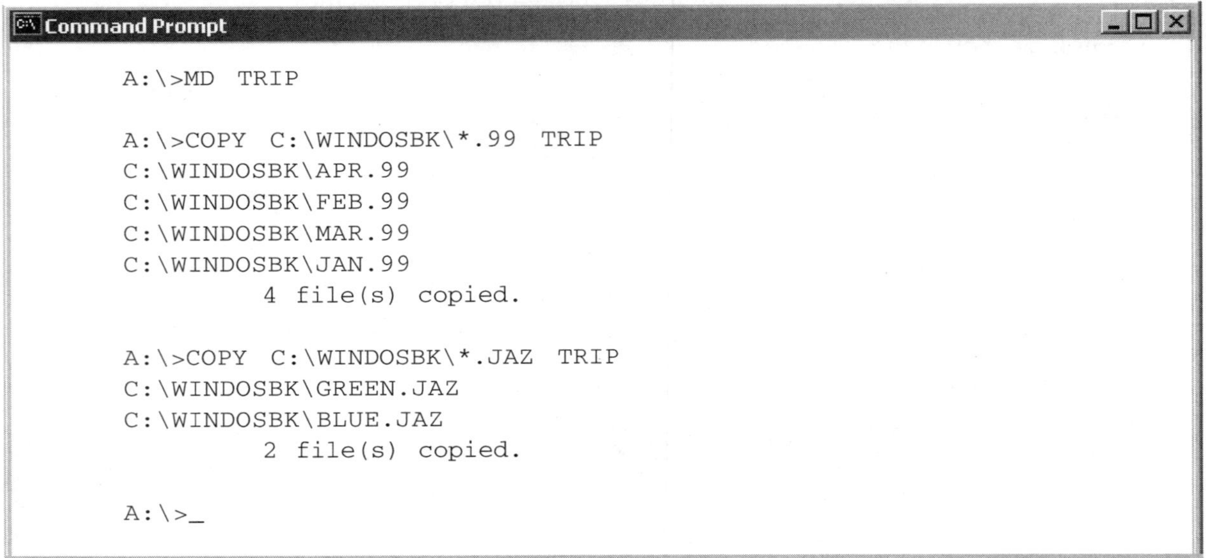

```
Command Prompt

A:\>MD TRIP

A:\>COPY C:\WINDOSBK\*.99 TRIP
C:\WINDOSBK\APR.99
C:\WINDOSBK\FEB.99
C:\WINDOSBK\MAR.99
C:\WINDOSBK\JAN.99
        4 file(s) copied.

A:\>COPY C:\WINDOSBK\*.JAZ TRIP
C:\WINDOSBK\GREEN.JAZ
C:\WINDOSBK\BLUE.JAZ
        2 file(s) copied.

A:\>_
```

You created another subdirectory on the DATA disk called **TRIP**. You then copied files from the **\WINDOSBK** subdirectory on the hard disk to the subdirectory called **TRIP** on the DATA disk. You used the COPY command. You had to specify where the source files were located, **C:\WINDOSBK**. However, for the destination of these files, since the default drive is A and the default directory is the root, the OS assumed the default, and you did not have to specify either the destination drive or the root directory in the destination. If you had not included the name of the subdirectory **TRIP**, where you wanted the files copied, the operating system would have assumed the default and copied the files to the root directory of the DATA disk. The longhand or absolute path version of the command is A:\>**COPY C:\WINDOSBK*.99 A:\TRIP*.99**.

Step 4 Key in the following: A:\>**DIR TRIP\JAN.99** Enter

```
Command Prompt

A:\>DIR TRIP\JAN.99
 Volume in drive A is DATA
 Volume Serial Number is 3330-1807

 Directory of A:\TRIP

10/10/1999  04:53p                    73 JAN.99
               1 File(s)             73 bytes
               0 Dir(s)       1,396,224 bytes free

A:\>_
```

WHAT'S HAPPENING? The file is there. You successfully copied it.

Step 5 Key in the following: A:\>**DEL TRIP\JAN.99** Enter

```
Command Prompt

A:\>DEL TRIP\JAN.99

A:\>_
```

WHAT'S HAPPENING? You had to provide the proper syntax to tell the DEL command where the **JAN.99** file was located. It was located in the subdirectory **TRIP** under the root directory on the DATA disk. Since the default drive is A, you did not need to include the drive letter. Since the default subdirectory is the root (\), the \ is assumed and does not need to be keyed in. However, the \ between the subdirectory **TRIP** and the file name **JAN.99** does need to be keyed in. In this case \ is used as a delimiter between the subdirectory name and the file name. Has the file been deleted?

Step 6 Key in the following: A:\>**DIR TRIP\JAN.99** Enter

```
Command Prompt

A:\>DIR TRIP\JAN.99
 Volume in drive A is DATA
 Volume Serial Number is 3330-1807

 Directory of A:\TRIP
```

```
File Not Found

A:\>_
```

WHAT'S HAPPENING? The file called **JAN.99** is gone from the subdirectory called **TRIP** on the DATA disk. Look at the display. The third line returned by the command, **Directory of A:\TRIP**, tells you that DIR looked only in the subdirectory called **TRIP**.

Step 7 Key in the following: A:\>**CD /D C:\WINDOSBK** Enter

Step 8 Key in the following: C:\WINDOSBK>**COPY HELLO.TXT A:** Enter

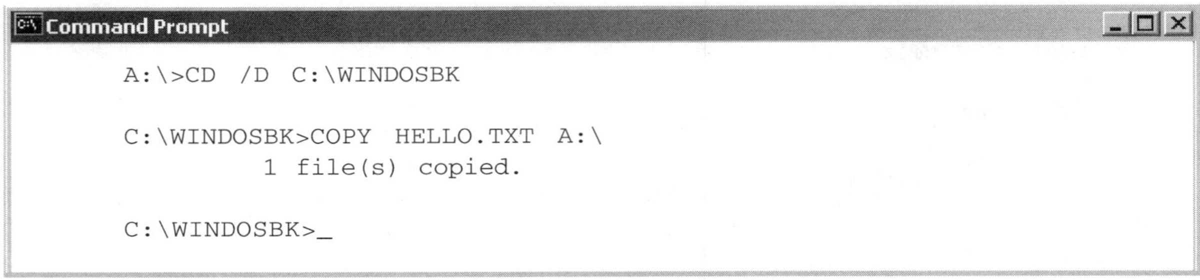

```
Command Prompt
A:\>CD /D C:\WINDOSBK

C:\WINDOSBK>COPY HELLO.TXT A:\
        1 file(s) copied.

C:\WINDOSBK>_
```

WHAT'S HAPPENING? You changed the default drive and the default subdirectory from the root of the hard disk to the subdirectory called **\WINDOSBK** on Drive C. You then copied the file called **HELLO.TXT** from the **\WINDOSBK** directory to the root directory of the DATA disk. The purpose of this activity is to have two identically named files on different drives.

Step 9 Key in the following: C:\WINDOSBK>**DIR HELLO.TXT** Enter

Step 10 Key in the following: C:\WINDOSBK>**DIR A:\HELLO.TXT** Enter

```
Command Prompt
C:\WINDOSBK>DIR HELLO.TXT
 Volume in drive C is 2000 PRO
 Volume Serial Number is C4A7-8571

 Directory of C:\WINDOSBK

05/30/2000  04:32p                  53 HELLO.TXT

            1 File(s)             53 bytes
            0 Dir(s)   1,121,550,336 bytes free

C:\WINDOSBK>DIR A:\HELLO.TXT
 Volume in drive A is DATA
 Volume Serial Number is 3330-1807

 Directory of A:\
```

```
05/30/2000  04:32p                    53 HELLO.TXT
             1 File(s)                53 bytes
             0 Dir(s)         1,396,224 bytes free

C:\WINDOSBK>_
```

You have two files called **HELLO.TXT**. One file is on the hard disk in the subdirectory **\WINDOSBK**. The other file is on the DATA disk. You want to delete the file on the DATA disk, *not* on the hard disk.

Step 11 Key in the following: C:\WINDOSBK>**DEL A:\HELLO.TXT** Enter

```
Command Prompt

C:\WINDOSBK>DEL  A:\HELLO.TXT

C:\WINDOSBK>_
```

You asked DEL to erase the file on the DATA disk called **HELLO.TXT**. The file should be gone from the DATA disk, but the file called **HELLO.TXT** on the hard disk (Drive C, subdirectory **\WINDOSBK**) should still be there.

Step 12 Key in the following: C:\WINDOSBK>**DIR HELLO.TXT** Enter

Step 13 Key in the following: C:\WINDOSBK>**DIR A:\HELLO.TXT** Enter

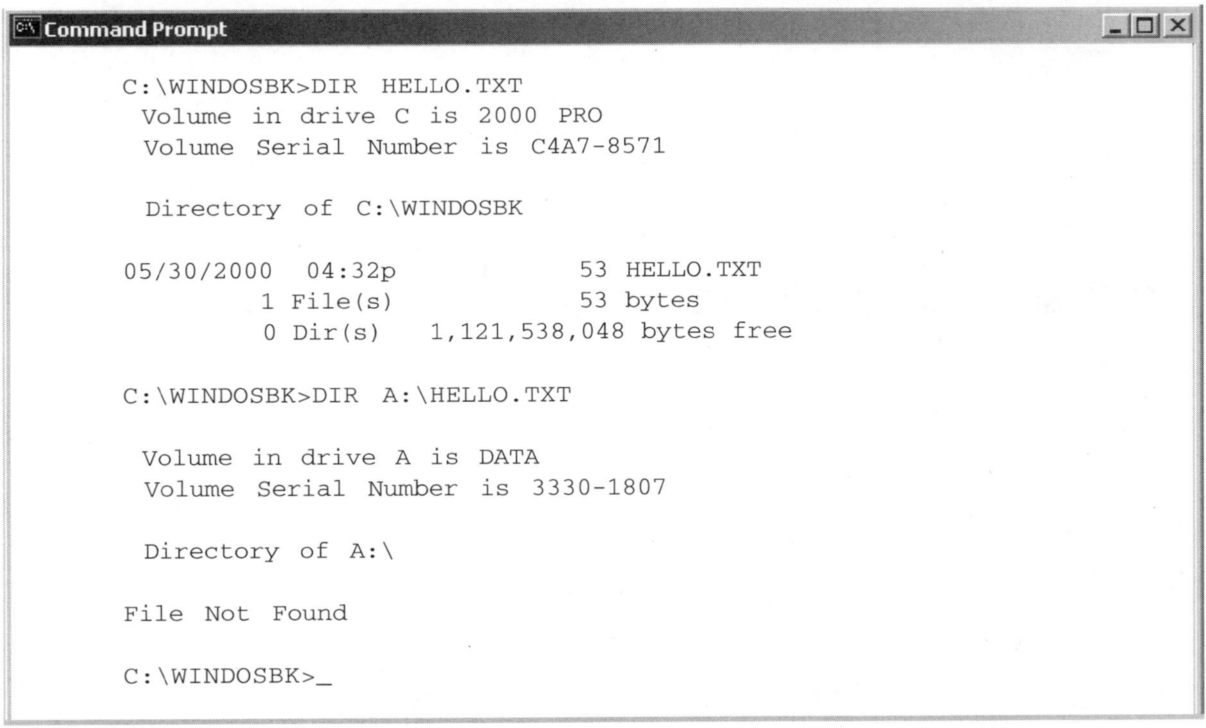

```
Command Prompt

C:\WINDOSBK>DIR  HELLO.TXT
 Volume in drive C is 2000 PRO
 Volume Serial Number is C4A7-8571

 Directory of C:\WINDOSBK

05/30/2000  04:32p              53 HELLO.TXT
             1 File(s)           53 bytes
             0 Dir(s)  1,121,538,048 bytes free

C:\WINDOSBK>DIR  A:\HELLO.TXT

 Volume in drive A is DATA
 Volume Serial Number is 3330-1807

 Directory of A:\

File Not Found

C:\WINDOSBK>_
```

The file called **HELLO.TXT** is still in the subdirectory **\WINDOSBK** on the hard disk, but the file called **HELLO.TXT** on the DATA disk is gone.

Step 14 Key in the following: C:\WINDOSBK>**DIR A:\TRIP\BLUE.JAZ** Enter

```
C:\WINDOSBK>DIR  A:\TRIP\BLUE.JAZ
 Volume in drive A is DATA
 Volume Serial Number is 3330-1807

 Directory of A:\TRIP

05/30/2000  04:32p              19 BLUE.JAZ
               1 File(s)             19 bytes
               0 Dir(s)       1,396,736 bytes free

C:\WINDOSBK>_
```

There is a file called **BLUE.JAZ** in the subdirectory **TRIP** on the DATA disk. To delete this file, you once again follow the syntax of the DEL command, substituting the values you want for the variable parameters.

Step 15 Key in the following: C:\WINDOSBK>**DEL A:\TRIP\BLUE.JAZ** Enter

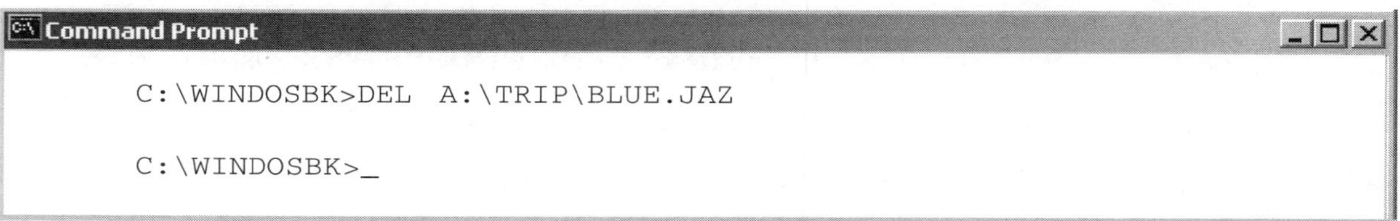
Command Prompt
C:\WINDOSBK>DEL A:\TRIP\BLUE.JAZ
C:\WINDOSBK>_

The syntax is DEL *names*. You used the drive letter of the DATA disk, then **TRIP** and **BLUE.JAZ** for the name. The second backslash was mandatory because you needed a delimiter between the file name and the subdirectory name. This backslash is similar to the period that you used to separate the file name from the file extension. Is the file gone?

Step 16 Key in the following: C:\WINDOSBK>**DIR A:\TRIP\BLUE.JAZ** Enter

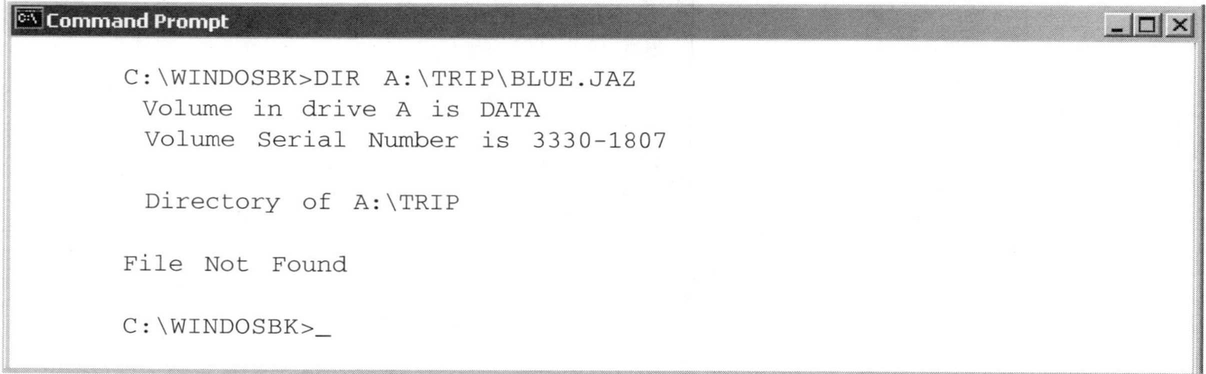
Command Prompt
C:\WINDOSBK>DIR A:\TRIP\BLUE.JAZ
Volume in drive A is DATA
Volume Serial Number is 3330-1807
Directory of A:\TRIP
File Not Found
C:\WINDOSBK>_

The file **BLUE.JAZ** from the directory **TRIP** on the DATA disk is gone.

Step 17 Key in the following: C:\WINDOSBK>**CD ** Enter

Step 18 Key in the following: C:\>**A:** Enter

```
Command Prompt

C:\WINDOSBK>CD \

C:\>A:

A:\>_
```

WHAT'S HAPPENING? You returned to the root directory of the hard disk. You then made the root directory of the DATA disk the default drive and directory.

6.7 USING WILDCARDS WITH THE DEL COMMAND

You have been erasing or deleting files one at a time. Often you want to erase many files. It is tedious to erase many files one at a time. You can use the wildcards with the DEL command to delete several files at one time. Wildcards allow you to erase a group of files with a one-line command. Although you can certainly delete files in My Computer, you must select each file to be deleted, which takes lots of time. It is simply quicker and easier deleting files from the command line. However, at the command line, be *exceedingly* careful when using wildcards with the DEL command. Once again, the strength of wildcards is also their weakness. A global file specification means global. You can eliminate a group of files very quickly. If you are not careful, you could erase files you want to keep. In fact, you probably will some day say, "Oh no, those files are gone." However, this does not mean you should never use wildcards. They are far too useful. Just be very, *very* careful.

6.8 ACTIVITY: USING THE DEL COMMAND

Note 1: The DATA disk is in Drive A. A:\> is displayed.

Note 2: If the **.TMP** files are not on the root of the DATA disk, they may be copied from the **\WINDOSBK** subdirectory.

Step 1 Key in the following: A:\>**DIR *.TMP** Enter

```
Command Prompt

A:\>DIR *.TMP
 Volume in drive A is DATA
 Volume Serial Number is 3330-1807

 Directory of A:\

04/23/2000  04:03p                  73 JAN.TMP
04/23/2000  04:03p                  75 FEB.TMP
04/23/2000  04:03p                  71 MAR.TMP
04/23/2000  04:18p                  72 APR.TMP
               4 File(s)            291 bytes
               0 Dir(s)       1,397,248 bytes free

A:\>_
```

You should see four files with **.TMP** as the file extension displayed on the screen. Prior to doing a global erase, it is always wise to key in DIR with the same global file specification you are going to use with the DEL command. In this way, you can see ahead of time *exactly* which files will be deleted. This process allows you to confirm visually that you are not going to erase a file you want to retain.

Step 2 Key in the following: A:\>**DEL *.TMP** Enter

You asked DEL to erase or delete every file with the **.TMP** file extension on the DATA disk in the root directory. The wildcard * represented any file name. Only the system prompt appears on the screen. The DEL command executed, erasing those ***.TMP** files quickly and permanently. To verify this, use the DIR command.

Step 3 Key in the following: A:\>**DIR *.TMP** Enter

```
Command Prompt

A:\>DIR *.TMP
 Volume in drive A is DATA
 Volume Serial Number is 3330-1807

 Directory of A:\

File Not Found

A:\>_
```

Those ***.TMP** files are, indeed, gone from the root directory on the DATA disk. They are not recoverable by the operating system. It must be emphasized that before you use a wildcard to delete a group of files you should use the DIR command to see the files you are going to delete. For instance, if you had a file called **TEST.TMP** that you had forgotten about and that you did not want to delete, the directory display would include it as follows:

```
Command Prompt
04/23/2000  04:03p                73 JAN.TMP
04/23/2000  04:03p                75 FEB.TMP
04/23/2000  04:03p                71 MAR.TMP
04/23/2000  04:18p                72 APR.TMP
05/01/1998  05:00p               500 TEST.TMP
               5 File(s)           787 bytes
```

You would have been made aware of the presence of the **TEST.TMP** file using the DIR command, and would thus have avoided losing a needed file. Using the DIR command with wildcards will let you display on the screen all the files that have been selected by ***.TMP**, which includes the **TEST.TMP** file that you do not want to erase. If you had keyed in **DEL *.TMP**, all those **.TMP** files would have been deleted. Remember, the computer does not come back and tell you, "Oh, by the way, **TEST.TMP** was included with the ***.TMP** files; did you want to erase that file?" The DEL command simply eliminates all the **.TMP** files because that is what you told it to do. You can also use wildcards when files are in a subdirectory.

Step 4 Key in the following: A:\>**DIR TRIP*.99** Enter

```
Command Prompt

A:\>DIR TRIP\*.99
 Volume in drive A is DATA
 Volume Serial Number is 3330-1807

 Directory of A:\TRIP

10/10/1999  04:53p                  72 APR.99
10/10/1999  04:53p                  75 FEB.99
10/10/1999  04:53p                  71 MAR.99
               3 File(s)            218 bytes
               0 Dir(s)       1,399,296 bytes free

A:\>_
```

WHAT'S HAPPENING? There are three files with the extension **.99** on the DATA disk in the subdirectory **TRIP**. The DEL command works the same way, but you must be sure to include the path name.

Step 5 Key in the following: A:\>**DEL TRIP*.99** Enter

```
Command Prompt

A:\>DEL TRIP\*.99

A:\>_
```

WHAT'S HAPPENING? You asked DEL to erase or delete every file on the DATA disk in the subdirectory **TRIP** that has any file name and has the file extension **.99**. The wildcard * represented any file name. Only the system prompt appears on the screen. The DEL command executed, erasing those ***.99** files quickly and permanently. To verify this, you can use the DIR command.

Step 6 Key in the following: A:\>**DIR TRIP*.99** Enter

```
Command Prompt

A:\>DIR TRIP\*.99
 Volume in drive A is DATA
 Volume Serial Number is 3330-1807
```

```
 Directory of A:\TRIP

File Not Found

A:\>_
```

WHAT'S HAPPENING? The ***.99** files are indeed gone from the **TRIP** directory.

6.9 THE /P AND /S PARAMETERS WITH THE DEL COMMAND

Prior to DOS 4.0, the DEL command provided no way for you to confirm deletions. The file was simply erased. In DOS 4.0 an enhancement was introduced—the /P parameter. This parameter allows you to tell the DEL command to prompt you with the file name prior to deleting the file. The syntax is:

```
DEL [/P] [/S] names
```

/P is one of the optional fixed parameters that work with the DEL command. Its purpose is to display each file name to verify that you really want to delete it. You can think of the P as standing for "prompt you for an answer." This parameter is particularly useful when you are using wildcards. It minimizes the risk of accidental file deletions. The /S parameter is also exceedingly useful, as it will traverse the directory tree so you do not have to delete files individually throughout your disk structure. Several new parameters were also added in Windows 2000 Professional. These include the ability to force the deletion of read-only files (/F), to delete files based on certain attributes (/A), and to not ask for confirmation of a deletion (/Q).

6.10 ACTIVITY: USING /P AND /S WITH THE DEL COMMAND

Note: The DATA disk is in Drive A. A:\> is displayed.

Step 1 Key in the following: A:\>**COPY C:\WINDOSBK*.99** Enter

Step 2 Key in the folloiwng: A:\>**MD TRIP\CHINA** Enter

Command Prompt

```
A:\>COPY C:\WINDOSBK\*.99
C:\WINDOSBK\APR.99
C:\WINDOSBK\FEB.99
C:\WINDOSBK\MAR.99
C:\WINDOSBK\JAN.99
        4 file(s) copied.

A:\>MD TRIP\CHINA

A:\>_
```

WHAT'S HAPPENING? You have copied the files with the **.99** extension from the **WINDOSBK** directory to the root of the DATA disk and kept the file names the same.

Step 3 Key in the following: A:\>**COPY *.99 TRIP** Enter

Step 4 Key in the following: A:\>**COPY *.99 TRIP\CHINA** Enter

Step 5 Key in the following: A:\>**DIR TRIP TRIP\CHINA** Enter

```
Command Prompt

A:\>COPY *.99 TRIP
APR.99
FEB.99
MAR.99
JAN.99
        4 file(s) copied.

A:\>COPY *.99 TRIP\CHINA
APR.99
FEB.99
MAR.99
JAN.99
        4 file(s) copied.

A:\>DIR TRIP TRIP\CHINA
 Volume in drive A is DATA
 Volume Serial Number is 3330-1807

 Directory of A:\TRIP

05/29/2001  10:11p      <DIR>          .
05/29/2001  10:11p      <DIR>          ..
05/30/2000  04:32p                  19 GREEN.JAZ
05/30/2001  12:14a      <DIR>          CHINA
10/10/1999  04:53p                  72 APR.99
10/10/1999  04:53p                  75 FEB.99
10/10/1999  04:53p                  71 MAR.99
10/10/1999  04:53p                  73 JAN.99
               5 File(s)            310 bytes

 Directory of A:\TRIP\CHINA

05/30/2001  12:14a      <DIR>          .
05/30/2001  12:14a      <DIR>          ..
10/10/1999  04:53p                  72 APR.99
10/10/1999  04:53p                  75 FEB.99
10/10/1999  04:53p                  71 MAR.99
10/10/1999  04:53p                  73 JAN.99
               4 File(s)            291 bytes
               2 Dir(s)       1,394,176 bytes free

A:\>_
```

You copied the files with the extension of **.99** to the **TRIP** and the **TRIP\CHINA** subdirectories on the DATA disk and confirmed that they are there. The file called **GREEN.JAZ** is also in that subdirectory. Next, you are going to choose *some* of the **.99** files to delete.

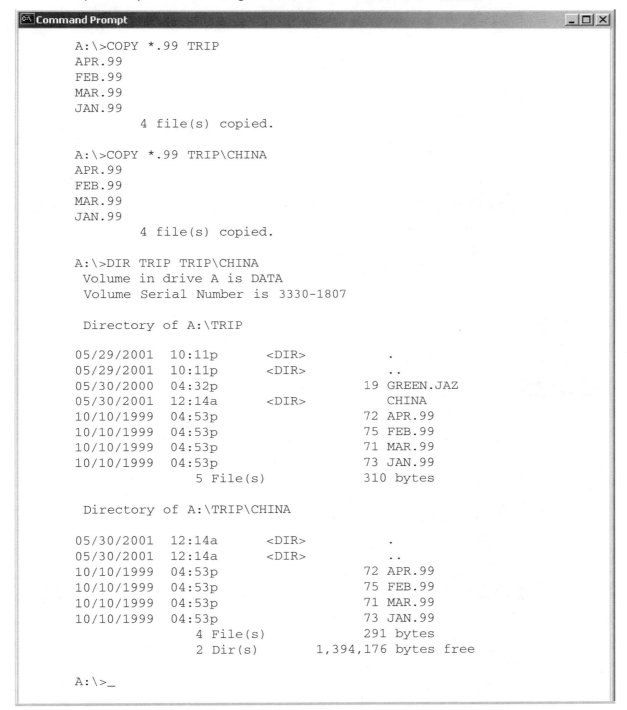

Step 6 Key in the following: A:\>**DEL TRIP*.99 /P** Enter

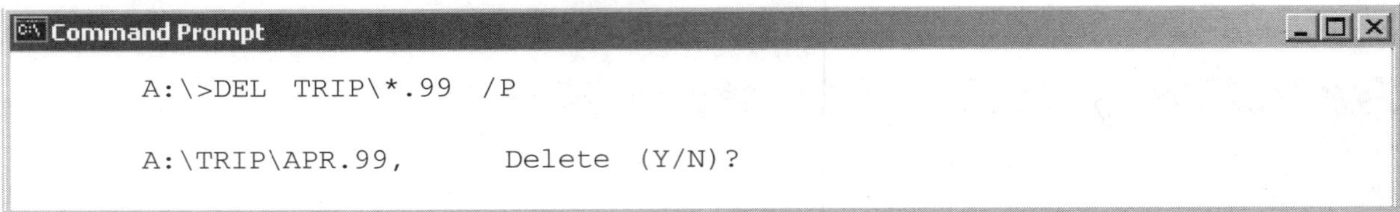
Command Prompt
A:\>DEL TRIP*.99 /P
A:\TRIP\APR.99, Delete (Y/N)?

WHAT'S HAPPENING? The **/P** parameter, when included in the command line, prompts you by asking if you want to delete the file called **APR.99** in the subdirectory **TRIP** on the DATA disk. When you have a **Y/N** choice, press either **Y** for "Yes" or **N** for "No." Pressing Enter takes no action.

Step 7 Key in the following: **N** Enter

```
Command Prompt
A:\>DEL TRIP\*.99 /P

TRIP\APR.99,     Delete (Y/N)?N
TRIP\FEB.99,     Delete (Y/N)?
```

WHAT'S HAPPENING? DEL found the next file and asked if you wanted to delete the file called **FEB.99**.

Step 8 Key in the following: **Y**

```
Command Prompt
A:\>DEL TRIP\*.99 /P

TRIP\APR.99,     Delete (Y/N)?N
TRIP\FEB.99,     Delete (Y/N)?Y
TRIP\MAR.99,     Delete (Y/N)?
```

WHAT'S HAPPENING? DEL found the next file and asked if you wanted to delete the file called **MAR.99**.

Step 9 Key in the following: **N**

```
Command Prompt
A:\>DEL TRIP\*.99 /P

TRIP\APR.99,     Delete (Y/N)?N
TRIP\FEB.99,     Delete (Y/N)?Y
TRIP\MAR.99,     Delete (Y/N)?N
TRIP\JAN.99,     Delete (Y/N)?
```

WHAT'S HAPPENING? DEL found the next file and asked you if you wanted to delete the file called **JAN.99**.

Step 10 Key in the following: **Y**

```
Command Prompt

TRIP\APR.99,      Delete  (Y/N)?N
TRIP\FEB.99,      Delete  (Y/N)?Y
TRIP\MAR.99,      Delete  (Y/N)?N
TRIP\JAN.99,      Delete  (Y/N)?Y

A:\>_
```

You were returned to the system prompt because there were no more files with the extension **.99** on the DATA disk in the subdirectory **TRIP**. You were able to delete files selectively. You deleted the files **JAN.99** and **FEB.99** but kept the files **MAR.99** and **APR.99**. You can verify this by using the DIR command.

Step 11 Key in the following: A:\>**DIR TRIP** Enter

```
Command Prompt

A:\>DIR TRIP
 Volume in drive A is DATA
 Volume Serial Number is 3330-1807

 Directory of A:\TRIP

05/29/2001  10:11p      <DIR>          .
05/29/2001  10:11p      <DIR>          ..
05/30/2000  04:32p                  19 GREEN.JAZ
05/30/2001  12:14a      <DIR>          CHINA
10/10/1999  04:53p                  72 APR.99
10/10/1999  04:53p                  71 MAR.99
               3 File(s)           162 bytes
               3 Dir(s)      1,393,200 bytes free

A:\>_
```

WHAT'S HAPPENING?

You retained the files **APR.99** and **MAR.99** but deleted **JAN.99** and **FEB.99**. The file **GREEN.JAZ** was not deleted because it did not have the file extension **.99**. You can use the /S parameter to traverse the directory tree. You can also use more than one parameter at a time.

Step 12 Key in the following: A:\>**DEL TRIP*.99 /P /S** Enter

Step 13 Key in **N** Enter, then **N** Enter again.

```
Command Prompt

A:\>DEL TRIP\*.99 /P /S
A:\TRIP\APR.99, Delete (Y/N)? N
A:\TRIP\MAR.99, Delete (Y/N)? N
A:\TRIP\CHINA\APR.99, Delete (Y/N)?
```

You answered "No, do not delete the files **APR.99** and **MAR.99** in the **TRIP** directory," but since you included the /S parameter, the DEL command continued down the tree looking for all files that ended in **.99**.

Step 14 Press **Y** and **Enter** until there are no more prompts.

```
A:\>DEL TRIP\*.99 /P /S
A:\TRIP\APR.99, Delete (Y/N)? n
A:\TRIP\MAR.99, Delete (Y/N)? n
A:\TRIP\CHINA\APR.99, Delete (Y/N)? y
Deleted file - A:\TRIP\CHINA\APR.99
A:\TRIP\CHINA\FEB.99, Delete (Y/N)? y
Deleted file - A:\TRIP\CHINA\FEB.99
A:\TRIP\CHINA\MAR.99, Delete (Y/N)? y
Deleted file - A:\TRIP\CHINA\MAR.99
A:\TRIP\CHINA\JAN.99, Delete (Y/N)? y
Deleted file - A:\TRIP\CHINA\JAN.99

A:\>_
```

Each time you pressed **Y**, you deleted the ***.99** files in the **TRIP\CHINA** directory. You also see a more complete error message that tells you which file has been deleted.

Step 15 Key in the following: A:\>**RD TRIP\CHINA** **Enter**

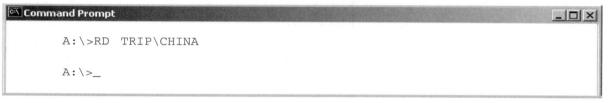

```
A:\>RD TRIP\CHINA

A:\>_
```

You have removed the **CHINA** directory.

6.11 CHANGING FILE NAMES

Often when working with files, you want to change a file name. For example, you may wish to change the name of a file to indicate an older version. You might also think of a more descriptive file name. As the contents of a file change, the old name may no longer reflect the contents. When you make a typographical error, you want to be able to correct it. One way to change the name of a file is to copy it to a different name. The COPY command can, in this way, help to change the name of a file. You could, for example, copy the file A:\JAN.99 to A:\TRIP\JAN.00. Actually, you did not change the name of an existing file—you created a new file with the same contents under a different name.

The operating system supplies a way to change existing file names using the internal command RENAME. RENAME does exactly what it says; it changes the name of a file. The contents of the file do not change, only the name of the file. The syntax for this command is:

```
RENAME [drive:][path][directoryname1 ¦ filename1]
    [directoryname2 ¦ filename2]
```

or

```
REN [drive:][path][directoryname1 ¦ filename1]
    [directoryname2 ¦ filename2]
```

RENAME does not let you specify a new drive or path for *filename2* or *directoryname2*. Remember, you are not making a copy of a file. It is like pasting a new label on an existing file folder. That file folder does not get moved in the process. You are dealing with only one file when using REN. In the syntax diagram, *filename1* and *filename2* refer to the same file—*filename1* will be changed to *filename2*. You are changing the file name only, not creating another copy of it with a new name.

The RENAME command has two forms, RENAME or REN, with exactly the same syntax. Most computer users choose REN, simply because it has fewer keystrokes. The syntax is the command REN, the first parameter (the old file name), and the second parameter (the new file name).

Renaming files at the command line is especially useful. In My Computer or Windows Explorer, renaming files is always a two-step process. First, you must select the file; then, you must rename it. At the command line, you can accomplish this task in one step.

6.12 ACTIVITY: USING THE REN COMMAND TO RENAME FILES

Note: The DATA disk is in Drive A. A:\> is displayed.

Step 1 Key in the following: A:\>**COPY C:\WINDOSBK\MEDIA\TV** Enter

Command Prompt

```
A:\>COPY C:\WINDOSBK\MEDIA\TV
C:\WINDOSBK\MEDIA\TV\COMEDY.TV
C:\WINDOSBK\MEDIA\TV\DRAMA.TV
        2 file(s) copied.

A:\>_
```

WHAT'S HAPPENING?

You copied two files from the subdirectory **\WINDOSBK\MEDIA\TV** from the hard disk to the root directory of the DATA disk. Notice that after **TV** you did not have to specify a file name. When you key in a command ending in the name of a directory rather than a file specification, ***.*** is assumed. The destination is also assumed. It is the default drive and directory—in this case the root directory of the DATA disk.

Step 2 Key in the following: A:\>**TYPE COMEDY.TV** Enter

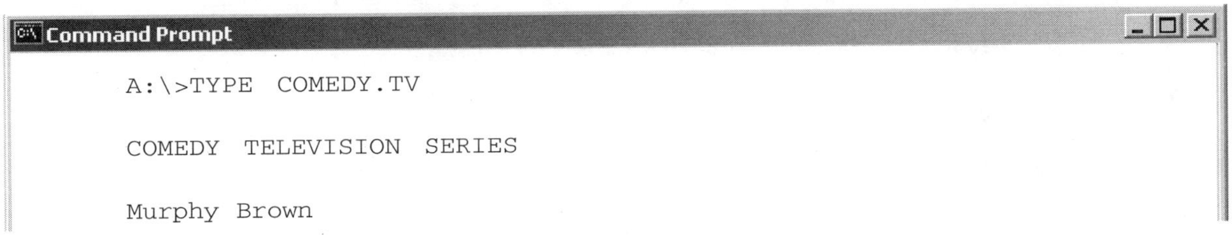

Command Prompt

```
A:\>TYPE COMEDY.TV

COMEDY TELEVISION SERIES

Murphy Brown
```

```
Suddenly Susan
Caroline in the City
Home Improvement
Seinfeld
I Love Lucy
Roseanne
TAXI
The Mary Tyler Moore Show
Wings
The Dick Van Dyke Show
Frasier
Third Rock From the Sun
A:\>_
```

WHAT'S HAPPENING? You are displaying the contents of the file called **COMEDY.TV** located in the root directory on the DATA disk. You opened the file folder called **COMEDY.TV** and looked inside.

Step 3 Key in the following: A:\>**REN COMEDY.TV FUNNY.TV** Enter

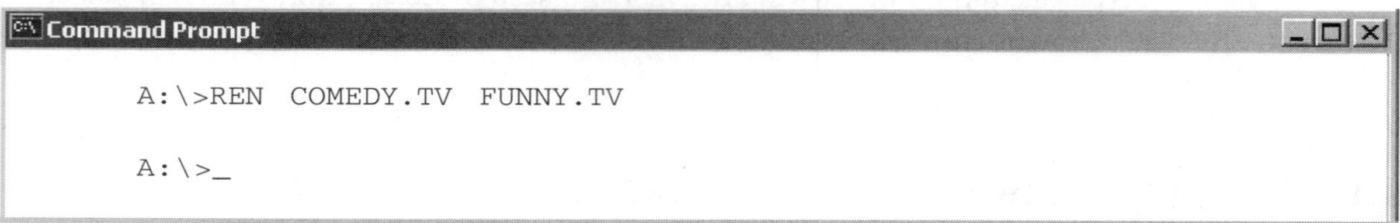

WHAT'S HAPPENING? Using the command REN changed the name of the file called **COMEDY.TV** to **FUNNY.TV**. Since the default was the DATA disk and the default directory was the root, the operating system looked only on the root directory of the DATA disk for the file called **COMEDY.TV**. Once you pressed Enter, you got back only the system prompt. Did anything happen?

Step 4 Key in the following: A:\>**DIR COMEDY.TV** Enter

```
Command Prompt

A:\>DIR COMEDY.TV
 Volume in drive A is DATA
 Volume Serial Number is 3330-1807

 Directory of A:\

File Not Found

A:\>_
```

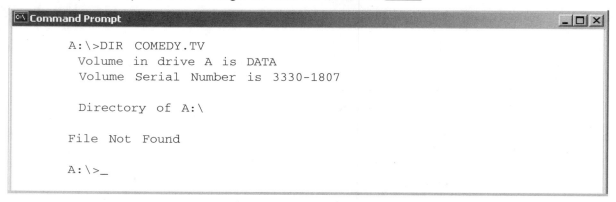

WHAT'S HAPPENING? Once you have renamed a file, it no longer exists under its old file name.

Step 5 Key in the following: A:\>**DIR FUNNY.TV** Enter

```
Command Prompt

A:\>DIR FUNNY.TV
 Volume in drive A is DATA
 Volume Serial Number is 3330-1807

 Directory of A:\

03/05/2000  04:41p                 232 FUNNY.TV
               1 File(s)            232 bytes
               0 Dir(s)       1,396,736 bytes free

A:\>_
```

WHAT'S HAPPENING? The above display demonstrates that the file called **FUNNY.TV** is on the DATA disk in the root directory. You know that the file named **COMEDY.TV** is no longer on the DATA disk. Are the contents of the file **FUNNY.TV** the same as the contents of the file that was named **COMEDY.TV**?

Step 6 Key in the following: A:\>**TYPE FUNNY.TV** Enter

```
Command Prompt

A:\>TYPE FUNNY.TV

COMEDY TELEVISION SERIES

Murphy Brown
Suddenly Susan
Caroline in the City
Home Improvement
Seinfeld
I Love Lucy
Roseanne
TAXI
The Mary Tyler Moore Show
Wings
The Dick Van Dyke Show
Frasier
Third Rock From the Sun

A:\>_
```

WHAT'S HAPPENING? As you can see, you changed the file name from **COMEDY.TV** to **FUNNY.TV**, but the contents of the file did not change. REN works the same way with a file in a subdirectory. You just have to follow the syntax (only the partial syntax, that which refers to renaming files, is shown here):

```
REN [drive:][path][filename1] [filename2]
```

Step 7 Key in the following: A:\>**DIR TRIP\GREEN.JAZ** Enter

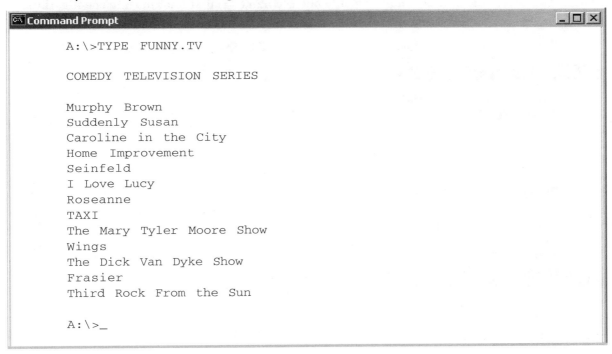

```
Command Prompt

A:\>DIR  TRIP\GREEN.JAZ
 Volume in drive A is DATA
 Volume Serial Number is 3330-1807

 Directory of A:\TRIP

05/30/2000  04:32p                  19 GREEN.JAZ
               1 File(s)             19 bytes
               0 Dir(s)       1,396,736 bytes free

A:\>_
```

WHAT'S HAPPENING? The file called **GREEN.JAZ** is in the subdirectory called **TRIP** on the DATA disk. Using REN is different from using COPY. The COPY syntax requires that you place the path name in front of the source file and the destination file. You are dealing with two files; thus, each file could be in a separate location. This situation is not true with REN. You are dealing with only one file and are changing only one file name. You are not moving the file; thus, the path name is placed in front of the source file only.

Step 8 Key in the following: A:\>**REN TRIP\GREEN.JAZ TRIP\RED.JAZ** Enter

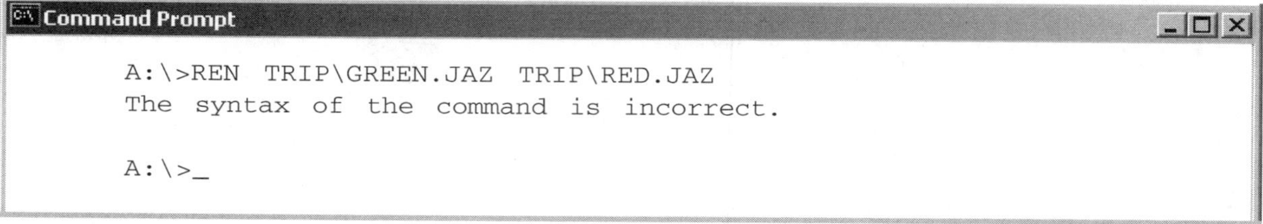

```
Command Prompt

A:\>REN  TRIP\GREEN.JAZ  TRIP\RED.JAZ
The syntax of the command is incorrect.

A:\>_
```

WHAT'S HAPPENING? The message is descriptive. The error message refers to **TRIP\RED.JAZ**. That portion of the command syntax is incorrect. It is incorrect because you placed a subdirectory before the new file name.

Step 9 Key in the following: A:\>**REN TRIP\GREEN.JAZ RED.JAZ** Enter

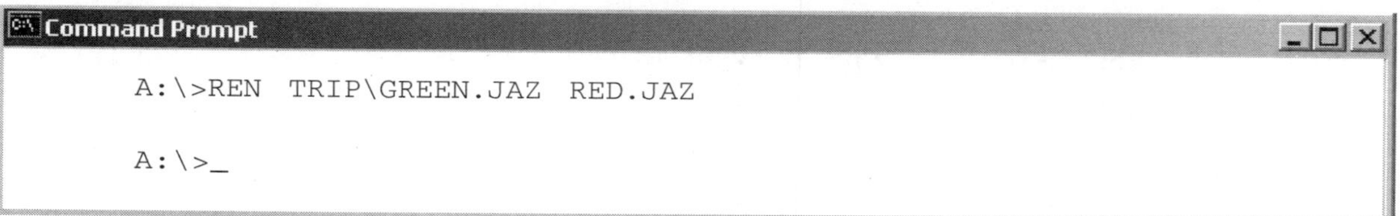

```
Command Prompt

A:\>REN  TRIP\GREEN.JAZ  RED.JAZ

A:\>_
```

WHAT'S HAPPENING? You received no error message, indicating that this command was executed. You will confirm that the file name was changed from **GREEN.JAZ** to **RED.JAZ** using the DIR command.

Step 10 Key in the following: A:\>**DIR TRIP*.JAZ** Enter

```
Command Prompt

A:\>DIR  TRIP\*.JAZ
 Volume in drive A is DATA
```

```
 Volume Serial Number is 3330-1807

 Directory of A:\TRIP

05/30/2000  04:32p                 19 RED.JAZ
           1 File(s)             19 bytes
           0 Dir(s)       1,396,736 bytes free

A:\>_
```

 You can see that the file in the **TRIP** subdirectory with the extension **.JAZ** is now called **RED.JAZ** instead of **GREEN.JAZ**.

6.13 CHANGING THE NAMES OF SUBDIRECTORIES

In previous versions of MS-DOS, the REN command worked only with files. With the release of Windows 95, it became possible to use the REN command to rename subdirectories. Previously, you used the MOVE command to rename subdirectories. Remember the syntax.

```
REN [drive:][path][directoryname1 ¦ filename1]
[directoryname2 ¦ filename2]
```

When renaming subdirectories, the partial syntax is:

```
REN [drive:][path][directoryname1] [directoryname2]
```

6.14 ACTIVITY: USING THE REN COMMAND TO RENAME SUBDIRECTORIES

Note: The DATA disk is in Drive A. A:\> is displayed as the default drive and the default directory.

Step 1 Key in the following: A:\>**MD NAMEONE** Enter

Step 2 Key in the following: A:\>**DIR N*.*** Enter

```
Command Prompt

A:\>MD NAMEONE

A:\>DIR N*.*
 Volume in drive A is DATA
 Volume Serial Number is 3330-1807

 Directory of A:\

05/30/2000  05:32p    <DIR>          NAMEONE
           0 File(s)              0 bytes
           1 Dir(s)       1,396,224 bytes free

A:\>_
```

You have created a new directory called **NAMEONE** on the root of the DATA disk in the A drive. You have verified its existence by using the DIR command. There is only one entry on the root of the DATA disk that begins with the letter **N**.

Step 3 Key in the following: A:\>**REN NAMEONE NAMETWO** Enter

```
Command Prompt

A:\>REN NAMEONE NAMETWO

A:\>_
```

You received no error messages, so the command executed. Was the subdirectory **NAMEONE** actually renamed to **NAMETWO**?

Step 4 Key in the following: A:\>**DIR N*.*** Enter

```
Command Prompt

A:\>DIR N*.*
 Volume in drive A is DATA
 Volume Serial Number is 3330-1807

 Directory of A:\

05/30/2001  05:32p      <DIR>          NAMETWO
            0 File(s)              0 bytes
            1 Dir(s)       1,396,224 bytes free

A:\>_
```

You have verified that the REN command successfully renamed the directory **NAMEONE** to **NAMETWO**. **NAMEONE** no longer exists under its original name. It is now **NAMETWO**. You can also rename subdirectories that are within other subdirectories.

Step 5 Key in the following: A:\>**MD NAMETWO\DIRONE** Enter

Step 6 Key in the following: A:\>**DIR NAMETWO** Enter

```
Command Prompt

A:\>MD NAMETWO\DIRONE

A:\>DIR NAMETWO
 Volume in drive A is DATA
 Volume Serial Number is 3330-1807

 Directory of A:\NAMETWO

05/30/2001  05:32p      <DIR>          .
05/30/2001  05:32p      <DIR>          ..
05/30/2001  05:33p      <DIR>          DIRONE
```

```
            0 File(s)              0 bytes
            3 Dir(s)       1,395,712 bytes free

A:\>_
```

You have created a subdirectory called **DIRONE** in the existing subdirectory **NAMETWO**. You have also used the DIR command to display the contents of the **NAMETWO** directory to verify the new subdirectory just created called **DIRONE**. You will now rename the new directory.

Step 7 Key in the following: A:\>**REN NAMETWO\DIRONE DIRTWO** Enter

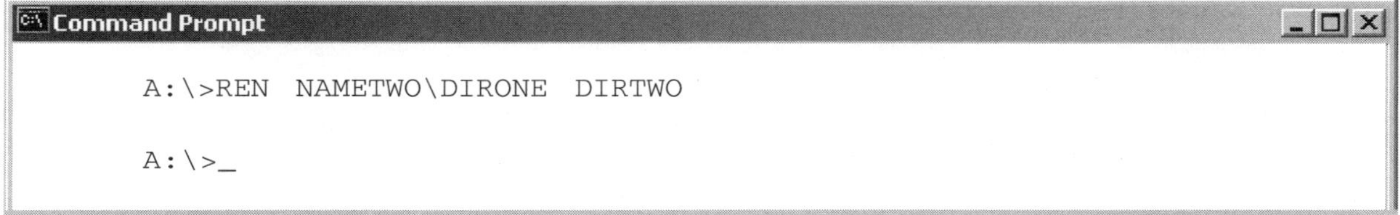
Command Prompt
A:\>REN NAMETWO\DIRONE DIRTWO
A:\>_

You have renamed the subdirectory **DIRONE** to **DIRTWO**. Again, you see no error messages, so the command executed. You can verify the change with the DIR command.

Step 8 Key in the following: A:\>**DIR NAMETWO** Enter

```
Command Prompt

A:\>DIR NAMETWO
 Volume in drive A is DATA
 Volume Serial Number is 3330-1807

 Directory of A:\NAMETWO

05/30/2001  05:32p      <DIR>          .
05/30/2001  05:32p      <DIR>          ..
05/30/2001  05:33p      <DIR>          DIRTWO
            0 File(s)              0 bytes
            3 Dir(s)       1,395,712 bytes free

A:\>_
```

You have used the DIR command to confirm that you have, indeed, renamed the subdirectory **DIRONE** to the new name of **DIRTWO**. This subdirectory structure will no longer be used. You will use the RD /S command, covered later in this chapter, to remove the entire structure.

Step 9 Key in the following: A:\>**RD NAMETWO /S** Enter

```
Command Prompt

A:\>RD NAMETWO /S
NAMETWO, Are you sure (Y/N)?
```

The RD /S command is asking you if you are sure you want to delete the **NAMETWO** subdirectory and all of its contents.

Step 10 Key in the following: **Y** Enter

Step 11 Key in the following: A:\>**DIR N*.*** Enter

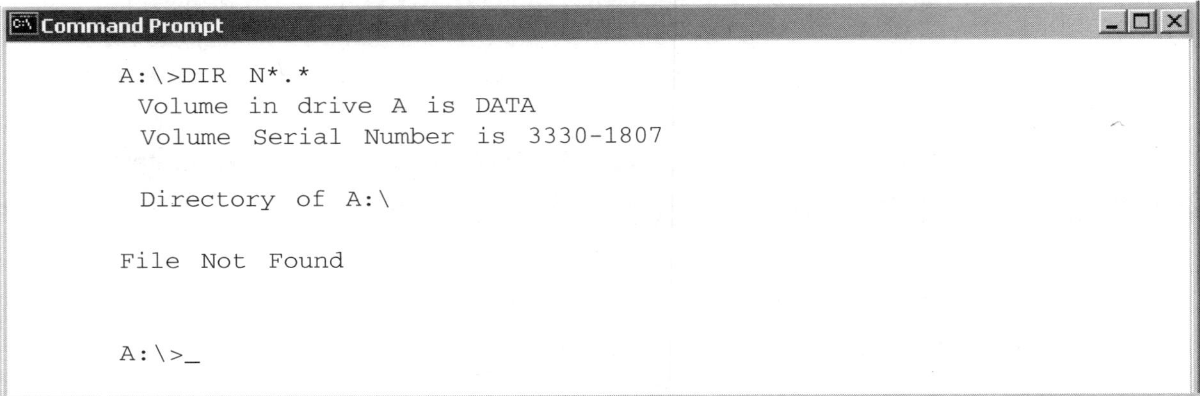
```
Command Prompt

A:\>DIR N*.*
 Volume in drive A is DATA
 Volume Serial Number is 3330-1807

 Directory of A:\

File Not Found


A:\>_
```

WHAT'S HAPPENING? As you can see with the DIR command, you have successfully removed the **NAMETWO** directory structure.

6.15 USING REN WITH WILDCARDS

When you wish to change the name of a single file or directory, you can use My Computer from the GUI. It is easy to do—just right-click the file or folder and choose Rename. If, however, you have numerous files to rename and they have something in common, such as they all have the .ABC file extension, using the command line is more efficient. You can use the REN or RENAME command with the wildcards ? and *, allowing you to change many file names with a one-line command.

The wildcards or global file specifications are so "global" that, prior to renaming files, it is wise to do a directory display with the wildcards you want to use so that you can see what files are going to be renamed, just as you use a directory display before you use the DEL command with wildcards. You do not want to rename a subdirectory accidentally along with a group of files. This can happen all too easily. Once a file is renamed, you can never find the file under its old name. This rule has caused havoc for users because it seems as if the file is lost. The file is still on the disk, and you can find it, but only under its new name.

6.16 ACTIVITY: USING REN WITH WILDCARDS

Note 1: The DATA disk is in Drive A. A:\> is displayed.
Note 2: This activity assumes you have files on the DATA disk with the file extension **.NEW**. If you do not, you may copy them from **\WINDOSBK** to the DATA disk.

Step 1 Key in the following: A:\>**DIR ???.NEW** Enter

```
Command Prompt

A:\>DIR ???.NEW
 Volume in drive A is DATA
 Volume Serial Number is 3330-1807

 Directory of A:\

04/23/2000  04:03p                  75 FEB.NEW
04/23/2000  04:03p                  73 JAN.NEW
04/23/2000  04:03p                  71 MAR.NEW
04/23/2000  04:18p                  72 APR.NEW
               4 File(s)            291 bytes
               0 Dir(s)       1,396,736 bytes free

A:\>_
```

WHAT'S HAPPENING? You have four files with file names of three characters and with the extension **.NEW**. You used **???** instead of *. When you used **???.NEW**, the **???** selected only files that had a file name of three characters or less. Had you used * instead of **???**, you would have selected all file names that had an extension of **.NEW**. That would have included such files as **BONJOUR .NEW**. Your objective is to rename these four files, keeping their file names but changing the file extension from **.NEW** to **.BUD**. You could rename these files one at a time, **REN FEB.NEW FEB.BUD**, then **REN JAN.NEW JAN.BUD**, then **REN MAR.NEW MAR.BUD**, and **REN APR.NEW APR.BUD**. However, this repetition becomes very tiresome. Using wildcards allows you to rename these four files at one time.

Step 2 Key in the following: A:\>**REN ???.NEW *.BUD** Enter

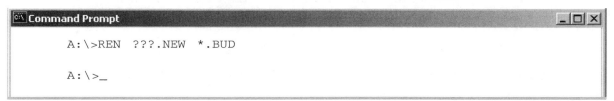

WHAT'S HAPPENING? All that is displayed is the system prompt. Was the work done? Are the files renamed? To verify that you did rename these files, use the DIR command.

Step 3 Key in the following: A:\>**DIR ???.NEW *.BUD** Enter

```
Command Prompt

A:\>DIR ???.NEW *.BUD
 Volume in drive A is DATA
 Volume Serial Number is 3330-1807

 Directory of A:\


 Directory of A:\
```

```
04/23/2000  04:03p                 75 FEB.BUD
04/23/2000  04:03p                 73 JAN.BUD
04/23/2000  04:03p                 71 MAR.BUD
04/23/2000  04:18p                 72 APR.BUD
               4 File(s)          291 bytes
               0 Dir(s)     1,396,224 bytes free

A:\>_
```

WHAT'S HAPPENING? Files with file names of three characters and the extension **.NEW** no longer exist on the DATA disk. With the REN command and the use of the wildcards, you renamed four files with one command. When you use multiple parameters on the command line, you do not see the message, **File Not Found**. You simply see the **A:** prompt with no file name following it. You can also use wildcards with subdirectories.

Step 4 Key in the following: A:\>**COPY *.BUD TRIP** Enter

```
Command Prompt

A:\>COPY *.BUD TRIP
JAN.BUD
MAR.BUD
APR.BUD
FEB.BUD
        4 file(s) copied.

A:\>_
```

WHAT'S HAPPENING? You copied files with the **.BUD** extension from the root directory of the DATA disk to a subdirectory called **TRIP** on the DATA disk.

Step 5 Key in the following: A:\>**REN TRIP*.BUD *.PEN** Enter

Step 6 Key in the following: A:\>**DIR TRIP*.BUD** Enter

Step 7 Key in the following: A:\>**DIR TRIP*.PEN** Enter

```
Command Prompt

A:\>REN TRIP\*.BUD *.PEN

A:\>DIR TRIP\*.BUD
 Volume in drive A is DATA
 Volume Serial Number is 3330-1807

 Directory of A:\TRIP

File Not Found

A:\>DIR TRIP\*.PEN
 Volume in drive A is DATA
 Volume Serial Number is 3330-1807

 Directory of A:\TRIP
```

```
04/23/2000  04:03p                75 FEB.PEN
04/23/2000  04:03p                73 JAN.PEN
04/23/2000  04:03p                71 MAR.PEN
04/23/2000  04:18p                72 APR.PEN
               4 File(s)             291 bytes
               0 Dir(s)        1,394,688 bytes free

A:\>_
```

You successfully renamed all the files with the **.BUD** extension in the subdirectory **TRIP** on the DATA disk to a new set of files with the same file name but with the file extension of **.PEN**.

6.17 USING RENAME ON DIFFERENT DRIVES AND DIRECTORIES

Since REN is an internal command, you can use it at any time, for any file, in any drive, and in any directory. If you wish to rename a file on a different drive, you must specify on which drive the old file is located. If you want the file renamed in a different directory, you must specify in which directory the file is located. In the syntax of REN OLDFILE.EXT NEWFILE.EXT, the operating system looks for OLDFILE.EXT on the designated drive and directory. It renames the file and leaves the file where it found it unless you preface OLDFILE.EXT with a drive letter. When you key in the command REN B:OLDFILE.EXT NEWFILE.EXT, only the disk in Drive B will be searched for the file called OLDFILE.EXT. If a directory is involved, you must also include its name, so the command would read:

```
REN C:\JUNK\OLDFILE.EXT  NEWFILE.EXT
```

There is a substantial difference between the COPY command and the REN command. With the COPY command, you can copy a file from one disk to another disk or one directory to another directory, ending up with two identical files in different locations. You *cannot* do this with the REN command because it changes the names of files in only one directory or disk at a time. Remember, with REN you are changing the name of an existing file in a specific location. REN finds a file by its name, which is the first parameter in the REN command, on the designated disk or directory. The second parameter must be the new name only, not including a repeat of the location. REN cannot move a file from one location to another, nor can it copy a file. It simply renames a file, leaving it where it found it.

6.18 ACTIVITY: USING RENAME ON DIFFERENT DRIVES

Note: The DATA disk is in Drive A. A:\> is displayed.

Step 1 Key in the following: A:\>**CD /D C:\WINDOSBK** Enter

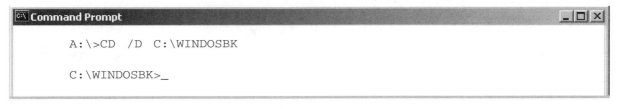

```
A:\>CD /D C:\WINDOSBK

C:\WINDOSBK>_
```

You have changed the default drive to **C:** and have made **\WINDOSBK** the default directory.

Step 2 Key in the following: C:\WINDOSBK>**DIR APRIL.TXT** Enter

Step 3 Key in the following: C:\WINDOSBK>**DIR A:\APRIL.TXT** Enter

Note: If you do not have **APRIL.TXT** on your DATA disk, copy it there from the **C:\WINDOSBK** directory now.

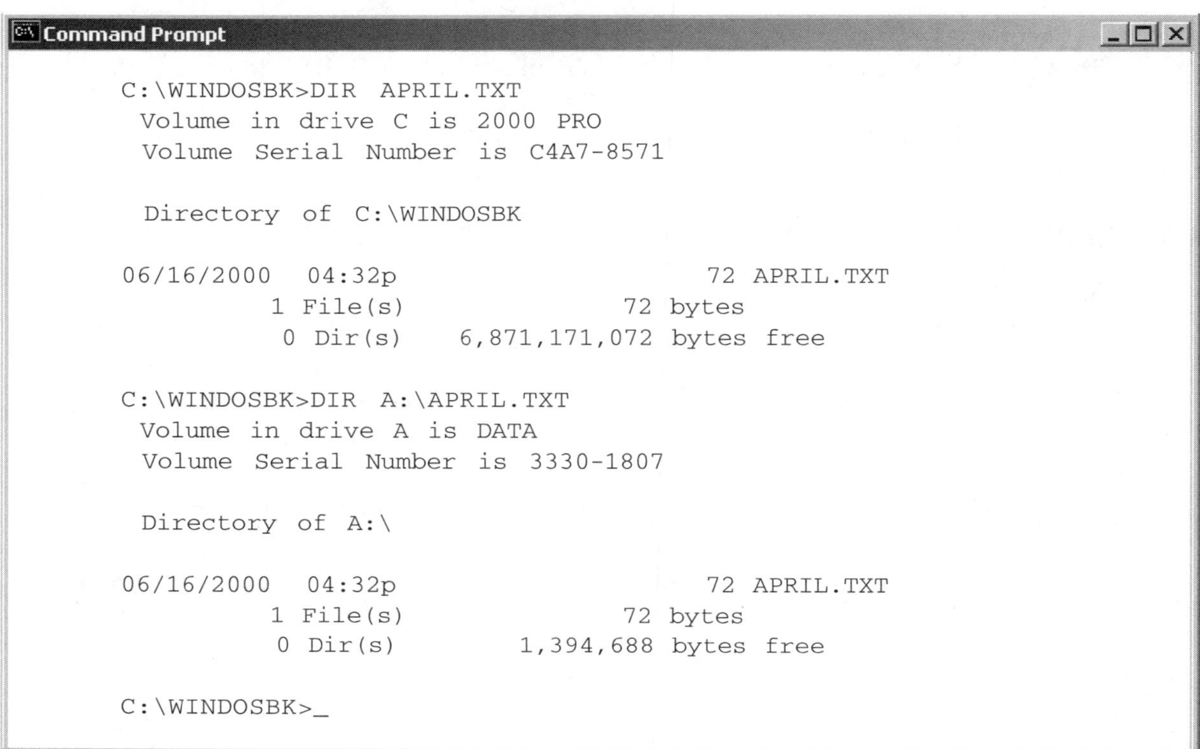

Command Prompt

```
C:\WINDOSBK>DIR APRIL.TXT
 Volume in drive C is 2000 PRO
 Volume Serial Number is C4A7-8571

 Directory of C:\WINDOSBK

06/16/2000  04:32p                  72 APRIL.TXT
               1 File(s)             72 bytes
               0 Dir(s)   6,871,171,072 bytes free

C:\WINDOSBK>DIR A:\APRIL.TXT
 Volume in drive A is DATA
 Volume Serial Number is 3330-1807

 Directory of A:\

06/16/2000  04:32p                  72 APRIL.TXT
               1 File(s)             72 bytes
               0 Dir(s)       1,394,688 bytes free

C:\WINDOSBK>_
```

The directory display tells you that the file called **APRIL.TXT** does exist on both the root of the DATA disk in the A drive and in the **\WINDOSBK** subdirectory on the C drive.

Step 4 Key in the following: C:\WINDOSBK>**TYPE A:\APRIL.TXT** Enter

Command Prompt

```
C:\WINDOSBK>TYPE A:\APRIL.TXT

This is my April file.
It is my fourth dummy file.
This is file 4.

C:\WINDOSBK>_
```

You used the TYPE command to see the contents of the file called **APRIL.TXT** located on the DATA disk.

Step 5 Key in the following: C:\WINDOSBK>**REN A:\APRIL.TXT A:\APR.TST** Enter

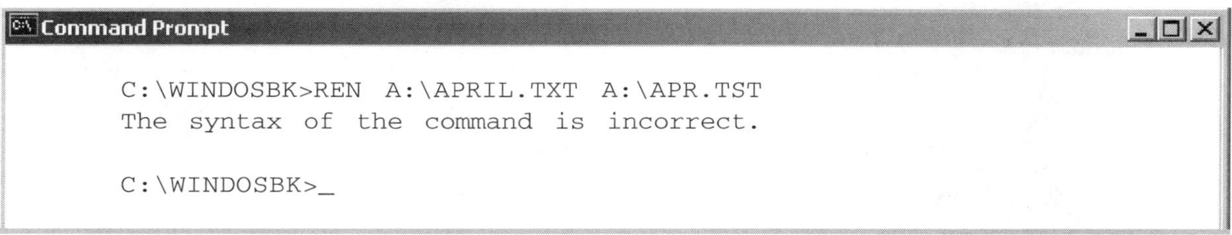

```
C:\WINDOSBK>REN  A:\APRIL.TXT  A:\APR.TST
The syntax of the command is incorrect.

C:\WINDOSBK>_
```

Remember, the syntax of this command is:

```
REN [drive:][path]oldfile.ext newfile.ext
```

Since the operating system knows you cannot change a file name on any other disk except where the original file is located, it will not allow you to put a drive designator before the new file name.

Step 6 Key in the following: C:\WINDOSBK>**REN A:\APRIL.TXT APR.TST** Enter

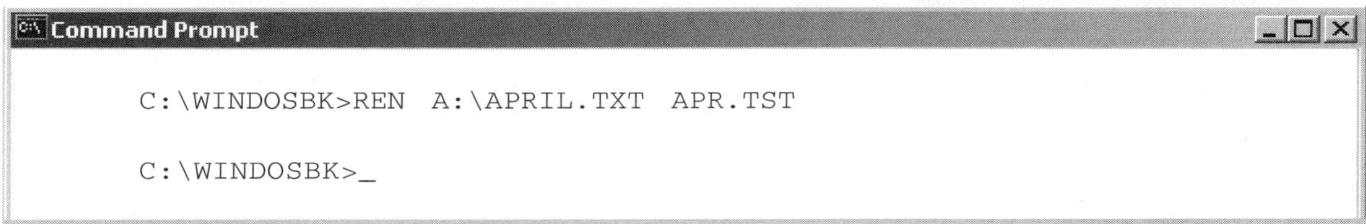

```
C:\WINDOSBK>REN  A:\APRIL.TXT  APR.TST

C:\WINDOSBK>_
```

You see no messages because the syntax of the command you issued is correct. The file called **APRIL.TXT** is in the root directory of the DATA disk. You requested that REN change the name of this file from **APRIL.TXT** to a new file name **APR.TST**.

Step 7 Key in the following: C:\WINDOSBK>**DIR APRIL.TXT** Enter

Step 8 Key in the following: C:\WINDOSBK>**DIR A:\APRIL.TXT** Enter

```
C:\WINDOSBK>DIR  APRIL.TXT
 Volume in drive C is 2000 PRO
 Volume Serial Number is C4A7-8571

 Directory of C:\WINDOSBK

06/16/2000  04:32p                  72 APRIL.TXT
            1 File(s)             72 bytes
            0 Dir(s)   1,121,439,744 bytes free

C:\WINDOSBK>DIR  A:\APRIL.TXT
 Volume in drive A is DATA
 Volume Serial Number is 3330-1807

 Directory of A:\

File Not Found

C:\WINDOSBK>_
```

You did not rename the file **APRIL.TXT** on the hard disk in the **\WINDOSBK** directory, only the one on the DATA disk. You got the message **File Not Found** for the DATA disk because the file no longer exists under the file name **A:\APRIL.TXT**.

Step 9 Key in the following: C:\WINDOSBK>**DIR A:\APR.TST** Enter

```
Command Prompt

C:\WINDOSBK>DIR A:\APR.TST
 Volume in drive A is DATA
 Volume Serial Number is 3330-1807

 Directory of A:\

06/16/2000  04:32p                  72 APR.TST
               1 File(s)             72 bytes
               0 Dir(s)       1,394,688 bytes free

C:\WINDOSBK>_
```

WHAT'S HAPPENING? You successfully renamed the file in the root directory of the DATA disk from **APRIL.TXT** to **APR.TST**. Does the file **APR.TST** have the same contents as **APRIL.TXT**? It should because renaming changes only the file name, not the contents. To verify this, you can use the TYPE command.

Step 10 Key in the following: C:\WINDOSBK>**TYPE A:\APR.TST** Enter

```
Command Prompt

C:\WINDOSBK>TYPE A:\APR.TST

This is my April file.
It is my fourth dummy file.
This is file 4.

C:\WINDOSBK>_
```

WHAT'S HAPPENING? If you check the screen display following Step 4, you will see that the file contents are identical. REN works the same way with subdirectories on other drives. In Activity 6.16, you copied the files with the **.BUD** extension to the subdirectory **TRIP** on the DATA disk; you then renamed them with the same file name but with the **.PEN** file extension.

Step 11 Key in the following: C:\WINDOSBK>**DIR A:\TRIP*.PEN** Enter

```
Command Prompt

C:\WINDOSBK>DIR A:\TRIP\*.PEN
 Volume in drive A is DATA
 Volume Serial Number is 3330-1807

 Directory of A:\TRIP

04/23/2000  04:03p                  75 FEB.PEN
```

```
04/23/2000  04:03p                 73 JAN.PEN
04/23/2000  04:03p                 71 MAR.PEN
04/23/2000  04:18p                 72 APR.PEN
               4 File(s)            291 bytes
               0 Dir(s)       1,394,688 bytes free

C:\WINDOSBK>_
```

The files are there in the subdirectory **TRIP** on the DATA disk.

Step 12 Key in the following: C:\WINDOSBK>**REN A:\TRIP*.PEN *.INK** Enter

Command Prompt

```
C:\WINDOSBK>REN A:\TRIP\*.PEN *.INK

C:\WINDOSBK>_
```

Once again, all that appears is the system prompt. Notice how you placed the drive and path in front of *only* the file names that you wanted to change (the old file names). These files can only be renamed on the DATA disk in the subdirectory **TRIP**. The REN command does not move files; it only changes file names.

Step 13 Key in the following: C:\WINDOSBK>**DIR A:\TRIP*.PEN** Enter

Step 14 Key in the following: C:\WINDOSBK>**DIR A:\TRIP*.INK** Enter

Command Prompt

```
C:\WINDOSBK>DIR A:\TRIP\*.PEN
 Volume in drive A is DATA
 Volume Serial Number is 3330-1807

 Directory of A:\TRIP

File Not Found

C:\WINDOSBK>DIR A:\TRIP\*.INK
 Volume in drive A is DATA
 Volume Serial Number is 3330-1807

 Directory of A:\TRIP

04/23/2000  04:03p                 75 FEB.INK
04/23/2000  04:03p                 73 JAN.INK
04/23/2000  04:03p                 71 MAR.INK
04/23/2000  04:18p                 72 APR.INK
               4 File(s)            291 bytes
               0 Dir(s)       1,394,688 bytes free

C:\WINDOSBK>_
```

You successfully renamed all the **.PEN** files in the subdirectory **TRIP** on the DATA disk. These files no longer exist with the **.PEN** file extension.

Step 15 Key in the following: C:\WINDOSBK>**CD ** Enter

Step 16 Key in the following: C:\>**A:** Enter

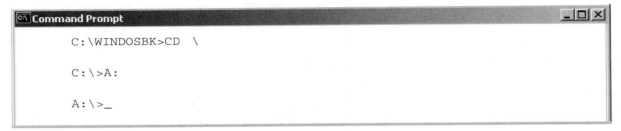

WHAT'S HAPPENING? You returned to the root directory of the hard disk and also changed the default drive to the DATA disk location.

6.19 MOVING FILES AND RENAMING DIRECTORIES

You learned in Chapter 4 that you could use the MOVE command to rename a directory. In this chapter, you learned to use the RENAME command for renaming both files and subdirectories. The REN command renames files and subdirectories; it does not move them from one location to another.

The MOVE command was introduced in DOS 6.0. MOVE allows you to move files and subdirectories from one location to another. If you move a file or subdirectory individually, you can change the name as you move it. If you move a group of files and/or subdirectories, you cannot change their names. The MOVE command includes a prompt that will warn you that you are about to overwrite a file. However, if you desire, you can turn off the warning. The full syntax diagram for the MOVE command is:

```
To move one or more files:
MOVE [/Y | /-Y] [drive:][path]filename1[,...] destination

To rename a directory:
MOVE [/Y | /-Y] [drive:][path]dirname1 dirname2

  [drive:][path]filename1   Specifies the location and name of the file or
                            files you want to move.
  destination               Specifies the new location of the file. Desti-
                            nation can consist of a drive letter and colon,
                            a directory name, or a combination. If you are
                            moving only one file, you can also include a
                            filename if you want to rename the file when
                            you move it.
  [drive:][path]dirname1    Specifies the directory you want to rename.
  dirname2                  Specifies the new name of the directory.

  /Y                        Suppresses prompting to confirm creation of a
                            directory or overwriting of the destination.
  /-Y                       Causes prompting to confirm creation of a di-
                            rectory or overwriting of the destination.
```

```
The switch /Y may be present in the COPYCMD environment variable. This may be
overridden with /-Y on the command line. Default is to prompt on overwrites
unless move command is being executed from within a batch script.
```

The MOVE command will not only move files and directories from one directory to another but will also allow you to move them from one drive to another. This feature is especially useful in maintaining your hard disk.

6.20 ACTIVITY: MOVING FILES AND RENAMING DIRECTORIES

Note: The DATA disk is in Drive A. A:\> is displayed.

Step 1 Key in the following: A:\>**MD FILES** Enter

Step 2 Key in the following: A:\>**COPY *.99 FILES*.FIL** Enter

Step 3 Key in the following: A:\>**MD FILES\ROOM** Enter

Step 4 Key in the following: A:\>**COPY GOODBYE.NEW FILES** Enter

```
Command Prompt

A:\>MD FILES

A:\>COPY *.99 FILES\*.FIL
APR.99
FEB.99
MAR.99
JAN.99
        4 file(s) copied.

A:\>MD FILES\ROOM

A:\>COPY GOODBYE.NEW FILES
        1 file(s) copied.

A:\>_
```

WHAT'S HAPPENING? You have created the **FILES** directory with a directory beneath it called **ROOM**. You copied some files from the root directory of the DATA disk into the **FILES** directory.

Step 5 Key in the following: A:\>**DIR FILES** Enter

```
Command Prompt

A:\>DIR FILES
 Volume in drive A is DATA
 Volume Serial Number is 3330-1807

 Directory of A:\FILES

06/01/2001  12:45p      <DIR>          .
06/01/2001  12:45p      <DIR>          ..
10/10/1999  04:53p                  72 APR.FIL
```

```
10/10/1999  04:53p                    75 FEB.FIL
10/10/1999  04:53p                    71 MAR.FIL
10/10/1999  04:53p                    73 JAN.FIL
06/01/2001  12:45p      <DIR>            ROOM
01/01/2002  04:32a                    34 GOODBYE.NEW
               5 File(s)          325 bytes
               3 Dir(s)     1,391,104 bytes free

A:\>_
```

WHAT'S HAPPENING? You have a subdirectory called **ROOM** under the **FILES** directory on the DATA disk. You decide that you no longer care for the name **ROOM** and wish to call the directory **MYROOM**.

Step 6 Key in the following: A:\>**MOVE FILES\ROOM FILES\MYROOM** Enter

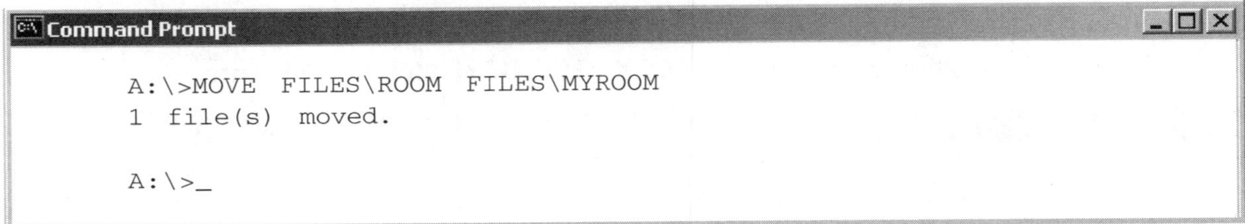
Command Prompt
A:\>MOVE FILES\ROOM FILES\MYROOM
1 file(s) moved.
A:\>_

WHAT'S HAPPENING? You have renamed a subdirectory from **FILES\ROOM** to **FILES\MYROOM**. Notice the difference between the MOVE and REN syntax. When using REN, you do not give the path with the new name. When using MOVE to rename a directory, you do give the full path with the new name.

Step 7 Key in the following: A:\>**REN FILES\MYROOM PLACE** Enter

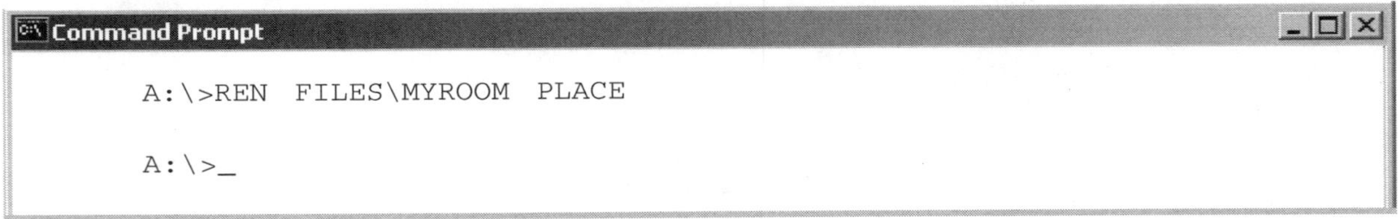
Command Prompt
A:\>REN FILES\MYROOM PLACE
A:\>_

WHAT'S HAPPENING? You can verify that the subdirectory **MYROOM** was, indeed, renamed to **PLACE**.

Step 8 Key in the following: A:\>**DIR FILES** Enter

```
Command Prompt

A:\>DIR FILES

 Volume in drive A is DATA
 Volume Serial Number is 3330-1807

 Directory of A:\FILES

06/01/2001  12:45p      <DIR>          .
06/01/2001  12:45p      <DIR>          ..
```

```
10/10/1999  04:53p                   72 APR.FIL
10/10/1999  04:53p                   75 FEB.FIL
10/10/1999  04:53p                   71 MAR.FIL
10/10/1999  04:53p                   73 JAN.FIL
06/01/2001  12:45p      <DIR>           PLACE
01/01/2002  04:32a                   34 GOODBYE.NEW
               5 File(s)            325 bytes
               3 Dir(s)       1,391,104 bytes free

A:\>_
```

The directory name has again changed. Now you want to move a file. You use MOVE to move files from one location to another. If you try to move a file in the same drive and the same directory, it has the effect of eliminating the first file and replacing the contents of the second file with the contents of the first file. In the next steps you will see the results of such a task.

Step 9 Key in the following: A:\>**TYPE FILES\APR.FIL** Enter

Step 10 Key in the following: A:\>**TYPE FILES\JAN.FIL** Enter

```
Command Prompt

A:\>TYPE FILES\APR.FIL

This is my April file.
It is my fourth dummy file.
This is file 4.

A:\>TYPE FILES\JAN.FIL

This is my January file.
It is my first dummy file.
This is file 1.

A:\>_
```

You can see that the contents are different as well as the file names.

Step 11 Key in the following: A:\>**MOVE FILES\APR.FIL FILES\JAN.FIL** Enter

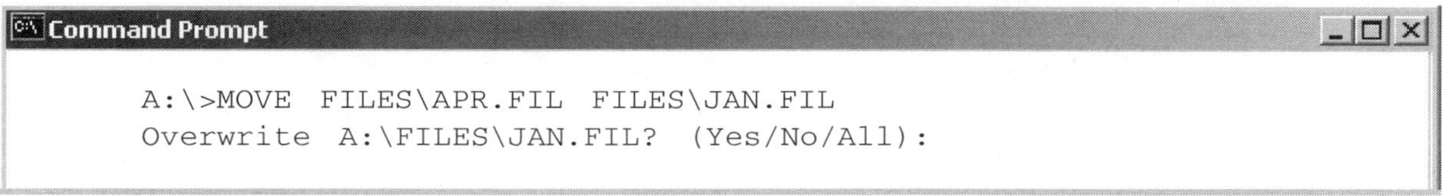

```
Command Prompt

A:\>MOVE FILES\APR.FIL FILES\JAN.FIL
Overwrite A:\FILES\JAN.FIL? (Yes/No/All):
```

This warning by the MOVE command tells you that you are about to overwrite a file.

Step 12 Press **Y** Enter

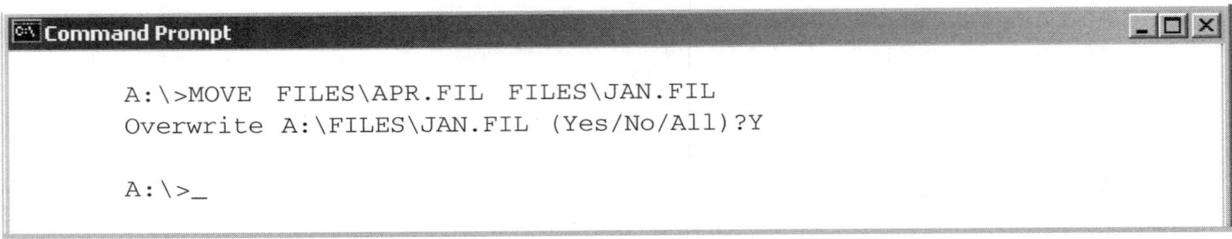

```
Command Prompt
A:\>MOVE FILES\APR.FIL FILES\JAN.FIL
Overwrite A:\FILES\JAN.FIL (Yes/No/All)?Y

A:\>_
```

WHAT'S HAPPENING? Because you entered **Y** for "yes," the file was overwritten.

Step 13 Key in the following: A:\>**TYPE FILES\APR.FIL** Enter

Step 14 Key in the following: A:\>**TYPE FILES\JAN.FIL** Enter

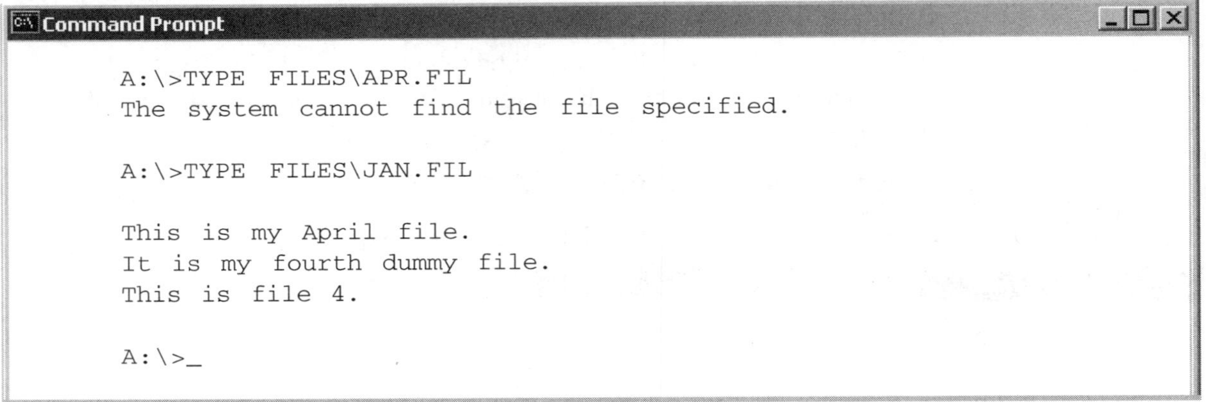

```
Command Prompt
A:\>TYPE FILES\APR.FIL
The system cannot find the file specified.

A:\>TYPE FILES\JAN.FIL

This is my April file.
It is my fourth dummy file.
This is file 4.

A:\>_
```

WHAT'S HAPPENING? The file **APR.FIL** no longer exists. It "moved" to a new file, **JAN.FIL**. Thus, **JAN.FIL** now holds the contents of the old **APR.FIL**. The old contents of **JAN.FIL** are gone. If this sounds confusing, it is. The lesson here is do not use MOVE when you mean REN. The following steps will show you how MOVE is useful when it is used wisely.

Step 15 Key in the following: A:\>**MOVE FILES\FEB.FIL FILES\PLACE\FEB.NEW** Enter

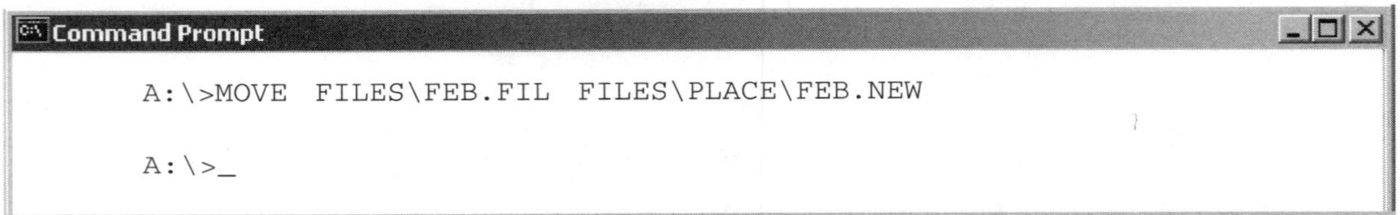

```
Command Prompt
A:\>MOVE FILES\FEB.FIL FILES\PLACE\FEB.NEW

A:\>_
```

WHAT'S HAPPENING? You have, in essence, accomplished three separate functions with one command. First, you copied the file called **FEB.FIL** located in the **FILES** directory to the **FILES\PLACE** directory. Second, you gave it a new name, **FEB.NEW**. Third, you deleted **FEB.FIL** from the **FILES** directory. All this occurred using one command, MOVE, not three—COPY, REN, and DEL. If you used Windows Explorer, you would have to take two steps: first move the file, and then rename it. The command line provided a one-step solution.

Step 16 Key in the following: A:\>**DIR FILES** Enter

Step 17 Key in the following: A:\>**DIR FILES\PLACE** Enter

```
Command Prompt

A:\>DIR FILES
 Volume in drive  A is DATA
 Volume Serial Number is 3330-1807

 Directory of A:\FILES

06/01/2001  12:45p      <DIR>          .
06/01/2001  12:45p      <DIR>          ..
10/10/1999  04:53p                  72 JAN.FIL
10/10/1999  04:53p                  71 MAR.FIL
06/01/2001  12:45p      <DIR>          PLACE
01/01/2002  04:32a                  34 GOODBYE.NEW
               3 File(s)            177 bytes
               3 Dir(s)       1,391,616 bytes free

A:\>DIR FILES\PLACE
 Volume in drive A is DATA
 Volume Serial Number is 3330-1807

 Directory of A:\FILES\PLACE

06/01/2001  12:45p      <DIR>          .
06/01/2001  12:45p      <DIR>          ..
10/10/1999  04:53p                  75 FEB.NEW
               1 File(s)             75 bytes
               2 Dir(s)       1,391,616 bytes free

A:\>_
```

WHAT'S HAPPENING? The file called **FEB.FIL** is no longer in the **FILES** directory. It is, however, in the **FILES\PLACE** directory with the name of **FEB.NEW**. MOVE also works well with wildcards. However, when you use wildcards with the MOVE command, you cannot change file names.

Step 18 Key in the following: A:\>**MOVE FILES*.FIL FILES\PLACE*.TXT** Enter

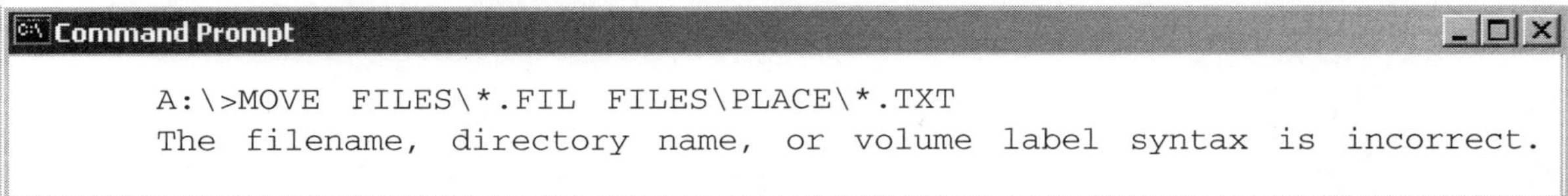

```
Command Prompt

A:\>MOVE FILES\*.FIL FILES\PLACE\*.TXT
The filename, directory name, or volume label syntax is incorrect.
```

WHAT'S HAPPENING? MOVE cannot combine the contents of files (concatenate files) and therefore cannot place these files into one file called ***.TXT**.

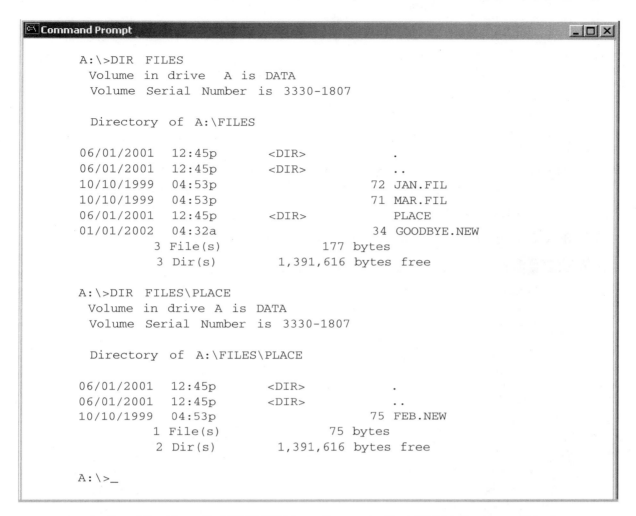

Step 19 Key in the following: A:\>**MOVE FILES*.FIL FILES\PLACE** Enter

```
Command Prompt

A:\>MOVE  FILES\*.FIL  FILES\PLACE
A:\FILES\MAR.FIL
A:\FILES\JAN.FIL

A:\>_
```

WHAT'S HAPPENING? Now that you have issued the command correctly, the files with the **.FIL** extension are no longer in the **FILES** directory but in the **PLACE** directory.

Step 20 Key in the following: A:\>**DIR FILES** Enter

Step 21 Key in the following: A:\>**DIR FILES\PLACE*.FIL** Enter

```
Command Prompt

A:\>DIR  FILES
 Volume  in  drive  A  is  DATA
 Volume  Serial  Number  is  3330-1807

 Directory  of  A:\FILES

06/01/2001   12:45p      <DIR>          .
06/01/2001   12:45p      <DIR>          ..
06/01/2001   12:45p      <DIR>          PLACE
01/01/2002   04:32a                  34 GOODBYE.NEW
               1 File(s)             34 bytes
               3 Dir(s)       1,391,616 bytes free

A:\>DIR  FILES\PLACE\*.FIL
 Volume  in  drive  A  is  DATA
 Volume  Serial  Number  is  3330-1807

 Directory  of  A:\FILES\PLACE

10/10/1999   04:53p                  72 JAN.FIL
10/10/1999   04:53p                  71 MAR.FIL
               2 File(s)            143 bytes
               0 Dir(s)       1,391,616 bytes free

A:\>_
```

WHAT'S HAPPENING? The files with the **.FIL** extension were successfully moved from one location to another. You can move files from one drive to another and from one directory to another.

Step 22 Key in the following: A:\>**MOVE FILES\PLACE*.FIL CLASS** Enter

```
Command Prompt

A:\>MOVE  FILES\PLACE\*.FIL  CLASS
A:\FILES\PLACE\MAR.FIL
A:\FILES\PLACE\JAN.FIL
A:\>_
```

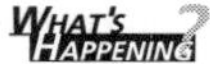

The files with the **.FIL** extension are no longer located in the **FILES\PLACE** directory but were moved to the **CLASS** directory, keeping the same file names.

Step 23 Key in the following: A:\>**DIR FILES\PLACE*.FIL** Enter

Step 24 Key in the following: A:\>**DIR CLASS*.FIL** Enter

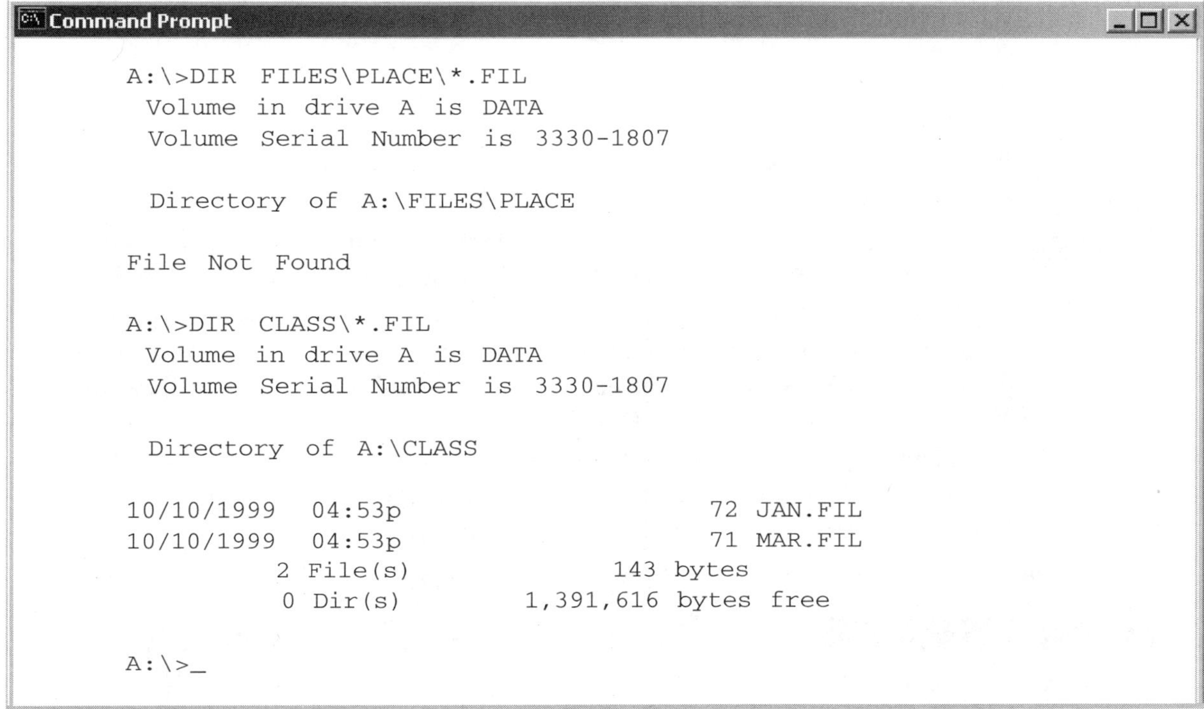

```
Command Prompt

A:\>DIR FILES\PLACE\*.FIL
 Volume in drive A is DATA
 Volume Serial Number is 3330-1807

 Directory of A:\FILES\PLACE

File Not Found

A:\>DIR CLASS\*.FIL
 Volume in drive A is DATA
 Volume Serial Number is 3330-1807

 Directory of A:\CLASS

10/10/1999  04:53p                      72 JAN.FIL
10/10/1999  04:53p                      71 MAR.FIL
               2 File(s)            143 bytes
               0 Dir(s)       1,391,616 bytes free

A:\>_
```

The files were successfully moved. You can see that the MOVE command is very useful and very powerful. You can move entire subdirectory structures, along with the files in them, with one command.

Step 25 Key in the following: A:\>**MD START** Enter

Step 26 Key in the following: A:\>**MD START\SUBDIR** Enter

Step 27 Key in the following: A:\>**COPY *.FIL START\SUBDIR** Enter

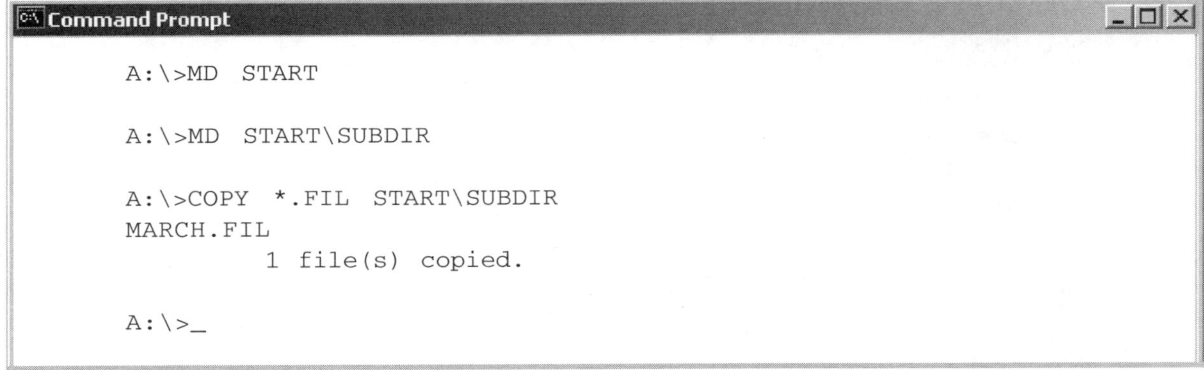

```
Command Prompt

A:\>MD START

A:\>MD START\SUBDIR

A:\>COPY *.FIL START\SUBDIR
MARCH.FIL
        1 file(s) copied.

A:\>_
```

You have created a new directory, **START**, that contains a child directory, **SUBDIR**, in which there is one file, **MARCH.FIL**. To see everything in the

START directory structure, you will use the DIR command with two of its parameters: /S to view all the contents in the subdirectories and /B to see only the file and subdirectory names with none of the other information.

Step 28 Key in the following: A:\>**DIR START /S /B** Enter

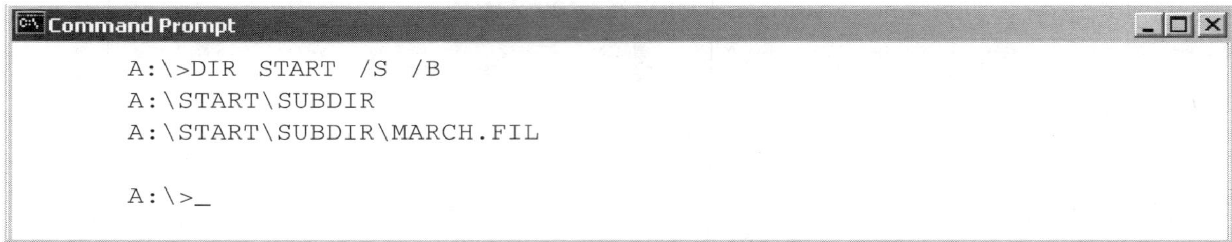

```
Command Prompt
A:\>DIR START /S /B
A:\START\SUBDIR
A:\START\SUBDIR\MARCH.FIL

A:\>_
```

You can see that with this bare (/B) display, you do not see "Volume in drive A is DATA," "Volume Serial Number is 3330-1807," or "Directory of A:\START." Nor do you see the amounts of drive space used or free. The bare display shows you directory names and file names only. You can see that the **START** directory contains only one subdirectory, **SUBDIR**, and no files. The subdirectory **SUBDIR** contains one file, **MARCH.FIL**. But you made a mistake. You actually wanted to place this entire directory structure beginning with **START** under the subdirectory **FILES**. You can move the entire structure with the MOVE command.

Step 29 Key in the following: A:\>**MOVE START FILES** Enter

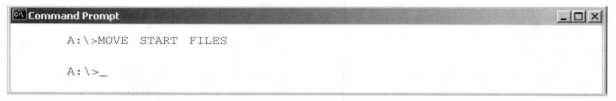

```
Command Prompt
A:\>MOVE START FILES

A:\>_
```

The command has properly executed. What actually happened? You can use the DIR command to verify that the **START** directory is no longer under the root, but that it and all of its contents are now under the **FILES** directory.

Step 30 Key in the following: A:\>**DIR START** Enter

Step 31 Key in the following: A:\>**DIR FILES** Enter

```
Command Prompt
A:\>DIR START
 Volume in drive A is DATA
 Volume Serial Number is 3330-1807

 Directory of A:\

File Not Found

A:\>DIR FILES
 Volume in drive A is DATA
 Volume Serial Number is 3330-1807
```

```
 Directory of A:\FILES

06/01/2001  12:45p    <DIR>          .
06/01/2001  12:45p    <DIR>          ..
06/01/2001  12:45p    <DIR>          PLACE
01/01/2002  04:32a                34 GOODBYE.NEW
06/01/2001  12:51p    <DIR>          START
               1 File(s)          34 bytes
               4 Dir(s)    1,390,080 bytes free

A:\>_
```

As you can see, the **START** subdirectory is no longer on the root of the DATA disk. It is now in the **FILES** directory. But has the entire subdirectory structure been moved? You can verify this further with the DIR /S /B command.

Step 32 Key in the following: A:\>**DIR FILES\START /S /B** Enter

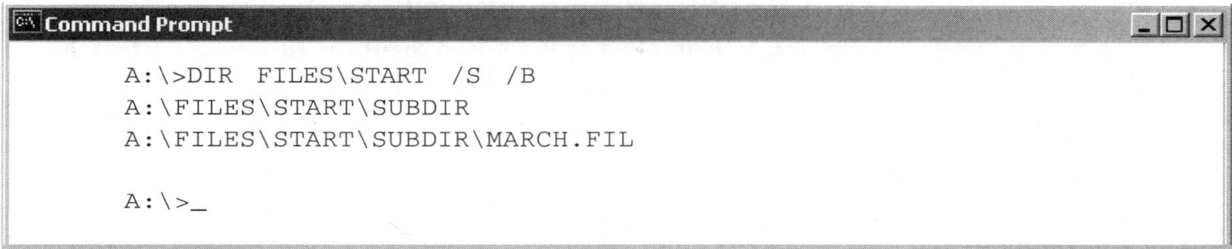
Command Prompt
A:\>DIR FILES\START /S /B
A:\FILES\START\SUBDIR
A:\FILES\START\SUBDIR\MARCH.FIL
A:\>_

WHAT'S HAPPENING? You can see that the entire **START** directory structure was moved successfully to the **FILES** directory.

6.21 RD /S REVISITED

In Chapter 4, you learned how to remove a directory. You could use the RD command with no parameters. This was the bottom-up approach. Since you create directories from the top down, you had to delete directories from the bottom up. If the subdirectory you wished to remove had more subdirectories beneath it, you had to remove those subdirectories first. RD with the parameter /S allows you to delete directories from the top down with one command. In addition, when you use RD on its own, you must first remove any subdirectories and any files that are in each subdirectory. Thus, removing directories with RD by itself is a two-step process—first delete files (DEL), then eliminate the directory (RD). Removing directories from the GUI is also a two-step process—delete and empty the Recycle Bin. RD /S has the advantage that in one fell swoop, you eliminate files and directories—no second step is required. It is a very powerful, but also very dangerous, command.

6.22 ACTIVITY: USING RD AND RD /S

Note: The DATA disk is in Drive A. A:\> is displayed.

Step 1 Key in the following: A:\>**RD FILES\PLACE** Enter

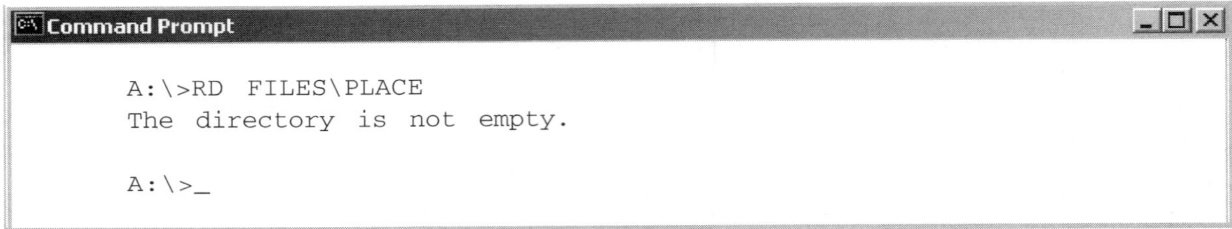

WHAT'S HAPPENING? The portion of the message that applies here is that the **FILES\PLACE** directory is not empty of files. Thus, you have to take a step preceding the RD command.

Step 2 Key in the following: A:\>**DEL FILES\PLACE** Enter

```
Command Prompt

A:\>DEL FILES\PLACE
A:\FILES\PLACE\*, Are you sure (Y/N)?
```

WHAT'S HAPPENING? You had to use the DEL command to eliminate the files. The command **DEL FILES\PLACE** implied or defaulted to all the files in the **PLACE** directory. You could have keyed in **DEL FILES\PLACE*.***, but ***.*** wasn't necessary since, if you do not use a value with DEL, the default is all files.

Step 3 Press **Y** Enter

Step 4 Key in the following: A:\>**RD FILES\PLACE** Enter

Step 5 Key in the following: A:\>**DIR FILES** Enter

```
Command Prompt

A:\>RD FILES\PLACE

A:\>DIR FILES
 Volume in drive A is DATA
 Volume Serial Number is 3330-1807

 Directory of A:\FILES

06/01/2001  12:45p      <DIR>          .
06/01/2001  12:45p      <DIR>          ..
06/01/2001  12:51p      <DIR>          START
01/01/2002  04:32a                  34 GOODBYE.NEW
               1 File(s)             34 bytes
               3 Dir(s)       1,392,104 bytes free

A:\>_
```

WHAT'S HAPPENING? Once you eliminated the files from the **PLACE** directory using DEL, you could remove the directory using the RD command without the /S parameter. Using RD /S is much faster because it is a one-step process. In addition, if you had any hidden or system files, they would be deleted as well.

Step 6 Key in the following: A:\>**RD FILES /S** Enter

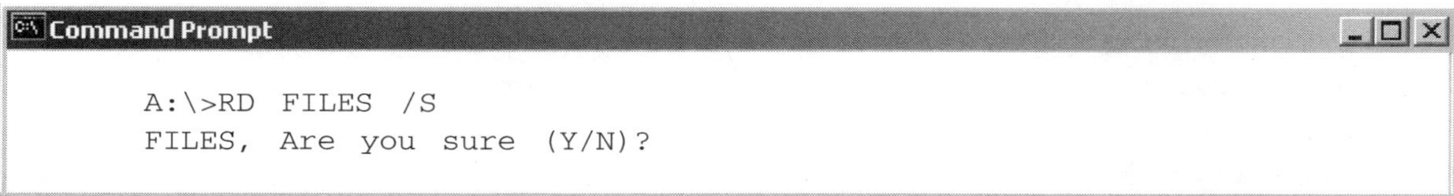

```
Command Prompt

A:\>RD FILES /S
FILES, Are you sure (Y/N)?
```

WHAT'S HAPPENING? As you can see, RD /S is offering to delete files and directories.

Step 7 Press **Y** Enter

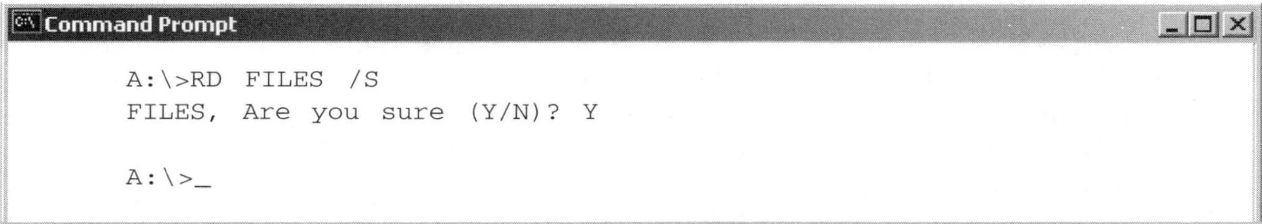

```
Command Prompt

A:\>RD FILES /S
FILES, Are you sure (Y/N)? Y

A:\>_
```

WHAT'S HAPPENING? You saw no message stating that the files or subdirectory were deleted. Were they?

Step 8 Key in the following: A:\>**DIR FILES** Enter

```
Command Prompt

A:\>DIR FILES
 Volume in drive A is DATA
 Volume Serial Number is 3330-1807

 Directory of A:\

File Not Found

A:\>_
```

WHAT'S HAPPENING? The directory **FILES** was removed. RD /S is fast, but keep in mind that "fast" can be "dangerous."

6.23 BACKING UP YOUR DATA DISK

You should get into the habit of backing up your data files so that if something happens to the original data, you have a copy of the original material. In data-processing circles, this habit is called "Disaster and Recovery Planning." It means exactly what it says. If there is a disaster—fire, flood, power surge, theft, head crash, coffee spilled on a disk—what is your plan to recover your programs and data?

Most application programs today come on a CD-ROM disc, but there are still programs that come on diskette. Backing up application program disks can be tricky, especially on ***copy-protected*** disks (which means you cannot back them up with regular operating system commands). You should never back up your program or software application disks until you understand how the application programs work. Application software that comes on diskettes provides documentation that instructs you how to back up the specific application program disk you own.

Backing up a hard disk is a special circumstance, using special operating commands and procedures. You cannot and should not back up the hard disk using the techniques that will be described here because the contents of a hard disk will not fit on one floppy disk or on a zip disk.

However, you can and should back up all the data on any data disk with the following techniques. There are three ways to back up data files. One way is to back up the entire data disk—this backs up all the files and all the subdirectories. To do this, you use the DISKCOPY command, which makes an identical copy of a disk, track for track and sector for sector. You can use DISKCOPY on floppy disks.

You can also use the COPY command, which backs up files from floppy disk to floppy disk or other storage media or specific files in specific directories on the hard disk. The third method, using the XCOPY command, will be discussed later. Never use the MOVE command for backup purposes. The MOVE command, although useful in placing files onto a floppy disk from a hard disk, removes the files from their original location. Thus, you end up with only one copy of your data files, which defeats the purpose of backing up.

Typically, data files are backed up at the end of every work session so that you can keep your data files current. It is very important to acquire a regular backup routine so that it becomes an automatic process.

Usually with application software you are not so worried about backing up the programs. If something happens to the hard disk, you can recover and reinstall the programs from the original, purchased CDs or disks. However, the data that you create is unrecoverable unless you have backed it up. A common technique to back up data from a hard disk is to purchase a device called a "tape backup." This device allows the user the ease of backing up the hard disk without having to sit in front of the computer and keep inserting blank floppy disks. However, the important message is that whatever technique you use, *back up your data files!*

In this text, you have been placing all your data files on a floppy disk. Backing up this disk is the easiest kind of backup to perform. It is also extremely useful. With a backup copy of the DATA disk, if you should have a problem, you would not have to go back to Chapter 2 and redo all the activities and homework. In the next activity, you will back up your DATA disk.

6.24 ACTIVITY: BACKING UP WITH THE DISKCOPY COMMAND

Note 1: The DATA disk is in Drive A. C:\> is displayed.
Note 2: DISKCOPY requires that media types be the same.

Step 1 If you are not at the C prompt, change to the C drive now. Get either a blank disk, a disk that has not been used, or a disk that has data on it that you no longer want. Label it "BACKUP DATA disk."

Step 2 Key in the following: C:\>**DISKCOPY A: A:** Enter

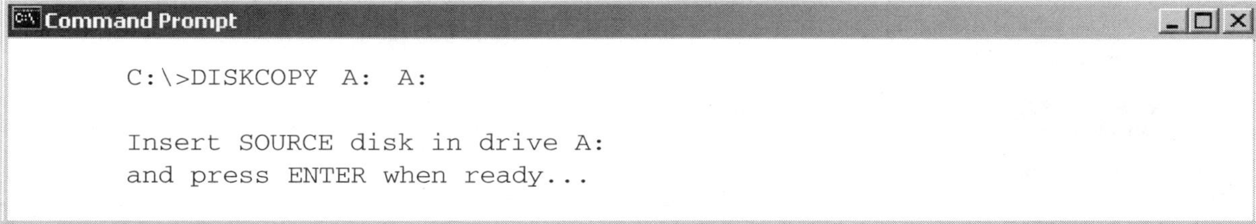

Command Prompt
C:\>DISKCOPY A: A:
Insert SOURCE disk in drive A:
and press ENTER when ready...

WHAT'S HAPPENING? You are asked to put the SOURCE disk that you wish to copy in Drive A. In this case, the DATA disk, which you want to copy, is already in Drive A. You keyed in two disk drives, **A** and **A**, to ensure that you do not accidentally copy the hard disk. You are telling DISKCOPY to make a copy from the disk in Drive A to the disk in Drive A.

Step 3 Press Enter

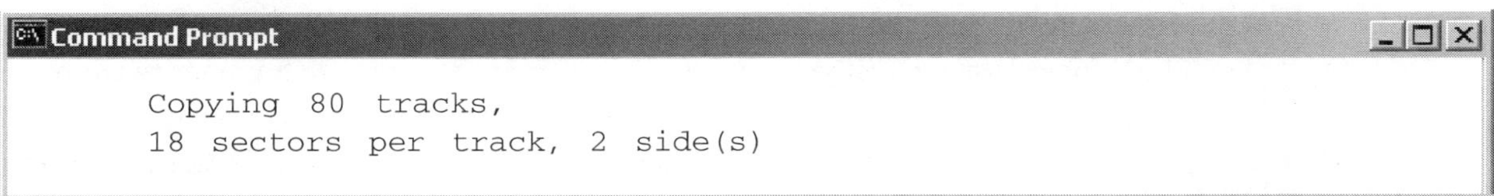

Command Prompt
Copying 80 tracks,
18 sectors per track, 2 side(s)

WHAT'S HAPPENING? The number of tracks and sectors will vary depending on the disk media type. The DISKCOPY command tells the operating system to copy everything on the disk in Drive A (the SOURCE) to RAM. While this program is doing the copying, the cursor flashes on the screen. When the command is completed or the program has finished executing (copying), you need to take another step. You receive the following prompt:

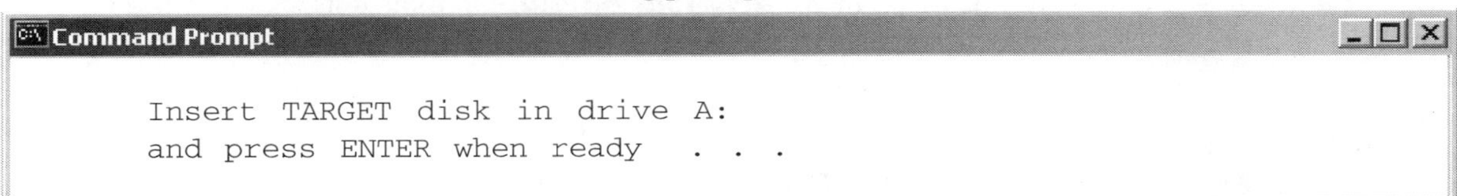

This prompt tells you to remove the SOURCE disk from Drive A and insert the blank or TARGET disk in Drive A so that the operating system has a place to copy the information.

Step 4 Remove your original DATA disk from Drive A. Insert the blank disk labeled "BACKUP DATA disk" into Drive A. This is your target disk. Close or latch the drive door. Press Enter

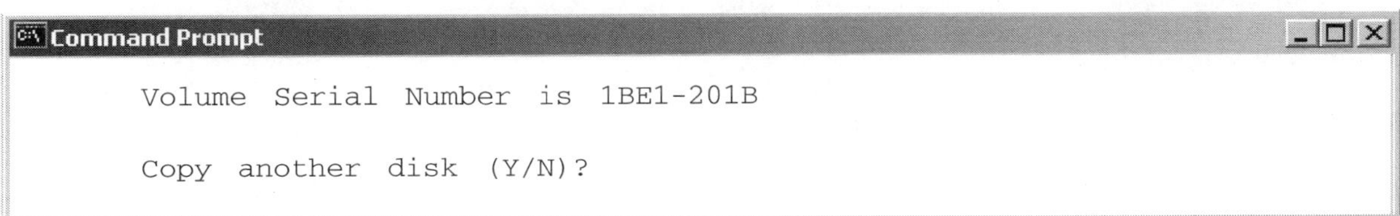

WHAT'S HAPPENING? You saw a flashing cursor while whatever was in RAM was being copied or written to the blank disk in Drive A. Now you see a question: Do you want to execute DISKCOPY again to copy another disk? In this case, you do not wish

to make another copy, so you key in **N**. The Volume Serial Number, by the way, changes each time you use the DISKCOPY command.

Step 5 Press **N**

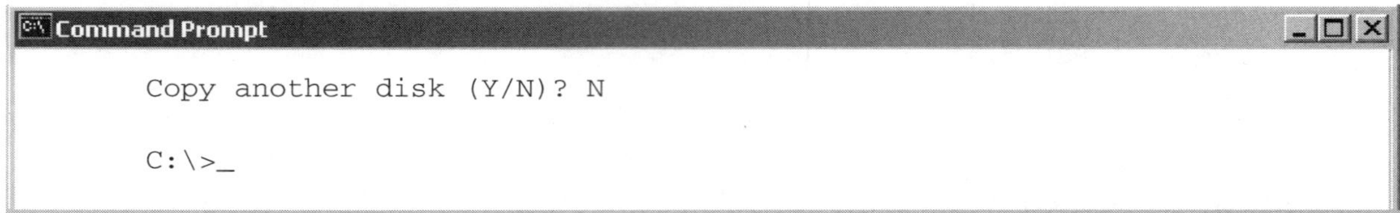

WHAT'S HAPPENING? Because of the DISKCOPY command, you now have two copies of the DATA disk, the original and the backup. At the end of each work session, you should follow these steps to back up your DATA disk. You do not need a new backup disk each time. Keep using the same backup disk over and over. You are merely keeping current; you do not need an archival or historical record of each day's work. You should also make a backup copy of your APPLICATION disk. However, if you wish to be prudent, it is wise to have more than one backup copy of your disks. As you can imagine, the only time you need your copy of the data is when something has gone wrong. This is not the time you want to find out that your only copy of the data is bad. It is also a good idea to check your backed up data periodically to ensure that it is good data and that you can recover it if you need to. Remember, DISKCOPY makes an exact duplicate of the source diskette. Anything that was previously on the target diskette is destroyed in this process.

Some organizations, such as banks and the IRS, may need to recreate records, so they will have not only a ***Disaster and Recovery Plan*** but also ***archival data*** or an ***archival backup***. This is sometimes called a "transaction history." Organizations like this need far more than a simple backup copy. For instance, if you go into the bank today and say you are missing the $100.00 deposit you made last week, the bank cannot tell you that they do not know what happened last week. The bank needs to be able to recreate all the transactions that occurred on the day in question. Just having a backup copy of your account for today or even yesterday is not sufficient. Most PC users, however, do not need archival data. Simply backing up their data is sufficient.

Step 6 Remove the disk labeled "BACKUP DATA disk" and keep it in a safe place until you need it again to make another backup.

WHAT'S HAPPENING? You now have a backup copy of your DATA disk. You may wish to repeat the steps with another disk to back up your APPLICATION disk too. Every time you complete a chapter, it is a good idea to update your backups so that they are kept current. In this way, if something happens to one of the original disks, you have lost only one chapter's work.

6.25 BACKING UP FILES WITH THE COPY COMMAND

Note: The following material is informational and meant *to be read only*. It is not an activity.

Using the DISKCOPY command backs up an entire floppy disk. More often than not, however, you need to back up only specific files, or you want to back up files from the hard disk to a floppy disk or a removable drive such as a Zip drive. Remember that you can also use the COPY command to back up specific files. The basic syntax does not change. It is as follows:

```
COPY [drive:][path]SOURCE.FIL [drive:][path]DESTINATION.FIL
```

You can also back up files from one floppy disk to another with the COPY command. Be sure that the destination disk is already formatted because COPY does not format a new disk as DISKCOPY does. Furthermore, COPY can be used only if you have two removable drives such as a floppy disk and a Zip drive. Since you are using two disk drives, COPY does not require identical disk media types. For example, you can copy from a 3½-inch, 1.44 MB disk to a Zip disk. You would place the source disk in Drive A and the destination disk in Drive H or whatever your removable drive letter is, and key in:

A:\>**COPY *.* H:**

A:\> is the default drive. COPY is the command. *.* means every file with every file extension—the first * represents any file name, the second * represents any file extension. COPY goes to the source disk to find each file in the root directory. As it copies the source file, it lists the file name on the screen. B:\ represents the root directory of the destination disk. Since you give no file names following B:\, COPY assumes that you want the same file names on the destination disk. If there is a file with the same name on the destination disk, COPY overwrites it.

If you want to back up files from a hard disk, you can also use the COPY command to copy the files in the individual subdirectories. However, you must be sure that there are not too many files in a subdirectory to fit on a floppy disk. Look at the following display:

```
Command Prompt

C:\WINDOSBK>DIR *.TMP
 Volume in drive C is 2000 PRO
 Volume Serial Number is C4A7-8571

 Directory of C:\WINDOSBK

04/23/2000  04:03p              72 APRIL.TMP
04/23/2000  04:03p              53 BONJOUR.TMP
04/23/2000  04:03p              75 FEB.TMP
01/01/2002  04:32a              34 GOODBYE.TMP
04/23/2000  04:03p              73 JANUARY.TMP
04/23/2000  04:03p              73 JAN.TMP
04/23/2000  04:03p              71 MAR.TMP
04/23/2000  04:03p              71 MARCH.TMP
04/23/2000  04:18p              72 APR.TMP
```

```
            9 File(s)                594 bytes
            0 Dir(s)     1,121,357,824 bytes free

C:\WINDOSBK>_
```

After **9 File(s)**, the number is **594 bytes**. This number tells you that these nine files require only 594 bytes and will easily fit on a floppy disk. On the other hand, you may get a display like the one that follows:

```
Command Prompt

 Volume in drive F is BETTES F
 Volume Serial Number is 2F4B-16FD

 Directory of F:\ENCARTA

04/23/2000  04:03p                    72 APRIL.TMP
07/03/2000  01:53p      <DIR>          WORKING
10/22/1997   4:31p      <DIR>          .
10/22/1997   4:31p      <DIR>          ..
08/12/1996   8:47p             2,681,344 ENCRES97.DLL
08/12/1996   2:34p               134,144 DECO_32.DLL
08/12/1996   2:40p                 1,434 E97SPAM.INI
08/12/1996   8:47p               355,328 ENCTITLE.DLL
08/12/1996   2:43p                13,204 YBBST97A.DAT
08/12/1996   2:34p               526,336 EEUIL10.DLL
08/12/1996   2:36p               212,992 SUBSCRIB.EXE
08/12/1996   8:45p                17,258 DISCS.HLP
08/12/1996   8:46p               863,913 ENC97.HLP
08/12/1996   8:45p                 6,429 ENC97.CNT
08/12/1996   2:36p                60,053 WEBTIPS.HLP
08/12/1996   2:34p                84,343 README.HLP
11/16/1997   3:42p                20,848 INST97A.LOG
08/12/1996   8:46p             1,520,354 ENC97F.STR
08/12/1996   8:46p             3,429,346 ENCART97.DAT
08/12/1996   8:53p                78,188 UNINSTAL.EXE
08/12/1996   8:45p             1,715,200 ENC97.EXE
10/05/1996  11:49a                     4 ENCART97.ANN
10/22/1997   4:31p      <DIR>          UPDATES
           18 File(s)     11,720,718 bytes
            3 Dir(s)     921,403,392 bytes free

F:\ENCARTA>_
```

The number is now **18 File(s)** that occupy **11,720,718 bytes**, which will not fit on a single floppy disk. However, the files would fit on a 100-MB Zip cartridge. Only if the files will fit on a floppy disk can you use the COPY command. Thus, if you wanted to back up the subdirectory \WINDOSBK, the command would be keyed in as:

```
C:\>COPY C:\WINDOSBK\*.* A:
```

This command, however, would not copy files in any subdirectories under the \WINDOSBK subdirectory, only the files in the \WINDOSBK directory. You would have to key in another command such as:

```
C:\>COPY \WINDOSBK\DATA\*.* A:
```

You cannot and must not copy all the files from a hard disk to a floppy disk with the COPY command. There are too many files on the hard disk, and they will not fit on a single floppy disk. There are backup utilities to back up large volumes, but they need a destination other than a floppy disk.

A question that arises is how often should you back up data? If you have backed up files to floppies or a tape and have not changed your original files, you do not need to back them up again. The files you are interested in backing up are those that have changed or those that are new. A rule of thumb to follow is to think of how long it would take you to recreate your data. If you think in those terms, you will make regular backups.

CHAPTER SUMMARY

1. DEL eliminates files.
2. Deleting files helps you manage your disks and directories.
3. The syntax for the DEL command is:

   ```
   DEL names
   ```

4. Wildcards can be used with DEL.
5. DEL does not eliminate the data on the disk, only the entry in the directory table.
6. Once a file has been deleted, it cannot be recovered except with special utility programs.
7. Before you use wildcards with DEL, it is wise to use the DIR command to see what is going to be erased.
8. The /P parameter prompts you to confirm whether or not you wish to delete a file, and the /S parameter allows you to delete files in the directory hierarchy.
9. You can change the names of files or directories with the RENAME or REN command.
10. The syntax for renaming is:

    ```
    RENAME [drive:][path][directoryname1 ¦ filename1]
    [directoryname2 ¦ filename2]
    REN [drive:][path][directoryname1 ¦ filename1]
    [directoryname2 ¦ filename2]
    ```

11. Renaming can be done only on one drive or directory. RENAME does not move files.
12. Renaming changes only file names, not contents of files.
13. With the REN command, you use the path only with the original file name and do not repeat it with the new file name.
14. Wildcards can be used with the REN command.
15. Before you use wildcards with the REN command, it is wise to use the DIR command to see what files are going to be affected by renaming.
16. Once a file is renamed, it cannot be found under its old name.
17. The MOVE command can be used either to change the name of a subdirectory or to move files from one location to another. When you use MOVE, two steps are taken: the files are copied to the new location and deleted from the old location.

18. You may remove directories with either RD or RD /S. With RD alone, you must remove files first and then any directories. RD /S does it all in one command.
19. It is wise to make backup copies of data files so that if something happens, you have another source of data.
20. You can back up a floppy disk with the DISKCOPY command, or you can back up files on your disk using the COPY command. The wildcard *.* allows you to back up all the files in a directory.

KEY TERMS

archival backup
archival data
copy-protected
Disaster and Recovery Plan

DISCUSSION QUESTIONS

1. Explain why you may want to eliminate files from a disk.
2. When you delete a file, the file is not actually removed from the disk. What really happens?
3. Give the syntax of the DEL command and explain each part of the syntax.
4. *The strength of wildcards is also a weakness*. Explain this statement, using DEL.
5. When deleting files, why should you key in DIR with global file specifications first?
6. Explain the purpose and function of the /P parameter with the DEL command. The /S?
7. Why would you want to change the name of a file?
8. Explain the purpose and function of the RENAME or REN command.
9. Give the syntax of the REN command and explain each part of the syntax.
10. What is the difference between the REN and RENAME commands?
11. What is the difference between the RENAME and COPY commands?
12. If you are using the REN command and get the message, "A duplicate file name exists, or the file name cannot be found," what could it mean?
13. What is the function and purpose of the MOVE command?
14. Give the syntax of the MOVE command and explain each part of the syntax.
15. Compare and contrast MOVE and COPY.
16. What is the difference between the MOVE and the REN commands?
17. Compare and contrast the RD /S command with the RD command without the /S parameter.
18. What process could you use to back up specific files?
19. What process could you use to back up a subdirectory?
20. Why would you not copy all the files from the hard disk to a floppy disk with the DISKCOPY command?
21. Why would you not copy all the files from a hard disk to a floppy disk with the COPY command?

TRUE/FALSE QUESTIONS

For each question, circle the letter T if the statement is true and the letter F if the statement is false.

T F 1. REN and RENAME perform identical functions.

T F 2. It is not possible to find a file that has been renamed if you do not know its new name.

T F 3. When using wildcards with the MOVE command, you cannot change the destination file name.

T F 4. You cannot use REN on subdirectories.

T F 5. If you use the command DEL TRIP and TRIP is a subdirectory name, the default parameter is all files (*.*).

COMPLETION QUESTIONS

Write the correct answer in each blank space.

6. One way to verify that a file has been deleted is to use the ________ command.
7. The REN command does not move files. Its only function is to ________ a file name.
8. The command for making an exact duplicate of a floppy disk is ___________.
9. After you complete a work session, an important procedure to follow to ensure not losing your data is to ________ your original disk.
10. The parameter that allows you to confirm whether or not you wish to delete a file is ________.

MULTIPLE CHOICE QUESTIONS

For each question, write the letter for the correct answer in the blank space.

☐ 11. DEL is a command that
   a. removes a subdirectory.
   b. can delete only one file at a time.
   c. can be used with wildcards.
   d. none of the above

☐ 12. Prior to using wildcards with the DEL command,
   a. it is a good idea to confirm visually the files to be erased using DIR.
   b. it is wise to remember that wildcards have opposite meanings when used with DIR and COPY.
   c. remember that only data files can be removed with the DEL command.
   d. remember that only program files can be removed with the DEL command.

☐ 13. When A:\> is the default and DEL CLASS.DBF is keyed in,
   a. the file CLASS.DBF will be deleted from the default drive.
   b. the file CLASS.DBF will be deleted from Drive C.
   c. nothing will happen.
   d. none of the above

14. Using the command RD *directory_name* /S only
    a. deletes the files from the specified directory.
    b. deletes the files from the specified directory and its child directories.
    c. deletes the specified directory and all subdirectories and files contained therein.
    d. deletes the subdirectories contained in the specified directory.
15. The MOVE command
    a. can be used to rename a directory.
    b. can be used to make multiple copies of files.
    c. can move an entire directory structure to a new location.
    d. both a and c

WRITING COMMANDS

Write the correct steps or commands to perform the required action as if you were at the computer. The prompt will indicate the default drive and directory.

16. Remove the file called **CATS** in the directory called **ANIMALS** located under the root directory of Drive A.

    `A:\TEST>`

17. Delete all the files with the **.OLD** file extension in the subdirectory **WHAT** located under the current directory on the default drive.

    `C:\JUNK>`

18. Change the extension of the **COLOR** file from **.DOT** to **.DOC**. The file is located in the **PAINT** directory under the root directory on Drive A.

    `C:\>`

19. Change the file extension from **.FIL** to **.TXT** for all the files in the **FURN** subdirectory located under the root directory on Drive C.

    `A:\>`

20. Eliminate the file called **MYFILE.TXT**, located in the subdirectory **JUNK** on Drive C.

    `C:\JUNK>`

APPLICATION ASSIGNMENTS

Note 1: Place the APPLICATION disk in Drive A. Be sure to work on the APPLICATION disk, not the DATA disk.

Note 2: The homework problems will assume Drive C is the hard disk and the APPLICATION disk is in Drive A. If you are using another drive, such as floppy Drive B or hard Drive D, be sure and substitute that drive letter when reading the questions and creating the answers.

Note 3: All subdirectories that are created will be under the root directory unless otherwise specified.

PROBLEM SET I

PROBLEM A

Note: If the DATA disk is in Drive A, remove it and place it in a safe place.

CAUTION!!! DO NOT USE THE DATA DISK FOR THESE APPLICATION PROBLEMS. USE THE APPLICATION DISK.

A-a Insert the APPLICATION disk into Drive A.

A-b Copy all the files from the **WINDOSBK\MEDIA\TV** subdirectory to the root directory of the APPLICATION disk.

A-c On the APPLICATION disk, rename the file called **DRAMA.TV** to **SERIOUS.TV**.

☐

1. Which command did you use to rename the file?
   a. REN DRAMA.TV SERIOUS.TV
   b. REN SERIOUS.TV DRAMA.TV
   c. COPY DRAMA.TV SERIOUS.TV
   d. COPY SERIOUS.TV DRAMA.TV

A-d Execute the DIR command looking only for the file called **DRAMA.TV**.

☐

2. What message is displayed?
   a. Invalid File Parameter
   b. File Not Found
   c. Required parameter missing
   d. no message is displayed

A-e Rename the file called **SERIOUS.TV** to **DRAMA.TV**.

☐

3. Which command did you use?
   a. REN DRAMA.TV SERIOUS.TV
   b. REN SERIOUS.TV DRAMA.TV
   c. COPY DRAMA.TV SERIOUS.TV
   d. COPY SERIOUS.TV DRAMA.TV

A-f Key in the following: **TYPE SERIOUS.TV** Enter

4. What message is displayed?
   a. The system cannot find the file specified
   b. File not found
   c. Required parameter missing
   d. no message is displayed

A-g Key in the following: **TYPE DRAMA.TV** Enter

5. What television series is displayed?
   a. The Rosie O'Donnell Show
   b. Seinfeld
   c. The Practice
   d. Dallas

PROBLEM B

Note: The exercises in Problem B assume the root directory of the APPLICATION disk is the default drive and directory.

B-a Copy all files from the **WINDOSBK** subdirectory that have the file extension of **.DOS** to the root directory of the APPLICATION disk, keeping the file names the same.

6. How many files were copied?
   a. one
   b. two
   c. three
   d. four

B-b Rename all the files that have a file extension of **.DOS** to the same file name but with **.WG** as the file extension (remember wildcards).

7. Which command did you use?
   a. COPY *.DOS *.WG
   b. REN *.DOS *.WG
   c. COPY ?.DOS ?.WG
   d. REN ?.DOS ?.WG

B-c Make copies of all the **.WG** files on the root of the APPLICATION disk keeping the same file name but with a new extension of **.RRR**.

8. Which command did you use?
   a. DIR *.RRR
   b. REN *.WG *.RRR
   c. DIR *.WG
   d. COPY *.WG *.RRR

B-d Make copies of all the **.WG** files on the APPLICATION disk keeping the same file names but with a new extension of **.MMM**.

9. What date is listed for the WILDTWO.MMM file?
   a. 02/13/00
   b. 12/31/01
   c. 12/31/00
   d. 02/13/99

B-e Using the relative path, move all the files with the **.RRR** file extension to the **PHONE** subdirectory.

10. What command did you use?
   a. COPY *.RRR PHONE
   b. REN *.RRR PHONE
   c. MOVE *.RRR PHONE
   d. MOVE PHONE *.RRR

B-f Execute the DIR command looking only for files in the root directory of the APPLICATION disk that have the **.RRR** file extension.

11. How many files were located?
   a. one
   b. two
   c. three
   d. zero

B-g Execute the DIR command looking only for files in the **PHONE** subdirectory that have the **.RRR** file extension.

12. How many files were located?
   a. one
   b. two
   c. three
   d. zero

B-h Rename all the files that have the extension of **.WG** to the same file name but with **.DOS** as the file extension. Use a wildcard.

13. Which command did you use?
   a. COPY *.DOS *.WG
   b. REN *.DOS *.WG
   c. COPY *.WG *.DOS
   d. REN *.WG *.DOS

B-i Key in the following: **MOVE WILDONE.MMM PHONE\OLD\WILD.MMM** **Enter**

14. What message is displayed?
    a. A:\WILDONE.MMM => a:\phone\old\wild.mmm [ok]
    b. The system cannot find the path specified.
    c. A:\WILDONE.MMM => a:\phone\old\wild.mmm [No such directory]
    d. no message is displayed

B-j Delete all the files with the **.MMM** extension. Use a wildcard.

15. Which command did you use?
    a. DEL *.MMM or DEL /S *.MMM
    b. DEL PHONE*.MMM or DEL /S PHONE*.MMM
    c. RD PHONE*.MMM or RD /S PHONE*.MMM
    d. MOVE *.MMM or MOVE /S *.MMM

16. What message is displayed when you have finished executing the command?
    a. Duplicate file name
    b. File not found
    c. Duplicate file name or file not found
    d. none of the above

B-k Using the relative path, delete all the files with the **.RRR** extension on the APPLICATION disk. Use a wildcard. (*Hint:* Remember DIR /S.)

17. Which command did you use?
    a. DEL /S *.RRR
    b. DEL PHONE*.RRR
    c. RD PHONE*.RRR
    d. MOVE *.RRR

PROBLEM C

Note: The exercises in Problem C assume the root directory of the APPLICATION disk is the default drive and directory.

C-a Copy the file from the **WINDOSBK\FINANCE** directory called **BALANCE.TKR** to the root of the APPLICATION disk.

C-b Create a subdirectory called **SERIES** under the root of the APPLICATION disk.

C-c Copy all the files on the root of the APPLICATION disk with the extension **.99** to the **SERIES** directory.

C-d Using the relative path, move the file called **BALANCE.TKR** from the root directory of the APPLICATION disk to the **SERIES** directory.

18. Which command did you use with BALANCE.TKR?
    a. COPY BALANCE.TKR SERIES
    b. DEL SERIES\BALANCE.TKR
    c. REN BALANCE.TKR SERIES
    d. MOVE BALANCE.TKR SERIES

19. The file BALANCE.TKR is now in
    a. only the SERIES directory on the APPLICATION disk.
    b. only the root of the APPLICATION disk.
    c. the WINDOSBK\FINANCE directory on the hard drive and the SERIES directory on the APPLICATION disk.
    d. none of the above

C-e From the root of the APPLICATION disk using the relative path, delete the file **BALANCE.TKR** on the APPLICATION disk.

20. Which command did you use?
    a. DEL BALANCE.TKR
    b. DEL SERIES\BALANCE.TKR
    c. MOVE BALANCE.TKR
    d. REN BALANCE.TKR

C-f Eliminate the **SERIES** directory from the APPLICATION disk *without* using the RD /S command.

21. Which command did you use *first?*
    a. RD SERIES or RD \SERIES*.*
    b. DEL SERIES or DEL \SERIES*.*
    c. DELETE SERIES or DELETE \SERIES*.*
    d. MOVE SERIES or MOVE \SERIES*.*

PROBLEM D

Note: The exercises in Problem D assume the root directory of the APPLICATION disk is the default drive and directory.

D-a You wish to use a wildcard, but you want to select only some files to eliminate in the **FILES** subdirectory that have the file extension **.FIL**.

22. What parameter would you use with the DEL command?
    a. /K
    b. /P
    c. /S
    d. /T

D-b Use the correct parameter from the above question with the DEL command to selectively eliminate the files with **JAN** or **FEB** as a file name and **.FIL** as a file extension from the **FILES** subdirectory.

23. Beside the file names, which message was displayed?
    a. Delete [ok]?
    b. Delete (Y/N)?
    c. Invalid parameter
    d. no message was displayed

D-c Rename all the files in the **FILES** subdirectory that have a file extension of **.FIL** to the same file name but with **.AAA** as the file extension.

24. Which command did you use?
    a. REN FILES*.FIL *.AAA
    b. REN FILES*.FIL FILES*.AAA
    c. REN FILES*.AAA FILES*.FIL
    d. REN FILES*.AAA *.FIL

PROBLEM E

Note: The root directory of the APPLICATION disk is the default drive and directory.

E-a Copy all the files from the **\WINDOSBK** directory that have the file extension of **.TMP** to the root directory of the APPLICATION disk.

25. How many files were copied?
    a. 3
    b. 6
    c. 9
    d. 12

E-b Rename all the files on the root of the APPLICATION disk with the **.TMP** file extension to have the same names with the file extension of **.FDP**. Use a wildcard.

26. Which command did you use?
    a. REN *.FDP *.TMP
    b. COPY *.FDP *.TMP
    c. REN *.TMP *.FDP
    d. COPY *.TMP *.FDP

E-c Eliminate all the **.FDP** files *except* **BONJOUR.FDP**.

27. Which command did you use?
    a. DEL *.FDP
    b. DEL *.FDP /P
    c. DEL *.FDP /Y
    d. DEL *.FDP /S

PROBLEM SET II—AT THE COMPUTER

Note 1: Before proceeding with these assignments, check with your lab instructor to see if there are any special procedures you should follow.

Note 2: The APPLICATION disk is in Drive A. The A:\> prompt is displayed as the default drive and the default directory. *All work will occur on the APPLICATION disk.*

Note 3: Make sure that **NAME.BAT**, **MARK.FIL**, **GETYN.COM**, and **GO.BAT** are all present in the root directory of the APPLICATION disk before proceeding with these problems.

Note 4: All files with the **.HW** extension *must* be created in the root directory of the APPLICATION disk.

Step 1 Key in the following: A:\>**NAME** Enter

Step 2 Here is an example to key in, but your instructor will have other information that applies to your class. Key in the following:

Bette A. Peat Enter (*Your* name goes here.)

CIS 55 Enter (*Your* class goes here.)

T-Th 8-9:30 Enter (*Your* day and time go here.)

Chapter 6 Applications Enter

Step 3 Press F6 Enter

Step 4 If the information is correct, press **Y** and you are back to A:\>.

WHAT'S HAPPENING? You have returned to the system level. You now have a file called **NAME.FIL** with your name and other pertinent information. *Hint*: Remember redirection.

TO CREATE 1.HW

- The root directory of the APPLICATION disk is the default drive and directory.
- Key in the following: **DIR EMP*.* > 1.HW** Enter
- Eliminate all the files that begin with **EMP** and have any file extension.
- Note the double >> and note that there is no space with between the two >>. Key in the following: **DIR EMP*.* >> 1.HW** Enter

TO CREATE 2.HW

- The root directory of the APPLICATION disk is the default drive and directory.
- Move all the files with a **.TV** extension to the **PHONE** directory.
- Locate only the files in the **PHONE** directory on the APPLICATION disk that have the extension of **.TV** and place the names of the files in a file called **2.HW**.

TO CREATE 3.HW

- The root directory of the APPLICATION disk is the default drive and directory.
- Locate all the files in the root directory of the APPLICATION disk that have an extension of **.TV**, if any, placing the output of the command in a file called **3.HW**.

TO CREATE 4.HW

- The root directory of the APPLICATION disk is the default drive and directory.
- Rename all the files in the **FILES** subdirectory that have the extension .**AAA** to the same name but with the extension of .**JOB**.
- Locate all the files in the **FILES** directory that have an extension of **.JOB**.
- Place the output of the command in a file called **4.HW**.

TO CREATE 5.HW

- The root directory of the APPLICATION disk is the default drive and directory.
- Eliminate all the files in the root directory of the APPLICATION disk that have the **.MAK** extension.
- Locate any files in the root directory of the APPLICATION disk with the **.MAK** extension, if any, and place the output of the command in a file called **5.HW**.

TO PRINT YOUR HOMEWORK

Step 1 Be sure the printer is on and ready to accept print jobs from your computer.

Step 2 Key in the following (be very careful to make no typing errors):
GO NAME.FIL 1.HW 2.HW 3.HW 4.HW 5.HW Enter

If the files you requested, **1.HW**, **2.HW**, etc., do not exist in the default directory, you will see the following message on the screen:

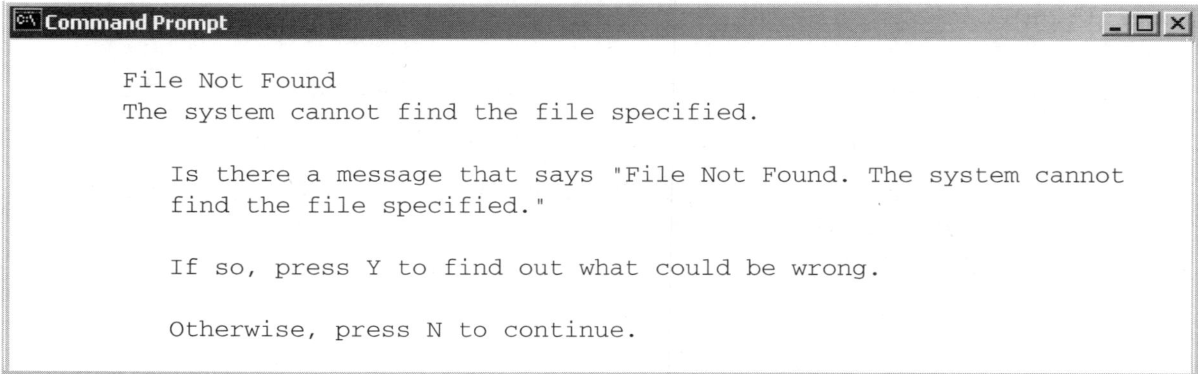
Command Prompt
File Not Found
The system cannot find the file specified.
Is there a message that says "File Not Found. The system cannot find the file specified."
If so, press Y to find out what could be wrong.
Otherwise, press N to continue.

WHAT'S HAPPENING? The operating system is telling you that the file cannot be found. If you see this screen, press **Y** to see what could be wrong, and repeat the print procedure after you have corrected the problem.

If the default directory contains the specified files, the following message will appear on the screen:

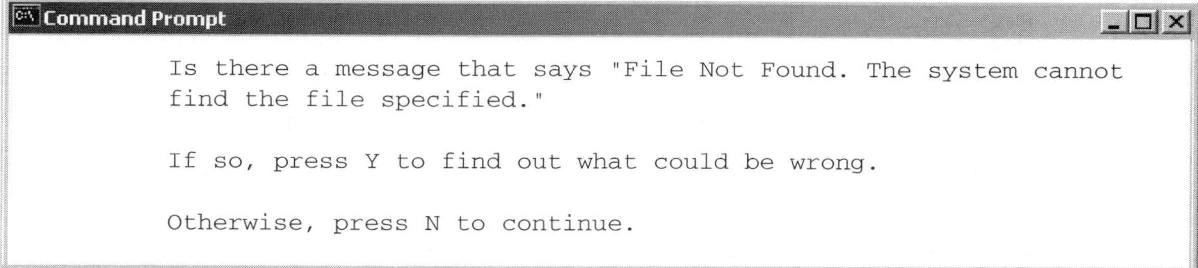

WHAT'S HAPPENING? You will need to press **N** once for each file you are printing.

Step 3 Follow the messages on the screen until the Notepad program opens with a screen similar to the following:

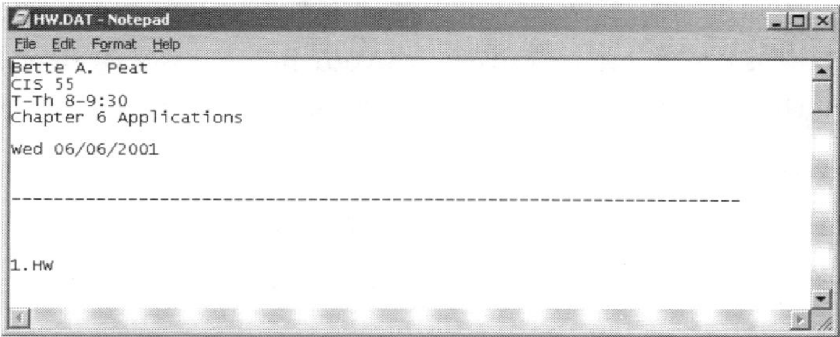

WHAT'S HAPPENING? All the requested files have been found and placed in a Notepad document. Your homework is now ready to print.

Step 4 On the Notepad menu bar, click **File**. Click **Print**.

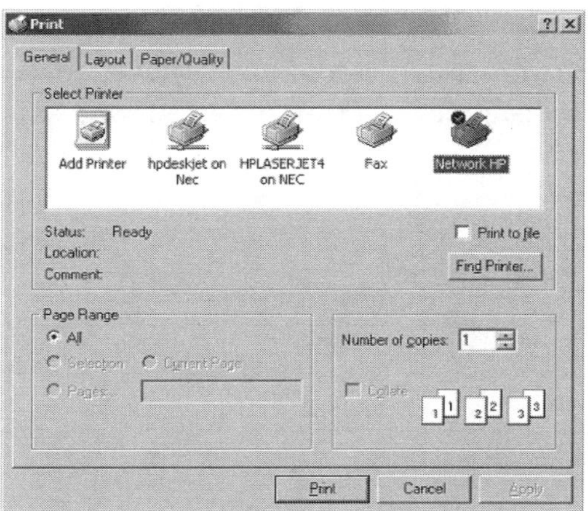

The print dialog box opens. If you have more than one printer, all your printer choices will be displayed. The default printer is the highlighted printer.

Step 5 Click the **Print** button.

Step 6 In the Notepad window, click **File**. Click **Exit**.

WHAT'S HAPPENING? The following will appear on the Command Prompt screen:

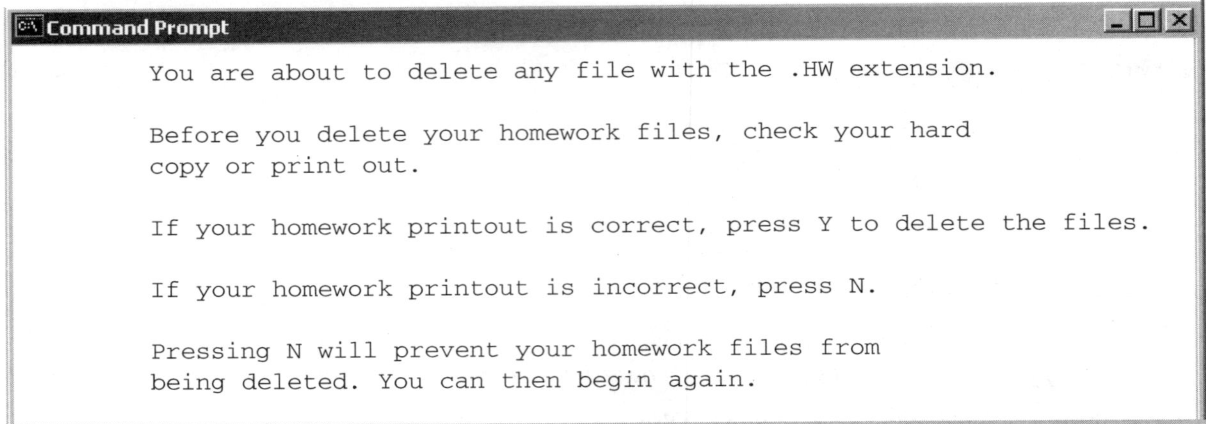
Command Prompt
You are about to delete any file with the .HW extension.
Before you delete your homework files, check your hard copy or print out.
If your homework printout is correct, press Y to delete the files.
If your homework printout is incorrect, press N.
Pressing N will prevent your homework files from being deleted. You can then begin again.

WHAT'S HAPPENING? At this point, look at your printout. If it is correct, you can press **Y** to delete the homework files for this chapter. If your printout is incorrect, you can press **N**. That will preserve your homework and you will need to redo only the problem that was incorrect and not all the homework assignments.

Step 7 Press **Y** **Enter**

WHAT'S HAPPENING? You have returned to the default prompt.

Step 8 Close the Command Prompt session.

PROBLEM SET III—BRIEF ESSAY

1. What are the advantages of using the commands REN, DEL, COPY, and MOVE from the command line instead of using Windows Explorer? What are the disadvantages?

2. *Deleting files and directories can have serious consequences and should never be done.* Agree or disagree with this statement and explain the rationale for your answer.

CHAPTER

7

USING ATTRIB, SUBST, XCOPY, DOSKEY, AND THE TEXT EDITOR

LEARNING OBJECTIVES

After finishing this chapter, you will be able to:

1. Explain the purpose and function of the ATTRIB command.
2. Explain the purpose and function of the SUBST command.
3. Explain the purpose and function of the XCOPY command.
4. Explain the purpose and function of DOSKEY.
5. Use the text editor to create and edit text files.

STUDENT OUTCOMES

1. Use the ATTRIB command to protect files.
2. Use the SUBST command to simplify long path names.
3. Use XCOPY to copy files and subdirectories.
4. Use the XCOPY parameters to copy hidden files and retain file attributes.
5. Use DOSKEY to be more efficient at the command line.
6. Create text files using the text editor.

CHAPTER OVERVIEW

By using different utility commands and programs, you can manipulate files and subdirectories to help make tasks at the command line much easier. You can make the DEL *.* command safer by using the ATTRIB command to hide files that you don't want to delete. You will learn what file attributes are and how to manipulate them with the ATTRIB command. You can copy files and subdirectories at the same time with the XCOPY command. You can even copy hidden files and empty subdirectories. By using DOSKEY, you can further use command line editing keys. By using the text editor, you can quickly create simple text files. In this chapter, you will take a look at these commands and programs.

7.1 FILE ATTRIBUTES AND THE ATTRIB COMMAND

The root directory keeps track of information about every file on a disk. This information includes the file name, file extension, file size, date and time the file was last modified, and a pointer to the file's starting cluster in the file allocation table. In addition, each file in the directory has attributes. Each attribute is a "bit" of information that is either on or off. A bit is ⅛ of a byte, and can store only a 1 or a 0, representing True or False, Yes or No, or On or Off. These attributes describe the status of a file. The attributes are represented by a single letter. These attributes include whether or not a file is a system file (S), a hidden file (H), a read-only file (R), or an archived file (A). Attributes are sometimes called flags.

The ***system attribute*** is a special signal to the operating system that the file is a system file. Files with this attribute are usually operating system files, but some application programs may set a bit to indicate that a particular program is a system file. The ***hidden attribute*** means that, when you use the DIR command, the file name is not displayed. Hidden files cannot be deleted with the DEL command, copied with the COPY command, or renamed. For example, hidden files such as the operating system files NTLDR and NTDETECT.COM are on a disk, but when you execute DIR, they are not displayed. The same is true in Windows Explorer or My Computer. Unless you change the folder options, hidden files are not displayed.

When a file is marked as read-only, it means exactly that. A user can only read the file, not modify or delete it. Sometimes application programs will set the ***read-only attribute*** bit to "on" for important files so that a user cannot delete them.

Finally, the ***archive attribute*** is used to indicate the backup history (archive status) of a file. When you create or modify a file, an archive bit is turned on or set. When a file has its archive bit turned on, that signifies that it has not been backed up. Certain commands and programs, such as those that back up, can modify the archive bit and reset it (turn it off or on).

The ATTRIB command allows you to manipulate ***file attributes***. You can view, set, and reset all the file attributes for one file or many files. ATTRIB is an external command. The syntax for the ATTRIB command is:

```
ATTRIB [+R ¦ -R] [+A ¦ -A] [+S ¦ -S] [+H ¦ -H] [[drive:][path]filename] [/S [/D]]
```

When you see a parameter in brackets, as you know, it is an optional parameter. When you see a parameter displayed as [+R ¦ -R], the bar (called a pipe) signifies that there is a choice. The parameter can be one thing or the other, not both—the choices are mutually exclusive. Thus, you can set a file with +R or -R, but not both at the same time. When you see two sets of brackets such as [/S [/D]], it means that the /S can be used alone but the /D must be used with the /S and cannot be used alone. The parameters are as follows:

+	Sets an attribute.
-	Clears an attribute.
R	Read-only file attribute.

A Archive file attribute.
S System file attribute.
H Hidden file attribute.
/S Processes matching files in the current folder and all subfolders.
/D Processes folders as well.

The attributes that you will find most useful to set or unset are read-only (R) and hidden (H). By making a file read-only, no one, including you, will be able to delete or overwrite the file accidentally. If a data file is marked read-only, even when you are in an application program, you cannot alter the data.

When you use the H attribute to make a file hidden, it will not be displayed when using the DIR command. If you cannot see a file displayed in the directory listing, you also cannot copy, delete, or rename it. This feature, as you will see, will allow you great flexibility in manipulating and managing files.

The A attribute is called the archive bit. The A attribute is a signal that the file has not been backed up. However, merely using the COPY command does not turn off the A attribute. You must use certain programs, such as XCOPY, which can read and manipulate the archive bit. Unlike COPY, XCOPY will determine whether or not a file has changed since the last time it was backed up, based on whether or not the archive bit is set. Then, XCOPY can make a decision on whether or not the file needs to be backed up. Rarely, if ever, will you use the ATTRIB command to change the attribute of a file marked as a system file (S).

You will find that, although you can change file attributes from Explorer, it is much easier to do these kinds of tasks from the command prompt.

7.2 ACTIVITY: USING ATTRIB TO MAKE FILES READ-ONLY

Note 1: Be sure you have opened the Command Prompt window.
Note 2: Be sure the DATA disk is in Drive A and A:\> is displayed.
Note 3: If specified files are not on your DATA disk, you can copy them from the **WINDOSBK** subdirectory.

Step 1 Key in the following: A:\>**ATTRIB *.99** Enter

```
Command Prompt

A:\>ATTRIB *.99
  A          APR.99
  A          FEB.99
  A          MAR.99
  A          JAN.99

A:\>_
```

You asked the ATTRIB command to show you all the files with the **.99** extension in the root directory of the DATA disk. The only file attribute that is visible or "on" for these files is A, the archive bit. The display tells you that the archive bit is set for each file that has a **.99** file extension.

Step 2 Key in the following: A:\>**ATTRIB C:*.*** Enter

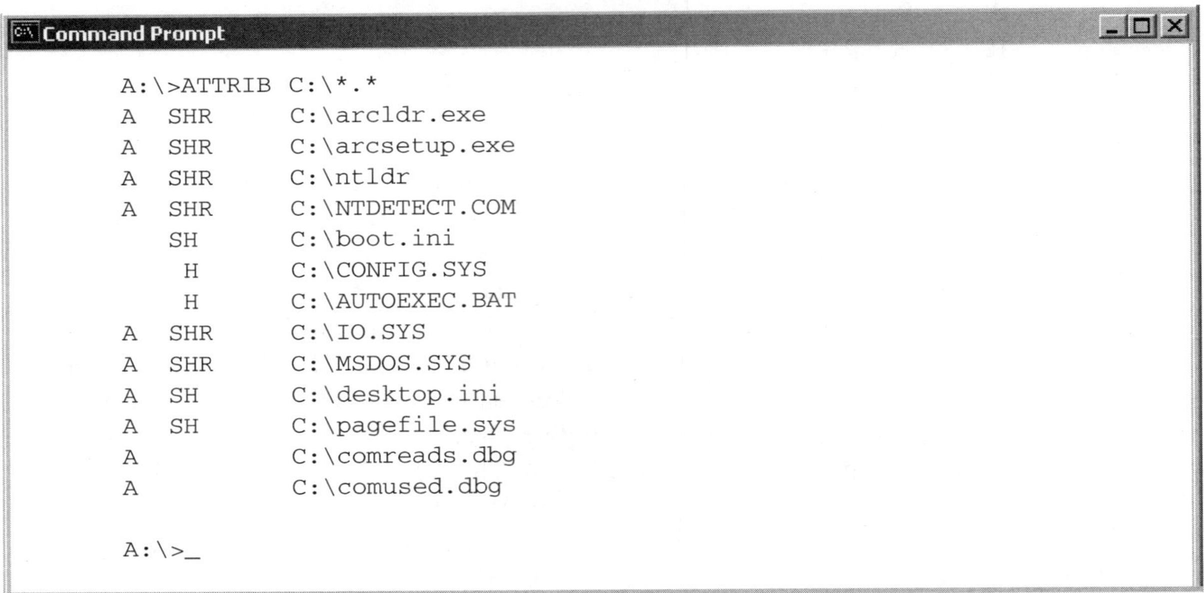

Command Prompt
A:\>ATTRIB C:*.*
A SHR C:\arcldr.exe
A SHR C:\arcsetup.exe
A SHR C:\ntldr
A SHR C:\NTDETECT.COM
SH C:\boot.ini
H C:\CONFIG.SYS
H C:\AUTOEXEC.BAT
A SHR C:\IO.SYS
A SHR C:\MSDOS.SYS
A SH C:\desktop.ini
A SH C:\pagefile.sys
A C:\comreads.dbg
A C:\comused.dbg
A:\>_

WHAT'S HAPPENING? You are looking at the files in the root directory of C. Your display will be different depending on what files are in your root directory. Also, if you are using a network drive instead of a local hard disk, you may not be able to access the root directory of the network drive. You can see that in this display, **ntldr** and **NTDETECT.COM** are marked with an S for the system attribute, an H for the hidden attribute, and an R for the read-only attribute. Since you cannot boot the computer from the hard disk without these files, they are triple-protected. Other critical files are marked with one or more of the S, H, and R attributes.

Step 3 Key in the following: A:\>**COPY C:\WINDOSBK*.FIL** Enter

Note: Overwrite any files if you are prompted to do so.

Command Prompt

```
A:\>COPY C:\WINDOSBK\*.FIL
C:\WINDOSBK\CASES.FIL
C:\WINDOSBK\STEVEN.FIL
C:\WINDOSBK\CAROLYN.FIL
C:\WINDOSBK\SECOND.FIL
C:\WINDOSBK\PERSONAL.FIL
C:\WINDOSBK\MARK.FIL
C:\WINDOSBK\FRANK.FIL
C:\WINDOSBK\NEWPRSON.FIL
C:\WINDOSBK\Y.FIL
        9 file(s) copied.

A:\>_
```

WHAT'S HAPPENING? You have copied all the files with the **.FIL** extension from the **\WINDOSBK** subdirectory to the DATA disk.

Step 4 Key in the following: A:\>**ATTRIB *.FIL** Enter

```
Command Prompt

A:\>ATTRIB *.FIL
  A          A:\MARCH.FIL
  A          A:\CASES.FIL
  A          A:\STEVEN.FIL
  A          A:\CAROLYN.FIL
  A          A:\SECOND.FIL
  A          A:\PERSONAL.FIL
  A          A:\MARK.FIL
  A          A:\FRANK.FIL
  A          A:\NEWPRSON.FIL
  A          A:\Y.FIL

A:\>_
```

WHAT'S HAPPENING? The only attribute that is set (turned on) for these files is the archive bit (A).

Step 5 Key in the following: A:\>**ATTRIB +R STEVEN.FIL** Enter

```
Command Prompt

A:\>ATTRIB +R STEVEN.FIL

A:\>_
```

WHAT'S HAPPENING? You asked the ATTRIB command to make **STEVEN.FIL** a read-only file.

Step 6 Key in the following: A:\>**ATTRIB STEVEN.FIL** Enter

```
Command Prompt

A:\>ATTRIB STEVEN.FIL
  A    R     A:\STEVEN.FIL

A:\>_
```

WHAT'S HAPPENING? Now you have flagged or marked **STEVEN.FIL** as a read-only file.

Step 7 Key in the following: A:\>**DEL STEVEN.FIL** Enter

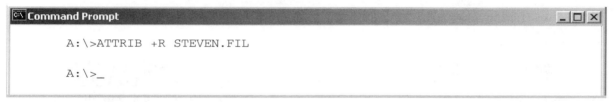

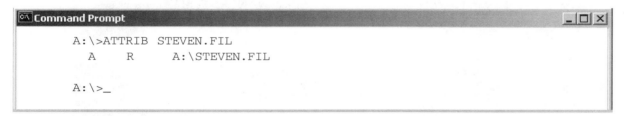

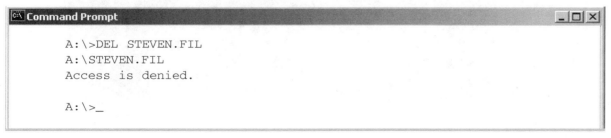

WHAT'S HAPPENING? You cannot delete this file because it is marked read-only. You can also protect against other kinds of file destruction. Once a file is marked read-only, even when you are in an application program, the operating system will stop you from overwriting the file.

Step 8 Key in the following: A:\>**CD /D C:\WINDOSBK\FINANCE** Enter

Step 9 Key in the following:
C:\WINDOSBK\FINANCE>**COPY HOMEBUD.TKR A:** Enter

Step 10 Key in the following:
C:\WINDOSBK\FINANCE>**ATTRIB +R A:\HOMEBUD.TKR** Enter

Step 11 Key in the following:
C:\WINDOSBK\FINANCE>**ATTRIB A:\HOMEBUD.TKR** Enter

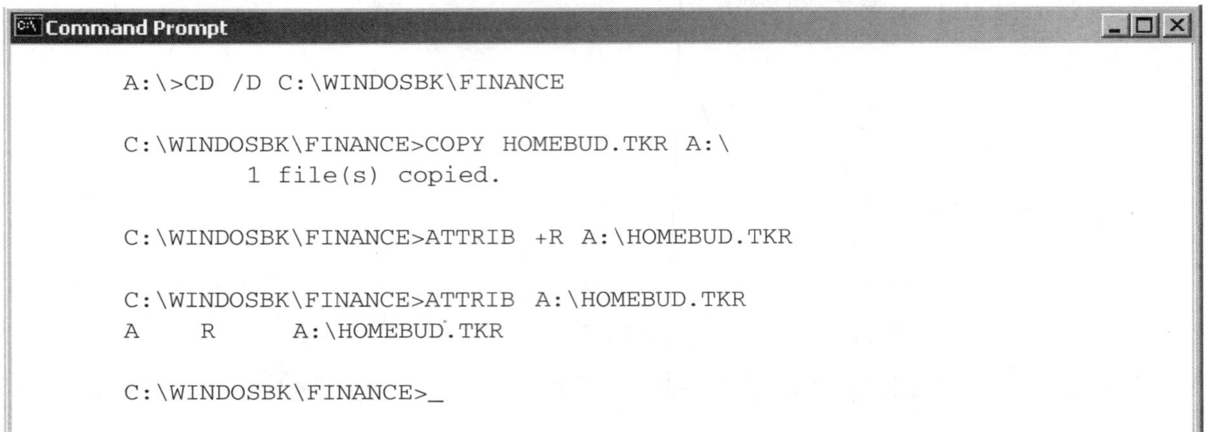
Command Prompt
A:\>CD /D C:\WINDOSBK\FINANCE
C:\WINDOSBK\FINANCE>COPY HOMEBUD.TKR A:\
1 file(s) copied.
C:\WINDOSBK\FINANCE>ATTRIB +R A:\HOMEBUD.TKR
C:\WINDOSBK\FINANCE>ATTRIB A:\HOMEBUD.TKR
A R A:\HOMEBUD.TKR
C:\WINDOSBK\FINANCE>_

WHAT'S HAPPENING? You have taken several steps. You changed your default drive to the hard disk. You changed directories. You then copied the **HOMEBUD.TKR** file to the DATA disk and made it a read-only file. Although you can alter the data in the file, if you try to save the altered file, the read-only attribute will prohibit you from overwriting the original data.

Step 12 Key in the following: C:\WINDOSBK\FINANCE>**THINK** Enter

Step 13 Press Enter

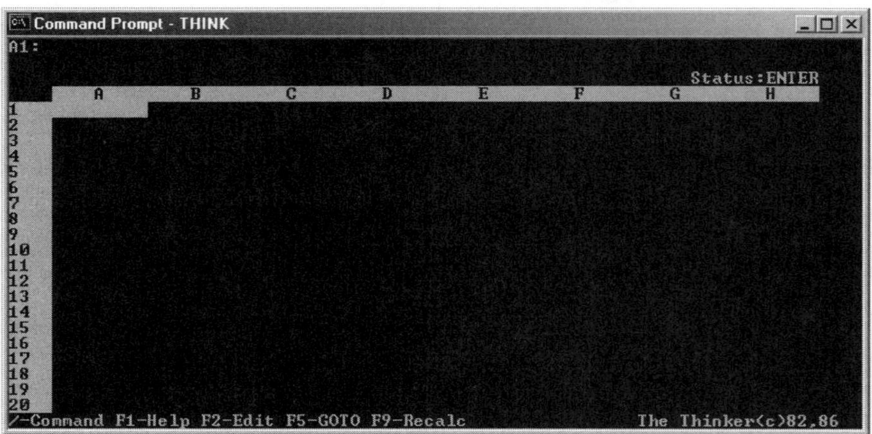
Command Prompt - THINK
A1:
Status:ENTER
A B C D E F G H
/-Command F1-Help F2-Edit F5-GOTO F9-Recalc
The Thinker(c)82,86

WHAT'S HAPPENING? You are in the Thinker program. You are going to load the read-only file from the DATA disk.

Step 14 Press **/**.

Step 15 Press **F**.

Step 16 Press **R**.

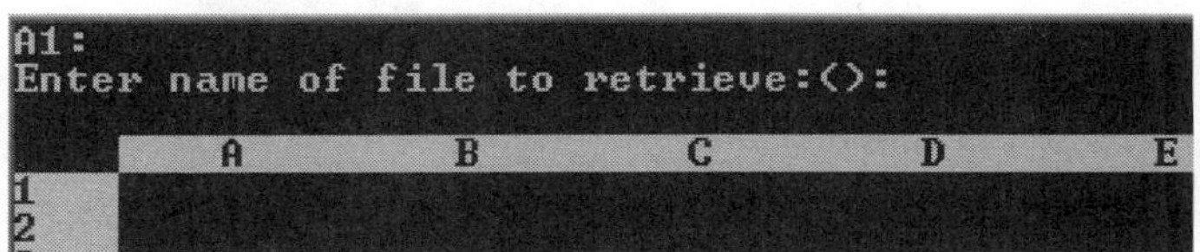

You issued the command to retrieve a file. Now you must enter the file name.

Step 17 Be sure to include the DATA disk drive letter in front of the file name. Key in the following: **A:\HOMEBUD** Enter

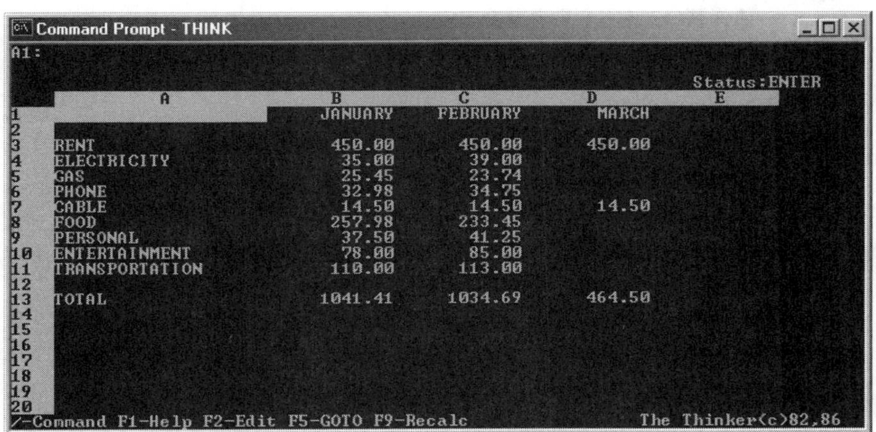

You have loaded the data file **HOMEBUD.TKR** from the DATA disk. You are going to change the file and try to save the changed file to the DATA disk.

Step 18 Key in the following: **TTTT** Enter

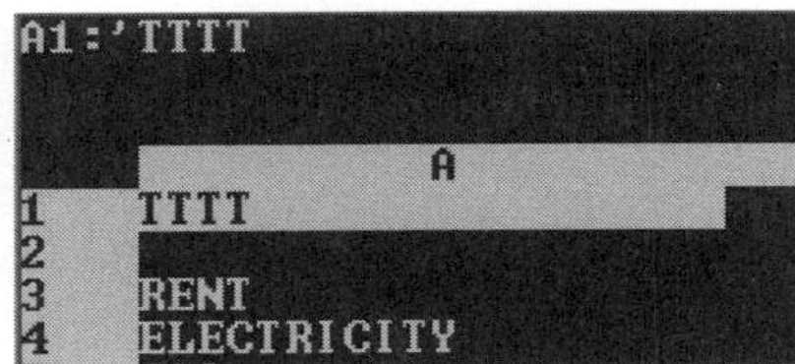

You have keyed in some characters, **TTTT**, changing the data file.

Step 19 Press **/**.

Step 20 Press **F**.

Step 21 Press **S**.

Step 22 Press Enter to accept the current file name.

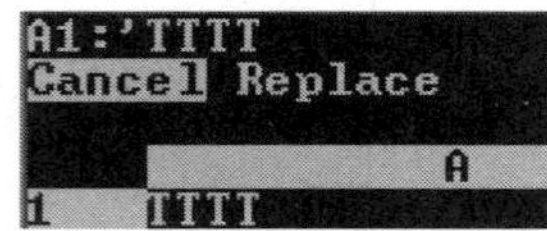

WHAT'S HAPPENING? This program asks if you want to replace an existing file.

Step 23 Press **R**.

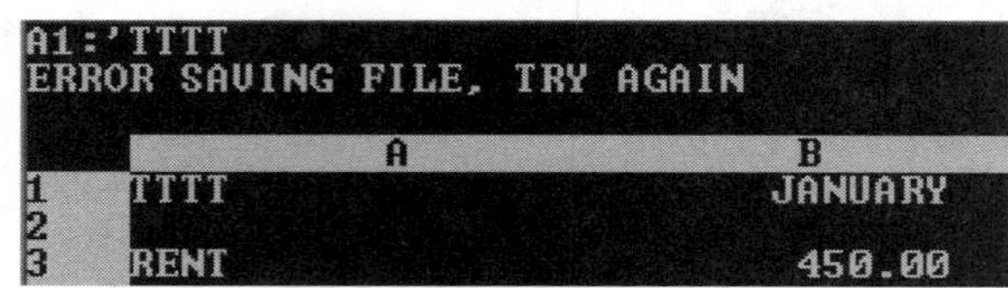

WHAT'S HAPPENING? The message indicates that on the DATA disk, the data file **A:\HOMEBUD.TKR** was flagged with the read-only attribute and cannot be overwritten.

Step 24 Press **/**.

Step 25 Press **Q**.

Step 26 Press **Y**.

WHAT'S HAPPENING? You have exited Thinker and returned to the system level. Your data file has not been changed on the DATA disk.

Step 27 Key in the following: C:\WINDOSBK\FINANCE>**CD ** Enter

Step 28 Key in the following: C:\>**A:** Enter

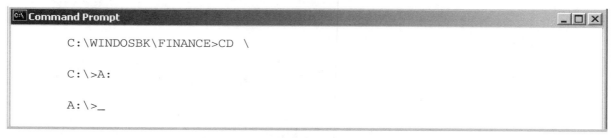

WHAT'S HAPPENING? You have returned to the root directory of the DATA disk. You may delete read-only files if you use the /F parameter with the DEL command.

Step 29 Key in the following: **A:\COPY STEVEN.FIL MARY.FIL** Enter

Step 30 Key in the following: **A:\>ATTRIB +R MARY.FIL** Enter

Step 31 Key in the following: **A:\>DEL MARY.FIL** Enter

Step 32 Key in the following: **A:\>DEL /F MARY.FIL** Enter

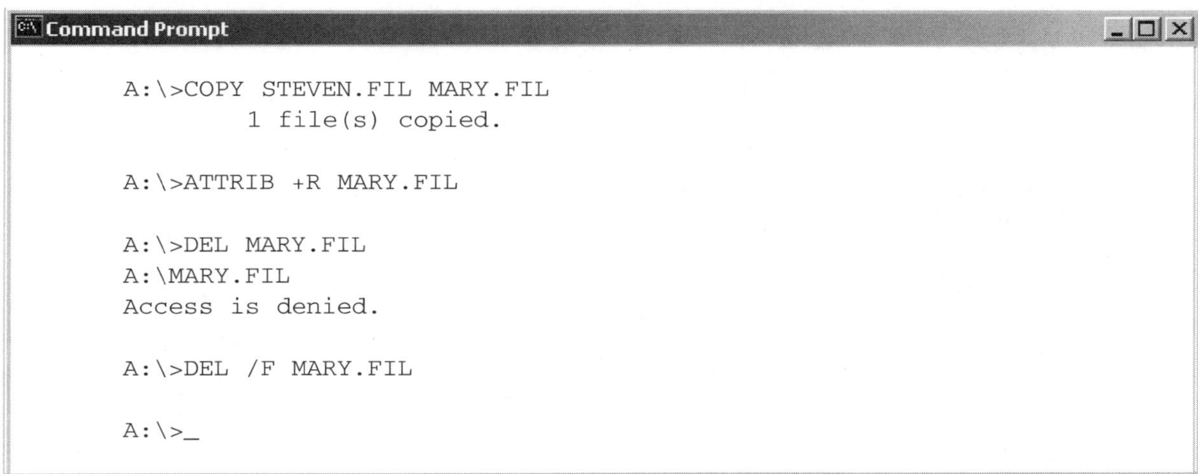

```
A:\>COPY STEVEN.FIL MARY.FIL
        1 file(s) copied.

A:\>ATTRIB +R MARY.FIL

A:\>DEL MARY.FIL
A:\MARY.FIL
Access is denied.

A:\>DEL /F MARY.FIL

A:\>_
```

You created a new file called **MARY.FIL**. You made it read-only and then attempted to delete it. Since it was read-only, you could not delete it with the DEL command ("Access is denied."). However, when you added the /F parameter to the DEL command to force deletion of a read-only file, you could successfully delete **MARY.FIL**.

7.3 USING THE HIDDEN AND ARCHIVE ATTRIBUTES WITH ATTRIB

The purpose of the H attribute is to hide a file so that when you use the DIR command, you will not see it displayed. Why would you want to hide a file? The most likely person you are going to hide the file from is yourself, and this seems to make no sense. The real advantage to using the hidden attribute is that it allows you to manipulate files. For instance, when you use the COPY or the MOVE command with wildcards, you may not want to move or copy specific files. When you hide files, neither COPY nor MOVE can see them so they are protected from manipulation. These are tasks you cannot perform in Windows Explorer. Although you can hide files and folders by right-clicking the file name, then clicking Properties, and then choosing the Hide attribute, it is much more difficult to perform file operations on groups of files simultaneously in Windows Explorer.

The A attribute uses certain commands to flag a file as changed since the last time you backed it up. These commands can read the attribute bit (A) and can identify if it has been set. If it is set (on), the commands that can read the archive bit know whether the file has changed since the last time it was copied. With the ATTRIB command, you can set and unset this flag to help identify what files you changed since the last time you backed them up. The following activity will demonstrate how you can use the H and A attributes.

7.4 ACTIVITY: USING THE H AND THE A ATTRIBUTES

Note: The DATA disk is in Drive A. A:\> is displayed.

Step 1 Key in the following: A:\>**COPY C:\WINDOSBK\FI*.*** Enter

Command Prompt

```
A:\>COPY C:\WINDOSBK\FI*.*
C:\WINDOSBK\FILE3.FP
C:\WINDOSBK\FILE3.SWT
C:\WINDOSBK\FILE4.FP
C:\WINDOSBK\FILE2.CZG
C:\WINDOSBK\FILE2.FP
C:\WINDOSBK\FILE2.SWT
C:\WINDOSBK\FILE3.CZG
        7 file(s) copied.

A:\>_
```

Step 2 Key in the following: A:\>**DIR F*.*** Enter

Command Prompt

```
A:\>DIR F*.*

 Volume in drive A is DATA
 Volume Serial Number is 3330-1807

 Directory of A:\

04/23/2000  04:03p                  75 FEB.BUD
04/23/2000  04:03p                  75 FEBRUARY.TXT
10/10/1999  04:53p                  75 FEB.99
03/05/2000  04:41p                 232 FUNNY.TV
07/31/1999  12:53p                  44 FRANK.FIL
12/06/2000  02:45p                  19 FILE3.FP
12/06/2000  02:45p                  19 FILE3.SWT
12/06/2000  02:45p                  19 FILE4.FP
12/06/2000  02:45p                  19 FILE2.CZG
12/06/2000  02:45p                  19 FILE2.FP
12/06/2000  02:45p                  19 FILE2.SWT
12/06/2000  02:45p                  19 FILE3.CZG
        12 File(s)            634 bytes
         0 Dir(s)      1,372,672 bytes free

A:\>_
```

WHAT'S HAPPENING? You copied all the files that begin with **FI** from the **WINDOSBK** subdirectory to the root directory of the DATA disk. Now you want to move all the files that begin with F to the **TRIP** subdirectory, but you do not want to move the files you just copied. The problem is that, if you use **MOVE F*.* TRIP**, all the files that begin with F will be moved, not just the ones you desire. You cannot say, "Move all the files that begin with F except the files that begin with FI." Here, the ability to hide files is useful.

Step 3 Key in the following: A:\>**ATTRIB +H FI*.*** Enter

Step 4 Key in the following: A:\>**DIR F*.*** Enter

```
Command Prompt

A:\>ATTRIB +H FI*.*

A:\>DIR F*.*

 Volume in drive A is DATA
 Volume Serial Number is 3330-1807

 Directory of A:\

04/23/2000  04:03p                  75 FEB.BUD
04/23/2000  04:03p                  75 FEBRUARY.TXT
10/10/1999  04:53p                  75 FEB.99
03/05/2000  04:41p                 232 FUNNY.TV
07/31/1999  12:53p                  44 FRANK.FIL
         5 File(s)            501 bytes
         0 Dir(s)       1,372,672 bytes free

A:\>_
```

WHAT'S HAPPENING? The files that begin with FI are hidden and will not be displayed by the DIR command. Now when you use the MOVE command, none of the hidden files, the **FI*.*** files, will be moved.

Step 5 Key in the following: A:\>**MOVE F*.* TRIP** Enter

```
Command Prompt

A:\>MOVE F*.* TRIP
A:\FEB.BUD
A:\FEBRUARY.TXT
A:\FEB.99
A:\FUNNY.TV
A:\FRANK.FIL


A:\>_
```

WHAT'S HAPPENING? You see that you accomplished your mission. The files you hid were not moved. What if you forget which files you hid? The /A parameter, which can be used with the DIR command, allows you to specify the kind of file you want to look for. The attribute choices are:

D	Directories	**H**	Hidden files
R	Read-only files	**A**	Files ready to archive

Step 6 Key in the following: A:\>**DIR /AH** Enter

```
Command Prompt

A:\>DIR /AH

 Volume in drive A is DATA
 Volume Serial Number is 3330-1807
```

```
 Directory of A:\

12/06/2000  02:45p                    19 FILE3.FP
12/06/2000  02:45p                    19 FILE3.SWT
12/06/2000  02:45p                    19 FILE4.FP
12/06/2000  02:45p                    19 FILE2.CZG
12/06/2000  02:45p                    19 FILE2.FP
12/06/2000  02:45p                    19 FILE2.SWT
12/06/2000  02:45p                    19 FILE3.CZG
               7 File(s)             133 bytes

        0 Dir(s)       1,372,672 bytes free

A:\>_
```

WHAT'S HAPPENING? The attribute you wanted to use was the hidden attribute (H). As you can see, the DIR /AH command displays only the hidden files. Now you can "unhide" the files.

Step 7 Key in the following: A:\>**ATTRIB -H FI*.*** Enter

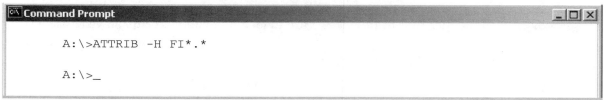

```
Command Prompt

A:\>ATTRIB -H FI*.*

A:\>_
```

WHAT'S HAPPENING? The **FI*.*** files are no longer hidden. You can manipulate other file attributes to assist you in managing your files. You can indicate what files have changed since the last time you copied them by changing the A, or archive, bit. When you create a file, the operating system automatically turns on the A attribute or "flags" it as new and not backed up. When you use certain commands, such as XCOPY, that command will turn off the A flag to indicate that the file has been backed up. Whenever you make a change to a file, the A attribute bit is turned on again or "re-flagged" to indicate that there has been a change since the last time you backed it up. You will learn later how this works when using the XCOPY command. You can also manipulate the archive bit directly with the ATTRIB command to let you know if you changed a file.

Step 8 Key in the following: A:\>**TYPE STEVEN.FIL** Enter

Step 9 Key in the following: A:\>**ATTRIB STEVEN.FIL** Enter

```
Command Prompt
A:\>TYPE STEVEN.FIL

Hi, my name is Steven.
What is your name?
```

```
A:\>ATTRIB STEVEN.FIL
  A    R     A:\STEVEN.FIL

A:\>_
```

WHAT'S HAPPENING? This file is protected with the R attribute. You can see the contents of it using the TYPE command. You set the R attribute. The operating system automatically set the A attribute.

Step 10 Key in the following: A:\>**ATTRIB -A -R STEVEN.FIL** Enter

Step 11 Key in the following: A:\>**ATTRIB STEVEN.FIL** Enter

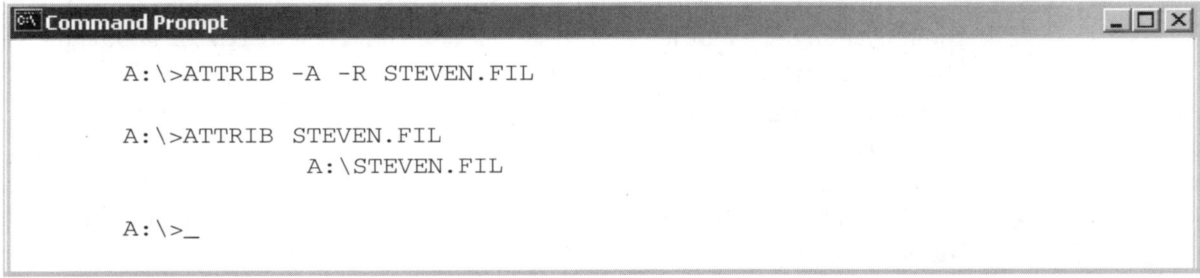

WHAT'S HAPPENING? You have turned off all the attributes of this file.

Step 12 Key in the following: A:\>**COPY TRIP\FRANK.FIL STEVEN.FIL** Enter

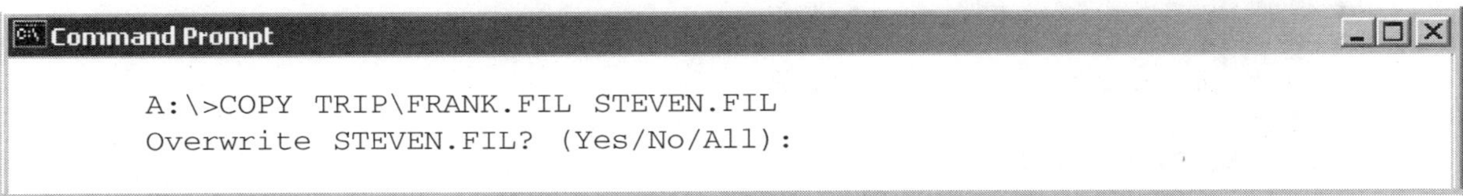

Command Prompt
A:\>COPY TRIP\FRANK.FIL STEVEN.FIL
Overwrite STEVEN.FIL? (Yes/No/All):

WHAT'S HAPPENING? Since the file is no longer read-only, you are asked if you want to overwrite the contents of **STEVEN.FIL** with **FRANK.FIL**.

Step 13 Press **Y** Enter

Step 14 Key in the following: A:\>**TYPE STEVEN.FIL** Enter

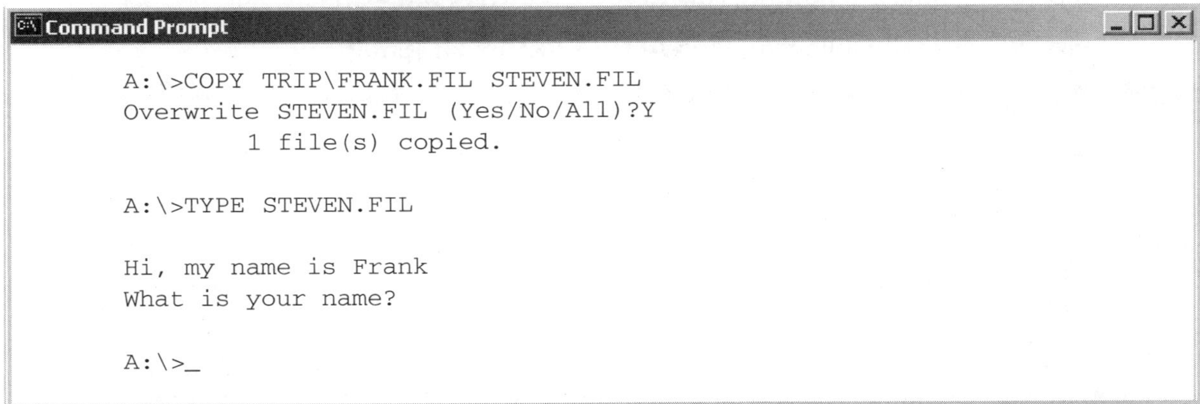

Command Prompt
A:\>COPY TRIP\FRANK.FIL STEVEN.FIL
Overwrite STEVEN.FIL (Yes/No/All)?Y
1 file(s) copied.
A:\>TYPE STEVEN.FIL
Hi, my name is Frank
What is your name?
A:\>_

WHAT'S HAPPENING? The file contents have clearly changed. This file is an ASCII or text file and can be read on the screen with the TYPE command. If this were a data file generated by a program, you could not use the TYPE command to see if the

contents had changed. By looking at the attributes of a data file, you could see that the file had changed.

Step 15 Key in the following: A:\>**ATTRIB STEVEN.FIL** Enter

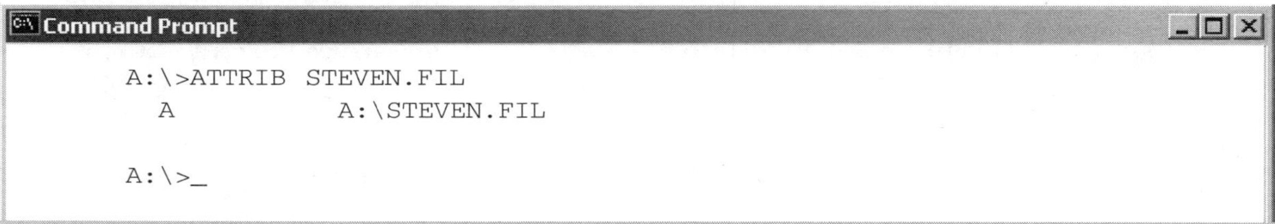
Command Prompt
A:\>ATTRIB STEVEN.FIL
A A:\STEVEN.FIL
A:\>_

WHAT'S HAPPENING? The A attribute or archive bit is once again turned on so that you know the file has changed. Another way of saying it is that **STEVEN.FIL** is flagged by the archive bit. If you had protected **STEVEN.FIL** with the read-only attribute, you would be protected from accidentally overwriting the file. Other operations do not work the same way. If you rename a file, it keeps the same file attributes, but if you copy the file, it does not carry the read-only attribute to the copy. Since this is a "new" file, the archive bit will be set automatically.

Step 16 Key in the following: A:\>**ATTRIB +R -A STEVEN.FIL** Enter

Step 17 Key in the following: A:\>**ATTRIB STEVEN.FIL** Enter

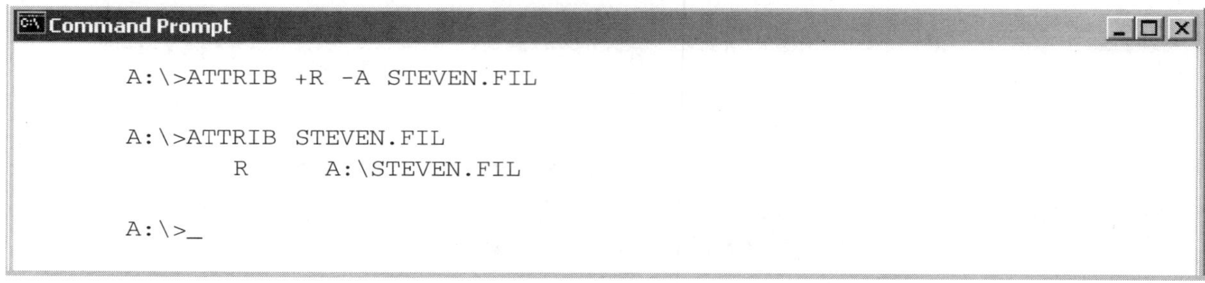
Command Prompt
A:\>ATTRIB +R -A STEVEN.FIL
A:\>ATTRIB STEVEN.FIL
R A:\STEVEN.FIL
A:\>_

WHAT'S HAPPENING? **STEVEN.FIL** is now read-only and has had the A flag turned off.

Step 18 Key in the following: A:\>**REN STEVEN.FIL BRIAN.FIL** Enter

Step 19 Key in the following: A:\>**ATTRIB BRIAN.FIL** Enter

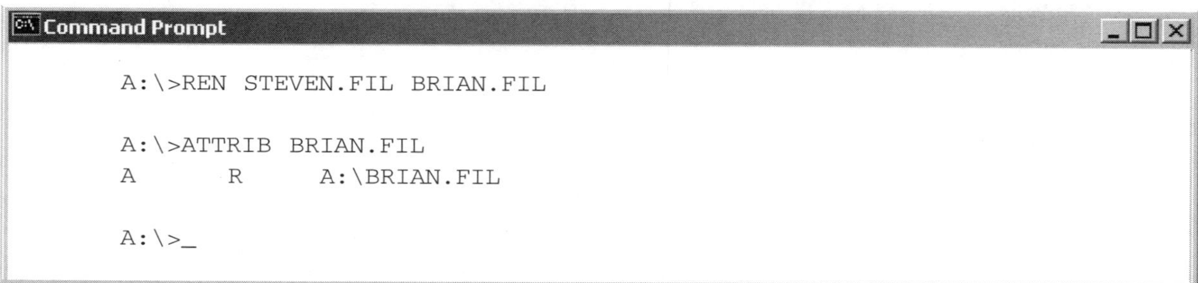
Command Prompt
A:\>REN STEVEN.FIL BRIAN.FIL
A:\>ATTRIB BRIAN.FIL
A R A:\BRIAN.FIL
A:\>_

WHAT'S HAPPENING? Even though you renamed **STEVEN.FIL** to **BRIAN.FIL**, **BRIAN.FIL** retained the read-only attribute that **STEVEN.FIL** had, plus the A attribute was added. It is the same file; you just renamed it. However, things change when you copy a file because you are creating a new file.

Step 20 Key in the following: A:\>**COPY BRIAN.FIL STEVEN.FIL** Enter

Step 21 Key in the following: A:\>**ATTRIB STEVEN.FIL** Enter

Step 22 Key in the following: A:\>**ATTRIB BRIAN.FIL** Enter

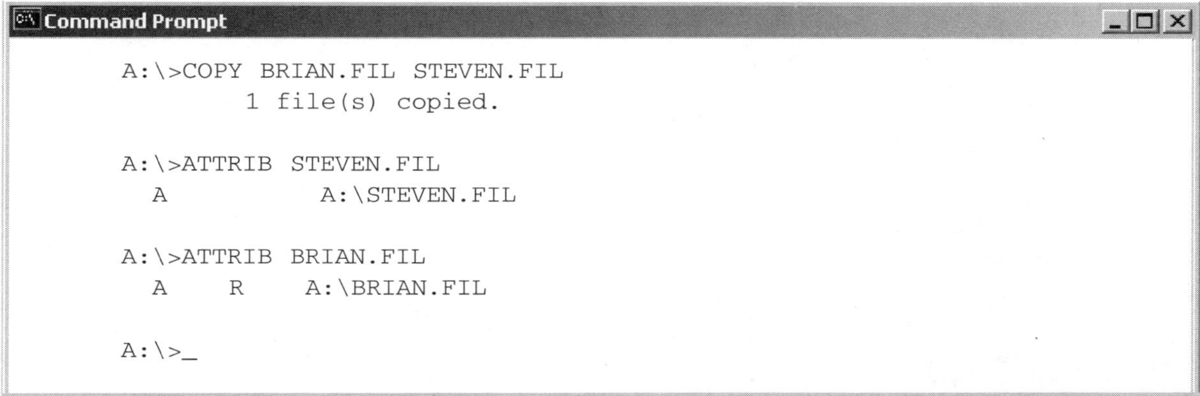
```
A:\>COPY BRIAN.FIL STEVEN.FIL
        1 file(s) copied.

A:\>ATTRIB STEVEN.FIL
  A           A:\STEVEN.FIL

A:\>ATTRIB BRIAN.FIL
  A    R     A:\BRIAN.FIL

A:\>_
```

When you copied **BRIAN.FIL**, which had a read-only file attribute, to a new file called **STEVEN.FIL**, the operating system removed the read-only attribute of the new file. **STEVEN.FIL** is not a read-only file. Thus, setting the read-only attribute is really most valuable for protecting you against accidental erasure of a file, not for any particular security reason. Remember that you set file attributes with the plus sign (+). You can unset file attributes with the minus sign (-). You can eliminate or add several file attributes with a one-line command, but there must be a space between each parameter, so follow the spacing of the command syntax carefully.

7.5 THE SUBST COMMAND

SUBST is an external command that allows you to substitute a drive letter for a path name. This command can be used to avoid having to key in a long path name. It can also be used to install programs that do not recognize a subdirectory but do recognize a disk drive. You can also use SUBST if you need information from a drive that a program does not recognize.

CAUTION!!! BE CAUTIOUS WHEN YOU USE SUBST WITH A NETWORK DRIVE. YOU MAY NOT BE ABLE TO USE SUBST ON THE NETWORK. AS NETWORKS USE LETTER DRIVE SPECIFICATIONS, BE SURE TO CHECK WITH YOUR LAB ADMINISTRATOR TO SEE IF YOU CAN USE THIS COMMAND SUCCESSFULLY, AND IF SO, WHAT DRIVE LETTER YOU ARE FREE TO USE.

On a stand-alone system, when you use SUBST and while a substitution is in effect, you should not use the commands LABEL, CHKDSK, FORMAT, DISKCOPY, DISKCOM, RECOVER, or FDISK. These commands expect a drive letter to represent an actual disk drive. The syntax for the SUBST command is:

```
SUBST [drive1: [drive2:]path]
```

or to undo a substitution:

```
SUBST   drive1: /D
```

and to see what you have substituted:

```
SUBST
```

7.6 ACTIVITY: USING SUBST

Note 1: You have the DATA disk in Drive A with A:\> displayed.

Note 2: If you have a Drive E on your own computer system you should pick a drive letter that is not being used, such as H: or K:. Remember that if you are in a lab environment you must check with your instructor to see if you can do this activity.

Step 1 Key in the following: A:\>**TYPE POLYSCI\USA\DRESS.UP** Enter

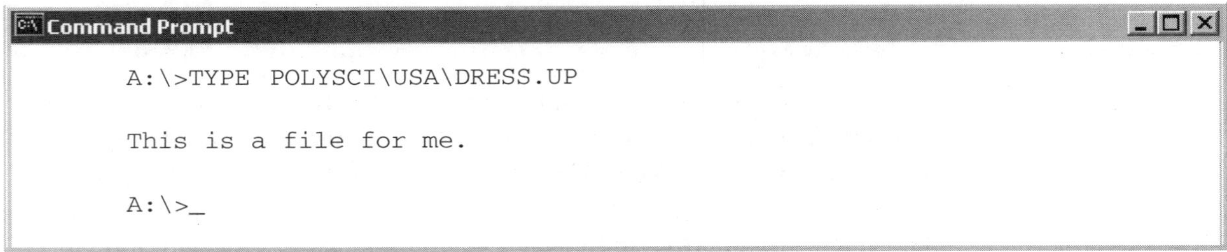

```
A:\>TYPE POLYSCI\USA\DRESS.UP

This is a file for me.

A:\>_
```

WHAT'S HAPPENING? You displayed the contents of the file called **DRESS.UP** in the subdirectory called **USA** under the subdirectory called **POLYSCI** in the root directory. Even though you left the first backslash off, since the default directory is the root, you still have a lot of keying in to do. If you use the SUBST command, you need to key in only the logical or virtual drive letter. In this example, E: is selected.

You are creating a virtual drive, one that exists temporarily. A virtual drive is also known as a logical drive. You are letting a drive letter represent an actual physical drive and path. Thus, you must be sure to use a drive letter that is not being used by an actual physical disk drive. If you have a floppy disk Drive A; a floppy disk Drive B; a hard disk that is logically divided into Drives C, D, and E; a removable drive such as a Zip drive that is Drive G; and a CD-ROM that is Drive H; your first available letter would be I. If, on the other hand, you had all the above drives except an actual physical Drive B, you could use B. Conceptually, this is how networks operate—a network takes a path name and substitutes a drive letter for the path. It appears to the user as a "real" drive and behaves like a real drive for COPY, MOVE, and other file and directory commands. However, since it is not a "real" drive, you cannot perform disk actions on it such as SCANDISK, format, or DISKCOPY. (*Note:* If you have a Drive E on your own computer system, you should pick a drive letter that is not being used, such as H: or K:. Remember, if you are in a lab environment, you must check with your instructor to see if you can do this activity.) Often, Drive B is not assigned to a drive letter and you may use B: instead of E:.

Step 2 Key in the following: A:\>**SUBST E: A:\POLYSCI\USA** Enter

Step 3 Key in the following: A:\>**TYPE E:DRESS.UP** Enter

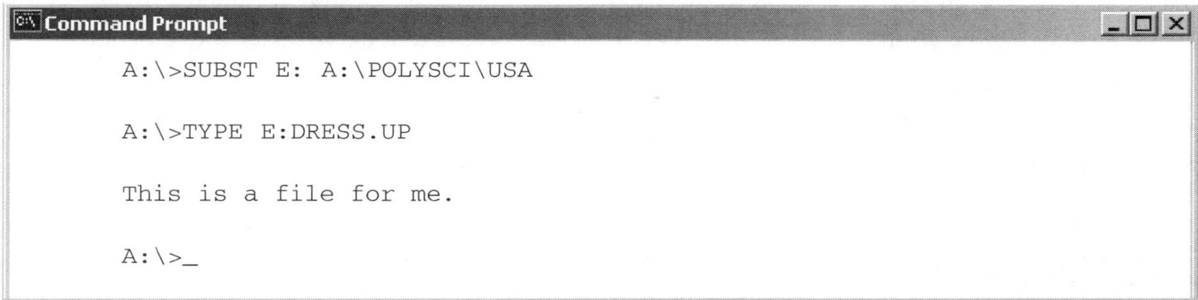

WHAT'S HAPPENING? You first set up the substitution. You said substitute the letter E for the path name **A:\POLYSCI\USA**. Now, every time you want to refer to the subdirectory called **A:\POLYSCI\USA**, you can just use the letter E, which refers to logical Drive E. You can use this logical drive just like a physical drive. You can use the DIR command, the COPY command, the DEL command, and just about any other command you wish.

Step 4 Key in the following: A:\>**SUBST** Enter

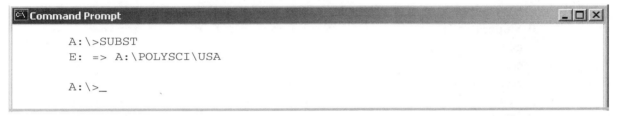

WHAT'S HAPPENING? SUBST, when used alone, tells you what substitution you have used.

Step 5 Key in the following: A:\>**SUBST E: /D** Enter

Step 6 Key in the following: A:\>**SUBST** Enter

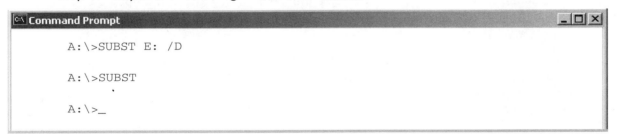

WHAT'S HAPPENING? The /D parameter disabled or "undid" the SUBST command so that logical Drive E no longer refers to the subdirectory **A:\POLYSCI\USA**. The SUBST that was keyed in with no parameters showed that no substitution was in effect. Most software today is quite sophisticated. For instance, if you have an older program that comes on a 5¼-inch disk and insists on running from Drive A but Drive A is a 3½-inch disk drive, you can solve the problem with SUBST. The biggest offenders are game programs and older installation programs. The solution would be as follows:

```
SUBST A: B:\
```

This command would reroute every disk request intended for Drive A to Drive B. The only tricky thing about this command is that you must include \ after **B:**. SUBST does not recognize a drive letter alone as a destination, so you must include the path.

7.7 THE XCOPY COMMAND

Although COPY is a useful internal command, it has some drawbacks, as you have seen. COPY copies one file at a time, even with wildcards, so it is a slow command. In addition, you cannot copy a subdirectory structure. If you have disks with different formats such as a 3½ inch disk and Zip disk, you cannot use DISKCOPY because the media types must be the same. You can, however, use XCOPY. Unlike COPY, XCOPY is an external command that allows you to copy files that exist in different subdirectories as well as the contents of a subdirectory, including both files and subdirectories beneath a parent subdirectory. It allows you to specify a drive as a source and assumes you want to copy all files on the drive in the default directory. With XCOPY you can copy files created on or after a certain date, or files with the archive bit set. XCOPY provides overwrite protection so that, if there is a file with the same name, XCOPY will request permission before overwriting the destination file with the source file. Furthermore, XCOPY operates faster than the COPY command. The COPY command reads and copies one file at a time, even if you use wildcards. XCOPY first reads all the source files into memory and subsequently copies them as one group of files. XCOPY will not, by default, copy system or hidden files.

XCOPY is a very powerful and useful command. With it you can copy files and subdirectories that have any attributes. You can also specify that the files and subdirectories copied *retain* their attributes. As you remember, when you use COPY to make a copy of a file, the copy does not have the same attributes as the source file. The attributes are lost when the file is copied. There are further advantages to using the command line over using Windows Explorer. When dragging and dropping to copy files and directory structures, it is easy to "miss" your destination. If you want to be specific, it is easier to key in commands than to drag and drop. In addition, you can perform file operations on a group of files rather than one file at a time.

There are many parameters available when using the XCOPY command. The full syntax is:

```
Copies files and directory trees.

XCOPY source [destination] [/A | /M] [/D[:date]] [/P] [/S [/E]] [/V] [/W]
                           [/C] [/I] [/Q] [/F] [/L] [/H] [/R] [/T] [/U]
                           [/K] [/N] [/O] [/X] [/Y] [/-Y] [/Z]
                           [/EXCLUDE:file1[+file2][+file3]...]

  source       Specifies the file(s) to copy.
  destination  Specifies the location and/or name of new files.
  /A           Copies only files with the archive attribute set,
               doesn't change the attribute.
  /M           Copies only files with the archive attribute set,
               turns off the archive attribute.
  /D:m-d-y     Copies files changed on or after the specified date.
```

```
              If no date is given, copies only those files whose
              source time is newer than the destination time.
  /EXCLUDE:file1[+file2][+file3]...
              Specifies a list of files containing strings.  When any of the
              strings match any part of the absolute path of the file to be
              copied, that file will be excluded from being copied.  For
              example, specifying a string like \obj\ or .obj will exclude
              all files underneath the directory obj or all files with the
              .obj extension respectively.
  /P          Prompts you before creating each destination file.
  /S          Copies directories and subdirectories except empty ones.
  /E          Copies directories and subdirectories, including empty ones.
              Same as /S /E. May be used to modify /T.
  /V          Verifies each new file.
  /W          Prompts you to press a key before copying.
  /C          Continues copying even if errors occur.
  /I          If destination does not exist and copying more than one file,
              assumes that destination must be a directory.
  /Q          Does not display file names while copying.
  /F          Displays full source and destination file names while copying.
  /L          Displays files that would be copied.
  /H          Copies hidden and system files also.
  /R          Overwrites read-only files.
  /T          Creates directory structure, but does not copy files. Does not
              include empty directories or subdirectories. /T /E includes
              empty directories and subdirectories.
  /U          Copies only files that already exist in destination.
  /K          Copies attributes. Normal Xcopy will reset read-only
              attributes.
  /N          Copies using the generated short names.
  /O          Copies file ownership and ACL information.
  /X          Copies file audit settings (implies /O).
  /Y          Suppresses prompting to confirm you want to overwrite an
              existing destination file.
  /-Y         Causes prompting to confirm you want to overwrite an
              existing destination file.
  /Z          Copies networked files in restartable mode.

The switch /Y may be preset in the COPYCMD environment variable.
This may be overridden with /-Y on the command line.
```

These parameters give XCOPY a great deal of versatility.

7.8 ACTIVITY: USING THE XCOPY COMMAND

Note: You have the DATA disk in Drive A with A:\> displayed.

Step 1 Key in the following: A:\>**DIR C:\WINDOSBK\MEDIA** Enter

Step 2 Key in the following: A:\>**DIR C:\WINDOSBK\MEDIA\BOOKS** Enter

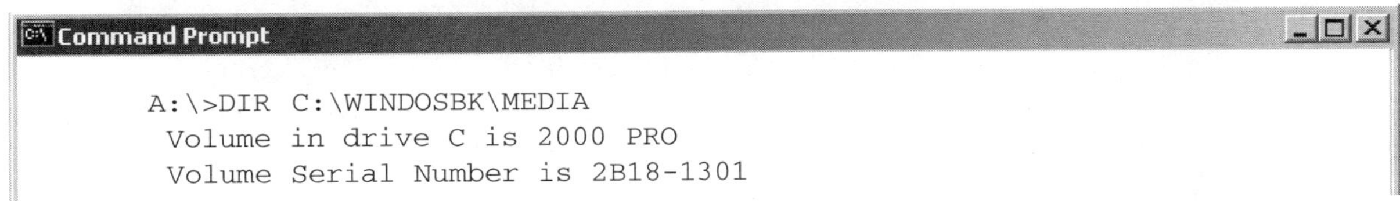


```
A:\>DIR C:\WINDOSBK\MEDIA
 Volume in drive C is 2000 PRO
 Volume Serial Number is 2B18-1301
```

```
Directory of C:\WINDOSBK\MEDIA

04/24/2001  09:40a      <DIR>          .
04/24/2001  09:40a      <DIR>          ..
07/03/2000  01:53p      <DIR>          BOOKS
07/03/2000  01:53p      <DIR>          TV
07/03/2000  01:53p      <DIR>          MOVIES

         0 File(s)              0 bytes
         5 Dir(s)   1,028,886,528 bytes free

A:\>DIR C:\WINDOSBK\MEDIA\BOOKS
 Volume in drive C is 2000 PRO
 Volume Serial Number is C4A7-8571

 Directory of C:\WINDOSBK\MEDIA\BOOKS

04/24/2001  09:40a      <DIR>          .
04/24/2001  09:40a      <DIR>          ..
08/08/2000  01:39p                 233 MYSTERY.BKS
08/08/2000  01:39p                 184 AME-LIT.BKS
08/08/2000  01:39p                 662 PULITZER.BKS

         3 File(s)          1,079 bytes
         2 Dir(s)   1,028,886,528 bytes free

A:\>_
```

WHAT'S HAPPENING? As you can see, the **MEDIA** subdirectory has three subdirectories: **BOOKS**, **TV**, and **MOVIES**. Each subdirectory has files in it as well. If you were going to use the COPY command to recreate this structure on your DATA disk, you would have to create the directories with the MD command and then copy the files in the **BOOKS**, **TV**, and **MOVIES** subdirectories. XCOPY can do all this work for you. You are still copying files, but you can consider XCOPY as a smart COPY command. When working with computers, you want the computer to do all the work, when possible.

Step 3 Key in the following: A:\>**XCOPY C:\WINDOSBK\MEDIA MEDIA /S** Enter

```
Command Prompt

A:\>XCOPY C:\WINDOSBK\MEDIA MEDIA /S
Does MEDIA specify a file name
or directory name on the target
(F = file, D = directory)?
```

WHAT'S HAPPENING? You asked XCOPY to copy all the files from the **WINDOSBK\MEDIA** subdirectory located on the hard disk to the **\MEDIA** subdirectory under the root directory of the DATA disk. In this case, XCOPY is a smart command. It asks you if you want to place all these files in one file or to create a subdirectory structure. In this case, you want to create the subdirectory structure. The /S parameter means to copy all the subdirectories and their files to the **MEDIA** subdirectory on the DATA disk. XCOPY is a command that does not care where you place /S. The command could have been written as **XCOPY /S C:\WINDOSBK\MEDIA MEDIA**, and it would also have been correct.

Step 4 Key in the following: **D**

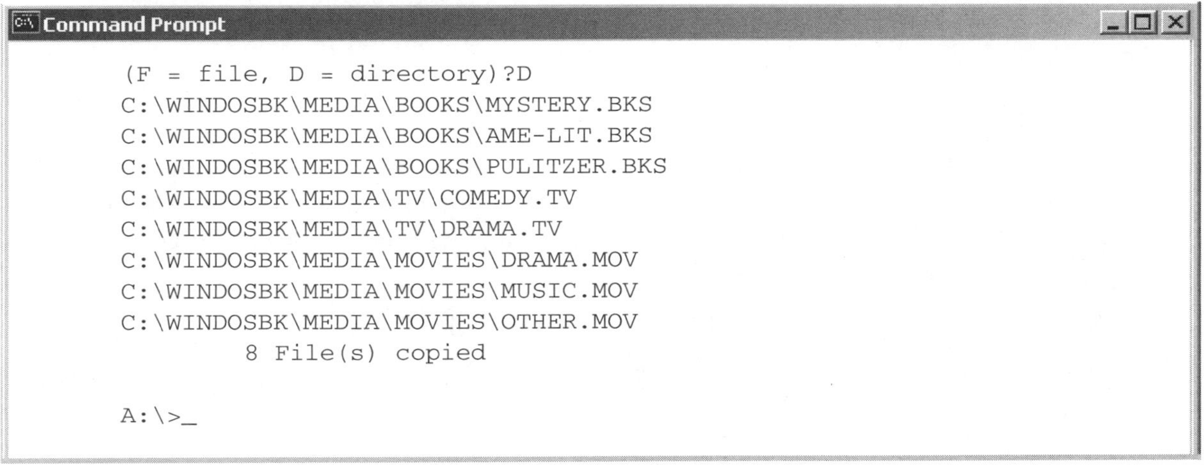

Command Prompt

```
(F = file, D = directory)?D
C:\WINDOSBK\MEDIA\BOOKS\MYSTERY.BKS
C:\WINDOSBK\MEDIA\BOOKS\AME-LIT.BKS
C:\WINDOSBK\MEDIA\BOOKS\PULITZER.BKS
C:\WINDOSBK\MEDIA\TV\COMEDY.TV
C:\WINDOSBK\MEDIA\TV\DRAMA.TV
C:\WINDOSBK\MEDIA\MOVIES\DRAMA.MOV
C:\WINDOSBK\MEDIA\MOVIES\MUSIC.MOV
C:\WINDOSBK\MEDIA\MOVIES\OTHER.MOV
        8 File(s) copied

A:\>_
```

WHAT'S HAPPENING? Since you included the /S parameter, XCOPY copied all the files from the subdirectory **\WINDOSBK\MEDIA**, including the subdirectories called **BOOKS**, **TV**, and **MOVIES** and their contents.

Step 5 Key in the following: A:\>**DIR MEDIA** Enter

Step 6 Key in the following: A:\>**DIR MEDIA\BOOKS** Enter

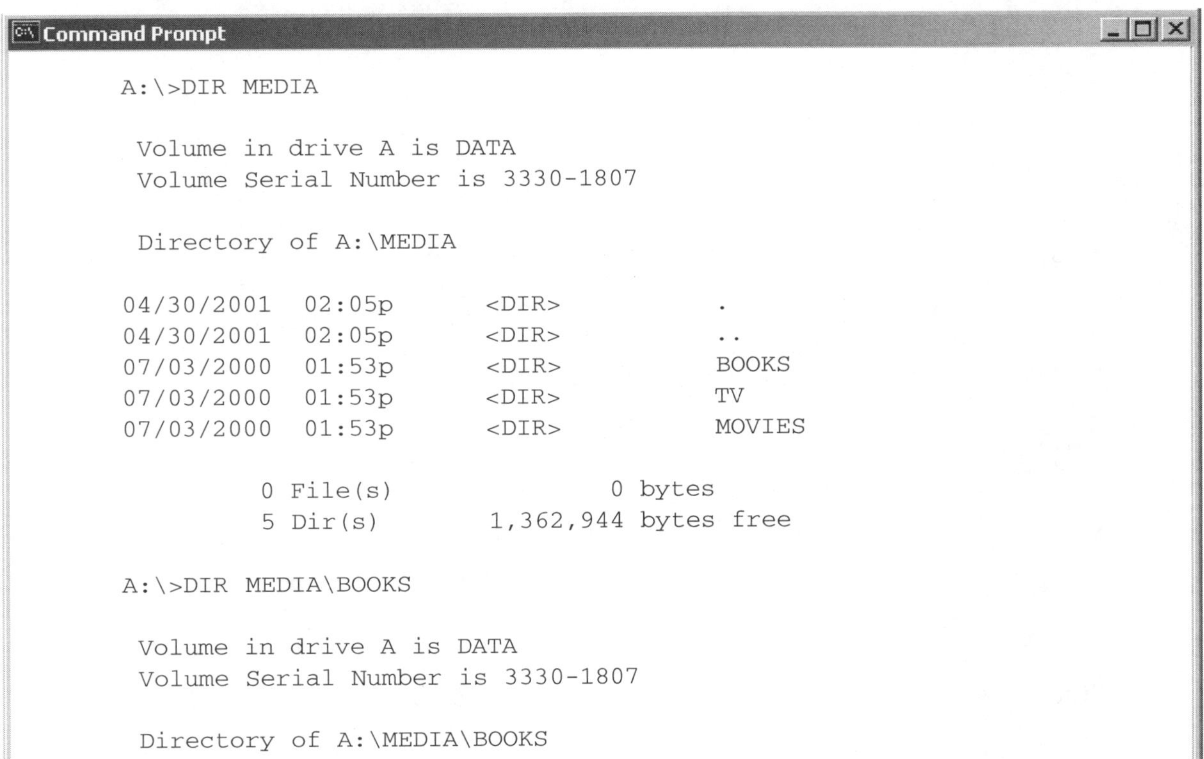

Command Prompt

```
A:\>DIR MEDIA

 Volume in drive A is DATA
 Volume Serial Number is 3330-1807

 Directory of A:\MEDIA

04/30/2001  02:05p      <DIR>          .
04/30/2001  02:05p      <DIR>          ..
07/03/2000  01:53p      <DIR>          BOOKS
07/03/2000  01:53p      <DIR>          TV
07/03/2000  01:53p      <DIR>          MOVIES

         0 File(s)              0 bytes
         5 Dir(s)       1,362,944 bytes free

A:\>DIR MEDIA\BOOKS

 Volume in drive A is DATA
 Volume Serial Number is 3330-1807

 Directory of A:\MEDIA\BOOKS
```

```
04/30/2001  02:05p      <DIR>          .
04/30/2001  02:05p      <DIR>          ..
08/08/2000  01:39p                 233 MYSTERY.BKS
08/08/2000  01:39p                 184 AME-LIT.BKS
08/08/2000  01:39p                 662 PULITZER.BKS

         3 File(s)        1,079 bytes
         2 Dir(s)      1,362,944 bytes free

A:\>_
```

WHAT'S HAPPENING? All the files and subdirectories were copied, and the subdirectory structure was retained. As you can see, XCOPY is a smart command with many useful parameters. One of the more useful ones is copying files modified or created after a certain date.

Step 7 Key in the following: A:\>**DIR C:\WINDOSBK*.TXT** Enter

```
Command Prompt

A:\>DIR C:\WINDOSBK\*.TXT
 Volume in drive C is 2000-PRO
 Volume Serial Number is C4A7-8571

 Directory of C:\WINDOSBK

01/01/2002  04:32a                  34 GOODBYE.TXT
06/16/2000  04:32p                  72 APRIL.TXT
06/16/2000  04:32p                  73 JANUARY.TXT
06/16/2000  04:32p                  75 FEBRUARY.TXT
06/16/2000  04:32p                  71 MARCH.TXT
05/30/2000  04:32p                  53 HELLO.TXT
05/30/2000  04:32p                  45 BYE.TXT
12/11/1999  04:03p                  72 DANCES.TXT
12/11/1999  04:03p                  65 TEST.TXT
11/16/2000  12:00p                  53 Sandy and Nicki.txt
11/16/2000  12:00p                  59 Sandy and Patty.txt
05/27/2001  10:08p                  81 LONGFILENAME.TXT
05/27/2001  10:42p                  97 LONGFILENAMING.TXT
05/27/2001  10:43p                  95 LONGFILENAMED.TXT
              14 File(s)            945 bytes
               0 Dir(s)     515,047,424 bytes free

A:\>_
```

WHAT'S HAPPENING? You want to copy all the **.TXT** files that were created on or after 05-01-00 to the root directory of the DATA disk. You do not want to copy the files **TEST.TXT** and **DANCES.TXT**. The XCOPY command allows you to make choices by date. In the following step, overwrite files if necessary.

Step 8 Key in the following: A:\>**XCOPY C:\WINDOSBK*.TXT /D:05-01-00** Enter

```
Command Prompt

A:\>XCOPY C:\WINDOSBK\*.TXT /D:05-01-00
C:\WINDOSBK\GOODBYE.TXT
C:\WINDOSBK\APRIL.TXT
Overwrite A:\JANUARY.TXT (Yes/No/All)?
```

WHAT'S HAPPENING? Remember the default for XCOPY is to confirm overwrites. The command is telling you that **JANUARY.TXT** already exists. In this case, you want to overwrite all the files.

Step 9 Press **A** Enter

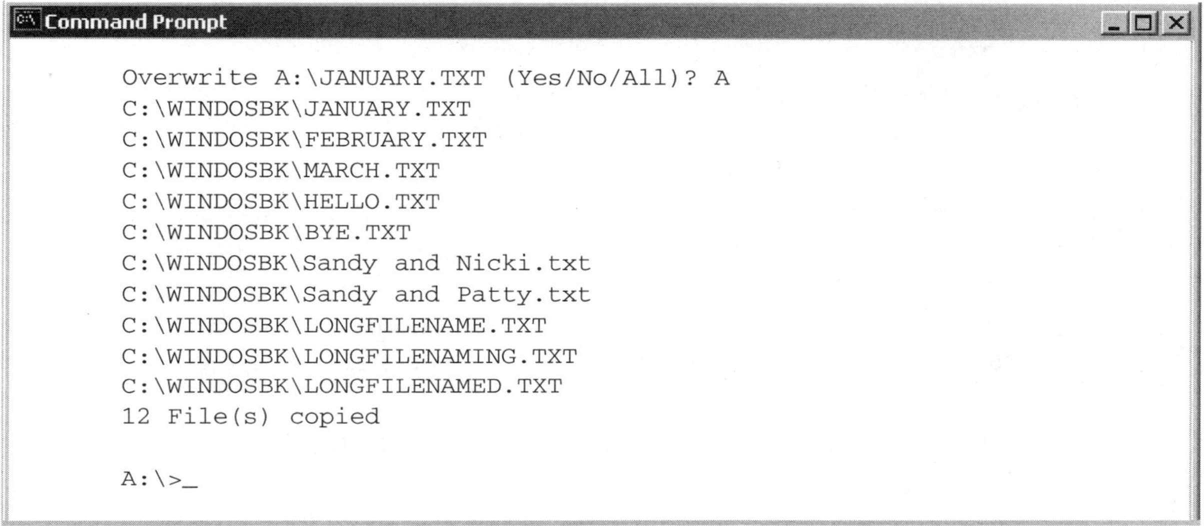

```
Command Prompt

Overwrite A:\JANUARY.TXT (Yes/No/All)? A
C:\WINDOSBK\JANUARY.TXT
C:\WINDOSBK\FEBRUARY.TXT
C:\WINDOSBK\MARCH.TXT
C:\WINDOSBK\HELLO.TXT
C:\WINDOSBK\BYE.TXT
C:\WINDOSBK\Sandy and Nicki.txt
C:\WINDOSBK\Sandy and Patty.txt
C:\WINDOSBK\LONGFILENAME.TXT
C:\WINDOSBK\LONGFILENAMING.TXT
C:\WINDOSBK\LONGFILENAMED.TXT
12 File(s) copied

A:\>_
```

WHAT'S HAPPENING? You copied only the 12 files of interest and not all 14 files that were in the **\WINDOSBK** subdirectory. Furthermore, you can use the XCOPY command to copy only files that have changed since the last time you copied them with XCOPY. Remember, XCOPY can manipulate the A attribute (archive bit).

Step 10 Key in the following: A:\>**ATTRIB *.BUD** Enter

Note: Do not be concerned if your files display in a different order than shown here.

```
Command Prompt

A:\>ATTRIB *.BUD
  A          A:\JAN.BUD
  A          A:\MAR.BUD
  A          A:\APR.BUD

A:\>_
```

WHAT'S HAPPENING? The files with the extension of **.BUD** have the archive attribute turned on.

Step 11 Key in the following: A:\>**XCOPY /M *.BUD CLASS** Enter

Step 12 Key in the following: A:\>**ATTRIB *.BUD** Enter

Command Prompt

```
A:\>XCOPY /M *.BUD CLASS
A:JAN.BUD
A:MAR.BUD
A:APR.BUD
        3 File(s) copied

A:\>ATTRIB *.BUD
             A:\JAN.BUD
             A:\MAR.BUD
             A:\APR.BUD

A:\>_
```

WHAT'S HAPPENING? When you used the /M parameter, it read the attribute bit for the ***.BUD** files and, as it copied each file to the **CLASS** directory, it turned off the archive bit on the source file.

To see how XCOPY can use the archive bit, you are going to make a change to the **APR.BUD** file by using COPY to copy over the contents of **APR.BUD** with the contents of **FILE2.FP**. You will then use the ATTRIB command to see that the A bit is back on because the file contents changed. When you next use XCOPY with the /M parameter, it will copy only the file that changed.

Step 13 Key in the following: A:\>**COPY FILE2.FP APR.BUD** Enter

Step 14 Press **Y** Enter

Step 15 Key in the following: A:\>**ATTRIB *.BUD** Enter

Command Prompt

```
A:\>COPY FILE2.FP APR.BUD
Overwrite APR.BUD (Yes/No/All)?Y
        1 file(s) copied.

A:\>ATTRIB *.BUD
             A:\JAN.BUD
             A:\MAR.BUD
  A          A:\APR.BUD

A:\>_
```

WHAT'S HAPPENING? Since **APR.BUD** already existed, COPY asked if you really wanted to overwrite it. You keyed in **Y** for "Yes." The **APR.BUD** file has changed since the last time you used XCOPY. When you used the ATTRIB command, you saw that the A bit for **APR.BUD** was turned back on.

Step 16 Key in the following: A:\>**XCOPY *.BUD CLASS /M** Enter

Step 17 Press **Y** Enter

Step 18 Key in the following: A:\>**ATTRIB *.BUD** Enter

```
Command Prompt

A:\>XCOPY *.BUD CLASS /M
Overwrite APR.BUD (Yes/No/All)?Y
        1 File(s) copied.

A:\>ATTRIB *.BUD
             A:\JAN.BUD
             A:\MAR.BUD
             A:\APR.BUD

A:\>_
```

WHAT'S HAPPENING? Once again, XCOPY informed you that you were about to overwrite an existing file in the **CLASS** subdirectory. You told XCOPY you wanted to do that. Notice that only one file was copied, **APR.BUD**, to the **CLASS** subdirectory. XCOPY read the attribute bit, saw that only **APR.BUD** had changed, and copied only one file, not all of the **.BUD** files. The XCOPY command then turned off the A attribute so that, if you make any further changes to any of the **.BUD** files, XCOPY will know to copy only the files that changed. XCOPY can also copy files that are hidden.

Step 19 Key in the following: A:\>**COPY C:\WINDOSBK*.TXT** Enter

Step 20 Key in the following: **A** Enter

```
Command Prompt

A:\>COPY A:\>COPY C:\WINDOSBK\*.TXT
C:\WINDOSBK\GOODBYE.TXT
Overwrite A:\GOODBYE.TXT? (Yes/No/All):A
C:\WINDOSBK\APRIL.TXT
C:\WINDOSBK\JANUARY.TXT
C:\WINDOSBK\FEBRUARY.TXT
C:\WINDOSBK\MARCH.TXT
C:\WINDOSBK\HELLO.TXT
C:\WINDOSBK\BYE.TXT
C:\WINDOSBK\DANCES.TXT
C:\WINDOSBK\TEST.TXT
C:\WINDOSBK\Sandy and Nicki.txt
C:\WINDOSBK\Sandy and Patty.txt
C:\WINDOSBK\LONGFILENAME.TXT
C:\WINDOSBK\LONGFILENAMING.TXT
C:\WINDOSBK\LONGFILENAMED.TXT
       14 file(s) copied.

A:\>_
```

WHAT'S HAPPENING? You have copied all the files with the extension **.TXT** from the **WINDOSBK** directory to the root of the DATA disk.

Step 21 Key in the following: A:\>**DIR *.TXT** Enter

Step 22 Key in the following: A:\>**ATTRIB +H SAN*.TXT** Enter

```
Command Prompt

A:\>DIR *.TXT
 Volume in drive A is DATA
 Volume Serial Number is 3330-1807

 Directory of A:\

06/16/2000  04:32p                  71 MARCH.TXT
06/16/2000  04:32p                  73 JANUARY.TXT
01/01/2002  04:32a                  34 GOODBYE.TXT
06/16/2000  04:32p                  72 APRIL.TXT
06/16/2000  04:32p                  75 FEBRUARY.TXT
05/30/2000  04:32p                  53 HELLO.TXT
05/30/2000  04:32p                  45 BYE.TXT
05/27/2001  10:08p                  81 LONGFILENAME.TXT
05/27/2001  10:42p                  97 LONGFILENAMING.TXT
05/27/2001  10:43p                  95 LONGFILENAMED.TXT
12/11/1999  04:03p                  72 DANCES.TXT
12/11/1999  04:03p                  65 TEST.TXT
11/16/2000  12:00p                  53 Sandy and Nicki.txt
11/16/2000  12:00p                  59 Sandy and Patty.txt
              14 File(s)            833 bytes
               0 Dir(s)       1,358,336 bytes free

A:\>ATTRIB +H SAN*.TXT

A:\>_
```

WHAT'S HAPPENING? You have used the DIR command to display all 14 files ending in **.TXT**. You have set the H attribute on for the two **.TXT** files that begin with SAN. Those files will no longer be listed by the DIR command.

Step 23 Key in the following: A:\>**DIR *.TXT** Enter

```
Command Prompt

A:\>DIR *.TXT
 Volume in drive A is DATA
 Volume Serial Number is 3330-1807

 Directory of A:\

06/16/2000  04:32p                  71 MARCH.TXT
06/16/2000  04:32p                  73 JANUARY.TXT
01/01/2002  04:32a                  34 GOODBYE.TXT
06/16/2000  04:32p                  72 APRIL.TXT
06/16/2000  04:32p                  75 FEBRUARY.TXT
05/30/2000  04:32p                  53 HELLO.TXT
05/30/2000  04:32p                  45 BYE.TXT
05/27/2001  10:08p                  81 LONGFILENAME.TXT
05/27/2001  10:42p                  97 LONGFILENAMING.TXT
05/27/2001  10:43p                  95 LONGFILENAMED.TXT
12/11/1999  04:03p                  72 DANCES.TXT
12/11/1999  04:03p                  65 TEST.TXT
```

```
                12 File(s)            833 bytes
                 0 Dir(s)       1,358,336 bytes free

A:\>_
```

WHAT'S HAPPENING? You have displayed all the files ending with **.TXT**, but only 12 files are displayed. The DIR command does not display hidden files.

Step 24 Key in the following: A:\>**MD HIDDEN** Enter

Step 25 Key in the following: A:\>**COPY *.TXT HIDDEN** Enter

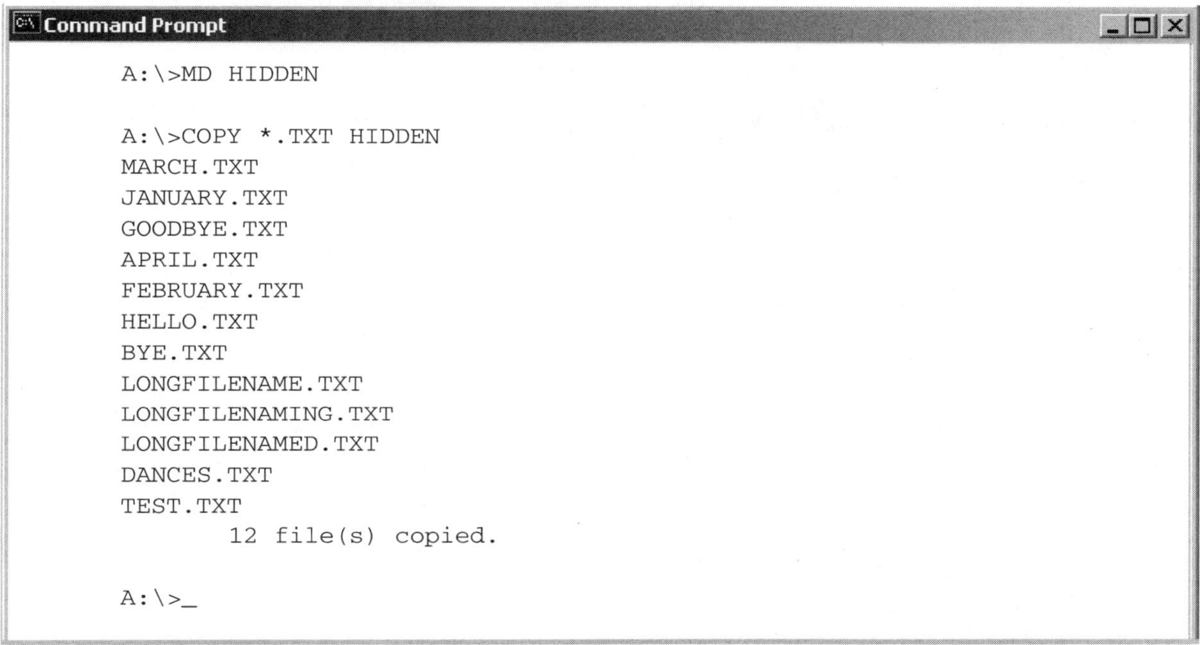

```
Command Prompt
A:\>MD HIDDEN

A:\>COPY *.TXT HIDDEN
MARCH.TXT
JANUARY.TXT
GOODBYE.TXT
APRIL.TXT
FEBRUARY.TXT
HELLO.TXT
BYE.TXT
LONGFILENAME.TXT
LONGFILENAMING.TXT
LONGFILENAMED.TXT
DANCES.TXT
TEST.TXT
        12 file(s) copied.

A:\>_
```

WHAT'S HAPPENING? Only 12 files were copied. The two hidden files were not copied.

Step 26 Key in the following: A:\>**XCOPY *.TXT HIDDEN /H** Enter

Step 27 Key in the following: **A** Enter

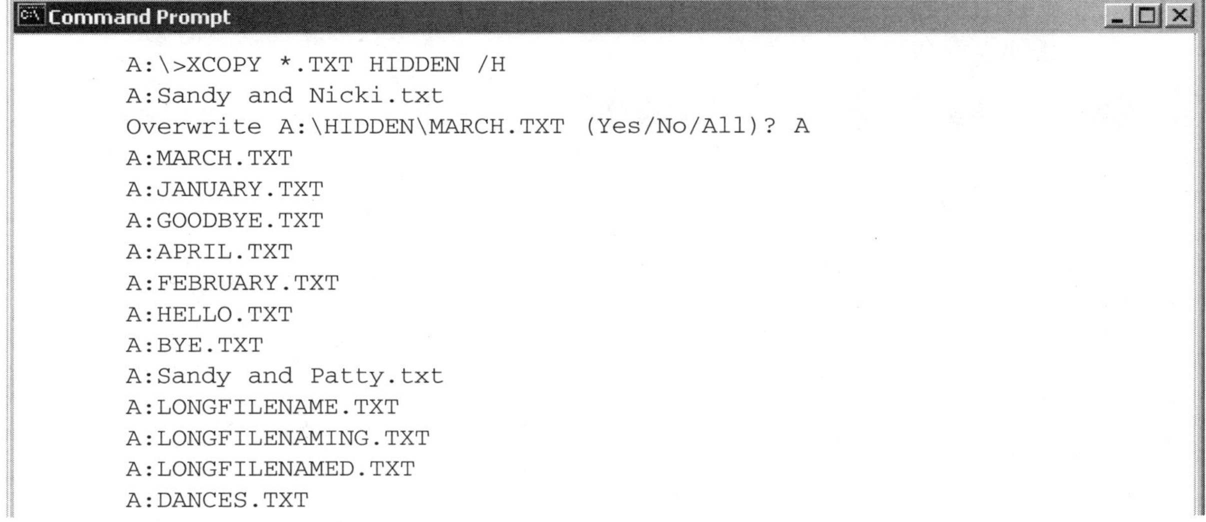

```
Command Prompt
A:\>XCOPY *.TXT HIDDEN /H
A:Sandy and Nicki.txt
Overwrite A:\HIDDEN\MARCH.TXT (Yes/No/All)? A
A:MARCH.TXT
A:JANUARY.TXT
A:GOODBYE.TXT
A:APRIL.TXT
A:FEBRUARY.TXT
A:HELLO.TXT
A:BYE.TXT
A:Sandy and Patty.txt
A:LONGFILENAME.TXT
A:LONGFILENAMING.TXT
A:LONGFILENAMED.TXT
A:DANCES.TXT
```

```
A:TEST.TXT
14 File(s) copied

A:\>_
```

WHAT'S HAPPENING? All the files ending with **.TXT** were copied, including the two files with the H attribute set.

Step 28 Key in the following: A:\>**CD HIDDEN** Enter

Step 29 Key in the following: A:\HIDDEN>**DEL *.*** Enter

Step 30 Key in the following: **Y** Enter

Step 31 Key in the following: A:\HIDDEN>**DIR** Enter

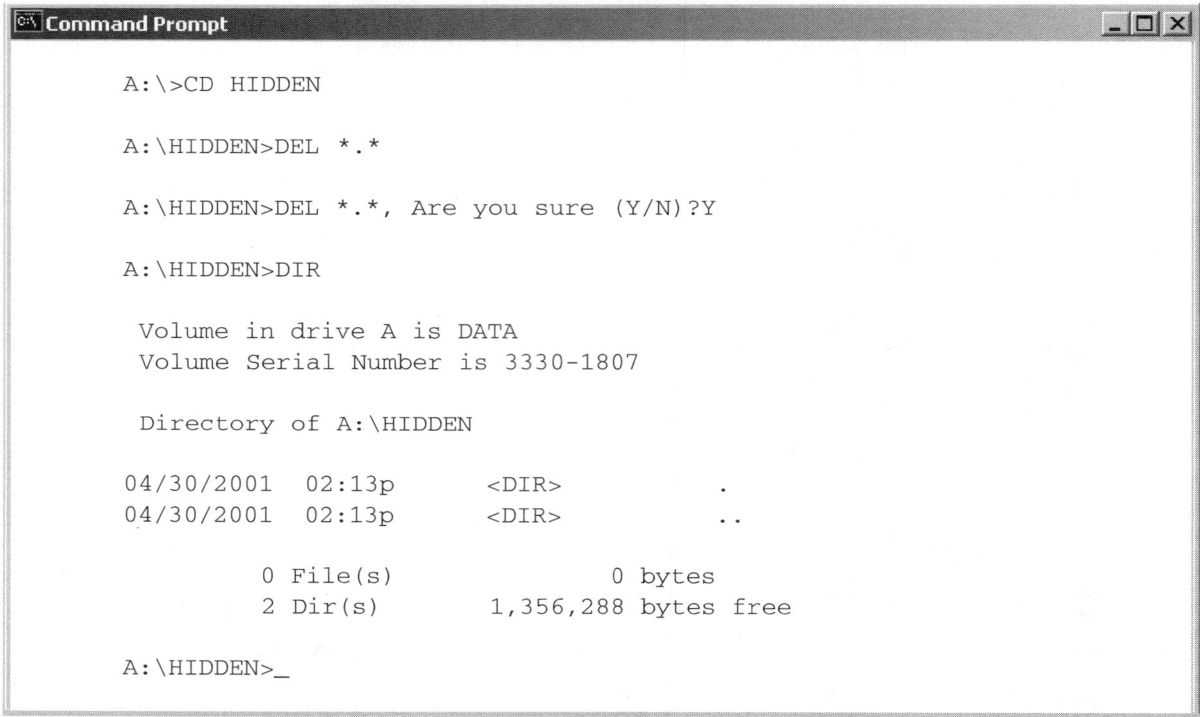

```
Command Prompt

A:\>CD HIDDEN

A:\HIDDEN>DEL *.*

A:\HIDDEN>DEL *.*, Are you sure (Y/N)?Y

A:\HIDDEN>DIR

 Volume in drive A is DATA
 Volume Serial Number is 3330-1807

 Directory of A:\HIDDEN

04/30/2001  02:13p      <DIR>          .
04/30/2001  02:13p      <DIR>          ..

         0 File(s)              0 bytes
         2 Dir(s)       1,356,288 bytes free

A:\HIDDEN>_
```

WHAT'S HAPPENING? It would appear that all the files have been deleted.

Step 32 Key in the following: A:\HIDDEN>**DIR /AH** Enter

```
Command Prompt

A:\HIDDEN>DIR /AH

 Volume in drive A is DATA
 Volume Serial Number is 3330-1807

 Directory of A:\HIDDEN

11/16/2000  12:00p                  53 Sandy and Nicki.txt
11/16/2000  12:00p                  59 Sandy and Patty.txt
```

```
               2 File(s)            112 bytes
               0 Dir(s)       1,356,288 bytes free

A:\HIDDEN>_
```

You have used the DIR command, asking it to display all files with the hidden attribute (/AH). You can see that there are still two files in the **HIDDEN** subdirectory. You did not delete them.

7.9 MULTIPLE XCOPY PARAMETERS

One of the advantages of using XCOPY is the ability to perform file operations on hidden, system, and even read-only files. You can use XCOPY to manipulate files that have one or more attributes set. As you become a more sophisticated computer user, you will find that you need to troubleshoot different kinds of computer problems to protect your Windows environment. Here you will find commands like XCOPY invaluable because you can accomplish tasks at the command line that you cannot accomplish in the graphical user interface.

In the last activity, in the A:\HIDDEN directory, there were two files that had the hidden attribute set. Now you want to copy these files to a new directory without removing the H attribute.

7.10 ACTIVITY: USING MULTIPLE XCOPY PARAMETERS

Note: The DATA disk is in Drive A and A:\HIDDEN> is displayed.

Step 1 Key in the following: A:\HIDDEN>**MD HOLD** Enter

Step 2 Key in the following: A:\HIDDEN>**XCOPY *.TXT HOLD /H** Enter

```
Command Prompt

A:\HIDDEN>MD HOLD

A:\HIDDEN>XCOPY *.TXT HOLD /H
A:Sandy and Nicki.txt
A:Sandy and Patty.txt
        2 File(s) copied

A:\HIDDEN>_
```

You can see from the display that the two hidden files were copied to the new **HOLD** directory. Did the copies of the files retain the hidden attribute?

Step 3 Key in the following: A:\HIDDEN>**DIR HOLD** Enter

```
Command Prompt

A:\HIDDEN>DIR HOLD

 Volume in drive A is DATA
 Volume Serial Number is 3330-1807
```

```
 Directory of A:\HIDDEN\HOLD

04/30/2001  02:15p      <DIR>          .
04/30/2001  02:15p      <DIR>          ..

         0 File(s)              0 bytes
         2 Dir(s)       1,354,752 bytes free

A:\HIDDEN>_
```

WHAT'S HAPPENING? There are no visible files in the **HOLD** directory.

Step 4 Key in the following: A:\HIDDEN>**DIR HOLD /AH** Enter

Command Prompt

```
A:\HIDDEN>DIR HOLD /AH

 Volume in drive A is DATA
 Volume Serial Number is 3330-1807

 Directory of A:\HIDDEN\HOLD

11/16/2000  12:00p                  53 Sandy and Nicki.txt
11/16/2000  12:00p                  59 Sandy and Patty.txt

         2 File(s)            112 bytes
         0 Dir(s)       1,354,752 bytes free

A:\HIDDEN>_
```

WHAT'S HAPPENING? The hidden attribute was retained. You can manipulate files with other attributes. You can also find out which files would be copied by using the /L parameter. The /L parameter tells you what files would be copied. It does not copy them.

Step 5 Key in the following: A:\HIDDEN>**XCOPY \FILE*.* /L** Enter

Command Prompt

```
A:\HIDDEN>XCOPY \FILE*.* /L
\FILE3.FP
\FILE3.SWT
\FILE4.FP
\FILE2.CZG
\FILE2.FP
\FILE2.SWT
\FILE3.CZG
7 File(s)

A:\HIDDEN>_
```

WHAT'S HAPPENING? Using /L with the XCOPY command lists the files that will be copied.

Step 6 Key in the following: A:\HIDDEN>**COPY \FILE*.*** Enter

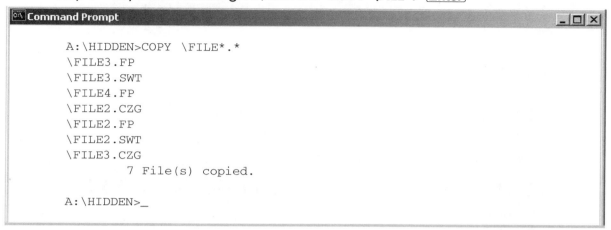

```
Command Prompt

A:\HIDDEN>COPY \FILE*.*
\FILE3.FP
\FILE3.SWT
\FILE4.FP
\FILE2.CZG
\FILE2.FP
\FILE2.SWT
\FILE3.CZG
        7 File(s) copied.

A:\HIDDEN>_
```

WHAT'S HAPPENING? Indeed, the files that were listed were copied. You have copied all the files that begin with FILE from the root directory to the **HIDDEN** subdirectory.

Step 7 Key in the following: A:\HIDDEN>**ATTRIB *.FP +R** Enter

Step 8 Key in the following: A:\HIDDEN>**ATTRIB +S *.CZG** Enter

Step 9 Key in the following: A:\HIDDEN>**ATTRIB *.SWT +S +H +R** Enter

```
Command Prompt

A:\HIDDEN>ATTRIB *.FP +R

A:\HIDDEN>ATTRIB +S *.CZG

A:\HIDDEN>ATTRIB *.SWT +S +H +R

A:\HIDDEN>_
```

WHAT'S HAPPENING? You have applied different attributes to the files you copied from the root directory. Notice that in Step 8, the file specification is listed last, while in Steps 7 and 9, it is listed first. Though this is not the case with most commands, with the ATTRIB command, the order of the parameters does not matter.

Step 10 Key in the following: A:\HIDDEN>**DIR** Enter

```
Command Prompt

A:\HIDDEN>DIR

 Volume in drive A is DATA
 Volume Serial Number is 3330-1807

 Directory of A:\HIDDEN

04/30/2001  02:13p      <DIR>          .
04/30/2001  02:13p      <DIR>          ..
```

```
04/30/2001  02:15p      <DIR>          HOLD
12/06/2000  02:45p                  19 FILE3.FP
12/06/2000  02:45p                  19 FILE4.FP
12/06/2000  02:45p                  19 FILE2.FP
               3 File(s)             57 bytes
               3 Dir(s)       1,350,144 bytes free

A:\HIDDEN>_
```

WHAT'S HAPPENING? Only the files ending with **.FP** are displayed. You can verify that all the files are there, as well as look at all the file attributes.

Step 11 Key in the following: A:\HIDDEN>**ATTRIB** Enter

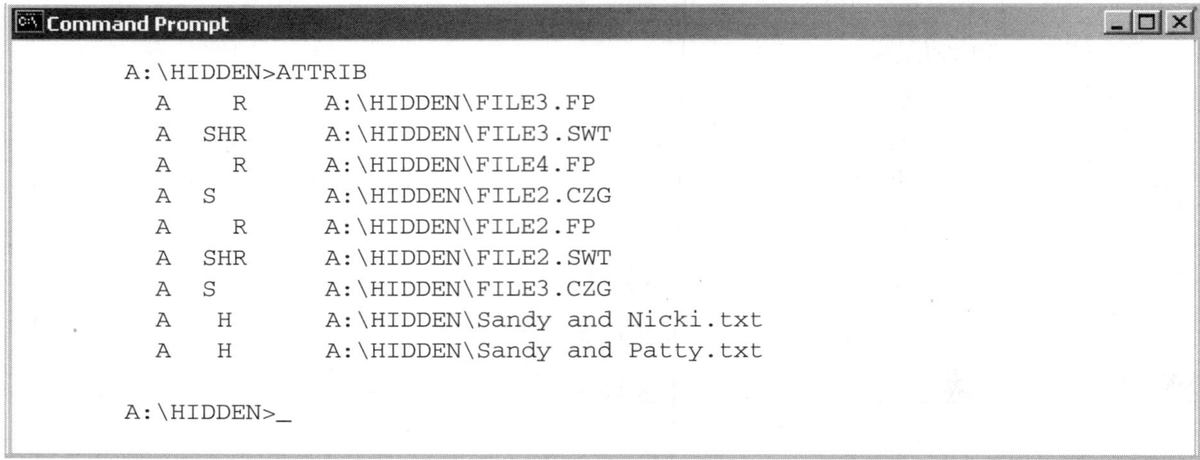

```
Command Prompt
A:\HIDDEN>ATTRIB
  A    R      A:\HIDDEN\FILE3.FP
  A  SHR      A:\HIDDEN\FILE3.SWT
  A    R      A:\HIDDEN\FILE4.FP
  A  S        A:\HIDDEN\FILE2.CZG
  A    R      A:\HIDDEN\FILE2.FP
  A  SHR      A:\HIDDEN\FILE2.SWT
  A  S        A:\HIDDEN\FILE3.CZG
  A   H       A:\HIDDEN\Sandy and Nicki.txt
  A   H       A:\HIDDEN\Sandy and Patty.txt

A:\HIDDEN>_
```

WHAT'S HAPPENING? You can see that all but five of the files have the hidden attribute set. You have discovered that files with only the S attribute set (the system attribute) are also hidden. Can you manipulate all of these files with different attributes at the same time?

Step 12 Key in the following: A:\HIDDEN>**CD ** Enter

Step 13 Key in the following: A:\>**MD HIDDEN2** Enter

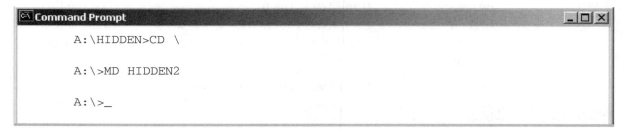

```
Command Prompt
A:\HIDDEN>CD \

A:\>MD HIDDEN2

A:\>_
```

WHAT'S HAPPENING? You have returned to the root of the DATA disk and created a new subdirectory named **HIDDEN2**.

You are going to copy the **HIDDEN** subdirectory with all its files and subdirectories to the new subdirectory **HIDDEN2**. To do this, you will use multiple parameters with the XCOPY command. The parameters you will use are as follows:

/S Copies directories and subdirectories except empty ones.
/H Copies hidden and system files.
/R Overwrites read-only files.
/I If the destination does not exist and you are copying more than one file, assumes that the destination must be a directory. If you do not include this parameter, you will be asked if you are copying to a directory or a file.
/E Copies directories and subdirectories, including empty ones.
/K Copies attributes. XCOPY will automatically reset read-only attributes.

These six parameters used together will copy everything, retaining all attributes. It may help you to remember them as SHRIEK. In this case, you had already created the directory, **HIDDEN2** so you did not need the /I. If you had not created it, you would have been queried whether the destination name was a file or a directory. Including the /I means that XCOPY will assume the destination is a directory.

Step 14 Key in the following:
A:\>**XCOPY HIDDEN HIDDEN2 /S /H /R /I /E /K** Enter

Command Prompt

```
A:\>XCOPY HIDDEN HIDDEN2 /S /H /R /I /E  /K
HIDDEN\FILE3.FP
HIDDEN\FILE3.SWT
HIDDEN\FILE4.FP
HIDDEN\FILE2.CZG
HIDDEN\FILE2.FP
HIDDEN\FILE2.SWT
HIDDEN\FILE3.CZG
HIDDEN\Sandy and Nicki.txt
HIDDEN\Sandy and Patty.txt
HIDDEN\HOLD\Sandy and Nicki.txt
HIDDEN\HOLD\Sandy and Patty.txt
       11 File(s) copied

A:\>_
```

WHAT'S HAPPENING? You copied all the files and subdirectories with one command. Did the copies of the files retain their attributes?

Step 15 Key in the following: A:\>**CD HIDDEN2** Enter

Step 16 Key in the following: A:\HIDDEN2>**ATTRIB /S** Enter

Command Prompt

```
A:\HIDDEN2>ATTRIB /S
  A    H      A:\HIDDEN2\HOLD\Sandy and Nicki.txt
  A    H      A:\HIDDEN2\HOLD\Sandy and Patty.txt
  A     R     A:\HIDDEN2\FILE3.FP
  A   SHR     A:\HIDDEN2\FILE3.SWT
```

```
  A    R      A:\HIDDEN2\FILE4.FP
  A  S        A:\HIDDEN2\FILE2.CZG
  A    R      A:\HIDDEN2\FILE2.FP
  A  SHR      A:\HIDDEN2\FILE2.SWT
  A  S        A:\HIDDEN2\FILE3.CZG
  A   H       A:\HIDDEN2\Sandy and Nicki.txt
  A   H       A:\HIDDEN2\Sandy and Patty.txt

A:\HIDDEN2>_
```

WHAT'S HAPPENING? You have verified that all the files you copied from the **HIDDEN** subdirectory to the **HIDDEN2** subdirectory have retained their attributes.

Step 17 Key in the following: A:\HIDDEN2>**CD ** Enter

Step 18 Key in the following: A:\\>**RD HIDDEN /S** Enter

Step 19 Key in the following: **Y** Enter

Step 20 Key in the following: A:\\>**RD HIDDEN2 /S** Enter

Step 21 Key in the following: **Y** Enter

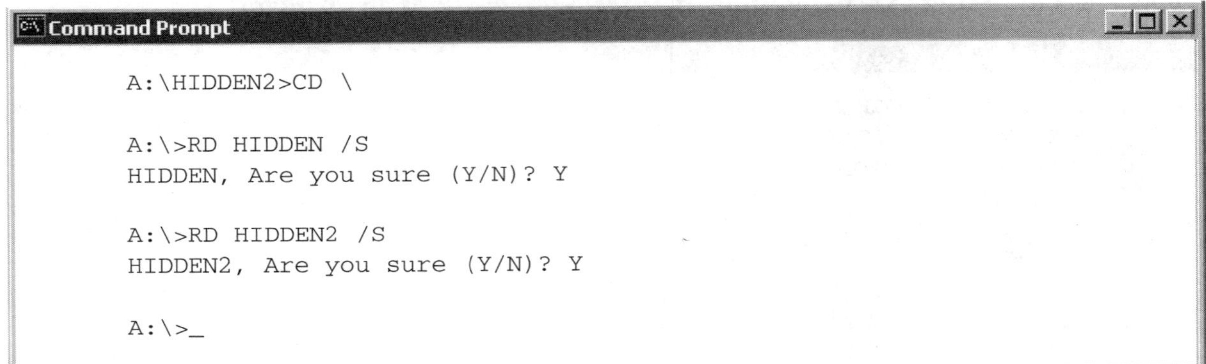

Command Prompt
A:\HIDDEN2>CD \
A:\>RD HIDDEN /S
HIDDEN, Are you sure (Y/N)? Y
A:\>RD HIDDEN2 /S
HIDDEN2, Are you sure (Y/N)? Y
A:\>_

WHAT'S HAPPENING? You returned to the root of the DATA disk and deleted the **HIDDEN** and **HIDDEN2** subdirectories along with all the files and subdirectories they contained.

Step 22 Close the Command Prompt window.

7.11 DOSKEY

DOSKEY enhances command line editing. You may already have used it to correct keystroke errors. DOSKEY is an external, memory-resident command that in Windows 2000 Professional is loaded automatically when you open a Command Prompt window. It keeps track of the last 50 commands that you enter when you are in the Command Prompt window and stores them in area of memory called the command history. You can, as you have been doing, recall those command from the command history and edit them. (See Table 2.1 in Chapter 2.) When you exceed 50 commands, the oldest commands are eliminated and replaced by the new commands. When you exit the Command Prompt window, all entries made during that work session are gone.

DOSKEY, though an external command, acts like an internal command, which means that you need not reload it from disk each time you wish to use it. Memory-resident commands are also referred to as ***TSR*** commands ***(Terminate Stay Resident)***. The normal process with any external command (program) is to execute it by keying in the command name. The operating system goes to the disk and looks for a program with that name, loads it into memory, and executes that program. When loaded, that program occupies and uses RAM. When you exit the program, the operating system reclaims the memory.

When you load a TSR, the process works initially as it does with any external command. You execute it by keying in the command name. The operating system goes to the specified or default drive and path and looks for the program with that name. The program is loaded into memory and executed. However, a TSR holds on to the memory it occupies, even while it is not actually being used or accessed. It does not release the memory for the duration of the Command Prompt work session. You may still load other programs, but the other programs will not use the memory that the TSR has claimed.

DOSKEY is loaded into memory when a Command Prompt window is opened. It remains there until you close the Command Prompt window. DOSKEY lets you recall command lines, edit them, keep a command history, and write macros. A macro is a command that you can define to automate a set of commands you often use. You may also increase the size the command history or see what is in the history file. The full syntax is as follows:

```
Edits command lines, recalls Windows 2000 commands, and creates macros.

DOSKEY [/REINSTALL] [/LISTSIZE=size] [/MACROS[:ALL | :exename]]
  [/HISTORY] [/INSERT | /OVERSTRIKE] [/EXENAME=exename] [/MACROFILE=filename]
  [macroname=[text]]

  /REINSTALL          Installs a new copy of Doskey.
  /LISTSIZE=size      Sets size of command history buffer.
  /MACROS             Displays all Doskey macros.
  /MACROS:ALL         Displays all Doskey macros for all executables which
                      have Doskey macros.
  /MACROS:exename     Displays all Doskey macros for the given executable.
  /HISTORY            Displays all commands stored in memory.
  /INSERT             Specifies that new text you type is inserted in old
                      text.
  /OVERSTRIKE         Specifies that new text overwrites old text.
  /EXENAME=exename    Specifies the executable.
  /MACROFILE=filename Specifies a file of macros to install.
  macroname           Specifies a name for a macro you create.
  text                Specifies commands you want to record.

UP and DOWN ARROWS recall commands; ESC clears command line; F7 displays
command history; ALT+F7 clears command history; F8 searches command
history; F9 selects a command by number; ALT+F10 clears macro definitions.

The following are some special codes in Doskey macro definitions:
$T     Command separator.  Allows multiple commands in a macro.
$1-$9  Batch parameters.  Equivalent to %1-%9 in batch programs.
$*     Symbol replaced by everything following macro name on command line.
```

7.12 ACTIVITY: USING DOSKEY

Note: A:\> is displayed and the path is set to **C:\WINNT\SYSTEM32**. The DATA disk is in Drive A.

Step 1 Open a new Command Prompt window.

Step 2 Key in the following:

C:\>**A:**
A:\>**DIR *.TXT** Enter
A:\>**DIR C:\WINDOSBK*.99** Enter
A:\>**VOL** Enter

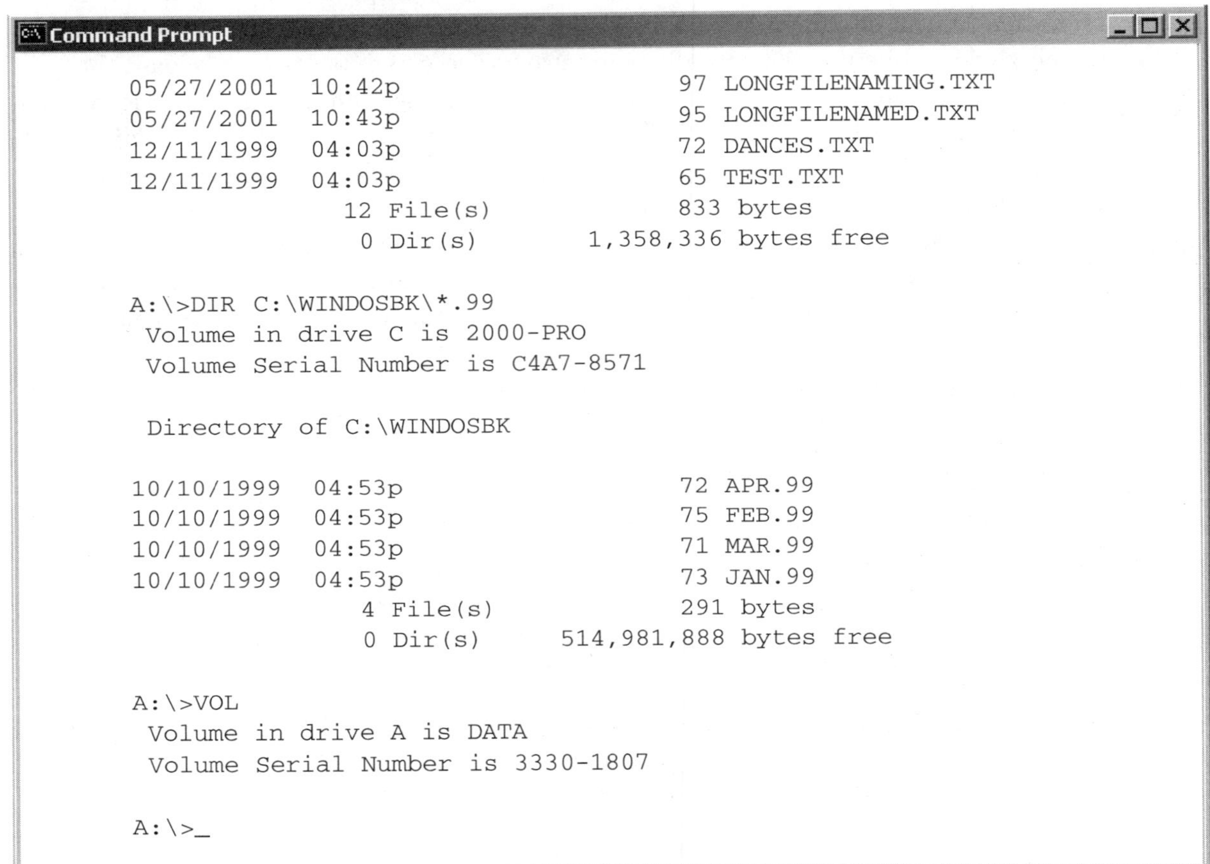

```
Command Prompt

05/27/2001  10:42p                    97 LONGFILENAMING.TXT
05/27/2001  10:43p                    95 LONGFILENAMED.TXT
12/11/1999  04:03p                    72 DANCES.TXT
12/11/1999  04:03p                    65 TEST.TXT
              12 File(s)             833 bytes
               0 Dir(s)        1,358,336 bytes free

A:\>DIR C:\WINDOSBK\*.99
 Volume in drive C is 2000-PRO
 Volume Serial Number is C4A7-8571

 Directory of C:\WINDOSBK

10/10/1999  04:53p                    72 APR.99
10/10/1999  04:53p                    75 FEB.99
10/10/1999  04:53p                    71 MAR.99
10/10/1999  04:53p                    73 JAN.99
               4 File(s)             291 bytes
               0 Dir(s)      514,981,888 bytes free

A:\>VOL
 Volume in drive A is DATA
 Volume Serial Number is 3330-1807

A:\>_
```

WHAT'S HAPPENING? (This graphic represents the tail end of what you see scroll by on your screen.) You have executed several commands and can now use the DOSKEY editing keys to recall and edit commands. If you want to see what is in the command history buffer, you can use the /HISTORY parameter.

Step 2 Key in the following: A:\>**DOSKEY /HISTORY** Enter

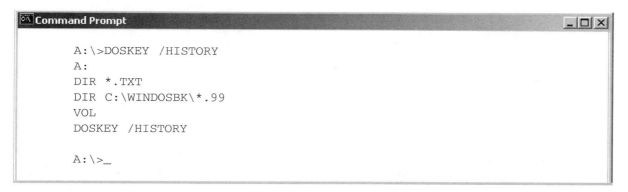

```
Command Prompt

A:\>DOSKEY /HISTORY
A:
DIR *.TXT
DIR C:\WINDOSBK\*.99
VOL
DOSKEY /HISTORY

A:\>_
```

You used the /HISTORY parameter to recall what commands you keyed in. Although this seems no different than using the **F7** key, there is one major advantage. Since this command writes the output to the screen, you could redirect the output to a file. If you do a certain series of repetitive tasks with a complicated set of commands, you can save those commands in a file. Later, when you learn about batch files, you could execute those series of commands with one command.

Step 4 Key in the following: A:\>**DOSKEY /HISTORY > TEST.BAT** **Enter**

Step 5 Key in the following: A:\>**TYPE TEST.BAT** **Enter**

```
Command Prompt

A:\>DOSKEY /HISTORY > TEST.BAT

A:\>TYPE TEST.BAT
A:
DIR *.TXT
DIR C:\WINDOSBK\*.99
VOL
DOSKEY /HISTORY
DOSKEY /HISTORY > TEST.BAT

A:\>_
```

You have saved the series of keystrokes you made in a file. You may also create a macro that will run a series of often-used commands. You, in essence, can create an alias for a command. You may also, in your macro, have more than one command on a line. You may actually have more than one command on a line in a Command Prompt window if you separate the commands with the &. If you wish to do this in a macro, you must use $T.

Step 6 Key in the following: A:\>**CD CLASS & DIR *.BUD & CD ** **Enter**

```
Command Prompt

A:\>CD CLASS & DIR *.BUD & CD \
 Volume in drive A is DATA
 Volume Serial Number is 3330-1807

 Directory of A:\CLASS
```

```
04/23/2000  04:03p                  73 JAN.BUD
04/23/2000  04:03p                  71 MAR.BUD
12/06/2000  02:45p                  19 APR.BUD
               3 File(s)           163 bytes
               0 Dir(s)      1,357,824 bytes free

A:\>_
```

WHAT'S HAPPENING? You issued more than one command on the command line using the & as a separator between the commands. Nonetheless, you needed to key all of the commands. If you used this command all the time, you could create a macro that would execute it for you.

Step 7 Key in the following:
A:\>**DOSKEY bb=CD CLASS$TDIR *.BUD$TCD ** Enter

Step 8 Key in the following: A:\>**bb** Enter

```
Command Prompt

A:\>DOSKEY bb=CD CLASS$TDIR *.BUD$TCD \

A:\>bb

A:\CLASS>

 Volume in drive A is DATA
 Volume Serial Number is 3330-1807

 Directory of A:\CLASS

04/23/2000  04:03p                  73 JAN.BUD
04/23/2000  04:03p                  71 MAR.BUD
12/06/2000  02:45p                  19 APR.BUD
               3 File(s)           163 bytes
               0 Dir(s)      1,357,824 bytes free

A:\CLASS>
A:\>_
```

WHAT'S HAPPENING? Since you saved those series of commands in a macro called **bb**, every time you wanted to execute those series of commands, you would only need to key in **bb**. However, once you close the Command Prompt window, those macros no longer exist. If you want to be able to reuse them, you can redirect the macros into a file.

Step 9 Key in the following: A:\>**DOSKEY /MACROS > b.bat** Enter

Step 10 Key in the following: A:\>**TYPE b.bat** Enter

```
Command Prompt

A:\>DOSKEY /MACROS > b.bat

A:\>TYPE b.bat
bb=CD CLASS$TDIR *.BUD$TCD \

A:\>_
```

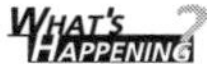

When you close the Command Prompt window, your macros are not saved. However, you have saved this macro in a batch file which you will edit in the next activity so you may reuse it.

7.13 THE COMMAND PROMPT TEXT EDITOR

There is no doubt that, for your writing needs, you will use a word-processing program such as Word or WordPerfect. Word-processing programs are extremely sophisticated and allow you full flexibility in creating and editing documents, including inserting graphics or using different fonts such as Century Schoolbook or Times New Roman. In order to retain all of your selections in your word-processing documents, there are special codes that only the word-processing program can read. These codes are entered as the document is formatted. Most word-processing programs will, however, allow you to save your document files as ASCII text, also referred to as text or as unformatted text, by stripping the formatting and saving only the keyed in text. This may puzzle you since, if you are creating a letter or a report, you want the formatting included when you print it. However, you will find that sometimes you need to "talk" to your computer. The only way you can talk to it or give the operating system instructions is by using a text file. Now you know why every operating system includes a ***text editor***.

The Windows operating system includes the applet called Notepad, which allows you to create text documents. If you are having troubles with Windows, you may need to edit certain text documents that the Windows operating system requires to operate. In addition, you will want to write batch files. These can be written only with a text editor. The command-line interface contains a text editor called Edit. It is a full-screen text editor for use in the Command Prompt window. It is not a word processor—it has no ability to format the data in documents. Edit cannot manipulate the environment with margin-size or page-length adjustments.

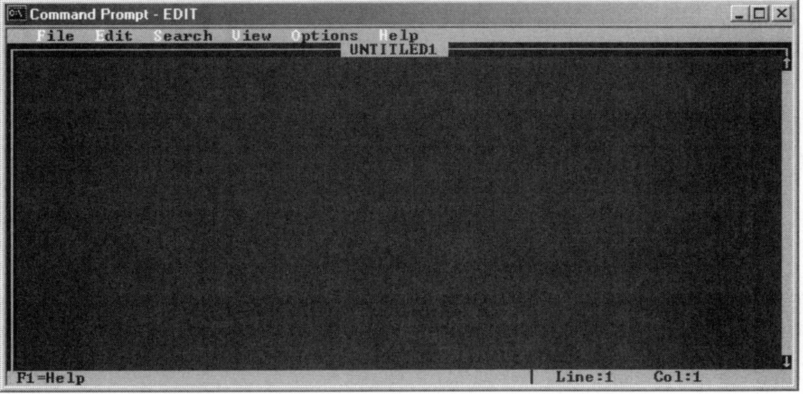

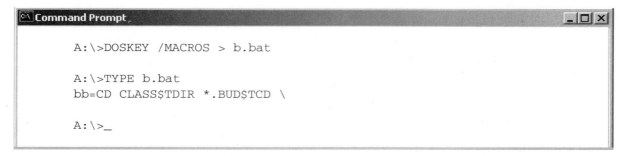

The Edit screen has a menu bar at the top and a status bar at the bottom. The status bar shows you the column and line where the cursor is currently positioned. Each menu contains further choices.

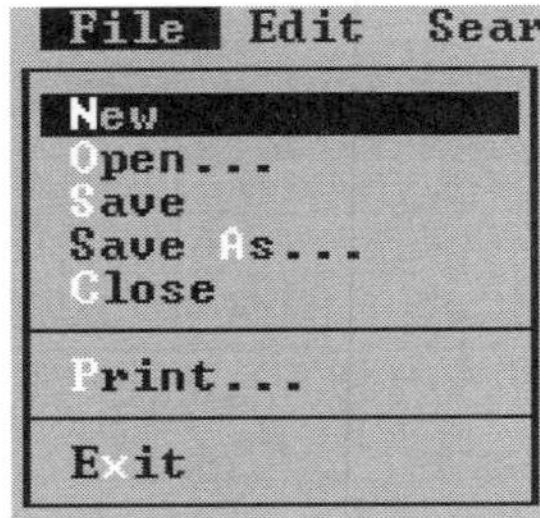

From the File menu, you can begin a New document, Open an existing document, Save a document, save a document under a new name (Save As), Print a document, and Exit the editor.

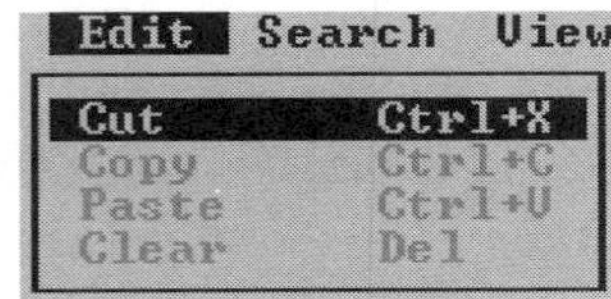

From the Edit menu, you can Cut selected text, Copy selected text, Paste previously cut or copied text, or Clear (delete) selected text.

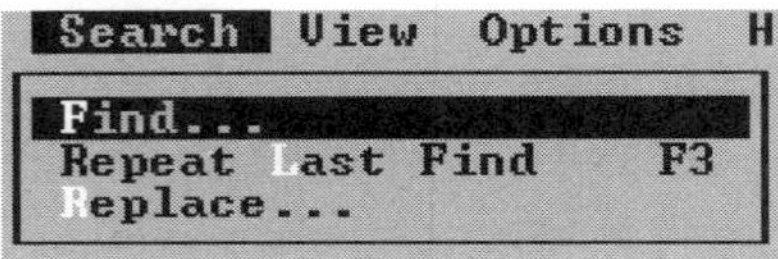

From the Search menu, you can Find a specified string of text, Repeat the Last Find, and search for a specified string of text and Replace it with another specified string of text.

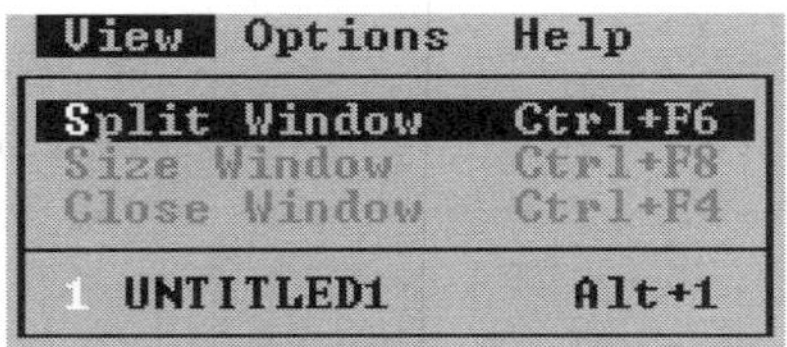

From the View menu, you can Split, Size, or Close the Edit window.

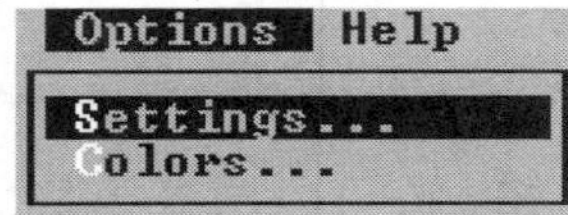

From the Options menu, you can change the Printer Port or the tab Stops and choose the Colors for the Edit window.

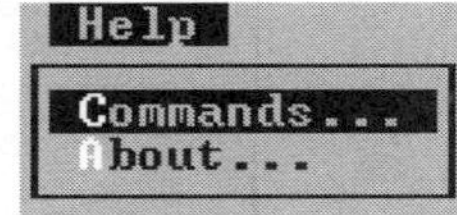

From the Help menu, you can click Commands to get a list of all available Edit commands and About to view the version information for Edit.

Aside from using the menus, there are many keystrokes you can use to edit a text file in the Edit window. Table 7.1 lists most of the cursor movement keys and shortcuts.

Cursor Action	Shortcut	Alternate Shortcut
Character left	←	Ctrl + S
Character right	→	Ctrl + D
Word left	Ctrl + →	Ctrl + A
Word right	Ctrl + ←	Ctrl + F
Line up	↑	Ctrl + E
Line down	↓	
Beginning of current line	Home	Ctrl + Q, S
End of current line	End	Ctrl + Q, D
Top of file	Ctrl + Home	
End of file	Ctrl + End	

TABLE 7.1 DESIRED CURSOR MOVEMENT KEY(S) TO USE KEYBOARD SHORTCUTS

7.14 ACTIVITY: USING THE COMMAND PROMPT TEXT EDITOR

Note: The DATA disk is in the A drive. A:\> is displayed.

Step 1 In order to make the mouse work in a window, you need to make some alterations to the properties of the window.

Step 2 Open a Command Prompt window. Right click the title bar. Click **Properties**.

Step 3 Click the **Options** tab.

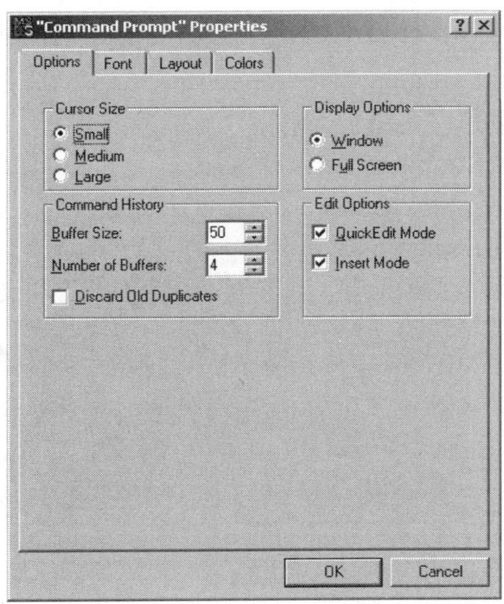

WHAT'S HAPPENING? If the QuickEdit Mode, under Edit Options has a check mark in it, the mouse will not work in Edit. The mouse will work in full-screen mode. But by clearing the QuickEdit Mode check box, you will always be able to use the mouse no matter if you are in a window or in full-screen mode.

Step 4 Clear the QuickEdit Mode check box by clicking it. Click **OK**.

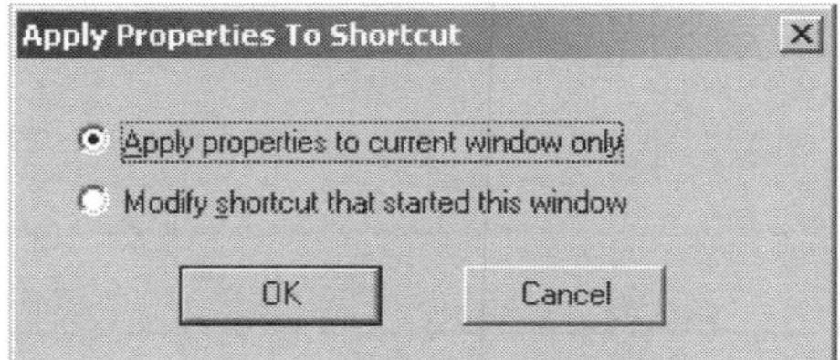

WHAT'S HAPPENING? You see another dialog box. You must choose the option of **Modify shortcut that started this window**. This will then allow the mouse to always work.

Step 5 Click **Modify shortcut that started in this window**. Click **OK**.

Step 6 Key in the following: **EDIT** Enter

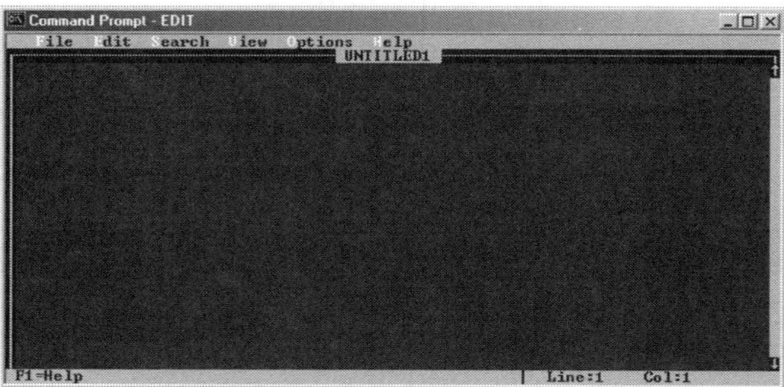

WHAT'S HAPPENING? This is the opening screen to the editor. If this is the first time the program has been executed, you will see a welcome message in the middle of the screen, with instructions on how to remove the welcome message.

Step 7 Close the welcome message so your screen is blank. Press Alt + Enter to go to the full-screen mode.

Step 8 Key in the following:

This is a test. Enter
This is more test data.

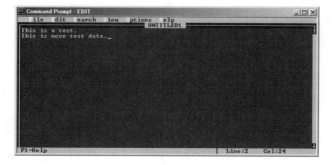

WHAT'S HAPPENING? You have keyed in some data. If you did not press **Enter** and kept keying in data, you would move to character column 25. If you look at the bottom of the screen, you see that the status line tells you what line and what character position you are in. As you can see, you are on the second line, and the cursor is in the 24th position.

You have two modes of operation: ***insert mode*** and ***overstrike mode***. Insert mode is the default. You can tell you are in insert mode because the cursor is a small blinking line. Insert mode means that, as you key in data on an existing line, any data following the cursor will not be replaced, just pushed along.

Step 9 Press **Ctrl** + **Home**

Step 10 Key in the following: **THIS IS MORE DATA.**

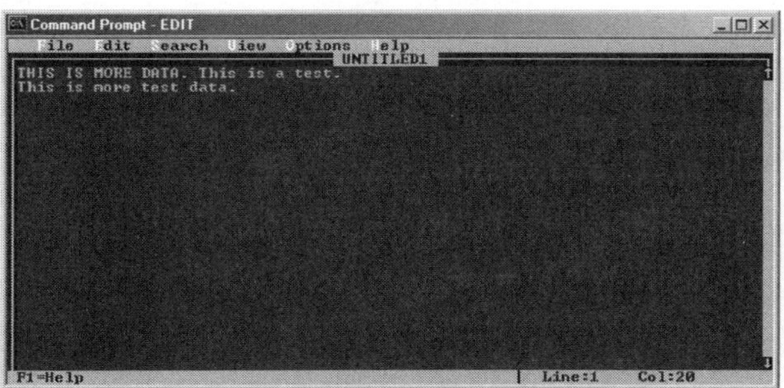

WHAT'S HAPPENING? The new data is there in front of the old data. Overstrike mode permits you to replace the characters that are there. You can toggle between overstrike mode and insert mode by pressing the **Insert** key.

Step 11 Press the **Insert** key.

Step 12 Key in the following: **My second**

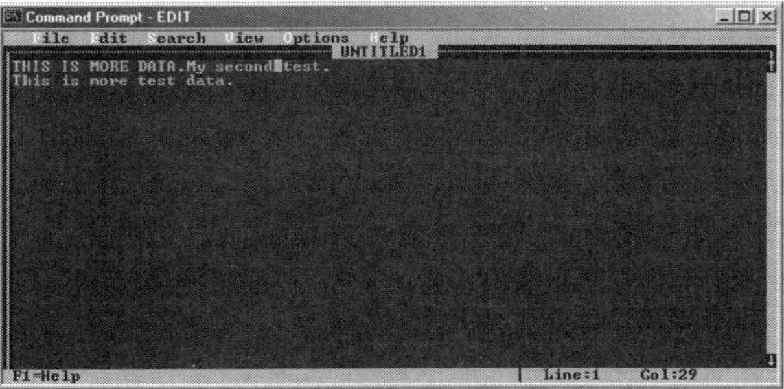

WHAT'S HAPPENING? Notice the shape of the cursor. It is a vertical rectangle. This cursor shape indicates that you are in overstrike mode. You have replaced old text data with new.

Step 13 Press the **Insert** key to return to insert mode.

WHAT'S HAPPENING? Full-screen editing can be done either with the cursor keys or with the mouse. You can position the mouse and click to reposition the point of insertion. You can select text by clicking the mouse at the beginning of the text you wish to select, holding down the left mouse button, and dragging it to the end of the text you wish to select.

Step 14 Click under the first **t** in the phrase **test data**.

Step 15 Hold down the left mouse button and drag to the end of the sentence.

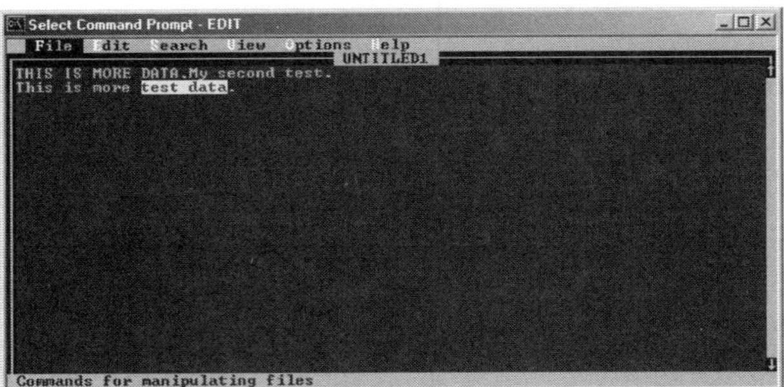

WHAT'S HAPPENING? You have selected the phrase **test data**.

Step 16 Press the **Delete** key.

Step 17 Key in the following: **meaningless data**

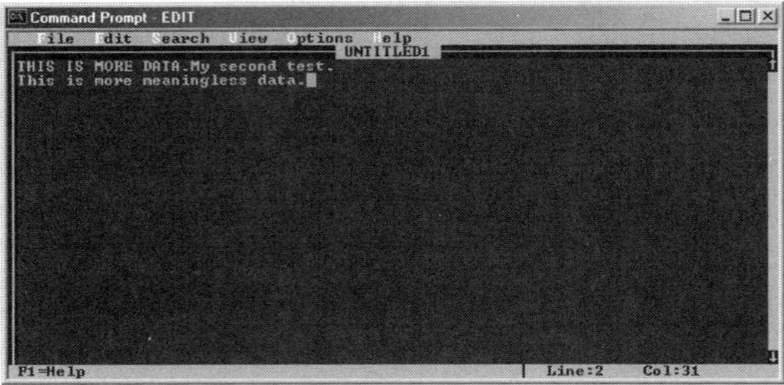

WHAT'S HAPPENING? You have used the mouse to edit data. You can also use the Command Prompt editor to edit existing files. *Note:* You can always use keystrokes if you do not want to use the mouse. Pressing the **Alt** key and the first letter of a menu will drop down the menu. Once you open the menu, you select the highlighted letter of the task you want to perform.

Step 18 On the menu bar at the top of the editor, click **File**.

Step 19 Click **Open**.

Step 20 Key in the following: **A:\PERSONAL.FIL Enter**

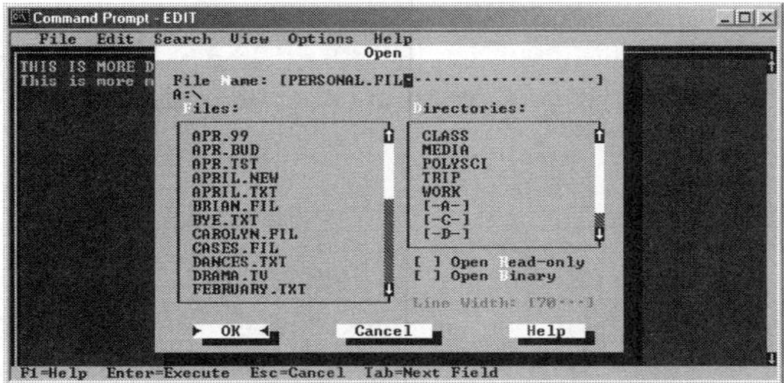

WHAT'S HAPPENING? You have chosen to open the **PERSONAL.FIL** file from the DATA disk in the A drive.

Step 21 Click **OK**.

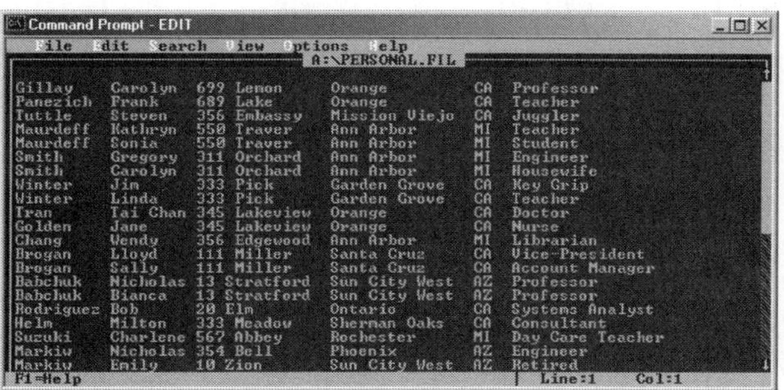

WHAT'S HAPPENING? You have opened the **PERSONAL.FIL** file in the editor. You can search for text strings in the editor. You are going to look for Ervin Jones.

Step 22 On the menu bar, click **Search**.

Step 23 Click **Find**.

Step 24 In the **Find What** area, key in **Jones**.

Step 25 Click **OK**.

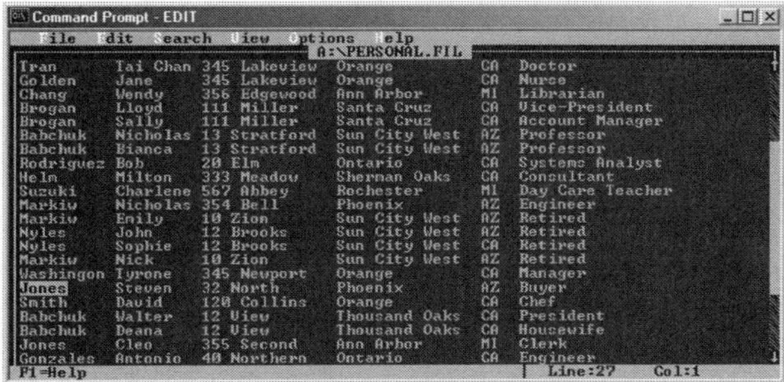

WHAT'S HAPPENING? You found a **Jones**, but not the right one. You can repeat the search with a function key.

Step 26 Press the F3 key three times.

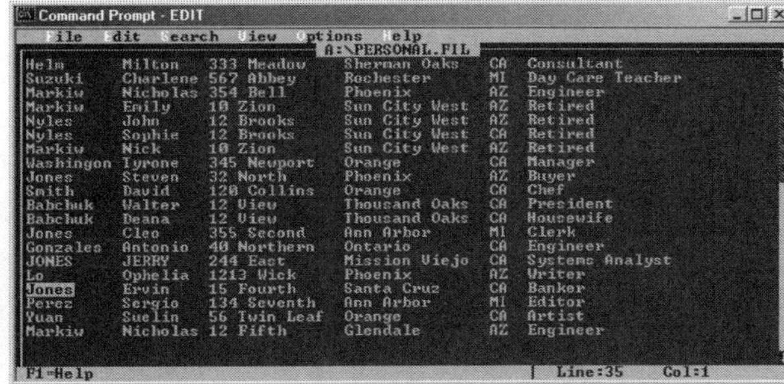

WHAT'S HAPPENING? You have cycled from Jones to Jones until you reached the one you were looking for. You can also add text to the file.

Step 27 Press the [↓] key four times.

Step 28 Key in the following (use [Space Bar] to align the data):

Peat	**Brian**	**125 Second**	**Vacaville**	**CA**	**Athlete**
Farneth	**Nichole**	**237 Arbor**	**Vacaville**	**CA**	**Dancer**

Step 29 On the menu bar, click **File**.

Step 30 Click **Exit**.

WHAT'S HAPPENING? A dialog box appears asking you if you want to save the file **UNTITLED1**. This file has the first data you keyed in. You do not want this file.

Step 31 Click **No**.

WHAT'S HAPPENING? You are now asked if you want to save **A:\PERSONAL.FIL**. You do want to save the changes you made.

Step 32 Click **Yes**.

WHAT'S HAPPENING? You have exited the editor and returned to the Command Prompt window.

Step 33 Open the Command Prompt editor.

Step 34 Click **File**. Click **Open**.

Step 35 Key in **A:\STEVEN.FIL** [Enter]

Step 36 Click **View**.

Step 37 Click **Split Window**.

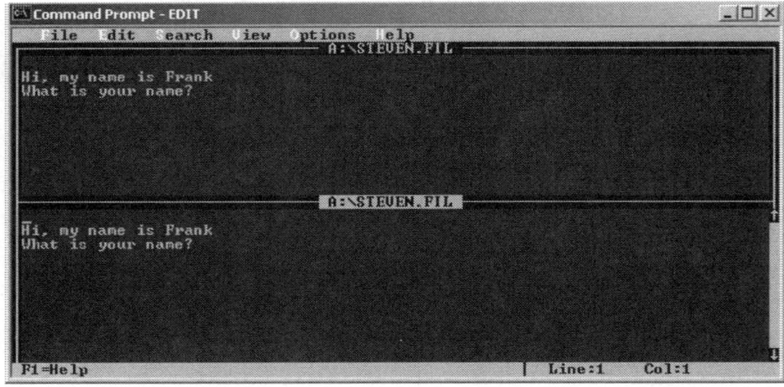

WHAT'S HAPPENING? You can see the file data displayed in two windows.

Step 38 Change the word **Frank** in the top screen to **Steven**.

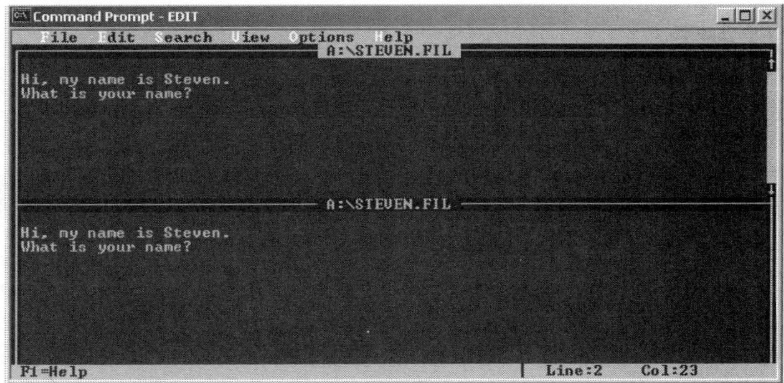

WHAT'S HAPPENING? You can see that the word was changed in both sections. When you split the screen, you can look at the same file data in both windows.

Step 39 Click **File**. Click **Save**.

Step 40 Click **File**. Click **Close**.

Step 41 Place your cursor in the top window. Click **File**. Click **Open**.

Step 42 Key in **A:\TEST.BAT**. Click **OK**.

Step 43 Place your cursor in the bottom window. Click **File**. Click **Open**.

Step 44 Key in **A:\B.BAT**. Click **OK**.

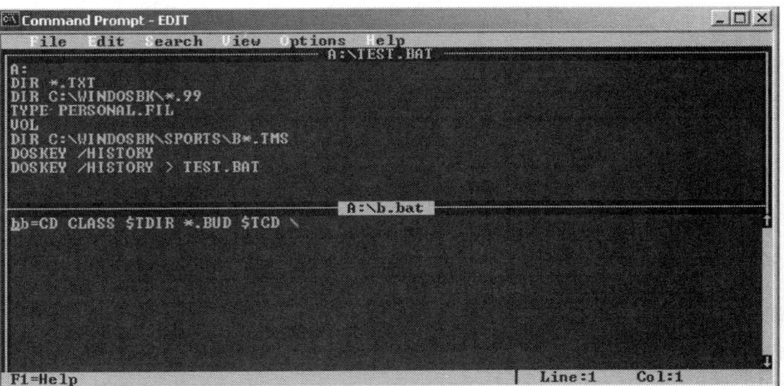

WHAT'S HAPPENING? You have opened two separate files and can view them simultaneously on the split screen.

Step 45 In the top window, delete the first line (**A:**) and the last two lines (**DOSKEY /HISTORY** and **DOSKEY /HISTORY > TEST.BAT**).

Step 46 In the bottom window, alter the line to read as follows:
**DOSKEY bb=CD CLASS $TDIR *.BUD$TCD **

Step 47 Save both files. Close both files. Exit the editor.

WHAT'S HAPPENING? You now have two batch files. Batch files, which will be covered in much more detail in Chapters 10 and 11, are programs that you can write. You execute a batch file by keying in its name. You have one batch file (**TEST.BAT**) that runs a series of commands. The other batch file (**B.BAT**) will set up a macro.

Step 48 Close the Command Prompt window. Open a Command Prompt window. Make **A:** the default drive.

Step 49 Key in the following: A:\>**bb** Enter

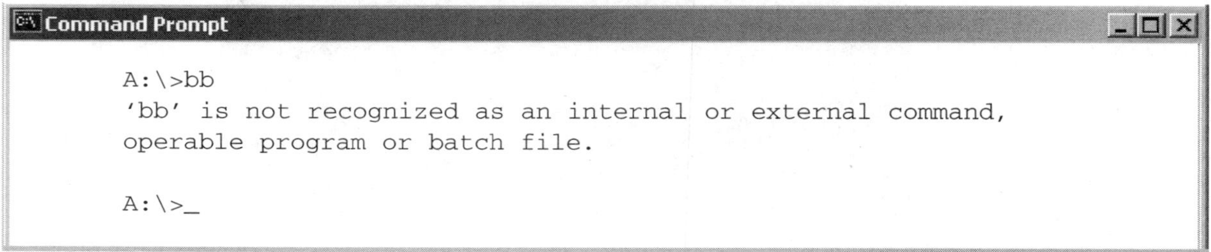

```
A:\>bb
'bb' is not recognized as an internal or external command,
operable program or batch file.

A:\>_
```

WHAT'S HAPPENING? Because you closed the Command Prompt window, your macros are no longer in effect.

Step 50 Key in the following: A:\>**B** Enter

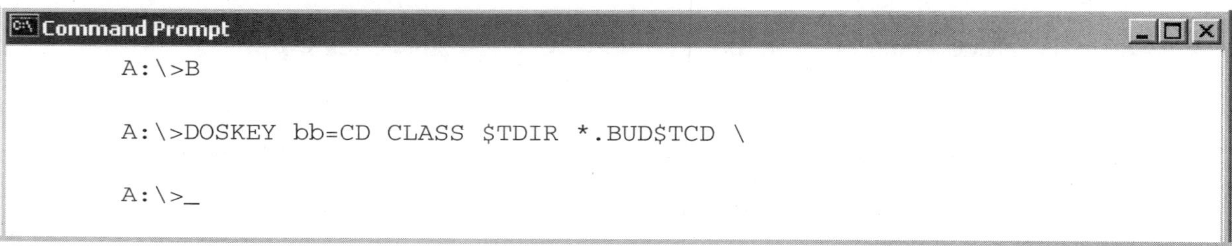

```
A:\>B

A:\>DOSKEY bb=CD CLASS $TDIR *.BUD$TCD \

A:\>_
```

WHAT'S HAPPENING? Since you executed your batch file, you enabled your macro. Now if you keyed in **bb**, you would see the screeen that follows Step 8 in Activity 7.12.

CHAPTER SUMMARY

1. File attributes are tracked by the operating system.
2. There are four file attributes: A (archive), H (hidden), S (system), and R (read-only).
3. The ATTRIB command allows you to manipulate file attributes.
4. The SUBST command allows you to substitute an unused drive letter for a long, unwieldy path name.
5. The XCOPY command allows you to copy files and subdirectories.
6. There are many parameters available to the XCOPY command. Among them are parameters that enable you to:
   a. copy by date (/D)
   b. copy hidden files (/H)
   c. copy subdirectories (/S)
   d. overwrite read-only files (/R)
   e. copy empty directories (/E)
   f. keep file attributes (/K)
7. DOSKEY is an external, memory-resident program that loads automatically in Windows 2000 Professional. It allows you to do command line editing.

8. A memory-resident program is commonly referred to as a TSR program. Once loaded into memory, it remains in memory for the duration of the session.
9. The arrow and function keys in DOSKEY allow you to do command-line editing by recalling and listing the previously keyed in commands.
10. You can create macros in a command line window.
11. On the desktop, you use Notepad to edit text files. In the Command Prompt window, you use the Edit editor.
12. Edit can be used to edit or create ASCII text files.
13. In Edit, you can use menus, the mouse, and keystrokes to edit text.

KEY TERMS

archive attribute
file attribute
hidden attribute
insert mode
overstrike mode
read-only attribute
system attribute
Terminate Stay Resident (TSR)
text editor

DISCUSSION QUESTIONS

1. What is the purpose and function of the ATTRIB command?
2. Give two parameters for the ATTRIB command and describe the function and purpose of each.
3. What are file attributes?
4. What effect does a file marked "hidden" have for a user? How can you "unhide" the file?
5. What does a file marked "read-only" mean to a user?
6. What is the function of the archive bit?
7. What is the purpose of the SUBST command?
8. Under what circumstances would the SUBST command be useful?
9. What is the purpose of the XCOPY command?
10. What advantages does the XCOPY command have over the COPY command?
11. List four XCOPY parameters, and explain their function and their syntax.
12. Explain the purpose and function of the DOSKEY command.
13. What is a memory-resident program, and how does it work?
14. Explain what a macro is and how you would create one.
15. Discuss how to execute commands from the history list.
16. Compare and contrast a word-processing program, Notepad, and Edit.

TRUE/FALSE QUESTIONS

For each question, circle the letter T if the statement is true and the letter F if the statement is false.

T F 1. The ATTRIB command allows you to add and remove file attributes.
T F 2. You should not use the DIR command when the drive letter has been assigned with the SUBST command.
T F 3. You cannot copy empty subdirectories with the XCOPY command.
T F 4. DOSKEY is a TSR program.
T F 5. The Edit editor can be used in place of Notepad.

COMPLETION QUESTIONS

Write the correct answer in each blank space.

6. If you key in the command ATTRIB +H THIS.ONE, you have marked the file THIS.ONE as ________.
7. The XCOPY parameter(s) that allow(s) you to copy hidden, system, and read-only files is/are __________.
8. To see what commands you have keyed in, key in ________________.
9. If you have to key in a long path name repeatedly, you can use the __________ command to assign a drive letter to the path.
10. To go to the beginning of a file in Edit, press __________.

MULTIPLE CHOICE QUESTIONS

For each question, write the letter for the correct answer in the blank space.

11. Once installed, a TSR acts like an
    a. external command.
    b. internal command.
    c. both a and b
    d. neither a nor b
12. The /D parameter of the SUBST command
    a. displays the true name of the logical drive.
    b. will have no effect on the SUBST command.
    c. will confirm that the substitution has occurred.
    d. will disable the SUBST command.
13. XCOPY will copy __________ than COPY.
    a. faster, with more options
    b. slower, with more options
    c. with fewer options
    d. none of the above
14. If you wanted to protect the file **MY.FIL** from being accidentally erased, you would key in the following:
    a. ATTRIB -R MY.FIL
    b. ATTRIB +R MY.FIL
    c. ATTRIB +S MY.FIL
    d. ATTRIB -S MY.FIL
15. To XCOPY a file marked read-only and to be sure that the destination file retained the read-only attribute, you would use the parameters
    a. /S /R
    b. /R /K
    c. /R /E
    d. /T /E

WRITING COMMANDS

Write the correct step(s) or command(s) necessary to perform the action listed as if you were at the keyboard.

16. Copy all the files and subdirectories, regardless of their attributes, from the TEMP directory on the root of the default directory to the OLDTEMP directory on the root directory of the disk in the A drive.

    `C:\>`

17. Create a macro called X that will allow you to change your drive to C: and your directory to the WINDOSBK.

    `A:\>`

18. Allow the letter J to stand for C:\WINDOSBK\SPORTS.

    `C:\>`

19. Prevent the DIR command from seeing all the files ending with .99 in the root directory of the disk in the A drive.

    `C:\TEST>`

20. In the Edit text editor, view and edit two text files simultaneously.

APPLICATION ASSIGNMENTS

Note 1: Be sure to work on the APPLICATION disk, not the DATA disk.

Note 2: The homework problems will assume Drive C is the hard disk and the APPLICATION disk is in Drive A. If you are using another drive, such as a floppy drive B or a hard drive D, be sure to substitute that drive letter when reading the questions and answers.

Note 3: All subdirectories that are created will be under the root directory unless otherwise specified.

PROBLEM SET I

Note: The prompt is A:\>.

PROBLEM A

A-a If necessary, remove the DATA disk and insert the APPLICATION disk in Drive A.

A-b Copy any files with the **.TV** extension from the **PHONE** directory to the root directory of the APPLICATION disk.

A-c Copy the file in the root directory called **DRAMA.TV** to a new file called **GRAVE.TV**, also in the root directory.

A-d Using the relative path, display the attributes of the **GRAVE.TV** file.

1. Which command did you use?
   a. DIR GRAVE.TV
   b. ATTRIB GRAVE.TV
   c. ATTRIB +R GRAVE.TV or ATTRIB GRAVE.TV +R
   d. ATTRIB -R GRAVE.TV or ATTRIB GRAVE.TV -R

2. What file attribute is *not* displayed?
   a. S
   b. H
   c. A
   d. both a and b

A-e Make the **GRAVE.TV** file read-only.

3. Which command did you use?
   a. DIR GRAVE.TV
   b. ATTRIB GRAVE.TV
   c. ATTRIB -R GRAVE.TV or ATTRIB GRAVE.TV -R
   d. ATTRIB +R GRAVE.TV or ATTRIB GRAVE.TV +R

A-f Key in the following: **DEL GRAVE.TV**

4. What message is displayed?
   a. Access is denied.
   b. This is a read-only file.
   c. This file is read-only, delete anyway?
   d. no message is displayed

A-g Display the attributes of the **GRAVE.TV** file.

5. Which attributes are set on the **GRAVE.TV** file?
   a. A and S
   b. A and R
   c. A and H
   d. A, H, and R

A-h Copy **GRAVE.TV** to **GRAVEST.TV**.

A-i Delete **GRAVE.TV** with the DEL command.

6. What parameter did you have to use with DEL?
   a. /X
   b. /P
   c. /F
   d. /Q

A-j Make **GRAVEST.TV** a hidden, read-only file.

7. Which command did you use?
   a. ATTRIB +A +R GRAVEST.TV
   b. ATTRIB +H +A GRAVEST.TV
   c. ATTRIB +H +R GRAVEST.TV
   d. ATTRIB +S +H +R GRAVEST.TV

A-k Use the DIR command (with no parameters) to display **GRAVEST.TV**.

8. Which of the following lines do you see on the screen?
   a. GRAVEST.TV is a hidden file.
   b. File Not Found.
   c. Not found - GRAVEST.TV.
   d. none of the above

PROBLEM B

B-a Make a subdirectory on the root of the APPLICATION disk called **FIRST**.

B-b From the root of the APPLICATION disk, make a subdirectory under **FIRST** called **SECOND**.

B-c From the root of the APPLICATION disk, make a subdirectory under **SECOND** called **THIRD**.

9. Which command did you use to make the THIRD subdirectory?
   a. MD THIRD
   b. MD FIRST\THIRD
   c. MD FIRST\SECOND\THIRD
   d. MD SECOND\THIRD

B-d Copy all the files ending in ***.99*** from the **WINDOSBK** directory on the C drive to **FIRST**.

B-e Copy the files in the **FIRST** subdirectory to the **SECOND** subdirectory keeping the same names but with the new file extension of **.BRI**.

B-f Copy the files in the **SECOND** subdirectory to the **THIRD** subdirectory keeping the same names but with the new file extension of **.NIC**.

B-g From the root of the APPLICATION disk, display all the files and subdirectories in and under the **FIRST** subdirectory, but not the entire disk.

10. Which command did you use?
    a. DIR /S
    b. DIR FIRST SECOND THIRD
    c. DIR FIRST /S
    d. DIR FIRST/SECOND/THIRD

B-h Make all the files in the **FIRST** directory read-only.

B-i Make all the files in the **THIRD** directory hidden.

11. Which command did you use to mark the files in the **THIRD** subdirectory as hidden?
    a. ATTRIB *.* +H THIRD
    b. ATTRIB THIRD +H
    c. ATTRIB FIRST\SECOND\THIRD*.* +H
    d. either a or b

B-j With the root directory of the APPLICATION disk as the default, make a directory called **FIRST-2**.

B-k With the root directory of the APPLICATION disk as the default, duplicate the **FIRST** subdirectory, including all files and subdirectories beneath it, to the subdirectory **FIRST-2**. (Be sure to duplicate all files and retain their attributes in **FIRST-2**.)

12. Which command and parameters did you use?
    a. XCOPY FIRST FIRST-2 /S /E
    b. XCOPY FIRST FIRST-2 /S /H /E /R /K
    c. XCOPY FIRST FIRST-2 /R /H /K
    d. XCOPY FIRST FIRST-2 /S /E

13. How many files were copied?
    a. 4
    b. 8
    c. 12
    d. 16

PROBLEM C

Note: Check with your lab administrator before proceeding with the next step.

C-a With the root directory of the APPLICATION disk as the default, assign the letter **E** to represent the path to the **THIRD** subdirectory on the APPLICATION disk under **FIRST**.

Note: If Drive E is not available, choose another drive letter and substitute it in the answers.

14. Which command did you use?
    a. SUBST E FIRST\SECOND\THIRD
    b. SUBST E: FIRST\SECOND\THIRD
    c. SUBST E THIRD
    d. SUBST E: THIRD

C-b Key in the following: **SUBST** Enter

15. What line is displayed on the screen?
    a. E:\: => A:\FIRST\SECOND\THIRD
    b. E = FIRST\SECOND\THIRD

c. E: = THIRD
d. none of the above

C-c With the root directory of the APPLICATION disk as the default, display the directory of the E drive.

16. How many files are displayed?
   a. zero
   b. two
   c. four
   d. eight

C-d With the root directory of the APPLICATION disk as the default and without using the ATTRIB command to determine which attributes are set, issue a command that will remove the attributes from the files in the **THIRD** directory.

17. Which command did you use?
   a. ATTRIB E:*.* -A -S -R -H
   b. ATTRIB -ALL E:
   c. ATTRIB -*.* E:
   d. none of the above

C-e Remove the virtual Drive E.

18. Which command did you use?
   a. SUBST /D
   b. SUBST E: /D
   c. SUBST E /D
   d. SUBST /D E

PROBLEM D

D-a Create a macro called FIRST that will display the directory of the FIRST directory and then will display the directory of the FIRST\SECOND\THIRD directory.

19. Which command did you use?
   a. DOSKEY /MACRO=FIRST=DIR FIRST & DIR FIRST\SECOND\THIRD
   b. DOSKEY DIR FIRST & DIR FIRST\SECOND\THIRD
   c. DOSKEY FIRST=DIR FIRST $TDIR FIRST\SECOND\THIRD
   d. DOSKEY /MACRO FIRST=DIR FIRST $TDIR FIRST\SECOND\THIRD

D-b Redirect the macro you created into a batch file called **FIRST.BAT**

20. Which command did you use?
    a. DOSKEY /MACRO > FIRST.BAT
    b. DOSKEY /HISTORY > FIRST.BAT
    c. DOSKEY > FIRST.BAT
    d. DOSKEY *.* > FIRST.BAT

D-c Edit the **FIRST.BAT** file so that it can be executed whenever you open a command prompt window. Delete any unnecessary lines.

21. What did you add to the batch file macro line?
    a. DOSKEY /MACROS
    b. DOSKEY
    c. DOSKEY /MACROS > FIRST.BAT
    d. none of the above

PROBLEM E

Note: The APPLICATION disk is in the A drive and A:\> is the default drive. If necessary, press **Alt** + **Enter** to operate in full-screen mode or clear the QuickEdit option button.

E-a Copy **FRANK.FIL** from the **WINDOSBK** directory to the root of the A drive.

E-b Copy **CAROLYN.FIL** from the **WINDOSBK** directory to the root of the A drive.

E-c Using Edit, edit **FRANK.FIL** to say "Hi, my name is Bob." instead of "Hi, my name is Frank."

E-d Save the file as **BOB.FIL**.

22. To save the file as **BOB.FIL**,
    a. you clicked File and then Save As, keyed in BOB.FIL, and clicked OK.
    b. you clicked File and then Save, keyed in BOB.FIL, and clicked OK.
    c. you clicked Edit and then Save As, keyed in BOB.FIL, and clicked OK.
    d. you clicked Edit and then Save, keyed in BOB.FIL, and clicked OK.

E-e Close the file.

E-f Open **CAROLYN.FIL** with the text editor.

E-g Edit the file to read:

```
Hi, my name is Bette.
I like learning about operating systems.
I hope you like it too.
```

E-h Save the file as **BETTE.FIL**.

E-i Close the editor.

☐ 23. The current contents of **CAROLYN.FIL** are:
   a. Hi, my name is Carolyn.
      What is your name?
   b. Hi, my name is Bette.
      What is your name?
   c. Hi, my name is Bette.
      I like learning about operating systems.
      I hope you like it too.
   d. none of the above

E-j Copy any files with the name **BYE** and any extension from the **\WINDOSBK** directory to the root of the A drive.

E-k Open the text editor and split the window into two sections.

☐ 24. After the editor was open, which procedure did you follow?
   a. Click File, click Two Windows.
   b. Click Edit, click Split Screen.
   c. Click View, click Split Window.
   d. Click Options, click Split View.

E-l With the cursor in the top window, open the file **APR.99** from the root of the A drive.

E-m Move the cursor to the bottom window and open the file **BYE.TYP** from the root of the A drive.

☐ 25. What is the last line in the bottom window?
   a. This is file 4.
   b. This is my April file.
   c. GOODBYE ALL
   d. YES!

E-n Close Edit.

PROBLEM SET II

Note 1: Before proceeding with these assignments, check with your lab instructor to see if there are any special procedures you should follow.

Note 2: The APPLICATION disk is in Drive A. The A:\> prompt is displayed as the default drive and the default directory. *All work will occur on the APPLICATION disk.*

Note 3: Make sure that **NAME.BAT**, **MARK.FIL**, **GETYN.COM**, and **GO.BAT** are all present in the root directory of the APPLICATION disk before proceeding with these problems.

Note 4: All files with the **.HW** extension *must* be created in the root directory of the APPLICATION disk.

Step 1 Key in the following: A:\>**NAME** Enter

Step 2 Here is an example to key in, but your instructor will have other information that applies to your class. Key in the following:

Bette A. Peat Enter (*Your* name goes here.)

CIS 55 Enter (*Your* class goes here.)

T-Th 8-9:30 Enter (*Your* day and time go here.)

Chapter 7 Applications Enter

Step 3 Press F6 Enter

Step 4 If the information is correct, press **Y** and you are back to A:\>.

WHAT'S HAPPENING? You have returned to the system level. You now have a file called **NAME.FIL** with your name and other pertinent information. (*Hint*: Remember redirection.)

TO CREATE 1.HW

- Display the names of all files in only the root of the APPLICATION disk that are hidden and redirect the output of the command to a file called **1.HW**.

TO CREATE 2.HW

- Remove the hidden attribute from all the files in only the root directory of the APPLICATION disk.
- Remove the **FIRST-2** subdirectory from the root of the APPLICATION disk.
- Change the default directory to **A:\FIRST**>.
- Remove all the attributes from all files and subdirectories *under* the **FIRST** subdirectory but not *in* the **FIRST** subdirectory.
- Key in the following: A:\FIRST>**ATTRIB /S > \2.HW** Enter

TO CREATE 3.HW

- Change the default directory to **A:\>**.
- Perform the step necessary to be able to refer to the directory **A:\FIRST\SECOND\THIRD** as **E:** or a drive letter you can use.
- Key in the following: A:\>**DIR E: > 3.HW** Enter
- Remove the virtual Drive E.

TO CREATE 4.HW

- Concatenate the files **BETTE.FIL** and **BOB.FIL** to a new file named **PEAT.FIL**.
- Open the file **PEAT.FIL** with the text editor and make sure there is a blank line between **I hope you like it too.** and **Hi, my name is Bob.**

- Add a new blank line to the bottom of the file, then add another line that reads: **Are we having fun yet?**
- Save the file and exit the text editor.
- Display the contents of **PEAT.FIL** and redirect it to a file called **4.HW**.

TO CREATE 5.HW

- From the root of the A drive, set the read-only and hidden attributes for all the files in the **FILES** subdirectory but not in any of the subdirectories of **FILES**.
- Make an exact duplicate of the **FILES** subdirectory and any subdirectories to another subdirectory off of the root called **MORFILES**. (*Hint:* You need to copy all files, regardless of their attributes, and the new files should retain their attributes.)
- Create a new file with the text editor on the root of the APPLICATION disk called **5.HW**. In the file, key in the command you used to copy **FILES** to **MORFILES** in the previous step.
- Remove any hidden or read-only attributes on any file on the entire APPLICATIONS disk.

TO PRINT YOUR HOMEWORK

Step 1 Be sure the printer is on and ready to accept print jobs from your computer.

Step 2 Key in the following (be very careful to make no typing errors):
GO NAME.FIL 1.HW 2.HW 3.HW 4.HW 5.HW Enter

If the files you requested, **1.HW, 2.HW**, etc., do not exist in the default directory, you will see the following message on the screen:

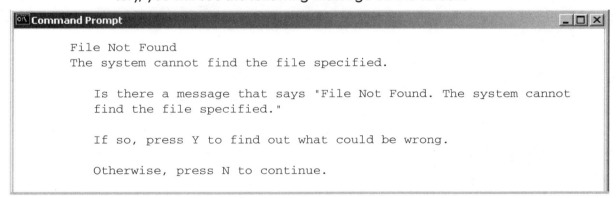

```
Command Prompt

    File Not Found
    The system cannot find the file specified.

       Is there a message that says "File Not Found. The system cannot
       find the file specified."

       If so, press Y to find out what could be wrong.

       Otherwise, press N to continue.
```

WHAT'S HAPPENING? The operating system is telling you that the file cannot be found. If you see this screen, press **Y** to see what could be wrong, and repeat the print procedure after you have corrected the problem.

If the default directory contains the specified files, the following message will appear on the screen:

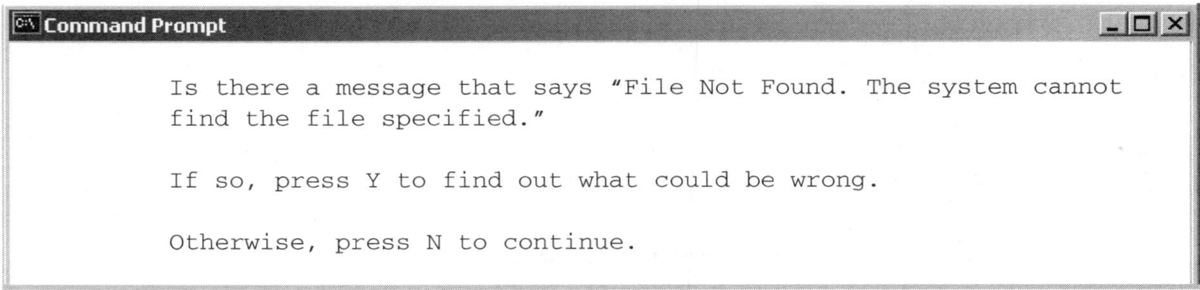

You will need to press **N** once for each file you are printing.

Step 3 Follow the messages on the screen until the Notepad program opens with a screen similar to the following:

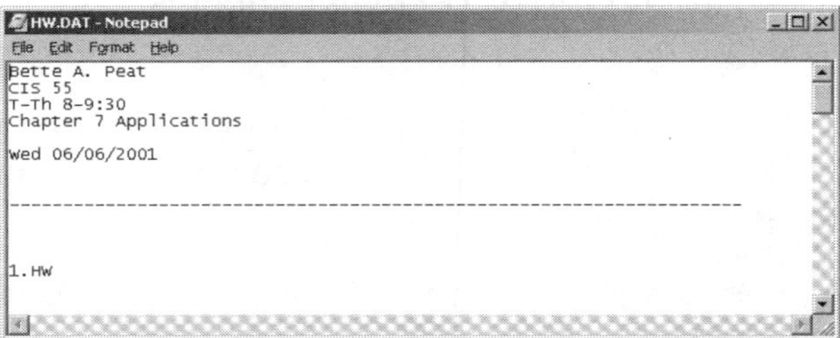

All the requested files have been found and placed in a Notepad document. Your homework is now ready to print.

Step 4 On the Notepad menu bar, click **File**. Click **Print**.

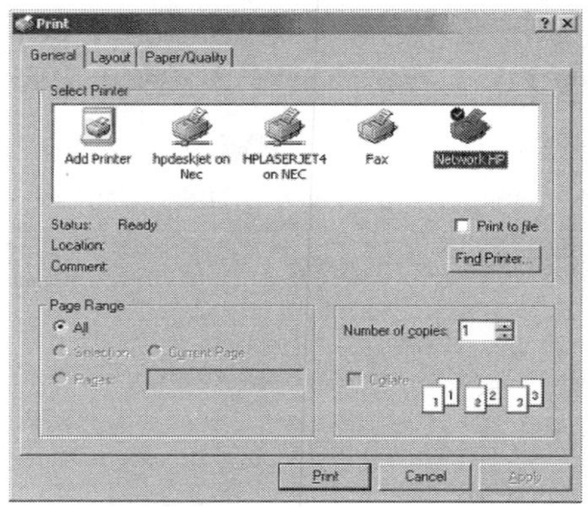

The print dialog box opens. If you have more than one printer, all your printer choices will be displayed. The default printer is the highlighted printer.

Step 5 Click the **Print** button.

Step 6 In the Notepad window, click **File**. Click **Exit**.

The following will appear on the Command Prompt screen:

Command Prompt

```
You are about to delete any file with the .HW extension.

Before you delete your homework files, check your hard
copy or print out.

If your homework printout is correct, press Y to delete the files.

If your homework printout is incorrect, press N.

Pressing N will prevent your homework files from
being deleted. You can then begin again.
```

WHAT'S HAPPENING? At this point, look at your printout. If it is correct, you can press **Y** to delete the homework files for this chapter. If your printout is incorrect, you can press **N**. That will preserve your homework and you will need to redo only the problem that was incorrect, not all the homework assignments.

Step 7 Press **Y** **Enter**

WHAT'S HAPPENING? You have returned to the default prompt.

Step 8 Close the Command Prompt session.

Step 9 Execute the shut-down procedure.

PROBLEM SET III—BRIEF ESSAY

1. The attributes most often set by the user are H and R. Describe two scenarios where you might find it advantageous to set the hidden and/or read-only attributes to a file or group of files.

2. The XCOPY command's many parameters make it a versatile command. Choose two of the parameters and describe, in detail, how, why, and when you would use them.

CHAPTER

ORGANIZING AND MANAGING YOUR HARD DISK

LEARNING OBJECTIVES

After completing this chapter, you will be able to:

1. Explain the purpose of organizing a hard disk.
2. Explain the purpose and function of the TREE command.
3. List criteria for organizing a hard disk efficiently and logically.
4. Explain the role XCOPY can play in organizing a hard disk.
5. Explain the difference between contiguous and noncontiguous files.
6. Explain the purpose and function of the CHKDSK command.
7. Explain lost clusters and cross-linked files.
8. Explain the ways you can repair a disk.
9. Explain the purpose and function of using the Disk Defragmenter program.

STUDENT OUTCOMES

1. Reorganize the DATA disk.
2. Use the TREE command to view the organization of a disk.
3. Use the XCOPY command with its parameters to copy files.
4. Use the CHKDSK command to elicit statistical information about disks and memory.
5. Interpret the statistical information obtained by using the CHKDSK command.
6. Use CHKDSK to see if files are contiguous.
7. Repair a disk, if possible.
8. Use the Disk Defragmenter utility program.

CHAPTER OVERVIEW

The more efficiently and logically a hard disk is organized, the easier it becomes for you to know where to store a new file or how to access an existing one. Subdirectories (folders that group files together under one heading) help you organize a hard disk so that you can easily locate a specific file.

An inefficient but typical hard disk organizational scheme is to divide the disk into major application programs (e.g., word-processing program, spreadsheet program, etc.) and place the data files for those applications in the same subdirectory. This organizational scheme can create problems when you try to locate a specific data file. To locate a specific data file, you have to remember under which program the data file was listed. It makes sense to never place program files and data files in the same subdirectory. Program files rarely change, and data files are always changing. The majority of computer users are working with application programs to help them do their work projects more easily and efficiently. It makes better sense to organize the disk the way most people work—by project, not by software application.

This chapter demonstrates ways to use the hard disk efficiently. You will learn how to organize a hard disk to serve your specific needs, use directories to keep track of the files on your disk, and determine the best command to use to locate a specific file. You will learn what a logical disk is and what commands can be used with a logical disk. In addition, you will learn some useful commands to manage the hard disk itself and keep it healthy.

8.1 WHY ORGANIZE A HARD DISK?

The initial response of most people with a hard disk, no matter what size, is to place program files and data files into the default directory. When they purchase a new program, such as Microsoft Office, there will be a default directory, My Documents, where the data files will be stored. All the files created with Word, Excel, and PowerPoint will end up in this directory. Within a relatively short period of time, there will be many, many files listed in that directory. Other application programs use the standard setup or install routines to place the application programs on the hard disk. These routines are programs that usually create a subdirectory for that application program and then copy the files from the floppy disks to the named subdirectory on the hard disk. Many application programs have such huge files that, when they are placed on the disk by the manufacturer, the files are compressed. In the process of copying the files to the named subdirectory, the setup or install programs must first decompress those program files. As part of the installation, these programs may or may not create a directory for data. If not, your data files may, by default, end up being saved to the directory that holds the application program files or to the My Documents folder.

If, when you use the DIR command, the many files and subdirectory names in the root directory scroll by endlessly, it becomes very difficult to know what files are on the hard disk and where they are located. You spend your time looking for data files instead of doing work with data files. This problem does not change in the Windows GUI. Even in a graphical environment, a disorganized disk does not look pretty.

If you install program files to the root directory of the hard disk instead of to a subdirectory, you are going to have a major problem knowing to which program those files belong. There are also technical reasons for not placing all files in the root directory on a hard disk if you are using FAT16. No matter what size a hard disk is, the root directory can hold only a limited number of file entries when using FAT16. If all files are placed in the root directory, it quickly becomes full. When the root directory table is full, then the operating system thinks the disk is full, even if there is actually room on the disk.

Remember, when you create a subdirectory, it counts as only one entry in the root directory, even though the subdirectory itself may hold hundreds of files. Your only storage limitation becomes the physical size of your hard disk. Most programs written for the Windows environment install themselves to the C:\Program Files subdirectory. As you can imagine, this directory fills rapidly. Other setup programs handle it differently. For example, when you install a program like WordPerfect using the setup program, a subdirectory is created called C:\Corel, and all products written by Corel are installed in that same directory. Most setup programs allow you to change the directory you wish to install in. If you have a second drive or partition with extra space on it, you will often want to install to a subdirectory of your own choosing. Perhaps you have three drawing programs, PCDraw, PCPaint, and PCPic. You might want to create a subdirectory called DRAW, and then install the programs in C:\DRAW\PCDraw, C:\DRAW\PCPaint, and C:\DRAW\PCPic, respectively. In this way, all your drawing programs would be in one place.

There can be, however, one disadvantage to choosing your own installation location. If you have technical problems with an installed program and need to call that company's tech support, the person you speak to will undoubtedly expect the software to be installed to the setup program's default directory. If you have installed it somewhere else, the support person may have difficulty helping you.

You typically have more than one program on your computer system. The programs may have come with the computer when you purchased it, or you may have purchased additional programs. For instance, a typical user might have a word-processing program (Word), a spreadsheet program (Lotus 1-2-3), a database program (FoxPro), the operating system (Windows 2000 Professional), and a checkbook management program (Quicken). If you were that user, your hard disk might look like Figure 8.1.

In Figure 8.1, an ellipsis (...) represents the rest of the files. You or the program would create each subdirectory and place the program files that belong to the application program in the proper subdirectory. Notice the Quicken program has automatically created a subdirectory for data files.

The point is you want to use the programs to do work. As an example, let's say you are a salesperson and you have two products to sell: widgets and bangles. You use Word to write letters to clients and to make proposals. You use Lotus 1-2-3 to do budget projections for clients. You use Quicken to manage your expenses. You use the operating system to manage your files and disks. You use FoxPro to manage your clients' names and addresses (a database). You know enough that you know you do not want the data files (such as REPORT.DOC or CLIENTS.DBF) in the root directory. You could use the MOVE command to move the REPORT.DOC file to the WINWORD subdirectory and to move CLIENTS.DBF to the FOXPRO subdirectory.

However, you now know that you do not want to place your data files in the program subdirectory either. There are several reasons for this. The major reason is that program files do not change. Data files are always changing as you add or delete information. Within this process you are also adding and deleting files. Thus, when you want to back up your data files, you would have to sort through many program files to do so.

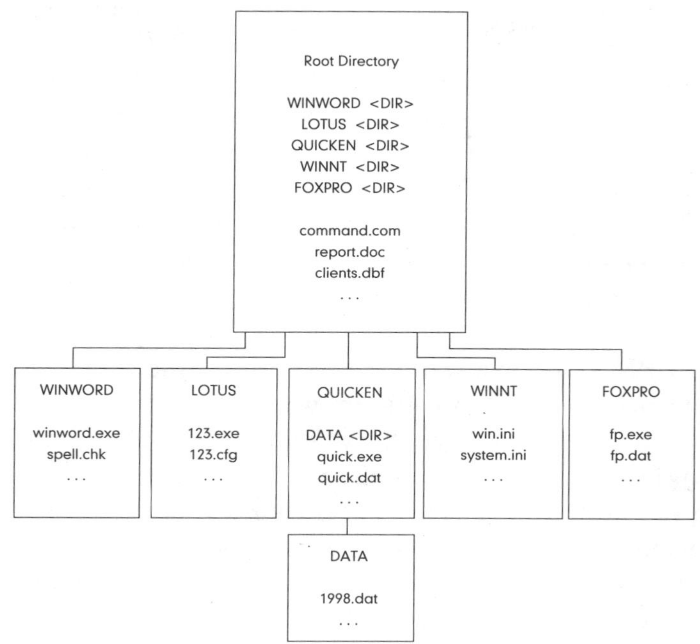

FIGURE 8.1 A TYPICAL HARD DISK CONFIGURATION

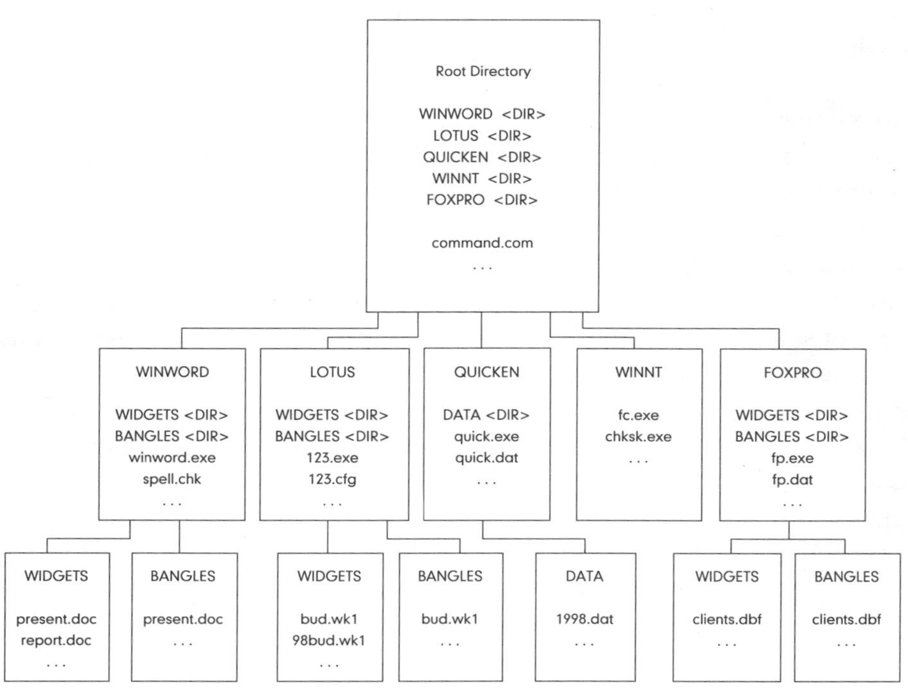

FIGURE 8.2 ORGANIZING A DISK BY SOFTWARE APPLICATION PACKAGE

Furthermore, part of the rationale for subdirectories is to categorize information—data files are information. It is easier to locate the file of interest if you know what subdirectory it might be in.

When creating file names, you always attempt to create a meaningful name. You want to have a naming convention so that when you create new files that fit into your scheme, you know what name you are going to give them. You should be able to identify a file's contents by its name. You do not want to have to open each file to see what its contents are. For example, you are using your database program and you want to keep track of your clients for the bangles product line. You name the data file CLIENTS.DBF. However, you have two products to sell, bangles and widgets. Each product has different clients, so each product requires a separate client file. You now have two files you want to call CLIENTS.DBF. You do not want to overwrite one file with another, so you must uniquely identify each file. An efficient way to do this is to create a subdirectory called BANGLES and a subdirectory called WIDGETS and place each CLIENTS.DBF file in the appropriate subdirectory. It is the subdirectory name that clarifies which product client file you work with. An example of an inefficient but typical hard disk organizational scheme with subdirectories for data might look like Figure 8.2.

Although the organizational scheme in Figure 8.2 is better than placing the data files in the root directory or in the program subdirectories, it is still very inefficient. There are too many repeated subdirectory names. In addition, every time you want a data file, you will have to remember not only what application you are working on, but also where the appropriate data file is located. Furthermore, at this point you must key in long path names. For example, when you want to retrieve REPORT.DOC in Word, you need to key in C:\WINWORD\WIDGETS\REPORT.DOC. In addition, when you need to find a file two or three levels down the hierarchical tree, the operating system must look at every subdirectory on the way down. The heads on the disk drive are constantly going back and forth reading the entries and looking for the files.

As you become a more sophisticated user, you will find that you can use data files in conjunction with different application programs. For instance, you can use FoxPro to generate a mailing list from your CLIENTS.DBF file so that you can use it with Word to send out a form letter. When you begin doing this, you end up with data in two places: the word-processing subdirectory and the database subdirectory. More importantly, when you find a new program you want to purchase, such as a presentation package like Harvard Graphics, you need to add a new subdirectory for that program, and you need to add further subdirectories for your products, bangles and widgets. Or you could decide that you want a different word processor, such as WordPerfect. How do you handle those data files in the WIDGETS and BANGLES subdirectories? You do not want to delete them because WordPerfect will be able to read them. An even worse nightmare is if you pick up a new product line such as beads. Now you have to create a BEADS subdirectory under each application program. You have created a logistical nightmare for finding out where files are located and deciding what data files should be kept.

The real problem with this all-too-typical organizational scheme is the logic behind it. Remember, programs are tools. Before computers, you still used tools—a pencil, a calculator, a typewriter. But did you file your output from these tools by the tool name? When you wrote a letter using a typewriter, did you file it in a folder labeled TYPEWRITER? When you calculated some numbers with your calculator, did you place your totals in a file folder called CALCULATOR? Of course not. It sounds silly to even suggest that. But in the above organizational scheme, that is *exactly* what you are doing!

Programs are simply tools. People do not work by software package; they work by projects. Software is a tool to help you do work easily and efficiently. Hence, it makes much better sense to organize a hard disk by the way you work rather than by the application package—the tool. In addition, with an efficient organizational scheme, it is easier to add and delete projects and software. The following section will recommend some guidelines to assist you in organizing your hard disk. However, you must always remember that any organizational scheme you devise is to assist you in saving, retrieving, and backing up your data files easily. A good organizational scheme for one user will not necessarily work for another.

8.2 METHODS OF ORGANIZING A HARD DISK

Certain criteria can give a hard disk an efficient and logical organization. These include the following suggestions:

- *The root directory should be a map to the rest of the disk.* The only files that should be in the root directory are the files placed there by the operating system. All other files in the root directory should be subdirectory listings. Look at the root directory as the index or table of contents to your entire hard disk. Ideally, when you execute the DIR command, you should not see more than a screenful of information. With today's very large hard disks, it is difficult to keep to this ideal. In reality, you may have 30 or more subdirectories off the root, which cannot fit on one screen. Nonetheless, the principle remains valid. Keep the root directory clear of unnecessary files.
- *Create subdirectories that are shallow and wide instead of compact and deep.* The reason is that it is easier for the operating system to find files that are not buried several levels down. Also, it is much easier for you to keep track of the subdirectories when the organizational scheme is simple. Remember the old programmer's principle: "KISS—Keep It Simple, Stupid." Short path names are easier to key in than long path names.
- *Plan the organization of your hard disk.* Think about the work you do and how it would be easiest for you to find your work files. This is especially true prior to installing new software.
- *Do not place data files in the same subdirectory as program files.* Although you are constantly changing, creating, and deleting data files, you rarely, if ever, create or delete program files.
- *Many small subdirectories with few files are better than a large subdirectory with many files.* Remember, you are categorizing data. If you begin to get too many files in a subdirectory, think about breaking the subdirectory into two or more subdirectories. It is easier to manage and update a subdirectory with a limited number of files because there is less likelihood of having to determine on a file-by-file basis which file belongs where. In addition, if you have too few files in many subdirectories, think about combining them into one subdirectory.
- *Keep subdirectory names short but descriptive.* Try to stay away from generic and meaningless subdirectory names such as DATA. The shorter the subdirectory name,

the less there is to key in. For instance, using the subdirectory name WIDGETS for your widgets data files is easy. If you simply use W, that is too short and cryptic for you to remember easily what the W subdirectory holds. On the other hand, the name WIDGETS.FIL is a little long to key in. You rarely, if ever, use extensions with subdirectory names. Again, remember you will be keying in these path names.

- *Create a separate subdirectory for batch files.* Batch files are files that you will learn to write to help automate processes you do often. Place the subdirectory for batch files under the root directory. A popular name for this subdirectory is BATCH.
- *Create a subdirectory called UTILS (utilities) in which you will create further separate subdirectories for each utility program you own or purchase.* As you work with computers, you start collecting utility software. Utility software programs provide commonly needed services. An example of this is Norton Utilities. Utility software would also include any shareware utilities that you might acquire from a download site on the World Wide Web. In many instances, utility software and shareware packages have similar file names, making it imperative that each has its own separate and readily identifiable subdirectory. You can place these subdirectories under the UTILS directory.
- *Learn how to install programs to your hard drive.* Typically programs will have a setup or install command. For instance, if you were going to install a file-compression program called WinZip, you would key in SETUP, and the setup program would tell you that it is going to install the program to C:\WINZIP. You can change that to C:\UTILS\WINZIP or D:\WINZIP. In other words, you can create your own organizational scheme and do not have to let the installation programs put the programs anywhere they wish.
- *Learn how to use the application package, and also learn how the application package works.* For instance, find out if the application package assigns a file extension. Lotus 1-2-3 assigns an extension of .WK1 for its files, whereas WordPerfect assigns a file extension of .WPD. If an application does not assign file extensions to data files, you can be extremely flexible and create file extensions that will apply to the work that you do with that application program's data files. For instance, you could assign the file extension .LET to letter files that deal with all your correspondence or .MYS to data files that deal with a mystery book you are writing. Most Windows programs will assign file extensions. With the addition of long file names introduced in Windows 95, you can name a file CHAPTER8.MYS in Word, and the .DOC extension will be added, leaving the full file name as CHAPTER8.MYS.DOC.
- *Find out how the application package works with subdirectories.* For instance, does it recognize subdirectories for data files? Very few programs today do not recognize subdirectories. However, most programs will have a default subdirectory where that program saves its data files. You should know what that subdirectory is and if you can change the default directory.
- *Analyze the way you work.* If you always use an application program's default data directory when you save and retrieve files, then organizing your hard disk around projects will not work for you. In that case, perhaps you do want to create data directories. Figure 8.3 is another way to organize your hard disk.

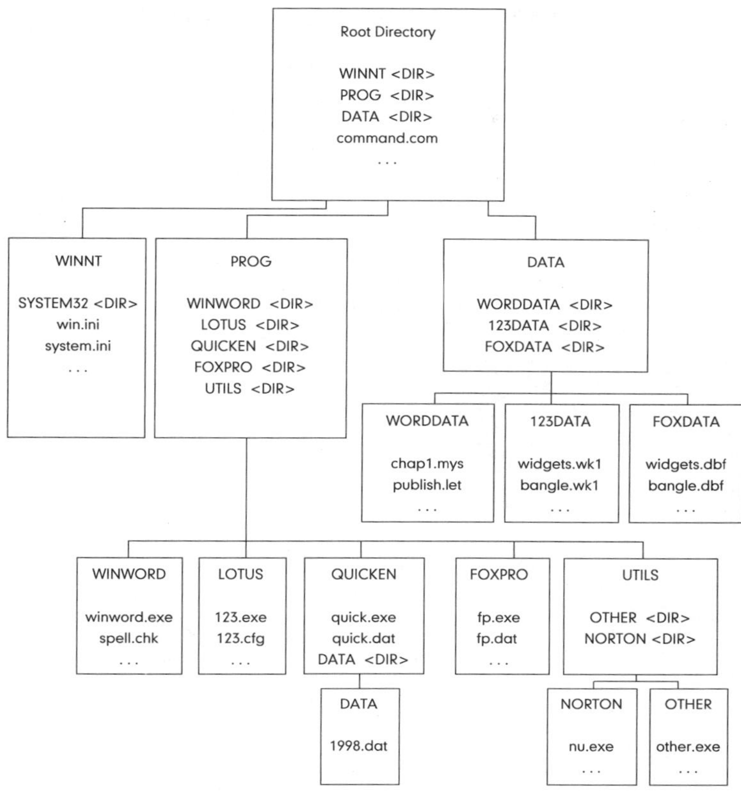

FIGURE 8.3 ANOTHER ORGANIZATIONAL SCHEME

- *Analyze your environment.* If, for instance, you are in an educational environment, organization by application package makes sense. You are teaching only that one application package, and all data created by students will be saved to floppy disks. Hence, your focus is the package, and organizing around the application package in this instance is logical.

An organizational scheme for a project-oriented environment based on our salesperson scenario could look something like Figure 8.4. In Figure 8.4, you know where all your software application programs are located. In addition, it is much easier to add a new software package or to update an existing one because all the program files are located in one place. For instance, when you want to add a presentation software application program, such as Harvard Graphics, you can create a subdirectory called C:\PROG\HG and install all the files in that location. If you have a suite of software, such as Corel Perfect Office or Microsoft Office, its installation makes subdirectories that act like PROG in the example. Microsoft creates MICROSOFT OFFICE under Program Files, and Corel creates COREL. Under these directories are subdirectories holding the individual programs. Also, since this scheme is organized by project, it is easy to add a new project or delete an old one. If, for example, you are now selling beads, you can create a subdirectory called C:\BEADS. If you no longer are selling widgets, you can use RD /S to eliminate the WIDGETS subdirectory. It is also easy to know which

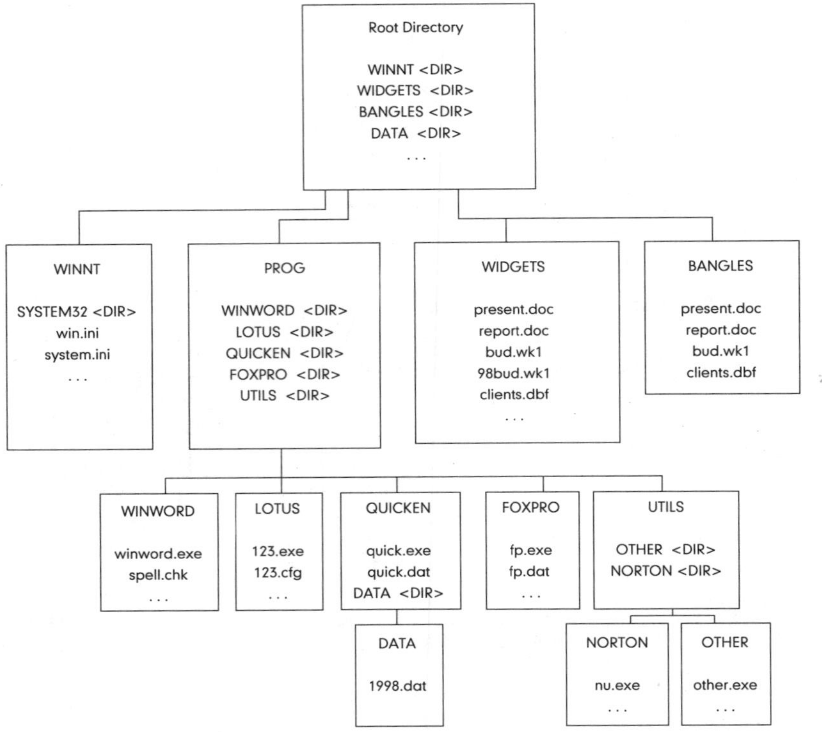

FIGURE 8.4 ORGANIZATION BY PROJECT

data files belong to what project. You also can tell which data files belong to which program by virtue of the file extension. In this example, if you look at the subdirectory called WIDGETS, you know that the data files PRESENT.DOC and REPORT.DOC were created with Word. You know that the data files BUD.WK1 and 98BUD.WK1 were created with Lotus 1-2-3, whereas CLIENTS.DBF was created with FoxPro. The same would be true for the BANGLES subdirectory. This example also shows that you leave the DATA subdirectory as is for Quicken because that is where Quicken prefers the data files.

This, of course, is not the only way to organize a hard disk. You can organize your hard disk any way you wish, but there should be organization. Although it may take some time in the beginning, ultimately organization will make more effective use of the hard disk. Primarily you want to organize your data files into meaningful directories. You do not want to save all your data files to a subdirectory called My Documents. You want to be able to go directly to the subdirectory that holds the files you wish to work on. Except when you create a new file, you will find that if you properly organize your data files, you will rarely use the Start/Programs menu. Instead, you will go directly to the directory that holds the files you wish to work on. For instance, if you were working with the bangles product line, you could open the directory BANGLES, which would have all of your files that deal with bangles, regardless of the application program that created them. The two major considerations for any organizational scheme are first, how do *you* work, and second, how do the *application programs* work?

8.3 ORGANIZING A DISK

Most users do not begin with an organized hard disk. What may seem organized to one user is chaos to another. In this instance, the user needs to reorganize the hard disk, a process that can be done without reformatting the hard disk. To master this process, you are going to take the DATA disk and reorganize it. This exercise will give you some idea of how the process works without having to worry about inadvertently deleting files from the hard disk. Prior to reorganizing it, however, you will update your backup copy of the DATA disk.

8.4 ACTIVITY: MAKING A COPY OF THE DATA DISK

Note 1: You are in Windows and have not shelled out to the command prompt.
Note 2: You will use My Computer to create a copy of the DATA disk.

Step 1 Double-click **My Computer**.

Step 2 Place the DATA disk in the A drive.

Step 3 Right-click the A drive icon.

Step 4 Point to **Copy Disk**.

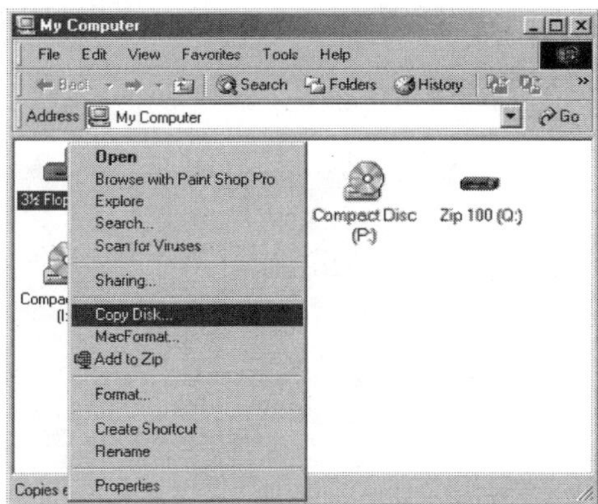

WHAT'S HAPPENING? You have started the process to copy a disk.

Step 5 Click **Copy Disk**.

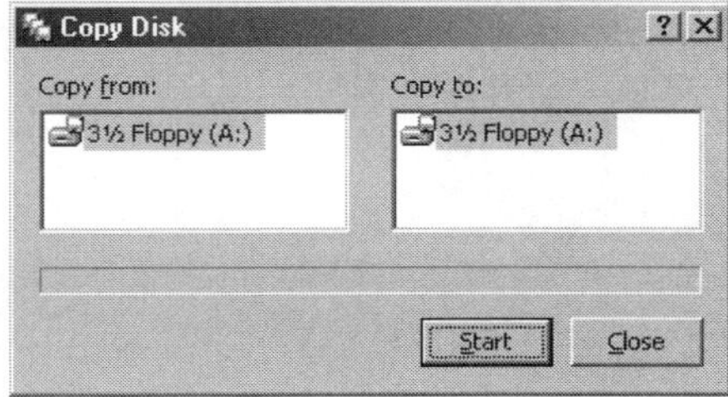

Step 6 Be sure both the **Copy from** and **Copy to** boxes have floppy Drive A selected.

Step 7 Click **Start**.

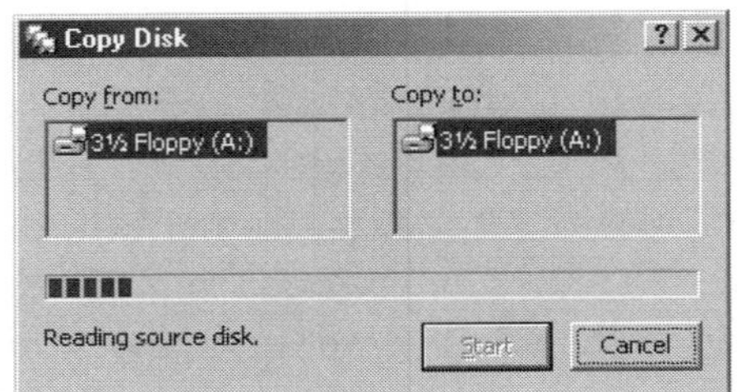

What's Happening? The copy process has started. Soon you will see:

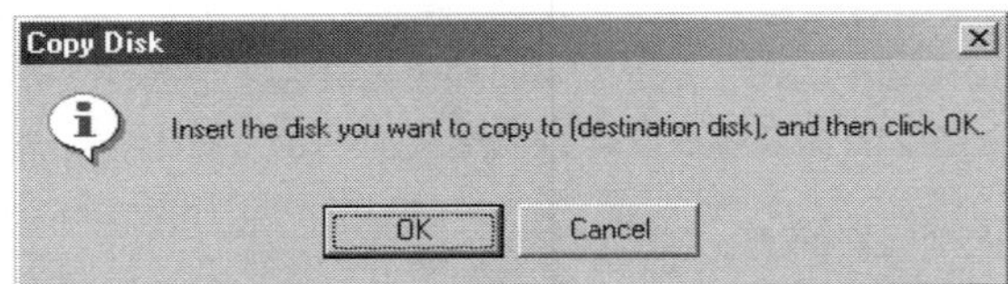

What's Happening? The information from the DATA disk is now in memory, and the operating system is waiting for the target disk.

Step 8 Replace the DATA disk with the BACKUP DATA disk you created in Chapter 6. Do not use the ACTIVITIES disk or the APPLICATION disk.

Step 9 Click the **OK** button.

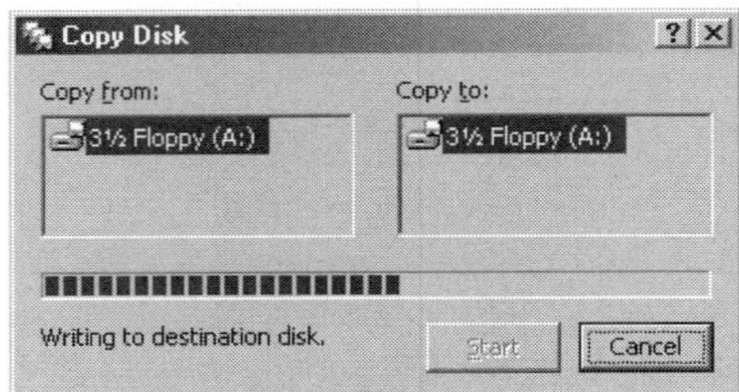

What's Happening? You see the message "Writing to destination disk." When the writing to disk is completed, you will see the following:

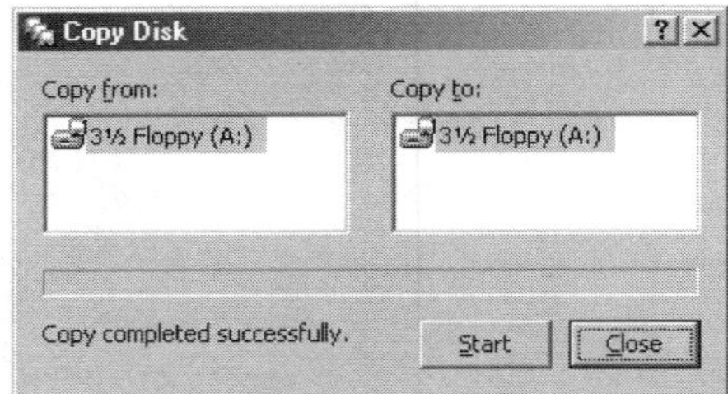

What's Happening? The copy process is completed.

Step 10 Click the **Close** button.

Step 11 Remove the BACKUP DATA disk from Drive A.

You now have updated your BACKUP DATA disk. Now you can safely work on the DATA disk because you have a current backup copy of it.

Step 12 Place the BACKUP DATA disk in a safe place. Insert the DATA disk into Drive A.

8.5 VIEWING THE DISK STRUCTURE WITH THE TREE COMMAND

You have looked at disk structures in the figures shown in this chapter. These have been pictorial representations of how a disk was organized. The TREE command allows you to see a graphic representation of the disk structure on the screen. The syntax of the TREE command is:

```
TREE [drive:][path] [/F] [/A]

  /F   Display the names of the files in each folder.
  /A   Use ASCII instead of extended characters.
```

Step 1 Open a Command Prompt window.

Step 2 Change to the **C:\WINDOSBK** directory.

Step 3 Key in the following: C:\WINDOSBK>**TREE** Enter

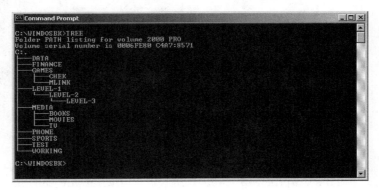

You can see a graphical representation of the folder structure under the **C:\WINDOSBK** directory. Your order may be different. The subdirectories **DATA**, **FINANCE**, **GAMES**, **LEVEL-1**, **MEDIA**, **PHONE**, **SPORTS**, **TEST**, and **WORKING** are directly under **WINDOSBK**. The subdirectories **CHECK** and **MLINK** are under **GAMES**; **LEVEL-2** is under **LEVEL-1**; **LEVEL-3** is under **LEVEL-2**; and **BOOKS**, **MOVIES**, and **TV** are all under **MEDIA**. With this graphic, it is easy to see how the **WINDOSBK** directory is organized.

Step 4 Key in the following: C:\WINDOSBK>**TREE /A** Enter

```
C:\WINDOSBK>TREE /A
Folder PATH listing for volume 2000 PRO
Volume serial number is 0006FE80 C4A7:8571
C:.
+---DATA
+---FINANCE
+---GAMES
|   +---CHEK
|   \---MLINK
+---LEVEL-1
|   \---LEVEL-2
|       \---LEVEL-3
+---MEDIA
|   +---BOOKS
|   +---MOVIES
|   \---TV
+---PHONE
+---SPORTS
+---TEST
\---WORKING

C:\WINDOSBK>
```

WHAT'S HAPPENING? You used the TREE command with the /A parameter. Instead of the solid graphic lines, you got only those lines that you could create with the keyboard using only ASCII characters, not the extended character set, which is able to draw solid, unbroken lines on the screen. The information displayed, however, is exactly the same.

Step 5 Key in the following: C:\WINDOSBK>**TREE /F** Enter

```
│           COMEDY.TV
│           DRAMA.TV
│
├───PHONE
│       FILE_ID.DIZ
│       HPB.CFG
│       HPB.DAT
│       HPB.EXE
│       HPB.SLC
│       README.HPB
│
├───SPORTS
│       BASKETBL.TMS
│       BSBALL-A.TMS
│       BSBALL-N.TMS
│       FOOT-COL.TMS
│       FOOT-PRO.TMS
│
├───TEST
│       NEW.FIL
│       SAMPLE.FIL
│
└───WORKING
C:\WINDOSBK>_
```

WHAT'S HAPPENING? (This graphic represents only part of what you see on your screen.) All the file names were listed within their respective directories. You can use redirection to place this information in a file, use the MORE filter, or simply scroll up and down the Command Prompt window using the scroll bar, as indicated below.

```
│   │   HELLO.TXT
│   │
│   └───LEVEL-2
│       │   HELLO.TXT
│       │
│       └───LEVEL-3
│               HELLO.TXT
│
├───MEDIA
│   ├───BOOKS
│   │       AME-LIT.BKS
│   │       MYSTERY.BKS
│   │       PULITZER.BKS
│   │
│   ├───MOVIES
│   │       DRAMA.MOV
│   │       MUSIC.MOV
│   │       OTHER.MOV
│   │
│   └───TV
│           COMEDY.TV
│           DRAMA.TV
│
├───PHONE
│       FILE_ID.DIZ
│       HPB.CFG
│       HPB.DAT
```

8.6 ORGANIZING THE DATA DISK

The DATA disk has minimal organization. The **. . .** in the figure below represents file names. (*Note:* If you did not do all the chapter activities, your disk could look different. It is not important that your disk is exactly as the one pictured. If you have additional files or are missing some files, you can delete, copy, or create files as needed. The contents of the text files do not matter.) Its structure is as follows:

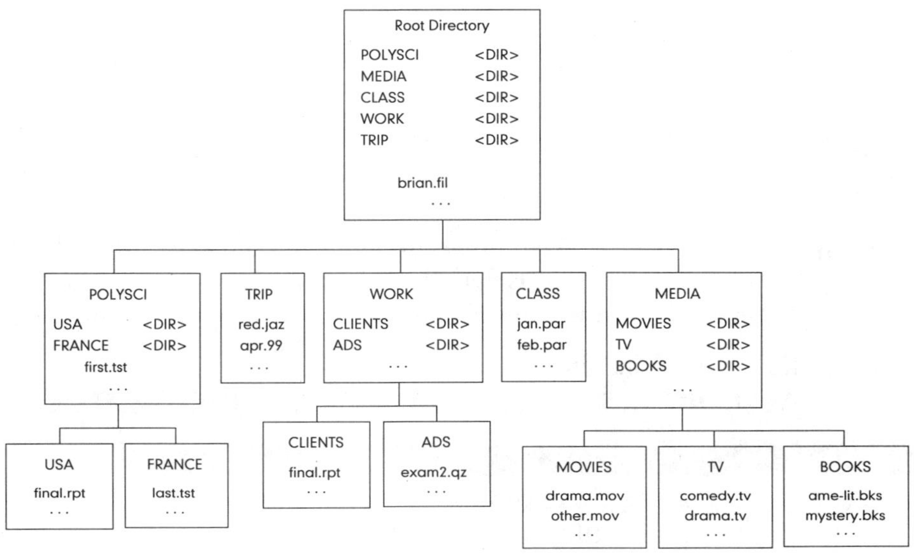

FIGURE 8.5 DISK ORGANIZATION

In addition to organizing this disk, you are also going to copy some programs from the \WINDOSBK directory to the disk so that there will be programs as well as data files on it. At this moment, you really cannot tell what is on this disk. There are so many files in the root directory that when you key in DIR, you see many, many files scrolling by on the screen. Therefore, you are going to reorganize the disk so that it will be easier to manage. You are going to create the necessary subdirectories and copy the appropriate files to the correct subdirectories. You will create a PROG subdirectory, which will be a map to the programs on the DATA disk. In the PROG subdirectory you will have the subdirectory GAMES for the different games you will copy from the \WINDOSBK directory and UTILS for the RNS.EXE program. (*Warning:* If you have installed programs on your hard disk, you do not move or copy them elsewhere. You may do so here as these are special examples.)

8.7 ACTIVITY: SETTING UP THE PROG SUBDIRECTORY

Note: The DATA disk is in Drive A. You have shelled out to the Command Prompt. C:\> is displayed as the default drive and the default directory.

Step 1 Key in the following: C:\>**A:** Enter

Step 2 Key in the following: A:\>**MD PROG** Enter

Step 3 Key in the following: A:\>**MD PROG\GAMES** Enter

Step 4 Key in the following: A:\>**MD PROG\UTILS** Enter

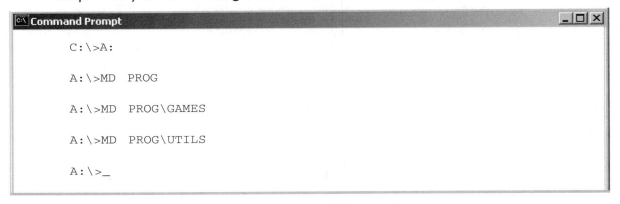

```
Command Prompt

C:\>A:

A:\>MD  PROG

A:\>MD  PROG\GAMES

A:\>MD  PROG\UTILS

A:\>_
```

WHAT'S HAPPENING? You created a generic program subdirectory and identified the specific subdirectories that reflect the programs you will have on the DATA disk. Now you need to copy the proper files to the proper subdirectory.

Step 5 Key in the following:
A:\>**COPY C:\WINDOSBK\GAMES\M*.* PROG\GAMES** Enter

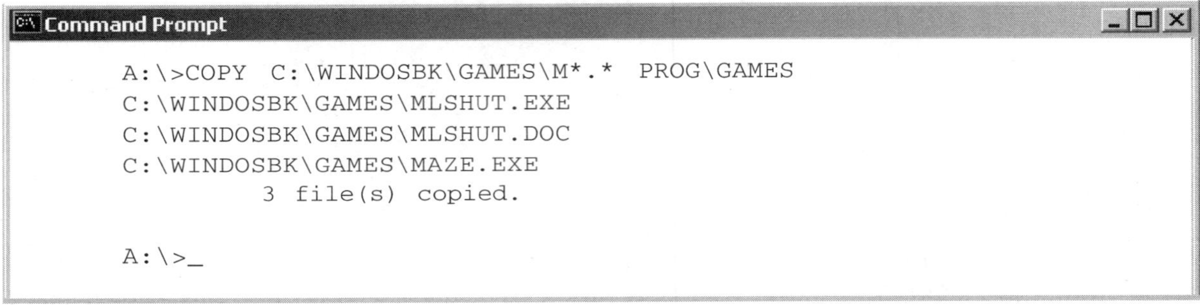

```
Command Prompt

A:\>COPY  C:\WINDOSBK\GAMES\M*.*  PROG\GAMES
C:\WINDOSBK\GAMES\MLSHUT.EXE
C:\WINDOSBK\GAMES\MLSHUT.DOC
C:\WINDOSBK\GAMES\MAZE.EXE
        3 file(s) copied.

A:\>_
```

WHAT'S HAPPENING? You copied all the programs that begin with M from the **\WINDOSBK\GAMES** directory to the **PROG\GAMES** subdirectory on the DATA disk.

Step 6 Key in the following: A:\>**DIR C:\WINDOSBK\GAMES** Enter

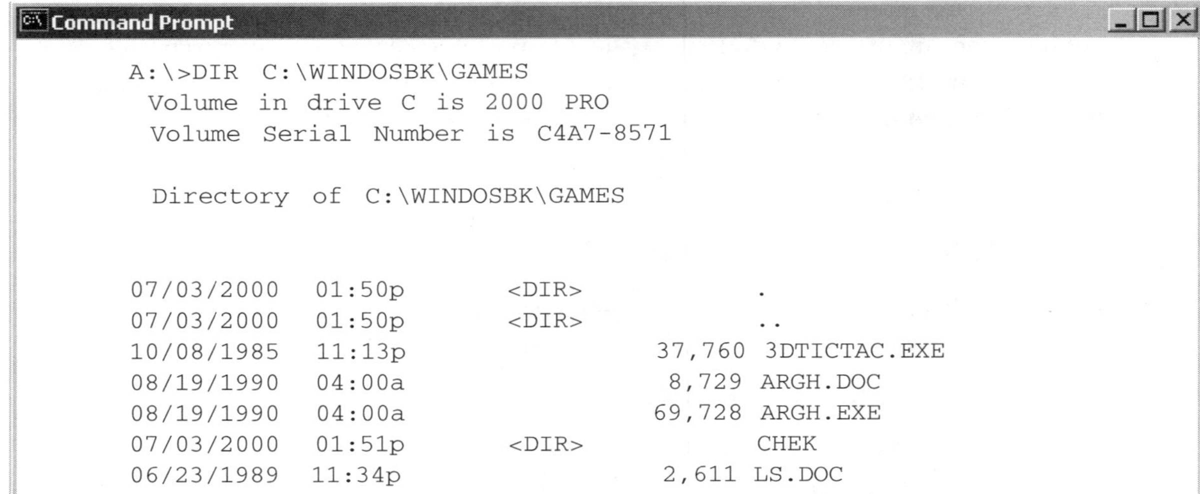

```
Command Prompt

A:\>DIR  C:\WINDOSBK\GAMES
 Volume in drive C is 2000 PRO
 Volume Serial Number is C4A7-8571

 Directory of C:\WINDOSBK\GAMES


07/03/2000  01:50p      <DIR>          .
07/03/2000  01:50p      <DIR>          ..
10/08/1985  11:13p              37,760 3DTICTAC.EXE
08/19/1990  04:00a               8,729 ARGH.DOC
08/19/1990  04:00a              69,728 ARGH.EXE
07/03/2000  01:51p      <DIR>          CHEK
06/23/1989  11:34p               2,611 LS.DOC
```

```
06/23/1989  11:40p                12,576 LS.EXE
06/23/1989  11:41p                 8,404 LS.PAS
05/09/1989  03:51p                34,645 MAZE.EXE
07/03/2000  01:51p      <DIR>            MLINK
08/14/1989  10:48p                15,049 MLSHUT.DOC
08/14/1989  10:31p                43,776 MLSHUT.EXE
                 9 File(s)        233,278 bytes
                 4 Dir(s)   6,849,961,984 bytes free

A:\>_
```

WHAT'S HAPPENING? You used the COPY command in Step 5 to request all the files that begin with M to be copied to the **PROG\GAMES** subdirectory, but the subdirectory called **MLINK** and the files in it were not copied to the DATA disk. COPY copies only files, not subdirectories. If you had wanted to copy everything that begins with M including the **MLINK** subdirectory, you would have used the XCOPY command.

Step 7 Key in the following: A:\>**DIR C:\WINDOSBK*.TXT** Enter

```
Command Prompt

A:\>DIR C:\WINDOSBK\*.TXT
 Volume in drive C is 2000 PRO
 Volume Serial Number is C4A7-8571

 Directory of C:\WINDOSBK

06/16/2000  04:32p                    72 APRIL.TXT
05/30/2000  04:32p                    45 BYE.TXT
12/11/1999  04:03p                    72 DANCES.TXT
06/16/2000  04:32p                    75 FEBRUARY.TXT
01/01/2002  04:32a                    34 GOODBYE.TXT
05/30/2000  04:32p                    53 HELLO.TXT
06/16/2000  04:32p                    73 JANUARY.TXT
05/27/2001  10:08p                    81 LONGFILENAME.TXT
05/27/2001  10:43p                    95 LONGFILENAMED.TXT
05/27/2001  10:42p                    97 LONGFILENAMING.TXT
06/16/2000  04:32p                    71 MARCH.TXT
11/16/2000  12:00p                    53 Sandy and Nicki.txt
11/16/2000  12:00p                    59 Sandy and Patty.txt
12/11/1999  04:03p                    65 TEST.TXT
              14 File(s)             945 bytes
                 0 Dir(s)   6,849,961,984 bytes free

A:\>_
```

WHAT'S HAPPENING? You displayed all the **.TXT** files in the **WINDOSBK** directory. You want to copy all the **.TXT** files that were created on or after 05-30-00 to the root directory of the DATA disk. You do not want to copy the files **TEST.TXT** or **DANCES.TXT**. XCOPY allows you to make choices by date.

Step 8 Key in the following: A:\>**ATTRIB -S -H -R A:*.*** Enter

You removed any system, hidden, and read-only attributes that were set for the files on the root of the A drive.

Step 9 Key in the following: A:\>**XCOPY C:\WINDOSBK*.TXT /D:05-30-00** Enter

```
A:\>XCOPY C:\WINDOSBK\*.TXT /D:05-30-00
Overwrite GOODBYE.TXT (Yes/No/All)?
```

Remember the default for XCOPY is to confirm overwrites. The command is telling you that **GOODBYE.TXT** already exists. In this case, you do want to overwrite all the files.

Step 10 Press **A** Enter

```
A:\>XCOPY C:\WINDOSBK\*.TXT /D:05-30-00
Overwrite GOODBYE.TXT (Yes/No/All)? A
C:\WINDOSBK\GOODBYE.TXT
C:\WINDOSBK\BYE.TXT
C:\WINDOSBK\FEBRUARY.TXT
C:\WINDOSBK\APRIL.TXT
C:\WINDOSBK\HELLO.TXT
C:\WINDOSBK\JANUARY.TXT
C:\WINDOSBK\LONGFILENAME.TXT
C:\WINDOSBK\LONGFILENAMED.TXT
C:\WINDOSBK\LONGFILENAMING.TXT
C:\WINDOSBK\MARCH.TXT
C:\WINDOSBK\Sandy and Nicki.txt
C:\WINDOSBK\Sandy and Patty.txt
12 File(s) copied

A:\>
```

You copied only the 12 files of interest, not all 14 that were in the **\WINDOSBK** subdirectory.

8.8 THE MOVE COMMAND REVISITED

When reorganizing your hard disk, you sometimes do need to copy files and/or subdirectory structures from one place to another and replace existing files. In terms of reorganizing your hard disk, you do not necessarily want to *copy* files and directories. Most often, what you really want to do is either move files from one location to another or simply rename the subdirectory.

You have used the MOVE command in previous chapters to move files from one directory to another. Clearly, using the MOVE command is an easy way to manipulate your files. However, there is an important precaution to take before moving files and directories wholesale. Moving *data* files and *data* directories is usually a safe and fool-proof procedure that rarely impacts your programs. However, moving *program* files and renaming *program* directories is not "safe." Windows registers program files, their names, and their locations in the Registry. If they are moved or renamed at the command prompt, the Registry will not be able to find them. Program files are not generally *copied* to a location—they are *installed* in a location with a setup program. Files pertaining to the program are placed in many different locations. Moving or renaming these Windows program files and directories will almost certainly cause the program to fail.

When dealing with small programs that are completely contained within one directory and were created to run under DOS rather than Windows, problems can still occur. Moving the entire directory or renaming it *may* be safe—the program may still run. If you do decide to manipulate program files and directories, be sure and take note of which directory the program files are in before you start. Does this mean that you should not organize your hard disk? It does not, but you must do it with caution. You can and will be primarily concerned with organizing your data files. These files can be easily and safely rearranged to meet your needs.

In the next activity you will move files and rename subdirectories so you can see how easy it is with data files.

8.9 ACTIVITY: USING MOVE TO ORGANIZE YOUR DISK

Note: You have the DATA disk in Drive A with A:\> displayed.

Step 1 Key in the following: A:\>**MOVE BON*.* POLYSCI\FRANCE** Enter

```
Command Prompt

A:\>MOVE BON*.* POLYSCI\FRANCE
A:\BONJOUR.NEW

A:\>_
```

WHAT'S HAPPENING? You quickly copied the **BONJOUR.NEW** file to the **POLYSCI\FRANCE** subdirectory and deleted it from the root directory at the same time. That is what the MOVE command does.

Step 2 Key in the following: A:\>**DIR M*.*** Enter

```
Command Prompt

A:\>DIR M*.*
 Volume in drive A is DATA
 Volume Serial Number is 3330-1807

 Directory of A:\

04/23/2000  04:03p                  71 MARCH.FIL
04/23/2000  04:03p                  71 MAR.BUD
```

```
04/23/2000  04:03p                   71 MARCH.NEW
06/16/2000  04:32p                   71 MARCH.TXT
04/30/2001  12:09p                  292 MONTHS.SAM
10/10/1999  04:53p                   71 MAR.99
08/12/2000  04:12p                   73 MARK.FIL
07/03/2000  01:53p      <DIR>          MEDIA
               7 File(s)            720 bytes
               1 Dir(s)       1,261,568 bytes free

A:\>_
```

WHAT'S HAPPENING? You want to move all the files that begin with M to the **POLYSCI\USA** directory. But you don't want to move the **MEDIA** subdirectory. In Windows 2000 Professional, the MOVE command will ignore subdirectories. This was not true in some previous versions of Windows.

Step 3 Key in the following: A:\>**MOVE M*.* POLYSCI\USA** Enter

```
Command Prompt

A:\>MOVE  M*.*  POLYSCI\USA
A:\MAR.99
A:\MARCH.FIL
A:\MAR.BUD
A:\MARCH.NEW
A:\MARCH.TXT
A:\MONTHS.SAM
A:\MARK.FIL
        7 File(s) moved.

A:\>_
```

WHAT'S HAPPENING? Notice that the **MEDIA** subdirectory was not moved. You can use the MOVE command to rename a subdirectory, but the REN command works on subdirectories as well as files.

Step 4 Key in the following: A:\>**REN TRIP NEWSTUFF** Enter

Step 5 Key in the following: A:\>**DIR TRIP** Enter

```
Command Prompt

A:\>REN  TRIP  NEWSTUFF

A:\>DIR  TRIP
 Volume  in  drive  A  is  DATA
 Volume  Serial  Number  is  3330-1807

 Directory  of  A:\

File  Not  Found

A:\>_
```

You successfully renamed the **TRIP** directory **NEWSTUFF**. In versions of DOS previous to Windows 95, the REN command would not rename subdirectories; you had to use the MOVE command. Using the MOVE command for this purpose was confusing given that, if you keyed it in one way, you moved files, but, if you keyed it another way, you renamed subdirectories. Because this was so confusing, there were utility programs created that rename subdirectories. One such program is **RNS.EXE**.

8.10 A UTILITY PROGRAM—RNS.EXE

There is always something that users want to do that cannot be done easily with the commands that come with the operating system. This is how third-party utilities are born. Some of these utility programs are given away, others are released as shareware, and others are commercially packaged and sold. One of the better-known commercial utility programs is Norton Utilities. Why do computer users buy utility programs? Each program does something useful that the operating system does not allow you to do.

The program RNS.EXE was written by Nick Markiw. It was written for versions of DOS previous to Windows 95 when the REN command could not be used to rename subdirectories. It is included on the ACTIVITIES disk. This program was given to you when you purchased this textbook to demonstrate how third-party utility programs can work with the operating system. The syntax for this program is:

```
RNS [drive:][path]oldname [drive:][path]newname
```

8.11 ACTIVITY: USING RNS, A SUBDIRECTORY RENAMING UTILITY

Note 1: You have the DATA disk in Drive A with A:\> displayed.

Note 2: You previously created the **PROG\UTILS** subdirectory on your DATA disk. If you do not have this directory structure, create it now.

Step 1 Key in the following: A:\>**COPY C:\WINDOSBK\RNS.EXE PROG\UTILS** Enter

Step 2 Key in the following: A:\>**DIR PROG\UTILS** Enter

Command Prompt

```
A:\>COPY C:\WINDOSBK\RNS.EXE PROG\UTILS
        1 File(s) copied.

A:\>DIR PROG\UTILS
 Volume in drive A is DATA
 Volume Serial Number is 3330-1807

 Directory of A:\PROG\UTILS

06/07/2001  08:34a      <DIR>          .
06/07/2001  08:34a      <DIR>          ..
11/22/1989  10:35p               7,269 RNS.EXE
               1 File(s)          7,269 bytes
               2 Dir(s)       1,253,888 bytes free

A:\>_
```

You copied the file **RNS.EXE** from the **\WINDOSBK** subdirectory to the **PROG\UTILS** subdirectory on the DATA disk. You should recognize any file with an **.EXE** extension as a program. You decide that **NEWSTUFF** is not a descriptive name for the subdirectory and want to change the subdirectory name from **NEWSTUFF** to **TRIP**.

Step 3 Key in the following: A:\>**CD PROG\UTILS** Enter

Step 4 Key in the following: A:\PROG\UTILS>**RNS \NEWSTUFF \TRIP** Enter

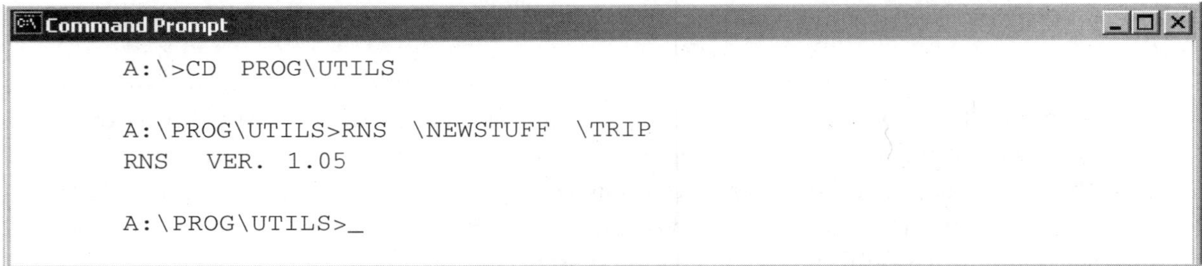

```
Command Prompt

A:\>CD  PROG\UTILS

A:\PROG\UTILS>RNS  \NEWSTUFF  \TRIP
RNS   VER. 1.05

A:\PROG\UTILS>_
```

You first changed the directory to the place where the program **RNS.EXE** is located so that you could execute it. You could have changed the path, but since this is a one-time experiment, you do not want to do that. Then you executed the RNS program to change the directory names. This seemed easy enough. Did it work?

Step 5 Key in the following: A:\PROG\UTILS>**DIR \TRIP** Enter

Step 6 Key in the following: A:\PROG\UTILS>**DIR \NEWSTUFF** Enter

```
Command Prompt

A:\PROG\UTILS>DIR  \TRIP
 Volume in drive A is DATA
 Volume Serial Number is 3330-1807

 Directory of A:\TRIP

05/29/2001  10:11p      <DIR>          .
05/29/2001  10:11p      <DIR>          ..
04/23/2000  04:03p                  71 MAR.INK
04/23/2000  04:03p                  75 FEB.BUD
04/23/2000  04:03p                  75 FEBRUARY.TXT
10/10/1999  04:53p                  75 FEB.99
03/05/2000  04:41p                 232 FUNNY.TV
05/30/2000  04:32p                  19 RED.JAZ
07/31/1999  12:53p                  44 FRANK.FIL
10/10/1999  04:53p                  72 APR.99
10/10/1999  04:53p                  71 MAR.99
04/23/2000  04:18p                  72 APR.INK
04/23/2000  04:03p                  75 FEB.INK
04/23/2000  04:03p                  73 JAN.INK
              12 File(s)            954 bytes
               2 Dir(s)       1,253,888 bytes free
```

```
A:\PROG\UTILS>DIR  \NEWSTUFF
 Volume in drive A is DATA
 Volume Serial Number is 3330-1807

 Directory of A:\

File Not Found

A:\PROG\UTILS>_
```

The RNS command did rename the subdirectory **\NEWSTUFF** to **\TRIP**. It is, of course, not necessary to use this command, as the REN command works as well. The RNS command is used here as an example of a third-party utility. People write utility programs like RNS to extend the power of the operating system. You will find that this is also true with Windows utilities. There are third-party utility programs available for Windows that extend and expand its capabilities. Although utility programs often have overlapping commands, users often purchase more than one utility program because each one has certain useful functions.

Step 7 Key in the following: A:\PROG\UTILS>**CD ** Enter

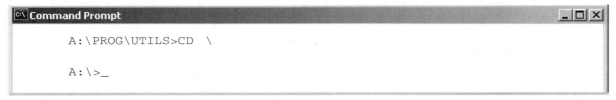

Command Prompt

```
A:\PROG\UTILS>CD  \

A:\>_
```

WHAT'S HAPPENING? You have returned to the root of the A drive.

8.12 CHECKING A DISK

CHKDSK is an operating system utility that dates back to very early versions of MS-DOS. CHKDSK is an external command stored in the C:\WINNT\SYSTEM32 subdirectory. CHKDSK can be used on disks with any file system supported by Windows 2000 Professional: FAT12 (floppy disks), FAT16, FAT32, and NTFS. CHKDSK examines disk space and use for the NTFS and FAT file systems. A status report is provided with information specific to the file system on the drive you checked. CHKDSK also locates errors on a disk and can correct those errors when you use the proper parameters.

The information provided by the reports is information you need to know about your disks. You need to know how much room is left on the disk so that you can add a new file. You want to know if there are any bad spots on a disk, which can mean the loss of a file. Bad spots can come from a variety of sources, such as a mishandled disk or a manufacturing defect. You may want to know if the files are being stored efficiently on a disk or if you have problems with the logical structure of the disk.

If your disk is using the FAT file system, the CHKDSK command analyzes both FATs (file allocation tables) on the disk, the directory table for the root directory, the directory structure, and the integrity of the files, including the validity of any long file names. Part of the process of checking the FAT includes tracing out the chain of data for each file. This ensures that the directory entries match the location and lengths of files with the file allocation table on the specified drive. It ensures that all the directories are readable. After checking the disk, CHKDSK reports how many files are on a disk and how much space is taken. CHKDSK establishes the space left on the disk for additional files.

As you learned in Chapter 3, NTFS uses an MFT (Master File Table) to track every file on the disk rather than a FAT. The CHKDSK utility when used with an NTFS file system works in three stages. Stage 1: CHKDSK looks at each file record segment in the MFT for consistency. It also identifies which file segments and clusters are currently being used. At the end of Stage 1, the CHKDSK command then compares the information it collected against the information that NTFS keeps on the disk. CHKDSK is looking for any discrepancies or problems. Stage 2: It verifies what NTFS calls "indexes" (directories), again checking for internal consistency. It ensures that every directory and file belongs to at least one directory and that the reference to that file in the MFT is valid. It also verifies file times and dates as well as file size. This is the most time-consuming portion of CHKDSK. Stage 3: CHKDSK checks and verifies the security for each directory and file. The security information includes the file's owner, permissions granted to users and groups, and any auditing that is to occur for that file or directory.

You should regularly run the CHKDSK command for each disk to ensure that your file structures have integrity. No files should be open when you run CHKDSK on a disk. This means you need to close all programs, including programs such as screen savers. If CHKDSK cannot lock the drive—prevent access—it will tell you that it will run CHKDSK the next time you start your system.

The syntax for CHKDSK is:

```
Checks a disk and displays a status report.


CHKDSK [volume[[path]filename]] [/F] [/V] [/R] [/X] [/I] [/C]
[/L[:size]]


  volume          Specifies the drive letter (followed by a colon),
                  mount point, or volume name.
  filename        FAT only: Specifies the files to check for
                  fragmentation.
  /F              Fixes errors on the disk.
  /V              On FAT/FAT32: Displays the full path and name of every
                  file on the disk.
                  On NTFS: Displays cleanup messages if any.
  /R              Locates bad sectors and recovers readable information
                  (implies /F).
  /L:size         NTFS only: Changes the log file size to the specified
                  number of kilobytes. If size is not specified, displays
                  current size.
  /X              Forces the volume to dismount first if necessary.
                  All opened handles to the volume would then be invalid
                  (implies /F).
  /I              NTFS only: Performs a less vigorous check of index entries.
```

```
  /C              NTFS only: Skips checking of cycles within the folder
                  structure.

The /I or /C switch reduces the amount of time required to run Chkdsk by
skipping certain checks of the volume.
```

Note that there are parameters that are valid only with FAT file systems and other parameters that are valid only with NTFS drives. In addition, on a hard disk, you need to have administrator privileges to run CHKDSK.

8.13 ACTIVITY: USING CHKDSK ON HARD AND FLOPPY DRIVES

Note: The DATA disk is in Drive A. A:\> is displayed.

Step 1 Key in the following: A:\>**C:** Enter

Step 2 Key in the following: C:\>**CD WINNT\SYSTEM32** Enter

Step 3 Key in the following: C:\WINNT\SYSTEM32>**DIR CHKDSK.*** Enter

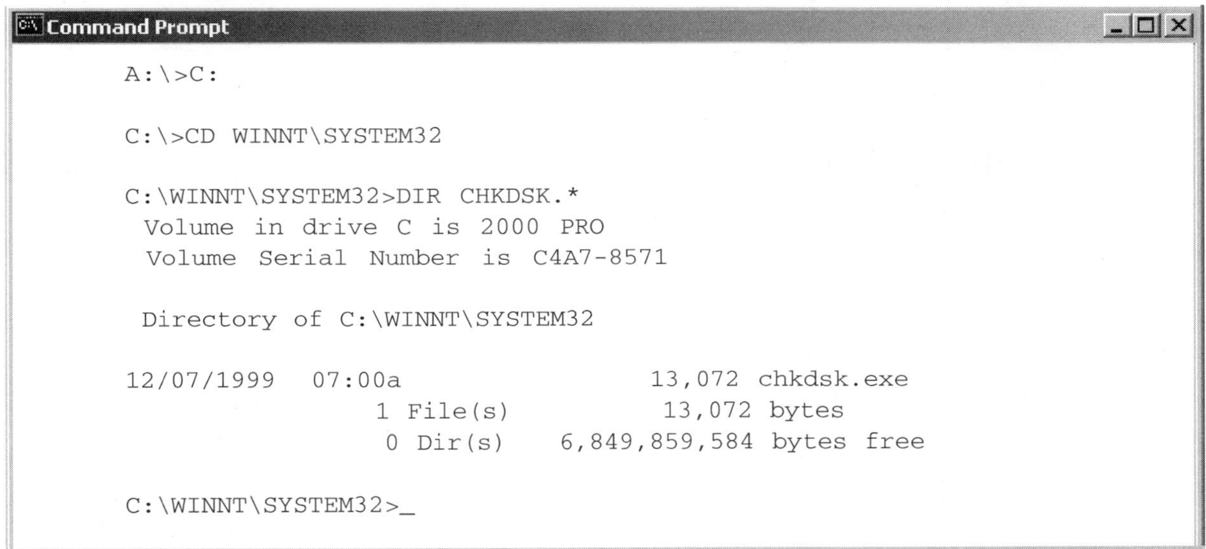

```
Command Prompt

A:\>C:

C:\>CD WINNT\SYSTEM32

C:\WINNT\SYSTEM32>DIR CHKDSK.*
 Volume in drive C is 2000 PRO
 Volume Serial Number is C4A7-8571

 Directory of C:\WINNT\SYSTEM32

12/07/1999  07:00a              13,072 chkdsk.exe
               1 File(s)         13,072 bytes
               0 Dir(s)   6,849,859,584 bytes free

C:\WINNT\SYSTEM32>_
```

WHAT'S HAPPENING? The DIR command told you that the program **CHKDSK.EXE** is indeed stored as a file in the **\WINNT\SYSTEM32** subdirectory.

Step 4 Key in the following: C:\WINNT\SYSTEM32>**CHKDSK** Enter

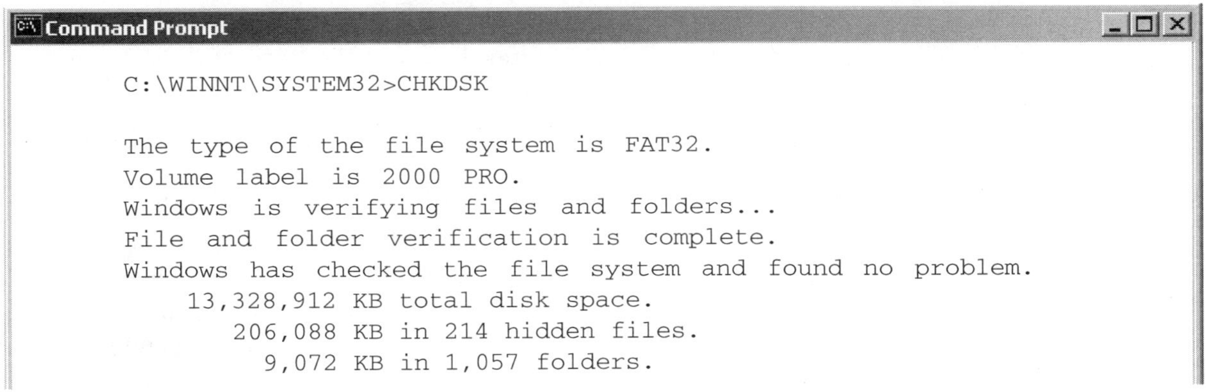

```
Command Prompt

C:\WINNT\SYSTEM32>CHKDSK

The type of the file system is FAT32.
Volume label is 2000 PRO.
Windows is verifying files and folders...
File and folder verification is complete.
Windows has checked the file system and found no problem.
    13,328,912 KB total disk space.
       206,088 KB in 214 hidden files.
         9,072 KB in 1,057 folders.
```

```
     2,213,272 KB in 32,682 files.
    10,900,472 KB are available.

          8,192 bytes in each allocation unit.
      1,666,114 total allocation units on disk.
      1,362,559 allocation units available on disk.

C:\WINNT\SYSTEM32>_
```

WHAT'S HAPPENING? The operating system tells you it has checked this file system (FAT32) for errors and found none. Valuable information has been provided. You know the total disk capacity (13,328,912KB), the remaining space (10,900,472KB), the total number of allocation units (1,666,114), the number of allocation units available for use (1,362,559), and the number of bytes in each allocation unit (8,192). Do not worry if you do not see the same numbers displayed on your screen. These numbers are related to how the disk was formatted, the size of the hard disk, and how much internal memory is installed in a specific computer. What is important is what the status report is telling you. Let us look at this example, line by line:

13,328,912 KB total disk space This number is the entire capacity of a specific disk.

206,088 KB in 214 hidden files What are hidden files? The Registry files are hidden files. Many Help files are hidden files, as well as system and information files from both the operating system and software applications. The number of hidden files will vary from disk to disk.

9,072 KB in 1,057 folders Nearly all hard disks have subdirectories. This number is for subdirectory entries only.

2,213,272 KB in 32,682 files These are the files that are stored on the disk. They are not necessarily files that you created. User files include all program or application files you have on a disk.

10,900,472 KB are available This line establishes how much room remains on the disk in Drive C for new data or program files in bytes. A KB is 1,024 bytes. A byte is one character. It can be the letter "b," the letter "c," the number "3," or the punctuation mark "?," for example. To give you a rough idea of what a byte means, a page of a printed novel contains about 3,000 bytes. Thus, a disk with a total capacity of 360,000 bytes could hold or store a maximum of about 120 pages of a novel. A 20-MB hard disk (1 megabyte means 1,000,000 bytes) would hold approximately 20,000,000 bytes or 6,667 pages of text; if the average novel has about 400 pages, you could store about 16½ novels. A 2-GB hard drive could hold about 1,800 books! This approximation is not entirely accurate because it does not take into account that often information is stored in such a way as to be compressed. However, it does give you an idea of the disk capacity in "human terms." As you work with computers, you become accustomed to thinking in bytes.

8,192 bytes in each allocation unit	As discussed earlier, the smallest unit that the OS actually reads is a cluster. A cluster is made up of sectors. A cluster is also referred to as an allocation unit. The number of sectors that make up a cluster (allocation unit) vary depending on the type of disk.
1,666,114 total allocation units on disk	This indicates the total number of clusters available. If you multiply 1,666,114 by 8,192, you get 13,648,805,880—or the capacity of this hard disk, a 13-GB hard disk.
1,362,559 allocation units available on disk	This line tells you how much room is available on the disk by cluster.

Sometimes you will see a line reporting how many bad sectors a disk may have. Having bad sectors is not uncommon on hard disks. If you had bad sectors, the line might read "65,536 bytes in bad sectors." The number would, of course, vary depending on the disk that is checked. On a 20-GB hard disk, for instance, 65,536 bytes in bad sectors is not that significant. However, if you had a smaller hard disk, the number would be significant and you might want to determine if your hard disk needs to be replaced. The next step cannot be done unless you have a disk that is formatted with NTFS. If you do not, simply read the steps.

Step 5 Key in the following: C:\WINNT\SYSTEM32>**CD ** Enter

Step 6 Key in the following: C:\>**CHKDSK E:** Enter

Command Prompt

```
C:\>CHKDSK E:
The type of the file system is NTFS.
Volume label is QUAN-2.

WARNING! F parameter not specified.
Running CHKDSK in read-only mode.

CHKDSK is verifying files (stage 1 of 3)...
File verification completed.
CHKDSK is verifying indexes (stage 2 of 3)...
Index verification completed.
CHKDSK is verifying security descriptors (stage 3 of 3)...
Security descriptor verification completed.
```

```
Windows found problems with the file system.
Run CHKDSK with the /F (fix) option to correct these.

   1040224 KB total disk space.
    804221 KB in 616 files.
       240 KB in 36 indexes.
         0 KB in bad sectors.
      8719 KB in use by the system.
      7264 KB occupied by the log file.
    227043 KB available on disk.

       512 bytes in each allocation unit.
   2080448 total allocation units on disk.
    454086 allocation units available on disk.

C:\>_
```

In order to repair a disk, you need to include a parameter, and CHKDSK informs you of that fact. Then each stage is executed. Then, again, you see the statistical report.

1040224 KB total disk space	This number is the entire capacity of a specific disk.
804221 KB in 616 files	These are the files that are stored on the disk. They are not necessarily files that you created. User files include all program or application files you have on a disk.
240 KB in 36 indexes	This refers to indexes, which are subdirectories.
0 KB in bad sectors	The report tells you that you have no bad sectors.
8719 KB in use by the system	This is information being used by the system.
7264 KB occupied by the log file	The log file is a transaction log of disk activities. Windows 2000 Professional uses this file so it can recover files if you have disk problems. It can even repair itself if necessary.
227043 KB available on disk	This line establishes how much room remains on the disk.
512 bytes in each allocation unit	As discussed earlier, the smallest unit that the OS actually reads is a cluster. A cluster is made up of sectors. A cluster is also referred to as an "allocation unit."
2080448 total allocation units on disk	This indicates the total number of clusters available. If you multiply 2,080,448 by 512, you get 1,065,189,376 bytes or the capacity of this hard disk, a 1-GB hard disk.

454086 allocation units available on disk	This line tells you how much room is available on the disk by cluster.

Step 7 Key in the following: C:\> **A:** Enter

Command Prompt
C:\>A:
A:\>_

WHAT'S HAPPENING? You have changed the default drive to the A drive. The DATA disk is in the A drive.

Step 8 Key in the following: A:\>**CHKDSK** Enter

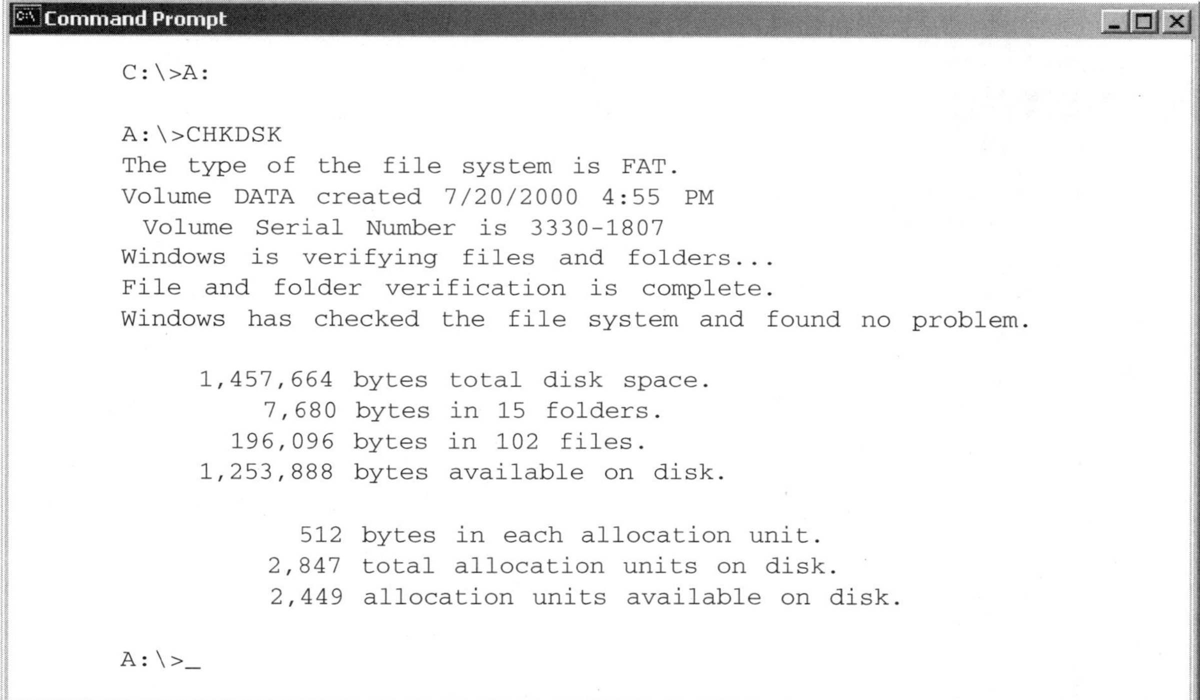
Command Prompt
C:\>A:
A:\>CHKDSK
The type of the file system is FAT.
Volume DATA created 7/20/2000 4:55 PM
Volume Serial Number is 3330-1807
Windows is verifying files and folders...
File and folder verification is complete.
Windows has checked the file system and found no problem.
1,457,664 bytes total disk space.
7,680 bytes in 15 folders.
196,096 bytes in 102 files.
1,253,888 bytes available on disk.
512 bytes in each allocation unit.
2,847 total allocation units on disk.
2,449 allocation units available on disk.
A:\>_

WHAT'S HAPPENING

This display looks similar to the screen displayed when you used CHKDSK on the FAT hard drive. The numbers are, of course, very different. You have 1,457,664 bytes total disk space because this is a 1.44-MB disk. The files and bytes available will vary based on what is on the DATA disk. If you placed another disk in Drive A, you would get different information about files and free bytes remaining on that particular disk.

8.14 THE VERBOSE PARAMETER WITH THE CHKDSK COMMAND

The CHKDSK command has a very useful parameter, /V. Using /V on a FAT drive is known as running in verbose mode. This parameter, in conjunction with the CHKDSK command, not only gives the usual status report, but also lists every file on the disk including hidden files. On an NTFS drive, it displays clean-up messages, if any.

An important thing to remember about parameters is that they are associated with specific commands and perform specific tasks for those commands. The same parameter does not do the same thing with other commands. For instance, if you use the parameter /V with the FORMAT command, it means put a volume label on the disk. However, when you use /V with the CHKDSK command, it displays all the files on the disk if it is FAT and displays clean-up messages if it is NTFS.

8.15 ACTIVITY: USING THE /V PARAMETER AND USING DIR PARAMETERS

Note 1: The DATA disk is in Drive A. A:\> is displayed.

Note 2: When you press Enter in Step 1, the screen display will scroll by too fast to see. Even hitting the Pause key immediately will not stop the screen.

Note 3: Your files may appear in a different order.

Note 4: To facilitate mouse usage, click on the Command Prompt icon, go to Properties, and disable QuickEdit mode.

Step 1 Key in the following: A:\>**CHKDSK /V** Enter

```
Command Prompt

\CLASS\JAN.FIL
93 percent completed.
\POLYSCI\USA
94 percent completed.
\POLYSCI\FIRST.TST
95 percent completed.
\POLYSCI\FRANCE
96 percent completed.
\POLYSCI\FRANCE\LAST.TST
\POLYSCI\USA\FINAL.RPT
97 percent completed.
\POLYSCI\USA\NOTE2.TMP
98 percent completed.
\POLYSCI\USA\NOTE3.TMP
99 percent completed.
\POLYSCI\USA\DRESS.UP
100 percent completed.
File and folder verification is complete.
Windows has checked the file system and found no problem.

    1,457,664 bytes total disk space.
        7,680 bytes in 15 folders.
      196,096 bytes in 102 files.
    1,253,888 bytes available on disk.

          512 bytes in each allocation unit.
        2,847 total allocation units on disk.
        2,449 allocation units available on disk.

A:\>_
```

The output from the command you entered scrolled by so quickly that you were unable to see that all the files on the disk were listed. You can see only the last few files and the statistical and memory information at the end of the display. In order to view the information returned by this command, you are going to use an operating system feature that will be covered in the next chapter—redirection. You have, however, used this feature in previous chapters to direct the Application Assignments to the printer. You will redirect the output of the CHKDSK /V command to a file instead of the screen, and then use the command line editor to see it.

Step 2 Key in the following: A:\>**CHKDSK /V > CHKDSK.TXT** Enter

Nothing is displayed on the screen. You have redirected the display to the file **CHKDSK.TXT** on the default drive.

Step 3 Key in the following: A:\>**EDIT CHKDSK.TXT** Enter

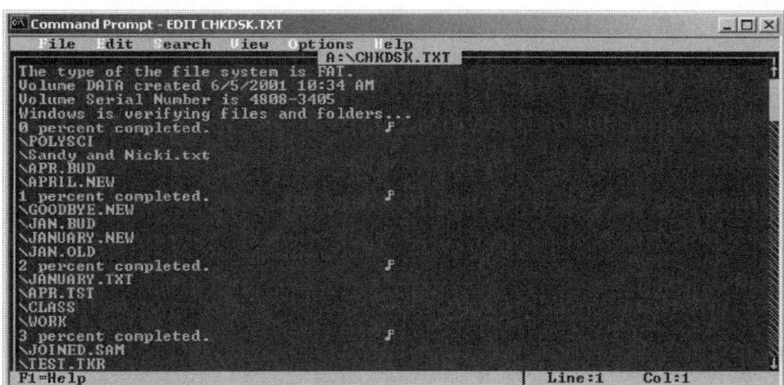

You can see the output of the CHKDSK /V command that you have redirected to the **CHKDSK.TXT** file.

Step 4 Move the scroll bar at the right edge of the screen approximately halfway down the screen, as shown in the following screen.

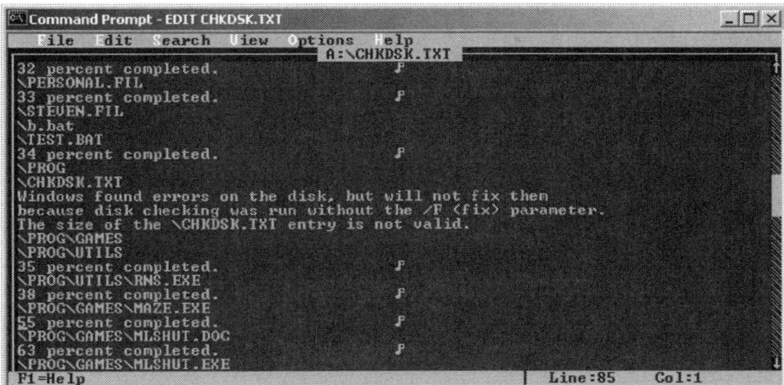

The subdirectory names are displayed, along with all the files each subdirectory contains. You can use this command on any FAT drive to see the files and directories. You could, for instance, key in **CHKDSK C: /V**. However, since the display on a hard disk is typically large, it is not as useful as you would like. The DIR command has the /S parameter, which allows you to look at all your subdirectories on any disk. Furthermore, the DIR command has the /P parameter to pause the display, and CHKDSK does not. Notice that Windows found errors on this disk. Your display may or may not report errors.

Step 5 On the Edit menu bar, click **File**. Click **Exit**.

You have closed the command line editor.

Step 6 Key in the following: A:\>**DIR /S /P** [Enter]

Step 7 Press [Enter]

Step 8 Press [Enter]

```
Command Prompt

  Directory of A:\MEDIA\TV

06/06/2001  11:49a      <DIR>          .
06/06/2001  11:49a      <DIR>          ..
03/05/2000  04:41p                 232 COMEDY.TV
07/03/2000  01:24p                 213 DRAMA.TV
               2 File(s)            445 bytes

  Directory of A:\PROG

Press any key to continue . . .
06/07/2001  08:33a      <DIR>          .
06/07/2001  08:33a      <DIR>          ..
06/07/2001  08:34a      <DIR>          GAMES
06/07/2001  08:34a      <DIR>          UTILS
               0 File(s)              0 bytes

  Directory of A:\PROG\GAMES

06/07/2001  08:34a      <DIR>          .
06/07/2001  08:34a      <DIR>          ..
05/09/1989  03:51p              34,645 MAZE.EXE
08/14/1989  10:48p              15,049 MLSHUT.DOC
08/14/1989  10:31p              43,776 MLSHUT.EXE
               3 File(s)         93,470 bytes

  Directory of A:\PROG\UTILS
```

```
06/07/2001  08:34a      <DIR>          .
06/07/2001  08:34a      <DIR>          ..
11/22/1989  10:35p               7,269 RNS.EXE
Press any key to continue . . .
```

WHAT'S HAPPENING? (This graphic represents a portion of the scrolling display.) This parameter allows you to view the files in all your directories and pause the display. You can also view specific files in all subdirectories.

Step 9 Press **Enter** until you reach the A:\> prompt.

Step 10 Key in the following: A:\>**DIR *.NEW /S** **Enter**

```
Command Prompt

A:\>DIR *.NEW /S
 Volume in drive A is DATA
 Volume Serial Number is 3330-1807

 Directory of A:\

04/23/2000  04:03p                  72 APRIL.NEW
01/01/2002  04:32a                  34 GOODBYE.NEW
04/23/2000  04:03p                  73 JANUARY.NEW
               3 File(s)           179 bytes

 Directory of A:\POLYSCI\USA

04/23/2000  04:03p                  71 MARCH.NEW
               1 File(s)            71 bytes

 Directory of A:\POLYSCI\FRANCE

04/23/2000  04:03p                  53 BONJOUR.NEW
               1 File(s)            53 bytes

     Total Files Listed:
               5 File(s)           303 bytes
               0 Dir(s)      1,259,280 bytes free

A:\>_
```

WHAT'S HAPPENING? This command allows you to be even more specific and locate a file anywhere on the disk by searching all the subdirectories. Thus, DIR /S supplants CHKDSK /V in its ability to show every file on the disk in every subdirectory.

The CHKDSK /V command can also show any hidden files, but the parameters in the DIR command are better for that purpose. Using the /A parameter (attribute) with the attribute you wish, you can determine what you will see. You can use D (directories), R (read-only files), H (hidden files), S (system files), and A (files ready to archive). If you use the - sign before an attribute, you can select all the files except those that have that attribute.

Step 11 Key in the following: A:\>**DIR /AD** Enter

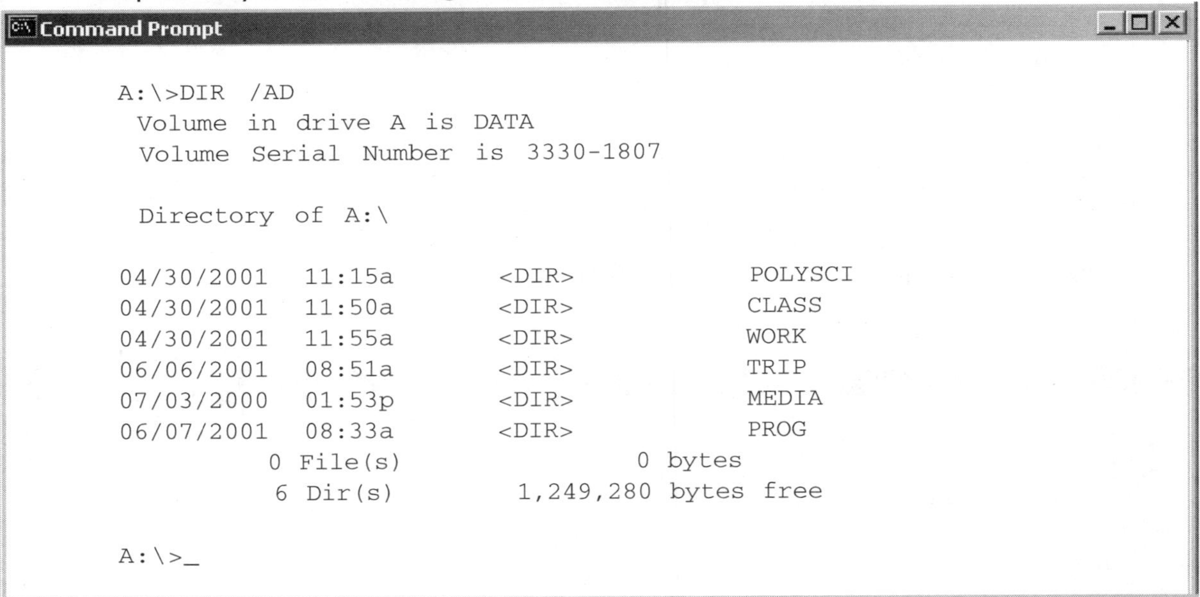

```
Command Prompt

A:\>DIR /AD
 Volume in drive A is DATA
 Volume Serial Number is 3330-1807

 Directory of A:\

04/30/2001  11:15a    <DIR>          POLYSCI
04/30/2001  11:50a    <DIR>          CLASS
04/30/2001  11:55a    <DIR>          WORK
06/06/2001  08:51a    <DIR>          TRIP
07/03/2000  01:53p    <DIR>          MEDIA
06/07/2001  08:33a    <DIR>          PROG
           0 File(s)              0 bytes
           6 Dir(s)       1,249,280 bytes free

A:\>_
```

WHAT'S HAPPENING? You selected the /A parameter and used the D attribute for directories to control the output of the DIR command. Remember, the order in which your directories and files are displayed may vary.

8.16 USING CHKDSK TO REPAIR DISK PROBLEMS

On a FAT disk, the file allocation table (FAT) and the directory work in conjunction. Every file has an entry in the directory table. The file entry in the directory table points to the starting cluster in the FAT. If the file is longer than one cluster, which it usually is, the file allocation table has a pointer that leads it to the next cluster, then the next cluster, and so on. These pointers ***chain*** all the data together in a file. If the chain is broken (i.e., there is a lost pointer), the disk ends up with lost clusters, which means that these clusters are marked as used in the FAT and not available for new data. Look at Figure 8.6; clusters 3, 4, and 6 are a chain, but the FAT does not know to which file this chain belongs. There is no entry in the root directory. Hence, these are ***lost clusters***.

Root Directory Table

File Name	File Extension	Date	Time	Other Info	Starting Cluster Number
MY	FIL	5-7-99	11:23a		1
HIS	DOC	5-7-99	11:50a		5
					3

Clusters 3, 4, and 6 have data, are linked together, but have no file entry in the directory table.

File Allocation Table

Cluster Number	Status
1	in use
2	in use
3	4
4	6
5	in use
6	end

FIGURE 8.6 LOST CLUSTERS

Since these lost clusters belong to no specific file, they cannot be retrieved. The data becomes useless, yet the operating system cannot write other data to these lost clusters. Thus, you lose space on the disk. This phenomenon occurs for a variety of reasons, the most common being a user who does not exit a program properly. If you simply turn off the computer, you are interrupting the shut-down process of the application program. Often, when you interrupt this process, the data will not be properly written to the disk. Other times power failures or power surges are the cause. Not exiting an application properly can be damaging to the operating system and can leave lost clusters on the hard disk.

On an NTFS disk, CHKDSK, in Stage 2, looks for orphaned files. An orphaned file is one that has an entry in the MFT but is not listed in any directory. It is similar to a lost cluster in the FAT file system.

If one of these events happens, you may not be able to boot back into Windows. You would then boot with your Windows boot disks and use your Emergency Repair disk to try to repair the damage. This will be covered in Chapter 13. When Windows 2000 Professional is running, you cannot run CHKDSK with the /F parameter and attempt to repair disk errors. When you execute the CHKDSK /F command, you will get a message at the beginning of the CHKDSK display similar to this:

```
C:\>CHKDSK /F
The type of the file system is FAT32.
Cannot lock current drive.

Chkdsk cannot run because the volume is in use by another
process.  Would you like to schedule this volume to be
checked the next time the system restarts? (Y/N)
```

This message means that you can schedule CHKDSK with the /F parameter to run when your computer starts up the next time. The utility will run *before* most of the system loads, eliminating the problem of other processes running. You can, however, use the /F and /R parameters with CHKDSK on a floppy disk. If you have multiple hard drives, you can run CHKDSK on a hard drive that is not the default drive. If you did use it on an active partition, it may report erroneous error messages since it cannot lock the drive. The /F is used to repair logical errors, and the /R is used to locate bad sectors and recover readable information. Using /R implies /F.

Be careful when running this utility program. First, you should always regularly back up your data files in case the "fix" behaves improperly. You could lose data. Actually, you should be backing up your hard disk on a regular basis. Secondly, if you use /F on a large disk or on a disk with a very large number of files (in the millions), CHKDSK can take a very, very long time (even days) to complete. During this time, you will not have access to the drive you are repairing since CHKDSK does not give up control of the disk until it is finished executing. If the drive (system volume) is being checked during the startup process, your computer will not be available to you until the CHKDSK process is complete.

Another type of error that occurs infrequently is cross-linked files. Cross-linked files usually occur on FAT disks. ***Cross-linked*** files are two files that claim the same cluster in the FAT.

Root Directory Table

File Name	File Extension	Date	Time	Other Info	Starting Cluster Number
MY	FIL	4-15-94	11:23		1
HIS	FIL	4-15-94	11:23		3

File Allocation Table

Cluster Number	Status
1	MY.FIL
2	MY.FIL
3	HIS.FIL
4	MY.FIL HIS.FIL
5	HIS FIL
6	MY.FIL

FIGURE 8.7 CROSS-LINKED FILES

In Figure 8.7, MY.FIL thinks it owns clusters 1, 2, 4, and 6. HIS.FIL thinks it owns clusters 3, 4, and 5. Thus, both MY.FIL and HIS.FIL think that cluster 4 is part of their chain. If you edit MY.FIL, the file will contain its own data as well as some part of HIS.FIL. Even worse, if you delete MY.FIL, you will be deleting part of the HIS.FIL data. Usually, to recover data from cross-linked files, you copy each file to a new location so they are no longer cross-linked. One of the files is usually bad, but at least you have one file that is good.

8.17 ACTIVITY: USING CHKDSK TO REPAIR DISK PROBLEMS

Note: The DATA disk is in Drive A. A:\> is displayed.

Step 1 Key in the following: A:>**CHKDSK /R** Enter

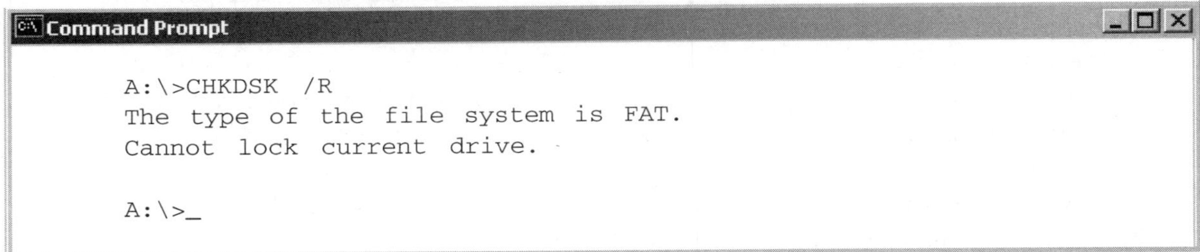
Command Prompt
A:\>CHKDSK /R
The type of the file system is FAT.
Cannot lock current drive.
A:\>_

WHAT'S HAPPENING? Windows 2000 Professional needs total access to the disk. Since your default drive is A, the OS cannot "lock" or gain total access to the drive so it cannot run CHKDSK.

Step 2 Key in the following: A:\>**C:** Enter

Step 3 Key in the following: C:\>**CHKDSK A: /R**

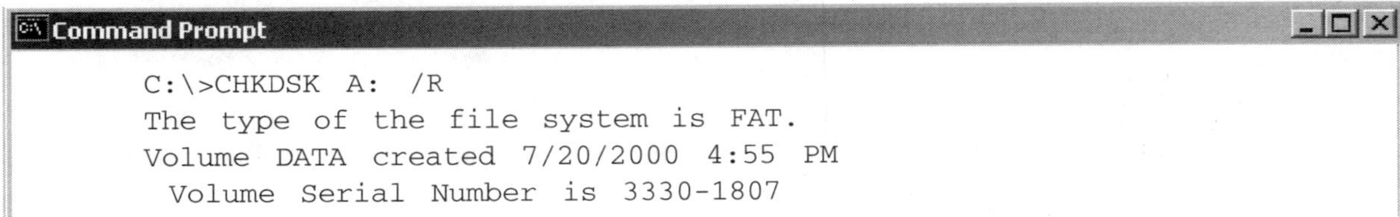
Command Prompt
C:\>CHKDSK A: /R
The type of the file system is FAT.
Volume DATA created 7/20/2000 4:55 PM
Volume Serial Number is 3330-1807

```
Windows is verifying files and folders...
File and folder verification is complete.
Windows is verifying free space...
Free space verification is complete.
Windows has checked the file system and found no problem.

    1,457,664 bytes total disk space.
        7,680 bytes in 15 folders.
      200,704 bytes in 103 files.
    1,249,280 bytes available on disk.

          512 bytes in each allocation unit.
        2,847 total allocation units on disk.
        2,440 allocation units available on disk.

C:\>_
```

WHAT'S HAPPENING? You needed to change drives so that CHKDSK could lock Drive A. The status reports that there is "no problem" with this drive. Again, if you do not have an NTFS drive (or one with errors), you cannot do the next steps. However, read the steps.

Step 4 Key in the following: C:\>**CHKDSK E:** Enter

```
Command Prompt

C:\>CHKDSK E:
The type of the file system is NTFS.
Volume label is QUAN-2.

WARNING!  F parameter not specified.
Running CHKDSK in read-only mode.

CHKDSK is verifying files (stage 1 of 3)...
File verification completed.
CHKDSK is verifying indexes (stage 2 of 3)...
Index verification completed.
CHKDSK is verifying security descriptors (stage 3 of 3)...
Security descriptor verification completed.
Windows found problems with the file system.
Run CHKDSK with the /F (fix) option to correct these.

   1040224 KB total disk space.
    804221 KB in 616 files.
       240 KB in 36 indexes.
         0 KB in bad sectors.
      8719 KB in use by the system.
      7264 KB occupied by the log file.
    227043 KB available on disk.

       512 bytes in each allocation unit.
   2080448 total allocation units on disk.
    454086 allocation units available on disk.

C:\>_
```

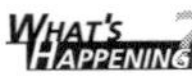

This disk has errors. It is recommending that you run CHKDSK with the /F parameter.

Step 5 Key in the following: C:\>**CHKDSK E: /F** Enter

```
Command Prompt

C:\>CHKDSK E: /F
The type of the file system is NTFS.
Volume label is QUAN-2.

CHKDSK is verifying files (stage 1 of 3)...
File verification completed.
CHKDSK is verifying indexes (stage 2 of 3)...
Index verification completed.
CHKDSK is verifying security descriptors (stage 3 of 3)...
Security descriptor verification completed.
Windows has made corrections to the file system.

  1040224 KB total disk space.
   804221 KB in 616 files.
      240 KB in 36 indexes.
        0 KB in bad sectors.
     8719 KB in use by the system.
     7264 KB occupied by the log file.
   227043 KB available on disk.

      512 bytes in each allocation unit.
  2080448 total allocation units on disk.
   454086 allocation units available on disk.

C:\>_
```

Windows made the corrections to the file system. If you had errors on a FAT disk, Windows 2000 Professional, would ask if you wanted to convert the lost files to fragments. You would see the following error message.

```
Convert lost chains to files (Y/N?)
```

FIGURE 8.8 MESSAGE TO CONVERT LOST CLUSTERS

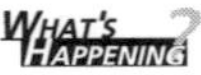

If you answered yes, then Windows would create directories called **FOUND.001**, **FOUND.002**, and so on. It then would place those file fragments in files labeled **FILE0000.CHK**, **FILE0001.CHK**, **FILE0002.CHK**, and so on, depending on how many chains were found. The directory listing would look as shown in Figure 8.9.

```
Command Prompt

C:\>DIR FOUND.001
 Volume in drive C is 2000 PRO
 Volume Serial Number is C4A7-8571

 Directory of C:\FOUND.001
```

```
06/07/2001     6:34P          <DIR>                 .
06/07/2001     6:34P          <DIR>                 ..
05/20/2001     6:34P         32,768   FILE0000.CHK
        1 File(s)                          32,768 bytes
        2 Dir(s)                     206,045,184 bytes free

C:\>_
```

FIGURE 8.9 DIRECTORY LISTING FOR LOST CLUSTERS

If you opened the file with a program like Notepad, you would likely see that the file was a garbage file, as shown in Figure 8.10.

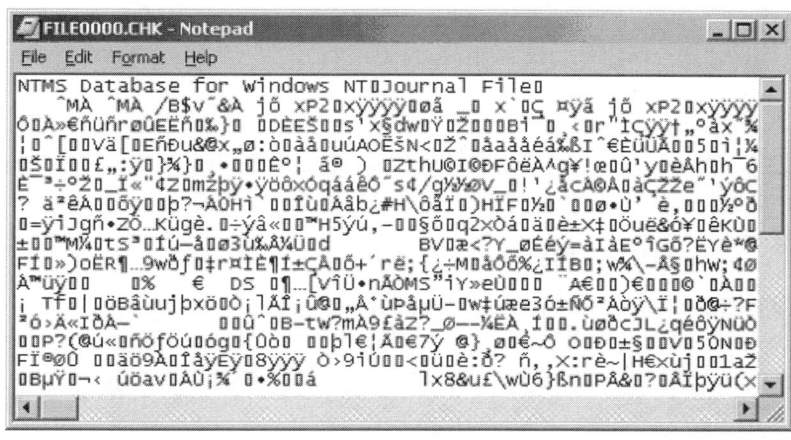

FIGURE 8.10 A LOST CLUSTER OPENED IN NOTEPAD

Normally those files are useless and can be safely deleted, as well as any **FOUND** directories.

8.18 CHECKING DISKS WITH SYSTEM TOOLS

Windows 2000 Professional provides another way to check a disk. You may use the GUI and use System Tools. The three system tools that are provided in the GUI are Error-checking (CHKDSK), Backup, and Defragmentation.

8.19 ACTIVITY: CHECKING DISKS WITH SYSTEM TOOLS

Note: The DATA disk is in the A drive.

Step 1 Key in the following: C:\>**EXIT** Enter

WHAT'S HAPPENING? You have terminated the command line session and returned to the Windows 2000 Professional "GUI" screen.

Step 2 Double-click **My Computer**.

Step 3 Right-click on the A drive icon.

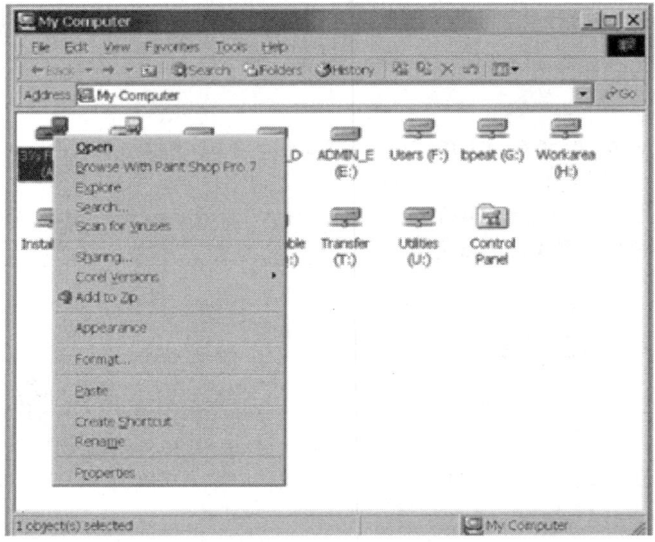

WHAT'S HAPPENING? You have opened the shortcut menu for the A drive.

Step 4 Click **Properties**. Click the **Tools** tab.

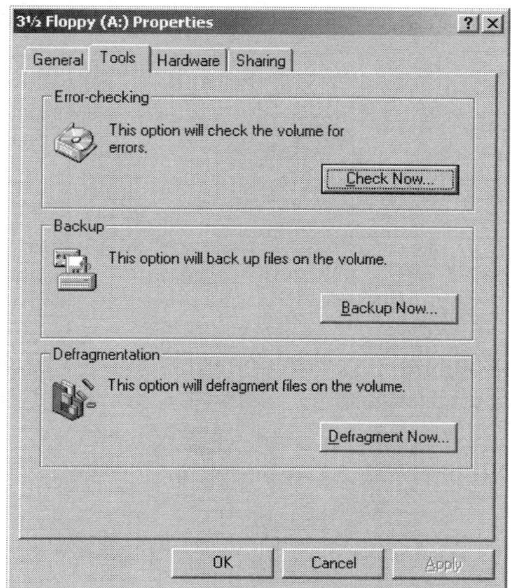

WHAT'S HAPPENING? You have displayed the Tools dialog box, showing you three options. You can check the disk for errors, back it up, or defragment it. Defragmenting will eliminate noncontiguous files from a hard disk. Error-checking will perform in a similar manner to CHKDSK.

Step 5 Click the **Check Now** button.

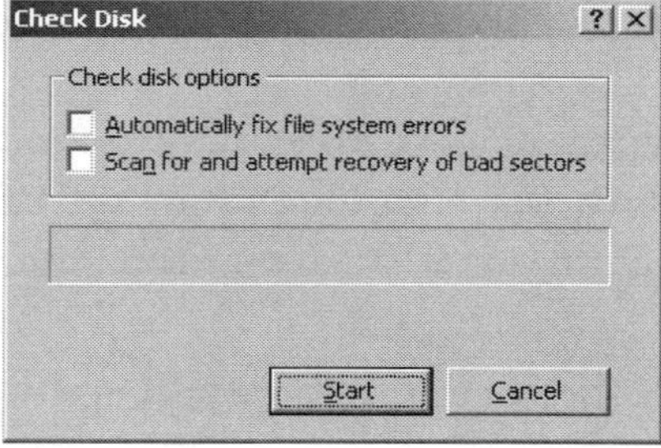

WHAT'S HAPPENING? You are give two options—to fix the errors if any are found and to try and fix any bad sectors discovered during the check. This second option is very time-consuming. In general, if there are bad sectors on a floppy disk, it is best to copy the files to another disk and throw the disk with bad sectors away. Floppy disks are very inexpensive, and data is very valuable.

Step 6 Click **Automatically fix file system errors**.

Step 7 Click **Start**.

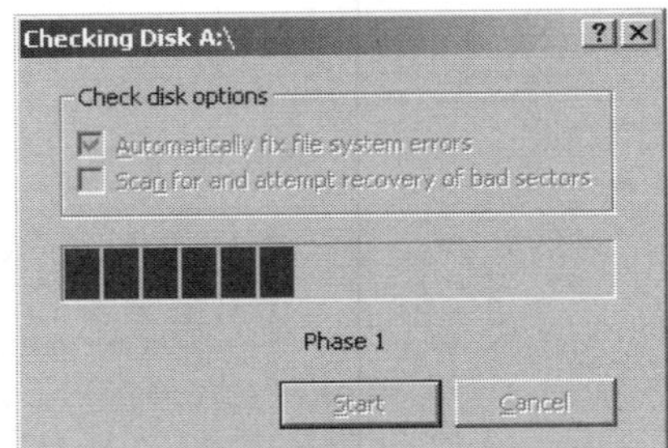

The disk checking begins. Phase 1 is checking for errors. Scanning for and attempting the recovery of bad sectors is Phase 2, which was not requested. The completion dialog box appears when the check is complete.

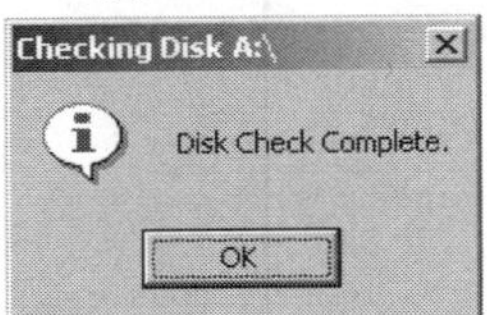

No errors were found, and the check is complete. These options are available on the property sheet for the hard drive as well, but if you attempt to check the hard drive, you will receive the following message:

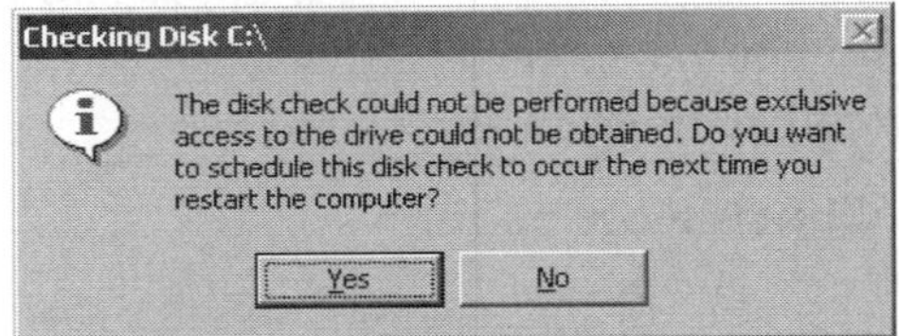

Just as at the command line, the checks cannot be performed while other processes are active. To check the hard drive, you would have to click **Yes** and shut down and restart your computer.

Step 8 Close all open windows.

8.20 CONTIGUOUS AND NONCONTIGUOUS FILES

"Contiguous" means being in contact with or touching. What does this have to do with files? As far as the operating system is concerned, data is a string of bytes that it keeps track of by grouping the data into a file. In order to manage storing and retrieving files, a disk is divided into numbered blocks called "sectors." Sectors are then grouped into clusters. A cluster is the smallest unit that the operating system deals with, and it is always a set of contiguous sectors. Clusters on a 1.44-MB floppy disk consist of one 512-byte sector. The number of sectors that make up a cluster on a hard disk varies depending on the size of the hard disk and the FAT being used. On a 2-GB hard disk, a sector consists of 32,768 bytes. Most often, a data file will take up more space on a disk than one cluster. Thus, the operating system has to keep track of the location of all the parts of the file that are on the disk. It does so by means of the directory and the FAT. If you are using NTFS, then it tracks the files by means of the MFT.

The original release of Windows 95 used the standard FAT—a 16-bit version. A 32-bit FAT was introduced with release B of Windows 95. From that version through Millennium, you have the choice of using the standard FAT or the 32-bit version, referred to as FAT32. Windows 2000 Professional also supports NTFS (New Technology File System), which was previously supported only by Windows NT. This file system allows local security. With NTFS, access to areas of the partition can be blocked to some users, and allowed for others. This is useful in an environment where more than one user has sensitive files stored on the same computer. It also can block access to the operating system files. The decision on which file system to use is made when the disk volume is originally partitioned. All floppy drives are FAT12.

The FAT keeps a record of the cluster numbers each file occupies. As the operating system begins to write files on a new disk, it makes an entry in the disk's directory for that file and updates the FAT with the cluster numbers used to store that file. Data is written to the disk based on the next empty cluster. Files being written to a disk are written in adjacent clusters. The operating system wants all the pieces of file information to be next to each other and tries to write to adjacent clusters whenever possible. It is easier to retrieve or store information when it is together. When this occurs, the file is considered contiguous. For example, if you began writing a letter to your United States senator, it would be stored on your disk in the manner shown in Figure 8.11.

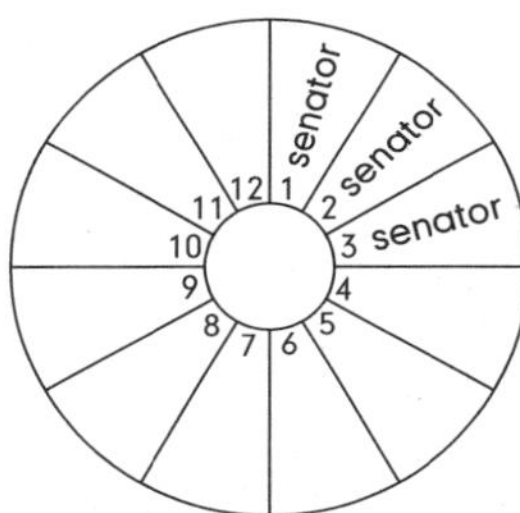

FIGURE 8.11 ONE FILE IN CLUSTERS

The clusters with nothing in them are simply empty spaces on the disk. If you now decide to write a letter to your mother, this new file is written to the next group of adjacent clusters, which would begin with cluster 4 as shown in Figure 8.12.

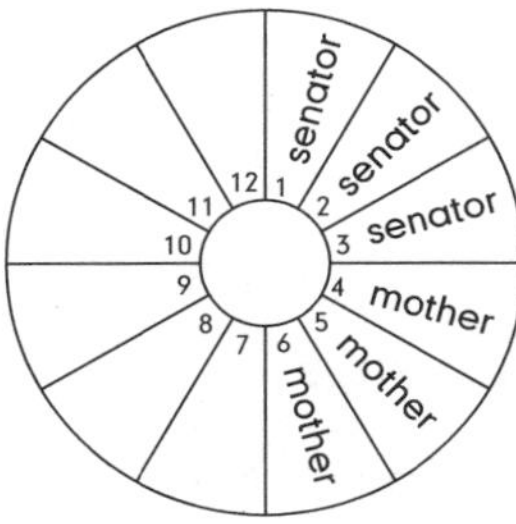

FIGURE 8.12 CONTIGUOUS FILES IN CLUSTERS

These two files, SENATOR and MOTHER, are contiguous. Each part of each file follows on the disk. Now you decide to add a comment to your senator letter, making the SENATOR file bigger. When the operating system goes to write the file to the disk, the FAT looks for the next empty clusters, which are clusters 7 and 8. The FAT would appear as shown in Figure 8.13.

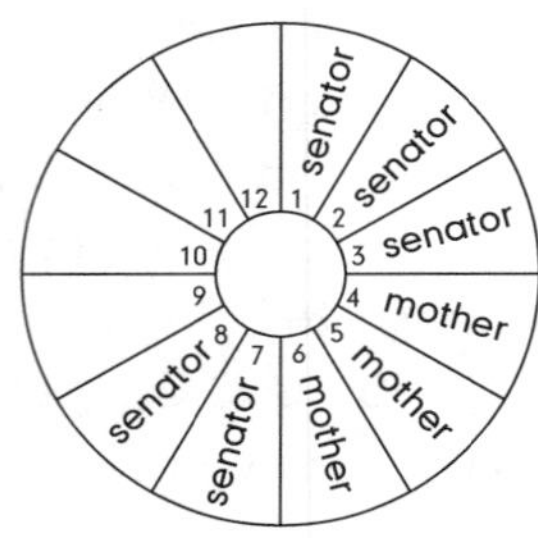

FIGURE 8.13 NONCONTIGUOUS FILES IN CLUSTERS

The parts of the file named SENATOR are separated, making this file noncontiguous, or fragmented. The process becomes more complicated as you add and delete files. For example, if you delete the file SENATOR, the FAT marks clusters 1, 2, 3, 7, and 8 as available even though the data actually remains on the disk. You then decide to develop a PHONE file, as shown in Figure 8.14.

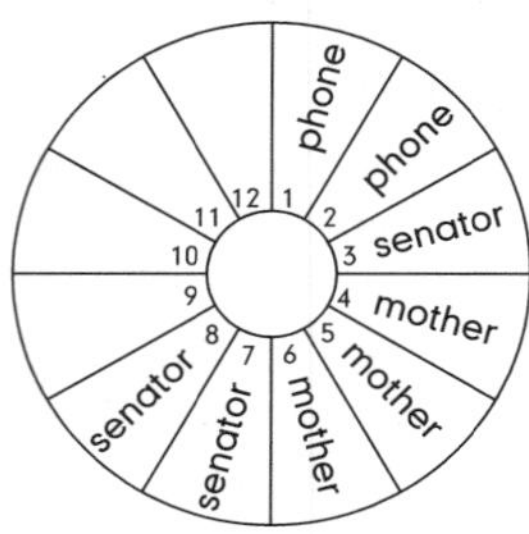

FIGURE 8.14 ADDING A FILE

Next, you decide to write a letter to your friend Joe, to write a letter to your friend Mary, to add to the PHONE file, and to add to the letter to your mother. The disk would look like Figure 8.15.

FIGURE 8.15 ADDING MORE FILES

The parts of these files are broken up and are no longer stored in adjacent clusters. They are now known as noncontiguous or ***fragmented files***. If the disk is comprised of noncontiguous files, it can be called a fragmented disk. It will take longer to read noncontiguous files because the read/write heads must move around the disk to find all the parts of a file. You can see if files are contiguous or noncontiguous by using a parameter with the CHKDSK command, but only on FAT volumes.

8.21 ACTIVITY: USING CHKDSK TO SEE IF FILES ARE CONTIGUOUS

Note: The DATA disk is in Drive A. You are shelled out to the Command Prompt. A:\> is displayed.

Step 1 Key in the following: A:\>**CHKDSK GOODBYE.TXT** Enter

```
Command Prompt

A:\>CHKDSK  GOODBYE.TXT
The type of the file system is FAT.
Volume DATA created 7/20/2000 4:55 PM
 Volume Serial Number is 3330-1807
Windows is verifying files and folders . . .
File and folder verification is complete.
Windows has checked the file system and found no problem.

     1,457,664 bytes total disk space.
         7,680 bytes in 15 folders.
       200,704 bytes in 103 files.
     1,249,280 bytes available on disk.

           512 bytes in each allocation unit.
         2,847 total allocation units on disk.
         2,440 available allocation units on disk.


All specified files are contiguous.

A:\>_
```

WHAT'S HAPPENING? The screen display supplies all the statistical information about the DATA disk and computer memory. In addition, the last line states, "All specified file(s) are contiguous." By adding the parameter of the file name **GOODBYE.TXT** after the CHKDSK command, you asked not only to check the disk but also to look at the file **GOODBYE.TXT** to see if all the parts of this file are next to one another on the DATA disk. Are they contiguous? The message indicates that they are.

Step 2 Key in the following: A:\>**CHKDSK *.TXT** Enter

```
Command Prompt

A:\>CHKDSK  *.TXT
The type of the file system is FAT.
Volume DATA created 7/20/2000 4:55 PM
 Volume Serial Number is 3330-1807
Windows is verifying files and folders...
File and folder verification is complete.
Windows has checked the file system and found no problem.

     1,457,664 bytes total disk space.
         7,680 bytes in 15 folders.
       200,704 bytes in 103 files.
     1,249,280 bytes available on disk.
```

```
             512 bytes in each allocation unit.
           2,847 total allocation units on disk.
           2,440 allocation units available on disk.
\CHKDSK.TXT contains 2 non-contiguous blocks.

A:\>_
```

WHAT'S HAPPENING? CHKDSK not only gave you the usual statistical information but also checked to see if all the files in the root directory that have **.TXT** as an extension are contiguous. By using wildcards, you can check a group of files with a common denominator. In this case, the common denominator is the file extension **.TXT**. The message on the screen verifies that one file, **CHKDSK.TXT** from all the files with the extension **.TXT**, has two noncontiguous blocks.

Step 3 Key in the following: A:\>**CHKDSK *.*** Enter

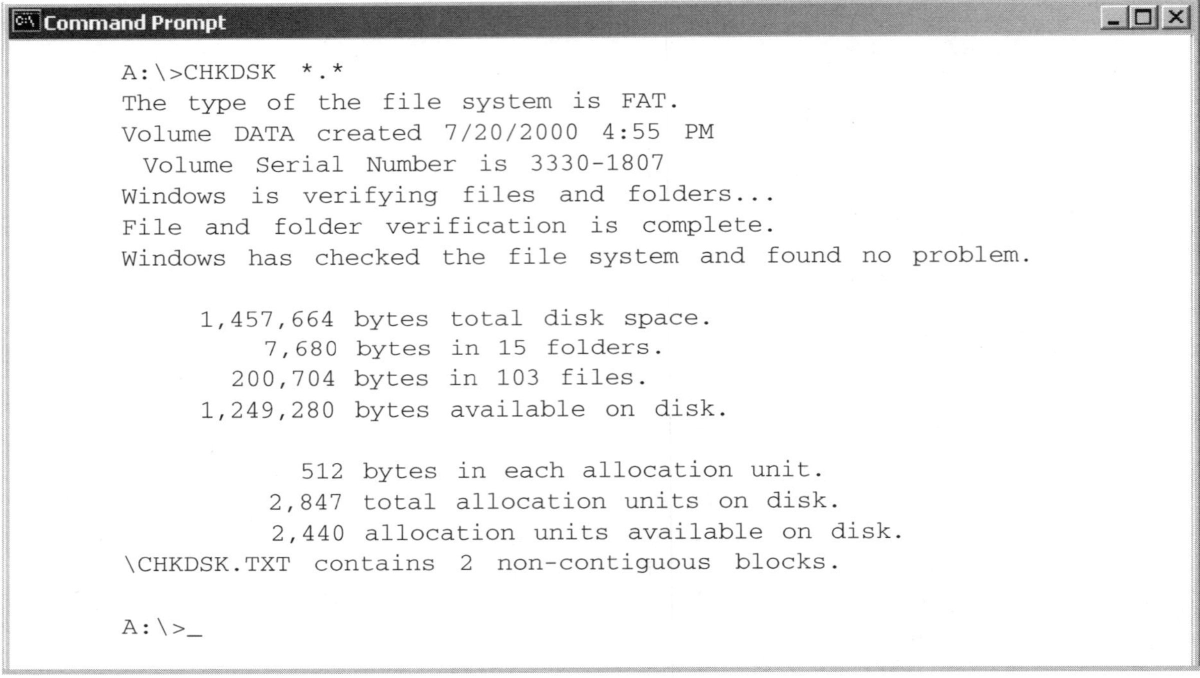

```
Command Prompt
A:\>CHKDSK *.*
The type of the file system is FAT.
Volume DATA created 7/20/2000 4:55 PM
 Volume Serial Number is 3330-1807
Windows is verifying files and folders...
File and folder verification is complete.
Windows has checked the file system and found no problem.

     1,457,664 bytes total disk space.
         7,680 bytes in 15 folders.
       200,704 bytes in 103 files.
     1,249,280 bytes available on disk.

             512 bytes in each allocation unit.
           2,847 total allocation units on disk.
           2,440 allocation units available on disk.
\CHKDSK.TXT contains 2 non-contiguous blocks.

A:\>_
```

WHAT'S HAPPENING? The screen display shows only the same noncontiguous file. If you had no fragmented files, you would have received the message, "All specified files are contiguous." The CHKDSK command, followed by star dot star (***.***), checked every file in the root directory on the DATA disk to see if all the files were contiguous. The ***.*** represents all files in the root directory.

Step 4 Key in the following: A:\>**CHKDSK CLASS*.*** Enter

```
Command Prompt
A:\>CHKDSK CLASS\*.*
The type of the file system is FAT.
Volume DATA created 7/20/2000 4:55 PM
 Volume Serial Number is 3330-1807
Windows is verifying files and folders...
```

```
File and folder verification is complete.
Windows has checked the file system and found no problem.

     1,457,664 bytes total disk space.
         7,680 bytes in 15 folders.
       200,704 bytes in 103 files.
     1,249,280 bytes available on disk.

           512 bytes in each allocation unit.
         2,847 total allocation units on disk.
         2,440 allocation units available on disk.
All specified files are contiguous.

A:\>_
```

You are checking to see if all the files in the subdirectory **CLASS** are contiguous. In this case, they are.

What difference does it make if files are contiguous or not? Only to the extent that noncontiguous files or a fragmented disk can slow performance. In other words, if a file is contiguous, all of its parts can be found quickly, minimizing the amount of time the heads need to read and write to the disk. If files are noncontiguous, the operating system has to look for all the parts of the file, causing the read/write heads to fly about the disk. The longer the disk is used, the more fragmented it becomes, slowing its performance. However, performance on a floppy disk is usually not that important because most of the time you are working on the hard disk.

You do notice a big decline in performance on a hard disk system. The solution most hard disk users opt for is to use the disk defragmenter program. This program is listed as Disk Defragmenter on the Start menu, under Programs, under Accessories, under System Tools. This program, referred to generically as a ***disk optimization*** program, rearranges the storage on the hard disk so that each file is stored in sequentially numbered clusters. Before using disk optimization, the disk must be free of errors.

8.22 DEFRAGMENTING YOUR HARD DISK

To make your programs run faster and better, you need to perform disk maintenance. One way to maintain your disk is to run the Defragmenter program from the Tools menu on the disks drive property sheet. The other is to run it from the Start Menu. Either way, it will rearrange files and unused space on your hard disk. Although the Windows operating system allows you to run Disk Defragmenter without closing all your programs, it is better, faster, and safer to close any open programs you have running, including any screen savers or virus-protection programs. You will discover it is no longer possible to defragment your floppy disk.

8.23 ACTIVITY: USING DISK DEFRAGMENTER

Step 1 Click **Start**.

Step 2 Point to **Programs**.

Step 3 Point to **Accessories**.

Step 4 Point to **System Tools**.

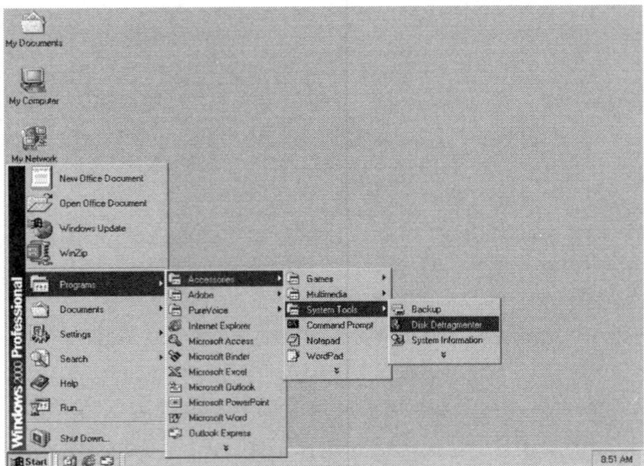

WHAT'S HAPPENING? You opened the System Tools menu. You will choose Disk Defragmenter.

Step 5 Click **Disk Defragmenter**.

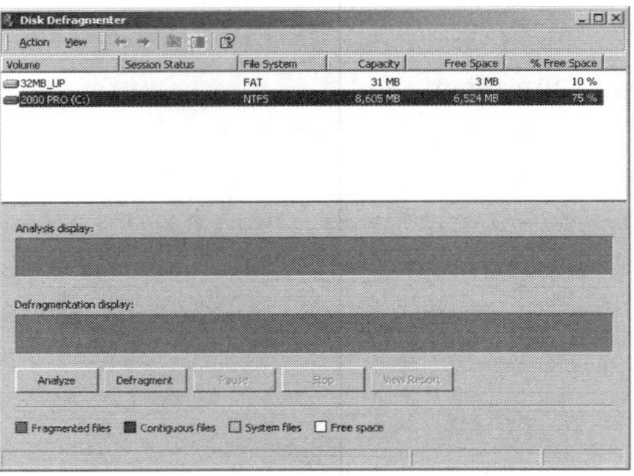

WHAT'S HAPPENING? Although this computer has both an A drive and a B drive, neither are listed in the Disk Defragmenter options box. Attempting to defragment the A drive from its property sheet menu would give the following results:

Step 6 Highlight your hard drive C and click **Analyze**.

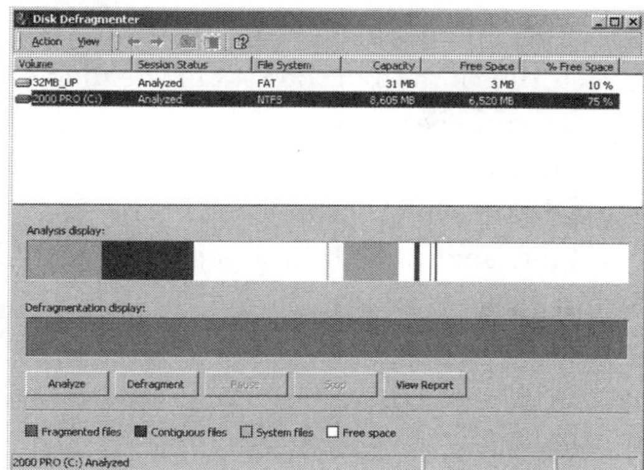

You will first see a graphical display of your disk, and then a dialog box where you can choose to defragment or to view the analysis report.

Step 7 Click **View Report**.

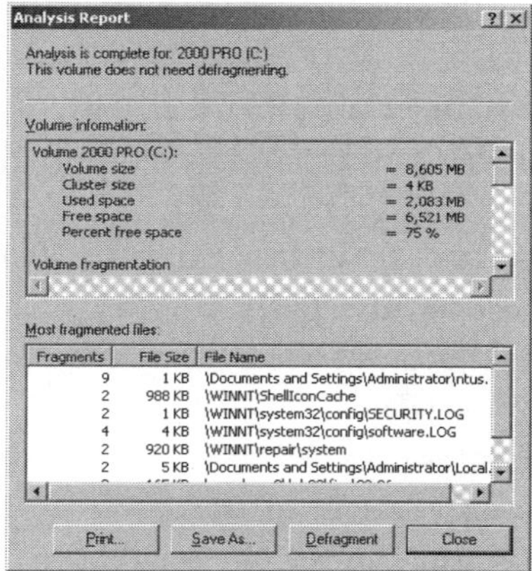

You can see the information on your hard drive. You can scroll up and down in the Volume information window and the Most fragmented files window, or you can click the Save As button and save the report for printing or examination at a later time. You will also get a recommendation to defragment or not to defragment. It is good practice to defragment your hard drive regularly, as it improves the performance of your system.

CHAPTER SUMMARY

1. All disks should be organized. You should not place all your programs and data in the root directory.
2. The root directory of a hard disk holds only 512 files if you are using FAT16.
3. Many users inefficiently organize their disk by application programs. This often leads to a repetition of subdirectory names, forcing users to remember where they placed their files and key in long path names. The operating system must search every subdirectory when accessing a file. It is difficult to add and delete application programs and data files in this scheme.

4. One way to organize a hard disk is by project.
5. Some guidelines to organizing a disk:
   a. The root directory is a map to the rest of the disk.
   b. Subdirectories should be shallow and wide.
   c. Plan the organization before installing software.
   d. Do not place data files in program subdirectories.
   e. It is better to have small subdirectories with only a few files.
   f. Have a file and directory naming scheme.
   g. Keep subdirectory names short and descriptive.
   h. Create a separate subdirectory for utility programs.
   i. Learn how each application program works.
   j. Analyze the way you work.
6. If a disk is unorganized, you can organize it by planning it, creating the new organizational scheme and any necessary subdirectories, copying files to the new subdirectories, and deleting those files from the old subdirectories.
7. The XCOPY command allows you to copy files and the subdirectories beneath them. You may choose:
   a. to be prompted (/P).
   b. to copy by date (/D).
   c. to be instructed to insert another disk (/W).
   d. to copy subdirectories and the files in them (/S).
   e. to create an empty subdirectory (/E).
   f. to verify that sectors are written correctly (/V).
   g. to copy files whose archive bit is set (/M).
   h. to copy only files that have been created or modified since the last backup (/A).
   i. to copy hidden files (/H).
   j. to keep file attributes (/K).
   k. to keep the read-only attribute (/R).
8. The command line editor is a full-screen editor that allows you to modify text files. It is a menu-driven program.
9. MOVE is used to move files. Although it can rename directories, it is better to use the REN command to rename objects and the MOVE command to move these objects. You must be cautious when you use MOVE to ensure you are performing the task that you wish.
10. Utility programs include the ones that come with the operating system, such as the external command MOVE.
11. There are software packages that add enhancements to the operating system. These are either given away, sold commercially, or are shareware.
12. RNS is an example of a third-party utility program that does not come with the operating system.
13. CHKDSK will search your drives for errors and give you a statistical report on the integrity of your drives.
14. You can use CHKDSK to check or repair FAT and FAT32 drives but it must not be the default drive.
15. You must not use CHKDSK /F while on a network drive or on any substituted drives or the default drive.

16. Disk Defragmenter is a program used to optimize performance of a disk by rewriting files so the clusters are contiguous. When files are contiguous, computer performance is enhanced.

KEY TERMS

chain
cross-linked files
disk optimization
fragmented file
lost cluster

DISCUSSION QUESTIONS

1. Why would you want to organize a hard disk?
2. What are the advantages and disadvantages of organizing a hard disk by application program rather than by project?
3. Why would you not want to place data files in a program subdirectory?
4. List five criteria that can be used for organizing a hard disk and explain the rationale for each.
5. What are two major considerations for any disk organizational scheme?
6. What are some of the drawbacks of using the COPY command for organizing your disk?
7. Why is moving program files and renaming program directories not as safe as moving data files and renaming data file directories?
8. What steps would you take to move a directory?
9. Why would you want to own utility programs that do not come with the operating system?
10. What is the purpose and function of programs like RNS.EXE?
11. What is the function and purpose of the CHKDSK command?
12. CHKDSK informs you of two types of errors. Explain.
13. What is a lost cluster? A cross-linked file? What impact does either of these have on available disk space?
14. Give the syntax for CHKDSK and explain two parameters when used with FAT volumes. With NTFS volumes.
15. What is verbose mode? Explain the use of the /V parameter with the CHKDSK command with a FAT file system and an NTFS file system.
16. Compare and contrast contiguous files with noncontiguous (fragmented) files.
17. Why would you use the parameter of the file name with the CHKDSK command?
18. What is the purpose and function of the /F parameter when it is used with the CHKDSK command, and under what circumstances would you use it?
19. Explain the function and purpose of disk-optimization programs.

TRUE/FALSE QUESTIONS

For each question, circle the letter T if the statement is true, and the letter F if the statement is false.

T F 1. The number of files that can be stored in the root of a hard drive is unlimited if the file system is FAT16.

T F 2. It is a good idea to have your data files and program files in the same subdirectory so you can keep track of your files easily.

T F 3. To repair FAT32 drives, you should use CHKDSK.

T F 4. The operating system writes files to disk based on the next available cluster.

T F 5. To optimize a disk, you should use CHKDSK.

COMPLETION QUESTIONS

Write the correct answer in each blank space.

6. To change the name of a subdirectory, you can use the _______ command or the ______ command.
7. Two commands that can help you organize your disk are _______ and ________.
8. When you use the MOVE *.* command, subdirectories contained in the default directory ___________ (*are* or *are not*) moved.
9. When you use the CHKDSK command, the parameter that will list every file on the disk, including hidden files, is the ______ parameter if the disk is using the FAT16 or FAT32 file system.
10. To solve the problem of having noncontiguous files on a disk, use ____________________________.

MULTIPLE CHOICE QUESTIONS

For each question, write the letter for the correct answer in the blank space.

☐ 11. A good rule of thumb when organizing a hard disk is
   a. to create compact and deep subdirectories rather than shallow and wide ones.
   b. to place data files in the same subdirectories with their associated program files.
   c. to use the root directory as a map to the rest of the disk.
   d. to have no files, only subdirectories, in the root directory.

☐ 12. When organizing a hard disk, XCOPY is ___________ to use than COPY.
   a. faster
   b. slower
   c. neither faster nor slower
   d. less reliable

☐ 13. CHKDSK will not
   a. tell how many files are on a floppy disk.
   b. tell whether or not a floppy disk has hidden files.
   c. remove damaged files from a floppy disk.
   d. tell how much room is left on a floppy disk.

14. A noncontiguous file is one that
    a. occupies more than one cluster.
    b. occupies nonconsecutive clusters.
    c. has a directory entry table that is missing certain numbers.
    d. contains a document that hasn't been finished.
15. To help your disk perform quickly and reliably, you should
    a. rename the directories that hold program files after they have been installed, so that they are all in the same directory.
    b. use deep subdirectories.
    c. run Disk Defragmenter.
    d. use long file names.

WRITING COMMANDS

Write the correct steps or commands to perform the required action as if you were at the computer. The prompt will indicate the default drive and directory. If there is no prompt indicated, assume you are at the desktop and not in the MS-DOS window.

16. You need statistical information about the disk in Drive A.

    C:\WINNT>

17. You want to see if the file called MARCH.TXT in the POLYSCI\USA directory on the disk in Drive A is contiguous.

    C:\WINNT>

18. You want to fix lost clusters and cross-linked files on the disk in Drive A.

    C:\WINNT>

19. You want to display all the files on the disk in Drive A. (Do not use the DIR command.)

    C:\>

20. You want to locate bad sectors and recover any readable information on Drive E.

    C:\>

APPLICATION ASSIGNMENTS

Note 1: Place the APPLICATION disk in Drive A. Be sure to work on the APPLICATION disk, not the DATA disk.

Note 2: The homework problems will assume that Drive C is the hard disk and the APPLICATION disk is in Drive A. If you are using another drive, such as floppy Drive B or hard Drive D, be sure and substitute that drive letter when reading the questions and answers.

Note 3: All subdirectories that are created will be under the root directory unless otherwise specified.

PROBLEM SET 1

PROBLEM A

A-a On the APPLICATION disk, under the subdirectory called **HISTORY**, create a subdirectory called **ROMAN**.

A-b With the root directory of the APPLICATION disk as the default, use the XCOPY command with the relative path to copy all the files in the root directory that begin with W to the subdirectory called **ROMAN** that you just created.

1. Which command did you use?
   a. XCOPY W*.* HISTORY
   b. XCOPY W*.* HISTORY\ROMAN
   c. XCOPY W*.* ROMAN\HISTORY
   d. XCOPY W*.* ROMAN

2. What message(s) was/were displayed on the screen?
   a. Reading source file(s).
   b. Copying source file(s).
   c. 3 File(s) copied
   d. none of the above

3. Are there any files that begin with W in the root directory of the APPLICATION disk?
   a. yes
   b. no

A-c With the root directory of the APPLICATION disk as the default, move all the files that begin with W to the subdirectory called **ROMAN** you created above.

4. Which command did you use?
   a. MOVE W*.* HISTORY\ROMAN
   b. MOVE W*.* ROMAN\HISTORY
   c. MOVE W*.* ROMAN
   d. none of the above

A-d Take the necessary steps to complete the move.

5. Are there any files that begin with W in the root directory of the APPLICATION disk?
   a. yes
   b. no

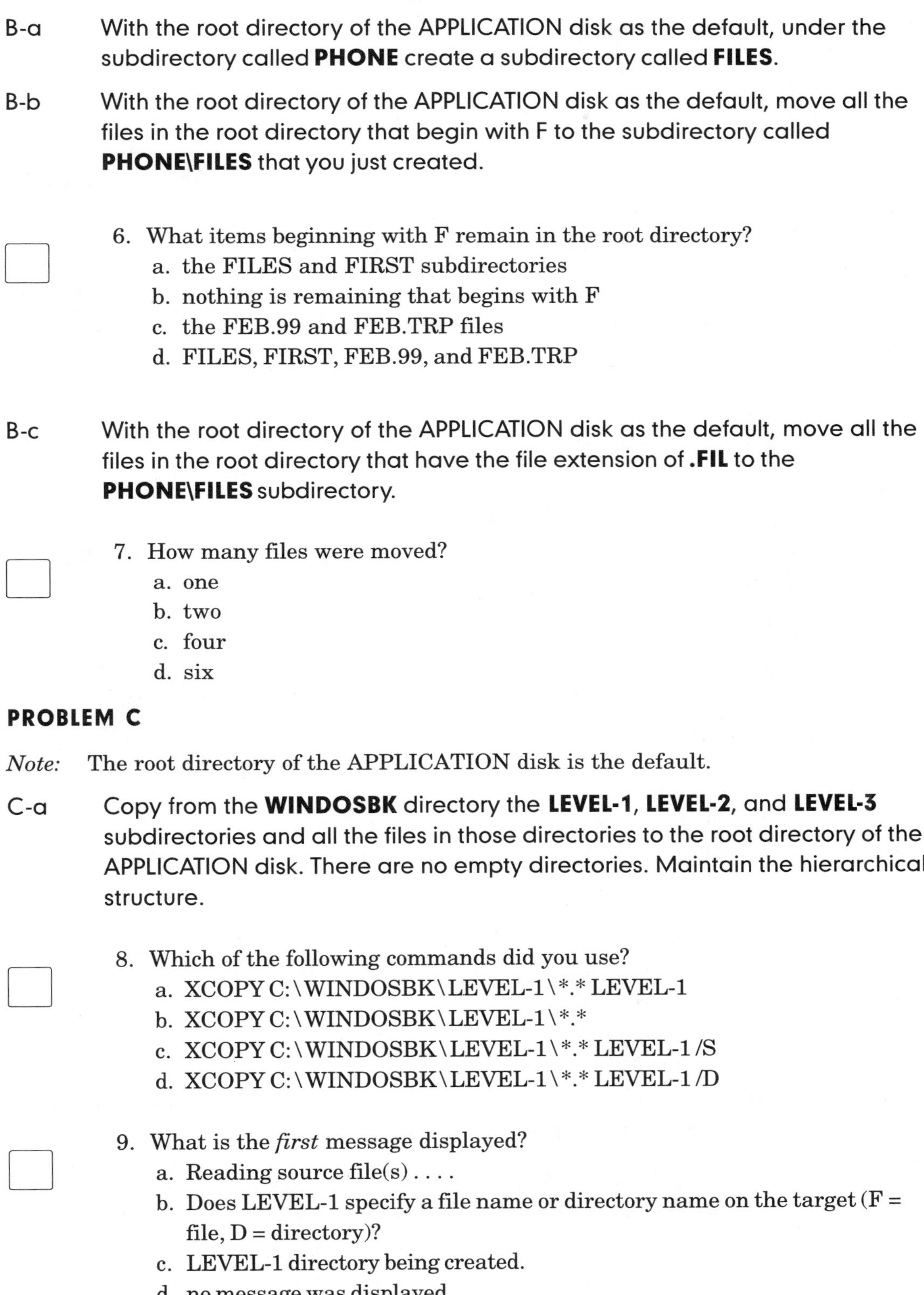

PROBLEM B

B-a With the root directory of the APPLICATION disk as the default, under the subdirectory called **PHONE** create a subdirectory called **FILES**.

B-b With the root directory of the APPLICATION disk as the default, move all the files in the root directory that begin with F to the subdirectory called **PHONE\FILES** that you just created.

6. What items beginning with F remain in the root directory?
   a. the FILES and FIRST subdirectories
   b. nothing is remaining that begins with F
   c. the FEB.99 and FEB.TRP files
   d. FILES, FIRST, FEB.99, and FEB.TRP

B-c With the root directory of the APPLICATION disk as the default, move all the files in the root directory that have the file extension of **.FIL** to the **PHONE\FILES** subdirectory.

7. How many files were moved?
   a. one
   b. two
   c. four
   d. six

PROBLEM C

Note: The root directory of the APPLICATION disk is the default.

C-a Copy from the **WINDOSBK** directory the **LEVEL-1**, **LEVEL-2**, and **LEVEL-3** subdirectories and all the files in those directories to the root directory of the APPLICATION disk. There are no empty directories. Maintain the hierarchical structure.

8. Which of the following commands did you use?
   a. XCOPY C:\WINDOSBK\LEVEL-1*.* LEVEL-1
   b. XCOPY C:\WINDOSBK\LEVEL-1*.*
   c. XCOPY C:\WINDOSBK\LEVEL-1*.* LEVEL-1 /S
   d. XCOPY C:\WINDOSBK\LEVEL-1*.* LEVEL-1 /D

9. What is the *first* message displayed?
   a. Reading source file(s) . . . .
   b. Does LEVEL-1 specify a file name or directory name on the target (F = file, D = directory)?
   c. LEVEL-1 directory being created.
   d. no message was displayed

C-b Complete the command. Then, with the root directory of the APPLICATION disk as the default, use Edit to create a new file called **DOWN.RED**. The contents of the file will be as follows:

```
This is a new red file.
I like the color red.
I like the softness of down.
```

C-c Make a directory called **TRAVEL** on the root of the APPLICATION disk.

C-d Copy all the files from the **WINDOSBK** directory ending with the extension **.RED** to the **TRAVEL** subdirectory on the APPLICATION disk.

C-e With the root directory of the APPLICATION disk as the default, move the **DOWN.RED** file to the **TRAVEL** subdirectory on the APPLICATION disk.

C-f With the root directory of the APPLICATION disk as the default, use Edit to alter and save the **DOWN.RED** file so that the contents read:

```
This is the last red file.
I am not so sure I like the color red.
```

C-g With the root directory of the APPLICATION disk as the default, use Edit to create a new file in the **TRAVEL** directory called **UP.RED**. The contents should read:

```
Maybe it wasn't the last red file after all!
```

☐ 10. How many files are on the root of the APPLICATION disk with the file extension of .RED?
   a. one
   b. two
   c. three
   d. zero

☐ 11. How many files are in the TRAVEL subdirectory with the file extension of .RED?
   a. two
   b. three
   c. four
   d. five

C-h With the root of the APPLICATION disk as the default, rename the file called **UP.RED** to **UPPER.RED** in the **TRAVEL** subdirectory.

C-i With the root of the APPLICATION disk as the default, copy all the files from the **TRAVEL** directory to the **BOOKS** subdirectory.

☐ 12. What is the total number of files with the extension .RED on the APPLICATION disk?
   a. 3
   b. 5
   c. 8
   d. 10

☐ 13. What command did you use to answer question 12?
   a. CHKDSK A:
   b. DIR *.RED
   c. DIR *.RED /S
   d. DIR *.RED TRAVEL BOOKS

PROBLEM SET II

Note 1: Before proceeding with these assignments, check with your lab instructor to see if there are any special procedures you should follow.

Note 2: The APPLICATION disk is in Drive A. A:\> is displayed as the default drive and the default directory. *All work will occur on the APPLICATION disk.*

Note 3: Make sure that **NAME.BAT**, **MARK.FIL**, **GETYN.COM**, **GO.BAT**, and **NAME.FIL** are all present in the root directory of the APPLICATION disk before proceeding with these problems. (**MARK.FIL** was moved from the root directory as part of a homework exercise—you will need to copy it to the root of the A drive from **WINDOSBK**.)

Note 4: All files with the **.HW** extension *must* be created in the root directory of the APPLICATION disk.

Step 1 Key in the following: A:\>**NAME** [Enter]

Step 2 Here is an example to key in, but your instructor will have other information that applies to your class. Key in the following:

Bette A. Peat [Enter] (*Your* name goes here.)

CIS 55 [Enter] (*Your* class goes here.)

T-Th 8-9:30 [Enter] (*Your* day and time go here.)

Chapter 8 Applications [Enter]

Step 3 Press [F6] [Enter]

Step 4 If the information is correct, press **Y** and you are back to A:\>.

WHAT'S HAPPENING? You have returned to the system level. You now have a file called **NAME.FIL** with your name and other pertinent information. (*Hint*: Remember redirection.)

TO CREATE 1.HW

- Key in the following: A:\> **MOVE PHONE\FILES\MARK.FIL** [Enter]
- Locate ***all*** of the files ending with **.RED** on the APPLICATION disk and place the results of the command in a file called **1.HW**.

TO CREATE 2.HW

- Copy only the files with the **.TXT** extension that were created on or after 5-30-00 in the **WINDOSBK** subdirectory to the root of the APPLICATION disk.
- Locate only the files in the root of the APPLICATION disk that have the extension **.TXT**. Place the names of the files in a file called **2.HW**.

TO CREATE 3.HW

- Copy all the files that have the extension **.RED** from the **BOOKS** subdirectory to the root of the APPLICATION disk.
- Edit the file **DOWN.RED** in the **TRAVEL** directory. Add the following line to the bottom of the file: **Does a down red file come from a red goose?**
- Display the contents (not the file name) of the **DOWN.RED** file you just edited to a file called **3.HW**.

TO CREATE 4.HW

- Locate ***all*** the files that have the extension **.TXT** on the APPLICATION disk and place the results of the command in a file called **4.HW**.

TO CREATE 5.HW

- See if the files that have the **.TRP** file extension are contiguous and place results of the command in a file called **5.HW**.

TO PRINT YOUR HOMEWORK

Step 1 Be sure the printer is on and ready to accept print jobs from your computer.

Step 2 Key in the following (be very careful to make no typing errors):
GO NAME.FIL 1.HW 2.HW 3.HW 4.HW 5.HW Enter

If the files you requested, **1.HW, 2.HW**, etc., do not exist in the default directory, you will see the following message on the screen:

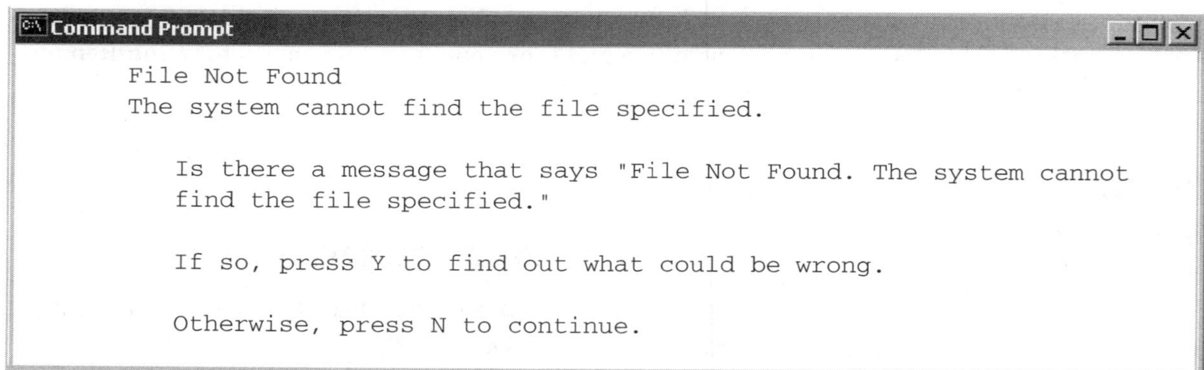
Command Prompt
File Not Found
The system cannot find the file specified.
Is there a message that says "File Not Found. The system cannot find the file specified."
If so, press Y to find out what could be wrong.
Otherwise, press N to continue.

The operating system is telling you that the file cannot be found. If you see this screen, press **Y** to see what could be wrong, and repeat the print procedure after you have corrected the problem.

If the default directory contains the specified files, the following message will appear on the screen:

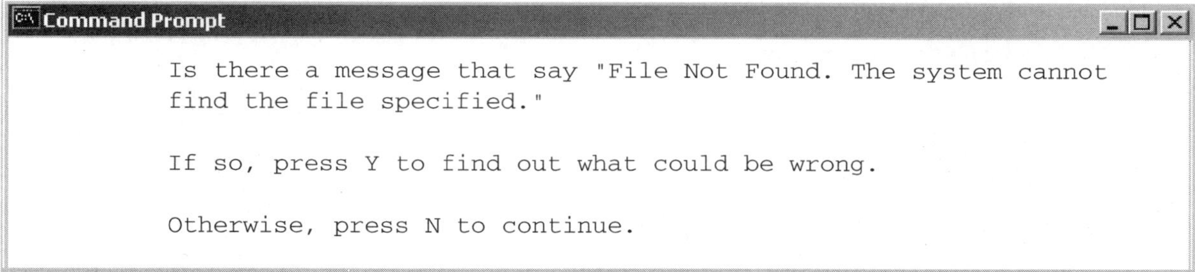

You will need to press **N** once for each file you are printing.

Step 3 Follow the messages on the screen until the Notepad program opens with a screen similar to the following:

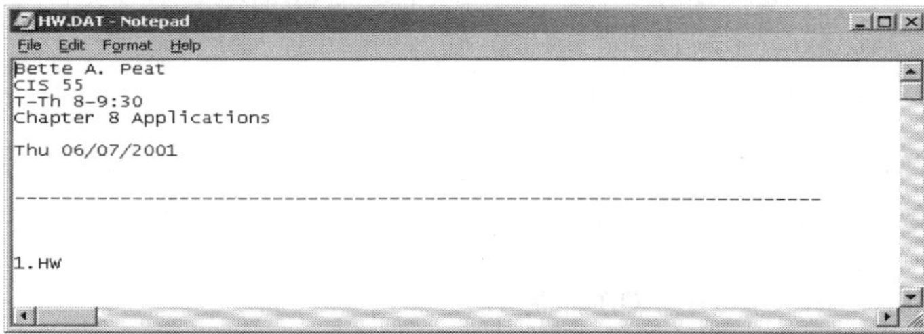

All the requested files have been found and placed in a Notepad document. Your homework is now ready to print.

Step 4 On the Notepad menu bar, click **File**. Click **Print**.

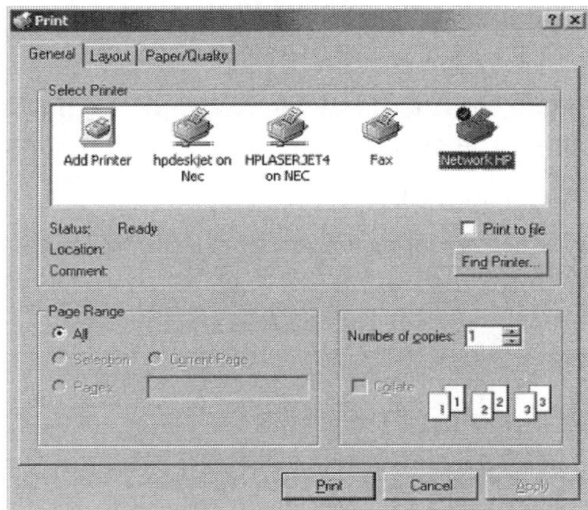

The print dialog box opens. If you have more than one printer, all your printer choices will be displayed. The default printer is the highlighted printer.

Step 5 Click the **Print** button.

Step 6 In the Notepad window, click **File**. Click **Exit**.

The following will appear on the Command Prompt screen:

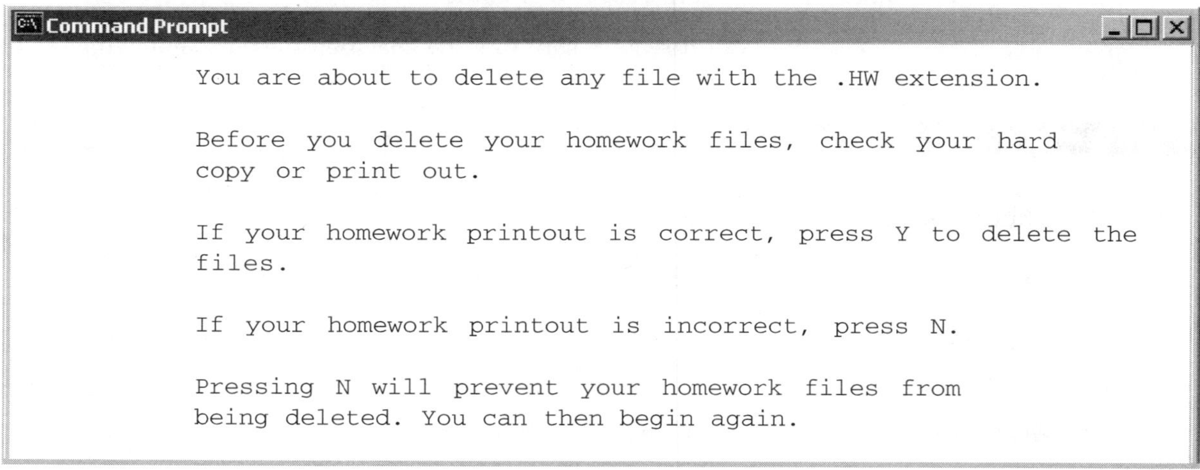
Command Prompt
You are about to delete any file with the .HW extension.
Before you delete your homework files, check your hard copy or print out.
If your homework printout is correct, press Y to delete the files.
If your homework printout is incorrect, press N.
Pressing N will prevent your homework files from being deleted. You can then begin again.

At this point, look at your printout. If it is correct, you can press **Y** to delete the homework files for this chapter. If your printout is incorrect, you can press **N**. That will preserve your homework and you will need to redo only the problem that was incorrect, not all the homework assignments.

Step 7 Press **Y** **Enter**

You have returned to the default prompt.

Step 8 Close the Command Prompt session.

Step 9 Execute the shut-down procedure.

PROBLEM SET III—BRIEF ESSAY

1. Plan and organize the APPLICATION disk *on paper only*. Write a brief explanation to justify your organizational scheme.

2. One way to organize a hard disk is by project. Another way to organize it is by program. Which way do you prefer? What advantages/disadvantages do you see to each method? Explain your answer.

CHAPTER

9

PIPES, FILTERS, AND REDIRECTION

LEARNING OBJECTIVES

After completing this chapter, you will be able to:

1. List the standard input and output devices.
2. Explain redirection.
3. Explain what filters are and when they are used.
4. Formulate and explain the syntax of the filter commands SORT, FIND, and MORE.
5. Explain when and how to use the SORT, FIND, and MORE commands.
6. Explain what shell extensions are and how you may use them.
7. Explain what pipes are and how they are used.

STUDENT OUTCOMES

1. Use > and >> to redirect standard output.
2. Use < to redirect standard input.
3. Use filter commands to manipulate information.
4. Enable shell extensions and use extended features.
5. Combine commands using pipes, filters, and redirection.

CHAPTER OVERVIEW

The operating system usually expects to read information from the keyboard. The keyboard is the standard input device. The standard output device, where the results of commands and the output of programs is displayed, is the screen. However, there are times when it is desirable to *redirect* input and output. Changing the standard input or output from one device to another is a process known as redirection. There are three external commands, called filters, which allow the user to manipulate data input and output. Pipes, used with filters, allow the user to link commands. Pipes, filters, and redirection give the user choices in determining where information is read from (input) and written to (output).

In this chapter you will learn how to use redirection. You will learn to use pipes to connect programs and filters to manipulate data.

9.1 REDIRECTION OF STANDARD I/O (INPUT/OUTPUT)

You have already used input and output. When you keyed in something on the keyboard, the operating system recognized it as input. After the input was processed, it was written to an output device—usually the screen. In other words, if you key in TYPE MYFILE.TXT, the input is what you key in. The output is the content of the file that is displayed on the screen. See Figure 9.1.

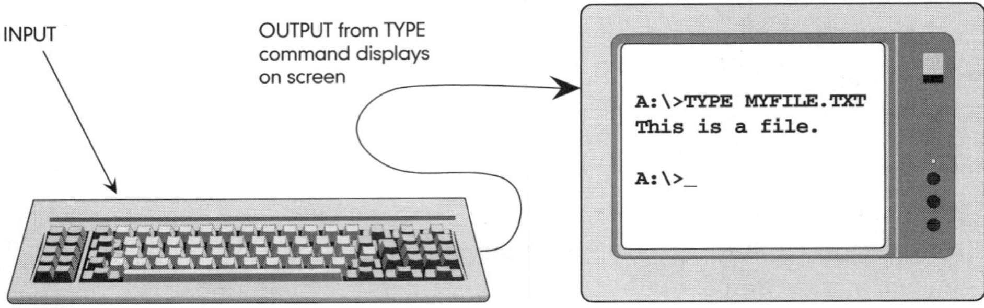

FIGURE 9.1 INPUT AND OUTPUT DEVICES

In the data processing world, this ***input/output*** process is commonly referred to as ***I/O***.

The operating system gets information from or sends information to three places: standard input, standard output, and standard error. ***Standard input*** is the keyboard. ***Standard output*** is the display screen. ***Standard error*** is the place from which the operating system writes error messages to the screen, e.g., "File Not Found."

Not all commands deal with standard input and standard output. For instance, the result or output of many of the commands you have used has been some action that occurred, such as copying a file with the COPY command. There is no standard input or output except the messages written to the screen. See Figure 9.2.

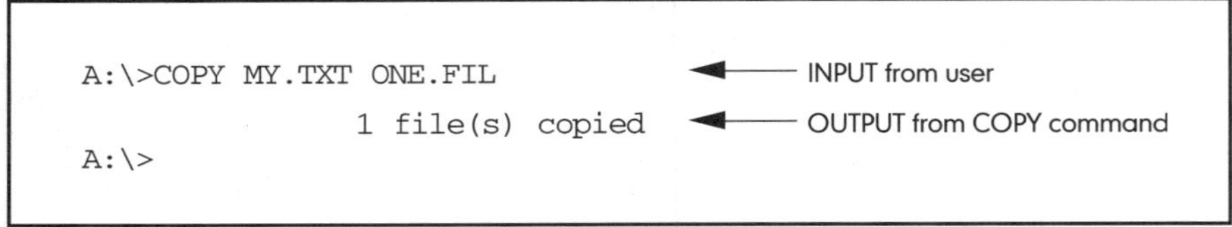

FIGURE 9.2 RESULTS OF COPY COMMAND

On the other hand, the output of commands like DIR has been a screen display of all the files on a disk. The information was received from the standard input device, the keyboard, and the results of the DIR command were sent to the standard output device, the screen. I/O ***redirection*** means that you tell the operating system you want information read from or written to a device *other than* the standard ones. With the DIR command, you can write the output to a file. This process is called redirecting the output of a command. See Figure 9.3.

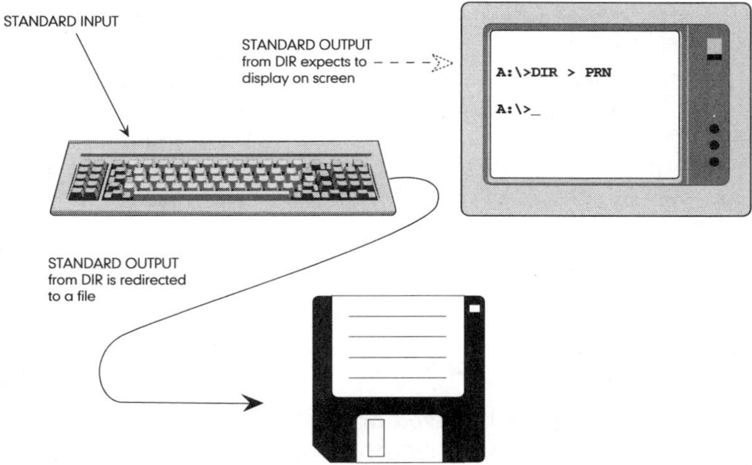

FIGURE 9.3 REDIRECTING STANDARD OUTPUT

Redirection works only when the command expects to send its results to the standard output device or receive the information from the standard input device.

The following symbols are used for redirection:

- \> The greater-than symbol redirects the output of a command to someplace other than the standard output.
- < The less-than symbol tells the operating system to get its input from somewhere other than the keyboard.
- \>> The double greater-than symbol redirects the output of a command but does not overwrite the existing file. It appends the output to the bottom of the existing file.

As a matter of fact, you have already used these redirection principles if you did the Application Assignments in prior chapters. You redirected output to a file and appended the files together.

9.2 ACTIVITY: USING > TO REDIRECT STANDARD OUTPUT

Note: The DATA disk is in Drive A wi th A:\> displayed.

Step 1 Key in the following: A:\>**DIR C:\WINDOSBK*.TXT** Enter

Command Prompt

```
A:\>DIR C:\WINDOSBK\*.TXT
 Volume in drive C is 2000 PRO
 Volume Serial Number is C4A7-8571

 Directory of C:\WINDOSBK

06/16/2000  04:32p                  72 APRIL.TXT
05/30/2000  04:32p                  45 BYE.TXT
12/11/1999  04:03p                  72 DANCES.TXT
```

```
06/16/2000  04:32p                  75 FEBRUARY.TXT
01/01/2002  04:32a                  34 GOODBYE.TXT
05/30/2000  04:32p                  53 HELLO.TXT
06/16/2000  04:32p                  73 JANUARY.TXT
05/27/2001  10:08p                  81 LONGFILENAME.TXT
05/27/2001  10:43p                  95 LONGFILENAMED.TXT
05/27/2001  10:42p                  97 LONGFILENAMING.TXT
06/16/2000  04:32p                  71 MARCH.TXT
11/16/2000  12:00p                  53 Sandy and Nicki.txt
11/16/2000  12:00p                  59 Sandy and Patty.txt
12/11/1999  04:03p                  65 TEST.TXT
              14 File(s)            945 bytes
                 0 Dir(s)   6,782,853,120 bytes free

A:\>_
```

WHAT'S HAPPENING? This command behaved in the "normal" way. You asked for a display of all the files in the **WINDOSBK** directory that had a **.TXT** file extension. The selected files were displayed on the screen. Because the DIR command writes its results to the screen, the standard output device, redirection can be used with this command.

Step 2 Key in the following: A:\>**DIR C:\WINDOSBK*.TXT > TXTFILES.TXT** Enter

Command Prompt

```
A:\>DIR C:\WINDOSBK\*.TXT > TXTFILES.TXT

A:\>_
```

WHAT'S HAPPENING? The output of the command has been sent to the file **TXTFILES.TXT** on the DATA disk. Nothing appears on the screen. When you key in **DIR C:\WINDOSBK*.TXT**, you normally see the directory listing of all the ***.TXT** files on the screen, as you did in the display following Step 1. The **>** sign tells the operating system that instead of sending the standard output to the screen, you want to redirect that output elsewhere. Redirection is very useful. For example, if you wanted a file copy of the directory of a disk, you could not key in **COPY DIR filename** because DIR is a command, not a file. You cannot copy a command to a file. COPY is for files only. Redirection used properly gets you that hard copy.

9.3 ACTIVITY: USING < TO REDIRECT STANDARD INPUT

Note: The DATA disk is in Drive A with A:\> displayed.

Step 1 Key in the following: A:\>**MD TEST** Enter

Step 2 Key in the following: A:\>**COPY C:\WINDOSBK*.NEW TEST** Enter

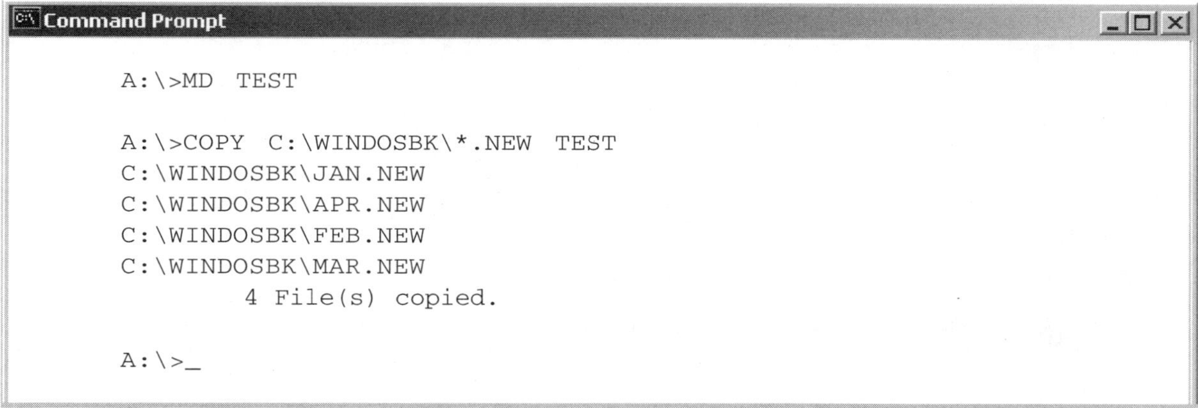

```
Command Prompt

A:\>MD  TEST

A:\>COPY  C:\WINDOSBK\*.NEW  TEST
C:\WINDOSBK\JAN.NEW
C:\WINDOSBK\APR.NEW
C:\WINDOSBK\FEB.NEW
C:\WINDOSBK\MAR.NEW
        4 File(s) copied.

A:\>_
```

You have a created a subdirectory called **TEST** on the DATA disk and copied four files into it.

Step 3 Key in the following: A:\>**DEL TEST*.*** Enter

```
Command Prompt

A:\>DEL  TEST\*.*
A:\TEST\*.*,  Are  you  sure  (Y/N)?
```

You asked the DEL command to delete all the files in the **TEST** subdirectory. DEL is asking you if you are really sure that you want to delete these files. DEL is expecting input from the standard input device, the keyboard.

Step 4 Key in the following: **N** Enter

```
Command Prompt

A:\>DEL  TEST\*.*
A:\TEST\*.*,  Are  you  sure  (Y/N)?N

A:\>_
```

You were returned to the system prompt without deleting the files in the **TEST** subdirectory because you answered **N** for "No, don't delete." As you can see, the operating system took no action until it received input from you via the keyboard, **N**. The input was **N**. You can prove that the files are still there by keying in **DIR TEST**.

Step 5 Key in the following: A:\>**DIR TEST** Enter

```
Command Prompt

A:\>DIR  TEST
 Volume  in  drive  A  is  DATA
 Volume  Serial  Number  is  3330-1807

 Directory  of  A:\TEST

06/08/2001   08:43a      <DIR>          .
06/08/2001   08:43a      <DIR>          ..
```

```
10/01/1999  02:53p                 74 APR.NEW
10/01/1999  02:53p                 75 FEB.NEW
10/01/1999  02:53p                 73 JAN.NEW
10/01/1999  02:53p                 71 MAR.NEW
               4 File(s)           293 bytes
               2 Dir(s)      1,245,696 bytes free

A:\>_
```

WHAT'S HAPPENING? From the display you can see that you did not delete the files in the **TEST** directory.

Step 6 Key in the following: A:\>**TYPE Y.FIL** Enter

```
Command Prompt

A:\>TYPE Y.FIL
Y

A:\>_
```

WHAT'S HAPPENING? The **Y.FIL** file is a simple file that contains the letter Y followed by a carriage return (Enter). If you do not have this file on the DATA disk, you can copy it from the **WINDOSBK** directory to the DATA disk.

Step 7 Key in the following: A:\>**DEL TEST*.* < Y.FIL** Enter

```
Command Prompt

A:\>DEL TEST\*.* < Y.FIL
A:\TEST\*.*, Are you sure (Y/N)?Y

A:\>_
```

WHAT'S HAPPENING? This time you told the operating system to get input from a file called **Y.FIL** (**< Y.FIL**), instead of from the standard input device, the keyboard. When **DEL TEST*.*** was executed and displayed the message "Are you sure (Y/N)?" it still needed input, a **Y** or **N** followed by Enter. The operating system found the file you told it to look for, **Y.FIL**, which had the "**Y** Enter" answer. This file provided a response to the question, so the operating system proceeded to delete the files in the subdirectory **TEST**.

You must be very careful with redirection of input. When you tell the operating system to take input from a file, any input from the keyboard will be ignored. In this example, if the **Y.FIL** contents were "X," this would not be a valid answer to the question posed, "Are you sure (Y/N)?" Only **Y** or **N** is an acceptable response. Any other letter would be unacceptable, and the question would be asked again, and then the system would assume the response was **N**. You would see the following on the screen:

```
A:\TEST\*.*, Are you sure (Y/N)?X
A:\TEST\*.*, Are you sure (Y/N)?
```

and the files would not have been deleted.

Step 8 Key in the following: A:\>**DIR TEST** Enter

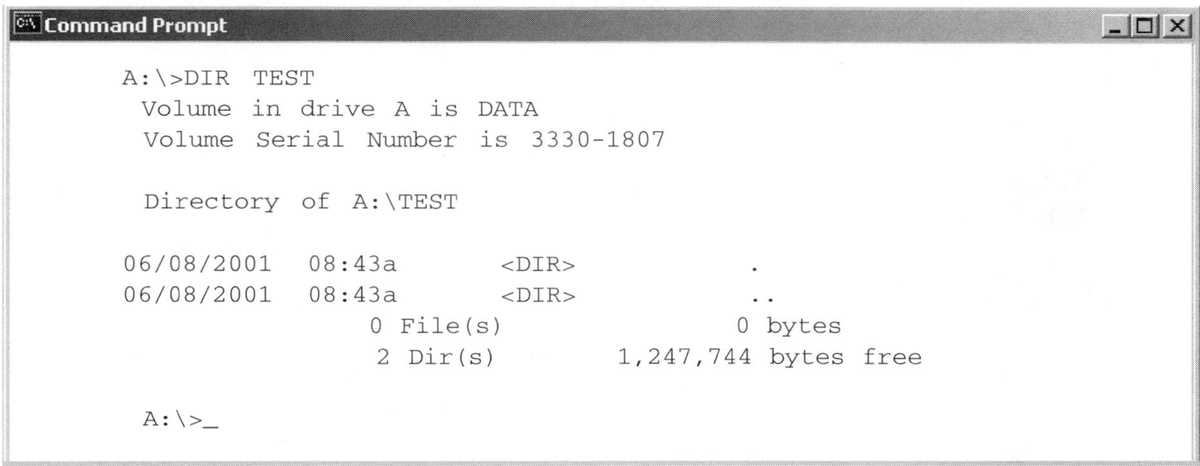

Command Prompt
A:\>DIR TEST
Volume in drive A is DATA
Volume Serial Number is 3330-1807
Directory of A:\TEST
06/08/2001 08:43a <DIR> .
06/08/2001 08:43a <DIR> ..
0 File(s) 0 bytes
2 Dir(s) 1,247,744 bytes free
A:\>_

WHAT'S HAPPENING? The files were deleted. You did it with one command line, and you did not have to key in the **Y**. The Y came from the file **Y.FIL**.

9.4 ACTIVITY: USING >> TO ADD REDIRECTED OUTPUT TO A FILE

Note: The DATA disk is in Drive A with A:\> displayed.

Step 1 Key in the following: A:\>**TYPE JANUARY.TXT** Enter

Step 2 Key in the following: A:\>**TYPE FEBRUARY.TXT** Enter

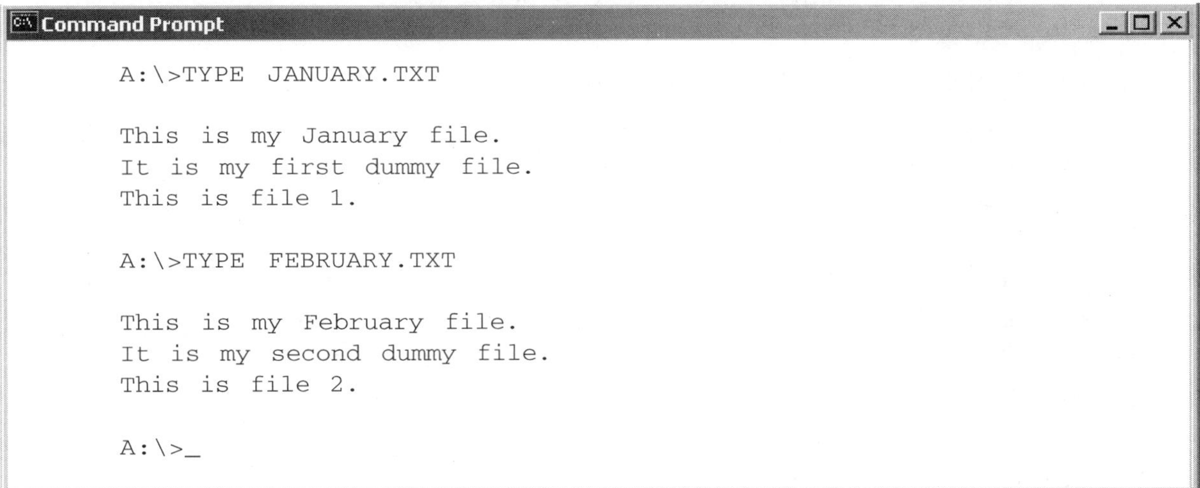

WHAT'S HAPPENING? You have two separate files. You want to add **FEBRUARY.TXT** to the end of **JANUARY.TXT**. If you keyed in **TYPE FEBRUARY.TXT > JANUARY.TXT**, you would *overwrite* the contents of **JANUARY.TXT** with the contents of **FEBRUARY.TXT**. To *append* to the end of an existing file, you use the double redirection symbol, >>.

Step 3 Key in the following: A:\>**TYPE FEBRUARY.TXT >> JANUARY.TXT** Enter

Step 4 Key in the following: A:\>**TYPE JANUARY.TXT** Enter

```
Command Prompt

A:\>TYPE FEBRUARY.TXT >> JANUARY.TXT

A:\>TYPE JANUARY.TXT

This is my January file.
It is my first dummy file.
This is file 1.

This is my February file.
It is my second dummy file.
This is file 2.

A:\>_
```

WHAT'S HAPPENING? Instead of overwriting the contents of **JANUARY.TXT** with the contents of **FEBRUARY.TXT**, the contents of **FEBRUARY.TXT** were added to the end of the **JANUARY.TXT** file.

9.5 FILTERS

Filter commands manipulate information. ***Filters*** read information from the keyboard (standard input), change the input in a specified way, and write the results to the screen (standard output). Filter commands function like filters in a water purification system. They remove the unwanted elements from the water (data) and send the purified water (data) on its way. There are three filters, all of which are external commands:

SORT Arranges lines in ascending or descending order.

FIND Searches for a particular group of characters, also called a ***character string***.

MORE Temporarily halts the screen display after each screenful.

The operating system creates temporary files while it "filters" data, so during this process it is important that there be access to the disk and the filters. You must be sure that the floppy disk is not write-protected. If a disk is write-protected, the operating system will not be able to execute filter commands.

9.6 THE SORT COMMAND

The SORT filter command arranges or sorts lines of input (text) and sends them to standard output (the screen), unless you redirect it. The default SORT is in ascending order (A to Z or lowest to highest numbers), starting in the first column. The SORT command has many parameters. The syntax for the command is:

```
SORT [/R] [/+N] [/M kilobytes] [/L locale] [/REC characters]
[[drive1:][path1]filename1] [/T [drive2:][path2]] [/O [drive3:][path3]filename3]
[command |] sort [/R] [/+N] [/M kilobytes] [/L locale] [/REC characters]
[[drive1:][path1]filename1] [/T [drive2:][path2]] [/O [drive3:][path3]filename3]
```

The full syntax is listed in the command summary in Appendix B.

9.7 ACTIVITY: USING SORT

Note 1: The DATA disk is in Drive A with A:\> displayed.
Note 2: Remember when you see F6, it means to press the F6 key.

Step 1 Key in the following: A:\>**SORT** Enter
BETA Enter
OMEGA Enter
CHI Enter
ALPHA Enter
F6 Enter

As you can see, the SORT command took input from the keyboard. When you pressed the F6 key (identical to pressing Ctrl + **Z**), you told the SORT command that you were finished entering data. Then the SORT command "filtered" the data and wrote the keyboard input alphabetically to the standard output device (the screen). See Figure 9.4 for a graphical representation of this filter.

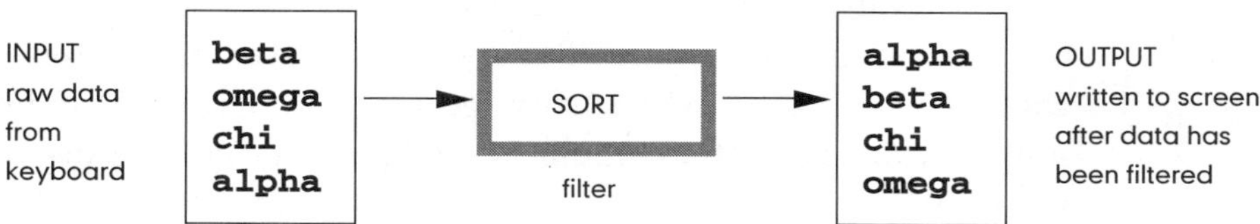

FIGURE 9.4 FILTERING DATA

Step 2 Key in the following: A:\>**SORT** Enter
333 Enter
3 Enter
23 Enter
124 Enter
F6 Enter

```
A:\>SORT
333
3
23
124
^Z
124
23
3
333

A:\>_
```

The SORT command does not seem very smart because these numbers are certainly not in order. Numbers, in this case, are really character data and not numeric values that are manipulated mathematically. Numbers are often used as character data. For instance, a zip code or a phone number, although they use numbers, really are character data and are not treated mathematically. You would not think of adding your address to your phone number and dividing by your zip code, for example.

Character data is sorted from left to right. Numeric data is sorted by units. Thus, if you look at "Smith" and "Smythe," you read character data from left to right and would place "Smith" before "Smythe." If you had the numbers 124, 222, 22, 23, 31, 9, and 6, the numeric order would be, of course, 6, 9, 22, 23, 31, 124, and 222. You first sort all the single-digit numbers. You then sort the two-digit numbers by looking at the first digit—thus you know that 22 and 23 come before 32. Since 22 and 23 have the same first digit, you then go to the second digit to determine that the 2 in 22 comes before the 3 in 23.

A human knows that 12 comes before 13 because that person has learned how numbers work. The operating system is different. It relies on something called the ***ASCII sort sequence***. ASCII is a standard code that assigns values to letters, numbers, and punctuation marks—from the *left*, in the same way we read characters. The ASCII sort sequence is determined by the number assigned to the ASCII character. The sort order is punctuation marks (including spaces), then numbers, then letters (lowercase preceding uppercase). If you had a series of characters such as BB, aa, #, 123, bb, 13, and AA, the ASCII sort order would be:

```
#     123   13    aa    AA    bb    BB
```

Notice that with the new sort sequence the relative position of aa and AA did not change, but the relative position of BB and bb did change.

There is another point about using the SORT command. Not only does it follow the ASCII sort sequence, but it also sorts entire lines from left to right. Thus, the sort sequence of "Carolyn Smith" and "Robert Nesler" is:

```
Carolyn  Smith
Robert Nesler
```

Because the SORT command looks at the entire line, "Carolyn" comes before "Robert."

In our numeric example, SORT looked at the entire line, and, since the "1" in "124" preceded the "2" in "23," it placed the "124" before the "23." You can force the operating system to sort numbers correctly using the spacebar to add the space character.

Step 3 Key in the following: A:\>**SORT** Enter
333 Enter
Space Bar Space Bar **3** Enter
Space Bar **23** Enter
124 Enter
F6 Enter

```
Command Prompt

A:\>SORT
333
  3
 23
124
^Z
  3
 23
124
333

A:\>_
```

WHAT'S HAPPENING? By entering spaces, you forced the lines to be the same length, placing the number digits in their proper position. Since spaces precede numbers in the ASCII sort sequence, the SORT command could sort the entire line and place it in proper numeric order. Indeed, you made numeric data character data. Essentially, you left-justify character data and right-justify numeric data.

9.8 FILTERS AND REDIRECTION

The standard output of filters is a screen display. Hence, you can redirect both the output and input of these filter commands. The filter commands are not usually used with actual keyboard input, but with input redirected from a file, a device, or another command.

9.9 ACTIVITY: USING THE SORT COMMAND WITH REDIRECTION

Note: The DATA disk is in Drive A with A:\> displayed.

Step 1 Key in the following: A:\>**COPY C:\WINDOSBK\STATE.CAP** Enter

Step 2 Key in the following: A:\>**SORT < STATE.CAP** Enter

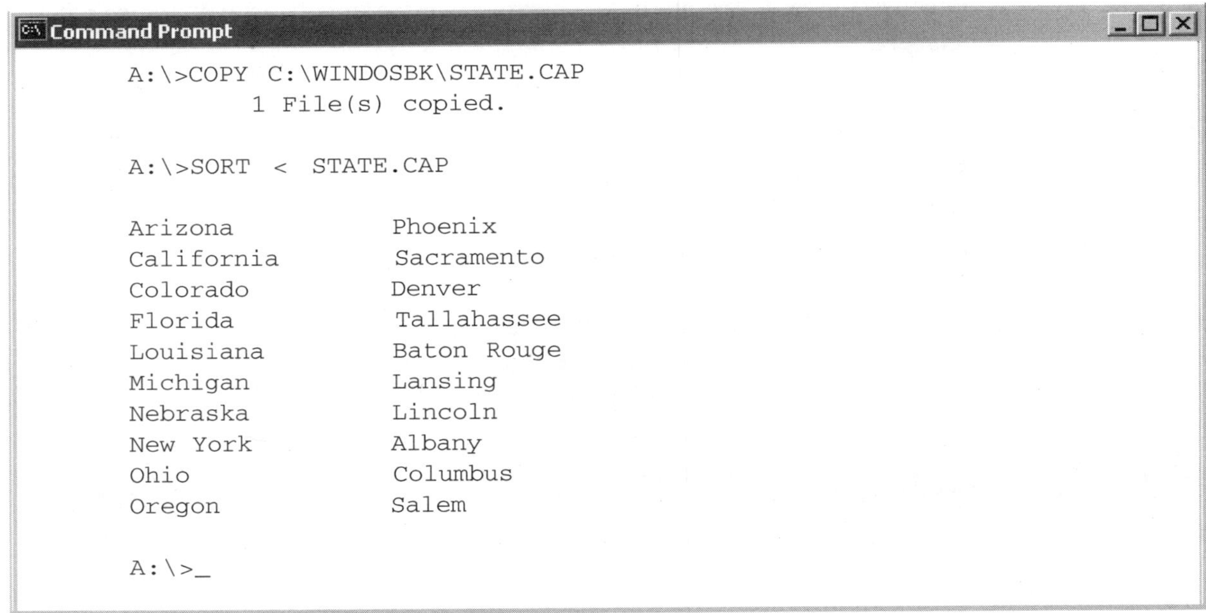

```
Command Prompt

A:\>COPY C:\WINDOSBK\STATE.CAP
        1 File(s) copied.

A:\>SORT  <  STATE.CAP

Arizona             Phoenix
California          Sacramento
Colorado            Denver
Florida             Tallahassee
Louisiana           Baton Rouge
Michigan            Lansing
Nebraska            Lincoln
New York            Albany
Ohio                Columbus
Oregon              Salem

A:\>_
```

WHAT'S HAPPENING? You copied the **STATE.CAP** file from the **WINDOSBK** directory to the DATA disk. You then keyed in the **SORT** command. You used the symbol **<** for taking data from a source other than the keyboard, the file called **STATE.CAP**, and fed it into the SORT command. Displayed on your screen (the standard output) is the **STATE.CAP** file arranged in alphabetical order, with **Arizona** and **Phoenix** at the top. Another SORT command feature is the /R parameter, which allows you to sort in reverse or descending order (Z to A). In Windows 2000 Professional, the SORT command no longer requires the < prior to the file being sorted.

Step 3 Key in the following: A:\>**SORT STATE.CAP** Enter

```
Command Prompt

A:\>SORT  STATE.CAP

Arizona             Phoenix
California          Sacramento
Colorado            Denver
Florida             Tallahassee
Louisiana           Baton Rouge
Michigan            Lansing
Nebraska            Lincoln
New York            Albany
```

```
Ohio            Columbus
Oregon          Salem

A:\>_
```

As you can see, the command worked the same even without the < symbol. SORT expects either keyboard input or a file.

Step 4 Key in the following: A:\>**SORT /R < STATE.CAP** Enter

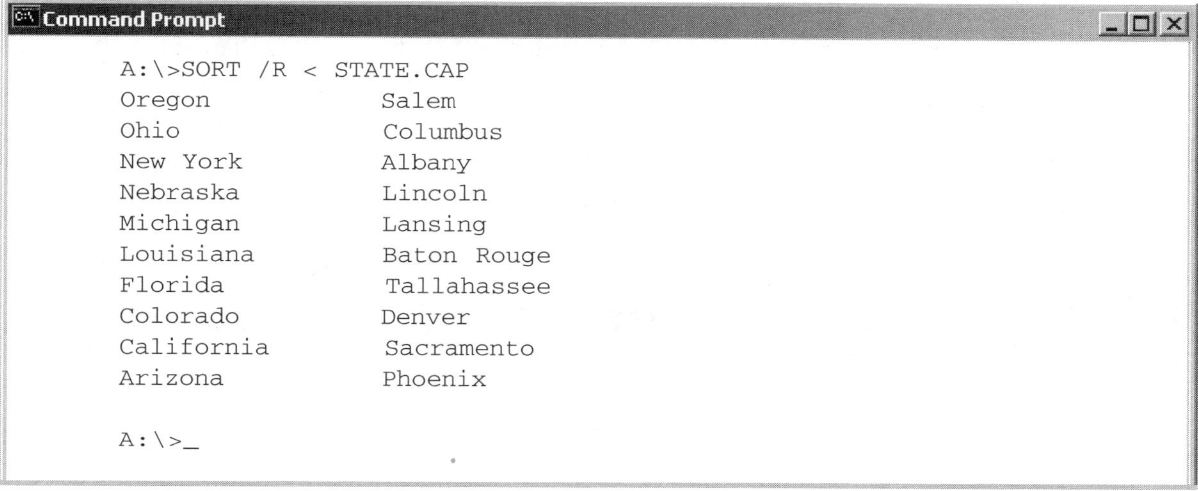

```
Command Prompt

A:\>SORT /R < STATE.CAP
Oregon          Salem
Ohio            Columbus
New York        Albany
Nebraska        Lincoln
Michigan        Lansing
Louisiana       Baton Rouge
Florida         Tallahassee
Colorado        Denver
California      Sacramento
Arizona         Phoenix

A:\>_
```

The file **STATE.CAP** that the SORT command used as input is displayed on the screen in reverse alphabetical order. The standard output, the results of the SORT command, is written to the screen. The SORT parameter that sorts by a column number is /+*n*. (A column, on the screen, is the place occupied by one character.)

Step 5 Key in the following: A:\>**SORT /+17 STATE.CAP** Enter

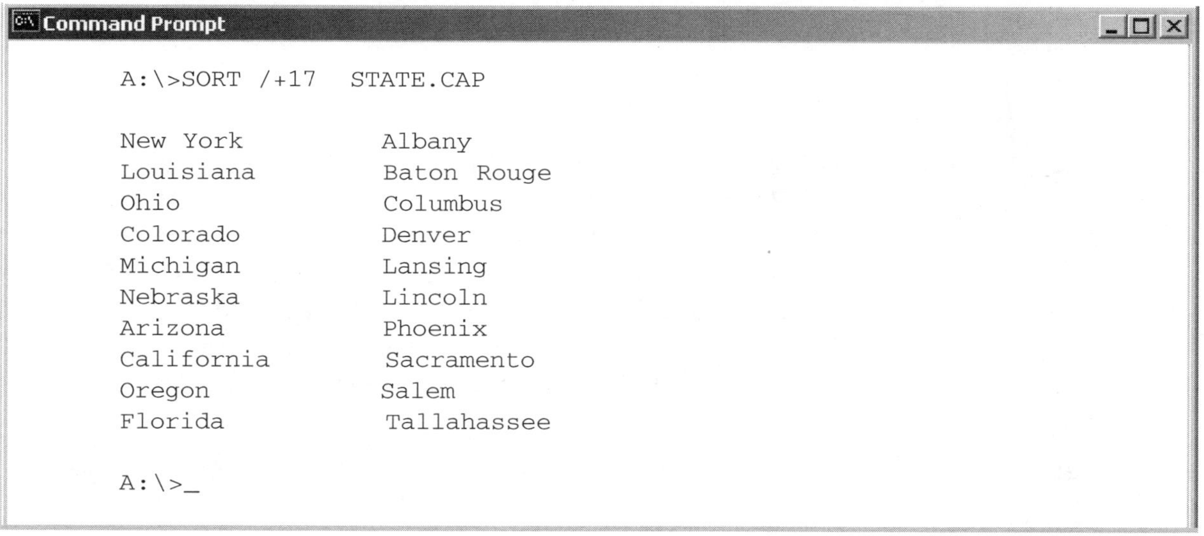

```
Command Prompt

A:\>SORT /+17  STATE.CAP

New York        Albany
Louisiana       Baton Rouge
Ohio            Columbus
Colorado        Denver
Michigan        Lansing
Nebraska        Lincoln
Arizona         Phoenix
California      Sacramento
Oregon          Salem
Florida         Tallahassee

A:\>_
```

This time you sorted by column number, the seventeenth position in the list in this example. The first letter of the city is in the seventeenth column. The

file is now ordered by city rather than by state. It is important to note that the SORT command does not understand columns in the usual sense. A person would say that the "city" column is the second column, going from left to right. The SORT command counts each character (letters and spaces) from left to right and counts each character as a column. Thus, "city" is located by counting the number of characters, including the spaces between the characters. The total number was 17.

In these examples, you have been "massaging the data." The actual data in **STATE.CAP** has not changed at all. It remains exactly as it was written. The only thing that has changed is the way it is displayed—the way you are *looking* at the data. This alphabetic arrangement is temporary. If you want to change the data in the file, you need to save the altered data to a new file.

Step 6 Key in the following: A:\>**SORT /+17 STATE.CAP > SORTED.CAP** Enter

Step 7 Key in the following: A:\>**TYPE SORTED.CAP** Enter

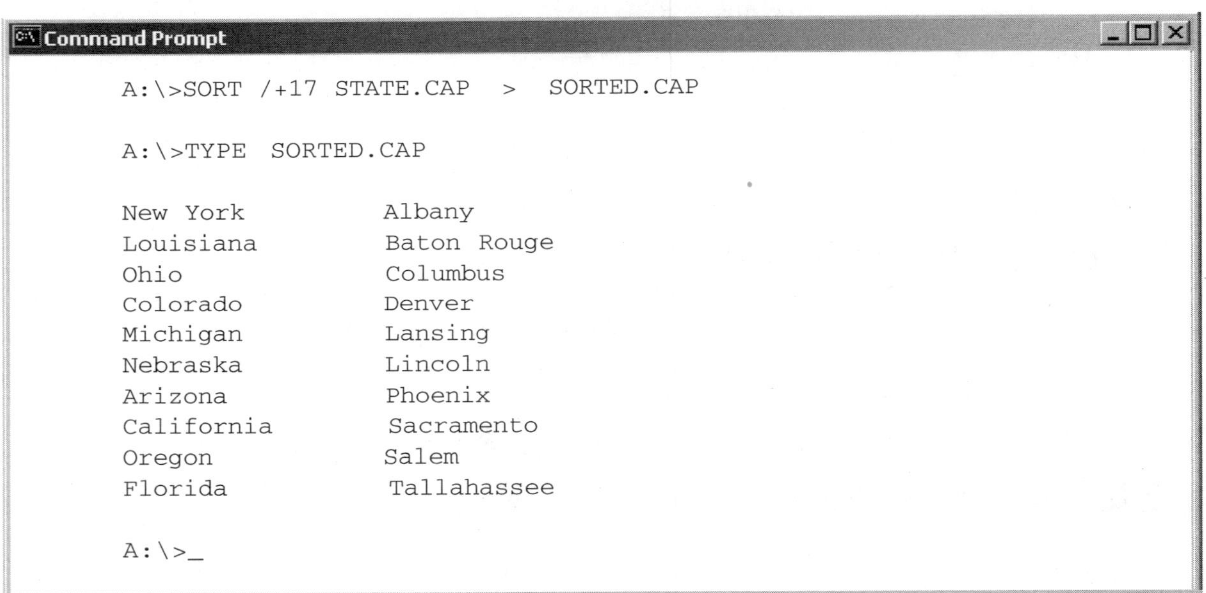
Command Prompt
A:\>SORT /+17 STATE.CAP > SORTED.CAP
A:\>TYPE SORTED.CAP
New York Albany
Louisiana Baton Rouge
Ohio Columbus
Colorado Denver
Michigan Lansing
Nebraska Lincoln
Arizona Phoenix
California Sacramento
Oregon Salem
Florida Tallahassee
A:\>_

You used redirectiona and saved the sorted output to a new file called **SORTED.CAP**. The standard output of the command **SORT STATE.CAP** will be written to the screen (the standard output device). Since standard output writes to the screen, you can redirect it to a file called **SORTED.CAP** with the command line **SORT STATE.CAP > SORTED.CAP**. You do need the > symbol. Otherwise SORT will not know what to do with the output. The SORT command includes a parameter to store the sorted data in a file that works faster than redirection. The parameter is /O.

Step 8 Key in the following. A:\>**SORT /+17 STATE.CAP /O BYCITY.CAP** Enter

Step 9 Key in the following. A:\>**TYPE SORTED.CAP** Enter

Step 10 Key in the following: A:\>**TYPE BYCITY.CAP** Enter

```
Command Prompt

A:\>SORT /+17 STATE.CAP /O BYCITY.CAP


A:\>TYPE  SORTED.CAP

New York          Albany
Louisiana         Baton Rouge
Ohio              Columbus
Colorado          Denver
Michigan          Lansing
Nebraska          Lincoln
Arizona           Phoenix
California        Sacramento
Oregon            Salem
Florida           Tallahassee

A:\>TYPE  BYCITY.CAP

New York          Albany
Louisiana         Baton Rouge
Ohio              Columbus
Colorado          Denver
Michigan          Lansing
Nebraska          Lincoln
Arizona           Phoenix
California        Sacramento
Oregon            Salem
Florida           Tallahassee

A:\>_
```

As you can see, both files are the same. With this small file, the time difference is not discernable, but with a large data file, using /O is considerably faster than using redirection.

9.10 THE FIND FILTER

The FIND command allows you to search a file for a specific character string by enclosing it in quotation marks. Although intended for use with ASCII text files, this command can be useful with some data files produced by application software. For example, let's say you used a program to create five documents. One of the documents was a paper on law enforcement in which you know you used the word "indictment" but you can't remember the name of the file. You could, of course, open each one of the five documents, or you could use the FIND command to search for the word "indictment." Although much of the document would appear as funny characters if you used the TYPE command, the FIND command might be able to tell you whether or not the word "indictment" is in the file.

On the desktop, there is a Search option in the Start menu, which can search files for textbook as well. In this text you are using the command line. Using the FIND command at the command line can help you find a file based on content.

The FIND command is ***case sensitive*** unless you use the parameter /I, which means ignore case. The syntax is:

```
FIND [/V] [/C] [/N] [/I] "string" [[drive:][path]filename[ ...]]

/V        Displays all lines NOT containing the specified string.
/C        Displays only the count of lines that contain the
          specified string.
/N        Precedes each line with the line number.
/I        Specifies that the search is not to be case sensitive.
"string"  Specifies the group of characters you want to search for.
[drive:][path]filename
          Specifies the location and name of the file
          in which to search for the specified string.
```

If a file name is not specified, FIND searches the text typed at the prompt or piped from another command.

9.11 ACTIVITY: USING THE FIND FILTER

Note 1: The DATA disk is in Drive A with the A:\> displayed.
Note 2: If **PERSONAL.FIL** is not on the DATA disk, it can be copied from the **WINDOSBK** directory to the DATA disk.
Note 3: You *must* use double quotes. Single quotes are invalid.

Step 1 Key in the following: A:\>**FIND "Smith" PERSONAL.FIL** Enter

```
Command Prompt

A:\>FIND "Smith" PERSONAL.FIL

---------- PERSONAL.FIL
Smith     Gregory   311 Orchard   Ann Arbor    MI   Engineer
Smith     Carolyn   311 Orchard   Ann Arbor    MI   Housewife
Smith     David     120 Collins   Orange       CA   Chef

A:\>_
```

The FIND command found every occurrence of the character string "Smith" in **PERSONAL.FIL** on the DATA disk. A character string must be enclosed in quotation marks. Since FIND is case sensitive, you must key in the word exactly as it appears in the file. The character string SMITH would not be found because FIND would be looking for uppercase letters. If you use the parameter /I, the command would find SMITH, smith, or Smith. The FIND command "filtered" the file **PERSONAL.FIL** to extract the character string that matched the specification. With the use of the /V parameter, you can search a file for anything *except* what is in quotation marks.

Step 2 Key in the following: A:\>**FIND /V "Smith" PERSONAL.FIL** Enter

```
Command Prompt

Babchuk   Bianca   13 Stratford  Sun City West  AZ  Professor
Rodriguez Bob      20 Elm        Ontario        CA  Systems Analyst
Helm      Milton   333 Meadow    Sherman Oaks   CA  Consultant
Suzuki    Charlene 567 Abbey     Rochester      MI  Day Care Teacher
Markiw    Nicholas 354 Bell      Phoenix        AZ  Engineer
Markiw    Emily    10 Zion       Sun City West  AZ  Retired
Nyles     John     12 Brooks     Sun City West  AZ  Retired
Nyles     Sophie   12 Brooks     Sun City West  CA  Retired
Markiw    Nick     10 Zion       Sun City West  AZ  Retired
Washingon Tyrone   345 Newport   Orange         CA  Manager
Jones     Steven   32 North      Phoenix        AZ  Buyer
Babchuk   Walter   12 View       Thousand Oaks  CA  President
Babchuk   Deana    12 View       Thousand Oaks  CA  Housewife
Jones     Cleo     355 Second    Ann Arbor      MI  Clerk
Gonzales  Antonio  40 Northern   Ontario        CA  Engineer
JONES     JERRY    244 East      Mission Viejo  CA  Systems Analyst
Lo        Ophelia  1213 Wick     Phoenix        AZ  Writer
Jones     Ervin    15 Fourth     Santa Cruz     CA  Banker
Perez     Sergio   134 Seventh   Ann Arbor      MI  Editor
Yuan      Suelin   56 Twin Leaf  Orange         CA  Artist
Markiw    Nicholas 12 Fifth      Glendale       AZ  Engineer
Peat      Brian    125 Second    Vacaville      CA  Athlete
Farneth   Nichole  237 Arbor     Vacaville      CA  Dancer

A:\>_
```

WHAT'S HAPPENING? (This graphic represents the last part of what you will see on your screen.) Though the output is so long it scrolled off the screen, you can see that FIND located everyone *except* Smith. Furthermore, you can find the specific line number of each occurrence by using the /N parameter.

Step 3 Key in the following: A:\>**FIND /N "Smith" PERSONAL.FIL** Enter

```
Command Prompt

A:\>FIND /N "Smith" PERSONAL.FIL

---------- PERSONAL.FIL
[7]Smith    Gregory  311 Orchard  Ann Arbor   MI  Engineer
[8]Smith    Carolyn  311 Orchard  Ann Arbor   MI  Housewife
[28]Smith    David    120 Collins  Orange      CA  Chef

A:\>_
```

WHAT'S HAPPENING? Displayed on the screen are not only all the people named Smith, but also the line numbers where their names appear in the file. You can also have a numeric count of the number of times a specific character string appears in a file. The FIND command will not display the actual lines, but it will tell you how many occurrences there are of that specific string.

Step 4 Key in the following: A:\>**FIND /C "Smith" PERSONAL.FIL** Enter

```
Command Prompt

A:\>FIND /C "Smith" PERSONAL.FIL

---------- PERSONAL.FIL: 3

A:\>_
```

WHAT'S HAPPENING? The number 3 follows the file name. The name Smith appears three times in the file **PERSONAL.FIL**. You can also tell the FIND command to ignore case.

Step 5 Key in the following: A:\>**FIND /I "Jones" PERSONAL.FIL** Enter

```
Command Prompt

A:\>FIND /I "Jones" PERSONAL.FIL

---------- PERSONAL.FIL
Jones      Steven   32 North     Phoenix        AZ  Buyer
Jones      Cleo     355 Second   Ann Arbor      MI  Clerk
JONES      JERRY    244 East     Mission Viejo  CA  Systems Analyst
Jones      Ervin    15 Fourth    Santa Cruz     CA  Banker

A:\>_
```

WHAT'S HAPPENING? By using the /I parameter, which told the FIND command to ignore the case, you found both Jones and JONES.

9.12 PIPES

Pipes allow the standard output of one program to be used as the standard input to the next program. When you use pipes, you are not limited to two programs. You may pipe together many programs. The term "pipe" reflects the flow of information from one command to the next. Pipes are used with filter commands. You may take any command that has standard output and pipe it to a filter. The filter will "do" something to the standard output of the previous command, such as sort it. Since filters always write to standard output, you may use pipes and filters to further refine your data. Essentially, you may use filters to transform data to meet your needs.

The pipe symbol is the vertical broken bar (¦) used between two commands. The standard output from a command is written to a temporary file. Then the next command in the pipeline, typically a filter, reads the temporary file as standard input. See Figure 9.5.

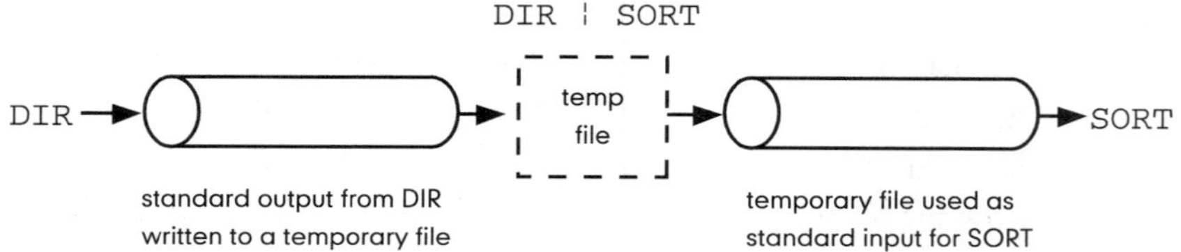

FIGURE 9.5 PIPING COMMANDS

On the original IBM keyboard, the pipe symbol is located between the Shift key and the letter Z. On some computers, the pipe symbol is located along with the backslash. Some other keyboards have the ¦ symbol next to the Ctrl and Alt keys on the right side of the keyboard. The location of the ¦ symbol is not standard and could appear in other locations. The symbol ¦ is the connection between two commands, like a pipe in a water system. Since filters are external commands, the operating system must be able to access the commands. If a disk is write-protected, filter commands will not work because these commands read and write temporary files to the disk.

After using pipes with filters, you may see some strange files on the directory listing labeled:

```
%PIPE1.$$$
%PIPE2.$$$
%PIPE3.$$$
```

or

```
11002649
1100274E
```

All files must be named—even temporary files. These are the names the operating system gives for the files that it creates when you use piping. These temporary files "hold" the data until the next command can process it. These temporary files are automatically deleted by the operating system when you have finished your chain of commands. You will not see these names displayed on the screen, and probably will not see them at all.

9.13 THE MORE FILTER

The MORE command displays one screenful of data at a time with a prompt that reads **-- More --**. The MORE command pauses after the screen is full. When any key is pressed, the MORE command displays the next screenful of information, once again pausing so you can read the screen display. When there is no more data in the file, the MORE command finishes by returning you to the system prompt. The purpose of the MORE command is to allow you to be able to read a long text file, one that would not fit onto the screen, one screenful at a time. Many new features have been added to the MORE command with Windows 2000 Professional. The syntax is:

```
MORE [/E [/C] [/P] [/S] [/Tn] [+n]] < [drive:][path]filename
command-name ¦ MORE [/E [/C] [/P] [/S] [/Tn] [+n]]
MORE /E [/C] [/P] [/S] [/Tn] [+n] [files]

  [drive:][path]filename    Specifies a file to display one
                            screen at a time.

  command-name              Specifies a command whose output
                            will be displayed.

  /E      Enable extended features
  /C      Clear screen before displaying page
  /P      Expand FormFeed characters
```

```
/S        Squeeze multiple blank lines into a single line
/Tn       Expand tabs to n spaces (default 8)

          Switches can be present in the MORE environment
          variable.

+n        Start displaying the first file at line n

files     List of files to be displayed. Files in the list
          are separated by blanks.
```

As the syntax diagram indicates, MORE can be both redirected and used with a pipe.

9.14 ACTIVITY: USING THE MORE FILTER

Note: The DATA disk is in Drive A with the A:\> displayed.

Step 1 You will use the pipe symbol ¦, so be sure you locate it on the keyboard. Key in the following: A:\>**DIR ¦ MORE** Enter

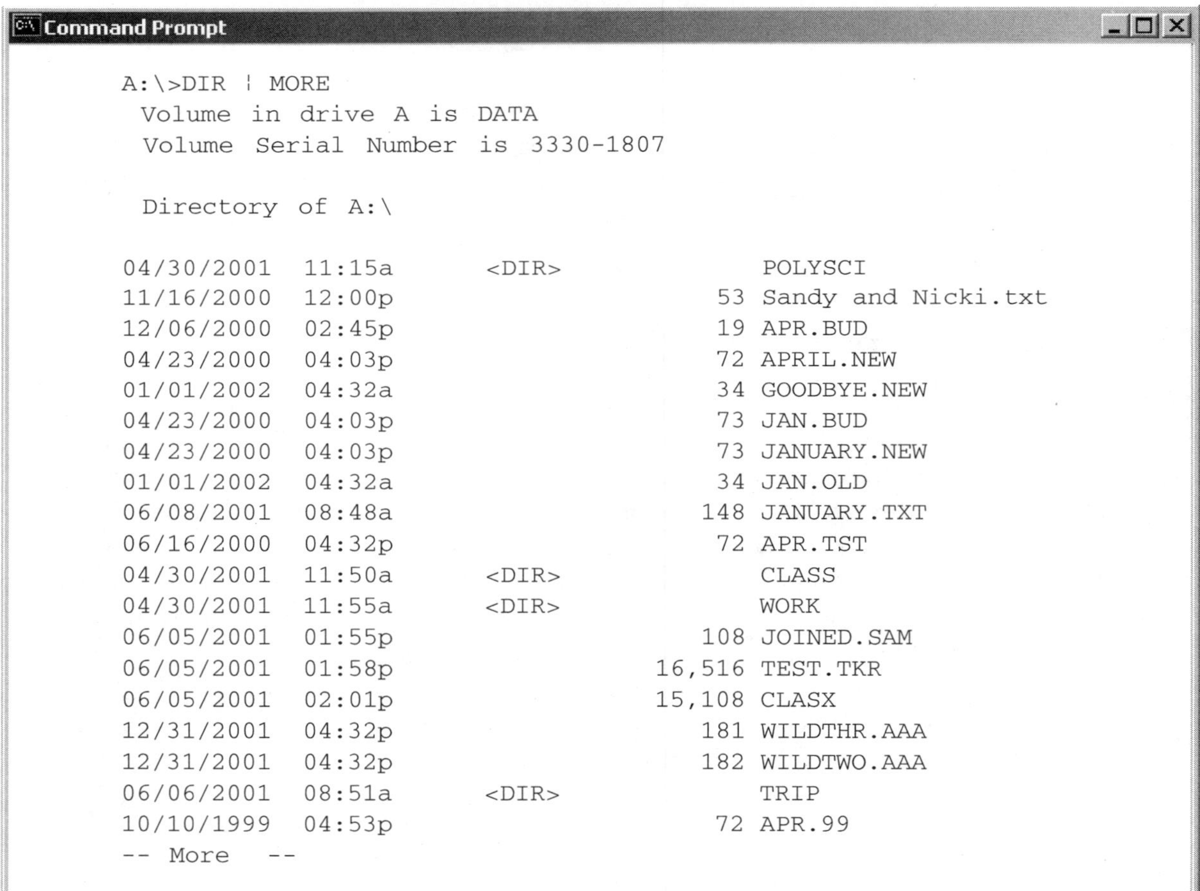

```
Command Prompt

A:\>DIR ¦ MORE
 Volume in drive A is DATA
 Volume Serial Number is 3330-1807

 Directory of A:\

04/30/2001  11:15a      <DIR>          POLYSCI
11/16/2000  12:00p                  53 Sandy and Nicki.txt
12/06/2000  02:45p                  19 APR.BUD
04/23/2000  04:03p                  72 APRIL.NEW
01/01/2002  04:32a                  34 GOODBYE.NEW
04/23/2000  04:03p                  73 JAN.BUD
04/23/2000  04:03p                  73 JANUARY.NEW
01/01/2002  04:32a                  34 JAN.OLD
06/08/2001  08:48a                 148 JANUARY.TXT
06/16/2000  04:32p                  72 APR.TST
04/30/2001  11:50a      <DIR>          CLASS
04/30/2001  11:55a      <DIR>          WORK
06/05/2001  01:55p                 108 JOINED.SAM
06/05/2001  01:58p              16,516 TEST.TKR
06/05/2001  02:01p              15,108 CLASX
12/31/2001  04:32p                 181 WILDTHR.AAA
12/31/2001  04:32p                 182 WILDTWO.AAA
06/06/2001  08:51a      <DIR>          TRIP
10/10/1999  04:53p                  72 APR.99
-- More  --
```

Your file listing may vary. By using the pipe symbol, you asked that the output of the DIR command be used as input to the MORE command. The **- - More - -** on the bottom of the screen tells you that there are more screens of data. Press any key and the next screen of data will display.

Step 2 Press the **Enter** key until you are back at the system prompt. You may have to press several times until you are returned to the system prompt. You can also use **Ctrl** + **C** to break into the command and return to the system prompt.

```
Command Prompt

    06/16/2000  04:32p                    75 FEBRUARY.TXT
    01/01/2002  04:32a                    34 GOODBYE.TXT
    05/30/2000  04:32p                    53 HELLO.TXT
    05/27/2001  10:08p                    81 LONGFILENAME.TXT
    05/27/2001  10:43p                    95 LONGFILENAMED.TXT
    05/27/2001  10:42p                    97 LONGFILENAMING.TXT
    11/16/2000  12:00p                    59 Sandy and Patty.txt
    12/11/1999  04:03p                    72 DANCES.TXT
    12/11/1999  04:03p                    65 TEST.TXT
    06/06/2001  01:39p                 2,428 PERSONAL.FIL
    06/06/2001  01:42p                    46 STEVEN.FIL
    06/06/2001  01:47p                    39 b.bat
    06/06/2001  01:47p                    88 TEST.BAT
    06/07/2001  08:33a      <DIR>          PROG
    06/07/2001  09:14a                 4,300 CHKDSK.TXT
    06/08/2001  08:43a                   947 TXTFILES.TXT
    06/08/2001  08:43a      <DIR>          TEST
    07/31/2000  04:32p                   260 STATE.CAP
    06/08/2001  09:02a                   260 SORTED.CAP
    06/08/2001  09:03a                   260 BYCITY.CAP
                  51 File(s)          53,759 bytes
                   7 Dir(s)        1,246,208 bytes free

    A:\>_
```

Note: The size (number of bytes) listed may be different from the display due to the difference in files you created.

You returned to the system level. You may ask yourself, why do this when I get the same effect by using DIR /P? There are two reasons. The first is that you can connect several commands with pipes and filters. The second is that /P works only with the DIR command.

Step 3 Key in the following: A:\>**DIR | SORT | MORE** **Enter**

```
Command Prompt

                   7 Dir(s)        1,246,208 bytes free
                  51 File(s)          53,759 bytes
     Directory of A:\
     Volume in drive A is DATA
     Volume Serial Number is 3330-1807
    01/01/1999  05:00a                 8,064 HOMEBUD.TKR
    01/01/2002  04:32a                    34 GOODBYE.NEW
    01/01/2002  04:32a                    34 GOODBYE.TXT
    01/01/2002  04:32a                    34 JAN.OLD
    04/23/2000  04:03p                    72 APRIL.NEW
```

```
04/23/2000  04:03p                   73 JAN.BUD
04/23/2000  04:03p                   73 JANUARY.NEW
05/27/2001  10:08p                   81 LONGFILENAME.TXT
05/27/2001  10:42p                   97 LONGFILENAMING.TXT
05/27/2001  10:43p                   95 LONGFILENAMED.TXT
05/30/2000  04:32p                   45 BYE.TXT
05/30/2000  04:32p                   53 HELLO.TXT
04/30/2001  11:55a     <DIR>            WORK
06/05/2001  01:55p                  108 JOINED.SAM
06/05/2001  01:58p               16,516 TEST.TKR
06/05/2001  02:01p               15,108 CLASX
04/30/2001  11:15a     <DIR>            POLYSCI
-- More  --
```

WHAT'S HAPPENING? You now have a sorted directory listing. The reason the blank lines, volume label, files, and numbers are at the top is that, as we discussed with the ASCII sort sequence, spaces are listed before numbers.

Step 4 Continue pressing the **Enter** key until you have returned to the system prompt.

```
Command Prompt

08/12/2000  04:12p                   75 SECOND.FIL
08/12/2000  04:12p                  314 CASES.FIL
10/10/1999  04:53p                   72 APR.99
10/10/1999  04:53p                   73 JAN.99
11/16/2000  12:00p                   53 Sandy and Nicki.txt
11/16/2000  12:00p                   59 Sandy and Patty.txt
12/06/2000  02:45p                   19 APR.BUD
12/06/2000  02:45p                   19 FILE2.CZG
12/06/2000  02:45p                   19 FILE2.FP
12/06/2000  02:45p                   19 FILE2.SWT
12/06/2000  02:45p                   19 FILE3.CZG
12/06/2000  02:45p                   19 FILE3.FP
12/06/2000  02:45p                   19 FILE3.SWT
12/06/2000  02:45p                   19 FILE4.FP
12/11/1999  04:03p                   65 TEST.TXT
12/11/1999  04:03p                   72 DANCES.TXT
12/31/2001  04:32p                  181 WILDTHR.AAA
12/31/2001  04:32p                  182 WILDTWO.AAA

A:\>_
```

WHAT'S HAPPENING? You returned to the system prompt. Pipes are extremely useful with long ASCII text files. Often a program will come with a **Read.me** or **Readme.txt** file and this command can be used to read the file. A Readme file holds late-breaking information about the program. If you have a text file that is more than one screenful of data, you cannot use **TYPE /P filename.ext** because /P is not a valid TYPE parameter. You can use the MORE command with a file as input. You can enter the name of the text file to be used with the MORE command, or you can pipe it. In the next step, the command used with the file name will be used first.

Step 5 Key in the following: A:\>**MORE PERSONAL.FIL** Enter

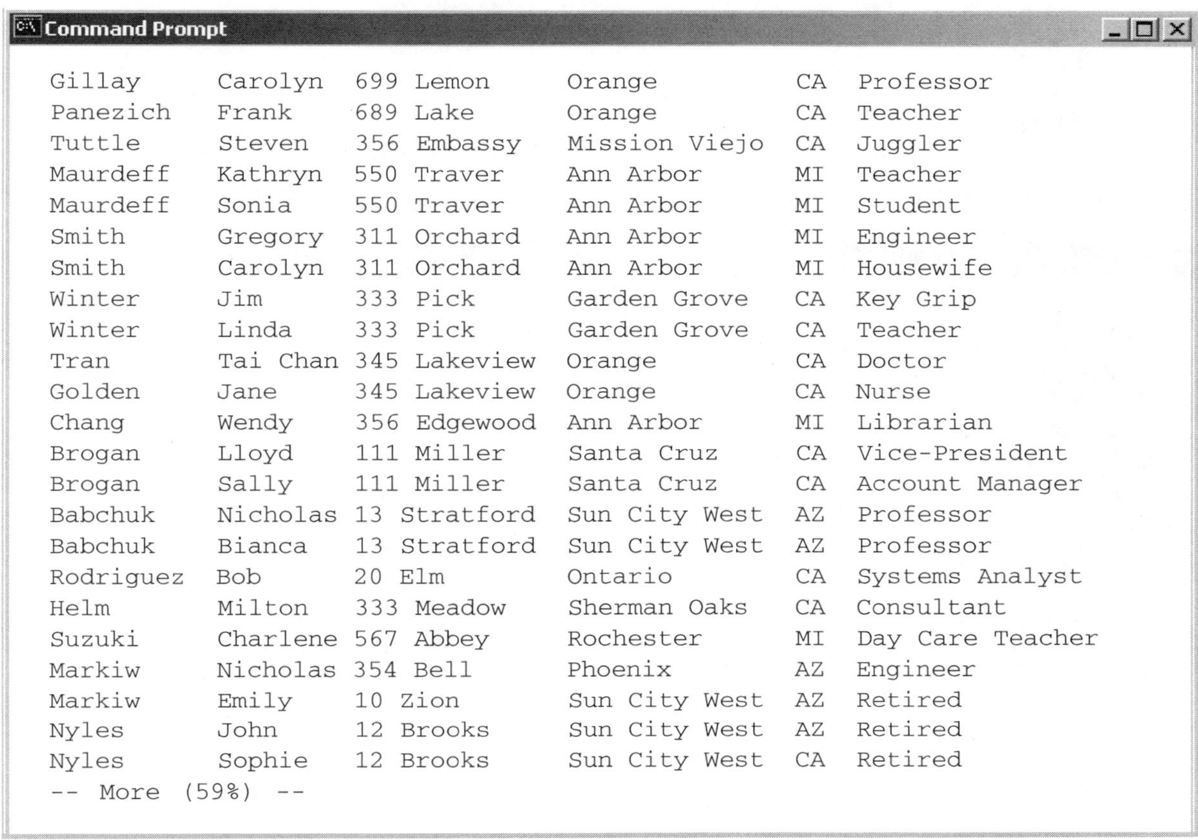

Command Prompt

```
Gillay     Carolyn  699 Lemon     Orange        CA  Professor
Panezich   Frank    689 Lake      Orange        CA  Teacher
Tuttle     Steven   356 Embassy   Mission Viejo CA  Juggler
Maurdeff   Kathryn  550 Traver    Ann Arbor     MI  Teacher
Maurdeff   Sonia    550 Traver    Ann Arbor     MI  Student
Smith      Gregory  311 Orchard   Ann Arbor     MI  Engineer
Smith      Carolyn  311 Orchard   Ann Arbor     MI  Housewife
Winter     Jim      333 Pick      Garden Grove  CA  Key Grip
Winter     Linda    333 Pick      Garden Grove  CA  Teacher
Tran       Tai Chan 345 Lakeview  Orange        CA  Doctor
Golden     Jane     345 Lakeview  Orange        CA  Nurse
Chang      Wendy    356 Edgewood  Ann Arbor     MI  Librarian
Brogan     Lloyd    111 Miller    Santa Cruz    CA  Vice-President
Brogan     Sally    111 Miller    Santa Cruz    CA  Account Manager
Babchuk    Nicholas 13 Stratford  Sun City West AZ  Professor
Babchuk    Bianca   13 Stratford  Sun City West AZ  Professor
Rodriguez  Bob      20 Elm        Ontario       CA  Systems Analyst
Helm       Milton   333 Meadow    Sherman Oaks  CA  Consultant
Suzuki     Charlene 567 Abbey     Rochester     MI  Day Care Teacher
Markiw     Nicholas 354 Bell      Phoenix       AZ  Engineer
Markiw     Emily    10 Zion       Sun City West AZ  Retired
Nyles      John     12 Brooks     Sun City West AZ  Retired
Nyles      Sophie   12 Brooks     Sun City West CA  Retired
-- More (59%) --
```

WHAT'S HAPPENING? You asked that the file from the DATA disk called **PERSONAL.FIL** be used as the file to be sent to the MORE command. The MORE command then displayed a screenful of this file.

Step 6 Continue to press the Enter key until you have returned to the system prompt or press Ctrl + **C**.

Command Prompt

```
Nyles      John     12 Brooks     Sun City West  AZ  Retired
Nyles      Sophie   12 Brooks     Sun City West  CA  Retired
Markiw     Nick     10 Zion       Sun City West  AZ  Retired
Washingon  Tyrone   345 Newport   Orange         CA  Manager
Jones      Steven   32 North      Phoenix        AZ  Buyer
Smith      David    120 Collins   Orange         CA  Chef
Babchuk    Walter   12 View       Thousand Oaks  CA  President
Babchuk    Deana    12 View       Thousand Oaks  CA  Housewife
Jones      Cleo     355 Second    Ann Arbor      MI  Clerk
Gonzales   Antonio  40 Northern   Ontario        CA  Engineer
JONES      JERRY    244 East      Mission Viejo  CA  Systems Analyst
Lo         Ophelia  1213 Wick     Phoenix        AZ  Writer
Jones      Ervin    15 Fourth     Santa Cruz     CA  Banker
Perez      Sergio   134 Seventh   Ann Arbor      MI  Editor
Yuan       Suelin   56 Twin Leaf  Orange         CA  Artist
Markiw     Nicholas 12 Fifth      Glendale       AZ  Engineer
Peat       Brian    125 Second    Vacaville      CA  Athlete
```

```
Farneth     Nichole  237 Arbor     Vacaville      CA  Dancer

A:\>_
```

WHAT'S HAPPENING? You returned to the system prompt. There is an alternative way to produce the same results. You can pipe the output of the file to the MORE command.

Step 7 Key in the following: A:\>**TYPE PERSONAL.FIL | MORE** Enter

```
Command Prompt
Gillay      Carolyn  699 Lemon     Orange         CA  Professor
Panezich    Frank    689 Lake      Orange         CA  Teacher
Tuttle      Steven   356 Embassy   Mission Viejo  CA  Juggler
Maurdeff    Kathryn  550 Traver    Ann Arbor      MI  Teacher
Maurdeff    Sonia    550 Traver    Ann Arbor      MI  Student
Smith       Gregory  311 Orchard   Ann Arbor      MI  Engineer
Smith       Carolyn  311 Orchard   Ann Arbor      MI  Housewife
Winter      Jim      333 Pick      Garden Grove   CA  Key Grip
Winter      Linda    333 Pick      Garden Grove   CA  Teacher
Tran        Tai Chan 345 Lakeview  Orange         CA  Doctor
Golden      Jane     345 Lakeview  Orange         CA  Nurse
Chang       Wendy    356 Edgewood  Ann Arbor      MI  Librarian
Brogan      Lloyd    111 Miller    Santa Cruz     CA  Vice-President
Brogan      Sally    111 Miller    Santa Cruz     CA  Account Manager
Babchuk     Nicholas 13 Stratford  Sun City West  AZ  Professor
Babchuk     Bianca   13 Stratford  Sun City West  AZ  Professor
Rodriguez   Bob      20 Elm        Ontario        CA  Systems Analyst
Helm        Milton   333 Meadow    Sherman Oaks   CA  Consultant
Suzuki      Charlene 567 Abbey     Rochester      MI  Day Care Teacher
Markiw      Nicholas 354 Bell      Phoenix        AZ  Engineer
Markiw      Emily    10 Zion       Sun City West  AZ  Retired
Nyles       John     12 Brooks     Sun City West  AZ  Retired
Nyles       Sophie   12 Brooks     Sun City West  CA  Retired
-- More  --
```

WHAT'S HAPPENING? You took the output from the TYPE command, which is normally a screen display, and piped it as input to the MORE command. The MORE command then displayed a screenful of this file. Remember that there must be a command on either side of the pipe. You could not key in **PERSONAL.FIL | MORE** because **PERSONAL.FIL** is a file and not a command.

Step 8 Continue to press the Enter key until you have returned to the system prompt.

```
Command Prompt
Nyles       Sophie   12 Brooks     Sun City West   CA  Retired
Markiw      Nick     10 Zion       Sun City West   AZ  Retired
Washingon   Tyrone   345 Newport   Orange          CA  Manager
Jones       Steven   32 North      Phoenix         AZ  Buyer
Smith       David    120 Collins   Orange          CA  Chef
Babchuk     Walter   12 View       Thousand Oaks   CA  President
Babchuk     Deana    12 View       Thousand Oaks   CA  Housewife
```

```
Jones       Cleo      355 Second     Ann Arbor       MI   Clerk
Gonzales    Antonio   40 Northern    Ontario         CA   Engineer
JONES       JERRY     244 East       Mission Viejo   CA   Systems Analyst
Lo          Ophelia   1213 Wick      Phoenix         AZ   Writer
Jones       Ervin     15 Fourth      Santa Cruz      CA   Banker
Perez       Sergio    134 Seventh    Ann Arbor       MI   Editor
Yuan        Suelin    56 Twin Leaf   Orange          CA   Artist
Markiw      Nicholas  12 Fifth       Glendale        AZ   Engineer
Peat        Brian     125 Second     Vacaville       CA   Athlete
Farneth     Nichole   237 Arbor      Vacaville       CA   Dancer

A:\>_
```

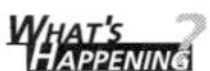

You returned to the system prompt. PERSONAL.FIL is more than one screenful of information. Lines of information in a data file are called records. Each person listed in the file, and all the information on that same line, is one record. MORE will allow you to start viewing the file at a specified line, or record number. Also, to help avoid confusion, you can clear the screen before the display begins.

Step 9 Key in the following: A:\>**MORE PERSONAL.FIL /C +20** Enter

```
Command Prompt

Markiw      Nicholas  354 Bell       Phoenix         AZ   Engineer
Markiw      Emily     10 Zion        Sun City West   AZ   Retired
Nyles       John      12 Brooks      Sun City West   AZ   Retired
Nyles       Sophie    12 Brooks      Sun City West   CA   Retired
Markiw      Nick      10 Zion        Sun City West   AZ   Retired
Washingon   Tyrone    345 Newport    Orange          CA   Manager
Jones       Steven    32 North       Phoenix         AZ   Buyer
Smith       David     120 Collins    Orange          CA   Chef
Babchuk     Walter    12 View        Thousand Oaks   CA   President
Babchuk     Deana     12 View        Thousand Oaks   CA   Housewife
Jones       Cleo      355 Second     Ann Arbor       MI   Clerk
Gonzales    Antonio   40 Northern    Ontario         CA   Engineer
JONES       JERRY     244 East       Mission Viejo   CA   Systems Analyst
Lo          Ophelia   1213 Wick      Phoenix         AZ   Writer
Jones       Ervin     15 Fourth      Santa Cruz      CA   Banker
Perez       Sergio    134 Seventh    Ann Arbor       MI   Editor
Yuan        Suelin    56 Twin Leaf   Orange          CA   Artist
Markiw      Nicholas  12 Fifth       Glendale        AZ   Engineer
Peat        Brian     125 Second     Vacaville       CA   Athlete
Farneth     Nichole   237 Arbor      Vacaville       CA   Dancer

A:\>_
```

Markiw's record is the twentieth record in **PERSONAL.FIL** (+20). The display began at that point in the file. Also, the screen was cleared (/C) before the display began. Notice, not even the command you keyed in is visible. You can use the MORE filter with more than one file.

Step 10 Key in the following: A:\>**MORE SORTED.CAP BYCITY.CAP /C** Enter

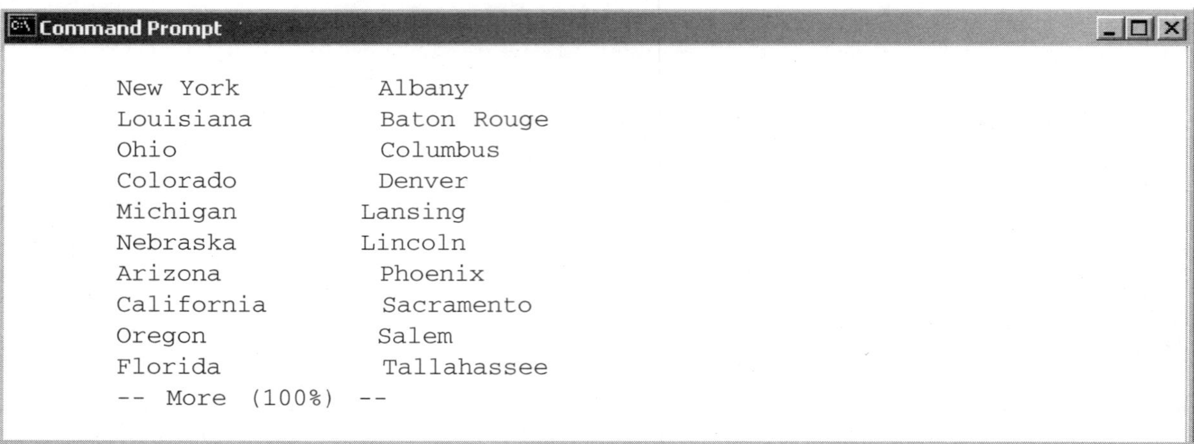

The command does not appear on the screen, as the /C parameter cleared the screen before the display began. The entire file, **SORTED.CAP** is on the screen, signified by the 100%.

Step 11 Press **Space Bar**

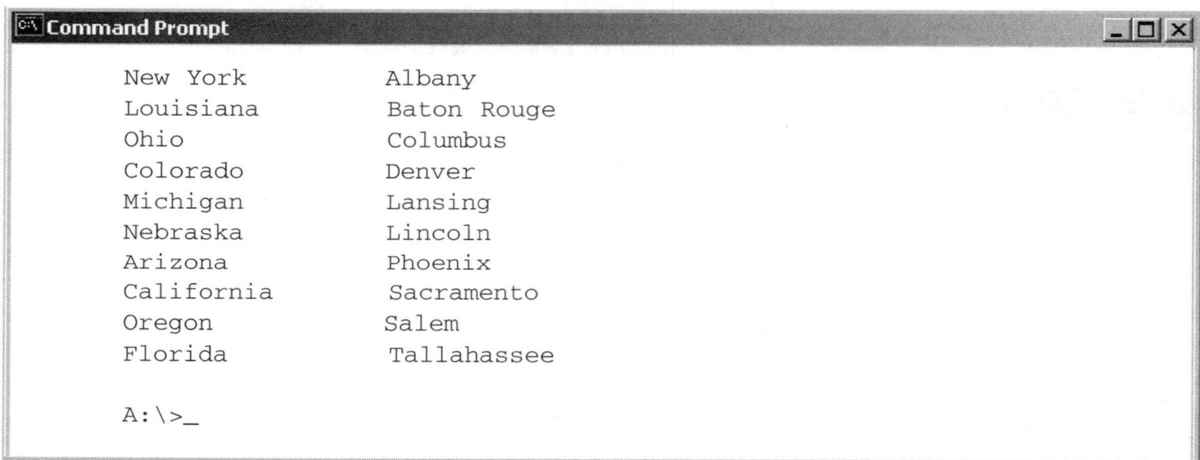

Because **SORTED.CAP** and **BYCITY.CAP** contained the same information and the /C parameter cleared the screen before each display, the information does not seem to have changed. There are times when clearing the screen can become confusing.

Step 12 Key in the following: A:\>**MORE SORTED.CAP BYCITY.CAP** **Enter**

Step 13 Press **Space Bar**

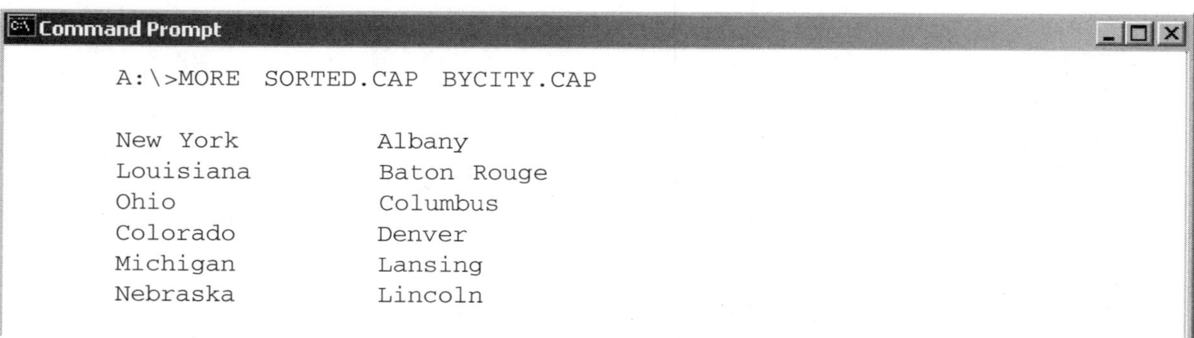

```
Arizona          Phoenix
California       Sacramento
Oregon            Salem
Florida           Tallahassee

New York          Albany
Louisiana         Baton Rouge
Ohio              Columbus
Colorado          Denver
Michigan          Lansing
Nebraska          Lincoln
Arizona           Phoenix
California        Sacramento
Oregon            Salem
Florida           Tallahassee

A:\>_
```

The first file displayed, and then the message **- - More (100%) - -** was displayed. When you pressed the space bar, the message disappeared, and the second file was displayed. In this case, not using the /C parameter made it possible to compare the two files.

Step 14 Close all open windows and return to the desktop environment, the GUI.

9.15 OTHER FEATURES OF MORE

If you look at the bottom of the syntax diagram of the MORE command,

```
If extended features are enabled, the following commands
are accepted at the -- More -- prompt:

  P n      Display next n lines
  S n      Skip next n lines
  F        Display next file
  Q        Quit
  =        Show line number
  ?        Show help line
  <space>  Display next page
  <ret>    Display next line
```

it states that if extended features are enabled, you have more choices available to you with the MORE command. ***Extensions*** in this case means that Windows 2000 Professional provides more features to CMD.EXE, which provides a richer, more powerful shell programming environment. When you open a Command Prompt window, you are running a shell. A shell is the command interpreter used to pass commands to the operating system. The Command Prompt, by default, enables the shell extensions. If your system did not, by default, enable shell extensions, you could do so by keying in CMD /X. If you wanted the shell extensions disabled, you could key in CMD /Y. The commands that use the shell extensions are DEL, COLOR, CD, MD, PROMPT, PUSHD, POPD, SET, SETLOCAL, ENDLOCAL, IF, FOR, CALL, SHIFT, GOTO, STARTS, ASSOC, and FTYPE. If you wanted full details on what you may do with each command, you would key in the command name with /? . In this case, you are going to use some of the extended features of the MORE command.

9.16 ACTIVITY: USING THE EXTENDED FEATURES OF MORE

Note: The DATA disk is in Drive A. You are on the desktop.

Step 1 Click **Start**. Click **Run**.

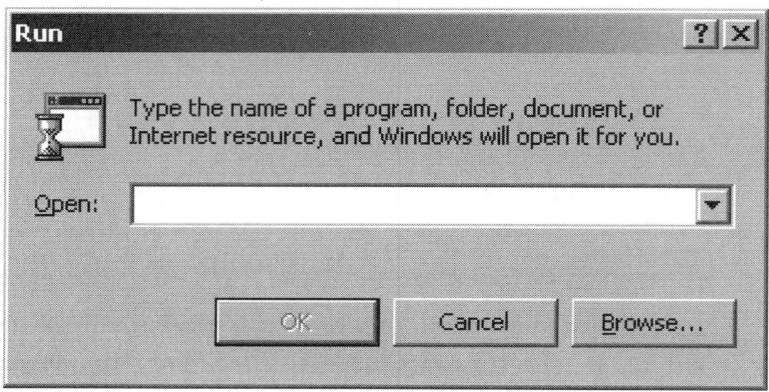

WHAT'S HAPPENING? You may run a program from the Run dialog box. You may have data already in the Open text box. Run remembers the last command that was keyed in. In this case, the command you want to execute is the shell, **CMD.EXE**.

Step 2 If there is any text in the Open text box, clear it. Then key in **CMD /X**.

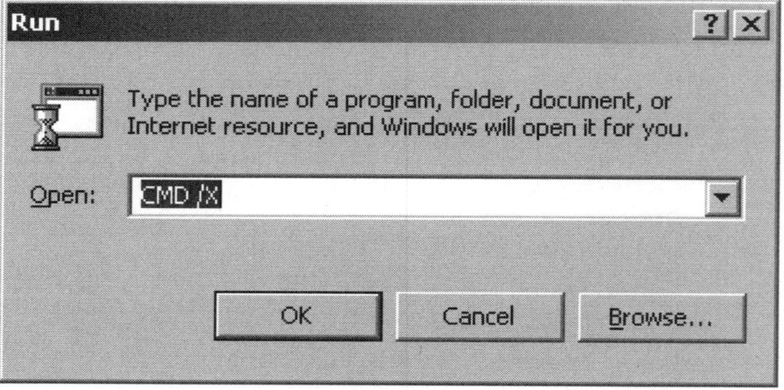

WHAT'S HAPPENING? You are now going to execute the program CMD /X. The /X ensures that you are going to be able to use the extensions to commands.

Step 3 Click **OK**.

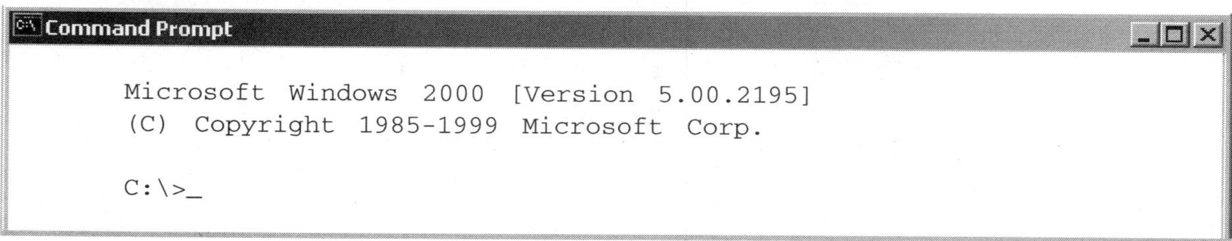

WHAT'S HAPPENING? You have opened a Command Prompt window.

Step 4 Key in the following: C:\>**A:** Enter

Step 5 Key in the following: A:\>**MORE PERSONAL.FIL** Enter

```
Command Prompt
 Gillay     Carolyn  699 Lemon     Orange        CA  Professor
 Panezich   Frank    689 Lake      Orange        CA  Teacher
 Tuttle     Steven   356 Embassy   Mission Viejo CA  Juggler
 Maurdeff   Kathryn  550 Traver    Ann Arbor     MI  Teacher
 Maurdeff   Sonia    550 Traver    Ann Arbor     MI  Student
 Smith      Gregory  311 Orchard   Ann Arbor     MI  Engineer
 Smith      Carolyn  311 Orchard   Ann Arbor     MI  Housewife
 Winter     Jim      333 Pick      Garden Grove  CA  Key Grip
 Winter     Linda    333 Pick      Garden Grove  CA  Teacher
 Tran       Tai Chan 345 Lakeview  Orange        CA  Doctor
 Golden     Jane     345 Lakeview  Orange        CA  Nurse
 Chang      Wendy    356 Edgewood  Ann Arbor     MI  Librarian
 Brogan     Lloyd    111 Miller    Santa Cruz    CA  Vice-President
 Brogan     Sally    111 Miller    Santa Cruz    CA  Account Manager
 Babchuk    Nicholas 13 Stratford  Sun City West AZ  Professor
 Babchuk    Bianca   13 Stratford  Sun City West AZ  Professor
 Rodriguez  Bob      20 Elm        Ontario       CA  Systems Analyst
 Helm       Milton   333 Meadow    Sherman Oaks  CA  Consultant
 Suzuki     Charlene 567 Abbey     Rochester     MI  Day Care Teacher
 Markiw     Nicholas 354 Bell      Phoenix       AZ  Engineer
 Markiw     Emily    10 Zion       Sun City West AZ  Retired
 Nyles      John     12 Brooks     Sun City West AZ  Retired
 Nyles      Sophie   12 Brooks     Sun City West CA  Retired
 -- More (59%) --
```

So far the MORE command is working in the usual way. With extensions enabled, if you press the Space Bar you will display the next page. If you press the Enter key, referred to as **<ret>** in the syntax diagram, you will display the next line in the file.

Step 6 Press Enter twice.

```
Command Prompt
 Panezich   Frank    689 Lake      Orange        CA  Teacher
 Tuttle     Steven   356 Embassy   Mission Viejo CA  Juggler
 Maurdeff   Kathryn  550 Traver    Ann Arbor     MI  Teacher
 Maurdeff   Sonia    550 Traver    Ann Arbor     MI  Student
 Smith      Gregory  311 Orchard   Ann Arbor     MI  Engineer
 Smith      Carolyn  311 Orchard   Ann Arbor     MI  Housewife
 Winter     Jim      333 Pick      Garden Grove  CA  Key Grip
 Winter     Linda    333 Pick      Garden Grove  CA  Teacher
 Tran       Tai Chan 345 Lakeview  Orange        CA  Doctor
 Golden     Jane     345 Lakeview  Orange        CA  Nurse
 Chang      Wendy    356 Edgewood  Ann Arbor     MI  Librarian
 Brogan     Lloyd    111 Miller    Santa Cruz    CA  Vice-President
 Brogan     Sally    111 Miller    Santa Cruz    CA  Account Manager
```

```
Babchuk    Nicholas 13 Stratford  Sun City West  AZ  Professor
Babchuk    Bianca   13 Stratford  Sun City West  AZ  Professor
Rodriguez  Bob      20 Elm        Ontario        CA  Systems Analyst
Helm       Milton   333 Meadow    Sherman Oaks   CA  Consultant
Suzuki     Charlene 567 Abbey     Rochester      MI  Day Care Teacher
Markiw     Nicholas 354 Bell      Phoenix        AZ  Engineer
Markiw     Emily    10 Zion       Sun City West  AZ  Retired
Nyles      John     12 Brooks     Sun City West  AZ  Retired
Nyles      Sophie   12 Brooks     Sun City West  CA  Retired
Markiw     Nick     10 Zion       Sun City West  AZ  Retired
Washingon  Tyrone   345 Newport   Orange         CA  Manager
-- More (64%) --
```

WHAT'S HAPPENING? By pressing **Enter** twice, you moved two lines down in the file. You may exit the MORE command by keying in **Q**.

Step 7 Press **Q**.

```
Command Prompt

Tuttle     Steven   356 Embassy   Mission Viejo  CA  Juggler
Maurdeff   Kathryn  550 Traver    Ann Arbor      MI  Teacher
Maurdeff   Sonia    550 Traver    Ann Arbor      MI  Student
Smith      Gregory  311 Orchard   Ann Arbor      MI  Engineer
Smith      Carolyn  311 Orchard   Ann Arbor      MI  Housewife
Winter     Jim      333 Pick      Garden Grove   CA  Key Grip
Winter     Linda    333 Pick      Garden Grove   CA  Teacher
Tran       Tai Chan 345 Lakeview  Orange         CA  Doctor
Golden     Jane     345 Lakeview  Orange         CA  Nurse
Chang      Wendy    356 Edgewood  Ann Arbor      MI  Librarian
Brogan     Lloyd    111 Miller    Santa Cruz     CA  Vice-President
Brogan     Sally    111 Miller    Santa Cruz     CA  Account Manager
Babchuk    Nicholas 13 Stratford  Sun City West  AZ  Professor
Babchuk    Bianca   13 Stratford  Sun City West  AZ  Professor
Rodriguez  Bob      20 Elm        Ontario        CA  Systems Analyst
Helm       Milton   333 Meadow    Sherman Oaks   CA  Consultant
Suzuki     Charlene 567 Abbey     Rochester      MI  Day Care Teacher
Markiw     Nicholas 354 Bell      Phoenix        AZ  Engineer
Markiw     Emily    10 Zion       Sun City West  AZ  Retired
Nyles      John     12 Brooks     Sun City West  AZ  Retired
Nyles      Sophie   12 Brooks     Sun City West  CA  Retired
Markiw     Nick     10 Zion       Sun City West  AZ  Retired
Washingon  Tyrone   345 Newport   Orange         CA  Manager

A:\>_
```

WHAT'S HAPPENING? By pressing **Q**, you exited the MORE command and returned to the system prompt.

Step 8 Key in the following:A:>**MORE PERSONAL.FIL** **Enter**

Step 9 Key in the following: **P**

```
Command Prompt

Nyles       Sophie    12 Brooks      Sun City West   CA   Retired
-- More (59%) -- Lines:
```

WHAT'S HAPPENING? By pressing **P** where MORE stopped, you can now request how many lines you want displayed.

Step 10 Key in the following: **5** **Enter**

```
Command Prompt

Nyles       Sophie    12 Brooks      Sun City West   CA   Retired
Markiw      Nick      10 Zion        Sun City West   AZ   Retired
Washingon   Tyrone    345 Newport    Orange          CA   Manager
Jones       Steven    32 North       Phoenix         AZ   Buyer
Smith       David     120 Collins    Orange          CA   Chef
Babchuk     Walter    12 View        Thousand Oaks   CA   President
-- More (72%) --
```

WHAT'S HAPPENING? You have displayed the next five lines.

Step 11 Press the = sign.

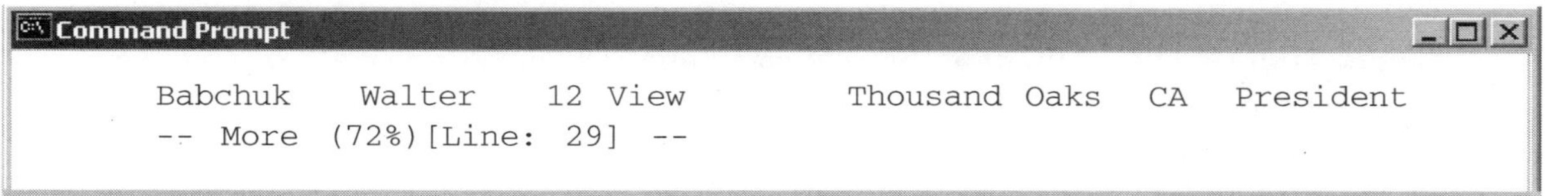

WHAT'S HAPPENING? Pressing the = sign displays which line number you are on.

Step 12 Press **S**.

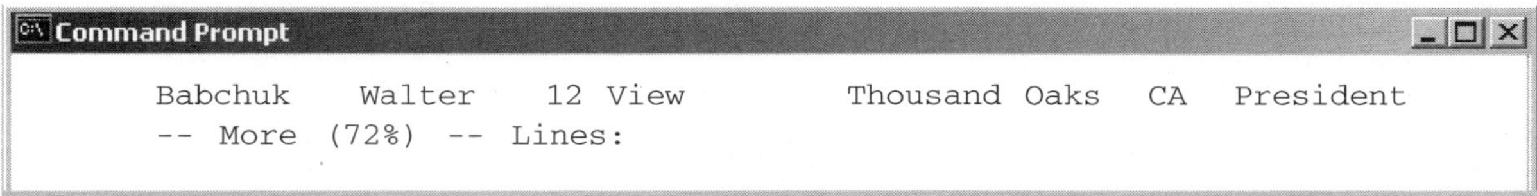

WHAT'S HAPPENING? You are asked how many lines you want to skip in your display.

Step 13 Key in the following: **3** **Enter**

```
Command Prompt

Brogan      Sally     111 Miller     Santa Cruz      CA   Account Manager
Babchuk     Nicholas  13 Stratford   Sun City West   AZ   Professor
Babchuk     Bianca    13 Stratford   Sun City West   AZ   Professor
Rodriguez   Bob       20 Elm         Ontario         CA   Systems Analyst
Helm        Milton    333 Meadow     Sherman Oaks    CA   Consultant
Suzuki      Charlene  567 Abbey      Rochester       MI   Day Care Teacher
Markiw      Nicholas  354 Bell       Phoenix         AZ   Engineer
Markiw      Emily     10 Zion        Sun City West   AZ   Retired
Nyles       John      12 Brooks      Sun City West   AZ   Retired
Nyles       Sophie    12 Brooks      Sun City West   CA   Retired
Markiw      Nick      10 Zion        Sun City West   AZ   Retired
```

```
Washingon   Tyrone    345 Newport   Orange          CA  Manager
Jones       Steven    32 North      Phoenix         AZ  Buyer
Smith       David     120 Collins   Orange          CA  Chef
Babchuk     Walter    12 View       Thousand Oaks   CA  President
JONES       JERRY     244 East      Mission Viejo   CA  Systems Analyst
Lo          Ophelia   1213 Wick     Phoenix         AZ  Writer
Jones       Ervin     15 Fourth     Santa Cruz      CA  Banker
Perez       Sergio    134 Seventh   Ann Arbor       MI  Editor
Yuan        Suelin    56 Twin Leaf  Orange          CA  Artist
Markiw      Nicholas  12 Fifth      Glendale        AZ  Engineer
Peat        Brian     125 Second    Vacaville       CA  Athlete
Farneth     Nichole   237 Arbor     Vacaville       CA  Dancer

A:\>_
```

WHAT'S HAPPENING? You skipped three lines, which in this case took you to the end of the file.

Step 14 Close all open windows.

WHAT'S HAPPENING? You have returned to the desktop.

9.17 COMBINING COMMANDS WITH PIPES AND FILTERS

You can use the pipe symbol to join commands where the standard output of one command is the standard input of the next command. The pipe symbol allows you to connect two or more programs and create a flow of data. When you use the pipe symbol, there must be a command on both sides of the actual symbol. If you use redirection with the "pipeline," a command does not have to be on either side of the > or >>. Remember, when you are redirecting output from a command, it is an "instead of" process. For instance, instead of writing the output of a command to the screen, you are redirecting the output to a file. When you combine the use of pipes and the >, the redirection becomes the end of the pipeline, the last step in the process.

9.18 ACTIVITY: COMBINING COMMANDS

Note 1: Open a Command Prompt window.
Note 2: The DATA disk is in Drive A. A:\> is displayed.

Step 1 Key in the following:
A:\>**FIND "Teacher" PERSONAL.FIL ¦ FIND "CA"** Enter

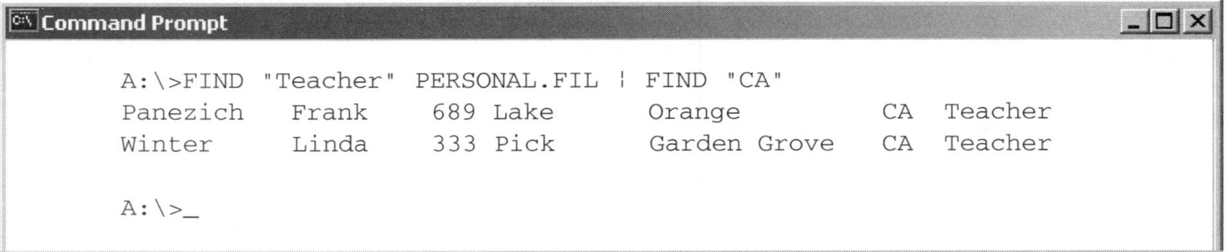
Command Prompt
A:\>FIND "Teacher" PERSONAL.FIL ¦ FIND "CA"
Panezich   Frank   689 Lake   Orange   CA Teacher
Winter   Linda   333 Pick   Garden Grove   CA Teacher
A:\>_

WHAT'S HAPPENING
You asked the FIND command to locate the lines that contained "Teacher" in the **PERSONAL.FIL**, and to take the output from that command and pipe it back through the FIND command again, locating the lines from that output

that contained "CA." The results were that only the teachers who live in California were displayed. Remember, the data in **PERSONAL.FIL** has not changed. You have merely searched that data so you could display only those lines, or records, that met your requirements. If you want to save the data you displayed, you must save it to a file.

Step 2 Key in the following:

A:\>**FIND "Teacher" PERSONAL.FIL | FIND "CA" > TEACHER.FIL** Enter

Step 3 Key in the following: A:\>**TYPE TEACHER.FIL** Enter

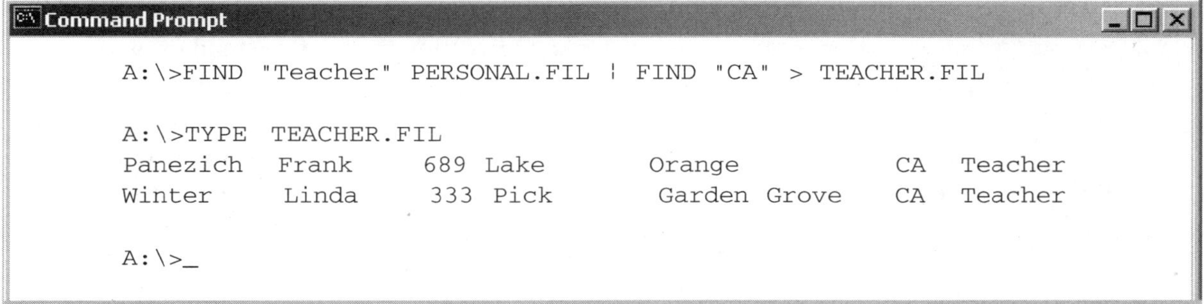

```
Command Prompt

A:\>FIND "Teacher" PERSONAL.FIL | FIND "CA" > TEACHER.FIL

A:\>TYPE TEACHER.FIL
Panezich  Frank    689 Lake       Orange          CA  Teacher
Winter    Linda    333 Pick       Garden Grove    CA  Teacher

A:\>_
```

You used FIND to locate all the teachers in California in the same way you did in Step 1. Since the FIND command sends its output to the screen, you were able to redirect it. The results of the command did not appear on the screen because you redirected the output to a file called **TEACHER.FIL**. You then used the TYPE command to display that file on the screen. You can use the same filter more than once in the same command line. You can also use filters in combination in the same command line.

Step 4 Key in the following:
A:\>**FIND "Professor" PERSONAL.FIL | FIND "AZ" | SORT** Enter

```
Command Prompt

A:\>FIND "Professor" PERSONAL.FIL | FIND "AZ" | SORT
Babchuk   Bianca    13 Stratford  Sun City West  AZ  Professor
Babchuk   Nicholas  13 Stratford  Sun City West  AZ  Professor

A:\>_
```

You asked FIND to locate all occurrences of "Professor" in the file called **PERSONAL.FIL**. You then piped (had the standard output of the FIND command sent as standard input to the next FIND command) to select only those who lived in Arizona ("AZ"). You then piped the standard output of FIND to the SORT command because you wanted all the professors who live in Arizona sorted in alphabetical order.

If you wanted a permanent copy of this list, you could have redirected the standard output (normally displayed on the screen) to a file. For instance, if you had keyed in the command as **FIND "Professor" PERSONAL.FIL | FIND "AZ" | SORT > AZ.FIL**, the output of the command would have been placed in a file called **AZ.FIL.**

Perhaps the easiest way to remember the rules of pipes, filters, and redirection is that, when you use a pipe, there must be a command on either side of the pipe. Remember, you are taking the standard output of a command and using it as standard input to the next command. Remember also that not every command has standard output. For instance, when you key in **DEL filename** at the system level, there is no output that appears or is written to the screen. The file is simply deleted. When you key in **COPY MYFILE YOURFILE**, the only item written to the screen is the message "1 file(s) copied." The standard output from the COPY command is that message. Nothing else is written to the screen.

Conversely, when you use redirection, it is an "instead of" action. Instead of the standard output being written to the screen, you are redirecting (sending) it somewhere else, such as a file or a device. You only get one output place. Since it is an "instead of" action, you cannot say instead of displaying the output of the DIR command on the screen, redirect the output to a file *and* redirect the output to the screen. Your choice is either the screen or a file, not both. The device name for the screen is CON. If you keyed in **DIR > CON > TESTFILE**, the output would not appear on the screen, but would go to the file **TESTFILE**. If you keyed in **DIR > TESTFILE > CON** the output would go to the screen. The output will go to the last place it is directed to go. The primary use of pipes and filters is manipulating the standard output and standard input of commands. You rarely use pipes and filters to sort or find data in text or data files.

Step 5 Key in the following: A:\>**DIR ¦ SORT /+39 ¦ MORE** Enter

```
Command Prompt

A:\>DIR ¦ SORT /+39 ¦ MORE

 Directory of A:\

 Volume Serial Number is 3330-1807
 Volume in drive A is DATA
10/10/1999  04:53p                  72 APR.99
12/06/2000  02:45p                  19 APR.BUD
06/16/2000  04:32p                  72 APR.TST
04/23/2000  04:03p                  72 APRIL.NEW
06/16/2000  04:32p                  72 APRIL.TXT
06/06/2001  01:47p                  39 b.bat
07/31/1999  12:53p                  44 BRIAN.FIL
06/08/2001  09:03a                 260 BYCITY.CAP
05/30/2000  04:32p                  45 BYE.TXT
07/31/1999  12:53p                  47 CAROLYN.FIL
08/12/2000  04:12p                 314 CASES.FIL
06/07/2001  09:14a               4,300 CHKDSK.TXT
06/05/2001  12:55p    <DIR>              CLASS
06/05/2001  02:01p              15,108 CLASX
12/11/1999  04:03p                  72 DANCES.TXT
07/03/2000  01:24p                 213 DRAMA.TV
06/16/2000  04:32p                  75 FEBRUARY.TXT
```

```
12/06/2000  02:45p                    19 FILE2.CZG
12/06/2000  02:45p                    19 FILE2.FP
-- More  --
```

Note: Your screen display will vary based on the work you did as well as the date and time you created the files.

You took the directory display and piped the output to the SORT command. You then sorted by the file name. You then piped the output to the MORE command so that you could see the output one screenful at a time. You can perform the same task with the parameters of the DIR command. The command line **DIR /ON /P** would provide the same results.

Step 6 Continue pressing **Enter** until you have returned to the system prompt.

Step 7 Key in the following: A:\>**DIR ¦ FIND "<DIR>" ¦ SORT /+39** **Enter**

```
Command Prompt

A:\>DIR ¦ FIND "<DIR>" ¦ SORT /+39
06/05/2001  12:55p      <DIR>          CLASS
07/03/2000  01:53p      <DIR>          MEDIA
04/30/2001  10:35a      <DIR>          POLYSCI
06/07/2001  08:33a      <DIR>          PROG
06/08/2001  08:43a      <DIR>          TEST
06/06/2001  08:51a      <DIR>          TRIP
04/30/2001  11:55p      <DIR>          WORK

A:\>_
```

You sent the output of DIR to FIND. You were looking for any file that had **<DIR>** in it. You used uppercase letters since that is how <DIR> is displayed. You had to use quotation marks to enclose <DIR>. Had you not done that, the command line would have read the < and the > as redirection symbols. By enclosing them, you ensured those symbols were read as character data. You then sent that output to the SORT command with the /+39 parameter. Now you have an alphabetical list of the subdirectories on your DATA disk. Again, you can do the same task with the parameters of the DIR command. The command line **DIR /AD /ON** would provide the same results, except you would see information about bytes and volume label.

CHAPTER SUMMARY

1. The redirection symbols are >, <, and >>.
2. The >> appends output to the end of a file.
3. Redirection, pipes, and filters have to do with standard input and standard output.
4. Any command that expects its input from the keyboard has standard input.
5. Any command that normally displays its output on the screen has standard output.
6. Standard error means that the operating system writes error messages to the screen.
7. You can redirect standard input and output to and from devices or files.
8. The pipe symbol is ¦.

9. The pipe takes standard output from one command and uses it as standard input for the next command.
10. You can pipe many programs together.
11. Filters take data, change it in some fashion, and send the output to the screen.
12. The three filters are SORT, FIND, and MORE.
13. Two of the SORT command parameters are /R for reverse order and /+n for column number.
14. FIND has four parameters: /V for everything except the specified item, /C for the number of occurrences of the item, /N for the line number where the item appears in the file, and /I for results regardless of case.
15. MORE lets you look at text files one screenful at a time. The parameter /C clears the screen before the display begins.
16. You may enable shell extensions in a command prompt window. Command extensions are on by default. Extensions give you more options with commands.
17. You must have a command on both ends of the pipe.
18. Redirection is the last action you can take. You write either to the screen or to a file, not to both. You either accept input from the keyboard or from a file.
19. You can string together pipes and filters to create your own commands.
20. Each part of a command must be able to stand alone on the command line.
21. Redirection performs an "instead of" action.

KEY TERMS

ASCII sort sequence
case sensitive
character string
extension
filter
input/output (I/O)
pipe
redirection
standard error
standard input
standard output

DISCUSSION QUESTIONS

1. Explain redirection.
2. Explain the terms standard input, standard output, and standard error.
3. Does every operating system command use standard input and standard output? If not, why not?
4. What is the difference between > and >> when redirecting output?
5. Explain how the symbol < is used.
6. Keying in **COPY DIR filename** will not give you a file containing the directory display. Why?
7. What are filters?
8. What do the three SORT parameters covered in this chapter—*/n, /O,* and */R*—represent?
9. Explain how the SORT command works. Describe any limitations of the SORT command.
10. Identify one place to which standard output can be written.
11. What is the purpose of the FIND command?
12. What are four parameters that can be used with the FIND command, and what do they represent?

13. Why must a character string be enclosed in quotation marks when using the FIND command?
14. What are pipes?
15. Are there any restrictions on the use of pipes? If so, what are they?
16. How is the MORE command used?
17. What are command line extensions?
18. Why would you want to be able to use command line extensions?

TRUE/FALSE QUESTIONS

For each question, circle the letter T if the statement is true or the letter F if the statement is false.

T F 1. All system commands use standard input and standard output.
T F 2. Standard output can be directed to a file.
T F 3. There are only two filter commands: FIND and SORT.
T F 4. You can use the FIND command to find data either with or without a specified word.
T F 5. The MORE command allows you to enter more data from the keyboard.

COMPLETION QUESTIONS

Write the correct answer in each blank space.

6. The standard input device is the ____________.
7. The standard output device is the ____________.
8. In the syntax SORT [/R] [/+*n*], the letter *n* represents a(n) ____________.
9. The filter command used to display information one screenful at a time is the ____________ command.
10. The redirection symbols are ____________ , ____________, and ____________.

MULTIPLE CHOICE QUESTIONS

For each question, write the letter for the correct answer in the blank space.

☐ 11. The command that redirects the output of the DIR command to the file **DIRTXT.TXT** is
 a. DIR ¦ DIRTXT.TXT
 b. DIR < DIRTXT.TXT
 c. DIR >DIRTXT.TXT
 d. COPY DIR DIRTXT.TXT

☐ 12. The parameter used with the command SORT to sort a list by the fifth column of data in a file (where the fifth column begins at character number 25) would be:
 a. /+5
 b. /+25
 c. /+5-25
 d. /+R=25

13. To display **MYFILE.FIL** one screenful at a time, you would use:
    a. MORE MYFILE.FIL
    b. TYPE MYFILE.FIL ¦ MORE
    c. COPY MYFILE.FIL > MORE
    d. either a or b
14. The command to display the files **FIRST.FIL** and **SECOND.FIL** on the screen, each one screenful at a time, is:
    a. MORE FIRST.FIL SECOND.FIL
    b. MORE > FIRST.FIL > SECOND.FIL
    c. FIRST.FIL >> SECOND.FIL >> MORE
    d. none of the above
15. When using the SORT command, if you key in 1234, 96, 4, and 789, the order returned would be:

a.	4	96	789	1234
b.	1234	789	96	4
c.	1234	4	789	96
d.	96	789	4	1234

WRITING COMMANDS

Note: If you find it necessary to perform some of the steps in order to write your answers, do the work on a new disk. If so, copy the files **\WINDOSBK\STATES.USA**, **\WINDOSBK\PERSONAL.FIL**, **\WINDOSBK\STEVEN.FIL**, and **\WINDOSBK\CASES.FIL** to the root of the new disk, named **APPS2**.

Write the step(s) or command(s) to perform the required action as if you were at the computer. The prompt will indicate the default drive and directory.

16. Make a directory on the A drive named **WORK**. Locate every occurrence of "Teacher" in the file **PERSONAL.FIL** located in the root directory of the disk in the A drive, and send the output to a file called **TEACHER.FIL**, which is in the **WORK** directory of the disk in the A drive.

    `C:\>`

17. Display the contents of **PERSONAL.FIL**, located on the root of the disk in the A drive, one screenful at a time.

    `C:\TEMP>`

18. Display the contents of **PERSONAL.FIL**, located on the root of the disk in the A drive, one screenful at a time beginning with the 25th record, on a clear screen.

    `A:\>`

19. Append the contents of **STEVEN.FIL** to the file called **CASES.FIL**. Both files are on the root of the disk in Drive A.

    `C:\>`

20. Find out how many occurrences of "Teacher" appear in the file **PERSONAL.FIL**, which is located on the root of the disk in Drive A.

    `C:\>`

APPLICATION ASSIGNMENTS

Note 1: Place the APPLICATION disk in Drive A. Be sure to work on the APPLICATION disk, not the DATA disk.

Note 2: The homework problems assume that Drive C is the hard disk and that the APPLICATION disk is in Drive A. If you are using another drive, such as floppy Drive B or hard Drive D, be sure to substitute that drive letter when reading the questions and answers.

Note 3: All subdirectories that are created will be under the root directory unless otherwise specified.

Note 4: The homework problems will use **C:\WINNT\SYSTEM32** as the directory where the system utility files are located.

Note 5: It is assumed that the path includes **C:\WINNT\SYSTEM32**.

Note 6: Do not save the output from the commands to a file unless specified.

PROBLEM SET I

PROBLEM A

A-a Place the APPLICATION disk in Drive A.

A-b Copy all the files from the **WINDOSBK\SPORTS** directory to the APPLICATION disk, maintaining the same directory structure on the APPLICATION disk. (*Hint*: Remember XCOPY.)

A-c With the root directory of the A drive as the default directory and using the relative path, sort the file called **BASKETBL.TMS** in the **SPORTS** subdirectory.

☐ 1. Which command(s) could you have used?
   a. SORT SPORTS\BASKETBL.TMS
   b. TYPE BAKSETBL.TMS ¦ SORT
   c. both a and b
   d. neither a nor b

☐ 2. What team is listed first?
   a. Atlanta Hawks
   b. Boston Celtics
   c. Charlotte Hornets
   d. Los Angeles Lakers

A-d Key in the following: A:\>**COPY \SPORTS*.TMS \SPORTS\ALL.SPT** Enter

A-e With the root directory of the APPLICATION disk as the default and using the relative path, display the contents of the **SPORTS\ALL.SPT** file one screenful at a time.

3. Which command did you use?
   a. TYPE SPORTS\ALL.SPT < MORE
   b. TYPE SPORTS\ALL.SPT /P
   c. MORE SPORTS\ALL.SPT
   d. MORE < TYPE SPORTS\ALL.SPT

A-f Press **Q** to exit.

A-g Sort the **ALL.SPT** file in reverse order and display the output one screenful at a time.

4. What team appeared first on the first screen display?
   a. Utah Jazz
   b. Washington Bullets
   c. USC Trojans
   d. Washington Redskins

A-h Press **Q** to exit.

A-i In the **ALL.SPT** file, find all the teams that have "Los" in their names. Do not ignore case.

5. What results are displayed?
   a. Los Angeles Lakers
   b. Los Angeles Dodgers
   c. neither a nor b appears
   d. both a and b appear

PROBLEM B

B-a Be sure you have the **ALL.SPT** file from Problem A above. In the **ALL.SPT** file, find all the teams that have "go" in their names. Do not ignore case.

6. What team appears that *is not* from Chicago?
   a. Michigan Gophers
   b. San Diego Padres
   c. San Diego Chargers
   d. all teams are from Chicago

B-b Copy **PERSONAL.FIL** from **C:\WINDOSBK** to **A:\TRAVEL**. Sort the **TRAVEL\PERSONAL.FIL** file in alphabetical order.

7. What name appears last?
   a. Winter
   b. Wyse
   c. Yuan
   d. Zola

B-c From **TRAVEL\PERSONAL.FIL**, create a file sorted by city (city starts in column 34) called **CALIF.FIL** that will be saved to the **TRAVEL** subdirectory. This file will contain only people who live in California. Begin your command with the FIND command.

☐ 8. What street name is listed *last* in **CALIF.FIL**?
   a. Brooks
   b. Lake
   c. Pick
   d. View

B-d Find anyone who is an engineer in **PERSONAL.FIL** but exclude anyone who lives in California. (*Hint:* Remember case.)

☐ 9. What state(s) is/are displayed?
   a. AZ
   b. CO
   c. MI
   d. both a and c

B-e Copy the **STATES.USA** file from the **WINDOSBK** directory to the subdirectory called **TRAVEL** on the APPLICATION disk keeping the same file name.

B-f In the **STATES.USA** file, find all the states that are located in the South and sort the output in reverse alphabetical order.

☐ 10. What state is displayed first?
   a. South Carolina
   b. North Carolina
   c. Louisiana
   d. Florida

PROBLEM SET II

Note 1: Before proceeding with these assignments, check with your lab instructor to see if there are any special procedures you should follow.

Note 2: The APPLICATION disk is in Drive A. A:\> is displayed as the default drive and the default directory. *All work will occur on the APPLICATION disk.*

Note 3: Make sure that **NAME.BAT**, **MARK.FIL**, **GETYN.COM**, **GO.BAT**, and **NAME.FIL** are all present in the root directory of the APPLICATION disk before proceeding with these problems.

Note 4: All files with the **.HW** extension *must* be created in the root directory of the APPLICATION disk.

Step 1 Key in the following: A:\>**NAME** Enter

Step 2 Here is an example to key in, but your instructor will have other information that applies to your class. Key in the following:

Bette A. Peat Enter (*Your* name goes here.)

CIS 55 Enter (*Your* class goes here.)

T-Th 8-9:30 Enter (*Your* day and time go here.)

Chapter 9 Applications Enter

Step 3 Press F6 Enter

Step 4 If the information is correct, press **Y** and you are back to A:\>.

WHAT'S HAPPENING? You have returned to the system level. You now have a file called **NAME.FIL** with your name and other pertinent information. (*Hint*: Remember redirection.)

TO CREATE 1.HW

- While the root directory of the APPLICATION disk is the default, locate all the people who live in Orange in the **TRAVEL\PERSONAL.FIL** file and sort them in descending order. (*Hint:* Z to A.)
- Save the output to a file called **1.HW**.

TO CREATE 2.HW

- Sort the files in the **TRAVEL** directory of the APPLICATION disk. Sort in file name order. Use the SORT command. File name begins in column 40. Save the output to a file called **2.HW**.
- Sort the files in the **SPORTS** directory of the APPLICATION disk. Sort in file name order. Use the SORT command. File name begins in column 40. Append the output to the file called **2.HW**.

TO CREATE 3.HW

- In the **SPORTS\ALL.SPT** file, find all the teams that have "in" within their names, and direct the output to a file called **3.HW**. (*Hint:* Remember case.)

TO CREATE 4.HW

- In the **TRAVEL\PERSONAL.FIL** file, find all occurrences, regardless of case, of the name Jones, and direct the output to a file called **4.HW**.

TO CREATE 5.HW

- In the **SPORTS\ALL.SPT** file, locate all the teams that *do not* have an "e" in their names, regardless of case, and direct the output to a file called **5.HW**.

TO PRINT YOUR HOMEWORK

Step 1 Be sure the printer is on and ready to accept print jobs from your computer.

Step 2 Key in the following (be very careful to make no typing errors):
GO NAME.FIL 1.HW 2.HW 3.HW 4.HW 5.HW Enter

If the files you requested, **1.HW**, **2.HW**, etc. do not exist in the default directory, you will see the following message on the screen:

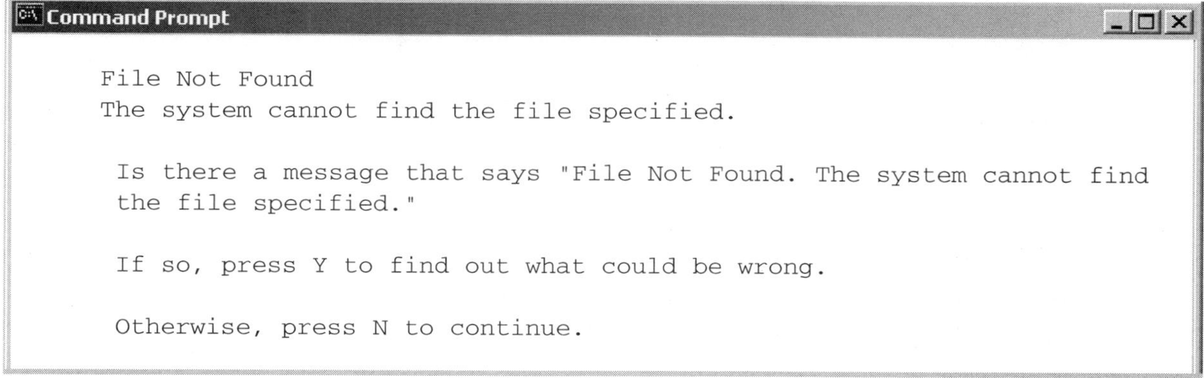
Command Prompt
File Not Found
The system cannot find the file specified.
Is there a message that says "File Not Found. The system cannot find the file specified."
If so, press Y to find out what could be wrong.
Otherwise, press N to continue.

WHAT'S HAPPENING? The operating system is telling you that the file cannot be found. If you see this screen, press **Y** to see what could be wrong, and repeat the print procedure after you have corrected the problem.

If the default directory contains the specified files, the following message will appear on the screen:

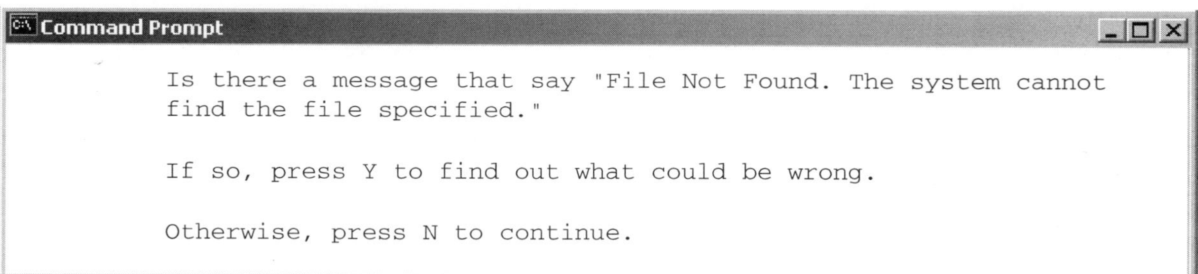
Command Prompt
Is there a message that say "File Not Found. The system cannot find the file specified."
If so, press Y to find out what could be wrong.
Otherwise, press N to continue.

You will need to press **N** once for each file you are printing.

Step 3 Follow the messages on the screen until the Notepad program opens with a screen similar to the following:

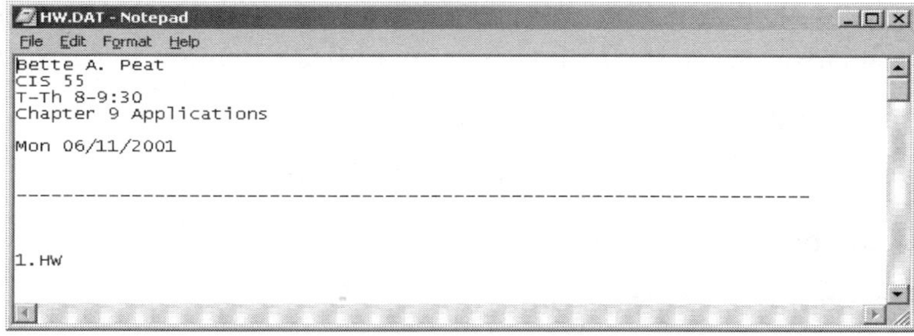
HW.DAT - Notepad
File Edit Format Help
Bette A. Peat
CIS 55
T-Th 8-9:30
Chapter 9 Applications
Mon 06/11/2001
1.HW

WHAT'S HAPPENING? All the requested files have been found and placed in a Notepad document. Your homework is now ready to print.

Step 4 On the Notepad menu bar, click **File**. Click **Print**.

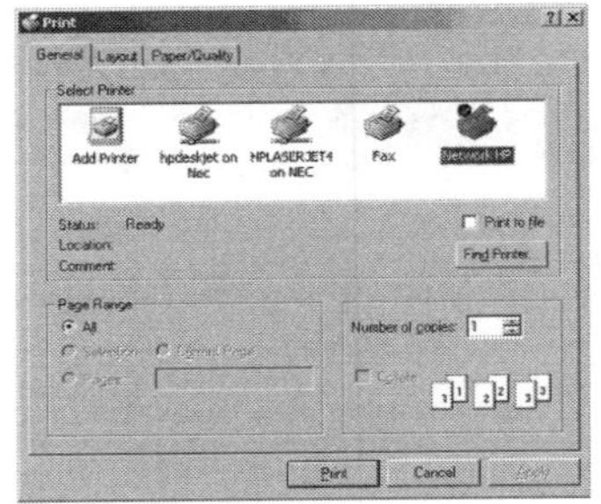

WHAT'S HAPPENING? The print dialog box opens. If you have more than one printer, your printer choices will be displayed. The default printer is the highlighted printer.

Step 5 Click the **Print** button.

Step 6 In the Notepad window, click **File**. Click **Exit**.

WHAT'S HAPPENING? The following will appear on the Command Prompt screen:

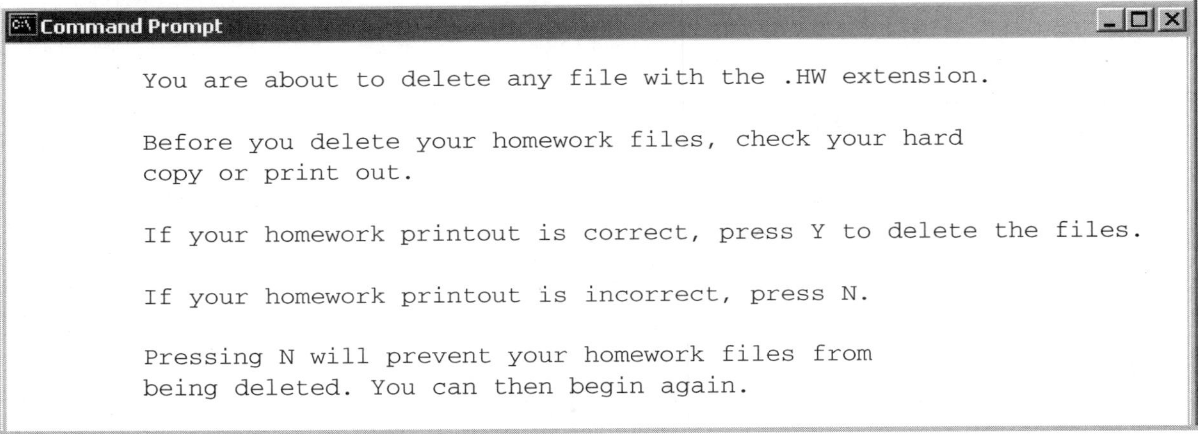
Command Prompt
You are about to delete any file with the .HW extension.
Before you delete your homework files, check your hard copy or print out.
If your homework printout is correct, press Y to delete the files.
If your homework printout is incorrect, press N.
Pressing N will prevent your homework files from being deleted. You can then begin again.

WHAT'S HAPPENING? At this point, look at your printout. If it is correct, you can press **Y** to delete the homework files for this chapter. If your printout is incorrect, you can press **N**. That will preserve your homework and you will need to redo only the problem that was incorrect, not all the homework assignments.

Step 7 Press **Y** **Enter**

WHAT'S HAPPENING? You have returned to the default prompt.

Step 8 Close the Command Prompt session.

Step 9 Execute the shut-down procedure.

PROBLEM SET III—BRIEF ESSAY

1. List and explain the syntax and at least two parameters for the three filter commands (FIND, SORT, and MORE). Also explain how redirection and piping can work with each of them.
2. Discuss two real-world scenarios where you would use pipes, a filters, and redirection. Include one example of a pipe, a filter, and a use of redirection.

CHAPTER

10

INTRODUCTION TO BATCH FILES

LEARNING OBJECTIVES

After completing this chapter you will be able to:

1. Compare and contrast batch and interactive processing.
2. Explain how batch files work.
3. Explain the purpose and function of the REM, ECHO, and PAUSE commands.
4. Explain how to stop or interrupt the batch file process.
5. Explain the function and use of replaceable parameters in batch files.
6. Explain the function of pipes, filters, and redirection in batch files.

STUDENT OUTCOMES

1. Use Edit to write batch files.
2. Use COPY CON to write batch files.
3. Write and execute a simple batch file.
4. Write a batch file to load an application program.
5. Use the REM, PAUSE, and ECHO commands in batch files.
6. Terminate a batch file while it is executing.
7. Write batch files using replaceable parameters.
8. Write a batch file using pipes, filters, and redirection.

CHAPTER OVERVIEW

You have used many command line commands throughout this textbook. Many of these commands are repeated in the same sequence. If more than one command is needed to execute a program, you have to key in each command at the system prompt. This repetitive, time-consuming process increases the possibility of human error.

A batch file is a text file that contains a series of commands stored in the order the user wants them carried out. It executes a series of commands with a minimum number of keystrokes. Batch files allow you to automate a process and, at the same time, create more powerful commands, which increases productivity.

In this chapter, you will learn to create batch files to automate a sequence of commands, to write and use batch files for complex tasks, to use batch file subcommands, to halt the execution of a batch file, and to write batch files using replaceable parameters. You will also learn how batch files can be used from the desktop.

10.1 CONCEPTS OF BATCH AND INTERACTIVE PROCESSING

Operating system commands used at the command line are programs that are executed or run when you key in the command name. If you wish to run more than one command, you need to key in each command at the system prompt. You can, however, customize and automate the sequence of commands by writing a command sequence, called a ***batch file*** or a command file, to be executed with a minimum number of keystrokes. Any command you can enter at the system prompt can be included in a batch file. You can even execute an application program from a batch file. When you string together a sequence of steps in an application program, it is called a "macro," which is conceptually similar to a batch file.

A batch file contains one or more commands. To create this file of commands, you write a text file using Edit, COPY CON, or a text editor such as Notepad. You can also use a word processor providing it has a "Save as text file" option. The file that you write and name will run any command that the operating system can execute. This file *must* have the file extension .BAT if you are using a version of Windows earlier than Windows 2000 Professional. If you are using Windows 2000 Professional, you may also use the extension .CMD. The file must be an ASCII file. Once you have written this command file, you execute or run it by simply keying in the name of the batch file, just as you key in the name of a command. The operating system reads and executes each line of the batch file, as if you were sitting at the terminal and separately keying in each command line. Once you start running a batch file, your attention or input is not needed until the batch file has finished executing.

Batch files are used for several reasons. They allow you to minimize keystrokes, and they minimize the possibility of errors, as you don't have to key in the commands over and over. Batch files are used to put together a complex sequence of commands and store them under an easily remembered name. They automate any frequent and/or consistent procedures that you always want to do in the same manner, such as backing up critical data to an alternate location. In addition, you can execute application programs by calling them with a batch file.

"Batch" is an old data-processing term. In the early days of computing, work was done by submitting a job (or all the instructions needed to run the job successfully) to a data-processing department, which would run these jobs in *batches*. There was no chance for anyone to interact with the program. The job was run, and the output was delivered. Thus, when you run a batch job, you are running a computer routine without interruption.

Batch jobs are still run today. An example of a batch job would be running a payroll—issuing paychecks. The computer program that calculates and prints paychecks is run without interruption. The output or results are the paychecks. This job can be run at any time. If a company decides that payday will be Friday, the data-processing department can run the payroll Thursday night. If the company decides payday will be Monday, the data-processing department can run the payroll Sunday night. This is ***batch processing***.

Batch processing is in contrast to an interactive mode of data processing. Sometimes called online or real time mode, interactive mode means you are interacting directly with the computer. An automated teller machine (ATM) that a bank uses so that you can withdraw or deposit money without human intervention is an example of ***interactive processing***. The bank needs instant updating of its records. It cannot wait until next week to run a batch job to find out how much money you have deposited or withdrawn. If you withdraw $100, the bank first wants to be sure that you have $100 in your account, and then it wants the $100 subtracted immediately from your balance. You are dealing with the computer in an interactive, real time mode—the data is processed without delay.

In the PC world, you can work in interactive mode, but this usually requires a connection to another computer, often over phone lines. The Internet allows you to communicate directly with other computers and perform such functions as reviewing airline flight schedules. Although interactive mode can be exciting, most of the time you are working one-on-one with your computer and are not in interactive mode. Hence, the batch mode is the area of emphasis.

10.2 HOW BATCH FILES WORK

You will be creating and executing batch files in this chapter. By now you should know that data and programs are stored as files, but how does the operating system know the difference between a data file and a program file? As mentioned in previous chapters, it knows the difference based on the file extension. When you key in something at the prompt, the operating system first checks in RAM to compare what you keyed in to the internal table of commands. If it finds a match, the program is executed. If what you keyed in does not match an internal command, the operating system looks on the default drive and directory for the extension .COM, meaning command file, first. Then the operating system looks for the file extension .EXE, meaning executable file (this extension is used for system utility programs and most application software).

If what you keyed in does not match either .COM or .EXE, the operating system looks on the default drive and directory for the file extension .BAT, meaning batch file. If it finds a match, it loads and executes the batch file, one line at a time. It then looks for .CMD, meaning command file. If it finds a match, it loads and executes the command file, one line at a time. If what you keyed in does not match any of the above criteria, it continues to search in your default directory for files with the following extensions: .VBS, .VBE, JS, JSE, WSF and WSH. Table 10.1 lists the search order for extensions.

Extension	Meaning
.COM	Command file
.EXE	Executable file
.BAT	Batch file
.CMD	Command script file
.VB	VBScript file (Visual Basic)
.VBE	VBScript Encoded Script file (Visual Basic)
.JS	JScript file (JavaScript)
.JSE	JScript Encoded Script file (JavaScript)
.WSF	Windows Script file
.WSH	Windows Script Host Settings file

TABLE 10.1 SEARCH ORDER FOR EXTENSIONS

If the command interpreter does not find any of these in your default drive and directory, it then searches your search path as set in the PATH statement, in the file extension order listed above. If your file name does not meet any of these criteria, then you see the error message, "*filename* is not recognized as an internal or external command, operable program or batch file."

What if you had files on a disk that had the same file name but three different file extensions, such as CHKDSK.COM, CHKDSK.EXE, and CHKDSK.BAT? How would the operating system know which program to load and execute? Priority rules are followed. The operating system looks for the program with the .COM file extension first and, if found, would never get to the other files. However, if you were more specific and keyed in both the file name *and* the file extension, such as CHKDSK.BAT, the operating system would then execute the file name you specified.

Remember that, since the batch file is a program, either the .BAT file must be on the default drive and directory or the path must be set to the location of the batch file so you may invoke it. Most importantly, each line in a batch file must contain only one command.

10.3 USING EDIT TO WRITE BATCH FILES

To write batch files, you need a mechanism to create an ASCII text file, since that is what a batch file is. You should remember that ASCII is a code used by the operating system to interpret the letters, numbers, and punctuation marks that you key in. In simple terms, if a file is readable with the TYPE command, it is an ASCII text file. You can use a word-processing program to write a batch file if it has a nondocument or text mode. However, most word-processing programs are quite large and take time to load into memory. Most batch files are not very long, nor do they need the features of a word processor. Using a word processor to write a batch file is like using a sledgehammer to kill a fly.

Having a small, simple text editor is so important that the operating system includes one as part of the system utility programs. This is the Command Prompt editor, called Edit. Edit is simple to use and universal. You will write some batch files using Edit. Remember, Edit is only a tool to create the file; it does not run or execute it. You execute the file when you key in the file name at the system prompt in the Command Prompt window. Each line in a batch file must contain only one command. A batch file can have any legal file name but the file extension must always be .BAT or .CMD.

If you are in the Windows interface, the text editor is Notepad. Like Edit, Notepad creates text-only files and may be used to write batch files. However, if you are having problems with Windows, you will not have Notepad available to you because you need a graphical user interface to use Notepad. Edit, on the other hand, can work at the command line. In fact, you will later see that when you create your startup disk, Edit is on the disk, but not Notepad. Thus, in the following activities, you will be using Edit.

10.4 ACTIVITY: WRITING AND EXECUTING A BATCH FILE

Note 1: The DATA disk is in Drive A. A:\> is displayed.

Note 2: Although you may use a mouse with the MS-DOS editor, the instructions will show the keystroke steps, not the mouse steps.

Note 3: In some systems, the mouse will not work in Edit unless you change the properties of Edit to open Edit in full-screen mode or clear the Quick Edit Mode check box in the Command Prompt property sheet (Options tab).

Note 4: The amount of space shown as remaining on the disk will vary, depending on the size and placement of the batch files on your disk.

Step 1 Key in the following: A:\>**EDIT EXAMPLE.BAT** Enter

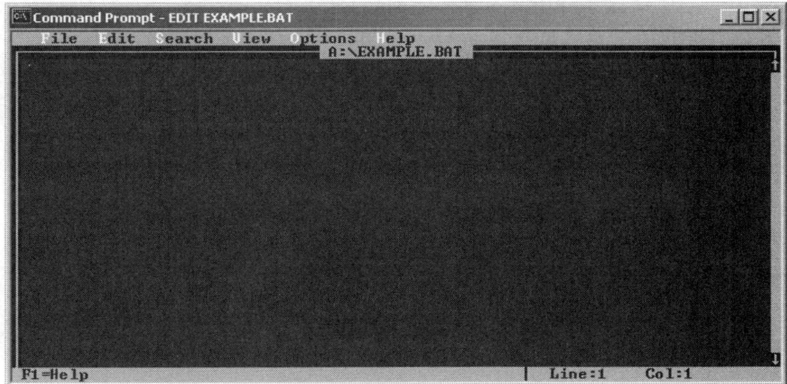

WHAT'S HAPPENING? You are now using the command prompt editor. You are going to create a batch file named **EXAMPLE**. The file extension must be **.BAT** or **.CMD**.

Step 2 Key in the following: **DIR *.99** Enter

Step 3 Key in the following: **DIR C:*.99** Enter

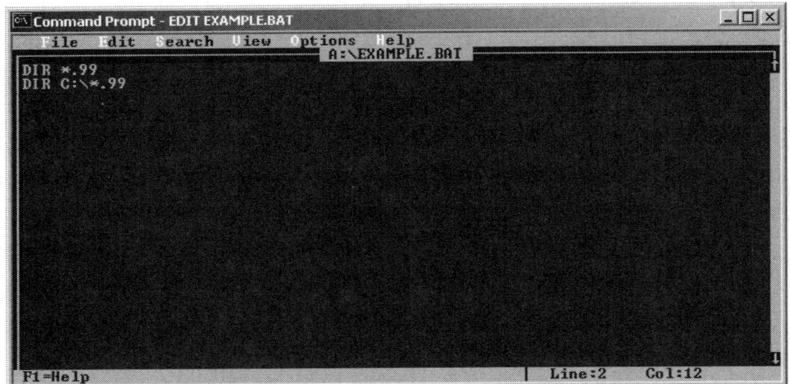

WHAT'S HAPPENING? Look at each line. Each one is a legitimate operating system command that could be keyed in at the prompt. Each command is on a separate line. The first line asks for a listing of all the files on the disk in the default drive that have the file extension **.99**. The second line asks for all the files in the root directory of C that have the file extension **.99**. At this point, you have written the batch file. Next, you need to exit Edit and save the file to disk.

Step 4 Press Alt + **F**.

Step 5 Press **X**.

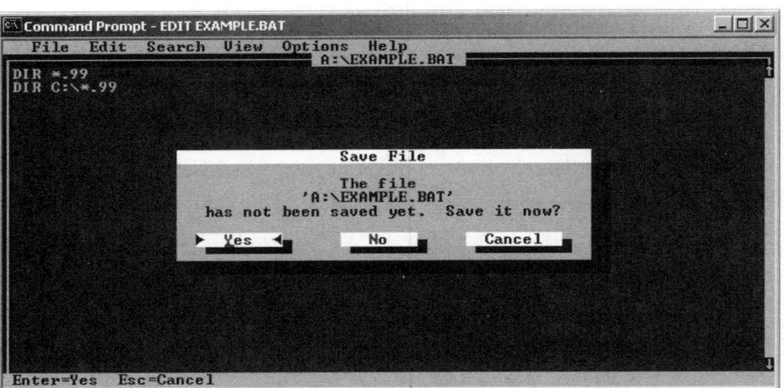

WHAT'S HAPPENING? Since you have not saved the file, Edit reminds you with a dialog box that, if you want this file on the disk, you must save it.

Step 6 Press **Y**.

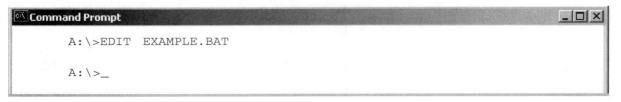

WHAT'S HAPPENING? You have saved your file, exited Edit, and returned to the system prompt.

Step 7 Key in the following: A:\>**DIR EXAMPLE.BAT** Enter

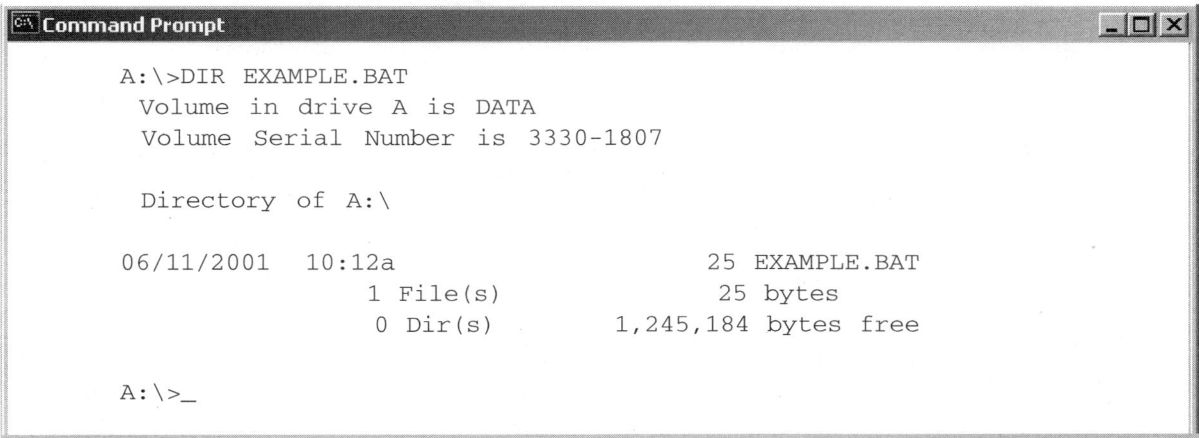

```
Command Prompt

A:\>DIR EXAMPLE.BAT
 Volume in drive A is DATA
 Volume Serial Number is 3330-1807

 Directory of A:\

06/11/2001  10:12a                  25 EXAMPLE.BAT
               1 File(s)            25 bytes
               0 Dir(s)      1,245,184 bytes free

A:\>_
```

WHAT'S HAPPENING? The **DIR EXAMPLE.BAT** command shows that there is a file on the DATA disk called **EXAMPLE.BAT**. It looks like any other text file.

How do you make the operating system treat it like a program so that you can execute it? You simply key in the name of the file at the prompt. You do not need to key in the extension, just the name. The operating system first looks for a file in its internal table called **EXAMPLE**. It does not find it. It then looks for a file called **EXAMPLE.COM** on the default disk, the DATA disk. No file exists called **EXAMPLE.COM**. Next, it looks for a file on the default disk called **EXAMPLE.EXE**. No file exists called **EXAMPLE.EXE**. It then looks for a file called **EXAMPLE.BAT** on the default disk. It does find a file by this name. It loads it into memory and executes each line, one at a time. Thus, to execute the batch file called **EXAMPLE**, key in the name of the file at the prompt. Watch what happens on the screen after you key in the file name.

Step 8 Key in the following: A:\>**EXAMPLE** Enter

```
Command Prompt

A:\>EXAMPLE

A:\>DIR *.99
 Volume in drive A is DATA
 Volume Serial Number is 3330-1807

 Directory of A:\

10/10/1999  04:53p                  72 APR.99
10/10/1999  04:53p                  73 JAN.99
               2 File(s)           145 bytes
               0 Dir(s)      1,245,184 bytes free

A:\>DIR C:\*.99
 Volume in drive C is 2000 PRO
 Volume Serial Number is C4A7-8571
```

```
 Directory of C:\

File Not Found
A:\>_
```

(*Note:* Part of the display may have scrolled off of your screen.) The operating system read and executed each line of the batch file you wrote, one line at a time. The screen displayed each command line and the results of the command line as it executed. Each line executed as if you had sat in front of the keyboard and keyed in each command individually. You did key in the commands when you wrote the batch file, but you had to key them in only once. The first line was **DIR *.99**. When the operating system read that line, it executed it and showed on the screen both files on the DATA disk with the file extension **.99**. It read the next line of the batch file and looked in the root directory of Drive C for any file that had the file extension **.99**. Since there were no files on that drive with the extension **.99**, it gave the message "File Not Found." Now that you have written the file **EXAMPLE.BAT**, you can execute this batch file's commands over and over again by keying in **EXAMPLE** at the prompt.

10.5 WRITING AND EXECUTING A BATCH FILE TO SAVE KEYSTROKES

The previous example showed you how to write and execute a batch file, but that file is not especially useful. The next batch file to be written will allow you to key in only one keystroke instead of seven. As you know, the command DIR /AD will quickly show you any subdirectories on the DATA disk. The /A switch means attribute, and the attribute you want displayed is D for directories. This command is composed of seven keystrokes, and you must have the proper parameters. With a batch file, you can do the same task by pressing only one key.

The DIR command has other parameters that are very useful. One of these is O for order. There are many kinds of order you can achieve. One kind that is useful is the arrangement of files by size. The command line would be DIR /OS. The O is for order, and the S is to arrange by size from the smallest to the largest file. If you wanted to reverse the order so that the files would be displayed from the largest to smallest, the command would be DIR /O-S. The O is still for order, but the - is for reverse order, placing smallest files at the end of the listing. The S is for file size. This command would take eight keystrokes. You can reduce it to one.

These batch files you are going to write are very small—one line. It seems like a lot of trouble to load Edit just to accomplish this task. If you would rather not load Edit, you can use the COPY command to write a simple ASCII file. The syntax is:

```
COPY CON filename
```

What you are doing here is copying what you key in (CON) to a file name. CON is the operating system's name for the keyboard/console devices of your computer. You are still following the syntax of the COPY command; it is just that now you are copying from a device—the console (CON)—to a file. Remember that in an early chapter, you copied to a device, the printer (COPY filename PRN). Just as PRN, LPT1, and LPT2 are reserved device names, so is CON.

When you are done keying in text, you must tell the COPY command you are finished. You do this by pressing the F6 key and then the Enter key. This writes the data you keyed in to the file name you specified. This is what you have been doing in your application assignments when you have entered data in NAME.FIL. The only problem with COPY CON, as it is informally referred to, is that you cannot correct errors once you press Enter at the end of a command line. Nor can you use COPY CON to correct errors in an existing file. To do that, you need an editor, such as Edit. But nothing is faster than using COPY CON.

10.6 ACTIVITY: WRITING AND EXECUTING A ONE-LETTER BATCH FILE

Note 1: The DATA disk is in Drive A. A:\> is displayed.

Note 2: For these examples, the use of COPY CON will be shown. If you make errors, you can either use COPY CON and key in all the data again or use the MS-DOS editor to correct the errors.

Note 3: In earlier chapters you may have used DOSKEY and the function keys to correct errors. Either of these methods will work with COPY CON.

Step 1 Key in the following: A:\>**COPY CON D.BAT** Enter

```
A:\>COPY CON D.BAT
_
```

WHAT'S HAPPENING? When you keyed in **COPY CON D.BAT**, you were informing the COPY command that you wanted to make the keyboard the source. The cursor is blinking right below the prompt, and the screen is blank.

Step 2 Key in the following: **DIR /AD** Enter

```
A:\>COPY CON D.BAT
DIR /AD
_
```

WHAT'S HAPPENING? You have one line. You are finished keying in data and you wish this line to be saved to a file called **D.BAT**. First, however, you must tell COPY you are finished.

Step 3 Press F6 Enter

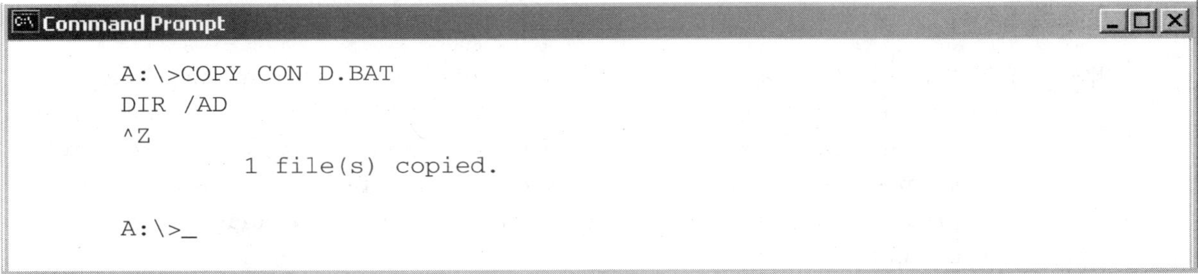

```
A:\>COPY CON D.BAT
DIR /AD
^Z
        1 file(s) copied.

A:\>_
```

By pressing F6 and then Enter, you sent a signal to COPY that you were done. The F6 appeared on the screen as **^Z**. Pressing Ctrl + **Z** will produce the same results as F6. You then got the message "1 file(s) copied" and were returned to the system level.

Step 4 Key in the following: A:\>**TYPE D.BAT** Enter

```
Command Prompt

A:\>TYPE D.BAT
DIR /AD

A:\>_
```

You wrote a one-line batch file named **D.BAT** with COPY CON and saved the file **D.BAT** to the disk. Once you returned to the system prompt, you displayed the contents of **D.BAT** with the TYPE command. The fact that you could display this file with the TYPE command is another indication that it is indeed an ASCII file. All COPY CON did was allow you to create the file, and TYPE merely displayed what is inside the file. To execute the file, you must key in the file name. Now, whenever you want to see the subdirectories on the DATA disk in Drive A, you only have to key in one letter to execute this command.

Step 5 Key in the following: A:\>**D** Enter

```
Command Prompt

A:\>DIR /AD
 Volume in drive A is DATA
 Volume Serial Number is 3330-1807

 Directory of A:\

04/30/2001  11:15a      <DIR>          POLYSCI
04/30/2001  11:50a      <DIR>          CLASS
04/30/2001  11:55a      <DIR>          WORK
06/06/2001  08:51a      <DIR>          TRIP
07/03/2000  01:53p      <DIR>          MEDIA
06/07/2001  08:33a      <DIR>          PROG
06/08/2001  08:43a      <DIR>          TEST
               0 File(s)              0 bytes
               7 Dir(s)       1,244,672 bytes free

A:\>_
```

Your display may vary based on what subdirectories are on the DATA disk and in what order they were created. As you can see, you set up a command sequence in a batch file called **D.BAT**. You can run this batch file whenever the need arises, simply by keying in the name of the batch file at the system prompt. You can also display the files by size, with the smallest file at the end of the list.

Step 6 Key in the following: A:\>**COPY CON S.BAT** Enter
DIR /O-S Enter
F6 Enter

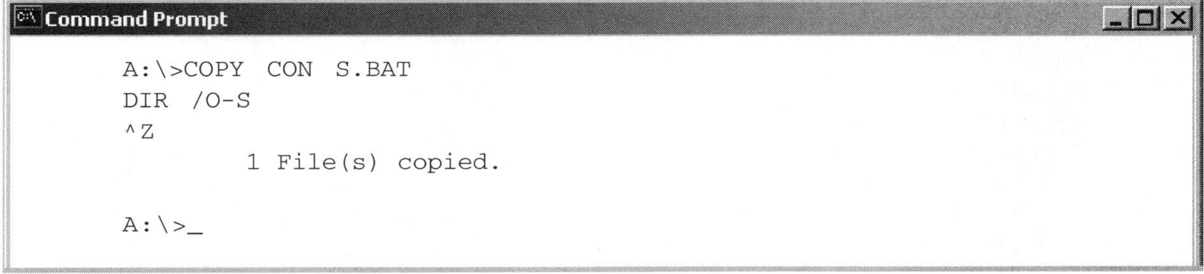

```
Command Prompt
A:\>COPY  CON  S.BAT
DIR  /O-S
^Z
        1 File(s) copied.

A:\>_
```

WHAT'S HAPPENING? You have written another simple one-line batch file and saved it to the default directory.

Step 7 Key in the following: A:\>**TYPE S.BAT** Enter

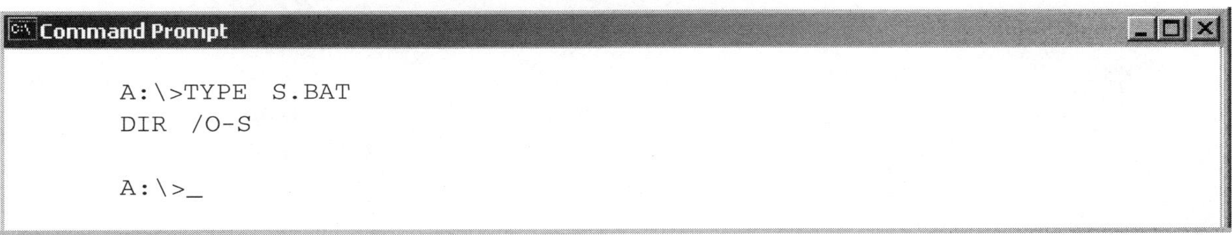

```
Command Prompt
A:\>TYPE  S.BAT
DIR  /O-S

A:\>_
```

WHAT'S HAPPENING? After saving the file to disk, you looked at its contents with the TYPE command. To execute the batch file, you must key in the batch file name (**S**) at the system prompt.

Step 8 Key in the following: A:\>**S** Enter

```
Command Prompt
A:\>S

A:\>DIR  /O-S
 Volume  in  drive  A  is  DATA
 Volume  Serial  Number  is  3330-1807

  Directory  of  A:\

06/05/2001  01:58p              16,516 TEST.TKR
06/05/2001  02:01p              15,108 CLASX
01/01/1999  05:00a               8,064 HOMEBUD.TKR
06/07/2001  09:14a               4,300 CHKDSK.TXT
07/31/1999  12:53p               2,672 NEWPRSON.FIL
06/06/2001  01:39p               2,428 PERSONAL.FIL
06/08/2001  08:43a                 947 TXTFILES.TXT
08/12/2000  04:12p                 314 CASES.FIL
---
12/06/2000  02:45p                  19 FILE3.FP
12/06/2000  02:45p                  19 FILE3.SWT
12/06/2000  02:45p                  19 FILE4.FP
12/06/2000  02:45p                  19 FILE2.SWT
```

```
12/06/2000  02:45p                   19 FILE2.FP
12/06/2000  02:45p                   19 FILE2.CZG
12/06/2000  02:45p                   19 APR.BUD
12/06/2000  02:45p                   19 FILE3.CZG
06/11/2001  10:23a                   10 S.BAT
06/11/2001  10:18a                    9 D.BAT
08/12/2000  04:12p                    3 Y.FIL
06/08/2001  08:43a      <DIR>           TEST
06/07/2001  08:33a      <DIR>           PROG
06/05/2001  01:05p      <DIR>           WORK
06/05/2001  12:55p      <DIR>           CLASS
07/03/2000  01:53p      <DIR>           MEDIA
06/05/2001  10:35a      <DIR>           POLYSCI
06/06/2001  08:51a      <DIR>           TRIP
              55 File(s)         53,714 bytes
               7 Dir(s)      1,244,160 bytes free

A:\>_
```

(The graphic represents the top and bottom of what you will see scroll by on your screen.) The files are listed by size, and all the subdirectories are grouped at the bottom of the display. Because directories have no size, they are listed last as the smallest files.

10.7 USING BATCH FILES TO LOAD APPLICATION SOFTWARE

Today, in the Windows environment, you typically launch application programs such as Word or Excel by either selecting them from a menu, clicking the program icon, or using a toolbar. These are, of course, application programs written for the Windows world. If you had an older program that was written for the DOS world only, it would have none of these choices. Thus, you could write a batch file to launch it, and then create an icon for your desktop. You will also find that there will be system activities you will want to run from the command line. Some of these activities will launch certain programs. The techniques you learn here can assist you in these matters.

You will first look at the use of batch files to load application software written to run under MS-DOS. Usually, application software programs are stored in a subdirectory. When you want to use a program, you have to change the directory to the proper subdirectory, load the program, and, when you are finished using the application program, return to the system level. You usually want to change the default subdirectory to the root directory. This process can be easier with a batch file. First you will run through the process of working with application software, and then you will create a batch file to load the application software.

10.8 ACTIVITY: USING THE HPB APPLICATION PACKAGE

Note: The DATA disk is in Drive A. A:\> is displayed.

Step 1 Key in the following: A:\>**XCOPY C:\WINDOSBK\PHONE*.* HPB** Enter

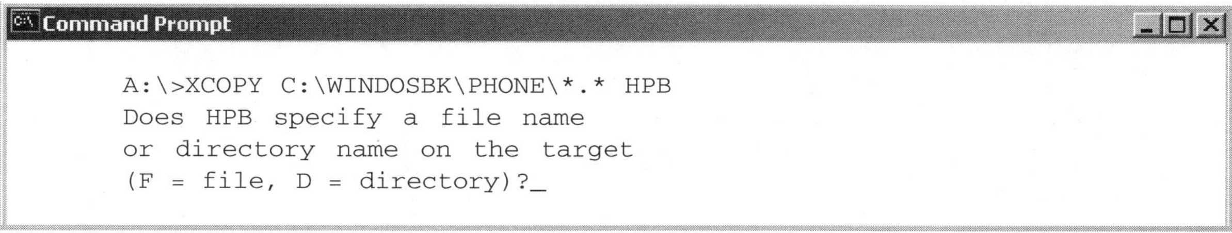

```
Command Prompt
A:\>XCOPY C:\WINDOSBK\PHONE\*.* HPB
Does HPB specify a file name
or directory name on the target
(F = file, D = directory)?_
```

WHAT'S HAPPENING? You are copying the **PHONE** directory and its files from the **\WINDOSBK** subdirectory to the DATA disk. You are placing the files in a subdirectory you called **HPB**.

Step 2 Press **D**.

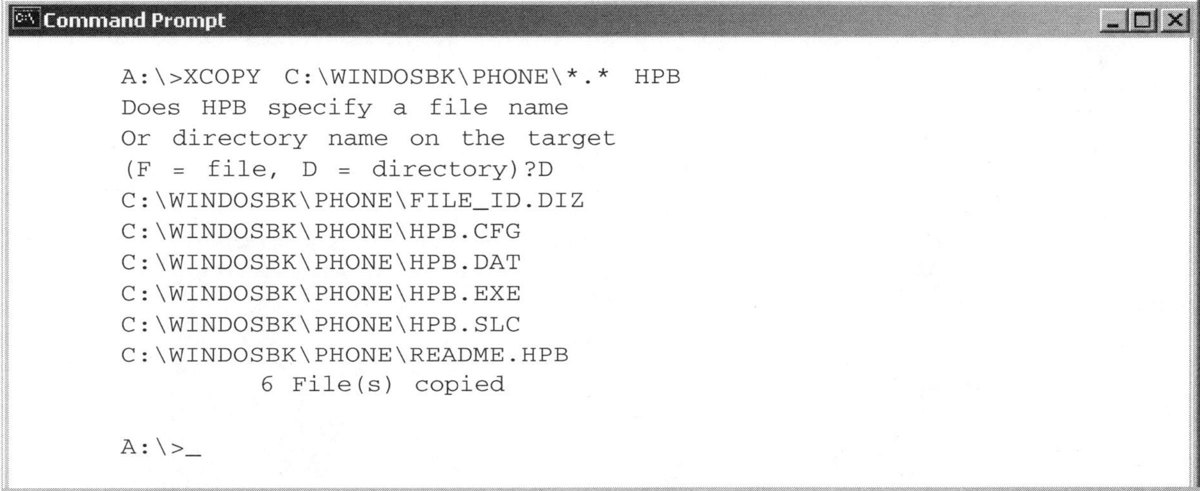

```
Command Prompt
A:\>XCOPY  C:\WINDOSBK\PHONE\*.*  HPB
Does HPB specify a file name
Or directory name on the target
(F = file, D = directory)?D
C:\WINDOSBK\PHONE\FILE_ID.DIZ
C:\WINDOSBK\PHONE\HPB.CFG
C:\WINDOSBK\PHONE\HPB.DAT
C:\WINDOSBK\PHONE\HPB.EXE
C:\WINDOSBK\PHONE\HPB.SLC
C:\WINDOSBK\PHONE\README.HPB
         6 File(s) copied

A:\>_
```

WHAT'S HAPPENING? You have copied the files to the new **HPB** subdirectory on the DATA disk.

Step 3 Key in the following: A:\>**CD HPB** Enter

Step 4 Key in the following: A:\HPB>**DIR HPB.EXE** Enter

Step 5 Key in the following: A:\HPB>**DIR HPB.DAT** Enter

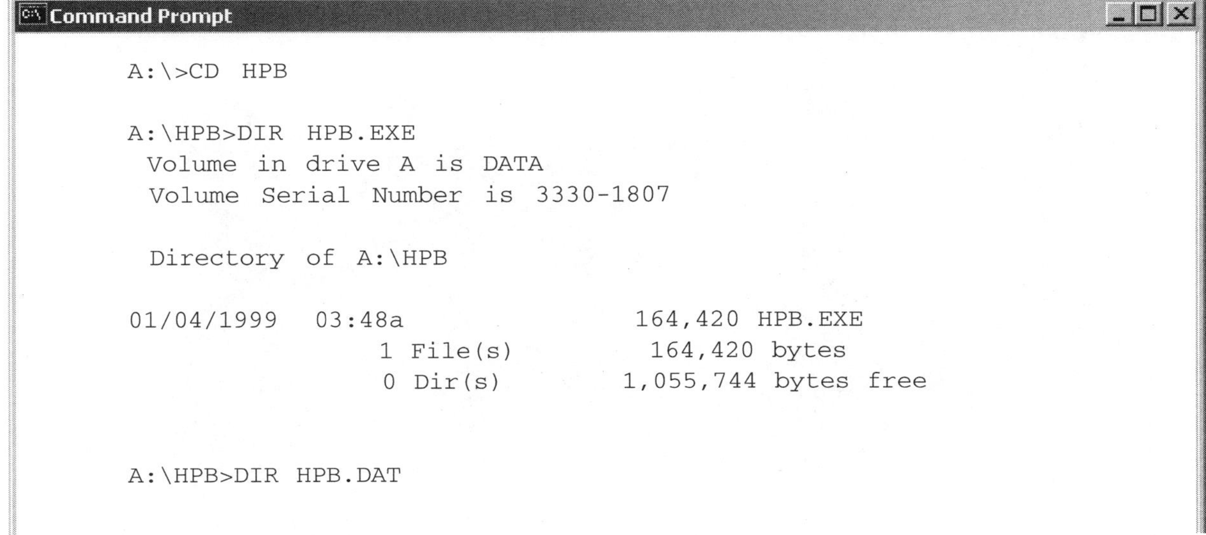

```
Command Prompt
A:\>CD  HPB

A:\HPB>DIR  HPB.EXE
 Volume in drive A is DATA
 Volume Serial Number is 3330-1807

 Directory of A:\HPB

01/04/1999   03:48a              164,420 HPB.EXE
                 1 File(s)         164,420 bytes
                 0 Dir(s)        1,055,744 bytes free


A:\HPB>DIR HPB.DAT
```

```
 Volume in drive A is DATA
 Volume Serial Number is 3330-1807

 Directory of A:\HPB

01/04/1999  03:48a               4,368 HPB.DAT
               1 File(s)          4,368 bytes
               0 Dir(s)       1,055,744 bytes free

A:\HPB>_
```

WHAT'S HAPPENING? You are looking at the file **HPB.EXE** in the subdirectory **HPB** on the DATA disk. You are going to load the program called **HPB.EXE**, which is a simple address book. You are going to use the data file called **HPB.DAT**, also in the subdirectory **HPB**. This program automatically loads its data file when you load the program.

Step 6 Key in the following: A:\HPB>**HPB** Enter

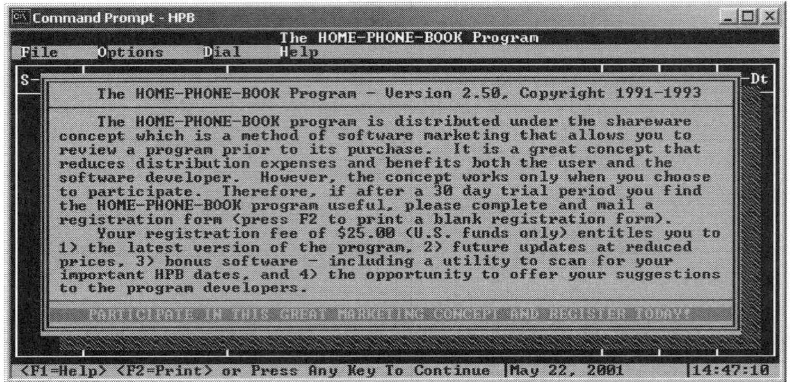

WHAT'S HAPPENING? You see the opening screen introducing you to shareware and to the details for registering the program.

Step 7 Press Enter

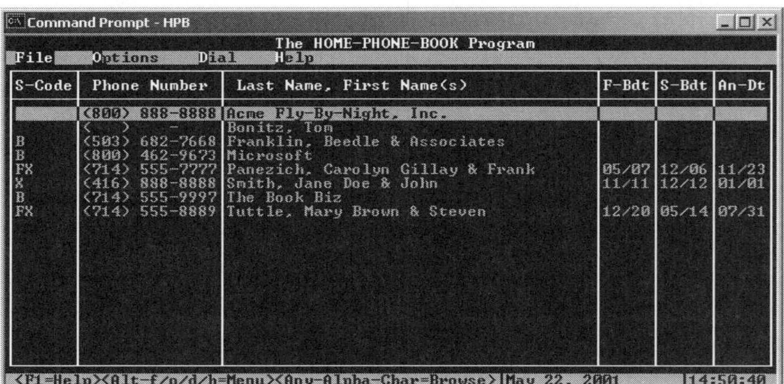

You see a quick message that this program is automatically loading the data file. The data file is called **HPB.DAT**. Then the above screen appears. This is a database program called Home Phone Book. It has a menu bar across the top with specific choices. To access the menu, you press the Alt key and the first letter of your menu choice.

Step 8 Press Alt + **O**.

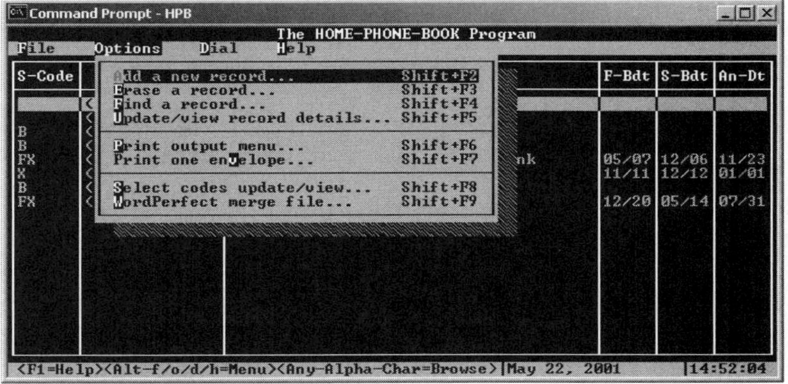

You dropped down the Options menu, which has many choices. A database program is comprised of records and fields. A record is a new entry in the file. **Add a new record** is already highlighted and is the default choice, so it is not necessary to select it. To add a new record, there is also a keyboard shortcut—pressing the Shift + F2 keys.

Step 9 Press Shift + F2

You are presented with a screen in which you can fill out information. Each item on the screen is a field. A collection of fields makes up a record, and a collection of records is the data file.

Step 10 In the **Last Name :** field, key in your last name.

Step 11 Press the Tab key. That will move you to **First Name :**.

Step 12 Key in your first name.

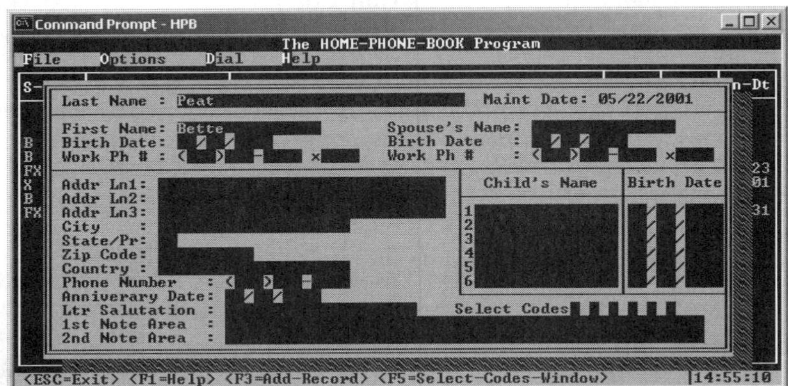

WHAT'S HAPPENING? You have keyed in some information in the appropriate fields. At the bottom of the screen are the instructions for using this program. You are going to choose **Add Record**. This means that you will save the information you just keyed in.

Step 13 Press the F3 key.

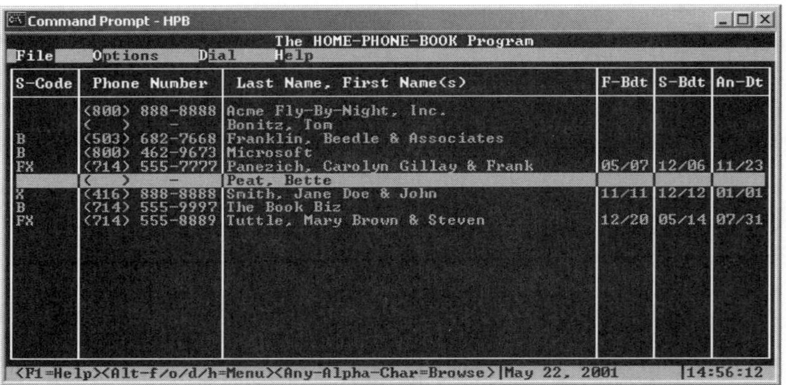

WHAT'S HAPPENING? You returned to the main screen. Your name should be highlighted. Now you are going to exit the program.

Step 14 Press Alt + **F**.

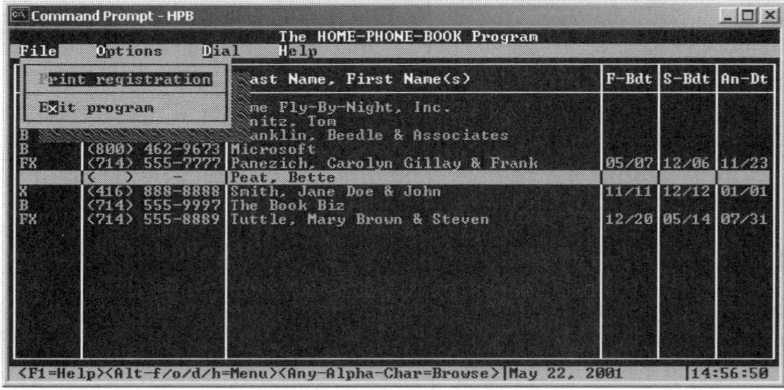

You have dropped down the File menu. From this menu, you know you simply press **X** to exit the program.

Step 15 Press **X**.

You briefly see what is called a housekeeping detail on the screen. The housekeeping here is placing the records in the file in order. Then you are returned to the Command Prompt window. However, you are still in the HPB subdirectory.

Step 16 Key in the following: A:\HPB>**CD ** Enter

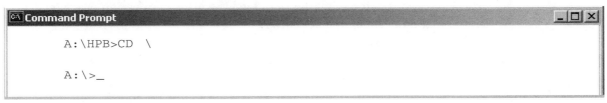

You returned to the root directory of the DATA disk so that you can do other work.

10.9 WRITING A BATCH FILE TO LOAD AN APPLICATION PROGRAM

In the previous activity, in order to execute the database program called HPB, you needed to take three steps. First (Step 3), you went from the root directory to the subdirectory called HPB. Second (Step 6), you had to load HPB.EXE. Third (Step 16), after you exited HPB, you returned to the root directory. A batch file is an ideal place to put all of these commands.

10.10 ACTIVITY: WRITING A BATCH FILE TO EXECUTE HPB

Note 1: The DATA disk is in Drive A. A:\> is displayed.

Note 2: You may use any text editor you wish for creating the batch files. You may use COPY CON, but when you have more than one line, using an editor is easier. Remember, you cannot edit lines when you use COPY CON. The Edit instructions for keyboard use will be shown, but if you prefer using a mouse, do so.

Step 1 Key in the following: A:\>**EDIT HPB.BAT** Enter

Step 2 Key in the following: **CD \HPB** Enter
HPB Enter
**CD **

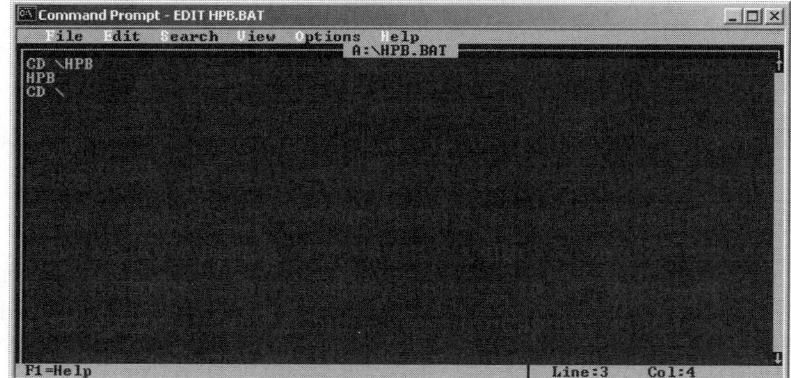

WHAT'S HAPPENING? You have just written a batch file to load the HPB application program. You can give the file the name **HPB.BAT**, because it is in the root directory of the DATA disk and **HPB.EXE** is in a subdirectory. The two file names will not conflict, and you will not have to be specific and key in **HPB.BAT**. Furthermore, the first line states **CD \HPB**. Although the backslash is not necessary in this instance, you want the batch file to run no matter where you are, so the CD command includes the \.

Step 3 Press Alt + **F**.

Step 4 Press **X**.

Step 5 Press **Y**.

Step 6 Key in the following: A:\>**TYPE HPB.BAT** Enter

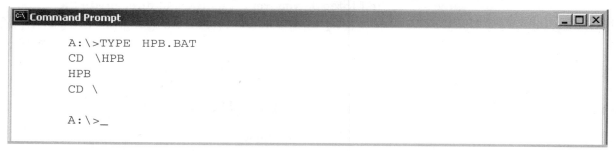

WHAT'S HAPPENING? You created the batch file **HPB.BAT** in Edit and then returned to the system prompt. Now you can execute this file.

Step 7 Key in the following: A:\>**HPB** Enter

Step 8 Press Enter

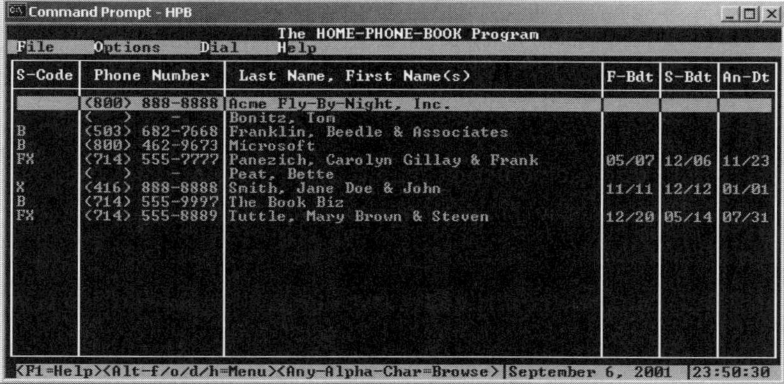

When you keyed in HPB at the root directory, the operating system looked for **HPB.BAT** and found it. It read the first line, which said to change the directory to the **HPB** subdirectory. It then read the second line, which told it to look for a program called **HPB.EXE**, and then it loaded HPB. The program HPB then appeared on the screen.

Step 9 Press **Alt** + **F**.

Step 10 Press **X**.

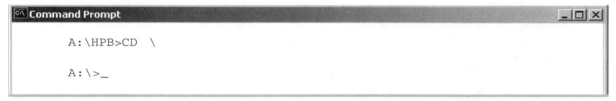

It does not matter if you are in the application program one minute, one hour, or one entire day. Whenever you exit the application program, the command prompt continues with the batch file where it last was and simply reads and executes the next line. The operating system finished executing your batch file by changing the directory to the root.

10.11 CREATING SHORTCUTS FOR BATCH FILES ON THE DESKTOP

Any batch file can be run from the Windows environment. One way to do it is to locate the batch file name in Windows Explorer or My Computer, then double-click the file name. You can also create a shortcut for it and place it on the desktop or in a folder. Again, once it is a shortcut, the shortcut can be clicked to execute the batch file. However, there are things that you can do with the shortcut that you cannot do in the command line interface. One of the things you may have noticed is that if you run a batch file from the GUI, it will open a command prompt window and leave you in the command prompt window. You can change the properties of a shortcut so the command prompt window is automatically closed. You can also change the icon for the shortcut.

10.12 ACTIVITY: CREATING A SHORTCUT ON THE DESKTOP

Note: The DATA disk is in Drive A. A:\> is displayed.

Step 1 Key in A:\>**EXIT** Enter

Step 2 On the desktop, double-click **My Computer**. Double-click the A drive icon to see the contents of the DATA disk.

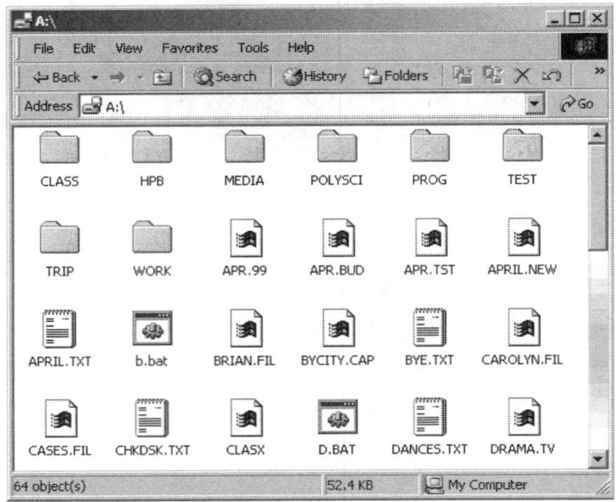

WHAT'S HAPPENING? You are looking at the contents of the DATA disk.

Step 3 Scroll down using the horizontal scroll bar until you locate **HPB.BAT**. Double-click it.

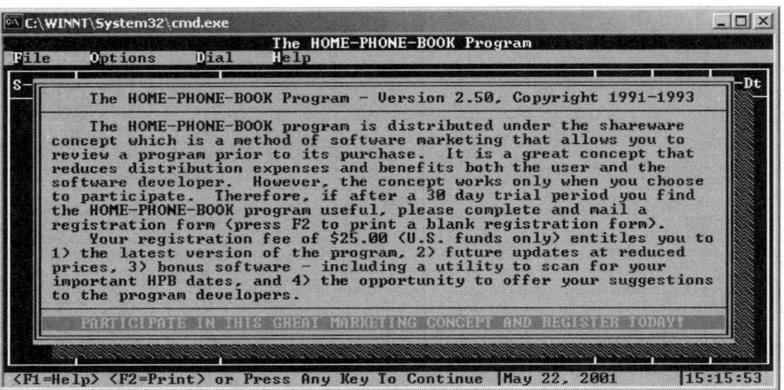

WHAT'S HAPPENING? You have just executed **HPB.BAT**.

Step 4 Press Enter. Press Alt + **F**. Press **X**.

WHAT'S HAPPENING? You are returned to the My Computer window.

Step 5 Select **HPB.BAT** in the My Computer window. Point to the HPB icon and hold down the right mouse button.

Step 6 Drag the icon to the desktop and release the right mouse button.

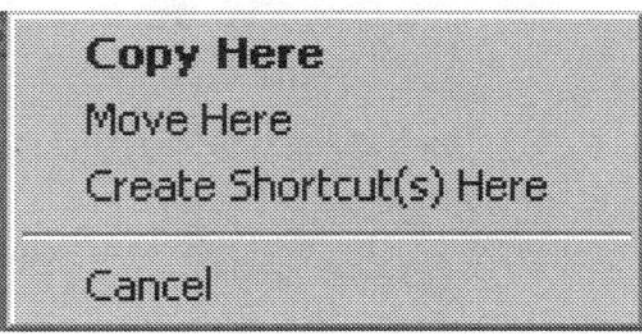

WHAT'S HAPPENING? The shortcut menu has **Copy Here** highlighted. You want a shortcut, not a copy.

Step 7 Click **Create Shortcut(s) Here**.

WHAT'S HAPPENING? You now have a shortcut to the batch file you created. If you clicked it, it would execute. You can change the icon so it is more distinctive.

Step 8 Close the My Computer window. Right-click the shortcut.

Step 9 Click **Properties**.

WHAT'S HAPPENING? You have opened the property sheet for the shortcut to **HPB.BAT**.

Step 10 Click the **Shortcut** tab, if it is not already selected.

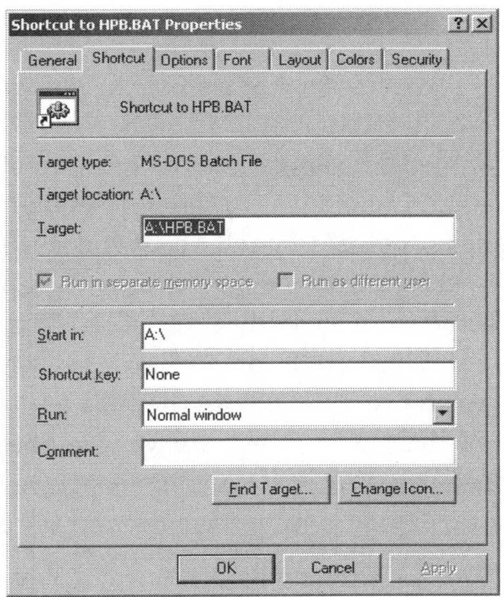

WHAT'S HAPPENING? You can see the command line listed in the Target text box.

Step 11 Click the **Change Icon** button.

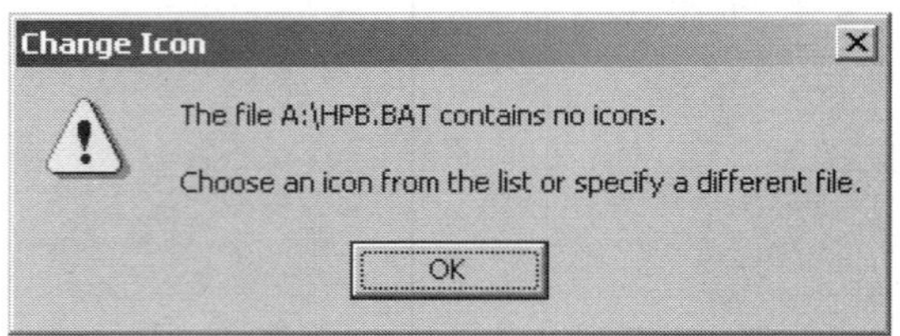

WHAT'S HAPPENING? As you can see, the batch file has no icons of its own.

Step 12 Click **OK**.

WHAT'S HAPPENING? Windows provides a set of icons in a file named **%SYSTEMROOT%\SYSTEM32\SHELL32.DLL**. The **%SYSTEMROOT%** is an ***environmental variable*** that represents the location of the Windows operating system files. The environment is an area in memory where Windows 2000 Professional keeps "notes" to itself about the settings it needs to run. For instance, Windows knows that the operating system files are located in a directory. The directory name could be **C:\WINNT** or **C:\WINDOWS**. When you boot the system, Windows locates where the system files are stored on your disk and stores the value of where the files are in the variable named **%SYSTEMROOT%**. Whenever you see the percent signs surrounding a name, the operating system will substitute a value for that variable. Other programs can also store information in the environment.

Step 13 Scroll until you see a tree icon. Click it. Click **OK**. Click **OK**.

WHAT'S HAPPENING? Now your shortcut to HPB is represented by the tree icon.

Step 14 Double-click the tree icon.

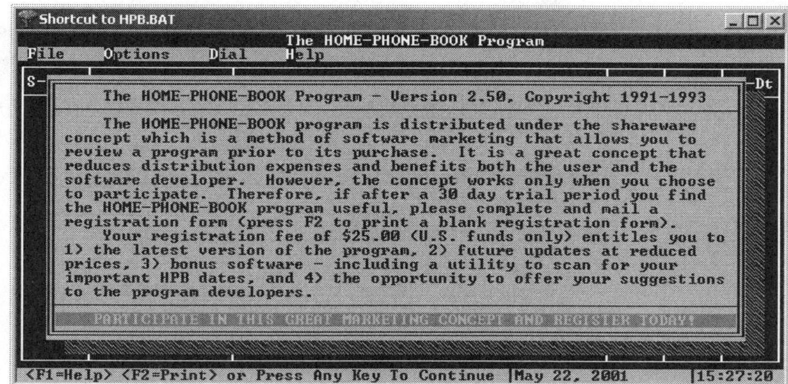

WHAT'S HAPPENING? You have opened the HPB program.

Step 15 Press **Enter**. Press **Alt** + **F**. Press **X**.

WHAT'S HAPPENING? You have returned to the desktop. The Command Prompt window closed automatically.

Step 16 Drag the shortcut to HPB to the **Recycle Bin**.

10.13 BATCH FILES TO RUN WINDOWS PROGRAMS

You can use a batch file to run the small programs that come with Windows, such as Notepad or Calculator. Perhaps you prefer to use Notepad when writing batch files, but find it bothersome to have to return to the GUI to start the Notepad program. You can create a batch file that will allow you to run the program without having to return to the desktop. You can also use special features of Notepad to create a log file that will add the current date and time to a file created with Notepad. In order to use this feature, you must create a file with Notepad whose first line is .LOG.

10.14 ACTIVITY: CREATING A BATCH FILE TO RUN NOTEPAD

Note: You have shelled out to the Command Prompt. The DATA disk is in Drive A. A:\> is displayed.

Step 1 Key in the following: A:\>**EDIT N.BAT** **Enter**
%SYSTEMROOT%\NOTEPAD.EXE **Enter**
A: **Enter**

Step 2 Key in the following: **Alt** + **F**. Press **X**.

Step 3 Key in the following: **Y** **Enter**

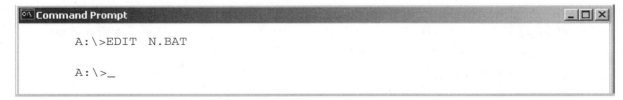

WHAT'S HAPPENING? You have written a batch file to start a Windows applet, Notepad. You used an environmental variable, **%SYSTEMROOT%**. Case does not matter. You could key in an absolute path such as **C:\WINDOWS\NOTEPAD.EXE** or **C:\WINNT\NOTEPAD.EXE** if you knew the name of your windows directory. However, if you use the environmental variable, Windows knows where the Windows files are located and will substitute the correct name.

Step 4 Key in the following: A:\>**N** Enter

WHAT'S HAPPENING? You have opened Notepad without returning to the desktop.

Step 5 Key in the following in the Notepad window: **.LOG** Enter

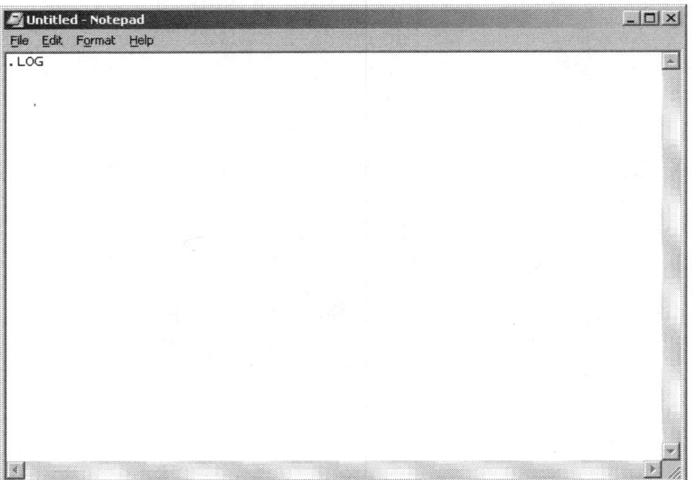

WHAT'S HAPPENING? You are creating a log file using Notepad. Here case does matter and you must use uppercase letters preceded by a period.

Step 6 Click **File**. Click **Save As**.

Step 7 In the File name text box, key in the following: **A:\LOG.TXT** Enter

Step 8 Click **Save**. Click **File**. Click **Exit**.

WHAT'S HAPPENING? You have closed Notepad and returned to the Command Prompt Window.

Step 9 Key in the following: **EDIT log.bat** Enter
%SYSTEMROOT%\NOTEPAD LOG.TXT Enter
DIR *.99 Enter

Step 10 Press Alt + **F**. Press **X**. Press **Y**.

Step 11 Key in the following: A:\>**LOG** Enter

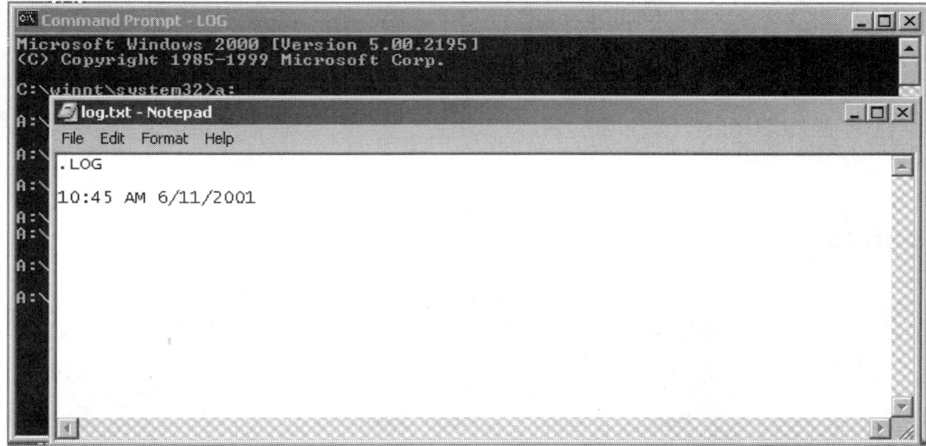

WHAT'S HAPPENING? When you supplied a file name with Notepad, it opened the file you specified. As you can see, Notepad has placed the current date and time in the **log.txt** file. However, your second command has not executed. Your batch file requires that you finish using Notepad before it will read the next line and execute it (**DIR *.99**).

Step 12 In Notepad, key in the following: **My first entry in my log file.** Enter

Step 13 Press Alt + **F**. Press **X**. Key in the following: **Y**.

```
Command Prompt
A:\>EDIT N.BAT

A:\>N

A:\>C:\WINNT\NOTEPAD.EXE

A:\>A:
A:\>EDIT LOG.BAT

A:\>LOG

A:\>C:\WINNT\NOTEPAD LOG.TXT

A:\>DIR *.99
 Volume in drive A is DATA
 Volume Serial Number is 4808-3405

 Directory of A:\

10/10/1999  04:53p                  72 APR.99
10/10/1999  04:53p                  73 JAN.99
               2 File(s)            145 bytes
               0 Dir(s)       1,048,064 bytes free

A:\>_
```

WHAT'S HAPPENING? Now that you exited Notepad, your other command could execute. There is a command called START that allows you to start a program in a new window and at the same time, continue executing your batch file in the previous window. You may also change the title of the Command Prompt window.

Step 14 Edit and save the LOG.BAT file so it reads as follows:
START NOTEPAD LOG.TXT
START "THE 99 FILES WINDOW" DIR *.99

WHAT'S HAPPENING? The START command will start a new command window so that LOG.TXT will open in one window. The second command accomplishes two tasks. It will open another window, and it will give the window the title enclosed in quotation marks.

Step 15 Key in the following: **LOG** Enter

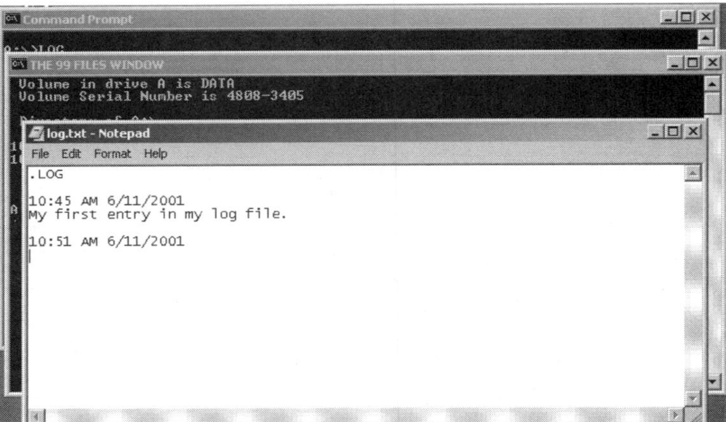

WHAT'S HAPPENING? You have three windows open, your original command prompt, your Notepad window and "THE 99 FILES WINDOW." THE 99 FILES WINDOW executed your directory command. The Notepad window is waiting for you to make an entry.

Step 16 Make the Notepad window active. In the Notepad window, key in the following: **My second entry in my log file.**

Step 17 Click **File**. Click **Save**. Click **File**. Click **Exit**.

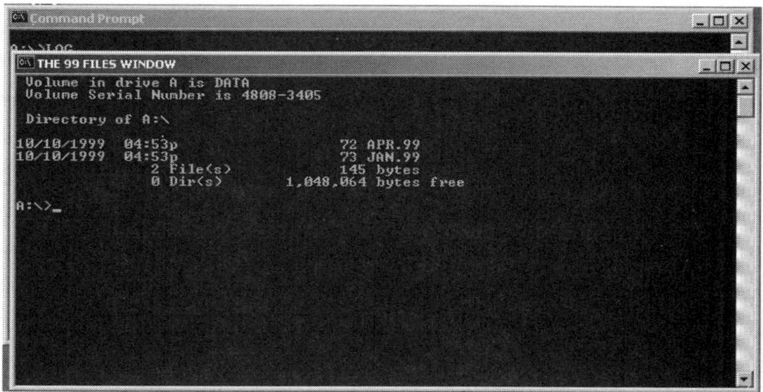

WHAT'S HAPPENING? You still have THE 99 FILES WINDOW open. The DIR command executed.

Step 18 Key in the following: **EXIT** Enter

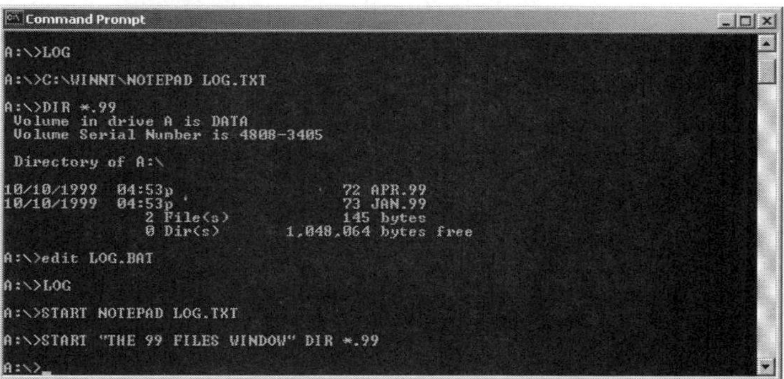

WHAT'S HAPPENING? You have returned to your original Command Prompt window where you executed your batch file.

Step 19 Key in the following: A:\>**EXIT** Enter

WHAT'S HAPPENING? You have closed the Command Prompt window.

10.15 SPECIAL BATCH FILE COMMANDS

There are commands specifically designed to be used in batch files. These commands can make batch files extremely versatile. They are listed in Table 10.2 below:

Command	Purpose
CALL	Calls one batch program from another without causing the first batch program to stop. The CALL command now accepts labels as the target of the call.
ECHO	Displays or hides the text in batch programs while the program is running. Also used to determine whether or not commands will be *echoed* to the screen while the program file is running.
ENDLOCAL	Ends localization of environment changes in a batch file, restoring environment variables to their values before the matching SETLOCAL command.
FOR	Runs a specified command for each file in a set of files. This command can also be used at the command line.
GOTO	Directs the operating system to a new line in the program that you specify with a label.
IF	Performs conditional processing in a batch program, based on whether or not a specified condition is true or false.
PAUSE	Suspends processing of a batch file and displays a message prompting the user to press a key to continue.
REM	Used to document your batch files. The operating system ignores any line that begins with REM, allowing you to place lines of information in your batch program or to prevent a line from running.
SETLOCAL	Begins localization of environmental variables in a batch file. Localization lasts until a matching ENDLOCAL command is encountered or the end of the batch file is reached.
SHIFT	Changes the position of the replaceable parameter in a batch program.

TABLE 10.2 BATCH FILE COMMANDS

You will examine and use some of these commands in the following activities.

10.16 THE REM COMMAND

The REM command, which stands for "remarks," is a special command that allows the user to key in explanatory text that will be displayed on the screen. Nothing else happens. REM does not cause the operating system to take any action, but it is very useful. When a line begins with REM, the operating system knows that anything following the REM is not a command and, thus, is not supposed to be executed, just displayed on the screen. REM allows a batch file to be ***documented***. In a data-processing environment, "to document" means to give an explanation about the purpose of a program. This process can be very important when there are many batch files on a disk, especially when someone who did not write the batch file would like to use it. The REM statements should tell anyone what the purpose of the batch file is. The remarks can also include the name of the batch file, the time and date it was last updated, and the author of the batch file.

10.17 ACTIVITY: USING REM

Note 1: You have shelled out to a Command Prompt window. The DATA disk is in Drive A. A:\> is displayed.

Note 2: If **JAN.BUD** is not on the DATA disk, you can copy **\WINDOSBK\JAN.TMP** to the DATA disk as **JAN.BUD**.

Step 1 Key in the following: A:\>**EDIT TEST2.BAT** Enter
REM This is a test file Enter
REM to see how the REM Enter
REM command works. Enter
TYPE JAN.BUD Enter
COPY JAN.BUD JAN.XYZ

You are using Edit to write another batch file called **TEST2.BAT**. You have inserted some text with REM preceding each line. You keyed in two command line commands, TYPE and COPY. Now you want to save this file to the disk and return to the system level.

Step 2 Press Alt +**F**. Press **X**. Press **Y**.

Step 3 Key in the following: A:\>**TYPE TEST2.BAT** Enter

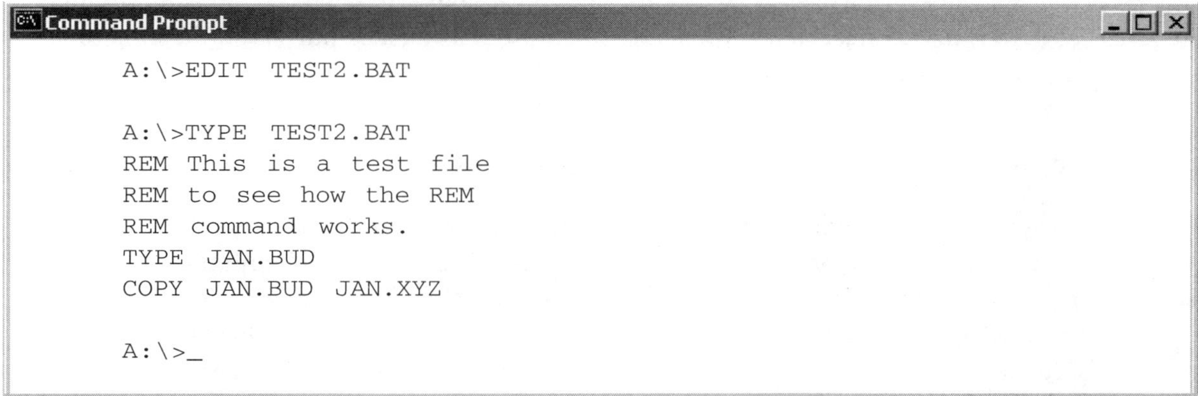

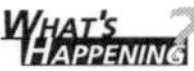

This batch file was created as a test case. The remarks just keyed in explain the purpose of this batch file. You created **TEST2.BAT** in Edit and returned to the system prompt. You then displayed **TEST2.BAT** with the TYPE command. To execute the **TEST2.BAT** batch file, you must run it.

Step 4 Key in the following: A:\>**TEST2** Enter

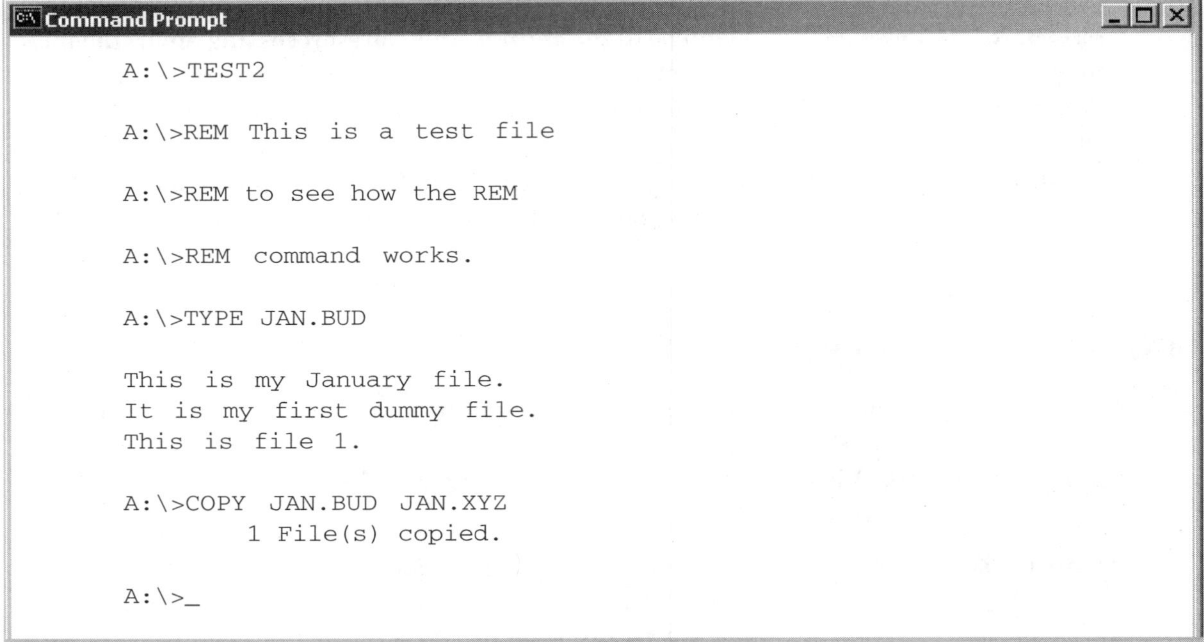

Command Prompt
A:\>TEST2
A:\>REM This is a test file
A:\>REM to see how the REM
A:\>REM command works.
A:\>TYPE JAN.BUD
This is my January file.
It is my first dummy file.
This is file 1.
A:\>COPY JAN.BUD JAN.XYZ
1 File(s) copied.
A:\>_

When you keyed in **TEST2**, the batch file was executed. The operating system read the first line of the batch file, *REM This is a test file*. It knew that it was supposed to do nothing but display the text following REM on the screen. Then the next line in the batch file was read, *REM to see how the REM*, and the same procedure was followed. The operating system kept reading and displaying the REM lines until it got to the line that had the command TYPE. To the operating system, TYPE is a command, so it executed or ran the TYPE command with the parameter JAN.BUD. Then the next line was read, which was another command, COPY, so it was executed. The file **JAN.BUD** was copied to a new file called **JAN.XYZ**. Then the operating system looked for another line in the batch file but could find no more lines, so it returned to the system level. The purpose of REM is to provide explanatory remarks about the batch file.

10.18 THE ECHO COMMAND

Notice in the above activity, when you ran TEST2.BAT you saw the command on the screen, and then the command executed. You saw TYPE JAN.BUD and then saw the typed-out file. Both the command and the output of the command were "echoed" to the screen. ECHO is a command that means display to the screen. The default value for ECHO is on. The ECHO command is normally always on. The only time it is off is if you turn it off. In a batch file, you can turn off the display of the command and see only the output of a command—not the command itself. For instance, COPY THIS.FIL

THAT.FIL is a command. The output of the command is **1 File(s) copied**. The work of the command is the actual copying of the file. See Table 10.3.

	Echo On Display	Echo Off Display
Command:	COPY THIS.FIL THAT.FIL	
Output:	1 File(s) copied	1 File(s) copied

TABLE 10.3 ECHO ON OR OFF

If the purpose of the REM command is to document a batch file, what is the purpose of the ECHO command? One of the purposes you saw in an earlier chapter was to redirect a special character to the printer so that the printer would eject a page. Another purpose of the ECHO command is to minimize screen clutter. For instance, although you want to use the REM command to document your batch file, you really do not need to see your documentation on the screen every time you run the batch file. ECHO OFF allows you to suppress the display of the commands.

10.19 ACTIVITY: USING ECHO

Note: The DATA disk is in Drive A. A:\> is displayed.

Step 1 Key in the following: A:\>**COPY TEST2.BAT TESTING.BAT** Enter

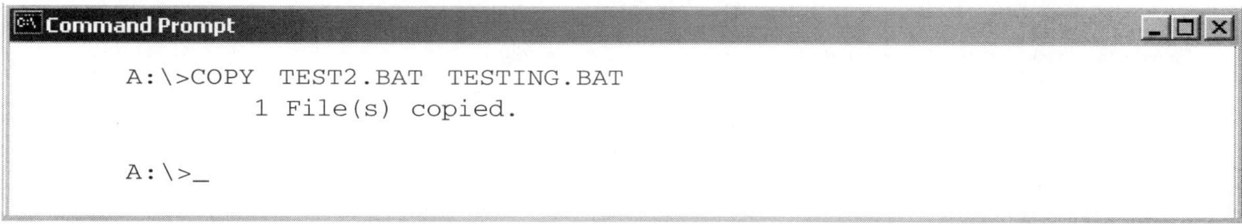

WHAT'S HAPPENING? You made a copy of the file **TEST2.BAT**.

Step 2 Key in the following: A:\> **EDIT TESTING.BAT** Enter

Step 2 At the top of the file, key in **ECHO OFF** Enter

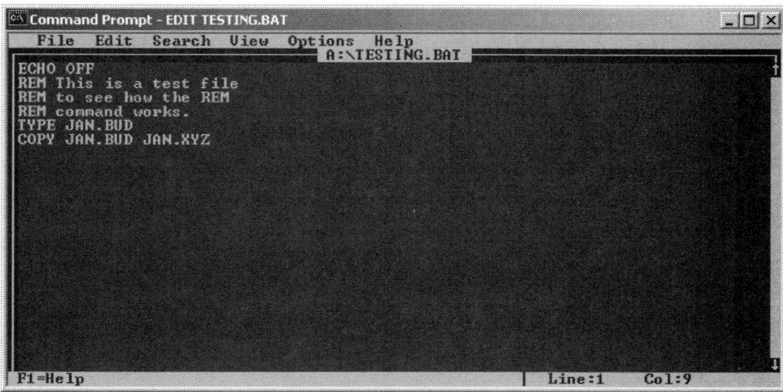

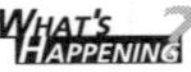

You are using a copy of the batch file from the previous activity. The only difference is that you added one line at the top of the batch file to turn ECHO off. You are going to run the batch file so that only the output of each command is displayed, not the actual commands. First you must exit Edit and save the file to the disk.

Step 4 Press **Alt** + **F**. Press **X**. Press **Y**.

Step 5 Key in the following: A:\>**TYPE TESTING.BAT** **Enter**

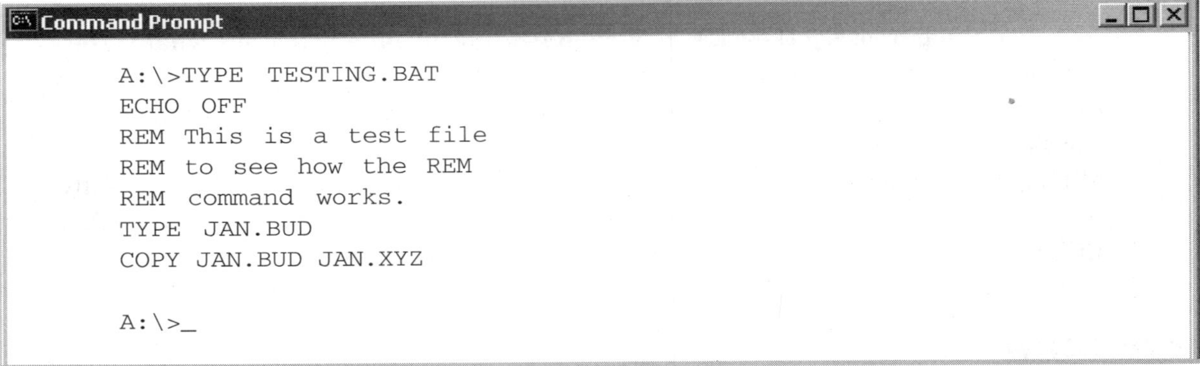

```
Command Prompt

A:\>TYPE TESTING.BAT
ECHO OFF
REM This is a test file
REM to see how the REM
REM command works.
TYPE JAN.BUD
COPY JAN.BUD JAN.XYZ

A:\>_
```

You saved the file as **TESTING.BAT** and displayed the contents on the screen. Now you wish to execute the file.

Step 6 Key in the following: A:\>**TESTING** **Enter**

```
Command Prompt

A:\>TESTING

A:\>ECHO OFF

This is my January file.
It is my first dummy file.
This is file 1.
        1 file(s) copied.
A:\>_
```

The batch file **TESTING.BAT** has the same commands as **TEST2.BAT**, but this time you saw only the output of the commands, not the actual commands themselves. You saw the ECHO OFF command on the screen, but you did not see the REM commands displayed on the screen. You saw the results of the TYPE JAN.BUD command, the contents of the file on the screen, but you never saw the TYPE JAN.BUD command on the screen. You also did not see the COPY JAN.BUD JAN.XYZ command, only the results of the command—the message "1 file(s) copied."

You already have a file by the name of **JAN.XYZ**, but, even though you are using the COPY command, it did not tell you that the file already exists (overwrite protection). The purpose of using a batch program would be defeated if there were interaction required by the user, so the warning is not there. The differences between ECHO ON and ECHO OFF are exemplified in Table 10.4.

	TEST2.BAT— ECHO ON Display	TESTING.BAT— ECHO OFF Display
Command:	ECHO ON	ECHO OFF
Command:	REM This is a test file	
Command:	REM to see how the REM	
Command:	REM command works.	
Command:	TYPE JAN.BUD	
Output:	This is my January file. It is my first dummy file. This is file 1.	This is my January file. It is my first dummy file. This is file 1.
Command:	COPY JAN.BUD JAN.XYZ	
Output:	1 File(s) copied	1 File(s) copied

(*Note:* Although commands and file names are shown as uppercase letters, the case does not matter.)

TABLE 10.4 ECHO ON AND ECHO OFF: A COMPARISON OF SCREEN DISPLAYS

The batch files **TEST2.BAT** and **TESTING.BAT** executed the same commands. The only difference is that when ECHO was on, which it was for **TEST2.BAT**, you saw the remarks as well as the commands. When you executed **TESTING.BAT**, you saw only the output of the commands displayed on the screen, not the actual commands, because ECHO was off. If you did not want to see ECHO OFF on the screen, you could have entered the command as @ECHO OFF. The @ suppresses the display of ECHO OFF.

10.20 THE PAUSE COMMAND

Another batch file command is PAUSE, which does *exactly* what its name implies: It tells the batch file to stop executing until the user takes some action. No other batch command will be executed until the user presses a key. The PAUSE command will wait forever until the user takes some action.

10.21 ACTIVITY: USING PAUSE

Note: The DATA disk is in Drive A. A:\> is displayed.

Step 1 Key in the following: A:\>**EDIT TEST2.BAT** Enter

Step 2 Press Ctrl + End

Step 3 Key in the following: **PAUSE You are going to delete JAN.XYZ** Enter
DEL JAN.XYZ

Step 4 Press **Alt** + **F**. Press **X**. Press **Y**.

Step 5 Key in the following: A:\>**TYPE TEST2.BAT** **Enter**

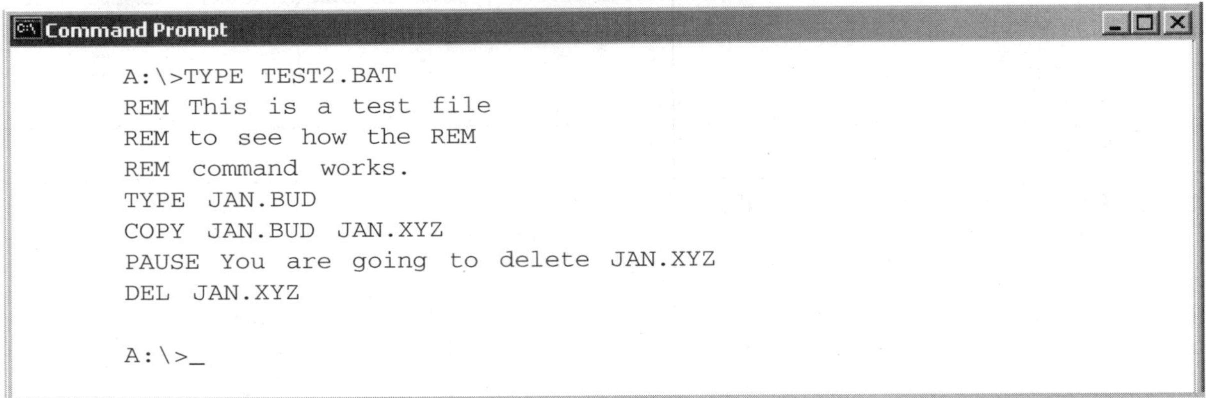

Command Prompt

```
A:\>TYPE TEST2.BAT
REM This is a test file
REM to see how the REM
REM command works.
TYPE JAN.BUD
COPY JAN.BUD JAN.XYZ
PAUSE You are going to delete JAN.XYZ
DEL JAN.XYZ

A:\>_
```

WHAT'S HAPPENING? You saved the file to disk with the changes you made. You then looked at the contents of the file with the TYPE command. You edited the batch file **TEST2.BAT**. When the file is executed, the first three lines of the file, the **REM** statements, explain the purpose of **TEST2.BAT**. Then the batch file displays the contents of **JAN.BUD** on the screen and copies the file **JAN.BUD** to a new file, **JAN.XYZ**. The PAUSE statement tells you that the file is going to be deleted and gives you a chance to change your mind. After you take action by pressing a key, the file **JAN.XYZ** is erased.

To execute **TEST2.BAT**, you must key in **TEST2** at the prompt.

Step 6 Key in the following: A:\>**TEST2** **Enter**

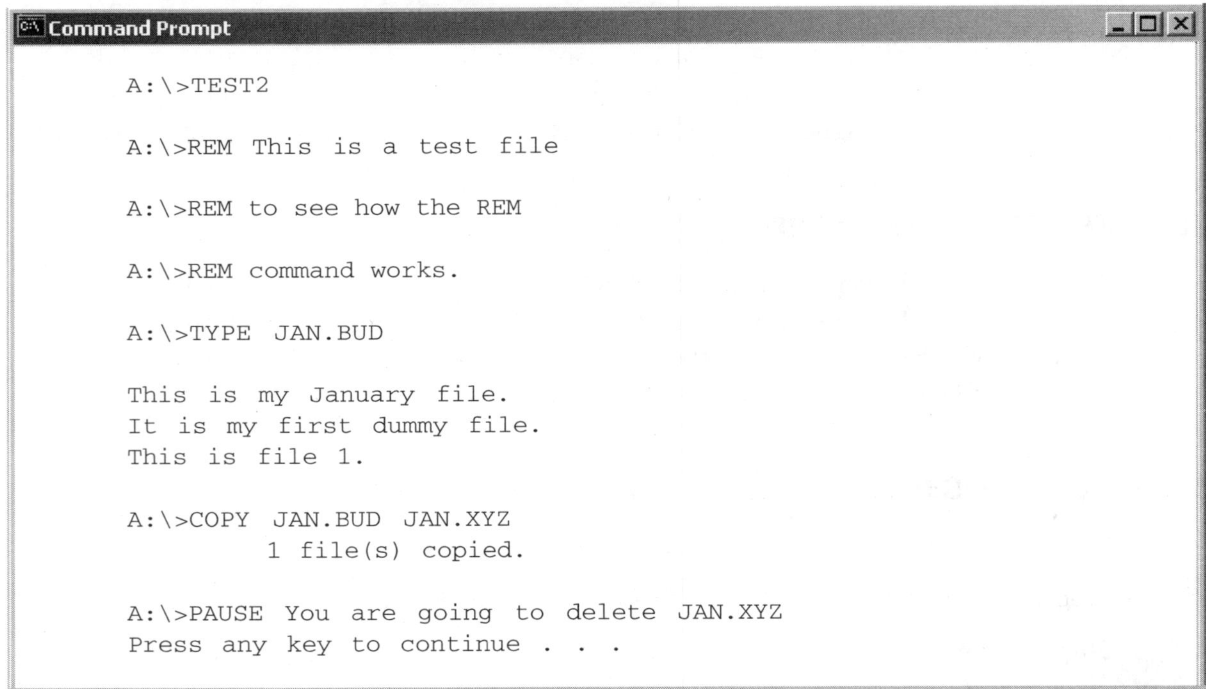

Command Prompt

```
A:\>TEST2

A:\>REM This is a test file

A:\>REM to see how the REM

A:\>REM command works.

A:\>TYPE JAN.BUD

This is my January file.
It is my first dummy file.
This is file 1.

A:\>COPY JAN.BUD JAN.XYZ
        1 file(s) copied.

A:\>PAUSE You are going to delete JAN.XYZ
Press any key to continue . . .
```

The batch file TEST2 has stopped running or "paused." It has halted execution until some action is taken. When you press a key, the operating system will read and execute the next line of the batch file. PAUSE just stops; it is not an order. If ECHO were off, all you would see is the message, "Press any key to continue ...". You would not see the message, "You are going to delete JAN.XYZ."

Step 7 Press **Enter**

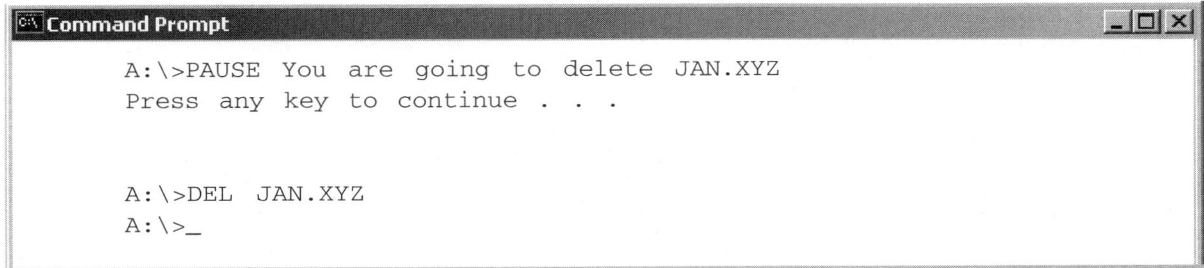


```
A:\>PAUSE You are going to delete JAN.XYZ
Press any key to continue . . .


A:\>DEL JAN.XYZ
A:\>_
```

The batch file continued executing all the steps and deleted the file called **JAN.XYZ**.

Step 8 Key in the following: A:\>**DIR JAN.XYZ** **Enter**

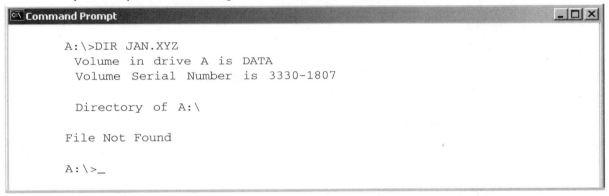

Command Prompt

```
A:\>DIR JAN.XYZ
 Volume in drive A is DATA
 Volume Serial Number is 3330-1807

 Directory of A:\

File Not Found

A:\>_
```

The file **JAN.XYZ** was deleted.

10.22 STOPPING A BATCH FILE FROM EXECUTING

In the above activity, you pressed a key after the PAUSE command was displayed so that the batch file continued to execute. What if you wanted to stop running the batch file? You can do this by interrupting or exiting from a running batch file. You do this by pressing the **Ctrl** key, and while pressing the **Ctrl** key, pressing the letter C (**Ctrl** + C or **Ctrl** + **Break**). At whatever point **Ctrl** + C is pressed, you leave the batch file and return to the system prompt. The rest of the lines in the batch file do not execute.

10.23 ACTIVITY: QUITTING A BATCH FILE

Note: The DATA disk is in Drive A. A:\> is displayed.

Step 1 Key in the following: A:\>**TEST2** **Enter**

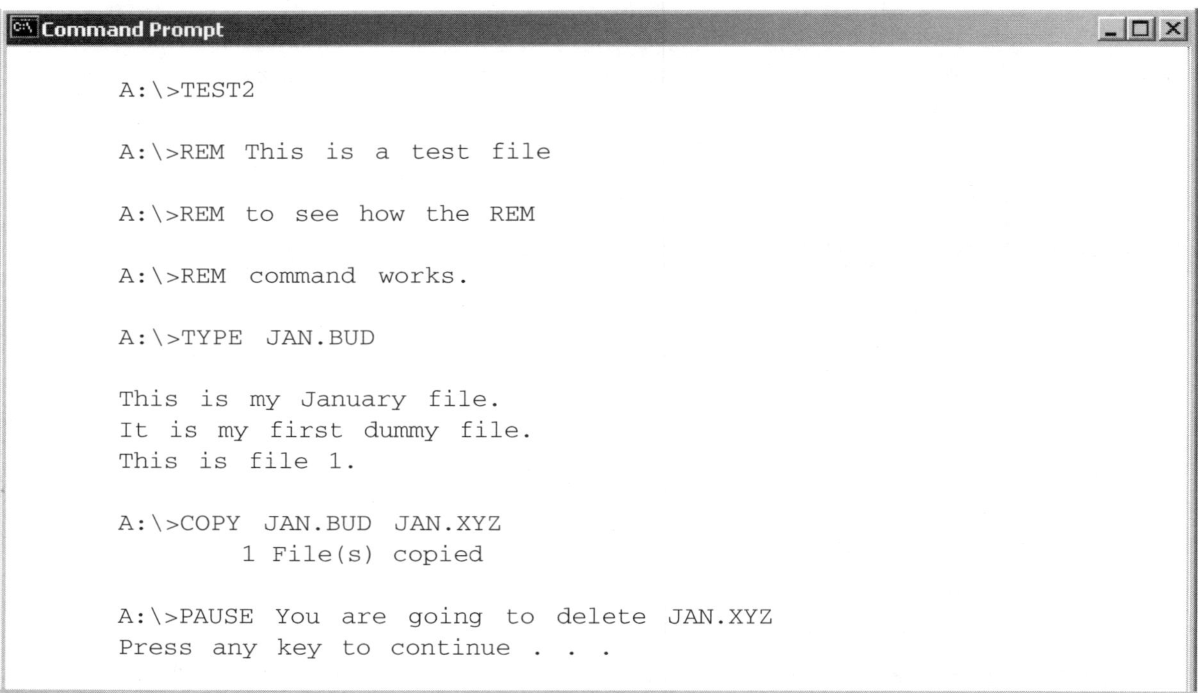

Command Prompt
A:\>TEST2
A:\>REM This is a test file
A:\>REM to see how the REM
A:\>REM command works.
A:\>TYPE JAN.BUD
This is my January file.
It is my first dummy file.
This is file 1.
A:\>COPY JAN.BUD JAN.XYZ
1 File(s) copied
A:\>PAUSE You are going to delete JAN.XYZ
Press any key to continue . . .

WHAT'S HAPPENING? You are at the same point as you were in the last activity. The batch file reached the PAUSE command. It has momentarily stopped running. You do not want to erase **JAN.XYZ**. You want the batch file to cease operation. Previous experience with the PAUSE command showed that pressing any key would continue running the program. If any key were pressed here, the next line in the file, DEL JAN.XYZ, would execute and the file **JAN.XYZ** would be erased. To stop this from happening, another action must be taken to interrupt the batch file process.

Step 2 Hold down the **Ctrl** key, and while it is down, press the letter **C**. Then release both keys.

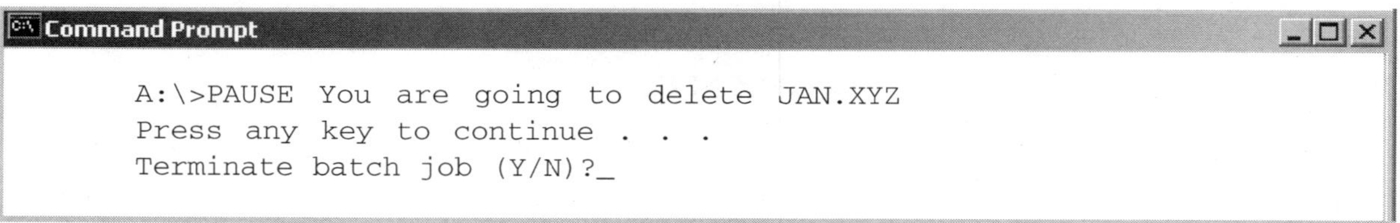

WHAT'S HAPPENING? The message is giving you a choice: either stop the batch file from running (**Y** for "yes") or continue with the batch file (**N** for "no"). If you press **Y**, the last line in the batch file, DEL JAN.XYZ, will not execute.

Step 3 Press **Y** **Enter**

Command Prompt

```
A:\>PAUSE You are going to delete JAN.XYZ
Press any key to continue . . .
Terminate batch job (Y/N)?Y

A:\>_
```

The system prompt is displayed. If the batch file was interrupted properly, **JAN.XYZ** should not have been deleted because the line, DEL JAN.XYZ should not have executed.

Step 4 Key in the following: A:\>**DIR JAN.XYZ** Enter

```
Command Prompt

A:\>DIR JAN.XYZ
 Volume in drive A is DATA
 Volume Serial Number is 3330-1807

 Directory of A:\

04/23/2000  04:03p                  73 JAN.XYZ
               1 File(s)             73 bytes
               0 Dir(s)       1,046,528 bytes free

A:\>_
```

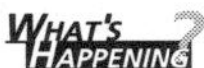

The file **JAN.XYZ** is still on the DATA disk. Pressing Ctrl + **C** at the line *PAUSE You are going to delete JAN.XYZ* broke into the batch file **TEST2.BAT** and stopped it from running. Because **TEST2.BAT** stopped executing and returned you to the system prompt, it never got to the command line DEL JAN.XYZ. Therefore, the file **JAN.XYZ** is still on the DATA disk. Although in this activity you broke into the batch file at the PAUSE statement, you can press Ctrl + **C** any time during the execution of a batch file. The batch file will stop when it has completed the current command before executing the next one. The problem is, with the speed of today's computers, it is difficult to ascertain how many lines of the batch file have been read by the operating system when you press Ctrl + **C**.

10.24 REPLACEABLE PARAMETERS IN BATCH FILES

In the same way that you use parameters with system commands, you can use parameters effectively in batch files. For instance, look at the command DIR A: /W.

```
Command      Command Line Parameter
DIR                A: /W
```

In the above example, the space and the / are delimiters. DIR is the command. A: and W are parameters that tell the operating system that you want a directory of A: and that you want it displayed in a wide mode. Parameters give the command additional instructions on what to do. When you use the DIR command as used above, the /W parameter is fixed; you cannot choose another letter to accomplish a wide mode display.

Many commands use ***variable*** or ***replaceable parameters***. An example of a command that uses a replaceable parameter is TYPE. TYPE requires one parameter, a file name, but the file name you use will vary; hence, it is a variable parameter. The TYPE command uses the parameter that you keyed in to choose the file to display on the screen. You can key in TYPE THIS.FIL or TYPE TEST.TXT or whatever file name you want. You replace the file name for the parameter, hence the term replaceable parameter.

```
Command          Replaceable Command Line Parameter
 TYPE                   THIS. FIL
```

or

```
Command          Replaceable Command Line Parameter
 TYPE                   TEST.TXT
```

Batch files can also use replaceable parameters, also called ***dummy parameters***, ***substitute parameters***, or ***positional parameters***. When you key in the name of the batch file to execute, you can also key in additional information on the command line that your batch file can use. What you are doing is parsing a command. To parse is to analyze something in an orderly way. In linguistics, to parse is to divide words and phrases into different parts in order to understand relationships and meanings. In computers, to parse is to divide the computer language statement into parts that can be made useful for the computer. In the above example, the TYPE command had the argument TEST.TXT passed to it so that it can display the contents of that variable. When you write the batch file, you supply the markers or place holders to let the batch file know that something, a variable, will be keyed in with the batch file name. The place holder, marker, or blank parameter used in a batch file is the percent sign (%) followed by a number from **0** through **9**. The % sign is the signal to the operating system that a parameter is coming. The numbers indicate what position the parameter is on the command line. Whatever is first is **%0**, usually the command itself. Thus, the command occupies %0.

The batch files that you have written so far deal with specific commands and specific file names, but the real power of batch files is their ability to use replaceable parameters. You are going to write a batch file in the usual way with specific file names, and then use the batch file to see how replaceable parameters work.

10.25 ACTIVITY: USING REPLACEABLE PARAMETERS

Note: The DATA disk is in Drive A. A:\> is displayed.

Step 1 Key in the following: A:\>**TYPE JAN.XYZ** Enter

Step 2 Key in the following: A:\>**DIR JAN.XYZ** Enter

Command Prompt

```
A:\>TYPE JAN.XYZ

This is my January file.
It is my first dummy file.
This is file 1.

A:\>DIR JAN.XYZ
 Volume in drive A is DATA
 Volume Serial Number is 3330-1807
```

```
 Directory of A:\

04/23/2000  04:03p                 73 JAN.XYZ
                1 File(s)             73 bytes
                0 Dir(s)       1,046,528 bytes free
A:\>_
```

WHAT'S HAPPENING? This file was created in the last activity. It has data in it and occupies 73 bytes of space on the disk. (Your file size may differ slightly.) If you remember, when you delete a file, the data is still on the disk. What if you wanted a way to delete the data completely so that it cannot ever be recovered? You can overwrite the file with new data. If you key in ECHO at the command line, you get a status report of whether ECHO is on or off. You can redirect the output of the ECHO command to your file, making it 13 bytes long and replacing the data in the file with the output of the ECHO command. You are going to first try this at the command line.

Step 3 Key in the following: A:\>**ECHO > JAN.XYZ** Enter

Step 4 Key in the following: A:\>**TYPE JAN.XYZ** Enter

Step 5 Key in the following: A:\>**DIR JAN.XYZ** Enter

```
Command Prompt

A:\>ECHO > JAN.XYZ

A:\>TYPE JAN.XYZ
ECHO is on.

A:\>DIR JAN.XYZ
 Volume in drive A is DATA
 Volume Serial Number is 3330-1807

 Directory of A:\

06/11/2001  11:16a                 13 JAN.XYZ
               1 File(s)              13 bytes
                0 Dir(s)       1,046,528 bytes free

A:\>_
```

WHAT'S HAPPENING? As you can see, it worked. You have really overwritten this file. Your data is no longer in the file to recover. This command would be useful when deleting files of a confidential nature. It would prevent most data recovery programs from being able to recover the data from your file. It can also be used in a batch file.

Step 6 Key in the following: A:\>**EDIT KILLIT.BAT** Enter
ECHO > JAN.XYZ Enter
DEL JAN.XYZ

Step 7 Press Alt + **F**. Press **X**.

Step 8 Press **Y**.

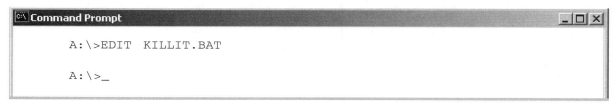

```
Command Prompt

A:\>EDIT  KILLIT.BAT

A:\>_
```

Edit is the tool you used to write the batch file. You created a simple batch file that sends data to **JAN.XYZ** and then deletes the file called **JAN.XYZ**. You then used the Edit menu to exit and save **KILLIT.BAT** to your disk.

Step 9 Key in the following: A:\>**TYPE KILLIT.BAT** Enter

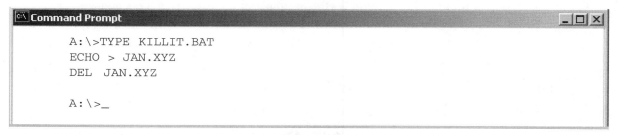

```
Command Prompt

A:\>TYPE KILLIT.BAT
ECHO > JAN.XYZ
DEL  JAN.XYZ

A:\>_
```

You displayed the contents of the **KILLIT.BAT** file. To execute this batch file, you must *call* it, which is another way of saying key in the command name—the name of the batch file.

Step 10 Key in the following: A:\>**KILLIT** Enter

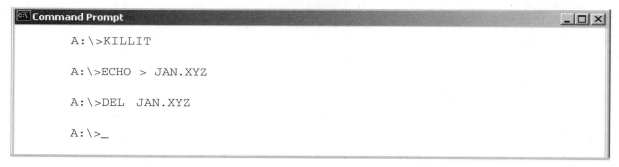

```
Command Prompt

A:\>KILLIT

A:\>ECHO > JAN.XYZ

A:\>DEL  JAN.XYZ

A:\>_
```

The batch file called **KILLIT** ran successfully. However, this batch file can be used only for the file called **JAN.XYZ**. You have deleted **JAN.XYZ** so now **KILLIT.BAT** is no longer useful.

What if you wanted to do the same sequence of commands for a file called **JAN.TMP** or **PERSONAL.FIL** or any other file on the disk? Until now, you would have to create another batch file using **JAN.TMP** instead of **JAN.XYZ**. You would write another batch file for **PERSONAL.FIL**. You can quickly clutter up your disks with many batch files, all doing the same thing but using different file names and having no value after they have executed. An easier way is to have a batch file that does the same steps—a generic batch file. When you execute it, you supply the specific parameter or file name that interests you. When you write this batch file, you need to supply a place for the name of the file. These places are called "replaceable parameters." They are percent signs followed by numbers.

You are going to edit **KILLIT.BAT** so that it uses replaceable parameters. In addition, you will document it and add some protection for yourself. When you key in the replaceable parameters, be sure to use the percent sign (%), then the number **1**, and not the lowercase of the letter L (**l**). Also note that there is no space between % and the number **1**.

Step 11 Key in the following:
A:\>**EDIT KILLIT.BAT** Enter
REM This batch file will make Enter
REM the data in a file difficult to recover. Enter
DIR %1 Enter
PAUSE You are going to kill the file, %1. Are you sure? Enter

Step 12 Replace **ECHO > JAN.XYZ** with **ECHO > %1**.

Step 13 Replace **DEL JAN.XYZ** with **DEL %1**.

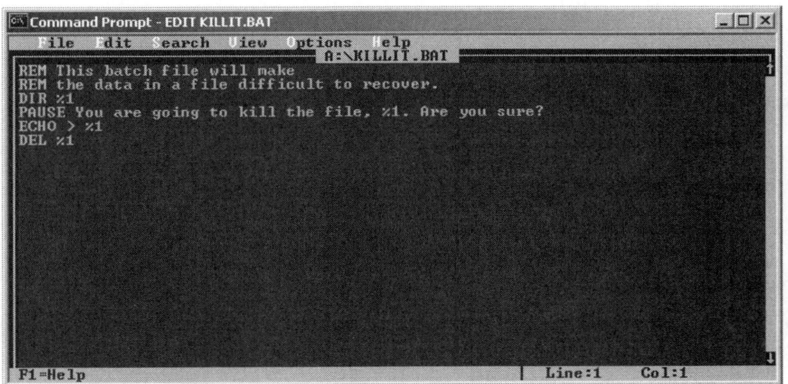

WHAT'S HAPPENING? Your edited file should look like the above screen. Remember, you must save the file to the disk.

Step 14 Press Alt + **F**. Press **X**.

Step 15 Press **Y**.

Step 16 Key in the following: A:\>**TYPE KILLIT.BAT** Enter

```
Command Prompt

A:\>TYPE KILLIT.BAT
REM This batch file will make
REM the data in a file difficult to recover.
DIR %1
PAUSE You are going to kill the file, %1. Are you sure?
ECHO > %1
DEL %1

A:\>_
```

You used Edit to edit the file **KILLIT.BAT**. You then saved it to the disk. You displayed the contents of the file on the screen. The contents of the batch file **KILLIT.BAT** are different from the previous version of **KILLIT.BAT**. By using the place holder **%1**, instead of a specific file name, you are saying that you do not yet know what file name (**%1**) you want these commands to apply to. When you run the batch file **KILLIT**, you will provide a value or parameter on the command line that the batch file will substitute for **%1**. For instance, if you key in on the command line, **KILLIT MY.FIL**, **KILLIT** is in the zero position on the command line (**%0**) and **MY.FIL** is in the first position on the command line (**%1**).

For you to understand the purpose of replaceable parameters, it is helpful to view them as *positional* parameters, their other name. The operating system gets the information or knows what to substitute by the position on the command line. The first piece of data on the command line is always in position 0; the second piece of data on the command line is always in position 1; the third piece of data on the command line is always in position 2, and so on.

Step 17 Key in the following: A:\>**KILLIT JAN.BUD** Enter

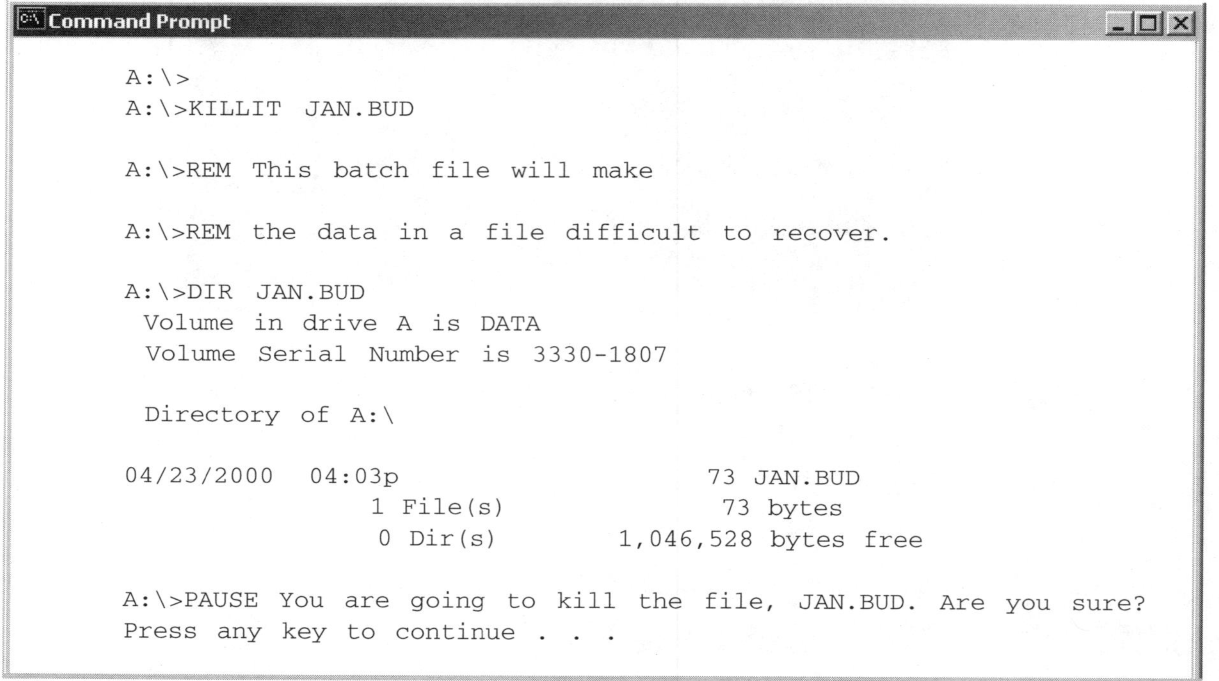

```
Command Prompt

A:\>
A:\>KILLIT JAN.BUD

A:\>REM This batch file will make

A:\>REM the data in a file difficult to recover.

A:\>DIR JAN.BUD
 Volume in drive A is DATA
 Volume Serial Number is 3330-1807

 Directory of A:\

04/23/2000  04:03p                  73 JAN.BUD
               1 File(s)             73 bytes
               0 Dir(s)       1,046,528 bytes free

A:\>PAUSE You are going to kill the file, JAN.BUD. Are you sure?
Press any key to continue . . .
```

What's Happening? In the command line **KILLIT JAN.BUD**, **KILLIT** is position 0 and **JAN.BUD** is position 1. The batch file **KILLIT** executed each command line. However, when it found **%1** in the batch file, it looked for the first position after **KILLIT** on the command line, which was **JAN.BUD**. It substituted **JAN.BUD** every time it found **%1**. You placed the **DIR %1** in the batch file to confirm that it is on the disk. The PAUSE statement allows you to change your mind. The **%1** in the PAUSE line identifies which file is to be killed.

Step 18 Press Enter

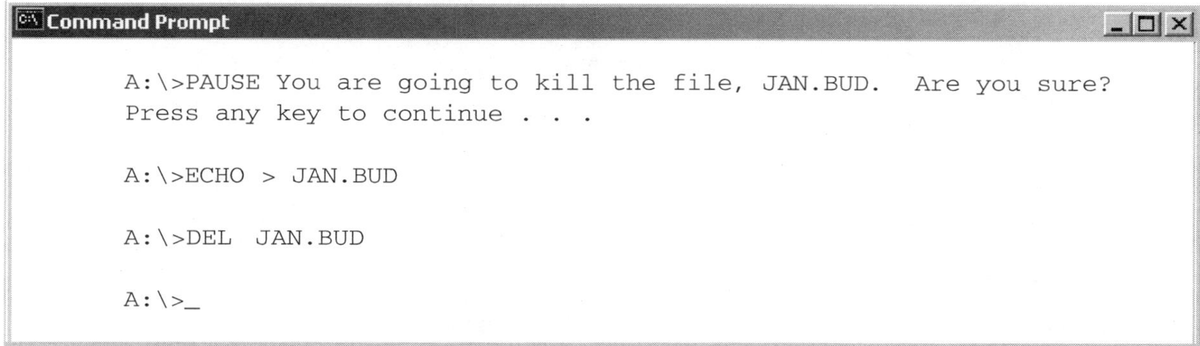

You have deleted the file. Even if you, or anyone else, try to recover it, the data is truly gone. You have written a generic or "plain wrap" batch file that allows you to use the same batch file over and over. All you have to supply is a value or parameter after the batch file name on the command line. Thus, you could key in **KILLIT BUSINESS.APP**, **KILLIT SALES.LET**, **KILLIT FEB.99**, **KILLIT TELE.SET**, or any other file name. The batch file will execute the same commands over and over, using the position 1 value (the file name) you key in after the batch file name. You can see that because this file is versatile, it is infinitely more useful than it was without positional parameters.

10.26 MULTIPLE REPLACEABLE PARAMETERS IN BATCH FILES

In the above example, you used one replaceable parameter. What happens if you need more than one parameter? For instance, if you want to include the COPY command in a batch file, COPY needs two parameters: *source* and *destination*. Many commands require more than one parameter. You may also use multiple parameters in batch files. You can have up to 10 dummy parameters (%0 through %9). Remember, replaceable parameters are sometimes called positional parameters because the operating system uses the position number in the command line to determine which parameter to use. The parameters are placed in order from left to right. For example, examine the command line:

```
COPY  MYFILE.TXT  YOUR.FIL
```

COPY is in the first position, %0 (computers always count beginning with 0, not 1). MYFILE.TXT is in the second position, %1, and YOUR.FIL is in the third position, %2.

The next activity will allow you to create a simple batch file with multiple replaceable parameters so you will see how the positional process works. Then you will write another batch file, and in it you will create a command that the operating system does not have. Your new command will copy all files *except* the ones you specify.

10.27 ACTIVITY: USING MULTIPLE REPLACEABLE PARAMETERS

Note: The DATA disk is in Drive A. A:\> is displayed.

Step 1 Key in the following:

A:\>**EDIT MULTI.BAT** Enter

REM This is a sample batch file Enter
REM using more than one replaceable parameter. Enter
TYPE %3 Enter
COPY %1 %2 Enter
TYPE %1

Step 2 Press Alt + **F**. Press **X**.

Step 3 Press **Y**.

Step 4 Key in the following: A:\>**TYPE MULTI.BAT** Enter

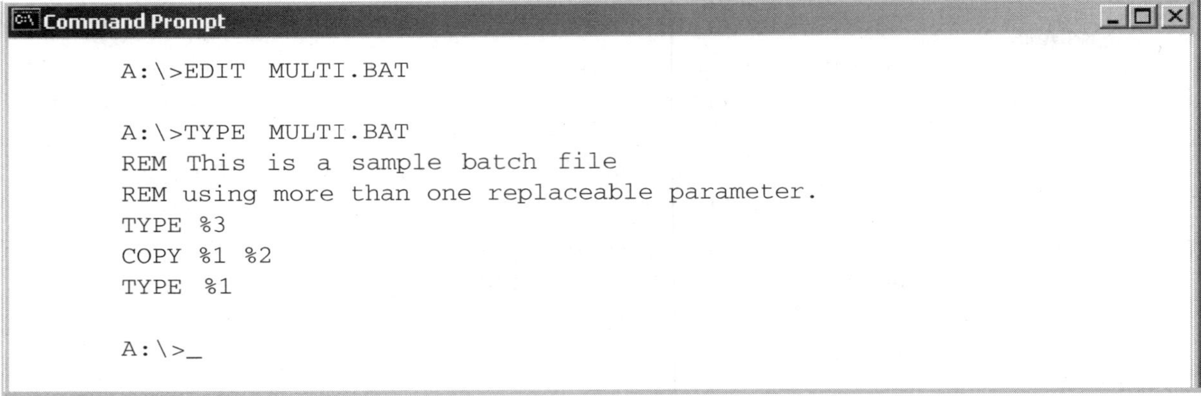

```
A:\>EDIT  MULTI.BAT

A:\>TYPE  MULTI.BAT
REM This is a sample batch file
REM using more than one replaceable parameter.
TYPE %3
COPY %1 %2
TYPE %1

A:\>_
```

WHAT'S HAPPENING? You keyed in and saved a batch file called **MULTI.BAT** on the root of the DATA disk. You then displayed the contents of **MULTI.BAT** on the screen. To execute it you must not only key in the command name **MULTI** but must also provide the command with the positional parameters that are referred to in the file. In the next step, you will key in **MULTI APR.99 LAST.ONE FILE2.SWT**. The batch file knows what to put in each percent sign because it looks at the position on the command line. It does not matter which order you use the %1 or %2 or %3 in the batch file, only the order you use on the command line. See Table 10.5.

Position 0 on the Command Line	Position 1 on the Command Line	Position 2 on the Command Line	Position 3 on the Command Line
MULTI	**APR.99**	**LAST.ONE**	**FILE2.SWT**
When the batch file needs a value for %0, it uses **MULTI**	When the batch file needs a value for %1, it uses **APR.99**	When the batch file needs a value for %2, it uses **LAST.ONE**	When the batch file needs a value for %3, it uses **FILE2.SWT**
Command	**Parameter**	**Parameter**	**Parameter**

TABLE 10.5 POSITIONAL PARAMETERS

Step 5 Key in the following: A:\>**MULTI APR.99 LAST.ONE FILE2.SWT** Enter

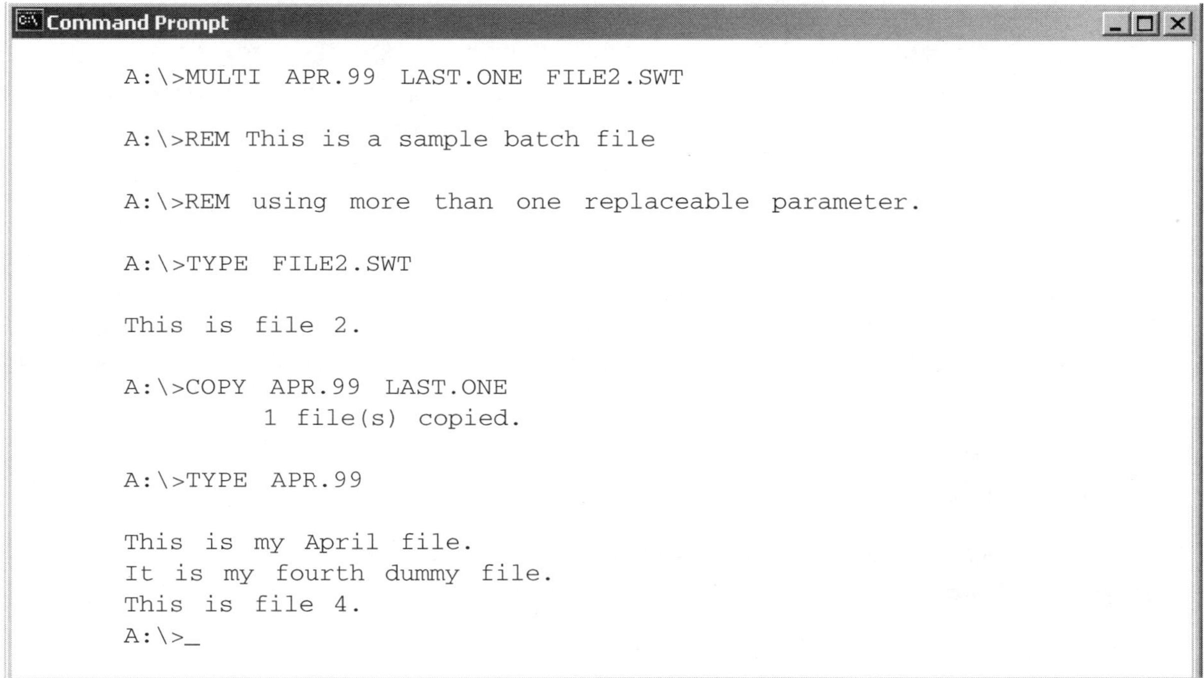

Command Prompt
A:\>MULTI APR.99 LAST.ONE FILE2.SWT
A:\>REM This is a sample batch file
A:\>REM using more than one replaceable parameter.
A:\>TYPE FILE2.SWT
This is file 2.
A:\>COPY APR.99 LAST.ONE
1 file(s) copied.
A:\>TYPE APR.99
This is my April file.
It is my fourth dummy file.
This is file 4.
A:\>_

Each time the batch file came to a command line and needed a value for a replaceable parameter (**%1**, **%2**, or **%3**), it looked to the command line as it was keyed in by you, and it counted over until it found the value to replace for the percent sign. **MULTI.BAT** is actually in the first position, which is counted as %0. The command itself is always first, or %0. Thus, to indicate the position of the replaceable parameters, %1 refers to the first position after the command, not the first item on the command line. %2 refers to the second position after the command, not the second item on the command line, and so on. Hence, when you refer to %1, you are referring to the first position after the command. When it needed a value for %1, it used **APR.99** because that was in the first position on the command line. When it needed a value for %2, it used **LAST.ONE** because that was in the second position on the command line, and, when it needed a value for %3, it used **FILE2.SWT** because that was in the third position on the command line. Instead of calling them replaceable parameters, it is easier to remember them as positional parameters because it is the position on the command line that matters, not where it occurs in the batch file. Although this batch file may show you how the positional parameters work, it is not very useful. It does not accomplish any logical task. You are going to use the same principle to create a command that the operating system does not have.

Step 6 Key in the following:

A:\>**EDIT NOCOPY.BAT** Enter
REM This batch file, NOCOPY.BAT, will hide specified files, Enter
REM then copy all other files from one location to another, Enter
REM then unhide the original files. Enter
ATTRIB +H %1 Enter
COPY %3*.* %2 Enter
ATTRIB -H %1

You created a batch file called **NOCOPY.BAT** using multiple positional parameters. You have created a command that the operating system does not have. It copies files selectively, allowing you to copy all files except those you hid. You must save the file to disk.

Step 7 Press Alt + **F**. Press **X**.

Step 8 Press **Y**.

Step 9 Key in the following: A:\>**TYPE NOCOPY.BAT** Enter

Command Prompt

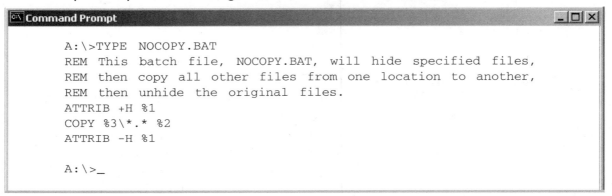

```
A:\>TYPE NOCOPY.BAT
REM This batch file, NOCOPY.BAT, will hide specified files,
REM then copy all other files from one location to another,
REM then unhide the original files.
ATTRIB +H %1
COPY %3\*.* %2
ATTRIB -H %1

A:\>_
```

You are displaying the contents of **NOCOPY.BAT**. To execute it, you must not only key in the command name—NOCOPY—but also provide the command with values for all the positional parameters. You want to copy all the files from the **CLASS** directory to the **TRIP** subdirectory except the files that have the **.ABC** file extension. Remember, parameters are separated by a space. On the command line you will key in **NOCOPY CLASS*.ABC TRIP CLASS**. The value *CLASS*.ABC* replaces parameter %1, *TRIP* replaces %2, and CLASS replaces %3. Notice that %1 will be used to represent a subdirectory and files ending with **.ABC**, while %2 and %3 will represent subdirectory names only.

Step 10 Key in the following: A:\>**NOCOPY CLASS*.ABC TRIP CLASS** Enter

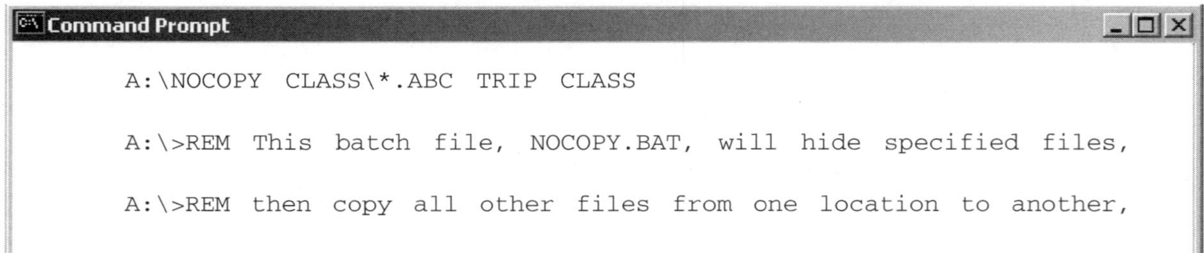

Command Prompt

```
A:\NOCOPY CLASS\*.ABC TRIP CLASS

A:\>REM This batch file, NOCOPY.BAT, will hide specified files,

A:\>REM then copy all other files from one location to another,
```

```
A:\>REM then unhide the original files.

A:\>ATTRIB +H CLASS\*.ABC

A:\>COPY CLASS\*.* TRIP
CLASS\JAN.PAR
CLASS\FEB.PAR
CLASS\MAR.PAR
CLASS\APR.PAR
CLASS\MAR.FIL
CLASS\JAN.FIL
CLASS\JAN.BUD
CLASS\MAR.BUD
CLASS\APR.BUD
        9 file(s) copied.

A:\>ATTRIB -H CLASS\*.ABC
A:\>_
```

WHAT'S HAPPENING? (*Note:* You may not see the command line you keyed in, as it may scroll off the screen.) You ran the batch file called **NOCOPY**. You substituted or provided the values: CLASS*.ABC (%1), TRIP (%2), and CLASS (%3). To check that the ***.ABC** files are not hidden in the **CLASS** directory and that they have not been copied to the **TRIP** directory, do the following:

Step 11 Key in the following: A:\>**DIR CLASS*.ABC** Enter

Step 12 Key in the following: A:\>**DIR TRIP*.ABC** Enter

Command Prompt

```
A:\>DIR CLASS\*.ABC
 Volume in drive A is DATA
 Volume Serial Number is 3330-1807

 Directory of A:\CLASS

04/23/2000  04:03p                  73 JAN.ABC
04/23/2000  04:03p                  75 FEB.ABC
04/23/2000  04:03p                  71 MAR.ABC
04/23/2000  04:18p                  72 APR.ABC
               4 File(s)            291 bytes
               0 Dir(s)       1,040,384 bytes free

A:\>DIR TRIP\*.ABC
 Volume in drive A is DATA
 Volume Serial Number is 3330-1807

 Directory of A:\TRIP

File Not Found

A:\>_
```

Your goal was achieved. To the operating system, the command sequence or string of commands looked like this:

```
ATTRIB +H CLASS\*.ABC
COPY CLASS\*.* TRIP
ATTRIB -H CLASS\*.ABC
```

When you keyed in **NOCOPY CLASS*.ABC TRIP CLASS**, you asked the operating system to load the batch file called **NOCOPY.BAT**. The first position after **NOCOPY** has the value of **CLASS*.ABC**. The second position has the value of **TRIP**, and the third position has the value of **CLASS**. Then the lines were executed in order:

1. **REM This batch file, NOCOPY.BAT, will hide specified files,**
   This line is documentation for you to know why you wrote this batch file.
2. **REM then copy all other files from one location to another,**
   This line is a continuation of the documentation for you to know why you wrote this batch file.
3. **REM then unhide the original files.**
   This line is a continuation of the documentation for you to know why you wrote this batch file.
4. **ATTRIB +H CLASS*.ABC**
   This line tells ATTRIB to hide all the files in the **CLASS** directory with the file extension of **.ABC**. The operating system knew which file and which directory were %1 and could substitute CLASS*.ABC for %1 because CLASS*.ABC held the first position (%1) after the command NOCOPY.
5. **COPY CLASS*.* TRIP**
   This line tells the operating system to copy files in a directory. It knew in which directory to get the files because CLASS was %3, so it substituted CLASS for %3. The operating system knew it could substitute CLASS for %3 because CLASS was in the third position after NOCOPY. It knew to copy all the files because you included *.*. It knew which directory to copy the files to because it substituted TRIP for %2. It could substitute TRIP for %2 because TRIP was in the second position after NOCOPY.
6. **ATTRIB -H CLASS*.ABC**
   This line tells the operating system to unhide all the files in the **CLASS** directory with the file extension of **.ABC**. It knew which files and which directory were %1 and could substitute CLASS*.ABC for %1 because CLASS*.ABC held the first position after the command NOCOPY.

This command, which you just wrote as a batch file with replaceable parameters, can be very useful. You can use it to copy files selectively from one disk to another or from one subdirectory to another. You do not need to take separate steps because all the steps are included in the batch file.

10.28 CREATING USEFUL BATCH FILES

Batch files are used to automate processes that otherwise take numerous commands in succession. With batch files you can, in essence, create new commands—commands that are not provided with the operating system.

The next batch file you will write will solve a problem. For backup purposes, you often have the same files on more than one subdirectory or floppy disk. You may want to compare which files are in which directory or on which disk. This normally would involve using the DIR command to view each directory or disk, or redirecting the output of the DIR command to the printer and comparing them. Why not let the computer do the work? You can do so with the FC command, which compares two files or sets of files and displays the differences between them. To be sure the DATA disk has all the necessary files, first you will copy the files from the \WINDOSBK\GAMES directory to the PROG\GAMES directory on the DATA disk.

10.29 ACTIVITY: WRITING USEFUL BATCH FILES

Note: The DATA disk is in Drive A with A:\> displayed.

Step 1 Key in the following:
A:\>**XCOPY C:\WINDOSBK\GAMES*.* A:\PROG\GAMES** Enter

Step 2 Press **D** to indicate a directory to be made. Press **A** to overwrite files when necessary.

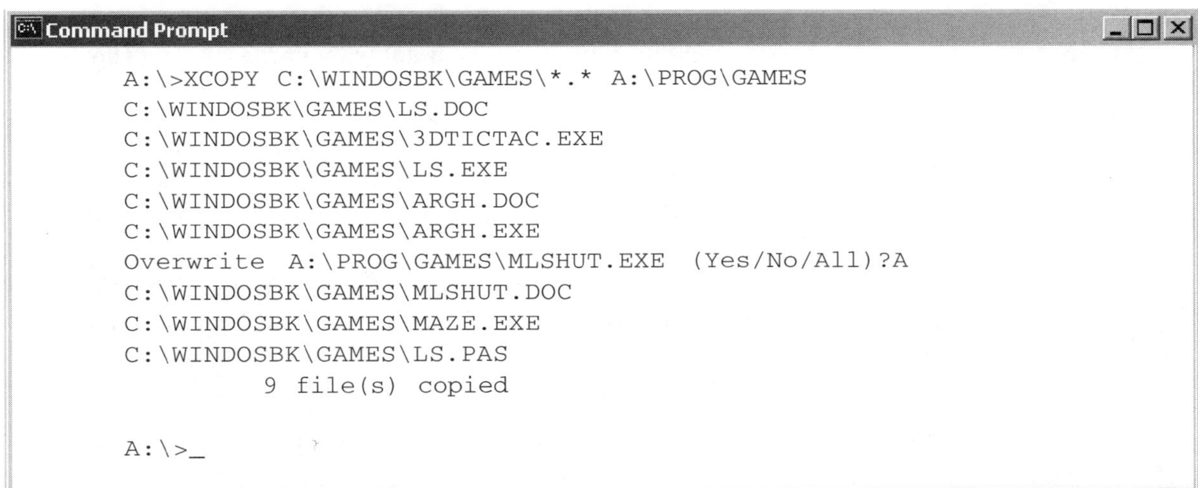

Command Prompt
A:\>XCOPY C:\WINDOSBK\GAMES*.* A:\PROG\GAMES
C:\WINDOSBK\GAMES\LS.DOC
C:\WINDOSBK\GAMES\3DTICTAC.EXE
C:\WINDOSBK\GAMES\LS.EXE
C:\WINDOSBK\GAMES\ARGH.DOC
C:\WINDOSBK\GAMES\ARGH.EXE
Overwrite A:\PROG\GAMES\MLSHUT.EXE (Yes/No/All)?A
C:\WINDOSBK\GAMES\MLSHUT.DOC
C:\WINDOSBK\GAMES\MAZE.EXE
C:\WINDOSBK\GAMES\LS.PAS
9 file(s) copied
A:\>_

WHAT'S HAPPENING? Though you have not copied all the files needed to play the games, you have copied all the files you will need to use with the batch file you will write.

Step 3 Key in the following:
A:\> **EDIT DCOMP.BAT** Enter
REM This batch file will compare the file names Enter
REM in two directories. Enter
DIR /A-D /B /ON %1 > SOURCE.TMP Enter
DIR /A-D /B /ON %2 > OTHER.TMP Enter
FC SOURCE.TMP OTHER.TMP ¦ MORE Enter
PAUSE You are about to delete SOURCE.TMP and OTHER.TMP Enter
DEL SOURCE.TMP Enter
DEL OTHER.TMP

Step 4 Press Alt + **F**. Press **X**.

Step 5 Press **Y**.

WHAT'S HAPPENING? This batch file uses the FC command to compare two files, each of which contains the file names in a different directory. Rather than writing the command line as **DIR ¦ SORT > SOURCE.TMP**, the command line was written as **DIR /A-D /B /ON %1 > SOURCE.TMP**. Why? You will examine each part of the line:

DIR /A-D This is the command used to display files that do not have the directory attribute, so any subdirectory names will not be displayed.

/B The /B parameter will eliminate all information in the directory display, such as

Volume in drive A is DATA
Volume Serial Number is 3330-1807
Directory of A:

as well as the file size, date, time, and long file name information.

/ON This parameter will order the display by name, sorting the display alphabetically.

> SOURCE.TMP This redirection character will send the output of the command line to the specified file, first **SOURCE.TMP**, and then **OTHER.TMP**. The files can now be compared to each other.

In addition, you took care to clean up by deleting both **SOURCE.TMP** and **OTHER.TMP** when the program finished executing. You are now going to test this batch file.

Step 6 Key in the following:
A:\>**DCOMP PROG\GAMES C:\WINDOSBK\GAMES** Enter

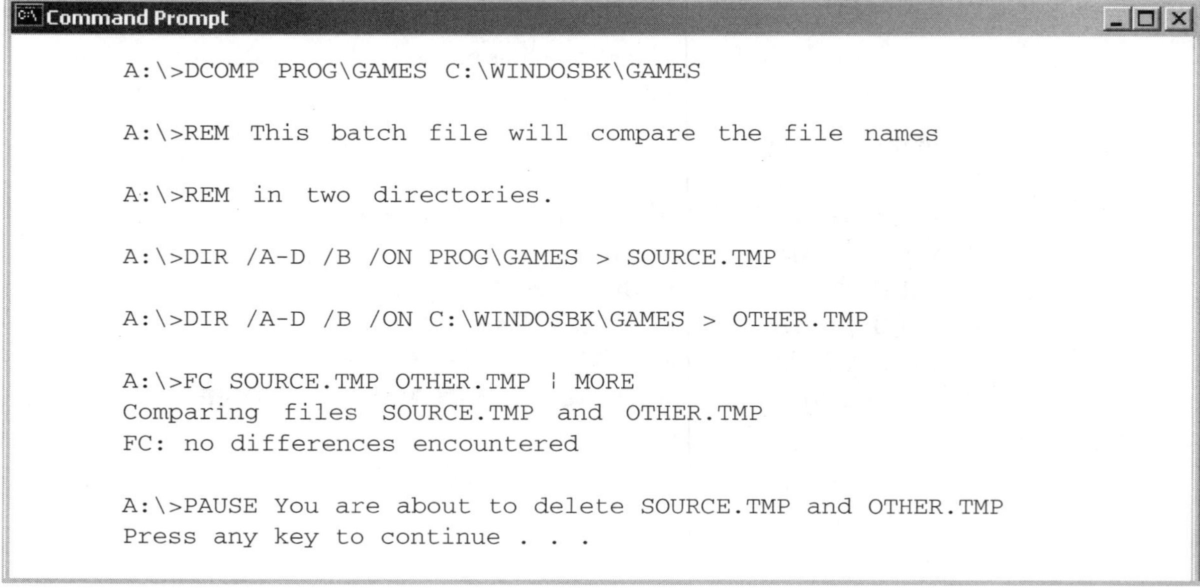
Command Prompt

```
A:\>DCOMP PROG\GAMES C:\WINDOSBK\GAMES

A:\>REM This batch file will compare the file names

A:\>REM in two directories.

A:\>DIR /A-D /B /ON PROG\GAMES > SOURCE.TMP

A:\>DIR /A-D /B /ON C:\WINDOSBK\GAMES > OTHER.TMP

A:\>FC SOURCE.TMP OTHER.TMP ¦ MORE
Comparing files SOURCE.TMP and OTHER.TMP
FC: no differences encountered

A:\>PAUSE You are about to delete SOURCE.TMP and OTHER.TMP
Press any key to continue . . .
```

The same files are on the DATA disk in the **PROG\GAMES** subdirectory and in the **C:\WINDOSBK\GAMES** subdirectory.

Step 7 Press **Enter**

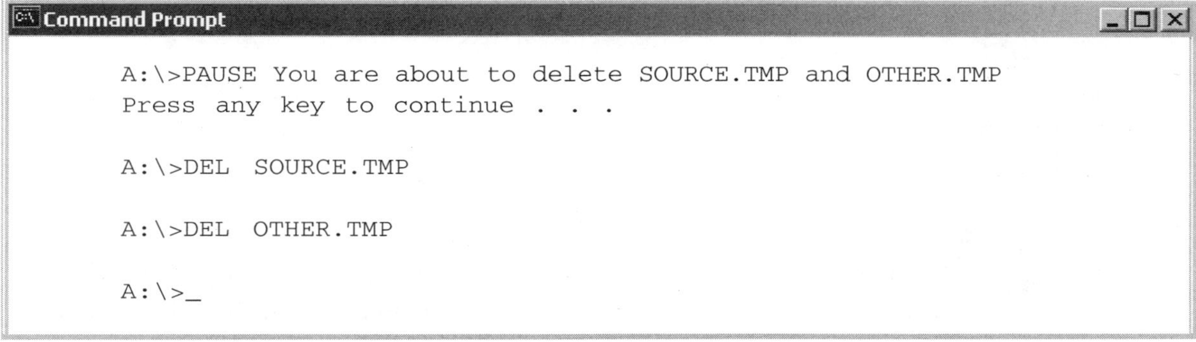

```
Command Prompt

A:\>PAUSE You are about to delete SOURCE.TMP and OTHER.TMP
Press any key to continue . . .

A:\>DEL  SOURCE.TMP

A:\>DEL  OTHER.TMP

A:\>_
```

You have deleted the **SOURCE.TMP** and **OTHER.TMP** files. What if there were differences?

Step 8 Key in the following: A:\>**DCOMP HPB C:\WINDOSBK\PHONE** **Enter**

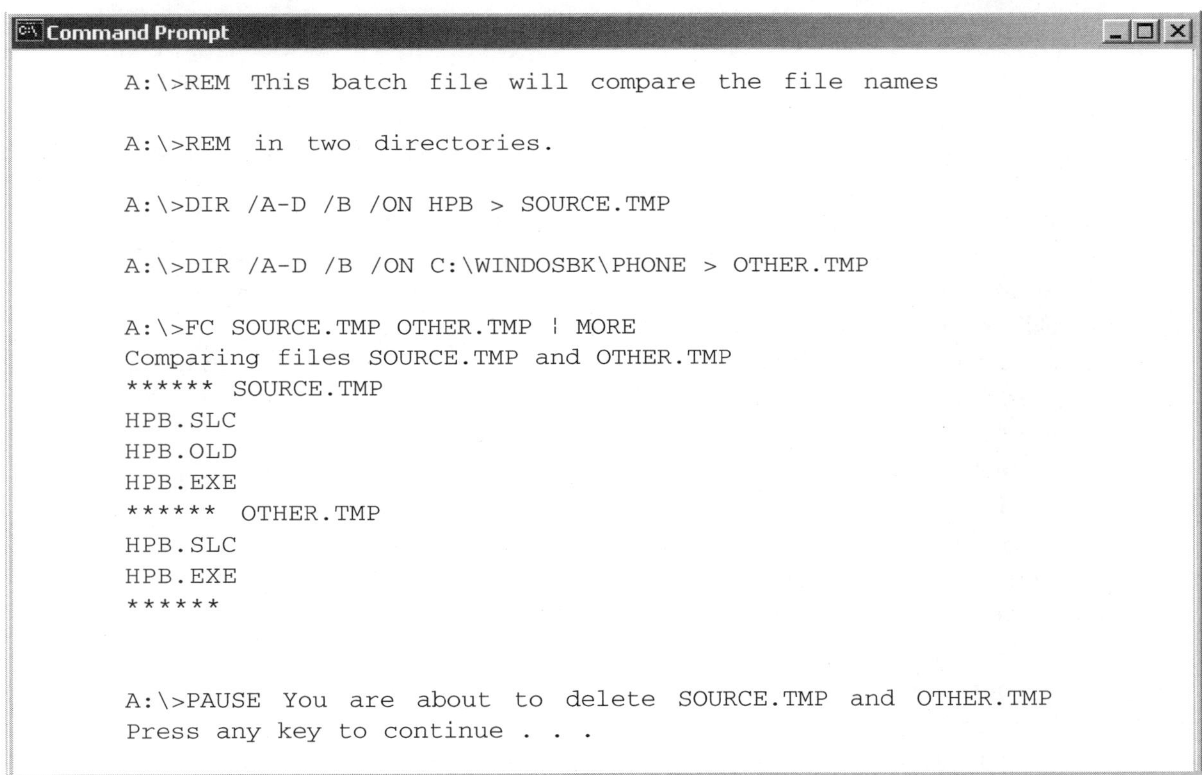

```
Command Prompt

A:\>REM This batch file will compare the file names

A:\>REM in two directories.

A:\>DIR /A-D /B /ON HPB > SOURCE.TMP

A:\>DIR /A-D /B /ON C:\WINDOSBK\PHONE > OTHER.TMP

A:\>FC SOURCE.TMP OTHER.TMP | MORE
Comparing files SOURCE.TMP and OTHER.TMP
****** SOURCE.TMP
HPB.SLC
HPB.OLD
HPB.EXE
****** OTHER.TMP
HPB.SLC
HPB.EXE
******


A:\>PAUSE You are about to delete SOURCE.TMP and OTHER.TMP
Press any key to continue . . .
```

There are differences. The DATA disk has one more file (**HPB.OLD**) than the **C:\WINDOSBK\PHONE** subdirectory.

Step 9 Press **Enter**

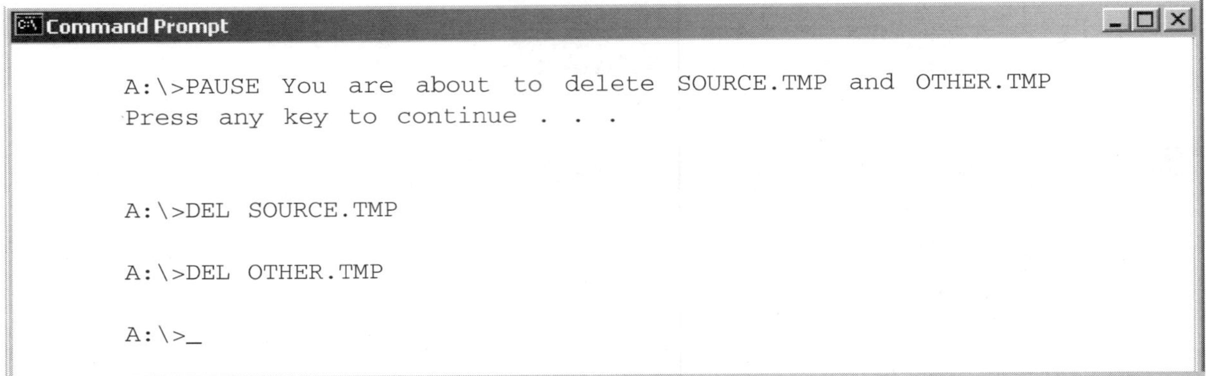
Command Prompt
A:\>PAUSE You are about to delete SOURCE.TMP and OTHER.TMP
Press any key to continue . . .
A:\>DEL SOURCE.TMP
A:\>DEL OTHER.TMP
A:\>_

WHAT'S HAPPENING

You have deleted the temporary files. You now have an easy way to compare the files in directories or on disks. You could add an @ECHO OFF statement at the beginning of the batch file so you would not see the REM statements and would see only the results of the command.

CHAPTER SUMMARY

1. Batch processing means running a series of instructions without interruption.
2. Interactive processing allows the user to interface directly with the computer and update records immediately.
3. Batch files allow a user to put together a string of commands and execute them with one command.
4. Batch files must have the .BAT or .CMD file extension.
5. Windows looks first internally for a command, then for a .COM file extension, then for a .EXE file extension, and finally for a .BAT or .CMD file extension.
6. Edit is a full-screen text editor used to write batch files.
7. A word processor, if it has a means to save files in ASCII, can be used to write batch files. ASCII files are also referred to as unformatted text files.
8. Batch files must be in ASCII.
9. A quick way to write an ASCII file is to use COPY CON. You copy from the console to a file.
10. Batch files are executed from the system prompt by keying in the batch file name.
11. Batch files are used for many purposes, such as to save keystrokes.
12. To "document" means to explain the purpose a file serves.
13. REM allows the user to document a batch file.
14. When the operating system sees REM, it displays on the screen whatever text follows REM. REM is not a command that executes.
15. ECHO OFF turns off the display of commands. Only the messages from the commands are displayed on the screen.
16. PAUSE allows the user to take some action before the batch file continues to execute.
17. PAUSE does not force the user to do anything. The batch file just stops running until the user presses a key.
18. To stop a batch file from executing, press the **Ctrl** key and the letter **C** (**Ctrl** + **C**).

19. Replaceable parameters allow the user to write batch files that can be used with many different parameters. The replaceable parameters act as place holders for values that the user will substitute when executing the batch file.
20. Replaceable parameters are sometimes called dummy, positional, or substitute parameters.
21. The percent sign (%) followed immediately by a numerical value, 0 to 9, indicates a replaceable parameter in a batch file.

KEY TERMS

batch file
batch processing
documented
dummy parameter
environmental variable
interactive processing
positional parameter
replaceable parameter
substitute parameter
variable

DISCUSSION QUESTIONS

1. Explain the purpose and function of batch files.
2. Compare and contrast batch processing with interactive processing.
3. You have a batch file called CHECK.BAT. You key in CHECK at the prompt. Where does it look for the file? What does the operating system then do?
4. What is an ASCII file? Why is it important in batch processing?
5. Under what circumstances can a word processor be used to write batch files?
6. Compare and contrast using Edit and COPY CON to write batch files.
7. Explain the purpose and function of the O and A parameters when used with the DIR command.
8. Explain the purpose and function of the REM command. What happens when the operating system sees REM in a batch file?
9. In a data-processing environment, what does it mean to document a batch file? Why would it be important to document a batch file?
10. Explain the purpose and function of the ECHO command.
11. Explain the purpose and function of the PAUSE command.
12. Why does the PAUSE command require user intervention?
13. How can you stop a batch file from executing once it has begun?
14. What are parameters?
15. What is a replaceable parameter? Describe how it might be used.
16. What indicates to the operating system that there is a replaceable parameter in a file?
17. What advantages are there to using replaceable parameters in a batch file?
18. Replaceable parameters are sometimes called positional parameters. Explain.
19. There appear to be two prompts when you do not use the ECHO OFF. Explain.

TRUE/FALSE QUESTIONS

For each question, circle the letter T if the statement is true and the letter F if the statement is false.

T F 1. Any command that can be keyed in at the system prompt can be included in a batch file.

T F 2. Each command in a batch file is on a separate line.

T F 3. Batch files should be written to complete a multicommand process that will need to be done one time only.

T F 4. The PAUSE command, when used in a batch file, requires user intervention.

T F 5. In the batch file line COPY MYFILE YOURFILE, COPY would be %1.

COMPLETION QUESTIONS

Write the correct answer in each blank space.

6. A word-processing program can be used to write batch files if it has a(n) ____________ output mode.
7. The maximum number of replaceable parameters in a batch file is ______.
8. In a data-processing environment, to explain the purpose of a batch file is to ______________ it.
9. Pressing the Ctrl and **C** keys simultaneously during the execution of a batch file will cause the file execution to __________.
10. If you wanted only the output of the command displayed on the screen and not the command itself, you would begin the batch file with the line ______________________.

MULTIPLE CHOICE QUESTIONS

For each question, write the letter for the correct answer in the blank space.

11. When searching a disk for an external command, the operating system will
    a. choose the command with the extension **.COM** before one with the extension **.BAT**.
    b. choose the command with the extension **.BAT** before one with the extension **.COM**.
    c. know automatically which file extension you are seeking.
    d. choose the extension **.BAT** before **.EXE**.
12. To execute a batch file called **THIS.BAT** at the prompt, key in:
    a. THIS %1
    b. %1
    c. THIS
    d. RUN BATCH THIS
13. In a batch file, to display the output of the command but not the command itself, use:
    a. ECHO ON
    b. ECHO OFF
    c. DISPLAY ON
    d. none of the above
14. Which of the following statements is true?
    a. Batch files cannot use variable parameters.
    b. Ctrl + **Z** interrupts the execution of a batch file.
    c. The PAUSE command will wait until the user takes some action.
    d. either a or b

15. Quitting a batch file by using Ctrl + C
    a. erases all the lines of the batch file that come after you quit.
    b. can be done only at a PAUSE during the batch file run.
    c. erases the batch files from the disk.
    d. can be done at any time while the batch file is running.

WRITING COMMANDS

Write five lines that would perform the following items in a batch file. Each question represents one line in the file.

16. Document the batch file, explaining that it is a demonstration file.

17. List the files in the **A:\TEMP** directory.

18. Display the contents of a file in the **A:\TEMP** directory that is specified when the batch file is called.

19. Rename the above file to **NAME.NEW**.

20. Display the contents of the **NAME.NEW** file.

APPLICATION ASSIGNMENTS

PROBLEM SET I

Note 1: Place the APPLICATION disk in Drive A. Be sure to work on the APPLICATION disk, not the DATA disk. On each batch file you write, be sure and include *your name*, the *name of the batch file*, and the *date* as part of the documentation.

Note 2: The homework problems will assume Drive C is the hard disk and the APPLICATION disk is in Drive A. If you are using another drive, such as floppy drive B or hard drive D, be sure and substitute that drive letter when reading the questions and answers.

Note 3: Test all of your batch files before submitting them to be sure they work correctly.

Note 4: To save a file with Edit under a new name, press Alt + **F** and choose **Save As**.

Note 5: It will be assumed that the root of the APPLICATION disk is the default drive and directory, unless otherwise specified.

Note 6: There can be more than one way to write a batch file. If your batch file works correctly, it is most likely written correctly.

PROBLEM A

TO CREATE DD.BAT

A-a Create a batch file called **DD.BAT**. This batch file should display the files on the root of the APPLICATION disk in date order with the most current date displayed first, and should pause so that the user may view the display one screenful at a time.

A-b Document **DD.BAT**. Remember to include *your name*, the *name of the batch file*, and the *date* as part of the documentation.

TO CREATE DDA.BAT

A-c Edit the batch file called **DD.BAT** and save it under the new name of **DDA.BAT**.

A-d Edit **DDA.BAT** so that it will look on any drive for files, using a replaceable parameter. It will still be displaying files in date order, with the most current date displayed first.

A-e Update the documentation.

TO CREATE SD.BAT

A-f Create a batch file called **SD.BAT** that will display subdirectories only, in order by name, on the root of the A drive.

A-g Document the file. Remember to include your name, the name of the batch file, and the date as part of the documentation.

TO CREATE SDD.BAT

A-h Edit **SD.BAT** created above and save the edited file as **SDD.BAT**. The **SDD.BAT** file will display subdirectories on a specified drive\directory in order by name.

A-i Use replaceable parameters.

A-j Document the file.

TO PRINT YOUR HOMEWORK

Step 1 Be sure the printer is on and ready to accept print jobs from your computer.

Step 2 Key in the following: A:\>**NAME** Enter

Step 3 Here is an example to key in, but your instructor will have other information that applies to your class. Key in the following:

Bette A. Peat Enter (*Your* name goes here.)

CIS 55 Enter (*Your* class goes here.)

T-Th 8-9:30 Enter (*Your* day and time go here.)

Chapter 10 Applications Enter

Problem A Enter

Step 4 Press F6 Enter

Step 5 If the information is correct, press **Y** and you are back to A:\>.

Step 6 Key in the following:
GO NAME.FIL DD.BAT DDA.BAT SD.BAT SDD.BAT Enter
(These files will not be deleted from your disk after printing.)

Step 7 In Notepad, click **File**. Click **Print**. Close Notepad.

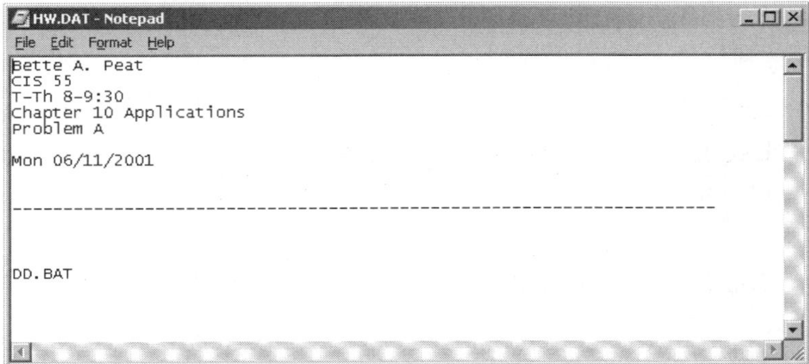

PROBLEM B

TO CREATE EXTRA.BAT

B-a Copy all the files with the **.TXT** extension from the **WINDOSBK** subdirectory to the root directory of the APPLICATION disk. (Overwrite existing files.)

B-b Create a batch file named **EXTRA.BAT** that will do the following:

- Clear the screen.
- Display the root directory of the APPLICATION disk for any file that has **.TXT** as a file extension.
- Make a copy of the file called **DANCES.TXT** and call the copy **NEWEST.DAN**.

- Display the contents of the file called **NEWEST.DAN**.
- Give the user time to read the file.
- Erase the file called **NEWEST.DAN**.

B-c Document **EXTRA.BAT**, including your name, the name of the file, and the date.

TO CREATE EXTRA2.BAT

B-d Edit **EXTRA.BAT** and save it as **EXTRA2.BAT**. It will do all that **EXTRA.BAT** does but will

- use replaceable parameters so that the user may choose what files to display. (Use only one parameter to represent the entire file specification, such as ***.FIL** or **MY.FIL**)
- allow any existing file to be copied to a new file that the user names.
- display the contents of the newly created file.
- provide a way for the user to change her or his mind and not delete any files.

TO PRINT YOUR HOMEWORK

Step 1 Be sure the printer is on and ready to accept print jobs from your computer.

Step 2 Use Edit to edit **NAME.FIL**. Change the last line from Problem A to Problem B.

Step 3 Key in the following:
GO NAME.FIL EXTRA.BAT EXTRA2.BAT Enter

Step 4 In Notepad, click **File**. Click **Print**. Close Notepad.

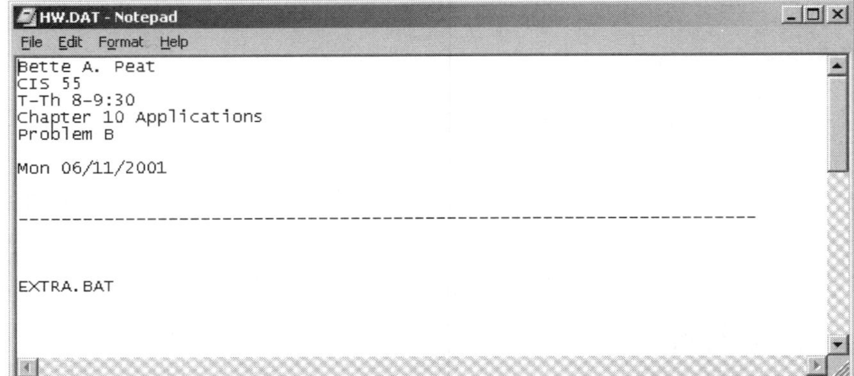

PROBLEM C

TO CREATE CHECKIT.BAT

C-a Write and document a batch file using replaceable parameters called **CHECKIT.BAT** that will

- check the status of a specified disk.
- see if any files are noncontiguous on that disk.
- do a wide display of the root directory of that disk.
- pause as necessary so users can view all of each display.

TO CREATE LIST.BAT

C-b Write and document a batch file called **LIST.BAT** that will use replaceable parameters to display the contents of three files, using the TYPE command, instead of only one file. (*Hint*: Think about how many replaceable parameters you will want to use.) Use **JAN.99**, **BYE.TXT**, and **DRAMA.TV** to test your file.

TO PRINT YOUR HOMEWORK

Step 1 Be sure the printer is on and ready to accept print jobs from your computer.

Step 2 Use Edit to edit **NAME.FIL**. Change the last line from Problem B to Problem C.

Step 3 Key in the following: **GO NAME.FIL CHECKIT.BAT LIST.BAT** Enter

Step 4 In Notepad, click **File**. Click **Print**. Close Notepad.

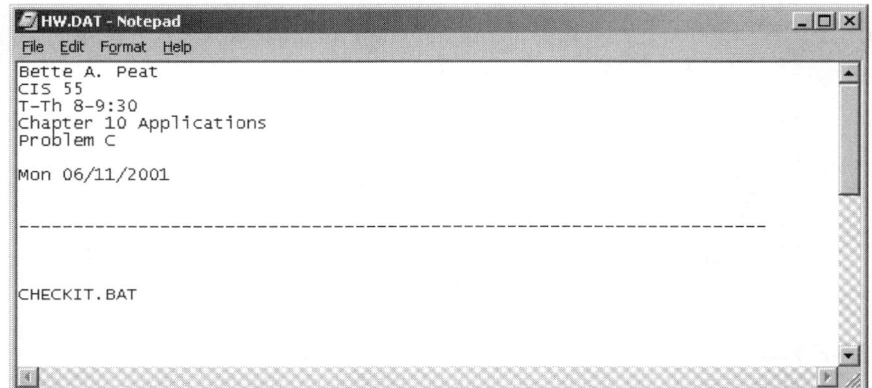

PROBLEM D: CHALLENGE ASSIGNMENTS

The following three batch file assignments use commands in combination that may not have been specifically discussed or shown by example in the chapter. Research and experimentation may be required in order to write these batch files.

TO CREATE CDD.BAT

D-a Write and document a batch file called **CDD.BAT** that will allow you to change drives and directories on one line (the line used to run the batch file).

TO CREATE NODEL.BAT

D-b Using **NOCOPY.BAT**, created in this chapter, as a model, write and document a batch file called **NODEL.BAT** that will

- allow you to delete all the files *except* the file(s) you hide in a specified subdirectory.
- view the files you are about to delete.
- clear the screen when necessary to make it easy for the user to read what is happening in the file.
- give the user an opportunity to cancel prior to deleting the files.
- delete the files.
- unhide the files.
- view which files remain.

D-c Document the batch file completely, explaining precisely what the file will do, and giving an example of how to run the file.

Hint 1: Create a practice subdirectory, such as **\TEMP**, on the APPLICATION disk. Use the **NODEL** batch file with the files that you copy into this temporary subdirectory, such as the ***.RED** files and the ***.FIL** files. If you make a mistake, you will not delete all the files on your APPLICATION disk.

Hint 2: If you do not want to be asked for confirmation from the DEL command, you can use the command DEL *.* < Y.FIL. You will need to copy **Y.FIL** from **\WINDOSBK** to the root directory of the APPLICATION disk.

TO CREATE NEWSUB.BAT

D-d Write and document a batch file called **NEWSUB.BAT**, using replaceable parameters, that will accomplish what is specified in the following documentation:

```
REM This file will allow the user to create a subdirectory
REM on a drive specified by the user, and with a name specified
REM by the user, and then copy files (both location and
REM file names specified by the user) to the new subdirectory.
REM This batch file is flexible, so any of the elements can be
REM changed by the user when executing this file.(Elements are
REM DESTINATION FOR NEW SUBDIRECTORY, NEW SUBDIRECTORY NAME,
REM LOCATION OF FILES TO BE COPIED, and FILES TO BE COPIED.)
REM The newly created subdirectory with its files will then be
REM displayed on the screen.
```

D-e Include the above lines in the documentation of the file.

D-f You may want to delete the **TEMP** directory created with the **NODEL.BAT** assignment, and use it again to write and debug **NEWSUB.BAT**.

TO PRINT YOUR HOMEWORK

Step 1 Be sure the printer is on and ready to accept print jobs from your computer.

Step 2 Use Edit to change the last two lines in **NAME.FIL** to read:

Chapter 10 Challenge Assignments

Problem D

Step 3 Key in the following:
GO NAME.FIL CDD.BAT NODEL.BAT NEWSUB.BAT Enter

Step 4 In Notepad, click **File**. Click **Print**. Close Notepad.

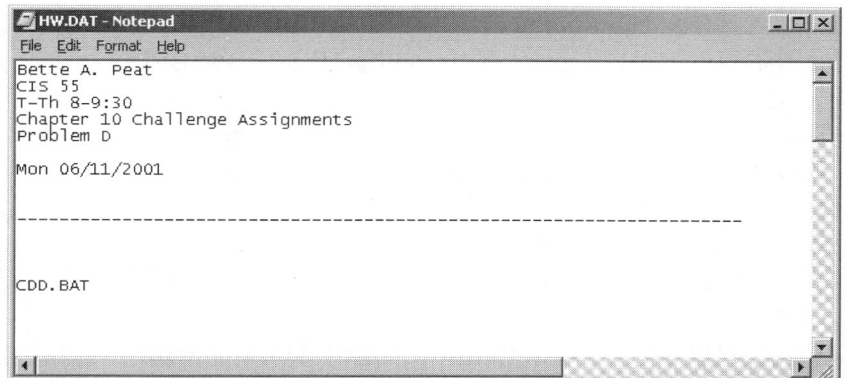

CAUTION! IF YOU CREATED A TEMP DIRECTORY ON THE APPLICATION DISK, DELETE THAT DIRECTORY BEFORE GOING ON TO CHAPTER 11.

PROBLEM SET II—BRIEF ESSAY

Discuss replaceable parameters, including how they work and why they are useful. Include the number of parameters available and the numbering sequence used to represent commands in your discussion.

CHAPTER

11

ADVANCED BATCH FILES

LEARNING OBJECTIVES

After completing this chapter you will be able to:

1. List commands used in batch files.
2. List and explain batch file rules.
3. Explore the function of the REM, PAUSE, and ECHO commands.
4. Explain the use of batch files with shortcuts.
5. Explain the purpose and function of the GOTO command.
6. Explain the purpose and function of the SHIFT command.
7. Explain the purpose and function of the IF command.
8. Explain the purpose and function of the IF EXIST/IF NOT EXIST command.
9. Explain the purpose and function of the IF ERRORLEVEL command.
10. Explain the purpose and function of writing programs.
11. Explain the purpose and function of the environment and environmental variables.
12. Explain the use of the SET command.
13. Explain the purpose and function of the FOR...IN...DO command.
14. Explain the purpose and function of the CALL command.

STUDENT OUTCOMES

1. Use the ECHO command to place a blank line in a batch file.
2. Use the GOTO command in conjunction with a label to create a loop.
3. Use a batch file with a shortcut.
4. Use the SHIFT command to move parameters.
5. Use the IF command with strings for conditional processing.

6. Test for null values in a batch file.
7. Use the IF EXIST/IF NOT EXIST command to test for the existence of a file or a subdirectory.
8. Use the SET command.
9. Use the environment and environmental variables in batch files.
10. Use the IF ERRORLEVEL command with XCOPY to write a batch file for testing exit codes.
11. Use the FOR...IN...DO command for repetitive processing.
12. Use the CALL command in a batch file.

CHAPTER OVERVIEW

You learned in Chapter 10 how to write simple batch files and use replaceable parameters. Some commands allow you write even more powerful batch files that act like sophisticated programs.

This chapter focuses on the remaining batch file commands, which will allow you to write sophisticated batch files. You will further refine your techniques in working with the environment.

11.1 BATCH FILE COMMANDS

A quick summary of batch file rules tells us that any batch file must have the file extension of .BAT or .CMD, it must always be an ASCII file, and it must include legitimate commands. In addition, you can use replaceable or positional parameters to create generic batch files. Batch file commands are not case sensitive. You may use any command in a batch file that you can use on the command line, as well as some specific batch file commands. See Table 11.1 for batch file commands.

Command	Purpose
CALL	Calls one batch program from another without causing the first batch program to stop. In Windows 2000 Professional, CALL now accepts labels as the target of the call.
ECHO	Displays or hides the text in batch programs while the program is running. Also used to determine whether commands will be “echoed” to the screen while the program file is running.
ENDLOCAL	Ends localization of environment changes in a batch file, restoring environment variables to their values before the matching SETLOCAL command. There is an implicit ENDLOCAL at the end of the batch file.
FOR	Runs a specified command for each file in a set of files. This command can also be used at the command line.
GOTO	Directs the operating system to a new line that you specify with a label.
IF	Performs conditional processing in a batch program, based on whether or not a specified condition is true or false.

PAUSE	Suspends processing of a batch file and displays a message prompting the user to press a key to continue.
REM	Used to document your batch files. The operating system ignores any line that begins with REM, allowing you to place lines of information in your batch program or to prevent a line from running.
SETLOCAL	Begins localization of environmental variables in a batch file. Localization lasts until a matching ENDLOCAL command is encountered or the end of the batch file is reached.
SHIFT	Changes the position of the replaceable parameter in a batch program.

TABLE 11.1 BATCH FILE COMMANDS

You have already used ECHO, PAUSE, and REM. You will now learn the remaining batch file commands, which allow you to create complex batch files. Using these commands is similar to using a programming language. Batch files have a limited vocabulary (the commands listed above), a syntax, and a programming logic. Batch files are also limited in the kinds of programming they can do. They do not have the power or the flexibility of a "real" programming language such as Visual Basic or C++. Batch files, however, accomplish many things in the Windows environment.

11.2 A REVIEW OF THE REM, PAUSE, AND ECHO COMMANDS

The REM command in a batch file indicates to the operating system that whatever text follows is to be displayed, but only if ECHO has *not* been turned off. If a command follows REM, it will be displayed but not executed. Remarks can be a string of up to 123 characters, and typically they document batch files. Placing REM in front of a command will allow you to execute a batch file or the CONFIG.SYS file without executing the command that follows it. This allows you to disable a line or lines without having to actually delete them.

The PAUSE command stops a batch file from continuing to execute until you press any key. It tells you to press any key to continue, but does not do any ***conditional processing***.

Remember, to interrupt a batch file, you can always press **Ctrl** + **C** or **Ctrl** + **Break**. Pressing this key combination will interrupt the execution of the batch file. There is one warning—if the batch file has called an external command and the operating system is in the middle of executing a command such as FORMAT or DISKCOPY, it will finish executing the command before exiting the batch file. **Ctrl** + **C** stops the execution of the batch file itself—it will not stop the execution of a .EXE or .COM program.

The ECHO command can be used either on a command line or in a batch file. It is a special command that turns on or turns off the echoing of commands to the screen. If you key in the command ECHO by itself on the command line or include it in a batch file, it will return the status of ECHO: either ECHO on or ECHO off. When ECHO is on, all the commands in a batch file are displayed on the screen. When ECHO is off, you see the output of the command, but not the command itself. Normally ECHO is on, which is particularly useful when you want to track the operation of a batch file. However, when a batch file runs successfully, the display of commands can clutter the screen.

In a batch file, if you do not wish to see each command on the screen, you can issue the command ECHO OFF. The batch file commands are not displayed, but any messages that a command such as COPY issues will be displayed, for example, "1 file(s) copied." Depending on your preferences, you can key in ECHO ON or ECHO OFF within the batch file to display or not display the commands. In addition, if you precede ECHO OFF with @, the words ECHO OFF will not appear on the screen.

11.3 ADVANCED FEATURES OF ECHO AND REM

There are some interesting features and variations you can implement with both REM and ECHO. One problem with REM is that the operating system recognizes it as a command and must take time to process it. A shortcut is to use a double colon (::) instead of REM in front of a remark, or documentation line. This will save valuable processing time because the operating system treats all lines beginning with a colon as a label and ignores them unless they are "called" elsewhere in the batch file. This will be further explained later.

When you turn ECHO off, you still get the display of messages such as "1 file(s) copied." Sometimes you do not wish to see messages. You can use redirection with standard output to redirect the output of a command to a device called NUL. As the name implies, NUL means send it to "nothing." When you send the output to NUL, it goes nowhere, and it is not displayed on the screen.

Although redirecting the output of a command to the NUL device will suppress messages such as "1 file(s) copied," it will not suppress a message generated by the operating system like "File not found."

You often want to place a blank line in a batch file for aesthetic purposes or to highlight particular commands. There is, of course, no such thing as a blank line. In the word-processing world, when you want a blank line, you press the [Enter] key, which places a carriage return in the document and prints as a blank line. This does not work in batch files. In a batch file, the operating system simply ignores it when you press [Enter]. Pressing [Enter] does not leave a blank line. If you use REM, you will see nothing if ECHO is off. If you place the word ECHO in the batch file, it will report whether ECHO is on or off. An easy method to get a blank line is to key in ECHO followed by a period. There can be no space between ECHO and the period.

11.4 ACTIVITY: USING ECHO AND NUL

Note: The DATA disk is in Drive A. Open a Command Prompt window. A:\> is displayed.

Step 1 Use an editor to create and save the following batch file called **ONE.BAT**, pressing the [Enter] key only where indicated.

:: This is a test of a batch file using [Enter]
:: different features. [Enter]
COPY CAROLYN.FIL BOOK.FIL [Enter]
[Enter]
TYPE BOOK.FIL [Enter]
ECHO [Enter]
DEL BOOK.FIL [Enter]
COPY NO.FIL BOOK.FIL [Enter]

Step 2 Close the editor and then key in the following: A:\>**TYPE ONE.BAT** Enter

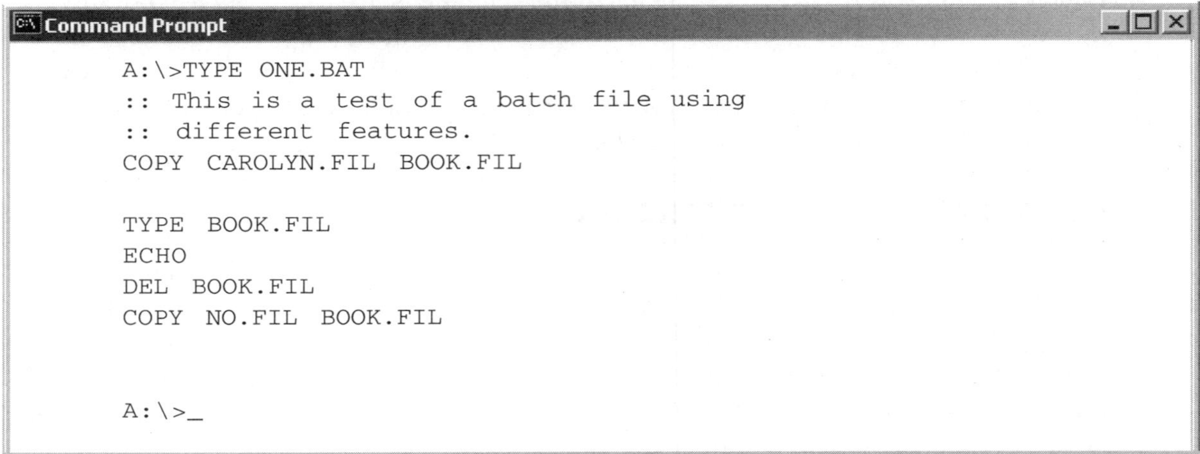

```
Command Prompt
A:\>TYPE ONE.BAT
:: This is a test of a batch file using
:: different features.
COPY CAROLYN.FIL BOOK.FIL

TYPE BOOK.FIL
ECHO
DEL BOOK.FIL
COPY NO.FIL BOOK.FIL


A:\>_
```

Step 3 Key in the following: A:\>**ONE** Enter

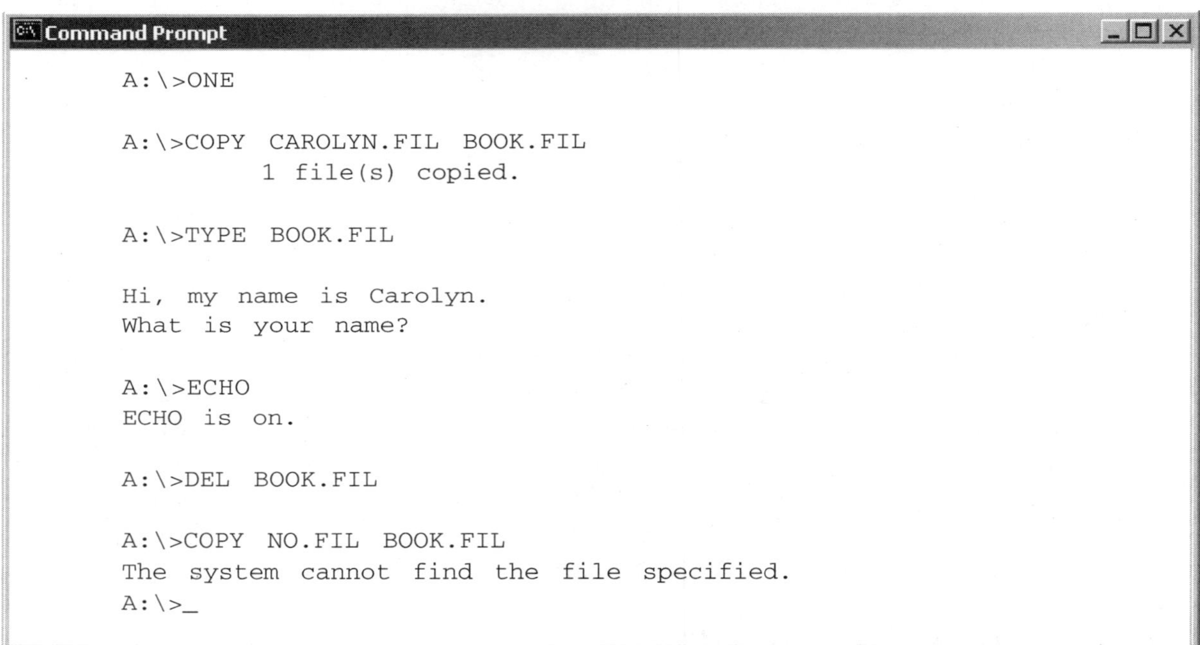

```
Command Prompt
A:\>ONE

A:\>COPY CAROLYN.FIL BOOK.FIL
        1 file(s) copied.

A:\>TYPE BOOK.FIL

Hi, my name is Carolyn.
What is your name?

A:\>ECHO
ECHO is on.

A:\>DEL BOOK.FIL

A:\>COPY NO.FIL BOOK.FIL
The system cannot find the file specified.
A:\>_
```

WHAT'S HAPPENING? You see messages as well as the output.

Step 4 Edit and save **ONE.BAT** so it looks as follows:

```
@ECHO OFF
:: This is a test of a batch file using
:: different features.
COPY CAROLYN.FIL BOOK.FIL > NUL
ECHO.
TYPE BOOK.FIL
ECHO.
DEL BOOK.FIL
COPY NO.FIL BOOK.FIL > NUL
```

Step 5 Key in the following: A:\>**ONE** Enter

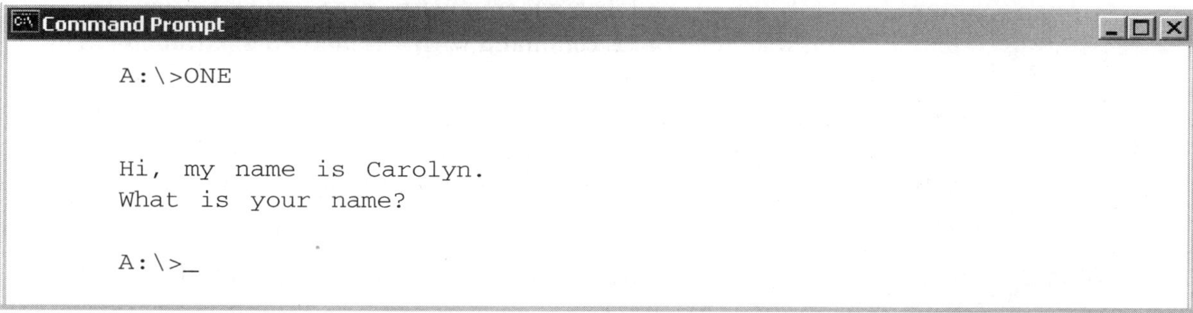
Command Prompt
A:\>ONE
Hi, my name is Carolyn.
What is your name?
A:\>_

WHAT'S HAPPENING? You now do not see your messages or remarks. You also get some blank lines. The COPY command could not find **NO.FIL** and the error message was redirected to the NUL device and was not displayed.

11.5 THE GOTO COMMAND

By using the GOTO command, a batch file can be constructed to behave like a program written in a programming language such as BASIC or C++. The GOTO command will branch to a specific part within a batch file, creating a loop. A ***loop*** is an operation that will repeat steps until you stop the loop either by using an IF statement or by breaking into the batch file with Ctrl + **C**.

The GOTO command works in conjunction with a label. This label is not to be confused with a volume label on a disk. A label is any name you choose to flag a location in a batch file. A label is preceded by a colon (:) and is ignored by the operating system until called with the GOTO command. A double colon (::), used earlier for REM statements, ensures that the operating system will always disregard the line since a colon may not be used as a label name. A label can be no longer than eight characters. The label itself is not a command, it just identifies a location in a batch file. When a batch file goes to a label, it carries out whatever command follows on the line after the label. GOTO has one parameter—GOTO label. Although it is not necessary that labels be exactly the same (i.e., the same case) it is still wise to make them the same case.

11.6 ACTIVITY: USING THE GOTO COMMAND

Note: The DATA disk should be in Drive A with A:\> displayed.

Step 1 Use any text editor to create and save a batch file called **REPEAT.BAT**. Key in the following using exactly the same case:

```
REM This file displays many times the contents
REM of a file.
:REPEAT
TYPE %1
PAUSE
GOTO REPEAT
```

WHAT'S HAPPENING? You have written a small batch file. The first two lines are remarks that will not execute. You are not including ECHO OFF, because you want to see what is happening in your batch file. Omitting ECHO OFF is a way to "debug" a batch file program. ***Debug*** means to see and repair any errors. The third line (:REPEAT) is a label, which must be preceded by a colon. The fourth line is a simple TYPE command with a replaceable parameter. The PAUSE command is placed on the fifth line so you may see what is happening. The sixth and last line is the loop. The GOTO tells the batch file to return to the label (:REPEAT). It will then return to line 4 and execute the TYPE command. It will then read lines 5 and 6 and continually repeat the process.

Step 2 You must be at the system prompt, not in the editor. Key in the following:
A:\>**REPEAT APRIL.TXT** Enter

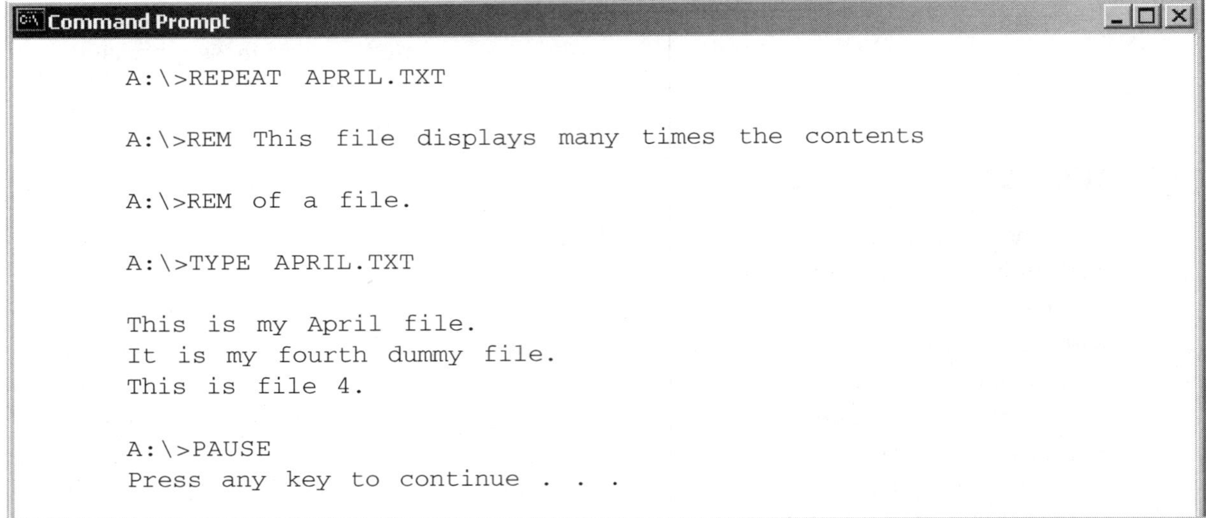

```
Command Prompt

A:\>REPEAT APRIL.TXT

A:\>REM This file displays many times the contents

A:\>REM of a file.

A:\>TYPE APRIL.TXT

This is my April file.
It is my fourth dummy file.
This is file 4.

A:\>PAUSE
Press any key to continue . . .
```

WHAT'S HAPPENING? The first two lines displayed are remarks. The label was ignored, but the TYPE command was executed. The next line has paused the batch file. You need to press Enter to continue.

Step 3 Press Enter

```
Command Prompt

A:\>PAUSE
Press any key to continue . . .


A:\>GOTO REPEAT

A:\>TYPE APRIL.TXT

This is my April file.
It is my fourth dummy file.
This is file 4.

A:\>PAUSE
Press any key to continue . . .
```

WHAT'S HAPPENING? The next line in the batch file was GOTO REPEAT. The batch file was sent back to the label :REPEAT. The batch file read the next line after the label, which was the TYPE command, then the next line, which was PAUSE. When you press a key, you will again be returned to the label. Now you see a loop in action.

Step 4 Press **Enter** a few times to see the loop in action. Then press **Ctrl** + **C** to break out of the batch file. It will ask you if you want to terminate the batch job. Key in **Y**, then **Enter** for yes. You will be returned to the A:\> prompt.

WHAT'S HAPPENING? A loop can be very useful. For instance, if you wanted to delete all the files from many floppy disks, you could write a batch file that would look like this:

```
@ECHO OFF
:TOP
CLS
ECHO Place the disk with the files you no longer want in
ECHO Drive A.
PAUSE
DEL /Q A:*.*
ECHO Press Ctrl + C to stop executing this batch file.
ECHO Otherwise, press any key to continue deleting files.
PAUSE > NUL
GOTO TOP
```

The /Q parameter makes it so the DEL command does not require a Y or N. You did not want to see the output of the PAUSE command, so you redirected it to the NUL device.

11.7 THE SHIFT COMMAND

When you have written a batch file with positional parameters, you key in the batch file name followed by a series of values. When the batch file is executed, the operating system looks to the command line for the values it needs to plug into the batch file. It does this based on the position of particular parameters in the command line. In the case of a batch file called LIST.BAT with the lines TYPE %1 %2 %3, you would key in the following command line:

```
LIST  APPIL.TXT  MAY.TXT  JUNE.TXT
```

With this generic batch file, you could key in only three file names. If you wanted more file names, you would have to re-execute the batch file. You are limited to 10 parameters on a command line—%0 through %9. Since %0 actually represents the batch file name itself, you can have only nine parameters. The SHIFT command allows you to shift the parameters to the left, one by one, making the number of parameters on a line limitless. As the SHIFT command shifts the contents of the parameters to the left, parameter 2 becomes parameter 1, parameter 3 becomes parameter 2, and so on. This allows the batch file to process all the parameters on the command line.

11.8 ACTIVITY: USING THE SHIFT COMMAND

Note: The DATA disk should be in Drive A with A:\> displayed.

Step 1 Key in the following: A:\>**ECHO a b c d e** Enter

```
Command Prompt

A:\>ECHO a b c d e
a b c d e

A:\>_
```

WHAT'S HAPPENING? ECHO on a command line just "echoed" what you keyed in. Thus, the parameters a, b, c, d, and e on the command line were repeated on the screen. If you wanted to display more than five parameters and place the echoing parameters in a batch file, you would need to use the SHIFT command.

Step 2 Use any text editor to create and save the file **ALPHA.BAT** as follows:

@ECHO OFF
ECHO %0 %1 %2 %3
SHIFT
ECHO %0 %1 %2 %3
SHIFT
ECHO %0 %1 %2 %3
SHIFT
ECHO %0 %1 %2 %3

WHAT'S HAPPENING? You have created a batch file with replaceable parameters. The purpose of the batch file is to demonstrate the SHIFT command. Remember that ECHO just echoes what you keyed in. In your command line, however, even though you have only four parameters (0 through 3), you want to key in more than four values.

Step 3 Remember, you must be at the system prompt, not in the editor. Key in the following: A:\>**ALPHA a b c d e f** Enter

```
Command Prompt

A:\>ALPHA a b c d e f
ALPHA a b c
a b c d
b c d e
c d e f

A:\>_
```

WHAT'S HAPPENING? Notice the output. In each case, when the batch file read SHIFT, it moved each parameter over by one position.

Batch File	Supplied Value from the Command Line	Screen Display
@ECHO OFF		
ECHO %0 %1 %2 %3	ALPHA is %0 a is %1 b is %2 c is %3	ALPHA a b c
SHIFT	ALPHA is dropped as %0 a becomes %0 b becomes %1 c becomes %2 d becomes %3	
ECHO %0 %1 %2 %3	a is %0 b is %1 c is %2 d is %3	a b c d
SHIFT	a is dropped as %0 b becomes %0 c becomes %1 d becomes %2 e becomes %3	
ECHO %0 %1 %2 %3	b is %0 c is %1 d is %2 e is %3	b c d e
SHIFT	b is dropped as %0 c becomes %0 d becomes %1 e becomes %2 f becomes %3	
ECHO %0 %1 %2 %3	c is %0 d is %1 e is %2 f is %3	c d e f

You should see that you are indeed shifting parameters, but how is this useful? You will write some batch files that use SHIFT so you can see how this technique can be used.

As you know, the operating system stamps each file with the current date and time when it is created or modified. Most often, this means that each file has a unique time and date based on the last time you modified or created the file. Sometimes, you want to place a specific time and date stamp on a file or group of files. For example, if you sell software and you have customers to whom you send files, you might like to ascertain which version of the file they have. By having a particular date and/or time on the file, you can easily keep a date log that is not dependent on the file modification date.

Commands such as XCOPY can back up files after or before a certain date. To ensure that you are backing up all the files you want, you can set the date and update the date stamp on your files. Then you can backup from that date. You need a way to update the dates. You can do this by using the following command:

```
COPY filename /b +
```

Remember, the + sign tells the operating system to concatenate files. The first thing that happens when copying files is a file name is created with the current time and date in the destination directory. At first, the new file is empty. Since there is no specific destination file name, COPY will default to the source file name. It then proceeds to concatenate (add) the existing file to the "new" file name and the new date and time. In essence, it is copying a file onto itself. Since it is a new entry in the directory table, it has the current date and time.

The /B switch tells the operating system to copy the file in binary mode. When you concatenate files with no switches, the files are copied in text mode. The COPY command knows the contents of the file have ended when it sees a special mark called an ***EOF (end-of-file) mark***. Typically, the EOF mark is Ctrl + **Z**. The instant COPY sees this special signal, it thinks there is no more information to copy and will place its own EOF mark at the end of the file—another Ctrl + **Z**. Unfortunately, this "extra" EOF mark is sometimes interpreted by a program or a data file as something other than the end of the file. Thus, you could be in the situation of not copying the entire file. The alternative is to copy the file in binary mode. When you choose this option—the /B switch—COPY will not read the file but will copy everything in the file, ensuring that the entire file contents are copied without adding an extra Ctrl **+ Z**. An extra Ctrl **+ Z** can create problems when you are trying to use the copied file.

Now that you know how and why to update file dates and times, it is easy to place these commands in a batch file. Since you may have more than one file you wish to "stamp," you want to allow for many file names by using the SHIFT command.

Step 4 Use any text editor to create and save a new file. Name the file **UPDATE.BAT** and then key in the following:

:DOIT
COPY %1 /B + > NUL
SHIFT
PAUSE
GOTO DOIT

Step 5 Key in the following: A:\>**DIR APR.99** Enter

Step 6 Key in the following: A:\>**DIR APR.BUD** Enter

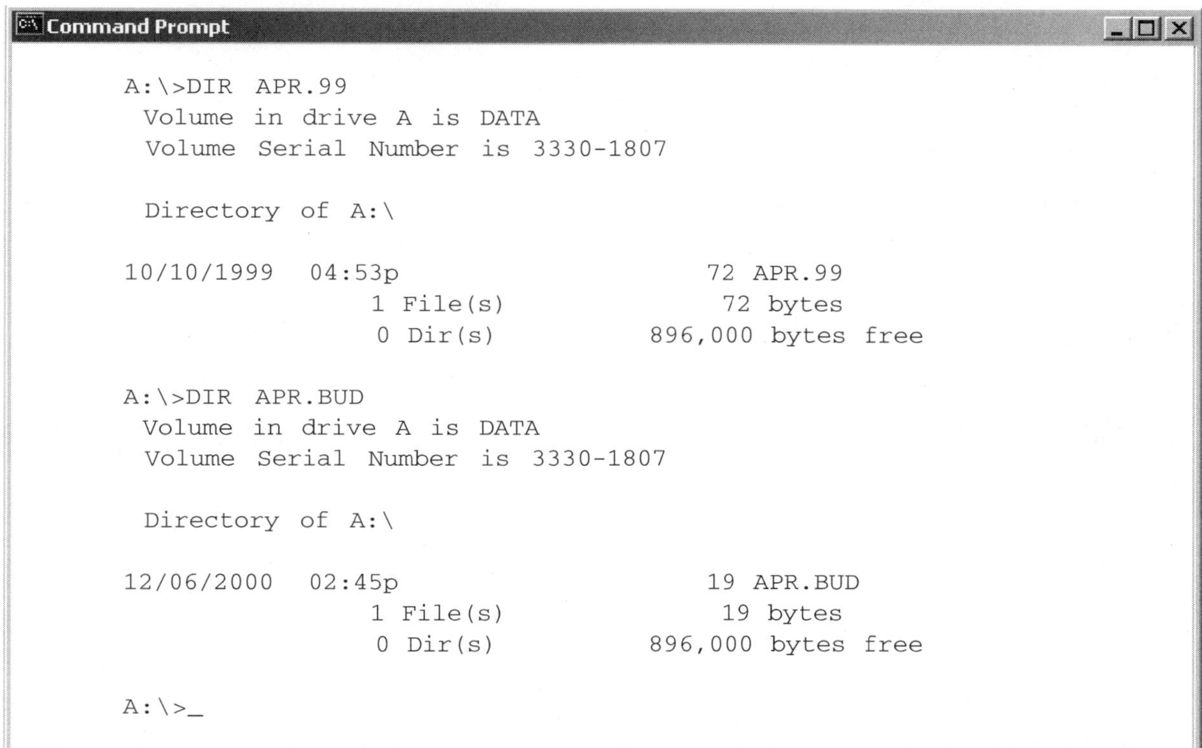

WHAT'S HAPPENING? You want the files **APR.99** and **APR.BUD** to have today's date and time on them.

Step 7 Key in the following: A:\>**UPDATE APR.99 APR.BUD** **Enter**>

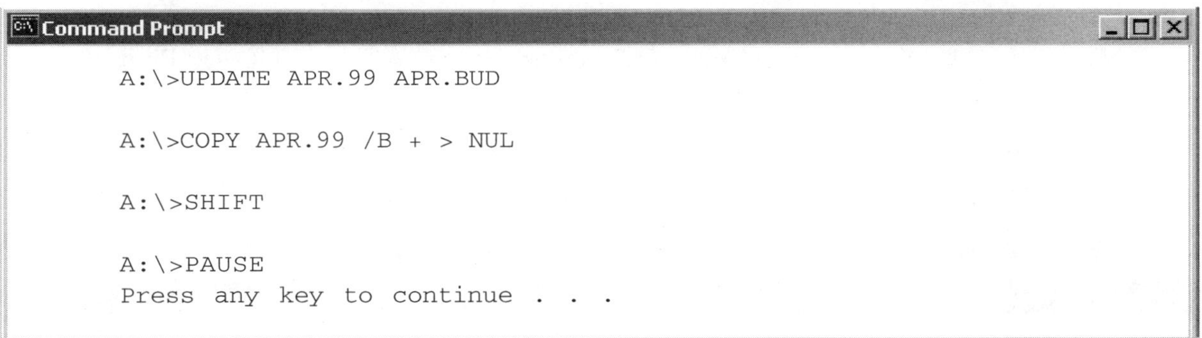

Command Prompt
A:\>UPDATE APR.99 APR.BUD
A:\>COPY APR.99 /B + > NUL
A:\>SHIFT
A:\>PAUSE
Press any key to continue . . .

WHAT'S HAPPENING? The batch file copied **APR.99**, went to SHIFT, and is now going to copy the next parameter it shifted, **APR.BUD**.

Step 8 Press **Enter**

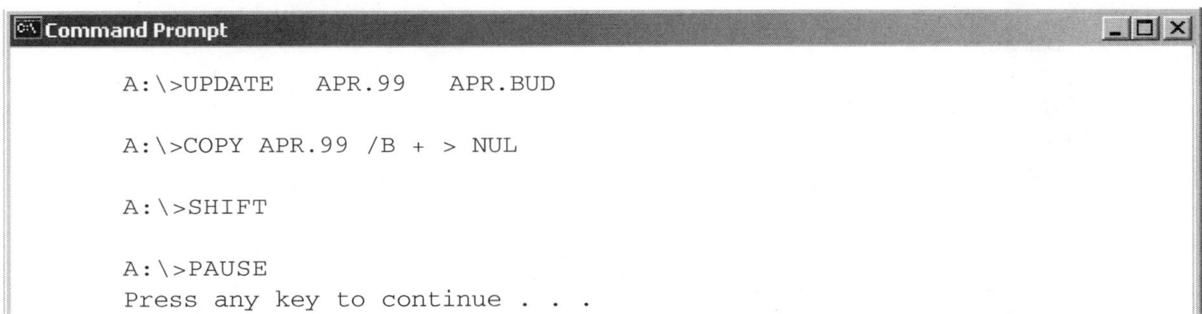

Command Prompt
A:\>UPDATE APR.99 APR.BUD
A:\>COPY APR.99 /B + > NUL
A:\>SHIFT
A:\>PAUSE
Press any key to continue . . .

```
A:\>GOTO DOIT

A:\>COPY APR.BUD /B + > NUL

A:\>SHIFT

A:\>PAUSE
Press any key to continue . . .
```

WHAT'S HAPPENING? It copied **APR.BUD**.

Step 9 Press **Enter**

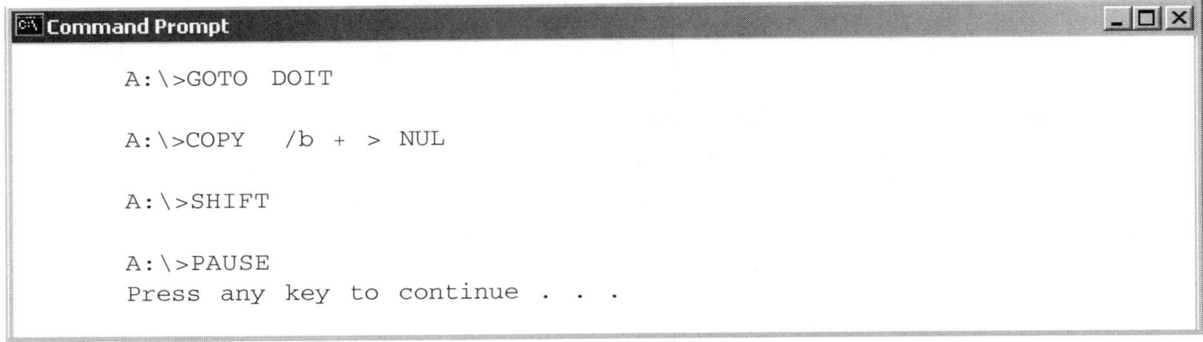

```
A:\>GOTO DOIT

A:\>COPY  /b + > NUL

A:\>SHIFT

A:\>PAUSE
Press any key to continue . . .
```

WHAT'S HAPPENING? This batch file seemed to work effectively when you first initiated it. It copied **APR.99**. It then shifted over to **APR.BUD** and copied that. However, you created an endless loop. When the batch file finished copying **APR.BUD**, it again shifted parameters, but there was nothing to shift to. The batch file is continually going to the label and then trying to execute the command. There is something missing here: a condition that you need to insert. First, though, you must break into the batch file.

Step 10 Press **Ctrl** + **C** and answer **Y** to the prompt.

Step 11 Key in the following: A:\>**DIR APR.99** **Enter**

Step 12 Key in the following: A:\>**DIR APR.BUD** **Enter**

```
Terminate batch job (Y/N)?Y

A:\>DIR APR.99
 Volume in drive A is DATA
 Volume Serial Number is 3330-1807

 Directory of A:\

06/11/2001  02:29p                   72 APR.99
               1 File(s)              72 bytes
               0 Dir(s)         896,000 bytes free

A:\>DIR APR.BUD
 Volume in drive A is DATA
 Volume Serial Number is 3330-1807
```

```
 Directory of A:\

06/11/2001   02:29p                    19 APR.BUD
                1 File(s)               19 bytes
                0 Dir(s)           896,000 bytes free

A:\>_
```

WHAT'S HAPPENING? The file worked—the date and time should be the current date and time. You can create a batch file and use SHIFT to identify the size and number of files in a directory so you can determine whether the files will fit on a floppy disk.

Step 13 Use any text editor to create and save a file named **SIZE.BAT** that contains the following:

:TOP
DIR %1 | FIND "Directory" >> TEMP.FIL
DIR %1 | FIND "bytes" | FIND /V "free" >> TEMP.FIL
SHIFT
GOTO TOP
TYPE TEMP.FIL
PAUSE
DEL TEMP.FIL

WHAT'S HAPPENING? Since you do not care about the names of the files, only the size and the directory they are in, you filtered the output from the DIR command to include only the items that you wanted. You used >> so that you would see both the name of the directory and the bytes in the directory. Had you not used >>, you would have *overwritten* **TEMP.FIL**. At the end of your work, delete **TEMP.FIL** so it will not take space on your disk.

Step 14 Key in the following: A:\>**SIZE CLASS TRIP** Enter

```
Command Prompt

A:\>GOTO  TOP

A:\>DIR TRIP | FIND "Directory" 1>>  TEMP.FIL

A:\>DIR TRIP | FIND "bytes" | FIND /V "free" 1>> TEMP.FIL

A:\>SHIFT

A:\>GOTO  TOP

A:\>DIR   | FIND "Directory" 1>>  TEMP.FIL

A:\>DIR   | FIND "bytes" | FIND /V "free" 1>> TEMP.FIL
```

WHAT'S HAPPENING? Your batch file is running endlessly. You again created an endless loop.

Step 15 Press Ctrl + **C** and answer **Y** to the prompt.

```
Command Prompt

A:\>DIR  | FIND "bytes" | FIND /V "free" 1>> TEMP.FIL

A:\>SHIFT

A:\>GOTO  TOP

A:\>DIR  | FIND "Directory" 1>>  TEMP.FIL

A:\>DIR  | FIND "bytes" | FIND /V "free" 1>> TEMP.FIL
^C

Terminate batch job (Y/N)? Y

A:\>_
```

WHAT'S HAPPENING? Your display may look different depending on where you broke into the batch file.

Step 16 Key in the following: A:\>**TYPE TEMP.FIL | MORE** Enter

```
Command Prompt

A:\>TYPE TEMP.FIL | MORE
 Directory of A:\CLASS
               13 File(s)            888 bytes

 Directory of A:\TRIP
               21 File(s)          1,551 bytes

 Directory of A:\
               71 File(s)         55,909 bytes

 Directory of A:\
               71 File(s)         55,977 bytes

 Directory of A:\
               71 File(s)         56,045 bytes
```

Step 17 Press Ctrl + **C** to stop the processing, if necessary.

WHAT'S HAPPENING? Your file may be shorter or longer, depending on the length of time before you "broke out" with Ctrl + **C**. In any case, you got more information than you wanted. You now know the size of the **CLASS** and **TRIP** directories, but the other information is useless. You are missing conditional processing. (The size of your directories may be different, depending on the work you have done on your DATA disk.)

11.9 THE IF COMMAND

The IF command allows for conditional processing. Conditional processing is a powerful tool in programming. Conditional processing allows a comparison between two items to determine whether the items are identical or whether one is greater than another. A comparison test will yield one of only two values—true or false. If the items are identical, the condition is true. If the items are not identical, the condition is false. Once you establish a true or false value, you can then direct the program to do something based on that value. Conditional processing is often expressed as IF the condition is true, THEN do something; IF the condition is false, THEN do nothing.

In batch files, the IF command will test for some logical condition and then, if the condition is true, the batch file will execute the command. If the test is false, the command will not be executed and the batch file will fall through to the next command line in the batch file. The IF command in batch file processing can check for three conditions:

1. Whether two sets of characters are or are not identical. The characters are called a string, as in a string of data (sometimes referred to as a character string).
2. Whether or not a file exists.
3. The value of the variable in ERRORLEVEL. ERRORLEVEL is a number that a program can set depending on the outcome of a process, such as checking a true/false condition. ERRORLEVEL can check that number.

The syntax for IF/IF NOT ERRORLEVEL is:

```
Performs conditional processing in batch programs.

IF [NOT] ERRORLEVEL number command
IF [NOT] string1==string2 command
IF [NOT] EXIST filename command

  NOT                   Specifies that Windows should carry out the command
                        only if the condition is false.
  ERRORLEVEL number     Specifies a true condition if the last program run
                        returned an exit code equal to or greater than the
                        number specified.
  command               Specifies the command to carry out if the condition
                        is met.
  string1==string2      Specifies a true condition if the specified text
                        strings match.
  EXIST filename        Specifies a true condition if the specified
                        filename exists.
```

11.10 THE IF COMMAND USING STRINGS

You can use the IF command with character strings to test whether or not one string is exactly the same as another. You can tell the IF statement to GOTO a label or to perform an operation when the strings match and the condition is true. Conversely, you can tell the IF statement to GOTO a label or perform an operation when the strings do *not* match and the condition is false. What is to be compared is separated by two equal signs (==).

11.11 ACTIVITY: USING THE IF COMMAND WITH STRINGS

Note: The DATA disk should be in Drive A. The default drive and directory should be A:\>.

Step 1 Use any text editor to create and save a file called **GREET.BAT**. (*Note:* There are no spaces between the two equal signs.) Key in the following:

```
IF %1==Carolyn GOTO Carolyn
IF %1==Bette GOTO Bette
ECHO Isn't anyone there?
GOTO FINISH
:Carolyn
ECHO Greetings, Ms. Carolyn.
GOTO FINISH
:Bette
ECHO Greetings, Ms. Bette.
:FINISH
```

WHAT'S HAPPENING? You have created a batch file to test the IF statement using character strings. You did not place ECHO OFF at the beginning of the file so you can see what happens when it executes.

Step 2 Key in the following: A:\>**GREET Carolyn** Enter

```
Command Prompt

A:\>GREET  Carolyn

A:\>IF Carolyn == Carolyn GOTO Carolyn

A:\>ECHO  Greetings,  Ms.  Carolyn.
Greetings,  Ms.  Carolyn.

A:\>GOTO  FINISH

A:\>_
```

WHAT'S HAPPENING? You keyed in **GREET Carolyn**. The first line in the batch file was executed. When Carolyn took the place of %1, the line read **IF Carolyn==Carolyn**, which is a true statement because the strings of data matched exactly. Since it is true, it performed the GOTO Carolyn command. The line after the label **:Carolyn** was then displayed: **Greetings, Ms. Carolyn.** The line following said **GOTO FINISH**, which it did. After the label **:FINISH**, there were no more lines, and you were returned to the system prompt.

Step 3 Key in the following: A:\>**GREET Bette** Enter

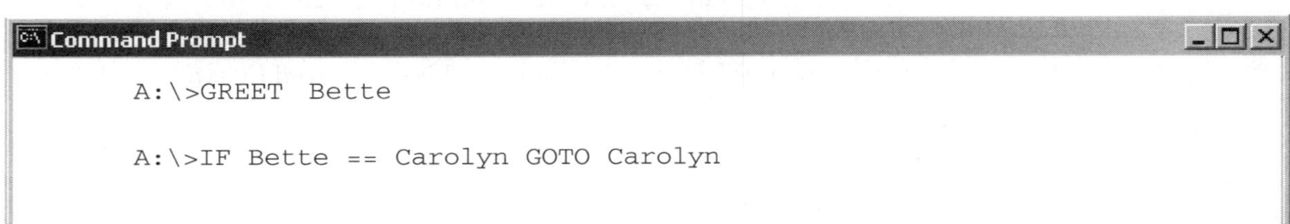
Command Prompt
A:\>GREET Bette
A:\>IF Bette == Carolyn GOTO Carolyn

```
A:\>IF Bette == Bette GOTO Bette

A:\>ECHO Greetings, Ms. Bette.
Greetings, Ms. Bette.

A:\>_
```

WHAT'S HAPPENING? When you keyed in **GREET Bette**, it read the first line as **IF Bette==Carolyn GOTO Carolyn**. Bette does not equal Carolyn, so it is a false statement. Therefore, the batch file did not go to the label **:Carolyn** but fell through to the next line. The line then read as **IF Bette==Bette**, which is a true statement because the strings of data match exactly. Since it is true, it performed the GOTO Bette command. The line after the label **:Bette** was then displayed: **Greetings, Ms. Bette.** The line following said **:FINISH**, which it did. After the label **:FINISH**, there were no more lines, and you were returned to the system prompt.

Step 4 Key in the following: A:\>**GREET Juan** Enter

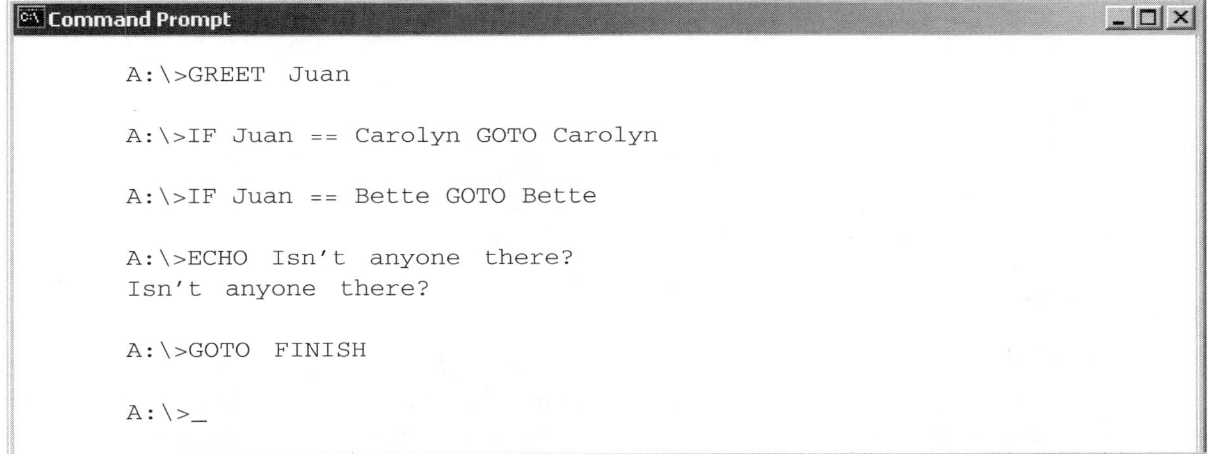
Command Prompt
A:\>GREET Juan
A:\>IF Juan == Carolyn GOTO Carolyn
A:\>IF Juan == Bette GOTO Bette
A:\>ECHO Isn't anyone there?
Isn't anyone there?
A:\>GOTO FINISH
A:\>_

WHAT'S HAPPENING? You keyed in **GREET Juan**. It read the first line as **IF Juan==Carolyn GOTO Carolyn**. Juan does not equal Carolyn, so it is a false statement. The batch file did not go to the label **:Carolyn** but fell through to the next line. The line then read as **IF Juan==Bette**. This is another false statement, so the batch file did not go to the label **:Bette** but fell through to the next line. The line following said **ECHO Isn't anyone there?** Thus, **Isn't anyone there?** was displayed (echoed) to the screen. It then fell through to the next line, which was **GOTO FINISH**. After the label **:FINISH**, there were no more lines, and you were returned to the system prompt.

Step 5 Key in the following: A:\>**GREET BETTE** Enter

```
Command Prompt

A:\>GREET BETTE

A:\>IF BETTE == Carolyn GOTO Carolyn

A:\>IF BETTE == Bette GOTO Bette
```

```
A:\>ECHO Isn't anyone there?
Isn't anyone there?

A:\>GOTO FINISH

A:\>_
```

You keyed in **GREET BETTE**. It read the first line as **IF BETTE==Carolyn GOTO Carolyn**. BETTE does not equal Carolyn, so it is a false statement. The batch file did not go to the label **:Carolyn** but fell through to the next line. The line then read **IF BETTE==Bette**, which is another false statement. Even though the word is the same, the case is different. Both sides of == must match *exactly*. Because it was not an exact match, the batch file did not go to the label **:Bette**, but fell through to the next line. The line following said **ECHO Isn't anyone there?** Thus, **Isn't anyone there?** was displayed (echoed) to the screen. It then fell through to the next line, which was **GOTO FINISH**. It did. After the label **:FINISH**, there were no more lines, and you were returned to the system prompt. If you wish to ignore case, you can add a parameter, the /I, which when included, tells the batch file to ignore case. The command would be written as

IF /I %1= =Carolyn GOTO Carolyn

IF /I %1= =Bette GOTO Bette

and so on. The /I must immediately follow the IF statement.

11.12 TESTING FOR NULL VALUES

In the above example, you tested for an exact match of character strings. What if you have nothing to test for? For example, in the batch files you wrote, UPDATE.BAT and SIZE.BAT, you used SHIFT. SHIFT kept shifting parameters until all of them were used. When there were no more parameters, you were in an endless loop. You can test to see if a string matches, but what if nothing is there? This is called testing for a ***null value***. You are literally testing for nothing. You must have "something" to test for "nothing." Thus, you place a value in the test that will give you nothing.

There are a variety of methods for testing for null values. One method is to use quotation marks so that your statement becomes IF "%1"=="" GOTO LABEL. The second set of quotation marks is keyed in with no spaces. This statement says, "If nothing is there, GOTO somewhere else." You may also make the line read IF %1void==void GOTO LABEL. If you keyed in GREET Carolyn, your line would then look like Carolynvoid==void. This is not true, so it would proceed to the next line. If there was no value, your line would look like void==void. Now this is true, and the GOTO label would execute. You may use any word; "void" was used in this example. Another method is to use \ so that the statement would become IF \%1\==\\ GOTO LABEL. If you keyed in GREET Carolyn, your line would then look like \Carolyn\==\\. This is not true, so it would proceed to the next line. If there were no value, your line would look like \\==\\. Now this *is* true and the GOTO label would execute.

11.13 ACTIVITY: USING NULL VALUES

Note: The DATA disk should be in Drive A. The default drive and directory should be A:\>.

Step 1 Edit and save the file called **UPDATE.BAT** to look as follows:

```
:DOIT
IF "%1"=="" GOTO END
COPY %1 /B + > NUL
SHIFT
PAUSE
GOTO DOIT
:END
```

Step 2 Key in the following: A:\>**DIR CAROLYN.FIL** Enter

```
Command Prompt

A:\>DIR CAROLYN.FIL
 Volume in drive A is DATA
 Volume Serial Number is 3330-1807

 Directory of A:\

07/31/1999  12:53p                  47 CAROLYN.FIL
               1 File(s)             47 bytes
              0 Dir(s)        893,952 bytes free

A:\>_
```

WHAT'S HAPPENING? The file called **CAROLYN.FIL** has a date of 7-31-99. You are going to update only the date on this file. SHIFT will still work and will shift "nothing" to %1, but now you are testing for a null value. Once the file is updated, you will go to :END.

Step 3 Key in the following: A:\>**UPDATE CAROLYN.FIL** Enter

```
Command Prompt

A:\>UPDATE CAROLYN.FIL

A:\>IF "CAROLYN.FIL" == "" GOTO END

A:\>COPY CAROLYN.FIL /B + > NUL

A:\>SHIFT

A:\>PAUSE
Press any key to continue . . .
```

WHAT'S HAPPENING? The batch file updated the file **CAROLYN.FIL**. Prior to your testing for a null value, the file looped endlessly. Now you will see if your test for "nothing" works. Remember, there is a SHIFT that will shift over nothing.

Step 4 Press **Enter**

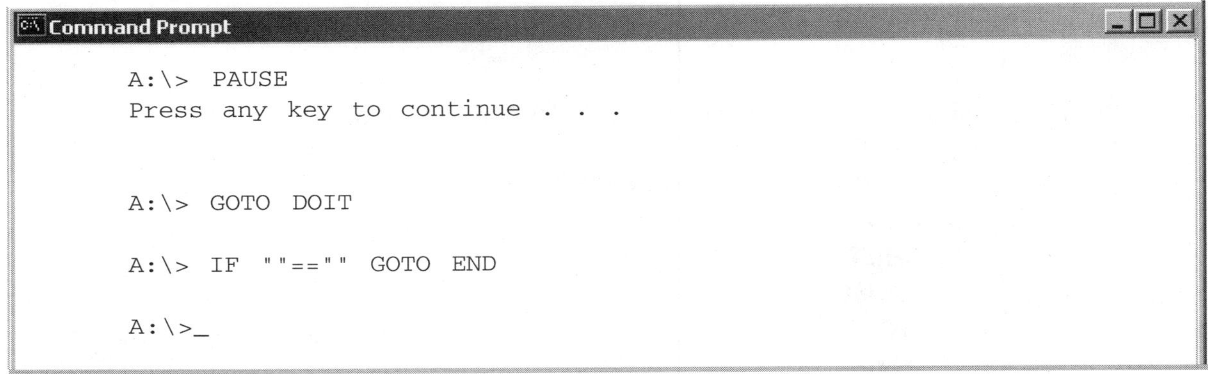

```
Command Prompt
A:\> PAUSE
Press any key to continue . . .


A:\> GOTO DOIT

A:\> IF ""=="" GOTO END

A:\>_
```

WHAT'S HAPPENING? Since nothing, or a null value, was there, it was a true condition, and GOTO told it to go to the label called :END. Thus, it skipped the lines and went directly to the end of the batch file.

Step 5 Key in the following: A:\>**DIR CAROLYN.FIL** **Enter**

```
Command Prompt
A:\>DIR CAROLYN.FIL
 Volume in drive A is DATA
 Volume Serial Number is 3330-1807

 Directory of A:\

06/11/2001  02:41p                  47 CAROLYN.FIL
               1 File(s)             47 bytes
               0 Dir(s)         893,952 bytes free

A:\>_
```

WHAT'S HAPPENING? The date did change to the current date (your date will be different), and you were not in an endless loop. You are now going to try another technique to test for a null value.

Step 6 Edit and save the file called **SIZE.BAT** to look as follows:

:TOP
IF %1nothing==nothing GOTO END
DIR %1 | FIND "Directory" >> TEMP.FIL
DIR %1 | FIND "bytes" | FIND /V "free" >> TEMP.FIL
SHIFT
GOTO TOP
TYPE TEMP.FIL
PAUSE
DEL TEMP.FIL
:END

Step 7 Key in the following: A:\>**DEL TEMP.FIL** **Enter**

WHAT'S HAPPENING? You wanted to eliminate **TEMP.FIL**, because the last time you ran this batch file, you were stuck in a loop and **TEMP.FIL** did not get deleted. You never reached that line in the batch file.

Step 8 Key in the following: A:\>**SIZE CLASS TRIP** Enter

```
Command Prompt

A:\>IF CLASSnothing == nothing GOTO END

A:\>DIR CLASS | FIND "Directory" 1>> TEMP.FIL

A:\>DIR CLASS | FIND "bytes" | FIND /V "free" 1>> TEMP.FIL

A:\>SHIFT

A:\>GOTO  TOP

A:\>IF TRIPnothing == nothing GOTO END

A:\>DIR TRIP | FIND "Directory" >> TEMP.FIL

A:\>DIR TRIP | FIND "bytes" | FIND /V "free" 1>> TEMP.FIL

A:\>SHIFT

A:\>GOTO  TOP

A:\>IF nothing == nothing GOTO END

A:\>_
```

WHAT'S HAPPENING? You did not have the problem of an endless loop, but, when you tested for a null value and there was a null value, you told the batch file to GOTO END. It did so, but, by going to the label :END, it never processed the other three lines in the batch file—the lines beginning with TYPE, PAUSE, and DEL. This is why writing batch files (and programs) is a complicated task. You have to think through what you are trying to do and what consequences your instructions will have.

Step 9 Key in the following: A:\>**TYPE TEMP.FIL** Enter

```
Command Prompt

A:\>TYPE  TEMP.FIL
  Directory of  A:\class
                13 File(s)              888 bytes

  Directory of  A:\trip
                21 File(s)            1,551 bytes

  Directory of  A:\
                71 File(s)           55,909 bytes
```

```
Directory of A:\
            71 File(s)          55,977 bytes

Directory of A:\
            71 File(s)          56,045 bytes

Directory of A:\CLASS
            13 File(s)             888 bytes

Directory of A:\TRIP
            21 File(s)           1,551 bytes
```

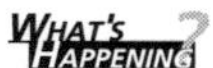

The batch file **SIZE.BAT** worked, to some degree. You got the information in the file **TEMP.FIL**, but the file was never displayed or deleted. Thus, you must find another solution to the problem.

11.14 THE IF EXIST/IF NOT EXIST COMMAND

The IF EXIST command uses a file specification for the test. If the file exists, then the condition is true. Processing then passes to the specified GOTO location or to the command that follows the IF statement. If the file does not exist, the condition is false and the operating system ignores the command in the IF clause. The batch process then reads the next line in the file. When you use IF NOT EXIST and the file does not exist, then the condition is true. Processing then passes to the specified GOTO location or to the command that follows the IF NOT statement. If the file does exist, the condition is false and the batch process will fall through to the next line in the batch file. *Note:* IF EXIST/IF NOT EXIST works only with file names and *not with directory names*.

11.15 ACTIVITY: USING IF EXIST TO TEST FOR A FILE

Note: The DATA disk should be in Drive A. The displayed prompt is A:\>.

Step 1 Use any text editor to create and save a file called **RENDIR.BAT**. Key in the following:

```
IF \%1\==\\ GOTO end
IF NOT \%2\==\\ GOTO next
ECHO You must include a destination name
ECHO for the new directory name.
GOTO end
:next
IF EXIST %1 GOTO message
REN %1 %2
GOTO end
:message
ECHO This is a file, not a directory.
:end
```

This batch file will ensure that you are renaming a directory and not a file. The following table analyzes the batch file one line at a time. The line numbers are for purposes of reference only.

```
1.  IF \%1\==\\ GOTO end
2.  IF NOT \%2\==\\ GOTO next
3.  ECHO You must include a destination name
4.  ECHO for the new directory name.
5.  GOTO end
6.  :next
7.  IF EXIST %1 GOTO message
8.  REN %1 %2
9.  GOTO end
10. :message
11. ECHO This is a file, not a directory.
12. :end
```

Batch File by Line Number	Test TRUE	Processing	Test FALSE
1. IF \%1\==\\ GOTO end	User keys in nothing for %1. Since test is true, action is to go to line 12.	Testing for null value.	User keys in value for %1. Since test is false, action is to go to line 2.
2. IF NOT \%2\==\\ GOTO next	User keys in nothing for %2. Since test is true, action is to go to line 3.	Testing for null value.	User keys in value for %2. Since test is false, action is to go to line 6.
3. ECHO You must include a destination name		Message for user that he or she did not include a value.	
4. ECHO for the new directory name.		Continuation of the message.	
5. GOTO end		Falls through to the GOTO end statement. Action is to go to line 12.	
6. :next		Label referred to in line 2.	
7. IF EXIST %1 GOTO message	User keys in file name for %1. Since test is true, action is to go to line 10.	Testing for value for %1. Is it a file or a directory?	User keys in directory for %1. Since test is false, action is to go to line 8.

8. REN %1 %2	Since %1 test is false (not a file), renaming directory can proceed.
9. GOTO end	After directory is renamed, falls through to GOTO end.
10. :message	Label referred to in line 2.
11. ECHO This is a file, not a directory.	Message that user used a file name, not a directory name.
12. :end	

Step 2 Key in the following: A:\>**RENDIR JAN.99 LAST** Enter

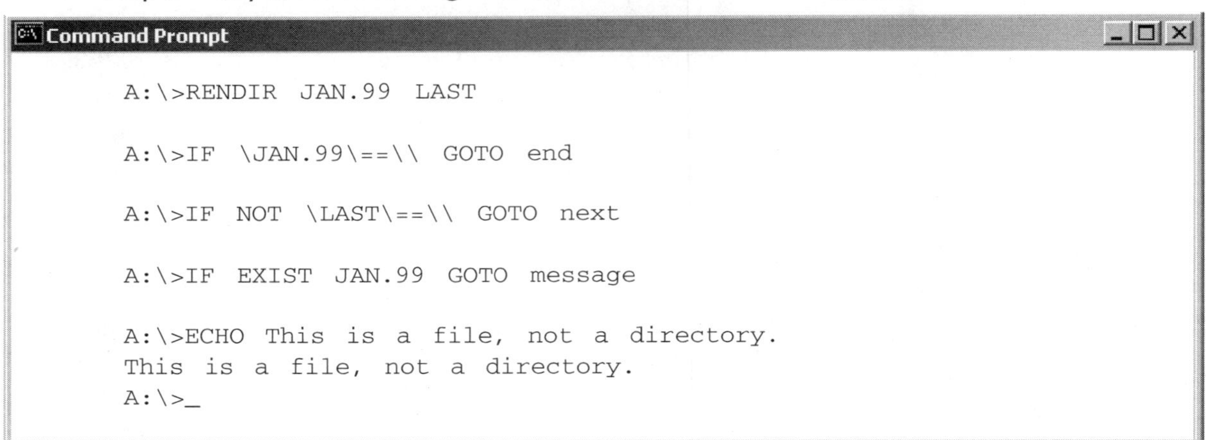

```
A:\>RENDIR JAN.99 LAST

A:\>IF \JAN.99\==\\ GOTO end

A:\>IF NOT \LAST\==\\ GOTO next

A:\>IF EXIST JAN.99 GOTO message

A:\>ECHO This is a file, not a directory.
This is a file, not a directory.
A:\>_
```

WHAT'S HAPPENING? Since **JAN.99** is a file, the line **IF EXIST JAN.99** is true. Since it is true, the batch file executed GOTO and went to the label **:message**. What if it is a directory and not a file?

Step 3 Key in the following: A:\>**RENDIR TEST OLDER** Enter

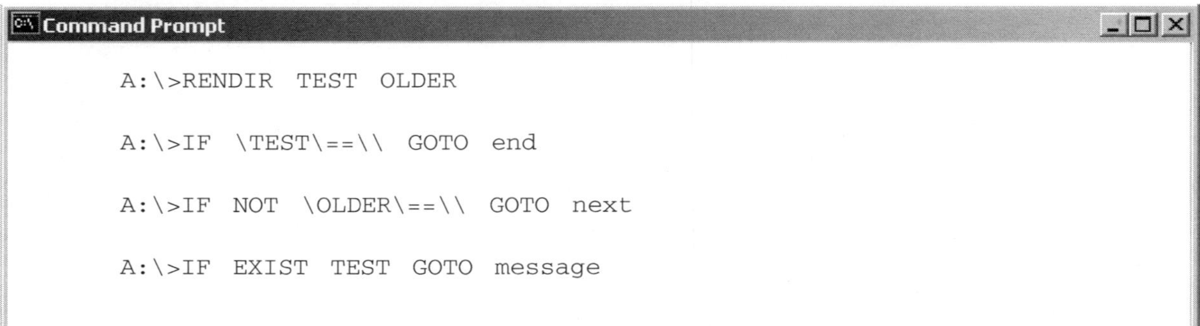

```
A:\>RENDIR TEST OLDER

A:\>IF \TEST\==\\ GOTO end

A:\>IF NOT \OLDER\==\\ GOTO next

A:\>IF EXIST TEST GOTO message
```

```
A:\>ECHO This is a file, not a directory.
This is a file, not a directory.
A:\>_
```

WHAT'S HAPPENING? The if statement identified TEST as a file and therefore went to the message. The directory was not renamed. You cannot use IF EXIST to check for the existence of a directory, as it only works with files. There is a way around this—you can "fool" the IF EXIST command. To check for the existence or nonexistence of a directory, you must use NUL. The null (NUL) device does exist in every directory. NUL is a device that discards anything sent to it. By using %1\NUL, you force IF EXIST/IF NOT EXIST to check for a directory name and not a file name. IF looks for a NUL file (or the nonexistence of a nothing file) in the directory represented by %1. If it cannot get through %1 to look for NUL, then %1 does not exist.

Step 4 Edit the **RENDIR.BAT** file so that you change the line **IF EXIST %1 GOTO message** to read **IF NOT EXIST %1\NUL GOTO message**.

Step 5 Key in the following: A:\>**RENDIR TEST OLDER** Enter

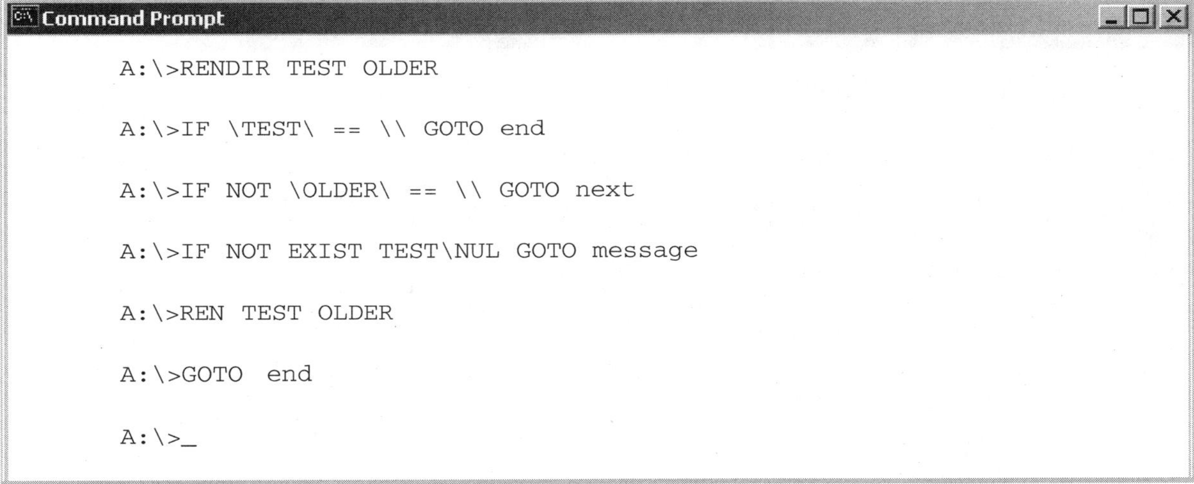
Command Prompt
A:\>RENDIR TEST OLDER
A:\>IF \TEST\ == \\ GOTO end
A:\>IF NOT \OLDER\ == \\ GOTO next
A:\>IF NOT EXIST TEST\NUL GOTO message
A:\>REN TEST OLDER
A:\>GOTO end
A:\>_

WHAT'S HAPPENING? The question asked with the IF NOT EXIST statement was testing whether TEST was a directory. If this statement were false (a file name), then the batch file would execute the command following IF (the GOTO message). Since TEST does exist (TEST\NUL) the statement is true, the command following IF is ignored, and the batch file falls through to the next line and renames the directory from TEST to OLDER. Using the logic you just learned, you can correct (debug) **SIZE.BAT** so that it processes all the lines in the batch file. There is one more piece of information you need.

Step 6 Edit and save the file called **SIZE.BAT** to look as follows:

```
IF EXIST TEMP.FIL DEL TEMP.FIL
:TOP
IF %1nothing==nothing GOTO END
IF NOT EXIST %1\NUL GOTO NEXT
DIR %1 | FIND "Directory" >> TEMP.FIL
DIR %1 | FIND "bytes" | FIND /V "free" >> TEMP.FIL
```

:NEXT
SHIFT
GOTO TOP
:END
TYPE TEMP.FIL
PAUSE
DEL TEMP.FIL

WHAT'S HAPPENING? The first line, IF EXIST TEMP.FIL DEL TEMP.FIL, looks for the file called **TEMP.FIL** and delete it if it exists. Then when you create **TEMP.FIL**, it will be a new file every time. The next addition, IF NOT EXIST %1\NUL GOTO NEXT, will see if a directory exists. That is the purpose of %1\NUL. If it is a file, the batch file will go to the :NEXT label, SHIFT, and go back to the :TOP label. The :TOP label is not at the top of the batch file because you want to delete **TEMP.FIL** only the first time you execute the batch file. Notice that you had to move the :END label. In its previous batch file location, you would not have been able to read **TEMP.FIL**.

Step 7 Key in the following: A:\>**SIZE CLASS JAN.99 TRIP** Enter

Command Prompt

```
A:\>SIZE CLASS JAN.99 TRIP

A:\>IF EXIST TEMP.FIL DEL TEMP.FIL

A:\>IF CLASSnothing == nothing GOTO END

A:\>IF NOT EXIST CLASS\NUL GOTO NEXT

A:\>DIR CLASS | FIND "Directory" 1>>TEMP.FIL

A:\>DIR CLASS | FIND "bytes" | FIND /V "free" 1>> TEMP.FIL

A:\>SHIFT

A:\>GOTO TOP

A:\>IF JAN.99nothing == nothing GOTO END

A:\>IF NOT EXIST JAN.99\NUL GOTO NEXT

A:\>SHIFT

A:\>GOTO TOP

A:\>IF TRIPnothing == nothing GOTO END

A:\>IF NOT EXIST TRIP\NUL GOTO NEXT

A:\>DIR TRIP | FIND "Directory" 1>>TEMP.FIL

A:\>DIR TRIP | FIND "bytes" | FIND /V "free" 1>> TEMP.FIL
```

```
A:\>SHIFT

A:\>GOTO TOP

A:\>IF nothing == nothing GOTO END

A:\>TYPE TEMP.FIL
 Directory of A:\CLASS
              13 File(s)            888 bytes

 Directory of A:\TRIP
              21 File(s)          1,551 bytes


A:\>PAUSE
Press any key to continue . . .
```

Your batch file worked correctly. It used **JAN.99**, knew it was a file, and did not include it in the output. The more complicated you want a batch file to be, the more you will have to analyze the logic of what you want to do and how to accomplish it.

Step 8 Press **Enter**

```
Command Prompt

A:\>PAUSE
Press any key to continue . . .

A:\>DEL TEMP.FIL
A:\>_
```

You have executed your batch file and returned to the system level.

11.16 THE IF ERRORLEVEL COMMAND TESTING

A program can set an ***exit code*** when it finishes executing. A batch file can test this exit code with the IF ERRORLEVEL statement. Actually, the name ERRORLEVEL is a misnomer because the number returned does not necessarily mean there was an error. For instance, the test IF ERRORLEVEL 3 will be true if the exit code is greater than or equal to 3. Thus, an exit code is not tested for a match with ERRORLEVEL, but to determine if it is greater than or equal to it. The test IF ERRORLEVEL 0 will *always* be true since every possible exit code is greater than or equal to 0. The trickiest thing about testing ERRORLEVELs in batch files is that the exit codes must be listed in *descending* order when you use IF ERRORLEVEL and in *ascending* order when you use IF NOT ERRORLEVEL. For instance, COPY will set one of the following exit codes:

```
0 Files were copied without error.
1 No files were found to copy.
```

You can write a batch file testing for exit codes.

11.17 ACTIVITY: USING IF ERRORLEVEL WITH COPY

Note: The DATA disk should be in Drive A. The displayed prompt is A:\>.

Step 1 Use any text editor to create and save a file called **ERROR.BAT**. Key in the following:

```
COPY %1 %2
IF ERRORLEVEL 1 GOTO NOTOK
IF ERRORLEVEL 0 GOTO OK
:NOTOK
ECHO There are no %1 files. Try again.
GOTO END
:OK
ECHO You copied the %1 files successfully.
:END
```

Step 2 Key in the following: A:\>**ERROR *.TXT OLDER** Enter

```
Command Prompt

A:\>ERROR *.TXT OLDER

A:\>COPY *.TXT OLDER
Sandy and Nicki.txt
JANUARY.TXT
APRIL.TXT
BYE.TXT
FEBRUARY.TXT
GOODBYE.TXT
HELLO.TXT
LONGFILENAME.TXT
LONGFILENAMED.TXT
LONGFILENAMING.TXT
Sandy and Patty.txt
DANCES.TXT
TEST.TXT
CHKDSK.TXT
TXTFILES.TXT
LOG.TXT
        16 file(s) copied.

A:\>IF ERRORLEVEL 1 GOTO NOTOK

A:\>IF ERRORLEVEL 0 GOTO OK

A:\>ECHO You copied the *.TXT files successfully.
You copied the *.TXT files successfully.
A:\>_
```

You successfully copied the **.TXT** files to the **OLDER** subdirectory. The exit code that was generated by COPY gave you the message that the copy was successful.

Step 3 Key in the following: A:\>**ERROR *.NON OLDER** Enter

```
A:\>ERROR *.NON OLDER

A:\>COPY *.NON OLDER
*.NON
The system cannot find the file specified.
        0 file(s) copied.

A:\>IF ERRORLEVEL 1 GOTO NOTOK

A:\>ECHO There are no *.NON files. Try again.
There are no *.NON files. Try again.

A:\>GOTO END

A:\>_
```

Again, the exit code was correctly read. As you can see, you can use the exit codes successfully in a batch file. Since programs like COPY give you a message anyway when it could not find the file or files, you may ask yourself, why go to the trouble of writing a batch file? The reason is that you can write a small program to test for other kinds of information.

11.18 WRITING PROGRAMS TO TEST FOR KEY CODES

Rather than being limited to the exit codes that are set by operating system programs, you can write a small program that will create an exit code based on some activity. For instance, a program can be written that will identify which key was pressed and report which key it was. You can do this because every time you press a key, it is identified by a one- or two-digit ***scan code***. Actually, two things are reported when you press any key on the keyboard. First, that you pressed a key. Second, that you released the key. The keyboard controller tells the CPU that some keyboard activity is occurring. The stream of bytes is converted into the scan code, which identifies the specific key (see Appendix C for a list of scan codes for all the keys).

You are going to write a program that will report the scan code for any key that is pressed on the keyboard. Once you know the reported code, you can test for a specific key using ERRORLEVEL in the batch file. The batch file can then act based on the reported code. In order to do this, you must write a program. Remember, to be executed, a program must be in "bits and bytes"—the 0s and 1s the computer understands.

There are several ways to write a program. One is to know a programming language and be able to turn the programming language program (source code) into executable code (object code). This is called compiling a program—turning a language into code. That task is beyond the scope of this text. Fortunately, there is an easier way that you can create a small program—using an operating system utility program called DEBUG.

DEBUG can directly modify bytes in a file. DEBUG allows you to test and debug executable files—those with a .COM or .EXE file extension. Remember, you cannot use TYPE to look at a file with the extension of .EXE or .COM because those file extensions indicate programs that are not ASCII-readable files. DEBUG is a small program that has its own commands and syntax. If you know the commands of the DEBUG program and the rules of programming, you could write a .COM program directly with DEBUG. Unless you are a programming expert, you will probably not want to do this.

The easiest way to use DEBUG is to create a script or a ***script file***. A script is a set of instructions that you can write in any ASCII editor. Once you have written the script, you can "feed" it to the DEBUG program via redirection (DEBUG < SCRIPT.FIL). DEBUG will then convert the script file to an executable program with a .COM file extension. Once you have a .COM file, you can execute it as you do any program. This process is the simplest way to create a file that will report the scan code for any key that is pressed. The program you create will be called REPLY.COM.

Since using DEBUG directly can be tricky, the example below shows a .COM program written with DEBUG that will return the scan code of a pressed key. If you want to try to use DEBUG directly, what appears on the screen in this example will be in *this typeface* and what you key in will be in **this typeface**. The hyphen (-) and the colon (:) are prompts presented to you by the DEBUG program. Instructions such as 100 assemble the program at memory address 100 (hexadecimal). 12B3 will vary from machine to machine. In the example shown here, 12B3:0100 represents segment/offset memory address. You must press Enter after each line and also when Enter is specified. The following is a summary of commands available within the DEBUG program:

```
assemble    A [address]
compare     C range address
dump        D [range]
enter       E address [list]
fill        F range list
go          G [=address] [addresses]
hex         H value1 value2
input       I port
load        L [address] [drive] [firstsector] [number]
move        M range address
name        N [pathname] [arglist]
output      O port byte
proceed     P [=address] [number]
quit        Q
register    R [register]
search      S range list
trace       T [=address] [value]
unassemble U [range]
write       W [address] [drive] [firstsector] [number]

allocate expanded memory          XA [#pages]
deallocate expanded memory        XD [handle]
map expanded memory pages         XM [Lpage] [Ppage] [handle]
display expanded memory status    XS
```

The following is shown as an example of how to use DEBUG, but you do not have to do this. If you do, note the differences between the letter l and the number 1. Be sure and check with your lab administrator before attempting to key in this example. Be very sure you are at the A:\> prompt.

A:\>**DEBUG**
-a 100 Enter
158E:0100 **mov ah,8** Enter
158E:0102 **int 21** Enter
158E:0104 **cmp al,0** Enter
158E:0106 **jnz 10a** Enter
158E:0108 **int 21** Enter
158E:010A **mov ah,4c** Enter
158E:010C **int 21** Enter
158E:010E Enter
-r cx Enter
CX 0000
:e Enter
-n reply.com Enter
-w Enter
Writing 0000E bytes
-q Enter

An easier way to create REPLY.COM is to create a script file. Again, a script file is merely a text file that contains a series of commands that can be redirected into DEBUG to create a .COM file. The script file is not the program. You use any text editor; name the file, in this case REPLY.SCR; and key in the following commands. Then, to make REPLY.SCR an executable program, you redirect it into DEBUG to create REPLY.COM. The next activity will show you how to create REPLY.SCR and REPLY.COM. (*Note:* You may want to check with your instructor to see if he or she has created REPLY.COM for you.)

11.19 ACTIVITY: WRITING A SCRIPT FILE

Note: The DATA disk should be in Drive A. The displayed prompt is A:\>.

Step 1 Use any text editor to create and save a file called **REPLY.SCR**. Key in the following:

e 100 b4 08 cd 21 3c 00 75 02 cd 21 b4 4c cd 21
rcx
e
n reply.com
w
q

WHAT'S HAPPENING? Now that you have written **REPLY.SCR**, you must now "assemble" it or convert it into the bytes that make it a program. You do this by redirecting the script file into DEBUG.

Step 2 Key in the following: A:\>**DEBUG < REPLY.SCR** Enter

```
Command Prompt

A:\>DEBUG < REPLY.SCR
-e 100  b4  08  cd  21  3c  00  75 02  cd  21  b4  4c  cd  21
-rcx
CX 0000
:e
-n  reply.com
-w
Writing 0000E bytes
-q

A:\>_
```

WHAT'S HAPPENING? You have compiled **REPLY.SCR** into a program called **REPLY.COM**.

Step 3 Key in the following: A:\>**DIR REPLY.COM** Enter

```
Command Prompt

A:\>DIR REPLY.COM
 Volume in drive A is DATA
 Volume Serial Number is 3330-1807

 Directory of A:\

06/11/2001  03:12p                  14 REPLY.COM
               1 File(s)             14 bytes
               0 Dir(s)         879,616 bytes free

A:\>_
```

WHAT'S HAPPENING? Now that you have written a program, you want to use it in a batch file.

Step 4 Use any text editor to create and save a file called **KEYING.BAT** that contains the following:

```
ECHO PRESS F1 TO CLEAR THE SCREEN.
ECHO PRESS F2 TO DISPLAY THE DIRECTORY.
ECHO PRESS ANY OTHER KEY TO EXIT.
REPLY
IF ERRORLEVEL 61 GOTO END
IF ERRORLEVEL 60 GOTO F2
IF ERRORLEVEL 59 GOTO F1
GOTO END
:F1
CLS
GOTO END
:F2
DIR
:END
```

WHAT'S HAPPENING? This is a simple batch file that checks the scan codes you generate by pressing a key. Checking IF ERRORLEVEL codes in descending order is *critical* because the command is tested to determine if the error code is equal to or greater than the value specified. In this program, if you press a key that returns a value of 61 or above, you exit the program. If you press F2, it returns a code of 60. If you press F1, it returns a code of 59. If none of those conditions exist, then you exit the batch file.

Step 5 Key in the following: A:\>**KEYING** Enter

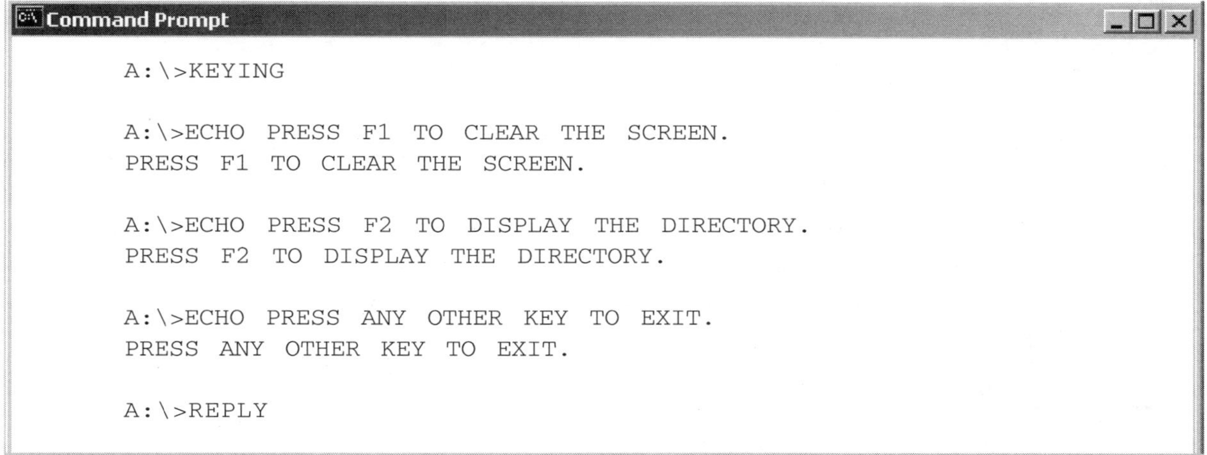

```
Command Prompt

A:\>KEYING

A:\>ECHO PRESS F1 TO CLEAR THE SCREEN.
PRESS F1 TO CLEAR THE SCREEN.

A:\>ECHO PRESS F2 TO DISPLAY THE DIRECTORY.
PRESS F2 TO DISPLAY THE DIRECTORY.

A:\>ECHO PRESS ANY OTHER KEY TO EXIT.
PRESS ANY OTHER KEY TO EXIT.

A:\>REPLY
```

You have executed the **KEYING** batch file. The program called **REPLY.COM** is waiting for you to press a key.

Step 6 Press F1

```
Command Prompt

A:\>GOTO END

A:\>_
```

Pressing F1 cleared the screen.

Step 7 Key in the following: A:\>**KEYING** Enter

Step 8 Press F2

```
Command Prompt

06/11/2001  10:33a          20 HPB.BAT
06/11/2001  10:43a          32 N.BAT
06/11/2001  10:53a         113 log.txt
06/11/2001  10:50a          61 log.bat
06/11/2001  11:05a         115 TESTING.BAT
06/11/2001  11:07a         157 TEST2.BAT
06/11/2001  11:20a         161 KILLIT.BAT
06/11/2001  11:24a         111 MULTI.BAT
10/10/1999  04:53p          72 LAST.ONE
06/11/2001  11:27a         203 NOCOPY.BAT
06/11/2001  11:36a         258 DCOMP.BAT
06/11/2001  02:14p         182 ONE.BAT
06/11/2001  02:16p         102 REPEAT.BAT
06/11/2001  02:20p         104 ALPHA.BAT
```

```
06/11/2001  02:38p                191 GREET.BAT
06/11/2001  02:41p                 80 UPDATE.BAT
06/11/2001  02:55p                252 RENDIR.BAT
06/11/2001  02:58p                258 SIZE.BAT
06/11/2001  03:03p                178 ERROR.BAT
06/11/2001  03:12p                 14 REPLY.COM
06/11/2001  03:11p                 76 REPLY.SCR
06/11/2001  03:14p                246 KEYING.BAT
              76 File(s)       56,646 bytes
               8 Dir(s)       879,104 bytes free

A:\>_
```

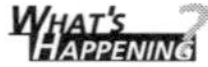

(The graphic represents only a portion of what scrolled by on your screen.) Pressing **F2** gave you a directory of your disk. As you can see, **REPLY.COM** checked the scan code returned by the key you pressed and followed the instruction in the batch file based on the key you pressed. Writing **.COM** programs can be difficult.

11.20 THE ENVIRONMENT

The environment is an area that the operating system sets aside in memory. It is like a scratch pad where notes are kept about important items that the operating system needs to know. The environment is like a bunch of post-it notes. Application programs can read any items in the environment and can post their own messages there. A ***variable*** is a value that can change, depending on conditions or on information passed to the program. Data consists of constants or fixed values that never change and variable values that do change. The ***environment*** is, in essence, an area in memory where data can be stored. When evaluating an expression in some environment, the evaluation of a variable consists of looking up its name in the environment and substituting its value. In programming, an ***expression*** is any legal combination of symbols that represents a value. These variables are used by the operating system to discover things about the environment it is operating in. Environment variables can be changed or created by the user or a program.

Programs can get the value of a variable and use it to modify their operation, much like you can use a value in a command line argument. The operating system has the ability to store data in memory. The stored data takes the form of two strings—one is the name of the variable, and the other is the value of the variable. An ***environmental variable*** is a name assigned to a string (value) of data. You can set your own environmental variables. However, there are some common environmental variables that are set when you start Windows. There are environmental variables that are commonly used which usually have short, easy-to-remember names. These environmental variables store information such as your user name (USERNAME); the location where, by default, your files are saved (USERPROFILE); the search path the operating system uses to look for commands (PATH); what is displayed in your prompt (PROMPT); as well as the name of your Windows directory—where the operating system files are kept (SystemRoot). It also includes the location of the file CMD.EXE. You can also leave messages there via batch files or from the command line. You do this with the SET command. Environmental variables set by the operating system will remain in effect throughout the entire work session at the computer. Those set in the Command Prompt window or in batch files executed in the Command Prompt window will remain in effect *only* during that command prompt session. While values are in effect, you can use the syntax %VARIABLENAME%, which will use the value of the environment variable. To view the value of an environmental variable, you can use the syntax of ECHO %ENVIRONMENTALVARIABLENAME%. The internal command SET allows you to display what is currently in the environment, set environmental variables, or delete environmental variables. If you use the SET command, followed by a letter, the SET command will list any environmental variables that begin with that letter. The basic syntax is:

```
SET [variable=[string]]

  variable      Specifies the environment-variable name.
  string        Specifies a series of characters to assign to the
                variable.

Type SET without parameters to display the current environment
variables.
```

11.21 ACTIVITY: USING SET AND THE ENVIRONMENTAL VARIABLES

Step 1 Key in the following: A:\>**SET | MORE** Enter

```
Command Prompt

ALLUSERSPROFILE=C:\Documents and Settings\All Users
APPDATA=C:\Documents and Settings\Carolyn Z. Gillay\Application Data
CommonProgramFiles=C:\Program Files\Common Files
COMPUTERNAME=DELLXPS
ComSpec=C:\WINNT\system32\cmd.exe
HOMEDRIVE=C:
HOMEPATH=\
LOGONSERVER=\\DELLXPS
NUMBER_OF_PROCESSORS=1
OS=Windows_NT
Os2LibPath=C:\WINNT\system32\os2\dll;
Path=C:\WINNT\system32;C:\WINNT;C:\WINNT\System32\Wbem
PATHEXT=.COM;.EXE;.BAT;.CMD;.VBS;.VBE;.JS;.JSE;.WSF;.WSH
PROCESSOR_ARCHITECTURE=x86
PROCESSOR_IDENTIFIER=x86 Family 6 Model 3 Stepping 4, GenuineIntel
PROCESSOR_LEVEL=6
PROCESSOR_REVISION=0304
ProgramFiles=C:\Program Files
PROMPT=$P$G
SystemDrive=C:
SystemRoot=C:\WINNT
TEMP=C:\DOCUME~1\CAROLY~1.GIL\LOCALS~1\Temp
TMP=C:\DOCUME~1\CAROLY~1.GIL\LOCALS~1\Temp
USERDOMAIN=DELLXPS
-- More --
```

Your values will differ from those shown. As you can see, Windows stores much information about your system (your environment) in the operating system environment. For instance, the environmental variable called ComSpec has a value, in this example, of C:\WINNT\system32\cmd.exe. This tells the operating system that the location of CMD.EXE is C:\WINNT\SYSTEM32. When you execute a program, Windows no longer needs the command processor in memory. However, when you exit the program and need to key in another command, Windows must reload the command processor from disk. In order to do so, it must know where it is located. It looks up the value of ComSpec to find that location. The PATH value tells Windows what directories and in what order it is to search for executable files. The value for SystemRoot, in this example, is C:\WINNT. That tells Windows the name of the directory that holds the Windows operating system files.

Step 2 Press **Enter**. Press the **Space Bar**

```
Command Prompt

HOMEDRIVE=C:
HOMEPATH=\
LOGONSERVER=\\DELLXPS
NUMBER_OF_PROCESSORS=1
OS=Windows_NT
Os2LibPath=C:\WINNT\system32\os2\dll;
Path=C:\WINNT\system32;C:\WINNT;C:\WINNT\System32\Wbem
PATHEXT=.COM;.EXE;.BAT;.CMD;.VBS;.VBE;.JS;.JSE;.WSF;.WSH
PROCESSOR_ARCHITECTURE=x86
PROCESSOR_IDENTIFIER=x86 Family 6 Model 3 Stepping 4, GenuineIntel
PROCESSOR_LEVEL=6
PROCESSOR_REVISION=0304
ProgramFiles=C:\Program Files
PROMPT=$P$G
SystemDrive=C:
SystemRoot=C:\WINNT
TEMP=C:\DOCUME~1\CAROLY~1.GIL\LOCALS~1\Temp
TMP=C:\DOCUME~1\CAROLY~1.GIL\LOCALS~1\Temp
USERDOMAIN=DELLXPS
USERNAME=Carolyn Z. Gillay
USERPROFILE=C:\Documents and Settings\Carolyn Z. Gillay
windir=C:\WINNT


A:\>_
```

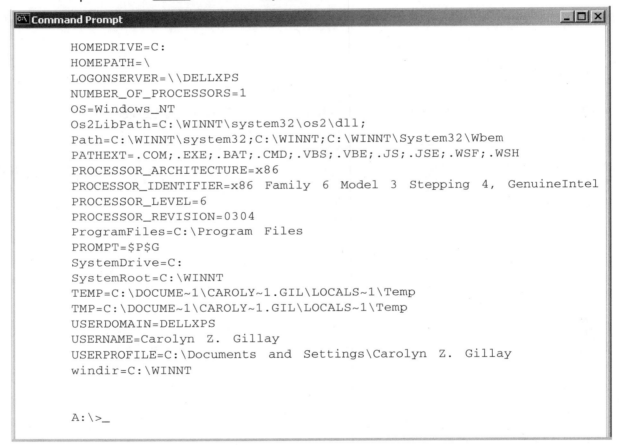

WHAT'S HAPPENING? When using MORE, pressing the **Enter** key moves you one line at time through the screen display whereas pressing the **Space Bar** moves you to the end of the file. Here you can see such environmental variables as what your user name is (Carolyn Z. Gillay in this example) as well as the default location for where your files will be saved (USERPROFILE).

Step 3 Key in the following: A:\>**SET U** **Enter**

Step 4 Key in the following: A:\>**SET S** **Enter**

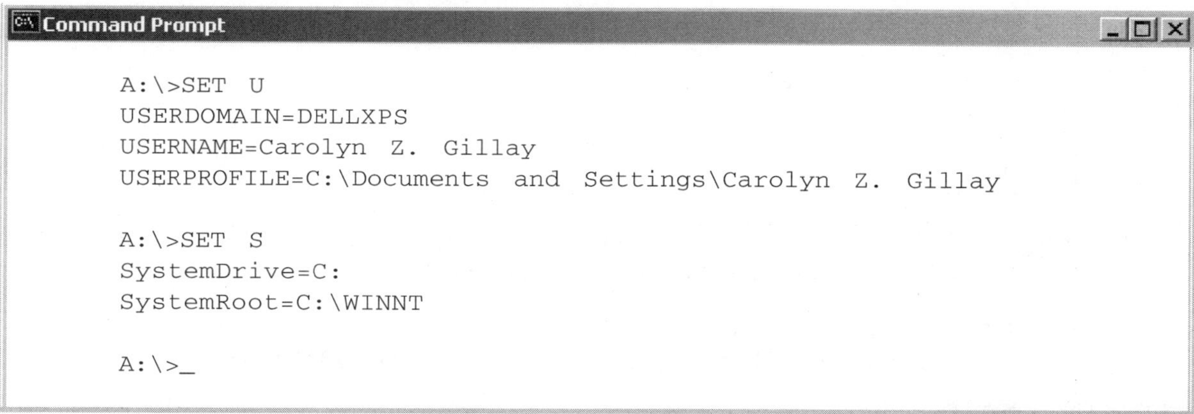

By using the SET command with a letter of the alphabet, all environmental variables that began with that letter were displayed. If you wanted to see the value of an environmental variable, you may do so with the ECHO command, provided that you enclose the environmental variable name you are seeking with percent signs.

Step 5 Key in the following: A:\>**ECHO %PATH%** Enter

Step 6 Key in the following: A:\>**ECHO %SystemRoot%** Enter

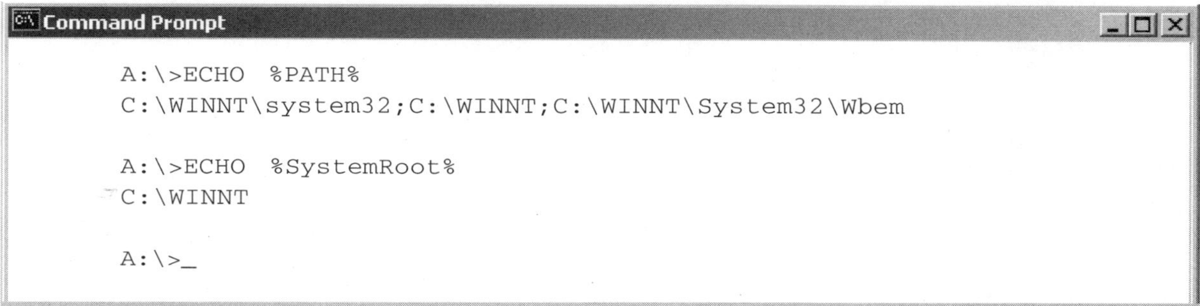

By surrounding the environmental name with percent signs, you see the value for the variable you requested. You may also use the environmental variable with commands.

Step 7 Key in the following: A:\>**C:** Enter

Step 8 Key in the following: C:\>**CD %SYSTEMROOT%** Enter

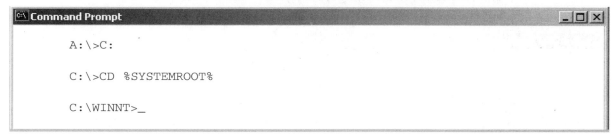

Instead of keying in CD \WINNT, you used the environmental variable %SYSTEMROOT%, which changed your location to the value held by the environmental variable %SYSTEMROOT%, in this case, C:\WINNT.

Step 9 Key in the following: C:\WINNT>**CD %USERPROFILE%** Enter

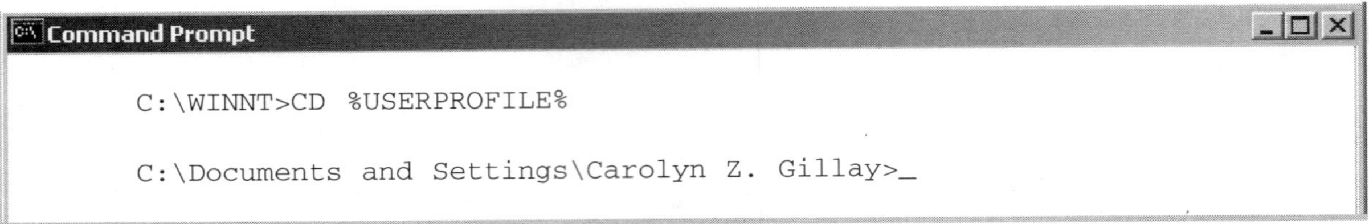

```
Command Prompt

C:\WINNT>CD %USERPROFILE%

C:\Documents and Settings\Carolyn Z. Gillay>_
```

WHAT'S HAPPENING? Again, you used an environmental variable to change directories. Using the environmental variables can be a useful shortcut.

Step 10 Key in the following:
C:\Documents and Settings\Carolyn Z. Gillay>**DIR /AH** Enter

```
Command Prompt

C:\Documents and Settings\Carolyn Z. Gillay>DIR /AH
 Volume in drive C is 2000 PRO
 Volume Serial Number is C4A7-8571

 Directory of C:\Documents and Settings\Carolyn Z. Gillay

05/22/2001  09:15a           1,126,400 NTUSER.DAT
02/26/2000  09:57p      <DIR>          Local Settings
02/26/2000  09:57p      <DIR>          Templates
02/26/2000  09:57p      <DIR>          SendTo
02/26/2000  09:57p      <DIR>          Recent
02/26/2000  09:57p      <DIR>          PrintHood
02/26/2000  09:57p      <DIR>          NetHood
02/26/2000  09:57p      <DIR>          Application Data
05/22/2001  09:15a               1,024 ntuser.dat.LOG
05/21/2001  10:47p                 180 ntuser.ini
               3 File(s)      1,127,604 bytes
               7 Dir(s)     564,199,424 bytes free

C:\Documents and Settings\Carolyn Z. Gillay>_
```

WHAT'S HAPPENING? Local Settings is a hidden directory that contains settings that are specific for this user.

Step 11 Key in the following (do not press Enter until you see Enter):
C:\Documents and Settings\Carolyn Z. Gillay>**DIR "LOCAL SETTINGS"\TEMP\~*.TMP** Enter

```
Command Prompt

 Volume in drive C is 2000 PRO
 Volume Serial Number is C4A7-8571

 Directory of C:\Documents and Settings\Carolyn Z. Gillay\local
settings\TEMP

04/13/2000  12:37a              16,384 ~DFCEDA.tmp
06/19/2000  09:57a              16,384 ~DFFBEF.tmp
03/16/2000  10:39p              74,928 ~WRS0000.tmp
03/16/2000  10:39p             180,224 ~WRF0001.tmp
```

```
03/24/2000  06:02p              6,188 ~WRS0001.tmp
03/24/2000  06:02p         11,309,056 ~WRC0002.tmp
05/22/2001  08:16a                512 ~DF1854.tmp
05/22/2001  09:16a                512 ~DFC6A4.tmp
05/26/2000  01:31a             16,384 ~DF4441.tmp
05/22/2001  08:16a                512 ~DF1DAF.tmp
05/22/2001  08:18a            124,416 ~WRS0002.tmp
05/22/2001  09:16a                512 ~DFC6C9.tmp
05/22/2001  09:16a                512 ~DFC6B4.tmp
05/22/2001  08:49a             22,016 ~WRC0005.tmp
05/22/2001  08:49a                512 ~DFA147.tmp
05/22/2001  09:20a                512 ~DFCA7C.tmp
              16 File(s)     11,769,564 bytes
               0 Dir(s)     564,199,424 bytes free

C:\Documents and Settings\Carolyn Z. Gillay>_
```

WHAT'S HAPPENING? You may have fewer files then those that are listed here (or no files). The TEMP directory is where Windows keeps temporary files that it is supposed to delete when you finish using a program. Often these files are not deleted. Rather than having to key in a long path name with the DEL command (DEL C:\W C:\Documents and Settings\Carolyn Z. Gillay\LOCAL SETTINGS\TEMP\~*.TMP, you can use the environmental variable name.

Step 12 Key in the following:
C:\Documents and Settings\Carolyn Z. Gillay>**DEL %TEMP%\~*.TMP** Enter

Step 13 Key in the following:
C:\Documents and Settings\Carolyn Z. Gillay>**DIR %TEMP%\~*.TMP** Enter

Command Prompt

```
C:\Documents and Settings\Carolyn Z. Gillay>DEL %TEMP%\~*.TMP

C:\Documents and Settings\Carolyn Z. Gillay>DIR %TEMP%\~*.TMP
 Volume in drive C is 2000 PRO
 Volume Serial Number is C4A7-8571

 Directory of C:\DOCUME~1\CAROLY~1.GIL\LOCALS~1\Temp

File Not Found

C:\Documents and Settings\Carolyn Z. Gillay>_
```

WHAT'S HAPPENING? You have quickly deleted the **~.TMP** files using an environmental variable.

Step 14 Key in the following:
C:\Documents and Settings\Carolyn Z.Gillay>**CD ** Enter

Step 15 Key in the following: C:\> **A:** Enter

WHAT'S HAPPENING? You have returned to the root of C, then returned to Drive A.

11.22 USING SET AND THE ENVIRONMENT IN BATCH FILES

You have been using the built-in environmental variables that Windows sets and uses. You can also set your own environmental variables, giving them both a name and a value in a batch file as well as at the command line. Once you set the variable, you may use it in a batch file. However, any variables that are set are only good for that session of the Command Prompt window. Once you exit the command prompt, those values are no longer available the next time you open the command prompt.

11.23 ACTIVITY: USING SET AND THE ENVIRONMENT IN BATCH FILES

Note: The DATA disk should be in Drive A. The displayed prompt is A:\>.

Step 1 Close the Command Prompt window, and reopen it to begin a new DOS session. Return to the A:\> prompt.

Step 2 Write and save the following batch file called **TESTIT.BAT**:

@ECHO OFF
ECHO %PATH%
ECHO.

Step 3 Key in the following: A:\>**TESTIT** Enter

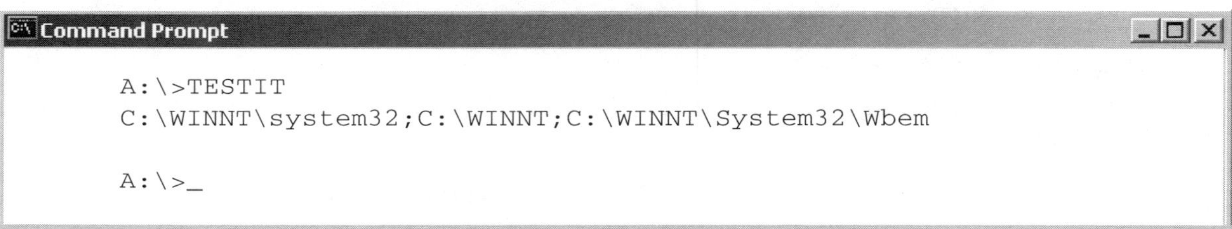

```
Command Prompt

A:\>TESTIT
C:\WINNT\system32;C:\WINNT;C:\WINNT\System32\Wbem

A:\>_
```

WHAT'S HAPPENING? The screen display created by this batch file showed the path used in a Command Prompt window on your system. Notice that it did not return the word PATH but the value stored in the environmental variable "PATH." You can set an environmental value and then use it in a batch file.

Step 4 Key in the following: A:\>**SET TODAY=C:\WINDOSBK*.99** Enter

Step 5 Key in the following: A:\>**SET** Enter

```
Command Prompt

HOMEDRIVE=C:
HOMEPATH=\
LOGONSERVER=\\DELLXPS
NUMBER_OF_PROCESSORS=1
OS=Windows_NT
Os2LibPath=C:\WINNT\system32\os2\dll;
Path=C:\WINNT\system32;C:\WINNT;C:\WINNT\System32\Wbem
PATHEXT=.COM;.EXE;.BAT;.CMD;.VBS;.VBE;.JS;.JSE;.WSF;.WSH
PROCESSOR_ARCHITECTURE=x86
PROCESSOR_IDENTIFIER=x86 Family 6 Model 3 Stepping 4, GenuineIntel
PROCESSOR_LEVEL=6
PROCESSOR_REVISION=0304
ProgramFiles=C:\Program Files
```

```
PROMPT=$P$G
SystemDrive=C:
SystemRoot=C:\WINNT
TEMP=C:\DOCUME~1\CAROLY~1.GIL\LOCALS~1\Temp
TMP=C:\DOCUME~1\CAROLY~1.GIL\LOCALS~1\Temp
TODAY=C:\WINDSOBK\*.99
USERDOMAIN=DELLXPS
USERNAME=Carolyn Z. Gillay
USERPROFILE=C:\Documents and Settings\Carolyn Z. Gillay
windir=C:\WINNT

A:\>_
```

WHAT'S HAPPENING? You now have a value for TODAY, which you set in the environment as **C:\WINDOSBK*.99**. Now, as long as you do not close the Command Prompt window, you can use it in a batch file. When you close the Command Prompt window, the environmental variables you set there will disappear.

Step 6 Write and save the following batch file called **SETTING.BAT**:

DIR %today%
ECHO %TODAY%

Step 7 Key in the following: A:\>**SETTING** Enter

```
Command Prompt

A:\>SETTING

A:\>DIR C:\WINDOSBK\*.99
 Volume in drive C is 2000 PRO
 Volume Serial Number is C4A7-8571

 Directory of C:\WINDOSBK

10/10/1999  04:53p                  72 APR.99
10/10/1999  04:53p                  75 FEB.99
10/10/1999  04:53p                  73 JAN.99
10/10/1999  04:53p                  71 MAR.99
               4 File(s)           291 bytes
               0 Dir(s)   6,776,516,608 bytes free

A:\>ECHO C:\WINDOSBK\*.99
C:\WINDOSBK\*.99

A:\>_
```

WHAT'S HAPPENING? Your batch file needed a value for %today%. The percent signs indicate that the value was in the environment. It substituted **C:\WINDOSBK*.99** for %today% and for %TODAY%. Case does not matter with environmental variables. You can use another value.

Step 8 Key in the following: A:\>**SET TODAY=C:\WINDOSBK*.TMP** Enter

Step 9 Key in the following: A:\>**SETTING** Enter

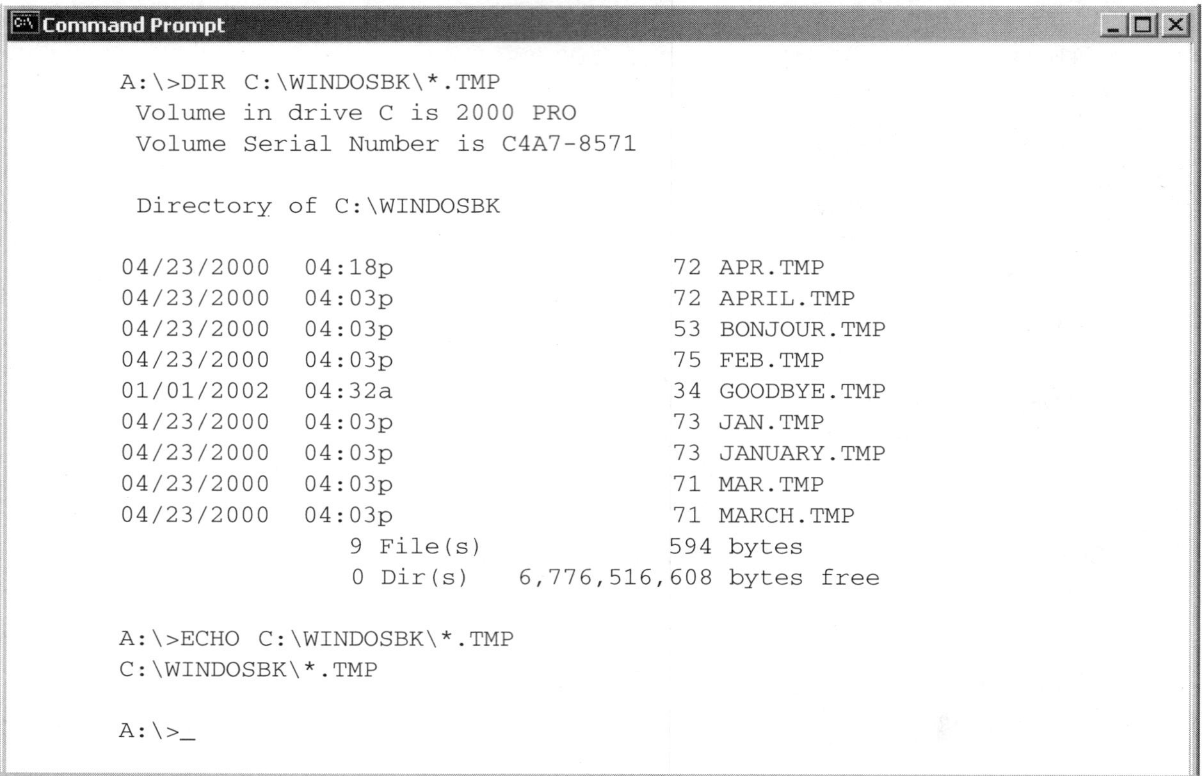

```
Command Prompt

A:\>DIR C:\WINDOSBK\*.TMP
 Volume in drive C is 2000 PRO
 Volume Serial Number is C4A7-8571

 Directory of C:\WINDOSBK

04/23/2000  04:18p                  72 APR.TMP
04/23/2000  04:03p                  72 APRIL.TMP
04/23/2000  04:03p                  53 BONJOUR.TMP
04/23/2000  04:03p                  75 FEB.TMP
01/01/2002  04:32a                  34 GOODBYE.TMP
04/23/2000  04:03p                  73 JAN.TMP
04/23/2000  04:03p                  73 JANUARY.TMP
04/23/2000  04:03p                  71 MAR.TMP
04/23/2000  04:03p                  71 MARCH.TMP
               9 File(s)           594 bytes
               0 Dir(s)   6,776,516,608 bytes free

A:\>ECHO C:\WINDOSBK\*.TMP
C:\WINDOSBK\*.TMP

A:\>_
```

WHAT'S HAPPENING? Since you changed the value of %TODAY% from **C:\WINDOSBK*.99** to **C:\WINDOSBK*.TMP**, the batch file knew to get only the value in the environment called %TODAY%. To eliminate the value, you must set it to nothing.

Step 10 Key in the following: A:\>**SET TODAY=** Enter

Step 11 Key in the following: A:\>**SET T** Enter

```
Command Prompt

A:\>SET TODAY=

A:\>SET T
TEMP=C:\DOCUME~1\CAROLY~1.GIL\LOCALS~1\Temp
TMP=C:\DOCUME~1\CAROLY~1.GIL\LOCALS~1\Temp

A:\>_
```

WHAT'S HAPPENING? You no longer have an environmental value called TODAY. That environmental variable would have been eliminated automatically if you had closed and reopened the Command Prompt window.

Step 12 Key in the following: A:\>**SET TODAY=FRIDAY** Enter

Step 13 Key in the following: A:\>**ECHO %TODAY%** Enter

Step 14 Key in the following: A:\>**SET T** Enter

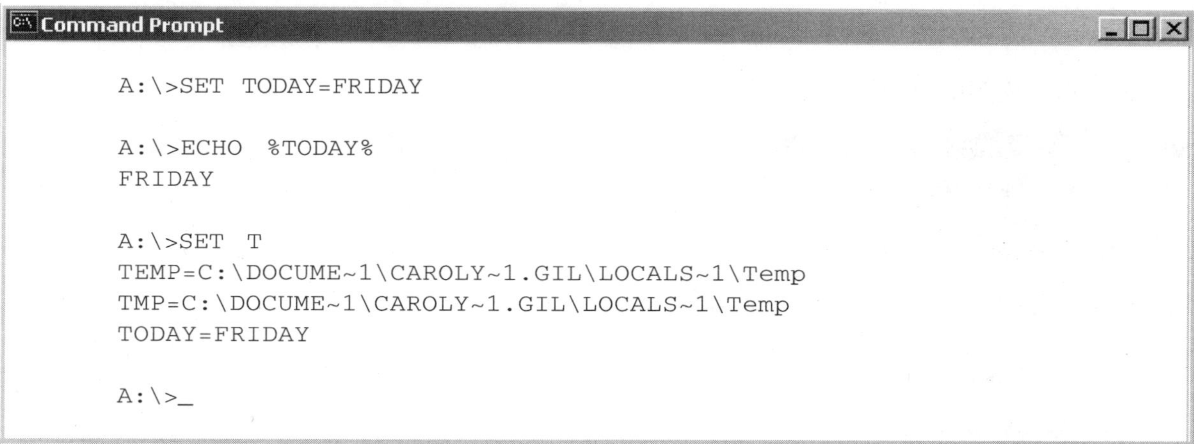


```
A:\>SET TODAY=FRIDAY

A:\>ECHO %TODAY%
FRIDAY

A:\>SET T
TEMP=C:\DOCUME~1\CAROLY~1.GIL\LOCALS~1\Temp
TMP=C:\DOCUME~1\CAROLY~1.GIL\LOCALS~1\Temp
TODAY=FRIDAY

A:\>_
```

WHAT'S HAPPENING? You have set a new environmental variable with the value of FRIDAY. You have used the variable syntax %VARIABLENAME% to display the value of the variable. You have also used the SET T command to see any current environment variables that begin with T.

Step 15 Close the Command Prompt window.

Step 16 Reopen the Command Prompt window, and return to the A prompt.

Step 17 Key in the following: A:\>**SET T** Enter

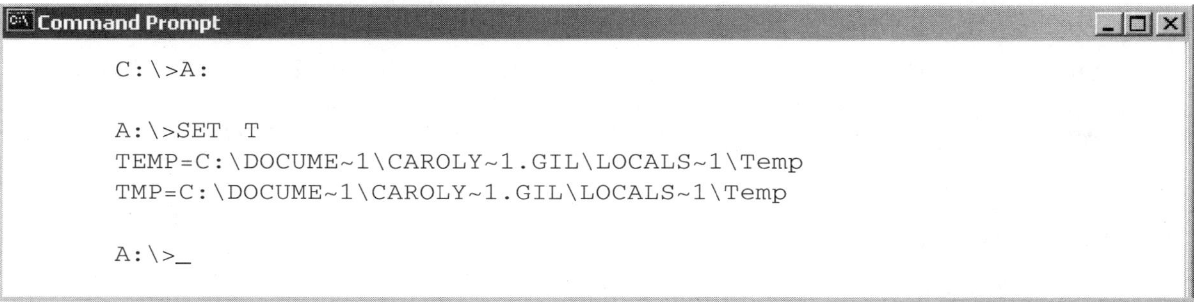


```
C:\>A:

A:\>SET T
TEMP=C:\DOCUME~1\CAROLY~1.GIL\LOCALS~1\Temp
TMP=C:\DOCUME~1\CAROLY~1.GIL\LOCALS~1\Temp

A:\>_
```

WHAT'S HAPPENING? The TODAY variable is no longer there. You can create a useful batch file that you can use during a DOS session. You don't often want to add a directory to your PATH statement, but perhaps you will be doing a lot of work at the Command Prompt using files that are in the root of the A drive. To do this by hand would involve keying in the entire path you currently have and adding your new directory to the end. There is an easier way to do it using the environment.

Note: The default prompt is A:\>.

Step 18 Write and save the following batch file called **ADD.BAT**:

```
IF "%1"= ="" GOTO END
PATH > OLDPATH.BAT
:TOP
PATH %PATH%;%1
SHIFT
IF NOT \%1\==\\ GOTO TOP
:END
```

Step 19 Key in the following: A:\>**PATH > ORIGPATH.BAT** [Enter]

Step 20 Key in the following: A:\>**ADD A:\PROG\GAMES** [Enter]

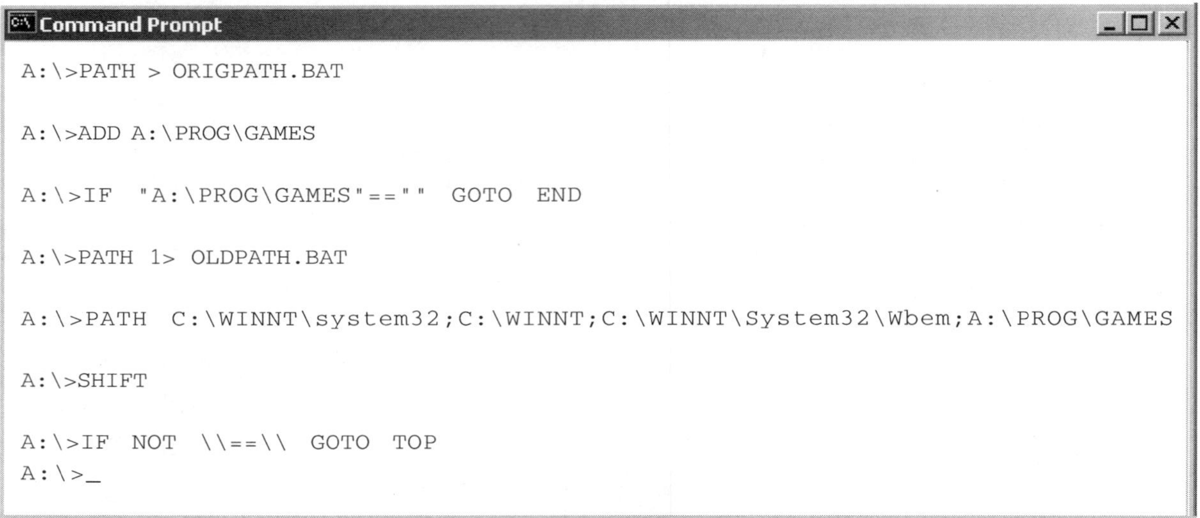

```
Command Prompt
A:\>PATH > ORIGPATH.BAT

A:\>ADD A:\PROG\GAMES

A:\>IF  "A:\PROG\GAMES"==""  GOTO  END

A:\>PATH 1> OLDPATH.BAT

A:\>PATH  C:\WINNT\system32;C:\WINNT;C:\WINNT\System32\Wbem;A:\PROG\GAMES

A:\>SHIFT

A:\>IF  NOT  \\==\\  GOTO  TOP
A:\>_
```

WHAT'S HAPPENING? To preserve your default path, you saved it to a file called **ORIGPATH.BAT**. You then used your new batch file, **ADD.BAT**, and added the **GAMES** directory to the path. You can add more than one directory.

Step 21 Key in the following: A:\>**ORIGPATH** [Enter]

Step 22 Key in the following: A:\>**ADD A:\PROG\UTILS OLDER CLASS** [Enter]

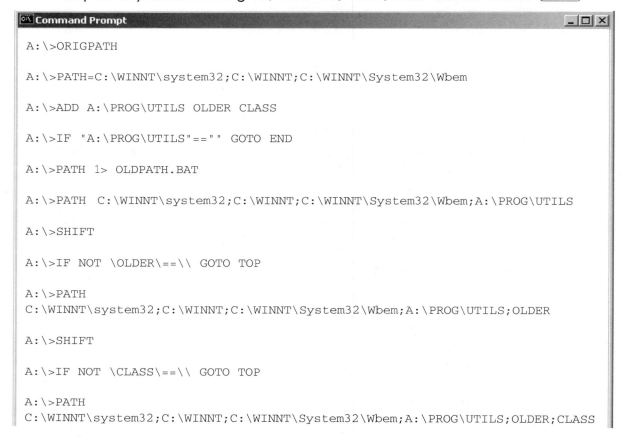

```
Command Prompt
A:\>ORIGPATH

A:\>PATH=C:\WINNT\system32;C:\WINNT;C:\WINNT\System32\Wbem

A:\>ADD A:\PROG\UTILS OLDER CLASS

A:\>IF "A:\PROG\UTILS"=="" GOTO END

A:\>PATH 1> OLDPATH.BAT

A:\>PATH  C:\WINNT\system32;C:\WINNT;C:\WINNT\System32\Wbem;A:\PROG\UTILS

A:\>SHIFT

A:\>IF NOT \OLDER\==\\ GOTO TOP

A:\>PATH
C:\WINNT\system32;C:\WINNT;C:\WINNT\System32\Wbem;A:\PROG\UTILS;OLDER

A:\>SHIFT

A:\>IF NOT \CLASS\==\\ GOTO TOP

A:\>PATH
C:\WINNT\system32;C:\WINNT;C:\WINNT\System32\Wbem;A:\PROG\UTILS;OLDER;CLASS
```

```
A:\>SHIFT

A:\>IF NOT \\==\\ GOTO TOP
A:\>_
```

WHAT'S HAPPENING? You have quickly added new directories to your path.

Step 23 Key in the following: A:\>**PATH** Enter

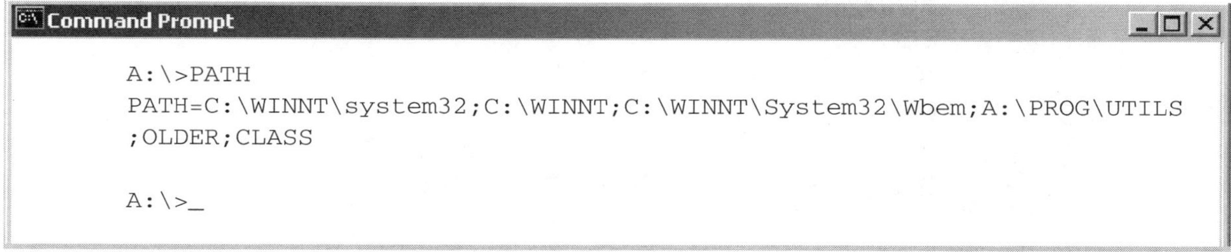

```
A:\>PATH
PATH=C:\WINNT\system32;C:\WINNT;C:\WINNT\System32\Wbem;A:\PROG\UTILS
;OLDER;CLASS

A:\>_
```

WHAT'S HAPPENING? You keyed in **PATH** to confirm that you added subdirectories. To return to your original path, you created **ORIGPATH.BAT**.

Step 24 Key in the following: A:\>**ORIGPATH** Enter

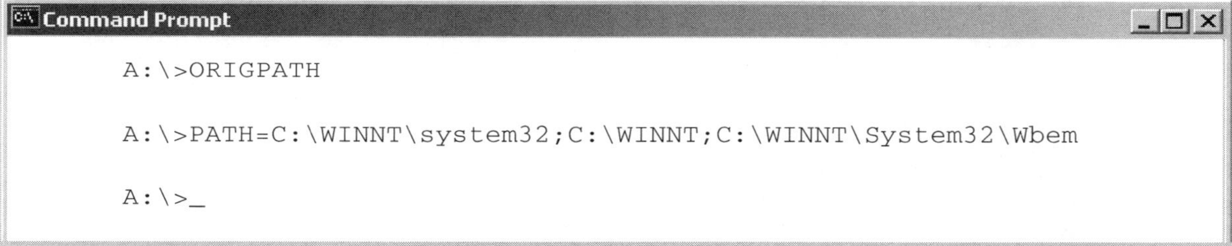

```
A:\>ORIGPATH

A:\>PATH=C:\WINNT\system32;C:\WINNT;C:\WINNT\System32\Wbem

A:\>_
```

11.24 THE DIRCMD ENVIRONMENTAL VARIABLE

As has been discussed, the environment is an area that is set aside in memory. In addition to being able to place and use variables in the environment, you can preset DIR command parameters and switches by including the SET command with the DIRCMD environmental variable. Keying in SET by itself will tell you what is in the environment. You can use the DIRCMD variable and ERRORLEVEL to write a batch file that will allow you to change the way DIR displays information for the current command prompt work session.

11.25 ACTIVITY: USING DIRCMD

Note: The DATA disk should be in Drive A. The displayed prompt is A:\>.

Step 1 Create the following batch file called **MY.BAT**:

@ECHO OFF
CLS
ECHO.
ECHO.
ECHO How do you want your directory displayed?
ECHO.

```
ECHO   1.   Files only arranged by file name.       A to Z
ECHO   2.   Files only arranged by file name.       Z to A
ECHO   3.   Files only arranged by file extension.  A to Z
ECHO   4.   Files only arranged by file extension.  Z to A
ECHO   5.   Directory displays in default mode.
ECHO.
ECHO PLEASE SELECT A NUMBER.
ECHO.
REPLY
ECHO.
IF ERRORLEVEL 49 IF NOT ERRORLEVEL 50 SET DIRCMD=/ON /A-D
IF ERRORLEVEL 50 IF NOT ERRORLEVEL 51 SET DIRCMD=/O-N /A-D
IF ERRORLEVEL 51 IF NOT ERRORLEVEL 52 SET DIRCMD=/OE /A-D
IF ERRORLEVEL 52 IF NOT ERRORLEVEL 53 SET DIRCMD=/O-E /A-D
IF ERRORLEVEL 53 IF NOT ERRORLEVEL 54 SET DIRCMD=
```

WHAT'S HAPPENING? You have created a batch file to set the DIRCMD environmental variable.

Step 2 Key in the following: A:\>**MY** Enter

```
Command Prompt

How do you want your directory displayed?

   1.      Files only arranged by file name.          A to Z
   2.      Files only arranged by file name.          Z to A
   3.      Files only arranged by file extension.     A to Z
   4.      Files only arranged by file extension.     Z to A
   5.      Directory displays in default mode.

PLEASE SELECT A NUMBER.
```

WHAT'S HAPPENING? The batch file is asking you to select how you want your batch files displayed. You want your files displayed in file extension order in descending order (Z–A).

Step 3 Key in the following: A:\>**4**

Step 4 Key in the following: A:\>**SET D** Enter

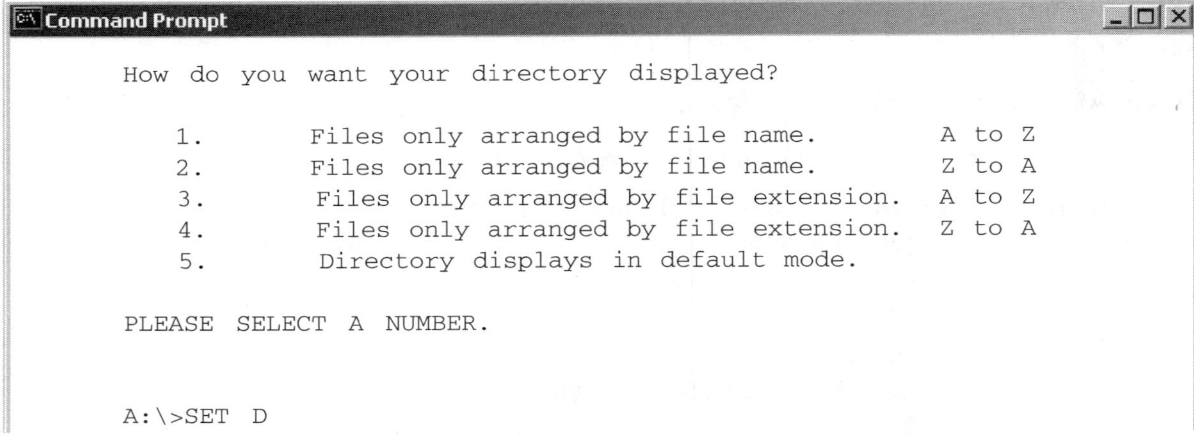
Command Prompt
How do you want your directory displayed?
1. Files only arranged by file name. A to Z
2. Files only arranged by file name. Z to A
3. Files only arranged by file extension. A to Z
4. Files only arranged by file extension. Z to A
5. Directory displays in default mode.
PLEASE SELECT A NUMBER.
A:\>SET D

```
DIRCMD=/O-E /A-D

A:\>_
```

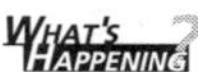

Now during this Command Prompt session, whenever you key in **DIR**, it will automatically arrange the files by extension in reverse order. You can see that you have established the environmental variable for DIRCMD to equal the switches /O-E and /A-D.

Step 5 Key in the following: A:\>**DIR CLASS** Enter

```
Command Prompt

ADIR CLASS
 Volume in drive A is DATA
 Volume Serial Number is F0F9-2830

 Directory of A:\CLASS

04/23/2000  04:03p                 71 MAR.PAR
04/23/2000  04:03p                 75 FEB.PAR
04/23/2000  04:18p                 72 APR.PAR
04/23/2000  04:03p                 73 JAN.PAR
10/10/1999  04:53p                 72 JAN.FIL
10/10/1999  04:53p                 71 MAR.FIL
04/23/2000  04:03p                 73 JAN.BUD
04/23/2000  04:03p                 71 MAR.BUD
12/06/2000  02:45p                 19 APR.BUD
04/23/2000  04:03p                 75 FEB.ABC
04/23/2000  04:03p                 73 JAN.ABC
04/23/2000  04:03p                 71 MAR.ABC
04/23/2000  04:18p                 72 APR.ABC
              13 File(s)           888 bytes
               0 Dir(s)        875,520 bytes free

A:\>_
```

WHAT'S HAPPENING?

The files are arranged by file extension in reverse alphabetical order. Until you change the values, or close this Command Prompt session, every time you issue the DIR command it will display file names in reverse alphabetical order by file extension.

Step 6 Key in the following: A:\>**MY** Enter

Step 7 Press **5**

Step 8 Key in the following: A:\>**SET D** Enter

```
Command Prompt

How do you want your directory displayed?

  1.      Files only arranged by file name.       A to Z
  2.      Files only arranged by file name.       Z to A
  3.      Files only arranged by file extension.  A to Z
```

```
  4.        Files only arranged by file extension.  Z to A
  5.        Directory displays in default mode.

PLEASE SELECT A NUMBER.


A:\>SET D
Environment variable D not defined

A:\>_
```

You returned the default DIRCMD environmental variable to its default value. DIRCMD is no longer defined.

11.26 THE FOR...IN...DO COMMAND

The FOR...IN...DO command can be issued at the command line or placed in a batch file. This command allows repetitive processing. FOR allows you to use a single command to issue several commands at once. The command can DO something FOR every value IN a specified set. The basic syntax at the command line is:

```
FOR %variable IN (set) DO command [command-parameters]

 %variable              Specifies a replaceable parameter.
 (set)                  Specifies a set of one or more files. Wildcards
                        may be used.
 command                Specifies the command to carry out for each file.
 command-parameters     Specifies parameters or switches for the specified
                        command.

To use the FOR command in a batch program, specify %%variable instead of
%variable.
```

The FOR command has been greatly expanded in Windows 2000 Professional. For full details, key in FOR /?.

The batch file variable is an arbitrary single letter. The double percent sign with a letter (%%a) distinguishes the batch file variable from the replaceable parameter (%1). The difference between a variable and a parameter is not complicated. The FOR statement tells the operating system to get a value from the set you have chosen. After it executes the command that appears after DO, the FOR command looks for the next value in the set. If it finds another value, %%a will represent something new, and the command will be executed with the new value. If there are no more values in the set, the FOR command stops processing.

If you consider the GOTO label as a *vertical* loop, you can consider the FOR...IN...DO as a *horizontal* loop. You do not need to use the letter a. You may use any letter—a, c, x, etc. The parameter value, on the other hand, is set before the batch file begins processing. Remember, the operating system gets the value from the position in the command line. The set is always enclosed in parentheses. The values in the set, either data or file names, will be used to DO some command. The items in the set must be separated by spaces or commas. You may also use wildcards in a set.

11.27 ACTIVITY: USING THE FOR...IN...DO COMMAND

Note 1: The DATA disk should be in Drive A. The displayed prompt is A:\>.

Note 2: Look at the command line you are going to use in Step 1. In English, the command says: Using the variable %a to hold each value in the set (what is in parentheses), do the command (TYPE) to each value in the set (%a).

Step 1 Key in the following: A:\>**FOR %a IN (*.99) DO TYPE %a** Enter

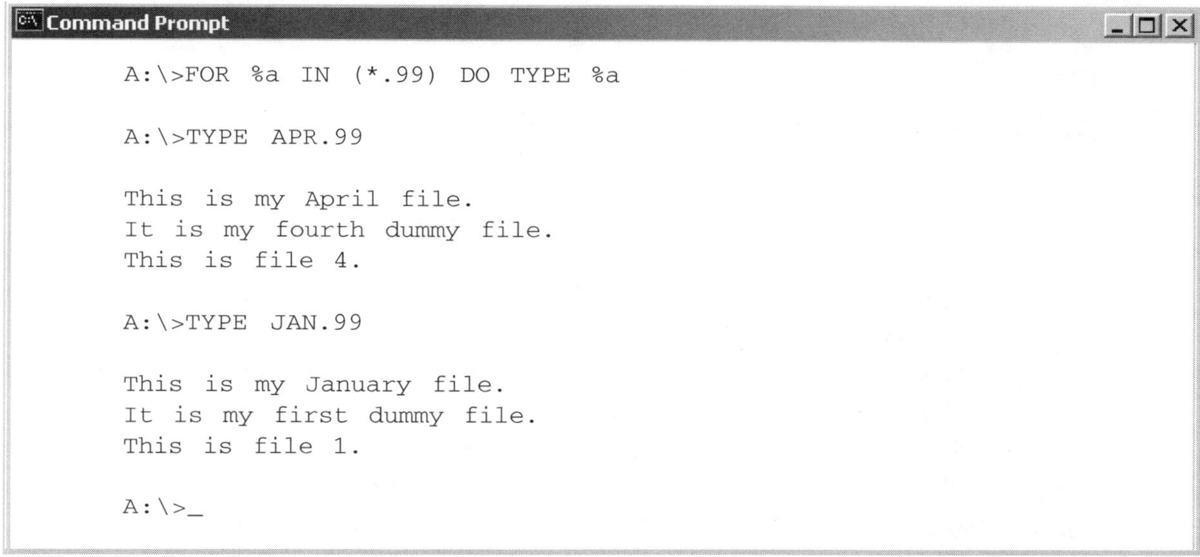

```
A:\>FOR %a IN (*.99) DO TYPE %a

A:\>TYPE APR.99

This is my April file.
It is my fourth dummy file.
This is file 4.

A:\>TYPE JAN.99

This is my January file.
It is my first dummy file.
This is file 1.

A:\>_
```

WHAT'S HAPPENING? FOR...IN...DO processed every item in the set as indicated below. Besides using wildcards, you can also be specific.

Step 2 Key in the following:
A:\>**FOR %x IN (APR.99 NOFILE.EXT D.BAT) DO TYPE %x** Enter

Step 3 Key in the following:
A:\>**FOR %y IN (APR.99,NOFILE.EXT,D.BAT) DO TYPE %y** Enter

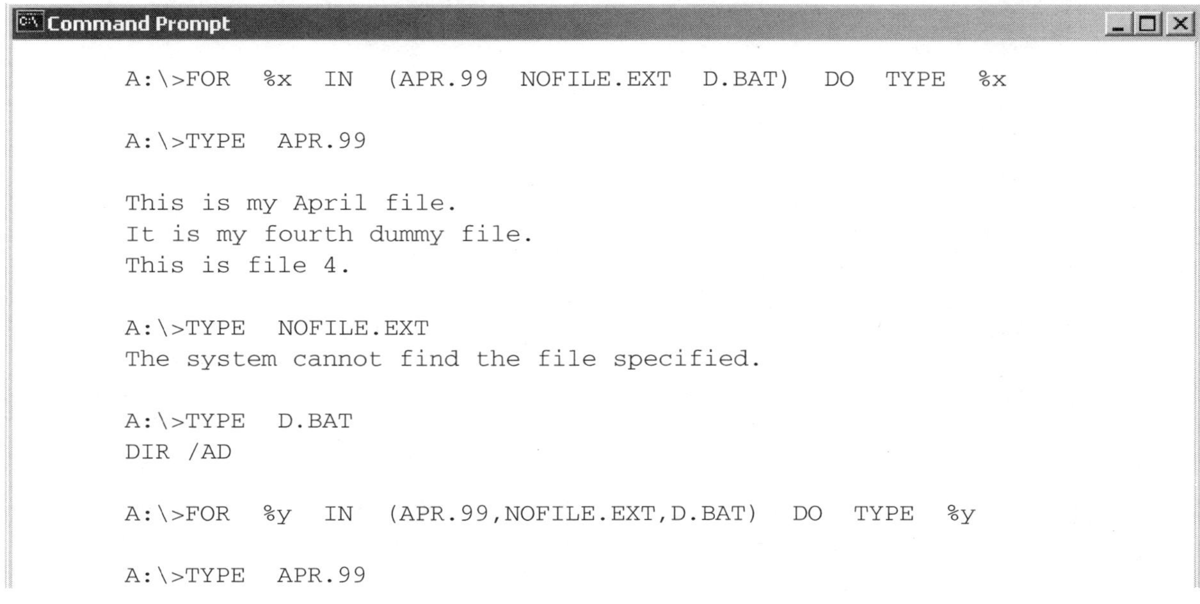

```
A:\>FOR %x IN (APR.99 NOFILE.EXT D.BAT) DO TYPE %x

A:\>TYPE APR.99

This is my April file.
It is my fourth dummy file.
This is file 4.

A:\>TYPE NOFILE.EXT
The system cannot find the file specified.

A:\>TYPE D.BAT
DIR /AD

A:\>FOR %y IN (APR.99,NOFILE.EXT,D.BAT) DO TYPE %y

A:\>TYPE APR.99
```

```
This is my April file.
It is my fourth dummy file.
This is file 4.

A:\>TYPE NOFILE.EXT
The system cannot find the file specified.

A:\>TYPE D.BAT
DIR /AD

A:\>_
```

There are some important things to notice about these command lines. First, both a space and a comma between items in a set work the same way. Second, the variable letter you choose is not important. In the first case, x was chosen—in the second, y. This command line is case sensitive. If you had keyed in **FOR %b IN (APR.99 NOFILE.EXT D.BAT) DO TYPE %B**, the difference between b and B would have made the command line invalid. Even when there was an invalid file (**NOFILE.EXT**), the command line continued processing the other file names in the command. You did not need to worry about testing for null values. This command works the same when placed in a batch file, only you must use %%. However, it appears that this works no differently than had you keyed in TYPE *.99 nofile.ext.

Step 4 Key in the following:A:\> **TYPE *.99 NOFILE.EXT** Enter

```
Command Prompt

A:\>TYPE *.99 NOFILE.EXT

APR.99



This is my April file.
It is my fourth dummy file.
This is file 4.

JAN.99



This is my January file.
It is my first dummy file.
This is file 1.
The system cannot find the file specified.
Error occurred while processing: NOFILE.EXT.

A:\>_
```

You see an error message since NOFILE.EXT does not exist. You can use a test to test for an existence of a file in conjunction with the FOR...IN...DO so

that the TYPE command will only display the files it finds and will not display any error messages.

Key in the following:
A:\>**FOR %a IN (*.99,NOFILE) DO IF EXIST %a TYPE %a** Enter

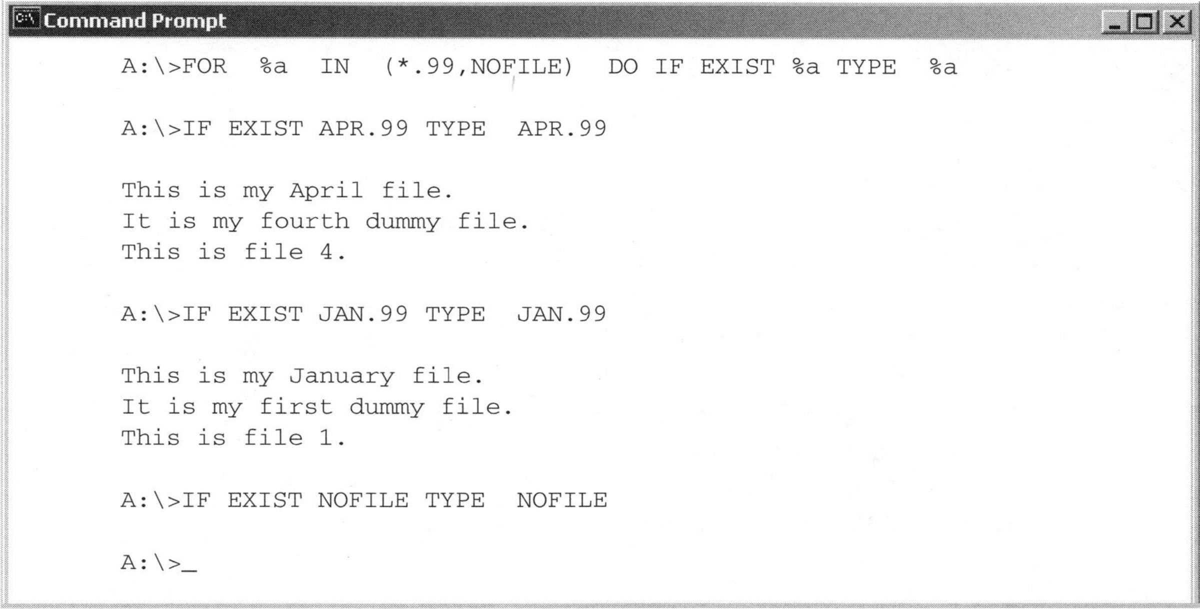

```
A:\>FOR  %a  IN  (*.99,NOFILE)  DO IF EXIST %a TYPE  %a

A:\>IF EXIST APR.99 TYPE  APR.99

This is my April file.
It is my fourth dummy file.
This is file 4.

A:\>IF EXIST JAN.99 TYPE  JAN.99

This is my January file.
It is my first dummy file.
This is file 1.

A:\>IF EXIST NOFILE TYPE  NOFILE

A:\>_
```

WHAT'S HAPPENING? Now that you checked to see if there is a file, you no longer see the error message. You can also test for character strings supplied in the set.

Step 6 Create and save the following batch file called **DO.BAT** and key in the following: **FOR %%v IN (Patty Nicki Sandy Brian) DO ECHO %%v**

Step 7 Key in the following: A:\>**DO** Enter

```
A:\>DO

A:\>FOR %v IN (Patty Nicki Sandy Brian) DO ECHO %v

A:\>ECHO  Patty
Patty

A:\>ECHO  Nicki
Nicki

A:\>ECHO  Sandy
Sandy

A:\>ECHO  Brian
Brian

A:\>_
```

As you can see, the ECHO command was carried out for each item in the set. It substituted each value (**Patty**, **Nicki**, **Sandy**, and **Brian**) for the replaceable parameter in the ECHO command. In this example, spaces were used to separate the values, but you could have also used commas. The advantage to using this command is that you do not have to write it with a command on each line, as in:

```
ECHO Patty
ECHO Nicki
ECHO Sandy
ECHO Brian
```

Another advantage of the FOR...IN...DO method is that you can set values in the environment and then use them in a batch file.

Step 8 Write and save a batch file called **PASS.BAT** and key in the following:

```
FOR %%a IN (%USERS%) DO IF "%1"=="%%a" GOTO OKAY
:NO
ECHO You, %1, are NOT allowed in the system.
GOTO END
:OKAY
ECHO Welcome %1 to my world of computers.
:END
```

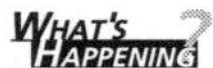

You have combined several features in this FOR..IN..DO statement. You have used an environmental variable in the set (**%USERS%**). The percent signs surrounding the value tell the FOR command to use the environmental variable called USERS. You have also used an IF statement. If what the user keys in is in the environment, then it is a true statement and the batch file will go to the :OKAY label. If what the user keys in is false and not equal to the environmental variable, then the batch file falls through to the next line. First, you need to set the environmental variable. (Use upper and lower case exactly as shown.)

Step 9 Key in the following: A:\>**SET USERS=Carolyn,Bette** Enter

Step 10 Key in the following: A:\>**PASS Bette** Enter

Command Prompt

```
A:\>PASS Bette

A:\>FOR %a IN (Carolyn,Bette) DO IF "Bette"=="%a" GOTO OKAY

A:\> IF "Bette"=="Carolyn" GOTO OKAY

A:\> IF "Bette"=="Bette" GOTO OKAY

A:\>ECHO Welcome Bette to my world of computers.
 Welcome Bette to my world of computers.
A:\>_
```

WHAT'S HAPPENING? You set the environmental values for USERS. You then executed the **PASS.BAT** batch file. It worked as directed because the statement was true. What if it were false?

Step 11 Key in the following: A:\>**PASS Denzel** Enter

```
Command Prompt

A:\>PASS Denzel

A:\>FOR %a IN (Carolyn,Bette) DO IF "Denzel"=="%a" GOTO OKAY

A:\> IF "Denzel"=="Carolyn" GOTO OKAY

A:\> IF "Denzel"=="Bette" GOTO OKAY

A:\>ECHO You, Denzel, are NOT allowed in the system.
 You, Denzel, are NOT allowed in the system.

A:\>GOTO END

A:\>_
```

WHAT'S HAPPENING? The statement was false and the batch file behaved accordingly. FOR..IN..DO can also be used with replaceable parameters, file names, and wildcards. You are going to take another look at **UPDATE.BAT**.

Step 12 Use any text editor and edit and save the **UPDATE.BAT** file so it looks as follows. Be sure you include two percent signs preceding "v."

:DOIT
IF "%1"=="" GOTO END
FOR %%v IN (%1) DO COPY %%v /b + > NUL
SHIFT
PAUSE
GOTO DOIT
:END

WHAT'S HAPPENING? You now can process any number of parameters that appear in the command line. There can be a problem with this batch file. As written, this batch file will copy the newly updated files to the current default directory. Thus, it is a good idea, in general, to place all your batch files in a subdirectory called **BATCH** and set your path to include the **BATCH** directory.

Step 13 Key in the following: A:\>**MD BATCH** Enter

Step 14 Key in the following: A:\>**ADD A:\BATCH** Enter

```
Command Prompt

A:\>MD BATCH

A:\>ADD A:\BATCH

A:\>IF "A:\BATCH"=="" GOTO END
```

```
A:\>PATH > OLDPATH.BAT

A:\>PATH C:\WINNT\system32;C:\WINNT;C:\WINNT\System32\Wbem;A:\BATCH

A:\>SHIFT

A:\>IF NOT \\==\\ GOTO TOP
A:\>_
```

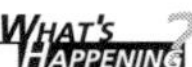

WHAT'S HAPPENING? You have created a subdirectory called **BATCH** and added it to your current path. Now you will move all the batch files, as well as the **REPLY** files, into the **BATCH** subdirectory.

Step 15 Key in the following: A:\>**MOVE *.BAT BATCH** Enter

Step 16 Key in the following: A:\>**MOVE REPLY*.* BATCH** Enter

Command Prompt

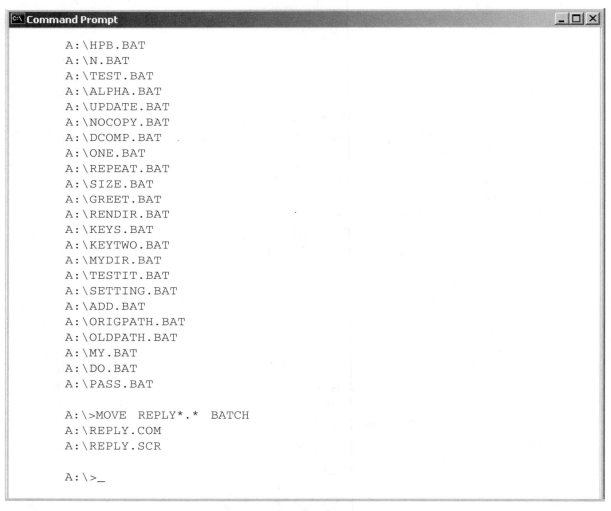

```
A:\HPB.BAT
A:\N.BAT
A:\TEST.BAT
A:\ALPHA.BAT
A:\UPDATE.BAT
A:\NOCOPY.BAT
A:\DCOMP.BAT
A:\ONE.BAT
A:\REPEAT.BAT
A:\SIZE.BAT
A:\GREET.BAT
A:\RENDIR.BAT
A:\KEYS.BAT
A:\KEYTWO.BAT
A:\MYDIR.BAT
A:\TESTIT.BAT
A:\SETTING.BAT
A:\ADD.BAT
A:\ORIGPATH.BAT
A:\OLDPATH.BAT
A:\MY.BAT
A:\DO.BAT
A:\PASS.BAT

A:\>MOVE REPLY*.* BATCH
A:\REPLY.COM
A:\REPLY.SCR

A:\>_
```

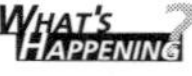

WHAT'S HAPPENING? You have moved all your batch files to the **BATCH** subdirectory and you included the **REPLY** files, because batch files use these programs. This grouping allowed you to clean up the root directory of the DATA disk. To ensure that you can use your batch files, you first added the **BATCH** subdirectory to the PATH statement.

CAUTION! IF YOU CLOSE THE COMMAND PROMPT WINDOW, YOU WILL HAVE TO ISSUE THE FOLLOWING COMMAND TO INCLUDE THE A:\BATCH DIRECTORY IN YOUR PATH: A:\BATCH>A:\BATCH\ADD A:\BATCH

Step 17 Key in the following: A:\>**DIR *.SWT** Enter

Step 18 Key in the following: A:\>**DIR *.CAP** Enter

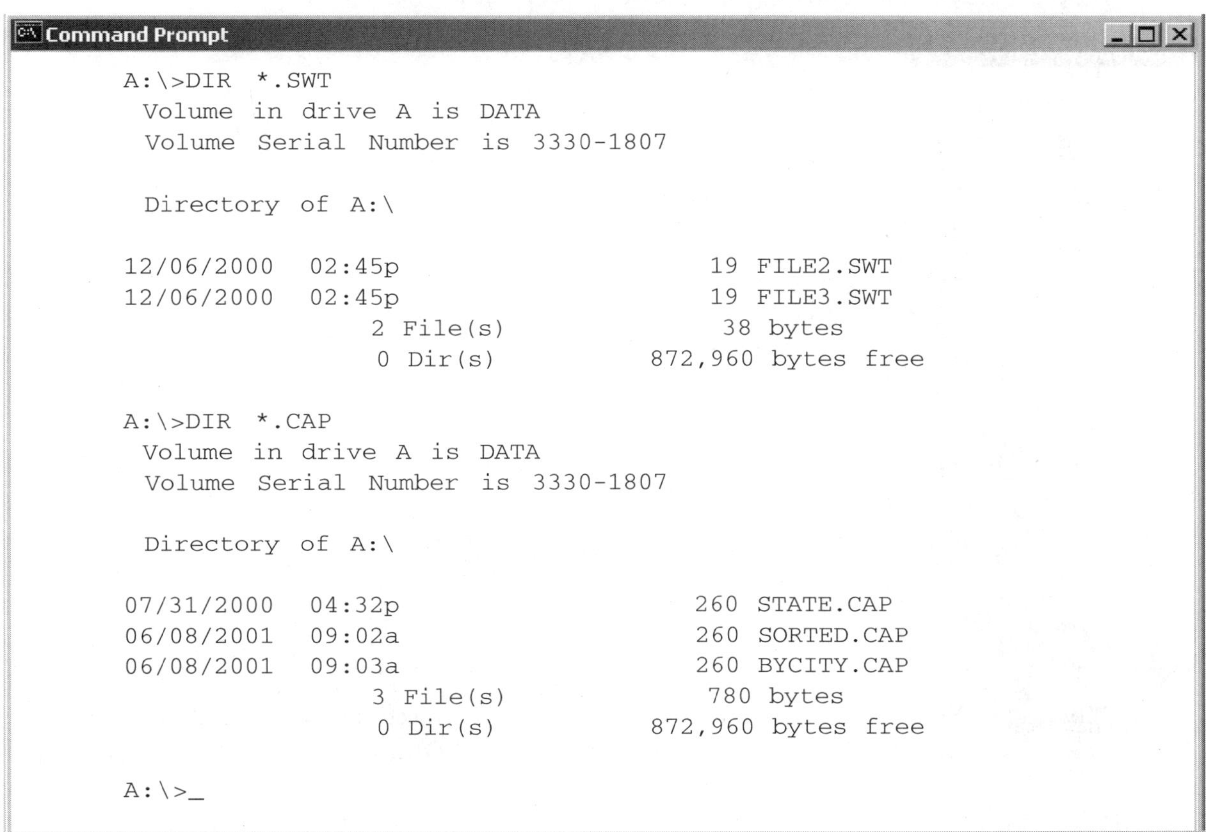

```
Command Prompt

A:\>DIR *.SWT
 Volume in drive A is DATA
 Volume Serial Number is 3330-1807

 Directory of A:\

12/06/2000  02:45p                  19 FILE2.SWT
12/06/2000  02:45p                  19 FILE3.SWT
               2 File(s)             38 bytes
               0 Dir(s)         872,960 bytes free

A:\>DIR *.CAP
 Volume in drive A is DATA
 Volume Serial Number is 3330-1807

 Directory of A:\

07/31/2000  04:32p                 260 STATE.CAP
06/08/2001  09:02a                 260 SORTED.CAP
06/08/2001  09:03a                 260 BYCITY.CAP
               3 File(s)            780 bytes
               0 Dir(s)         872,960 bytes free

A:\>_
```

WHAT'S HAPPENING? You can see the dates on these files. Now you are going to update them to the current date.

Step 19 Key in the following: A:\>**UPDATE *.SWT *.CAP** Enter

```
Command Prompt

A:\>UPDATE *.SWT *.CAP

A:\>IF "*.SWT" == "" GOTO END

A:\>FOR %v IN (*.SWT) DO COPY %v /b +  >NUL

A:\>COPY FILE2.SWT /b +  >NUL

A:\>COPY FILE3.SWT /b +  >NUL

A:\>SHIFT

A:\>PAUSE
Press any key to continue . . .
```

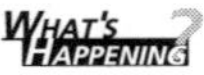

You can see how FOR processed each item in the set, which it got from the command line (%1 was ***.SWT**). Each file that had a **.SWT** file extension was updated. Now the batch file is going to SHIFT and process the new item in the set (***.CAP**).

Step 20 Keep pressing **Enter** until you are back at the command prompt.

Step 21 Key in the following: A:\>**DIR *.SWT *.CAP** **Enter**

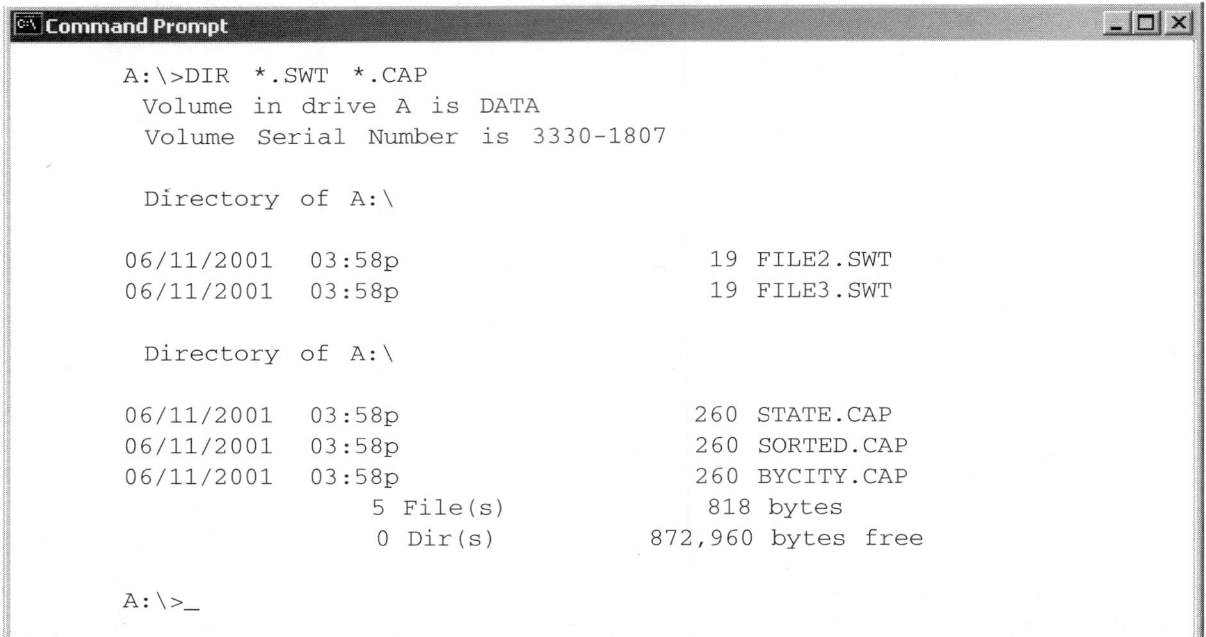

```
Command Prompt

A:\>DIR *.SWT *.CAP
 Volume in drive A is DATA
 Volume Serial Number is 3330-1807

 Directory of A:\

06/11/2001  03:58p                 19 FILE2.SWT
06/11/2001  03:58p                 19 FILE3.SWT

 Directory of A:\

06/11/2001  03:58p                260 STATE.CAP
06/11/2001  03:58p                260 SORTED.CAP
06/11/2001  03:58p                260 BYCITY.CAP
               5 File(s)            818 bytes
               0 Dir(s)         872,960 bytes free

A:\>_
```

WHAT'S HAPPENING? Your dates will be different, but you have successfully changed the dates of the files. You have successfully used the FOR.. IN..DO command.

11.28 NEW FEATURES OF THE FOR...IN...DO COMMAND

Some new features in of the FOR...IN...DO command is that you may list environmental variables so that they are divided and appear on separate lines. You may also use the special tilde operator (~) to perform such tasks as stripping a file name of quotation marks and to expand a variable. You may also use the /R parameter. The /R parameter is a recursive parameter. Recursive means that the command will search and perform actions on all subdirectories beneath it. You may also select specific text from ASCII files.

11.29 ACTIVITY: USING THE NEW FEATURES OF THE FOR...IN...DO COMMAND

Step 1 Key in the following: A:\>**SET PATHEXT** **Enter**

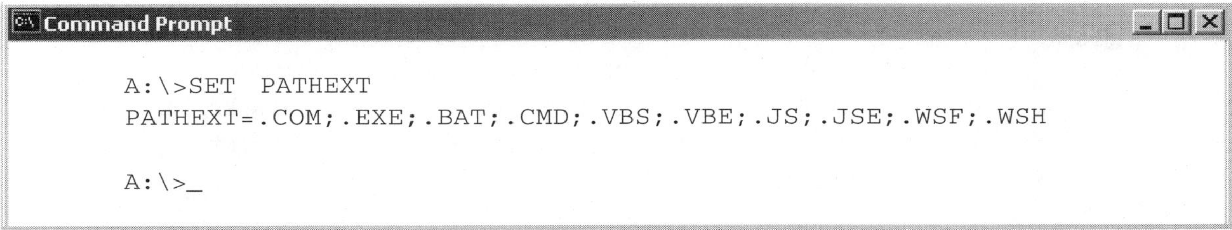
Command Prompt
A:\>SET PATHEXT
PATHEXT=.COM;.EXE;.BAT;.CMD;.VBS;.VBE;.JS;.JSE;.WSF;.WSH
A:\>_

WHAT'S HAPPENING? The above list is a list of the file extensions that Windows 2000 Professional has associated with the application programs on your system. Your list may be different. This list is separated by semicolons and appears on one line, sometimes making it difficult to read. You can use FOR...IN...DO to display the list one line at a time.

Step 2 Key in the following: A:\>**FOR %a IN (%pathext%) DO @ECHO %a** Enter

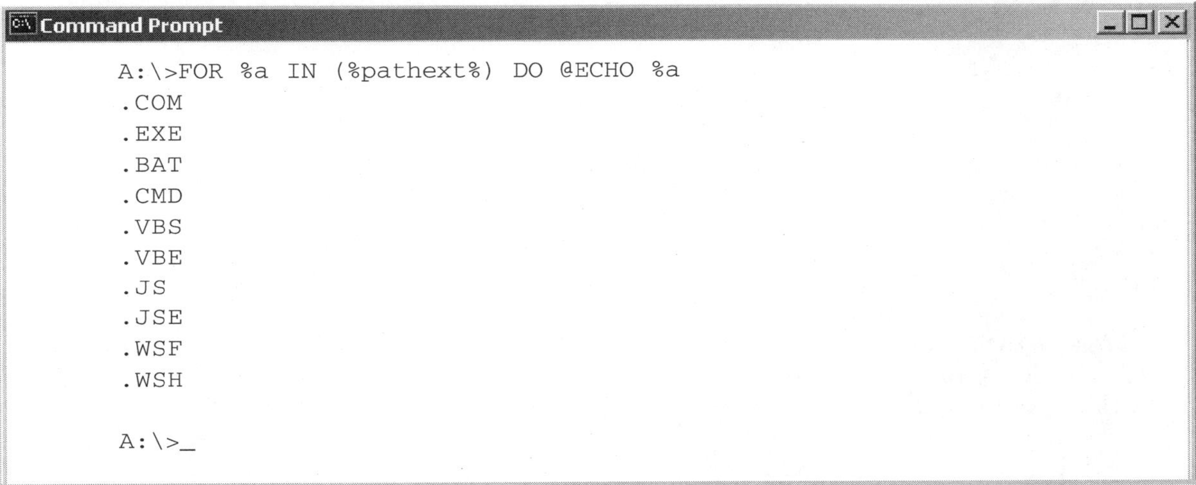
Command Prompt
A:\>FOR %a IN (%pathext%) DO @ECHO %a
.COM
.EXE
.BAT
.CMD
.VBS
.VBE
.JS
.JSE
.WSF
.WSH
A:\>_

WHAT'S HAPPENING? Now your extensions are listed one line at a time. Files with spaces in their names provide certain challenges at the command line as well as in batch files.

Step 3 Key in the following:
A:\>**FOR %a IN ("Sandy and Patty.txt", APRIL.TXT) DO @ECHO %a** Enter

Step 4 Key in the following:
A:\>**FOR %a IN ("Sandy and Patty.txt", APRIL.TXT) DO @ECHO %~a** Enter

Command Prompt

```
A:\>FOR %a IN ("Sandy and Patty.txt",APRIL.TXT) DO @ECHO %a
"Sandy and Patty.txt"
APRIL.TXT

A:\>FOR %a IN ("Sandy and Patty.txt",APRIL.TXT) DO @ECHO %~a
Sandy and Patty.txt
APRIL.TXT

A:\>_
```

In the second command, you added a tilde prior to the variable, a. This stripped the file name of its quotation marks. When you want to add a prefix or suffix to a long file name, you need to use quotation marks. However, if, in the set, you use quotation marks, when you try to rename a file, you will end up with extra quotation marks.

Step 5 Key in the following:
A:\>**FOR %a IN ("Sandy and Patty.txt", APRIL.TXT) DO @REN %a "CZG %a"** Enter

Step 6 Key in the following:
A:\>**FOR %a IN ("Sandy and Patty.txt", APRIL.TXT) DO @ECHO %~a** Enter

Step 7 Key in the following: A:\>**DIR CZG*.*** Enter

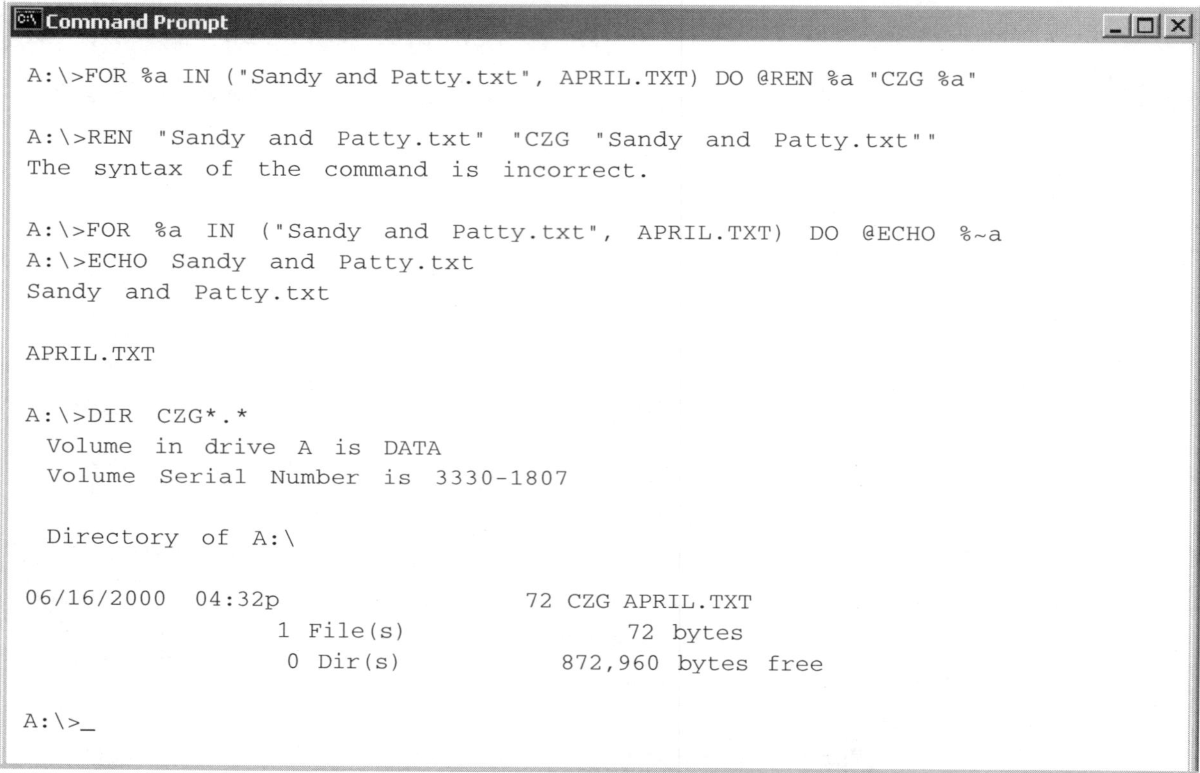

```
Command Prompt

A:\>FOR %a IN ("Sandy and Patty.txt", APRIL.TXT) DO @REN %a "CZG %a"

A:\>REN "Sandy and Patty.txt" "CZG "Sandy and Patty.txt""
The syntax of the command is incorrect.

A:\>FOR %a IN ("Sandy and Patty.txt", APRIL.TXT) DO @ECHO %~a
A:\>ECHO Sandy and Patty.txt
Sandy and Patty.txt

APRIL.TXT

A:\>DIR CZG*.*
 Volume in drive A is DATA
 Volume Serial Number is 3330-1807

 Directory of A:\

06/16/2000  04:32p                  72 CZG APRIL.TXT
               1 File(s)             72 bytes
               0 Dir(s)         872,960 bytes free

A:\>_
```

The file name with quotation marks did not get renamed because the syntax was incorrect. You had too many quotation marks.

Step 8 Key in the following: A:\>**DEL CZG*.*** Enter

Step 9 Key in the following (do not press Enter until you see Enter):
A:\>**FOR %a IN ("Sandy and Patty.txt", JANUARY.TXT) DO REN %a "CZG %~a"** Enter

```
Command Prompt

A:\>DEL CZG*.*

A:\>FOR %a IN ("Sandy and Patty.txt",JANUARY.TXT) DO REN %a "CZG %~a"

A:\>REN "Sandy and Patty.txt" "CZG Sandy and Patty.txt"
```

```
A:\>REN JANUARY.TXT "CZG JANUARY.TXT"

A:\>_
```

WHAT'S HAPPENING? Because you stripped out the quotation marks, you could successfully rename your files. In Step 10, overwrite the files.

Step 10 Key in the following: A:\>**COPY C:\WINDOSBK*.TXT TRIP** Enter

Step 11 Key in the following: A:\>**FOR /R %a IN (SANDY*.*) DO @ECHO %a** Enter

Step 12 Key in the following:
A:\>**FOR /R %a IN (SANDY*.*) DO @ECHO %~nxa** Enter

Command Prompt

```
A:\>COPY C:\WINDOSBK\*.TXT TRIP
C:\WINDOSBK\APRIL.TXT
C:\WINDOSBK\BYE.TXT
C:\WINDOSBK\DANCES.TXT
C:\WINDOSBK\FEBRUARY.TXT
Overwrite TRIP\FEBRUARY.TXT? (Yes/No/All): A
C:\WINDOSBK\GOODBYE.TXT
C:\WINDOSBK\HELLO.TXT
C:\WINDOSBK\JANUARY.TXT
C:\WINDOSBK\LONGFILENAME.TXT
C:\WINDOSBK\LONGFILENAMED.TXT
C:\WINDOSBK\LONGFILENAMING.TXT
C:\WINDOSBK\MARCH.TXT
C:\WINDOSBK\Sandy and Nicki.txt
C:\WINDOSBK\Sandy and Patty.txt
C:\WINDOSBK\TEST.TXT
        14 file(s) copied.

A:\>FOR /R %a IN (SANDY*.*) DO @ECHO %a
A:\Sandy and Nicki.txt
A:\TRIP\Sandy and Nicki.txt
A:\TRIP\Sandy and Patty.txt
A:\older\Sandy and Nicki.txt
A:\older\Sandy and Patty.txt

A:\>FOR /R %a IN (SANDY*.*) DO @ECHO %~nxa
Sandy and Nicki.txt
Sandy and Nicki.txt
Sandy and Patty.txt
Sandy and Nicki.txt
Sandy and Patty.txt

A:\>_
```

WHAT'S HAPPENING? You copied files to the **TRIP** directory. You then looked for those files that began with "SANDY." The /R parameter searched all the directories on your disk. However, it showed you the entire path name. If you want to use commands such as REN, you need only the file name. The options preceded by the tilde allowed you to do so. The n forces the variable to expand to only the file name whereas the x forces the expansion only of the file extension. You can use these features to write a batch file that will allow you to precede any file name with any prefix you wish.

Step 13 In your batch file directory, create the following batch file called **PREFIX.BAT**. Remember that in a batch file, variable names need to be preceded by two percent signs. Use your name instead of "Carolyn Z. Gillay."

```
@ECHO OFF
REM  Carolyn Z. Gillay
REM  Purpose of batch file is to add a new prefix to any file name.
IF "%1"=="" GOTO MESSAGE
IF "%2"=="" GOTO MESSAGE2
FOR /R %%a IN (%2) DO REN "%%~a"  "%1 %%~nxa"
GOTO END
:MESSAGE
ECHO You must include a prefix you wish to use.
ECHO Syntax is PREFIX  prefix  filename
GOTO END
:MESSAGE2
ECHO You must include a file name you wish to rename.
ECHO Syntax is PREFIX  prefix  filename
:END
```

Step 14 Be sure that the **BATCH** directory is in your path. You can use **ADD.BAT** to include it.

Step 15 Be sure you are in the root of A:\. Key in the following:
A:\>**DIR Sandy*.* /S** Enter

```
A:\>DIR SANDY*.* /S
 Volume in drive A is DATA
 Volume Serial Number is 3330-1807

 Directory of A:\

11/16/2000  12:00p                  53 Sandy and Nicki.txt
               1 File(s)            53 bytes

 Directory of A:\TRIP

11/16/2000  12:00p                  53 Sandy and Nicki.txt
11/16/2000  12:00p                  59 Sandy and Patty.txt
               2 File(s)           112 bytes

 Directory of A:\OLDER
```

```
11/16/2000  12:00p                  53 Sandy and Nicki.txt
11/16/2000  12:00p                  59 Sandy and Patty.txt
               2 File(s)            112 bytes

     Total Files Listed:
               5 File(s)            277 bytes
                0 Dir(s)        865,792 bytes free

A:\>_
```

You have three files that have SANDY as the first characters in their names, one in the root of A and the others in a subdirectory called **TRIP**. You are going to modify those files so that their names will be preceded by SWT.

Step 16 Key in the following: A:\>**PREFIX SWT SANDY*** Enter

Step 17 Key in the following: A:\>**DIR *SANDY* /S** Enter

Command Prompt

```
A:\>PREFIX  SWT  SANDY*

A:\>DIR  *SANDY*  /S
 Volume in drive A is DATA
 Volume Serial Number is 3330-1807

 Directory of A:\

11/16/2000  12:00p                  53 SWT Sandy and Nicki.txt
11/16/2000  12:00p                  59 CZG Sandy and Patty.txt
               2 File(s)            112 bytes

 Directory of A:\TRIP

11/16/2000  12:00p                  53 SWT Sandy and Nicki.txt
11/16/2000  12:00p                  59 SWT Sandy and Patty.txt
               2 File(s)            112 bytes

 Directory of A:\OLDER

11/16/2000  12:00p                  53 SWT Sandy and Nicki.txt
11/16/2000  12:00p                  59 SWT Sandy and Patty.txt
               2 File(s)            112 bytes

     Total Files Listed:
               6 File(s)            336 bytes
               0 Dir(s)         865,792 bytes free

A:\>_
```

You successfully renamed your files. You may also strip out specific fields in a text file. The FOR command also allows you to use the /F parameter. The /F parameter allows you to extract specific data from a text file. It lets you set the rules by which you will extract the data. The basic syntax is:

```
FOR /F "USERBACKQ=option TOKENS=list" %%variable IN ("set") DO command
```

Using USERBACKQ, you may specify what delimiter you are going to use. If you do not specify a delimiter, then spaces or tabs are used. The TOKENS is a series of numbers telling the command which token on the text line is to be assigned the next %%variable.

Step 18 Create the following batch file called **PERSON.BAT** in the **BATCH** directory:
@ECHO OFF
FOR /F "TOKENS=1,2,7" %%a IN (%1) DO ECHO %%b %%a, %%c

Step 19 Key in the following: A:\BATCH>**CD ** Enter

Step 20 Key in the following: A:\>**TYPE PERSONAL.FIL** Enter

```
Command Prompt

Babchuk    Nicholas 13 Stratford Sun City West  AZ  Professor
Babchuk    Bianca   13 Stratford Sun City West  AZ  Professor
Rodriguez  Bob      20 Elm       Ontario        CA  Systems Analyst
Helm       Milton   333 Meadow   Sherman Oaks   CA  Consultant
Suzuki     Charlene 567 Abbey    Rochester      MI  Day Care Teacher
Markiw     Nicholas 354 Bell     Phoenix        AZ  Engineer
Markiw     Emily    10 Zion      Sun City West  AZ  Retired
Nyles      John     12 Brooks    Sun City West  AZ  Retired
Nyles      Sophie   12 Brooks    Sun City West  CA  Retired
Markiw     Nick     10 Zion      Sun City West  AZ  Retired
Washingon  Tyrone   345 Newport  Orange         CA  Manager
Jones      Steven   32 North     Phoenix        AZ  Buyer
Smith      David    120 Collins  Orange         CA  Chef
Babchuk    Walter   12 View      Thousand Oaks  CA  President
Babchuk    Deana    12 View      Thousand Oaks  CA  Housewife
Jones      Cleo     355 Second   Ann Arbor      MI  Clerk
Gonzales   Antonio  40 Northern  Ontario        CA  Engineer
JONES      JERRY    244 East     Mission Viejo  CA  Systems Analyst
Lo         Ophelia  1213 Wick    Phoenix        AZ  Writer
Jones      Ervin    15 Fourth    Santa Cruz     CA  Banker
Perez      Sergio   134 Seventh  Ann Arbor      MI  Editor
Yuan       Suelin   56 Twin Leaf Orange         CA  Artist
Markiw     Nicholas 12 Fifth     Glendale       AZ  Engineer

A:\>_
```

Here you have a text file. In the batch file you just wrote, you are going to use the /F option. The tokens that you specified are in the first, second, and seventh positions. In other words, you want the first name, last name, and profession extracted from this file. The last name will be a, the first name will be b, and the profession will be c. These are assigned by the FOR command. You will display them so that you see first name, then last name, then profession.

Step 21 Key in the following: A:\>**PERSON PERSONAL.FIL** Enter

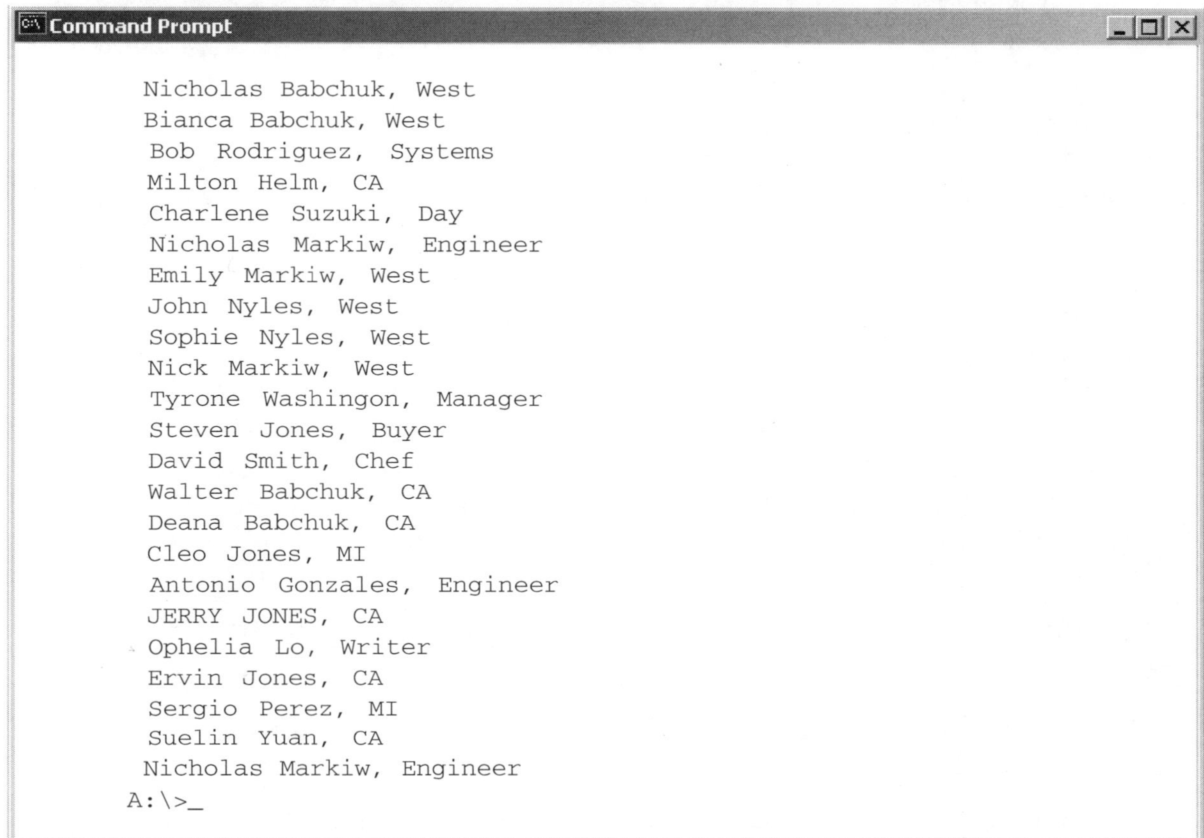

```
Command Prompt

Nicholas Babchuk, West
Bianca Babchuk, West
Bob Rodriguez, Systems
Milton Helm, CA
Charlene Suzuki, Day
Nicholas Markiw, Engineer
Emily Markiw, West
John Nyles, West
Sophie Nyles, West
Nick Markiw, West
Tyrone Washingon, Manager
Steven Jones, Buyer
David Smith, Chef
Walter Babchuk, CA
Deana Babchuk, CA
Cleo Jones, MI
Antonio Gonzales, Engineer
JERRY JONES, CA
Ophelia Lo, Writer
Ervin Jones, CA
Sergio Perez, MI
Suelin Yuan, CA
Nicholas Markiw, Engineer
A:\>_
```

WHAT'S HAPPENING? As you can see, you extracted the fields you wanted in the order that you wanted. You can make your batch file more sophisticated by creating the output in sorted order.

Step 22 Edit the **PERSON.BAT** file in the **BATCH** directory as follows:

@ECHO OFF
SORT < %1 > %2
FOR /F "TOKENS=1,2,7" %%a IN (%2) DO ECHO %%b %%a, %%c
DEL %2

Step 23 Key in the following: A:\>**PERSON PERSONAL.FIL TEMP.FIL** Enter

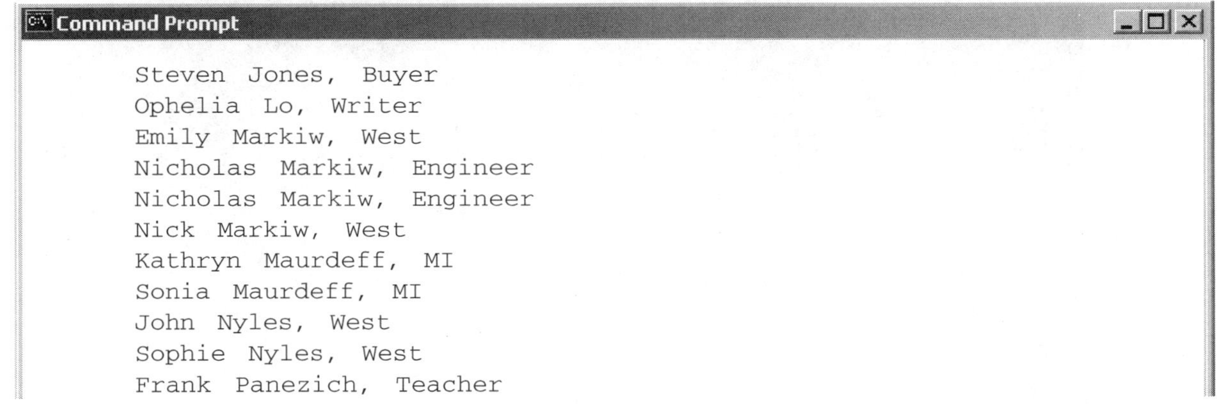

```
Command Prompt

Steven Jones, Buyer
Ophelia Lo, Writer
Emily Markiw, West
Nicholas Markiw, Engineer
Nicholas Markiw, Engineer
Nick Markiw, West
Kathryn Maurdeff, MI
Sonia Maurdeff, MI
John Nyles, West
Sophie Nyles, West
Frank Panezich, Teacher
```

```
Sergio Perez, MI
Bob Rodriguez, Systems
Carolyn Smith, MI
David Smith, Chef
Gregory Smith, MI
Charlene  Suzuki,  Day
Tai  Tran,  CA
Steven  Tuttle,  CA
Tyrone  Washingon,  Manager
Jim  Winter,  CA
Linda  Winter,  CA
Suelin  Yuan,  CA
A:\>_
```

WHAT'S HAPPENING? You have a sorted list of people and their professions. However, there is a problem. If you look at the bottom line, you see CA, the state, instead of the profession. The batch file you wrote looks at a space as a delmiter. If you looked at the original data, the seventh position varies, depending on the address.

DATA	**Yuan**	**Suelin**	**56**	**Twin**	**Leaf**	**Orange**	**CA**	**Artist**
Position	**1**	**2**	**3**	**4**	**5**	**6**	**7**	**8**

The problem here is the data. You can alter the data and choose a delimiter that will set off the fields as fields.

Step 24 Edit the **PERSONAL.FIL** and select the first five lines. Copy them into a new file called **SHORT.FIL**.

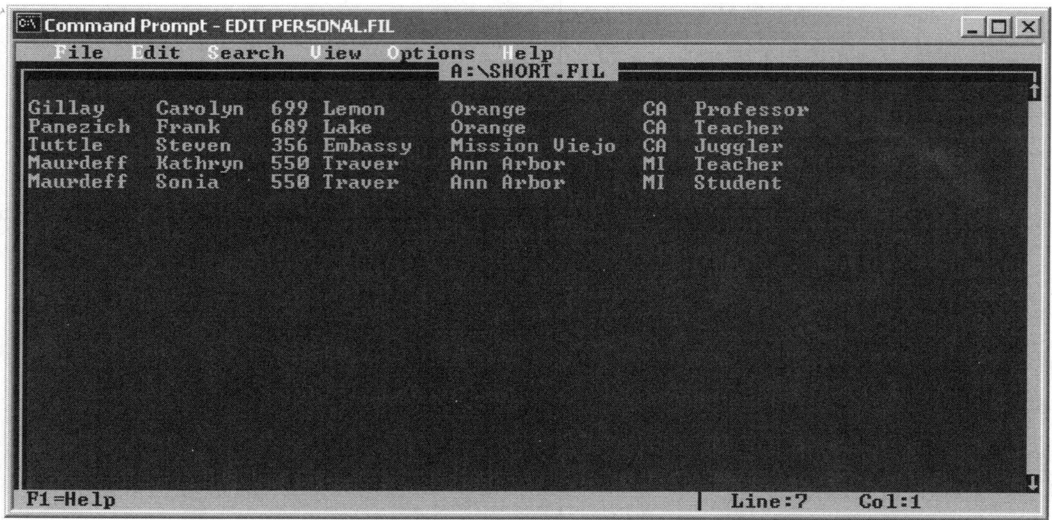

WHAT'S HAPPENING? You have a smaller sample of data.

Step 25 Exit Edit and key in the following: A:\>**PERSON SHORT.FIL TEMP.FIL** Enter

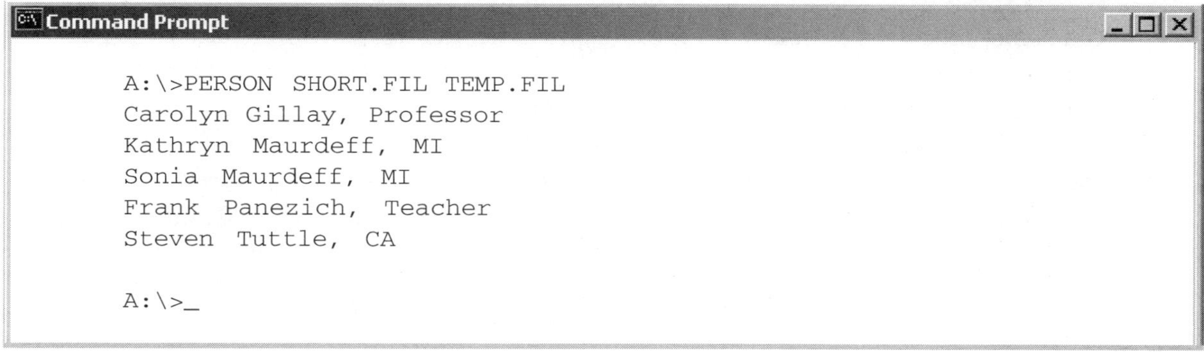

```
A:\>PERSON SHORT.FIL TEMP.FIL
Carolyn Gillay, Professor
Kathryn Maurdeff, MI
Sonia Maurdeff, MI
Frank Panezich, Teacher
Steven Tuttle, CA

A:\>_
```

WHAT'S HAPPENING? You are not getting the results that you want. You are going to edit the file, using semicolons to separate the fields.

Step 26 Edit the **SHORT.FIL** file as follows:

Gillay;Carolyn;699 Lemon;Orange;CA;Professor
Panezich;Frank;689 Lake;Orange;CA;Teacher
Tuttle;Steven;356 Embassy;Mission Viejo;CA;Juggler
Maurdeff;Kathryn;550 Traver;Ann Arbor;MI;Teacher
Maurdeff;Sonia;550 Traver;Ann Arbor;MI;Student

WHAT'S HAPPENING? You now have a delimited file. Each field is set off with a semicolon. You could have used any character. If you had used commas, it would be considered a comma-delimited file. But you have to alter your batch file so that it knows that the character you selected is a semicolon. Note that tokens change from 1,2,7 to 1,2,6.

Step 27 Edit **PERSON.BAT** so it looks as follows:

```
@ECHO OFF
SORT < %1 > %2
FOR /F "usebackq delims=; TOKENS=1,2,6" %%a IN (%2) DO ECHO %%b %%a, %%c
DEL %2
```

WHAT'S HAPPENING? The statement "usebackq delims" stated that you were going to use the ; as your delimiter. You also had to change the token. The last token is now 6, not 7.

Step 28 Key in the following: A:\>**PERSON SHORT.FIL TEMP.FIL** Enter

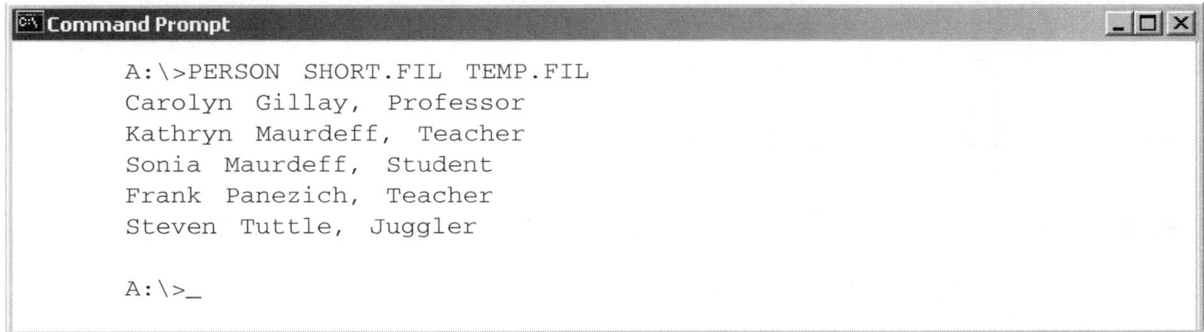

```
A:\>PERSON SHORT.FIL TEMP.FIL
Carolyn Gillay, Professor
Kathryn Maurdeff, Teacher
Sonia Maurdeff, Student
Frank Panezich, Teacher
Steven Tuttle, Juggler

A:\>_
```

WHAT'S HAPPENING? Your data is delimited, and your output is displayed the way you want it.

11.30 THE CALL COMMAND

You sometimes need to be able to execute one batch file from within another. If the second batch file is the last line in the original batch file, there is no problem. The second batch file is "invoked" from the first batch file. But invoking a second batch file, executing it, and upon completion of the second file, returning to the first batch file, is not so simple. When the operating system finishes executing a batch file, it returns control to the system level and never returns to the original batch file. There is a solution to this problem, the CALL command. It allows you to call (execute) another batch file and then return control to the next line in the first (calling) batch file.

11.31 ACTIVITY: USING CALL

Note: The DATA disk should be in Drive A. The displayed prompt is A:\>. You have executed the command A:\BATCH\>**ADD A:\BATCH** at some point during the current Command Prompt session.

Step 1 Key in the following: A:\>**CD BATCH** Enter

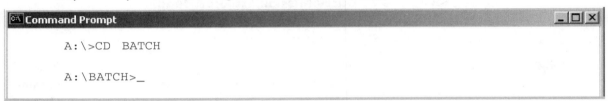

```
A:\>CD  BATCH

A:\BATCH>_
```

WHAT'S HAPPENING? Your default directory is now the **BATCH** subdirectory. One of the things that you can create is a "noise" to get a user's attention. You can use Ctrl + **G** to make a noise. All computers will not make a noise—most do. Although the noise you create sounds like a beep, it is referred to as a bell because in the ASCII character set, Ctrl + **G** is labeled **BEL**. By using Ctrl + **G** with ECHO you "ring a bell." Remember that when you see Ctrl + **G**, it means press the Ctrl key and the letter **G**. When you see F6, it means press the F6 function key. Today's computers are very fast—200–400 MHz is commonplace. The beep sound is very short, and may be difficult to hear. Therefore we will repeat the beep command four times, making it easier for you to hear the generated sound. Even if you cannot hear the sound, you will not get an error message.

Step 2 Key in the following: A:\BATCH>**COPY CON BELL.BAT** Enter
ECHO Ctrl + **G** Enter
ECHO Ctrl + **G** Enter
ECHO Ctrl + **G** Enter
ECHO Ctrl + **G** Enter
F6 Enter

Command Prompt

```
A:\BATCH>COPY CON BELL.BAT
ECHO ^G
ECHO ^G
ECHO ^G
```

```
ECHO ^G
^Z
        1 file(s) copied.

A:\>BATCH_
```

WHAT'S HAPPENING? Now that you have written **BELL.BAT**, you can execute it.

Step 3 Key in the following: A:\BATCH>**BELL** Enter

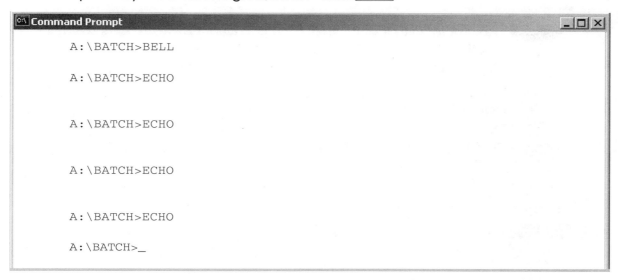

```
A:\BATCH>BELL

A:\BATCH>ECHO


A:\BATCH>ECHO


A:\BATCH>ECHO


A:\BATCH>ECHO

A:\BATCH>_
```

WHAT'S HAPPENING? You should have heard the bell beeping or clicking as you ran the program.

Step 4 Use any text editor to create and save a batch file called **BELLING.BAT** in the **BATCH** directory. Key in the following:
COPY *.99 *.XYZ
DEL *.XYZ
BELL
(Be sure to hit Enter after **BELL**.)

WHAT'S HAPPENING? This batch file will copy the **.99** files to the **BATCH** subdirectory, delete them, and then ring a bell.

Step 5 Key in the following: A:\BATCH>**BELLING** Enter

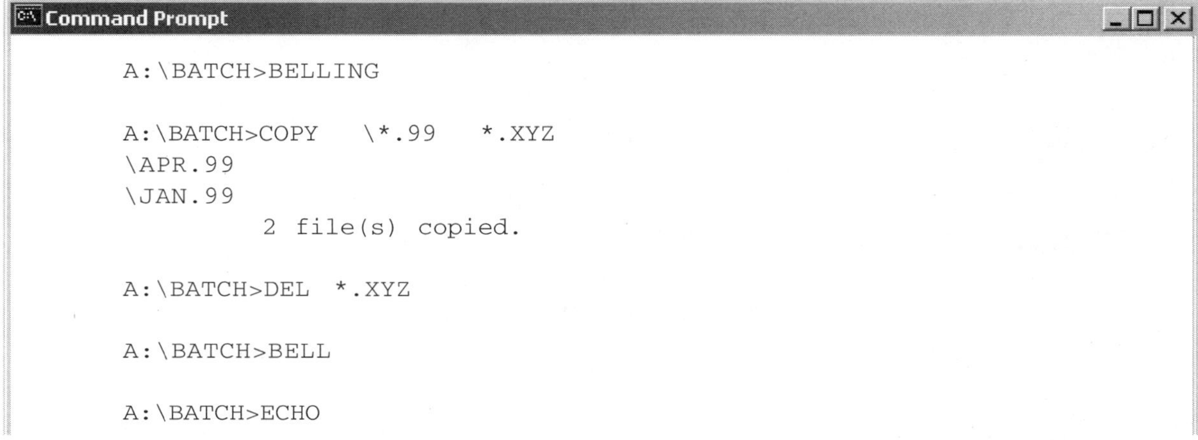

```
A:\BATCH>BELLING

A:\BATCH>COPY  \*.99  *.XYZ
\APR.99
\JAN.99
        2 file(s) copied.

A:\BATCH>DEL *.XYZ

A:\BATCH>BELL

A:\BATCH>ECHO
```

```
A:\BATCH>ECHO


A:\BATCH>ECHO


A:\BATCH>ECHO

A:\BATCH>_
```

WHAT'S HAPPENING? You called one batch file from another. You ran **BELLING**. Its last line was BELL. **BELL** was called and it executed as expected. However, perhaps you would like the bell to sound before the files are deleted.

Step 6 Edit and save **BELLING.BAT** to look as follows:
COPY *.99 *.XYZ
BELL
REM You are about to delete the *.XYZ files. Are you sure?
PAUSE
DEL *.XYZ

Step 7 Key in the following: A:\BATCH>**BELLING** Enter

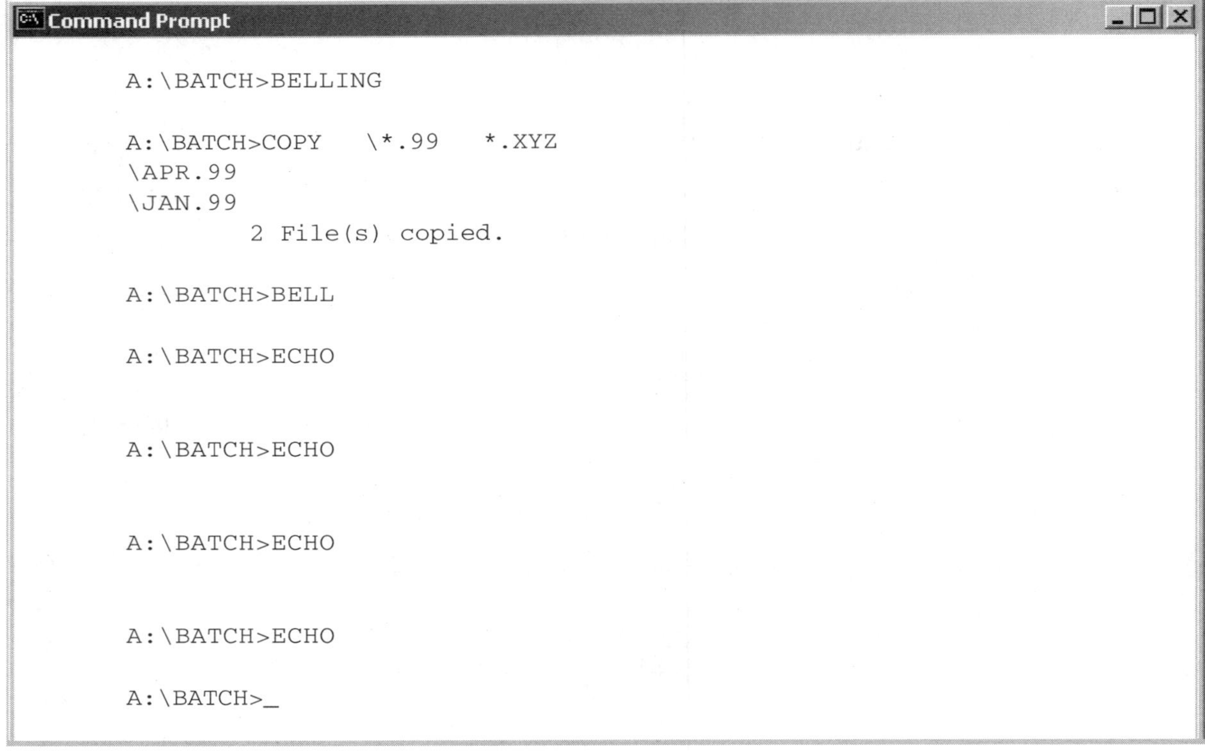

Command Prompt

```
A:\BATCH>BELLING

A:\BATCH>COPY   \*.99   *.XYZ
\APR.99
\JAN.99
        2 File(s) copied.

A:\BATCH>BELL

A:\BATCH>ECHO


A:\BATCH>ECHO


A:\BATCH>ECHO


A:\BATCH>ECHO

A:\BATCH>_
```

WHAT'S HAPPENING? When the **BELLING** batch file reached the line BELL, it called and executed **BELL**. It turned control over to **BELL.BAT**. Once **BELL.BAT** had control, it never returned to **BELLING**. Since it never returned to **BELLING.BAT**, your ***.XYZ** files were not deleted, nor did you see a message.

Step 8 Key in the following: A:\BATCH>**DIR *.XYZ** Enter

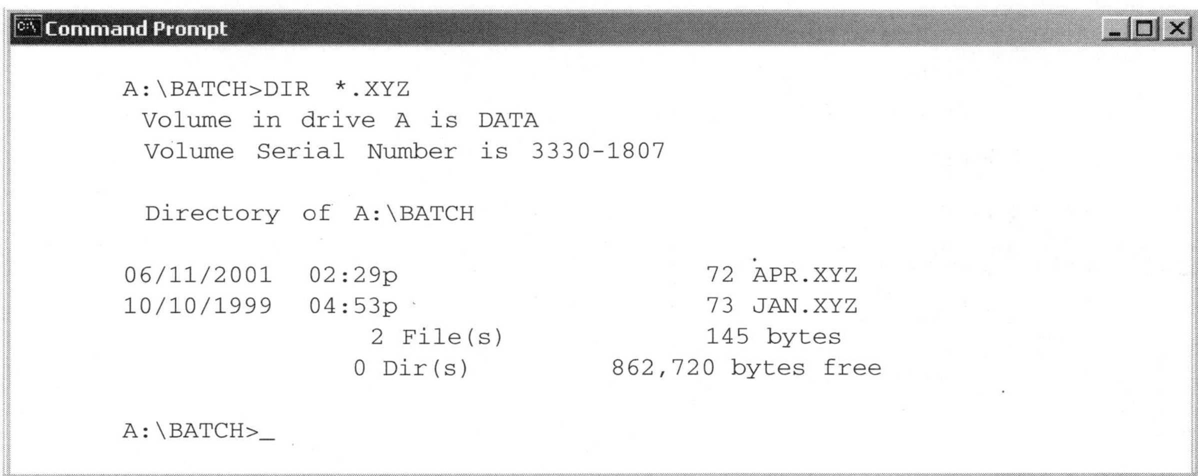

```
Command Prompt

A:\BATCH>DIR  *.XYZ
 Volume in drive A is DATA
 Volume Serial Number is 3330-1807

 Directory of A:\BATCH

06/11/2001  02:29p                  72 APR.XYZ
10/10/1999  04:53p                  73 JAN.XYZ
               2 File(s)            145 bytes
              0 Dir(s)          862,720 bytes free

A:\BATCH>_
```

WHAT'S HAPPENING? Indeed, the files are there. This is why you need the CALL command. CALL will process the batch file **BELL**, but it will then return control to **BELLING** so that the other commands in **BELLING** can be executed.

Step 9 Edit and save **BELLING.BAT** to look as follows:
COPY *.99 *.XYZ
CALL BELL
REM You are about to delete the *.XYZ files. Are you sure?
PAUSE
DEL *.XYZ

Step 10 Key in the following: A:\BATCH>**BELLING** Enter

```
Command Prompt

A:\batch>BELLING

A:\BATCH>COPY  \*.99  *.XYZ
\APR.99
\JAN.99
        2 file(s) copied.

A:\batch>CALL BELL

A:\batch>ECHO

A:\batch>ECHO

A:\batch>ECHO

A:\BATCH>ECHO

A:\BATCH>REM You are about to delete the *.XYZ files. Are you sure?

A:\BATCH>PAUSE
Press any key to continue . . .
```

WHAT'S HAPPENING

Since you added CALL in front of BELL, the bell sounded. Once **BELL** was finished executing, it passed control back to **BELLING** so that the next commands could be executed.

Step 11 Press Enter

Step 12 Key in the following: A:\BATCH>**DIR *.XYZ** Enter

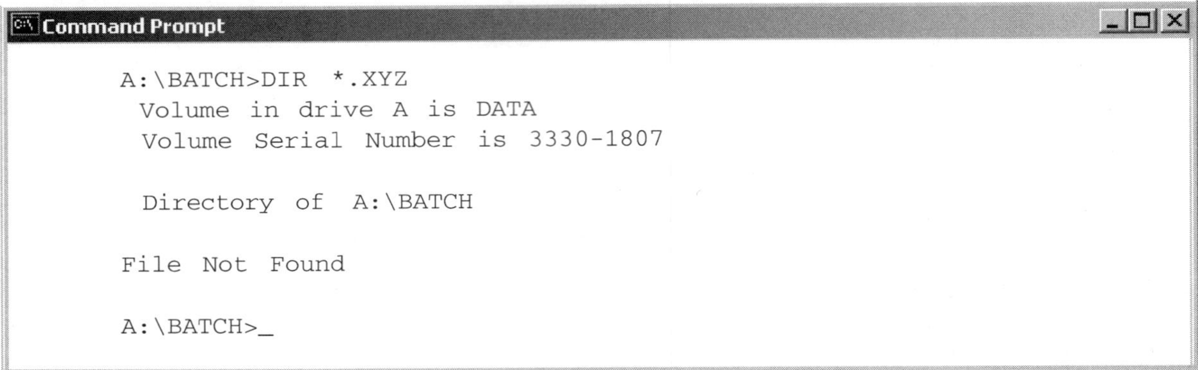
Command Prompt
A:\BATCH>DIR *.XYZ
Volume in drive A is DATA
Volume Serial Number is 3330-1807
Directory of A:\BATCH
File Not Found
A:\BATCH>_

WHAT'S HAPPENING

The CALL command worked as promised. Your **.XYZ** files are gone. A more practical example of using CALL can be seen in the next group of batch files you are going to write. You may find, as you move among directories, that you want to go "home" again. In other words, you want to return to the directory where you were previously. You can create a series of batch files that will remember the directory you were in and return you to it.

Note: In the next file, it is important to press the F6 immediately after the command *before* you press Enter. Do not press Enter, then F6. Create the file in the BATCH directory.

Step 13 Use COPY CON to create and save **HOME.DAT**. Key in the following:
COPY CON HOME.DAT Enter
SET HOME=F6 Enter

Step 14 Use any editor to create and save a batch file called **HOMETO.BAT**. Key in the following:
COPY A:\BATCH\HOME.DAT A:\BATCH\HOMESAVE.BAT
CD >> A:\BATCH\HOMESAVE.BAT
CALL HOMESAVE.BAT
DEL A:\BATCH\HOMESAVE.BAT

WHAT'S HAPPENING

The **HOME.DAT** data file you created will create an environmental variable called HOME. The batch file **HOMETO.BAT** that you just created will be used to set the environmental variable to wherever you want HOME to be. The batch file, line by line, breaks down as follows:

Line 1: Copies the contents of the data file to the batch file. **HOME.DAT** now contains SET HOME=. **HOMESAVE.BAT** now contains SET HOME=.

Line 2: Takes whatever directory you are in and appends it to **HOMESAVE.BAT**. If your current directory is **GAMES**, **HOMESAVE.BAT** now has the contents of SET HOME=A:\GAMES.

Line 3: Executes the batch file. **HOMESAVE.BAT** now executes and sets the variable of **HOME** to **A:\GAMES**.

Line 4: Deletes the batch file. Now that you have set the environmental variable, you no longer need the batch file **HOMESAVE.BAT**.

Step 15 Use any editor to create and save a batch file called **HOME.BAT** that contains the following:
CD %HOME% Enter

The batch file **HOME.BAT** will change your directory to whatever value is in the environmental variable **HOME** at the time the batch file is executed. In order for this procedure to work correctly, you must include A:\BATCH in your path statement.

Step 16 Key in the following: **PATH** Enter

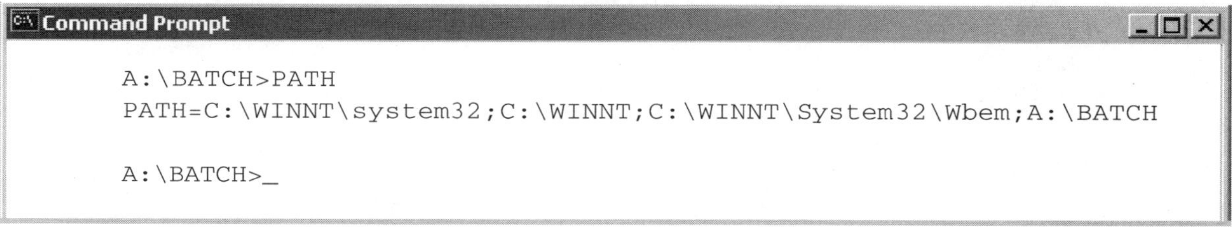

In this example, A:\BATCH is indeed included in the path. If it is not included in your path, run ADD A:\BATCH before proceeding.

Step 17 Key in the following: A:\BATCH>**SET H** Enter

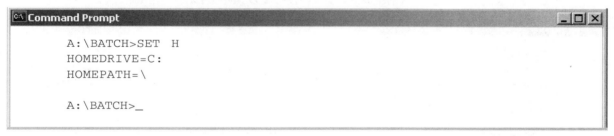

A:\BATCH is included in the path. There is no environmental variable HOME displayed. You are now ready to test "going home."

Step 18 Key in the following: A:\BATCH>**CD ** Enter

Step 19 Key in the following: A:\>**CD WORK\ADS** Enter

Step 20 Key in the following: A:\WORK\ADS>**HOMETO** Enter

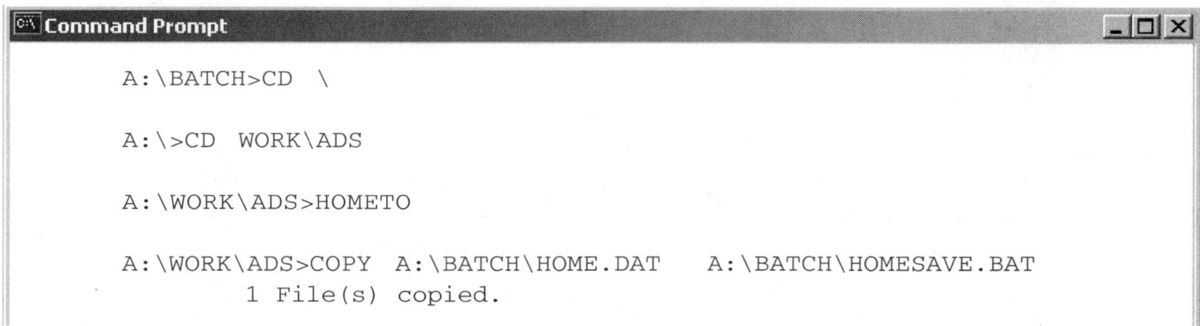

```
A:\WORK\ADS>CD  1>>A:\BATCH\HOMESAVE.BAT

A:\WORK\ADS>CALL  HOMESAVE.BAT

A:\WORK\ADS>SET  HOME=A:\WORK\ADS

A:\WORK\ADS>DEL  A:\BATCH\HOMESAVE.BAT
A:\WORK\ADS>_
```

You wanted the subdirectory **\WORK\ADS** to be your home directory so you keyed in **HOMETO**.

Step 21 Key in the following: A:\WORK\ADS>**SET H** Enter

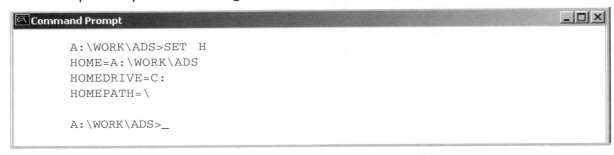

You now have an environmental variable named HOME whose value is **A:\WORK\ADS**. You will go to another directory and then return to **A:\WORK\ADS** by using the HOME command you just wrote.

Step 22 Key in the following: A:\WORK\ADS>**CD \MEDIA\TV** Enter

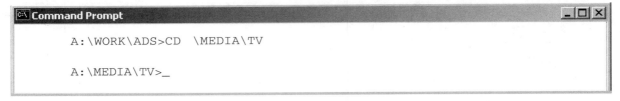

Your default directory is now **A:\MEDIA\TV**. You want to return home, which is **A:\WORK\ADS**.

Step 23 Key in the following: A:\MEDIA\TV>**HOME** Enter

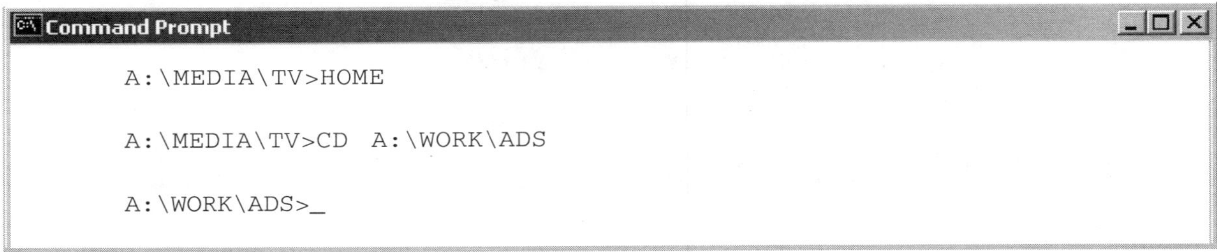

You went home—home being the value set in the HOME variable. At any time during the Command Prompt session, you can change the value of home by running HOMETO while in the directory you want home to be, and you can return to it at any time by simply keying in **HOME**.

Step 24 Key in the following: A:\WORK\ADS>**CD ** Enter

Step 25 Key in the following: A:\>**ORIGPATH** Enter

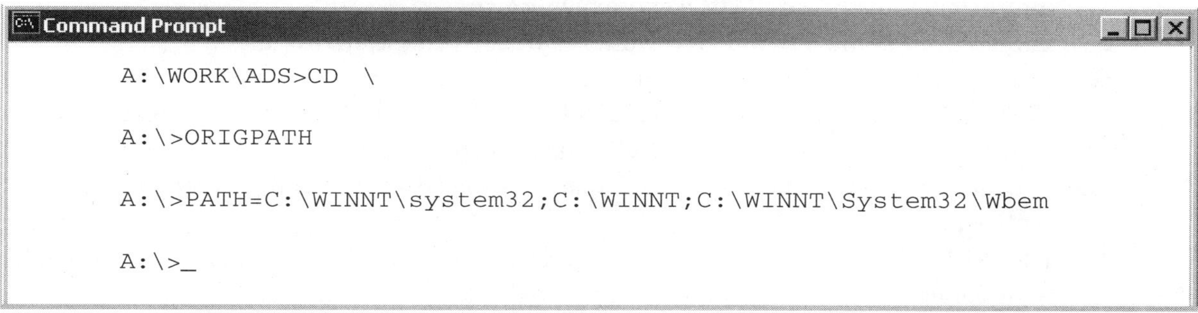
```
A:\WORK\ADS>CD  \

A:\>ORIGPATH

A:\>PATH=C:\WINNT\system32;C:\WINNT;C:\WINNT\System32\Wbem

A:\>_
```

WHAT'S HAPPENING? You have returned to the root directory of the DATA disk and reset the default path.

CHAPTER SUMMARY

1. You may substitute a double colon (::) for the REM statement.
2. To place a blank line in a batch file, use the ECHO command followed immediately by a period (ECHO.).
3. The GOTO command used in conjunction with a label creates a loop. The GOTO will process the command following the label.
4. The label in a batch file is not a command, but identifies a location in the batch file.
5. The SHIFT command shifts over command line parameters to the left one position at a time.
6. The SHIFT command is typically used in conjunction with GOTO and a label.
7. The IF command will test for some logical condition. If the condition is true, the command will be processed. If the condition is false, the batch file will fall through to the next line of the batch file.
8. The IF command can test whether or not two character strings are identical.
9. The IF command can test whether or not a file exists.
10. The IF command checks ERRORLEVEL.
11. You may also use IF with NOT. The IF NOT command will test for a NOT condition. If a condition is not true, then the command will process. If the command is true, then the batch file will fall through to the next line in the batch file.
12. You can test for a null value by using quotation marks, a word, or backslashes.
13. To use IF EXIST and to test for the existence of a subdirectory, you may use IF %1\NUL.
14. Many programs set an exit code when finished executing. The IF ERRORLEVEL in a batch file will test if an exit code is equal to or greater than the one in the test.
15. When you use IF ERRORLEVEL in a batch file, the codes must be listed in descending order.
16. When you use IF NOT ERRORLEVEL in a batch file, the codes must be listed in ascending order.
17. You may write programs with DEBUG to set exit codes.
18. You can write programs directly in DEBUG, or you may write a script file that supplies input for DEBUG to create a program.
19. The environment is an area in memory where the operating system leaves messages to itself, including the path and the prompt values.

20. You can create environmental variables that can be used in batch files. When using the variable in a batch file, the syntax is *%variable%*.
21. The SET command lets you view what is currently in the environment.
22. Environmental variables set in other batch files or at the command line remain in effect only during the current Command Prompt session. When the Command Prompt window is closed, the variable disappears.
23. The DIRCMD command can be used to preset the DIR command parameters and switches.
24. The FOR...IN...DO command allows repetitive processing. The command will execute some command for every value in a specified set.
25. When you use FOR...IN...DO at the command line, the syntax is FOR *%variable* IN (*set*) DO *command* [*command-parameter*].
26. The /R when used with FOR...IN...DO allows recursive processing. Recursive means that the command will search all the directories.
27. Using the /F parameter allows you to select specified text using delimiters that you can set.
28. The CALL command allows you to call one batch file from another. When the second batch file is finished executing, it returns control to the first batch file.

KEY TERMS

debug
EOF (end-of-file) mark
exit code
conditional processing
environment
environmental variable
expression
loop
null value
scan code
script file
variable

DISCUSSION QUESTIONS

1. What is the function of the REM, ECHO, and PAUSE commands?
2. What happens in a batch file if ECHO is set to OFF?
3. What happens in a batch file if you precede the ECHO OFF switch with @?
4. What is a NUL device? Why would you use a NUL device?
5. How can you place a blank line in a batch file?
6. How can you create a loop in a batch file? How can you stop a loop from processing in a batch file?
7. What is the purpose and function of the GOTO command?
8. What is a label in a batch file?
9. What is the purpose and function of the SHIFT command?
10. Why is it useful to shift parameters?
11. How can you determine whether or not a file exists?
12. What is the purpose and function of the IF command?
13. Give the syntax of the IF command and explain each part of the syntax.
14. What does it mean to test for a null value?
15. How can you test for a null value? Why would you test for a null value?
16. What is the purpose and function of the IF EXIST/IF NOT EXIST command?
17. Explain the purpose and function of the IF ERRORLEVEL command.
18. What is a script file? How can you create one?

19. What is a scan code?
20. Give the syntax of the SET command and explain each part of the syntax.
21. Explain the purpose and function of the DIRCMD environmental variable.
22. What is the purpose and function of the FOR...IN...DO command?
23. Name two parameters you can use with the FOR...IN...DO command.
24. Describe the purpose of those parameters.
25. Give the syntax of the FOR...IN...DO command and explain each part of the syntax.
26. Explain the purpose and function of the CALL command.

TRUE/FALSE QUESTIONS

For each question, circle the letter T if the statement is true and the letter F if the statement is false.

T F 1. The SHIFT command may be used only in batch files.

T F 2. Environmental variables set at the command line remain in effect until the computer is turned off.

T F 3. You may alter the way DIR displays by changing the values in DIRCMD.

T F 4. Keying in SET at the command line shows the correct date and time.

T F 5. In order to run a batch file from another batch file and then return to the original batch file, you must use the CALL command.

COMPLETION QUESTIONS

Write the correct answer in each blank space.

6. In a batch file, to see whether or not the file called MY.FIL is a valid file, you must have the line IF __________ MY.FIL.
7. In a batch file, the line IF "%1"= ="" GOTO END is testing for a(n)__________.
8. You can use the ________ parameter or switch with the FOR command to look at files in different directories.
9. When you key in SET THIS=DIR *.TXT, you are setting a(n) __________________.
10. When you use the GOTO command, you must also use a(n) __________.

MULTIPLE CHOICE QUESTIONS

For each question, write the letter for the correct answer in the blank space.

11. If ECHO. (ECHO followed immediately by a period) is entered into a batch file, it will
    a. display the status of ECHO.
    b. create a blank line.
    c. do nothing.
    d. cause the following command not to execute.

12. ECHO %PATH% (keyed in at the command line) will
    a. produce an error message.
    b. display the contents of the file named PATH.
    c. display the path for the current session.
    d. display the environmental variables set in the current session.

13. The following command in a batch file—IF %1none==none GOTO TOP—will
    a. test for a null value.
    b. test for the existence of a file.
    c. test for ERRORLEVEL.
    d. all of the above
14. A valid batch file label consists of a
    a. percent sign (%) and text chosen by the user.
    b. colon (:) and text chosen by the user.
    c. double colon (::) and text chosen by the user.
    d. any of the above
15. So that %3 becomes %2, and %2 becomes %1, you must use the _________ command in a batch file.
    a. ROTATE %1
    b. SHIFT %1
    c. SHIFT
    d. none of the above

APPLICATION ASSIGNMENTS

Note 1: Place the APPLICATION disk in Drive A. Be sure to work on the APPLICATION disk, not the DATA disk.

Note 2: The homework problems will assume Drive C is the hard disk and the APPLICATION disk is in Drive A. If you are using another drive, such as floppy drive B or hard drive D, be sure and substitute that drive letter when reading the questions and answers.

Note 3: Test all of your batch files before submitting them to be sure they work correctly.

Note 4: To save a file under a new name with Edit, press Alt + **F** and choose **Save As**.

Note 5: There can be more than one way to write a batch file. If your batch file works correctly, it is most likely written correctly.

SETUP

Step 1 Place the APPLICATION disk in Drive A.

Step 2 Create a **BATCH** subdirectory on the APPLICATION disk and move any batch files from the root directory into the **BATCH** subdirectory.

Step 3 Move **GO.BAT** and **NAME.BAT** from the **BATCH** subdirectory to the root of the APPLICATION disk.

Step 4 Create a subdirectory called **CHAP11** off the root directory of the APPLICATION disk.

PROBLEM SET I

PROBLEM A

A-a Make **CHAP11** the default directory.

A-b Create and save a batch file in the **CHAP11** subdirectory called **DELBAK.BAT** that has the following line in it:

```
FOR %%h IN (*.BAK) DO IF EXIST %%h DEL %%h
```

1. The DELBAK.BAT file will
   a. delete any file in the default drive and directory.
   b. delete any file in the default drive and directory with the .BAK extension.
   c. first check whether or not any files with the .BAK file extension exist in the current drive and directory.
   d. both b and c

2. If you wanted to use the previous batch file command on the command line, what would you have to do?
   a. change %%h to %h
   b. change %%h to %h%
   c. change *.BAK to %h%
   d. none of the above

A-c Create the following batch file in the **CHAP11** subdirectory and save it as **LIST.BAT**:

```
@ECHO OFF
ECHO.
FOR %%v IN (%PATH%) DO ECHO %%v
ECHO.
ECHO.
```

3. The **LIST.BAT** file will
   a. display the directory names in the current path.
   b. use an environmental variable.
   c. both a and b
   d. neither a nor b

PROBLEM B

Note: If you are in a lab environment, there may not be a correct answer listed for questions 4 and 5.

B-a Be sure that **CHAP11** is the default directory on the APPLICATION disk.

B-b In the **CHAP11** subdirectory, create and save a batch file called **PASSING.BAT** that has the following lines in it:

```
@ECHO OFF
FOR %%a IN (%USERNAME%) DO IF "%1"=="%%a" GOTO DISPLAY
:NOT
ECHO You used %1. This is not your correct login name.
GOTO END
:DISPLAY
DIR %homepath% /p
:END
```

B-c Execute **PASSING.BAT** using your logon name.

4. When you used PASSING.BAT you
   a. displayed the files in the current default directory.
   b. displayed the files in the root of the APPLICATION disk.
   c. displayed the files in the root of Drive C.
   d. displayed the message, "You used Bette. This is not your correct login name."

B-d Execute **PASSING.BAT** using Bette.

5. When you used PASSING.BAT with Bette, you
   a. displayed the files in the current default directory.
   b. displayed the files in the root of the APPLICATION disk.
   c. displayed the files in the root of Drive C.
   d. displayed the message, "You used Bette. This is not your correct login name."

PROBLEM C

C-a Be sure that **CHAP11** is the default directory on the APPLICATION disk.

Note: The following batch file is called **SWAP.BAT**. Its purpose is to allow the user to swap file names between two existing files. If the user keyed in **SWAP MY.OLD MY.NEW**, the file **MY.OLD** would then be named **MY.NEW** and the file **MY.NEW** would then be named **MY.OLD**. However, this batch file has a problem and does not work properly.

C-b In the **CHAP11** subdirectory, create and save a batch file called **SWAP.BAT** that has the following lines in it:

```
@ECHO OFF
IF NOT EXIST %1 GOTO NOFILE1
IF NOT EXIST %2 GOTO NOFILE2
REN %1 HOLD
REN %2 %1
REN HOLD %2
GOTO END
:NOFILE1
ECHO Cannot find file %1
:NOFILE2
ECHO Cannot find file %2
:END
```

C-c If you do not have a subdirectory called **\SPORTS**, create it now. Then copy any file with a **.99** extension from the **WINDOSBK** subdirectory to the **\SPORTS** subdirectory on the APPLICATION disk.

C-d Key in the following:
A:\CHAP11>**SWAP \SPORTS\APR.99 \SPORTS\JAN.99** Enter

☐ 6. When you used **SWAP.BAT**, you received an error message and **SWAP.BAT** did not work. Why?
   a. You cannot name a file **HOLD**.
   b. The file **\SPORTS\APR.99** does not exist.
   c. The syntax of the REN command is incorrect.
   d. You were immediately sent to the :END label.

☐ 7. Did any file get renamed in the **\SPORTS** directory?
   a. yes
   b. no

PROBLEM SET II

Note 1: The APPLICATION disk is in Drive A and A:\> is displayed as the default drive and the default directory. All work will occur on the APPLICATION disk.

Note 2: If **NAME.BAT**, **MARK.FIL**, **GETYN.COM**, and **GO.BAT** are not in the root directory, copy them from the **WINDOSBK** directory before proceeding.

Step 1 Key in the following: A:\>**NAME** [Enter]

Step 2 Here is an example to key in, but your instructor will have other information that applies to your class. Key in the following:

Bette A. Peat [Enter]	(*Your* name goes here.)
CIS 55 [Enter]	(*Your* class goes here.)
T-Th 8–9:30 [Enter]	(*Your* day and time go here.)
Chapter 11 Applications [Enter]	
Problem A [Enter]	

Step 3 Press [F6] [Enter]. If the information is correct, press **Y** and you are back to A:\>.

Step 4 Begin a new Command Prompt session by closing any existing Command Prompt windows and opening a new window.

Step 5 Make A:\> the default directory.

Step 6 Key in the following: A:\>**PATH > MYPATH.BAT** [Enter]

PROBLEM A

A-a Make **CHAP11** the default directory.

A-b The following batch file is called **SETPATH.BAT**. Its purpose is to allow the user to add a path to either the front or the back of the existing path. Any number of subdirectory names can be added. When the user keys in **SETPATH /F subdirectory1 subdirectory2** or **SETPATH /f subdirectory1 subdirectory2**, the /F or /f tells the batch file to add the subdirectory name in front of the existing path. If the SETPATH command is keyed in without /F or /f, each subdirectory listed will be added to the end of the path.

A-c Analyze the following batch file:

```
IF "%1"=="" GOTO DEFAULT
IF "%1"== "/f" GOTO FRONT
IF "%1"== "/F" GOTO FRONT
:ADD
IF "%1"== "" GOTO END
PATH= %PATH%;%1
SHIFT
GOTO ADD
:FRONT
SHIFT
IF "%1"== "" GOTO END
PATH=%1;%PATH%
GOTO FRONT
:DEFAULT
PATH=C:\WINNT\SYSTEM32
:END
```

A-d In the **CHAP11** subdirectory, create and edit a batch file called **SETPATH.BAT** based on the model above.

A-e Document it with your name and date, and explain the purpose of the batch file.

A-f Copy the file called **REPLY.COM** that you wrote in Activity 11.19 to the **CHAP11** directory. Then begin the batch file so that you may give the user the opportunity to choose help on how to use this command. The user will press **Y** or **y** if they want help or **N** or **n** if they do not want help. If the user chooses help, provide help on syntax as well as a description on how to use **SETPATH.BAT**. After displaying the description, the user should exit from the batch file. *Note:* The scan code value for Y is 89 and for y is 121. The scan code value for N is 78 and for n is 110.

A-g Change the :DEFAULT section so that it calls whatever your original path was, rather than **PATH C:\WINNT\SYSTEM32**. (*Hint*: Remember, **MYPATH.BAT** is in the root directory of the APPLICATION disk, created in Problem A.)

A-h Key in the following: A:\CHAP11>**CD** Enter

A-i Key in the following:
A:\>**GO NAME.FIL CHAP11\SETPATH.BAT \CHAP11\SETPATH.TXT** Enter

A-j In Notepad, click **File**. Click **Print**. Click **File**. Click **Exit**.

PROBLEM B

B-a Make **CHAP11** the default directory.

B-b Use **SETPATH**, created in Problem A, to add the **A:\CHAP11** and the **A:\BATCH** subdirectories to the path.

B-c Using as a model **MY.BAT** from Activity 11.25, create and save a batch file called **DIRS.BAT** in the **CHAP11** subdirectory.

B-d Document it with your name and date and explain the purpose of the batch file.

B-e Have the following choices in **DIRS.BAT**:

- Look at directories only, arranged alphabetically by name in the root directory. (Call this Root Directory Only.)
- Look at directories only, arranged alphabetically by name on the entire disk beginning with the root directory. (Call this All Directories.)
- Look at file names only—no dates, no directory information—on the root directory in reverse alphabetic order. (*Hint:* Remember /b.) (Call this **File Names Only**.)
- Look at files only in the root directory arranged by date/time. (Call this **Files by Date/Time**.) *Note:* Do not use date alone in an ECHO line. If you do, you are asking that the DATE command be executed.
- The scan code value for 1 is 49, 2 is 50, 3 is 51, and 4 is 52. If you want to use other key choices, see Appendix C for the scan code values.
- Remove any other choices.
- Be sure no command lines are displayed, only the results of the commands.

B-f Key in the following: A:\CHAP11>**CD** Enter

B-g Use Edit to modify **NAME.FIL**, changing Problem A to Problem B.

B-h Key in the following: A:\>**GO NAME.FIL CHAP11\DIRS.BAT** Enter

B-i In Notepad, click **File**. Click **Print**. Click **File**. Click **Exit**.

PROBLEM C

C-a Make **CHAP11** the default directory.

C-b Check the path to see if **CHAP11** is in the path. If not, use **SETPATH**, created in Problem A, to add the A:**CHAP11** subdirectory to the path. Add the **A:\BATCH** subdirectory to the path as well.

Note: The following batch file is called **WORD.BAT**. Its purpose is to allow the user to key in WORD *filename.ext*. If the file already exists, the user is immediately taken into Edit with the named file. If, however, the file is a new file, the user will be told to key in WORD and the new file name at the command line. This batch file, as written, has a fatal flaw. Every time the user keys in WORD *newfile.nam* he or she is kicked out of the batch file.

C-c Analyze the following batch file:

```
:START
IF EXIST %1 GOTO PROCEED
IF NOT EXIST %1 GOTO NEWFILE
:PROCEED
```

```
EDIT %1
GOTO END
:NEWFILE
ECHO This is a new file, %1. If you
ECHO wish to create a new file, you must
ECHO key in WORD and the new file name at the command line.
ECHO The syntax is:
ECHO WORD new.fil
:END
```

C-d Edit and save a batch file called **WORD.BAT** in the **CHAP11** subdirectory based on the above model. Document it with your name and date and explain the purpose of the batch file.

- If the user keys in WORD with no file name, the batch file should tell the user what was done wrong and return the user to the system level.
- If the user keys in WORD filename.ext and it is an existing file, the file should go directly into Edit using that file name. However, if the file does not exist, offer the user two choices—either to not create a new file and exit the batch file or to create a new file and be taken back to the PROCEED label. You will use REPLY and ERRORLEVEL so this choice can be made. *Note:* The scan code value for Y is 89 and for y is 121. The scan code value for N is 78 and for n is 110.

C-e Key in the following: A:\CHAP11>**CD ** Enter

C-f Use Edit to modify **NAME.FIL**, changing Problem B to Problem C.

C-g Key in the following: A:\>**GO NAME.FIL CHAP11\WORD.BAT** Enter

C-h In Notepad, click **File**. Click **Print**. Click **File**. Click **Exit**.

PROBLEM D: CHALLENGE ASSIGNMENT

The following batch file change is difficult, so do it only if you want a challenge.

D-a Make **CHAP11** the default directory.

D-b Check the path to see if **CHAP11** is in the path. If not, use **SETPATH**, created in Problem A, to add the **CHAP11** subdirectory to the path.

Note: The following batch file is called **COMPILE.BAT**. Its purpose is to allow the user to make a list of all the files in all the subdirectories on a specific removable disk. You will need to ascertain which are your removable disk drive letters. You obviously will have Drive A but if you have a Zip drive or CD-ROM drive, you will need to know the drive letter for each device. Once the user keys in **COMPILE**, the REPLY command in the batch file asks which drive the user wants to use to compile a list of files. You will have to use the scan codes in Appendix C to determine which keys the user may press depending on the drive letters on your system. The user may also quit once the list of files is completed. All the information from all the disks that are cataloged is collected in one file called **TEMP.TXT**.

D-c Analyze the following batch file:

```
@ECHO OFF
CLS
ECHO.
ECHO   Key in a Drive letter to compile a list of files on Drive A.
ECHO   Use Q to quit. Use A for Drive A.
ECHO.
REPLY
IF ERRORLEVEL 65 IF NOT ERRORLEVEL 66 GOTO DRIVEA
IF ERRORLEVEL 81 IF NOT ERRORLEVEL 82 GOTO END
IF ERRORLEVEL 97 IF NOT ERRORLEVEL 98 GOTO DRIVEA
IF ERRORLEVEL 113 IF NOT ERRORLEVEL 114 GOTO END
:DRIVEA
SET DRV=A
GOTO LIST
:LIST
CLS
ECHO You are now compiling a list of all the files on Drive %DRV%
ECHO Listing files for Drive %DRV%
ECHO. >> TEMP.TXT
DIR %DRV%:\ /S /A /ON >> TEMP.TXT
ECHO. >> TEMP.TXT
ECHO You have compiled a list of all the files on Drive %DRV%
ECHO to a file called TEMP.TXT on the default drive.
PAUSE
:END
```

D-d Edit and create a batch file called **COMPILE.BAT** in the **CHAP11** subdirectory based on the above model.

D-e Document it with your name and date and explain the purpose of the batch file.

D-f **The file TEMP.TXT should first be deleted in the batch file.**

D-g Following REPLY, add more choices for the user. The additional choices will allow the user to choose any removable drive. The user should be able to return to the REPLY line to decide which drive to accumulate more files from. This will give the user the opportunity to either choose a different removable drive, or to choose the same one and place a new disk or CD in it. (*Hint:* Remember, adding choices also means adding more IF ERRORLEVEL.)

D-h Use the same REPLY in the batch file to allow the user to view the **TEMP.TXT** file on the screen. Remember, the file will be long and you want the user to be able to view the entire file. When finished viewing, the user should be returned to REPLY to either compile more files or to quit. (*Hint:* Remember, every time you add a choice, you must add more IF ERRORLEVEL statements.)

D-i Key in the following: A:\CHAP11>**CD ** Enter

D-j Use EDIT to modify **NAME.FIL**, changing Problem C to Problem D.

D-k Key in the following: A:\>**GO NAME.FIL CHAP11\COMPILE.BAT** Enter

D-l In Notepad, click **File**. Click **Print**. Click **File**. Click **Exit**.

PROBLEM E: CHALLENGE ASSIGNMENT

The following batch file change is difficult, so do it only if you want a challenge.

E-a Make **CHAP11** the default directory.

E-b Copy **SWAP.BAT** (created in Problem Set I—Problem C) to a new file called **SWAP2.BAT**.

E-c Document it with your name and date and explain the purpose of the batch file.

E-d The batch file should perform as follows:

- When you key in SWAP2 *dirname filename1 filename2*, the file names will be reversed in the specified directory. The batch file will change to the specified directory prior to performing the "swap."
- One of the items you wish to test for is the existence of a directory. (*Hint*: Remember %1\Nul.) If you key in a subdirectory name where a file name is expected, the batch file should take you to a message that tells you that you keyed in a directory name, not a file name.
- If you key in only SWAP2, the batch file will take you to a message that tells the user how to use the command correctly.
- Be sure the batch file returns the user to the **CHAP11** subdirectory.

E-e Key in the following: A:\CHAP11>**CD ** Enter

E-f Use Edit to modify **NAME.FIL**, changing Problem C to Problem D.

E-g Key in the following: A:\>**GO NAME.FIL \CHAP11\SWAP2.BAT** Enter

E-h In Notepad, click **File**. Click **Print**. Click **File**. Click **Exit**.

PROBLEM F: CHALLENGE ASSIGNMENT

The following batch file change is very difficult, so do it only if you want a *real* challenge.

F-a In the **CHAP11** directory, copy **SWAP2.BAT** to **SWAP3.BAT**.

F-b Change **SWAP3.BAT** to allow the user to key in either **SWAP3 *dirname file1 file2*** or **SWAP3 *file1 file2 dirname.***

F-c Use Edit to modify **NAME.FIL**, changing Problem D to Problem E.

F-d Key in the following: A:\>**GO NAME.FIL \CHAP11\SWAP3.BAT** Enter

F-e In Notepad, click **File**. Click **Print**. Click **File**. Click **Exit**.

PROBLEM SET III—BRIEF ESSAY

1. The following is a batch file called **TEST.BAT**:

```
@ECHO OFF
:AGAIN
IF \%1\==\\ GOTO END
IF %1==LIFE ECHO LIFE
IF %1==MINE ECHO MINE
IF %1==YOURS ECHO YOURS
IF \%1\==\\ GOTO END
IF NOT EXIST %1 GOTO NEXT
TYPE %1
:NEXT
SHIFT
GOTO AGAIN
:END
```

   LIFE, MINE, and YOURS are variables. **MY.FIL** is a file that is on the disk. Analyze this file and describe what will happen anzd why when you key in each of the following at the command line:

   a. **TEST LIFE**
   b. **TEST MINE**
   c. **TEST YOURS**
   d. **TEST MY.FIL**
   e. **TEST life**
   f. **TEST my.fil**

2. The following is a batch file. The batch file is called **COPI.BAT**. The purpose of this batch file is so that the user may copy many different files to any floppy disk that the user specifies. Thus, if the user keyed in COPY A:*.TXT *.NEW, all the **.TXT** files and all the **.NEW** files would be copied to the disk in Drive A. The contents of **COPI.BAT** are:

```
IF "%1"=="" GOTO END
FOR %%a IN (a A) DO IF "%%a"=="%1" GOTO drivea
FOR %%b IN (b B) DO IF "%%b"=="%1" GOTO driveb
:drivea
SHIFT
:newa
IF "%1"=="" GOTO END
ECHO copying %1
COPY %1 A:
SHIFT
GOTO newa
:driveb
SHIFT
:newb
```

```
IF "%1"=="" GOTO END
ECHO copying %1
COPY %1 B:
SHIFT
GOTO newb
:END
```

Analyze this file and describe what will happen and why when you key in each of the following at the command line:

a. **COPI**
b. **COPI A C:\WINDOSBK*.TMP C:\WINDOSBK*.99**
c. **COPI B C:\WINDOSBK*.TMP C:\WINDOSBK*.99**
d. **COPI A:**
e. **COPY B:**

Since most people no longer have a Drive B, how could you modify this batch file so you could use a removable Zip drive with the drive letter of H:?

CHAPTER

12

CONNECTIVITY

LEARNING OBJECTIVES

1. Explain the following terms: client, server, resources, LAN, and WAN.
2. Compare and contrast server-based networks and peer-to-peer networks.
3. List and explain two reasons for setting up a network.
4. Compare and contrast setting up a peer-to-peer network using bus topology and using star topology.
5. Explain how to set up a peer-to-peer network using Windows 2000 Professional.
6. Explain the purposes of sharing a printer, a folder on a hard drive, and an entire hard drive.
7. Explain the purpose and function of a mapped drive.
8. Explain how to use direct cable connections to share files.
9. Explain the purpose and function of the Internet.
10. Compare and contrast the Internet and the World Wide Web.
11. Explain the following terms: Web page, home page, hyperlinks, and search engines.
12. Explain three ways to connect to the Internet.
13. Explain the roles that TCP/IP can play in computer communication.
14. Explain the purpose and function of an IP address.
15. Explain the function and purpose of the Domain Name System.
16. Explain the purpose and function of a URL.
17. Explain how the TCP/IP utilities can be used to troubleshoot problems and offer connections to non-Microsoft hosts.
18. Explain the purpose and function of FTP
19. Explain the purpose and function of Telnet

STUDENT OUTCOMES

1. Create a network connection.
2. Identify a computer and its workgroup on a network.
3. Share a printer, a folder on a hard drive, and an entire hard drive.
4. Map a drive on a network.
5. Use Internet Explorer to navigate a local area network and the World Wide Web.
6. Examine ways to customize Internet Explorer.
7. Use TCP/IP Utilities.

CHAPTER OVERVIEW

In the computer world, connectivity is a reality. Connectivity can mean connecting to other computers in your home or office. It can mean sharing resources such as printers or files on your computer or accessing those resources from another computer. It can also mean connecting to resources throughout the world using the Internet. Networks provide these connections. Windows 2000 Professional is designed for networking; it allows you to network with others to collect information, exchange files, and share resources.

This chapter introduces the basic concepts of networking. It explains the terminology used in the networking world, such as client, server, peer-to-peer network, LAN, WAN, and more. If you have the appropriate hardware, it will show you how to set up a peer-to-peer network and then how to share resources on your network. You will also learn about direct cable connections so that, if you want to merely copy files from one computer to another, you may do so without a network.

Networking also encompasses the Internet. You will be introduced to the basic protocols of the Internet. If you have the appropriate setup, you will learn how to connect to and navigate the Internet. You will learn how Windows 2000 Professional lets you automatically update any new features or fixes to Windows 2000 Professional. You will also learn how to customize Internet Explorer to meet your needs.

12.1 NETWORKS (LANS AND WANS)

Today it is more and more common for a small business or even a home to have more than one computer. In this world of so many computers, you will probably want to connect computers together. When you connect computers together, you create what is called a ***LAN*** (***local area network***). In networks, there are servers and clients. A ***server*** is a computer that provides shared resources to network users. A ***client*** is a computer that accesses the shared network resources provided by the server. ***Resources*** refers to the elements that are shared, such as a disk drive, a printer, a file, or a folder. A ***server-based network*** is one in which security and other network functions are provided by a ***dedicated server***. A dedicated server's sole function is to provide network resources.

Client/Server-based networks have become the standard model for networks serving more than 10 users. The key here is 10 or more users. There are many environments that have fewer than 10 users, but would still benefit from a network. Thus, there is an alternative to a server-based network. It is called a ***peer-to-peer network***, or a ***workgroup***. A peer-to-peer network has neither a dedicated server nor a hierarchy among the computers. All the computers are equal and therefore peers. Each computer can function as either a client or a server.

There are many advantages to setting up a network. If you have only one printer, CD-ROM drive, or Zip drive, every computer in the LAN can use that hardware. If you and others are working on the same document, you can access the document without having to copy it to your own computer. If you have several people working on a customer list, for instance, and you can keep that information on one computer, all users can access that information and know that they are working with the most current information. You can set up local email so that you can send messages to any user on the network. If you have notebook computers (portables), you can attach or detach them from the network and update information as you need. If you are away from the office, you can dial in to your network and access the resources you need.

You may also hear the term ***WAN*** (***wide area network***). A WAN consists of computers that use long-range telecommunication links such as modems or satellites to connect over long distances. The ***Internet*** is a WAN. It is a worldwide network of networks that connects millions of computers.

In order to have any kind of network, including a peer-to-peer network, you must have a ***network interface card***, referred to as an ***NIC***, installed into a slot in each computer so that a LAN cable connecting all the computers can be installed. One of the most common network cards is an Ethernet card. The card must fit the bus architecture slot you have available, typically an ISA (industry standard architecture) or a PCI (peripheral component interconnect) slot on a desktop computer and a PCMCIA (Personal Computer Memory Card International Association) slot on a notebook computer. The card must support the type of cable you will be using to connect the computers. Furthermore, you must consider what design is the most appropriate for your network. A network design is called a ***topology***. The two most common topologies for a peer-to-peer network are the ***bus topology*** and the ***star topology***.

The bus topology uses a single ***coaxial cable*** and is commonly called Thin Ethernet, 10BASE-2, or ***Thinnet***. If you use this method, you also need ***T-connectors*** and ***terminator plugs***. All the computers connect to a single cable, which is why this topology is called a bus. A T-connector has one end plugged into a network interface card and two open ends (like a T) for connecting the cables that go to other computers. Once the cables are connected to the computers using the T-connectors, each end of the cable uses a terminator plug to complete the networking. Every cable end must be plugged into the network or have a terminator to complete the connection. There can be no end that is unattached. See Figure 12.1.

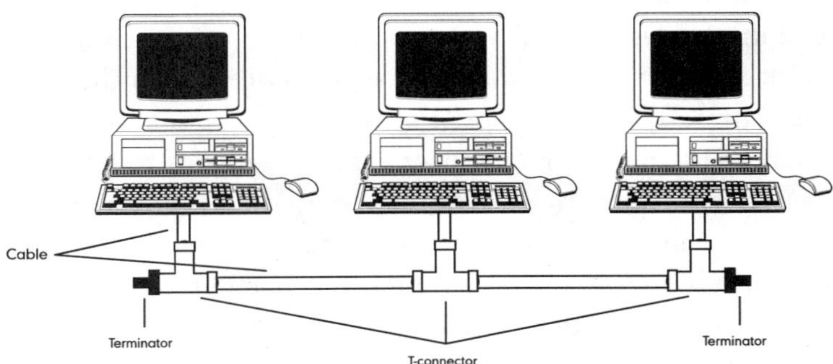

FIGURE 12.1 A PEER-TO-PEER NETWORK WITH A BUS TOPOLOGY

The advantages to using a bus topology are that it is easy to install and relatively inexpensive. It is also easy to expand a bus network by adding another length of cable between the terminators. A disadvantage is that if you have three or more components on the bus and one segment of the cable fails, the entire network will fail.

The other way to create a peer-to-peer network is to use an Ethernet hub. This method is considered a star topology. Each connection is like a spoke of a bicycle wheel: one end connects to the hub and the other end connects to a computer or a device such as a printer. In this case, you use the type of cable called ***twisted-pair cable***. This topology is also known as 10BASE-T, twisted pair, twisted-pair Ethernet, 10BT, TPE, or RJ-45. See Figure 12.2.

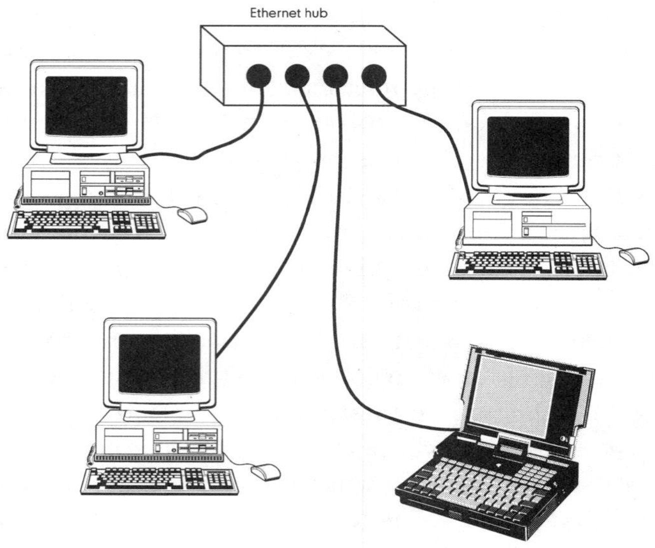

FIGURE 12.2 A PEER-TO-PEER NETWORK WITH A STAR TOPOLOGY

With a star topology, a single piece of defective cabling affects only the computer it connects, unless it is the hub itself. This kind of problem is known as a ***single point of failure***. Each computer would still work, but there would be no network connection to the computer on the segment of cable that failed. The disadvantages to a star topology are many. It is more expensive than a bus topology because you must purchase additional hardware, the hub. Expansion of the network may require the purchase of an additional hub if you have used all the connections on the existing hub. Also, the wiring can become unwieldy, especially if you cannot run cable through your walls.

With either topology, you can use a networkable printer, or any resource, by connecting it directly to a cable or to a hub. Only the computer that needs to use the printer must be on; no other computers on the network must be turned on. The printer must have a network interface card installed. Most laser printers can have an NIC added, but the common, inexpensive inkjet printers cannot. In that case, the printer must be connected to one of the computers on the network and that computer must be turned on for the printer to be used by any station.

In a server-based network you must also have software that tells the computers how to communicate with one another. The software is known as a ***network operating system*** (***NOS***). The two most popular network operating systems are Novell NetWare and Microsoft Windows NT. Windows NT, however, is being replaced by Windows 2000 Server. An up-and-coming NOS is Linux, a version of an older network operating system, Unix. The server (the computer that serves the other computers on the network) uses this software. In a generic sense, a network operating system is the software you need to make your networked hardware communicate.

You have been introduced to hardware and software. There is a trilogy in networking. The third component is the ***network administrator***, sometimes called the system administrator. The administrator is the person who decides how the hardware and software will be used and who will have access to what devices and resources on the network. The administrator also manages the day-to-day operation of the hardware, the network operating system, and the resources of the network.

A server-based network is beyond the scope of this textbook. However, a peer-to-peer network is not. Any computer that is running Windows has the built-in peer-to-peer software to create and administer a small network. A small network still needs the appropriate hardware, software, and administration. In a peer-to-peer network, either each computer can be administered by its user, or there can be a single administrator. The selection of the topology, network interface card, and cable is beyond the scope of this textbook. This textbook makes the assumption that these hardware decisions have been made. In this chapter you will use a peer-to-peer LAN with the built-in networking software that comes with Windows.

12.2 SETTING UP A NETWORK

When Windows 2000 Professional is installed, it will detect your network card and install the default components. You will have to name your computer. All computers must have a unique name even if they are not on a network. The setup program will provide a cryptic name for your computer. You may override this. Often, a good computer name is the name of the brand of the computer. If you had two computers with the same brand name, you could differentiate between them numerically, such as DellXPS-1 and DellXPS-2. You will also have to enter an administrator password. The administrator password is the most important password in Windows, so be sure to use a secure password as well as write it down and store it in a safe place. This password is what allows you to administer your computer. See Figure 12.3.

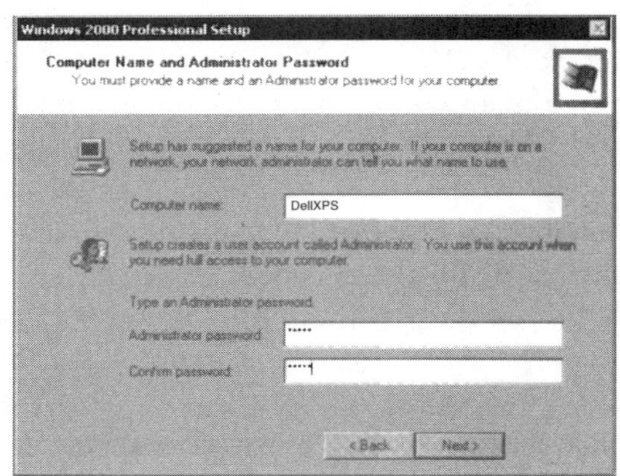

FIGURE 12.3 ENTERING A COMPUTER NAME AND AN ADMINISTRATOR PASSWORD

You will then see Figure 12.4, which is where you will specify whether you are a member of a domain or workgroup. For a peer-to-peer network, you are a member of a workgroup. Each computer in the workgroup must have the same workgroup name. The computer will restart and then prompt you with your logon options. See Figure 12.5.

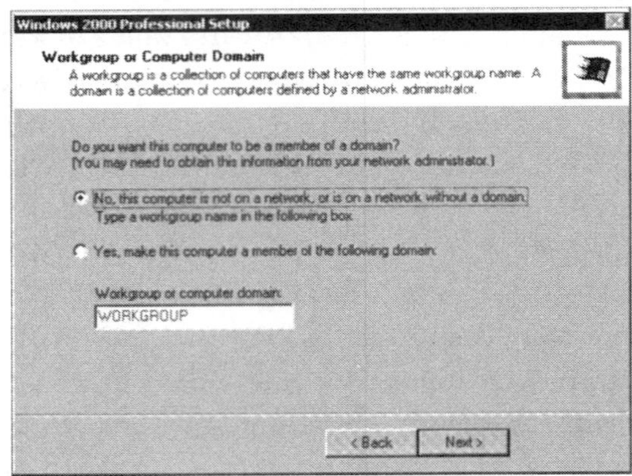

FIGURE 12.4 MEMBER OF A DOMAIN OR WORKGROUP

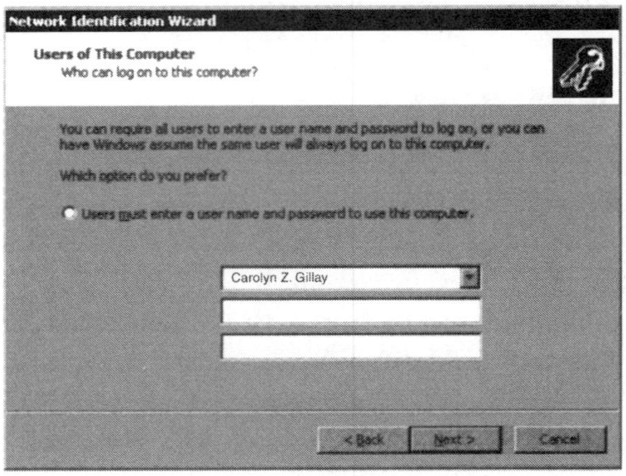

FIGURE 12.5 USER LOGON

You do not want to log on each time as the administrator. It is best to select **Users must enter a user name and password to use this computer**. If you choose the other option, Windows always assumes that the default user has logged on to this computer, and you defeat the entire purpose of a secure operating system. You will want each user to have a logon name. User names are commonly in the form of first initial and last name, such as Cgillay or Bpeat, or last name and first initial, such as GillayC or PeatB. If you like, you can use your entire name, such as Carolyn Z. Gillay or Bette A. Peat. You will also be asked to key in a password. Select one that you will not forget. You will then be asked to key in your password a second time to confirm its spelling and case. Passwords are case sensitive. Your password should be difficult to guess, but not so difficult that you will forget it. For this reason, you should avoid obvious passwords such as your user name, name, children's names, address, or social security number. Too often a user creates a password and then leaves it on a note taped to the computer—obviously defeating the purpose of any security.

Once you have logged on, you will see a new icon on your desktop, My Network Places:

My Network Places is your map to your network. The activities that follow are based on a specific computer configuration. These activities are meant to act as a guide to accomplishing these tasks on your system. You will have to interpret the screen examples to match your specific computer network. Unfortunately, most schools do not have the hardware, software, or support staff to allow you to do these tasks in a lab environment. If this is the case, only read the activities, do not do them. *Again, do not attempt to do these activities in a lab environment.*

12.3 ACTIVITY: IDENTIFYING A COMPUTER TO A NETWORK

Note 1: It is assumed that you have successfully installed the necessary software and hardware.

Note 2: The activity is based on a specific computer configuration. This configuration is a simple bus topology with three computers and two printers. Your display will be different.

Step 1 Right-click **My Network Places**. Click **Properties**. Right-click **Local Area Connection**. Click **Properties**.

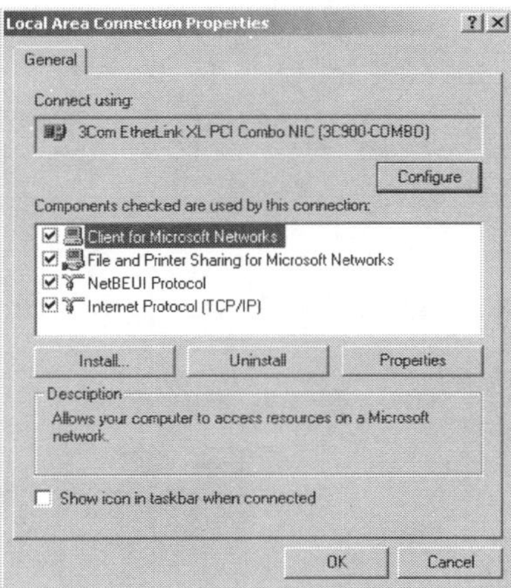

The Local Area Connection Properties sheet appears. This computer system is on a peer-to-peer network. When you are on a peer-to-peer network, you have only one tab, General. The dialog box lists the network clients, adapters, protocols, and services that are installed on your computer. The client software allows you to use files and printers shared on other networked computers. The adapter is the network interface card that physically connects you to the network. A ***protocol*** is a set of rules that allows computers to connect with one another and to exchange information. Computers on a network must use the same protocol in order to communicate. ***Services*** allow you to share your files and printers with other computers on the network. Besides sharing files and printers, there are other services as well, such as automatically backing up the system and remotely administering the Registry. The following items are listed:

- Client for Microsoft Networks
- File and Printer Sharing for Microsoft Networks
- Internet Protocol (TCP/IP)
- NetBEUI (pronounced "net-booey") Protocol
- Your network interface card (in the above example, 3Com EtherLink XL PCI Combo NIC (3C900-COMBO))

Step 2 Click **Cancel**. Close the Network and Dial-Up Connections window.

Step 3 Click Start. Point to **Settings**. Click **Control Panel**. Double-click **System**. Click the **Network Identification** tab.

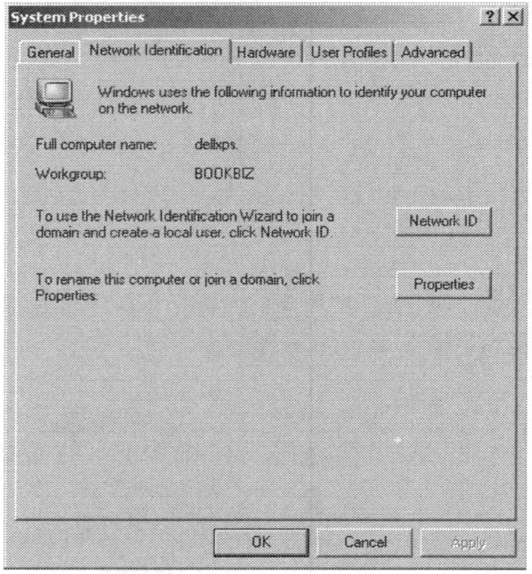

WHAT'S HAPPENING? Here you see the name of your computer and the workgroup you belong to.

Step 4 Click **Properties**.

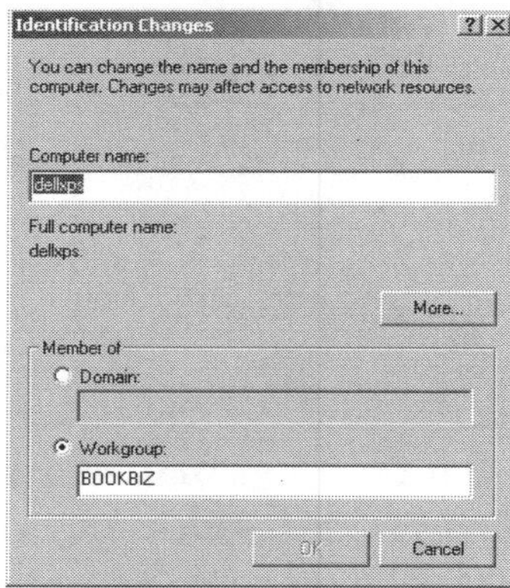

WHAT'S HAPPENING? The computer name and workgroup have been filled in. Here is where you could make changes if you desired. The computer name can be any name you wish, but each computer on the network needs to have a unique name. The name can be longer than 15 characters, but it is best to remain under 15 characters with no spaces. This is because on other network protocols names are limited to 15 characters. Again, for the name of your computer you could use the brand of the computer. But be sure to choose a name that will clearly identify which computer is which on the network. Here, this computer is identified by its brand name.

All computers on your peer-to-peer network *must* use the same workgroup name. But a workgroup name cannot be the same name as the computer. The workgroup name must be identical in case and spelling on all computers. Again, you can have up to 15 characters with no spaces. Only computers with the same workgroup name can share resources. In this example, the workgroup name is BOOKBIZ.

Step 5 Click **Cancel**. Click **Network ID**.

WHAT'S HAPPENING? Had you not created your network connection when you installed Windows 2000 Professional, you could do so at this time, using Network Identification Wizard.

Step 6 Click **Cancel**. Click **Cancel**. Close the Control Panel window.

Step 7 Repeat these steps for each computer on the network.

Step 8 Be sure that all your computers are on. Sit at one computer. Double-click **My Network Places**. Double-click **Computers Near Me**.

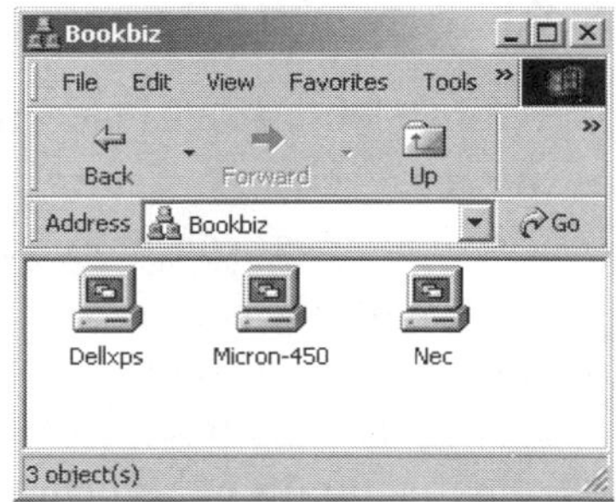

You see the names for every computer on your network. This window is in Large Icons view. Your view may be different. Be a little patient. It takes some time for the computers to see each other. Each is broadcasting its availability. (*Note:* If you do not see My Network Places or if My Network Places is empty, chances are you have a problem with your network installation, either with the hardware or with the protocols and services. Network troubleshooting is beyond the scope of this textbook. However, a simple mistake that users often make when setting up a network is that they have different workgroup names on each computer. You can correct this easily on each computer by opening System in Control Panel, choosing Networking Identification, and then choosing Properties and ensuring that the workgroup name is the same.)

Step 9 (*Note:* Remember that this activity refers to a specific computer configuration. Your computer network will *not* look exactly like this example.) Double-click the Nec computer.

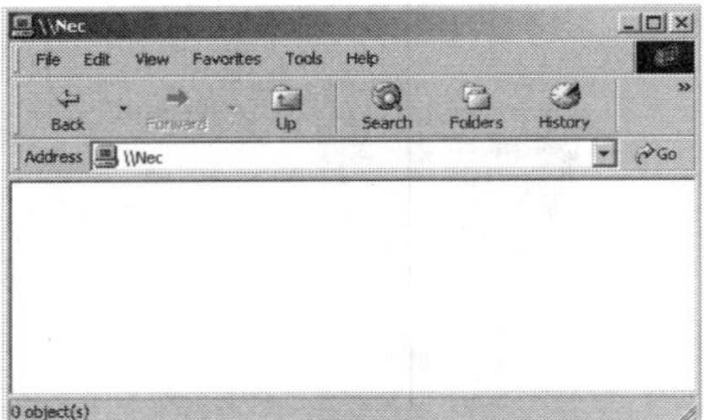

Windows 2000 Professional uses a window like Internet Explorer's. Internet Explorer is a ***browser*** (a tool to search the Internet). However, the Nec window is empty because you have not shared any of the resources. Also, note the address in the window. Nec is listed as \\Nec. The double backslash is the ***UNC*** (***universal naming convention***) for locating the path to a network resource. It specifies the share name of a particular computer. The computer name is limited to 15 characters, and the share name is usually limited to 15 characters. The address takes the format of *\\computer name\share name[\optional path]*. (Brackets are used to indicate items that are optional. They are not actually included in the name.)

Step 10 Close all windows.

12.4 SHARING PRINTERS ON A NETWORK

There are always two parts to sharing resources—the client and the server. The server is the computer that has the resource you wish to share. The client is the computer that wishes to access the resource. The most common items to share are a printer, a folder on a hard drive, and an entire hard drive.

When you share a printer, any computer on the network can use that printer. If you do not have a hub, the printer, of course, needs to be connected physically to a computer on the network. That computer then becomes the ***print server***. Often, in a large network, there will be one computer dedicated to handling printing, and it will be called the print server. In a small network, the print server is not dedicated only to printing. It can be any computer on the network that has the printer connected to it. Furthermore, if you have more than one printer, each can be shared. Look at Figure 12.6.

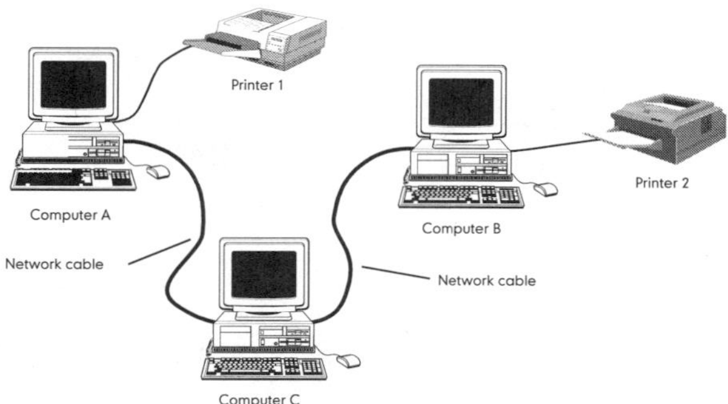

FIGURE 12.6 PRINTER SHARING ON A NETWORK

Computers A, B, and C are networked in a simple bus. Computer A has Printer 1 attached to it. If you are sitting at Computer C and want to print, you are the client who wants to use the resource (Printer 1) of Computer A. Computer A, in this case, is the print server because Printer 1 is attached to Computer A. If you wanted to use the printer attached to Computer B, then Computer B would be the print server because Printer 2 is attached to Computer B. Any computer on this network can use any printer attached to the network. However, the computer attached to the printer must be turned on. If you were sitting at Computer C and Computer A were not turned on, you would not be able to use the printer attached to Computer A. You also have the choice of using a printer ***locally***. If you were sitting at Computer A, you could use Printer 1 locally. Locally means without using a network. You could use Printer 1 because it is physically attached to the computer. You would not need to be on the network.

12.5 ACTIVITY: SHARING PRINTERS ON A NETWORK

Note: The following activity is based on a specific computer configuration. Your display will be different.

Step 1 Go to the computer that has the printer physically attached to it (the print server). In this example, it is the NEC computer. In this example, the NEC computer is running Windows 98. You can run different operating systems on the different computers on your network.

Step 2 Open **My Computer**. Open **Control Panel**. Open the **Printers** folder. Right-click the printer you wish to share. In this example, it is the HPLaserJet 4 Plus.

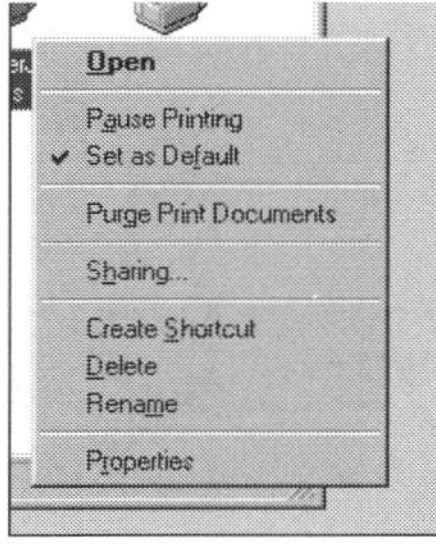

In order for others to use this printer, you need to share it. The context menu has a Sharing choice.

Step 3 Click **Sharing**. Click the **Shared As** button.

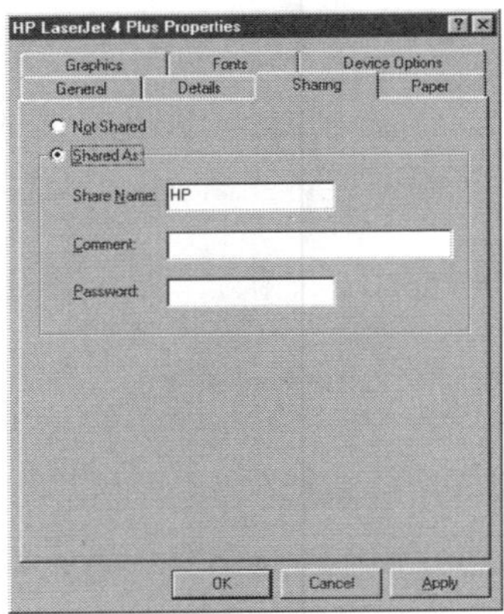

Here you give a name to your shared printer. You again must use the same name across the network.

Step 4 In this example, key in **HPLASER**.

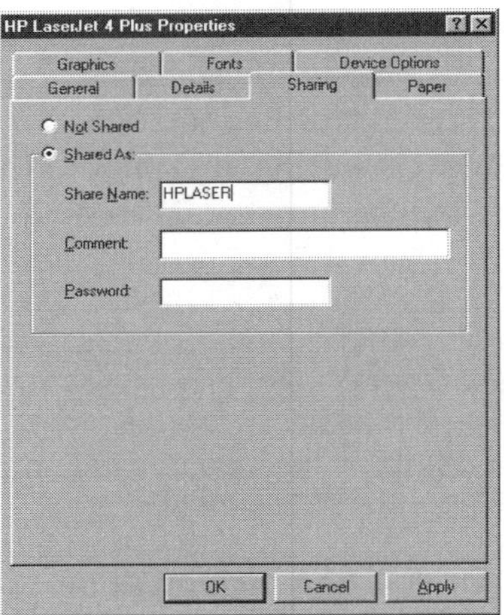

You have named your shared printer. If you wanted, you could include a password. However, if you did that, any user who wanted to use this printer would need to know the password.

Step 5 Click **OK**.

Your printer now has a hand icon under it, indicating that the printer is shared. Now you need to go to each printer client to set up the shared printer. A printer client is any computer on your network that you want to have access to the shared printer. (*Note:* You may need your Windows CD if the printer driver is not installed on the client computer.)

Step 6 Go to a client computer (in this example, the Dellxps). Open **My Computer**. Open **Control Panel**. Open the **Printers** folder. Double-click the **Add Printer** icon. Click **Next**.

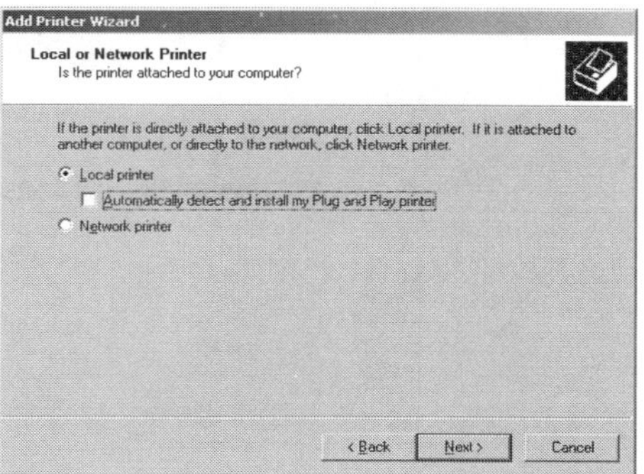

You are asked whether this is a local printer or a network printer. In this case, you want to select Network printer.

Step 7 Click **Network printer**. Click **Next**.

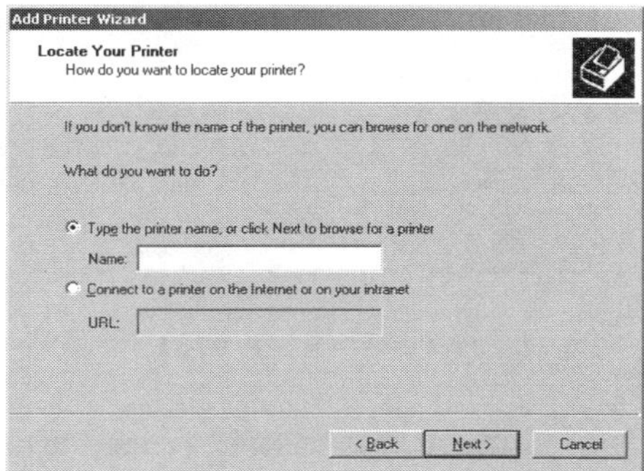

Now you must locate your computer. If you know the name, its URL, you can key it in. Or you can browse for the printer you wish to use.

Step 8 Click **Next**.

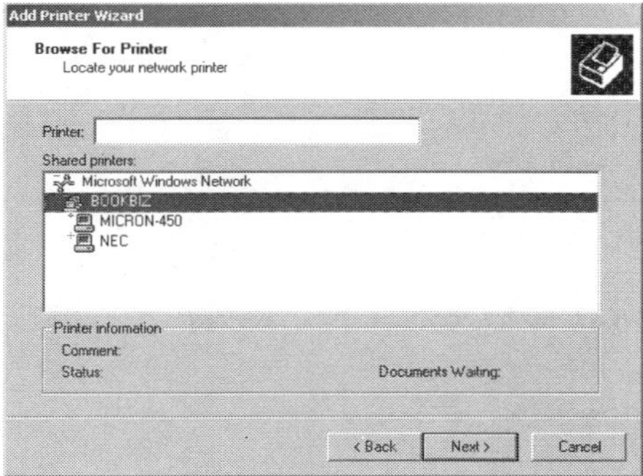

WHAT'S HAPPENING? You are looking at your network. You need to find the computer with the printer attached.

Step 9 Double-click **NEC**. This is the computer to which the printer is physically attached.

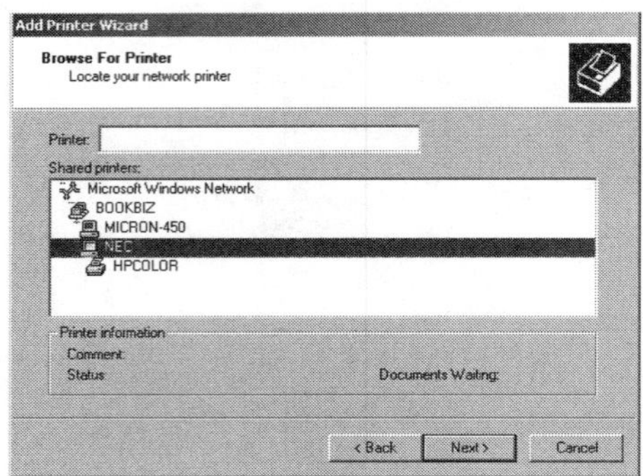

WHAT'S HAPPENING? You can see the shared resource, the HPCOLOR printer.

Step 10 Click the printer to select it. Click **Next**.

WHAT'S HAPPENING? You may see the following dialog box (Figure 12.7). This dialog box is telling you that you do not have the printer drivers installed for this printer. If you see this dialog box, click **OK**. You will then be led through choosing the printer driver.

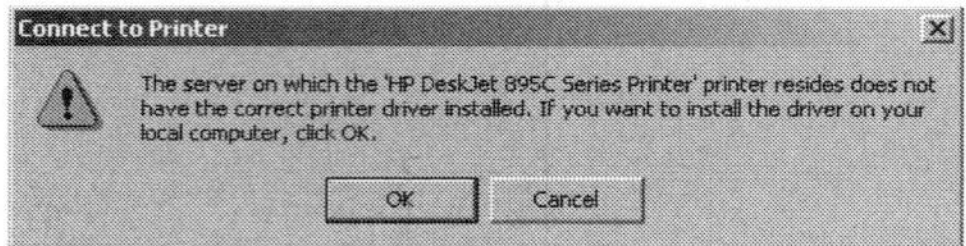

FIGURE 12.7 THE CONNECT TO PRINTER DIALOG BOX

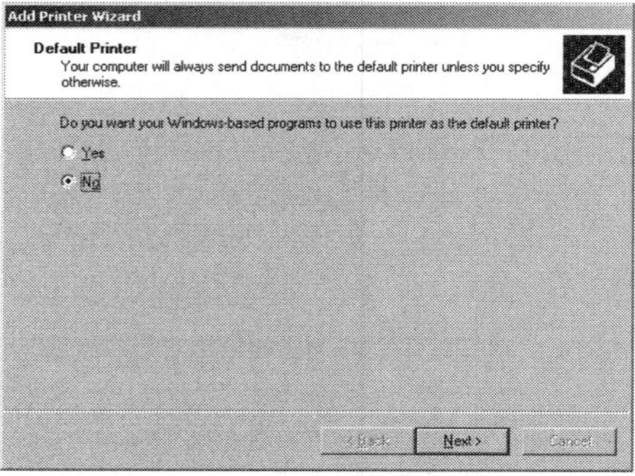

WHAT'S HAPPENING? You are asked if you want this to be the default printer.

Step 11 Be sure **No** is selected. Click **Next**.

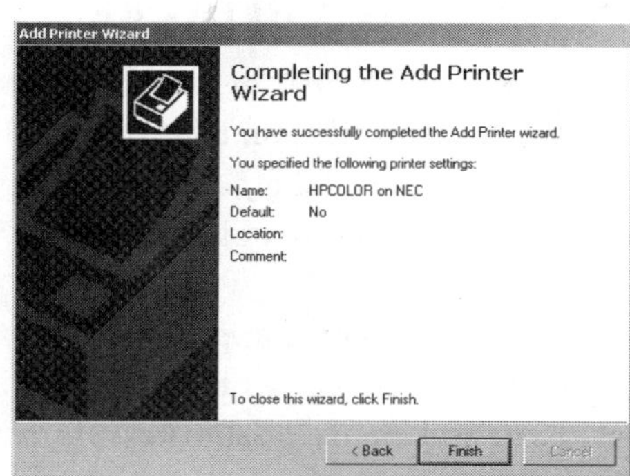

You see a summary of your printer choice.

Step 12 Click **Finish**.

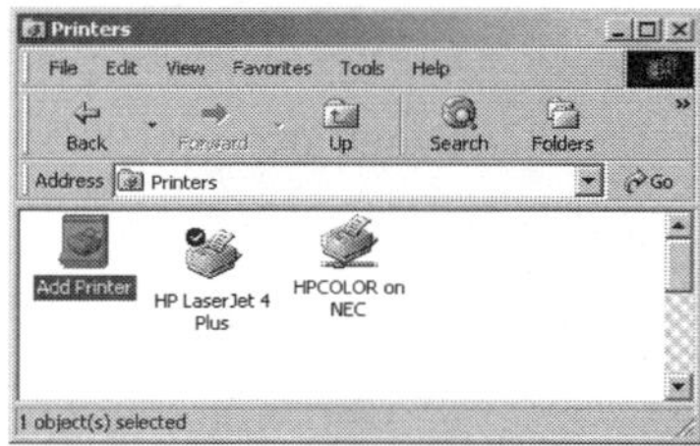

You see your added printer. You know it is a network printer because the icon has the printer on a cable.

Step 13 Right-click the HPCOLOR printer. Click **Properties**. Click **Ports**.

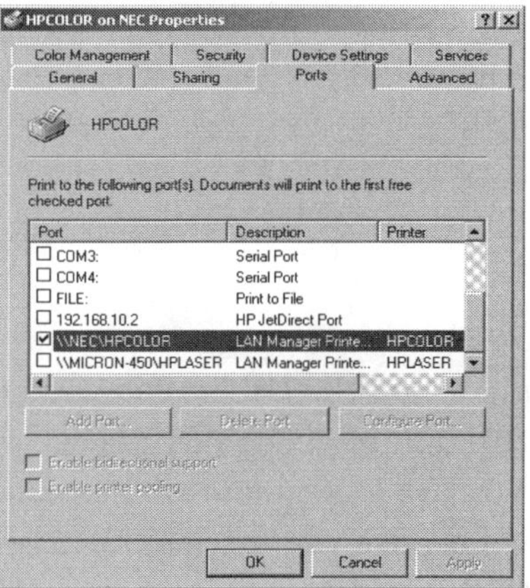

You now see your network path. Notice the format—\\NEC\HPCOLOR. The network path always begins with the double backslash (\\). It is in the format of *computer name**share name*.

Step 14 Click **Cancel**. Close the Printers window.

You have installed your network printer. You would have to take these steps for each client computer that you wished to access the shared printer.

12.6 SHARING A HARD DRIVE ON A NETWORK

When you share a drive, just like a printer, any computer on the network can look into that drive and use the folders and files on that drive. The computer with the drive you wish to share is taking on the role of the ***file server***. Again, in a large network, often there will be one computer dedicated to being a file server. In a small network, typically, there is no dedicated file server.

In a peer-to-peer network any computer on the network can share its drive, but first the drive on the server computer has to be shared in the same manner that the printer is shared. You have the choice of sharing an entire drive or selected folders. The process requires two steps. You must go to the server computer, which contains the drive you wish to share, and set up the drive so that you can share it. Then you go to the client computer and access the shared drive via My Network Places.

12.7 ACTIVITY: SHARING DRIVES ON A NETWORK

Note: The following activity is based on a specific computer configuration. Your display will be different.

Step 1 Go to the computer with a drive you wish to share. In this example, it is the Dell computer.

Step 2 Open My **Network Places**. Open **Computers Near Me**. Open the Dellxps.

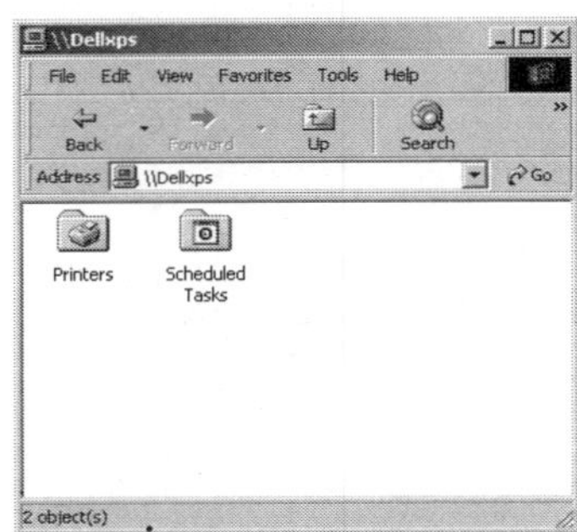

In this example, you are logged onto the Dellxps computer. You see only the Printers folder and the Scheduled Tasks folder. You don't see any drives available through My Network Places, even though you are looking at the computer you are logged on to. The reason that you don't see any drives available is because you are looking at your own computer through the network. Nothing has been shared on the network.

Step 3 Click the **Back** button. Click the Micron-450 computer icon.

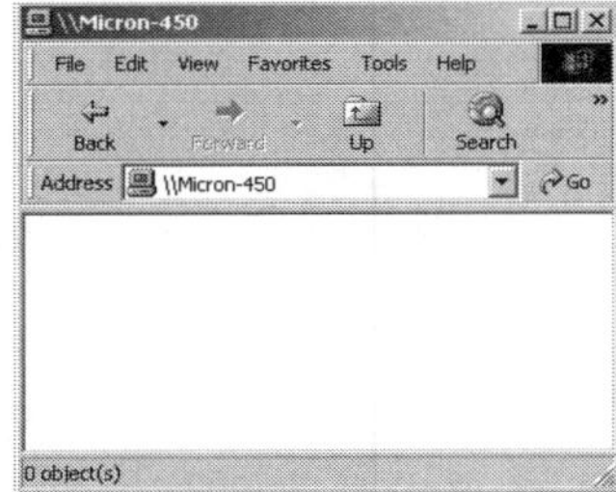

If you see a flashlight icon, that icon indicates that Windows is looking for the network connection. Once it finds it, you will see the empty window. Again, no drive has been shared on the Micron-450, so no drive is visible in My Network Places.

Step 4 Close My Network Places. Open **My Computer**. Right-click Drive C. Click **Sharing**. Click the **Share this folder** button.

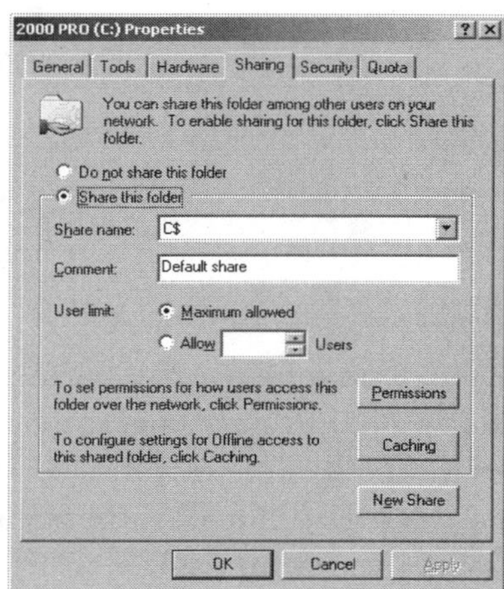

In Windows 2000 Professional, all drives on your computer, such as Drive C or D, are automatically shared using the syntax of ***drive letter$***, such as **D$** or **E$**. This is known as an administrative share. This type of share allows administrators to connect to the root directory of a drive over the network. These drives are not shown in either My Computer or Windows Explorer. These drives are also hidden when users connect to your computer remotely. But if any user knows your computer name, user name, and password and if that user is a member of the Administrators, Backup Operators, or Server Operators group, that user can gain access to your computer over a network or the Internet.

Step 5 Click **New Share**.

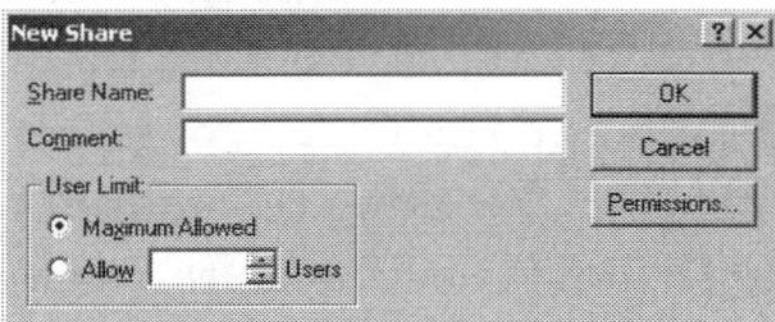

You may name the shared drive anything you like. However, simply calling it C is not a good idea. All computers have a C drive. You want to name it uniquely so that it can be identified on the network as the Dellxps's Drive C. You may also set how many users may be allowed to share this drive at one time (User Limit).

Step 6 Click **Permissions**.

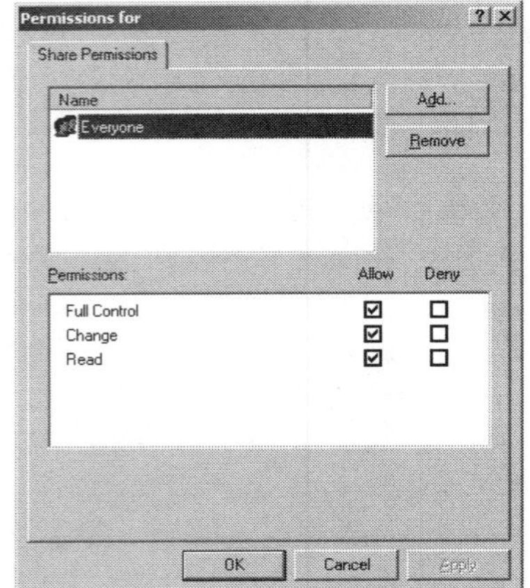

WHAT'S HAPPENING? As you can see, Everyone has full permission to do anything to the shared drive. Windows 2000 Professional provides these groups, whose membership is controlled by the administrator: Users, Power Users, and Administrators. There is another group called Authenticated Users, whose membership is controlled by the operating system or by the domain, if you are on a domain. Authenticated Users is the same as the Everyone group. By default in Windows 2000 Professional, any authenticated user is a member of the Users group. Often, an administrator will remove the Everyone group and add specific groups who may access the information so that the environment is more secure. At the moment, you will simply allow Everyone access to this drive.

Step 7 Click **Cancel**. In the Share Name text box, key in **Dellxps-C**.

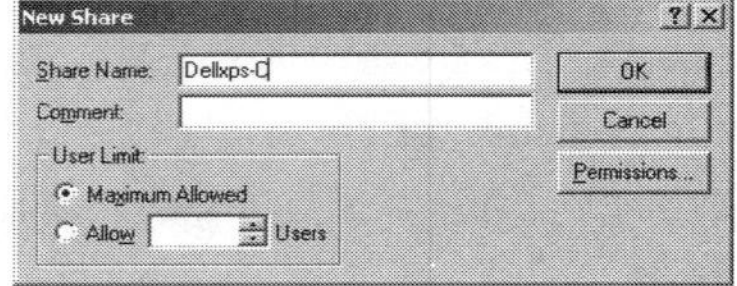

In this case, you chose to name the drive by the computer brand, and you gave full access to your drive. Note that there is no space between the computer brand and the C. A hyphen was used. A space in a share name can cause problems in accessing the shared resource. To avoid problems, avoid spaces. The Dellxps is acting as the server computer. Remember that this is an example. Your drive names and availability will differ from the example.

Step 8 Click **OK**. Click **OK**.

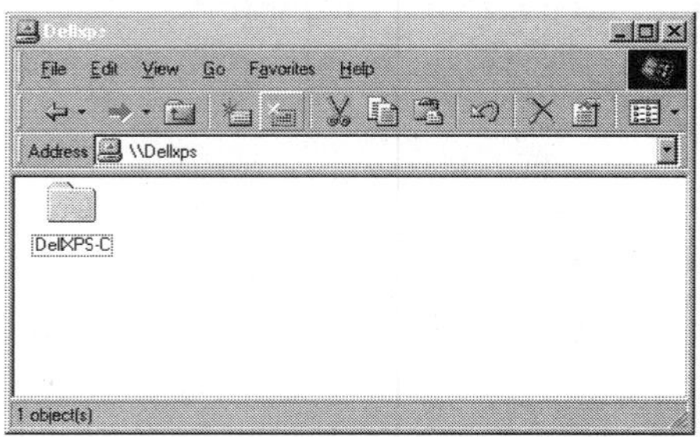

WHAT'S HAPPENING? Now on the Dellxps, you have shared Drive C. You can tell by the hand under the drive icon.

Step 9 Close My Computer. Open **My Network Places**. Double-click **Computers Near Me**. Double-click **Dellxps**.

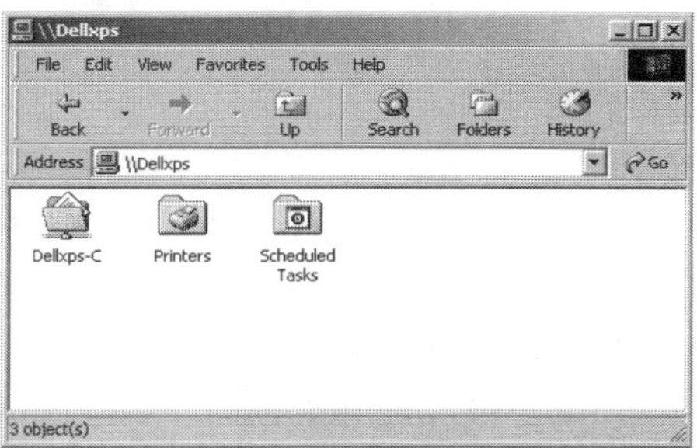

WHAT'S HAPPENING? Now you see your drive represented as a folder icon. You are still the server. To test that you have made the Dellxps's Drive C available to others on the network, you need to go to a client computer.

Step 10 Close My Network Places. Go to a client computer, in this case, the Micron-450. The Micron-450 is using Windows 98. Thus, you open **Network Neighborhood**.

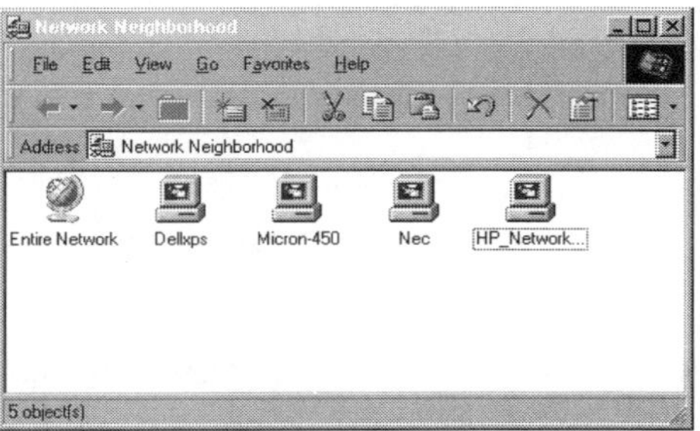

WHAT'S HAPPENING? You are now on the Micron-450 computer, the client, and wish to access the drive on the Dellxps computer. You should be able to because it is shared.

Step 11 Double-click the **Dellxps**.

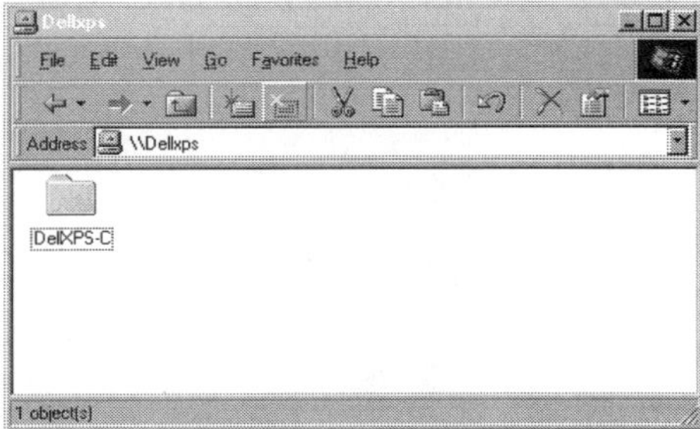

WHAT'S HAPPENING? Now you have access to Drive C on the Dellxps computer.

Step 12 Double-click **DellXPS-C**.

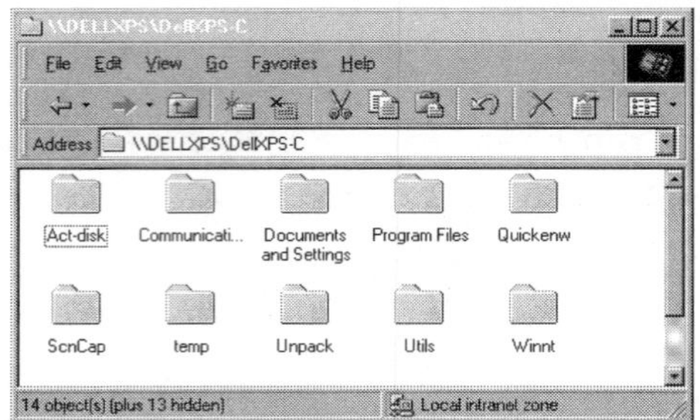

WHAT'S HAPPENING? You have full access to Drive C on the Dellxps. Both the title bar and the address tell you what computer you are accessing. You have been acting as the client computer, because you are logged on to the Micron-450 computer and you are able to access any shared resources (Drive C) of the Dellxps computer, in this case, the server. However, on a peer-to-peer network, you can switch roles and become the server and share your drives so that other users on the network can access your drives.

Step 13 Click the **Back** button twice. Double-click the **Micron-450** computer.

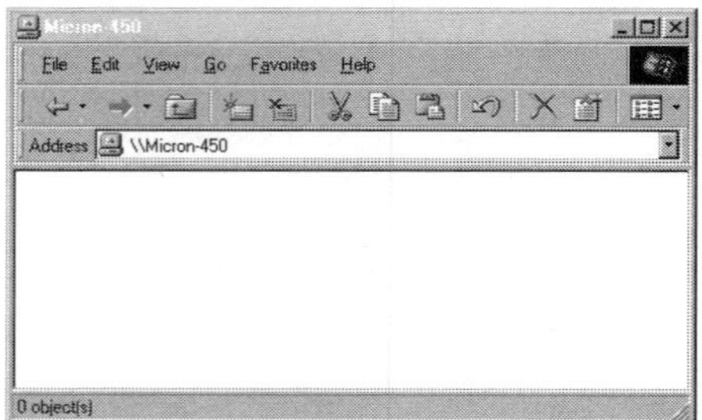

WHAT'S HAPPENING? Even though you are sitting at the client computer, the Micron-450, you cannot see any of your drives because you are looking at the Micron-450 computer through Network Neighborhood. Since no drives are shared on the Micron-450 computer, no drives on the Micron-450 computer can be seen through Network Neighborhood.

Step 14 Close Network Neighborhood. Open **My Computer** on the Micron-450. Right-click Drive C. Click **Sharing**. Click the **Shared As** button. Key in **Micron-C**. Click the **Full** option button.

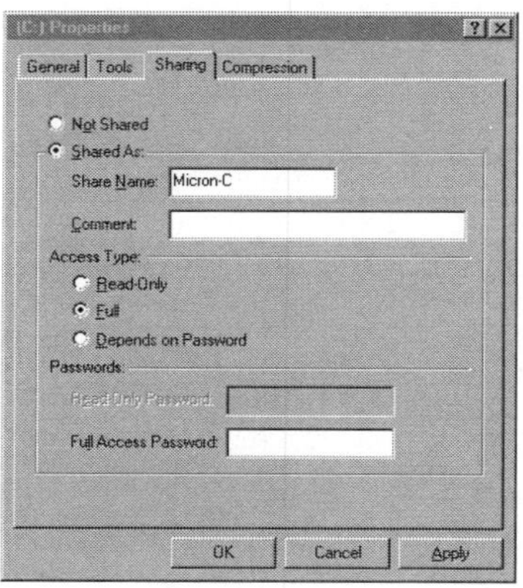

Since the Micron is a Windows 98 computer, you do not have any permissions to set by users, as you do in Windows 2000 Professional. Your only choices are Read-Only, Full, or Depends on Password. Depends on Password only means that you can restrict specific users to Read-Only or to Full.

Step 15 Click **Apply**. Click **OK**.

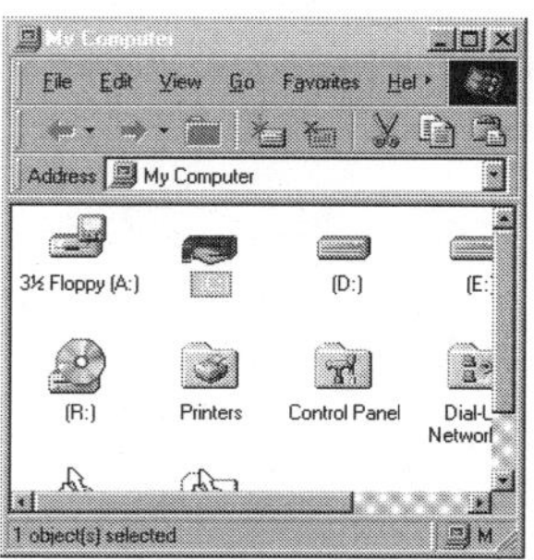

You now see that on the Micron computer, Drive C is shared. Now anyone on another computer connected to the network can access Drive C on the Micron computer. You have just acted as the server.

Step 16 Close My Computer. Open the **Network Neighborhood** window. Double-click **Micron-450**.

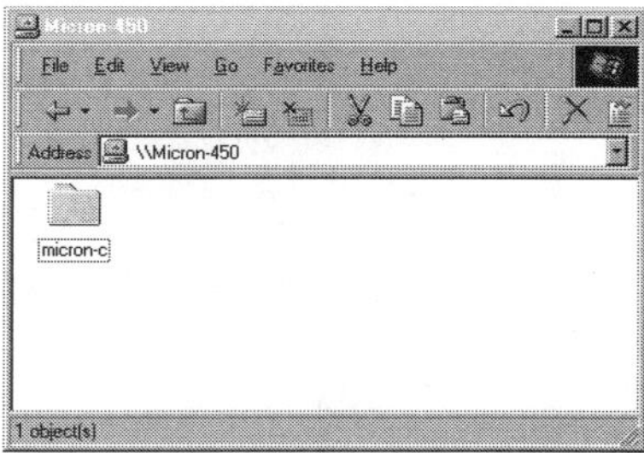

As you can see, now the Micron-450 drive is available through Network Neighborhood.

Step 17 Close Network Neighborhood.

12.8 SHARING ONLY A FOLDER ON A HARD DRIVE ON A NETWORK

You do not need to share your entire hard drive. You can elect to share only a folder and limit other users on the network to accessing only that folder, not your entire hard drive. In fact, that is often what users do. They opt to share a folder or folders on their hard drive but do not want to let other users access their entire hard drive.

Again, the process requires two steps. You must go to the server computer, which contains the folder you wish to share, and share it. Then you go to the client computer and access the shared drive via My Network Places (or Network Neighborhood in Windows 98).

12.9 ACTIVITY: SHARING A FOLDER ON A NETWORK

Note: The following activity is based on a specific computer configuration. Your display will be different.

Step 1 Go to the computer that has the folder you wish to share, in this case the Dellxps computer.

Step 2 Open **My Network Places**. Click on **Computers Near Me**. Open the Dellxps computer.

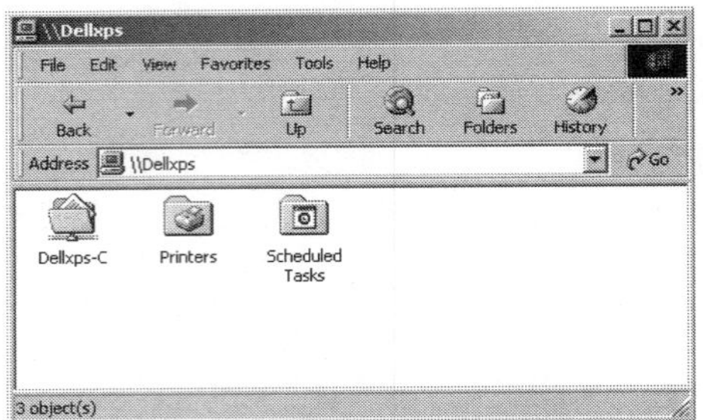

As you can see, Drive C is shared. You can tell by the network connection under the Dellxps-C icon.

Step 3 Close My Network Places. Open **My Computer**. Right-click Drive C. Click **Sharing**. Click the down arrow in the Share name drop-down list box. Select **DellXPS-C**. Click **Do not share this folder**.

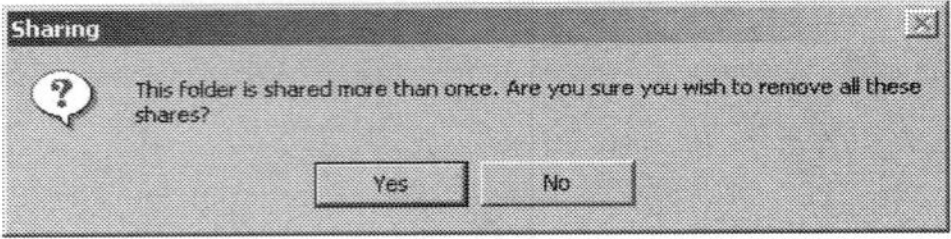

Since this folder is shared, you are reminded that you are removing access to the shared drive. What you are also doing is removing the administrative share (C$). Although you could recreate it (New Share/C$), it is not necessary, because each time you reboot, the administrative share is always recreated.

Step 4 Click **Yes**. Click **Apply**. Click **OK**.

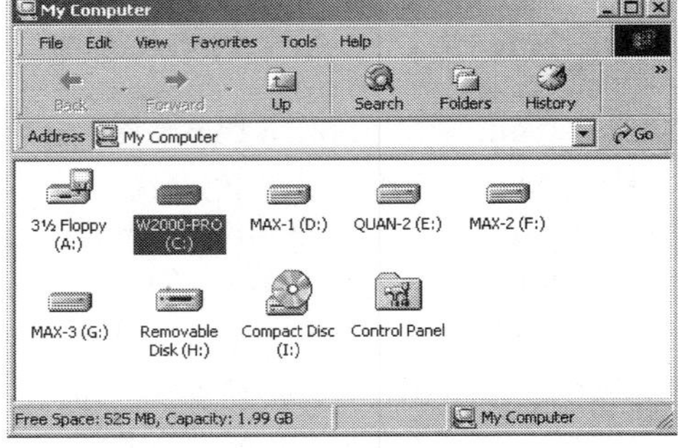

Drive C is no longer shared.

Step 5 Open **My Network Places**. Open the Dellxps computer.

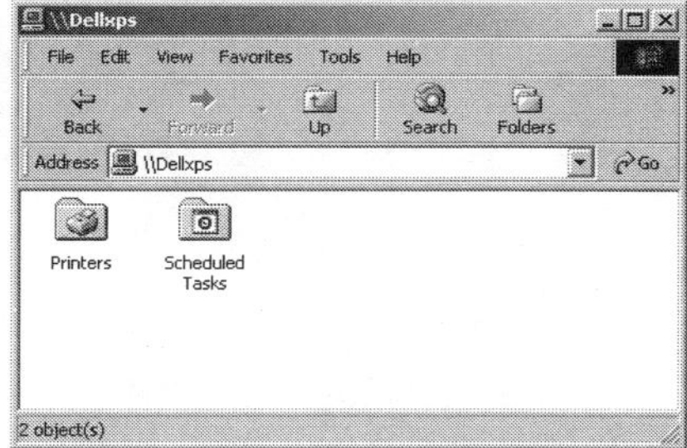

WHAT'S HAPPENING? You can see that Drive C is no longer available to the network.

Step 6 Close the Dellxps window. Click the **My Computer** window to make it active. Open Drive C. Right-click the **WINDOSBK** folder. Click **Sharing**. Click **Share this folder**.

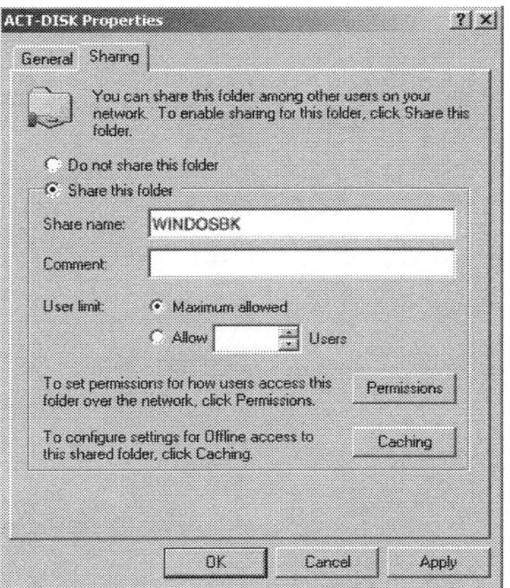

WHAT'S HAPPENING? You are going to share the **WINDOSBK** folder. The folder name is **WINDOSBK** and the default is full for everyone. You are giving other users full access to that folder only.

Step 7 Click **Apply.** Click **OK**. Close all open windows. Open **My Network Places**. Open the Dellxps computer.

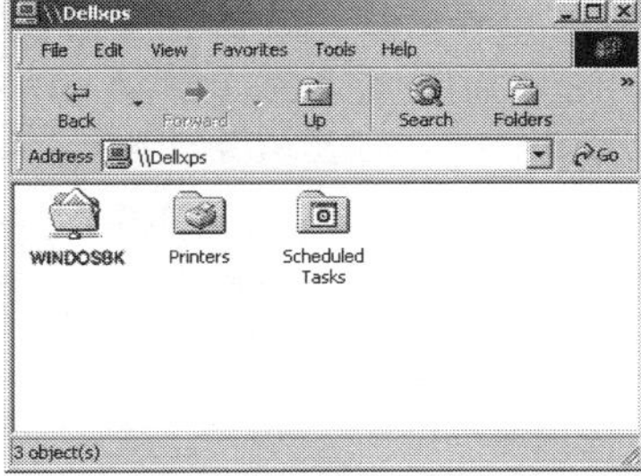

WHAT'S HAPPENING? As you can see, the only item that is available for other users on the network is the folder **WINDOSBK** on Drive C.

Step 8 Close My Network Places. Open **My Computer**. Right-click Drive C. Click **Sharing**. Click **Share this folder**.

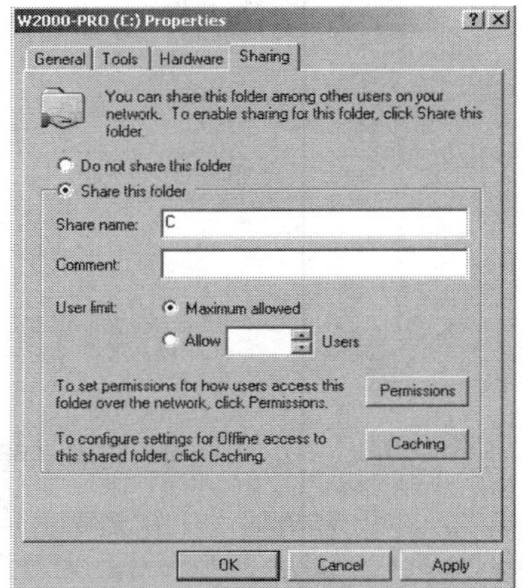

If you are continuing the activities without rebooting, you will see that there is no New Share command button and the share name is C. If you rebooted, you would see the administrative C$ share.

Step 9 If you have a **New Share** button, click it. Then key in the name **Dellxps-C**. Otherwise, in the Share name text box, key in **Dellxps-C**. Click **OK**. Click **OK**.

You have now shared the **WINDOSBK** folder as well as the entire C drive.

Step 10 Close My Computer.

12.10 MAPPING DRIVES

Once a drive or folder is shared, you may map a drive letter to the shared drive or folder. A ***mapped drive*** is a network drive or folder (one that has been shared) that you assign a local drive letter. When you map a drive or a folder, it appears as a drive on client computers in Windows Explorer and My Computer. You no longer need to browse My Network Places to have access to that shared drive or folder. You access directly from My Computer using the assigned, or *mapped,* letter. Most often you will map folders rather than entire drives.

Windows 2000 Professional lets you use My Network Places to map drives using the Internet Explorer–like window. In order to see the mapped drive icons, you can use the customization feature in My Computer. Windows 2000 Professional also allows you to map a drive by right-clicking the My Computer icon or the My Network Places icon and choosing Map Network Drive. You may also use the Tools menu in My Computer or Windows Explorer.

12.11 ACTIVITY: MAPPING DRIVES ON A NETWORK

Note: The following activity is based on a specific computer configuration. Your display will be different.

Step 1 In this example, you are going to begin with the Micron computer—the computer with a drive you wish to map.

Step 2 Share the Micron drive as Micron-C with full access. Return to the Dellxps computer.

Step 3 Right-click **My Network Places**.

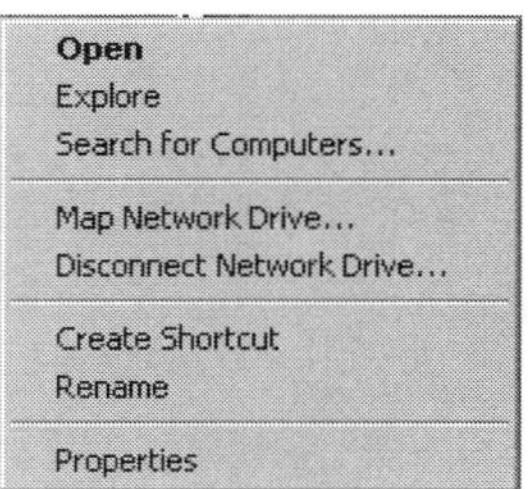

WHAT'S HAPPENING? You see a shortcut menu listing your choices. The one you are interested in is Map Network Drive.

Step 4 Click **Map Network Drive**.

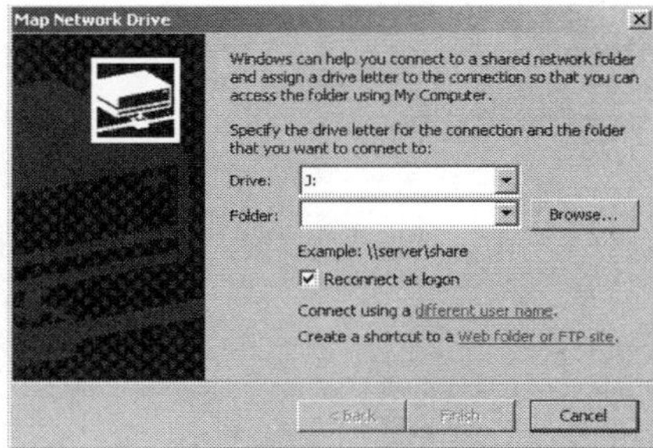

WHAT'S HAPPENING? The drive listed, in this case, is J:, the first available drive letter not assigned to any real device on this computer. The path is the UNC path to the drive that you want. If you check the Reconnect at logon box, every time you connect to the network, Drive J on your local computer (the Dellxps, in this example) will actually point to Drive C on the Micron-450 computer.

Step 5 Key in **\\Micron-450\Micron-C**. Click **Finish**.

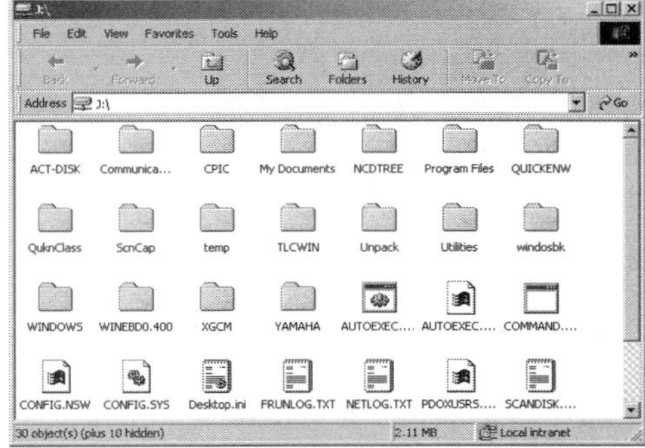

You see your Drive J, which is really Drive C on the Micron-450.

Step 6 Close the window. Open **My Computer**. Be in Large Icons view. Click Drive J.

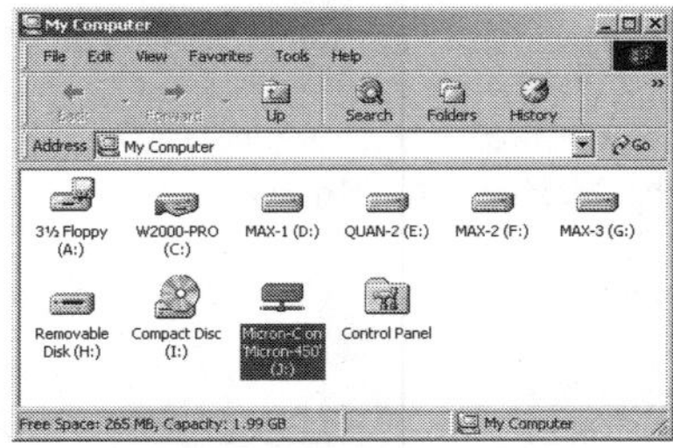

WHAT'S HAPPENING? You can see that Drive J appears in My Computer as if it were a drive on your system. You may access it in the usual way, by clicking it. You can tell it is a network drive by the icon, which looks like a regular drive icon connected to a cable. See Figure 12.8.

FIGURE 12.8 A MAPPED DRIVE ICON

Step 7 Click **Tools** on the menu bar. Click **Disconnect Network Drive**.

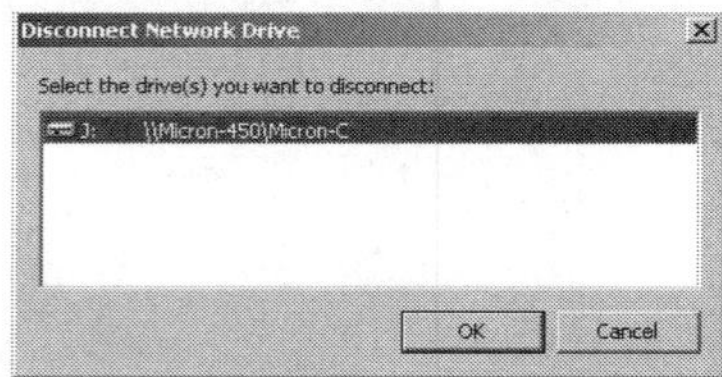

WHAT'S HAPPENING? You see a dialog box that tells you which drives are connected. In this case, you have only one. If you had more than one mapped drive, each would be listed and you could select what drives to disconnect.

Step 8 Be sure the Micron drive is selected. Click **OK**.

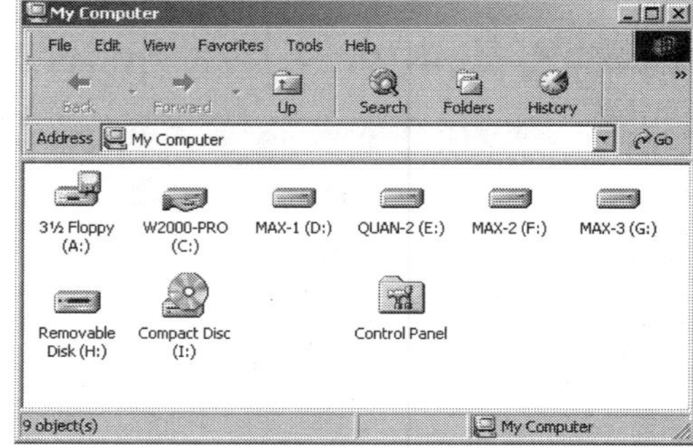

WHAT'S HAPPENING? Your mapped drive is no longer available. The drive icon with a cable is gone.

Step 9 Close My Computer. Open My Network Places. Open **Computers Near Me**. Open the **Micron-450 computer**. Open Drive C.

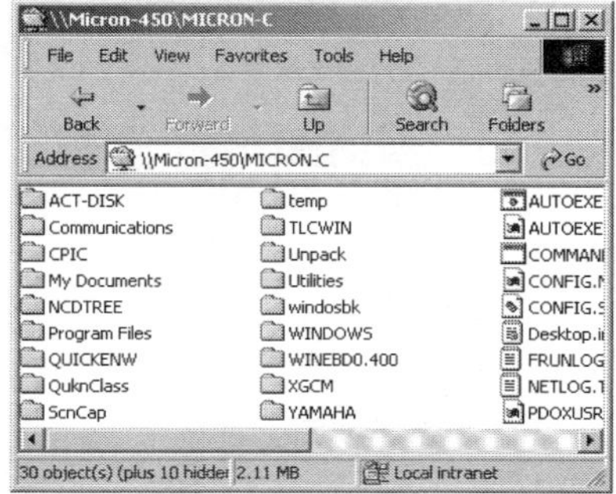

WHAT'S HAPPENING? Since the entire drive is shared, the **WINDOSBK** folder is available. You may map a folder as well.

Step 10 Click on the [»] on the right side of the toolbar.

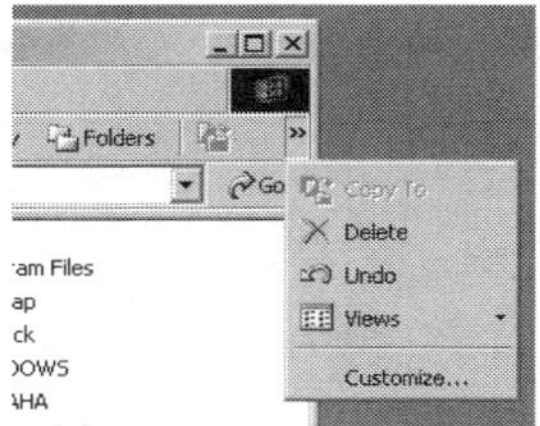

WHAT'S HAPPENING? You have dropped down a menu, but Map Network Drive is not listed. Your available choices may be different. You need to customize this menu.

Step 11 Click **Customize**.

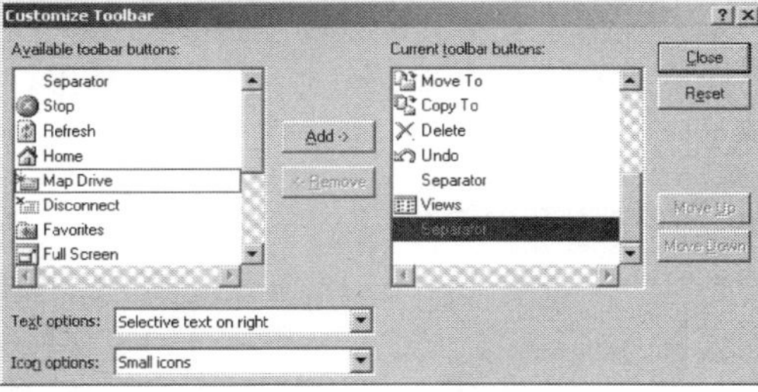

WHAT'S HAPPENING? You can add or delete toolbar buttons.

Step 12 Under Available toolbar buttons, click **Map Drive**. Click **Add**.

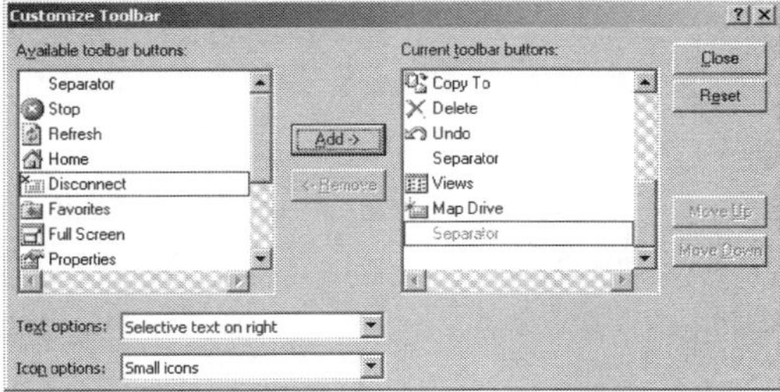

WHAT'S HAPPENING? Map Drive now appears in the Current toolbar buttons window.

Step 13 Under Available toolbar buttons, click **Disconnect**. Click **Add**. Click **Close**.

Step 14 Click the Map Drive icon.

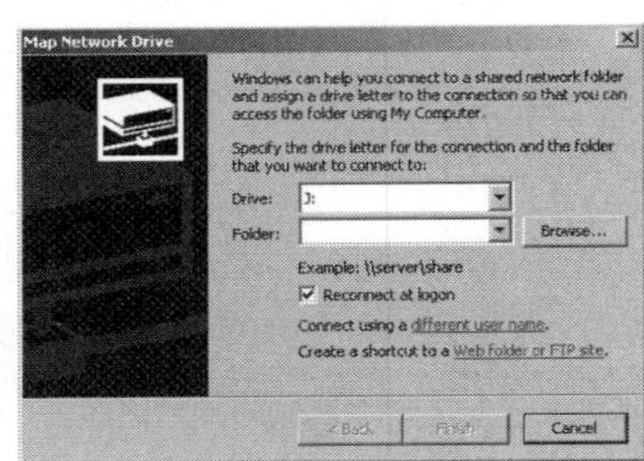

WHAT'S HAPPENING? Drive J is available and needs to be mapped to the folder **WINDOSBK**. Again, note that the UNC will be **\\Micron-450\Micron-C\WINDOSBK**.

Step 15 Key in **\\Micron-450\Micron-C\WINDOSBK**. Click **Finish**.

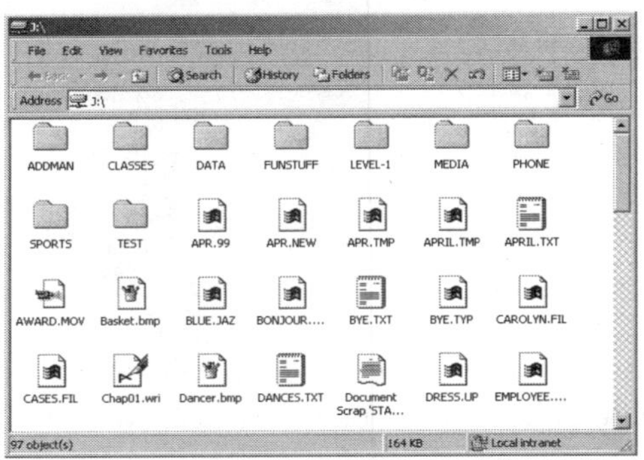

WHAT'S HAPPENING? Since you shared the drive, you shared all the folders on the drive and could map Drive J (in this example) to the **WINDOSBK** folder on the Micron's Drive C.

Step 16 Close the Drive J window.

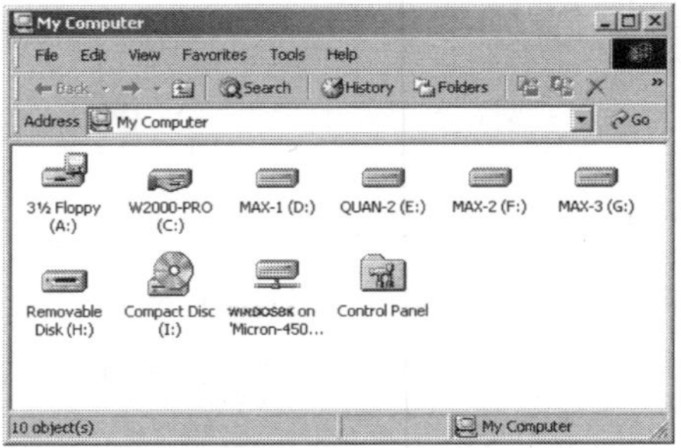

WHAT'S HAPPENING? Now Drive J, a network drive, really refers only to the folder **WINDOSBK** on the Micron-450 computer. Notice that the description of the icon tells you this information.

Step 17 Select the **WINDOSBK on Micron-450** icon. Click **Tools**. Click **Disconnect Network Drive**. Click **OK**.

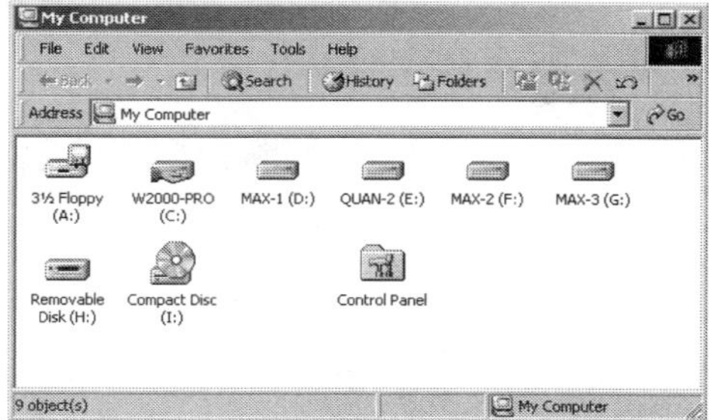

What's Happening? You no longer have a mapped drive letter representing the **WINDOSBK** folder on the Micron computer.

Step 18 Close all open windows. Open Windows Explorer. On the menu bar, click **Tools**.

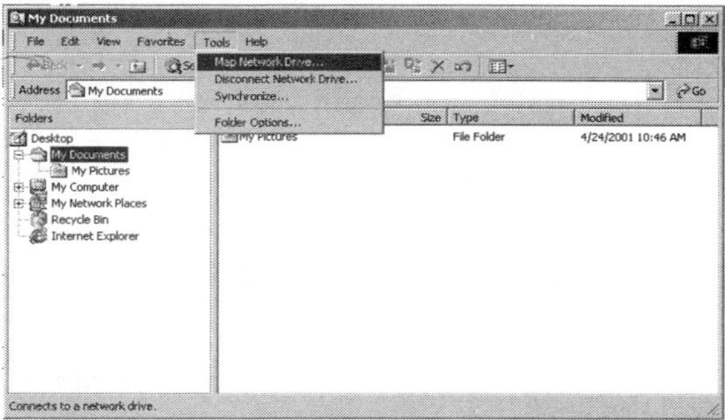

What's Happening? Here you can either map a drive or disconnect a network drive.

Step 19 Close Windows Explorer.

What's Happening? You have returned to the desktop.

12.12 MAPPING DRIVES WITH THE NET USE COMMAND

The Net Use command is a very powerful Command Line utility that gives you information and allows you to manipulate your shares. Some of the options are applicable to larger Local Area Networks, and are in reference to passwords and HOME directories. Those options are outside the scope of this text. The following abbreviated syntax and options are applicable to a small peer-to-peer network.

```
NET USE [devicename | *] [\\computername\sharename[\volume] [password | *]]
```

NET USE can be used at the command line or, as with all command line commands, in a batch file.

Note 1: This activity is based on a specific computer network. Your own environment will be significantly different. You musts have mapped a drive to see any entries.

Note 2: Be sure and check with your instructor and/or lab technician before attempting to use NET USE in a lab environment.

Step 1 Open a Command Line window. You are at the **C:\WINNT>** prompt.

Step 2 Key in the following: **NET USE** Enter

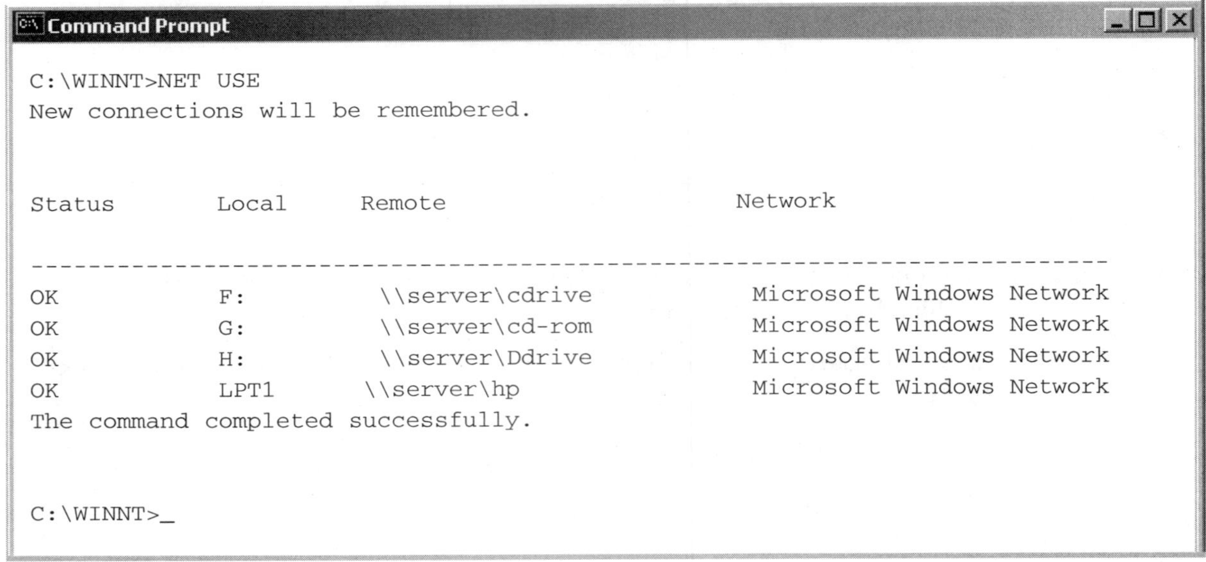

```
Command Prompt

C:\WINNT>NET USE
New connections will be remembered.


Status       Local     Remote                    Network

-------------------------------------------------------------------------------
OK           F:        \\server\cdrive           Microsoft Windows Network
OK           G:        \\server\cd-rom           Microsoft Windows Network
OK           H:        \\server\Ddrive           Microsoft Windows Network
OK           LPT1      \\server\hp               Microsoft Windows Network
The command completed successfully.


C:\WINNT>_
```

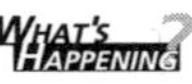

You see under Local name that you have three drives mapped, and the name of the connected printer device, HP, is visible.You must select a name that appears on your list.

Step 3 Key in the following: C:\WINNT>**NET USE T: \\Server\srvtemp** Enter

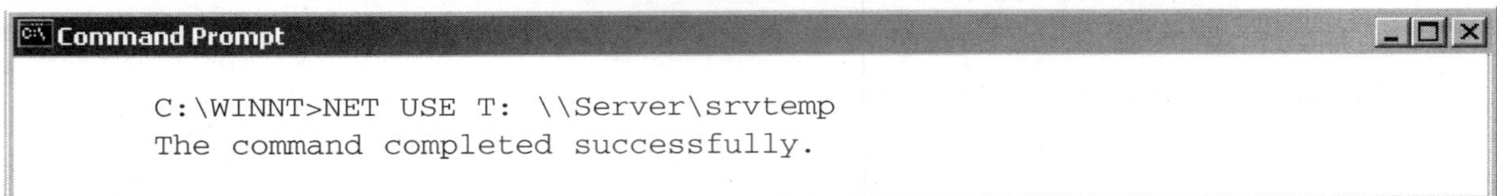

```
Command Prompt

C:\WINNT>NET USE T: \\Server\srvtemp
The command completed successfully.
```

You see confirmation that the command worked.

Step 4 Minimize the Command Line window.

Step 5 Open **My Computer**.

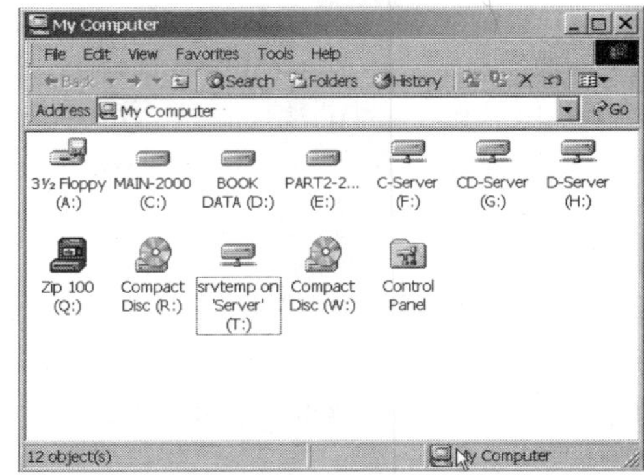

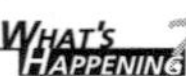

You can see the new T drive. Notice the drive icons under F, G, H, and the new T have cables. This indicates that these drives are not on the local computer, but are available across the network.

STEP 6 Close My Computer and restore the Command Line window.

STEP 7 Key in the following: C:\WINNT>**T:** Enter

STEP 8 Key in the following: T:\>**DIR** Enter

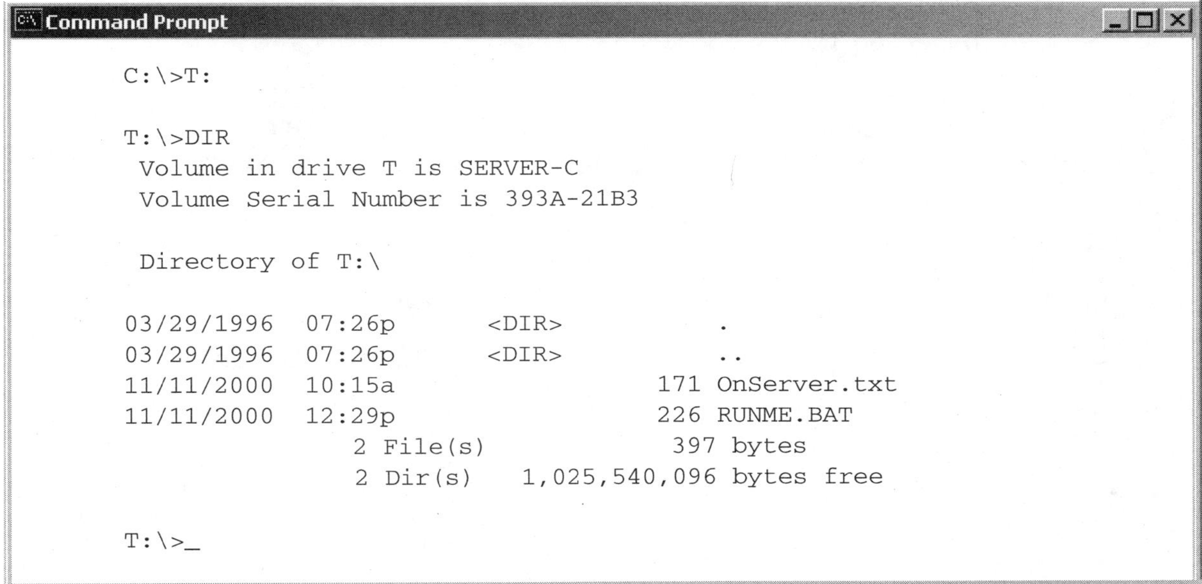

```
Command Prompt

C:\>T:

T:\>DIR
 Volume in drive T is SERVER-C
 Volume Serial Number is 393A-21B3

 Directory of T:\

03/29/1996  07:26p      <DIR>          .
03/29/1996  07:26p      <DIR>          ..
11/11/2000  10:15a                 171 OnServer.txt
11/11/2000  12:29p                 226 RUNME.BAT
               2 File(s)            397 bytes
               2 Dir(s)   1,025,540,096 bytes free

T:\>_
```

WHAT'S HAPPENING? As you can see, you can access a mapped drive from the Command Line prompt just as if it was a local drive.

STEP 9 Key in the following: T:\>**C:** Enter

STEP 10 Key in the following: C:\WINNT>**NET USE T: /DELETE** Enter

STEP 11 Key in the following: C:\WINNT>**DIR T:** Enter

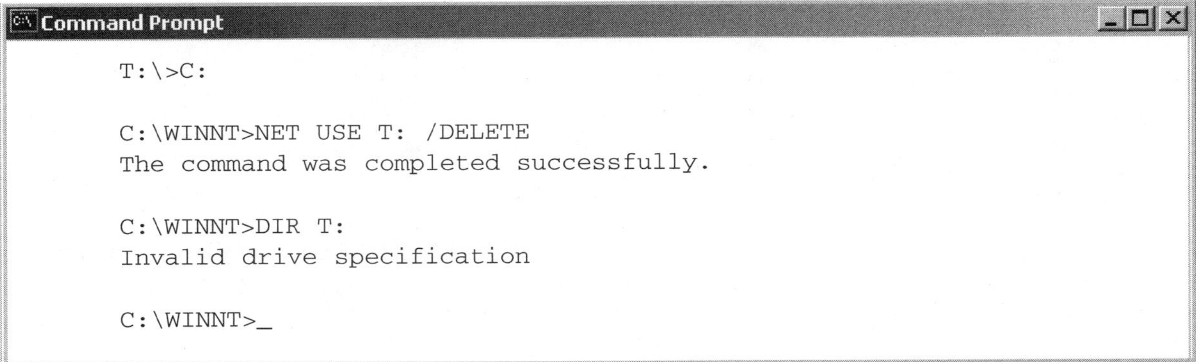

```
Command Prompt

T:\>C:

C:\WINNT>NET USE T: /DELETE
The command was completed successfully.

C:\WINNT>DIR T:
Invalid drive specification

C:\WINNT>_
```

WHAT'S HAPPENING? The message may read, **The system cannot find the path specified**. You have successfully disconnected the drive mapping of **T:** to **\\Server\srvtemp**. However, it is *ever-so-much* more convenient to place drive mapping commands into batch files and place shortcuts to the batch files on the Desktop.

STEP 12 Place the DATA disk in the A drive.

STEP 13 Key in the following: C:\WINNT>**A:** Enter

STEP 14 Key in the following: A:\>**MD CHAP12** Enter

STEP 15 Key in the following: A:\>**CD CHAP12** Enter

STEP 16 Using the Command Line editor, create the following two batch files in the CHAP12 subdirectory on the DATA disk. Be sure to use a valid network connection, not the name shown here.

MAP-T.BAT
@ECHO OFF
NET USE T: \\SERVER\SRVTEMP
PAUSE

UNMAP-T.BAT
@ECHO OFF
NET USE T: /DELETE
PAUSE

STEP 17 Close the Command Line prompt window.

STEP 18 Right-click the Desktop, Click **New**, Click **Shortcut**.

STEP 19 Click **Browse**. Go to the A drive. Go to the **CHAP12** directory.

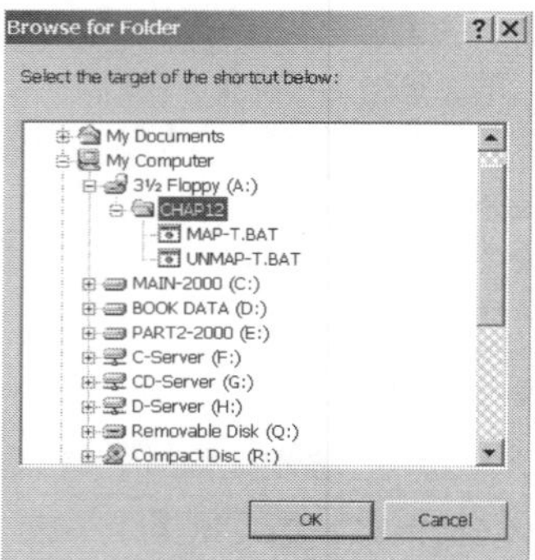

WHAT'S HAPPENING? You can see both of the batch files.

STEP 20 Click on **MAP-T.BAT** and **OK**.

STEP 21 Click **Next**, Click **Finish**.

WHAT'S HAPPENING? You have a new icon on the Desktop, pointing to the batch file that will map the **T** drive to the **Temp** directory on the server computer's C drive.

STEP 22 Right-click the **MAP-T.BAT** icon.

STEP 23 Click **Properties**.

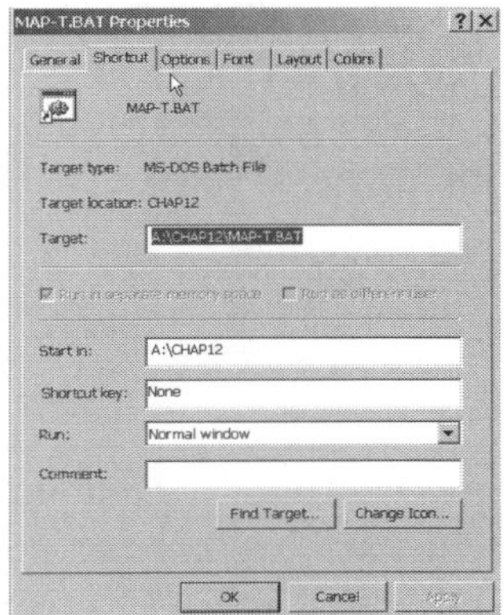

WHAT'S HAPPENING? You have opened the property sheet for the **MAP-T.BAT** file.

STEP 24 Click the **Change Icon** button.

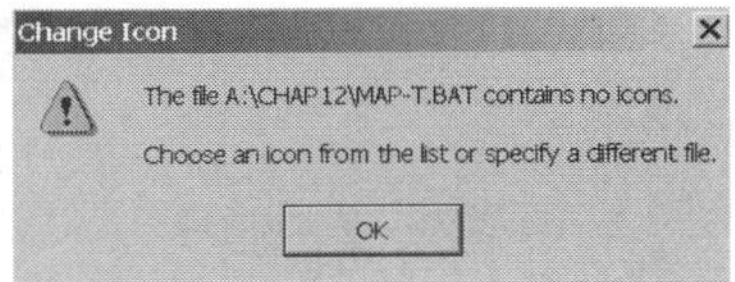

WHAT'S HAPPENING? This messages tells you that there are no built-in icons in the **MAP-T.BAT** file.

STEP 25 Click **OK**.

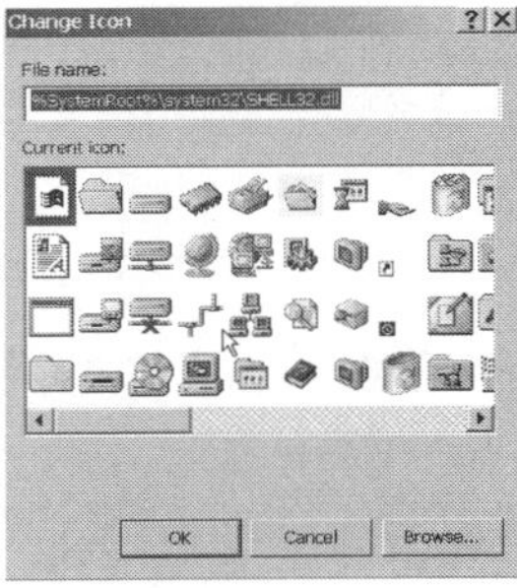

WHAT'S HAPPENING? You have opened the Windows icon library file.

STEP 26 Select an icon and click **OK** twice.

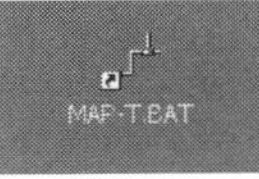

WHAT'S HAPPENING? You have given your shortcut a new icon.

STEP 27 Repeat steps 18 through 26 for the **UNMAP-T.BAT** file, choosing a different icon.

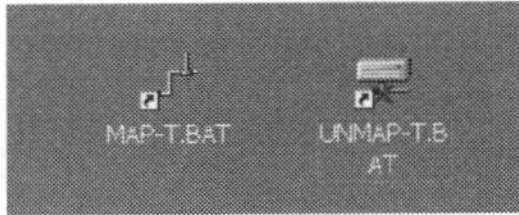

WHAT'S HAPPENING? You now have icons to both MAP and disconnect the T: drive mapping.

Step 28 Double click the **MAP-T.BAT** icon.

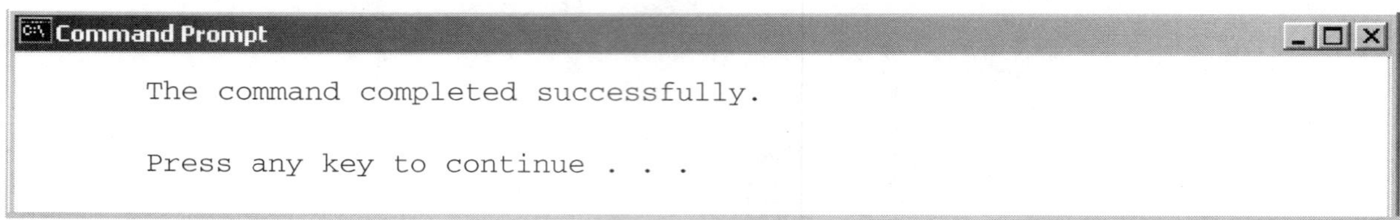

WHAT'S HAPPENING? You get the message that the command was successfully completed. The Command prompt window has not closed, as there is a PAUSE command holding the batch file for user intervention. If not for the PAUSE command, the window would close immediately. If there had been a problem with the mapping, you would have no opportunity to view the error message.

Step 29 Make sure the Command Prompt window is active and press any key.

WHAT'S HAPPENING? The batch file finishes, and the window closes.

Step 30 Open **My Computer**.

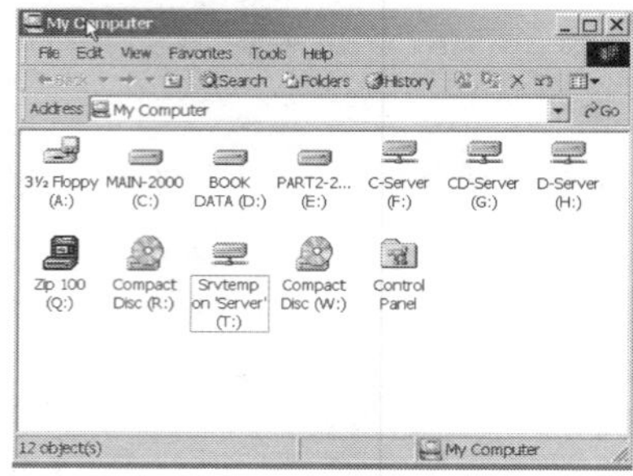

WHAT'S HAPPENING? You can see the **T** drive is available.

Step 31 Close My Computer and issue the **NET USE** command in the Command Prompt window.

```
Command Prompt

C:\>NET USE
New connections will be remembered.


Status       Local     Remote                    Network

-------------------------------------------------------------------------------
OK           F:        \\server\cdrive           Microsoft Windows Network
OK           G:        \\server\cd-rom           Microsoft Windows Network
OK           H:        \\server\Ddrive           Microsoft Windows Network
OK           T:        \\SERVER\SRVTEMP          Microsoft Windows Network
OK           LPT1      \\server\hp               Microsoft Windows Network
The command completed successfully.


C:\>_
```

WHAT'S HAPPENING? The NET USE command registers the drive mapping **T:**.

Step 32 Close the Command Prompt window.

Step 33 Double-click the **UNMAP-T.BAT** icon.

Step 34 Press the **Space Bar** when you see the message that the command was successful.

Step 35 Open **My Computer**.

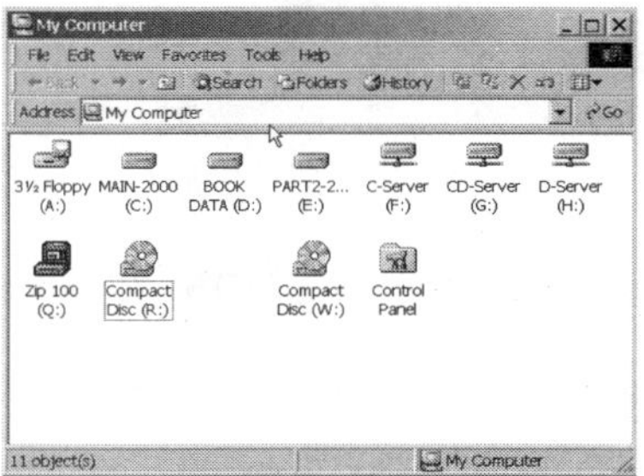

 The batch file window closed, and the **T** drive disappeared from the My Computer window.

Step 36 Close all open windows. Delete the two shortcuts you created.

 There are endless combinations of useful ways to use drive letter mappings to shared devices. If you have a graphic package with two CDs, you could place one in each computer, map a drive letter to the second computer, and be able to access them quickly without switching disks. You can make backups of critical data "on the fly" by mapping a letter to a subdirectory on the remote computer and doing a second save to the remote drive. Each situation is different, and only you know the optimum method for your system.

12.13 UNDERSTANDING DIRECT CABLE CONNECTIONS

Although setting up a network is certainly useful, if what you want to do is transfer many files from your notebook to your desktop computer, the network solution is overkill. But copying data to floppy disks or a removable disk is slow and unwieldy when you have many files to copy. Fortunately, Windows 2000 Professional has a solution. You can purchase a cable, connect two computers together using the serial or parallel ports, and copy or move files quickly and easily from one computer to the other. And if your computers have infrared ports, you do not even need a cable. Windows 2000 Professional supports standard serial null modem (RS-232) cables and the following parallel cables:

- Standard or basic 4-bit parallel cables, including Laplink and Interlink cables.
- Extended Capabilities Port (ECP) cables. If your computer has ECPs, these cables are faster than standard parallel cables. ECP cables provide the fastest performance but they require an ECP-enabled parallel port on both computers.
- Universal Fast parallel cable.

You can set up a direct cable connection with Network Connection Wizard. The following is an example setup of a cable connection:

- Click **Start**, then point to **Settings** and select **Network and Dial-up Connections**. Double-click **Make New Connection**. See Figure 12.9.

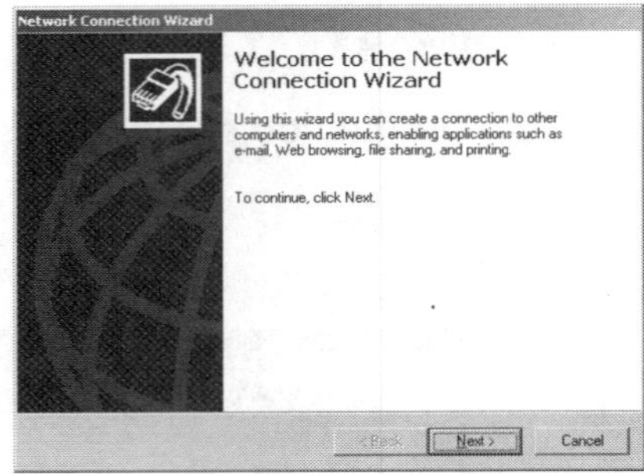

FIGURE 12.9 THE NETWORK CONNECTION WIZARD

- You then click **Next**. See Figure 12.10.

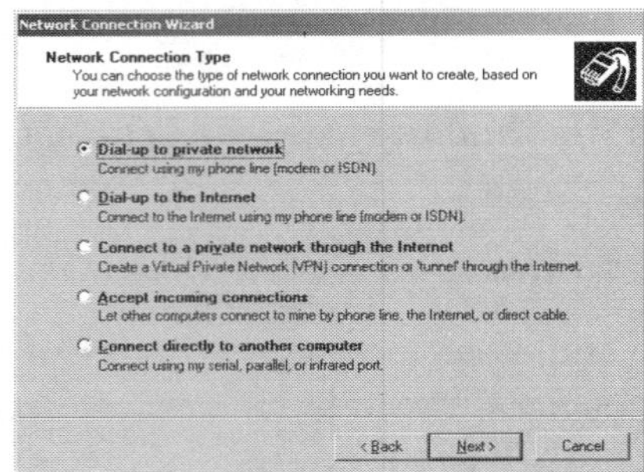

FIGURE 12.10 CHOOSING YOUR NETWORK CONNECTION TYPE

- You choose **Connect directly to another computer** and click **Next**. See Figure 12.11.

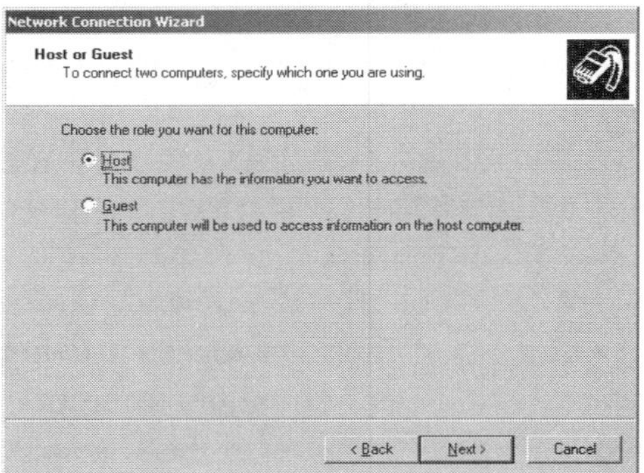

FIGURE 12.11 DESIGNATING THE HOST AND GUEST COMPUTERS

One computer needs to be designated as the host (where the resources that you want to access are) and the other as the guest (where you want the resources to end up). You select one of those, **Host**, for instance, and then click **Next**. You are then asked which port you plan to use. At this time, you make sure your cable is connected between the two computers. See Figure 12.12.

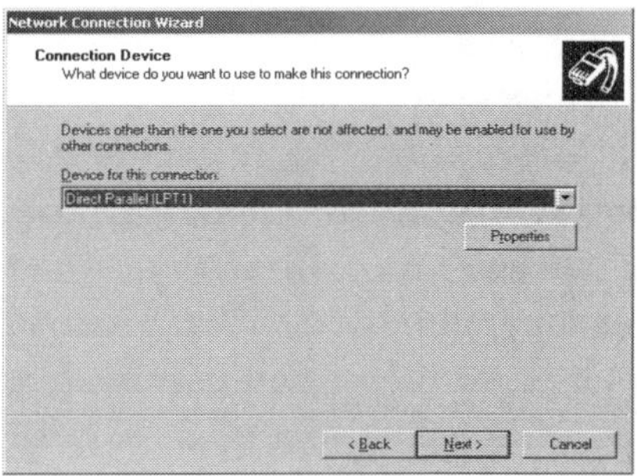

FIGURE 12.12 CHOOSING A PORT

Once you have chosen a port and connected your computers, you have almost completed your connection but you must still assign permissions and rights. See Figure 12.13.

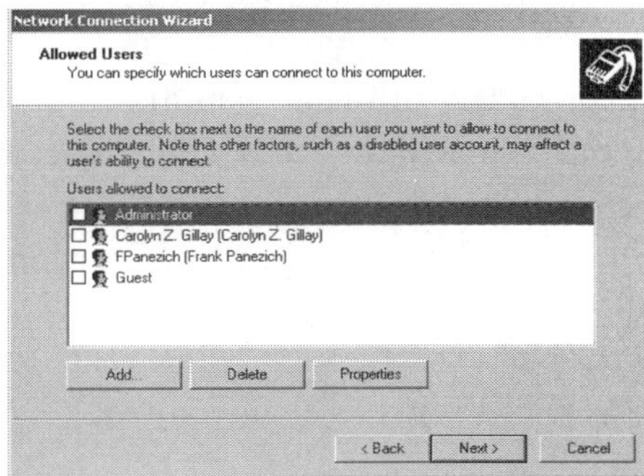

FIGURE 12.13 SETTING PERMISSIONS

Once you have set your permissions, click **Next**.

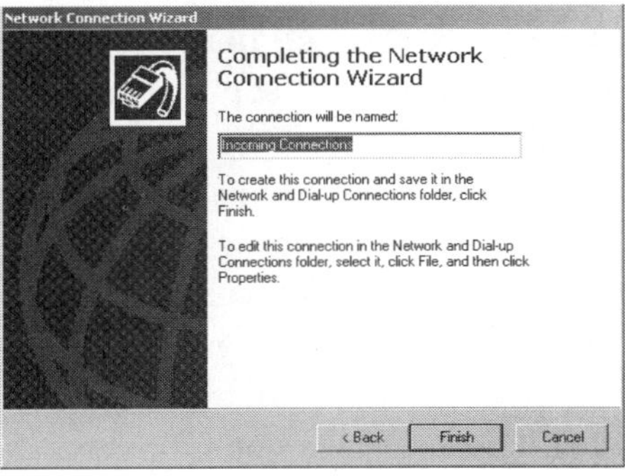

FIGURE 12.14 A FINISHED CONNECTION

Your connection is named. Click **Finish**. You have successfully set up one computer. However, you must still run Network Connection Wizard on the other computer. Since you designated this computer as a host, the other computer must be designated as a guest. Network Connection Wizard is intended for occasional file transfers. It is much slower than a network connection. However, if you only occasionally need to transfer a lot of data between computers, this tool will be adequate.

12.14 THE INTERNET

The Internet is an enormous, worldwide network of computers. Most simply stated, it is a network of networks. More than 400 million people and organizations are connected to the Internet (**http://www.nua.ie/surveys/how_many_online/world.html**). By accessing this network, you can communicate with all the people who sit at those computers. You can connect to various public and private institutions in order to gather information, do research, explore new ideas, and purchase items. You can access the government, museums, companies, colleges, and universities.

The Internet is part of the ***information superhighway***, a term popularized by the media. The Internet is also referred to as ***cyberspace***. William Gibson, who coined the term "cyberspace" in his book *Neuromancer*, defined it as "a consensual hallucination experienced daily by billions of legitimate operators, in every nation, by children being taught mathematical concepts. A graphic representation of data abstracted from the banks of every computer in the human system. Unthinkable complexity. Lines of light ranged in the nonspace of the mind, clusters and constellations of data. Like city lights, receding . . ."

When you log on to the Internet, you are in cyberspace. You can use the Internet to communicate by email (electronic mail), chat lines, and forums, which are like bulletin boards where you leave notes or read information about a topic of interest. Email allows you to send letters and notes instantly. Chat lines let you talk to people around the world on any subject of interest, such as computers, sewing, or Ukrainian culture. You are sure to find people who share your interests on the "net." You may connect to the ***World Wide Web*** (***WWW***) through the Internet. You may even publish your own documents.

For most people, the best-known aspect of the Internet is the Web, an informal expression for the World Wide Web. The Web is a collection of standards and protocols used to access information on the Internet. It is an interconnected collection of more than 15 million ***Web sites***. It is a virtual space accessible from the Internet that holds pages of text and graphics in a format recognizable by Web browsers. These pages are linked to one another and to individual files. Using the Web requires a browser to view and navigate through links. The most popular browsers today are Netscape Navigator and Microsoft Internet Explorer.

The World Wide Web is the graphical interface developed at the European Laboratory for Particle Physics in Geneva, Switzerland, by Tim Berners-Lee as a means for physicists to share papers and data easily. Tim Berners-Lee disseminated these tools for free, not taking any personal profit from this world-changing event. He even won a MacArthur "genius" award for the development of the WWW.

The Web and the Internet are not synonymous. The Internet is the actual network used to transport information. The Web is a graphical interface to the Internet. The Web uses three standards: ***URLs*** (***uniform resource locators***), which tell the location of documents; ***HTML*** (***Hypertext Markup Language***), which is the programming language used to create Web documents; and the protocols used for information transfer. Most Web traffic uses the protocol ***HTTP*** (***Hypertext Transfer Protocol***).

URLs are a standard means for identifying locations on the Internet. URLs specify three types of information needed to retrieve a document—the protocol to be used, the server address with which to connect, and the path to the information. The URL syntax is *protocol://server name/path*; examples of URLs are

http://www.netscape.com/netcenter and **ftp://microsoft.com**. ***FTP*** stands for ***File Transfer Protocol***, and it is used to download or upload files. HTTP is the major protocol used to transfer information within the World Wide Web.

A Web site resides on a server. It is both the virtual and the physical location of a person's or an organization's Web pages. A ***Web page*** is a single screen of text and graphics that usually has links to other pages. A Web site has an address, its URL. A ***home page*** is the first page of a Web site. A home page can be thought of as a gateway page that starts you on your search through that Web site.

Web pages usually have hypertext links, referred to as hyperlinks or links. A hypertext link is a pointer to a Web page on the same site or on a different site anywhere in the world. When you click on a link, your browser takes you to the page indicated by the link. If you were at a site about companies that provide electronic commerce solutions for businesses and saw a link called "Reference Desk," you could click it to see what references were available. From the Reference Desk page, you could see a hypertext link to a document called "United States Government Electronic Commerce Policy." Clicking that could take you to the Web site of the Department of Commerce, where you could read the article "Surfing the Net."

A Web site's type is indicated by the "dot" part of its address. Common types include commercial sites, which end in **.com**; educational sites, which end in **.edu**; government sites, which end in **.gov**; military sites, which end in **.mil**; and nonprofit organizations' sites, most of which end in **.org**. Since addresses are being depleted due to the rapid growth of the Internet, new "dots" are being developed, even ones longer than three characters.

Since so much information exists on the Internet, a category of sites called search engines has been developed to help you find what you want. These are essentially indexes to indexes. Popular search engines include Yahoo! (**http://www.yahoo.com**), AltaVista (**http://altavista.com**), Go.com (**http://www.guide.infoseek.com**), Google (**http://www.google.com**), Ask Jeeves (**http://www.askjeeves.com**), Lycos (**http://www.lycos.com**), and WebCrawler (**http://www.webcrawler.com**). Many companies and organizations position themselves as ***portals***. A portal is an entry to the Web. Yahoo! and Excite are now expanding beyond being just search engines and are positioning themselves as portals.

There are many ways to access information on the Internet. One common way is to have a modem, communication software, and an online provider. You set up your dial-up network in Network and Dial-up Connections, found in Control Panel. You use your modem to dial out through your telephone line. In order to establish your dial-up account, you have to decide what service you are going to use. You could choose to connect to the Internet by belonging to a service such as MSN (Microsoft Network) or AOL (America Online). Each of these providers would give you detailed instructions on how to set up your dial-up account and would supply you with a local telephone number. If you used a service such as AOL or MSN, you would probably use its preferred browser, although you certainly could use any browser. Both MSN and AOL are now considered portals.

Another popular way to connect to the Internet is to use an ISP. ***ISPs*** (***Internet service providers***), also called ***IAPs (Internet access providers)*** or service providers, are companies or organizations that provide a gateway or link to the Internet for a fee. EarthLink and Concentric Network are examples of this kind of company. You would be given explicit instructions from your provider how to create your dial-up account. You may choose your browser. Most people choose either Netscape Navigator or Microsoft Internet Explorer. The ISP is simply the link to the Internet. On your browser, you can have a home page, the first page that opens when you launch your browser. With some ISPs you can have your own Website, with a home page and one or more Web pages. Many ISPs charge a fee to create a Website, but some provide this service at no additional cost.

There are other ways to connect to the Internet. Some cable companies provide direct cable connections. In this case, you would not use your telephone line. You would always be connected to the Internet and would not have to dial up when you wished to surf the Net. You could use Netscape Navigator or Internet Explorer as your browser, or you could use the cable company's supplied browser. The advantage of a cable connection is speed. Some people joke that when the Internet is accessed over a telephone line, WWW stands for World Wide Wait. A cable connection, on the other hand, is extremely fast.

Another choice is to use an ISDN (Integrated Services Digital Network), which is a high-speed digital phone line that transfers data at a rate five to six times faster than that of a 28.8-kilobits-per-second modem. The phone company must lay the ISDN line to your home or business, and you must have a special modem. A DSL (digital subscriber line) is yet another choice, if available. Here a user can purchase bandwidth that is potentially 10 times faster than a 28.8-kilobits-per-second modem, but still slower than cable. You may be fortunate enough to have your connection through a business or educational institution that has a T1 or T3 leased line, which provides a faster connection than any of the above choices. Another way, not that common yet, is connecting via satellites. This connection provides truly high-speed communications, but it is, at this point, not readily available.

DSL is becoming more and more popular. In many areas there are waiting lists to have DSL installed. When you have DSL installed, the company will usually provide you with a special modem and will run a line directly into your house that looks just like a normal telephone line. They may also provide the network interface card. The installers will "activate" your line with the local company. Some companies will do the software installation as well as the hardware installation.

To your computer, the DSL connection is just another link on a LAN. The company will provide you with the IP addresses that you require.

DSL uses a static connection. "Static" refers to the fact that the IP address of this computer does not change. This is not the usual home connection, however. Most companies assign a temporary IP address to your computer as you connect.

12.15 ABOUT DSL

The acronym "DSL" stands for Digital Subscriber Line. It is used to refer both categories of DSL—ADSL and SDSL. Both operate over existing copper telephone lies and both need to be relatively close to a central telephone office. Usually you are required to be within 20,000 feet.

ADSL stands for Asymmetrical Digital Subscriber Line. It uses a special modem and a technology that allows more data to be sent on existing phone lines. This is the type that is currently extremely popular.

SDSL stands for Symmetrical Digital Subscriber Line. It also requires a special modem. This technology is being used primarily in Europe. It uses high frequency digital pulsing, and since high frequencies are not used by the human voice, SDSL can operate simultaneously with voice on the same line.

When you speak on a phone line, your voice is transmitted on analog signals. Computers "speak" digital, not analog. Old modems MOdulated digital signals from a computer into analog signals to transmit, and then, at the other end DEModulated back to digital for the receiving computer. Hence the word MODEM. DSL knows that the data does not require change to analog form and back, but can be transmitted directly as sent from one computer to another. This technology allows for speeds up to 50 times greater than over a 56k modem. For example, to download a needed upgrade for software on a 56k modem would take over 45 minutes. Using DSL, the same upgrade would take less than two minutes.

12.16 SETTING UP A DSL ACCOUNT

Note 1: This is a read-only activity, and is presented here for demonstration purposes.

Note 2: It is assumed that the TCP/IP protocol has been added to the Network properties, as demonstrated previously in this chapter.

STEP 1 Right-click **My Network Places**. Click **Properties**.

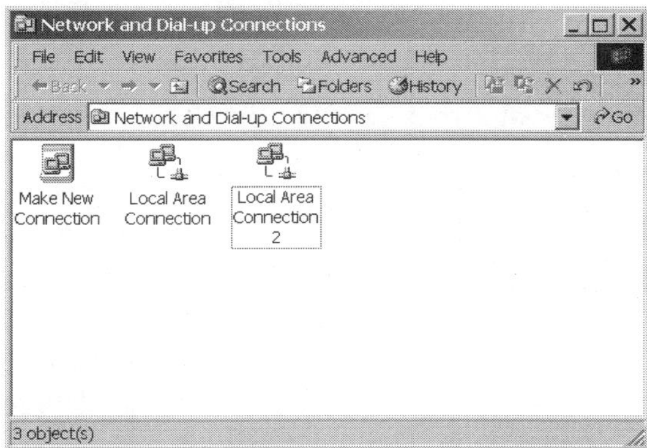

Notice there are two Local Area Connection icons. This computer has two NICs, one connecting to the **Server** computer, and one for the DSL connection to the Internet. To get to the property sheet of each NIC, you must right-click each local area connection and click Properties. Both property sheets are shown here together.

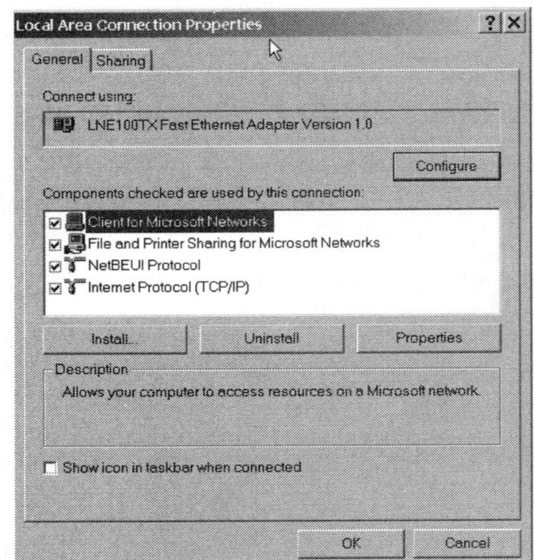

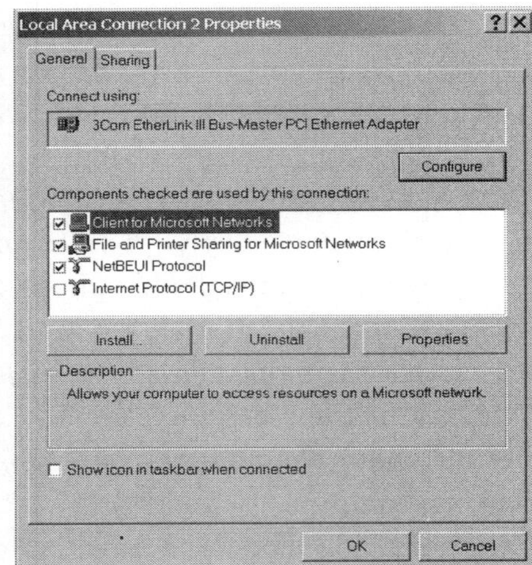

WHAT'S HAPPENING? You have opened the Local Area Connection property sheets and are looking at the General tabs. You can see the two NICs (network interface cards) installed: 3Com Ethterlink III and LNE 100 TX. There are also two protocols installed—TCP/IP and NetBEUI. When protocols are installed, they are installed to a specific NIC, not to the network in general. This is referred to as "binding" the protocol to the NIC. The 3Com card has only one protocol bound to it—NetBEUI. This is the card that is used to connect Admin to Server, the two PCs on the LAN. The LNE card is the card provided by the DSL provider and has NETBEUI and TCP/IP bound to it. TCP/IP is the protocol used for the Internet.

Step 2 Close the **Local Area Connection** property sheet for the 3Com card.

Step 3 On the **Local Area Connection** property sheet for the LNE card, click **Internet Protocol (TCP/IP)**.

Step 4 Click **Properties**.

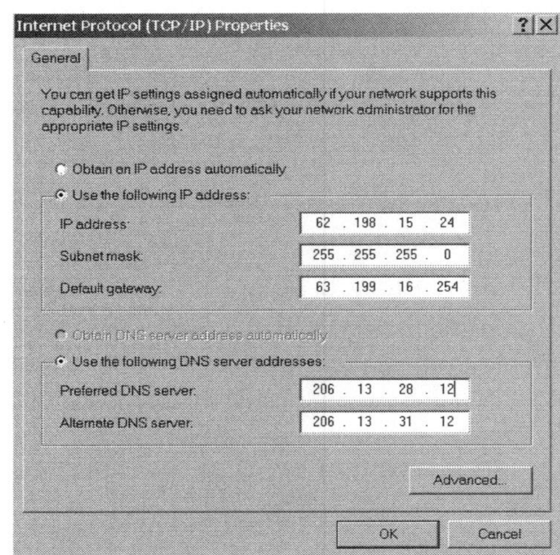

WHAT'S HAPPENING? You are looking at the TCP/IP property sheets for the DSL NIC. **Use the following IP address:** is selected. In most cases, you would choose **Obtain an IP address automatically**. The Subnet Mask is used to mask off a portion of the IP address so that TCP/IP can distinguish the network ID from the host ID. The most common is 255.255.255.0. This number will be given to you by your provider. The default gateway IP address will be given to you by your provider. This is the address of the router used to handle the packets of information sent to remote networks–destinations not physically connected to each other. The preferred and alternate DNS servers' IP addresses will also be given to you by your provider. They are the addresses of your provider's Internet servers.

STEP 5 At this point, you would click **OK** to return to the properties box and click **OK** again to start the process of implementing your changes. You would be told you needed to reboot your computer for the changes to take effect.

This has been a demonstration of the installation of DSL as provided by a specific company. Details may vary slightly from different providers, but the basic principles will remain the same.

12.17 ACTIVITY: A BRIEF LOOK AT INTERNET EXPLORER

Step 1 Open **My Computer**. Open **Control Panel**. Open **Network and Dial-up Connections**.

Note: In a lab environment or if you have DSL or cable, your connection is already established. If so, go directly to your browser, key in the address shown in Step 6, and go on to Step 8.

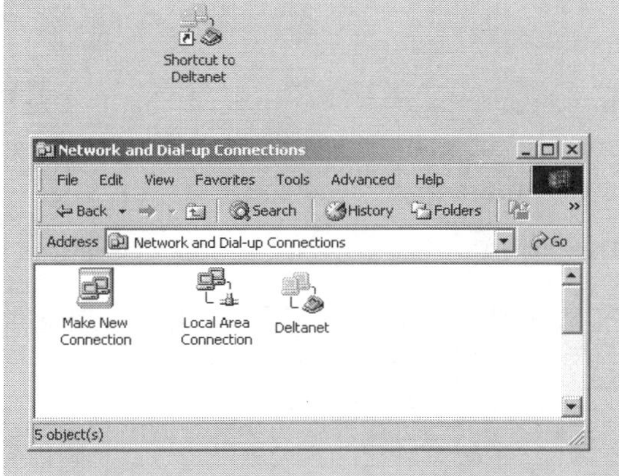

WHAT'S HAPPENING? In this example, there is one Local Area Connection and one dial-up account. Deltanet is the name of an Internet service provider. Look above the Network and Dial-Up Connections window. You see a shortcut. Rather than having to open this window, using the shortcut is easier and faster. Once you have chosen your type of connection, you must access it.

Step 2 Double-click **Deltanet**.

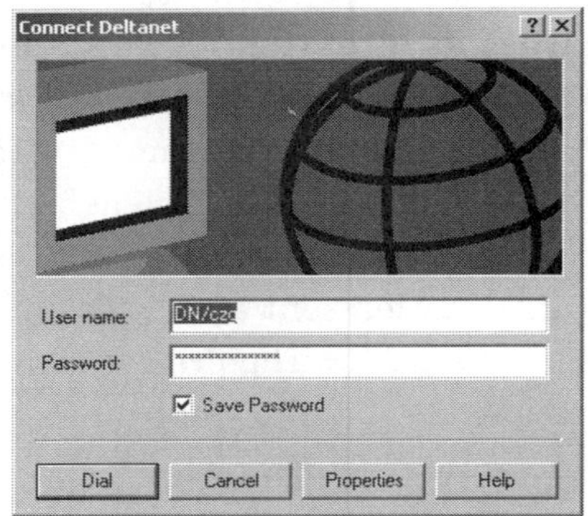

WHAT'S HAPPENING? You see the Connect Deltanet dialog box.

Step 3 Click **Dial**.

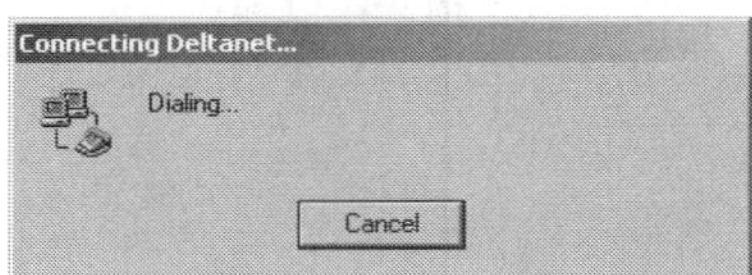

WHAT'S HAPPENING? A dialog box indicates that you are connecting to the service.

WHAT'S HAPPENING? You have connected. If you look at the status bar, you can see the icon indicating that you are connected. You can right-click this icon at any time to either disconnect or to see the status of your connection.

Step 4 Click **OK**. Open your browser. In this case, it is Internet Explorer.

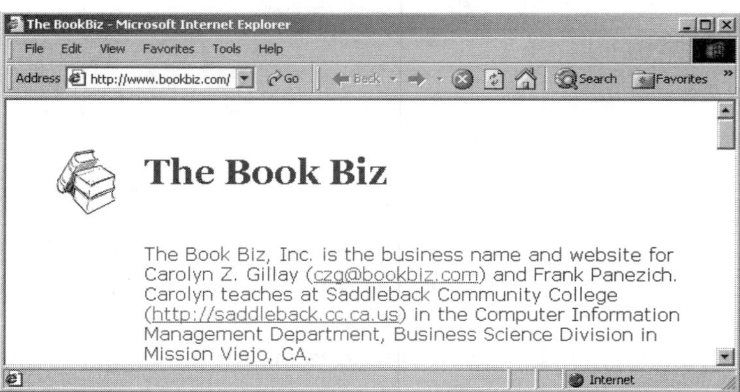

WHAT'S HAPPENING? You have opened Internet Explorer and you have connected to the Internet. You can now explore the Internet. The **Address** text box shows my "home," which is **http://www.bookbiz.net**, the address that I will come home to.

STEP 5 Click **File** on the menu bar. Click **Open**

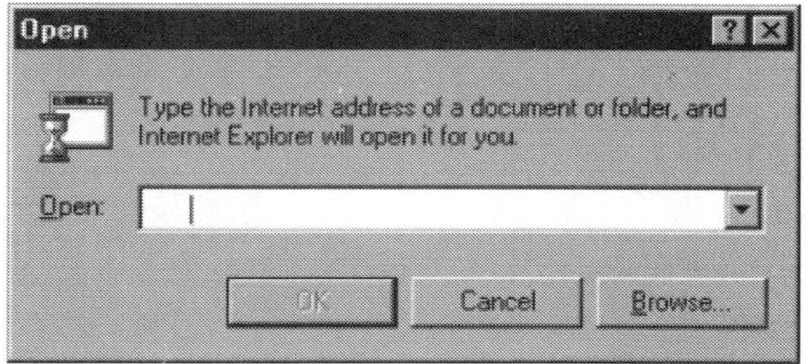

WHAT'S HAPPENING? If you know where you want to go, you can key in the address here.

STEP 6 In the **Open** text box, key in the following: **http://www.yahoo.com**

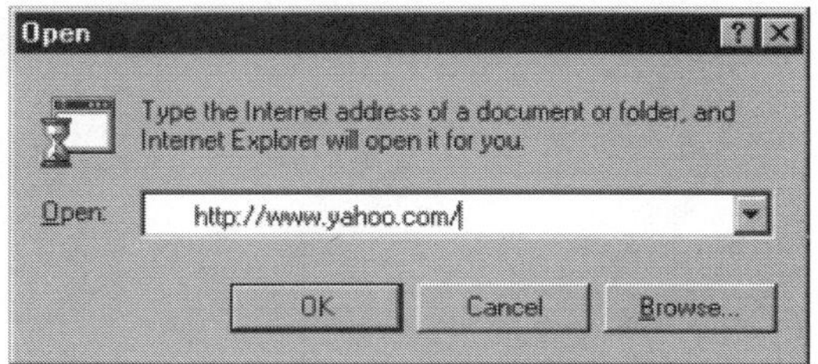

WHAT'S HAPPENING? You will find that Internet Explorer can complete a URL address once you start keying it in if you have previously visited the site. You have keyed in the URL.

STEP 7 Click **OK**.

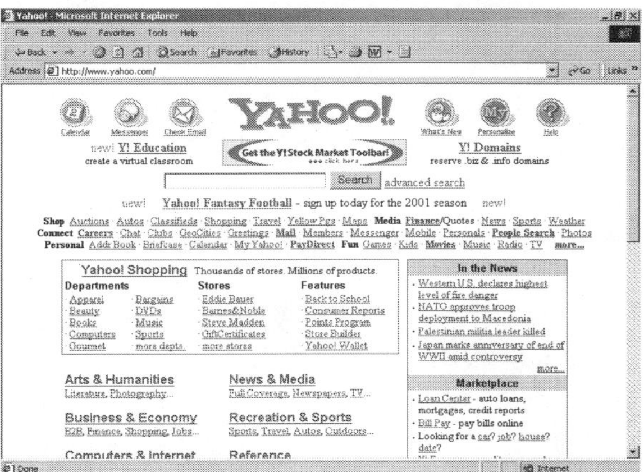

WHAT'S HAPPENING? You have gone to the Yahoo! Web site. Yahoo! is an index to the different sites on the net. Each time you click an underlined term, called a hypertext link, you will be taken to an index of sites.

STEP 8 Scroll until you can see **Computers & Internet**. Click **Computers & Internet**.

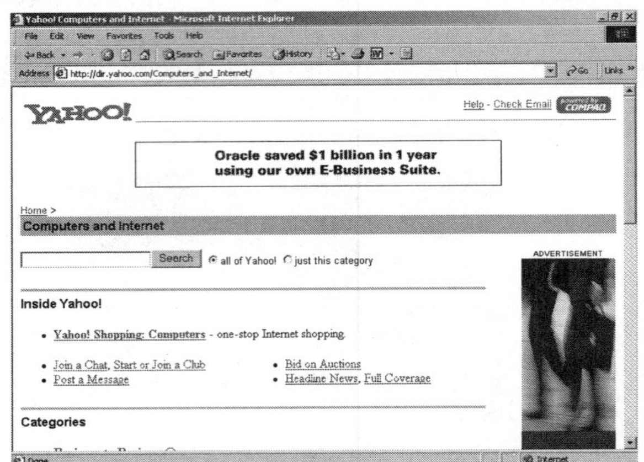

WHAT'S HAPPENING? You have gone to the page of your selected topic, **Computers & Internet**.

STEP 9 Scroll down until you see the topic **Humor@**.

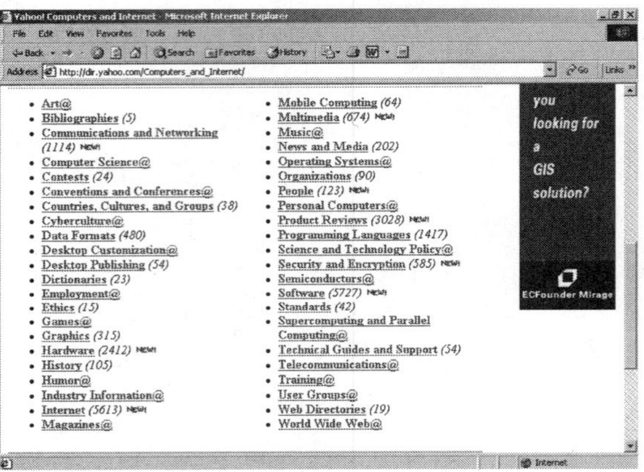

WHAT'S HAPPENING? Each one of these topics will take you to another topic. You can tell because it is underlined. The number in parentheses after the site name tells you the number of entries.

STEP 10 Click **Humor@**. Scroll so you can see the categories.

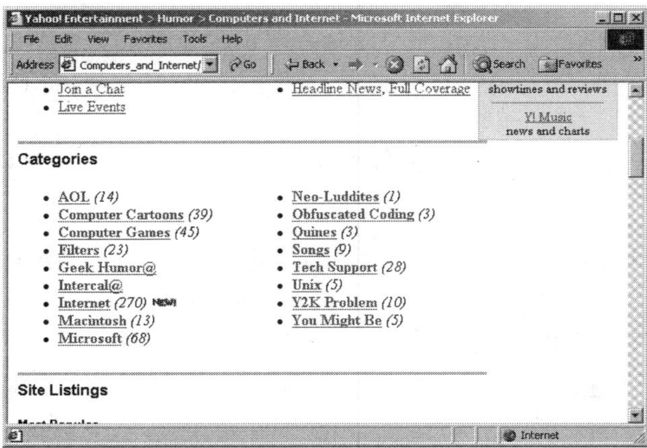

As you can see, each click takes you to another site. You can also back up one page at a time. You are backed up in the reverse order in which you accessed the pages.

STEP 11 Click the **Back** button twice.

You have returned to the first page, **yahoo.com**. If you wanted to go here often, you could add it to your favorites.

Step 12 Click **Favorites**. Click **Add to Favorites**.

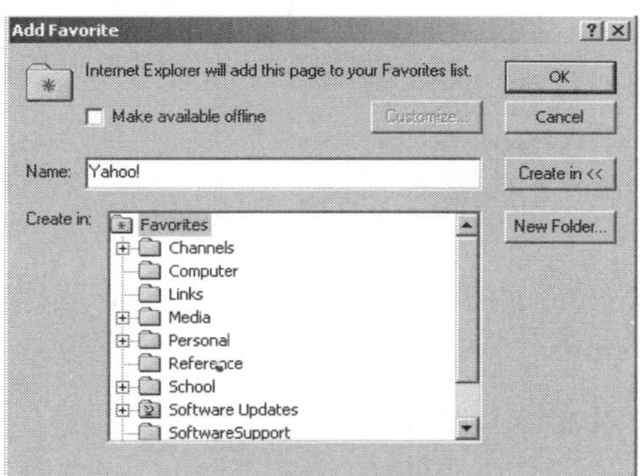

WHAT'S HAPPENING? Yahoo is being added to the menu under its common name (**Yahoo!**), which you can use instead of having to remember the URL of the Web site. If you want to add a new favorite, whenever you find a page you like you click **Add to Favorites**. To delete or change your favorites, you would choose **Organize Favorites**. You can also quickly return to your home page.

STEP 13 Click **Cancel**. Click the **Home** button on the toolbar.

You have returned to your home page. To go to another site, you can key in the address in the **Address** text box.

STEP 14 Select the address in the **Address** text box, in this case **bookbiz.com**

WHAT'S HAPPENING? You need to select only the part you wish to change because typing will replace what is highlighted, leaving the un-highlighted portion as it is.

STEP 15 Key in the following: **fbeedle.com**

WHAT'S HAPPENING? You have the URL of the home page of the publisher of this book, Franklin, Beedle and Associates.

STEP 16 Press **Enter**.

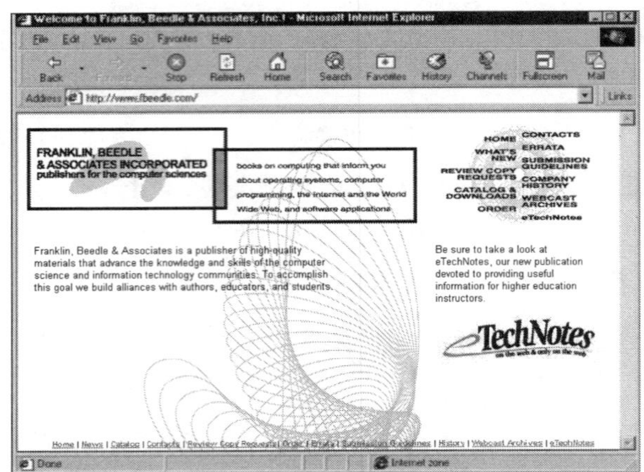

WHAT'S HAPPENING? You can write to the publisher, see the available books, and order books on the Franklin, Beedle and Associates Web site.

STEP 17 Click the **Home** button.

WHAT'S HAPPENING? You have returned to your home page.

Step 18 Close the Browser window. Disconnect if necessary by right-clicking the connect icon on the taskbar( ).

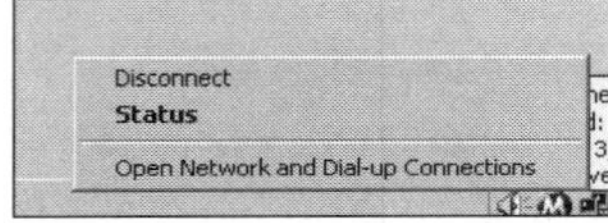

WHAT'S HAPPENING? You have opened a shortcut menu that allows you to Disconnect.

Step 19 Click **Disconnect**.

WHAT'S HAPPENING? You have disconnected from the Internet.

12.18 AN OVERVIEW OF TCP/IP

When discussing communication, especially the Internet, you will hear the term TCP/IP (Transmission Control Protocol/Internet Protocol). TCP/IP is truly the protocol of the Internet. Data is transferred over the Internet through the protocols called TCP/IP.

Using the Internet is not unlike making a telephone call from Los Angeles to your mother in Phoenix. You know that you do not have a direct phone line connection to your mother's home. You dial and the phone company decides the best way to route your call. If Los Angeles is very busy, the phone company may send your call to Phoenix through Denver because Denver is not as busy and can process the data you are sending faster. It is not important to you how the phone company manages communication as long as you can talk to your mother.

On the Internet, data usually travels through several networks before it gets to its destination. Each network has a ***router***, a device that connects networks. Data is sent in ***packets***, units of information. A router transfers a packet to another network only when the packet is addressed to a station outside of its own network. The router can make intelligent decisions as to which network provides the best route for the data.

The rules for creating, addressing, and sending packets are specified by the TCP/IP protocols. TCP and IP have different jobs and are actually two different protocols. TCP is what divides the data into packets and then numbers each packet so it can be reassembled correctly at the receiving end. IP is responsible for specifying the addresses of the sending and receiving computers and sending the packets on their way. An ***IP address*** tells routers where to route the data. Data is divided into packets for two major reasons. The first is to ensure that sending a large file will not take up all of a network's time, and the second is to ensure that the data will be transferred correctly. Each packet is verified as having been received correctly. If a packet is corrupt, only the corrupted packet has to be resent, not the entire file.

A large company, college, or university will maintain a permanent open connection to the Internet (a T1 or T3 line), but this is not the case for a small office or a standalone PC. As mentioned previously, a single user often accesses the Internet through a dial-up, cable, or DSL connection instead. This procedure provides a temporary connection known as a ***PPP*** (***Point-to-Point Protocol***) connection. Another older protocol that accomplishes the same task is ***SLIP*** (***Serial Line Internet Protocol***). This connection provides full access to the Internet as long as you are online. However, if you are using a cable modem or a DSL connection, you do not need to dial up; you are always connected to your provider (the cable company or phone company). The connection is more like a LAN. You are always connected to the server, which in turn is connected to the gateway to the Internet.

Each computer connected to the Internet must have the TCP/IP protocols installed, as well as a unique IP address. The IP address identifies the computer on the Internet. If you are connected to the Internet through a permanent connection, the IP address remains a static (constant) address. If you have a dial-up account, a cable modem account, or other type of connection, you typically get a dynamic (temporary) IP address. It is a leased address and will change depending on how long the hosting server runs its leases for.

The Internet Corporation for Assigned Names and Numbers (ICANN, **http://www.icann.org/general/abouticann.htm**) is the non-profit corporation that was formed to assume responsibility for the IP address space allocation, protocol parameter assignment, domain name system management, and root server system management functions previously performed under U.S. Government contract by IANA (Internet Assigned Numbers Authority, **http://www.ican.org**) and other entities. It is a nonprofit organization established for the purpose of administration and registration of IP numbers for the geographical areas previously managed by Network Solutions, Inc. When an organization applies for IP addresses, ICANN assigns a range of addresses appropriate to the number of hosts on the asking organization's network.

An IP address is made up of four numbers separated by periods. An IP address is 32 bits long, making each of the four numbers 8 bits long. These 8-bit numbers are called ***octets***. The largest possible octet is 11111111. In decimal notation, that is equal to 255. So the largest possible IP address is 255.255.255.255. This format is called dotted decimal notation, also referred to as "dotted quad." See Figure 12.15.

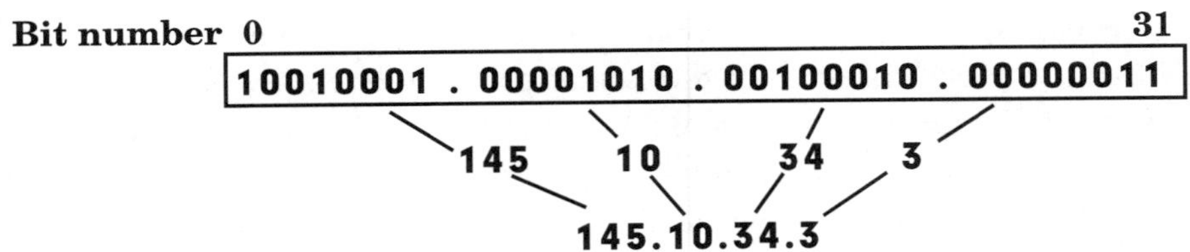

FIGURE 12.15 A DOTTED QUAD ADDRESS

As originally designed, IP address space was divided into three different address classes: Class A, Class B, and Class C. A Class A network receives a number that is used in the first octet of the address. Class A network numbers range from 0 to 127. If an organization was assigned 95 as its network address, the hosts in the network would have IP addresses like 95.0.0.1, 95.0.0.2, 95.0.0.3, and so forth. There are no Class A network addresses remaining. Class A networks are now referred to as /8 (pronounced "slash eight") or sometimes just 8 since they have an 8-bit network prefix.

A Class B network has its network address assigned as the first two octets. The first octet can range between 128 and 191. The second octet can range between 0 and 255. If an organization was assigned 145.21, the hosts in the network would have IP addresses like 145.21.0.1, 145.21.0.2, 145.21.0.3, and so on. Class B networks are now referred to as /16 since they have a 16-bit network prefix. There are also no Class B network addresses remaining.

Today, Class C network addresses are still available. These are assigned the first three octets as their network address. The first octet can range from 192 to 254. If an organization was assigned 199.91.14, the hosts in the network would have IP addresses like 199.91.14.1, 199.91.14.2, 199.91.14.3, and so on. Class C networks are now referred to as /24 since they have a 24-bit network prefix.

There are two additional classes: Class D, which is used to support multicasting, and Class E, which is reserved for experimental use. With the explosive expansion of the Internet, IP addresses are going to be depleted. The appropriate parties are working on a solution to this problem by developing a new standard, called IP Next Generation (IPv6). In the meantime, the current system remains in place.

Even with the current system, if you had an organization with a large number of computers, you would still run out of IP addresses fairly quickly. A solution is to not assign a permanent (static) IP address to a computer, but rather to assign an IP address to be used for the current work session only when the computer goes online (a dynamic IP address). In this system, when you log off, your IP address is returned to the list of available addresses, and, since not everyone is online at the same time, not as many IP addresses are needed. The server that manages dynamic IP addresses is called a dynamic host configuration protocol (DHCP) server. Some ISPs (Internet service providers) use this method to assign IP addresses to their dial-up clients. Others assign the address to the modem you dial into.

It would be difficult for most people to remember a numeric IP address. People remember names better than numbers. Phone numbers such as 1-800-FLOWERS or 1-800-URENTIT became popular for this very reason. Although you may not name your personal computer, computers in organizations are named so one computer can be distinguished from another. Organizations may choose names such as *pc1*, *pc2*, *mac1*, *mac2* or do it by department such as *sales*. Often, a computer's name will reflect its major role in the company. Thus, a computer devoted to handling electronic mail is often named *mail,* whereas a computer devoted to running the company's World Wide Web service is often called *www*. Both are easy-to-remember host names. These are in-house business names, not IP addresses for the Internet. If the computer is on the Internet, it has an IP address. An IP address can change, but typically it is not an organization's name. To give Internet addresses easy-to-remember names like this, the Internet is divided into domains. A domain is a general category that a computer on the Internet belongs to. A domain name is an easy-to-understand name given to an Internet host, as opposed to the numerical IP address. A user or organization applies for a ***domain name*** through the Internet Network Information Center (InterNIC) to ensure that each name is unique. InterNIC is now not the only organization responsible for assigning domain names. Some examples of domain names are **saddleback.cc.ca.us**, **solano.cc.ca.us**, **fbeedle.com**, **unl.edu**, **loyola.edu**, **ces.sdsu.edu**, **uci.edu**, **bookbiz.com**, **dell.com**, and **microsoft.com**.

A fully qualified domain name (FQDN) is the host name plus the domain name. As an example, a host name could be **mail** and the domain name could be **fbeedle.com**. The FQDN would be **mail.fbeedle.com**. Another host name could be **www** with a domain name of **microsoft.com**; thus the FQDN would be **www.microsoft.com**. A fully qualified domain name must be resolved into the numeric IP address in order to communicate across the Internet.

The ***Domain Name System*** (***DNS***) provides this name resolution. It ensures that every site on the Internet has a unique address. Part of its job is to divide the Internet into a series of networks called domains. Each site attached to the Internet belongs to a domain. Large domains are divided into smaller domains, with each domain responsible for maintaining unique addresses in the next lower-level domain or subdomain. DNS maintains a distributed database. When a new domain name is assigned, the domain name and its IP address are placed into a database on a top-level domain name server (domain root server), which is a special computer that keeps information about addresses in its domain. When a remote computer tries to access a domain name and does not know the IP address, it queries its DNS server. If that DNS server does not have the IP address in its database, it contacts a root DNS server for the authoritative server responsible for that domain. Then, the DNS server goes directly to the authoritative server to get the IP address and other needed information, updates its database, and informs the remote computer of the domain name's IP address.

When you use a browser to access a site on the Internet, you key in the URL (uniform resource locator). The browser program contacts the remote server for a copy of the requested page. The server on the remote system returns the page, tells the browser how to display the information, and gives a URL for each item you can click on the page. Figure 12.16 describes the parts of a URL.

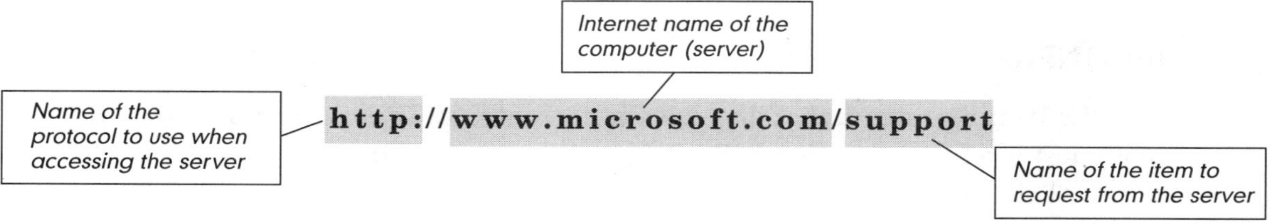

FIGURE 12.16 THE PARTS OF A URL

The URL in the above figure is for the page that gives you support for Microsoft products.

This somewhat technical discussion is not intended to confuse you, but to give you some idea of Internet jargon. Terms like IP address, URL, and domain name are commonly used in conjunction with the Internet. Having some understanding and familiarity with the terms will help you navigate the Internet.

12.19 TCP/IP UTILITIES—THE COMMAND LINE INTERFACE WITH THE INTERNET

Although the program you will normally use with the Internet is a browser such as Netscape Navigator, Windows also provides a series of commands, also called utility programs, that run at the command line. These are actually TCP/IP commands and are a set of tools that can help you troubleshoot problems as well as offer you connections to computers not connected to the Web, such as Unix system computers. These utilities are automatically installed when you install the TCP/IP network protocol. These tools are as follows:

Command	Purpose
ARP	Displays and modifies the IP to Ethernet translation tables.
FTP	Transfers files to and from a node running FTP services.
IPCONFIG	Displays the IP address and other configuration information.
NETSTAT	Displays protocol statistics and current TCP/IP connections.
PING	Verifies connections to a remote host or hosts.
ROUTE	Manually controls network-routing tables.
TELNET	Starts terminal emulation with a remote system running a Telnet service.
TRACERT	Determines the route taken to a destination.

TABLE 12.1 COMMAND LINE COMMANDS FOR THE INTERNET

If you want help on any of these commands, at the command line, you key in the command name, a space, and then **/?**, such as **ping /?**. In the next activities, you will look at some of these utilities.

12.20 IPCONFIG

IPCONFIG is a program that displays the current TCP/IP configurations and allows you to request a release or renewal of a DHCP-assigned IP address.

This tool presents all the TCP/IP configuration settings in one place. If you have a dial-up service and you dial in, you are assigned an IP address that you might need to know if you are trying to Telnet into a restricted server. Telnet is the utility that emulates a video display terminal. You use it to connect to character-based computers on a TCP/IP network, typically a computer running the Unix operating system. When you Telnet, you log in and use a remote computer interactively. A restricted server denies everyone entry except those who are explicitly permitted into the system. The administrator of the remote system might need to know your IP address in order to allow you into the system.

12.21 ACTIVITY: USING IPCONFIG

STEP 1 Open a Command Prompt window. Key in the following:
C:\WINNT>**ipconfig** Enter

```
Command Prompt

C:\WINNT>IPCONFIG

Windows 2000 IP Configuration

Ethernet adapter Local Area Connection:

        Connection-specific DNS Suffix  . :
        IP Address. . . . . . . . . . . . : 63.199.16.15
        Subnet Mask . . . . . . . . . . . : 255.255.255.0
        Default Gateway . . . . . . . . . : 63.199.16.254

C:\WINNT>_
```

You can see all the information on the Internet adapter that has TCP/IP bound to it. This computer is on a static DSL connection, so is always on the Web. Consequently, it always has an IP addresses. If you were not connected and logged on, no IP address would be reported.

12.22 PING

If you are using your browser and cannot connect to a site, ping is an easy diagnostic tool for checking to see if the computer you are trying to reach is up and running. You can use ping (Packet InterNet Groper) to check out your connection to your service provider or to another computer. Ping sends out a request to see if a computer at the address you specified is there. It affirms whether that computer is up and running. You can ping either the IP address or the host name of the computer you are trying to reach. Ping sends four packets of data to the specified computer. If your ping is successful, you see four replies on the screen display. If any of the packets did not successfully reach their destination or were returned to your computer, you will see a "Request timed out" message. If the IP address is verified but the host name is not, there is some kind of name resolution problem. You can also ping yourself using the special loopback address discussed earlier (127.0.0.1). However, you should be aware that pings are not always reliable. Some servers do not allow themselves to be "pinged," because the server would then be wasting its time responding to pings. Furthermore, some organizations also do not respond to pings for security reasons.

12.23 ACTIVITY: USING PING

Note: This activity assumes you are logged on.

STEP 1 Open a Command Prompt window.

STEP 2 Key in the following: C:\WINNT>**ping fbeedle.com** Enter

```
Command Prompt

C:\WINNT>ping fbeedle.com

Pinging fbeedle.com [207.202.148.200] with 32 bytes of data:

Reply from 207.202.148.200: bytes=32 time=68ms TTL=243
Reply from 207.202.148.200: bytes=32 time=68ms TTL=243
Reply from 207.202.148.200: bytes=32 time=83ms TTL=243
Reply from 207.202.148.200: bytes=32 time=82ms TTL=243

Ping statistics for 207.202.148.200:
    Packets: Sent = 4, Received = 4, Lost = 0 (0% loss),
Approximate round trip times in milli-seconds:
    Minimum = 68ms, Maximum =  83ms, Average =  75ms

C:\WINNT>_
```

WHAT'S HAPPENING? You have successfully pinged the publisher of this book. Note the IP address.

STEP 3 Key in the following: C:\WINNT>**ping 207.202.148.200** Enter

```
Command Prompt

C:\WINNT>ping 207.202.148.200

Pinging 207.202.148.200 with 32 bytes of data:

Reply from 207.202.148.200: bytes=32 time=69ms TTL=243
Reply from 207.202.148.200: bytes=32 time=83ms TTL=243
Reply from 207.202.148.200: bytes=32 time=82ms TTL=243
Reply from 207.202.148.200: bytes=32 time=83ms TTL=243

Ping statistics for 207.202.148.200:
    Packets: Sent = 4, Received = 4, Lost = 0 (0% loss),
Approximate round trip times in milli-seconds:
    Minimum = 69ms, Maximum =  83ms, Average =  79ms

C:\WINNT>_
```

WHAT'S HAPPENING? You have pinged both the IP address and the host name. You now know this site is up and running.

STEP 4 Key in the following: C:\WINNT>**ping 127.0.0.1** Enter

```
Command Prompt

C:\WINNT>ping 127.0.0.1

Pinging 127.0.0.1 with 32 bytes of data:

Reply from 127.0.0.1: bytes=32 time<10ms TTL=128
Reply from 127.0.0.1: bytes=32 time<10ms TTL=128
Reply from 127.0.0.1: bytes=32 time<10ms TTL=128
Reply from 127.0.0.1: bytes=32 time<10ms TTL=128

Ping statistics for 127.0.0.1:
    Packets: Sent = 4, Received = 4, Lost = 0 (0% loss),
Approximate round trip times in milli-seconds:
    Minimum = 0ms, Maximum =  0ms, Average =  0ms

C:\WINNT>_
```

WHAT'S HAPPENING? You have just "pinged" yourself. Remember that 127.0.0.1 is the loopback address and is the IP address of your computer.

STEP 5 Key in the following: **ping microsoft.com** Enter

```
Command Prompt

C:\WINNT>ping microsoft.com

Pinging microsoft.com [207.46.230.229] with 32 bytes of data:

Request timed out.
Request timed out.
Request timed out.
Request timed out.

Ping statistics for 207.46.230.229:
    Packets: Sent = 4, Received = 0, Lost = 4 (100% loss),
Approximate round trip times in milli-seconds:
    Minimum = 0ms, Maximum =  0ms, Average =  0ms

C:\WINNT>_
```

WHAT'S HAPPENING? Microsoft has "blocked" your ping. However, you did attain some information, as the ping did resolve the address. (207.46.230.229)

STEP 6 Close the Command Prompt window.

STEP 7 If you are going to continue with the activities, remain logged on. Otherwise, log off the system.

12.24 TRACERT

Tracert, pronounced "trace route," is a utility that traces the route on which your data is moving. It is a diagnostic utility that determines the route to the destination computer by sending packets containing time values (TTL—Time to Live). Each router along the path is required to decrease the TTL value by 1 before forwarding it. When the value of the TTL is 0, the router is supposed to send back a message to the originating computer. When you use the command, it returns a five-column display. The first column is the hop number, which is the TTL value. Each of the next three columns contains the round-trip times in milliseconds. The last column is the host name and IP address of the responding system. An asterisk (*) means that the attempt timed out. If nothing else, it is fascinating to see the way your data travels. Since tracert uses pings, you may not be able to trace a route if the server you are looking for does not allow pinging.

12.25 ACTIVITY: USING TRACERT

Note: It is assumed you are logged on.

STEP 1 Open a Command Prompt window.

STEP 2 Key in the following: C:\WINNT>**tracert www.bookbiz.com** Enter

Command Prompt

```
C:\WINNT>tracert www.bookbiz.com

Tracing route to www.bookbiz.com [204.210.20.241]
over a maximum of 30 hops:

  1    30 ms    30 ms    30 ms  adsl-63-199-16-254.dsl.snfc21.pacbell.net
[63.199.16.254]

  2    10 ms    20 ms    20 ms  core4-g3-0.snfc21.pbi.net [216.102.187.130]
  3    10 ms    20 ms    20 ms  edge1-ge2-0.snfc21.pbi.net [209.232.130.71]
  4    10 ms    20 ms    20 ms  sl-gw25-stk-8-3.sprintlink.net [160.81.16.21]
  5    30 ms    30 ms    30 ms  sl-servcocox-1-0.sprintlink.net [160.81.16.14]
  6    30 ms    30 ms    40 ms  ubr3-POS2-0.san.rr.com [24.25.192.53]
  7    30 ms    30 ms    40 ms  mcr3.san.rr.com [24.25.192.58]
  8   140 ms    60 ms    40 ms  dt031nf1.san.rr.com [204.210.20.241]

Trace complete.

C:\WINNT>
```

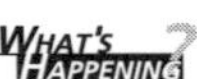

Your display will be different. In this example, the sending computer is in Fairfield, California. The Web site, **bookbiz.com**, is on a computer in San Diego. It is part of the **bookbiz.net** domain. If you look at the rightmost column, you can see what computers the packets are traveling on. The packets go out first on **pacbell.net**, which is this user's ISP. Notice the ADSL notation, reporting the use of ADSL by this computer. It then goes to "pbi" network, to some connections in San Francisco, then to Sprintlink, and eventually to San Diego. As you can see, the packets traveled up and down the California coast in milliseconds.

STEP 3 Key in: **tracert www.fbeedle.com** Enter

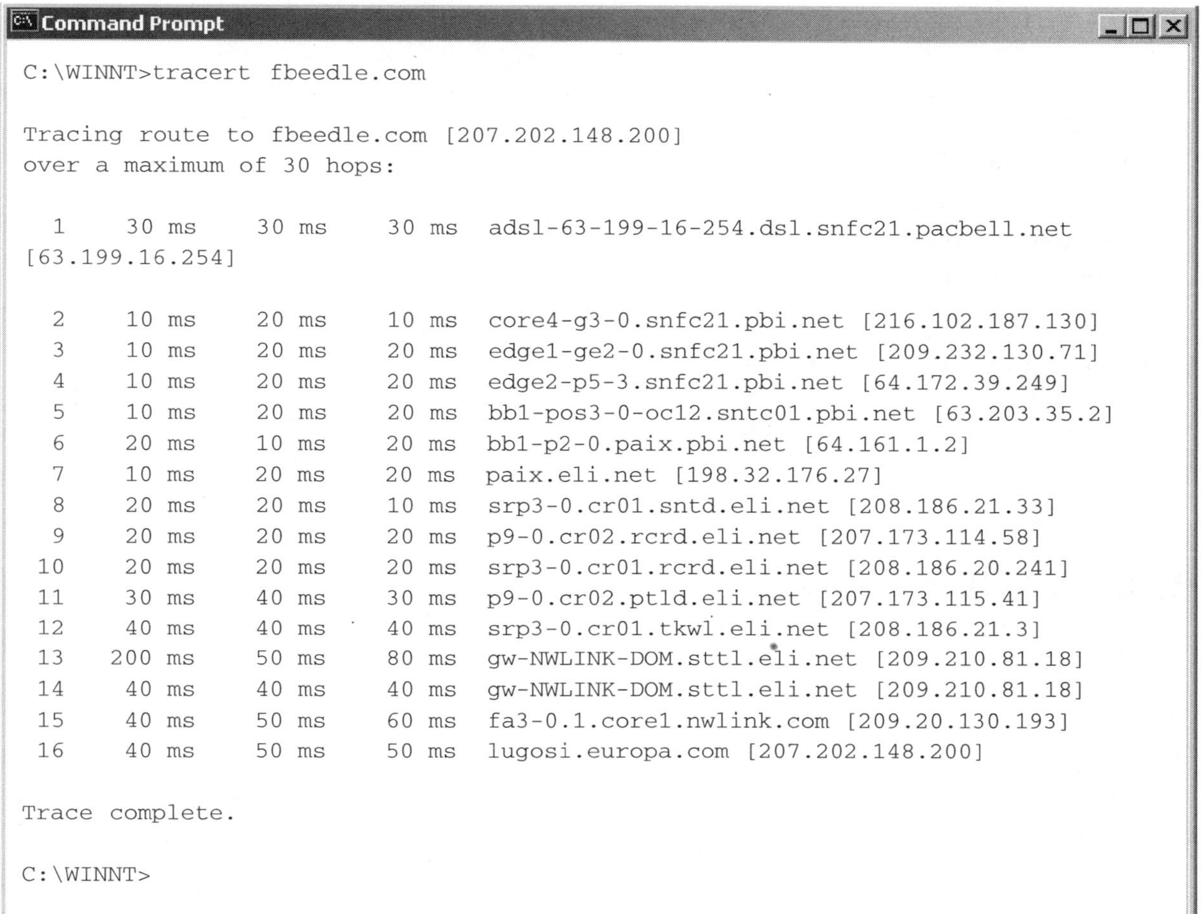

Command Prompt

```
C:\WINNT>tracert fbeedle.com

Tracing route to fbeedle.com [207.202.148.200]
over a maximum of 30 hops:

  1    30 ms    30 ms    30 ms  adsl-63-199-16-254.dsl.snfc21.pacbell.net
[63.199.16.254]

  2    10 ms    20 ms    10 ms  core4-g3-0.snfc21.pbi.net [216.102.187.130]
  3    10 ms    20 ms    20 ms  edge1-ge2-0.snfc21.pbi.net [209.232.130.71]
  4    10 ms    20 ms    20 ms  edge2-p5-3.snfc21.pbi.net [64.172.39.249]
  5    10 ms    20 ms    20 ms  bb1-pos3-0-oc12.sntc01.pbi.net [63.203.35.2]
  6    20 ms    10 ms    20 ms  bb1-p2-0.paix.pbi.net [64.161.1.2]
  7    10 ms    20 ms    20 ms  paix.eli.net [198.32.176.27]
  8    20 ms    20 ms    10 ms  srp3-0.cr01.sntd.eli.net [208.186.21.33]
  9    20 ms    20 ms    20 ms  p9-0.cr02.rcrd.eli.net [207.173.114.58]
 10    20 ms    20 ms    20 ms  srp3-0.cr01.rcrd.eli.net [208.186.20.241]
 11    30 ms    40 ms    30 ms  p9-0.cr02.ptld.eli.net [207.173.115.41]
 12    40 ms    40 ms    40 ms  srp3-0.cr01.tkwl.eli.net [208.186.21.3]
 13   200 ms    50 ms    80 ms  gw-NWLINK-DOM.sttl.eli.net [209.210.81.18]
 14    40 ms    40 ms    40 ms  gw-NWLINK-DOM.sttl.eli.net [209.210.81.18]
 15    40 ms    50 ms    60 ms  fa3-0.1.core1.nwlink.com [209.20.130.193]
 16    40 ms    50 ms    50 ms  lugosi.europa.com [207.202.148.200]

Trace complete.

C:\WINNT>
```

WHAT'S HAPPENING? In this example, your route goes from Fairfield, California, to Portland, Oregon. It is not always easy to know where the route actually goes. You can recognize sfn as San Francisco, and sttl as Seattle, but quite often, the location remains a mystery.

STEP 4 Close the Command Prompt window.

12.26 FTP

FTP (file transfer protocol) servers store files that Internet users can download (copy) to their own computers. FTP is the communications protocol that these computers use to transfer files. It allows you to transfer text and binary files between a host computer and your computer. FTP requires you to log on to the remote host for user identification. Many FTP servers, however, let you log on as anonymous and use your email address as your password so that you can acquire free software and documents. Most FTP servers contain text files that describe the layout of their entire directory structure to help you find what you need. You can transfer files in either text or binary mode but you must first choose the mode. Text (ASCII) is the default.

One of the major advantages to FTP is that you do not care what operating system is on these remote computers because they all have TCP/IP. The ability to transfer files to and from computers running different operating systems is one of the greatest benefits of FTP. There are still computers out there that only have the character-based interface.

FTP has many commands. To get help from within FTP, you key in **HELP** *command*, where *command* is the name of the command for which you seek help. For a list of the commands, you simply key in **HELP**.

12.27 ACTIVITY: USING FTP

Note: It is assumed you are logged on.

STEP 1 Open a Command Prompt window. Be at the A:\> prompt.

STEP 2 Key in the following: A:\>**ftp ftp.microsoft.com** Enter

```
Command Prompt

A:\>ftp ftp.microsoft.com
Connected to ftp.microsoft.com.
220 CPMSFTFTPA06 Microsoft FTP Service (Version 5.0).
User (ftp.microsoft.com:(none)):
```

You have just contacted the FTP server at Microsoft. It is asking for a user name. This server allows anonymous logins.

STEP 3 Key in the following: **anonymous** Enter

```
Command Prompt

User (ftp.microsoft.com:(none)): anonymous
331 Anonymous access allowed, send identity (e-mail name) as password.
Password:
```

It asks for your password and tells you that your email name can be used. When you key in your email address, you will not see it on the screen. You may key in anything for the password; you do not really need to key in your email address.

STEP 4 Key in the following: **aaaa** Enter (*Note:* The cursor will appear frozen when you key this in, but when you press Enter you will continue on.)

```
Command Prompt

Password:
230-This is FTP.MICROSOFT.COM  Please see the dirmap.txt
230-file for more information.
230 Anonymous user logged in.
ftp>
```

What's Happening? You are logged into the site.

STEP 5 Key in the following: **help** Enter

```
Command Prompt

ftp> help
Commands may be abbreviated. Commands are:

!               delete          literal         prompt          send
?               debug           ls              put             status
append          dir             mdelete         pwd             trace
ascii           disconnect      mdir            quit            type
bell            get             mget            quote           user
binary          glob            mkdir           recv            verbose
bye             hash            mls             remotehelp
cd              help            mput            rename
close           lcd             open            rmdir
ftp>
```

What's Happening? These are the FTP commands. For syntax on any command, you would key in **help** plus the command name.

STEP 6 Key in the following: **help bye** Enter

```
Command Prompt

ftp> help bye
bye             Terminate ftp session and exit
ftp>
```

What's Happening? The command BYE is how you can terminate the FTP session. You can use commands you are familiar with already, like DIR, to see what is in the directory.

STEP 7 Key in the following: **dir** Enter

```
Command Prompt

ftp> dir
200 PORT command successful.
150 Opening ASCII mode data connection for /bin/ls.
dr-xr-xr-x   1 owner    group               0 Feb 13 20:02 bussys
dr-xr-xr-x   1 owner    group               0 May 21 15:41 deskapps
dr-xr-xr-x   1 owner    group               0 Apr 20 15:41 developr
-r-xr-xr-x   1 owner    group               0 Nov 27  2000 dirmap.htm
dr-xr-xr-x   1 owner    group               0 Feb 25  2000 kbhelp
```

```
dr-xr-xr-x   1 owner    group              0 Jan 20 23:04 misc
dr-xr-xr-x   1 owner    group              0 Feb 25  2000 peropsys
dr-xr-xr-x   1 owner    group              0 Jan  2 14:43 products
dr-xr-xr-x   1 owner    group              0 Sep 21  2000 reskit
dr-xr-xr-x   1 owner    group              0 Feb 25  2000 services
dr-xr-xr-x   1 owner    group              0 Feb 25  2000 softlib
dr-xr-xr-x   1 owner    group              0 Feb 25  2000 solutions
226 Transfer complete.
ftp: 820 bytes received in 0.01Seconds 82.00Kbytes/sec.
ftp>
```

WHAT'S HAPPENING? You see a list of files and directories. Your listing may be different. Files that have the extension **.txt** are ASCII files. You can recognize directories by locating a **dr** on the far left. **Softlib** is a directory that contains Microsoft software files. Files that have a **.ZIP** extension are compressed. You need a utility like PKZIP to unpack the file. If you key in the command **get** *filename*, it will transfer the file to your default directory. If you key in **get** *filename* **-**, the file name followed by a hyphen acts just like the TYPE command. These commands are Unix commands. As you can see, MS-DOS commands borrow much from Unix commands. If you wanted to transfer a binary file (**.EXE**), you would key in

binary
get file.exe
ascii

You key in **ascii** to return to text-file mode. In the next step, be sure to follow the file name with a hyphen.

STEP 8 Key in the following: **cd deskapps** Enter

STEP 9 Key in the following: **dir** Enter

Command Prompt

```
ftp> cd deskapps
250 CWD command successful.
ftp> dir
200 PORT command successful.
150 Opening ASCII mode data connection for /bin/ls.
dr-xr-xr-x   1 owner    group              0 Feb 25  2000 access
dr-xr-xr-x   1 owner    group              0 Feb 25  2000 dosword
dr-xr-xr-x   1 owner    group              0 Feb 25  2000 excel
dr-xr-xr-x   1 owner    group              0 Mar 20  2000 games
dr-xr-xr-x   1 owner    group              0 Feb 25  2000 gen_info
dr-xr-xr-x   1 owner    group              0 Feb 25  2000 homeapps
dr-xr-xr-x   1 owner    group              0 Feb 25  2000 ie
dr-xr-xr-x   1 owner    group              0 Feb 25  2000 kids
dr-xr-xr-x   1 owner    group              0 May 21 16:08 macofficeten
dr-xr-xr-x   1 owner    group              0 Feb 25  2000 miscapps
dr-xr-xr-x   1 owner    group              0 Feb 25  2000 mmapps
dr-xr-xr-x   1 owner    group              0 Feb 25  2000 money
dr-xr-xr-x   1 owner    group              0 Feb 25  2000 office
dr-xr-xr-x   1 owner    group              0 Feb 25  2000 powerpt
dr-xr-xr-x   1 owner    group              0 Feb 25  2000 project
```

```
dr-xr-xr-x   1 owner    group              0 Feb 25  2000 publishr
-r-xr-xr-x   1 owner    group           1791 Aug 30  1994 readme.txt
dr-xr-xr-x   1 owner    group              0 Feb 25  2000 word
dr-xr-xr-x   1 owner    group              0 Feb 25  2000 works
226 Transfer complete.
ftp: 1282 bytes received in 0.13Seconds 9.86Kbytes/sec.
ftp>
```

WHAT'S HAPPENING? You changed directories to **deskapps** and are now seeing the contents of that directory.

STEP 10 Key in the following: **get readme.txt** Enter

```
Command Prompt
ftp> get readme.txt
200 PORT command successful.
150 Opening ASCII mode data connection for readme.txt(1791 bytes).
226 Transfer complete.
ftp: 1791 bytes received in 0.01Seconds 179.10Kbytes/sec.
ftp>
```

WHAT'S HAPPENING? You have downloaded the **readme.txt** file to the default directory.

STEP 11 Key in the following: **bye** Enter

```
Command Prompt
ftp> bye
221 Thank you for using FTP.MICROSOFT.COM!

A:\>_
```

WHAT'S HAPPENING? You have logged off from the FTP site at Microsoft as well as quit the FTP program.

STEP 12 Key in the following: A:\> **TYPE README.TXT | MORE** Enter

```
Command Prompt
Welcome to the Microsoft FTP Server. This machine offers the
following materials and information for systems and network products:

- Selected knowledge-base articles
- Selected product fixes
- Updated drivers
- Utilities
- Documentation

The deskapps directory is maintained by Microsoft Product Support. Products
represented here are Access, Word (for MS-DOS and Windows), Excel, Flight
Simulator, Creative Writer, Fine Artist, Office, PowerPoint, Project,
Publisher, Works and Money.

Each has its own directory, with appropriate sub-directories below. See
```

```
the readme.txt in each directory for more information.

Please report any problems with this area to "ftp@microsoft.com". Sorry,
individual replies to this alias may not be possible, but all mail will be
read. Please, this is not a product support alias!


              ftp> quote site dirstyle

======================================================================

THE INFORMATION IS PROVIDED "AS IS" WITHOUT WARRANTY
OF ANY KIND. MICROSOFT DISCLAIMS ALL WARRANTIES, EITHER
EXPRESSED OR IMPLIED, INCLUDING THE WARRANTIES OF MERCHANTABILITY
AND FITNESS FOR A PARTICULAR PURPOSE. IN NO EVENT SHALL
MICROSOFT CORPORATION OR ITS SUPPLIERS BE LIABLE FOR ANY
DAMAGES WHATSOEVER INCLUDING DIRECT, INDIRECT, INCIDENTAL,
CONSEQUENTIAL, LOSS OF BUSINESS PROFITS OR SPECIAL DAMAGES, EVEN IF
MICROSOFT CORPORATION OR ITS SUPPLIERS HAVE BEEN ADVISED OF THE
POSSIBILITY OF SUCH DAMAGES. SOME STATES DO NOT ALLOW THE EXCLUSION
OR LIMITATION OF LIABILITY FOR CONSEQUENTIAL OR INCIDENTAL DAMAGES
-- More --
```

WHAT'S HAPPENING? You are seeing the file you downloaded from Microsoft's ftp site.

STEP 13 Press **Enter** until you reach the bottom of the file.

STEP 14 Close the Command Prompt Window.

12.28 TELNET

Telnet is a connection to a remote computer which makes your computer act like a terminal on the remote machine. This connection type is used for real time exchange of text. Telnet makes your computer into a dumb terminal. It is called a dumb terminal because each time your press a key on your computer, your computer does nothing except transmit your keystroke to some other computer on the Internet. The software performing the commands actually runs at the remote computer and not on your computer. Telnet operates in a client/server environment in which one host (the computer you are using running Client Telnet) negotiates opening a session on another computer (the remote host, running Server Telnet). During the behind-the-scenes negotiation process, the two computers agree on the parameters governing the session. Technically, Telnet is the protocol and is the terminal handler portion of the TCP/IP protocol suite. It tells the remote computer how to transfer commands from the local computer, on which you are working, to another computer in a remote location. Thus, Telnet lets you become a user on a remote computer. Both computers must support the telnet protocol. The incoming user must have permission to use the remote computer by providing a user name and password. Telnet can be used by a system administrator or other professionals to log on to your computer and troubleshoot problems on your computer. However, Telnet is also most commonly used for connecting to libraries and other informational public databases. You can use a Telnet client to access hundreds of library and government databases. You begin the session in a Command Prompt window.

12.29 ACTIVITY: USING TELNET

STEP 1 Open a Command Prompt window. The A:\> prompt is displayed.

STEP 2 Key in the following: A:>**telnet**.

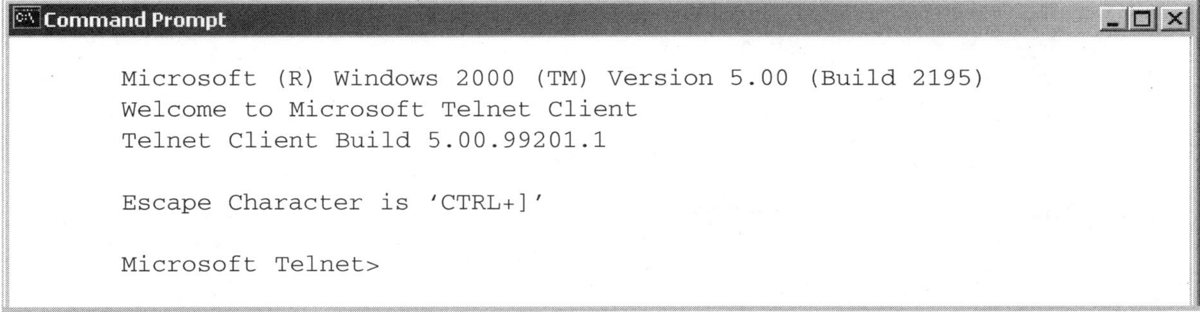

You have started the Telnet program. You need to know the useable commands:

STEP 3 Key in the following: **?/help** Enter

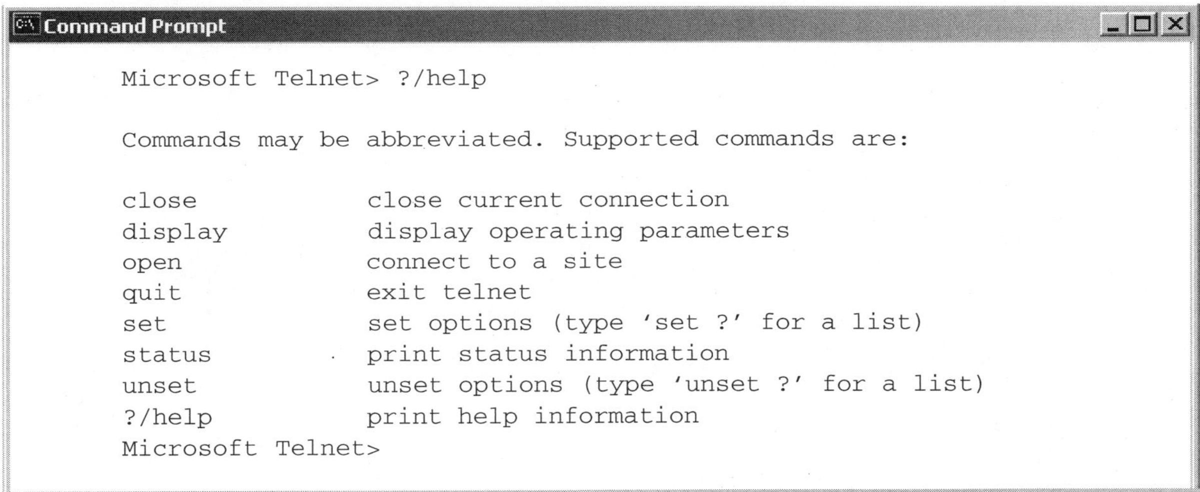

Command Prompt
Escape Character is 'CTRL+]'
You may SEARCH for library materials by any of the following:
Microsoft Telnet> ?/help
Commands may be abbreviated. Supported commands are:
close close current connection
display display operating parameters
open connect to a site
quit exit telnet
set set options (type 'set ?' for a list)
status print status information
unset unset options (type 'unset ?' for a list)
?/help print help information
Microsoft Telnet>

You see a list of commands you can use in the Telnet environment.

STEP 4 Key in the following: **open antpac.lib.uci.edu** Enter

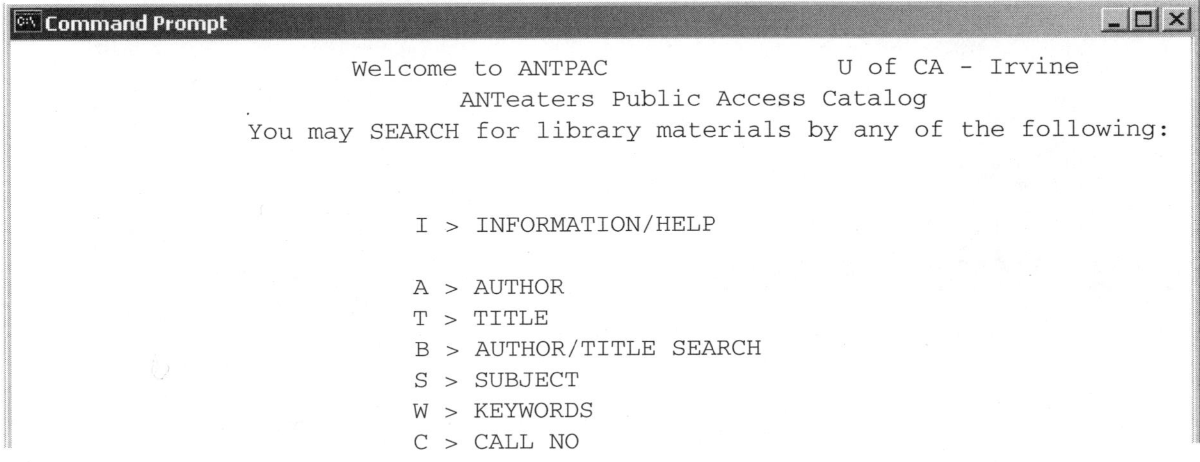

B > AUTHOR/TITLE SEARCH
S > SUBJECT
W > KEYWORDS

```
                 E > STANDARD NO
                 P > Repeat PREVIOUS Search
                 R > RESERVE Lists
                 L > Inter-Library LOAN requests
                 D > CONNECT to MELVYL(R) for Interlibrary Loan
                 V > VIEW your circulation record
                 F > DISCONNECT

                   Choose one (I,A,T,B,S,W,C,E,P,R,L,D,V,F)
```

You have just connected to the University of California at Irvine (UCI) Library Catalog. You are in the public access area and can look up information and make requests to this library.

STEP 5 Key in: **A**.

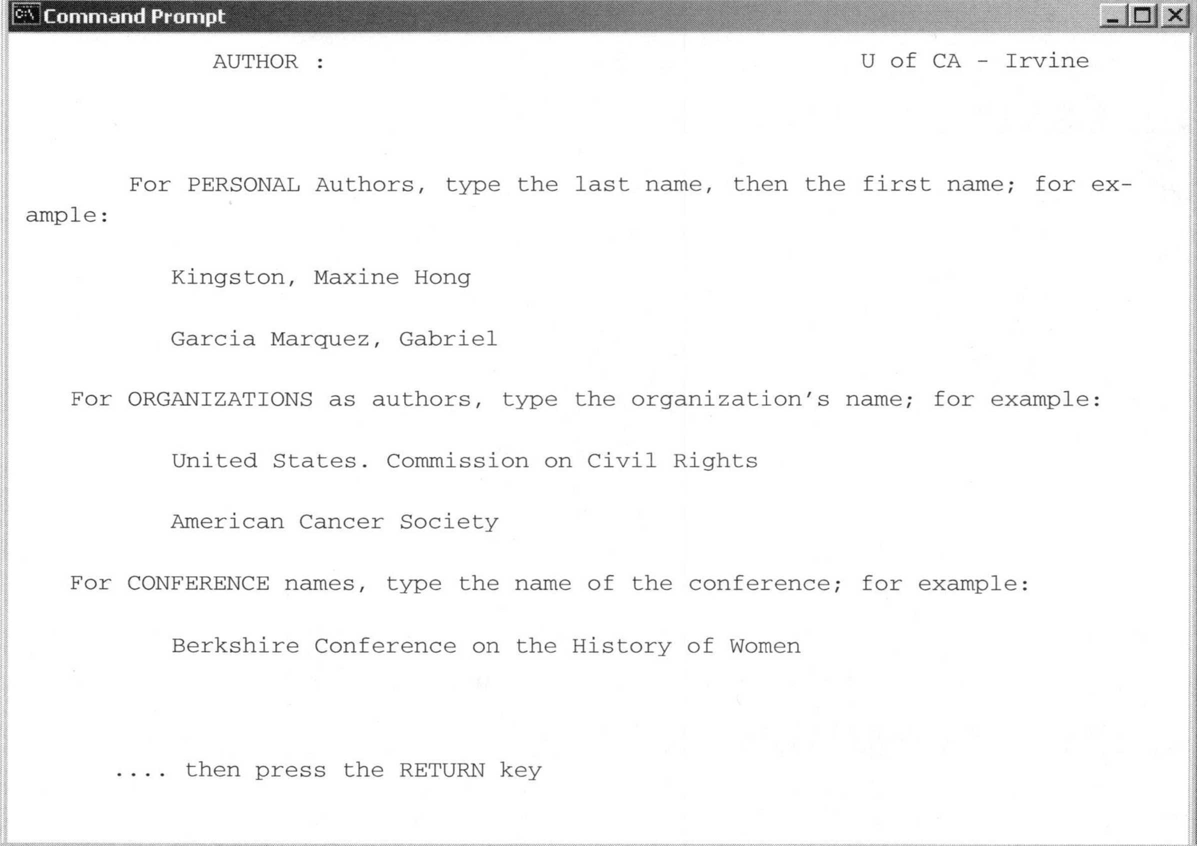

```
Command Prompt
           AUTHOR :                                     U of CA - Irvine



      For PERSONAL Authors, type the last name, then the first name; for ex-
ample:

          Kingston, Maxine Hong

          Garcia Marquez, Gabriel

   For ORGANIZATIONS as authors, type the organization's name; for example:

          United States. Commission on Civil Rights

          American Cancer Society

   For CONFERENCE names, type the name of the conference; for example:

          Berkshire Conference on the History of Women



     .... then press the RETURN key
```

You are on the Author page.

STEP 6 At AUTHOR, key in the following: **Babchuk, Nicholas** Enter

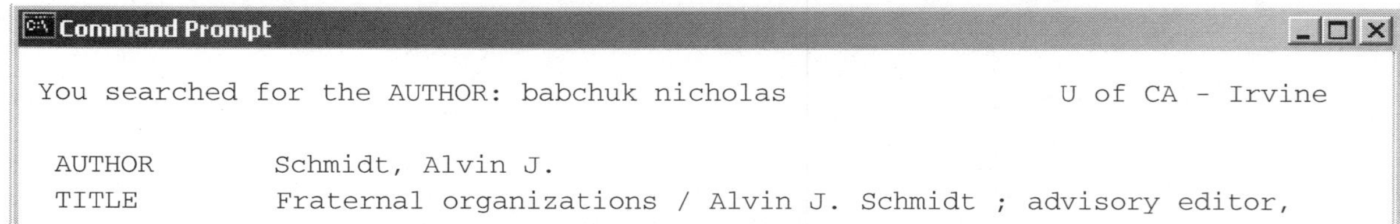

```
Command Prompt
You searched for the AUTHOR: babchuk nicholas                 U of CA - Irvine

 AUTHOR        Schmidt, Alvin J.
 TITLE         Fraternal organizations / Alvin J. Schmidt ; advisory editor,
```

```
                 Nicholas Babchuk.
 IMPRINT         Westport, Conn. : Greenwood Press, c1980.
 DESCRIPTION     xxxiii, 410 p. ; 25 cm.
 SERIES          Greenwood encyclopedia of American institutions ; 3.
 SUBJ-LCSH       Friendly societies -- United States -- History.
                 Friendly societies -- Canada -- History.
                 Friendly societies -- United States -- Directories.
                 Friendly societies -- Canada -- Directories.
                 Voluntarism -- United States.
                 Voluntarism -- Canada.
 ADD AUTHOR      Babchuk, Nicholas.
 NOTE(S)         Includes index.
 ISBN            0313214360.

lqqqqqqqqqqqqqqqqqqqqqqqqqqqqqqqqqqqqqqqqqqqqqqqqqqqqqqqqqqqqqqqqqqqqqqqqqqqqqqk
x    LOCATION                CALL NO.                    STATUS                x
x1 > MAIN-Ref                HS17 .S3                    LIB USE ONLY          x
mqqqqqqqqqqqqqqqqqqqqqqqqqqqqqqqqqqqqqqqqqqqqqqqqqqqqqqqqqqqqqqqqqqqqqqqqqqqqqqj
R > Browse Nearby Entries                       S > SHOW SIMILAR items
N > NEW Search                                  G > Request Item
A > ANOTHER Search by AUTHOR
Z > Show Items Nearby on Shelf
Choose one (R,N,A,Z,S,G)
```

WHAT'S HAPPENING? You have found a book, *Fraternal Organizations*, where Dr. Nicholas Babchuk, a renowned sociologist, was the advisory editor. You see the call number, the location, and the status. You could continue to search the UCI catalog for more articles or books. Instead, you will log out. The qqqqqqqqqqqqqqqqqq is the ASCII representation of whatever character they have used in their menu.

STEP 7 Press **N**. Press **F**.

Command Prompt
Connection to host lost
Press any key to continue. . .

WHAT'S HAPPENING? You have logged out.

Step 8 Key in the following: **quit** Enter

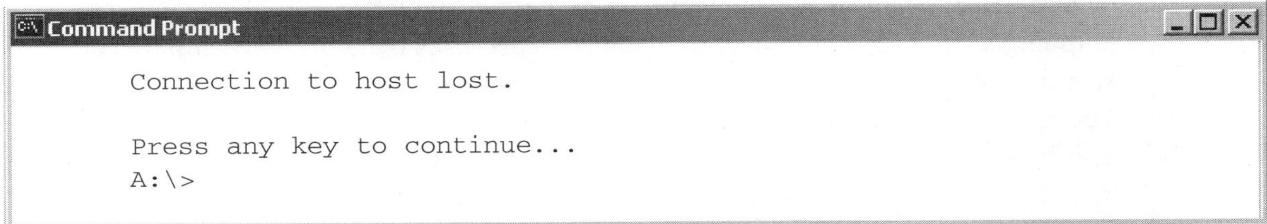
Command Prompt
Connection to host lost.
Press any key to continue...
A:\>

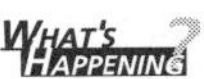
You have had a brief introduction to Telnet.

CHAPTER SUMMARY

1. When you connect computers together, you create what is known as a LAN (local area network).
2. A server is a computer that provides shared resources. A client is a computer that accesses the shared resources provided by a server. Resources are the parts of the computer you share.
3. The standard model for networks with more than 10 users is a server-based network. It is one in which network functions are provided by a computer that is a dedicated server.
4. For networks with fewer than 10 users, the model is a peer-to-peer network, in which all computers are equal. Each computer can function as either a client or server.
5. A WAN (wide area network) consists of computers that use long-range telecommunication links to connect the networked computers over long distances.
6. A network interface card (NIC) is required to set up a network.
7. The NIC must match your bus architecture slot as well as the type of cable used to connect your network.
8. You must have the proper networking software for your network to work.
9. A simple network has three parts: the hardware, the software, and the network administrator.
10. Setting up a peer-to-peer network using Windows usually requires that you have the original system disk.
11. You must install the correct protocols. All computers on the network must use the same protocol. A protocol is a set of rules that allows computers to connect with one another and exchange information.
12. In a peer-to-peer network, you must have these settings in the Configuration tab of the Network dialog box: Client for Microsoft Networks, NetBEUI, and your network interface card. You may add or delete items through My Network Places..
13. In a peer-to-peer network, you must be sure to enable file and print sharing.
14. In a peer-to-peer network, you must name your computer as well as your workgroup. The workgroup name must be identical on all computers in the workgroup.
15. There are two parts to sharing resources: the client and the server. The server has the resource. The client is the computer that wishes to access the resource.
16. When you share a device, any computer on the network can use that device.
17. Common shared devices include printers, drives, and folders.
18. The computer that has the resource must first share it so that others on the network can access it. You must name your shared resource. Others on the network will access it by its shared name.
19. My Network Places is a tool to browse the network.
20. Once a drive has been shared, you may assign a drive letter to it. This act is called mapping a drive. If you map a drive, you can access it through My Computer or Windows Explorer and need not use My Network Places.
21. You can use the NET USE command to map drives.
22. The Internet is a network of networks. You can use the Internet to use email and access chat lines and forums. You may connect to the World Wide Web.
23. The Web is an interconnected collection of Web sites that holds pages of text and graphics in a form recognized by the Web. These pages are linked to one another and

to individual files. The Web is a collection of standards and protocols used to access information on the Internet. Using the Web requires a browser.

24. The Web uses three standards: URL (uniform resource locator), HTML (hypertext markup language), and a method of access such as HTTP (hypertext transfer protocol).
25. URLs are a standard format for identifying locations on the Internet.
26. A Web site is both the physical and virtual location of a person's or organization's Web page(s).
27. A Web page is a single screen of text and graphics that usually has hypertext links to other pages.
28. In order to access the Internet, you usually need a modem, communication software, and an online provider.
29. Online providers includes services such as AOL (America Online) or MSN (Microsoft Network). You may also use an IAP (Internet access provider) or an ISP (Internet service provider).
30. You can connect to the Internet using a phone line, a special phone line (ISDN), DSL, through your cable company, or via satellite.
31. TCP/IP is the protocol of the Internet.
32. Protocols are "bound" to specific Network Interface Cards
33. Each network has a router, which is a device that connects networks. A router can make intelligent decisions on which network to use to send data.
34. TCP divides data into packets and numbers each packet.
35. IP specifies the addresses of the sending and receiving computers and sends the packets on their way.
36. A single user will typically access the Internet thorough a dial-up, cable, or DSL connection. This provides a temporary connection, usually a PPP (point-to-point protocol) connection.
37. Each computer on the Internet uses TCP/IP and must have a unique IP address.
38. An IP address is made up of four numbers separated by periods. This format is called dotted-decimal notation. Each section is called an octet.
39. IP address space is divided into three major address classes: A, B, and C.
40. Each site attached to the Internet belongs to a domain. A user or organization applies for a domain name so that each domain name is unique.
41. Fully qualified domain names are an alphabetic alias to the IP address.
42. The DNS (domain name system) resolves the domain name into the IP address.
43. When you connect to the Internet, you use the URL of the site to which you wish to connect. If you know the IP address, you may use that as well.
44. Included with TCP/IP is a set of command line utilities that can help you troubleshoot problems as well as offer you connections to computers not connected to the Web, such as Unix system computers. These tools are as follows:

Command	Purpose
ARP	Displays and modifies the IP to Ethernet translation tables.
IPCONFIG	Displays the IP address and other configuration information.

FTP	Transfers files to and from a node running FTP services.
NETSTAT	Displays protocol statistics and current TCP/IP connections.
PING	Verifies connections to a remote host or hosts.
ROUTE	Manually controls network-routing tables.
TELNET	Starts terminal emulation with a remote system running a Telnet service. Windows Millennium Edition provides a graphical version of this utility.
TRACERT	Determines the route taken to a destination.

If you want help on any of these commands, at the command line you key in the command name, a space, and then **/?**.

KEY TERMS

browser
bus topology
client
coaxial cable
cyberspace
dedicated server
DNS (domain name system)
domain name
file server
FTP (file transfer protocol)
home page
HTML (hypertext markup language)
HTTP (hypertext transfer protocol)
IAP (Internet access provider)
information superhighway
Internet
IP address
ISP (Internet service provider)
LAN (local area network)
locally
mapped drive
network administrator
NOS (network operating system)
NIC (network interface card)
octet
packet
peer-to-peer network
portal
PPP (point-to-point protocol)
print server
protocol
resources
router
server
server-based network services
services
single point of failure
SLIP (serial-line Internet protocol)
star topology
T-connectors
terminator plug
Thinnet
topology
twisted-pair cable
UNC (universal naming convention)
URL (uniform resource locator)
WAN (wide area network)
Web page
Web site
workgroup
WWW (World Wide Web)

DISCUSSION QUESTIONS

1. Define the following terms: *client, server, resources,* and *LAN.*
2. Compare and contrast a client computer and a server computer.
3. Compare and contrast a server-based network and a peer-to-peer network.

4. List and explain three reasons you might set up a network.
5. Compare and contrast a LAN and a WAN.
6. What is the purpose and function of a network interface card?
7. List the steps necessary to set up a peer-to-peer network.
8. Explain the purpose and function of the network clients, adapters, protocols, and services found in the Local Area Connection properties sheet.
9. Explain the purpose and function of a protocol. Why must computers on a network use the same protocol?
10. Why is it important that all computers in a peer-to-peer network use the same workgroup name?
11. Compare and contrast a print server and a file server on a server-based network and a peer-to-peer network.
12. List and explain the steps you need to take in order to share your drive on a peer-to-peer network.
13. Give the syntax of the network path and explain each part of the syntax.
14. When sharing your drive with another computer, why is it unwise for your share name to be C?
15. Explain the purpose and function of a mapped drive.
16. What is the purpose and function of the Internet?
17. How can the Internet be used?
18. Compare and contrast the Internet and the World Wide Web.
19. Explain the purpose of URLs, HTML, and HTTP.
20. List the three types of information a URL needs to retrieve a document.
21. What is a Web site?
22. Compare and contrast a Web site with a Web page.
23. The type of Web site is indicated by its "dot" address. Explain.
24. What is a hypertext link?
25. List and explain three ways a computer user can connect to the Internet.
26. Why is TCP/IP considered the protocol of the Internet?
27. What is a router?
28. Compare and contrast the purposes and functions of TCP and IP.
29. Data is divided into packets when it is transferred over the Internet. Why?
30. What is the purpose of an IP address?
31. Compare and contrast a static versus a dynamic IP address.
32. Why is the format of an IP address called dotted-decimal notation?
33. Describe the format of a Class A, Class B, and Class C IP address.
34. What is a loopback address?
35. Explain the purpose and function of the domain name system.
36. What is the purpose of name resolution?
37. Why can computers have both an IP address and a domain name?
38. Define each part of the following URL: **http://www.amazon.com/books**.
39. Explain the purposes and functions of two utilities that are automatically installed when TCP/IP network protocol is installed.
40. How can you receive help on the TCP/IP utilities?
41. What is the purpose and function of IPCONFIG?
42. What is the purpose and function of ping?
43. What is the purpose and function of tracert?

44. What is the purpose and function of FTP?
45. What is the purpose and function of Telnet?

TRUE/FALSE QUESTIONS

For each question, circle the letter T if the question is true or the letter F if the question is false.

T F 1. My Network Places allows you to browse all the resources on your network.

T F 2. On a peer-to-peer network, anyone may access any resource on the network, even if it has not been shared.

T F 3. Netscape Navigator is an example of a protocol.

T F 4. You may map both folders and drives.

T F 5. The World Wide Web (WWW) and the Internet are synonyms.

COMPLETION QUESTIONS

Write the correct answer in each blank space.

6. The global system of networked computers is called the ___________.
7. In order to connect to a Web site on the WWW, you must key in the address, known as the ___________.
8. An IP address expressed in terms of 121.22.34.44 is called ___________ notation.
9. A TCP/IP utility that allows you to check out your connection to another computer is the ___________ utility.
10. A network in which security and other network functions are provided by a dedicated computer is called a(n) ___________ network.

MULTIPLE CHOICE QUESTIONS

For each question, write the letter for the correct answer in the blank space.

☐ 11. What protocol is used to connect Windows to the Internet?
   a. PPP
   b. NetBIOS
   c. NetBEUI
   d. TCP/IP

☐ 12. If you wish to access information in a folder on another computer, you must, on the server computer, first
   a. map the folder.
   b. share the folder.
   c. open My Network Places.
   d. both a and c

☐ 13. In the URL **http://www.yahoo.com/computers**, **www.yahoo.com** is an example of the
   a. protocol used.
   b. name of computer on which the server is running.
   c. name of computer on which the client is running.
   d. name of item to request from the server.

14. Many FTP servers allow you to log on as
    a. anonymous.
    b. user.
    c. an email address.
    d. none of the above
15. You can connect to an ISP using
    a. DSL.
    b. cable.
    c. telephone lines with a modem.
    d. all of the above

APPLICATION ASSIGNMENTS

PROBLEM SET I—AT THE COMPUTER

Note: To do these two activities, you must have access to the Internet as well as a browser to access the World Wide Web.

1. If you have access to the Internet, visit the site of the magazine Scientific American (**http://www.sciam.com**). You will be taken to the home page. Click **Past Issues**. Click **Issues from 1999**. Click **December 1999**. Scroll till you see **Technology and Business**. Read the article entitled **Cable-Free** and write a brief report on what it says.
2. To know where things are going, it is helpful to know where they have been. Visit Hobbes' Internet Timeline (**http://www.zakon.org**). Once you reach the site, click on **Hobbes' Internet Timeline**. Scroll through the page. Find **1993**. Read it. Write a brief report describing one 1993 happening (from the timeline, not your memory).

PROBLEM SET II—BRIEF ESSAY

1. You are a small advertising company with three employees: Mary Brown, Jose Rodriquez, and Jin-Li Yu. The office has three computers, a scanner, a laser printer, and a color printer. You have already set up a peer-to-peer network. Mary's computer is connected to the laser printer. Jose's computer is connected to the color printer, and Jin-Li's computer is attached to the scanner. Mary needs to access the color printer but not the scanner. Jose needs only the color printer. Jin-Li needs access to the color printer. Describe what you need to do to accomplish these goals.
2. Briefly describe the importance and use of an IP address. Describe what it is and how it is used. Include in your discussion why a domain name must be resolved. Describe how a name is resolved.

CHAPTER

13

PROTECTING YOUR SYSTEM

LEARNING OBJECTIVES

1. Explain why it is necessary to back up your data and system files.
2. Explain the purpose and function of the Backup wizard.
3. Explain the purpose and function of scheduling backups.
4. Compare and contrast the five types of backups.
5. Describe the boot process.
6. Explain the need for a set of setup boot disks.
7. Compare and contrast the different options when booting into Safe Mode.
8. Explain the purpose and function of the Emergency Repair Disk (ERD).
9. Explain the purpose and function of the Registry.
10. Explain the purpose and function of the Recovery Console.

STUDENT OUTCOMES

1. Back up selected files.
2. Restore selected files.
3. Boot into Safe Mode, if permitted.
4. Make and use a set of setup boot disks, if permitted.
5. Create an Emergency Repair Disk (ERD).
6. Back up the Registry.
7. Install the Recovery Console, if permitted.
8. Use Recovery Console commands, if permitted.

CHAPTER OVERVIEW

It is important to protect your system. One way to protect your data and programs is to back up your files and programs to a different media, such as a tape or a removable disk. This chapter shows how to use the Backup program supplied by Windows. The Backup program allows you to back up and restore files for data protection and create an Emergency Repair Disk (ERD). If you have problems starting your computer, the ERD can assist you in trying to fix the problems. However, in order to use the ERD, you must also be able to boot into Windows.

In the days when DOS was the operating system and Windows was an environment that sat on top of it, protecting your system was very simple and straightforward. You made several bootable DOS disks that contained some utilities. In addition, you kept current copies of your .INI and .GRP files. With these items, you could correct 90 percent of the problems that could develop on your computer. Now that Windows *is* the operating system, protecting your system gets a bit more complicated. Now you must create setup boot disks so that you can boot into Windows 2000 Professional.

Windows 2000 Professional boots differently than previous MS-DOS or Windows operating systems. This chapter will help you understand how the boot process works. In addition, you will learn about Safe Mode and the different menu options available to you should you have a problem with your system.

The Registry keeps track of all of your object linking and embedding (OLE) operations. It stores all your hardware configuration information. It also tracks and contains all the preferences for each user of the computer system. Typically, you do not have to deal directly with the Registry. Preferably, you make changes using tools such as Control Panel. However, if your Registry becomes corrupt, there are methods to restore it. You will look at some of these options.

One of the options you will look at is the Recovery Console. This is a command line interface that should be used only by experienced Windows users. You must be an administrator or have administrator privileges to use the Recovery Console. It allows you, with a limited set of administrative commands, to repair errors to your system. You can use it to start and stop services, repair a Master Boot Record, or format a disk. You must install it using the Windows 2000 Professional CD. You may start it from the Windows 2000 Professional setup disks or from your hard disk, if you install it there.

13.1 BACKING UP YOUR DATA

Backing up data is a critical task that users too often neglect. When things go wrong, either through your error or the computer's, rather than having to try to recreate data, you can turn to your backups, but only if you have created them. A ***backup*** is nothing more than a duplicate of the file or files that are on a disk copied to a medium such as a floppy, CD-R, CD-RW, Zip disk, or a tape. You retrieve the files by restoring them, which means copying them back to the original medium. When you copy a file to a floppy disk, you are in effect backing it up. Windows 2000 Professional provides a tool called Backup, located in System Tools, which is a graphical tool that allows you to back up files, restore files, create an Emergency Repair Disk, and to schedule these tasks automatically.

The importance of backing up cannot be overstated. As you use your computer and programs, you create data. For instance, imagine you are writing a book and you create your first chapter and save it as a file to the hard disk. You back up in January. It is now April, and you have completed 10 chapters. You accidentally delete the folder that contains your chapters. You do not want to rewrite those chapters and, furthermore, you cannot. You turn to your backup, but you have a major problem. The only file you can restore is that first chapter you created in January. The rest of your work is gone. To say the least, backing up your data files regularly is critical. The reason for backing up your entire hard drive may not be as obvious, but it is equally important.

As you work with Windows 2000 Professional, you create settings, install new programs, and delete old programs. You are also adding and making changes to the system Registry that controls the Windows 2000 Professional environment. If the Registry becomes corrupt, you will not be able to boot Windows 2000 Professional. The system itself is ever-changing. If, for instance, you install a new program and it does something to your hard drive, such as cause another program not to work (or worse), you would like to return to the working system you had prior to your installation. If the problem is serious, you might have to reformat your hard drive. It can literally take hours, if not days, to reinstall all of your software. If you have backed up your system, you can simply restore what you had before, and a major catastrophe becomes a minor inconvenience.

There are many reasons to use Backup rather than just make a copy of your files. You often want to back up your entire hard disk, which includes all your files and all your folders, as well as the Windows system files stored in what is called the Registry. Although you can back up your entire hard disk to floppy disks, it is very laborious and time-consuming in this era of 15-gigabyte or larger hard drives. Most users opt to have a tape backup unit or a removable drive such as a CD-RW, Zip, or Jaz drive. Special tapes must be purchased for use in a tape drive, cartridges for a removable drive. Furthermore, COPY or XCOPY does not back up the Windows system files. Another advantage of using Backup instead of the COPY or XCOPY command is that a backup file can span multiple disks. When one disk is full, you are directed to insert another empty disk into the drive.

The Backup utility helps you protect your data from accidental loss. Backup provides many ways to protect your data and your computer system. Major options with Backup include:

- Backing up selected files and folders on your hard disk.
- Restoring the backed up files and folders to your hard disk or any other disk you can access.
- Creating an Emergency Repair Disk (ERD). An ERD allows you to repair system files if they become corrupt or are accidentally erased. Without the proper system files, your system will not boot.
- Make a copy of your computer's System State. The System State is a collection of computer-specific data that can be backed up and restored. It includes such things as the Registry, the boot files, and the system files. The Registry is a database for information about your computer's configuration that Windows 2000 Professional constantly references during your use of the computer. The boot files are the system files that Windows 2000 Professional needs to start Windows. The system files are

the additional files that Windows needs to load, configure, and run the operating system.
- Schedule regular backups to keep your backed-up data up to date.

13.2 TYPES OF BACKUPS

The Backup utility supports five methods of backing up data on your computer. These are copy, daily, differential, incremental, and normal. As you will see, you use a combination of these types of backups, depending on what you wish to do.

- Copy—A ***copy backup*** copies all selected files but does not mark each file as having been backed up. This method is actually no different than using the COPY or XCOPY command. Remember the archive bit. It is a file attribute and is also called the archive flag or the archive attribute. Depending on what choice you make with Backup, Backup uses the archive bit to determine whether or not a file needs to be backed up. If the bit is on, the file needs to be backed up. After the file is backed up, the archive bit may be set to off so that Backup knows that the file has been backed up. If you make any changes to the file, the archive bit is automatically turned on, indicating that the file has changed since the last backup. A copy backup does not clear the archive attribute.
- Daily—A ***daily backup*** copies all selected files that have been altered on the day you perform the daily backup. Again, the archive bit is not cleared. This provides you with the advantage of backing up whatever it is you worked on during the current day's activities.
- Differential—A ***differential backup*** copies files created or changed since the last normal or incremental backup. Again, the archive attribute is not cleared. If you are performing a combination of normal and differential backups, you must restore your files and folders by using the last normal backup as well as the last differential backup.
- Incremental—An ***incremental backup*** backs up only those files created or changed since the last normal or incremental backup. It marks the files and folders as backed up, which means that it clears the archive attribute. In this case, if you use a combination of normal and incremental backups, you will need to have the last normal backup set as well as all incremental backup sets in order to restore your data.
- Normal—A ***normal backup,*** sometimes referred to as a ***full backup,*** copies all selected files and clears the archive attribute. With normal backups, you need only the most recent copy of the backup file or tape to restore all of the files. You usually perform a normal backup the first time you create a backup set.

Using a combination of normal backups and incremental backups requires the least amount of storage space and takes the least amount of time to back up. But when you restore your files, this method is the most time-consuming and difficult, as you will need all the disks or tapes that you used. Using a combination of normal backups and differential backups takes more time to perform. But restoring your files is much easier and faster because your data will be stored on a few disks or tapes.

13.3 PLANNING BACKUPS

You should have a regular backup schedule. The timing of your backups depends on how much you use your computer and how often you change things. A typical backup schedule might be that once a week you perform a full backup and every day you perform an incremental backup. If you need to restore your data, you need all of the backups, both the normal and the incremental. If you are on a network, the network administrator will take care of the full backup; you need to be concerned about your data files only.

When you do backups, it is a good idea to have more than one copy of your backup or backup set. For instance, if you did a normal system backup once a week and incremental backups daily, you would want at least two sets of backups. One week, you would back up on one set; the following week you would use the other set. Thus, if Murphy's law was in effect for you—your hard disk and your backup were both corrupted—you would be able to restore files from the other week's backup. The files would not be the most current, but at least you would not have to recreate everything from scratch. Another word of warning: Store at least one copy of your backup away from your computer. If you have your backup tapes at the office and you have a fire or theft, you will lose everything. If you have another set at home, you can recover what was lost at work. The most important thing about backing up is to **DO IT**. Don't just do it, do it on a regularly scheduled basis.

To access Backup, you may right-click a drive, choose Properties, choose the Tools tab, and select the Backup Now command button. You may also access Backup from the Programs submenus. Backup also has other uses. You can use Backup to ***archive data***. If your hard disk starts filling up and you want to make more room on it, you can use Backup to copy seldom-used files to a backup medium and then delete them from the hard drive. If you need these files at a later date, you can restore them. You can also use Backup to transfer programs and files to other computers. If you purchase a new computer, you can back up your old computer and restore to your new computer. This way, your new system will look the same as your old system, including the arrangement of your desktop.

13.4 ACTIVITY: USING BACKUP

Note 1: Since Backup requires writing information to the hard disk, and since each system is unique, these steps are only one example of how to use Backup. Should you choose to complete this activity on your own computer, be aware that you are going to do only an incremental backup of some files. Under no circumstances should you do this activity if you are on a network, nor are you able to do it on a network.

Note 2: You should have a new formatted floppy disk. Do not use your ACTIVITIES disk, your DATA disk, or your APPLICATIONS disk for this activity.

Step 1 Click **Start**. Point at **Programs**. Point at **Accessories**. Point at **System Tools**. Click **Backup**.

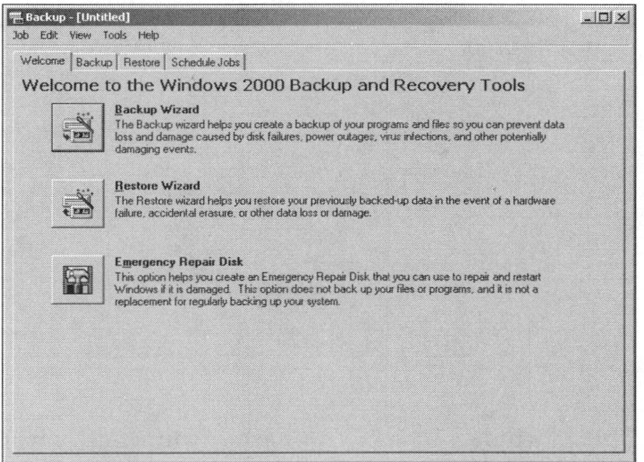

The Backup window opens and you see the Welcome page. There are three available command buttons: Backup Wizard, Restore Wizard, and Emergency Repair Disk.

Step 2 Click the **Backup Wizard** button.

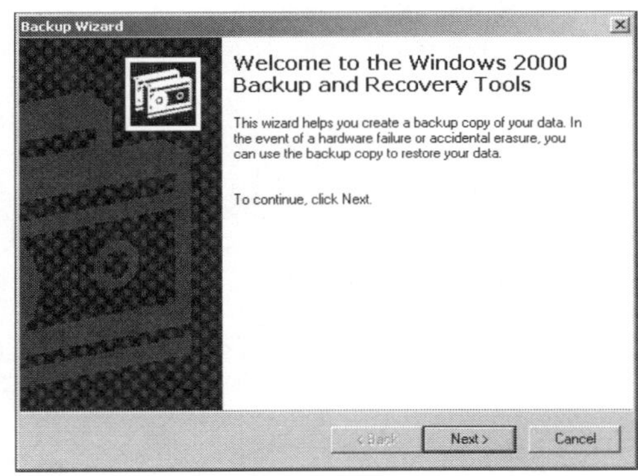

The Backup Wizard window informs you of the purpose of Backup. Since this is a wizard, it will lead you through the steps of backing up your files.

Step 3 Click **Next**.

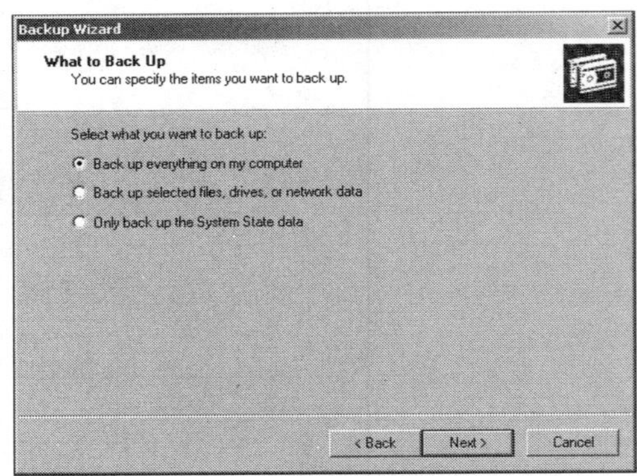

WHAT'S HAPPENING? This is where you specify whether you want to back up everything on your computer; only selected files, drives, or network data; or only the System State data. For Windows 2000 Professional, the System State data includes only the Registry, the COM+ Class Registration database, and boot files. The default setting is to back up everything on your computer. You are going to choose **Back up selected files, drives, or network data**.

Step 4 Click **Back up selected files, drives, or network data**. Click **Next**.

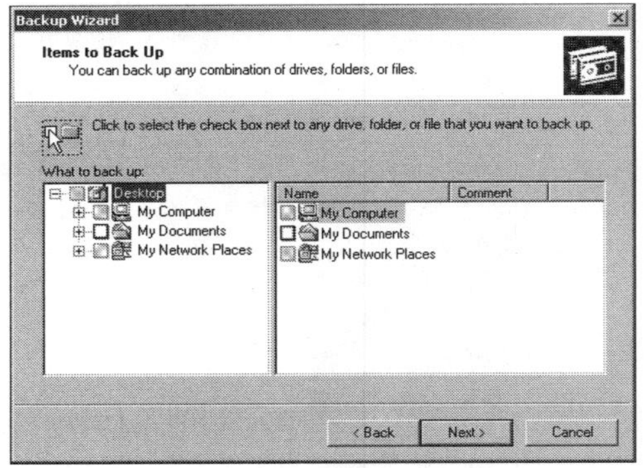

WHAT'S HAPPENING? The listings include your computer, the folder My Documents, and your data on a network. However, if you are on network, you may not have the proper permissions to back up network items.

Step 5 Click the plus sign next to **My Computer**. Click the plus sign next to **Drive C:** to expand it. Scroll in the left pane until you locate the **WINDOSBK** folder. Click on the plus sign to expand it. Click **WINDOSBK** in the left pane. Be sure not to place a checkmark in the box.

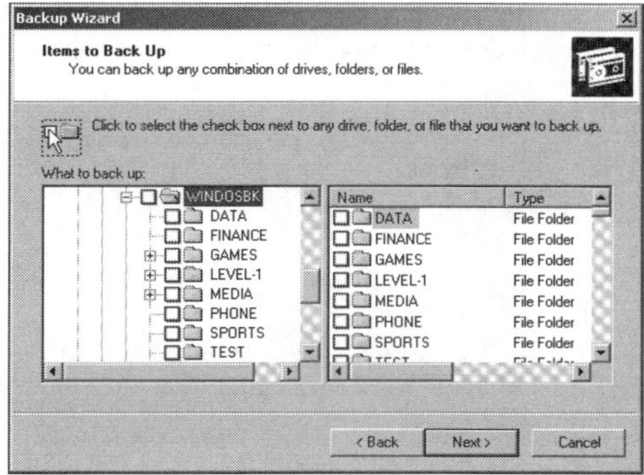

The Backup Wizard window looks somewhat like the Windows Explorer window. The left pane is the structure of your disk, and the right pane shows the folders as well as the files in the folders. In front of each item is an empty check box. To select an item for backing up, click in the check box. To expand an entry, double-click it or click the plus sign next to it. In this example, the left pane shows the structure of the **WINDOSBK** directory. The right pane shows the contents of the **WINDOSBK** directory. Placing a checkmark in the check box next to **WINDOSBK** would indicate that you wanted to back up the entire **WINDOSBK** folder. You only want to back up some files.

Step 6 Scroll in the right pane until you can see the April files. Click the check box in front of **APR.99**, **APR.NEW**, **APR.TMP**, **APRIL.TMP**, and **APRIL.TXT**.

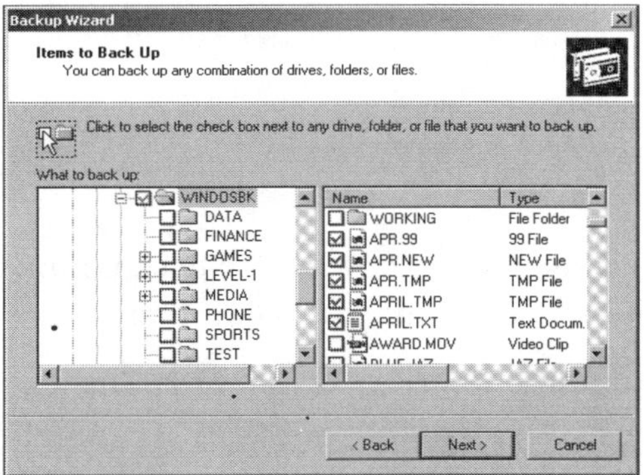

You have selected the files you wish to back up by placing a checkmark in each box.

Step 7 Click **Next**.

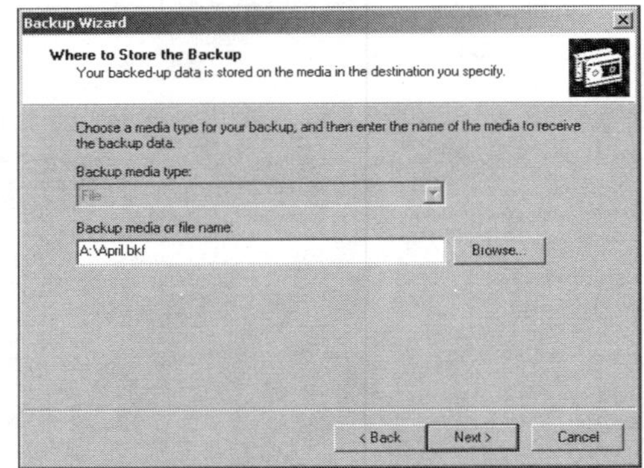

WHAT'S HAPPENING? The wizard wants to know where to store the backup. If you had a tape drive or another backup media type, you could select it here. In this case, since you are backing up to a floppy disk, your only choice is File. Backup creates a file, and you need to tell it what device and what file name you are going to use. In this example, the default is **A:\april.bkf** since on this system, these files were previously backed up. If you have never backed up before or if you had a different file set, your name would be different.

Step 8 Place the formatted disk in Drive A. Click the **Browse** command button. In the Look in drop-down list box, select Drive A.

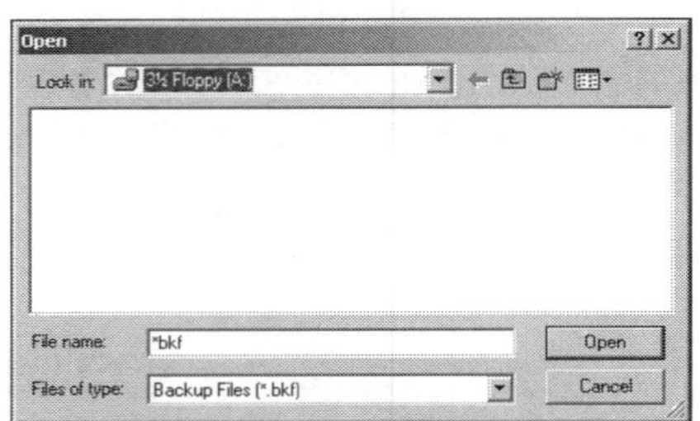

WHAT'S HAPPENING? You had your choice of where to back up the files and what to call the file. You chose Drive A. At this point, there is nothing on the disk in Drive A.

Step 9 In the File name textbox, key in: **april.bkf**

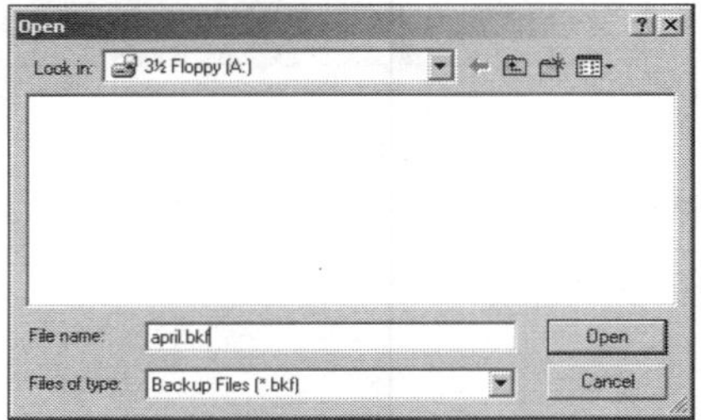

WHAT'S HAPPENING? You have named your backup set.

Step 10 Click **Open**.

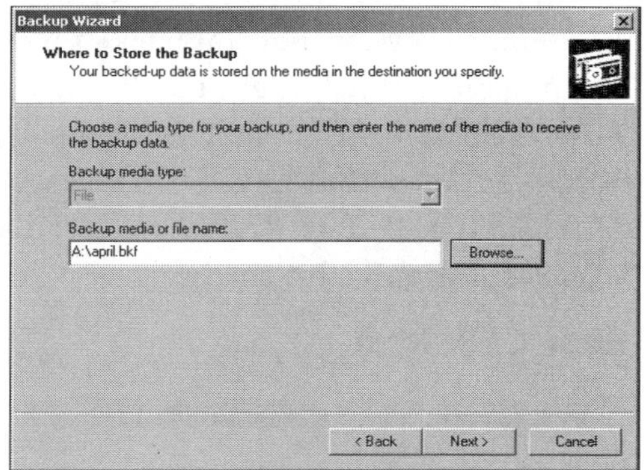

You are returned to the Backup Wizard, and the location and name of your backup set appears in the text box.

Step 11 Click **Next**.

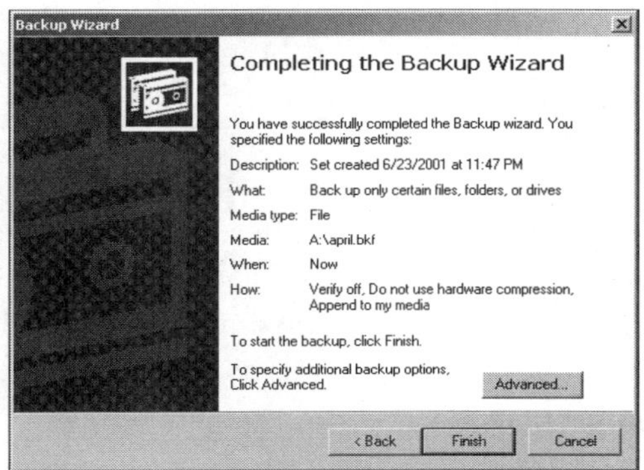

This screen summarizes your current selections. The How entry indicates whether the Backup program is going to verify the files when they are copied, use hardware compression, and append or replace data on the floppy disk.

Step 12 Click the **Advanced** command button. Click the down arrow in the drop-down list box.

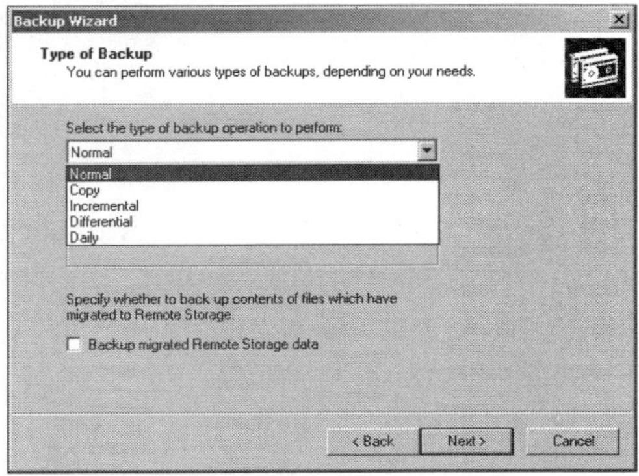

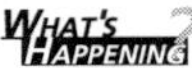

You have all the choices that were described earlier. The default choice is Normal. Again, to review, normal backs up every file you selected and turns off the archive bit for each file. Copy backs up the selected files but does not turn off the archive bit. Incremental backs up only selected files that have not been backed up or that have been changed and clears the archive bit of each backed up file. Differential is the same as incremental, but does not alter the current archive bit setting.

Step 13 Click **Normal**. Click **Next**.

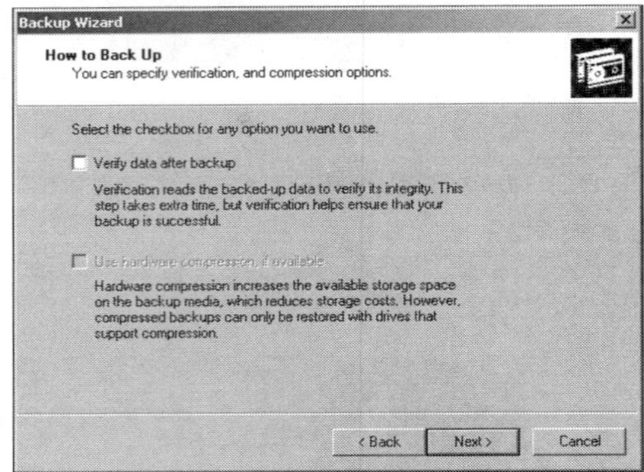

You are asked to make another decision. Windows can verify the data after the backup by reading it and comparing it to the original data, and it can save space on the backup media by compressing the data. In this example, hardware compression is not available, because the drive being backed up is not compressed.

Step 14 Be sure both options are off by clearing the check boxes. Click **Next**.

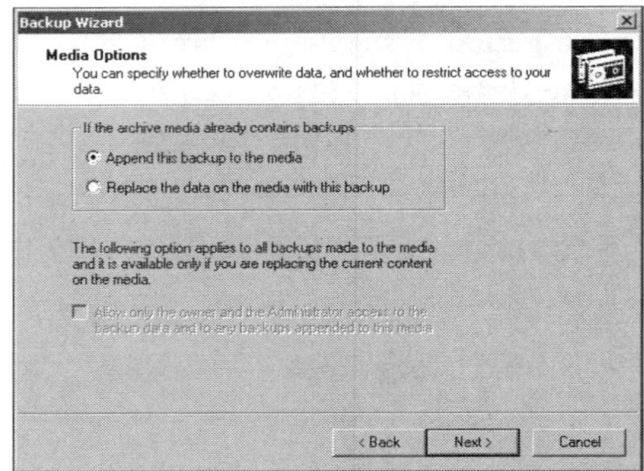

You must decide if you want this backup set to be appended to the data on the backup disk or if it should replace the data on the disk. Your formatted disk should be empty. If you append the data, your backups can become very large. By replacing the data, you are sure you only have one copy of your backup.

Step 15 Click **Replace the data on the media with this backup**.

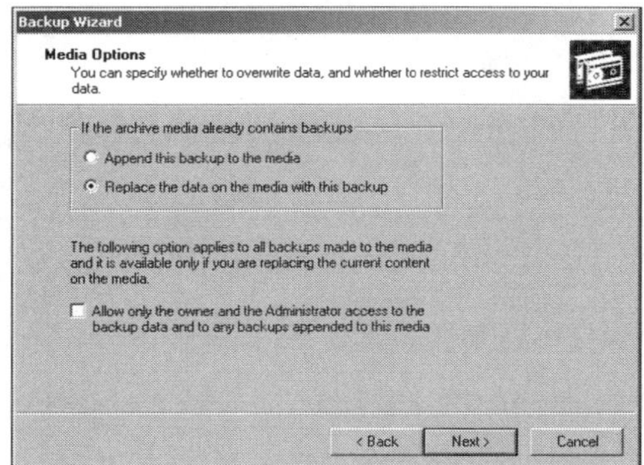

WHAT'S HAPPENING? You are asked to specify who can have access to your backup data.

Step 16 Click **Next**.

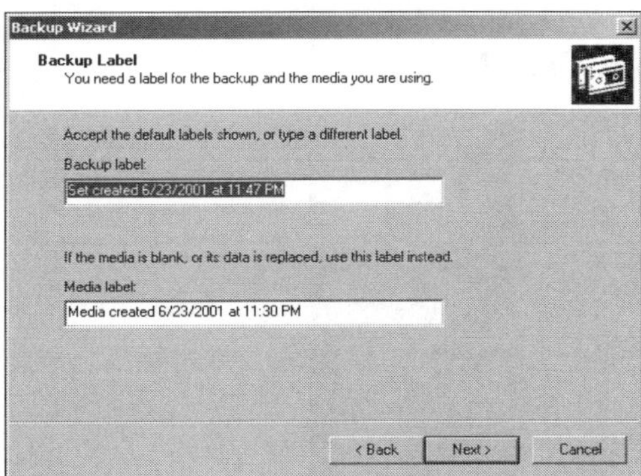

WHAT'S HAPPENING? You are asked to supply a backup label or use the default labels shown. The default name is **Set created *date* at *time***. The backup label is a file that defines your backup. It includes a list of the files you want to include in your backup and any options you selected, including the kind of backup you used and the destination drive and folder for the backup files. This is what is listed in the What, When, and How areas.

Step 17 In the Backup label text box, key in **Testing**.

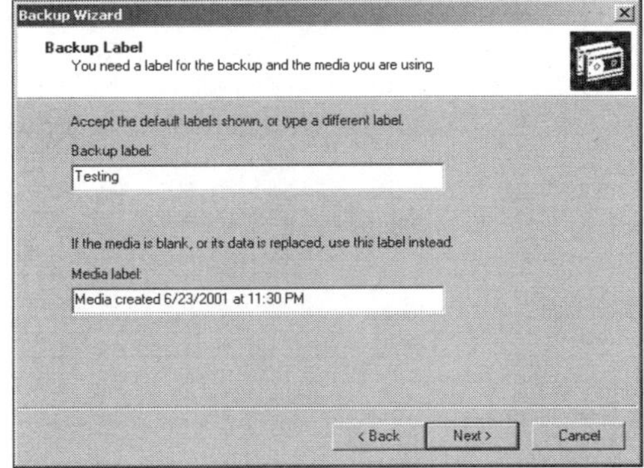

You have named the backup job.

Step 18 Click **Next**.

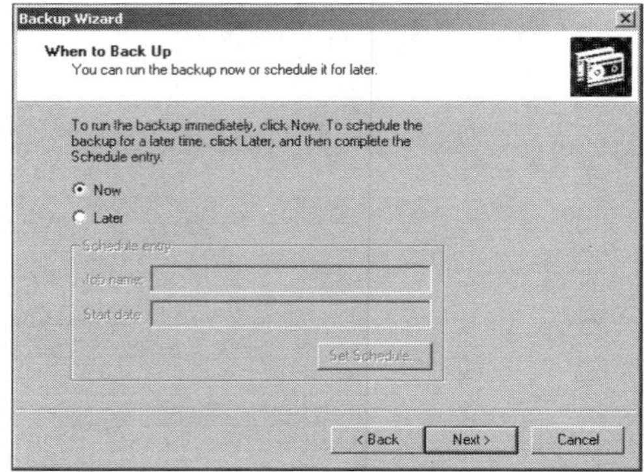

You can run Backup now or specify a later date and time.

Step 19 Click **Now**. Click **Next**.

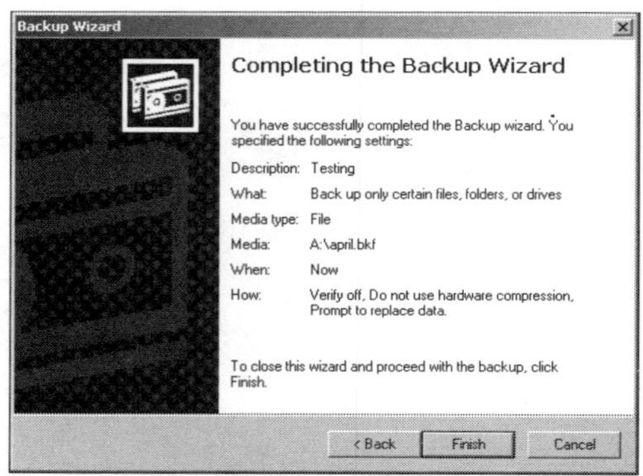

A revised summary appears that includes your new options.

Step 20 Click **Finish**.

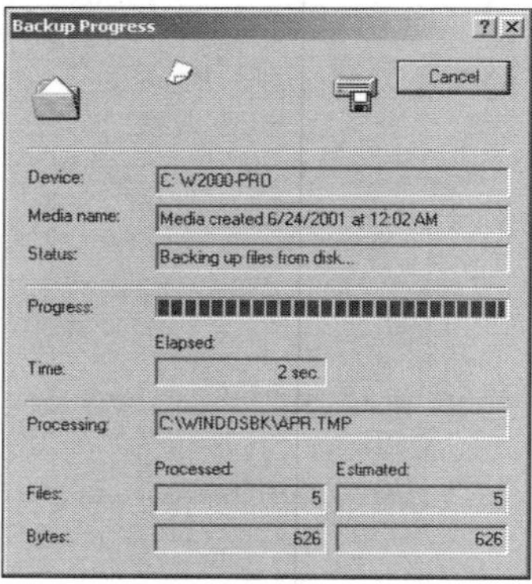

A window tells you that Backup is getting ready to do its job. Another window shows the progress of the backup. When it is complete, you see the following information box:

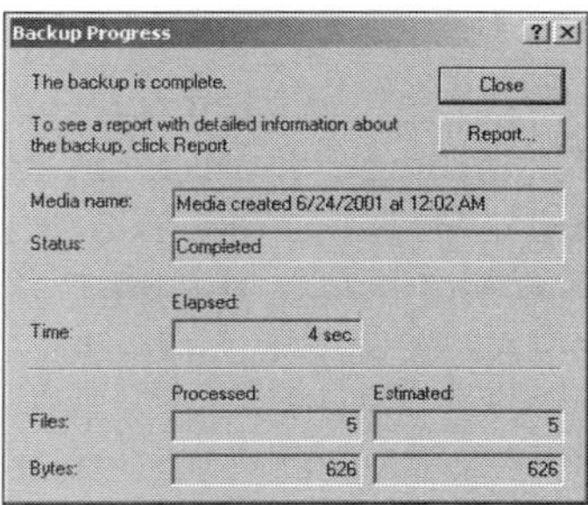

Step 21 Click the **Report** button.

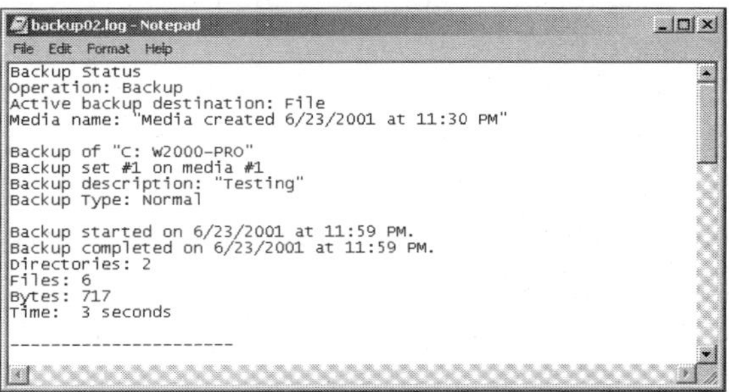

WHAT'S HAPPENING? You have opened a document in Notepad that has all the information about your backup in it.

Step 22 Close Notepad. Click **Close**. Close the Backup window.

Step 23 Open **Windows Explorer**. Open Drive A.

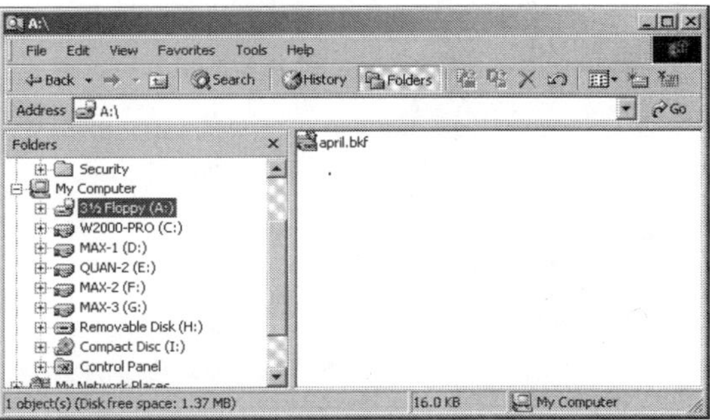

WHAT'S HAPPENING? Here is your backup file set. You have successfully backed up the April files. However, you cannot use this file or open it except with the Restore portion of the Backup utility.

Step 24 Close the Drive A window.

WHAT'S HAPPENING? Your backup is complete. You have returned to the desktop.

13.5 RESTORE

Backup has a ***Restore*** wizard, so that you can copy some or all of your files to your original disk, another disk, or another directory. Restore lets you choose which backup set to copy from. Restoring files is as easy as backing them up with the Backup program. You merely choose Restore and choose the kind of restoration you want. You can use Restore Wizard, which will lead you through the process of restoring your system.

13.6 ACTIVITY: RESTORING FILES

Note 1: Since using Restore requires writing information to the hard disk and since each system is unique, these steps are one example of how to restore. Should you choose to complete this activity on your own computer, be aware that you are only going to do an incremental restoration of some files. Under no circumstances should you do this activity if you are on a network, nor are you able to do it on a network.

Note 2: You should have the disk to which you just backed up your files in Drive A. Do not use your ACTIVITIES disk, your DATA disk, or your APPLICATIONS disk for this activity.

Step 1 Click **Start**. Point at **Programs**. Point at **Accessories**. Point at **System Tools**. Click **Backup**.

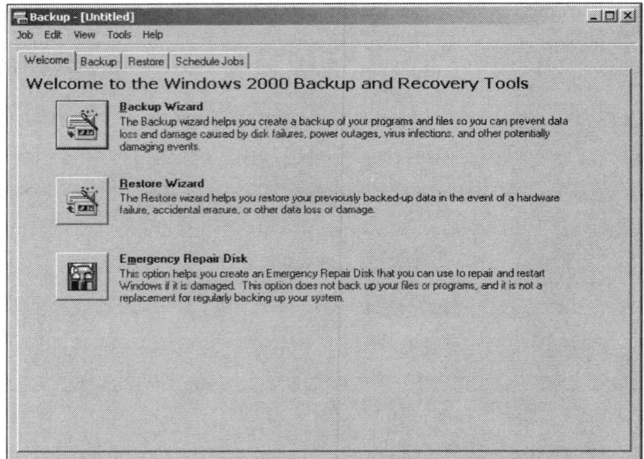

This screen is the same introduction you saw in the last activity. In this case, you are going to restore the files on the floppy disk to the hard disk.

Step 2 Click the **Restore Wizard** button. Click **Next**.

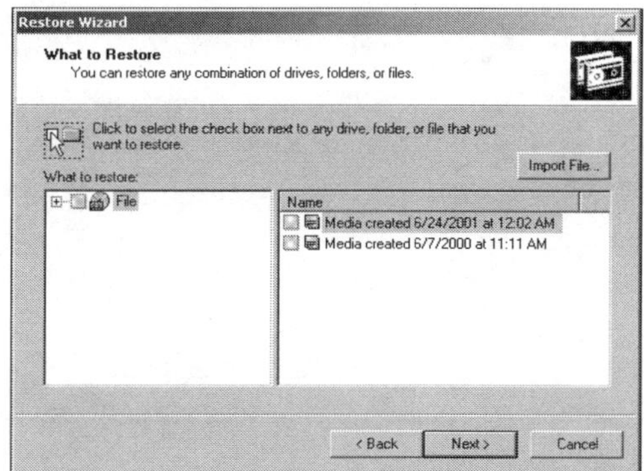

WHAT'S HAPPENING? Restore Wizard is asking you what you want to restore. If the Backup program was previously run on your computer, you may have several items listed.

Step 3 Click the plus sign in the left pane. In the left pane, double-click the date that you used when you created the backup set in Activity 13.4.

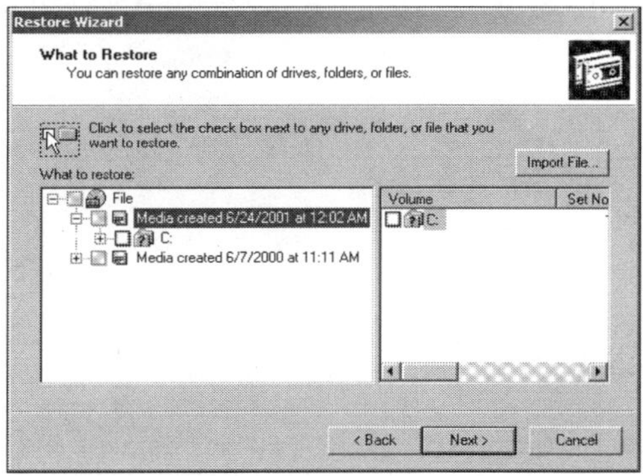

WHAT'S HAPPENING? The backup that you created in Activity 13.4 is selected.

Step 4 In the left pane click the plus sign to the left of **C:**.

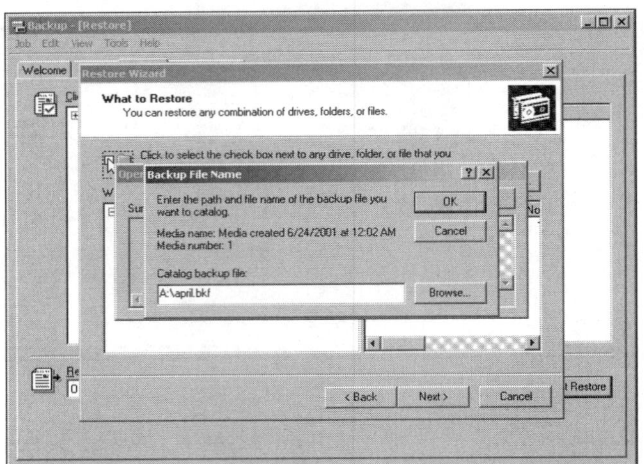

The Backup File Name dialog box appears. The last backup file name appears in the text box.

Step 5 Be sure that **A:\april.bkf** appears in the text box. Click **OK**.

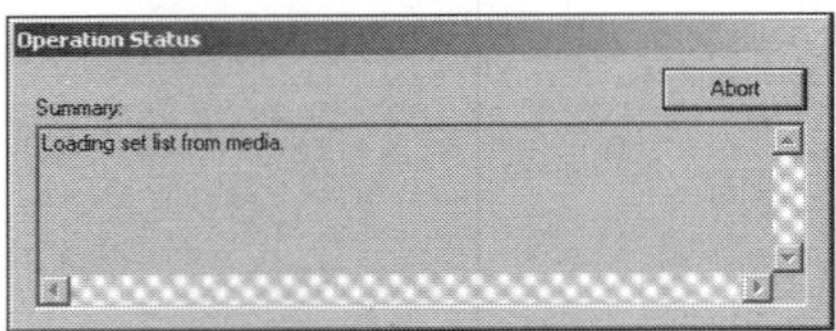

The Operation Status dialog box flashes on the screen followed by the Restore Wizard dialog box. The **WINDOSBK** folder has been located.

Step 6 In the left pane, click the check box to the left of **WINDOSBK**.

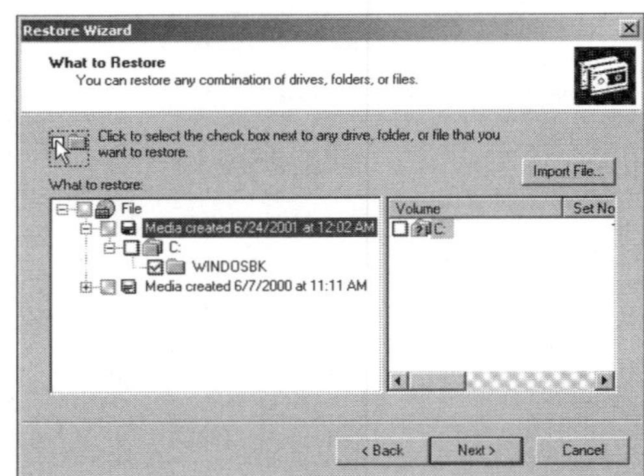

You have selected what to restore and where you want it restored.

Step 7 Click **Next**.

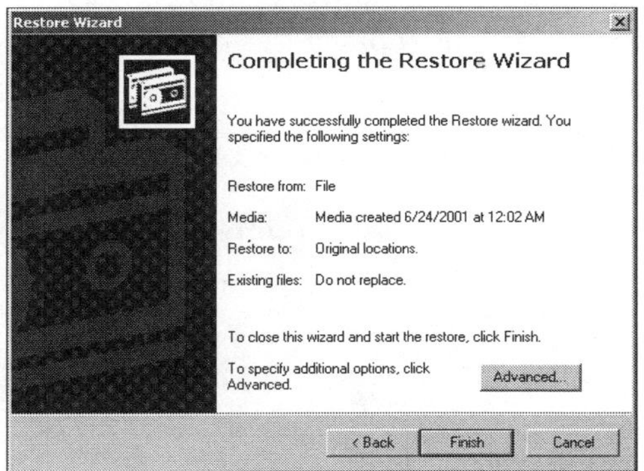

WHAT'S HAPPENING? You have begun the restoration process. The Advanced command button allows you to further define the task.

Step 8 Click the **Advanced** command button. Click the **Restore files to** drop-down list box.

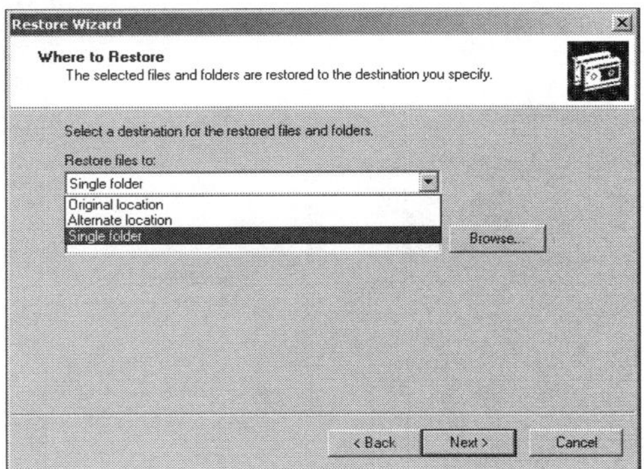

WHAT'S HAPPENING? You can restore the files to their original location, an alternate location, or to a single folder.

Step 9 Click **Original location**. Click **Next**.

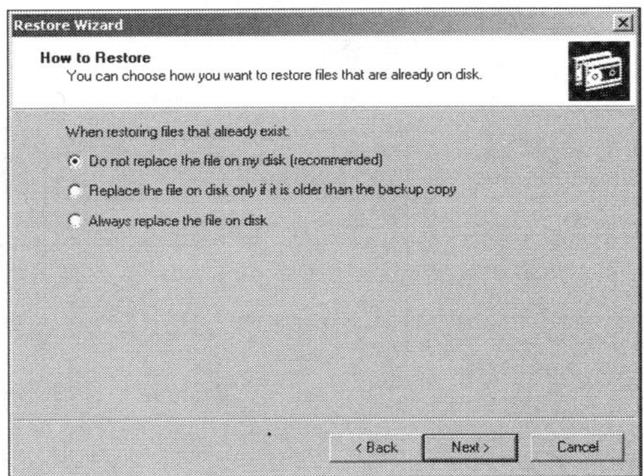

WHAT'S HAPPENING? Three option buttons allow you to select how to restore files that are already on the disk: do not replace the files, replace older files, and always replace the files.

Step 10 Click **Always replace the file on disk**. Click **Next**.

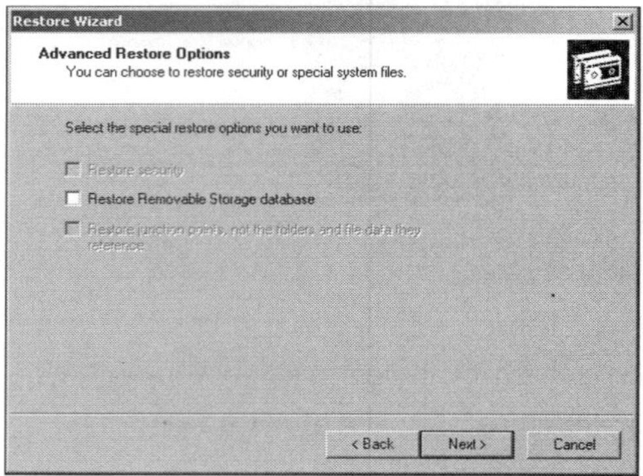

WHAT'S HAPPENING? Some options to restore security or special files may be available. In this instance, they do not apply.

Step 11 Clear all check boxes. Click **Next**.

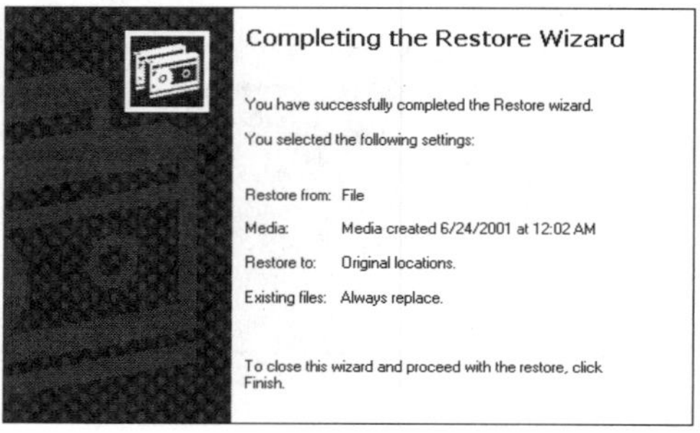

WHAT'S HAPPENING? The summary information appears and indicates that existing files are always replaced.

Step 12 Click **Finish**.

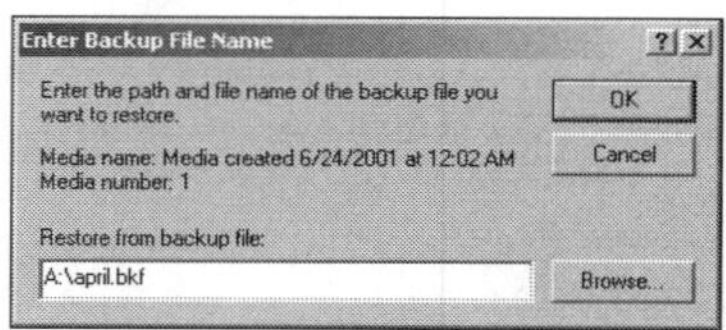

WHAT'S HAPPENING? You want to verify the name of the file to restore.

Step 13 Be sure the text box contains **A:\april.bfk**. Click **OK**.

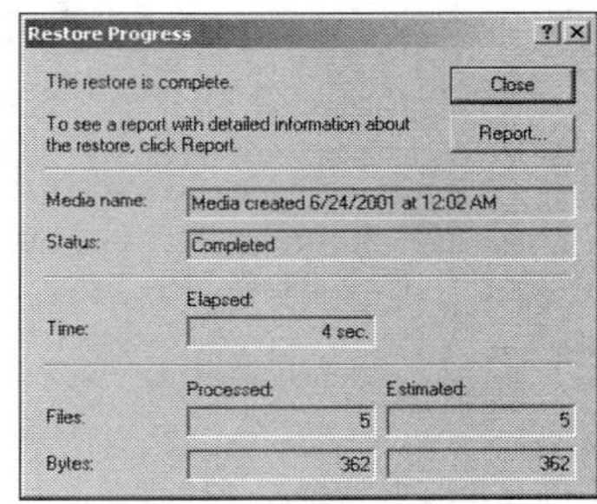

WHAT'S HAPPENING? The Restore Progress dialog box appears on the screen. It shows the task's progress followed by the summary information.

Step 14 Click the **Report** command button.

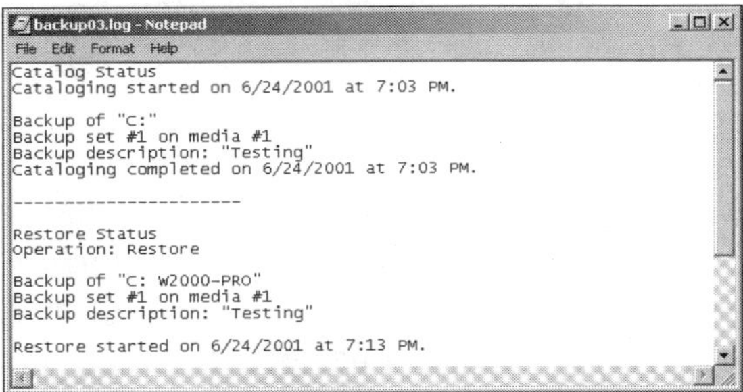


```
Catalog Status
Cataloging started on 6/24/2001 at 7:03 PM.

Backup of "C:"
Backup set #1 on media #1
Backup description: "Testing"
Cataloging completed on 6/24/2001 at 7:03 PM.

----------------------

Restore Status
Operation: Restore

Backup of "C: W2000-PRO"
Backup set #1 on media #1
Backup description: "Testing"

Restore started on 6/24/2001 at 7:13 PM.
```

WHAT'S HAPPENING? The report indicates that the backup set has been restored.

Step 15 Close Notepad. Close the Restore Progress dialog box.

Step 16 Click the **Schedule Jobs** tab.

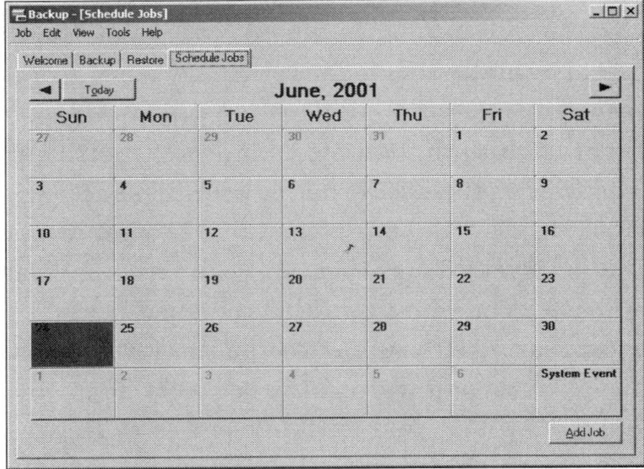

WHAT'S HAPPENING? You do not have to use the wizards to backup and restore files. You can use the options on the Backup and Restore pages. You can also schedule when Windows will perform the Backup task. Clicking the Add Job command button starts the Backup Wizard so that you can enter your backup settings and schedule the backup job.

Step 17 Close the Backup window.

WHAT'S HAPPENING? You have returned to the desktop.

13.7 TROUBLESHOOTING

Backing up your data is a critical task that must be done on a regular basis. If something happens to your files, you can use Restore to fix the problem. But if your computer system will not start or "boot," then you have a different problem. Windows 2000 Professional as an operating system has tools to assist you if your computer does not start correctly or start at all. In order to use these tools, it is important to have some understanding of what happens when you boot your computer.

13.8 THE BOOT PROCESS

When you power on a computer, the processor locates and executes startup routines (programs) that are stored in ***BIOS (Basic Input Output System)***. These essential routines that test your hardware at startup, begin the loading of the operating system, and support the transfer of data among your hardware devices are all controlled by BIOS. BIOS is stored in ROM (read-only memory) on a chip called ***ROM-BIOS***, so that these tasks can be executed.

When you turn on your computer, the POST (Power-On Self Test) checks for hardware errors such as a bad keyboard or memory errors. If it finds an error, it lets you know by either a series of beeps or a numeric error code. You would need to either have a reference manual for your computer to interpret the meaning of these codes or use the Internet to locate this information.

The next startup routine that runs is checking the first boot device for the operating system. Normally this is Drive A. The booting order of your drives is set in ***CMOS (complementary metal-oxide semiconductor)***. CMOS, pronounced "see moss," is a semiconductor (a chip) that stores your system settings such as what hardware you have installed as well as the boot order of your disks. The boot order simply determines the order in which drives will be searched for the operating system.

If you have a system disk (boot disk) in Drive A, then the system is started from Drive A. A ***boot disk*** is one that contains the most basic of the operating system files to get your computer started. If you have computer problems, such as your computer won't start or you have a virus, you will want a bootable floppy disk so that you can boot from Drive A. Normally, however, your system boots from Drive C.

When you boot from Drive C, the BIOS locates and loads the ***MBR (Master Boot Record)*** into memory. The MBR, which is located on the first sector of the hard disk, contains a small amount of executable code and the partition table, which stores information about the disk's primary and extended partitions. A ***boot loader***, the executable code in the MBR, locates the boot partition and then starts the process of loading the operating system. First to be loaded is a hidden system file located in the root of Drive C called NTLDR. The file name comes from Windows NT (NT loader). The process then switches operation from real mode to protected mode. ***Real mode*** remains from the original PC's operation, can only address up to 1 MB of memory, and cannot use extended memory. Real mode was used with DOS. It allowed other programs to directly deal with memory and communicate with devices. This can cause problems in running programs. Instead, protected mode "protects" the system. All programs must use the operating system to gain access to memory or devices. In addition, ***protected mode*** allows addressing of more than 1 MB of memory, supports the use of virtual memory (the ability to use hard disk space as memory), protects memory so that no two programs can access the same address space in memory, uses 32-bit processing instead of the old 16-bit processing, and supports multitasking.

The NTLDR file then uses settings located in the file called BOOT.INI, also located in the root of Drive C. Figure 13.1 shows an example of a BOOT.INI file.

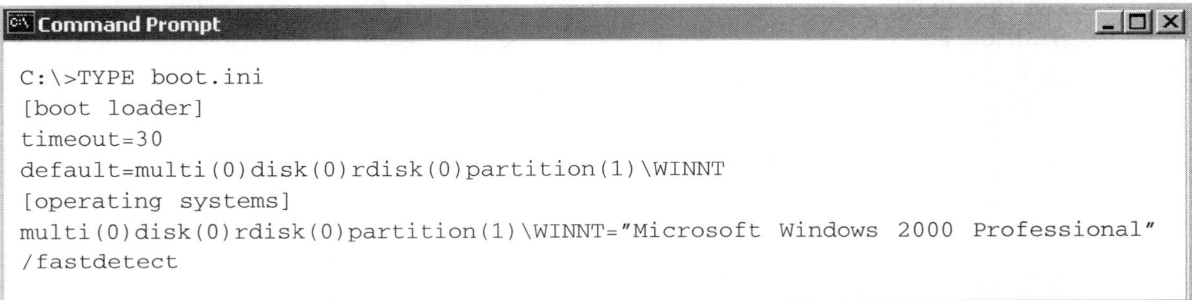

Command Prompt

```
C:\>TYPE boot.ini
[boot loader]
timeout=30
default=multi(0)disk(0)rdisk(0)partition(1)\WINNT
[operating systems]
multi(0)disk(0)rdisk(0)partition(1)\WINNT="Microsoft Windows 2000 Professional"
/fastdetect
```

FIGURE 13.1 A BOOT.INI FILE

In this example, the boot loader section indicates a timer of 30 seconds. If you had multiple operating systems, you would have 30 seconds to select one. If you did not select one in 30 seconds, then Windows 2000 Professional would continue to boot. In the next section, default refers to the path name and identifies the location of the Windows 2000 Professional partition. The syntax is multi(W)disk(X)rdisk(Y)partition(Z) \systemroot. Table 13.1 lists the meanings of the variables.

Parameter	Multiparameter Definition
W	The number of the adapter, usually 0.
X	Always 0.
Y	The number for the disk on the adapter, usually between 0 and 3.
Z	The partition number. All partitions that are in use receive a number. Primary partitions are numbered before logical drives. The first valid number for Z is 1. W, X, and Y start at 0.
systemroot	The name of the Windows directory where the Windows files are kept.

TABLE 13.1 THE SYNTAX OF THE BOOT.INI FILE

In this example, rdisk(0) refers to the first IDE controller on the hard drive and partition(1) refers to the first partition number of the drive. WINNT is the name of the directory where the Windows system files are located. The next section indicates which operating systems are available and which is the default. In this example, there is only one operating system, Windows 2000 Professional.

Then NTLDR loads and runs NTDECTECT.COM, a hidden system file located in the root of C, which checks the hardware on your computer so that it is configured correctly. Then the rest of the operating system files are loaded, such as the ***kernel*** (NTOSKNRL.EXE) and HAL.DLL, located in the Windows system directory, as well as all the device driver files needed to run your devices.

13.9 THE BOOTING TOOLS

When you start Windows, you have an opportunity to interrupt the boot process. When you see the opening screen, as shown in Figure 13.2, you have the opportunity to press the F8 key and boot into ***Safe Mode***. However, you must press it very quickly or Windows will boot. In addition, when you press F8, you must be patient, as it takes a very long time to boot in Safe Mode.

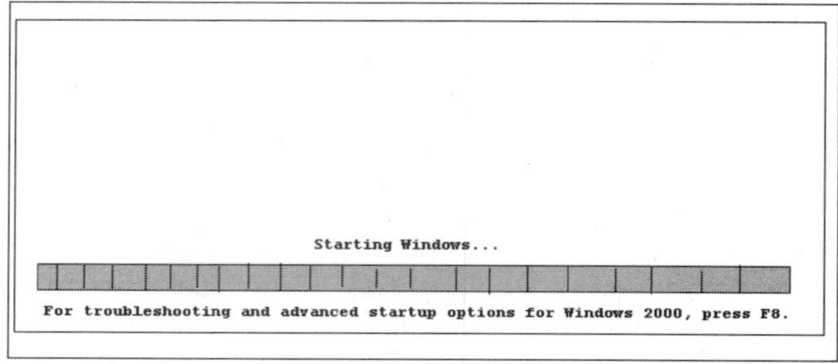
Starting Windows...
For troubleshooting and advanced startup options for Windows 2000, press F8.

FIGURE 13.2 THE OPENING SCREEN

When you press the F8 key, you open the Advanced Option menu, as shown in Figure 13.3.

Command Prompt

```
Windows 2000 Advanced Options
Please select an option:

        Safe Mode
        Safe Mode with Networking
        Safe Mode with Command Prompt

        Enable Boot Logging
        Enable VGA Mode
        Last Known Good Configuration
        Directory Services Restore Mode (Windows 2000 domain controllers only)
        Debugging Mode

        Boot Normally
```

```
Use ↑ and ↓ to move the highlight to your choice.
Press Enter to choose.
```

FIGURE 13.3 THE ADVANCED OPTIONS MENU

This menu provides a list of booting choices and gives you different ways to boot your computer. Choices on this menu can vary depending on your computer. Remember that booting will be very slow. The choices listed above provide the following three Safe Mode options: Safe Mode, Safe Mode with Networking, and Safe Mode with Command Prompt. When you choose Safe Mode or Safe Mode with Networking, Windows 2000 Professional will boot but first tell you that it is in Safe Mode. See Figure 13.4.

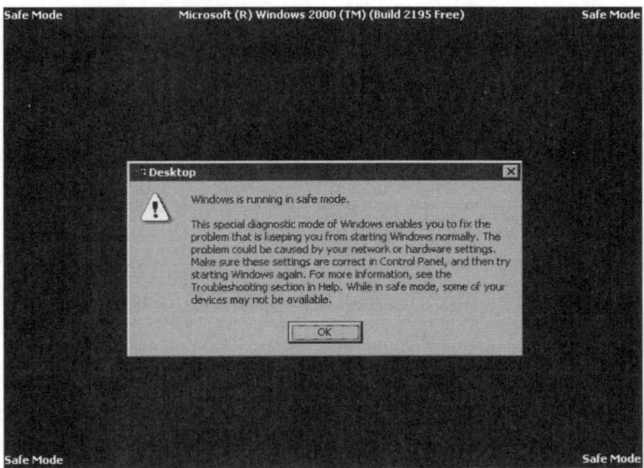

FIGURE 13.4 THE SAFE MODE OPTION

When you click OK, you then see the desktop in the lowest resolution, 640 by 480. When you choose either Safe Mode or Safe Mode with Networking, you first see this screen:

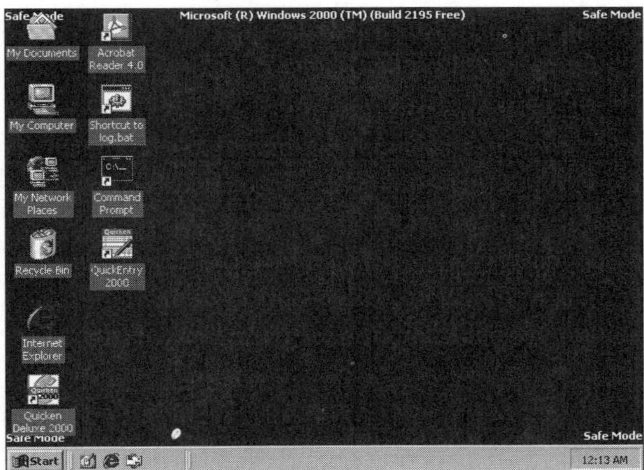

FIGURE 13.5 THE DESKTOP IN SAFE MODE

In Safe Mode, only the bare minimum set of files and drivers are loaded. Both Safe Mode and Safe Mode with Networking load the Windows 2000 Professional desktop. The only difference between these two modes is that if you are on a network, the second choice allows you access to your network. Windows 2000 Professional may boot to Safe Mode if there is a problem with newly installed software, with an upgrade of the operating system, or with newly installed hardware. Using Safe Mode, you may change settings in hardware or software and then attempt to reboot to see if you boot normally into Windows 2000 Professional. If you do, then you have solved your problem. Booting in Safe Mode is particularly valuable when newly installed software or device drivers do not allow your system to boot normally. It allows you an opportunity to repair the problem. It is also valuable when you are booting and the booting process stalls for an extended period of time or when Windows 2000 Professional is not behaving correctly.

Choosing Safe Mode with Command Prompt takes you to a Command Prompt window. See Figure 13.6.

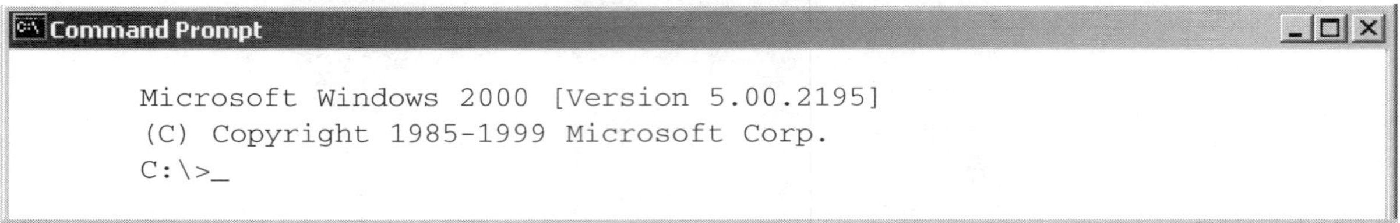
Command Prompt
Microsoft Windows 2000 [Version 5.00.2195]
(C) Copyright 1985-1999 Microsoft Corp.
C:\>_

FIGURE 13.6 SAFE MODE WITH COMMAND PROMPT

This option allows you to use all the commands that you have learned during the course of this textbook to fix problems. You may also use any Windows GUI program during this mode by keying in the command name, such as NOTEPAD or "C:\PROGRAM FILES\WINDOWS NT\ACCESSORIES\WORDPAD". Note that in the second example the full path name of the program is entered along with the quotation marks to include the spaces in the path name of the program.

The Enable Boot Logging choice boots Windows 2000 Professional normally but creates or updates a file called NTBTLOG.TXT. This file is saved in the WINDOWS directory and tracks all device drivers and services that load or do not load. A service is a program or process that provides support to other programs. By creating this file, you can look at it in any text editor and potentially identify any problem areas.

The Enable VGA Mode option is also a very valuable choice, as it starts Windows 2000 Professional using the basic VGA driver for your monitor. This mode is used if you have installed a new driver for your video card and you no longer can access your monitor. If this happens, you have no way to correct the settings in the GUI or in any other way. This option loads the most basic VGA drivers so that you can make the appropriate changes to your video settings.

The ***Last Known Good Configuration*** choice starts Windows 2000 Professional using the Registry information that Windows saved during your last successful boot and shutdown. If you have incorrectly installed a driver, you can recover and return to when your computer worked correctly. Any changes that you made since your last successful boot would be lost. This only works in case of an incorrect configuration and does not solve a problem with a missing or corrupt driver file.

Directory Services Restore Mode is not applicable for Windows 2000 Professional. It is only used with Windows 2000 Server. Debugging Mode will start Windows 2000 Professional and send debugging information through a serial cable to another computer. This will allow a technical support person to see what your problem is. Boot Normally is the default option and boots Windows 2000 Professional in the usual way.

13.10 MAKING BOOT DISKS

If you cannot start your computer system using these options, you have another choice—booting from a set of floppies. ***Setup disks*** allow you to reinstall or repair Windows 2000 Professional. In order to create setup disks, you must have the original Windows 2000 Professional CD. On this disk is a directory called BOOTDISK. You change directories to BOOTDISK and then run the program called MAKEBOOT.EXE, which is executed as MAKEBOOT A:. You also need four, blank, formatted floppy disks, which should be labeled Setup Boot 1, Setup Boot 2, Setup Boot 3, and Setup Boot 4. It is also useful to place the current date on your label so that you know when you created the disks.

The first disk in the series contains the necessary files for booting, BIOSINFO.INF, DISK101, NTDETECT.COM, NTKRNLMP.EX~, SETUPLDR.BIN, and TXTSETUP.SIF. The BIOSINFO.INF file contains information about using setup for your version of Windows and for your BIOS. Any file with a .INF extension is related to your specific computer configuration. The DISK101 file identifies which floppy disk you are using in your series of setup disks. The NTDETECT.COM file checks your computer configuration during the boot process so that Windows 2000 Professional can manage and configure your hardware. NTKRNLMP.EX~ is a compressed file that provides support for any computer with multiprocessors. Whenever you see a ~ in a file name, it indicates a compressed file. A compressed file is a file whose size has been reduced so it fits in a smaller area, such as on a floppy disk. Using the setup disks will automatically uncompress the files. You could also use a program called EXTRACT. SETUPLDR.BIN is the file that loads the Windows 2000 Professional setup. TXTSETUP.SIF contains detailed information on installing Windows 2000 Professional and provides support for your hardware devices such as your mouse. The other disks in the setup series primarily contain compressed files that are necessary to load Windows 2000 Professional. When you need to use the setup disks, you place the disk labeled Setup Boot 1 in Drive A and then turn on the computer. If your computer is set to boot from Drive C, you will have to change your CMOS settings to have it first read Drive A. The setup program will then prompt you to insert the other floppy disks as needed.

You may create the setup disks from the Run command from the desktop, from a Command Prompt window, by double-clicking the file name (MAKEBOOT) on the Windows 2000 Professional CD in Windows Explorer or My Computer, or by booting into Safe Mode from the Command Prompt.

13.11 ACTIVITY: MAKING BOOT DISKS FROM THE COMMAND PROMPT

Note 1: If you do not have access to the Windows 2000 Professional CD, you will not be able to do this activity. If that is the case, just read the steps in the activity.

Note 2: Have four blank formatted disks available, labeled Setup Boot 1, Setup Boot 2, Setup Boot 3, and Setup Boot 4.

Note 3: Use the drive letter of your CD-ROM drive. In this example, the CD-ROM drive is Drive I. Your drive letter probably will be different.

Step 1 Place the Windows 2000 Professional CD in your CD drive.

Step 2 Open a Command Prompt window and key in the following: C:\>**I:** Enter

Step 3 Key in the following: I:\>**CD BOOTDISK** Enter

Step 4 Key in the following: I:\BOOTDISK>**MAKEBOOT A:** Enter

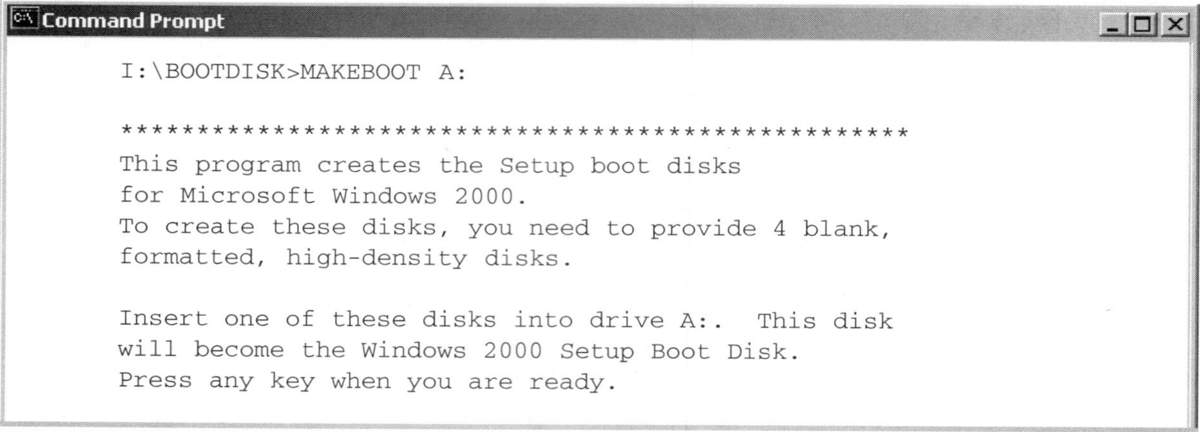

WHAT'S HAPPENING? As you can see, you are now going to create the setup boot disks. You are prompted to place your first labeled disk in Drive A.

Step 5 Place the first disk, labeled Setup Boot 1, in Drive A and press Enter

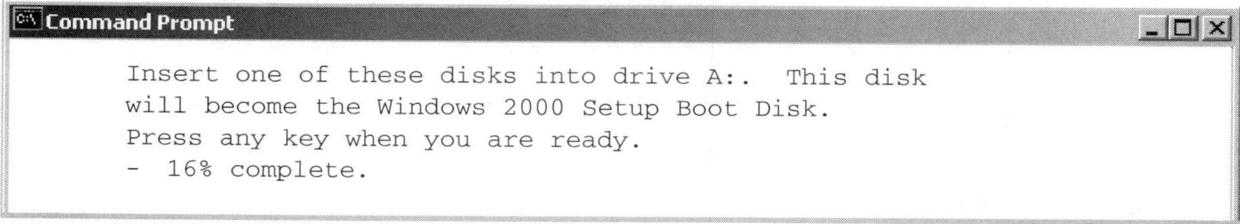

WHAT'S HAPPENING? As the disk is prepared, you see a progress indicator. When the first disk is done, you see the following screen.

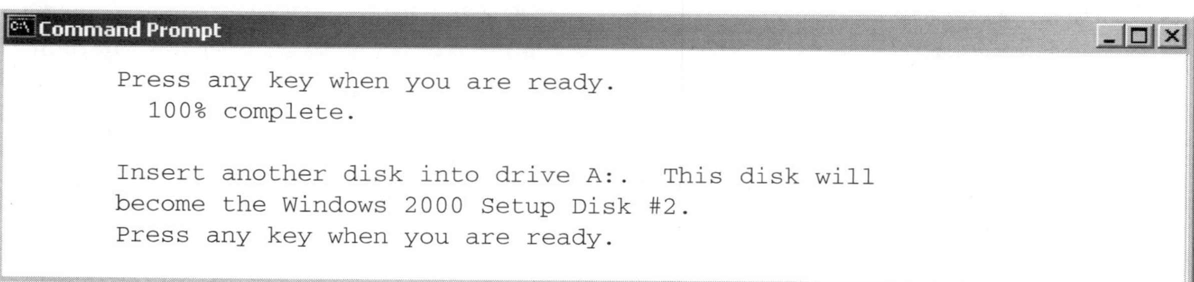

Step 6 Place your second disk in Drive A and continue the process. Keep inserting the disks as you are prompted until your setup disk set is complete. At the completion of your activity, your screen will look as follows:

```
Command Prompt

I:\BOOTDISK>MAKEBOOT A:

****************************************************
This program creates the Setup boot disks
for Microsoft Windows 2000.
To create these disks, you need to provide 4 blank,
formatted, high-density disks.

Insert one of these disks into drive A:.  This disk
will become the Windows 2000 Setup Boot Disk.
Press any key when you are ready.
  100% complete.

Insert another disk into drive A:.  This disk will
become the Windows 2000 Setup Disk #2.
Press any key when you are ready.
  100% complete.

Insert another disk into drive A:.  This disk will
become the Windows 2000 Setup Disk #3.
Press any key when you are ready.
  100% complete.

Insert another disk into drive A:.  This disk will
become the Windows 2000 Setup Disk #4.
Press any key when you are ready.
  100% complete.

The setup boot disks have been created successfully.
****************************************************

I:\BOOTDISK>
I:\BOOTDISK>_
```

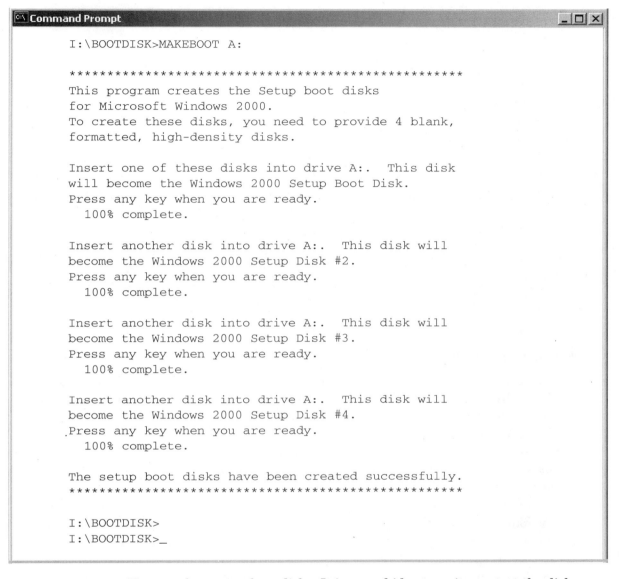

WHAT'S HAPPENING? You now have your boot disks. It is a good idea to write-protect the disks so that the files will not be overwritten and to protect them against viruses.

Step 7 Key in the following: I:\BOOTDISK>**CD ** Enter

Step 8 Key in the following: I:\>**C:** Enter

Step 9 Remove the Windows 2000 Professional CD and the last floppy disk. Insert the disk labeled Setup Boot 1.

Step 10 Key in the following: C:\>**DIR A:** Enter

```
Command Prompt

C:\>DIR A:
 Volume in drive A is W2PFPB1_EN
 Volume Serial Number is 2752-16F2

 Directory of A:\
```

```
12/07/1999  12:00p                3 DISK101
12/07/1999  12:00p           34,468 NTDETECT.COM
12/07/1999  12:00p          717,749 NTKRNLMP.EX_
12/07/1999  12:00p          229,264 SETUPLDR.BIN
12/07/1999  12:00p          356,925 TXTSETUP.SIF
12/07/1999  12:00p           20,949 BIOSINFO.INF
               6 File(s)      1,359,358 bytes
               0 Dir(s)          96,768 bytes free

C:\>_
```

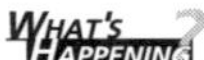

Here are the files that you need to boot the system. When you boot with the first floppy disk, the system will prompt you when you need the other disks. However, even though you can boot the system, you want to create another disk that will help you restore the system. It is the ERD (Emergency Repair Disk). It is important to note that the setup boot disks and the ERD that you create are machine-specific. You can use these disks only on the machine that created them. You cannot use them on a different computer.

13.12 EMERGENCY REPAIR DISK

Windows 2000 Professional has a built-in repair system for solving problems such as a corrupt Registry or a nonbooting system. This repair system relies on the creation of an ***Emergency Repair Disk (ERD)***. This is created in the Backup utility. This disk, along with the CD-ROM used to install Windows 2000 Professional, can fix a corrupt Registry. However, you must be able to boot into Windows. You cannot do so with the ERD alone nor with the Windows 2000 Professional CD, unless your system is set up to boot from the CD-ROM drive. The ERD is not a substitute for backing up your data. The ERD is for system problems. It can only restore the system as it was when the ERD was made. It is like a snapshot of your system at a specific point in time. Any time that you make a change to your system, such as installing new programs or hardware, you should update your ERD. The emergency repair process also relies on data saved in the %SystemRoot%\Repair folder. The notation %SystemRoot% indicates a variable name. You should substitute the name of your Windows folder, such as \WINDOWS\REPAIR or \WINNT\REPAIR.

To repair a damaged version of Windows 2000 Professional, you need both the Emergency Repair Disk *and* a Windows 2000 Professional installation CD or your setup boot disks. You would boot the system from the CD if your system allows or from your set of setup disks. Once you boot, you will then see the following screen.

```
Command Prompt

Windows 2000 Professional Setup

  Welcome to Setup

  This portion of the Setup program prepares Microsoft(R)
  Windows 2000 (TM) to run on your computer.
```

```
· To setup Windows 2000 now, press ENTER.

· To repair a Windows 2000 installation, press R.

· To quit Setup without installing Windows 2000, press F3.


  ENTER=Continue  R=Repair     F3=Quit
```

FIGURE 13.6 THE WINDOWS 2000 PROFESSIONAL SETUP SCREEN

Here you are asked if you want to install Windows 2000 Professional or repair a damaged version. To repair, you would press R. You would then see the following screen.

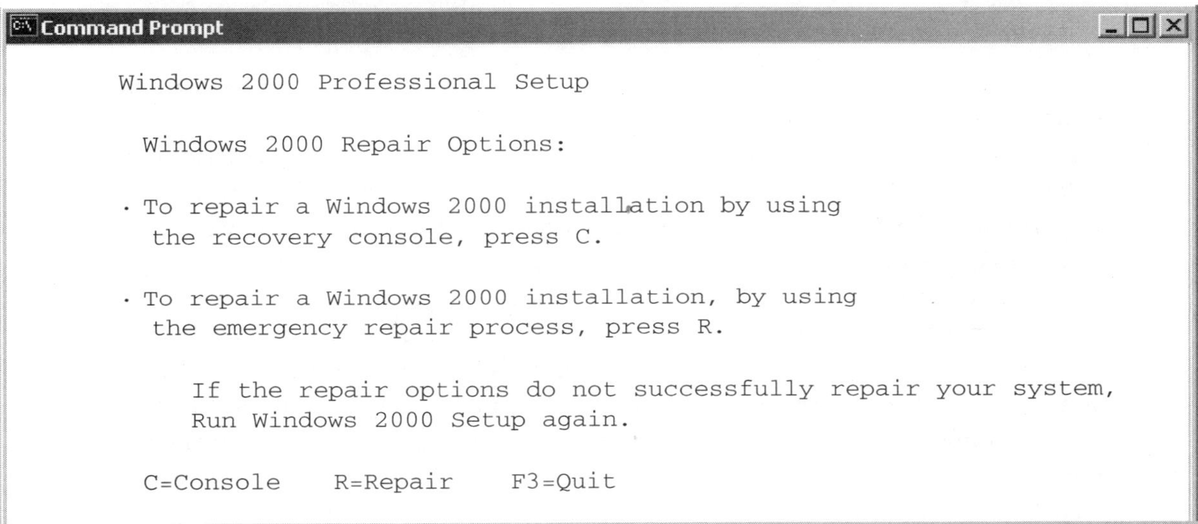

FIGURE 13.7 WINDOWS 2000 PROFESSIONAL REPAIR OPTIONS

This screen offers you the choice of using the Recovery Console or the Emergency Repair Disk. The Windows 2000 Recovery Console is a command line interface that you can start from the Windows 2000 setup program; it uses a set of administrative commands that are useful for repairing a computer. Using the Recovery Console, you can perform such tasks as starting and stopping services or formatting drives. Because the Recovery Console is quite powerful, it should only be used by advanced users who have a thorough knowledge of Windows 2000. In addition, you must be an administrator to use the Recovery Console.

In this case, to use your ERD, you would press R. You then would be presented with the following screen.

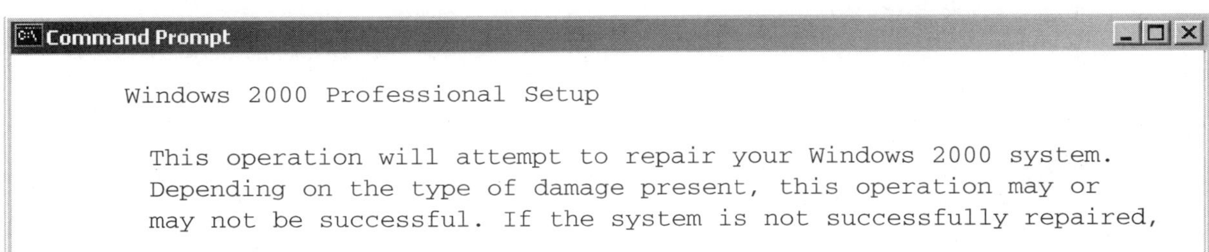

Command Prompt
Windows 2000 Professional Setup
This operation will attempt to repair your Windows 2000 system. Depending on the type of damage present, this operation may or may not be successful. If the system is not successfully repaired,

```
  restart Setup and choose the option to recover a destroyed system
  or system disk.

Select one of the following repair options.

· Manual Repair: To choose from a list of repair options, press M.

· Fast Repair: To perform all repair options, press F.

· To repair a Windows 2000 installation, by using


  M=Console     F=Fast Repair     ESC=Cancel     F3=Quit
```

FIGURE 13.8 MANUAL OR FAST REPAIR

Here you are asked to select a type of repair. Manual Repair allows you to repair system files, troubleshoot partition boot sector problems, and diagnose startup environment problems, but does not solve Registry problems. Fast Repair, as its name implies, is faster than Manual Repair and requires no user intervention. Unfortunately, Fast Repair will restore the Registry to what it was when you originally installed Windows 2000 Professional. Thus, any changes you have made would be lost.

If you choose Manual Repair, then you are presented with further choices. You will be instructed when to insert the ERD. If the repair program decides that a file is not the original file that was copied to your disk when you originally installed it, it will ask you if you want to repair that file only, skip the file, not repair it, or repair all files. In general, unless you know exactly what you are doing, it is wisest to skip the file and do not repair it. This is because, in general, you probably have newer files or newer versions of files on your hard disk that were not originally there. These current files are the ones you want to retain. Hopefully, by skipping the files, the repair process will solve your problems without overwriting files. When the repair process is complete, you will be prompted to remove the ERD and reboot the computer.

13.13 ACTIVITY: CREATING AN ERD

Note: You should have the disk to which you backed up files in Drive A. You last used this disk in Activity 13.6. Do not use your ACTIVITIES disk, your DATA disk, or your APPLICATIONS disk for this activity.

Step 1 Format the disk you used in the Backup and Restore activities.

Step 2 Click **Start**. Point at **Programs**. Point at **Accessories**. Point at **System Tools**. Click **Backup**.

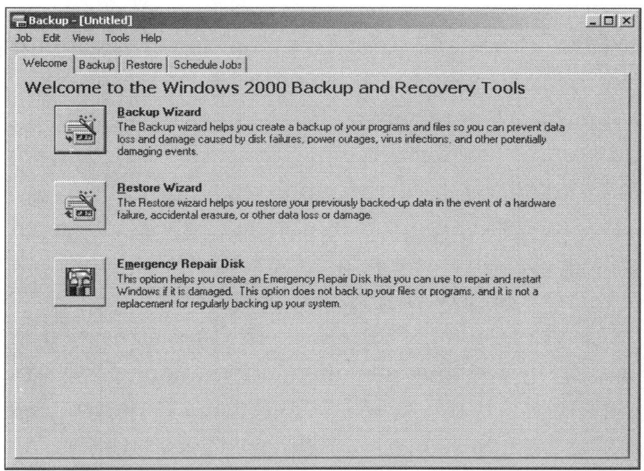

WHAT'S HAPPENING? The Backup window opens.

Step 3 Click the **Emergency Repair Disk** button.

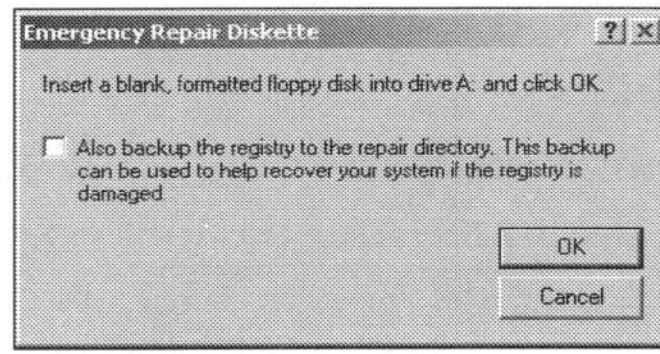

WHAT'S HAPPENING? You will need a blank, formatted 1.44-MB floppy disk to create the ERD. You should also back up the Registry. Remember, the Registry has information about the settings of your computer, such as which programs are installed, file associations, and other related information. If you do not back up the Registry, if you need to restore your system, you will be taken back to the original installation of Windows 2000 Professional without your software installed or your user preferences.

Step 4 Click the **Also backup the registry to the repair directory** check box. Click **OK**.

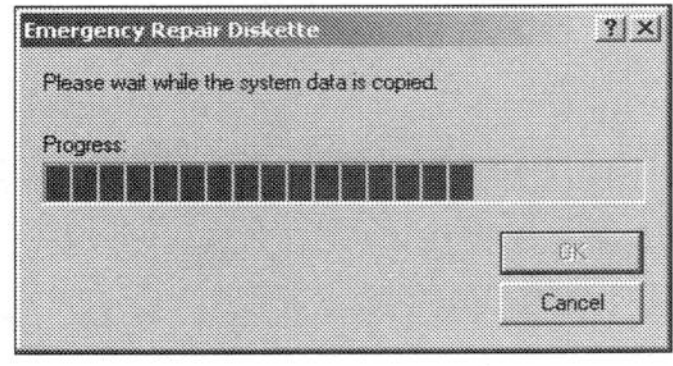

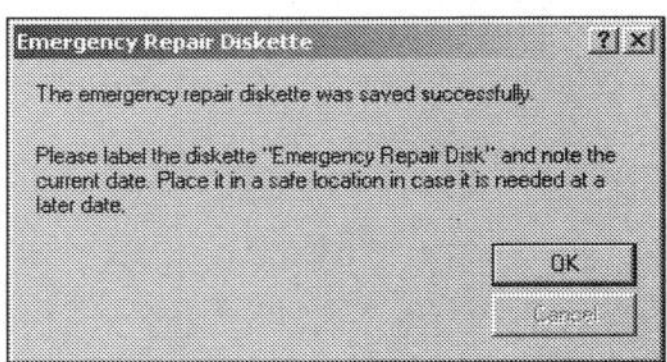

WHAT'S HAPPENING? A dialog box showing the task's progression briefly appears on the screen. When the disk is completed, the dialog box directs you to label the diskette, date it, and place it a safe location.

Step 5 Click **OK**. Close the Backup window. Remove the disk from Drive A and label it **Emergency Repair Disk**.

13.14 INITIALIZATION FILES

The Windows 2000 Professional environment is very customizable. You may have different users for one computer, each with his or her own desktop settings, menus, and icons. When you install new hardware, the operating system must know about the new hardware and any drivers for those hardware devices. You can double-click a document icon in Windows to open the correct application program, because, when you install an application program, the program "registers" its extension with Windows. As you can see, the operating system has much information to keep track of. All of this information is called the ***configuration information***.

In previous versions of Windows, the operating system and most application programs used ***.INI files*** to store information about the users, environmental parameters, and necessary drivers. The .INI extension is derived from ***initialization files***. The initialization files were broken into two types: system initialization files and private initialization files. Windows itself created the system .INI files such as WIN.INI and SYSTEM.INI, and application programs created private .INI files. These configuration files contained the information that Windows needed to run itself, as well as run the programs that were installed on a specific computer. The private .INI files were often added to the Windows directory and kept track of the state of the application, containing such information as the screen position or the last-used files.

The .INI files could specify many items that vary from one computer to the next. Thus, there could not be one set of .INI files that were common to all users. These files contained such items as the name and path of a specific file that is required by Windows, some user-defined variable, or some hardware or software configuration.

Windows itself had two primary initialization files, WINI.INI and SYSTEM.INI. WIN.INI was the primary location for information pertaining to the software configuration and specific system-wide information added by application software. The SYSTEM.INI file was the primary location for system information that had to do with the computer hardware. One might say that WIN.INI had information for how your system behaved, whereas SYSTEM.INI pointed the Windows operating system to the correct hardware and software components such as device drivers. In order to run Windows, these two files had to be present. The other initialization files that Windows used were PROGMAN.INI, WINFILE.INI, CONTROL.INI, and PROTOCAL.INI. PROGMAN.INI contained the settings for Program Manager. WINFILE.INI contained the settings for File Manager. CONTROL.INI contained such items as driver and pattern descriptions. These files were not required to start Windows, as was the case with WIN.INI and SYSTEM.INI. PROTOCAL.INI was added to Windows for Workgroups and contained the information for Windows networking.

The last file that Windows used was a file called REG.DAT. This file was the ***registration database***; it was not an ASCII file and could only be edited by a special application program, REGEDIT. It contained information about how various applications would open, how some of them would print, the information that was needed about file extensions associations, and how OLE (object linking and embedding) objects were handled.

13.15 THE REGISTRY

Instead of using SYSTEM.INI for hardware settings, WIN.INI for user settings, REG.DAT for file associations and object linking and embedding, and all the various private initialization files, Windows 2000 Professional uses a single location, called the ***Registry***, for hardware, system software, and application configuration information. Windows 2000 Professional does retain support for both WIN.INI and SYSTEM.INI, although Windows no longer uses these files, so they are available to any legacy application programs that might need to refer to them. Registry information comes from installing Windows 2000 Professional, booting Windows 2000 Professional, using applications, and interacting with the system. Every part of Windows 2000 Professional uses the Registry, without exception. The Registry files are kept in the directory %SystemRoot%\System32\Config. The Registry files that are backed up are kept in %SystemRoot%\Repair\RegBack. The files are the following:

- AUTOEXEC.NT Used to initialize the MS-DOS environment.
- CONFIG.NT Also used to initialize the MS-DOS environment.
- SETUP.LOG The file that contains a record of all the files that were installed with Windows 2000 Professional.

These above three files are copied to the ERD when you create it. The following files are the actual Registry files and have no file extensions.

- DEFAULT The default Registry file.
- SAM The Security Accounts Manager Registry file.
- SECURITY The security Registry file.
- SOFTWARE The application software Registry file.
- SYSTEM The system Registry file.

Another important file is SYSTEM.ALT, which is a duplicate of the SYSTEM file. There may also be other files in the %SystemRoot%\System32\Config folder that contain duplicate information or saved files.

These five files contain all of the system configuration and data settings. These are required during system startup to load the device drivers, to determine what hardware you have, and to handle the registration of file types. Although the ERD allows you to boot your system, if you do not restore the Registry, you would have to reinstall all of your software and any drivers you had added or any custom changes you had made. The ERD restores the original Registry created during setup.

13.16 THE RECOVERY CONSOLE

As mentioned previously, the ***Recovery Console*** is a command line repair tool that you can start when you boot the system using the setup boot disks. Once you boot with your system and choose R for repair, you see the following screen:

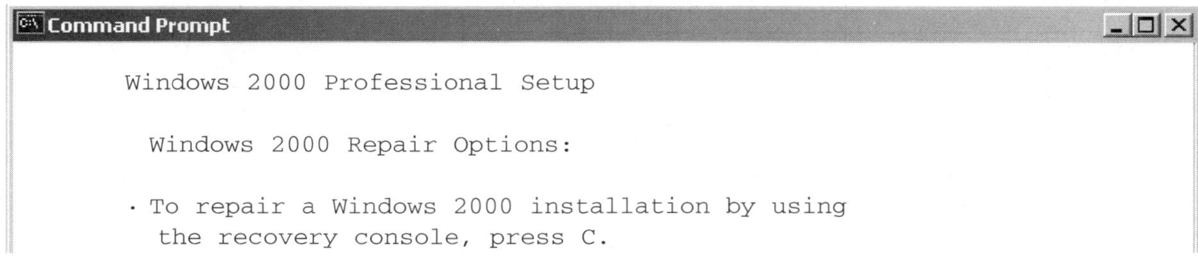

Command Prompt
Windows 2000 Professional Setup
Windows 2000 Repair Options:
• To repair a Windows 2000 installation by using
the recovery console, press C.

```
· To repair a Windows 2000 installation, by using
  the emergency repair process, press R.

     If the repair options do not successfully repair your system,
     Run Windows 2000 Setup again.

 C=Console    R=Repair    F3=Quit
```

FIGURE 13.9 THE RECOVERY CONSOLE

Once you start the Recovery Console, you use a set of commands that are separate from those used in the Command Prompt window. However, you will find that many of the commands are identical in syntax and in usage. When you are in Recovery Console mode, you can perform such tasks as starting and stopping services, formatting drives, reading and writing data on a local drive (which includes drives using NTFS), and performing many other administrative tasks. You should use Recovery Console only if you are an advanced user. You must either be an administrator or have administrator privileges.

There are two ways to start the Recovery Console. One way is to use the setup boot disks or the Windows 2000 Professional CD if you can boot from your CD-ROM drive. This is a valuable choice, since if your system will not boot at all, the setup boot disks will allow you to boot. The other way, which is the way that Microsoft recommends, is to install the Recovery Console on your hard disk to make it available in case you are unable to restart your system. This is where you would press the F8 key when you see the Starting Windows message. When you can boot your system, this method is faster and easier than booting from either the setup boot disks or the Windows 2000 Professional CD. You will then get the Startup menu. At that time, you can select Recovery Console from the Startup menu.

Once you start the Recovery Console, you will have to select which drive you want to log on to if you have a multiple boot system, and you will have to log on with the administrator password. Once you are in the Recovery Console, you can get help at the command line by keying in HELP. Table 13.5 lists the available commands with brief descriptions. Remember that the Recovery Console commands are more limited in terms of parameters and options than those in the Command Prompt window.

Command	Action
ATTRIB	Changes the attributes of a single file or directory. You may not use wildcards.
BATCH	Executes commands placed in a text file.
CD	Changes to a specific directory.
CHDIR	Same as CD.
CHKDSK	Checks a disk and, if needed, repairs or recovers it.
CLS	Clears the screen.

COPY	Copies one file at a time. You may not use wildcards.
DEL	Deletes one file at a time. You may not use wildcards.
DELETE	Same as DEL.
DIR	Displays files and directories and includes attributes. You may use wildcards.
DISABLE	Disables a Windows system service or driver.
DISKPART	Manages your hard drive partitions.
ENABLE	Enables a Windows service or driver.
EXIT	Quits Recovery Console and reboots.
EXPAND	Expands compressed files.
FIXBOOT	Rewrites a hard disk boot sector.
FIRXMBR	Repairs the Master Boot Record (MBR) by rewriting it.
FORMAT	Formats a disk.
HELP	Provides help for specific commands. Used alone, lists all commands.
LISTSVC	Lists all available services, drivers, and their start type. Use with DISABLE and ENABLE.
LOGON	Restarts Recovery Console.
MAP	Lists all drive letters (maps the physical devices) that are currently active.
MD	Creates a directory.
MKDIR	Same as MD.
MORE	Displays the contents of a file. Same as TYPE.
RD	Removes a directory.
REN	Renames a file or directory. You may not use wildcards.
RENAME	Same as REN.
RMDIR	Same as RD.
SYSTEMROOT	Changes the default directory to the directory that holds the Windows system files. Usually WINNT or WINDOWS.
TYPE	Displays the contents of a file. Same as MORE.

TABLE 13.4 RECOVERY CONSOLE COMMANDS

13.17 ACTIVITY: INSTALLING AND LAUNCHING THE RECOVERY CONSOLE (A READ-ONLY ACTIVITY)

Note 1: It is unlikely that you will be able to do this activity in a lab environment. Remember, to install the Recovery Console, you must have the original Windows 2000 Professional CD as well as have administrator privileges.

Note 2: Use the drive letter of your CD-ROM drive. In this example, the CD-ROM drive is Drive I. Your drive letter probably will be different.

Note 3: If the Windows 2000 setup CD window automatically opens, close it.

Step 1 Open a Command Prompt window.

Step 2 Place the Windows 2000 Professional CD in the CD-ROM drive.

Step 3 Key in the following: C:\>**I:** Enter

Step 4 Key in the following: I:\>**\i386\winnt32 /cmdcons** Enter

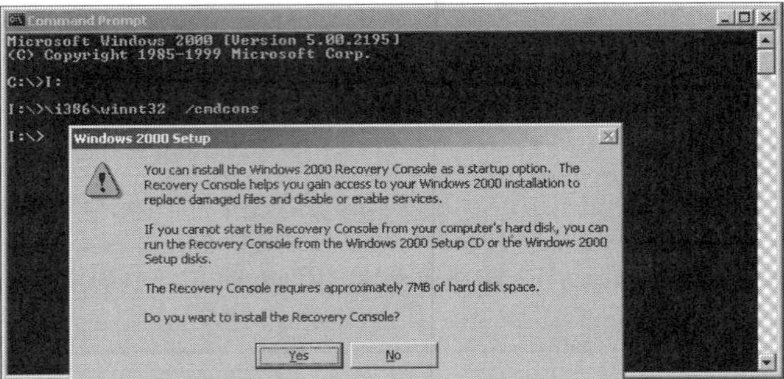

You changed drives to your CD-ROM drive. You then keyed in the command name, giving the entire path to the program you wanted to run, /cmdcons, the command console. This program requires about 7 MB of hard disk space. Now you have the opportunity to install the Recovery Console.

Step 5 Click **Yes**.

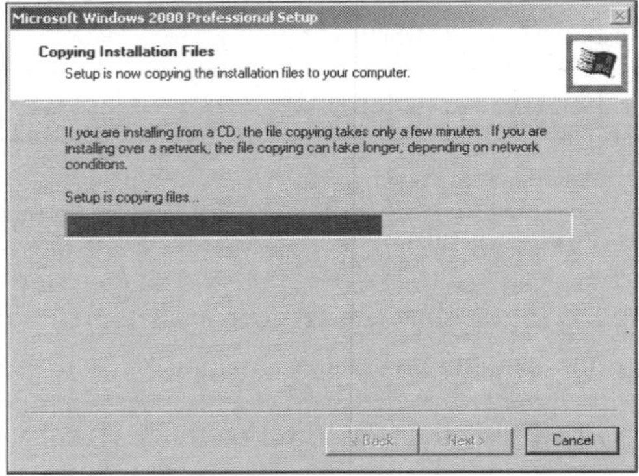

You see the progress of the program as it is copied to your hard disk. You then see the following message:

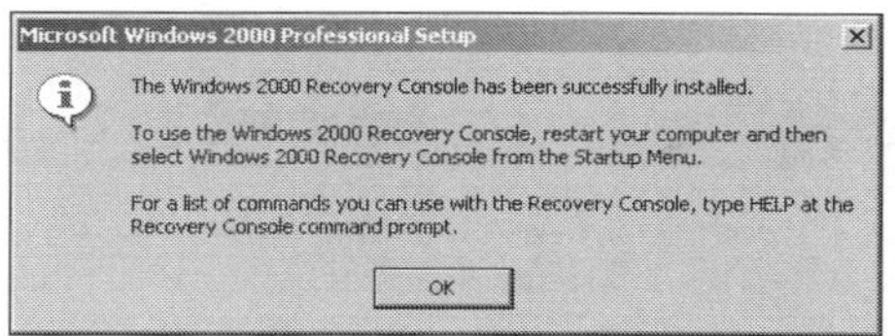

Microsoft Windows 2000 Professional Setup
The Windows 2000 Recovery Console has been successfully installed.
To use the Windows 2000 Recovery Console, restart your computer and then select Windows 2000 Recovery Console from the Startup Menu.
For a list of commands you can use with the Recovery Console, type HELP at the Recovery Console command prompt.
OK

Step 6 Click **OK**.

WHAT'S HAPPENING? You have now installed the Recovery Console. To use it, you must restart your computer.

Step 7 Close the Command Prompt window. Remove all disks from all drives. Click **Start**. Click **Shut Down**. In the Shut Down Windows dialog box, click in the drop-down list box and choose **Restart**. Click **OK**.

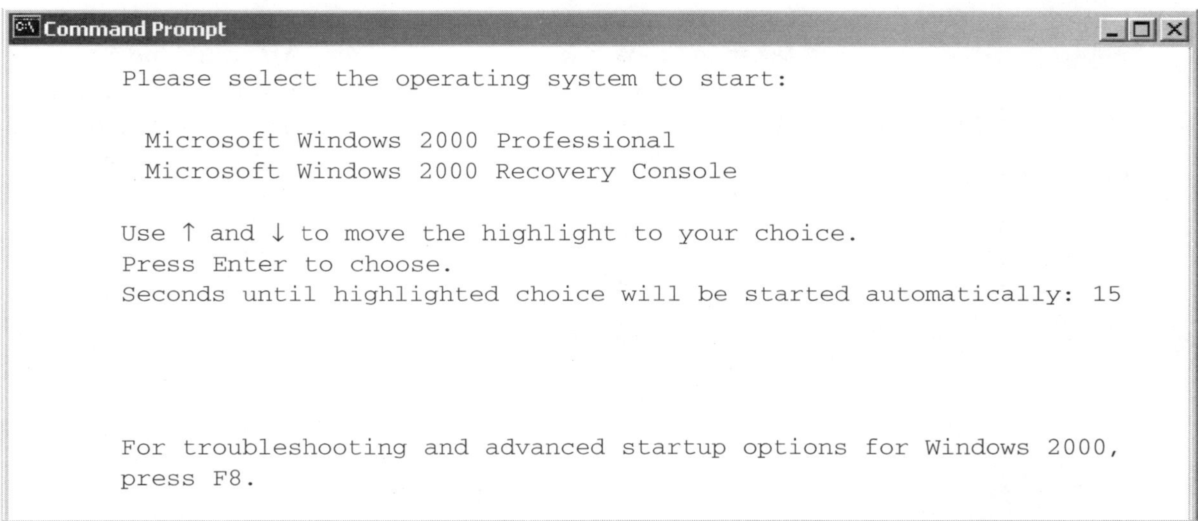

Command Prompt
The Recovery Console provides system repair and recovery functionality.
Please select the operating system to start:
Microsoft Windows 2000 Professional
Microsoft Windows 2000 Recovery Console
Use ↑ and ↓ to move the highlight to your choice.
Press Enter to choose.
Seconds until highlighted choice will be started automatically: 15
For troubleshooting and advanced startup options for Windows 2000, press F8.

WHAT'S HAPPENING? When you reboot, you now have the choices of starting Windows 2000 Professional normally or choosing the Recovery Console.

Step 8 Select **Microsoft Windows 2000 Recovery Console** and press Enter

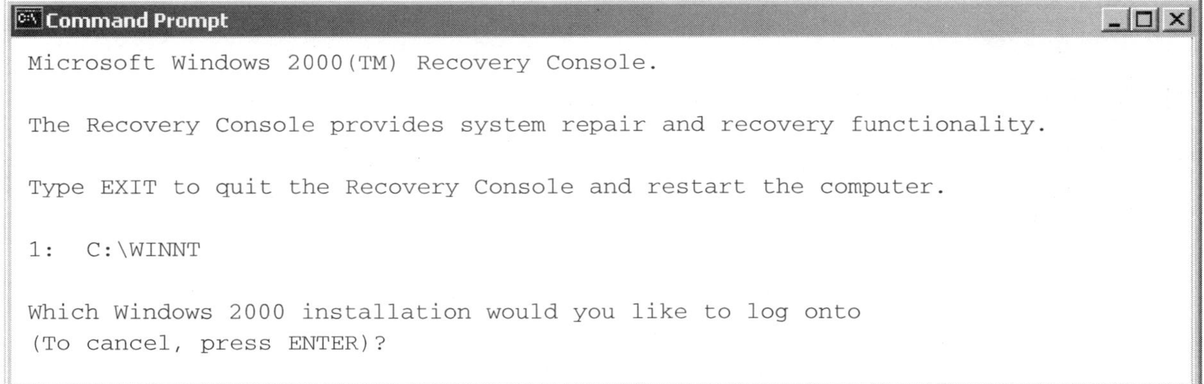

WHAT'S HAPPENING? The Recovery Console wants to know where you want to start it. Normally you select 1.

Step 9 Key in **1**. Press [Enter]

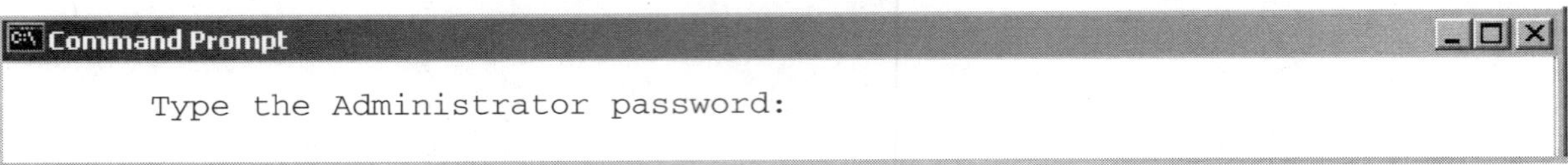

You must know the administrator password. Here is where you key it in.

Step 10 Key in your administrator password.

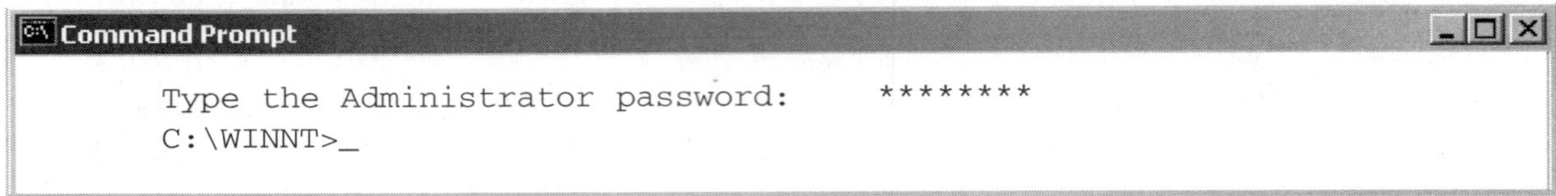

You do not see the password, only asterisks representing what you keyed in. You are then taken to the Windows system directory. You could have launched the Recovery Console from the boot disk or boot CD, but it is faster to do it the way you just did. In addition, every time you now boot your system, you will always have to choose whether you want to run Windows 2000 Professional or the Recovery Console. The default choice is Windows 2000 Professional.

Step 11 Key in the following: C:\WINNT>**HELP** [Enter]

Command Prompt

```
For more information on a specific command, type
Command-name /? Or HELP command-name.

ATTRIB
BATCH
CD
CHDIR
CHKDSK
CLS
COPY
DEL
DELETE
DIR
DISABLE
DISKPART
ENABLE
EXIT
EXPAND
FIXBOOT
FIRXMBR
FORMAT
HELP
LISTSVC
LOGON
MAP
MD
MKDIR
```

```
MORE
RD
REN
RENAME
More:      ENTER=Scroll <Line>   SPACE=Scroll <Page> ESC=Stop
```

WHAT'S HAPPENING? When you keyed in HELP, the commands stopped when you filled a screen. To move one line at a time, you press **Enter**. To move one page at a time, you press **Space Bar**.

Step 12 Press **Enter**. Press **Space Bar**

Command Prompt

```
RMDIR
SYSTEMROOT
TYPE

C:\WINNT>_
```

WHAT'S HAPPENING? Although many of the commands look familiar, they are not identical in usage to the commands you have learned.

Step 13 Key in the following: C:\WINNT>**DIR /?** **Enter**

Command Prompt

```
C:\WINNT>DIR /?

Displays a list of files and subdirectories in a directory.

DIR [drive:][path][filename]

  [drive:][path][filename]
              Specifies drive, directory, and/or files to list.

DIR lists all files, including hidden and system files.

Files may have the following attributes:

  D  Directory                R     Read-only
  H  Hidden file              A     Files ready for archiving
  S  System file              C     Compressed
  E  Encrypted                P     Reparse Point

DIR only operates within the system directories of the current
Windows installation, removable media, the root directory of any hard
disk partition, or the local installation sources.

C:\WINNT>_
```

As you can see, you have fewer parameters. You are also restricted to a few directories, most importantly the Windows system directory and any of its subdirectories. Remember, Recovery Console is used primarily for making a failed Window 2000 Professional installation work again, so that is why your access is restricted.

Step 14 Key in the following: C:\WINNT>**CD \WINDOSBK** Enter

```
Command Prompt
C:\WINNT>CD \WINDOSBK
Access is denied.
```

What's Happening? This is not a system or Windows directory so you cannot change directories to this location.

Step 15 Key in the following: C:\WINNT>**DIR SETUPLOG.TXT** Enter

```
Command Prompt
C:\WINNT>DIR SETUPLOG.TXT
 The volume in drive C is W2000-PRO
 The volume Serial Number is 2234-1CF8

 Directory of C:\WINNT\SETUPLOG.TXT

02/26/2000  10:27p  -a------      225,540 setuplog.txt
               1 File(s)        225,540 bytes
               477,331,456 bytes free

C:\WINNT>_
```

What's Happening? The DIR display now shows the file attributes for the selected file.

Step 16 Key in the following: C:\WINNT>**MORE NTBTLOG.TXT** Enter

```
Command Prompt
Microsoft (R) Windows 2000 (R) Version 5.0 (Build 219
 6 24 2001 23:56:22.500
Loaded driver \WINNT\System32\ntoskrnl.exe
Loaded driver \WINNT\System32\hal.dll
Loaded driver \WINNT\System32\BOOTVID.DLL
Loaded driver pci.sys
Loaded driver isapnp.sys
Loaded driver intelide.sys
Loaded driver \WINNT\System32\DRIVERS\PCIIDEX.SYS
Loaded driver MountMgr.sys
Loaded driver ftdisk.sys
Loaded driver Diskperf.sys
Loaded driver \WINNT\System32\Drivers\WMILIB.SYS
Loaded driver dmload.sys
Loaded driver dmio.sys
Loaded driver PartMgr.sys
Loaded driver atapi.sys
Loaded driver disk.sys
Loaded driver \WINNT\System32\DRIVERS\CLASSPNP.SYS
Loaded driver Fastfat.sys
```

```
Loaded driver KSecDD.sys
Loaded driver NDIS.sys
Loaded driver Mup.sys
Loaded driver agp440.sys
Did not load driver Audio Codecs
Did not load driver Legacy Audio Drivers
Did not load driver Media Control Devices
Did not load driver Legacy Video Capture Devices
Did not load driver Video Codecs
Did not load driver WAN Miniport (L2TP)
Did not load driver WAN Miniport (IP)
Did not load driver WAN Miniport (NetBEUI, Dial In)
Did not load driver WAN Miniport (NetBEUI, Dial In)
MORE: ENTER=Scroll {Line)  SPACE=Scroll (Page)  ESC=STOP
```

By looking at the **NTBTLOG.TXT** file, you can see what drivers were loaded or not loaded. In addition, note that the MORE command works the same as the TYPE command.

Step 17 Press the Esc key.

Step 18 Key in the following: C:\WINNT>**HELP SYSTEMROOT** Enter

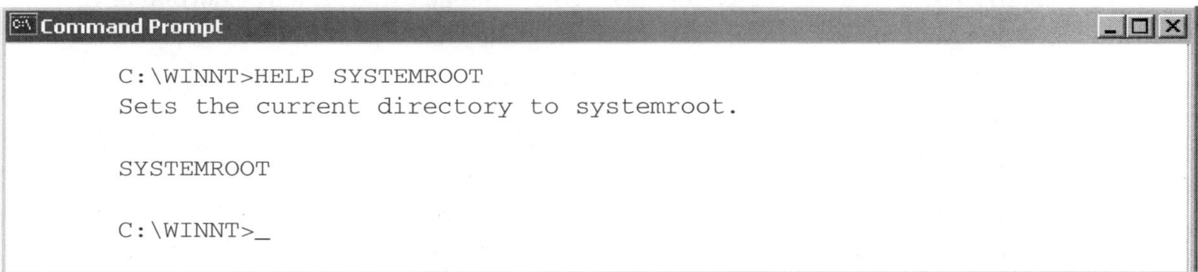

```
Command Prompt

C:\WINNT>HELP SYSTEMROOT
Sets the current directory to systemroot.

SYSTEMROOT

C:\WINNT>_
```

The SYSTEMROOT command changes your default directory to wherever the Windows system files are kept. In this case, **WINNT** is the directory where those files are kept.

Step 19 Key in the following: C:\WINNT>**CD ** Enter

Step 20 Key in the following: C:\>**SYSTEMROOT** Enter

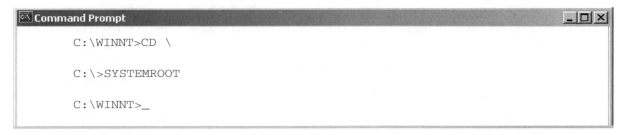

```
Command Prompt

C:\WINNT>CD \

C:\>SYSTEMROOT

C:\WINNT>_
```

You first changed the directory to the root of the hard disk. You then keyed in **SYSTEMROOT**, which returned you to the **C:\WINNT** directory where the windows system files are located.

Step 21 Key in the following: C:\WINNT>**EXIT** Enter

When you keyed in EXIT, your system rebooted. You will have to choose Microsoft Windows 2000 Professional from the operating system menu to reboot into Windows.

Step 22 Log into Windows 2000 Professional in the usual way.

13.18 REMOVING THE RECOVERY CONSOLE

If you no longer wish to have the operating system menu appear, you must remove the Recovery Console. The simplest way to do it is to use Help. Then in the Index, key in **Recovery Console**. Double-click **removing** and then follow the instructions listed.

CHAPTER SUMMARY

1. Backing up data is critical. A backup is a duplicate of what is on your hard disk.
2. A copy backup copies all selected files but does not mark each file as having been backed up.
3. A daily backup copies all selected files that have been altered on the day you perform the daily backup. The archive bit is not cleared.
4. A differential backup copies files created or changed since the last normal or incremental backup. The archive attribute is not cleared.
5. An incremental backup backs up only those files created or changed since the last normal or incremental backup. The archive attribute is cleared.
6. A normal backup, sometimes referred to as a full backup, copies all selected files. The archive bit is cleared.
7. Using Backup with a combination of normal backups and incremental backups requires the least amount of storage space and takes the least amount of time to back up. However, when restoring your files, this is the most time-consuming and difficult since you will need all the disks or tapes that you used.
8. If you choose to back up using a combination of normal backups and differential backups, the backup will take more time to perform, but it will be much easier and faster to restore because your data will be stored on a few disks or tapes.
9. You should have a regular backup schedule, as well as more than one copy of your backup media. Furthermore, at least one copy should be stored off-site.
10. The Windows backup program is called Backup and is located in System Tools.
11. Archiving data is removing data from the hard drive and keeping the data on an alternate media source. You may use the Backup program for this procedure.
12. You may back up selected files or all files.
13. You may use Backup Wizard, which leads you through the steps you need to take to use the Backup program.
14. The data saved using the Backup program cannot be read or used except by the Backup program.
15. Restoring files allows you to copy your files back to your hard drive from your backup media.
16. Restore is part of the Backup program located in System Tools.
17. You may use Restore Wizard, or you may go directly to the files you wish to back up.
18. You may use the Schedule Jobs tab in Backup to automatically schedule backups.

19. In using the Microsoft Backup tool, the Registry is not backed up unless you select the Windows folder.
20. When you power on a computer, the processor locates and executes startup routines that are stored in BIOS (Basic Input Output System). These essential routines test your hardware at startup, begin the loading of the operating system, support the transfer of data among your hardware devices, and are all controlled by BIOS.
21. The booting order of your drives is set in CMOS.
22. A boot disk is one that contains the most basic of the operating system files to get your computer started.
23. When you boot from Drive C, the BIOS locates and loads the MBR (Master Boot Record) into memory.
24. Real mode remains from the original PC's operation, can only address up to 1 MB of memory, and cannot use extended memory.
25. Protected mode mandates that all programs use the operating system to gain access to memory or devices.
26. Protected mode allows addressing of more than 1 MB of memory, supports the use of virtual memory (the ability to use hard disk space as memory), protects memory so that no two programs can access the same address space in memory, uses 32-bit processing instead of the old 16-bit processing, and supports multitasking.
27. When you start Windows, you have an opportunity to interrupt the boot process by pressing the F8 key when you see the message "Starting Windows." This takes you to the Advanced Options menu.
28. Once in the Advanced Options menu, you can select to boot into Safe Mode, Safe Mode with Networking, or Safe Mode with Command Prompt.
29. The default in the Advanced Options menu is to Boot normally.
30. The Enable VGA Mode option in the Advanced Options menu starts Windows 2000 Professional using the basic VGA driver for your monitor.
31. Last Known Good Configuration starts Windows 2000 Professional using the Registry information that Windows saved during your last successful boot and shutdown.
32. You may create the setup disks from the Run command from the desktop, from a Command Prompt window, by double-clicking the file name (MAKEBOOT) on the Windows 2000 Professional CD in Windows Explorer or My Computer, or by booting into Safe Mode from the Command Prompt. You must have the Windows 2000 Professional CD to create these disks.
33. To create the boot disks, you must go to the BOOTDISK directory and use the command MAKEBOOT A: It requires four blank, formatted floppy disks.
34. Windows uses a single location, called the Registry, for all hardware, system software, and application configuration information.
35. The ERD (Emergency Repair Disk), created in the Backup utility, allows you to repair a corrupt Registry.
36. The ERD, along with the CD-ROM used to install Windows 2000 Professional, can fix a corrupt Registry. However, you must be able to boot into the system. The ERD does not let you boot into the system.
37. The Registry files are kept in the directory %SystemRoot%\System32\Config.
38. The Registry files that are backed up are kept in %SystemRoot%\Repair\RegBack.
39. The Windows 2000 Recovery Console is a command line repair tool that you can start when you boot the system using the setup boot disks.

40. Once you start the Recovery Console, you use a set of commands that are separate from those used in the Command Prompt window. However, you will find that many of the commands are identical in syntax and in usage.
41. When you are in Recovery Console mode, you can perform such tasks as starting and stopping services, formatting drives, reading and writing data on a local drive (which includes drives using NTFS), and performing many other administrative tasks.
42. You should use Recovery Console only if you are an advanced user. You must either be an administrator or have administrator privileges.
43. You may install Recovery Console to your hard disk.
44. Once you install Recovery Console to your hard disk, you will always get a menu choice as to whether you want to load Windows 2000 Professional or the Recovery Console.
45. If you no longer wish to have the operating system menu appear, you must remove the Recovery Console.

KEY TERMS

.INI files
archive data
backup
Basic Input Output System (BIOS)
boot disk
boot loader
complementary metal-oxide semiconductor (CMOS)
configuration information
copy backup
daily backup
differential backup
ERD (Emergency Repair Disk)
full backup
incremental backup
initialization files
kernel
last known good configuration
Master Boot Record (MBR)
normal backup
protected mode
real mode
Recovery Console
registration database
Registry
Restore
ROM-BIOS
Safe Mode
setup disks

DISCUSSION QUESTIONS

1. Explain the purpose and the function of the Backup Wizard.
2. Why is it important to back up data? Programs?
3. Compare and contrast at least three types of backups.
4. Why is it wise to have more than one copy of your backup?
5. Two purposes of backing up files are to recover files after a disaster and to archive files. Explain.
6. Explain how you can restore files.
7. Briefly descibe the boot process.
8. What is a boot disk? Why would you want a boot disk?
9. Compare and contrast real and protected mode.
10. In the BOOT.INI file, there is the following entry:
    default=multi(0)disk(0)rdisk(0)partition(1)\WINNT.
    Briefly discuss each part of the entry.
11. What purpose does Safe Mode provide? How can you boot to Safe Mode?

12. Compare and contrast three options in the Advanced Options menu when you boot into Safe Mode.
13. Descibe the steps needed to create the setup disks.
14. What is the purpose and function of the Emergency Repair Disk?
15. What is the purpose and function of the Registry?
16. Why is it important to back up the Registry to the Repair directory?
17. If you want to use the ERD, what steps must you take?
18. What are .INI files?
19. Briefly descibe the purpose and function of the Recovery Console.
20. The commands used in Recovery Console differ from the commands used in the Command Prompt window. Explain.

TRUE/FALSE QUESTIONS

For each question, circle the letter T if the statement is true and the letter F if the statement is false.

T F 1. Windows does not provide a backup program for program files. In order to back up your program files, you must purchase a third-party program.

T F 2. You may restore files to the original folder or to a different folder.

T F 3. POST checks for hardware errors when you boot the system..

T F 4. To boot to Safe Mode, you hold down the **Alt** key when you see the message "Starting Windows."

T F 5. You may only create the setup boot disks from the Command Prompt.

COMPLETION QUESTIONS

Write the correct answer in each blank space.

6. A backup that backs up only the files changed or newly created since the last normal backup is called a(an) ____________ backup.
7. The Registry files are kept in the ____________ directory.
8. When you boot from the hard disk, the BIOS locates the ____________ (the first sector on the hard disk) and reads it into memory.
9. If you want to return to the configuration saved by Windows from your last successful boot, choose the ____________ booting option.
10. To use the Recovery Console, you must log on as the ____________ or have ____________ privileges.

MULTIPLE CHOICE QUESTIONS

For each question, write the letter for the correct answer in the blank space.

☐ 11. Which combination of backups takes the least time to create but the most time to restore?

a. Normal and differential.
b. Normal and incremental.
c. Normal and daily.
d. Copy and differential.

12. If your system is not working correctly and you suspect that the Registry may be corrupt, what can you do?
    a. Format your hard drive.
    b. Boot into Safe Mode and choose Boot normally.
    c. Boot with your boot disks and choose Repair.
    d. none of the above
13. Which of the following statements is true?
    a. Creating an ERD will automatically create a copy of the Registry.
    b. If you make changes to your system, you do not need to update your ERD.
    c. If you make changes to your system, you should create a new ERD.
    d. Using the Backup wizard will automatically restore and repair the Registry.
14. If you create a(n) ___________, you may reinstall or repair your Windows 2000 Professional operating system on your hard disk.
    a. Registry
    b. ERD disk only
    c. Last Know Good Configuration.
    d. set of setup boot disks
15. In Recovery Console, the DIR command displays the ___________ of each file and directory.
    a. size
    b. attributes
    c. both a and b
    d. neither a nor b

APPLICATION ASSIGNMENTS

1. Develop a plan for backing up your system. Include backing up your data files, your system files, and the Registry. Describe the time sequencing; i.e., how often you would back up what. Describe the tools and media you would use. Explain how you would go about backing up the critical files on your computer, including which files you would back up.
2. You are the owner of a small business. You have an accounting program installed on the computer. The accounting program is kept in a directory called Quicken. You keep your accounting data files in a directory called Accounting. You are using a word-processing program called Word. The program files are kept in a folder called Winword. You have business letters created in Word that are kept in a folder called Letters. You also use Word to create invoices and you keep those data files in a directory called Invoices. Develop a backup plan for this scenario. Include which files and directories you will backup and your backup schedule.
3. Explain the purpose and function of a set of boot disks. Describe how you would create a set of boot disks.
4. *It is critical to create an ERD disk. It is used when ___________.* Complete the fill-in portion of the question. Agree or disagree with these statements. Give your reasons for your choice.

5. Describe the purpose and function of the Recovery Console. Include in your answer at least two ways you can start the Recovery Console, as well as two methods for installing the Recovery Console. In addition, compare and contrast commands used in Recovery Console with those used in the Command Prompt window.

CHAPTER

14

ADVANCED TROUBLESHOOTING— CMOS, MEMORY, AND THE REGISTRY

LEARNING OBJECTIVES

1. Explain the importance of the CMOS Setup Utility.
2. List and explain the various types of memory.
3. Determine the available memory on a Windows computer.
4. Explain the purpose and function of the paging file.
5. Explain the purpose and function of the Registry.
6. Explain the structure of the Registry.
7. Compare and contrast Regedit and Regedt32.
8. Explain how to modify the Registry using Regedit.

STUDENT OUTCOMES

1. Use the CMOS Setup Utility, if possible.
2. Use the MEM command to determine available memory.
3. Configure virtual memory for optimum performance.
4. Explain how to modify the location of the paging file.
5. Use System Information to learn about your computer and its resources.
6. Use Regedit to modify the Registry.

CHAPTER SUMMARY

A CMOS (Complementary Metal-Oxide Semiconductor) is a computer chip built into your computer system. It is specific to your computer system. It is powered by a battery and retains all of your computer settings. Since the CMOS settings are so critical to the operation of your computer, it is a good idea to know how to access the CMOS and how to make changes to the settings.

The Windows operating system manages your computer's memory. Most of the time, you need not be concerned with the particulars of how this is done—you can let Windows handle it. However, understanding the concepts of how physical memory works and how virtual memory is implemented is necessary to a good overall understanding of the Windows operating system. This chapter will explore ways for you to discover information about your hardware.

There is another critical part of protecting your system, and that is dealing with and understanding the Registry. The Registry is the central database for all Windows configuration information. The Registry stores all of the configuration information about the hardware on a specific computer. It also tracks and contains all of the preferences for each user of the computer system. Typically, a user does not have to deal directly with the Registry; it is recommended that you make changes to it by using tools such as the Control Panel.

Nonetheless, even though you can corrupt the Registry by editing it, there are some problems that can be solved only by editing or modifying the Registry. Also, if your Registry becomes corrupt, you need to be able to restore it. This chapter deals with different ways of protecting and backing up your Registry as well as how to modify certain settings to improve the functionality of your operating system.

14.1 AN OVERVIEW OF CMOS

A ***CMOS (Complementary Metal-Oxide Semiconductor)*** is a computer chip built into your computer system. It is specific to your computer system. It is powered by a battery and retains all of your computer settings. It is battery-powered so that even if there is a power outage, your computer retains its settings. The batteries usually last five to seven years. The CMOS contains the settings that identify the type and specifications of your disk drives—how many and what kind, the assigned drive letters, and any password options. The CMOS also includes the ***boot sequence***. The boot sequence is the order in which the BIOS searches drives in order to locate and load the operating system. The normal boot sequence is to search for the operating system on Drive A, then Drive C, and then, on some systems, the CD-ROM. This order can be changed. However, if, for instance, Drive C is set as the only drive to be searched, if your system cannot boot, you cannot use boot floppies to boot the system, as it will never look for Drive A. The CMOS also contains any settings for power management, languages, and so on.

Since the CMOS settings are so critical to the operation of your computer, it is a good idea to know how to access this CMOS as well as how to change the settings. You should also either print the settings, if you can, or write them down. If your battery should ever fail or you have other problems, knowing what the CMOS settings are will allow you to repair your system.

Accessing your CMOS varies from computer to computer, as the CMOS is hardware-dependent, not software-dependent. Usually, when you boot your system, you will see a message displayed telling you what key or combination of keys to press to enter the CMOS utility program, often called Setup. Common keys used are the **Delete** key, the **F2** key or the **Ctrl** and **Alt** keys. On some computer systems, you see no information displayed on your monitor as you boot (during the POST—Power on Self-Test) until the system says "Starting Windows." Once you see "Starting Windows," you no longer have access to the CMOS utility. If this is the case on your system, and you want to see the POST, often pressing the **Esc** key when your computer starts to boot will display the POST information and the key or keys necessary to launch the CMOS utility. There are even computer systems that require you to insert a special start-up disk in Drive A to access the CMOS utility.

When you launch the CMOS utility, you must be exceedingly careful. You do not want to accidently change settings that might stop your computer from working or booting. In most lab environments, the computers will have their CMOS utility programs password-protected so that no one except the network administrator can make changes to the system. Because of this, the next activity is a read-only activity. The activity will describe some functions of two CMOS utilities, but you will not have to do the activity. You are going to look at the opening screen and the screen that allows you to change the boot order. Then you will learn how to exit from the CMOS utility.

14.2 ACTIVITY: LOOKING AT THE CMOS (A READ-ONLY ACTIVITY)

Step 1 Turn your computer on.

Step 2 Immediately press the F2 key (or watch the screen for which key(s) to press).

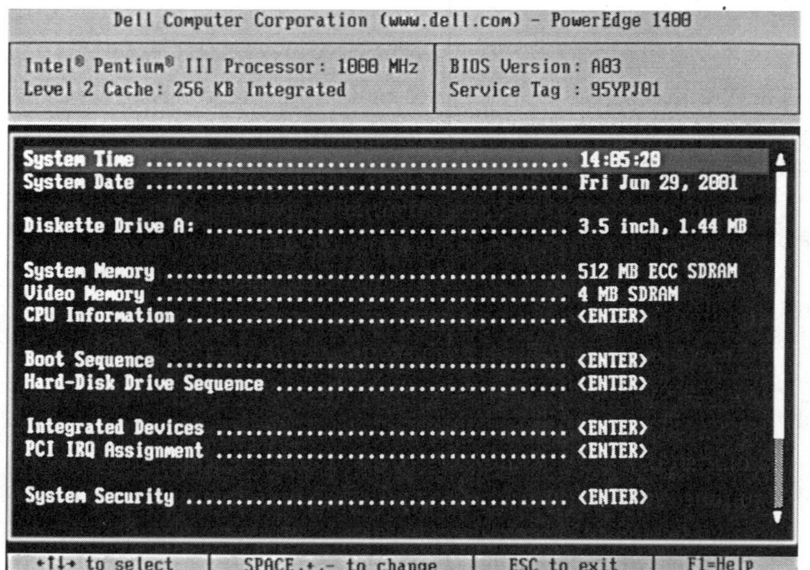

FIGURE 14.1 PENTIUM BIOS SETUP UTILITY

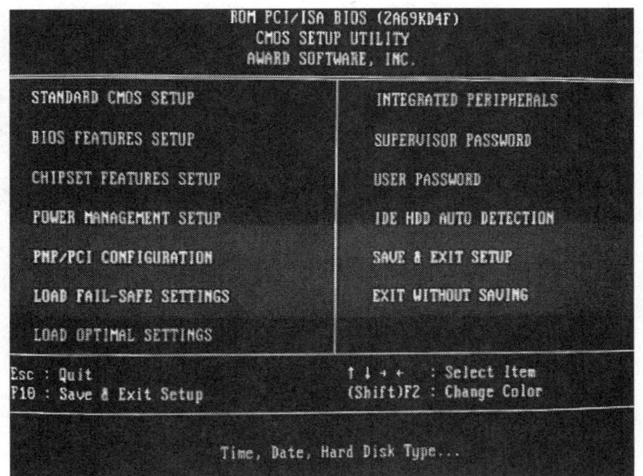

FIGURE 14.2 AWARD BIOS SETUP UTILITY

WHAT'S HAPPENING? Shown above are two common BIOS setup screens. The Pentium BIOS Setup Utility opening screen display gives you information about the memory, the language you are using, the system, and other information that is computer-specific. In the Award BIOS Setup Utility, you must use the up- and down-arrow keys to select an item. To see memory information and so on, you would select **CHIPSET FEATURES SETUP**. In both cases, you are interested in the boot order.

Step 3 In a Pentium Processor setup, arrow over to the **Boot** choice on the menu. In an Award BIOS Setup Utility, down-arrow to **BIOS FEATURE SETUP** and press Enter.

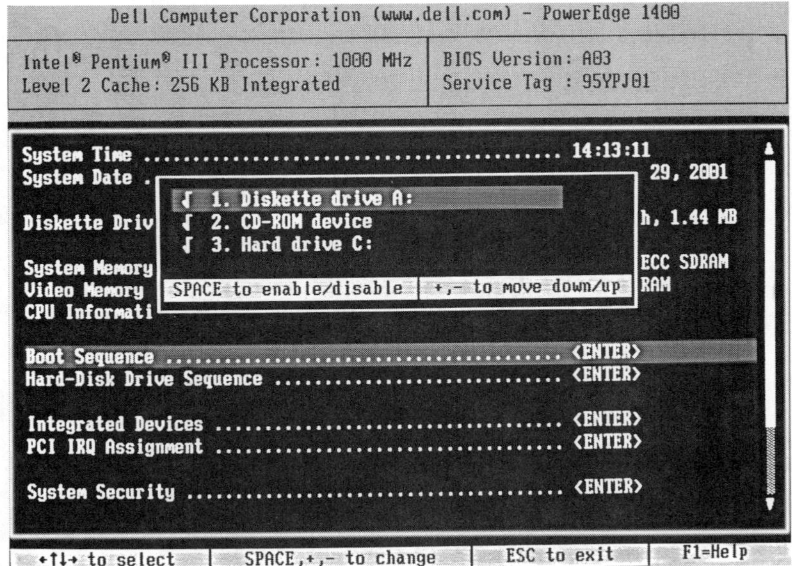

FIGURE 14.3 PENTIUM BIOS BOOT SCREEN

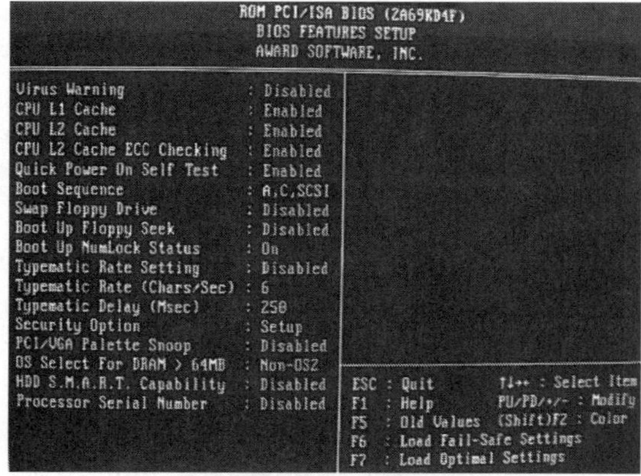

FIGURE 14.4 AWARD BIOS BOOT SCREEN

WHAT'S HAPPENING? The Pentium BIOS screen shows you the boot order on this computer. You use the ↑ and ↓ to select an item and then use the + and − keys to cycle through the available choices. Once you have made your selection, you would press **Esc** to exit.

In the Award BIOS window, the boot order is listed. In this example, the boot order is first Drive A, then Drive C, then a SCSI drive. In this utility, you would use the down- and up-arrow keys to move to the item of interest, then use the **PgUp** and **PgDn** within that item to make changes. Once you had selected an item, the **PgUp** and **PgDn** keys would cycle through the available choices for that item.

In either example, you could change the boot order so that it might check Drive C first, then Drive A. However, you always want to be able to check Drive A for the operating system so that if you have a problem with Drive C, you can use the different recovery tools available from Drive A.

Step 4 Using either BIOS Setup Utility screen, press **Esc**.

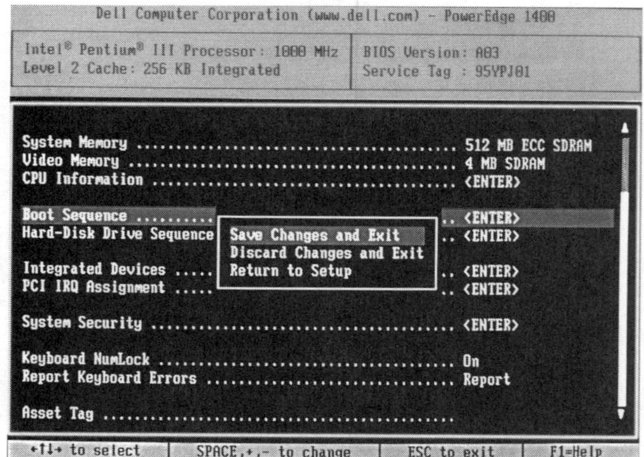

FIGURE 14.5 PENTIUM BIOS

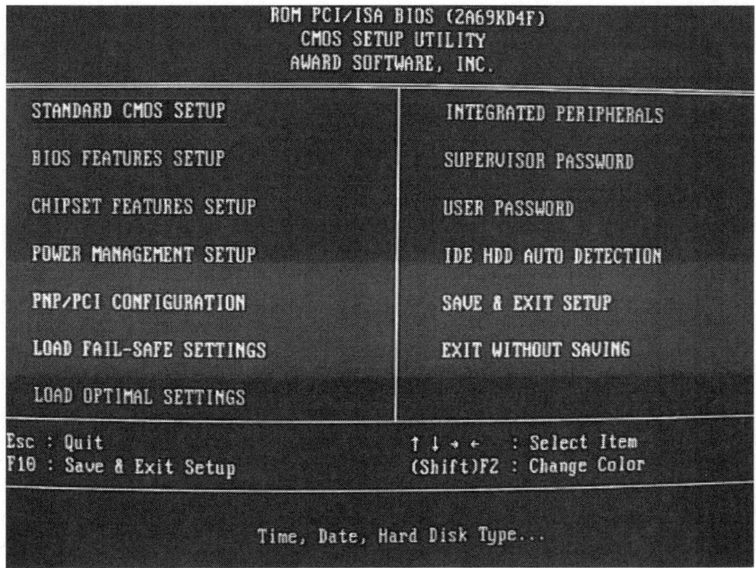

FIGURE 14.6 THE AWARD BIOS EXIT SCREEN

In the Pentium Exit Screen, the default choice is to save the changes. If you want to save the changes, you would press **Enter**. In the Award BIOS, the **Save & Exit** choice is selected. This will automatically save the changes you made. Note that regardless of the type of BIOS Setup Utility you have, you may restore the default settings. Since you are only looking at the CMOS, you do not want to make any changes.

Step 5 In the Pentium Processor Exit Screen, use the down arrow key to select **Discard Changes and Exit**. Press Enter. In the Award BIOS Exit Screen, down arrow to **Exit without Saving** and press Enter.

Your system will reboot.

14.3 MEMORY

There are two different types of memory to be understood: physical memory—the actual memory chips in the computer; and virtual memory (also known as logical memory)—which does not physically exist. This section will examine physical memory.

Memory is organized like a bank of mail boxes at the post office. Each box has a unique address. You do not know if there is anything in the mail boxes, but you can locate any mail box by its address. The same is true with memory. It also has addresses that are specific locations.

Personal computers use different microprocessor chips identified by number. Very early personal computers used the 8086 or 8088 Intel chip, which had 20 address pins. Address pins connect electrically to the rest of the system. Each address pin, when combined with other pins, can "map" or look at many addresses. Remember, all work on a computer uses only 0s or 1s; this is known as a "binary numbering system." The number of available addresses then becomes 2^{20}. The calculation is based on the base-2 number system “powered” to the number of address pins. If you multiply out 2^{20}, your final total is 1,048,576 unique addresses (1 MB of address space). The Intel 80386 chip had 30 lines, so the mathematical calculation is 2^{30}. This computes to 4 gigabytes. A gigabyte is a billion bytes; thus, 4 GB is 4 billion bytes. Though 4 GB of memory seems to be more than we will ever use, it was once thought that no one would ever need more than 640K of RAM! Today, 128 MB is standard with 256 MB and more becoming desirable.

However, one is still left with the legacy of the original CPU 1 MB limit. The 20-bit address bus allows for addresses between 00000H and FFFFH (0 and 1,048,575). The addresses are expressed in hexadecimal notation, meaning a base-16 number system. One reason for using hexadecimal notation is that binary numbers become extremely cumbersome. Base-16 uses the digits 0 through 9 and the letters A through F to represent numbers. As you know, the later processors can access up to 4 GB of addresses with their 32-bit addresses. When running MS-DOS, all of these processors must use a mode that emulates the original 8086 processor, which is in real mode. Only when the processor can access all available memory does it run in protected mode.

The real-mode processors divide addressable memory into segments. The 8086 and 286 processors and 486-and-above virtual 8086 mode were 16-bit processors with 16-bit registers. All addresses had to fit into 16-bit quantities. The processors used two registers to hold the address of the memory item being used—one to hold the segment address, the other to hold the offset in the segment that the particular addresses occupied. Addresses in this form are expressed as the segment address listed first, separated from the offset by a colon, as in CFFF:A3F1. The segmented form of an address can be converted to a physical address by shifting the segment address to the left and adding in the offset.

Why should you care about this “technogeek” discussion? Memory is your work area. The larger the work area, the more you can place there. More memory means that you will be able to work with enormous spreadsheets or large documents. It also means that your computer can handle larger and much more powerful application programs.

When you are running the Command Prompt, memory comes in three flavors: conventional, extended, and expanded, although today expanded memory is rare.

14.3.1 CONVENTIONAL MEMORY

Conventional memory is the first 640 KB of memory on the computer. All DOS application programs must think they are running in conventional memory. In the Windows operating system, they run in a virtual machine, so the program thinks it has its own 640 KB of conventional memory. A ***virtual machine*** is a software emulation of a physical computer environment.

Conventional memory cannot exceed 640K. The area of memory which begins at the end of conventional memory (640K) and ends at the beginning of ***extended memory*** (over 1 MB) is called the ***adapter segment***. Today, it is more commonly called the ***upper memory area*** or ***UMA***. It is also sometimes referred to as reserved memory.

The adapter segment, or upper memory, contains room for such things as ROM-BIOS routines, display adapters, and network adapters. Before DOS 5.0, this is where memory ended.

14.3.2 EXTENDED MEMORY

Extended memory is the region above the high memory area (covered later) through the end of physical memory. Extended memory is memory above 1 MB, which could not be addressed until the introduction of DOS 5.0. Extended memory is required by the Windows operating system. An 8086 or 8088 computer cannot have extended memory, nor can it handle the Windows operating system. Extended memory is managed by a real-mode ***memory manager***. This manager is ***HIMEM.SYS***.

14.3.3 EXPANDED MEMORY

Windows 2000 Professional will allot extended memory as ***expanded memory*** if legacy software needs it. An expanded memory manager is usually not required, but one is provided when you run a DOS-based program. It will establish a ***page frame*** in an empty area of the upper memory area. Each 16 KB is called a page, and the area of memory that receives the page is called a "page frame." The page frame is the storage place for the addresses in extended memory that contain data. The memory manager manages these pages with a page register and updates the page register to make the page frame point to the data in extended memory. The data then becomes available via the page frame so that older DOS programs can access it. This process is called ***bank switching***. Very few programs today actually require bank switching; instead, most will use the expanded memory allotted by the Windows operating system directly.

14.3.4 UPPER MEMORY AREA

There is another kind of memory called the upper memory area, the area immediately adjacent to the 640 KB of conventional memory. This area in reserved memory is not considered part of conventional memory. It is normally reserved for running hardware such as a monitor or a network card. However, information can be "mapped" from another kind of memory to the upper memory areas that are not being used by your system. The unused portions are called ***upper memory blocks (UMBs)***.

Upper memory addresses are also one of the critical system resources that are managed by plug and play. Memory between A0000H and C0000H is usually used for video memory.

14.3.5 HIGH MEMORY

The ***high memory*** area is the first 64 KB of extended memory. By enabling this area of memory, a portion of the OS that would be resident in real mode in conventional memory can be loaded into the HMA (high memory area).

14.3.6 MEMORY MANAGER—HIMEM.SYS

In order to use extended, expanded, or upper memory, Windows installs a memory manager, HIMEM.SYS. A memory manager is a software program that controls the access to the kind of memory you have.

HIMEM.SYS provides access to the memory above 1 MB on your computer. HIMEM.SYS ensures that no two programs will simultaneously use the same portion of extended memory. The Windows operating system will not load in protected mode without HIMEM.SYS.

How can you learn about the memory in your system? You can check the documentation for your computer to see what you have, but there is also a utility that will help you. There is an external command called MEM that will tell you about the memory in your machine when you are in the DOS window.

14.4 THE MEM COMMAND

The CHKDSK command gives you a report about disks and conventional memory. Because users always need more information about memory, the MEM command was introduced in DOS 4.0. The MEM command reports the amount of used and unused memory. It will report extended memory if memory above 1 MB is installed and will report all memory available for allotting as expanded memory. The syntax is:

```
MEM [/PROGRAM ¦ /DEBUG ¦ /CLASSIFY]

  /PROGRAM or /P          Displays the status of programs currently loaded
                          in memory.
  /DEBUG or /D            Displays the status of programs, internal drivers,
                          and other information.
  /CLASSIFY or /C         Classifies programs by memory usage. Lists the
                          size of programs, provides a summary of memory
                          in use, and lists largest memory block available.
```

The MEM command displays the amount of used and free memory in your system.

14.5 ACTIVITY: USING THE MEM COMMAND

Note: You are in the Command Prompt window with C:\> displayed as the default drive and directory.

Step 1 Key in the following: C:\>**MEM** Enter

```
Command Prompt

C:\>MEM


      655360 bytes total conventional memory
      655360 bytes available to MS-DOS
      633920 largest executable program size

     1048576 bytes total contiguous extended memory
           0 bytes available contiguous extended memory
      941056 bytes available XMS memory
             MS-DOS resident in High Memory Area

C:\>_
```

WHAT'S HAPPENING? Your display will vary depending on the amount of RAM in your machine. Compare the lines showing conventional and extended memory. In this example, you have a lot of extended memory, and very little of it is being used. This computer has 128 MB of RAM. Notice that MEM is reporting all the memory in the computer as extended memory (XMS).

Step 2 Key in the following: C:\>**MEM /C** Enter

```
Command Prompt

C:\>MEM /C

Conventional Memory :

  Name              Size in Decimal          Size in Hex
-------------     ---------------------    -------------
  MSDOS              12496       ( 12.2K)       30D0
  KBD                 3280       (  3.2K)        CD0
  HIMEM               1248       (  1.2K)        4E0
  COMMAND             3344       (  3.3K)        D10
  FREE                 112       (  0.1K)         70
  FREE              634704       (619.8K)      9AF50

Total  FREE :       634816       (619.9K)

Upper Memory :

  Name              Size in Decimal          Size in Hex
-------------     ---------------------    -------------
  SYSTEM            167920       (164.0K)      28FF0
  MOUSE              12528       ( 12.2K)       30F0
  MSCDEXNT             464       (  0.5K)        1D0
  REDIR               2672       (  2.6K)        A70
  DOSX               34848       ( 34.0K)       8820
  FREE                 784       (  0.8K)        310
  FREE               59168       ( 57.8K)       E720

Total  FREE :        59952       ( 58.5K)

Total bytes available to programs (Conventional+Upper): 694768
(678.5K)
Largest executable program size :                       633920 (619.1K)
Largest available upper memory block :                  59168   (57.8K)

    1048576 bytes total contiguous extended memory
          0 bytes available contiguous extended memory
     941056 bytes available XMS memory
            MS-DOS resident in High Memory Area

C:\>_
```

If your Command Prompt window was too small to display the entire output, you could have piped it to more (MEM /C ¦ MORE). By looking at this report, you can see that on this computer there is 128 MB of memory and that MS-DOS is resident in the high memory area.

14.6 THE PAGING FILE

One of the items that has the most impact on the performance of your computer system, other than the processor itself, is the amount of physical memory you have installed. To improve performance, Windows 2000 Professional uses space on the hard drive as virtual memory. When you run out of physical memory, Windows writes data from physical memory to a hidden file on your disk. When it needs that information again, it reads it back from what used to be called the ***swap file*** (which is now called the ***paging file***). The name "swap file" came from the fact that Windows “swaps” information to and from the hard disk when needed. This process is called ***demand paging***. This file is dynamic—it can shrink and/or grow as needed.

Let's say you are writing a book and have an 80-page chapter with color pictures. Such a document can be 20 to 24 MB in size. Even a computer with 128 MB of RAM does not have that much memory available—with the drivers, the running program, and other overhead—to keep a document of that size in memory. So, while you are looking at pages 7 and 8, pages 60 through 80 may be written out to the swap file to free up needed RAM. The swap slows down performance but gives the user more “room” in which to operate.

However, paging does impede performance since any disk activity is always slower than using memory. It is possible to set the place and size of the paging file yourself, but it is strongly recommended by Microsoft that you let Windows manage the paging file. There are, however, some instances where it may be advisable to specify where you want the swap file to be. Perhaps you have a second hard drive that is free of executable programs. There would be little I/O (input/output) to this drive. You may want to place your paging file on that drive, freeing up the read/write heads on your main drive. Also, if you elect to modify the placement of your swap file, be sure you are placing it on your fastest hard drive (the drive with the fastest access time). You may also have a large hard drive that has little information on it. In that case, you may wish to place the swap file on that drive and increase the paging file size.

14.7 READ-ONLY ACTIVITY: SETTING UP YOUR PAGING FILE

Note: The following activity is read-only. It is specific to the machines used for the demonstration. *Do not do this activity.*

Step 1 Right-click **My Computer**.

Step 2 Click **Properties**.

Step 3 Click the **Advanced** tab.

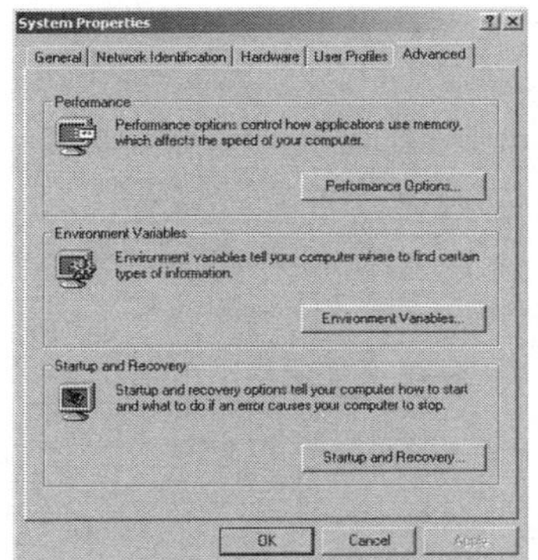

WHAT'S HAPPENING? You are looking at the property sheet for your system.

Step 4 Click the **Performance Options** command button.

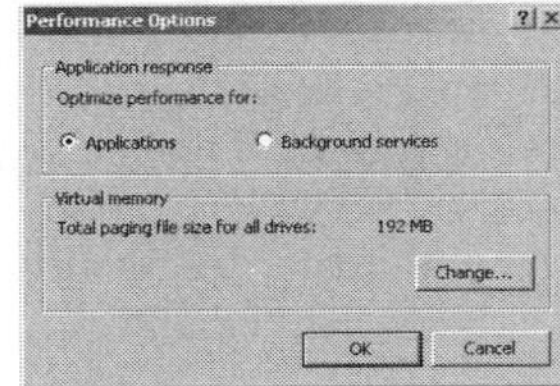

WHAT'S HAPPENING? The Performance Options dialog box tells you the current total paging file size for all drives. You can change this.

Step 5 Click the **Change** command button.

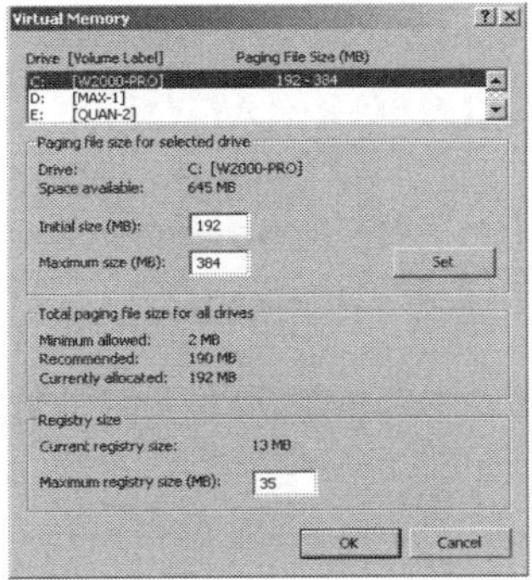

WHAT'S HAPPENING? You can set the paging file size and the Registry file size. In this example, the Recommended total paging file size is 190 MB, and it is currently allocated 192 MB.

Step 6 Click the question mark in the title bar, then click the Initial Size text box.

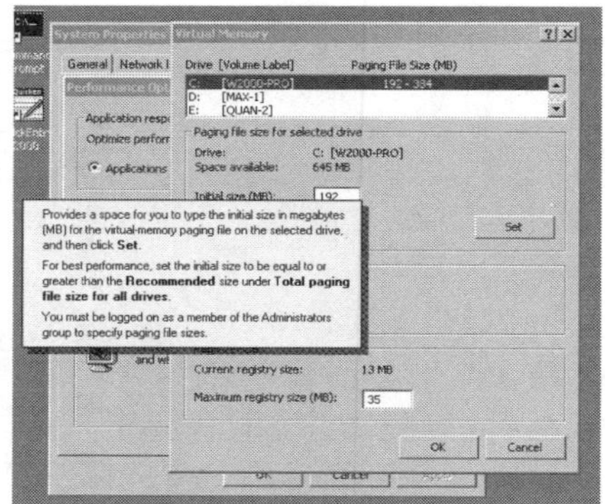

WHAT'S HAPPENING? As you can see, it is recommended that for best performance you follow Windows' suggestion and set the initial size to be equal to or greater than the Recommended size. You must also be an administrator to make any changes.

Step 7 Click **Cancel**. Click **Cancel**. Click **Cancel**.

WHAT'S HAPPENING? You have, in this instance, let Windows manage the paging file.

14.8 SYSTEM INFORMATION

You have used the MEM command at the Command Prompt. You have looked at your paging files. Windows 2000 Professional also has more tools to show you memory addresses and other system information.

14.9 ACTIVITY: SYSTEM INFORMATION

Step 1 Click **Start**. Point to **Programs**. Point to **Accessories**. Point to **System Tools**. Click **System Information**.

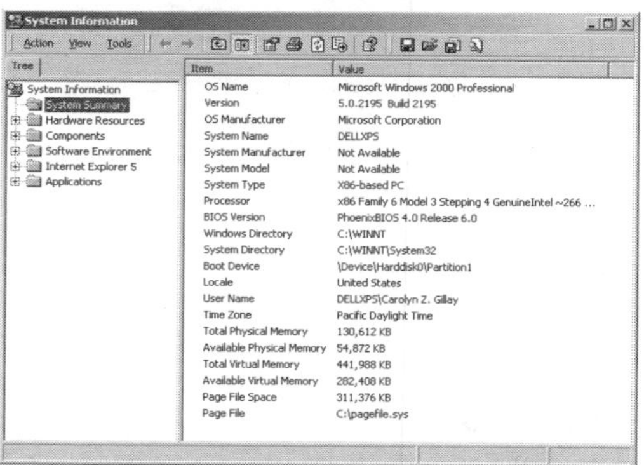

WHAT'S HAPPENING? Windows 2000 Professional provides additional tools to assist you in learning about your computer and its resources. You can see your physical memory, your virtual memory, and information on your paging files.

Step 2 Click the plus sign next to Hardware Resources to expand it.

Step 3 Click **Memory**.

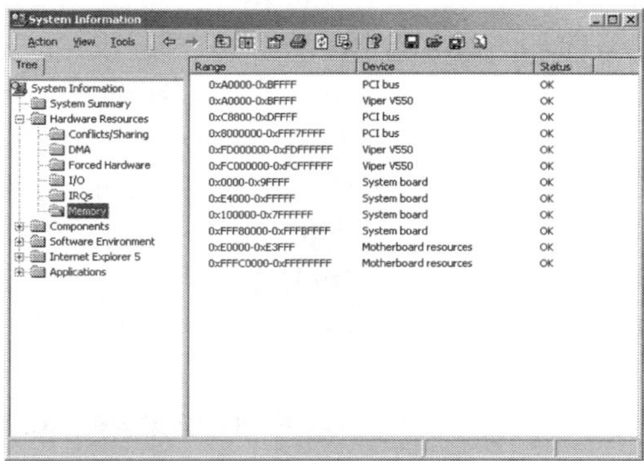

WHAT'S HAPPENING? Once again, you have a view of what hardware resources are occupying which areas in memory.

Step 4 Close the System Information window.

14.10 THE REGISTRY

The Registry stores all configuration data, including the system configuration, the hardware configuration, the configuration of most Windows-based applications, and all Windows 2000 Professional user preferences. Although the Registry is logically one database, it is not one large file. It is, in fact, stored as a number of files (at least six). You cannot use or look at these files in their native format but must use the tools that Microsoft supplies.

The simplest, safest, and recommended way to make changes to the Registry is to use Control Panel. When you activate any icon in Control Panel and make changes to an object, you are indeed making changes to the Registry. When you use Add/Remove Hardware or run setup programs for hardware, this information is placed in the Registry. When you use the Open With dialog box, you may change the registered file type. These methods are easy ways to update the Registry. You may also open Windows Explorer and use Tools/Folder Options/File Types to alter Registry settings for registered file types.

Some applications programs store their settings in the Registry. You can update these settings by changing the options in the application program's property sheet. You may use Device Manager to make changes to system hardware and resource settings. Device Manager displays all the hardware on your computer. It gets this information directly from the Registry. There is also a tool provided by Microsoft called "Tweak UI" that lets you set some of the most popular entries, such as an entry that controls window animation. You can go the Microsoft Website to locate and download Tweak UI.

The last choice, and the most dangerous, is to modify the Registry by using the provided tools—Regedit and Regedt32. When you install Windows, Regedit is stored in the WINNT directory and Regedt32 is stored in the WINNT\SYSTEM32 directory. The Registry can also be modified by a system administrator who can access your computer; this makes it possible to diagnose and repair computer problems from a remote site.

There are four primary users and consumers of the data in the Registry. These include the Windows 2000 Professional operating system, the other software that is installed on your computer, the hardware that is installed on your computer, and your own additions to or deletions from the Registry. You must be an administrator or a power user in order to make changes to the Registry. An ordinary user cannot. In addition, if you are on a network, the system administrator may have taken precautions that prevent you from making changes to the Registry. You should also be aware that the software applications and the hardware that you install are not forced into using the Registry. It is up to the software or hardware developer to decide if and what data will be stored in the Registry.

The major uses of the Registry include hardware management, security, software configuration, and user preferences. Hardware management includes such information as the device drivers, the I/O ports, and the BIOS information used by your computer. The security area stores information such as the different users, their account information, and the groups to which they belong. Information stored in the software configuration information varies from one application to another. However, typical software configuration information can include the location of the program, the user preferences, what languages are to be used, and licensing information. Windows 2000 Professional stores user preferences in the Registry, including such information as the printers available, color choices, wallpaper choices, and the mouse double-click speed.

Working with the Registry can be, to say the least, fraught with danger. It is not for the faint of heart. If you in any way damage the Registry files, you will not be able to boot into Windows 2000 Professional. Your entire computer system will be inoperable. Nonetheless, Windows 2000 Professional provides tools so that you may change the Registry files. This feature seems to be a contradictory position on the part of Microsoft. What Microsoft knows is what all computer users know. At one point or another, something will happen to your computer, and it will not work. If you cannot solve the problems yourself, your only alternative will be to take the computer to a repair facility (at $100 or more an hour) and hope for the best.

However, with the techniques you learn here, you will find that there is much you can do to solve your computer problems. You will also find that, as you use your computer, there will be things that you will want to fix. For instance, if you want to delete a program, you will find that it is not as simple as deleting the directory that holds the files. Windows 2000 Professional application programs leave footprints all over the Registry. To remove a program completely from your disk, you will need to delete the files and modify the Registry to remove all references to the program. There will also be certain types of customizations you may want to do that can only be done by modifying the Registry. For instance, you may wish to add or remove an item from a context or shortcut menu. In order to do so, you will need to modify the Registry.

This section differs from most of the other materials in the textbook. It will provide activities with step-by-step instructions, but, if you are in a lab environment or on a network, you will not be able to, nor should you, do any of these activities. No system administrator would ever let changes be made to the system, since one change could bring down the entire lab or the entire network in a company. This section is intended only to be read. *Read the section, but **do not** do any of the activities.* If you are using your own computer, you can do the activities. However, remember, until you know what you are doing, you run a great risk of destroying your computer system and making it totally inoperable. So if you choose to do the activities, proceed at your own risk!

14.11 BACKING UP THE REGISTRY

Given that the Registry is so critical to the operation of Windows 2000 Professional, it is imperative that it be backed up. Although most of the time the Registry and, hence, Windows 2000 Professional, works successfully, the Registry can become corrupted in many ways. How does the Registry become corrupted or "go bad"? The three most common ways the Registry becomes corrupted are as follows:

1. You add new application programs or new drivers to your system.
2. You (or the hardware installation software) make hardware changes from new settings, or your hardware fails.
3. You make changes to the Registry.

Your best protection is to back up the Registry. There are five major techniques to backing up the Registry. These include:

1. Creating an Emergency Repair Disk and choosing the option to back up the Registry, as you were shown in Chapter 13. Do not forget to make a set of setup boot disks as well.
2. The Regedit program provides a tool that allows you to export the Registry (or a part of the Registry).
3. Using Microsoft Backup or any commercial backup program to perform a full backup of your entire computer system. However, you could have a problem in restoring your system—you might not be able to start Backup and use Restore since you must be able to boot to the desktop to do this.
4. Using the Recovery Console, also demonstrated in Chapter 13. Again, remember you want a current version of your ERD.
5. Boot to Safe Mode and choosing Last Known Good Configuration. If your problem is a misinstalled application or driver, then this could solve your problem. But if you have a corrupt or missing file, this will not solve the problem.

14.12 STRUCTURE OF THE REGISTRY

The Registry is designed as a hierarchical structure, not unlike Windows Explorer. Keys and subkeys are similar to folders and subfolders in Windows Explorer. The Registry contains three types of objects: ***keys***, ***values***, and ***data***. At the top of the hierarchy are the Registry keys. Registry keys can also have several keys or ***subkeys***. The top-level keys are also known as ***hives*** and as ***predefined keys***. Keys can contain one or more other keys and values. When this occurs, it is known as ***nesting***. Each key and value must have a unique name within a key or subkey. Keys are case aware but not case sensitive. A key name cannot use backslashes. Backslashes are used as delimiters.

Keys and subkeys contain at least one value with a special name "(Default)". If the default value has no data, it is read as "value not set." Values have three parts: the data name, the data type, and the data value itself. A value has data like a file has data. There are nine types of data as listed in Table 14.1 Registry Data Types.

Data Type	Description
REG_BINARY	Binary data. In some cases, you will be able to edit this type of data, such as a value that indicates a true or false condition (0 for false or 1 for true).

REG_DWORD	A double word value is 4 bytes on an 8086, Pentium, or Pentium Pro computers. This is a lot of data. It will be displayed in either hexadecimal or decimal value.
REG_SZ	This data type is used to store string information. A string of data is a variable-length set of characters. String data is often enclosed in quotation marks.
REG_EXPAND_SZ	This data type is the same as REG_SZ except that it can contain expressions, macros, or environmental variables that would "expand" beyond what is shown if the entry were written out completely. Thus, an entry of %systemroot%\system32 would be interpreted as C:\WINNT\SYSTEM32.
REG_MULTI_SZ	This data type is used to store multiple string values (REG_SZ) for a single entry. Each string value is separated by the Null character.
REG_DWORD_LITTLE_ENDIAN	Same as REG_DWORD except that the least significant byte of a value is stored first.
REG_DWORD_BIG_ENDIAN	Same as REG_DWORD except that the most significant byte of a value is stored first.
REG_QWORD	This data type is 64-bit.
REG_RESOURCE_LIST	This data type is reserved for the use of device drivers to store a list of resources they will use.

TABLE 14.1 REGISTRY DATA TYPES

When you open the Registry Editor, you can see the structure of the Registry. My Computer is at the top. Then, in the left pane, you see the hierarchy of the structure with the keys and subkeys. The plus or minus in front of each entry indicates, as in Windows Explorer, whether an item is expanded or collapsed. The right pane shows the current setting of the selected entry or the value. See Figure 14.7 Registry Organization.

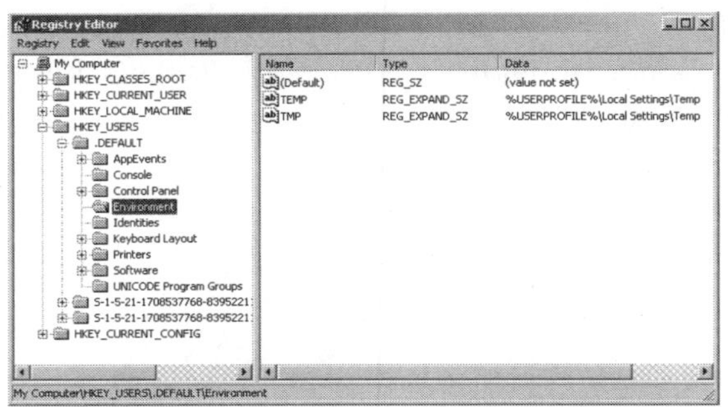

FIGURE 14.7 REGISTRY ORGANIZATION

There are five root keys. Each root key begins with ***HKEY***. HKEY is an abbreviation for "handle or hive to a KEY." Although there are five HKEYs that appear, in reality, there are only two keys: HKEY_LOCAL_MACHINE and HKEY_USERS. The other HKEYs are aliases for those two keys. Any change that is made in the aliases is changed in either HKEY_LOCAL_MACHINE or HKEY_CURRENT_USER. Table 14.2 Root Keys lists the predetermined keys.

Pre-Determined (Root)	Description
HKEY_CLASSES_ROOT	This is an alias for HKEY_LOCAL_MACHINE. It contains settings for shortcuts, dragging and dropping, and file associations.
HKEY_CURRENT_USER	This stores user preferences and desktop configuration details for the currently logged-on user. The information stored here is reflected in a user's profile. It includes such items as the shortcuts on the user's desktop, the contents of the Start menu, and the contents of the Favorites menu. It is an alias to either the .DEFAULT user or to the current user in HKEY_USERS.
HKEY_LOCAL_MACHINE	This contains configuration data that is specific to your computer, such as what hardware you have installed and what your program settings are. The information in this key applies to every user who uses this computer.
HKEY_USERS	This is the other major key that contains the configuration information for any user who logs on to the computer. In addition to maintaining information that applies to all users on the machine, it also contains information that is specific to each user. There will be a subkey for each user who has a profile. If a user does not have a profile, the .DEFAULT key will be used. The .DEFAULT is the minimum information Windows 2000 Professional needs to define the workspace when it boots. It is used as a template when a user logs on for the first time.
HKEY_CURRENT_CONFIG	This is also an alias for HKEY_LOCAL_MACHINE, which contains the current configuration for your computer.

TABLE 14.2 ROOT KEYS

HKEY_CLASSES_ROOT is an alias for HKEY_LOCAL_MACHINE. In this hive, you will see the file associations that associate specific classes with different file extensions. In the example shown below, WinZip is associated with the .ARC file extension.

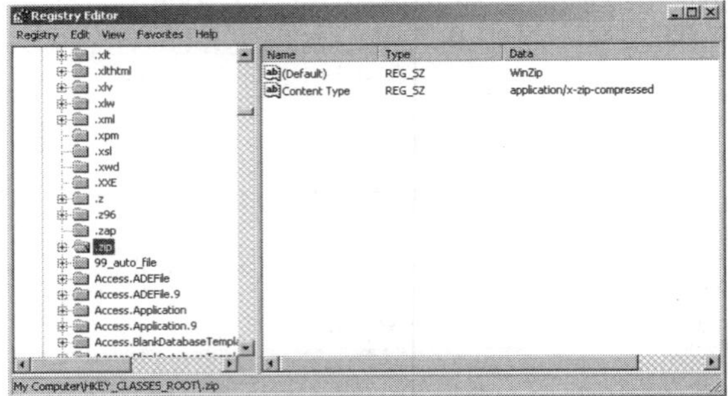

This key also includes class definitions that describe all of the actions associated with a file's class, such as open or print. In addition, you will find information about the icon that is used, any shell extensions installed, and the OLE information.

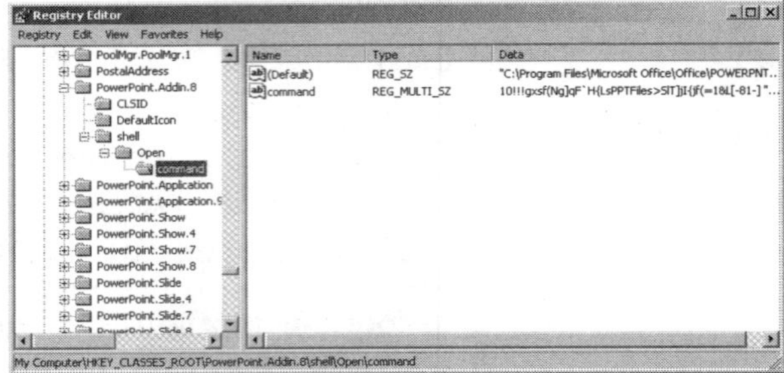

HKEY_CURRENT_USER is an alias for the current user in HKEY_USERS. If there is only one user on a computer, this will point to the (Default) subkey. If there is more than one user who maintains a configuration, this key will indicate who is currently logged on.

HKEY_LOCAL_MACHINE relates to the configuration data for this specific machine. This root key information applies to the computer itself, not to each user. This relationship is the reason you would never want to copy the Registry files from one computer to another. In this key, you will find individual program settings, such as the path to a program, that would apply to any user who logs on. You would find information about the drive letter assignments for your CD-ROM and removable drives. You would also find information about all the hardware on the computer. Furthermore, you would find data indicating where a program was installed from—the installation path. There are many subkeys which are also aliased by other root keys.

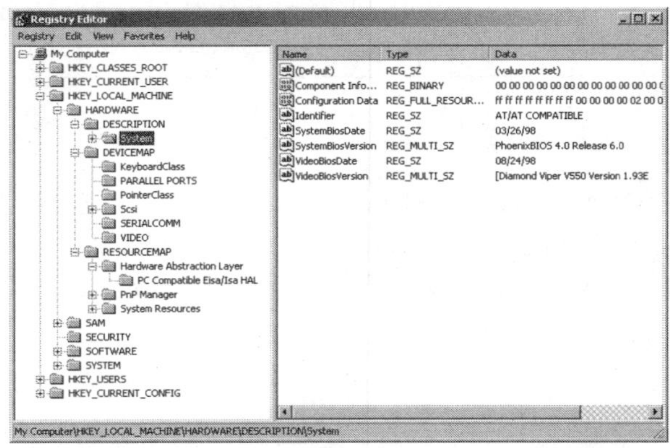

Some of the major subkeys include the System, which stores the data that Windows needs to boot your computer; the Security, which stores all security specific data for this local machine such as users, groups and so on; and the Software subkey, which contains all of the information about the software installed on the computer, including file associations and program settings. This data is computer-specific as opposed to user-specific, which means that you can see all of the software installed on this specific machine no matter which user is accessing the software.

HKEY_USERS contains the .DEFAULT subkey, which is the minimum amount of information Windows 2000 Professional needs. It also contains some very long numbers. The first is the Current User SID (Security Identification) for the user who is currently logged on. The last key contains any file extension associations or component embedding that override the default settings.

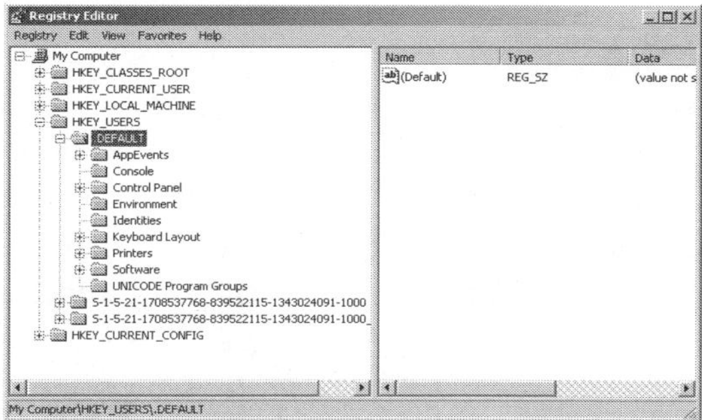

Each of the subkeys contains preferences that are specific to a user. Information is written here when you use Control Panel to make changes or when you create settings for specific programs.

HKEY_CURRENT_CONFIG is an alias for the currently used hardware configuration found in HKEY_LOCAL_MACHINE.

14.13 REGEDIT

Although Microsoft feels that changes should not be made directly to the Registry, there is a tool to make changes. The tool is Regedit.EXE. Regedit offers a particular view of the Registry. It is the best general-purpose tool for browsing and modifying the Registry. You may also back up the Registry from here. However, it is often a very large file, so it is best if you back it up to either a hard disk, a CD-RW, or a Zip disk.

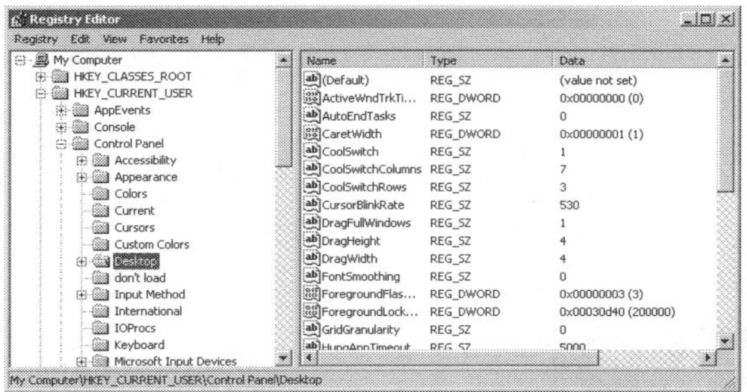

As you can see, the left pane displays the keys, and the right pane displays the values for a key. The status line shows where you are in the Registry. The split bar allows you to alter the size of the left and right panes. In the Value pane, one of two icons is displayed. The ab icon indicates the text data type, whereas the icon indicates the binary data type. The display of data in Regedit is static rather than dynamic. In other words, the display is showing you the Registry at the specific moment in time that Regedit was opened. Any changes made to the Registry after you have opened Regedit will not be reflected in the display.

There are only five menu choices: Registry, Edit, View, Favorites, and Help.

14.13.1 REGISTRY MENU

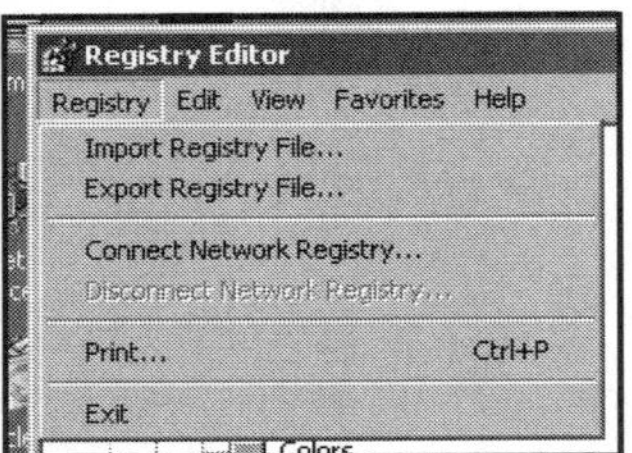

You can import and export the entire Registry or a branch of the Registry to a text file by using the Import and Export commands. To export the entire Registry, you would highlight My Computer at the top of the tree, choose Export Registry File, and then choose All. There are reasons for exporting the Registry. One of these is that, if you export the Registry to a text file, you can safely edit it. However, there is one warning. Windows 2000 Professional will write the Registry file in a Unicode format (each character is two bytes long). Some text editors do not understand Unicode. To convert the Unicode file to a regular text file, you would key in TYPE regfile.reg > regfile.txt. That way, any editor can read it. You can then import the altered file back into the Registry. These files have the .REG extension. This process can be *very* dangerous. If you double-click any file with a .REG extension, the file will *automatically* update the Registry. You can also export the Registry before you install a program or make changes, and then export it again after you have made these changes to see the differences. Exporting the Registry is another way to back up the Registry.

14.13.2 EDIT MENU

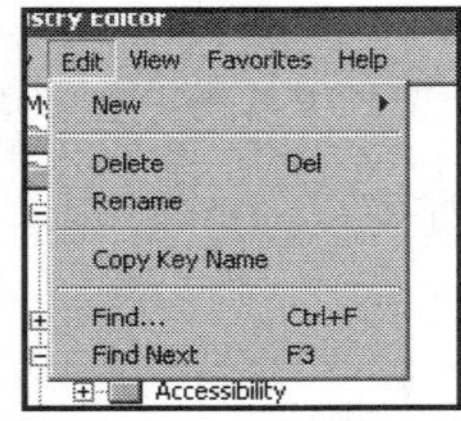

This menu allows you to delete or rename an existing key; copy a key; and find a value, key, or data in the Registry. Find has a submenu. To use Find Next, you either press F3 or click Edit/Find Next.

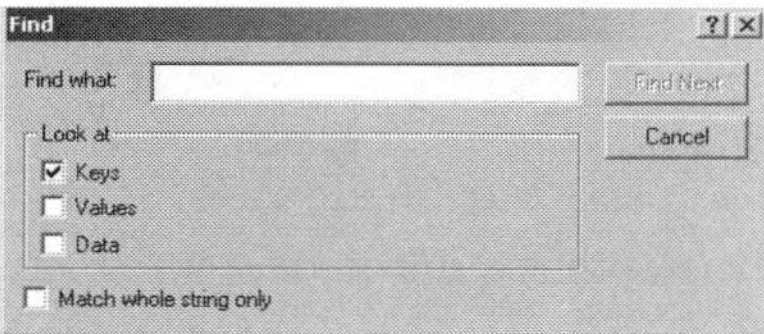

The Find and Find Next option is one reason users prefer Regedit to Regedt32. Regedt32 has no Find Next feature. It also limits its searches to keys only.

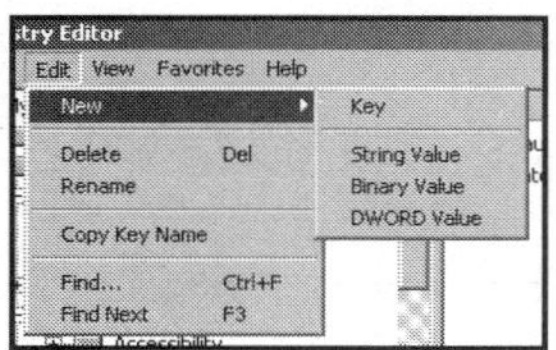

The New option has a submenu that also allows you to create a new key.

14.13.3 VIEW MENU

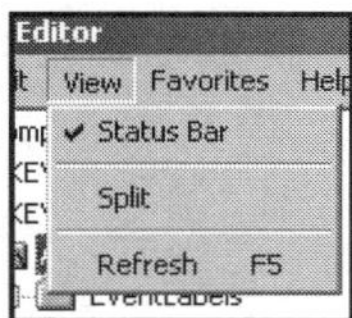

The View menu allows you to turn the status bar on or off, to adjust the size of the panes with the keyboard, and to force a rereading of the Registry (Refresh).

14.13.4 FAVORITES MENU

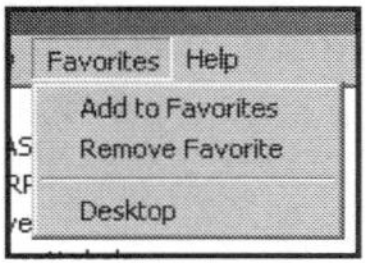

The Favorites menu allows you to quickly return to an item that you often use in the Registry. In this example, there is a favorite—Desktop. You add or remove favorites with the items on the menu.

14.14 REGEDT32

The other tool to edit the Registry is Regedt32.EXE. It is similar to Regedit but displays its information in separate windows. You may back up various hives, but it does not have an option to back up the entire Registry. You may place Regedt32 in read-only mode so no changes take place. You may also alter Security settings in Regedt32.

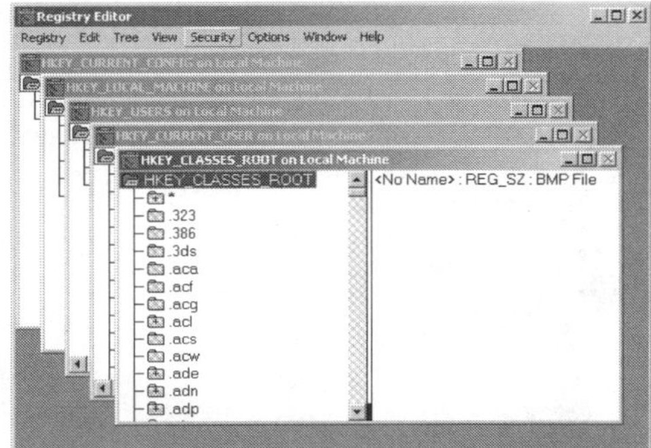

Each hive or predetermined key is in a separate window. You use either the Window command on the menu or click the window you wish to be active.

14.14.1 REGISTRY MENU

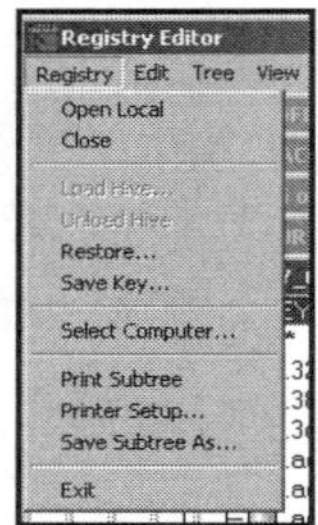

You can open your local or a remote computer. You can also save a key or a subtree.

14.14.2 THE EDIT MENU

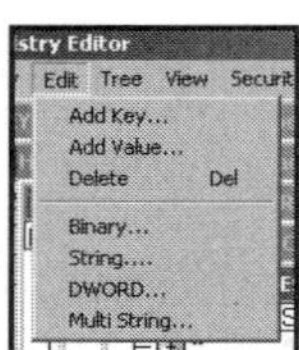

The Edit menu allows you to add keys and values.

14.14.3 THE VIEW MENU

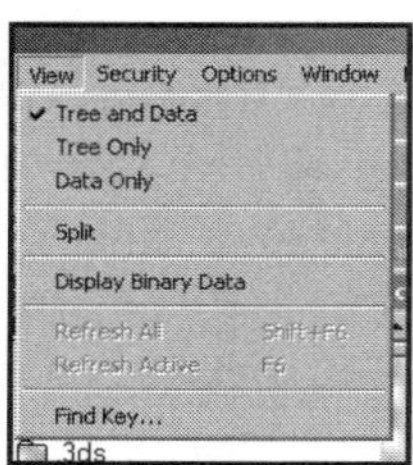

The View menu allows you to change the way you look at the data. Note that Find only finds a key, not values or other data.

14.14.4 SECURITY

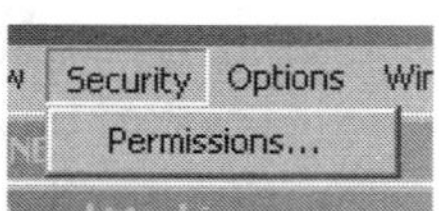

The Security menu allows you to alter permissions for users.

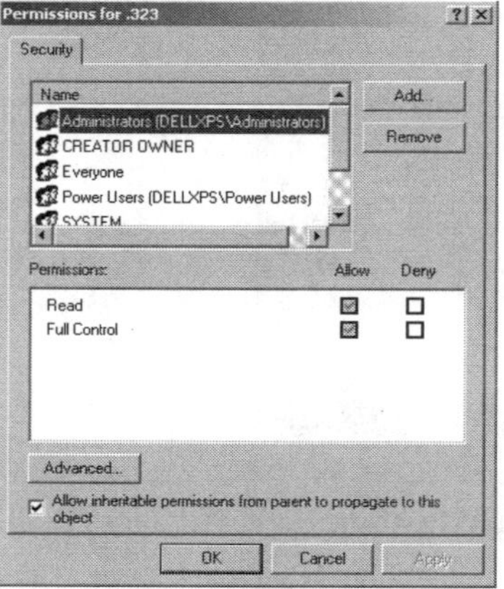

Here you see what groups and individuals have permissions to make changes. As you can see, if you are an administrator or a power user, you can grant or deny permissions.

14.14.5 THE OPTIONS MENU

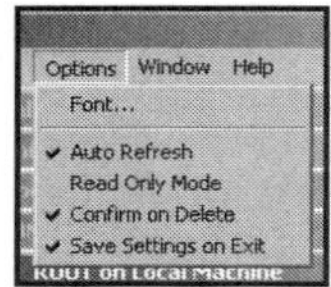

Here you can change the Font, place the Registry in Read Only Mode, and be sure you are asked to confirm before you delete a key or if you want to save your settings on exit.

14.14.6 THE WINDOW MENU

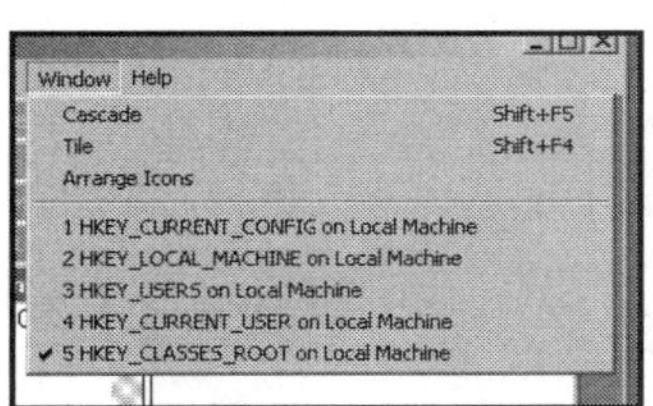

The Window menu lets you see what window is active and arrange your open windows.

14.15 USING REGEDIT TO ADD ACTIONS TO A CONTEXT MENU

You can use Regedit to add items to context menus. A common reason for this is that only one file extension can be associated with a specific application program. As an example, if you create a document with WordPad but also have Word, the .DOC extension is assigned to Word first. Thus, if you double-click the WordPad document icon, you will open Word, not WordPad. If you right-click the document icon, your menu choices will include Open With. Then you must open the submenu to choose with which program you want to open your document. Then you choose among programs that are installed on your system. You can add another choice to the context menu, Open with WordPad, so you do not have to use the submenus. Then you will have the choice of opening Word or WordPad on the menu. This problem also occurs frequently with graphic packages that have common file extensions such as JPEG, TIF, and so on.

14.16 ACTIVITY: USING REGEDIT TO OPEN WORDPAD

Note: The following activity assumes that you have Office 2000 (Word 8). Also, remember that, if you make a mistake working with the Registry, you can make your system inoperable. If you have not backed up the Registry, do so now.

Step 1 Place your DATA disk in Drive A. Open WordPad.

Step 2 Key in the following: **This is a test of altering the Registry.**

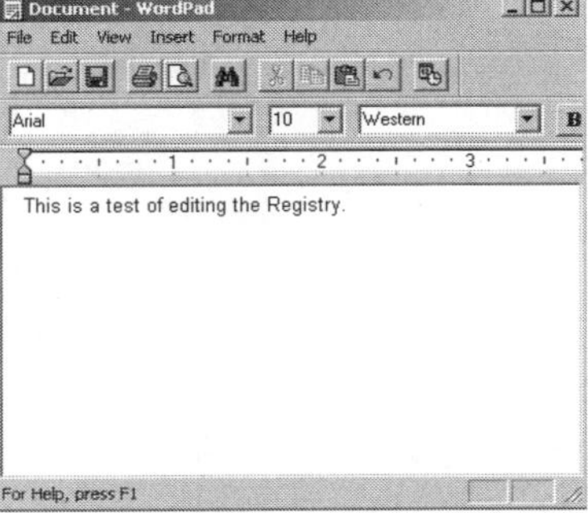

You have created a test file.

Step 3 Click **File**. Click **Save**. In the Save As dialog box, in the File name box, key in: **A:\Maryb.doc**

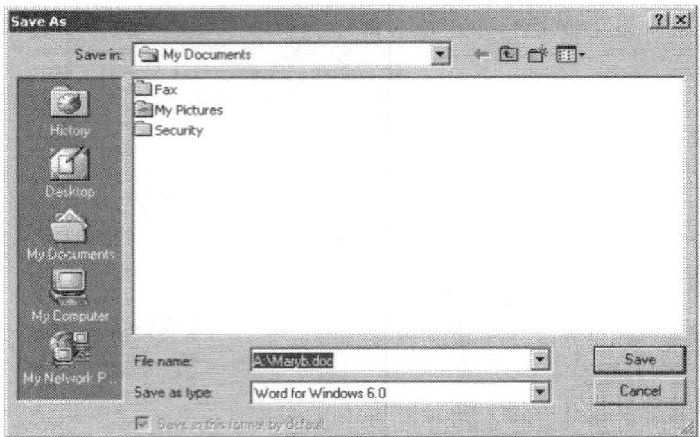

You are saving the file to the DATA disk.

Step 4 Click **Save**. Close WordPad.

Step 5 Click **Start**. Point to **Search**. Click **Files or Folders**. In the Search for Files and Folders text box, key in **A:\Maryb.doc**. Click **Search Now**.

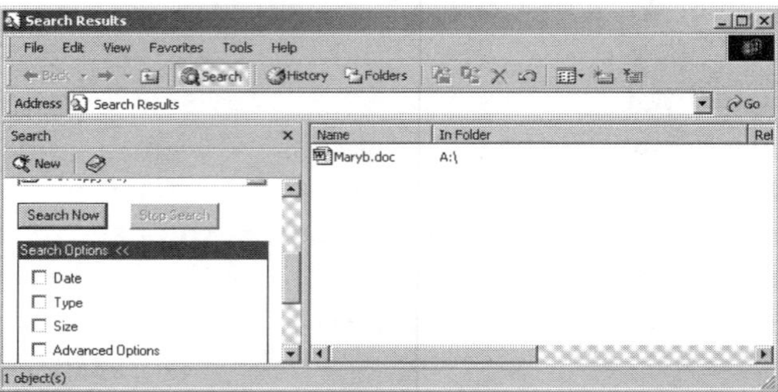

You have located the file. If you clicked the file, you would open Word, not WordPad.

Step 6 Right-click the **Maryb.doc** file.

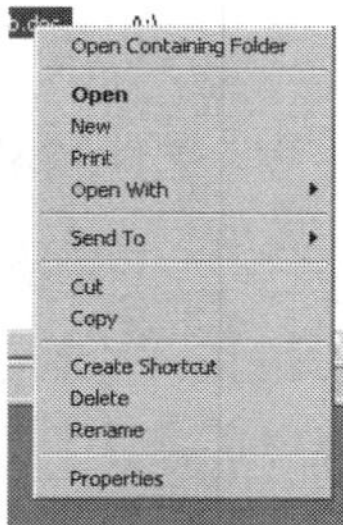

On the context (shortcut) menu, Open is available. Open opens this document in Word. You could also choose Open With, then choose WordPad. You cannot choose Open With WordPad from this menu.

Step 7 Close the Search Results dialog box. Click **Start**. Click **Run**. In the Run dialog box, key in: **Regdit**. Click **OK**.

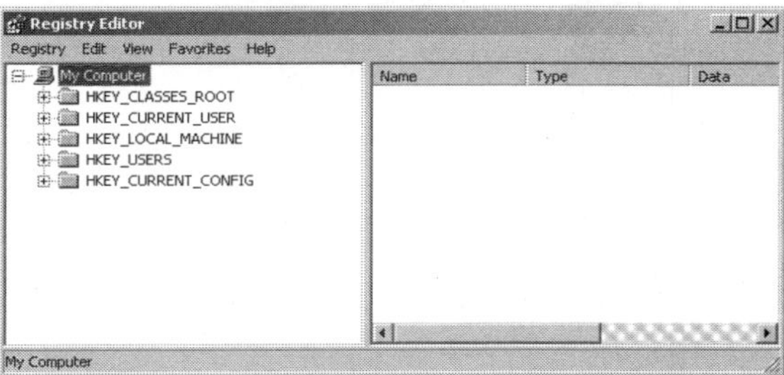

You have opened Regedit. If the hives are not collapsed (looking like the above screen), collapse them now.

Step 8 Click **My Computer** to select it. Click **Edit**. Click **Find**.

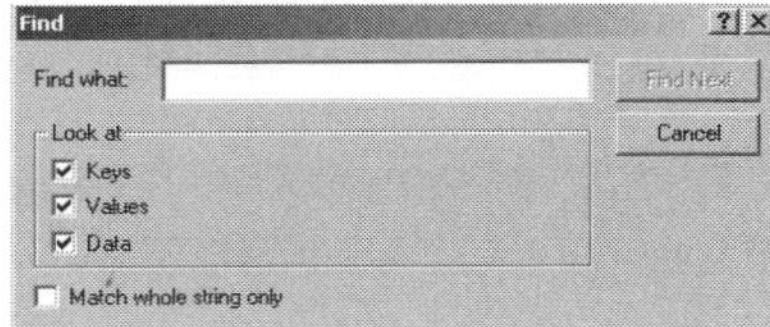

The Find dialog box is going to look at all the keys, values, and data for whatever you key in the Find what text box.

Step 9 Clear the Values and Data check boxes. In the Find what: text box, key in **Word.Document.8**

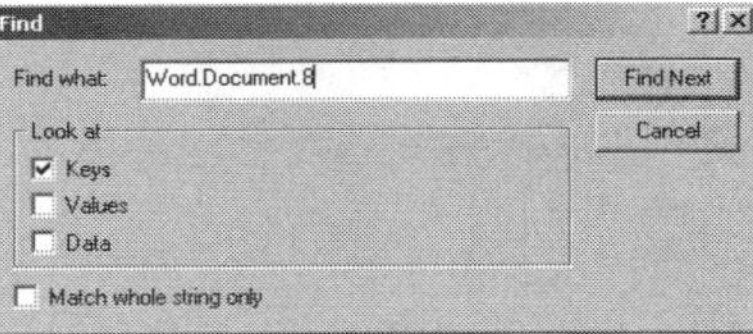

You are going to look for your key, **Word.Document.8**, in Office 97 or Office 2000. If you had an earlier version of Office, you would use Word.Document.7 or Word.Document.6.

Step 10 Click **Find Next**.

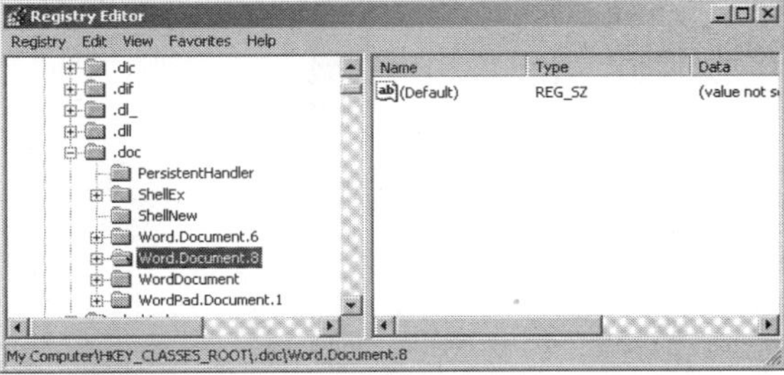

Find found the first occurrence of **Word.Document.8**. This is *not* the one you want. This is the .DOC file extension. You need to go to the shell.

Step 11 Click **Edit**. Click **Find Next** or press the F3 key.

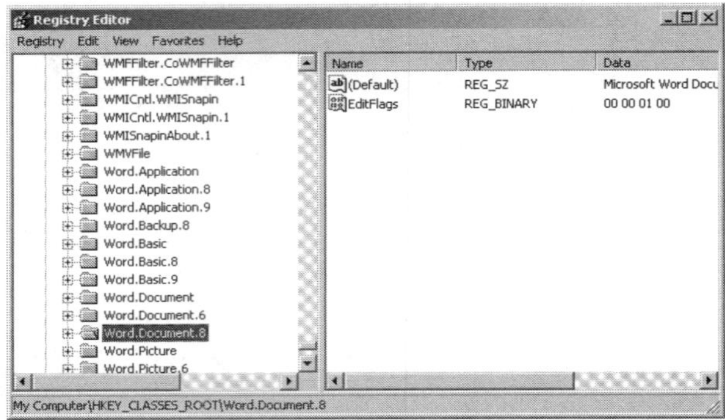

WHAT'S HAPPENING? Here is the key you are looking for.

Step 12 Click the + sign next to **Word.Document.8** to expand it. Click the **+** sign next to shell to expand it. Click **shell** to select it.

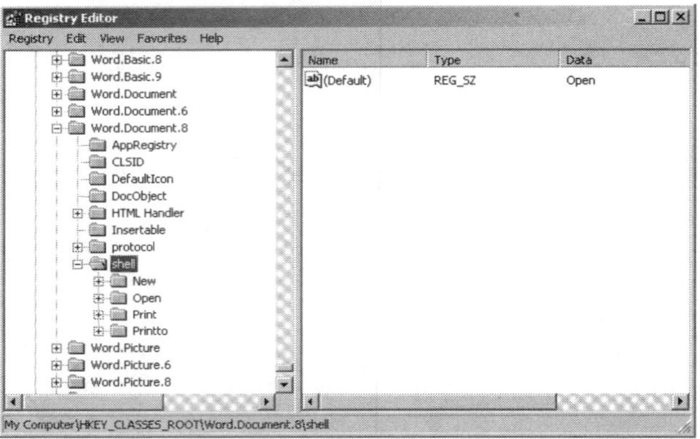

WHAT'S HAPPENING? You are ready to add your new subkey.

Step 13 Click **Edit**. Click **New**. Click **Key**.

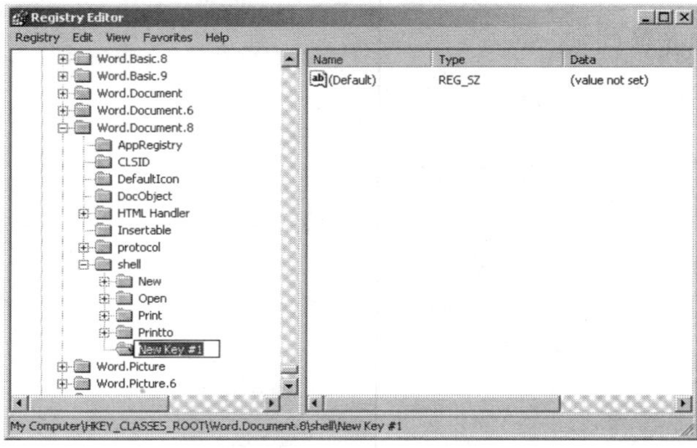

WHAT'S HAPPENING? You can now create your subkey.

Step 14 In the dotted lined box, key in **Open with WordPad**.

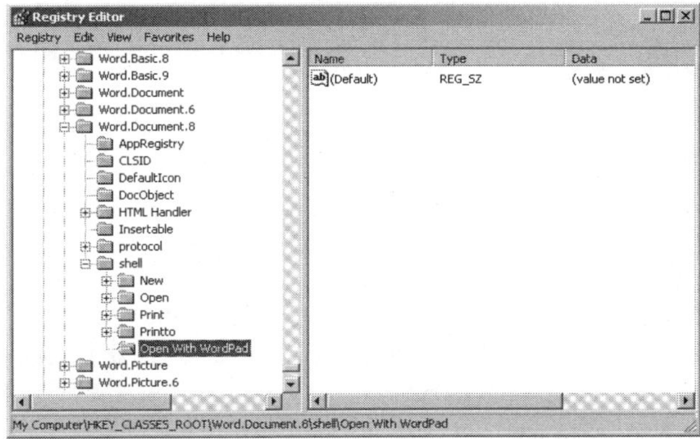

WHAT'S HAPPENING? Now you need to create the action.

Step 15 Click **Open with WordPad** to select it. Click **Edit**. Click **New**. Click **Key**.

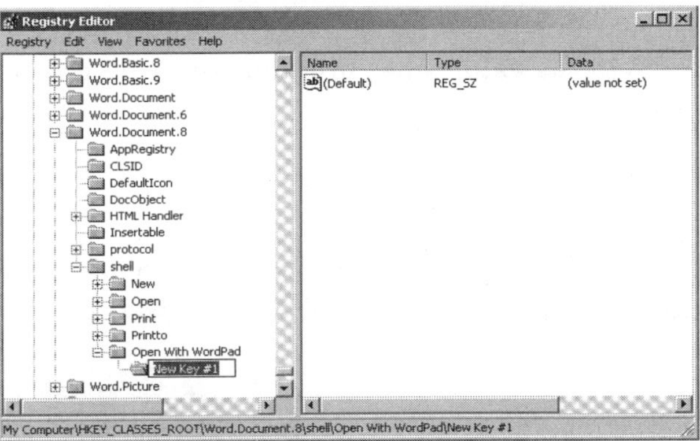

WHAT'S HAPPENING? You now want to create the action.

Step 16 In the New Key #1, key in **command**.

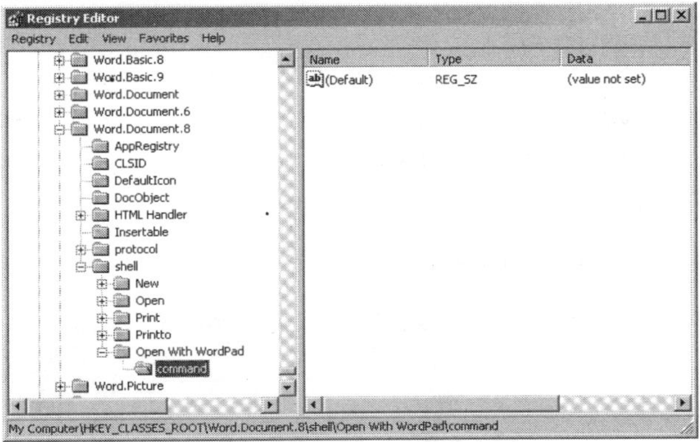

WHAT'S HAPPENING? Now, you have to tell it what value you want.

Step 17 In the Value pane, double-click **(Default)**.

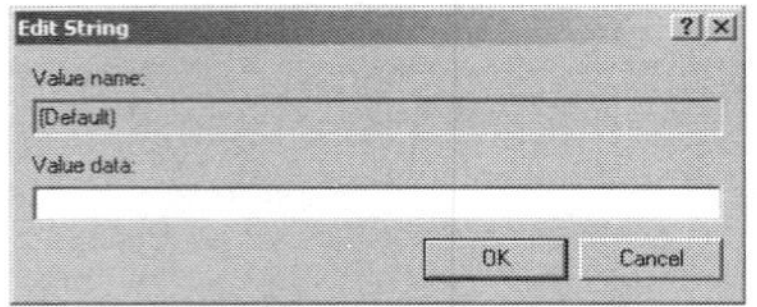

You are going to tell it what program you want to use. Note that there is a space between Program and Files and a space between Windows and NT.

Step 18 In the Value data text box, key in the following:
C:\Program Files\Windows NT\Accessories\WordPad.exe "%1"
Note that there is a space between Program and Files and a space between Windows and NT.

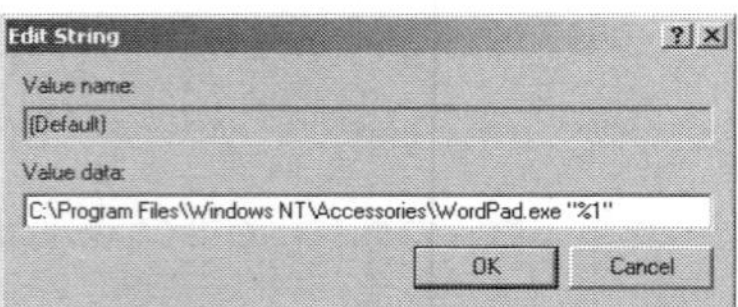

You told the value what program and where it was located, and you used the variable parameter **%1** enclosed by quotation marks so that WordPad will substitute your file name for the **%1**.

Step 19 Click **OK**. Close the Registry.

Step 20 Click **Start**. Point to **Search**. Click **Files or Folders**. In the Search for Files or Folders named text box, key in **A:\Maryb.doc**. Click **Search Now**. Right-click **A:\Maryb.doc**.

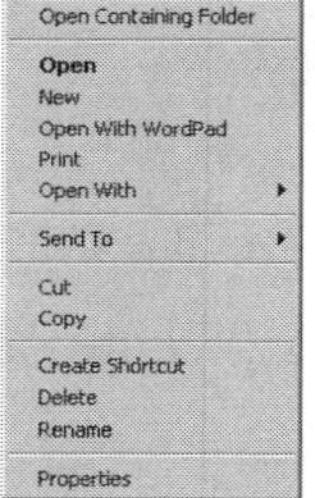

Notice your new choice on the context menu, **Open with WordPad**. Now you can choose to open any file that has the .DOC extension in either Word or WordPad from the shortcut menu.

Step 21 Click **Open with WordPad**.

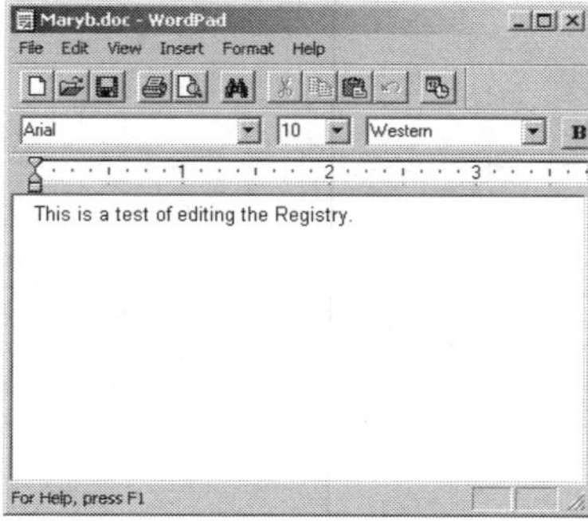

Indeed, your file opened with WordPad, not Word. Now, you are going to remove the key you just created.

Step 22 Close WordPad. Close the Search Results dialog box.

Step 23 Click **Start**. Click **Run**. In the Run dialog box, key in **Regedit**. Click **OK**.

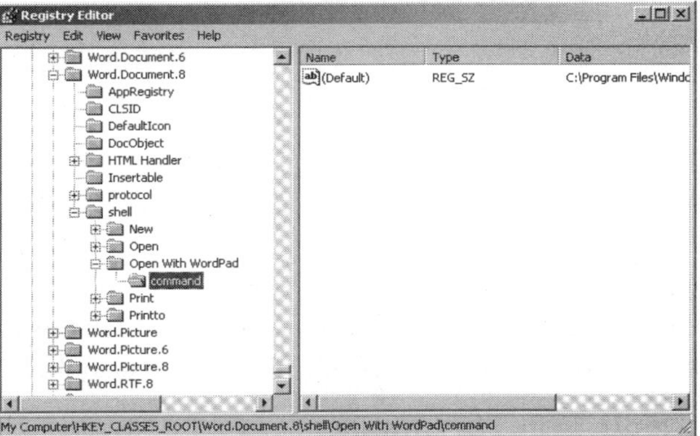

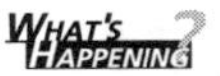

Regedit remembered the last place you were. However, just to ensure that you are selecting the correct key, you are going to collapse the structure and start at the top.

Step 24 Collapse the structure so that you are at My Computer. Select **My Computer**.

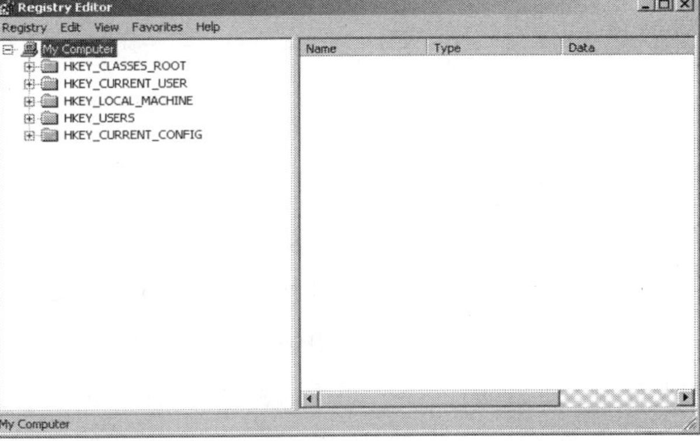

Step 25 Click **Edit**. Click **Find**.

Step 26 Clear the Values and Data check boxes. In the Find what: text box, key in **Word.Document.8**

Step 27 Click **Find Next**.

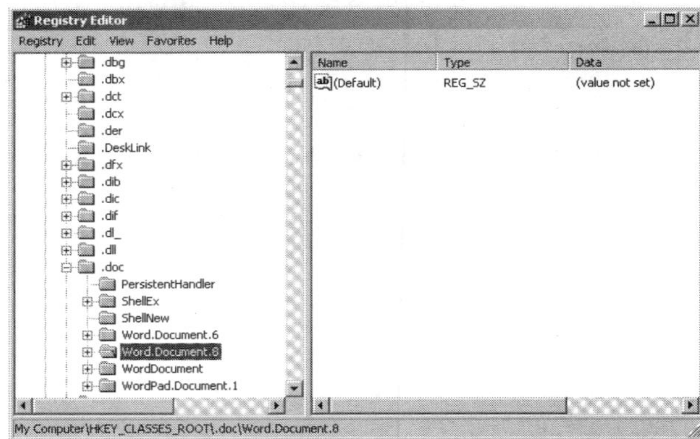

WHAT'S HAPPENING? Find found the first occurrence of **Word.Document.8**. Remember, this is *not* the one you want. This is the .DOC file extension. You need to go to the shell.

Step 28 Click **Edit**. Click **Find Next** or press F3.

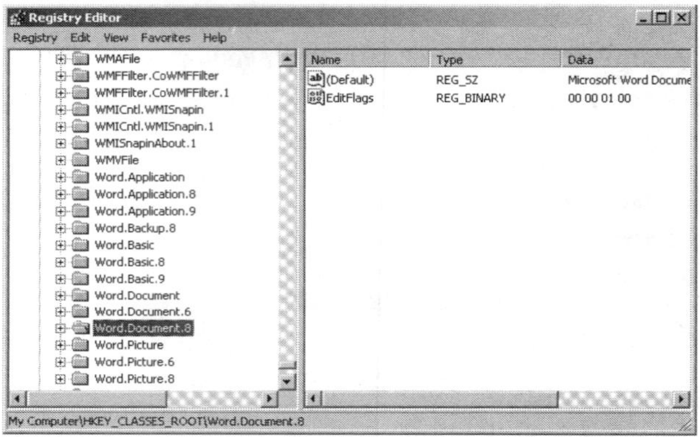

WHAT'S HAPPENING? This is the key you are looking for.

Step 29 Click the + sign next to **Word.Document.8** to expand it. Click the + sign next to **shell** to expand it. Click **shell** to select it. Click **Open with WordPad** to select it.

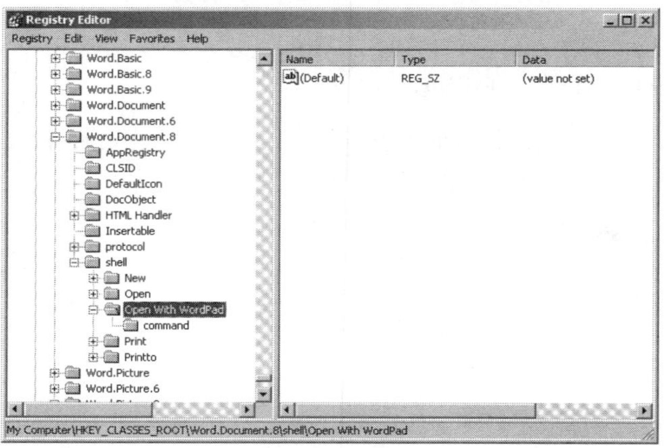

WHAT'S HAPPENING? You are going to delete the key that you created. Be sure that **Open with WordPad** is selected.

Step 30 Click **Edit**. Click **Delete**.

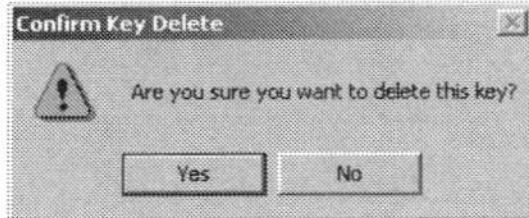

WHAT'S HAPPENING? You are being asked to confirm your key deletion.

Step 31 Click **Yes**.

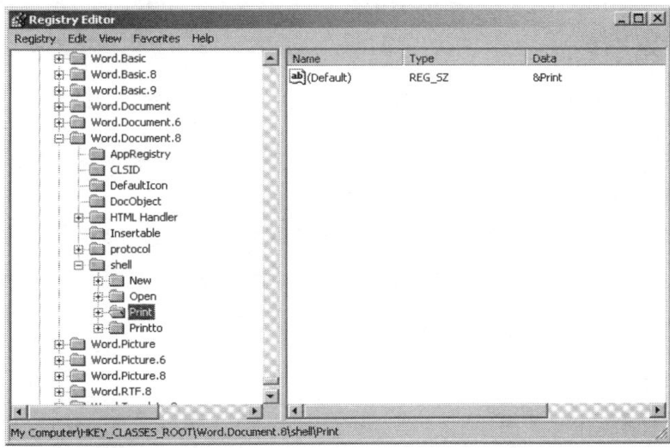

WHAT'S HAPPENING? Your key is gone.

Step 32 Close Regedit.

14.17 USING REGEDIT TO SEE YOUR BITMAP ICONS

If you have many bitmap files and you want to see the pictures they hold, you will have to open each file individually, which can get tedious. You can change this situation by making the document icon show the image rather than just a generic .BMP icon. You can do this without having to change each view in each window and selecting Thumbnails. If you have installed software that has changed or altered the bitmap image file type or the .BMP file extension associations, the following example may not work.

14.18 ACTIVITY: USING REGEDIT TO SEE YOUR BITMAP ICONS

Step 1 Open Windows Explorer. Open the **\WINNT** directory. Click **View**. Click **Large Icons**.

Step 2 Click **View**. Point to **Arrange Icons**. Click **by Type**. Scroll until you can see the files with the **.BMP** file extension. (If the file extensions are not visible, click **Tools**. Click **Folder Options**. Click the **View** tab. Clear the Hide File extensions for known file types check box.)

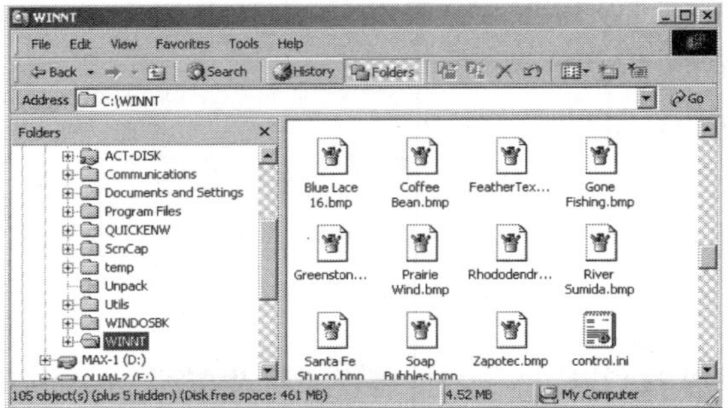

What's Happening? As you can see, it is hard to tell what each icon actually is. Even if you clicked View/Thumbnails, you would still not actually see the graphic image.

Step 3 Close Windows Explorer. Open Regedit.

Step 4 Collapse any trees and move to the top of the Registry. Select **My Computer**.

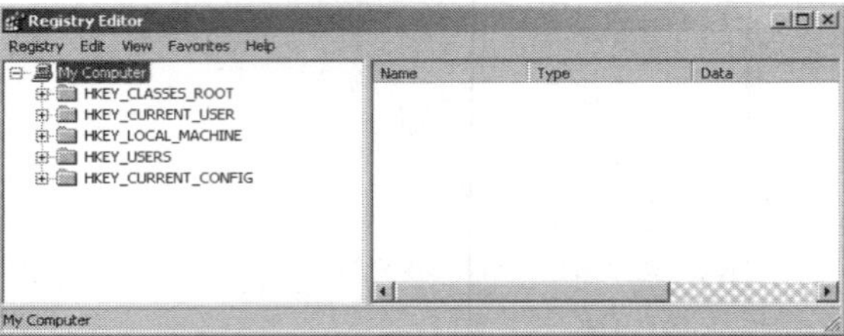

What's Happening? You have moved to the top of the tree in the Registry Editor.

Step 5 Click **Edit**. Click **Find**. Clear the Values and Data check boxes. Key in the following: **Paint.Picture**

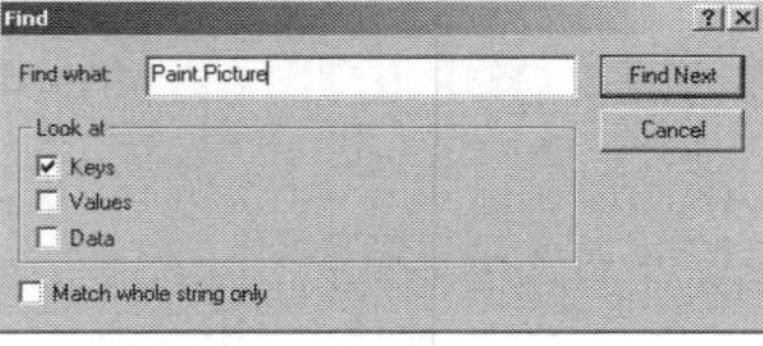

What's Happening? You are looking for a subkey.

Step 6 Click **Find Next**.

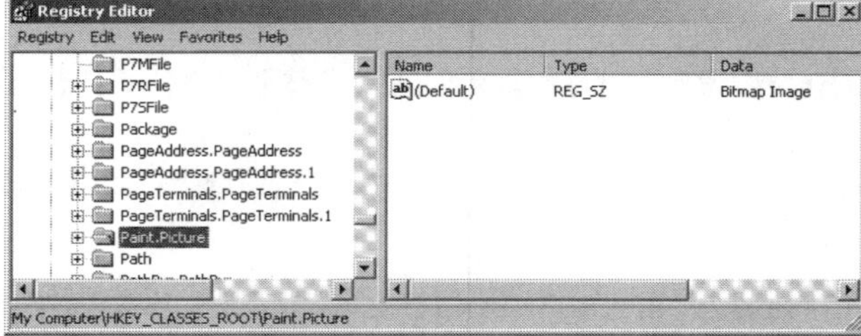

What's Happening? Here is the entry you are looking for.

Step 7 Click the plus sign next to **Paint.Picture** to expand it. Click **DefaultIcon** to select it.

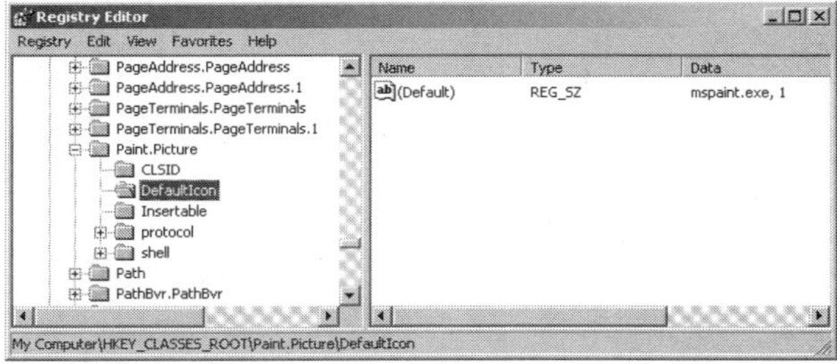

WHAT'S HAPPENING? Now you are going to change the value. Before you do so, write down the current value because, when you finish, you are going to return it to the original value.

Step 8 Double-click **(Default)** in the Value pane.

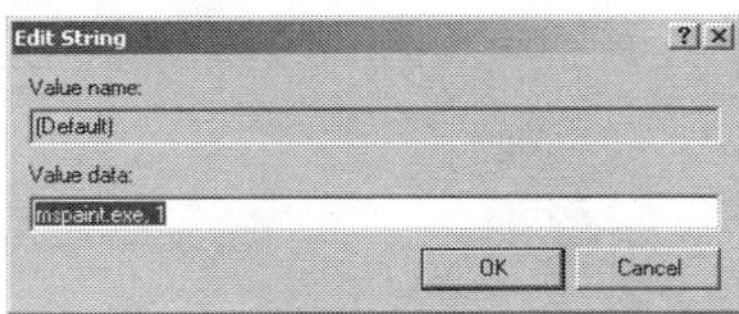

WHAT'S HAPPENING? You are going to replace this value.

Step 9 Key in **%1**

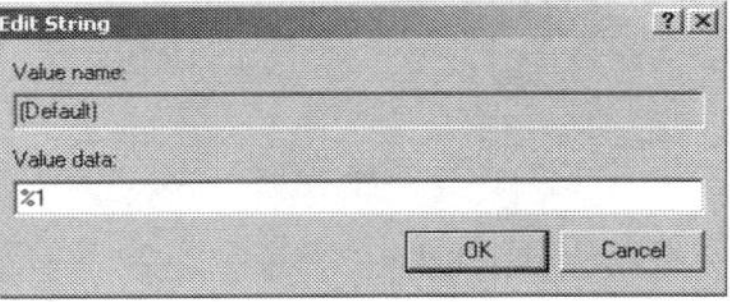

WHAT'S HAPPENING? You have changed the value.

Step 10 Click **OK**. Close Regedit.

WHAT'S HAPPENING? In order for this change to take effect, you need to restart Windows.

Step 11 Click **Start**. Click **Shut Down**. Click **Restart**.

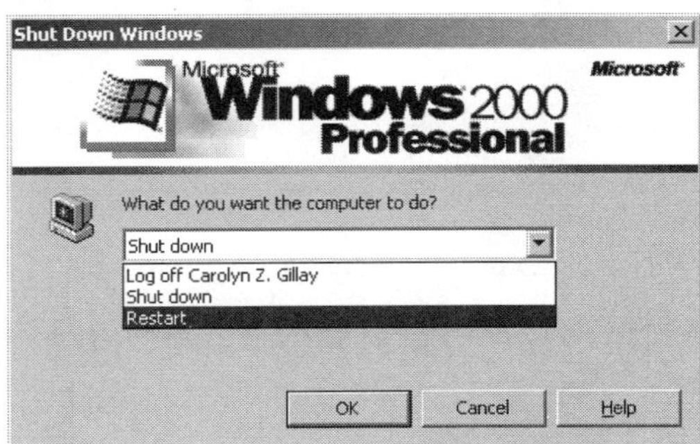

WHAT'S HAPPENING? You want to Restart the computer.

Step 12 Click **OK**.

Step 13 After Windows has restarted, open Windows Explorer. Open the **WINNT** directory. Click **Show Files**. Click **View**. Click **Large Icons**.

Step 14 Click **View**. Point to **Arrange Icons**. Click **by Type**. Scroll until you can see the files with the **.BMP** file extension.

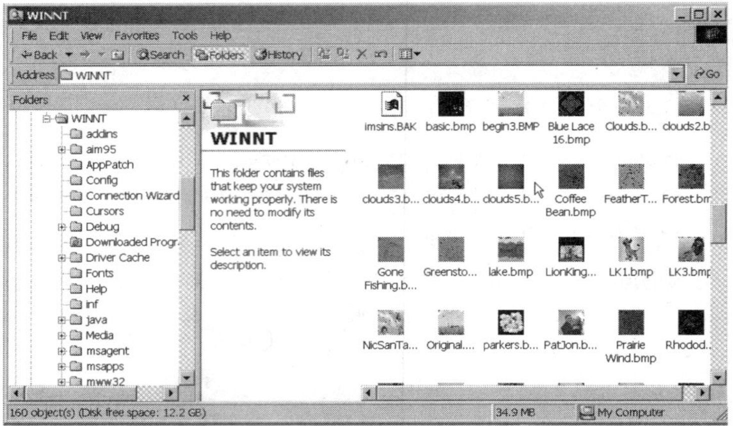

Now, you can actually see what the picture is. In this example, **Use Windows Classic Folders** was not selected. You can right-click the desktop, click **Properties**, click the **Effects** tab, click the Use Large Icons check box and click **apply**. Your display will look as follows:

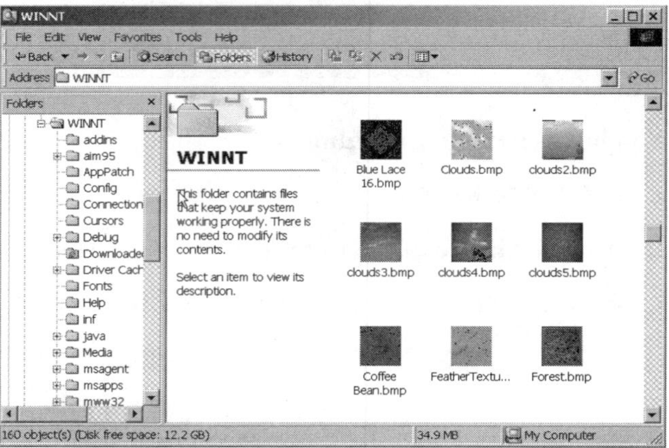

Step 15 Close Windows Explorer. Open Regedit.

Step 16 Hold the Ctrl key and press the Home key to return to the top of the Registry.

Step 17 Click **Edit**. Click **Find**. Clear the Values and Data check boxes. Key in the following: **Paint.Picture**

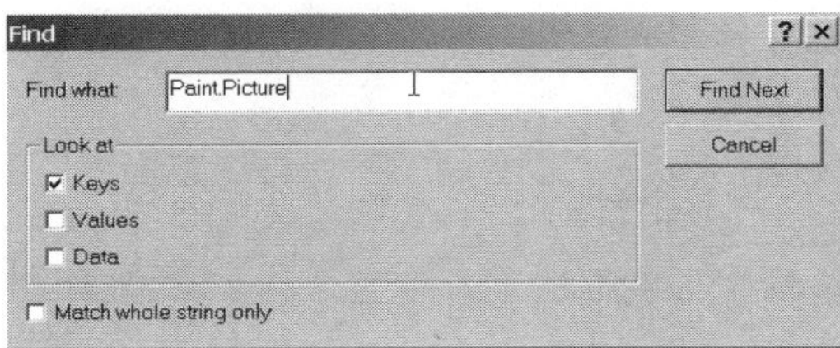

WHAT'S HAPPENING? You are looking for a subkey.

Step 18 Click **Find Next**.

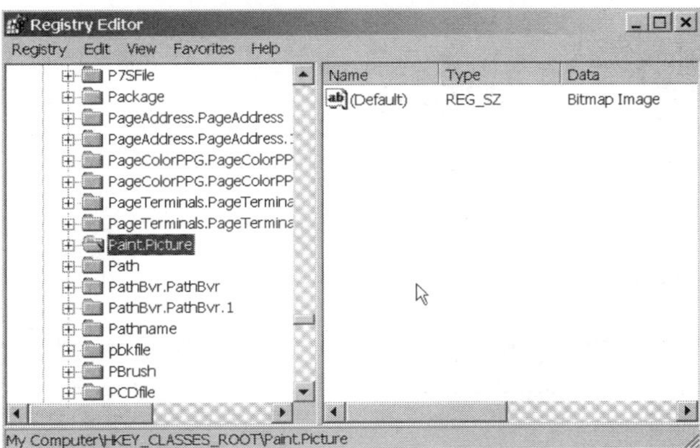

WHAT'S HAPPENING? Here is the entry you are looking for.

Step 19 Click the plus sign next to Paint.Picture to expand it. Click **DefaultIcon** to select it.

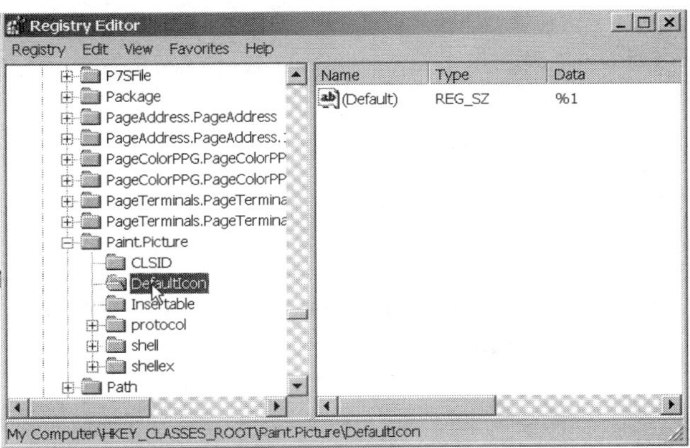

WHAT'S HAPPENING? You are going to change the value.

Step 20 Double-click **(Default)** in the Value pane.

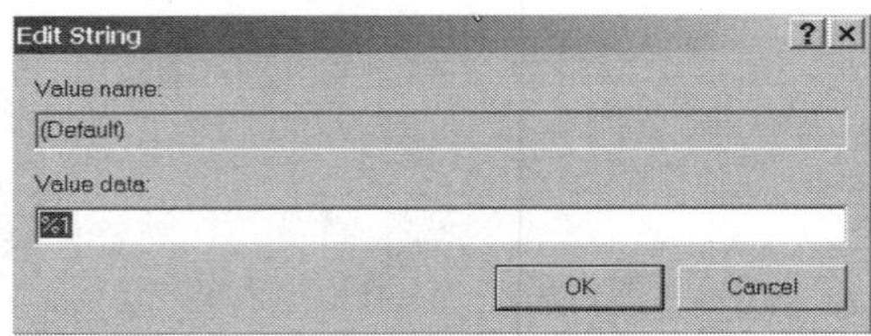

WHAT'S HAPPENING? Refer to the value you wrote down prior to changing it.

Step 21 Key in the original value.

WHAT'S HAPPENING? You have replaced the value.

Step 22 Click **OK**.

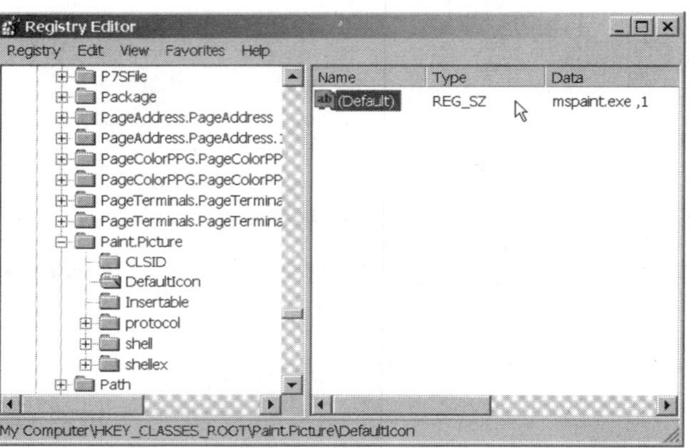

WHAT'S HAPPENING? You have changed the value.

Step 23 Close Regedit.

WHAT'S HAPPENING? You have returned to the desktop. Remember, for this to take effect, you need to restart Windows.

CHAPTER SUMMARY

1. A CMOS (Complementary Metal-Oxide Semiconductor) is a computer chip built into your computer system and is specific to your computer system.
2. The CMOS contains the settings that identify the type and specifications of your disk drives, the assigned drive letters, and any password options, as well as the boot sequence.
3. The boot sequence is the order in which the BIOS searches drives in order to locate and load the operating system.

4. CMOS is hardware dependent. When you boot your system, you will see a message that tells you what keys you must press to enter the CMOS Setup Utility program.
5. There are three types of memory: conventional, extended, and expanded. Conventional memory is the first 640 KB of memory, extended memory is memory above the first 1 MB.
6. The UMA (upper memory area) is the area between conventional memory and extended memory. Unused portions of this memory are called memory blocks (UMB).
7. The high memory area (HMA) is the first 64 KB of extended memory.
8. The MEM command makes it possible for you to display information about the memory available in a system.
9. You can verify use of the HMA and UMA in your system by using the MEM command with the /C and /P parameters.
10. Virtual memory is space on a hard drive used to simulate an environment in which more RAM is made available than actually exists on the system board.
11. Additional RAM is simulated by means of a virtual swap file on the hard disk, called a paging file.
12. It is advisable to let Windows manage your virtual memory paging file.
13. The System Information command also allows you to see memory addresses and other system information.
14. The Registry is the storage area for configuration information in Windows.
15. The best way to make changes to the Registry is to use the Control Panel icons.
16. The Registry is a tree-shaped hierarchy. It is stored in many files.
17. The Registry maintains three types of objects: keys, values, and data. The Registry keys can have subkeys, a procedure known as nesting.
18. Windows refers to the top-level keys as hives and predefined keys.
19. Keys and subkeys contain at least one value with a special name called "(Default)."
20. Values have three parts: the data type, the name, and the value.
21. There are five root keys: HKEY_LOCAL_MACHINE, HKEY_CLASSES_ROOT, HKEY_CURRENT_CONFIG, HKEY_USERS, and HKEY_CURRENT_USER. There are actually only two keys—HKEY_LOCAL_MACHINE and HKEY_USERS. The other keys are aliases for these two keys.
22. HKEY_LOCAL_MACHINE contains configuration information specific to the computer.
23. HKEY_USER contains the .DEFAULT subkey that is used for user preferences unless profiles have been enabled. In that case, there is a subkey for each user.
24. Regedit or Regedt32 are the tools that allow you to change the Registry directly.
25. Regedt32 shows a different window for each key. You can only search for keys in this utility.
26. Regedit has the keys in the left pane with the values in the right pane.
27. The icon in the right pane indicates whether it is a text data or binary data type.
28. You can import and export the entire Registry or a branch to a text file by using the Import/Export command. If you have a text file of the Registry, you can edit it safely and import it back into the Registry.
29. Do not double-click any file with the .REG extension, as this will automatically update the Registry.
30. Some changes do not take effect until you reload the Registry by restarting Windows.

KEY TERMS

adapter segment
bank switching
boot sequence
CMOS (Complementary Metal-Oxide Semiconductor)
conventional memory
data
demand paging
expanded memory
extended memory
high memory
HIMEM.SYS
hives
HKEY
HKEY_CLASSES_ROOT
HKEY_CURRENT_CONFIG
HKEY_CURRENT_USER
HKEY_LOCAL_MACHINE
HKEY_USERS
keys
memory manager
nesting
page frame
paging file
predefined key
subkeys
swap file
upper memory area (UMA)
upper memory blocks (UMBs)
values
virtual machine

DISCUSSION QUESTIONS

1. Describe the purpose and function of the CMOS.
2. Describe the steps you would take to use the CMOS Setup Utility.
3. What is physical memory?
4. What is the purpose and function of conventional memory?
5. What is the purpose and function of extended memory?
6. What is the UMA, and how is it used?
7. What is the purpose and function of the MEM command?
8. Define virtual memory.
9. What is a paging file?
10. Explain some of the advantages and disadvantages of paging.
11. Describe a set of circumstances in which you would take over the management of your machine's virtual memory paging file.
12. Why is it important to understand the purpose and function of the Registry?
13. Compare and contrast the safest and most dangerous methods of modifying the Registry.
14. Describe the structure of the Registry.
15. List the major keys of the Registry.
16. List and explain the three types of objects found in the Registry.
17. What is nesting?
18. Explain the purpose of two of the major keys found in the Registry.
19. List and explain the function of values in the Registry.
20. List and identify the three parts of a value.
21. List and identify at least three types of data in a value.
22. Explain the purpose and function of a Registry Editor.
23. Compare and contrast Regedit and Regedt32.
24. Explain the purpose and function of importing or exporting the Registry using Regedit.
25. Explain how to add an item to a context menu using Regedit.

TRUE/FALSE QUESTIONS

For each question, circle the letter T if the statement is true and the letter F if the statement is false.

T F 1. To change the booting sequence, you must use the CMOS Setup Utility.

T F 2. The MEM command provides information on the existence and usage of your computer's memory.

T F 3. Virtual memory refers to additional memory chips on the system board.

T F 4. If you have one physical hard drive in your computer, you should probably not manage your swap disk from the Windows operating system.

T F 5. You may edit the Registry using either Regedit or Regedt32.

COMPLETION QUESTIONS

Write the correct answer in each blank space.

6. The computer chip that retains the boot sequence of your computer is the _______.
7. If Windows runs out of physical memory on your computer, it uses _______ memory that is swapped to the hard drive.
8. When you boot your computer, Windows reads the information in the ________ to configure your computer properly.
9. The Registry is organized by _________, each of which usually has _________.
10. HKEY_CURRENT_CONFIG is an alias for _______________.

MULTIPLE CHOICE QUESTIONS

For each question, write the letter for the correct answer in the blank space.

☐ 11. An example of a memory manager is
   a. CMOS.
   b. HIMEM.SYS.
   c. REGEDIT.
   d. MEM.

☐ 12. Virtual memory is
   a. disk space used as memory where data is swapped in and out of RAM.
   b. memory space used as storage where data is swapped on and off of the hard drive.
   c. chips on the system board.
   d. none of the above

☐ 13. If you want to search the Registry for a specific value, the best tool to use is
   a. REGEDIT.
   b. REGEDT32.
   c. both a and b
   d. neither a nor b

☐ 14. REG_DWORD is an example of a
   a. hive.
   b. key.
   c. value.
   d. data type.

15. Which key stores the configuration data that is specific to your computer, such as what hardware you have installed and what your program settings are?
    a. HKEY_CLASSES_ROOT
    b. HKEY_USERS
    c. HKEY_LOCAL_MACHINE
    d. HKEY_CURRENT_USER

APPLICATION ASSIGNMENTS

For all essay questions, use Notepad or WordPad for your answer. Print your answer.

1. Compare and contrast virtual memory with physical memory.
2. Compare and contrast at least two types of memory.
3. You see the following display. Briefly describe the purpose and function of each section.

Command Prompt

```
C:\>MEM /C | MORE

Conventional Memory :

  Name                Size in Decimal       Size in Hex
      -------------    ---------------------  -------------

  MSDOS              12496      ( 12.2K)        30D0
  KBD                 3280      (  3.2K)         CD0
  HIMEM               1248      (  1.2K)         4E0
  COMMAND             3344      (  3.3K)         D10
  FREE                 112      (  0.1K)          70
  FREE              634704      (619.8K)       9AF50

Total  FREE :       634816      (619.9K)

Upper Memory :

  Name                Size in Decimal       Size in Hex
-------------       ---------------------  -------------

  SYSTEM            167920      (164.0K)       28FF0
  MOUSE              12528      ( 12.2K)        30F0
  MSCDEXNT             464      (  0.5K)         1D0
  REDIR               2672      (  2.6K)         A70
  DOSX               34848      ( 34.0K)        8820
  FREE                 784      (  0.8K)         310
  FREE               59168      ( 57.8K)        E720

Total  FREE :        59952      ( 58.5K)

Total bytes available to programs (Conventional+Upper):  694768  (678.5K)
Largest executable program size :                        633920  (619.1K)
Largest available upper memory block :                    59168  ( 57.8K)
```

```
   1048576 bytes total contiguous extended memory
         0 bytes available contiguous extended memory
    941056 bytes available XMS memory
           MS-DOS resident in High Memory Area


C:\>_
```

4. You have files that have the .BMP file extension. Every time you double-click a document with that extension, the Paint program opens. However, now you also have another program that you would like to be able to open instead of Paint. What could you do to solve this problem?

APPENDIX

A

INSTALLING THE WINDOSBK DIRECTORY AND SHAREWARE REGISTRATION

A.1 THE WINDOSBK DIRECTORY

The disk supplied with this textbook provides programs and files for you to use as you work through the book. The textbook assumes that the WINDOSBK directory has been installed on Drive C. If you wish to install the WINDOSBK directory on a hard drive other than Drive C, you must substitute the correct drive letter in these instructions. If you are working on your own computer, you must be in MS-DOS at the command line, not in Windows. You must be at the root of C and the default drive and directory must be A:\.

If you are in a lab environment, the lab instructors should have installed the WINDOSBK directory on the hard disk. The lab instructors, particularly if the lab is on a network, will have to give you instructions as to the location of the WINDOSBK directory if it is not on Drive C. The instructor will inform you if you need to install the WINDOSBK directory.

A.2 INSTALLING THE WINDOSBK DIRECTORY

Step 1 Have no disk in any drive. Turn on the monitor and computer.

WHAT'S HAPPENING? You are at the Windows desktop.

Step 2 Click **Start**. Point to **Programs**. Point to **Accessories**. Point to **Command Prompt**

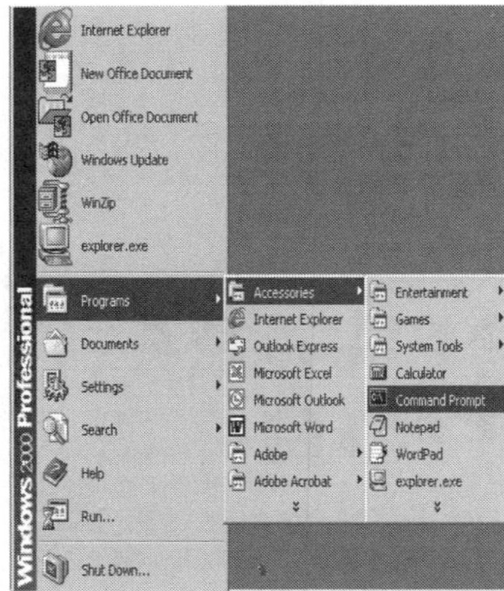

WHAT'S HAPPENING? You are going to open the Command Prompt window.

Step 3 Click **Command Prompt**

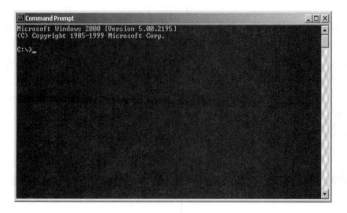

WHAT'S HAPPENING? You have opened a Command Prompt window. Your directory may differ. In this example, it is C:\WINDOWS>.

Step 4 Key in the following: C:\WINDOWS>**CD ** Enter

```
Command Prompt

Microsoft Windows 2000 [Version 5.00.2195]
(C) Copyright 1985-1999 Microsoft Corp.

C:\WINDOWS>CD \

C:\>_
```

You are now at the root of Drive C. If you wanted this folder to be on a drive other than C, you would substitute that drive letter for C.

Step 5 Place the ACTIVITIES disk that came with the textbook into Drive A.

Step 6 Key in the following: C:\>**A:** Enter

Command Prompt
C:\>A:
A:\>_

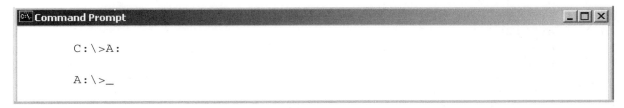

You have made the root of A the default drive and directory.

Step 7 Key in the following: A:>**XCOPY A:*.* /S /E C:\WINDOSBK**

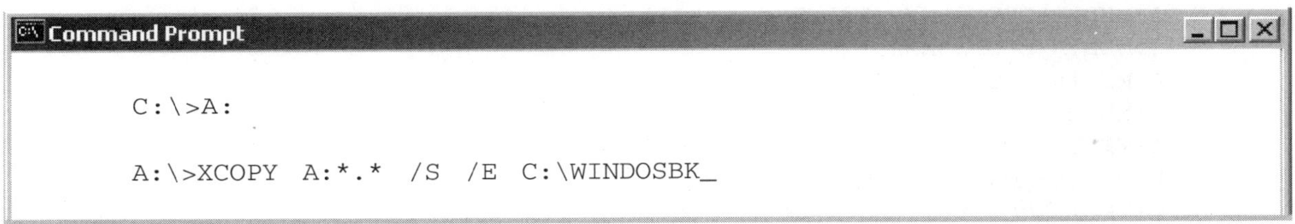
Command Prompt
C:\>A:
A:\>XCOPY A:*.* /S /E C:\WINDOSBK_

Be sure that this is what you have keyed in. Now you can begin executing the program by pressing Enter.

Step 8 Press Enter

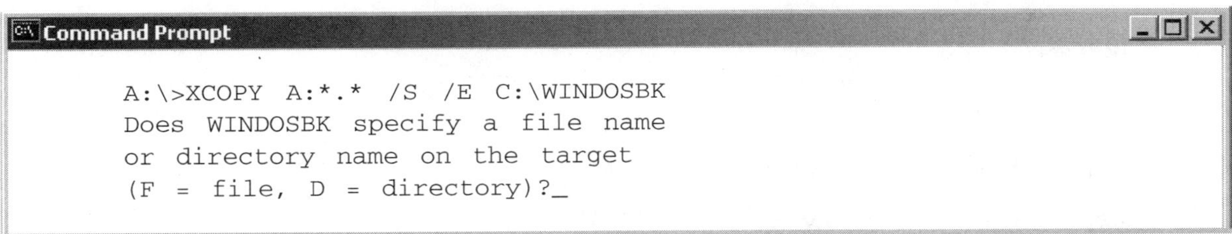
Command Prompt
A:\>XCOPY A:*.* /S /E C:\WINDOSBK
Does WINDOSBK specify a file name
or directory name on the target
(F = file, D = directory)?_

The XCOPY command is asking you if you want to create a directory or file called **WINDOSBK**. In this case you want to create a directory so you must specify that by pressing the letter **D**. Once you press **D**, the files will be copied to Drive C to the directory called **WINDOSBK**.

Step 9 Press **D** Enter

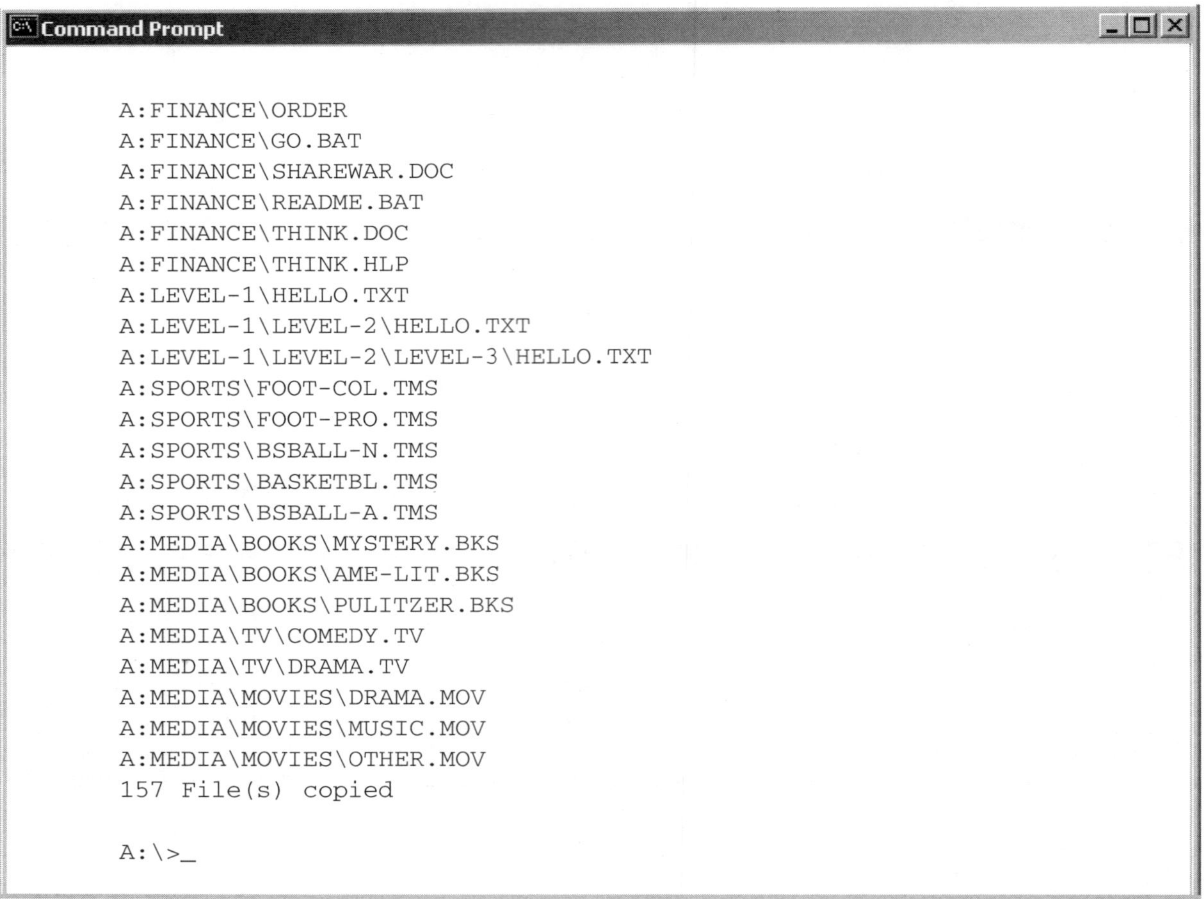

```
Command Prompt

A:FINANCE\ORDER
A:FINANCE\GO.BAT
A:FINANCE\SHAREWAR.DOC
A:FINANCE\README.BAT
A:FINANCE\THINK.DOC
A:FINANCE\THINK.HLP
A:LEVEL-1\HELLO.TXT
A:LEVEL-1\LEVEL-2\HELLO.TXT
A:LEVEL-1\LEVEL-2\LEVEL-3\HELLO.TXT
A:SPORTS\FOOT-COL.TMS
A:SPORTS\FOOT-PRO.TMS
A:SPORTS\BSBALL-N.TMS
A:SPORTS\BASKETBL.TMS
A:SPORTS\BSBALL-A.TMS
A:MEDIA\BOOKS\MYSTERY.BKS
A:MEDIA\BOOKS\AME-LIT.BKS
A:MEDIA\BOOKS\PULITZER.BKS
A:MEDIA\TV\COMEDY.TV
A:MEDIA\TV\DRAMA.TV
A:MEDIA\MOVIES\DRAMA.MOV
A:MEDIA\MOVIES\MUSIC.MOV
A:MEDIA\MOVIES\OTHER.MOV
157 File(s) copied

A:\>_
```

WHAT'S HAPPENING? You now have a directory on Drive C called **WINDOSBK**. You need to have this directory placed on Drive C in order to complete the exercises, activities, and homework.

Step 10 Key in the following: A:\>**C:** Enter

Step 11 Key in the following: C:\>**DIR WINDOS*.*** Enter

```
Command Prompt

C:\>DIR WINDOS*.*
 Volume in drive C is W2000-PRO
 Volume Serial Number is 2234-1CF8

 Directory of C:\

08/06/2001  06:56p      <DIR>          WINDOSBK
               0 File(s)              0 bytes
               1 Dir(s)     470,482,944 bytes free

C:\>_
```

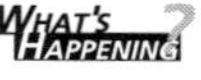

You have successfully installed the **WINDOSBK** directory on Drive C. Installed means that you created the **WINDOSBK** directory on Drive C and copied all the files on the disk in Drive A to the newly created directory called **WINDOSBK**.

Step 12 Key in the following: C:\>**Exit** Enter

You have closed the Command Prompt window and returned to the Windows desktop.

A.3 REMOVING THE WINDOSBK DIRECTORY FROM THE HARD DISK

Note 1: If you are working in a lab environment, do not take these steps. However, if you are working on your own computer, when you have completed the textbook you will probably want to take the WINDOSBK directory and the files it contains off your hard drive. You may, of course, use Explorer. You would select the WINDOSBK folder, then press the Delete key. If you would like to delete these files at the command line, you may use the RMDIR command.

Note 2: It is assumed that you have booted the system and are on the Windows desktop.

Step 1 Click **Start**. Point to **Programs**. Point to **Accessories**. Point to **Command Prompt**

Step 2 Key in the following: C:\WINDOWS>**CD ** Enter

```
Command Prompt

Microsoft Windows 2000 [Version 5.00.2195]
(C) Copyright 1985-1999 Microsoft Corp.

C:\WINDOWS>CD \

C:\>_
```

You are now at the root of Drive C.

Step 3 Key in the following: C:\>**RMDIR /S \WINDOSBK** Enter

Command Prompt
C:\>RMDIR /S \WINDOSBK

Be sure you have correctly keyed in the directory name.

Step 4 Press Enter

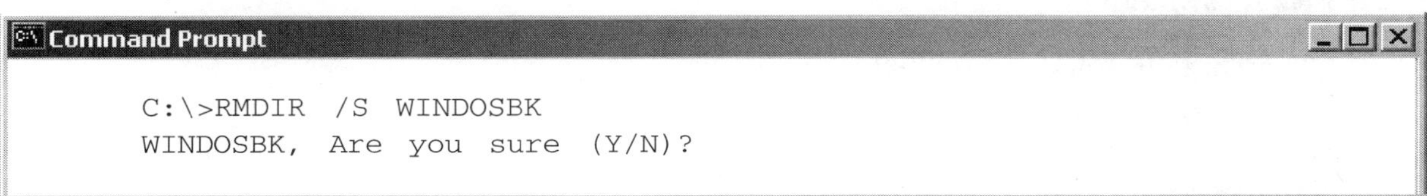
Command Prompt
C:\>RMDIR /S WINDOSBK
WINDOSBK, Are you sure (Y/N)?

You are being asked to confirm if you really want to delete the directory called **WINDOSBK** and all the files and directories that are in it.

Step 5 Press **Y** Enter

Step 6 Key in the following: C:\>**DIR WINDOS*.*** Enter

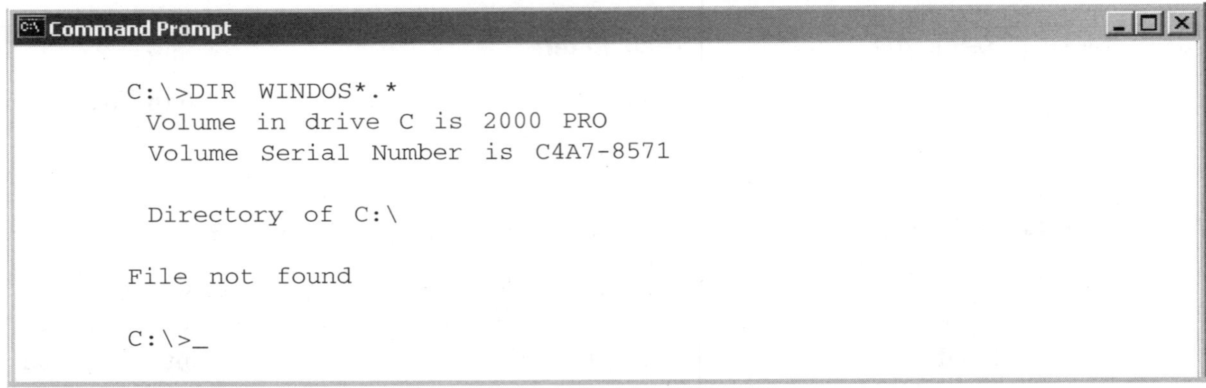

Command Prompt
C:\>DIR WINDOS*.*
Volume in drive C is 2000 PRO
Volume Serial Number is C4A7-8571
Directory of C:\
File not found
C:\>_

You have successfully deleted the **WINDOSBK** directory.

Step 7 Key in the following: C:\>**Exit** Enter

You have closed the Command Prompt window and returned to the Windows desktop.

A.4 SHAREWARE PROGRAMS PROVIDED WITH THE TEXTBOOKN

Several programs on the ACTIVITIES disk that are installed to the **WINDOSBK** directory are shareware programs. Shareware programs are for trial purposes only. If you find you like the programs and would like to keep them, you must register them and pay the registration fee.

HOME PHONE BOOK SHAREWARE PROGRAM

Home Phone Book, Version 2.5
This shareware program is provided by:

Thomas E. Bonitz
7903 Kona Circle
Papillion, NE 68046

If you like Home Phone Book, please send $20.00 to Thomas E. Bonitz at the above address.

THE THINKER SHAREWARE PROGRAM

The Thinker, Version 3.0-0788
This shareware program is provided by:

Alan C. Elliott
TexaSoft
P.O. Box 1169
Cedar Hill, TX 75104

If you like The Thinker, please send $35.00 plus shipping and handling to Alan C. Elliott at the above address. Phone orders: (214) 291–2115 or 1–800–955–TEXAS; FAX: (214) 291–3400. You may also print a copy of the order form by keying in PRINT \WINDOSBK\FINANCE\ORDER. The order form will allow you to specify your desired disk size.

MICROLINK SHAREWARE PROGRAMS

SHUT THE BOX, YAHT, OTRA, LOYD, PUSH YOUR LUCK, AND CRUX

These shareware programs are provided by:

Bob Lancaster
P. O. Box 5612
Hacienda Heights, CA 91745

If you like any of these games, please send $5.00 for each game to Bob Lancaster at the above address.

CHEKKERS SHAREWARE PROGRAM

CHEKKERS, Version 4.1
This shareware program is provided by:

J & J Software
P.O. Box 254
Matamoras, PA 18336

If you like CHEKKERS, please send $15.00 to J & J Software at the above address.

ARGH SHAREWARE PROGRAM

ARGH, Version 4.0
This shareware program is provided by:

David B. Howorth
1960 S.W. Palatine Hill Road
Portland, OR 97219

If you like ARGH, please send $10.00 to David B. Howorth at the above address.

COMMAND SUMMARY

APPEND Allows programs to open data files in specified directories as if they were in the current directory.

APPEND [[drive:]path[;...]] [/X[:ON ¦ :OFF]] [/PATH:ON ¦ /PATH:OFF] [/E] APPEND ;

[drive:]path	Specifies a drive and directory to append.
/X:ON	Applies appended directories to file searches and application execution.
/X:OFF	Applies appended directories only to requests to open files. /X:OFF is the default setting.
/PATH:ON	Applies appended directories to file requests that already specify a path. /PATH:ON is the default setting.
/PATH:OFF	Turns off the effect of /PATH:ON.
/E	Stores a copy of the appended directory list in an environment variable named APPEND. /E may be used only the first time you use APPEND after starting your system.

Type APPEND ; to clear the appended directory list. Type APPEND without parameters to display the appended directory list.

ARP Displays and modifies the IP-to-Physical address translation tables used by address resolution protocol (ARP).

ARP -s inet_addr eth_addr [if_addr]
ARP -d inet_addr [if_addr]
ARP -a [inet_addr] [-N if_addr]

-a	Displays current ARP entries by interrogating the current protocol data. If inet_addr is specified, the IP and Physical addresses for only the specified computer are displayed. If more than one network interface uses ARP, entries for each ARP table are displayed.
-g	Same as -a.
inet_addr	Specifies an Internet address.
-N if_addr	Displays the ARP entries for the network interface specified by if_addr.
-d	Deletes the host specified by inet_addr. inet_addr may be wildcarded with * to delete all hosts.
-s	Adds the host and associates the Internet address inet_addr with the Physical address eth_addr. The Physical address is given as 6 hexadecimal bytes separated by hyphens. The entry is permanent.
eth_add	Specifies a physical address.
if_addr	If present, this specifies the Internet address of the interface whose address translation table should be modified. If not present, the first applicable interface will be used.

Example:
> arp -s 157.55.85.212 00-aa-00-62-c6-09 .... Adds a static entry.
> arp -a .... Displays the ARP table.

ASSOC Displays or modifies file extension associations.

ASSOC [.ext[=[fileType]]]

.ext	Specifies the file extension to associate the file type with.
fileType	Specifies the file type to associate with the file extension.

Type ASSOC without parameters to display the current file associations. If ASSOC is invoked with just a file extension, it displays the current file association for that file extension. Specify nothing for the file type and the command will delete the association for the file extension.

AT Schedules commands and programs to run on a computer at a specified time and date. The Schedule service must be running to use the AT command.

AT [\\computername] [[id] [/DELETE] ¦ /DELETE [/YES]]
AT [\\computername] time [/INTERACTIVE] [/EVERY:date[,...] ¦ /NEXT:date[,...]] "command"

\\computername	Specifies a remote computer. Commands are scheduled on the local computer if this parameter is omitted.
id	Is an identification number assigned to a scheduled command.
/DELETE	Cancels a scheduled command. If id is omitted, all the scheduled commands on the computer are canceled.
/YES	Used with cancel all jobs command when no further confirmation is desired.
time	Specifies the time when command is to run.
/INTERACTIVE	Allows the job to interact with the desktop of the user who is logged on at the time the job runs.
/EVERY:date[,...]	Runs the command on each specified day of the week or month. If date is omitted, the current day of the month is assumed.
/NEXT:date[,...]	Runs the specified command on the next occurrence of the day (for example, next Thursday). If date is omitted, the current day of the month is assumed.
"command"	Is the command or batch program to be run.

ATMADM Monitors connections and addresses registered by the ATM Call Manager on an asynchronous transfer mode (ATM) network. You can use the utility to display statistics for incoming and outgoing calls on ATM adapters.

Usage: atmadm [options]
where options are one or more of the following:
-c Lists all connections.
-a Lists all registered addresses.
-s Displays Statistics.

ATTRIB Displays or changes file attributes.

ATTRIB [+R ¦ -R] [+A ¦ -A] [+S ¦ -S] [+H ¦ -H] [[drive:] [path] filename][/S [/D]]

+	Sets an attribute.
-	Clears an attribute.
R	Read-only file attribute.
A	Archive file attribute.
S	System file attribute.
H	Hidden file attribute.
/S	Processes matching files in the current folder and all subfolders.
/D	Processes folders as well.

BREAK Sets or clears extended Ctrl+C–checking on DOS systems.

This is present for compatibility with DOS systems. It has no effect under Windows 2000.

If Command Extensions are enabled, on the Windows 2000 platform, the BREAK command will enter a hard coded breakpoint if being debugged by a debugger.

CACLS Displays or modifies access control lists (ACLs) of files.

CACLS filename [/T] [/E] [/C] [/G user:perm] [/R user [...]]
[/P user:perm [...]] [/D user [...]]

filename	Displays ACLs.
/T	Changes ACLs of specified files in the current directory and all subdirectories.
/E	Edits ACL instead of replacing it.
/C	Continues on access denied errors.
/G user:perm	Grants specified user access rights. perm can be: R Read W Write C Change (write) F Full control
/R user	Revokes specified user's access rights (only valid with /E).
/P user:perm	Replaces specified user's access rights. perm can be: N None R Read W Write C Change (write) F Full control
/D user	Denies specified user access.

Wildcards can be used to specify more than one file in a command. You can specify more than one user in a command.

CALL Calls one batch program from another.

CALL [drive:][path]filename [batch-parameters]

batch-parameters Specifies any command line information required by the batch program.

If Command Extensions are enabled CALL changes as follows:

The CALL command now accepts labels as the target of the CALL. The syntax is the following:

CALL :label arguments

A new batch file context is created with the specified arguments and control is passed to the statement after the label specified. You must "exit" twice by reaching the end of the batch script file twice. The first time you read the end, control will return to just after the CALL statement. The second time you will exit the batch script. Type GOTO /? for a description of the GOTO :EOF extension that will allow you to "return" from a batch script.

In addition, expansion of batch script argument references (%0, %1, etc.) have been changed as follows:

%* in a batch script refers to all the arguments (e.g., %1 %2 %3 %4 %5 ...)

Substitution of batch parameters (%*n*) has been enhanced. You can now use the following optional syntax:

%~1	Expands %1 removing any surrounding quotes (").
%~f1	Expands %1 to a fully qualified path name.
%~d1	Expands %1 to a drive letter only.
%~p1	Expands %1 to a path only.
%~n1	Expands %1 to a file name only.
%~x1	Expands %1 to a file extension only.
%~s1	Expanded path contains short names only.
%~a1	Expands %1 to file attributes.
%~t1	Expands %1 to date/time of file.
%~z1	Expands %1 to size of file.
%~$PATH:1	Searches the directories listed in the PATH environment variable and expands %1 to the fully qualified name of the first one found. If the environment variable name is not

defined or the file is not found by the search, then this modifier expands to the empty string.

The modifiers can be combined to get compound results:

%~dp1	Expands %1 to a drive letter and path only.
%~nx1	Expands %1 to a file name and extension only.
%~dp$PATH:1	Searches the directories listed in the PATH environment variable for %1 and expands to the drive letter and path of the first one found.
%~ftza1	Expands %1 to a DIR-like output line.

In the above examples %1 and PATH can be replaced by other valid values. The %~ syntax is terminated by a valid argument number. The %~ modifiers may not be used with %*.

CD or CHDIR Displays the name of or changes the current directory.

CHDIR [/D] [drive:][path]
CHDIR [..]
CD [/D] [drive:][path]
CD [..]

.. Specifies that you want to change to the parent directory.

Type CD drive: to display the current directory in the specified drive. Type CD without parameters to display the current drive and directory.

Use the /D switch to change the current drive in addition to changing the current directory for a drive.

If Command Extensions are enabled CHDIR changes as follows:

The current directory string is converted to use the same case as the on-disk names. So CD C:\TEMP would actually set the current directory to C:\Temp if that is the case on the disk.

The CHDIR command does not treat spaces as delimiters, so it is possible to CD into a subdirectory name that contains a space without surrounding the name with quotes. For example:

cd \winnt\profiles\username\programs\start menu

is the same as

cd "\winnt\profiles\username\programs\start menu"

which is what you would have to type if extensions were disabled.

CHCP Displays or sets the active code page number.

CHCP [nnn]

nnn Specifies a code page number.

Type CHCP without a parameter to display the active code page number.

CHKDSK Checks a disk and displays a status report.

CHKDSK [volume[[path]filename]] [/F] [/V] [/R] [/X] [/I]
[/C] [/L[:size]]

volume	Specifies the drive letter (followed by a colon), mount point, or volume name.
filename	FAT only: Specifies the files to check for fragmentation.
/F	Fixes errors on the disk.
/V	On FAT/FAT32: Displays the full path and name of every file on the disk. On NTFS: Displays cleanup messages if any.
/R	Locates bad sectors and recovers readable information (implies /F).
/L:size	NTFS only: Changes the log file size to the specified number of kilobytes. If size is not specified, displays current size.

/X	Forces the volume to dismount first if necessary. All opened handles to the volume would then be invalid (implies /F).
/I	NTFS only: Performs a less vigorous check of index entries.
/C	NTFS only: Skips checking of cycles within the folder structure.

The /I or /C switch reduces the amount of time required to run CHKDSK by skipping certain checks of the volume.

CHKNTFS Displays or modifies the checking of a disk at boot time.

CHKNTFS volume [...]
CHKNTFS /D
CHKNTFS /T[:time]
CHKNTFS /X volume [...]
CHKNTFS /C volume [...]

volume	Specifies the drive letter (followed by a colon), mount point, or volume name.
/D	Restores the machine to the default behavior; all drives are checked at boot time and CHKDSK is run on those that are dirty.
/T:time	Changes the AUTOCHK initiation countdown time to the specified amount of time in seconds. If time is not specified, displays the current setting.
/X	Excludes a drive from the default boot-time check. Excluded drives are not accumulated between command invocations.
/C	Schedules a drive to be checked at boot time; CHKDSK will run if the drive is dirty.

If no switches are specified, CHKNTFS will display if the specified drive is dirty or scheduled to be checked on next reboot.

CIPHER Displays or alters the encryption of directories (files) on NTFS partitions.

CIPHER [/E ¦ /D] [/S:dir] [/A] [/I] [/F] [/Q] [/H] [/K] [pathname [...]]

/E	Encrypts the specified directories. Directories will be marked so that files added afterward will be encrypted.
/D	Decrypts the specified directories. Directories will be marked so that files added afterward will not be encrypted.
/S	Performs the specified operation on directories in the given directory and all subdirectories.
/A	Operation for files as well as directories. The encrypted file could become decrypted when it is modified if the parent directory is not encrypted. It is recommended that you encrypt the file and the parent directory.
/I	Continues performing the specified operation even after errors have occurred. By default, CIPHER stops when an error is encountered.
/F	Forces the encryption operation on all specified objects, even those that are already encrypted. Already-encrypted objects are skipped by default.
/Q	Reports only the most essential information.
/H	Displays files with the hidden or system attributes. These files are omitted by default.
/K	Create new file encryption key for the user running CIPHER. If this option is chosen, all the other options will be ignored.
pathname	Specifies a pattern, file, or directory.

Used without parameters, CIPHER displays the encryption state of the current directory and any files it contains. You may use multiple directory names and wildcards. You must put spaces between multiple parameters.

CLUSTER You can use cluster commands to administer server clusters from the Windows 2000 command prompt.

CLUSTER /LIST[:domain-name]
CLUSTER [[/CLUSTER:]cluster-name] <options>

<options> =
/PROP[ERTIES] [<prop-list>]
/PRIV[PROPERTIES] [<prop-list>]

/PROP[ERTIES][:propname[,propname ...] /USEDEFAULT]
/PRIV[PROPERTIES][:propname[,propname ...] /USEDEFAULT]
/REN[AME]:cluster-name
/VER[SION]
/QUORUM[RESOURCE][:resource-name] [/PATH:path] [/MAXLOGSIZE:max-size-kbytes]
/SETFAIL[UREACTIONS][:node-name[,node-name ...]]
/REG[ADMIN]EXT:admin-extension-dll[,admin-extension-dll ...]
/UNREG[ADMIN]EXT:admin-extension-dll[,admin-extension-dll ...]
NODE [node-name] node-command
GROUP [group-name] group-command
RES[OURCE] [resource-name] resource-command
{RESOURCETYPE ¦ RESTYPE} [resourcetype-name] resourcetype-command
NET[WORK] [network-name] network-command
NETINT[ERFACE] [interface-name] interface-command

<prop-list> =
name=value[,value ...][:<format>] [name=value[,value ...][:<format>] ...]

<format> =
BINARY ¦ DWORD ¦ STR[ING] ¦ EXPANDSTR[ING] ¦ MULTISTR[ING] ¦ SECURITY ¦ ULARGE

CMD Starts a new instance of the Windows 2000 command interpreter.

CMD [/A ¦ /U] [/Q] [/D] [/E:ON ¦ /E:OFF] [/F:ON ¦ /F:OFF] [/V:ON ¦ /V:OFF] [[/S] [/C ¦ /K] string]

/C	Carries out the command specified by the string and then terminates.
/K	Carries out the command specified by the string but remains.
/S	Modifies the treatment of the string after /C or /K (see below).
/Q	Turns echo off.
/D	Disables the execution of AutoRun commands from the Registry (see below).
/A	Causes the output of internal commands to a pipe or file to be ANSI.
/U	Causes the output of internal commands to a pipe or file to be Unicode.
/T:fg	Sets the foreground/background colors (see COLOR /?).
/E:ON	Enables command extensions (see below).
/E:OFF	Disables command extensions (see below).
/F:ON	Enables file and directory name completion characters (see below).
/F:OFF	Disables file and directory name completion characters (see below).
/V:ON	Enables delayed environment variable expansion using c as the delimiter. For example, /V:ON would allow !var! to expand the variable var at execution time. The var syntax expands variables at input time, which is quite a different thing when inside of a FOR loop.
/V:OFF	Disables delayed environment expansion.

Note that multiple commands separated by the command separator '&&' are accepted for string if surrounded by quotes. Also, for compatibility reasons, /X is the same as /E:ON, /Y is the same as / E:OFF, and /R is the same as /C. Any other switches are ignored.

If /C or /K is specified, then the remainder of the command line after the switch is processed as a command line, where the following logic is used to process quote (") characters:

1. If all of the following conditions are met, then quote characters on the command line are preserved:

   - no /S switch
   - exactly two quote characters
   - no special characters between the two quote characters, where special is one of: &<>()@^ ¦
   - there are one or more whitespace characters between the two quote characters
   - the string between the two quote characters is the name of an executable file

2. Otherwise, old behavior is to see if the first character is a quote character and if so, strip the leading character and remove the last quote character on the command line, preserving any text after the last quote character.

If /D was NOT specified on the command line, then when CMD.EXE starts, it looks for the following REG_SZ/REG_EXPAND_SZ registry variables, and if either or both are present, they are executed first.

HKEY_LOCAL_MACHINE\Software\Microsoft\Command Processor\AutoRun

and/or

HKEY_CURRENT_USER\Software\Microsoft\Command Processor\AutoRun

Command Extensions are enabled by default. You may also disable extensions for a particular invocation by using the /E:OFF switch. You can enable or disable extensions for all invocations of CMD.EXE on a machine and/or user logon session by setting either or both of the following REG_DWORD values in the registry using REGEDT32.EXE:

HKEY_LOCAL_MACHINE\Software\Microsoft\Command Processor\EnableExtensions

and/or

HKEY_CURRENT_USER\Software\Microsoft\Command Processor\EnableExtensions

to either 0x1 or 0x0. The user-specific setting takes precedence over the machine setting. The command line switches take precedence over the Registry settings.

The command extensions involve changes and/or additions to the following commands:

DEL or ERASE
COLOR
CD or CHDIR
MD or MKDIR
PROMPT
PUSHD
POPD
SET
SETLOCAL
ENDLOCAL
IF
FOR
CALL
SHIFT
GOTO
START (also includes changes to external command invocation)
ASSOC
FTYPE

To get specific details, type commandname /?.

Delayed environment variable expansion is NOT enabled by default. You can enable or disable delayed environment variable expansion for a particular invocation of CMD.EXE with the /V:ON or /V:OFF switch. You can enable or disable completion for all invocations of CMD.EXE on a machine and/or user logon session by setting either or both of the following REG_DWORD values in the Registry using REGEDT32.EXE:

HKEY_LOCAL_MACHINE\Software\Microsoft\Command Processor\DelayedExpansion

and/or

HKEY_CURRENT_USER\Software\Microsoft\Command Processor\DelayedExpansion

to either 0x1 or 0x0. The user-specific setting takes precedence over the machine setting. The command line switches take precedence over the Registry settings.

If delayed environment variable expansion is enabled, then the exclamation character can be used to substitute the value of an environment variable at execution time.

File and directory name completion is NOT enabled by default. You can enable or disable file name completion for a particular invocation of CMD.EXE with the /F:ON or /F:OFF switch. You can enable or disable completion for all invocations of CMD.EXE on a machine and/or user logon session by setting either or both of the following REG_DWORD values in the Registry using REGEDT32.EXE:

HKEY_LOCAL_MACHINE\Software\Microsoft\Command Processor\CompletionChar
HKEY_LOCAL_MACHINE\Software\Microsoft\Command Processor\PathCompletionChar

and/or

HKEY_CURRENT_USER\Software\Microsoft\Command Processor\CompletionChar
HKEY_CURRENT_USER\Software\Microsoft\Command Processor\PathCompletionChar

with the hex value of a control character to use for a particular function (e.g., 0x4 is Ctrl-D and 0x6 is Ctrl-F). The user-specific settings take precedence over the machine settings. The command line switches take precedence over the Registry settings.

If completion is enabled with the /F:ON switch, the two control characters used are Ctrl-D for directory name completion and Ctrl-F for file name completion. To disable a particular completion character in the Registry, use the value for space (0x20) as it is not a valid control character.

Completion is invoked when you type either of the two control characters. The completion function takes the path string to the left of the cursor, appends a wildcard character to it if none is already present, and builds up a list of paths that match. It then displays the first matching path. If no paths match, it just beeps and leaves the display alone. Thereafter, repeated pressing of the same control character will cycle through the list of matching paths. Pressing the Shift key with the control character will move through the list backwards. If you edit the line in any way and press the control character again, the saved list of matching paths is discarded and a new one generated. The same occurs if you switch between file and directory name completion. The only difference between the two control characters is that the file completion character matches both file and directory names, while the directory completion character only matches directory names. If file completion is used on any of the built-in directory commands (CD, MD, or RD) then directory completion is assumed.

The completion code deals correctly with file names that contain spaces or other special characters by placing quotes around the matching path. Also, if you back up and then invoke completion from within a line, the text to the right of the cursor at the point completion was invoked is discarded.

COLOR Sets the default console foreground and background colors.

COLOR [attr]

attr Specifies color attribute of console output.

Color attributes are specified by TWO hex digits. The first corresponds to the background; the second the foreground. Each digit can be any of the following values:

0 = Black	8 = Gray
1 = Blue	9 = Light Blue
2 = Green	A = Light Green
3 = Aqua	B = Light Aqua
4 = Red	C = Light Red
5 = Purple	D = Light Purple
6 = Yellow	E = Light Yellow
7 = White	F = Bright White

If no argument is given, this command restores the color to what it was when CMD.EXE started. This value comes from the current console window, the /T command line switch, or the DefaultColor Registry value.

The COLOR command sets ERRORLEVEL to 1 if an attempt is made to execute the COLOR command with a foreground and background color that are the same.

Example: "COLOR fc" produces light red on bright white

COMP Compares the contents of two files or sets of files.

COMP [data1] [data2] [/D] [/A] [/L] [/N=number] [/C]

data1 Specifies location and name of first file to compare.

data2	Specifies location and name of second file to compare.
/D	Displays differences in decimal format.
/A	Displays differences in ASCII characters.
/L	Displays line numbers for differences.
/N=number	Compares only the first specified number of lines in each file.
/C	Disregards case of ASCII letters when comparing files.

To compare sets of files, use wildcards in the data1 and data2 parameters.

COMPACT Displays or alters the compression of files on NTFS partitions.

COMPACT [/C ¦ /U] [/S[:dir]] [/A] [/I] [/F] [/Q] [filename [...]]

/C	Compresses the specified files. Directories will be marked so that files added afterward will be compressed.
/U	Uncompresses the specified files. Directories will be marked so that files added afterward will not be compressed.
/S	Performs the specified operation on files in the given directory and all subdirectories. By default, "dir" is the current directory.
/A	Displays files with the hidden or system attributes. These files are omitted by default.
/I	Continues performing the specified operation even after errors have occurred. By default, COMPACT stops when an error is encountered.
/F	Forces the compress operation on all specified files, even those that are already compressed. Already-compressed files are skipped by default.
/Q	Reports only the most essential information.
filename	Specifies a pattern, file, or directory.

Used without parameters, COMPACT displays the compression state of the current directory and any files it contains. You may use multiple file names and wildcards. You must put spaces between multiple parameters.

CONVERT Converts FAT volumes to NTFS.

CONVERT volume /FS:NTFS [/V]

volume	Specifies the drive letter (followed by a colon), mount point, or volume name.
/FS:NTFS	Specifies that the volume be converted to NTFS.
/V	Specifies that CONVERT should be run in verbose mode.

COPY Copies one or more files to another location.

COPY [/V] [/N] [/Y ¦ /-Y] [/Z] [/A ¦ /B] source [/A ¦ /B]
[+ source [/A ¦ /B] [+ ...]] [destination [/A ¦ /B]]

source	Specifies the file or files to be copied.
/A	Indicates an ASCII text file.
/B	Indicates a binary file.
destination	Specifies the directory and/or file name for the new file(s).
/V	Verifies that new files are written correctly.
/N	Uses the short file name, if available, when copying a file with a non-8.3 name.
/Y	Suppresses prompting to confirm you want to overwrite an existing destination file.
/-Y	Causes prompting to confirm you want to overwrite an existing destination file.
/Z	Copies networked files in restartable mode.

The switch /Y may be preset in the COPYCMD environment variable. This may be overridden with /-Y on the command line. The default is to prompt on overwrites unless the COPY command is being executed from within a batch script.

To append files, specify a single file for destination, but multiple files for source (using wildcards or file1+file2+file3 format).

CSCRIPT Runs scripts using the command line–based script host.

CSCRIPT scriptname.extension [option...] [arguments...]

Options:

//B	Batch mode: Suppresses script errors and prompts from displaying.
//D	Enables Active Debugging.
//E:engine	Uses engine for executing script.
//H:CScript	Changes the default script host to CScript.exe.
//H:WScript	Changes the default script host to WScript.exe (default).
//I	Activates interactive mode (default, opposite of //B).
//Job:xxxx	Executes a WS job.
//Logo	Displays logo (default).
//Nologo	Prevents logo display: No banner will be shown at execution time.
//S	Saves current command line options for this user.
//T:nn	Times out in seconds: Maximum time a script is permitted to run.
//X	Executes script in debugger.
//U	Uses Unicode for redirected I/O from the console.

DATE Displays or sets the date.

DATE [/T ¦ date]

Type DATE without parameters to display the current date setting and a prompt for a new one. Press Enter to keep the same date.

If Command Extensions are enabled the DATE command supports the /T switch, which tells the command to just output the current date, without prompting for a new date.

DEBUG Runs DEBUG, a program testing and editing tool.

DEBUG [[drive:][path]filename [testfile-parameters]]

[drive:][path]filename	Specifies the file you want to test.
testfile-parameters	Specifies the command line information required by the file you want to test.

After DEBUG starts, type ? to display a list of debugging commands.

DEL or ERASE Deletes one or more files.

DEL [/P] [/F] [/S] [/Q] [/A[[:]attributes]] names
ERASE [/P] [/F] [/S] [/Q] [/A[[:]attributes]] names

names	Specifies a list of one or more files or directories. Wildcards may be used to delete multiple files. If a directory is specified, all files within the directory will be deleted.
/P	Prompts for confirmation before deleting each file.
/F	Forces the deletion of read-only files.
/S	Deletes specified files from all subdirectories.
/Q	Activates quiet mode—does not ask if okay to delete on global wildcard.
/A	Selects files to delete based on attributes.
attributes	R Read-only files S System files H Hidden files A Files ready for archiving - Prefix meaning not

If Command Extensions are enabled DEL and ERASE change as follows:

The display semantics of the /S switch are reversed in that it shows you only the files that are deleted, not the ones it could not find.

DIR Displays a list of files and subdirectories in a directory.

DIR [drive:][path][filename] [/A[[:]attributes]] [/B] [/C] [/D] [/L] [/N] [/O[[:]sortorder]] [/P] [/Q] [/S] [/T[[:]timefield]] [/W] [/X] [/4]

[drive:][path][filename]	Specifies the drive, directory, and/or files to list.
/A	Displays files with specified attributes.
attributes	D Directories R Read-only files H Hidden files A Files ready for archiving S System files - Prefix meaning not
/B	Uses bare format (no heading information or summary).
/C	Displays the thousand separator in file sizes. This is the default. Use /-C to disable display of separator.
/D	Same as wide but files are sorted by column.
/L	Uses lowercase.
/N	Displays in new long list format where file names are on the far right.
/O	Lists by files in sorted order.
sortorder	N By name (alphabetic) S By size (smallest first) E By extension (alphabetic) D By date/time (oldest first) G Group directories first - Prefix to reverse order
/P	Pauses after each screenful of information.
/Q	Displays the owner of the file.
/S	Displays files in the specified directory and all subdirectories.
/T	Controls which time field is displayed or used for sorting.
timefield	C Creation A Last Access W Last Written
/W	Uses wide list format.
/X	Displays the short names generated for non-8.3 file names. The format is that of /N with the short name inserted before the long name. If no short name is present, blanks are displayed in its place.
/4	Displays four-digit years.

Switches may be preset in the DIRCMD environment variable. Override preset switches by prefixing any switch with - (hyphen), for example, /-W.

DISKCOMP Compares the contents of two floppy disks.

DISKCOMP [drive1: [drive2:]]

DISKCOPY Copies the contents of one floppy disk to another.

DISKCOPY [drive1: [drive2:]] [/V]

/V Verifies that the information is copied correctly.

The two floppy disks must be the same type. You may specify the same drive for drive1 and drive2.

DISKPERF Controls the types of counters that can be viewed using System Monitor.

DISKPERF [-Y[D¦V] ¦ -N[D¦V]] [\\computername]

-Y	Sets the system to start all disk performance counters when the system is restarted.
-YD	Enables the disk performance counters for physical drives when the system is restarted.
-YV	Enables the disk performance counters for logical drives or storage volumes when the system is restarted.
-N	Sets the system to disable all disk performance counters when the system is restarted.
-ND	Disables the disk performance counters for physical drives.

-NV	Disables the disk performance counters for logical drives.
\\computername	Is the name of the computer you want to see set disk performance counter use.

DOSKEY Edits command lines, recalls Windows 2000 commands, and creates macros.

DOSKEY [/REINSTALL] [/LISTSIZE=size] [/MACROS[:ALL ¦ :exename]] [/HISTORY] [/INSERT ¦ /OVERSTRIKE] [/EXENAME=exename] [/MACROFILE=filename] [macroname=[text]]

/REINSTALL	Installs a new copy of DOSKEY.
/LISTSIZE=size	Sets the size of the command history buffer.
/MACROS	Displays all DOSKEY macros.
/MACROS:ALL	Displays all DOSKEY macros for all executables that have DOSKEY macros.
/MACROS:exename	Displays all DOSKEY macros for the given executable.
/HISTORY	Displays all commands stored in memory.
/INSERT	Specifies that new text you type is inserted in old text.
/OVERSTRIKE	Specifies that new text overwrites old text.
/EXENAME=exename	Specifies the executable.
/MACROFILE=filename	Specifies a file of macros to install.
macroname	Specifies a name for a macro you create.
text	Specifies commands you want to record.

Up and down arrows recall commands; Esc clears command line; F7 displays command history; Alt+F7 clears command history; F8 searches command history; F9 selects a command by number; Alt+F10 clears macro definitions.

The following are some special codes in DOSKEY macro definitions:

$T	Command separator. Allows multiple commands in a macro.
$1–$9	Batch parameters. Equivalent to %1–%9 in batch programs.
$*	Symbol replaced by everything following macro name on command line.

ECHO Displays messages or turns command-echoing on or off.

ECHO [ON ¦ OFF]
ECHO [message]

Type ECHO without parameters to display the current echo setting.

EDLIN Starts EDLIN, a line-oriented text editor.

EDLIN [drive:][path]filename [/B]

/B Ignores end-of-file (Ctrl+Z) characters.

ENDLOCAL Ends localization of environment changes in a batch file. Environment changes made after ENDLOCAL has been issued are not local to the batch file; the previous settings are not restored on termination of the batch file.

ENDLOCAL

If Command Extensions are enabled ENDLOCAL changes as follows:

If the corresponding SETLOCAL enabled or disabled command extensions using the new ENABLEEXTENSIONS or DISABLEEXTENSIONS options, then after the ENDLOCAL, the enabled/disabled state of command extensions will be restored to what it was prior to the matching SETLOCAL command execution.

EXIT Quits the CMD.EXE program (command interpreter) or the current batch script.

EXIT [/B] [exitCode]

/B	Specifies to exit the current batch script instead of CMD.EXE. If executed from outside a batch script, it will quit CMD.EXE.
exitCode	Specifies a numeric number. If /B is specified, sets ERRORLEVEL to that number. If quitting CMD.EXE, sets the process exit code with that number.

EXPAND Expands one or more compressed files.

EXPAND [-r] source destination
EXPAND -r source [destination]
EXPAND -D source.cab [-F:files]
EXPAND source.cab -F:files destination

-r	Renames expanded files.
-D	Displays a list of the files in source.
source	Source file specification. Wildcards may be used.
-F:files	Name of files to expand from a .CAB.
destination	Destination file ¦ path specification. Destination may be a directory.

If source is multiple files and -r is not specified, destination must be a directory.

FC Compares two files or sets of files and displays the differences between them.

FC [/A] [/C] [/L] [/LBn] [/N] [/T] [/U] [/W] [/nnnn]
    [drive1:][path1]filename1
    [drive2:][path2]filename2
FC /B [drive1:][path1]filename1 [drive2:][path2]filename2

/A	Displays only first and last lines for each set of differences.
/B	Performs a binary comparison.
/C	Disregards the case of letters.
/L	Compares files as ASCII text.
/LBn	Sets the maximum consecutive mismatches to the specified number of lines.
/N	Displays the line numbers on an ASCII comparison.
/T	Does not expand tabs to spaces.
/U	Compare files as Unicode text files.
/W	Compresses white space (tabs and spaces) for comparison.
/nnnn	Specifies the number of consecutive lines that must match after a mismatch.

FIND Searches for a text string in a file or files.

FIND [/V] [/C] [/N] [/I] “string” [[drive:][path]filename[...]]

/V	Displays all lines NOT containing the specified string.
/C	Displays only the count of lines containing the string.
/N	Displays line numbers with the displayed lines.
/I	Ignores the case of characters when searching for the string.
“string”	Specifies the text string to find.
[drive:][path]filename	Specifies a file or files to search.

If a path is not specified, FIND searches the text typed at the prompt or piped from another command.

FINDSTR Searches for strings in files.

FINDSTR [/B] [/E] [/L] [/R] [/S] [/I] [/X] [/V] [/N] [/M] [/O] [/P] [/F:file] [/C:string] [/G:file] [/D:dir list] [/A:color attributes] [strings] [[drive:][path]filename[...]]

/B	Matches pattern if at the beginning of a line.
/E	Matches pattern if at the end of a line.
/L	Uses search strings literally.
/R	Uses search strings as regular expressions.
/S	Searches for matching files in the current directory and all subdirectories.
/I	Specifies that the search is not to be case-sensitive.
/X	Prints lines that match exactly.

/V — Prints only lines that do not contain a match.
/N — Prints the line number before each line that matches.
/M — Prints only the file name if a file contains a match.
/O — Prints character offset before each matching line.
/P — Skip files with nonprintable characters
/A:attr — Specifies color attribute with two hex digits. See "color /?".
/F:file — Reads file list from the specified file (/ stands for console).
/C:string — Uses specified string as a literal search string.
/G:file — Gets search strings from the specified file (/ stands for console).
/D:dir — Searches a semicolon-delimited list of directories.
strings — Text to be searched for.
[drive:][path]filename — Specifies a file or files to search.

Use spaces to separate multiple search strings unless the argument is prefixed with /C. For example, 'FINDSTR "hello there" x.y' searches for "hello" or "there" in file x.y. 'FINDSTR /C:"hello there" x.y' searches for "hello there" in file x.y.

Regular expression quick reference:

. — Wildcard: any character
* — Repeat: zero or more occurances of previous character or class
^ — Line position: beginning of line
$ — Line position: end of line
[class] — Character class: any one character in set
[^class] — Inverse class: any one character not in set
[x-y] — Range: any characters within the specified range
\x — Escape: literal use of metacharacter x
\<xyz — Word position: beginning of word
xyz\> — Word position: end of word

For full information on FINDSTR regular expressions refer to the online Command Reference.

FOR — Runs a specified command for each file in a set of files.

FOR %variable IN (set) DO command [command-parameters]

%variable — Specifies a replaceable parameter.
(set) — Specifies a set of one or more files. Wildcards may be used.
command — Specifies the command to carry out for each file.
command-parameters — Specifies parameters or switches for the specified command.

To use the FOR command in a batch program, specify %%variable instead of %variable. Variable names are case sensitive, so %i is different from %I.

If Command Extensions are enabled, the following additional forms of the FOR command are supported:

FOR /D %variable IN (set) DO command [command-parameters]

If set contains wildcards, then it specifies to match against directory names instead of file names.

FOR /R [[drive:]path] %variable IN (set) DO command [command-parameters]

Walks the directory tree rooted at [drive:]path, executing the FOR statement in each directory of the tree. If no directory specification is specified after /R then the current directory is assumed. If set is just a single period (.) character then it will just enumerate the directory tree.

FOR /L %variable IN (start,step,end) DO command [command-parameters]

The set is a sequence of numbers from start to end, by step amount. So (1,1,5) would generate the sequence 1 2 3 4 5 and (5,-1,1) would generate the sequence (5 4 3 2 1).

FOR /F ["options"] %variable IN (file-set) DO command [command-parameters]
FOR /F ["options"] %variable IN ("string") DO command [command-parameters]
FOR /F ["options"] %variable IN ('command') DO command [command-parameters]

or, if usebackq option present:

FOR /F ["options"] %variable IN (file-set) DO command [command-parameters]
FOR /F ["options"] %variable IN ('string') DO command [command-parameters]
FOR /F ["options"] %variable IN (`command`) DO command [command-parameters]

filenameset is one or more file names. Each file is opened, read, and processed before going on to the next file in filenameset. Processing consists of reading in the file, breaking it up into individual lines of text, and then parsing each line into zero or more tokens. The body of the for loop is then called with the variable value(s) set to the found token string(s). By default, /F passes the first blank separated token from each line of each file. Blank lines are skipped. You can override the default parsing behavior by specifying the optional "options" parameter. This is a quoted string that contains one or more keywords to specify different parsing options. The keywords are the following:

eol=c	Specifies an end-of-line comment character (just one).
skip=n	Specifies the number of lines to skip at the beginning of the file.
delims=xxx	Specifies a delimiter set. This replaces the default delimiter set of space and tab.
tokens=x,y,m-n	Specifies which tokens from each line are to be passed to the for body for each iteration. This will cause additional variable names to be allocated. The m-n form is a range, specifying the *m*th through the *n*th tokens. If the last character in thetokens= string is an asterisk, then an additional variable is allocated and receives the remaining text on the line after the last token parsed.
usebackq	Specifies that the new semantics are in force, where a back quoted string is executed as a command and a single quoted string is a literal string command and allows the use of double quotes to quote file names in filenameset.

FORCEDOS Starts the specified program in the MS-DOS subsystem. This command is necessary only for those MS-DOS programs not recognized as such by Windows 2000.

FORCEDOS [/D directory] filename [parameters]

/D directory	Specifies the current directory for the specified program to use.
filename	Specifies the program to start.
parameters	Specifies parameters to pass to the program.

FORMAT Formats a disk for use with Windows 2000.

FORMAT volume [/FS:file-system] [/V:label] [/Q] [/A:size] [/C] [/X]
FORMAT volume [/V:label] [/Q] [/F:size]
FORMAT volume [/V:label] [/Q] [/T:tracks /N:sectors]
FORMAT volume [/V:label] [/Q] [/1] [/4]
FORMAT volume [/Q] [/1] [/4] [/8]

volume	Specifies the drive letter (followed by a colon), mount point, or volume name.
/FS:filesystem	Specifies the type of the file system (FAT, FAT32, or NTFS).
/V:label	Specifies the volume label.
/Q	Performs a quick format.
/C	Files created on the new volume will be compressed by default.
/X	Forces the volume to dismount first if necessary. All opened handles to the volume would no longer be valid.
/A:size	Overrides the default allocation unit size. Default settings are strongly recommended for general use. NTFS supports 512, 1024, 2048, 4096, 8192, 16K, 32K, 64K. FAT supports 512, 1024, 2048, 4096, 8192, 16K, 32K, 64K (128K, 256K for sector size > 512 bytes). FAT32 supports 512, 1024, 2048, 4096, 8192, 16K, 32K, 64K (128K, 256K for sector size > 512 bytes). Note that the FAT and FAT32 file systems impose the following restrictions on the number of clusters on a volume: FAT: Number of clusters <= 65526 FAT32: 65526 < Number of clusters < 268435446 Format will immediately stop processing if it decides that the above requirements cannot be met using the specified cluster size.

	NTFS compression is not supported for allocation unit sizes above 4096.
/F:size	Specifies the size of the floppy disk to format (160, 180, 320, 360, 640, 720, 1.2, 1.23, 1.44, 2.88, or 20.8).
/T:tracks	Specifies the number of tracks per disk side.
/N:sectors	Specifies the number of sectors per track.
/1	Formats a single side of a floppy disk.
/4	Formats a 5.25-inch 360K floppy disk in a high-density drive.
/8	Formats eight sectors per track.

FTP Transfers files to and from a computer running an FTP server service (sometimes called a daemon). FTP can be used interactively. This command is available only if the TCP/IP protocol has been installed. FTP is a service, that, once started, creates a sub-environment in which you can use FTP commands, and from which you can return to the Windows 2000 command prompt by typing the QUIT subcommand. When the FTP sub-environment is running, it is indicated by the FTP command prompt.

FTP [-v] [-n] [-i] [-d] [-g] [-s:filename] [-a]
[-w:windowsize] [computer]

-v	Suppresses display of remote server responses.
-n	Suppresses auto-login upon initial connection.
-i	Turns off interactive prompting during multiple file transfers.
-d	Enables debugging, displaying all FTP commands passed between the client and server.
-g	Disables file-name globbing, which permits the use of wildcard characters (* and ?) in local file and path names. (See the GLOB command in the online Command Reference.)
-s:filename	Specifies a text file containing FTP commands; the commands automatically run after FTP starts. No spaces are allowed in this parameter. Use this switch instead of redirection (>).
-a	Uses any local interface when binding data connection.
-w:windowsize	Overrides the default transfer buffer size of 4096.
computer	Specifies the computer name or IP address of the remote computer to connect to. The computer, if specified, must be the last parameter on the line.

FTYPE Displays or modifies file types used in file extension associations.

FTYPE [fileType[=[openCommandString]]]

fileType	Specifies the file type to examine or change.
openCommandString	Specifies the open command to use when launching files of this type.

Type FTYPE without parameters to display the current file types that have open command strings defined. When FTYPE is invoked with just a file type, it displays the current open command string for that file type. Specify nothing for the open command string and the FTYPE command will delete the open command string for the file type. Within an open command string %0 or %1 are substituted with the file name being launched through the association. %* gets all the parameters and %2 gets the 1st parameter, %3 the second, etc. %~n gets all the remaining parameters starting with the *n*th parameter, where *n* may be between 2 and 9, inclusive. For example:

ASSOC .pl=PerlScript
FTYPE PerlScript=perl.exe %1 %*

would allow you to invoke a Perl script as follows:

script.pl 1 2 3

If you want to eliminate the need to type the extensions, then do the following:

set PATHEXT=.pl;%PATHEXT%

and the script could be invoked as follows:

script 1 2 3

GOTO Directs CMD.EXE to a labeled line in a batch program.

GOTO label

label Specifies a text string used in the batch program as a label.

You type a label on a line by itself, beginning with a colon.

If Command Extensions are enabled GOTO changes as follows:

The GOTO command now accepts a target label of :EOF, which transfers control to the end of the current batch script file. This is an easy way to exit a batch script file without defining a label. Type CALL /? for a description of extensions to the CALL command that make this feature useful.

GRAPHICS Loads a program that can print graphics.

GRAPHICS [type] [[drive:][path]filename] [/R] [/B] [/LCD]
[/PRINTBOX:STD ¦ /PRINTBOX:LCD]

type	Specifies a printer type (see User's Guide and Reference).
[drive:][path]filename	Specifies the file containing information on supported printers.
/R	Prints white on black as seen on the screen.
/B	Prints the background in color for COLOR4 and COLOR8 printers.
/LCD	Prints using LCD aspect ratio.
/PRINTBOX:STD ¦ /PRINTBOX:LCD	Specifies the print-box size, either STD or LCD.

HELP Provides help information for Windows 2000 commands.

HELP [command]

command Displays help information on that command.

IF Performs conditional processing in batch programs.

IF [NOT] ERRORLEVEL number command
IF [NOT] string1==string2 command
IF [NOT] EXIST filename command

NOT	Specifies that Windows 2000 should carry out the command only if the condition is false.
ERRORLEVEL number	Specifies a true condition if the last program run returned an exit code equal to or greater than the number specified.
string1==string2	Specifies a true condition if the specified text strings match.
EXIST filename	Specifies a true condition if the specified file name exists.
command	Specifies the command to carry out if the condition is met. The command can be followed by the ELSE command, which will execute the command after the ELSE keyword if the specified condition is FALSE.

The ELSE clause must occur on the same line as the command after the IF. For example:

```
IF EXIST filename. (
del filename.
) ELSE (
echo filename. missing.
)
```

The following would NOT work because the del command needs to be terminated by a newline:

```
IF EXIST filename. del filename. ELSE echo filename. missing
```

Nor would the following work, since the ELSE command must be on the same line as the end of the IF command:

```
IF EXIST filename. del filename.
ELSE echo filename. missing
```

The following would work if you want it all on one line:

```
IF EXIST filename. (del filename.) ELSE echo filename. missing
```

If Command Extensions are enabled IF changes as follows:

```
IF [/I] string1 compare-op string2 command
IF CMDEXTVERSION number command
IF DEFINED variable command
```

where compare-op may be one of the following:

```
EQU    Equal
NEQ    Not equal
LSS    Less than
LEQ    Less than or equal
GTR    Greater than
GEQ    Greater than or equal
```

and the /I switch, if specified, says to do case-insensitive string compares. The /I switch can also be used on the string1==string2 form of IF. These comparisons are generic, in that if both string1 and string2 are comprised of all numeric digits, then the strings are converted to numbers and a numeric comparison is performed.

The CMDEXTVERSION conditional works just like ERRORLEVEL, except it is comparing against an internal version number associated with the Command Extensions. The first version is 1. It will be incremented by one when significant enhancements are added to the Command Extensions. CMDEXTVERSION conditional is never true when Command Extensions are disabled.

The DEFINED conditional works just like EXISTS except it takes an environment variable name and returns true if the environment variable is defined.

%ERRORLEVEL% will expand into a string representation of the current value of ERRORLEVEL, provided that there is not already an environment variable with the name ERRORLEVEL, in which case you will get its value instead. After running a program, the following illustrates ERRORLEVEL use:

```
goto answer%ERRORLEVEL%
:answer0
echo Program had return code 0
:answer1
echo Program had return code 1
```

You can also using the numerical comparisons above:

```
IF %ERRORLEVEL% LEQ 1 goto okay
```

%CMDCMDLINE% will expand into the original command line passed to CMD.EXE prior to any processing by CMD.EXE, provided that there is not already an environment variable with the name CMDCMDLINE, in which case you will get its value instead.

%CMDEXTVERSION% will expand into a string representation of the current value of CMDEXTVERSION, provided that there is not already an environment variable with the name CMDEXTVERSION, in which case you will get its value instead.

IPCONFIG Displays all current TCP/IP network configuration values.

Windows 2000 IP Configuration

```
IPCONFIG [/? ¦ /all ¦ /release [adapter] ¦ /renew [adapter] ¦ /flushdns ¦ /registerdns
¦ /showclassid adapter ¦ /setclassid adapter [classidtoset]]
```

adapter Full name or pattern with '*' and '?' to 'match', * matches any character, ? matches one character.

Options:

/? Displays this help message.

/all	Displays full configuration information.
/release	Releases the IP address for the specified adapter.
/renew	Renews the IP address for the specified adapter.
/flushdns	Purges the DNS Resolver cache.
/registerdns	Refreshes all DHCP leases and re-registers DNS names.
/displaydns	Displays the contents of the DNS Resolver Cache.
/showclassid	Displays all the dhcp class IDs allowed for adapter.
/setclassid	Modifies the dhcp class id.

The default is to display only the IP address, subnet mask, and default gateway for each adapter bound to TCP/IP.

For Release and Renew, if no adapter name is specified, then the IP address leases for all adapters bound to TCP/IP will be released or renewed.

For SetClassID, if no class id is specified, then the classid is removed.

Examples:

> ipconfig	Shows information.
> ipconfig /all	Shows detailed information.
> ipconfig /renew	Renews all adapaters.
> ipconfig /renew EL*	Renews adapters named EL...
> ipconfig /release *ELINK?21*	Releases all matching adapters, e.g., ELINK-21, myELELINKi21adapter.

JVIEW Runs a command line Loader for Java.

Usage: JView [options] <classname> [arguments]

Options:

/?	Displays usage text.
/cp <classpath>	Sets class path.
/cp:p <path>	Prepends path to class path.
/cp:a <path>	Appends path to class path.
/n <namespace>	Namespace in which to run.
/p	Pauses before terminating if an error occurs.
/v	Verifies all classes.
/d:<name>=<value>	Defines system property.
/a	Executes AppletViewer.
/vst	Prints verbose stack traces (requires debug classes).
/prof[:options]	Enables profiling (/prof:? for help).
classname:	.CLASS file to be executed.
arguments:	Command-line arguments to be passed on to the class file.

LABEL Creates, changes, or deletes the volume label of a disk.

LABEL [drive:][label]
LABEL [/MP] [volume] [label]

drive:	Specifies the drive letter of a drive.
label	Specifies the label of the volume.
/MP	Specifies that the volume should be treated as a mount point or volume name.
volume	Specifies the drive letter (followed by a colon), mount point, or volume name. If volume name is specified, the /MP flag is unnecessary.

LOADFIX Loads a program above the first 64K of memory, and runs the program.

LOADFIX [drive:][path]filename

Use LOADFIX to load a program if you have received the message “Packed file corrupt” when trying to load it in low memory.

LPQ Displays the state of a remote lpd queue.

Usage: lpq -S server -P printer [-l]

Options:

-S server	Name or ipaddress of the host providing lpd service.
-P printer	Name of the print queue.
-l	Verbose output.

LPR Sends a print job to a network printer.

Usage: lpr -S server -P printer [-C class] [-J job][-o option][-x][-d] filename

Options:

-S server	Name or ipaddress of the host providing lpd service.
-P printer	Name of the print queue.
-C class	Job classification for use on the burst page.
-J job	Job name to print on the burst page.
-o option	Indicates type of the file (by default assumes a text file) Use "-o l" for binary (e.g., PostScript) files.
-x	Compatibility with SunOS 4.1.x and prior.
-d	Sends data file first.

MAKECAB Loads Cabinet Maker.

MAKECAB [/V[n]] [/D var=value ...] [/L dir] source [destination]
MAKECAB [/V[n]] [/D var=value ...] /F directive_file [...]

source	File to compress.
destination	File name to give compressed file. If omitted, the last character of the source file name is replaced with an underscore (_) and used as the destination.
/F directive_file	A file with MakeCAB directives (may be repeated).
/D var=value	Defines variable with specified value.
/L dir	Location to place destination (default is current directory).
/V[n]	Verbosity level (1–3).

MEM Displays the amount of used and free memory in your system.

MEM [/PROGRAM ¦ /DEBUG ¦ /CLASSIFY]

/PROGRAM or /P	Displays status of programs currently loaded in memory.
/DEBUG or /D	Displays status of programs, internal drivers, and other information.
/CLASSIFY or /C	Classifies programs by memory usage. Lists the size of programs, provides a summary of memory in use, and lists largest memory block available.

MKDIR or MD Creates a directory.

MKDIR [drive:]path
MD [drive:]path

If Command Extensions are enabled MKDIR changes as follows:

MKDIR creates any intermediate directories in the path, if needed.
For example, assume \a does not exist then:

```
mkdir \a\b\c\d
```

is the same as:

```
mkdir \a
chdir \a
mkdir b
chdir b
mkdir c
chdir c
mkdir d
```

which is what you would have to type if extensions were disabled.

MODE Configures system devices.

Serial port: MODE COMm[:] [BAUD=b] [PARITY=p] [DATA=d] [STOP=s] [to=on¦off] [xon=on¦off] [odsr=on¦off] [octs=on¦off] [dtr=on¦off¦hs] [rts=on¦off¦hs¦tg] [idsr=on¦off]

Device status: MODE [device] [/STATUS]
Redirect printing: MODE LPTn[:]=COMm[:]
Select code page: MODE CON[:] CP SELECT=yyy
Code page status: MODE CON[:] CP [/STATUS]
Display mode: MODE CON[:] [COLS=c] [LINES=n]
Typematic rate: MODE CON[:] [RATE=r DELAY=d]

MORE Displays output one screen at a time.

MORE [/E [/C] [/P] [/S] [/Tn] [+n]] < [drive:][path]filename
command-name ¦ MORE [/E [/C] [/P] [/S] [/Tn] [+n]]
MORE /E [/C] [/P] [/S] [/Tn] [+n] [files]

[drive:][path]filename Specifies a file to display one screen at a time.
command-name Specifies a command whose output will be displayed.
/E Enables extended features.
/C Clears screen before displaying page.
/P Expands FormFeed characters.
/S Squeezes multiple blank lines into a single line.
/Tn Expands tabs to n spaces (default 8).

Switches can be present in the MORE environment variable.

+n Starts displaying the first file at line n.
files List of files to be displayed. Files in the list are separated by blanks.

If extended features are enabled, the following commands are accepted at the --More-- prompt:

P n Displays next n lines.
S n Skips next n lines.
F Displays next file.
Q Quits.
= Shows line number.
? Shows help line.
<space> Displays next page.
<ret> Displays next line.

MOVE Moves files and renames files and directories.

To move one or more files:
MOVE [/Y ¦ /-Y] [drive:][path]filename1[,...] destination

To rename a directory:
MOVE [/Y ¦ /-Y] [drive:][path]dirname1 dirname2

[drive:][path]filename1 Specifies the location and name of the file or files you want to move.
destination Specifies the new location of the file. Destination can consist of a drive letter and colon, a directory name, or a combination. If you

	are moving only one file, you can also include a file name if you want to rename the file when you move it.
[drive:][path]dirname1	Specifies the directory you want to rename.
dirname2	Specifies the new name of the directory.
/Y	Suppresses prompting to confirm you want to overwrite an existing destination file.
/-Y	Causes prompting to confirm you want to overwrite an existing destination file.

The switch /Y may be present in the COPYCMD environment variable. This may be overridden with /-Y on the command line. The default is to prompt on overwrites unless the MOVE command is being executed from within a batch script.

NBTSTAT Displays protocol statistics and current TCP/IP connections using NBT (NetBIOS over TCP/IP).

NBTSTAT [[-a RemoteName] [-A IP address] [-c] [-n] [-r] [-R] [-RR] [-s] [-S] [interval]]

-a (adapter status)	Lists the remote machine's name table given its name.
-A (Adapter status)	Lists the remote machine's name table given its IP address.
-c (cache)	Lists NBT's cache of remote [machine] names and their IP addresses.
-n (names)	Lists local NetBIOS names.
-r (resolved)	Lists names resolved by broadcast and via WINS.
-R (Reload)	Purges and reloads the remote cache name table.
-S (Sessions)	Lists sessions table with the destination IP addresses.
-s (sessions)	Lists sessions table converting destination IP addresses to computer NETBIOS names.
-RR (ReleaseRefresh)	Sends Name Release packets to WINs and then starts Refresh.
RemoteName	Remote host machine name.
IP address	Dotted decimal representation of the IP address.
interval	Redisplays selected statistics, pausing interval seconds between each display. Press Ctrl+C to stop redisplaying statistics.

NET Many Windows 2000 networking commands begin with the word NET. These NET commands have some common properties. You can see a list of all available NET commands by typing net /?.

NET /? results in:

NET [ACCOUNTS ¦ COMPUTER ¦ CONFIG ¦ CONTINUE ¦ FILE ¦ GROUP ¦ HELP ¦ HELPMSG ¦ LOCALGROUP ¦ NAME ¦ PAUSE ¦ PRINT ¦ SEND ¦ SESSION ¦ SHARE ¦ START ¦ STATISTICS ¦ STOP ¦ TIME ¦ USE ¦ USER ¦ VIEW]

You can get syntax help at the command line for a NET command by typing NET HELP *command*. For example, for help with the NET USE command, type NET HELP USE. See results of this command below. (For help with the other commands listed above, key in NET HELP *command* at the command line.)

NET USE Connects a computer to a shared resource or disconnects a computer from a shared resource. When used without options, it lists the computer's connections.

NET USE [devicename ¦ *] [\\computername\sharename[\volume] [password ¦ *]]
[/USER:[domainname\]username]
[/USER:[dotted domain name\]username]
[/USER:[username@dotted domain name]
[[/DELETE] ¦ [/PERSISTENT:{YES ¦ NO}]]

NET USE {devicename ¦ *} [password ¦ *] /HOME

NET USE [/PERSISTENT:{YES ¦ NO}]

devicename	Assigns a name to connect to the resource or specifies the device to be disconnected. There are two kinds of device names: disk drives (D: through Z:) and printers (LPT1: through LPT3:). Type an asterisk instead of a specific device name to assign the next available device name.

\\computername	The name of the computer controlling the shared resource. If computername contains blank characters, enclose the double backslash (\\) and computername in quotation marks (" "). The computername may be from 1 to 15 characters long.
\sharename	The network name of the shared resource.
\volume	Specifies a NetWare volume on the server. You must have Client Services for Netware (Windows Workstations) or Gateway Service for Netware (Windows Server) installed and running to connect to NetWare servers.
password	The password needed to access the shared resource.
*	Produces a prompt for the password. The password is not displayed when you type it at the password prompt.
/USER	Specifies a different user name with which the connection is made.
domainname	Specifies another domain. If domain is omitted, the current logged on domain is used.
username	Specifies the user name with which to log on.
/HOME	Connects a user to the home directory.
/DELETE	Cancels a network connection and removes the connection from the list of persistent connections.
/PERSISTENT	Controls the use of persistent network connections. The default is the setting used last.
YES	Saves connections as they are made, and restores them at next logon.
NO	Does not save the connection being made or subsequent connections; existing connections will be restored at next logon. Use the /DELETE switch to remove persistent connections.

NETSH

The NetShell utility (NETSH) is a command line, scripting interface for configuring and monitoring Windows 2000.

Usage: NETSH [-a AliasFile] [-c Context] [-r RemoteMachine] [Command ¦ -f ScriptFile]

The following commands are available:

?	Displays a list of commands.
add	Adds a configuration entry to a list of entries.
delete	Deletes a configuration entry from a list of entries.
dump	Displays a configuration script.
exec	Runs a script file.
help	Displays a list of commands.
interface	Changes to the "interface" context.
ras	Changes to the "ras" context.
routing	Changes to the "routing" context.
set	Updates configuration settings.
show	Displays information.

NETSTAT

Displays protocol statistics and current TCP/IP network connections.

NETSTAT [-a] [-e] [-n] [-s] [-p proto] [-r] [interval]

-a	Displays all connections and listening ports.
-e	Displays Ethernet statistics. This may be combined with the -s option.
-n	Displays addresses and port numbers in numerical form.
-p proto	Shows connections for the protocol specified by proto; proto may be TCP or UDP. If used with the -s option to display per-protocol statistics, proto may be TCP, UDP, or IP.
-r	Displays the routing table.
-s	Displays per-protocol statistics. By default, statistics are shown for TCP, UDP, and IP; the -p option may be used to specify a subset of the default.
interval	Redisplays selected statistics, pausing interval seconds between each display. Press Ctrl+C to stop redisplaying statistics. If omitted, NETSTAT will print the current configuration information once.

PATH Displays or sets a search path for executable files.

PATH [drive:]path[;...][;%PATH%]
PATH ;

Type PATH ; to clear all search-path settings and direct CMD.EXE to search only in the current directory.
Type PATH without parameters to display the current path.
Including %PATH% in the new path setting causes the old path to be appended to the new setting.

PATHPING Loads a route-tracing tool.

Usage: pathping [-n] [-h maximum_hops] [-g host-list] [-p period]
[-q num_queries] [-w timeout] [-T] [-R] [-r] target_name

Options:

-n	Do not resolve addresses to host names.
-h maximum_hops	Maximum number of hops to search for target.
-g host-list	Loose source route along host-list.
-p period	Wait period milliseconds between pings.
-q num_queries	Number of queries per hop.
-w timeout	Wait timeout milliseconds for each reply.
-T	Test connectivity to each hop with Layer-2 priority tags.
-R	Test if each hop is RSVP-aware.

PAUSE Suspends processing of a batch program and displays the message “Press any key to continue . . .”

PENTNT Reports on whether the local computer exhibits Intel Pentium floating point division error.

pentnt [-?] [-H] [-h] [-C] [-c] [-F] [-f] [-O] [-o]

Run without arguments this program will tell you if the system exhibits the Pentium floating point division error and whether floating point emulation is forced and whether floating point hardware is disabled.

-? Prints this help message.

-c Turns on conditional emulation. This means that floating -C point emulation will be forced on if and only if the system detects the Pentium floating point division error at boot. Rebooting is required before this takes effect. This is what should generally be used.

-f Turns on forced emulation. This means that floating -F point hardware is disabled and floating point emulation will always be forced on, regardless of whether the system exhibits the Pentium division error. Useful for testing software emulators and for working around floating point hardware defects unknown to the OS. Rebooting is required before this takes effect.

-o Turns off forced emulation. Re-enables floating point hardware if present. Rebooting is required before this takes effect.

The floating point division error that this program addresses only occurs on certain Intel Pentium processors. It only affects floating point operations. The problem is described in detail in a white paper available from Intel. If you are doing critical work with programs that perform floating point division and certain related functions that use the same hardware (including remainder and transcendental functions), you may wish to use this program to force emulation.

PING Verifies connections to a remote computer or computers. This command is available only if the TCP/IP protocol has been installed.

ping [-t] [-a] [-n count] [-l size] [-f] [-i TTL] [-v TOS] [-r count] [-s count] [[-j host-list] ¦ [-k host-list]] [-w timeout] destination-list

-t Pings the specified host until stopped. To see statistics and continue, type Ctrl+Break; to stop, type Ctrl+C.

-a Resolves addresses to host names.
-n count Number of echo requests to send.
-l size Sends buffer size.
-f Sets Don't Fragment flag in packet.
-i TTL Time To Live.
-v TOS Type Of Service.
-r count Records route for count hops.
-s count Timestamp for count hops.
-j host-list Loose source route along host-list.
-k host-list Strict source route along host-list.
-w timeout Timeout in milliseconds to wait for each reply.

PRINT Prints a text file.

PRINT [/D:device] [[drive:][path]filename[...]]

/D:device Specifies a print device.

POPD Changes to the directory stored by the PUSHD command.

POPD

If Command Extensions are enabled the POPD command will delete any temporary drive letter created by PUSHD when you POPD that drive off the pushed directory stack.

PROMPT Changes the CMD.EXE command prompt.

PROMPT [text]

text Specifies a new command prompt.

Prompt can be made up of normal characters and the following special codes:

$A & (Ampersand)
$B ¦ (Pipe)
$C ((Left parenthesis)
$D Current date
$E Escape code (ASCII code 27)
$F) (Right parenthesis)
$G > (Greater-than sign)
$H Backspace (erases previous character)
$L < (Less-than sign)
$N Current drive
$P Current drive and path
$Q = (Equal sign)
$S (Space)
$T Current time
$V Windows 2000 version number
$_ Carriage return and linefeed
$$ $ (Dollar sign)

If Command Extensions are enabled the PROMPT command supports the following additional formatting characters:

$+ zero or more plus sign (+) characters depending upon the depth of the PUSHD directory stack, one character for each level pushed.

$M Displays the remote name associated with the current drive letter or the empty string if current drive is not a network drive.

PUSHD Stores the current directory for use by the POPD command, then changes to the specified directory.

PUSHD [path ¦ ..]

path	Specifies the directory to make the current directory.

If Command Extensions are enabled the PUSHD command accepts network paths in addition to the normal drive letter and path. If a network path is specified, PUSHD will create a temporary drive letter that points to that specified network resource and then change the current drive and directory, using the newly defined drive letter. Temporary drive letters are allocated from Z: on down, using the first unused drive letter found.

RCP Copies files to and from a computer running the RCP service.

RCP [-a ¦ -b] [-h] [-r] [host][.user:]source [host][.user:] path\destination

-a	Specifies ASCII transfer mode. This mode converts the EOL characters to a carriage return for UNIX and a carriage return/line feed for personal computers. This is the default transfer mode.
-b	Specifies binary image transfer mode.
-h	Transfers hidden files.
-r	Copies the contents of all subdirectories; destination must be a directory.
host	Specifies the local or remote host. If host is specified as an IP address or if the host name contains dots, you must specify the user.
.user:	Specifies a user name to use, rather than the current user name.
source	Specifes the files to copy.
path\destination	Specifies the path relative to the logon directory on the remote host. Use the escape characters (\ , “, or ‘) in remote paths to use wildcard characters on the remote host.

RECOVER Recovers readable information from a bad or defective disk.

RECOVER [drive:][path]filename

Consult the online Command Reference in Windows 2000 Help before using the RECOVER command.

REM Records comments (remarks) in a batch file or CONFIG.SYS.

REM [comment]

REN or RENAME Renames a file or files.

RENAME [drive:][path]filename1 filename2
REN [drive:][path]filename1 filename2

Note that you cannot specify a new drive or path for your destination file.

REPLACE Replaces files.

REPLACE [drive1:][path1]filename [drive2:][path2] [/A] [/P] [/R] [/W]
REPLACE [drive1:][path1]filename [drive2:][path2] [/P] [/R] [/S] [/W] [/U]

[drive1:][path1]filename	Specifies the source file or files.
[drive2:][path2]	Specifies the directory where files are to be replaced.
/A	Adds new files to the destination directory. Cannot use with the /S or /U switch.
/P	Prompts for confirmation before replacing a file or adding a source file.
/R	Replaces read-only files as well as unprotected files.
/S	Replaces files in all subdirectories of the destination directory. Cannot use with the /A switch.
/W	Waits for you to insert a disk before beginning.
/U	Replaces (updates) only files that are older than source files. Cannot use with the /A switch.

RMDIR or RDRemoves (deletes) a directory.

RMDIR [/S] [/Q] [drive:]path
RD [/S] [/Q] [drive:]path

/S	Removes all directories and files in the specified directory in addition to the directory itself. Used to remove a directory tree.
/Q	Quiet mode, do not ask if okay to remove a directory tree with /S.

ROUTE Manipulates network routing tables.

ROUTE [-f] [-p] [command] [destination]
[MASK netmask] [gateway] [METRIC metric] [IF interface]

-f	Clears the routing tables of all gateway entries. If this is used in conjunction with one of the commands, the tables are cleared prior to running the command.	
-p	When used with the ADD command, makes a route persistent across boots of the system. By default, routes are not preserved when the system is restarted. Ignored for all other commands, which always affect the appropriate persistent routes. This option is not supported in Windows 95.	
command	PRINT	Prints a route.
	ADD	Adds a route.
	DELETE	Deletes a route.
	CHANGE	Modifies an existing route.
destination	Specifies the host.	
MASK	Specifies that the next parameter is the netmask value.	
netmask	Specifies a subnet mask value for this route entry. If not specified, it defaults to 255.255.255.255.	
gateway	Specifies gateway.	
interface	The interface number for the specified route.	
METRIC	Specifies the metric, i.e., the cost for the destination.	

All symbolic names used for destination are looked up in the network database file NETWORKS. The symbolic names for gateway are looked up in the host name database file HOSTS.

If the command is PRINT or DELETE. Destination or gateway can be a wildcard (wildcard is specified as a star '*'), or the gateway argument may be omitted.

If Dest contains a * or ?, it is treated as a shell pattern, and only matching destination routes are printed. The '*' matches any string, and '?' matches any one char. Examples: 157.*.1, 157.*, 127.*, *224*.

Diagnostic Notes:
Invalid MASK generates an error, that is when (DEST & MASK) != DEST.
Example> route ADD 157.0.0.0 MASK 155.0.0.0 157.55.80.1 IF 1
The route addition failed: The specified mask parameter is invalid. (Destination & Mask) != Destination.

Examples:

```
> route PRINT
      > route ADD 157.0.0.0 MASK 255.0.0.0 157.55.80.1 METRIC 3 IF 2
      destination^     ^mask      ^gateway     metric^    ^ interface^
If IF is not given, it tries to find the best interface for a given gateway.
> route PRINT
> route PRINT 157*       .... Only prints those matching 157*
> route DELETE 157.0.0.0
> route PRINT
```

RSH Runs commands on remote hosts running the RSH service.

RSH host [-l username] [-n] command

host	Specifies the remote host on which to run the command.
-l username	Specifies the user name to use on the remote host. If omitted, the logged on user name is used.
-n	Redirects the input of RSH to NULL.
command	Specifies the command to run.

RUNAS Allows a user to run specific tools and programs with different permissions than the user's current logon provides.

RUNAS USAGE:
RUNAS [/profile] [/env] [/netonly] /user:<UserName> program

/profile	If the user's profile needs to be loaded.
/env	Uses current environment instead of user's.
/netonly	Use if the credentials specified are for remote access only.
/user	<UserName> should be in form USER@DOMAIN or DOMAIN\USER.
program	Command line for EXE. See below for examples.

Examples:

```
> runas /profile /user:mymachine\administrator cmd
> runas /profile /env /user:mydomain\admin "mmc %windir%\system32\dsa.msc"
> runas /env /user:user@domain.microsoft.com "notepad \"my file.txt\""
```

Note: Enter user's password only when prompted.
Note: USER@DOMAIN is not compatible with /netonly.

SET Displays, sets, or removes CMD.EXE environment variables.

SET [variable=[string]]

variable	Specifies the environment variable name.
string	Specifies a series of characters to assign to the variable.

Type SET without parameters to display the current environment variables.

If Command Extensions are enabled SET changes as follows:

The SET command invoked with just a variable name, no equal sign or value, will display the value of all variables whose prefix matches the name given to the SET command. For example:

SET P would display all variables that begin with the letter 'P'

The SET command will set the ERRORLEVEL to 1 if the variable name is not found in the current environment.

The SET command will not allow an equal sign to be part of the name of a variable.

Two new switches have been added to the SET command:

SET /A expression
SET /P variable=[promptString]

The /A switch specifies that the string to the right of the equal sign is a numerical expression that is evaluated. The expression evaluator is pretty simple and supports the following operations, in decreasing order of precedence:

()	grouping
* / %	arithmetic operators
+ -	arithmetic operators
<< >>	logical shift
&	bitwise and

^	bitwise exclusive or
¦	bitwise or
= *= /= %= += -=	assignment
&= ^= ¦= <<= >>=,	expression separator

If you use any of the logical or modulus operators, you will need to enclose the expression string in quotes. Any non-numeric strings in the expression are treated as environment variable names whose values are converted to numbers before using them. If an environment variable name is specified but is not defined in the current environment, then a value of zero is used. This allows you to do arithmetic with environment variable values without having to type all those % signs to get their values. If SET /A is executed from the command line outside of a command script, then it displays the final value of the expression. The assignment operator requires an environment variable name to the left of the assignment operator. Numeric values are decimal numbers, unless prefixed by 0x for hexadecimal numbers, and 0 for octal numbers. So 0x12 is the same as 18 is the same as 022. Please note that the octal notation can be confusing: 08 and 09 are not valid numbers because 8 and 9 are not valid octal digits.

The /P switch allows you to set the value of a variable to a line of input entered by the user. Displays the specified promptString before reading the line of input. The promptString can be empty.

Environment variable substitution has been enhanced as follows:

```
%PATH:str1=str2%
```

would expand the PATH environment variable, substituting each occurrence of "str1" in the expanded result with "str2". "str2" can be the empty string to effectively delete all occurrences of "str1" from the expanded output. "str1" can begin with an asterisk, in which case it will match everything from the begining of the expanded output to the first occurrence of the remaining portion of str1.

May also specify substrings for an expansion.

```
%PATH:~10,5%
```

would expand the PATH environment variable, and then use only the five characters that begin at the eleventh (offset 10) character of the expanded result. If the length is not specified, then it defaults to the remainder of the variable value. If either number (offset or length) is negative, then the number used is the length of the environment variable value added to the offset or length specified.

```
%PATH:~-10%
```

would extract the last 10 characters of the PATH variable.

```
%PATH:~0,-2%
```

would extract all but the last two characters of the PATH variable.

Finally, support for delayed environment variable expansion has been added. This support is always disabled by default, but may be enabled/disabled via the /V command line switch to CMD.EXE. See CMD /?.

Delayed environment variable expansion is useful for getting around the limitations of the current expansion that happens when a line of text is read, not when it is executed. The following example demonstrates the problem with immediate variable expansion:

```
set VAR=before
if "%VAR%" == "before" (
set VAR=after;
if "%VAR%" == "after" @echo If you see this, it worked
)
```

would never display the message, since the %VAR% in both IF statements is substituted when the first IF statement is read, since it logically includes the body of the IF, which is a compound statement. So the IF inside the compound statement is really comparing "before" with "after," which will never be equal. Similarly, the following example will not work as expected:

```
set LIST=
for %i in (*) do set LIST=%LIST% %i
echo %LIST%
```

in that it will not build up a list of files in the current directory, but instead will just set the LIST variable to the last file found. Again, this is because the %LIST% is expanded just once when the FOR statement is read, and at that time the LIST variable is empty. So the actual FOR loop we are executing is:

```
for %i in (*) do set LIST= %i
```

which just keeps setting LIST to the last file found.

Delayed environment variable expansion allows you to use a different character (the exclamation mark) to expand environment variables at execution time. If delayed variable expansion is enabled, the above examples could be written as follows to work as intended:

```
set VAR=before
if "%VAR%" == "before" (
set VAR=after
if "!VAR!" == "after" @echo If you see this, it worked
)

set LIST=
for %i in (*) do set LIST=!LIST! %i
echo %LIST%
```

If Command Extensions are enabled, then there are several dynamic environment variables that can be expanded but which don't show up in the list of variables displayed by SET. These variable values are computed dynamically each time the value of the variable is expanded. If the user explicitly defines a variable with one of these names, then that definition will override the dynamic one described below:

%CD%	Expands to the current directory string.
%DATE%	Expands to current date using same format as DATE command.
%TIME%	Expands to current time using same format as TIME command.
%RANDOM%	Expands to a random decimal number between 0 and 32767.
%ERRORLEVEL%	Expands to the current ERRORLEVEL value.
%CMDEXTVERSION%	Expands to the current Command Processor Extensions version number.
%CMDCMDLINE%	Expands to the original command line that invoked the Command Processor.

SETLOCAL Begins localization of environment changes in a batch file. Environment changes made after SETLOCAL has been issued are local to the batch file. ENDLOCAL must be issued to restore the previous settings. When the end of a batch script is reached, an implied ENDLOCAL is executed for any outstanding SETLOCAL commands issued by that batch script.

SETLOCAL

If Command Extensions are enabled SETLOCAL changes as follows:

SETLOCAL batch command now accepts optional arguments:
ENABLEEXTENSIONS / DISABLEEXTENSIONS: Enables or disables command processor extensions. See CMD /? for details.
ENABLEDELAYEDEXPANSION / DISABLEDELAYEDEXPANSION: Enables or disables delayed environment variable expansion. See SET /? for details.

These modifications last until the matching ENDLOCAL command, regardless of their setting prior to the SETLOCAL command.

The SETLOCAL command will set the ERRORLEVEL value if given an argument. It will be zero if one of the two valid arguments is given and one otherwise. You can use this in batch scripts to determine if the extensions are available, using the following technique:

```
VERIFY OTHER 2>nul
SETLOCAL ENABLEEXTENSIONS
IF ERRORLEVEL 1 echo Unable to enable extensions
```

This works because on old versions of CMD.EXE, SETLOCAL does NOT set the ERRORLEVEL value. The VERIFY command with a bad argument initializes the ERRORLEVEL value to a non-zero value.

SETVER Sets the version number that MS-DOS reports to a program.

Display current version table:	SETVER [drive:path]
Add entry:	SETVER [drive:path] filename n.nn
Delete entry:	SETVER [drive:path] filename /DELETE [/QUIET]

[drive:path]	Specifies location of the SETVER.EXE file.
filename	Specifies the file name of the program.
n.nn	Specifies the MS-DOS version to be reported to the program.
/DELETE or /D	Deletes the version-table entry for the specified program.
/QUIET	Hides the message typically displayed during deletion of version-table entry.

SHIFT Changes the position of replaceable parameters in a batch file.

SHIFT [/n]

If Command Extensions are enabled the SHIFT command supports the /n switch, which tells the command to start shifting at the *n*th argument, where *n* may be between zero and eight. For example:

SHIFT /2

would shift %3 to %2, %4 to %3, etc., and leave %0 and %1 unaffected.

SORT Reads input, sorts data, and writes the results to the screen, to a file, or to another device.

SORT [/R] [/+n] [/M kilobytes] [/L locale] [/RE recordbytes]
[[drive1:][path1]filename1] [/T [drive2:][path2]]
[/O [drive3:][path3]filename3]

/+n	Specifies the character number, *n*, to begin each comparison. /+3 indicates that each comparison should begin at the third character in each line. Lines with fewer than *n* characters collate before other lines. By default comparisons start at the first character in each line.
/L[OCALE] locale	Overrides the system default locale with the specified one. The ""C"" locale yields the fastest collating sequence and is currently the only alternative. The sort is always case insensitive.
/M[EMORY] kilobytes	Specifies amount of main memory to use for the sort, in kilobytes. The memory size is always constrained to be a minimum of 160 kilobytes. If the memory size is specified the exact amount will be used for the sort, regardless of how much main memory is available.

The best performance is usually achieved by not specifying a memory size. By default the sort will be done with one pass (no temporary file) if it fits in the default maximum memory size. Otherwise the sort will be done in two passes (with the partially sorted data being stored in a temporary file) such that the amounts of memory used for both the sort and merge passes are equal. The default maximum memory size is 90% of available main memory if both the input and output are files, and 45% of main memory otherwise.

/REC[ORD_MAXIMUM] characters	Specifies the maximum number of characters in a record (default 4096, maximum 65535).
/R[EVERSE]	Reverses the sort order; that is, sorts Z to A, then 9 to 0.
[drive1:][path1]filename1	Specifies the file to be sorted. If not specified, the standard input is sorted. Specifying the input file is faster than redirecting the same file as standard input.
/T[EMPORARY] [drive2:][path2]	Specifies the path of the directory to hold the sort's working storage, in case the data does not fit in main memory. The default is to use the system's temporary directory.
/O[UTPUT] [drive3:][path3]filename3	Specifies the file where the sorted input is to be stored. If not specified, the data is written to the standard output. Specifying the output file is faster than redirecting standard output to the same file.

START Starts a separate window to run a specified program or command.

START ["title"] [/Dpath] [/I] [/MIN] [/MAX] [/SEPARATE ¦ /SHARED] [/LOW ¦ /NORMAL ¦ /HIGH ¦ /REALTIME ¦ /ABOVENORMAL ¦ /BELOWNORMAL] [/WAIT] [/B] [command/program] [parameters]

"title"	Title to display in window title bar.
path	Starting directory
B	Starts application without creating a new window. The application has ^C handling ignored. Unless the application enables ^C processing, ^Break is the only way to interrupt the application.
I	The new environment will be the original environment passed to the CMD.EXE and not the current environment.
MIN	Starts window minimized.
MAX	Starts window maximized.
SEPARATE	Starts 16-bit Windows program in separate memory space.
SHARED	Starts 16-bit Windows program in shared memory space.
LOW	Starts application in the IDLE priority class.
NORMAL	Starts application in the NORMAL priority class.
HIGH	Starts application in the HIGH priority class.
REALTIME	Starts application in the REALTIME priority class.
ABOVENORMAL	Starts application in the ABOVENORMAL priority class.
BELOWNORMAL	Starts application in the BELOWNORMAL priority class.
WAIT	Starts application and wait for it to terminate command/program.

If it is an internal command or a batch file, then the command processor is run with the /K switch to CMD.EXE. This means that the window will remain after the command has been run.

If it is not an internal command or batch file then it is a program and will run as either a windowed application or a console application.

parameters These are the parameters passed to the command program

If Command Extensions are enabled, external command invocation through the command line or the START command changes as follows:

Nonexecutable files may be invoked through their file association just by typing the name of the file as a command. (For example, WORD.DOC would launch the application associated with the .DOC file extension.) See the ASSOC and FTYPE commands for how to create these associations from within a command script.

When executing an application that is a 32-bit GUI application, CMD.EXE does not wait for the application to terminate before returning to the command prompt. This new behavior does NOT occur if executing within a command script.

When executing a command line whose first token is the string "CMD" without an extension or path qualifier, then "CMD" is replaced with the value of the COMSPEC variable. This prevents picking up CMD.EXE from the current directory.

When executing a command line whose first token does NOT contain an extension, then CMD.EXE uses the value of the PATHEXT environment variable to determine which extensions to look for and in what order. The default value for the PATHEXT variable is:

```
.COM;.EXE;.BAT;.CMD
```

Notice the syntax is the same as the PATH variable, with semicolons separating the different elements.

When searching for an executable, if there is no match on any extension, then looks to see if the name matches a directory name. If it does, the Start command launches Explorer on that path. If done from the command line, it is the equivalent to doing a CD /D to that path.

SUBST — Associates a path with a drive letter.

SUBST [drive1: [drive2:]path]
SUBST drive1: /D

drive1:	Specifies a virtual drive to which you want to assign a path.
[drive2:]path	Specifies a physical drive and path you want to assign to a virtual drive.
/D	Deletes a substituted (virtual) drive.

Type SUBST with no parameters to display a list of current virtual drives.

TELNET — Provides user support for the Telnet protocol, a remote access protocol you can use to log on to a remote computer, network device, or private TCP/IP network.

telnet [host [port]]

host	Specifies the host name or IP address of the remote computer to connect to.
port	Specifies the port number or service name.

TIME — Displays or sets the system time.

TIME [/T ¦ time]

Type TIME with no parameters to display the current time setting and a prompt for a new one. Press Enter to keep the same time.

If Command Extensions are enabled the TIME command supports the /T switch, which tells the command to just output the current time, without prompting for a new time.

TITLE — Sets the window title for the command prompt window.

TITLE [string]

string	Specifies the title for the command prompt window.

TRACERT — This diagnostic utility determines the route taken to a destination by sending Internet Control Message Protocol (ICMP) echo packets with varying Time-To-Live (TTL) values to the destination. Each router along the path is required to decrement the TTL on a packet by at least 1 before forwarding it, so the TTL is effectively a hop count. When the TTL on a packet reaches 0, the router is supposed to send back an ICMP Time Exceeded message to the source system. Tracert determines the route by sending the first echo packet with a TTL of 1 and incrementing the TTL by 1 on each subsequent transmission until the target responds or the maximum TTL is reached. The route is determined by examining the ICMP Time Exceeded messages sent back by intermediate routers. However, some routers silently drop packets with expired TTL values and are invisible to TRACERT.

tracert [-d] [-h maximum_hops] [-j computer-list] [-w timeout] target_name

-d	Specifies not to resolve addresses to computer names.
-h maximum_hops	Specifies maximum number of hops to search for target.
-j computer-list	Specifies loose source route along computer-list.
-w timeout	Waits the number of milliseconds specified by timeout for each reply.
target_name	Name of the target computer.

TREE — Graphically displays the folder structure of a drive or path.

TREE [drive:][path] [/F] [/A]

/F	Displays the names of the files in each folder.
/A	Uses ASCII instead of extended characters.

TYPE Displays the contents of a text file or files.

TYPE [drive:][path]filename

VER Displays the Windows 2000 version number.

VER

VERIFY Tells CMD.EXE whether to verify that your files are written correctly to a disk.

VERIFY [ON ¦ OFF]

Type VERIFY without a parameter to display the current VERIFY setting.

VOL Displays the disk volume label and serial number, if they exist.

VOL [drive:]

XCOPY Copies files and directory trees.

XCOPY source [destination] [/A ¦ /M] [/D[:date]] [/P] [/S [/E]] [/V] [/W] [/C] [/I] [/Q] [/F] [/L] [/H] [/R] [/T] [/U]
[/K] [/N] [/O] [/X] [/Y] [/-Y] [/Z] [/EXCLUDE:file1[+file2][+file3]...]

source	Specifies the file(s) to copy.
destination	Specifies the location and/or name of new files.
/A	Copies only files with the archive attribute set, doesn't change the attribute.
/M	Copies only files with the archive attribute set, turns off the archive attribute.
/D:date	Copies files changed on or after the specified date. If no date is given, copies only those files whose source time is newer than the destination time.
/EXCLUDE:file1[+file2][+file3]...	Specifies a list of files containing strings. When any of the strings match any part of the absolute path of the file to be copied, that file will be excluded from being copied. For example, specifying a string like \obj\ or .obj will exclude all files underneath the directory obj or all files with the .obj extension, respectively.
/P	Prompts you before creating each destination file.
/S	Copies directories and subdirectories except empty ones.
/E	Copies directories and subdirectories, including empty ones. Same as /S /E. May be used to modify /T.
/V	Verifies each new file.
/W	Prompts you to press a key before copying.
/C	Continues copying even if errors occur.
/I	If destination does not exist and copying more than one file, assumes that destination must be a directory.
/Q	Does not display file names while copying.
/F	Displays full source and destination file names while copying.
/L	Displays files that would be copied.
/H	Copies hidden and system files also.
/R	Overwrites read-only files.
/T	Creates directory structure, but does not copy files. Does not include empty directories or subdirectories. /T /E includes empty directories and subdirectories.
/U	Copies only files that already exist in destination.
/K	Copies attributes. Normal XCOPY will reset read-only attributes.
/N	Copies using the generated short names.
/O	Copies file ownership and ACL information.
/X	Copies file audit settings (implies /O).
/Y	Suppresses prompting to confirm you want to overwrite an existing destination file.
/-Y	Causes prompting to confirm you want to overwrite an existing destination file.
/Z	Copies networked files in restartable mode.

The switch /Y may be preset in the COPYCMD environment variable. This may be overridden with /-Y on the command line.

ANSI.SYS KEYBOARD SCANCODE VALUES

Key	Standard	With Shift	With Ctrl	With Alt
A	97	65	1	0;30
B	98	66	2	0;48
C	99	67	3	0;46
D	100	68	4	0;32
E	101	69	5	0:18
F	102	70	6	0;33
G	103	71	7	0;34
H	104	72	8	0;35
I	105	73	9	0;23
J	106	74	10	0;36
K	107	75	11	0;37
L	108	76	12	0;38
M	109	77	13	0;50
N	110	78	14	0;49
O	111	79	15	0;24
P	112	80	16	0;25
Q	113	81	17	0;16
R	114	82	18	0;19
S	115	83	19	0;31
T	116	84	20	0;20
U	117	85	21	0;22
V	118	86	22	0;47
W	119	87	23	0;17

Key	Standard	With Shift	With Ctrl	With Alt
X	120	88	24	0;45
Y	121	89	25	0;21
Z	122	90	26	0;44
1	49	33	N/A	0;120
2	50	64	0	0;121
3	51	35	N/A	0;122
4	52	36	N/A	0;123
5	53	37	N/A	0;124
6	54	94	30	0;125
7	55	38	N/A	0;126
8	56	42	N/A	0;126
9	57	40	N/A	0;127
0	48	41	N/A	0;129
–	45	95	31	0;130
=	61	43	N/A	0;131
[	91	123	27	0;26
]	93	125	29	0;27
Space Bar	92	124	28	0;43
;	59	58	N/A	0;39
’	39	34	N/A	0;40
,	44	60	N/A	0;51
.	46	62	N/A	0;52
/	47	63	N/A	0;53
‘	96	126	N/A	0;41
Enter (keypad)	13	N/A	10	0;166
/ (keypad)	47	47	0;142	0;74
* (keypad)	42	0;144	0;78	N/A
- (keypad)	45	45	0;149	0;164
+ (keypad)	43	43	0;150	0;55
5 (keypad)	0;76	53	0;143	N/A
F1	0;59	0;84	0;94	0;104
F2	0;60	0;85	0;95	0;105
F3	0;61	0;86	0;96	0;106
F4	0;62	0;87	0;97	0;107
F5	0;63	0;88	0;98	0;108
F6	0;64	0;89	0;99	0;109

Key	Standard	With Shift	With Ctrl	With Alt
F7	0;65	0;90	0;100	0;110
F8	0;66	0;91	0;101	0;111
F9	0;67	0;92	0;102	0;112
F10	0;68	0;93	0;103	0;113
F11	0;133	0;135	0;137	0;139
F12	0;134	0;136	0;138	0;140
Home	0;71	55	0;119	N/A
↑	0;72	56	0;141	N/A
PgUp	0;73	57	0;132	N/A
←	0;75	52	0;115	N/A
→	0;77	54	0;116	N/A
End	0;79	49	0;117	N/A
↓	0;80	50	0;145	N/A
PgDn	0;81	51	0;118	N/A
Insert	0;82	48	0;146	N/A
Delete	0;83	46	0;147	N/A
Print Screen	N/A	N/A	0;114	N/A
Pause	N/A	N/A	0;0	N/A
Backspace	8	8	127	0
Enter	13	N/A	10	0
Tab	9	0;5	0;148	0;165
Home (directional keypad)	224;71	224;71	224;119	224;151
↑ (directional keypad)	224;72	224;72	224;141	224;152
PgUp (directional keypad)	224;73	224;73	224;132	224;153
← (directional keypad)	224;75	224;75	224;115	224;155
→ (directional keypad)	224;77	224;77	224;116	224;157
End (directional keypad)	224;79	224;79	224;117	224;159
↓ (directional keypad)	224;80	224;80	224;145	224;154
PgDn (directional keypad)	224;81	224;81	224;118	224;161
Insert (directional keypad)	224;82	224;82	224;146	224;162
Delete (directional keypad)	224;83	224;83	224;147	224;163

USING FDISK TO PARTITION THE HARD DISK

Note: Disk partitioning in Windows 2000 Professional is a part of the Disk Management tool. To partition a new hard drive without using Windows 2000 Professional Disk Management requires the FDISK program from a previous version of Windows; you should use either Windows 98 or Windows Millennium Edition so that you may have the option of using FAT32.

PARTITIONING THE HARD DISK

A hard disk is comprised of multiple physical disks called "drive platters." Each platter is divided into concentric rings (tracks), and each track is divided into sectors. On a hard disk, a three-dimensional cylinder is formed by connecting the track-sector "pie wedges" from all the platters.

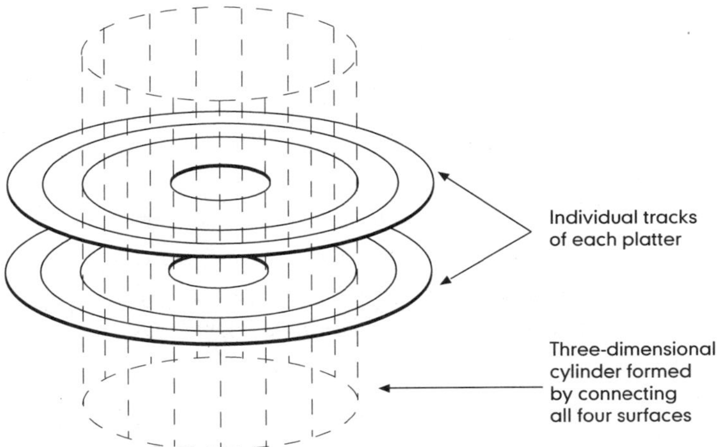

Low-level formatting tells the computer where the cylinders and sectors lie on the disk. This process creates the sectors and cylinders by writing the ID numbers of the sectors to the disk surface so that each sector is located and numbered. This identification, or "address," tells the hard-disk controller where the requested information is on the disk.

The numbering of each sector provides two primary benefits (besides the obvious one of giving the controller a place to find the information on the disk). These include the sector *interleave* and the identification of bad sectors on a disk. The sector interleave matches the rotation of the disk to the rate at which the disk controller can physically process data passing underneath the drive head. Thus, sectors will not be consecutively numbered on the disk. This occurs because computers cannot read a sector, write the data to RAM, and get ready to read the next sector by the time the next consecutively numbered sector arrives at the drive head. Rather than waiting for another entire revolution, the sectors are spaced so that when the head is ready to read the next sector, the next consecutively numbered sector is under the drive head. In this way, when the controller is ready to read, it is in the proper place.

Low-level formatting also marks any bad sectors on the disk so that they will not be used to store information. Usually, a disk is low-level formatted only once, at the factory. Rarely, if ever, will an end-user have to deal with low-level formatting.

FDISK

After low-level formatting, and before the formatting and installation of the operating system, the hard disk must be partitioned. A partition defines what part of the hard disk belongs to which operating system. With some operating systems, you may choose to have more than one operating system on a hard disk. For instance, you could have both DOS and Windows 95 on the same disk in different partitions. They "get along" very well. However, note that only one operating system can be used at one time.

There are three types of partitions: the primary DOS partition, the extended DOS partition, and the non-DOS partition. If you wish to use the Windows operating system on a hard disk, at least one partition is required; this is called the primary DOS partition. The primary DOS partition *must* exist in order to boot from the hard disk. It is the first partition on the disk. Using FAT (FAT16), the primary partition is limited in size to 2 GB. Using FAT32 (in Windows 95B, 95C, OSR2, Windows 98, and Windows Me), the primary partition no longer limited. (Note: In older computers, the hardware may limit the partition size to 7.9 GB.)

Many recommend that when creating the primary booting partition, FAT16 should be used instead of FAT32. The reason is that DOS 6.22 and previous versions of DOS do not recognize a disk partitioned to FAT32, and if there is "trouble," you would be unable to boot to DOS on a floppy and "see" the C drive. However, if you use a boot disk created with the same computer you are trying to boot, this should not be a problem.

After hard disk is partitioned, you can either format it or allow the Windows installation Setup program to format for it you. Please note, however, that formatting the partitions prior to the installation of the Windows operating system speeds up the installation process considerably.

HOW TO USE FDISK

Note 1: These steps are an example ONLY. The specifics will vary, depending on the exact version of the OS you are using and the size of your hard drive.

Note 2: This example assumes that you have a brand new hard disk drive in a computer that contains no other hard drives. You will need to have a boot disk that contains the FDISK.COM file and the FORMAT.EXE file.

Step 1 Boot with your booting disk. Run FDISK. You will see the following screen:

```
Your computer has a disk larger than 512 MB.
This version of Windows includes improved support for large
disks, resulting in more efficient use of disk space on large
drives, and allowing disks over 2 GB to be formatted as a
single drive.

IMPORTANT: If you enable large disk support and create any new
drives on this disk, you will not be able to access the new
drive(s) using other operating systems, including some versions
of Windows 95 and Windows NT, as well as earlier versions of
Windows and MS-DOS. In addition, disk utilities that were not
designed explicitly for the FAT32 file system will not be able
to work with this disk. If you need to access this disk with
other operating systems or older disk utilities, do not enable
large drive support.

Do you wish to enable large disk support (Y/N)..........? [Y]
```

Here you need to decide if you wish to use FAT32. In this example, the answer is **Yes**. After answering **Y** or **N**, you will see the following screen:

```
                    Microsoft Windows Millennium
                      Fixed Disk Setup Program
              (C)Copyright Microsoft Corp. 1983 - 2000

                           FDISK Options

    Current fixed disk drive: 1

    Choose one of the following:

    1. Create DOS partition or Logical DOS Drive
    2. Set active partition
    3. Delete partition or Logical DOS Drive
    4. Display partition information

    Enter choice: [1]
    Press Esc to exit FDISK
```

If you had more than one hard drive in your computer, there would be a fifth option.

```
    5. Change current fixed disk drive
```

Step 2 Select **4** to display the partition information.

You should get a message telling you no partitions are defined.

Step 3 Press **Esc** to return to the main menu.

Step 4 Choose **1** to create a primary partition.

WHAT'S HAPPENING? You will be asked if you wish to use the maximum size for a DOS partition and to make the partition active.

Step 5 Press **N** for no.

WHAT'S HAPPENING? You will be told the size of the drive, and you can key in what size (either in bytes or by percentage of total drive space) you wish to use for the primary partition.

At this point, you will decide how much space you wish to allocate to each partition. This example will partition the hard drive into two equal halves, and then split the second partition into two equal logical drives.

Step 6 Key in **50%** and press Enter

WHAT'S HAPPENING? There will now be a choice on the menu to set the active partition.

Step 7 Choose **Set the active partition** and set the number **1** partition as the active (booting) partition.

Step 8 Select **Create DOS partition or Logical DOS Drive** once again.

Step 9 Select **Create Extended DOS partition**.

Step 10 Choose **all the available space**.

WHAT'S HAPPENING? Once the partition is created, you will get a message saying **No logical drives defined**.

You will now divide the space that you have created as an extended DOS partition into more than one logical (as opposed to physical) drive. You will split this partition into the logical drives D and E, using 50 percent of the available space for each logical drive.

Step 11 Press Esc to exit from FDISK and reboot the system. (Note: Your booting disk is still in the A drive.)

Step 12 Format the C drive with the system on it.

WHAT'S HAPPENING? You *would not* need to place the system on the disk if you were actually preparing the disk for the installation of the OS. The installation process would do this. However, for the purposes of this demonstration, you will place the system on the C drive during formatting.

Step 13 Format the D drive.

WHAT'S HAPPENING? At this point, if you formatted the disk with the system, you would be able to boot the computer from the Primary DOS partition (drive C) of the new drive.

GLOSSARY

absolute path The direct route from the root directory through the hierarchical structure of a directory tree to the subdirectory of interest.

active desktop object A piece of Web content placed on the desktop that needs to be updated on a regular basis, such as stock market prices or a weather map.

active window The window that is currently in use when multiple windows are open.

ActiveX A set of technologies that enables software components to interact with one another in a networked environment, regardless of the language in which the components were created. ActiveX is used primarily to develop interactive content for the World Wide Web, although it can be used in other kinds of programs.

adapter card A printed circuit board that is installed in a computer to allow the installation and control of some type of device, such as a monitor.

add-on An accessory or utility program designed to work with, extend, and increase the capabilities of an original product.

allocation unit See *cluster*.

alphanumeric keys The keys on a keyboard that are letters (A–Z), numbers (0–9), and other characters such as punctuation marks.

ANSI An acronym for American National Standards Institute. A coding scheme used for transmitting data between a computer and peripherals. Each character has a numerical equivalent in ANSI.

app See *application package*.

application package A computer program that is user-oriented and is usually for a specific job, such as word processing. Application packages are also called *packages, off-the-shelf software, canned software,* or *apps*.

application program See *application package*.

application software See *application package*.

application window The window of the application that is currently open and on the desktop. An application window may also contain a document window.

archival backup A backup procedure in which all the files on a hard disk are backed up by being copied to floppy disks or some other backup medium.

archival data Information that is stored in archive files.

archive attribute See *archive bit*.

archive bit A file attribute that gives the backup history of a file (whether or not a file has been backed up). Archiving to save a file usually refers to long-term storage.

archiving a file Removing a file from a hard disk and storing it on another medium for historical purposes.

arithmetic/logic unit The circuitry that a computer uses for mathematical and logical functions and is an integral part of a microprocessor chip.

ASCII An acronym for American Standard Code for Information Interchange. A coding scheme used for transmitting data between a computer and peripherals. Each character has a numerical equivalent in ASCII.

ASCII editor A program that is similar to a word-processing program but is unable to perform any special editing. No embedded codes are inserted into documents. ASCII editors can only edit ASCII text files, also called text files or unformatted text files. ASCII editors are also called *text editors*.

asynchronous Not synchronized; not happening at regular time intervals.

asynchronous communication A form of data transmission that uses only two wires for communication between computers (generally for communicating via modems). Data is transmitted by the sending of one character at a time with variable time intervals between characters and a start bit and a stop bit to mark the beginning and end of the data.

attachment An external document included as part of an email message.

AutoPlay The feature that causes an audio CD placed in a CD-ROM drive to play automatically. To bypass this, hold the **Shift** key down when inserting the disc.

AutoRun The feature that causes a program CD placed in a CD-ROM drive to execute automatically. To bypass this, hold the **Shift** key down when inserting the disc.

background color The color that is in the background in Paint. It is not the current drawing color.

background printing Printing a document in the background while another program is being worked on in the foreground.

background program In Windows 98, which has multitasking capabilities, background program refers to a program that is being executed in the background at the same time that the user is working with another program in the foreground. For example, printing one document (background program) while at the same time editing another document (foreground program).

backup The process in which the user makes a copy of an original file or files for safekeeping.

bandwidth The data transfer capacity of a digital communications system.

batch file A text file of DOS commands. When its name is keyed in at the DOS system level, the commands in the batch file are executed sequentially.

batch processing A manner of running programs without interruption. Programs to be executed are collected and placed into prioritized batches, and then the programs are processed one after another without user interaction or intervention.

baud rate Measure of how fast a modem can transmit data. Named after the French telegrapher and engineer J.M.E. Baudot.

beta test A formal process of pretesting hardware and software that is still under development with selected "typical" users to see whether any operational or utilization errors (bugs) still exist in the program before the product is released to the general public.

binary value A binary value is a variable-length set of hexadecimal digits.

BIOS An acronym for basic input/output system. A program that controls input/output devices.

BIOS bootstrap A process that occurs before booting. The program that controls this process is in the BIOS chip and the CMOS setup of the computer. A POST (power-on self test) is performed, wherein the computer checks its physical health. Plug-and-play devices are identified and configured, and a bootable partition is executed.

bit The smallest unit of information, expressed in binary numbers 0 and 1, that a computer can measure. Eight bits make a byte.

bitmap font A font that a printer creates dot by dot. When displayed on the monitor, bitmap fonts are created pixel by pixel.

bootable disk A disk containing the operating system files.

booting the system The process of powering on a computer. When first turned on (a cold boot) or reset (a warm boot), a computer executes the software that loads and starts the computer's operating system. The computer can be said to pull itself up by its own bootstrap.

boot record If a disk is a system disk, the boot record contains the bootstrap routine used for loading. Otherwise, the disk will present a message that the disk is a nonsystem disk. Every disk has a boot record. The boot record also contains such information as the type of media, the number of tracks and sectors, and so forth.

boot sector The first sector on every logical drive.

boot sector virus A virus that replaces a disk's original boot sector with its own and then loads itself into memory. Once in memory, it infects other disks.

bootstrap The process a computer uses to get itself ready for loading the operating system into memory. It pulls itself up by its bootstraps.

browser An application software package that allows you to easily explore the Internet and the World Wide Web.

buffer A temporary holding area for data in memory.

bug An error in software that causes the program to malfunction or to produce incorrect results.

built-in font A resident font that comes with a printer.

bulletin board service (BBS) A service that users link to using their modems. Some BBSs allow users to read and post messages, download program fixes or other programs, and much more.

bundled Describes programs included with a larger program to make the larger program more attractive or functional. It is also used to describe a purchase of hardware that includes all devices as well as installed software.

bus A set of hardware lines (wires) that are used for data transfer among the elements of a computer system.

bus topology A topology (network design) for a local area network in which all computers or peripherals (nodes) are connected to a main communications line (bus). On a bus network, each node monitors activity on the line.

byte A unit of measurement that represents one character (a letter, number, or punctuation mark). A byte is comprised of eight bits. Computer storage and memory are measured in bytes.

cache A place in memory where data can be stored for quick access.

cache memory A place in memory where data can be stored for quick access.

caching A process where Windows sets up a reserved area in RAM where it can quickly read and write frequently used data without having to read from or write to the disk.

card A short name for an adapter card.

cascaded Windows layered on top of one another.

cascading menu A menu that opens another menu. A secondary menu will open as a result of a command issued on the first or primary menu. A right-pointing arrow next to the primary menu indicates that a cascade menu is available. Also called a hierarchical menu.

case sensitive Describes a program that distinguishes between upper- and lowercase characters.

CD-ROM An acronym for compact disc–read-only memory. It usually refers to a disc that plays in a CD-ROM device.

central processing unit (CPU) The central processing unit (CPU) is the brain of the computer. It carries out the instructions or commands given to it by a program.

chain When referring to the file allocation table, a pointer that links clusters together.

channel A Web site that has been expressly designed for push technology so that content can be delivered to your computer system.

character set A grouping of alphabetic, numeric, and other characters that have some relationship in common. A font file has character definitions.

character string A set of letters, symbols, and control characters that are treated as a unit.

checkbox A box that is clicked to either set or unset a feature.

child directory An analogous title given to offshoots (subdirectories) of any root or subdirectory.

child menu A menu in a hierarchical menu structure that is under the parent menu above it. Each subsequent child menu becomes a parent to the next menu in the hierarchy.

child window A window that belongs to a parent window. A child window can have only one parent but one or more child windows of its own..

clicking Pressing and releasing the left mouse button once.

client In networking, a client is a computer that accesses the shared network resources provided by the server.

client application An application program that is receiving an object from the server application.

clip art A collection of proprietary or public-domain photographs, maps, drawings, and other graphics that can be "clipped" from the collection and incorporated into other documents.

Clipboard A special memory area used by Windows that stores a copy of the last information that was copied or cut. A paste operation passes data from the Clipboard to the current program. The Clipboard allows information to be transferred from one program to another, provided the second program can read data generated by the first.

Close button A button that shuts down a window and closes an application package or dialog box.

cluster The smallest unit of disk space that DOS or Windows 95/98 can write to or read from. It is comprised of one or more sectors. A cluster can also be called an *allocation unit*.

cluster overhang Since clusters are made up of one or more 512-byte sectors and Windows 95/98 reads to or writes from only one cluster at a time, a file will occupy more space than it needs for its data, causing cluster overhang.

CMD.EXE That part of the operating system that the user actually communicates and interacts with. It processes and interprets what has been keyed in. It is also known as the command processor or the command interpreter.

CMOS An acronym for complementary metal-oxide semiconductor. CMOS, maintained by a battery pack, is memory that is used to store parameter values, such as the size and type of the hard disk and the number and type of floppy drives, the keyboard, and display type, that are used to boot PCs.

coaxial cable A type of cable used in connecting network components.

Color box In Paint, the box that displays the foreground and background colors you may use in your drawing.

combo box A combination text box and list box.

command An instruction that is a program that the user keys in at the command line prompt. This instruction executes the selected program.

command button A button that, when selected by the user, performs the desired action.

command interpreter See *command processor*.

command processor That portion of an operating system that interprets what the user keys in.

command syntax The vocabulary, order, and punctuation necessary to execute a command properly.

communication protocol A set of communication rules that enable computers to exchange information.

compact disc–read-only memory See *CD-ROM*.

compound document A document that contains information, data, or other objects created from more than one application program.

compressed file A file written (utilizing a file compression utility) to a special disk format that minimizes the storage space needed.

computer virus A computer program designed as a prank or sabotage that can replicate itself by attaching to other programs and spreading unwanted and often damaging operations. A virus can be spread to other computers by floppy disk and/or through electronic bulletin boards.

conditional processing A comparison of two items that yields a true or false value. Once the value is determined, a program can be directed to take some action based on the results of the test.

configuration information Information about your system such as the hardware applications and user preferences.

context menu A menu that opens with a right-click of the mouse. It is also referred to as a pop-up menu or a shortcut menu.

contiguous Describes elements that are next to each other. Contiguous files are those files that are written to adjacent clusters on a disk.

control Provides a way the user can interact (provide input) with available choices. Usually a control is a way to initiate an action, display information, or set the values that you are interested in. Example of controls include command buttons, options buttons, drop-down list boxes, and text boxes.

Control key The key labeled Ctrl on the keyboard that, when held down with another key, causes the other key to have another meaning.

controller A board that goes into the computer and is needed to operate a peripheral device.

control menu Has an icon, located in the upper-left corner of a window, that can be opened to provide commands to manipulate the window. These commands are usually keyboard oriented rather than mouse oriented. The icon is referred to as the control-menu icon.

control-menu icon In Windows, the icon that can be clicked to provide a drop-down menu with additional commands. It is also called the control-menu box.

conventional memory The first 640KB of memory, where programs and data are located while the user is working.

cookie On the World Wide Web, a block of data that a Web server stores on your computer system. When you return to the same Web site, your browser sends a copy of the cookie back to the server. Cookies are used to identify users, instruct the server to send a customized version of the requested Web page, or submit account information for the user.

CPU See *central processing unit (CPU).*

cross-linked files Two files that claim the same sectors in the file allocation table (FAT).

current directory The default directory.

cursor The location where the user can key in information.

cyberspace A term used when referring to the Internet; a virtual place where computers can connect and individuals or organizations can communicate.

cylinder The vertical measurement of two or more disk platters that have the track aligned. It is used when referring to hard disks.

data Information, in the widest possible sense. Usually it refers to the numbers and text used by a computer to do the work requested by the user.

database A collection of related information (data) stored on a computer, organized, and structured so that the information can be easily manipulated.

database management program An application program that allows for manipulation of information in a database.

data bits A group of bits used to represent a single character for transmission over a modem. A start bit and stop bit must be used in transmitting a group of data.

data file A file that is usually composed of related data created by the user with an application program. They are organized in a specific manner and usually can be used only by this program.

debugging Finding and correcting problems in a program. Debug is also a program usable at the command line interface.

dedicated server A computer in a server-based network that is devoted to providing network resources.

default What the computer system or computer program "falls back to" if no other specific instructions are given.

default drive The disk drive that the OS looks on to locate commands or files if no other instructions are given.

default folder The folder data will be read to or written from unless you change it.

default subdirectory The subdirectory that the computer "falls back to" when no other specific instructions are given.

defragger A means to optimize performance on a disk. Running the Disk Defragmenter program rearranges the storage of files on a disk so that they are contiguous.

delimiter A special character that is used to separate information so that an operating system such as Windows 2000 Professional can recognize where one part of a parameter ends and the next one begins.

designated drive See *default drive.*

desktop The on-screen work area that emulates the top of a desk.

destination file The desired file that data is to be sent to.

device A piece of computer equipment, such as a disk drive or a printer, that performs a specific job.

device driver Software necessary for the use of a hardware device. The program controls the specific peripheral device.

device icon A small graphic that represents a device such as a printer or a disk drive.

device name A reserved name that the operating system assigns to a device, such as PRN for printer.

dialog box In a graphical user interface, a box that either conveys information to or requests information from the user.

differential backup A differential backup backs up all the selected files that have changed since the last time an All selected files backup was used.

directional keys Keys used to move the cursor in various directions.

directory The location or container where documents, program files, devices, and other folders are stored on your disk. The terms *folders* and *directories* are synonymous.

directory tree The structure of the current disk drive.

disk A magnetically coated disk that allows permanent storage of computer data.

disk buffer Acts as the go-between for a disk and RAM.

disk cache An area in memory where Windows 2000 Professional looks for information prior to reading from or writing to the disk for the purpose of optimizing performance.

disk compression program A means to increase disk space by fooling the operating system into thinking that there is more space on the disk.

disk drive A device that rotates a disk so that the computer can read information from and write information to the disk.

disk file A file that is stored on a disk.

disk optimization program A means to optimize performance on a disk. Usually the user runs the Disk Defragmenter program that rearranges the storage of files on a disk so that they are contiguous. It is also called a *disk defragger*.

docucentric Describes a paradigm or model that designs a computer system or program around the fact that what is most important to the user is the data (the document), not the program that created it.

document A self-contained piece of work created with an application program and, if saved on a disk, given a unique file name by which it can be retrieved.

documentation Written instructions that inform the user how to use hardware and/or software.

document file A data file whose information was created in an application file and saved to a disk.

documenting Writing the purpose of and instructions for a computer program.

document window A window that belongs to a program window and is always contained within a program window.

domain name An alphabetic alias to the IP address. Some examples of domain names are saddleback.cc.ca.us and daedal.net.

Domain Name System (DNS) The system by which domain names are translated into their IP numeric addresses.

DOS An acronym for disk operating system, the character-based operating system commonly used on microcomputers. It is also a shorthand way of referring to the command line interface.

dot A subdirectory marker; a shorthand name; the . for the specific subdirectory name.

dot-matrix printer A printer that produces text characters and graphics by creating them with a series of closely spaced dots. It uses a print head, platen, and ribbon to form the characters.

dot pitch In printers, the distance between dots in a dot matrix. In video displays, a measure of image clarity. In a video display, the dot pitch is the vertical distance, expressed in millimeters, between like-colored pixels. A smaller dot pitch generally means a sharper image.

double-clicking Pressing and releasing the left mouse button twice in rapid succession.

downloading Receiving a file from a remote computer while connected by a modem, another outside connection, or a network.

downward compatible Describes software/hardware that can be used on older computer systems.

dragging Placing the pointer over an object, holding down the left mouse button, and moving the object to another location.

dragging and dropping Moving or manipulating an object or document across the desktop and dropping it in another location.

drawing area In Paint, the area where you create your drawing.

drive letter A letter of the alphabet that identifies a specific disk drive.

driver A piece of software that tells a piece of hardware how to work.

drop-down list box A box that contains a default selection. However, if the user clicks on the down arrow, a list box drops down and displays further choices.

drop-down menu A menu that presents choices that drop down from the menu bar when requested and remain open on the screen until the user chooses a menu item or closes the menu.

DVD An enhancement to CD-ROM technology. It provides the next generation of optical disc storage technology. It encompasses audio, video, and computer data. DVD is not an acronym but a trademark.

dynamic data exchange (DDE) A set of standards that supports data exchange among application programs.

dynamic link library (DLL) A feature that allows executable routines to be stored separately as files with DLL extensions and to be loaded only when needed by a program. A DLL file does not consume any memory until it is used. Since a DLL file is separate, a programmer can make corrections or improvements to only that module without affecting other programs or other DLLs. Also, the same dynamic link library can be used with other programs.

dynamic RAM (DRAM) Memory chips that hold data for a short time. DRAM is less expensive than SRAM and thus, most memory is DRAM. See also *static RAM*.

ellipsis Three dots that can appear after a menu item or on a command button. If you choose the item, a dialog box will open.

email Short for electronic mail. Email is a note or message that is sent between different computers that use telecommunications services or are on a network.

Emergency Repair Disk A bootable disk that has critical system files on it.

end-of-file (EOF) marker A symbol that alerts the operating system when a file has no more data.

enhancement Increases the capabilities of a computer by adding or updating hardware or software.

event An action performed by you or by your program that your computer can notify you of. Usually the notification is a sound, such as a beep if you press an incorrect key.

executable Refers to programs that place instructions in memory. The instructions are followed by the computer.

executing a program A process where instructions are placed in memory and then followed by the computer.

expansion slot An empty slot or space inside a system unit that can be used for adding new boards or devices to expand the computer's capabilities.

exporting Using an existing file or data in the file and sending it to another file.

extension See *file extension*.

external command A program that resides on a disk and must be read into RAM before it can be used.

external storage media Storage devices that are outside the computer system. Floppy, CD-ROM, and removable drives are the most common external storage media.

FAT See *file allocation table (FAT)*.

FAT file system The system originally used by MS-DOS to organize and manage files. The FAT (file allocation table) is a data structure is created on a disk when the disk is formatted. When a file is stored on a formatted disk, the operating system places information about the stored file in the FAT so that the operating system (DOS) can retrieve the file later. Windows 98 can use the FAT file system.

file A program or a collection of related information stored on a disk.

file allocation table (FAT) A map of the disk that keeps track of all the clusters on a disk. It is used in conjunction with the directory table.

file attributes Attributes are stored as part of a file's directory entry and describe and give other information about the file.

file extension The last portion of a file name following the last period. Usually file extensions describe the type of data in the file. See also *file type*.

file format A special format used to construct a file so an application program can read the data. It consists of special codes that only the creating application program understands.

file infector virus Adds programming instructions to files that run programs. The virus then becomes active when you run the program.

file name A label used to identify a file. When most users refer to the file name, they are referring to the file specification.

file server On a network, a file storage device that stores files. On a large network, a file server is a sophisticated device that no only stores files but also manages them and maintains order as network users request files and make changes to the files.

file specification The complete name of a file, including the file name and the file extension (file type).

file type The last portion of a file name following the last period in a file name. Usually file types describe the type of data in the file. See also *file extension.*

firewall A security system intended to protect an organization's network against external threats, such as hackers. A firewall prevents computers in the organization's network from communicating directly with computers external to the network and vice versa.

fixed disk See *hard disk.*

fixed parameter A parameter whose values are specific and limited.

flag A marker of some type used to process information. File attributes are commonly called flags because they indicate a particular condition of a file.

floating Describes a toolbar or taskbar that can be positioned anywhere on the screen and does not have to be anchored to a window.

floppy disk A magnetically coated disk that allows permanent storage of data.

floppy disk drive See *disk drive.*

folder The location or container where documents, program files, devices, and other folders are stored on your disk. The terms *folders* and *directories* are synonymous.

folder icon The graphic representation of a folder that will open when you double-click it.

Folders pane The left pane of the Explorer window.

font A typeface (set of characters) that consists of several parts, such as the type size and weight (i.e., bold or italic).

footer One or more identifying lines printed at the bottom of a page.

foreground Describes the application or window that the user is currently working on.

foreground application An application or window that the user is currently working on. It is also referred to as the foreground window or active window.

foreground window An application or window in which the user is currently working. It is also referred to as the foreground window or active window.

formatting Preparing a disk for use. It can also refer to the way data looks in a document.

form feed An operation that advances the hard copy on the printer to the next page.

fragmented See *fragmented disk.*

fragmented disk A disk that has many noncontiguous files on it.

fragmented file A file that is written to a disk in noncontiguous clusters. See also *noncontiguous.*

freeware A computer program given away free of charge and often made available on the Internet or through newsgroups.

FTP (File Transfer Protocol) A protocol that allows files to be transferred to and from a node running FTP services.

full backup A backup procedure that backs up every file on a disk, regardless of whether a file has changed or not.

full system backup A backup procedure that backs up every file on a disk, including special system files, regardless of whether a file has changed or not.

function keys Programmable keys on a keyboard. F1 and F2 are examples of function keys. Function keys are program dependent.

gig A colloquial term for gigabyte.

gigabyte (GB) A unit of measurement equal to approximately one billion bytes.

glide pad An input device that is a small, smooth object on which you move your finger to control the action of the pointer.

global file specifications The symbols * and ?, also called wildcards, that are used to represent a single character (?) or a group of characters (*) in a file name.

graphic file Pictures and drawings that can be produced on the screen or printer and are saved in a file.

grid of cells Two sets of lines or linear elements at right angles to each other. A spreadsheet is a grid of rows and columns; a graphics screen is a grid of horizontal and vertical lines of pixels. In optical character recognition, a grid is used for measuring or specifying characters.

GUI (graphical user interface) A display format that allows the user to interact with the computer by using pictorial representations and menu choices to manage the computer resources and work with application programs.

hard copy A printed paper copy of information that is created when using the computer. It can also be referred to as a printout.

hard disk A disk that is permanently installed in a computer system and has a larger capacity to store files than a floppy disk. Hard disks are measured in megabytes or gigabytes.

hard disk drive See *hard disk*.

hard return Generated when **Enter** is pressed. The system will not move a hard return, but will move a soft return.

hardware Physical computer components.

hardware interrupt A request for service or a signal from peripherals to the CPU for attention so the device may be serviced.

head crash A hard disk failure in which a read/write head, normally supported on a cushion of air, comes into contact with the platter, damaging the magnetic coating in which data is recorded.

header In word processing or printing, text that is to appear at the top of pages.

head slot Exposes the disk surface to the read/write heads via an opening in the jacket of a floppy disk.

hexadecimal A numbering system that uses a base of 16 consisting of the digits 0–9 and the letters A–F.

hidden file A file that is not displayed in Explorer or My Computer or when the DIR command is used in the DOS window.

hierarchical menu A menu that opens another menu. A secondary menu will open as a result of a command issued on the first or primary menu. A right-pointing arrow next to the primary menu indicates that a cascade menu is available. It is also called a cascading menu.

hierarchical structure The logical grouping of files and programs based on pathways between root directories and their subsequent directories. It is also called a tree-structured directory.

hierarchy A group of things that are ordered by rank. In a disk's structure, it is a dependent relationship where one folder is dependent on the folder above it. Every disk begins with the root directory (folder), with subsequent folders branching from the root.

high-capacity disk See *high-density disk*.

high-density disk A floppy disk that can store up to 1.2 MB on a 5¼-inch disk or 1.44 MB on a 3½-inch disk.

high-level formatting Also known as logical formatting. The process that Windows 98 uses to structure a disk so that files can be stored or retrieved.

highlighting The process of selecting an object, text, or an icon. Objects must be selected before they can be acted upon. Highlighting is indicated by reverse video.

home page On a server, the first screen that appears when you select a Web site.

housekeeping task Any number of routines to keep the environment where programs run in good working order.

hovering A mouse technique that highlights objects with an underline as you drag your mouse, which indicates that you have selected an object.

HTML (Hypertext Markup Language) The programming language with which Web documents are created.

HTTP (Hypertext Transfer Protocol) A common protocol used to access sites on the Internet.

hypertext A means to easily jump from one logically related topic to the next.

IAP Internet access provider.

icon A symbol that represents a more simple access to a program file, a data file, or a task.

impact printer A type of printer that transfers images onto paper through a mechanism that strikes a ribbon and transfers the images to paper. It is similar to a typewriter.

importing Bringing information from one program into another. You can import an entire file or part of a file.

incremental backup A backup process that only backs up files that have changed since the last full or incremental backup.

information superhighway Refers to the Internet. A worldwide network of networks that provides the ability to gather information, do research, explore ideas, purchase items, send email, and chat with people around the world. See also *cyberspace.*

initialization files Files that initialize a program or process. In earlier versions of Windows, the operating system and most application programs stored information about the users, environmental parameters, and necessary drivers in .INI files. The .INI extension is derived from initialization files.

initializing Getting a medium (a disk or a file) ready for use.

initializing a disk Getting a disk ready for use. It is another term for formatting a disk.

inkjet printer A nonimpact printer that prints by spraying a matrix of dots onto the paper.

input Refers to data or information entered into the computer.

input device A means to get information into RAM by communicating with the computer. Typical input devices include the keyboard and the mouse.

input/output The process of data and program instructions going into and out of the CPU (central processing unit). It is also referred to as I/O.

insert A mode that allows the user to enter data in which new text is inserted at the cursor, pushing all text that follows to the right.

install Copying files (programs) from a CD or floppy disk onto the hard disk.

integrated circuit An electronic device that combines thousands of transistors on a small wafer of silicon (chip). Such devices are the building blocks of computers.

integrated pointing device An input device that is an eraser-like object on the keyboard that you can manipulate to control the cursor.

interactive Describes the ability to update data within the computer system instantaneously.

interactive processing Sometimes called online or real-time mode, interactive means interacting directly with the computer.

interface Hardware and/or software needed to connect computer components. Also used as a synonym for interacting with a computer.

interface card The circuit board that is needed to connect computer components.

interlaced A technique used in some monitors in which the electron beam refreshes (updates) all odd-numbered scan lines in one vertical sweep of the screen and all even-numbered scan lines in the next sweep. The picture on these monitors tends to flicker. See also *noninterlaced.*

Internet A network of networks that connects computer users around the world.

intranet A network designed for information processing within a company or organization.

I/O See *input/output*.

IP address A unique numeric address that identifies a computer on the Internet.

ISP (Internet service provider) A company or organization that provides a gateway or connection to the Internet, usually for a fee. It is also called an access provider or a service provider.

keyboard A major device used for entering data into a computer consisting of a typewriter-like collection of labeled keys.

kilobyte (KB) A unit of measurement equal to 1,024 bytes.

LAN See *local area network (LAN).*

landscape A printing orientation that prints horizontally (sideways) on the paper.

laser printer A high-resolution nonimpact printer that provides letter-quality output of text and graphics. Laser printers are based on a technology in which characters are formed by a laser and made visible by the same technology used by photocopy machines.

legacy hardware Hardware that is not plug-and-play compatible.

legacy software Older versions of software that were designed to run on earlier versions of operating system, such as DOS.

light pen A pointing device (connected to the computer by a cable and resembling a pen) that is used to provide input to the computer by writing, sketching, or selecting commands on a special monitor designed to respond to the light pen.

line feed An operation that advances the hard copy to the next line of text whether or not the line is full.

list box A box that presents the user with a list of options. It is used in menus and dialog boxes.

loading Placing information (data or programs) from storage into memory.

local area network (LAN) A network of computer equipment located in one room or building and connected by a communication link that enables any device to interact with any other in the network, making it possible for users to exchange information, share peripherals, and draw on common resources.

local bus See *bus*.

locally In a networked environment, this means that you are not using the network, but only your own local computer.

local printer A printer physically attached to your computer.

logical device A device named by the logic of a software system regardless of its physical relationship to the system.

logical disk drive A drive named by the logic of the software (operating) system. It is an "imaginary drive" that acts exactly like a real disk drive.

logical formatting See *high-level formatting*.

logical view A view of items that are represented by icons rather then by their physical presence.

logo A distinctive signature or trademark that usually functions as a graphical representation of a company.

long file name (LFN) The term used in Windows 98 to indicate that file names are no longer limited to the 8.3 character file names. In Windows 95 and in Windows 98, file names cannot exceed 255 characters.

loop back The address 127.0.0.1, which is used to send data to your own computer without using the network card. The data "loops back."

lost cluster Clusters that have no directory entry in the directory table and do not belong to any file. They are debris that results from incomplete data, and they should be cleaned up periodically with Check Disk.

low-level formatting Also known as physical formatting. The process of numbering the tracks and sectors of a disk sequentially so that each can be identified. On a hard disk, this process is done by the manufacturer of the hard disk.

macro A short key code command which stands for a sequence of saved instructions that when retrieved will execute the commands to accomplish a given task.

mandatory parameter A parameter that must be used with a command.

mapped drive A network drive or folder (one that has been shared) that you may assign a local drive letter.

master boot record (MBR) Used before booting. It determines the location of the bootable partition of the hard disk and gives control over to it.

Maximize button A button that makes the current window fill the entire screen.

meg A colloquial term for *megabyte*.

megabyte (MB) A unit of measurement that is roughly equal to one million bytes.

megahertz (MHz) A unit of measurement used to compare clock speeds of computers.

memory The temporary workspace of the computer where data and programs are kept while they are worked on. It is also referred to as *RAM (random access memory)*. Information in RAM is lost when the computer is turned off, which is why memory is considered volatile.

menu A list of choices (selections) displayed on the screen from which the user chooses a course of action.

menu bar A rectangular bar, usually in a program, in which the names of the available, additional menus are shown. The user chooses one of these menus and a list of choices for that menu is shown.

message box A type of dialog box that informs you of a condition.

microcomputer A personal computer that is usually used by one person. It is also referred to as a desktop computer or a stand-alone computer.

microfloppy disk A 3½-inch floppy disk encased in a hard plastic shell.

MIDI (Musical Instrument Digital Interface) A way to get input from your musical instruments into a computer and then modify and store the sounds you recorded.

minicomputer A mid-level computer larger than a microcomputer but smaller than a mainframe computer. It is usually used to meet the needs of a small company or department.

minifloppy disk A 5¼-inch floppy disk.

Minimize button A button that reduces the current window to a button on the taskbar.

modem Short for modulator/demodulator. A device that provides communication capability between computers using phone lines. Modems are typically used to access online services, such as AOL (America Online) or an ISP.

monitor A device similar to a television screen that displays the input and output of the computer. It is also called a *screen, display screen, cathode-ray terminal,* or *VDT (video display terminal).*

monospaced typeface A typeface that gives all characters in the set the same width.

motherboard The main computer board that holds the memory and CPU, as well as slots for adapter cards. The power supply plugs directly into the motherboard. It is also called a *system board.*

mouse A small, hand-held device that is equipped with one or more control buttons and is housed in a palm-sized case. It is used to control cursor movement.

mouse pointer An onscreen pointer that is controlled by the movement of the mouse.

mouse trail A "ghost" of the mouse pointer that follows the movement of the mouse around the screen. It is used to improve the visibility of the cursor.

MS-DOS An abbreviation for *Microsoft disk operating system,* a character-based operating system for computers that use the 8086 or above microprocessor.

multitasking Describes the ability to work on more than one task or application program at a time.

naming convention A logical naming scheme for files and folders for facilitating the saving and retrieving of files and folders.

Net A colloquial name for the *Internet*.

netiquette A combination of the words *network* and *etiquette*. It is a set of principles of courtesy that should be observed when sending electronic messages such as email and newsgroup postings.

network A group of computers connected by a communication facility called a server, which permits the sharing and transmission of data. In addition, it allows the sharing of resources, such as a hard drive or a printer.

network administrator The person who decides how the hardware and software will be used on a network.

network interface card (NIC) An expansion card used to connect a computer to a local area network.

network operating system (NOS) An operating system installed on a server in a local area network that coordinates the activities of providing services to the computers and other devices attached to the network.

NIC See *network interface card.*

nonbootable disk A disk that does not contain the operating system files. The computer cannot boot from it.

noncontiguous Describes files that are written to a disk in nonadjacent clusters or clusters that are not next to one another.

nonimpact printer A type of printer that transfers images onto paper by means of ink-jet sprayers, melting ink, or lasers.

noninterlaced A display method on monitors in which the electron beam scans each line of the screen once during each refresh cycle. Monitors that are noninterlaced generally have clearer images and do not flicker. See also *interlaced*.

NOS See *network operating system*.

null value A test for nothing (no data).

numeric keypad A separate set of keys next to the main keyboard that contains the digits 0 through 9. It also includes an alternate set of commands that can be toggled such as PgUp and the arrow keys. These functions are program dependent.

object Most items in Windows are considered objects. Objects can be opened, have properties, and be manipulated. Objects can also have settings and parameters.

octet Refers to one of the four sections of the dotted-decimal notation address.

offline Describes a printer that may be attached to the computer but is not activated and ready to print. It also refers to not being connected to a network or the Internet.

online Describes a printer that is not only attached to the computer but also activated and ready for operation. When referring to communication, it refers to being attached to another computer, a network, or the Internet.

online help On-screen assistance consisting of advice or instructions on utilizing the program's features. It can be accessed without interrupting the work in progress.

open scroll area An area on a scroll bar to the right or left of the scroll box that will move you in large increments through a document.

operating system (OS) A master control program or set of programs that manages the operation of all the parts of a computer. An operating system, known as *system software,* is loaded into memory when the computer is booted. It must be loaded prior to any application software.

optional parameter A parameter that may be used with a command but is not mandatory.

option button Part of a list of choices presented to the user. Only one option can be selected at a time. Option buttons provide mutually exclusive choices.

overtype See *typeover*.

overwrite mode The mode in which newly typed characters replace existing characters to the right of the cursor.

overwriting Replacing data by writing over old data with new data. Usually when you copy a file from one location to another, the file that is copied overwrites the file that was there.

packet A unit of information transferred between computers via a network or a modem.

pane A division in a window.

parallel In data transmission, it refers to sending one byte (eight bits) at a time.

parallel port An input/output connector for parallel interface devices.

parameter A qualifier or modifier that can be added to a command and will specify the action to be taken.

parent directory The subdirectory above the current subdirectory. The parent directory is always one step closer to the root than the child.

parent menu A menu in a hierarchical menu structure that is at the top of the menu system. A parent menu may have a child menu; a child menu may become a parent and have child windows of its own.

parent window A window that is the owner of any objects in it. If there is a folder in the window, it is a child to that parent. A child window can have only one parent, but it can have one or more child windows of its own.

parity Parity bit is a simple method used to check for transmission errors. An extra bit is added to be sure that there is always either an even or an odd number of bits.

partitioning Physically dividing a section of the hard disk from other sections of the disk and then having the operating system treat that section as if it were a separate unit.

password A unique set of text or numbers that identifies the user. Passwords are used when logging onto networks and when Windows 98 has user profiles set up.

path Tells Windows where to look for programs and files on a disk that has more than one directory.

path name Information that tells the operating system where to look for program files on a disk that has more than one folder (directory).

peer-to-peer network A network that has no dedicated servers or a hierarchy among the computers. All the computers are equal, and therefore peers. Each computer can function as either client or server.

pel See *pixel*.

peripheral device Any device, such as a keyboard, monitor, or printer, that is connected to and controlled by the CPU.

physical formatting See *low-level formatting*.

physical memory The actual memory chips in a computer.

physical view A view of folders that shows the hierarchy of a file system, indicating drives and where they are located.

pixel The smallest element on the display screen grid that can be stored or displayed. Pixels are used to create or print letters, numbers, or graphics. The more pixels, the higher the resolution.

Plug and Play A feature of Windows that automatically detects and configures a new hardware device when it is added to a computer system.

point Fonts are measured in points. The more points, the larger the font. A point is $^1/_{72}$ of an inch.

pointer An arrow or other indicator on the screen which represents the current cursor (mouse) location.

pointing Placing the mouse pointer over an object.

Point-to-Point Protocol (PPP) A temporary dial-up connection that uses this protocol provides full access to the Internet as long as you are online.

pop-up menu A menu that opens with a right-click of the mouse. It is also referred to as a *shortcut* or *context menu*.

port A location or place on a CPU to connect other devices to a computer. It allows the computer to send information to and from the device.

portal An entry point to the World Wide Web (WWW). It is sometimes called a gateway. Search engines such as Yahoo! and service providers such as MSN are positioning themselves as portals.

portrait The most common printing mode for letters and other documents. This mode prints with the narrower side of the page across the top.

power cycle Physically turning the computer off, waiting at least five seconds, and turning the computer back on.

PPP See *Point-to-Point Protocol*.

primary mouse button The mouse button used for most operatins, usually configured as the left mouse button.

printer A computer peripheral that produces a hard copy of text or graphics on paper.

printer driver Software used to send correct codes to the printer. It is also called *driver software* since it drives the printer.

printer font A font that a printer is capable of printing.

print job A print job usually consists of a single document, which can be one page or hundreds of pages long.

print queue A list of files that have been sent to the printer by various applications. The print manager sends the files to the printer as the printer becomes available.

print server On a network, a computer that is dedicated only to printing.

print spooler A program that compensates for differences in rates of the flow of data by temporarily storing data in memory and then doling it out to the printer at the proper speed.

process An executable program or part of a program that is a coherent set of steps. The process consists of the program itself, the memory address space it uses, the system resources it uses, and at least one thread.

program A set of step-by-step instructions that tells the computer what to do.

program approach A paradigm of treating programs as central. In order to use data, you must first open your program and then open your file. See also *docucentric*.

program file A file containing an executable computer program. See also *application software* and *application program*.

progress bar control See *progress bar indicator*.

progress bar indicator A control that is a visual representation of the progress of a task.

prompt A symbol on the screen that tells the user that the computer is ready for the next command. In the DOS window, the prompt usually consists of the letter of the current drive followed by a greater-than sign (e.g. A>, B>, C>).

property sheet A special kind of dialog box that allows the user to view or change the properties (characteristics) of an object.

proportional typeface A typeface that varies the space given to each character. For instance, the *M* will take more space than the *I*.

protected mode An operating mode in which different parts of memory are allocated to different programs so that when programs are running simultaneously they cannot invade each other's memory space and can access only their own memory space.

protocol A set of rules or standards designed to enable computers to connect with one another and to exchange information.

push technology A method of distributing information over the Web by automatically sending updates from Web sites.

queue A line up of items waiting for processing.

random access memory (RAM) See *memory*.

read-cache Intercepts, makes a copy of, and places into memory the file that has been read. When a program makes a request, Windows checks to see if the data is already in the read-cache. Read-cache is used to optimize performance.

read-only attribute Prevents a file from being changed or deleted.

read-only memory (ROM) Memory that contains programs written on ROM chips, retained when the computer is turned off. ROM often controls the startup routines of the computer.

real mode A single-task working environment. DOS runs in real mode.

real time The actual amount of time the computer uses to complete an operation.

rebooting Reloading the operating system from a disk.

redirection A process in which a character-based operating system or the command line in Windows takes standard input or output from devices and sends it to a nonstandard input or output device. The redirection symbol is >.

Registry A mechanism in Windows that stores user information, application program information, and information about the specific computer. The Registry centralizes and tracks all this information. It is critical to the running of Windows.

relative path The path from where you are to where you want to go in relation to the directory tree hierarchical structure.

required parameter See *mandatory parameter*.

resident font A font stored in a printer.

resolution The sharpness and clarity of detail attained by a printer or a monitor in producing an image.

resources In a network environment, resources are what are provided by the server. Resources are the parts of the computer you share, such as a device or file.

Restore button A button on a window's title bar that returns the window to its previous size.

restoring Copying some or all of your files to your original disk, another disk, or another directory from your backup media.

Rich Text Format (RTF) A file format that allows different applications to use formatted text documents.

right-clicking Pressing the secondary mouse button, usually the right mouse button.

right-dragging Dragging while holding the secondary mouse button, usually the right mouse button.

ROM See *read-only memory (ROM)*.

ROM-BIOS (read-only memory–basic input/output system) A chip built into the hardware of a system. Its functions include running self-diagnostics, loading the boot record, and handling low-level system tasks.

root directory The directory that Windows creates on each disk when the disk is formatted. The backslash symbol (\) is used to represent the root directory.

router A device that connects networks. A router can make intelligent decisions about which network to use to send data.

RTF See *Rich Text Format (RTF).*

sample box In a dialog box, an area where a preview of your selections can be seen.

sans serif font A typeface with no serifs.

scale Various sizes a font can be made to print in.

scanner A device that enables a computer to read a handwritten or printed page.

screen capture A picture of a screen. To capture the screen to the Clipboard, you press the Print Screen key. To capture the active window, you press Alt + Print Screen. See also *screen dump*.

screen dump A transfer of the data on the monitor to a printer or another hard-copy device. See also *screen capture*.

screen font A font that is used to display text and graphics on the monitor.

screen saver An image that prevents screen burn-in and provides a modicum of security if passwords are used.

scroll bar A feature used to move through a window when the entire contents will not fit.

scroll box The box in a scroll bar that shows you your relative position in a window or document. It can be dragged with the mouse to move rapidly through the window or document.

scrolling Vertical movement through text.

search criteria The instructions or limitations for a search for files or folders.

search path The set path for searching for program files.

secondary storage media Data storage media other than RAM. Typically disks, tapes, or removable drives such as ZIP drives.

sector Data is stored on a disk in concentric circles (tracks) that are divided into sectors. A sector is a portion of a track. A sector is 512 bytes long, based on industry standards.

Serial Line Internet Protocol (SLIP) An older protocol that provides a temporary dial-up connection for full access to the Internet as long as you are online.

serial port A communications port to which a device, such as a modem or a serial printer, can be attached. Data is transmitted and received one bit at a time.

serif font A font with thin lines (serifs) at the ends of each letter.

server On a network, a computer that provides shared resources to network users. It is also used to refer to an application that provides data or an object in object linking and embedding.

server application An application program that provides data (an object) in object linking and embedding. It is also known as the source application.

server-based network A network model in which security and other network functions are provided by a dedicated server.

services A way to allow you to share files and devices on a network. There are other services such as being able to remotely administer a network.

shareware Software that is free on a trial basis with the option to either purchase it or remove it from your hard disk.

shortcut An icon that is created to represent commonly used objects. The icon is placed on the desktop or another location for easy access. A shortcut provides a pointer to the actual object, and it can usually be recognized by a right-bent arrow on top of the object's normal icon or by the word *shortcut.*

shortcut menu A menu that opens with a right-click of the mouse. It is also referred to as a *pop-up* or *context menu*.

single point of failure Desribes how, if the hub in a star topology fails, the entire network goes down.

sizing buttons Allow the user to minimize or maximize a window.

slider A control that allows you to adjust or set values when there is a range of values. You move the slider with the mouse.

SLIP See *Serial Line Internet Protocol (SLIP).*

soft return A code that is automatically inserted when the end of a line is reached in a document. Unlike a hard return, if text is inserted or removed, software will automatically adjust the text to fit within the margins.

software Programs that tell the computer what to do.

software package See *application package*.

spin box A control that allows you to either key in a number or click on the up or down arrow to increase or decrease a quantity. Usually a control that has numeric quantities to choose will be a spin box.

spinner A synonym for a *spin box*. See also *spin box*.

splash screen The first screen that appears when you boot the system or load a program. It is often a decorative screen to look at while the program or system is loading.

split bar In Explorer, a bar that divides the window to enable the user to see the structure of a disk on the left and the contents on the right.

spool file Stores a data document in a queue while it waits to be printed. The Windows print manager intercepts a print job on its way to the printer and sends it to disk or memory instead, where the print job is held until the printer is ready for it. The term *spool* comes from "simultaneous peripheral operations online."

spreadsheet program A program for budget management and financial projections.

standard A set of detailed technical guidelines used to establish conformity in software or hardware development.

standard error A process in which a character-based operating system or the command line in Windows writes error messages to the screen.

standard input A process in which a character-based operating system or the command line in Windows expects to receive information, usually from the keyboard.

standard output A process in which a character-based operating system or the command line in Windows expects to send information, usually to the screen.

star topology A local area network (LAN) design in which each device (node) is connected to a central point.

Start button The first button on the taskbar. Clicking the Start button opens the Start menu, which opens further menus for the user to access programs and data.

static RAM (SRAM) Memory chips that can hold data until the computer is turned off. See also *dynamic RAM*.

status area An area located at the right side of the taskbar that is used by Windows and other programs to place information or notification of events. If you were printing, for example, an icon of a printer would appear in the status area.

status bar A bar that supplies information about the current window.

string A string of data is a variable-length set of characters. String values are always enclosed in quotation marks.

stroke weight The thickness of a font.

subdirectory The location or container where documents, program files, devices, and other folders are stored on a disk. The terms *subfolders, folders, directories,* and *subdirectories* are used interchangeably.

subfolder A folder beneath a folder. The terms *subfolders, folders, directories,* and *subdirectories* are used interchangeably.

subscription Sets up a Web browser to check a Web page for new content. The program can then either notify the user about the new content or automatically download it to the user's computer.

supporting Describes a program's ability to read from and write to a specific file format.

surfing the Net Exploring the Internet by moving from topic to topic.

surge protector A device that prevents surges from reaching a computer or other kinds of electronic equipment. It is also called a *surge suppressor*.

surge suppressor See *surge protector*.

switch A modifier that controls the execution of a command. Typically the forward slash (/) is used to indicate a switch. See also *parameter*.

synchronizing files Updating files and folders that are duplicated. It is used with My Briefcase.

syntax The proper order or sequence of a computer's language and commands.

syntax diagram A graphic representation of a command and its syntax.

sysing a disk Placing the operating system files on a disk without removing the data that is there. The command is SYS.

system board Also known as a *motherboard,* it is the main circuit board controlling the major components of a computer system.

system configuration The components that make up a specific computer system.

system date The current date kept by the computer system.

system disk See *bootable disk*.

system prompt A symbol on the screen that tells the user that the computer is ready for the next command. It is used in the command line interface and usually consists of the current drive letter followed by the greater-than sign, as in C:\>.

system resources An area in memory that Windows uses for critical operating system tasks, such as drawing windows on the screen, using fonts, or running applications.

system software A set of programs that coordinates the operations of the hardware components.

system time The current time kept by the computer.

taskbar The bar on the screen that lets you move between any open programs, files, folders, or windows by displaying a button for each open item. The taskbar includes the Start button as well as the status area where Windows and other programs can place notification of events.

taskbar button The button on the taskbar that indicates an open program, file, or window. Clicking the specific button on the taskbar will activate that choice.

T-connector A device used in a network which has one end plugged into the network card and two open ends (like a T) for connecting the cables that go to the computers.

terminator plug A device used with T-connectors so that there is no unplugged end in a network.

text box A place where the user can key in information.

text editor A program that is similar to a word-processing program but is unable to perform any special editing. No embedded codes are inserted into documents. ASCII editors can only edit ASCII text files, also called *text files* or *unformatted text files*. Text editors are also called *ASCII editors*.

text file A file that contains text. It consists of data that can be read, such as letters and numbers, with an ASCII editor such as Notepad or in the DOS window.

Thinnet A single coaxial cable.

tiled A display mode that divides the screen equally among the open windows.

title bar A bar located at the top of a window that contains the name of the program.

toggle switch A switch that turns a function on or off like a light switch.

token A binary shorthand for repetitive words or phrases. When a file is decompressed, the tokens are read and the original characters are restored.

toolbar A toolbar appears in a window or on the desktop and provides shortcuts for entering menu commands. Rather than access the menu, you click a button on the toolbar.

ToolTip A brief description of a button. The user activates a ToolTip by pausing the mouse pointer over a button on a toolbar or the taskbar.

topology A design or configuration formed by the connections between devices on a local area network (LAN).

track A concentric circle on a disk where data is stored. Each track is further divided into sectors. All tracks and sectors are numbered so that the operating system can quickly locate information.

trackball A device used to move the cursor on the monitor. It usually consists of a stationary box that holds a ball that the user rotates to move the cursor.

tracking speed The rate at which the mouse pointer moves across the screen.

transparent to the user Describes a program or process that works so smoothly and easily that it is invisible to the user.

tree structure The organizational properties of a tree that relate to the structure of a disk from the root directory down.

troubleshooter A step-by-step guide to assist you in analyzing and solving a problem.

TrueType font A font that is provided with Windows and is capable of printing on any printer. The font usually looks on the screen like it will when it is printed. See *WYSIWYG*.

tweaking a system Making final changes and fine-tuning a system to improve performance.

twisted-pair cable A type of cable also known as 10BASET, 10BT, Ethernet, TPE, or RJ-45.

typeface The design of a group of letters, numbers, and punctuation, such as Arial or Times New Roman.

typeover The process of deleting existing characters as you key in new ones.

typing replaces selection The process of deleting existing characters by selecting them and keying in data. What you key in replaces your selection.

UNC See *universal naming convention (UNC)*.

unformatted text file See *text file*.

Unicode A 16-bit character set intended to accommodate all the commonly used characters in all languages.

uniform resource locator (URL) A standard format for identifying locations on the Internet. URLs specify three types of information needed to retrieve a document: the protocol to be used, the server address with which to connect, and the path to the information. The URL syntax is *protocol/servername/path;* an example of a URL address is **http://www.netscape.com**.

uninterruptible power supply (UPS) A device that ensures electrical flow to the computer is not interrupted because of a blackout and that protects the computer against potentially damaging events, such as power surges and brownouts. All UPS units are equipped with a battery and a loss-of-power sensor; if the sensor detects a loss of power, it switches over to the battery so that the user has time to save his or her work and shut off the computer.

universal naming convention (UNC) A convention used to locate the path to a network resource. It specifies the share name on a particular computer. The computer name is limited to 15 characters, and the share name is usually limited to 15 characters. It takes the format of *computername**sharename*[*optional path*].

universal serial bus (USB) The latest bus standard. It is an external bus standard for the computer that brings plug-and-play capability. It eliminates the need to install cards into dedicated computer slots and to reconfigure the system.

upgrading Purchasing the latest version of software and replacing your existing version with it.

uploading Sending a file to another computer while connected by a modem, another outside connection, or a network.

UPS See *uninterruptible power supply*.

URL See *uniform resource locator*.

user profiles In Windows, enabling profiles allows more than one user to use the same computer and retain his or her own personal settings on the desktop.

utility A program for carrying out specific, vital functions that assist in the operation of a computer or software.

utility program See *utility*.

variable parameter Value/information provided by the user.

vector font A font in which the characters are drawn using arrangements of line segments rather than arrangements of bits.

version A numbering scheme that indicates the progressive enhancements and improvement of software.

VFAT (virtual file allocation table) file system An extension of the file allocation table, with which it is compatible. It provides the ability to handle long file names. See also *file allocation table (FAT)*.

video card A circuit board that controls the capabilities of the video display.

virtual Describes a device, service, or sensory input that is perceived but is not real.

virtual machine (VM) An environment in memory that, from the application's point of view, looks like a separate computer, complete with all the resources available on the physical computer.

virus A program that has damaging side effects. Sometimes the side effects are intentionally damaging, other times not.

volume label An electronic label for a disk that the user can assign when it is formatted.

volume serial number A number randomly assigned to a disk when it is formatted.

wallpaper A graphic image file that serves as a background on the desktop, behind all open windows.

WAN See *wide area network (WAN).*

Web A colloquial expression for the World Wide Web (WWW).

Web browser A software program for navigating the Internet. Two popular programs are Netscape Navigator and Microsoft Internet Explorer.

Web page On the Internet, a single screen of text and graphics that usually has hypertext links to other pages.

Web site Both the physical and virtual location of a person's or an organization's Web page.

What's This? A feature that allows the user to right-click an item to obtain a brief description of it.

wide area network (WAN) A network that consists of computers using long-range telecommunication links.

wildcards The symbols * and ?, also called global file specifications, that are used to represent a character (?) or a group of characters (*) in a file name.

window A defined work area (rectangular frame) on the screen that is moveable and sizeable; information with which the user can interact is displayed in it.

Wintel A computer that uses the Microsoft Windows operating system and an Intel central processing unit (CPU).

wizard A program that uses step-by-step instructions to lead the user through the execution and completion of a Windows task.

word-processing program Software that allows the user to write, edit, and print any type of text.

word wrap A feature in software that automatically moves text to the next line when the current line is full.

workgroup Another name for a peer-to-peer network.

World Wide Web (WWW) A virtual space accessible from the Internet that holds pages of text and graphics in a recognizable format. These pages are linked to one another and to individual files. The Web is a collection of standards and protocols used to access information on the Internet.

wrapping Continuing a movement, with the cursor or a search operation, to the beginning or to a new starting point rather than stopping when the end of a series is reached. In a window, a title or an icon label would have additional lines created for the text to be displayed, if necessary.

write-protected disk A floppy disk that can be only read from, not written to.

WWW See *World Wide Web (WWW).*

WYSIWYG An acronym for *what you see is what you get*. It is displayed on the screen in the manner in which it will be printed.

zip A type of file. Its contents have been compressed by a special utility program, usually PKZIP or WinZip, so that it occupies less space on a disk or other storage device.

INDEX

F

G–H

I–J

K–L

M

N